# NEW!

## Achieve
## for Psychology

**Supporting Every Instructor.** | **Setting the New Standard for Teaching and Learning.**

**Achieve for Psychology** sets a whole new standard for integrating **assessments**, **activities**, and **analytics** into your teaching. It brings together all of the features that instructors and students loved about our previous platform, LaunchPad—interactive e-book, LearningCurve adaptive quizzing and other assessments, interactive learning activities, extensive instructor resources—in a powerful new platform that offers:

- A cleaner, more intuitive, **mobile-friendly** interface.
- Powerful analytics.
- Self-regulated learning and goal-setting surveys.
- A fully integrated iClicker classroom response system, with questions available for each unit or the option to integrate your own.
- A **NEW Video Collection for Introductory Psychology!**

Our resources were **co-designed with instructors and students**, on a foundation of *years* of **learning research**, and rigorous testing over multiple semesters. The result is superior content, organization, and functionality. Achieve's pre-built assignments engage students both *inside and outside of class*. And Achieve is effective for students of *all levels* of motivation and preparedness, whether they are high achievers or need extra support.

Macmillan Learning offers **deep platform integration** of Achieve with all LMS providers, including Blackboard, Brightspace, Canvas, and Moodle. With integration, students can access course content and their grades through one sign-in. And you can pair Achieve with course tools from your LMS, such as discussion boards and chat and gradebook functionality. LMS integration is also available with Inclusive Access. For more information, visit MacmillanLearning.com/College/US/Solutions/LMS-Integration or talk to your local sales representative.

Achieve was built with accessibility in mind. Macmillan Learning strives to create products that are usable by all learners and meet universally applied accessibility standards. In addition to addressing product compatibility with assistive technologies such as screen reader software, alternative keyboard devices, and voice recognition products, we are working to ensure that the content and platforms we provide are fully accessible. For more information visit https://www.macmillanlearning.com/college/us/our-story/accessibility

# Achieve for Psychology:    Assessments

## LearningCurve Adaptive Quizzing

Based on extensive learning and memory research, and proven effective for hundreds of thousands of students, LearningCurve focuses on the core concepts in every chapter, providing individualized question sets and feedback for correct and incorrect responses. The system adapts to each student's level of understanding, with follow up quizzes targeting areas where the student needs improvement. Each question is tied to a learning objective and linked to the appropriate section of the e-book to encourage students to discover the right answer for themselves. LearningCurve has consistently been rated the #1 resource by instructors and students alike.

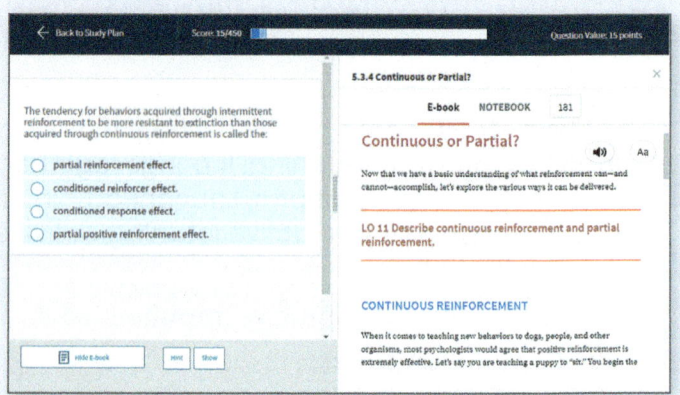

- LearningCurve's game-like quizzing promotes retrieval practice through its unique delivery of questions and its point system.

- Students with a firm grasp on the material get plenty of practice but proceed through the activity relatively quickly.

- Unprepared students are given more questions, therefore requiring that they do what they should be doing anyway if they're unprepared—practice some more.

- Instructors can monitor results for each student and the class as a whole, to identify areas that may need more coverage in lectures and assignments.

## E-book

Macmillan Learning's e-book is an interactive version of the textbook that offers highlighting, bookmarking, and note-taking. Built-in, low-stakes Show What You Know and Test Prep self-assessments allow students to test their level of understanding along the way, and learn even more in the process thanks to the *testing effect*. Students can download the e-book to read offline or to have it read aloud to them. Achieve allows instructors to assign chapter sections as homework.

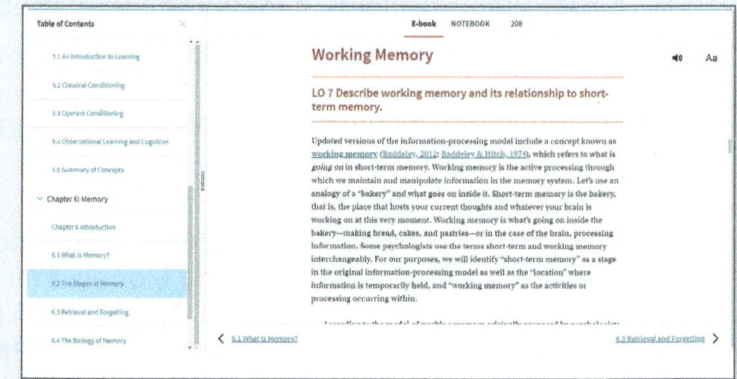

## Test Bank

Test banks for Macmillan Learning's psychology textbooks offer thousands of questions, all meticulously reviewed. Instructors can assign out-of-the-box exams or create their own by:

- Choosing from thousands of questions in our database.

- Filtering questions by type, topic, difficulty, and Bloom's level.

- Customizing multiple-choice questions.

- Integrating their own questions into the exam.

Exam/Quiz results report to a gradebook that lets instructors monitor student progress individually and classwide.

## Practice Quizzes

Practice Quizzes mirror the experience of a quiz or test, with questions that are similar but distinct from those in the test bank. Instructors can use the quizzes as is or create their own, selecting questions by question type, topic, difficulty, and Bloom's level.

## Achieve for Psychology:     Activities

Achieve is designed to support and encourage active learning by connecting familiar activities and practices out of class with some of the most effective and approachable in-class activities, curated from a variety of active learning sources.

### New! Video Collection for Introductory Psychology

This collection offers classic as well as current, in-demand clips from high-quality sources, with original content to support *Presenting Psychology*, Third Edition.

PBS Newshour/boclips

Accompanying assessment makes these videos assignable, with results reporting to the Achieve gradebook. Our faculty and student consultants were instrumental in helping us create this diverse and engaging set of clips. All videos are closed-captioned and found only in **Achieve**.

### Immersive Learning Activities

Focusing on student engagement, these immersive learning activities invite students to apply what they are learning to their own lives, or to play the role of researcher—exploring experimental methods, analyzing data, and developing scientific literacy and critical thinking skills.

Instructors want to make sure that students develop psychological literacy and acquire the critical-thinking skills needed for success in real-life situations. *Your Scientific World* was created with such goals in mind. These immersive learning activities place students in role-playing scenarios requiring them to think critically and apply their knowledge of psychological science to solve real-world problems.

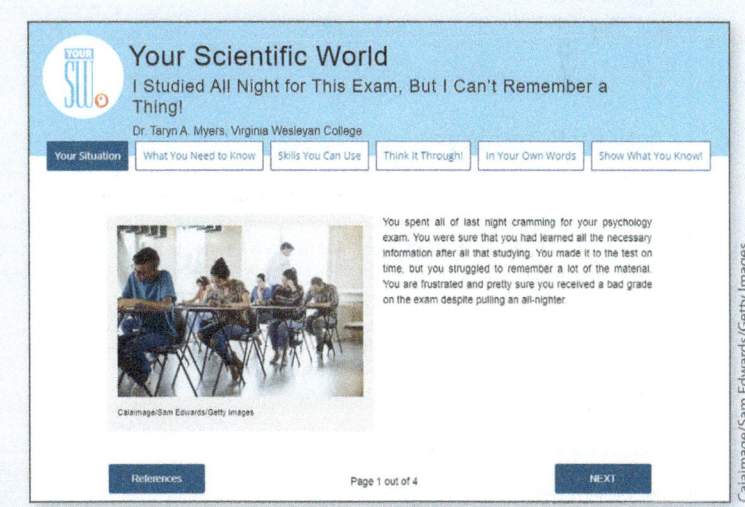

Caiaimage/Sam Edwards/Getty Images

## Concept Practice Tutorials

Achieve includes dozens of these dynamic, interactive mini-tutorials that teach and reinforce the course's foundational ideas. Each of these brief activities (only 5 minutes to complete) addresses one or two key concepts, in a consistent format—review, practice, quiz, and conclusion.

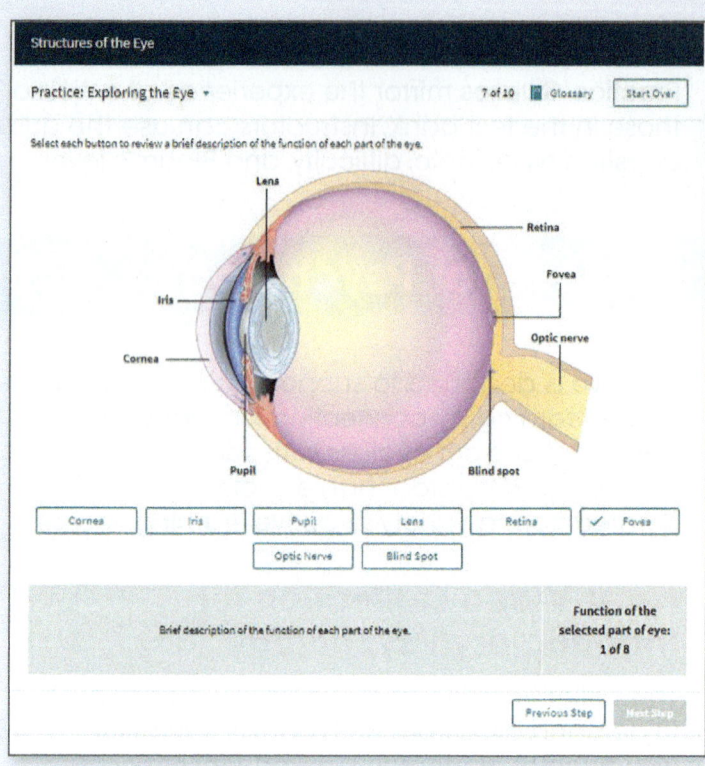

## Instructor Activity Guides

Instructor Activity Guides provide instructors with a structured plan for using Achieve's active learning opportunities in both face-to-face and remote learning courses. Each guide offers step-by-step instructions—from pre-class reflection to in-class engagement to post-class follow-up. The guides include suggestions for discussion questions, group work, presentations, and simulations, with estimated class time, implementation effort, and Bloom's taxonomy level for each activity.

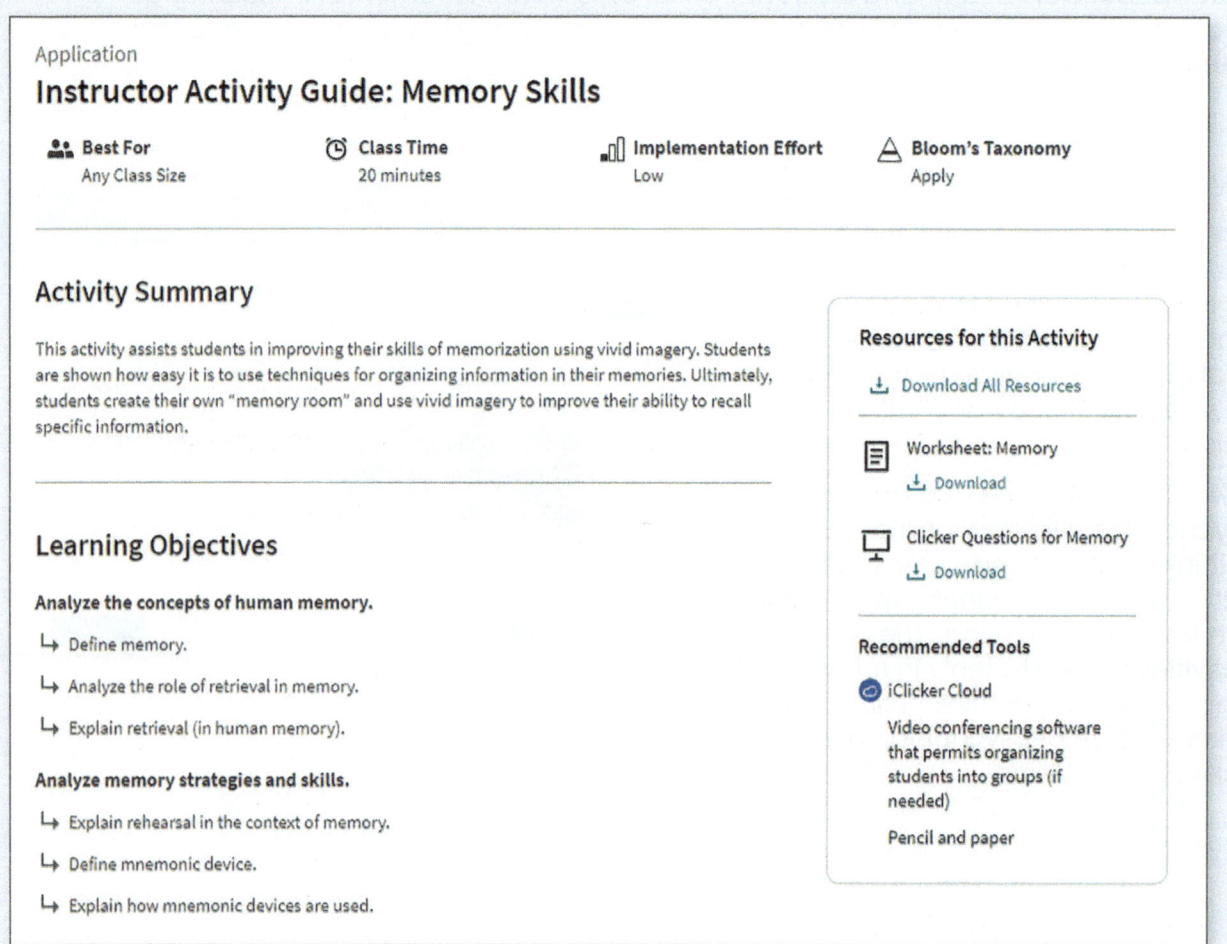

## iClicker Classroom Response System

Achieve seamlessly integrates iClicker, Macmillan Learning's highly acclaimed classroom response system. iClicker can help make any classroom—in person or virtual—more lively, engaging, and productive:

- iClicker's attendance feature helps you make sure students are actually attending in-person classes.

- Instructors can choose from flexible polling and quizzing options to engage students, check their understanding, and get their feedback in real time.

- iClicker allows students to participate using laptops, mobile devices, or in-class remotes.

- iClicker easily integrates your instructors' existing slides and polling questions—there is no need to re-enter them.

- Instructors can take advantage of the questions in our In-Class Activity Guides and our book-specific questions within Achieve to improve the opportunities for all students to be active in class.

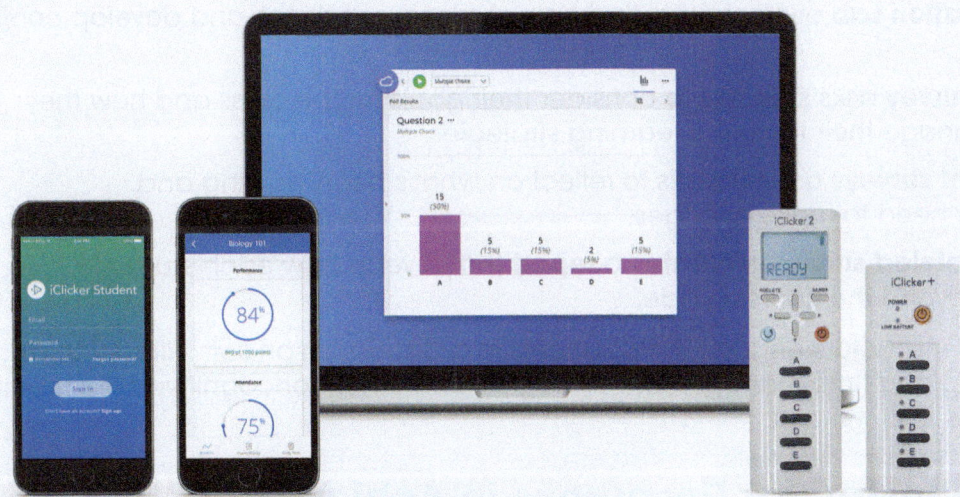

## Achieve for Psychology:   Analytics

### Learning Objectives, Reports, and Insights

Content in Achieve is tagged to specific Learning Objectives, aligning the coursework with the textbook and with the APA Learning Goals and Outcomes. Reporting within Achieve helps students see how they are performing against objectives, and it helps instructors determine if any student, group of students, or the class as a whole needs extra help in specific areas. This enables more efficient and effective instructor interventions.

Achieve provides reports on student activities, assignments, and assessments at the course level, unit level, subunit level, and individual student level, so instructors can identify trouble spots and adjust their efforts accordingly. Within Reports, the Insights section offers snapshots with high-level data on student performance and behavior, to answer such questions as:

- What are the top Learning Objectives to review in this unit?

- What are the top assignments to review?

- What's the range of performance on a particular assignment?

- How many students aren't logging in?

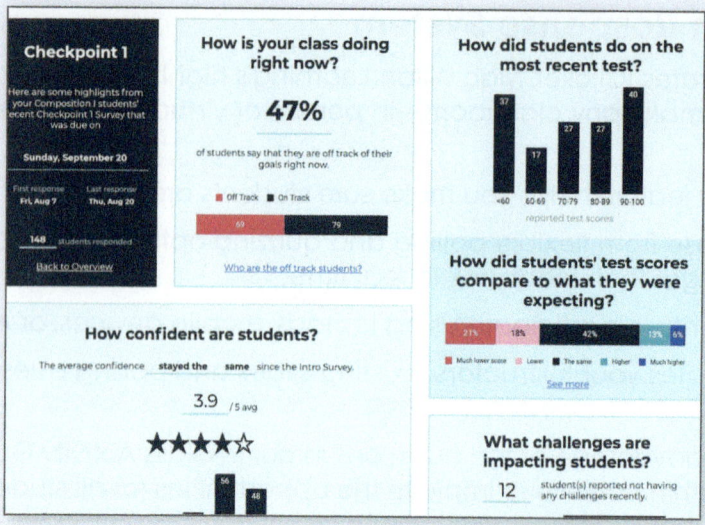

Achieve's **Innovation Lab** offers surveys that help students self-direct, and develop confidence in, their own learning:

- The **Intro Survey** asks students to consider their goals for the class and how they plan to manage their time and learning strategies.

- **Checkpoint surveys** ask students to reflect on what's been working and where they need to make changes.

- **Each completed survey generates a report** that reveals how each student is doing, beyond the course grade.

These tools help instructors engage their students in a discussion on soft skills, such as metacognition, effective learning and time management strategies, and other noncognitive skills that impact student success.

---

# Additional Instructor Resources in Achieve: All Within One Place

## Image Slides and Tables

Presentation slides feature chapter photos, illustrations, and tables and can be used as is or customized to fit an instructor's needs. Alt text for images is available upon request via WebAccessibility@Macmillan.com

## Instructor's Resource Manuals

Downloadable PDF manuals include a range of resources, such as chapter outlines or summaries, teaching tips, discussion starters, sample syllabi, assignment suggestions, and remote-friendly classroom activities.

## Lecture Slides

Accessible, downloadable presentation slides provide support for key concepts and themes from the text and can be used as is or customized to fit an instructor's needs.

---

# Customer Support

Our Achieve Client Success Team—dedicated platform experts—provides collaboration, software expertise, and consulting to tailor each course to fit your instructional goals and student needs. Start with a demo at a time that works for you to learn more about how to set up your customized course. Talk to your sales representative or visit https://www.macmillanlearning.com/college/us/contact-us/training-and-demos for more information.

Pricing and bundling options are available at the Macmillan student store: store.macmillanlearning.com/

# Presenting
# Psychology

### Third Edition

## Deborah M. Licht

Pikes Peak Community College, Colorado

PhD, Harvard University

## Misty G. Hull

Pikes Peak Community College, Colorado

MA, Colorado Christian University

## Coco Ballantyne

MS, Columbia University

worth publishers

Macmillan Learning

New York

· A PARTNERSHIP BETWEEN ·

WORTH PUBLISHERS & SCIENTIFIC AMERICAN

Executive Vice President, General Manager: Charles Linsmeier
Program Director, Social Sciences: Shani Fisher
Senior Executive Program Manager: Carolyn Merrill
Senior Development Editor: Lukia Kliossis
Editorial Assistant: Allison Curley
Executive Marketing Manager: Kate Nurre
Director of Media Editorial and Assessment, Social Sciences: Noel Hohnstine
Executive Media Editor: Laura Burden
Associate Media Editor: Stephanie Matamoros
Lead Media Project Manager: Joseph Tomasso
Director, Content Management Enhancement: Tracey Kuehn
Senior Managing Editor: Lisa Kinne
Senior Workflow Project Supervisor: Susan Wein
Senior Content Project Manager: Martha Emry
Director of Design, Content Management: Diana Blume
Design Services Manager: Natasha Wolfe
Interior Designers: Tamara Newnam, Marsha Cohen
Cover Design Manager: John Callahan
Art Manager: Matthew McAdams
Executive Permissions Editor: Cecilia Varas
Compositor: Lumina Datamatics, Ltd.
Infographic Designer: DeMarinis Design LLC
Infographic Illustrator: Anne DeMarinis
Illustrations: Todd Buck, Evelyn Pence, and Eli Ensor
Printing and Binding: King Printing Co., Inc.
Cover Designer: Michael Di Biase
Cover Images: Skydiver: vadimmmus/Shutterstock; Kaynen Brown Portrait: Celine Marie A. de la Rosa; Fish Toy:
    Pavel V Mukhin/Shutterstock; Brain: Sebastian Kaulitzki/Shutterstock; Mouse: Julius Lab at UCSF, Illustrations:
    Michael Di Biase
Integrated Thematic Features Icons: Finger snapping: kosmofish/Shutterstock; Profile of heads: Bloomicon/
    Shutterstock; Human head silhouette: Fresh_Studio/Shutterstock; Arrows: GzP_Design/Shutterstock; Colorful
    silhouettes of heads: grmarc/Shutterstock; Figures at table: linear_design/Shutterstock; Smartphone with
    hashtag: Paola Crash/Shutterstock; Lightning bolt: Maksym Drozd/Shutterstock; Leaves in hand: Gardashov
    Javidan/Shutterstock; Social relationship logo: stockfish/Shutterstock

Library of Congress Control Number: 2021936444

ISBN-13: 978-1-319-24720-1
ISBN-10: 1-319-24720-2

Printed in the United States of America
5   6   7               27   26   25

Worth Publishers
120 Broadway
New York, NY 10271
www.macmillanlearning.com

To all the individuals whose lives were tragically cut short by Covid, and to those they left behind. We remember and honor you.

# About the Authors

Edee Chesire.

Steve Hull.

Margherita Monti.

**Deborah Licht** is a professor of psychology at Pikes Peak Community College in Colorado Springs, Colorado. She received a BS in psychology from Wright State University, Dayton, Ohio; an MA in clinical psychology from the University of Dayton; and a PhD in psychology (experimental psychopathology) from Harvard University. She has three decades of teaching and research experience in a variety of settings, ranging from a small private university in the Midwest to a large public university in Copenhagen, Denmark. Deborah has taught introductory psychology, psychology of the workplace, abnormal psychology, the history of psychology, child development, and elementary statistics, in traditional, online, and hybrid courses. Working with community college students for nearly two decades has been very inspiring to Deborah; the great majority of students who attend community colleges often must overcome many challenges in pursuit of their dreams. Deborah continues to be interested in research on causal beliefs, particularly in relation to how college students think about their successes and failures as they pursue their degrees.

**Misty Hull** is a professor of psychology at Pikes Peak Community College in Colorado Springs, Colorado. She has taught a range of psychology courses at Pikes Peak Community College, including introductory psychology, human sexuality, and social psychology in a variety of delivery formats (traditional, online, and hybrid). Her love of teaching comes through in her dedication to mentoring new and part-time faculty in the teaching of psychology. She received her BS in human development and family studies from Texas Tech University in Lubbock, Texas, and an MA in professional counseling at Colorado Christian University in Lakewood, Colorado. Misty has held a variety of administrative roles at Pikes Peak Community College, including interim associate dean and coordinator of the Student Crisis Counseling Office. In addition, she served as the state psychology discipline chair of the Colorado Community College System from 2002 to 2010. One of her many professional interests is research on the impact of student persistence in higher education.

**Coco Ballantyne** is a New York–based journalist and science writer with a special interest in psychology. Before collaborating with Misty Hull and Deborah Licht on the *Scientific American: Psychology* series, Coco worked as a reporter for *Scientific American* online, covering the health, medicine, and neuroscience beats. She has also written for *Discover* magazine and *Nature Medicine.* Coco earned an MS from the Columbia University School of Journalism, where she received a Horgan Prize for Excellence in Critical Science Writing. Prior to her journalistic career, Coco worked as a teacher and tutor, helping high school and college students prepare for standardized tests such as the SAT, GRE, and MCAT. She also worked as a physics and math teacher at Eastside College Preparatory School in East Palo Alto, California, and as a human biology course associate at Stanford University, where she earned a BA in human biology.

# Preface

## A Product of Research

*Scientific American: Presenting Psychology* is built upon two pillars of research, the first and most important being the study of behavior and mental processes. The field of psychology is supported by a vast fund of scientific evidence, and this textbook is designed to reflect that. Flipping through the pages of this Third Edition, you will encounter thousands of citations, the great majority referencing studies published in academic journals. We select these articles with great care, weighing the quality of evidence, the credibility of the publication, and the credentials of the authors. The process involves a lot of critical thinking—an academic skill that we try to cultivate throughout the text and in our classrooms.

*Scientific American: Presenting Psychology* also rests on a strong pillar of market research. Before we even embarked on this edition, the *Scientific American: Psychology* series had already been formally reviewed by well over 1,300 instructors and students. This edition benefited from in-depth reviews by an additional 140 instructors and almost 600 students—all of this in addition to the semester-by-semester feedback we have been gathering from our own students. Over time, we have also met with our colleagues in more than 30 focus groups, listening to their feedback and brainstorming ways to address unmet needs in the classroom. This feedback, along with the extensive market research conducted by the publisher, has helped us identify the greatest challenges that emerge in the introductory course. The most critical of these challenges are outlined in the pages to come.

Our evidence-based approach also aligns seamlessly with the *American Psychological Association (APA) Introductory Psychology Initiative.* The IPI encourages instructors to use these *seven Integrative Themes* to help students (1) adapt their thinking in response to empirical evidence; (2) recognize general principles but individual differences; (3) acknowledge biological, psychological, and social-cultural influences; (4) respect diversity, equity, inclusion; (5) be aware of perceptual and thinking errors; (6) apply psychology's principles to improve their own lives and communities; and (7) value psychology's ethical principles. *Achieve for Scientific American: Presenting Psychology, Third Edition* offers instructors interested implementing these new recommendations a complete package of relevant and inclusive content, engaging learning activities, and rich assessment.

> **"**This is perhaps the best introductory textbook I have encountered that achieves the goal of not only providing students with relevant and practical applications, but also doing so in a very engaging way!**"**
>
> Anita Tam, *Clemson University*

# Creating Relevance and Student Engagement

### COVID COMES TO VEGAS

Summer, 2020: It was a quiet day in the Las Vegas emergency room (ER) where nurse Kaynen Brown worked. The halls and waiting areas were empty. Usually there are people milling around, but COVID-19 had changed everything. Except for caregivers of hospitalized children, family members of patients were barred from entering the hospital. Nevada was experiencing its first major wave of the coronavirus pandemic, and health-care professionals were just beginning to understand how this novel pathogen spread and created mayhem in the human body.

**Essential Worker**
Nurse Kaynen Brown was 26 years old when he began fighting on the front lines of the coronavirus pandemic. Like health-care workers all around the world, Kaynen faced an entirely new set of stressors: fighting a novel pathogen with no specific treatments, lacking adequate personal protective equipment (PPE), witnessing patients suffer and die without family members nearby, and fearing for the safety of himself and his loved ones.

## Real People, Real Stories

Our market research strongly suggests that the greatest challenge of teaching introductory psychology is generating student interest and engagement in the subject matter. We also know from our own teaching experience that students learn and remember material better when they see how it applies to the lives of real people. We capture the student's interest from the get-go, launching each chapter with a story about a person (or people) whose experiences help us understand and apply psychological concepts. Unlike the isolated case studies and opening vignettes commonly seen in other textbooks, our *Integrated Stories* are written in a journalistic style and *woven throughout* the chapters, offering memorable examples that reinforce important concepts at key intervals. These stories have been selected to represent people from all walks of life, providing a mosaic of gender, culture, race, age, nationality, and occupation. See Chapter 12 for a new integrated story about emergency room nurse Kaynen Brown (who is also featured on our cover), which explores health-care worker stress during the COVID-19 pandemic.

The chapter stories are accompanied by *Online Video Profiles,* which are embedded in the Achieve e-book. These custom videos bring our story subjects to life and provide valuable insights into their characters. Assessable versions of the videos provide thoughtful questions that tighten the link between the story and chapter content, creating a more relevant and memorable learning experience. Many instructors find these unique videos to be an excellent prelecture activity and assignment resource.

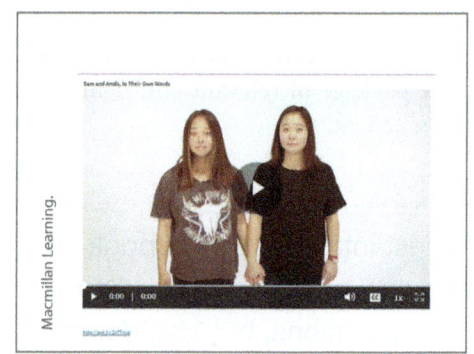

Macmillan Learning.

## Put Your Heads Together

Another source of engagement is the *Put Your Heads Together* feature, which prompts students to apply material and generate ideas in small groups. These activities are interspersed throughout the text. Put Your Heads Together was created in response to instructors' requests for more active learning exercises and recent research confirming the impact of such activities on concept understanding and retention. In our own classrooms, we have noted that these "learning by doing" tools are very effective and growing in popularity.

**Put Your Heads Together**

The link between consciousness and attention is not fully understood, but we do know that our attentional capacity—and therefore our ability to multitask effectively—is limited. In your group, discuss and record examples of A) when multitasking is advantageous to you and B) when multitasking could be risky or problematic. C) Decide if the benefits outweigh the risks.

## Integrated Thematic Features

Students want to know why studying psychology is important. How does it relate to their lives, and when will they ever use it? We explore topical, high-interest subjects with real-world relevance in our *Integrated Thematic Features.* Organized around key themes in psychology, these features are seamlessly woven into the running text (not relegated to "boxes" that students will skip over). Look for these titles: Relationships, Across the World, Apply This, Believe It . . . Or Not, Career Connections, Didn't See That Coming, Social Media and Psychology, Think Critically.

**NEW**

 **Relationships** Explains how psychology research can help us understand relationships with family, friends, and partners.

 **Across the World** Explores the impact of culture on human thoughts, emotions, and behaviors.

 **Apply This** Illustrates how psychology concepts readily apply to our daily experiences and observations.

 **Believe It . . . Or Not** Examines surprising findings and provocative issues in the psychological community.

 **Career Connections** Demonstrates how psychology concepts are relevant and applicable to a variety of careers.

 **Didn't See That Coming** Presents unexpected, high-interest, and newsworthy developments related to the chapter's focus.

 **Social Media and Psychology** Highlights research showing how Instagram, Twitter, and other forms of social media impact thoughts, emotions, and behaviors.

 **Think Critically** Challenges students to hone their critical thinking skills by evaluating research and questioning commonly held beliefs ("myth busting").

# Demonstrating Psychology Is a Science

In Chapters 0 and 1, we establish that psychology is a rigorous science, detailing the steps of the scientific method and emphasizing the importance of critical thinking. Using a variety of tools and features (some shown here), we continue to emphasize the scientific process in all subsequent chapters, encouraging students to evaluate research claims and consider the strengths and limitations of different methodologies.

**Think Critically**

6 SLEEP MYTHS

HAVE YOU FALLEN FOR ANY OF THEM?

- **Drinking alcohol before bed helps you sleep better:** Alcohol helps you fall asleep, but it undermines sleep quality and may cause you to awaken in the night (American Psychological Association, 2020; Caldwell et al., 2019).

- **Yawning means you are exhausted:** It likely means you are hot. Yawning appears to be related to temperature and functions to help cool the brain (Massen et al., 2014).

- **Everyone needs 8 hours of sleep each night:** Experts recommend that we get more than 7 hours of sleep each night (Watson et al., 2015), but sleep needs can range greatly from person to person. Some people do fine with 6 hours; others genuinely need 9 or 10 (Schoenborn et al., 2013).

- **Losing sleep during the week is no big deal, as long as you catch up on the weekend:** Sleep deprivation is associated with metabolic changes that can lead to weight gain, and "weekend recovery sleep" does not appear to cancel these effects (Depner et al., 2019).

- **Pressing snooze is a good way to catch a few more minutes of rest:** Because we need more than a few minutes of sleep to feel rested, hitting snooze is a good indication that you are not getting enough sleep (Oexman, 2013).

- **Sleep aids are totally safe:** When taken according to prescription, sleep aids are relatively safe and effective, although they do not guarantee a normal night of sleep. That being said, research has linked some of these medications to serious health problems (DeKosky & Williamson, 2020; Kripke et al., 2012), as well as an increased risk of sleep eating, sleep sex, and "driving while not fully awake" (U.S. Food and Drug Administration, n.d., para. 5).

**Apply This ↓**
DON'T BELIEVE EVERYTHING YOU READ

**Hyped Up Associations?**
Does eating meat cause people to experience better mental health outcomes ... or does evidence suggest a correlation between two variables? If you see a headline claiming "x causes y," immediately turn on your critical-thinking skills. Media reports sometimes suggest causation when the findings are based only on correlations.

**CORRELATION OR CAUSATION?**

As you venture deeper into the study of psychology, you may find yourself becoming increasingly skeptical of media reports on research relating to psychological phenomena. We encourage a healthy dose of skepticism. Although many news stories on scientific findings are accurate and balanced, others are distorted and exaggerated. Look at these headlines about a 2020 study investigating the relationship between food and psychological health:

"Study claims eating meat can help improve mental health" (Cortes, 2020)
"Eating meat may IMPROVE mental health and one in three vegetarians are depressed, study suggests" (Pinkstone, 2020)

It sounds as if meat-based diets are *causing* better mental health, while vegetarian diets create psychological problems. We must have a cause-and-effect relationship, right? Wrong. The following is a rough description of the research, which was actually a review of many studies published in the journal *Critical Reviews in Food Science and Nutrition*. Researchers combed through the scientific literature, looking for studies examining links between meat consumption (or meat avoidance) and variables related to mental health. Eighteen studies met the researchers' criteria for inclusion. Taken together, the results point to an association between meat avoidance and higher levels of anxiety and depression (Dobersek et al., 2020).

Provocative as these findings may be, they do not allow us to conclude that eating meat causes less anxiety and depression. In fact, the authors are careful to point this out: "Across all studies, there was no evidence to support a causal relation between the consumption or avoidance of meat and any psychological outcomes" (Dobersek et al., 2020, p. 9).

Isn't it possible that some third variable is at work, driving both eating behaviors and mental health symptoms? For example, research suggests that many people choose to become vegetarian for health reasons (Hopwood et al., 2020). Could it be that concerns about health are driving both anxiety and decisions to eliminate meat? Another factor to consider is the direction of causation. When we see headlines like those above, we tend to assume that cutting out meat *leads* to mental health issues. But what if the reverse is true, that is, experiencing anxiety or depression makes people more inclined to stop eating meat (Dobersek et al., 2020)? The take-home message: If a news report claims that *X causes Y*, **don't automatically assume** that the media has it right. In this case, the research has only demonstrated a correlation between variables, not a cause-and-effect relationship.

**CONNECTIONS**
In **Chapter 0**, we explained that psychology is driven by critical thinking, a process that involves synthesizing evidence, thinking beyond definitions, and being open-minded but skeptical at the same time. Here, we emphasize the importance of thinking critically about media reports of research findings; news stories can sometimes be misleading or inaccurate.

**NEW**

The new *Research Connections* feature links content in Chapters 2–14 to research concepts presented in Chapter 1.

applications are extremely broad (Wixted, 2020). Suppose a physician is evaluating a patient for potential lung cancer. The doctor must make important decisions (like whether to refer a patient for cancer treatment) amid the **"noise" of variables** related to their years of experience and workplace standards (Kostopoulou et al., 2019). In a health-care context, the ability to sense and perceive may have life or death implications.

How might signal detection theory apply to your everyday life? Imagine your phone rings as you stand on a busy street corner. Whether you hear the ringtone depends on many external factors, such as competing sounds from traffic and nearby voices. It also depends on internal factors, including how tired or alert you may be. Have you ever "heard" your ringtone when no one is calling? Signal detection theory can help explain that, too. Neurons in our sensory systems sometimes fire spontaneously, even

**Research CONNECTIONS**
Here, the "noise" of variables relates to the potential bias of the doctor, and how that bias might impact their decisions related to patient care. In **Chapter 1**, we discussed how bias can change the outcome of experiments. Expectations, attitudes, and value systems can influence a person's observations (observer bias). Researcher expectations can also impact results, but this experimenter bias often can be controlled with double-blind studies.

**NEW**

**THE PSYCHOLOGICAL TOLL OF RUDE E-MAILS**
Research reveals the subtle ways that impolite electronic communication at work brings you down.

From the SCIENTIFIC pages of AMERICAN

Imagine waking up on Monday morning to an e-mail in your inbox that was written entirely in capital letters—an e-mail that jolts you awake far quicker than the cup of coffee in your hand: "IS THIS A JOKE??? ARE YOU KIDDING ME?!" With the caps lock key and the stroke of an exclamation point, your co-worker has just done the equivalent of shouting at you across the office. Yet these days this kind of encounter is almost commonplace. Whether they come in all caps, exclamation marks, silence or snark, rude e-mails are on the rise.

For a civilized society, we're not always so civil. In fact, rudeness is a pervasive problem. In a 2002 report on a study conducted with a large representative sample of 2,013 adults, 88 percent of the general public indicated they had come across rude and disrespectful people on a daily basis. And the workplace is no escape. As the sheer volume of electronic communications has skyrocketed, the problem of "nasty e-mail" is becoming nonnegligible. In fact, more than 90 percent of professionals surveyed in a 2009 study said that they had experienced disrespectful e-mail exchanges at work. [. . .]

And being on the receiving end of such impoliteness can have a lasting effect. Studies have shown that dealing with rude e-mails at work can create lingering stress and take a toll on the recipient's well-being. In a simulated work experiment, participants who received such a message from their boss experienced more negative emotions, found it harder to stay engaged in work tasks and answered fewer questions correctly than the control group. The stress associated with e-mail rudeness can creep into family life as well. A diary study that surveyed employees twice a day over five workdays found that when employees received impolite messages during a workday, they were likely to report more stress symptoms both in the evening and the following morning. [. . .]

Our exclusive partnership with the highly respected publication *Scientific American* tacitly reinforces the notion that psychology is a science. Equally important, it provides us with the opportunity to feature the work of leading science journalists. Every chapter includes a From the Pages of *Scientific American* feature that describes impactful research in the field. In Achieve, instructors can assign quizzes on the content presented in the From the Pages of *Scientific American* features.

# Helping Students See the "Big Picture"

To help students see conceptual links across chapters, we have strategically placed *Connections* features in the margins. More detailed than typical cross-references, these brief summaries complement what many instructors do in the classroom—point out the relationships between topics currently being presented and material previously covered. Many students won't automatically make a connection between perception and memory, or see how epigenetics might play a role in the development of disorders, but the Connections spell it out without requiring readers to flip back pages and locate the linked topic. Because making connections is so crucial (not only to us, but to the hundreds of instructors who have used and reviewed this text), we have included assessment questions directly related to these links in our *Test Bank*.

**CONNECTIONS**

In **Chapter 2,** we described neurotransmitters and their role in the nervous system. Acetylcholine is a neurotransmitter that relays messages from motor neurons to muscles, enabling movement. Here, we see how drugs can block the normal activity of acetylcholine, causing the paralysis that is useful during surgery.

The Versed kicks in; you start to feel relaxed and sleepy; and before you know it, you're in the operating room, hooked up to all sorts of tubes and monitors. Dr. Chander lulls you into unconsciousness with a drug called propofol, and blunts your perception of pain with a powerful narcotic such as fentanyl. She also paralyzes your muscles with drugs such as rocuronium or vecuronium, whose effects are readily reversible. These drugs are modern derivatives of curare, an arrowhead poison used by South American natives. Curare works by blocking the activity of the neurotransmitter **acetylcholine**, which stimulates muscle contractions in the body. But curare does not cross into the brain, and therefore it does not have the power to transport you to another level of consciousness (Czarnowski et al., 2007).

**CONNECTIONS**

In **Chapter 8,** we discussed epigenetic changes, or alterations to the chemical compounds surrounding DNA. Epigenetic changes can be triggered by environmental factors (exposure to toxins, for example) and may influence the expression of genes that contribute to the development of autism.

and elevated blood pressure in the pregnant mother are risk factors (Zeliadt, 2018). Still other research has focused on teratogens, or prenatal exposure to environmental toxins such as pesticides, lead, and air pollutants; however, these results are somewhat inconclusive (Arora et al., 2017; Havdahl et al., 2021). The etiology of this disorder remains a puzzle, but researchers emphasize the importance of both genes and environmental factors, and **epigenetic** changes that could mediate their interaction (Forsberg et al., 2018).

**CONNECTIONS**

In **Chapter 7,** we described the availability heuristic. With this heuristic, we predict the probability of something happening based on how easily we can recall a similar event from the past. The false consensus effect may result partly from using the availability heuristic. We rely on information about ourselves because it is easy to recall, and thus overestimate the degree to which other people think and act like we do.

**FALSE CONSENSUS EFFECT**    When trying to decipher the causes of other people's behaviors, we **over-rely on knowledge about ourselves.** This can lead to the **false consensus effect,** which is the tendency to overestimate the degree to which others think or act like we do (Ross, Greene, et al., 1977). For example, people tend to believe that their favorite celebrities are more popular than they really are: *I love Taylor Swift, as does everyone else!* (Collisson et al., 2021). The false consensus effect may also be apparent in beliefs about vaccines: *I think the flu shot is dangerous, and most of my friends agree* (Bruine de Bruin et al., 2020). We seem to make such mistakes because we have an overabundance of information about ourselves, and often limited information about others.

**CONNECTIONS**

In **Chapter 10,** we discussed locus of control, or patterns of beliefs about where control resides. People with an internal locus of control believe they have control over their lives. Those who fall prey to the self-serving bias appear to have an internal locus of control when it comes to explaining the reasons for their successes.

**SELF-SERVING BIAS**    People who attribute their successes to **internal characteristics** and their failures to environmental factors may be prone to the **self-serving bias.** As research reveals, people exhibit "a generalized tendency to attribute positive outcomes to themselves and negative outcomes to others," and this can impact the way they learn and interpret events (Dorfman et al., 2019, p. 523).

One of the reasons Dennis was so drawn to Alexa was her apparent *lack* of self-serving bias. She was humble about her academic accomplishments, and she took

# Teaching and Mastering the Toughest Concepts

We understand that difficult concepts require multiple examples underscoring connections with everyday life; we also know that students benefit from expanded assessment opportunities. But sometimes more narrative examples and intensive assessment are not enough; in order for things to really "click," a student must see the information presented in a new light. This is why we use Infographics, tables, figures, and photos to tackle challenging topics throughout the text.

There are 57 Infographics appearing in this book. Patterned after the visual features in *Scientific American,* these full-page visual presentations combine concepts and/or data into a single storyboard format. Most illuminate concepts identified through research as the most challenging for instructors to teach and students to master. The Infographics have received some of the most enthusiastic feedback from our student reviewers. Interactive versions of the Infographics and their associated quizzes are available in Achieve.

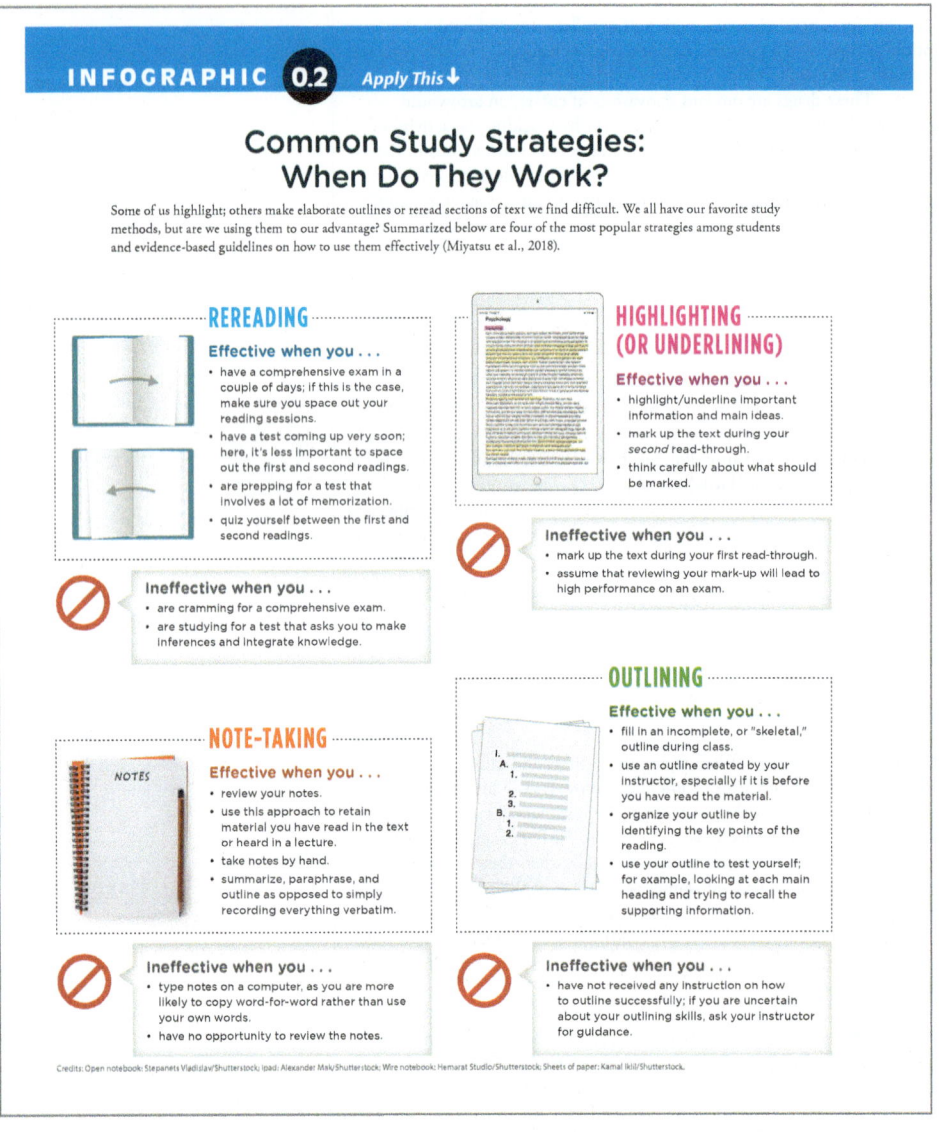

**INFOGRAPHIC 0.2**    *Apply This ↓*

## Common Study Strategies: When Do They Work?

Some of us highlight; others make elaborate outlines or reread sections of text we find difficult. We all have our favorite study methods, but are we using them to our advantage? Summarized below are four of the most popular strategies among students and evidence-based guidelines on how to use them effectively (Miyatsu et al., 2018).

**REREADING**

Effective when you . . .
- have a comprehensive exam in a couple of days; if this is the case, make sure you space out your reading sessions.
- have a test coming up very soon; here, it's less important to space out the first and second readings.
- are prepping for a test that involves a lot of memorization.
- quiz yourself between the first and second readings.

Ineffective when you . . .
- are cramming for a comprehensive exam.
- are studying for a test that asks you to make inferences and integrate knowledge.

**HIGHLIGHTING (OR UNDERLINING)**

Effective when you . . .
- highlight/underline important information and main ideas.
- mark up the text during your *second* read-through.
- think carefully about what should be marked.

Ineffective when you . . .
- mark up the text during your first read-through.
- assume that reviewing your mark-up will lead to high performance on an exam.

**NOTE-TAKING**

Effective when you . . .
- review your notes.
- use this approach to retain material you have read in the text or heard in a lecture.
- take notes by hand.
- summarize, paraphrase, and outline as opposed to simply recording everything verbatim.

Ineffective when you . . .
- type notes on a computer, as you are more likely to copy word-for-word rather than use your own words.
- have no opportunity to review the notes.

**OUTLINING**

Effective when you . . .
- fill in an incomplete, or "skeletal," outline during class.
- use an outline created by your instructor, especially if it is before you have read the material.
- organize your outline by identifying the key points of the reading.
- use your outline to test yourself; for example, looking at each main heading and trying to recall the supporting information.

Ineffective when you . . .
- have not received any instruction on how to outline successfully; if you are uncertain about your outlining skills, ask your instructor for guidance.

Credits: Open notebook: Stepanets Vladislav/Shutterstock; Ipad: Alexander Mak/Shutterstock; Wire notebook: Hemarat Studio/Shutterstock; Sheets of paper: Kamal Ikili/Shutterstock.

# What's New in This Edition?

This is our first edition to be rolled out with Achieve for Psychology, Macmillan Learning's new online platform. Achieve includes everything needed to teach the course: an e-book, learning activities, assessment tools such as LearningCurve adaptive quizzing, gradebook, insights and reporting, and integration options. For more information, go to https://achieve.macmillanlearning.com.

Achieve is not the only thing new to *Scientific American: Presenting Psychology*. As with every new edition, we have added numerous research updates, fresh examples, and new illustrations. Additionally, there are several chapter-specific changes outlined below:

## Chapter 0: Are You Ready for This?

- New integrated story about a soccer team in Thailand that became trapped in a cave in 2018 and the dramatic effort to rescue them
- New Online Video Profile to accompany the story of the Thai soccer team
- New Career Connections feature about psychology's relevance in a broad array of professions
- Expanded coverage of commonsense myths
- New table outlining the characteristics of critical thinkers
- New Put Your Heads Together on thinking critically about folk wisdom
- New Think Critically about astrology and other pseudosciences
- New Infographic about how to maximize the utility of common study strategies

## Chapter 1: Introduction to the Study of Psychology

- New Think Critically feature on twin research
- Expanded coverage of the history of psychology, with increased emphasis on diversity
- Updated scientific method Infographic
- New figure illustrating a representative sample
- New From the Pages of *Scientific American* article about the psychological impact of rude e-mails
- Two revamped and one new Put Your Heads Together features
- New Relationships feature about correlations between social support and physical health
- Revamped Apply This feature on how to think critically about media reports on psychological findings
- New Career Connections feature about communicating scientific findings to the public

## Chapter 2: Biology and Behavior

- Brighter and higher-contrast figures illustrating the nervous system and endocrine system
- New From the Pages of *Scientific American* feature about head injuries in women athletes
- New Think Critically feature exploring the "tend-and-befriend" response to stress in males and females
- New Relationships feature on neurotransmitter activity associated with love
- Revamped Social Media and Psychology feature examining the brain's threshold for social media "friends"
- New Put Your Heads Together feature
- New Research Connections feature

## Chapter 3: Sensation and Perception

- New From the Pages of *Scientific American* feature explaining illusions like the "blue dress" that ignited a global internet debate
- Revamped coverage of signal detection theory
- New Relationships feature on chronic pain
- New Across the World feature about how environmental factors influence color perception
- New Career Connections feature about the application of perceptual principles in artistic professions
- Three New Put Your Heads Together features
- New Research Connections feature

## Chapter 4: Consciousness

- Revamped introduction to consciousness
- New figure illustrating the neurological correlates of conscious experiences
- New Career Connections feature on shift work
- New figure illustrating the suprachiasmatic nucleus
- New From the Pages of *Scientific American* feature about the stigma of addiction
- New Relationships feature on perceptions of women and men drinking alcohol
- Two New Put Your Heads Together features
- New Research Connections feature

## Chapter 5: Learning

- Updated discussion on classical conditioning and advertising
- Two New Put Your Heads Together features
- New Social Media and Psychology feature about the brain activity underlying social media reinforcement

- New Believe It . . . Or Not feature exploring the scientific debate about whether violent video games promote aggression
- New From the Pages of *Scientific American* feature examining how uncommon behaviors can quickly evolve into social norms
- New Research Connections feature

## Chapter 6: Memory

- New Relationships feature about how working memory contributes to the resolution of relationship problems
- New From the Pages of *Scientific American* feature about the memory reliability of drunk eyewitnesses
- Updated and reorganized coverage of memory distortions in legal situations
- Inclusion of exercise as a strategy to improve memory
- New Research Connections feature

## Chapter 7: Cognition, Language, and Intelligence

- New Social Media and Psychology feature on "fake news" and confirmation bias
- New Relationships feature examining the connection between dishonesty and emotional intelligence
- New discussion about IQ tests and scientific racism
- New From the Pages of *Scientific American* feature about perceptions of leaders with exceptionally high IQs
- Revamped Think Critically feature on the cognitive abilities of females and males
- Two new Put Your Heads Together features
- New Research Connections feature

## Chapter 8: Human Development

- New Think Critically feature on epigenetics
- New Believe It . . . Or Not feature about the purported "30-million-word gap" between children from high- and low-income families
- New table outlining the sequence of language development
- New From the Pages of *Scientific American* feature about the classic "marshmallow test" and related research
- Expanded coverage of attachment styles
- Two new Put Your Heads Together features
- New Apply This feature about how exercise could help slow the aging process
- New Research Connections feature

## Chapter 9: Motivation and Emotion

- New table presenting terms used to describe gender identity and sexual orientation
- New From the Pages of *Scientific American* feature about growing from the experience of failure
- Updated treatment of same-sex attraction and the sexual orientation continuum
- New Relationships feature about detecting dishonesty in others
- New Put Your Heads Together feature
- New Research Connections feature

## Chapter 10: Personality

- New From the Pages of *Scientific American* feature on the personality traits of animals
- New Relationships feature about the long-term impact of parents showing children conditional regard
- New Put Your Heads Together feature
- New Research Connections feature

## Chapter 11: Social Psychology

- Expanded coverage of the fundamental attribution error
- New figure illustrating the neural correlates of the bystander effect
- New From the Pages of *Scientific American* feature about the link between air pollution and increased rates of violent crime
- New Relationships feature on the so-called "love at first sight" phenomenon
- New Across the World feature on behaviors aimed at curbing the spread of COVID-19, and how culture may play a role
- New Put Your Heads Together feature
- New table on microaggressions
- New Research Connections feature

## Chapter 12: Stress and Health

- New integrated story about emergency room nurse Kaynen Brown, which explores health-care worker stress during the COVID-19 pandemic
- New Online Video Profile to accompany the story of Kaynen
- New From the Pages of *Scientific American* feature explaining why stress drives us toward sweet foods
- Revised coverage of the "blue zones," regions of the world where people enjoy exceptional health and longevity

- New figure highlighting the geographic locations of the blue zones
- New Relationships feature about the stress-fighting power of social support
- New Put Your Heads Together feature
- New Research Connections feature

## Chapter 13: Psychological Disorders

- New Didn't See That Coming feature exploring the link between exposure to a common parasite and the development of certain disorders
- New figure illustrating thoughts and behaviors frequently experienced by people with obsessive-compulsive disorder (OCD)

- New From the Pages of *Scientific American* feature examining some of the reasons people die by suicide
- New figure showing thinning of the brain's cortex associated with bipolar disorder
- New Put Your Heads Together feature
- New Research Connections feature

## Chapter 14: Treatment of Psychological Disorders

- New From the Pages of *Scientific American* feature about short-course treatments for anxiety disorders
- Expanded coverage of biomedical treatments for depression
- New Put Your Heads Together feature
- New Research Connections feature

# Alignment with APA Learning Guidelines 2.0

| Alignment with APA Learning Guidelines 2.0 | |
|---|---|
| **Goal 1: Knowledge Base in Psychology**<br>AMERICAN PSYCHOLOGICAL ASSOCIATION LEARNING OUTCOMES | |
| **1.1** Describe key concepts, principles, and overarching themes in psychology | **1.2** Develop a working knowledge of psychology's content domains<br>**1.3** Describe applications of psychology |
| *Scientific American: Presenting Psychology,* **Third Edition, Learning Objectives/Substantive Content** | |
| **CHAPTER 0:** LO 1–LO 5<br>**CHAPTER 1:** LO 1–LO 10<br>**CHAPTER 2:** LO 1–LO 16<br>**CHAPTER 3:** LO 1–LO 14<br>**CHAPTER 4:** LO 1–LO 12<br>**CHAPTER 5:** LO 1–LO 15<br>**CHAPTER 6:** LO 1 –LO 15<br>**CHAPTER 7:** LO 1–LO 11<br>**CHAPTER 8:** LO 1–LO 17<br>**CHAPTER 9:** LO 1–LO 13<br>**CHAPTER 10:** LO 1–LO 14<br>**CHAPTER 11:** LO 1–LO 12<br>**CHAPTER 12:** LO 1–LO 12<br>**CHAPTER 13:** LO 1–LO 11<br>**CHAPTER 14:** LO 1–LO 12 | **APPENDIX A:** Introduction to Statistics<br>**APPENDIX B:** Careers in Psychology<br>**INTEGRATED THEMATIC FEATURES** in each chapter<br>**CONNECTIONS** in Chapters 0–14<br>**CAREER CONNECTIONS** in Chapters 1–14 and Appendix A<br>**RESEARCH CONNECTIONS** in Chapters 1–14<br>**INFOGRAPHICS** in each chapter and on the inside front and back covers<br>**TRY THIS** application activities throughout<br>**PUT YOUR HEADS TOGETHER** activities in each chapter<br>**YOUR SCIENTIFIC WORLD** interactive, problem-based learning activities for each chapter<br>**ACHIEVE RESOURCES**<br>**LEARNINGCURVE**<br>**INSTRUCTOR'S RESOURCE MANUAL** |
| **Goal 2: Scientific Inquiry and Critical Thinking**<br>AMERICAN PSYCHOLOGICAL ASSOCIATION LEARNING OUTCOMES | |
| **2.1** Use scientific reasoning to interpret psychological phenomena<br>**2.2** Demonstrate psychology information literacy | **2.3** Engage in innovative and integrative thinking and problem solving<br>**2.4** Interpret, design, and conduct basic psychological research<br>**2.5** Incorporate sociocultural factors in scientific inquiry |

## Alignment with APA Learning Guidelines 2.0 (Continued)

*Scientific American: Presenting Psychology,* **Third Edition, Learning Objectives/Substantive Content**

**CHAPTER 0:** Infographic 0.1: How to Read a Scientific Article; Infographic 0.2: Common Study Strategies: When Do They Work?; Infographic 0.3: You've Got the Power; *Think Critically:* Was It Written in the Stars?; Table 0.2: What Critical Thinkers Do; Table 0.3: 21st Century Skills; *Career Connections:* Psychology Is Going to Help You

**CHAPTER 1:** LO 5 through LO 10; *From the Pages of Scientific American:* Flooding the Senses; Infographic 1.1: The Scientific Method; Infographic 1.2: Critical Thinking; *Relationships:* Is Your Social Life Affecting Your Health?; Infographic 1.3: The Correlation Coefficient: What's in a Number?; Infographic 1.4: The Experimental Method: Are You in Control?; *Think Critically:* Nature and Nurture; *From the Pages of Scientific American:* The Psychological Toll of Rude E-Mails; Figure 1.4: Real-World Correlations; *Didn't See That Coming:* SpongeBob on the Brain; *Apply This:* Don't Believe Everything You Read; *Career Connections:* Communicating with the Public; *Didn't See That Coming:* Introducing Happiness

**CHAPTER 2:** LO 2 and 10; Infographic 2.1: Ways to Study the Living Brain; *From the Pages of Scientific American:* Heading Off Injury; *Think Critically:* Where's My Morning Antagonist?; *Relationships:* Your Romantic Brain; *Think Critically:* Tend and Befriend; *Apply This:* Table 2.3: Food for Thought?

**CHAPTER 3:** LO 6 and 11; *From the Pages of Scientific American:* A Pair of Crocks to Match the Dress; *Apply This:* How Powerful are Subliminal Influences?; *Across the World:* Colors and Culture; *Believe It . . . Or Not:* Sexy Smells?; Infographic 3.4: Gestalt Organizing Principles: The Whole Is Greater

**CHAPTER 4:** *Didn't See That Coming:* Are Screens Ruining Your Rhythm?; *Career Connections:* The Challenges of Shift Work; *Think Critically:* 6 Sleep Myths; *Think Critically:* America's Opioid Epidemic; Infographic 4.3: Marijuana in the United States; *From the Pages of Scientific American:* The Stigma of Addiction; *Social Media and Psychology:* Can't Get Enough; *Believe It . . . Or Not:* False Claims About Hypnosis

**CHAPTER 5:** LO 14; Infographic 5.1: Learning Through Classical Conditioning; *Didn't See That Coming:* Rescuing Animals with Classical Conditioning; Infographic 5.2: Learning Through Operant Conditioning; *Think Critically:* Chickens Can't Play Baseball; *Social Media and Psychology:* Tapping into the Brain's "Reward Circuitry"; *From the Pages of Scientific American:* Masks Reveal New Social Norms: What a Difference a Plague Makes; *Across the World:* Mind Your Manners; *Believe It . . . Or Not:* Do Kids Learn Aggression from Media?

**CHAPTER 6**: *Across the World:* Memory and Culture; *Didn't See That Coming:* Highly Superior Autobiographical Memory; *From the Pages of Scientific American:* Drunk Witnesses Remember a Surprising Amount; Infographic 6.1: Study Smarter: Methods of Improving Your Memory; Infographic 6.3: Chronic Traumatic Encephalopathy

**CHAPTER 7:** LO 11; Infographic 7.1: Concepts and Prototypes; Infographic 7.2: Problem Solving; *Social Media and Psychology:* Confirmation Bias and Fake News; Infographic 7.4: How Smart Are Intelligence Tests?; *From the Pages of Scientific American:* Ineffective Geniuses?; *Think Critically:* His and Her Brain Differences—Do They Matter?; Figure 7.8: Guilford's Alternate Uses Task

**CHAPTER 8:** Infographic 8.1: Research Methods in Developmental Psychology; *Think Critically:* What Is Epigenetics?; *Believe It . . . Or Not:* Is There a "30-Million-Word Gap"?; Infographic 8.3: Piaget's Theory of Cognitive Development; Infographic 8.4: Erikson's Eight Stages; *Social Media and Psychology:* Have Teens Gone Overboard?; *From the Pages of Scientific American:* A Simple Test Predicts What Kindergarteners Will Earn As Adults; Table 8.4: Kohlberg's Stages of Moral Development; *Apply This:* Can You Slow the Aging Process?; *Across the World:* Death in Different Cultures

**CHAPTER 9:** LO 2, 4, 5, 6, 10, 11, and 13; *Social Media and Psychology:* Trying to Meet Needs Online; *From the Pages of Scientific American:* Failing Successfully; Infographic 9.2: Theories of Emotion; *Relationships:* Can You Spot a Liar?; *Believe It . . . Or Not:* Just How Accurate Are Polygraph Tests?; *Across the World:* When to Reveal, When to Conceal; *Didn't See That Coming:* Going with the Flow; Infographic 9.3: The Anatomy of Fear; Infographic 9.4: Pathways to Happiness

**CHAPTER 10:** LO 11–14; *Believe It . . . Or Not:* How Birth Order May— Or May Not—Affect Your Personality; *Think Critically:* The Funny Thing About Personality; *From the Pages of Scientific American:* Killer Whales and Chimpanzees Have Similar Personalities; *Across the World:* Culture and Personality; *Relationships:* I Love You . . . When You Do What I Want; Infographic 10.1: Ego Defense Mechanisms; Infographic 10.2: The Social-Cognitive Perspective on Personality; Infographic 10.3: Examining the Unconscious: Projective Personality Tests; *Social Media and Psychology:* A Picture Is Worth a Thousand Words

**CHAPTER 11:** LO 4, 7, and 8; *Social Media and Psychology:* What's in a Selfie?; Infographic 11.2: Milgram's Shocking Obedience Study; *From the Pages of Scientific American:* Darker Skies, Darker Behaviors; Infographic 11.3: Thinking About Other People; *Believe It . . . Or Not:* The Stanford "Prison"; *Across the World:* Pandemic Responses and Culture; *Relationships:* Is "Love at First Sight" Really a Thing?

**CHAPTER 12:** LO 2 and 3; Infographic 12.1: Stressed Out; *Think Critically:* Does Poverty Change the Brain?; *Across the World:* The Stress of Starting Anew; Infographic 12.2: Physiological Responses to Stress; *From the Pages of Scientific American:* Why Do We Crave Sweets When We're Stressed?; Infographic 12.3: Health Psychology; Infographic 12.4: The Process of Coping; *Across the World:* What's Going On in the "Blue Zones"?

**CHAPTER 13:** LO 8; *Think Critically:* The Insanity Plea; *Believe It . . . Or Not:* A Label Can Change Everything; *Didn't See That Coming:* What Do Cats Have to Do with It?; *From the Pages of Scientific American:* Why Do People Kill Themselves?; *Believe It . . . Or Not:* Four Sisters with Schizophrenia

**CHAPTER 14:** LO 9 and 11; *Didn't See That Coming:* Virtual Reality Exposure Therapy; Infographic 14.2: Classical Conditioning in Behavior Therapy; *From the Pages of Scientific American:* Psychotherapy in a Flash; Figure 14.3: Biomedical Therapies; *Across the World:* Know Thy Client; *Didn't See That Coming:* Has Covid Changed Therapy Forever?

**APPENDIX A:** Introduction to Statistics

**DIVERSE CHARACTER** profiles integrated throughout each chapter

**CONNECTIONS** in Chapters 0–14

**CAREER CONNECTIONS** in Chapters 1–14 and Appendix A

**RESEARCH CONNECTIONS** in Chapters 1–14

**TRY THIS** application activities throughout

**PUT YOUR HEADS TOGETHER** activities in each chapter

**YOUR SCIENTIFIC WORLD** interactive, problem-based learning activities for each chapter

**ACHIEVE RESOURCES**

**LEARNINGCURVE**

**INSTRUCTOR'S RESOURCE MANUAL**

## Alignment with APA Learning Guidelines 2.0 (Continued)

### Goal 3: Ethical and Social Responsibility in a Diverse World
#### AMERICAN PSYCHOLOGICAL ASSOCIATION LEARNING OUTCOMES

| | |
|---|---|
| **3.1** Apply ethical standards to evaluate psychological science and practice | **3.2** Build and enhance interpersonal relationships<br>**3.3** Adopt values that build community at local, national, and global levels |

#### *Scientific American: Presenting Psychology,* **Third Edition, Learning Objectives/Substantive Content**

**CHAPTER 0:** Infographic 0.1: How to Read a Scientific Article; Table 0.2: What Critical Thinkers Do; Table 0.3: 21st Century Skills; *Think Critically:* Was It Written in the Stars?

**CHAPTER 1:** LO 10; *Think Critically:* Nature and Nurture; *Relationships:* Is Your Social Life Affecting Your Health?; *Didn't See That Coming:* Introducing Positive Psychology; *Apply This:* Don't Believe Everything You Read; *From the Pages of Scientific American:* The Psychological Toll of Rude E-Mails; Figure 1.4: Real-World Correlations; Infographic 1.2: Critical Thinking

**CHAPTER 2:** *From the Pages of Scientific American:* Heading Off Injury; *Relationships:* Your Romantic Brain; *Think Critically:* Tend and Befriend; *Social Media and Psychology:* A Magical Number 150?

**CHAPTER 3:** *Apply This:* How Powerful Are Subliminal Influences?; *Across the World:* Colors and Culture; *Relationships:* Know Someone with Chronic Pain?

**CHAPTER 4:** *Career Connections:* The Challenges of Shift Work; *Think Critically:* America's Opioid Epidemic; *Relationships:* See That Woman Holding a Beer?; *Social Media and Psychology:* Can't Get Enough; *From the Pages of Scientific American:* The Stigma of Addiction; *Believe It . . . Or Not:* False Claims About Hypnosis

**CHAPTER 5:** *Didn't See That Coming:* Rescuing Animals with Classical Conditioning; *Social Media and Psychology:* Tapping into the Brain's "Reward Circuitry"; *Career Connections:* Reinforcement Is Golden; *Across the World:* Mind Your Manners

**CHAPTER 6:** LO 10–12; *Relationships:* What's Love Got to Do with Working Memory?; *Across the World:* Memory and Culture

**CHAPTER 7:** LO 6; *Social Media and Psychology:* Confirmation Bias and Fake News; *From the Pages of Scientific American:* Ineffective Geniuses?; *Relationships:* Little Lies, Big Problems?; *Think Critically:* His and Her Brain Differences—Do They Matter?

**CHAPTER 8:** LO 14; *Believe It . . . Or Not:* Is There a "30-Million-Word Gap"?; *From the Pages of Scientific American:* A Simple Test Predicts What Kindergarteners Will Earn as Adults; *Across the World:* Death in Different Cultures

**CHAPTER 9:** *Relationships:* Can You Spot a Liar; *Across the World:* When to Reveal, When to Conceal; *Didn't See That Coming:* Going with the Flow; Infographic 9.1: Theories of Motivation; Infographic 9.4: Pathways to Happiness

**CHAPTER 10:** *Across the World:* Does Culture Influence Personality; *Relationships:* I Love You . . . When You Do What I Want; *Social Media and Psychology:* A Picture Is Worth a Thousand Words

**CHAPTER 11:** LO 5, 8, 11, and 12; *Social Media and Psychology:* What's in a Selfie?; Infographic 11.3: Thinking About Other People; *Think Critically:* Something Doesn't Feel Right; *From the Pages of Scientific American:* Darker Skies, Darker Behaviors; *Believe It . . . Or Not:* The Stanford "Prison"; *Across the World:* Pandemic Responses and Culture; *Relationships:* Is "Love at First Sight" Really a Thing?

**CHAPTER 12:** *Across the World:* The Stress of Starting Anew; *Across the World:* What's Going On in the "Blue Zones"?

**CHAPTER 13:** *Across the World:* A Cross-Cultural Look at Eating Disorders

**CHAPTER 14:** LO 9; *Across the World:* Know Thy Client; *Didn't See That Coming:* Has Covid Changed Therapy Forever?

**DIVERSE CHARACTER** profiles integrated throughout each chapter

**PUT YOUR HEADS TOGETHER** activities in each chapter

**TEST BANK QUESTIONS** both essay and multiple-choice questions connected to ethical and social responsibility

### Goal 4: Communication
#### AMERICAN PSYCHOLOGICAL ASSOCIATION LEARNING OUTCOMES

| | |
|---|---|
| **4.1** Demonstrate effective writing for different purposes | **4.2** Exhibit effective presentation skills for different purposes<br>**4.3** Interact effectively with others |

#### *Scientific American: Presenting Psychology,* **Third Edition, Learning Objectives/Substantive Content**

**CHAPTER 0:** Infographic 0.1: How to Read a Scientific Article; Infographic 0.2: Common Study Strategies: When Do They Work?; *Think Critically:* Was It Written in the Stars?

**CHAPTER 1:** Infographic 1.2: Critical Thinking; *From the Pages of Scientific American:* The Psychological Toll of Rude E-Mails; *Career Connections:* Communicating with the Public

**CHAPTER 4:** *Social Media and Psychology:* Can't Get Enough

**CHAPTER 7:** LO 7 and 8; Infographic 7.3: The Building Blocks of Language

**CHAPTER 8:** LO 7; *Social Media and Psychology:* Have Teens Gone Overboard?

**CHAPTER 9:** LO 13; *Social Media and Psychology:* Trying to Meet Needs Online; *Across the World:* When to Reveal, When to Conceal

**CHAPTER 10:** *Social Media and Psychology:* A Picture Is Worth a Thousand Words

**CHAPTER 11:** LO 3, 6, and 12; *Social Media and Psychology:* What's in a Selfie?; Infographic 11.1: Errors in Attribution; Infographic 11.3: Thinking About Other People

**CHAPTER 12:** Infographic 12:3: Health Psychology

**CHAPTER 14:** LO 8 and 9; *Across the World:* Know Thy Client; *Didn't See That Coming:* Has Covid Changed Therapy Forever?

**SHOW WHAT YOU KNOW** and **TEST PREP: ARE YOU READY?** assessment questions in each chapter

**PUT YOUR HEADS TOGETHER** activities in each chapter

**TEST BANK QUESTIONS** both essay and multiple-choice questions designed to assess communication skills

**YOUR SCIENTIFIC WORLD** interactive, problem-based learning activities for each chapter

**ACHIEVE RESOURCES**

**LEARNINGCURVE**

**INSTRUCTOR'S RESOURCE MANUAL**

## Alignment with APA Learning Guidelines 2.0 (Continued)

### Goal 5: Professional Development
#### AMERICAN PSYCHOLOGICAL ASSOCIATION LEARNING OUTCOMES

| | |
|---|---|
| **5.1** Apply psychological content and skills to career goals | **5.4** Enhance teamwork capacity |
| **5.2** Exhibit self-efficacy and self-regulation | **5.5** Develop meaningful professional direction for life after graduation |
| **5.3** Refine project-management skills | |

*Scientific American: Presenting Psychology,* Third Edition, Learning Objectives/Substantive Content

**CHAPTER 0:** LO 4; Infographic 0.1: How to Read a Scientific Article; *Career Connections:* Psychology Is Going to Help You; Table 0.2: What Critical Thinkers Do; Table 0.3: 21st Century Skills; Infographic 0.2: Common Study Strategies: When Do They Work?; Infographic 0.3: You've Got the Power

**CHAPTER 1:** LO 5; Infographic 1.2: Critical Thinking; *From the Pages of Scientific American:* The Psychological Toll of Rude E-Mails; *Career Connections:* Communicating with the Public

**CHAPTER 2:** *Think Critically:* Where's My Morning Antagonist?; *Think Critically:* Tend and Befriend; *Apply This:* Table 2.3: Food for Thought

**CHAPTER 3:** *Apply This:* Table 3.1: Protecting Your Senses; *Career Connections:* Is Art in Your Future?

**CHAPTER 4:** Table 4.1: Be Smart About Multitasking; *Didn't See That Coming:* Are Screens Ruining Your Rhythm?; *Career Connections:* The Challenges of Shift Work; *Think Critically:* 6 Sleep Myths; Table 4.4: How to Get a Good Night's Sleep

**CHAPTER 5:** *Social Media and Psychology:* Tapping into the Brain's "Reward Circuitry"; *Career Connections:* Reinforcement Is Golden; *Across the World:* Mind Your Manners

**CHAPTER 6:** *Social Media and Psychology:* Multitasking and Memory; Infographic 6.1: Study Smarter: Methods of Improving Your Memory; Table 6.1: Study Smart (and Often)

**CHAPTER 7:** LO 4, 5, and 6; *From the Pages of Scientific American:* Ineffective Geniuses?; Infographic 7.2: Problem Solving; *Social Media and Psychology:* Confirmation Bias and Fake News

**CHAPTER 8:** *Social Media and Psychology:* Have Teens Gone Overboard?; *From the Pages of Scientific American:* A Simple Test Predicts What Kindergarteners Will Earn as Adults

**CHAPTER 9:** LO 2 and 5; *Put Your Heads Together:* Trying to Meet Needs Online; *From the Pages of Scientific American:* Failing Successfully; *Didn't See That Coming:* Going with the Flow; Infographic 9.1: Theories of Motivation; Infographic 9.4: Pathways to Happiness

**CHAPTER 10:** Table 10.4: Are You a Self-Actualizer?; *Career Connections:* Personality Tests at Work

**CHAPTER 11:** LO 2, 6, 8, 10, and 12; *Across the World:* Pandemic Responses and Culture

**CHAPTER 12:** LO 7, 9, and 11; *Across the World:* The Stress of Starting Anew; Infographic 12.1: Stressed Out; Infographic 12.3: Health Psychology; Infographic 12.4: The Process of Coping

**CHAPTER 14:** LO 11 and 12; *Didn't See That Coming:* Virtual Reality Exposure Therapy; *Across the World:* Know Thy Client; *Didn't See That Coming:* Has Covid Changed Therapy Forever?

**APPENDIX B:** Careers in Psychology

**PUT YOUR HEADS TOGETHER** activities in each chapter

**TEST BANK QUESTIONS** both essay and multiple-choice questions assessing professional development skills

**ACHIEVE RESOURCES**

**LEARNINGCURVE**

**INSTRUCTOR'S RESOURCE MANUAL**

# Acknowledgments

More than a decade ago, the three authors came together to discuss the possibility of creating a bold new psychology textbook. We dreamed of creating an introductory text that would bring relevance and student engagement to a whole new level. We believe that dream has materialized, but it would not have been possible without the hard work and talent of reviewers, focus group attendees, students, interview subjects, contributors, and editors.

The early years were arduous, but we had many champions in our corner: a special thanks to Erik Gilg and the late Jim Strandberg. Catherine Woods, you have been with us from the beginning, and we are thankful for your ongoing support and oversight. Rachel Losh, you picked up this project and ran with it in all the right directions. Dan McDonough and Matt Wright, you provided much-needed support and enthusiasm during some difficult revisions.

Brad Rivenburgh and Glenn and Meg Turner of Burrston House, you came to this project just when we were in great need of your extensive publishing experience and vast fund of research knowledge. Although we are no longer working together, your legacy remains a potent force. The book continues to benefit from the extensive feedback you gathered through reviews and focus groups. Your unwavering support and love for this project continue to guide us, and it always will. We have said it a million times, and we will say it again: We never could have made this book without Burrston House. You have been our greatest champions, our trusted advisors, and our dear friends.

Executive Vice President, General Manager Charles Linsmeier, thank you for believing in this project and advocating for us. We appreciate your hard work behind the scenes. Program Director Shani Fisher, we are grateful to you for keeping the train moving even when it feels like it may run us over! Your oversight and direction do not go unnoticed. Senior Executive Program Manager Carolyn Merrill and Senior Development Editor Lukia Kliossis, you joined this team with fresh energy and open minds. Carolyn, thank you for being so responsive to our concerns; we appreciate your straightforward and efficient style. You know how to get things done! Lukia, it is wonderful to have you back on the project (you were with us in the very beginning), now playing such a critical role. We will remember the times you went out of your way to get things right (e.g., the stoplight photo comes to mind!). The book will be much stronger as a result of these efforts. Editorial Assistant Allison Curley, thank you for juggling many responsibilities associated with this project. We haven't had much direct contact (apart from the Zoom calls), but we understand that your role is essential, and we are grateful.

Anne DeMarinis, Dawn Albertson, and Matt McAdams, thank you for making the Infographics come to life so elegantly. Executive Permissions Editor Cecilia Varas, the photos keep getting better with every edition, thanks to your tireless efforts to track down images and secure permissions. We know that some of our requests require you to jump through hoops, but you are always willing to take on the challenge, and the results are outstanding. We are so lucky to have you on our team!

Producing a high-quality college textbook is a formidable task, but we had the best in the business: Senior Content Project Manager Martha Emry. We consider ourselves a perfectionist author team, yet there are details we have overlooked—and Martha, you caught them! You have a remarkable ability to see both the big picture and the minute elements. Director of Content Management Enhancement Tracey Kuehn, you made the transition from development to production more manageable—and perhaps more importantly, you kept us sane during that first production experience. Copy editor Deb Heimann, we are grateful to you for keeping the style consistent and answering our innumerable questions about copy issues. Sarah Wales-McGrath, you have done an excellent job keeping track of all the citations; your amazing attention to detail does not go unnoticed. Proofreader Daniel Nighting, thank you for carefully checking the page proofs and helping us identify typos and other problems as we prepared for publication. Chris Hunt, your work on the index continues to be exceptional. Director of Design Diana Blume, and Design Services Manager Natasha Wolfe, you have done a remarkable job presenting densely packed information in a clear and stimulating visual format. Thank you for taking the time to listen to our thoughts; this collaboration between the designers and the authors has made a huge difference, and we look forward to working together in the future. Cover designer Michael Di Biase, your artistry rivals no other. Our students are exposed to so much visual information, and you have produced a design that is both interesting and mnemonic.

To all the managers, designers, illustrators, editors, and other team members with whom we did not have direct contact, please know that we are thoroughly impressed with your work; we are grateful to have had you on our team. A huge thanks to Senior Workflow Project Supervisor Susan Wein, Senior Managing Editor Lisa Kinne, Art Manager Matt McAdams, and illustrators Todd Buck, Evelyn Pence, and Eli Ensor.

Peter Levin, John Philp, and Barbara Parks of Splash Studios, your videos give us goose bumps, and some of them move us to tears. Thank you for conveying the chapter stories in a way that is real, yet respectful of the interview subjects. No one could have done it better.

Noel Hohnstine, Laura Burden, Lauren Samuelson, and Stephanie Matamoros, you have provided essential support in the development and refinement of our supplements and online learning activities. We have been so impressed with your efficiency and dedication to our project. Scott Cohn, Program Assessment Lead, we have been looking for you for years, and finally you have joined our team! The outstanding work on the Test Bank by you, Laura Lauzen-Collins of Moraine Valley Community College, Vicki Ritts of St. Louis Community College–Meramec, and Kurt Nolin of Bittner Development Group speaks for itself. The four of you understand and appreciate our vision, and that is priceless. Charity Peak, your work on the Instructor's Resource Manual is critical; thank you for sharing your expertise.

Executive Marketing Manager Kate Nurre, all of our work would be futile if it weren't for you and your sales team ensuring that our book reaches students and instructors. We are grateful for all that you do.

We have benefited in countless ways from an exceptional group of academic reviewers. Some have been our greatest champions, and others our sharpest critics. We needed both. Thank you for the hundreds of hours you spent examining this text, writing thoughtful critiques, and offering bright ideas—many of which we have incorporated into the text. This is your book, too.

Michelle Bannoura, *Hudson Valley Community College*

Jeanmarie Bianchi, *Pima Community College*

Sherry Blakey, *Austin Community College–Northridge*

Stefanie Drew, *California State University–Northridge*

Michael Figuccio, *Farmingdale State College*

Ahni Fritton, *Lesley University*

Julie Hernandez, *Rock Valley College*

Nancy Honeycutt, *Almance Community College*

Becky Howell, *Forsyth Technical Community College*

Anika Hunter, *Prince George's Community College*

Amy Kausler, *Jefferson College*

Dana Kuehn, *Florida State College at Jacksonville–Deerwood*

Eric Mania, *Quinsigamond Community College*

Elizabeth Moseley, *Cleveland State Community College*

Darlene Mosley, *Pensacola State College*

Amie Muldong, *West Coast University–Orange County Campus*

Jodi Price, *University of Alabama in Huntsville*

Deninne Pritchett, *Central Piedmont Community College*

Sadhana Ray, *Delgado Community College*

Sabrina Rieder, *SUNY Rockland Community College*

Vicki Ritts, *St. Louis Community College–Meramec*

Ronald Salazar, *University of New Mexico, Valencia*

JoAnne Shayne, *Southern New Hampshire University*

Madhura Sohani, *Bellevue College*

Cari Stevenson, *Kankakee Community College*

Anita Tam, *Clemson University*

Margot Underwood, *Joliet Junior College*

Shawn Ward, *Le Moyne College*

Larolyn Zylicz, *Cape Fear Community College*

There is one "unofficial" reviewer whose contributions cannot be quantified. Working behind the scenes from start to finish, reading every line of this text alongside us was Dr. Eve Van Rennes. Dr. Van Rennes, thank you for your intelligent critiques and unwavering support—you have been our trusted advisor for more than 10 years now.

It goes without saying that this project would not have been possible without the hard work and dedication of our author team. Every sentence in this textbook has been a group effort: We have written and reviewed everything together. Our minds work differently and we have distinct skill sets, but we recognize and appreciate those in each other. Writing this book was a grueling task (who knew three women could live on just a few hours of sleep every night?), but we have encouraged and supported each other along the way. We are more than a work team—we are lifelong friends. We should also acknowledge that none of us would have written these words if it hadn't been for our parents and grandparents, who made our education their top priority.

Last, but certainly not least, we would like to thank the extraordinary people whose life stories are woven throughout these chapters. We selected you because your stories touched and inspired us. Learning about your lives has helped us become more thoughtful and compassionate people. We believe you will have the same effect on college students across the country.

Deborah M. Licht
Misty G. Hull
Coco Ballantyne

# Contents

## Chapter 0      0-1

## Are You Ready for This?

## Chapter 1      1

## Introduction to the Science of Psychology

## Chapter 2      41

## Biology and Behavior

| Chapter 6 | 208 |
| --- | --- |

# Memory

| Chapter 7 | 249 |
| --- | --- |

# Cognition, Language, and Intelligence

| Chapter 8 | 287 |
| --- | --- |

# Human Development

## Chapter 9     334

# Motivation and Emotion

## Chapter 10     375

# Personality

## Chapter 11     412

# Social Psychology

| Chapter 12 | 452 |

# Stress and Health

| Chapter 13 | 484 |

# Psychological Disorders

| Chapter 14 | 526 |

# Treatment of Psychological Disorders

## Check Your Answers

All of your hard work will soon pay off.

Image Source/Getty Images.

# Are You Ready for This?

## Welcome to Psychology

**TRAPPED IN A FLOODED CAVE, A GROUP OF YOUNG SOCCER PLAYERS FACED DEATH . . . and how their remarkable story relates directly to this course**  June 23, 2018: The Wild Boars soccer team of Northern Thailand had just finished their Saturday practice. The monsoon season was about to begin, but the prospect of heavy rain didn't deter the boys and their coach from an afternoon adventure. Twelve players, ranging in age from 11 to 16, hopped on their bicycles and headed for Thailand's longest cave, Tham Luang Nang Non. Their coach, 25-year-old Ekkapol Chantawong ("Coach Ek"), had brought them to the legendary cave on previous occasions. Exploring its 6-mile-long system of tunnels was somewhat of a rite of passage for those joining the team (BBC, 2018; Gutman & Winsor, 2018; Watcharasakwet et al., 2018).

Led by Coach Ek, the boys entered the cave carrying flashlights, water, and snacks. They intended to stay for just an hour, but on the way out, they encountered the unexpected; part of the passageway had filled with water. Coach Ek dove in and assessed the situation: The tunnel was totally flooded. Most of the boys could not swim, so continuing toward the exit was not an option. They tried digging drainage tunnels to offset the deluge, but water was pouring into the cave too fast, the result of rainfall outside. As the water level climbed, the group moved deeper into the cave and found an elevated resting spot. Sitting in the darkness, bellies empty, the boys

### Adventure Gone Wrong

On June 23, 2018, the Wild Boars soccer team (right) became trapped in Thailand's longest cave, Tham Luang Nang Non. Family members came looking for the boys and found their bikes abandoned outside the cave (left).

felt frightened. They missed their parents, and some of them cried (Watcharasakwet et al., 2018). Outside, rain threatened to flood the cave even further.

## How Is It Relevant?

At this point, you may be wondering how the story of a stranded soccer team relates to the study of psychology. Like any human story, the Thai cave ordeal has *everything* to do with psychology. In fact, many of its themes relate directly to content in the coming chapters. You could study the boys' experience from a *stress and health* perspective (look in Chapter 12), exploring how being trapped in the cave impacted their health and well-being, or how their behaviors were *motivated* by a variety of needs (see Chapter 9). You might examine how the boys' *personalities* impacted their behaviors (Chapter 10), or take the *social psychology* perspective by investigating relationships and group dynamics (Chapter 11). *Memory* is another angle, as traumatic memories may increase the risk of developing a *psychological disorder,* which could lead to the need for *treatment* (Chapters 6, 13, and 14). To study any of these phenomena, you would need to understand the research methods described in Chapter 1. As you continue through Chapters 1–14, you will see how psychology is relevant to all human stories, including your own.

You may want to know why this book begins with a Chapter 0. Before learning about psychological concepts and research, you must have a basic understanding of what psychology is, and how it relates to real life. Chapter 0 was created to lay this groundwork for you. More specifically, it aims to accomplish the following:

1. address misconceptions about psychology, including the belief that psychology is largely based on common sense
2. establish an understanding that psychology is a research-driven science
3. convey the importance of critical thinking
4. convey psychology's high level of relevance to your academic and career success, and life in general

Now it's time to get working on these goals. We'll begin by introducing you to the discipline and its practitioners.

## This Is the Field, and These Are the Players

**What Is an LO?**
Throughout this book, you will find callouts like this one. LO stands for Learning Objective, which is a statement pointing to essential content you should understand and be able to apply.

**LO 1**    Define psychology.

*Psychology* is the scientific study of behavior and mental processes. Yelling, crying, and trembling are observable behaviors the soccer players might have displayed when they realized they were trapped in the cave. The boys' mental processes included thoughts (*Are my parents coming to look for me? Will I survive this ordeal?*)

and emotions (fear, sadness, anxiety). All these phenomena are potential research topics in psychology.

*Psychologists* are scientists who work in a variety of fields, each of which centers on the study of behavior and underlying mental processes. People often associate psychology with therapy, and many psychologists do provide therapy. These *counseling psychologists* and *clinical psychologists* might also research the causes and treatments of psychological disorders (see Chapters 13 and 14). But clinical practice is just one slice of the gigantic psychology pie. (In the Careers in Psychology appendix, you can learn more about the variety of careers in the mental health field.) There are psychologists who spend their days in the lab studying interactions between people, and those who assess the performance of children learning in schools and online. Others may be found poring over brain scans in major medical centers, studying crimes and their perpetrators, or analyzing how humans interact with products and technology. Psychologists play a key role during crises, studying human responses and offering evidence-based tips for managing stress. When the coronavirus pandemic gathered momentum in early 2020, psychologists began exploring crucial questions: Why do people share false information on social media, and what can be done to reduce this behavior (Pennycook et al., 2020)? What leads some people to embrace social distancing while others reject it (Palmer, 2020)? In addition to researching questions like these, mental health professionals offered advice about working from home, coping with upsetting news, and fighting disease stigma (APA, 2020, March 25; Greenbaum, 2020; Weir, 2020), and thousands provided free counseling through hotlines (Rahhal, 2020).

In the United States, psychology has two major professional organizations devoted to advancing the field and sharing the benefits of psychological knowledge. The American Psychological Association (APA) has over 50 divisions representing various subdisciplines and areas of interest (APA, n.d.-d). The Association for Psychological Science (APS), another major professional organization, publishes a list of over 100 different societies, organizations, and agencies with some connection to the field (APS, n.d.-a). These organizations are affiliated with many groups that represent ethnic minority cultures, such as the Association of Black Psychologists, the National Latinx Psychological Association, and the Society of Indian Psychologists.

Psychology is a broad scientific discipline that includes various perspectives and subfields (**FIGURE 0.1**). In fact, many of these subfields correspond to chapters in

**What Is This?**

In every chapter, you will find reference information like this. These research citations tell you the source of research or findings being discussed—in this case, an article published by Gordon Pennycook and colleagues in 2020. If you want to know more about a topic, you can look in the alphabetized reference list at the end of the textbook. There you will find the full citation of the original article or book you want to read: In this case, you would search for Pennycook, McPhetres, Zhang, Lu, & Rand (2020) on page R-51. Failing to cite the proper source of information is considered plagiarism—a serious academic offense. There are many systems and formats for citing sources, but this textbook uses the APA style established by the American Psychological Association (APA, 2020). See **INFOGRAPHIC 0.1** "How to Read a Scientific Article" on the next page; learning how to read academic articles will help you in many classes, including psychology.

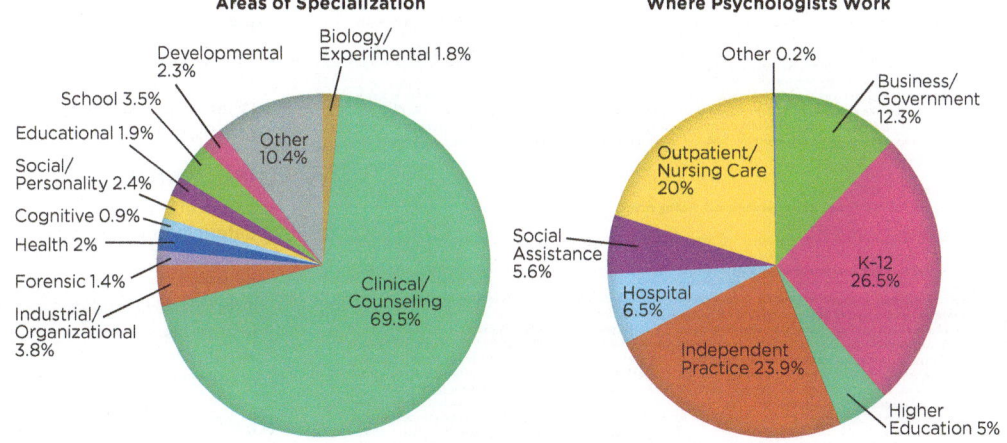

**Areas of Specialization**

- Developmental 2.3%
- Biology/Experimental 1.8%
- School 3.5%
- Educational 1.9%
- Social/Personality 2.4%
- Cognitive 0.9%
- Health 2%
- Forensic 1.4%
- Industrial/Organizational 3.8%
- Other 10.4%
- Clinical/Counseling 69.5%

**Where Psychologists Work**

- Other 0.2%
- Business/Government 12.3%
- Outpatient/Nursing Care 20%
- Social Assistance 5.6%
- Hospital 6.5%
- Independent Practice 23.9%
- K-12 26.5%
- Higher Education 5%

## FIGURE 0.1
### Fields of Psychology

These pie charts show the primary place of work for psychologists with master's and doctoral degrees working in 2016, and the areas of specialty for members of the American Psychological Association in 2017. (Note that this data excludes "not specified" responses.) As you can see, psychologists work in diverse contexts and specialize in many subfields. You can read about this multitude of career options in the Careers in Psychology appendix. In the photo on the right, sport psychologist Rebecca Symes talks with Stuart Meaker, who plays for the Surrey County Cricket Club in the United Kingdom. Data from: APA Center for Workforce Studies, 2017; Bureau of Labor Statistics, 2018.

Nigel French—EMPICS/Getty Images.

# How to Read a Scientific Article

Psychologists publish their research findings in peer-reviewed, scientific journals. Scientific journal articles are different from news articles or blog posts you would find through a typical internet search. When you read news articles or blog posts about scientific research, you can't assume these sources accurately interpret the study's findings or appropriately emphasize what the study's original authors think is important. For a full description of the background, methodology, results, and application of a study's findings, you must read a scientific article. (*Note:* The "article" below is fictitious and solely created for pedagogical purposes.)

## How Do I Find a Scientific Article?

You can find scientific journal articles through online journal databases such as PsycINFO, available through your school library. Search results can provide references that follow a standard format, such as APA style, shown here:

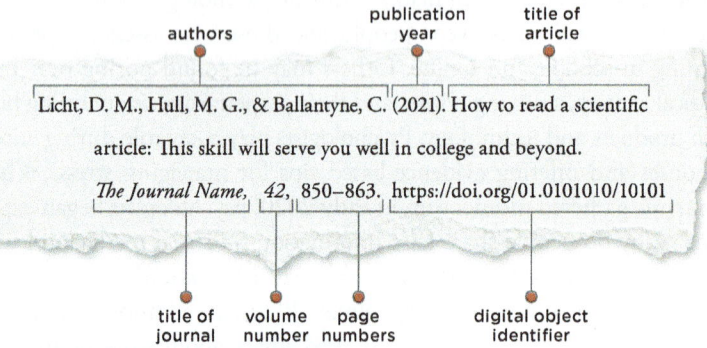

Licht, D. M., Hull, M. G., & Ballantyne, C. (2021). How to read a scientific article: This skill will serve you well in college and beyond. *The Journal Name, 42,* 850–863. https://doi.org/01.0101010/10101

- authors
- publication year
- title of article
- title of journal
- volume number
- page numbers
- digital object identifier

## What's in a Scientific Article?

At first glance, scientific articles can seem overwhelming. It helps to know what you will find in a typical article. Scientific articles follow a specific organizational style and include the following elements:

**TITLE**

**AUTHORS**

**ABSTRACT**
- ✔ Brief description of entire article.
- ✔ Helps you quickly decide if the article describes research you are interested in.

**KEYWORDS**
- ✔ Identify themes or topics in article.
- ✔ Can be used to search for similar articles.

**INTRODUCTION**
- ✔ Explains topic of study, relevant previous research, and specific goals and hypotheses.

*Other elements not shown here:*

**METHOD**
- ✔ Describes how study was conducted.
- ✔ Provides details about participants, materials, and procedures, allowing the study to be replicated.

**RESULTS**
- ✔ Describes data collected and outcome of study.
- ✔ Often includes tables, graphs, or figures.

**DISCUSSION**
- ✔ Interprets results to determine support or lack of support for the research hypotheses.
- ✔ Often reports study's limitations, contributions, and implications for future research.

**REFERENCES**
- ✔ Listing of all articles cited.
- ✔ A *great* place to look for additional research articles!

Credits: Ripped paper, robynmac/thinkstock/Getty images; White rip paper with clip, iStockphoto/thinkstock.

To learn more about using APA Style (APA, 2020), please visit the APA Style blog (APA, n.d.-b): https://apastyle.apa.org/blog.

this book. For example, Chapter 1 examines the methods psychologists use to conduct research, and Chapter 2 focuses on biological psychology, exploring the physiological underpinnings of behavior. As you familiarize yourself with these subfields, you will begin to see how knowledge of psychology is useful to everyone, regardless of their profession (Vespia, 2019).

## CAREER CONNECTIONS

### PSYCHOLOGY IS GOING TO HELP YOU

Planning to pursue a career in nursing or medicine? You should know the difference between EEG, MRI, PET, and CAT technologies, along with other concepts related to biology and behavior, covered in Chapter 2. Perhaps you have an artistic bent and are leaning toward graphic design, architecture, or animation. If so, you need to be familiar with the depth perception cues introduced in Chapter 3 (Liao et al., 2018; Vishwanath, 2020). Do you love animals and dream of training service dogs or protecting endangered species? The operant and classical conditioning principles described in Chapter 5 will help you succeed (Dollion et al., 2019; Frederick, 2019). If you're planning to work in law or law enforcement, take a careful look at Chapter 6; you will discover why eyewitness testimonies and confessions by criminal suspects are sometimes inaccurate (Kassin, 2017a; Smalarz et al., 2020). Planning to teach schoolchildren or work with older people in retirement communities? Then you must understand the social, emotional, and cognitive changes occurring throughout the human life span (Chapter 8). If marketing and sales is more your style, you can learn about the "foot-in-the-door" or "door-in the-face" routes to persuasion in Chapter 11. We could go on and on, but you get the idea: Concepts learned in this course can have immediate relevance to virtually any profession.

**COLD, HUNGRY, AND WAITING**    As the 12 boys and their coach shivered on a ledge more than 2 miles into the cave, their families began to wonder why they hadn't come home. Some parents went searching and discovered bicycles, backpacks, and soccer cleats left at the cave's entrance (BBC, 2018). Officials launched a search-and-rescue effort, while relatives held a vigil and set up camp at the site (Paddock & Jirenuwat, 2018).

Meanwhile, inside the cave, 11-year-old "Titan" cried for his parents. Coach Ek took the young player into his arms and told him he needed to stay strong (CBS News, 2018). He also helped Titan and the other boys stay relaxed through meditation, a skill he had learned while living at a Buddhist monastery for much of his life (Watcharasakwet et al., 2018).

## Isn't Psychology Just Common Sense?

You may be wondering how meditation could help a group of young soccer players stranded in a cave. Isn't meditation for adults? And how could you sit cross-legged in such a cramped environment? Both of these assumptions—that meditation is for adults and that it must be carried out in a special pose—are flawed. Children can benefit from this practice, and one can meditate in various positions, including lying down (de Bruin et al., 2020; Shanok et al., 2020; Vollbehr et al., 2020). When it comes to meditation, or any human behavior, misconceptions abound.

**LET'S BUST SOME MYTHS**    Have you ever been told that dyslexia is caused by seeing letters backward? Or that sugar makes kids inattentive? Research suggests these types of mistaken beliefs are relatively common (Ferguson, 2015b; Im et al., 2018;

Macdonald et al., 2017; Stanovich, 2019). Before taking psychology, students believe about 50% of the psychological myths they have heard; for example, "you only use 10% of your brain" (we essentially use all of it); "humans have five senses" (we have more than five senses); and "suicides are especially likely during the Christmas holidays" (the rate of suicide reaches a low point in the month of December; Furnham & Hughes, 2014, pp. 258–259; Hofstra et al., 2018). Through careful research, psychologists have determined that many prevalent assumptions about behaviors are simply not true. Discover some of these popular misconceptions in **TABLE 0.1.** Have you fallen for any of them?

In addition to clinging to misconceptions, many students assume that psychology is simply "common sense," or a collection of knowledge that any reasonably smart person can pick up through everyday experiences. The problem is that common sense and "popular wisdom" are not always correct (Lilienfeld, 2012). For example, common sense might suggest that bystanders are more inclined to help a person in distress when others are nearby; the more people present, the more likely someone will offer aid. But research on the "bystander effect" has repeatedly shown that the opposite can occur—bystanders are less likely to offer aid when many people are around (with some exceptions, which we will explore in Chapter 11 on social psychology; Hortensius & de Gelder, 2018).

**TABLE 0.1    10 Common Misconceptions**

| Misconception | Let's Look at Some Evidence |
|---|---|
| Social media is bad for teenagers' mental health. | The effects differ from person to person and depend on the type of social media use, but large studies suggest the overall impact is small (Denworth, 2019). |
| Kids with autism aren't really interested in socializing. | Children with autism spectrum disorder (ASD) often want friends, have friends, and value their friendships (Clark & Adams, 2020; Denworth, 2020). |
| We all have different learning styles. | Although we have different skills and areas of interest, little evidence suggests that people possess specific learning styles. Actually, many of us learn well when we see information presented in a variety of forms, rather than just one (May, 2018; Nancekivell et al., 2020). |
| Most older people live sad and solitary lives. | People actually become happier with age (Dzau et al., 2019; Lilienfeld et al., 2010). |
| American children get plenty of sleep. | The majority of kids in the United States do not get enough sleep, putting them at increased risk for obesity and psychological problems (Williamson et al., 2020). |
| Posttraumatic stress disorder (PTSD) only affects veterans. | Although PTSD is more common in veterans (especially female veterans), anyone exposed to trauma can potentially develop PTSD (Lehavot et al., 2018). |
| Punishment is a great way to change behavior in the long term. | Punishment can lead to unwanted results (see Chapter 5). Myths like this can have lasting impact on perceptions of discipline (Furnham & Hughes, 2014). |
| Eating "comfort foods" makes you feel happier. | So-called comfort foods are not unique in their mood-enhancing effects; it appears that a wide variety of foods can improve our mood (Finch et al., 2019; Wagner et al., 2014). |
| Listening to Mozart and other classical music will make an infant smarter. | There is no solid evidence that infants who listen to Mozart are smarter than those who do not (Hirsh-Pasek et al., 2003). |
| Children are "colorblind." They don't see race. | By preschool, children are already displaying racial bias, meaning race-related "stereotypes, prejudices, and discriminatory behaviors," both outside and inside their awareness (Qian et al., 2017, p. 845). |

Here are a few examples of misconceptions that have been debunked by psychological research.

**LO 2** Describe the hindsight bias and how it leads to misconceptions about psychology.

**HINDSIGHT BIAS** The impression that psychological findings are obvious might be related to the *hindsight bias,* or the "I knew it all along" feeling (see Chapter 7). When a student learns about the results of a psychology study, they may believe they knew it all along because it seems logical in retrospect. But could they have predicted the outcome beforehand? Not necessarily. We fall prey to the hindsight bias in part because we are constantly seeking to explain events. Once something occurs (for example, we hear about the findings of a study), we come up with a way to explain it, and then everything seems to make sense (Lilienfeld, 2012). If you like sports, you may fall prey to the hindsight bias when you "Monday morning quarterback," that is, point out how players and coaches could have avoided mistakes in a game you watched. Sure, you may come up with solutions that never occurred to the coaches and players, but unlike you, they did not have the luxury of thinking about it after the fact! In other words, they did not have hindsight.

**ANECDOTAL EVIDENCE** Students sometimes insist that life has already taught them all they need to know about psychology. Learning from experience is a critical ability that helps us survive and adapt, but it cannot take the place of scientific findings. Suppose you're talking with friends about the health effects of smoking. You say smoking causes lung cancer, but your friend disagrees, saying "My 95-year-old uncle has smoked two packs of cigarettes a day for most of his life, and he never developed lung disease." This type of *anecdotal evidence,* or personal observation, is valuable, but it is not the same as studying cigarette smoking and lung disease like an objective scientist. As you learn more about the human mind, you will see that it is quite prone to errors (see Chapters 6 and 7).

## It's a Science

Unlike common sense, which often is based on individual experiences, psychology is a science in the true sense of the word. *Science* is a systematic approach to gathering knowledge through careful observation and experimentation. It requires analyzing data and sharing results in a manner that permits others to duplicate and therefore verify work. Just like chemistry, biology, and all scientific disciplines, psychology is grounded in research using the scientific method. Did you know that many colleges categorize psychology as a part of their STEM (science, technology, engineering, and math) programs? As you read through this textbook, you will encounter examples of how psychology employs many of the essential components of science, including the peer-review process, evidence with citations, replication of research, and the use of theories, hypotheses, and statistical analyses. (Be on the lookout for a feature called *Research Connections,* which emphasizes some of the most important elements of psychological science.)

Now that we have established what psychology is and isn't, why not get a sense of your knowledge coming into the course? How much do you really know about the science of psychology?

Bill O'Leary/The Washington Post via Getty Images.

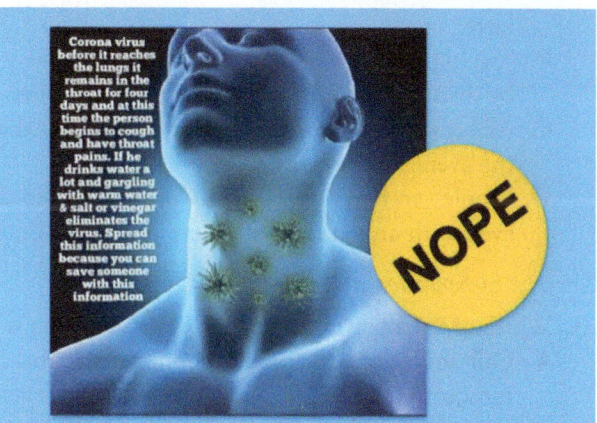

**Can You Spot Fake News?**
Some U.S. high schools are offering classes on "fighting fake news" (top; Contrera, 2017). Despite such efforts, researchers have found that teens still have trouble evaluating the credibility of information they see online (Breakstone et al., 2019). Why do people fall for social media rumors, like the one pictured above suggesting that gargling salt water or vinegar gets rid of the novel coronavirus (SARS-CoV-2)? A cognitive error called *confirmation bias* may be contributing to the problem: People tend to look for evidence that upholds their beliefs and overlook information that contradicts it. If the story reaffirms something we already think is true, we may fall prey to this confirmation bias (Chapter 7).

# Didn't See That Coming

## WHAT DO YOU KNOW?

Many students are surprised to discover how often their commonsense knowledge is at odds with scientific findings. See how much you know by taking the quiz below, and then checking your answers on the next page:

Chapter 1: *Introduction to the Science of Psychology*

1. Who is considered the "father" of psychology?
   A. Sigmund Freud       C. Wilhelm Wundt
   B. William James        D. Edward Titchener

Chapter 2: *Biology and Behavior*

2. Which of the following statements about the brain is FALSE?
   A. People are born with all the brain cells they will ever have.
   B. "Seeing stars" after a blow to the head is likely caused by disruption of activity in the occipital lobes.
   C. Albert Einstein's brain weighed the same as that of the average person.
   D. People can function normally in their day-to-day lives even with an entire hemisphere of their brain missing.

Chapter 3: *Sensation and Perception*

3. Which of the following statements about sensation is FALSE?
   A. Our ability to detect faint stimuli (the sound of a mosquito buzzing, for example) is partly dependent on our psychological state.
   B. The human eye has a blind spot.
   C. Advertisers can get people to buy products by using subliminal messages.
   D. Male testosterone levels are affected by the smell of female armpit secretions.

Chapter 4: *Consciousness*

4. Which of the following statements about sleep is TRUE?
   A. Drinking alcohol helps you get better sleep.
   B. The blue light emitted by smartphones and tablets interferes with the activity of the sleep hormone melatonin.
   C. Yawning indicates that someone is exhausted.
   D. Everyone needs 8 hours of sleep each night.

Chapter 5: *Learning*

5. Research suggests that childhood exposure to media violence is associated with later aggressive behaviors. This is an example of a:
   A. cause-and-effect relationship.
   B. prosocial relationship.
   C. correlation.
   D. conditioned emotional response.

Chapter 6: *Memory*

6. Which of the following statements about memory is FALSE?
   A. Adults can "remember" events that never happened after viewing doctored photos that portray the fake events.
   B. Memories are located in a specified area of the brain.
   C. Researchers study sea slugs to learn about the neural changes underlying memory formation.
   D. Memories are not always reliable records of past events.

Chapter 7: *Cognition, Language, and Intelligence*

7. When comparing the cognitive abilities of males and females, researchers have found that:
   A. girls tend to be better than boys at mental rotation tasks.
   B. boys tend to perform better than girls on tests of verbal ability.
   C. men and women differ significantly in their cognitive abilities.
   D. men and women are far more alike than different in their cognitive abilities.

Chapter 8: *Human Development*

8. Which of the following statements about human development is FALSE?
   A. There are times in fetal development when the brain is producing approximately 250,000 new neurons per minute.
   B. Happiness generally decreases with age, and negative emotions are more frequent in the elderly.
   C. By the age of 6, most children have a vocabulary that represents learning about one new word every 2 hours awake.
   D. Poor attachment during infancy can have long-term health consequences, influencing the development of illnesses like asthma and diabetes.

Chapter 9: *Motivation and Emotion*

9. Which of the following statements about happiness is NOT true?
   A. Paying for services that save you time, such as grocery delivery, has no effect on happiness.
   B. The simple act of smiling can make a person feel happier.
   C. Being completely absorbed in challenging tasks can promote happiness.
   D. Recording positive thoughts and feelings of gratefulness can increase happiness.

Chapter 10: *Personality*

**10.** Which of the following statements about birth order is TRUE?
   **A.** Firstborn children are conscientious and high achieving, and become leaders in the workforce.
   **B.** Youngest children are coddled by their parents, but tend to be rebellious as they grow up.
   **C.** Middle children get lost in the family shuffle, so they learn to be self-sufficient.
   **D.** Researchers have been unable to find any consistent connections between birth order and specific personality characteristics.

Chapter 11: *Social Psychology*

**11.** Social psychology research suggests all the following EXCEPT:
   **A.** People working in groups are more likely to slack off when individual contributions are hard to ascertain.
   **B.** People are more likely to comply with a request when given a reason—even if the reason doesn't make sense.
   **C.** Attractive people are generally perceived as being more intelligent.
   **D.** Women and men show similar degrees of physical aggression.

Chapter 12: *Stress and Health*

**12.** Which of the following is NOT a characteristic of people living in areas with the highest number of centenarians?
   **A.** strong social support
   **B.** alcohol abstinence
   **C.** eating a diet that is mainly plant-based
   **D.** eating until one feels 80% full

Chapter 13: *Psychological Disorders*

**13.** Insanity is a legal determination of the degree to which people are responsible for their criminal behaviors. Those deemed legally insane are thought to have little or no control over their behaviors at the time they committed their crimes. In what percentage of U.S. criminal cases is the insanity defense used?
   **A.** 1%          **C.** 10%
   **B.** 5%          **D.** 15%

Chapter 14: *Treatment of Psychological Disorders*

**14.** Which of the following statements about psychological treatment is TRUE?
   **A.** Only medical doctors can prescribe medications for people with psychological disorders.
   **B.** Neurosurgery is no longer used as a treatment for psychological disorders.
   **C.** Some antidepressants increase the risk of suicidal thoughts and behaviors among a small number of teenagers.
   **D.** Self-help groups such as Alcoholics Anonymous are typically run by licensed psychologists. ⊕

ANSWERS: 1. C; 2. A; 3. C; 4. B; 5. C; 6. B; 7. D; 8. B; 9. A; 10. D; 11. D; 12. B; 13. A; 14. C

# This Is Critical

How did you do? If you are like most students entering the class, you did not pass with flying colors, and that is 100% okay! The point of introductory psychology is for students to learn core concepts and develop psychological literacy, or "the ethical application of psychological skills and knowledge" (Murdoch, 2016, p. 189)—an important goal, according to the American Psychological Association (APA, 2013a, 2016). A student who has achieved psychological literacy can responsibly apply the lessons learned in psychology to everyday life. Suppose someone tells you the following: "People with mental illness are dangerous and prone to committing violent crimes." If you have a high degree of psychological literacy, you will not automatically accept this as truth, but draw on your psychology knowledge and thoughtfully assess the claim: *Actually, the research suggests that only a small percentage of crimes are clearly attributable to symptoms of psychological disorders; in fact, there is evidence that people who struggle with mental illness are more likely to be victims of violence than perpetrators of violence* (Bhavsar et al., 2019; Desmarais et al., 2014; Skeem et al., 2016). Psychological literacy is not just about tapping into acquired knowledge; it also hinges on *critical thinking*.

**"Birds of a Feather?"**
Do opposites really attract, as the saying goes? Put on your critical thinking cap, and you may begin to question this piece of commonsense "wisdom." Psychological research suggests that similarity is a better predictor of romantic attraction, as we are drawn to those who share our interests, viewpoints, and values. Age, education, occupation, and even personality tend to be similar among those who are close (Brooks & Neville, 2017; Lott & Lott, 1965; Youyou et al., 2017).

Peathegee Inc/Getty Images.

# Are You a Critical Thinker?

**LO3**  Describe critical thinking and evaluate its relationship to pseudopsychology.

*Critical thinking* involves weighing pieces of evidence, and considering the source and quality of information before accepting it as valid. But it goes far beyond verifying the facts (Davies, 2015; Yanchar et al., 2008). The process also entails synthesizing evidence (bringing it together), thinking beyond definitions, focusing on underlying concepts and applications, and being open-minded and skeptical at the same time. Like any scientific discipline, psychology is driven by critical thinking—disciplined thinking that is clear, rational, and always open to the consideration of new ideas. Infographic 1.2 on page 17 shows how critical thinking is useful for tackling problems, even ones that may at first seem unrelated to psychology.

Critical thinking is an invaluable skill, whether you are a psychologist planning an experiment, a citizen preparing to vote in an election, or a student trying to earn a good grade in psychology class. Has anyone ever told you that choosing "C" on a multiple-choice question is your best bet when you don't know the answer? Or that taking notes on your computer during class (as opposed to writing them on paper) is an effective way to learn material? According to research, these are not necessarily winning strategies (Morehead et al., 2019; Mueller & Oppenheimer, 2014; Skinner, 2009). Accepting academic advice without thinking critically can be a barrier to developing effective learning approaches (more about this soon). So next time you're offered a tempting bit of folk wisdom, think before you bite: Is there solid scientific evidence to back it up? **TABLE 0.2** explains how a critical thinker would evaluate a commonsense claim.

## Put Your Heads Together

 In your group, **A)** discuss folk wisdom that you learned as a child. **B)** Pick a claim and evaluate it using the critical-thinking model presented in Table 0.2 as a guide.

**TABLE 0.2**  What Critical Thinkers Do

| Is it true that "opposites attract"? In other words, are people really drawn to romantic partners different from themselves? To evaluate this claim with critical thinking, you must do the following: | |
|---|---|
| Be skeptical. | Why should I believe this? Is there any supporting evidence? |
| Think deeply. | What is meant by "opposites"? Are we referring to people with dissimilar personalities, interests, ethnic backgrounds, educational levels, socioeconomic status? |
| Draw on existing knowledge. | My psychology professor recently lectured on interpersonal attraction. What did I learn from that presentation? |
| Ask questions. | What factors are most important in determining whom we find attractive? Can these factors change as we age? |
| Consider alternative explanations. | Maybe the opposite is true: People are attracted to those who are similar. Do "birds of a feather flock together"? |
| Reflect on your own emotional reactions. | I am attracted to people who are different from me. But my personal experience does not constitute scientific evidence. |
| Tolerate uncertainty. | The rules of attraction may not be universal, and they could fluctuate over a person's lifetime. |
| Keep an open mind. | The idea that "opposites attract" is generally not supported by scientific research; however, it may be true for certain traits or certain people. |

The American Psychological Association (APA) views critical thinking as an essential skill for all undergraduate psychology majors. To achieve the APA's goal of Scientific Inquiry and Critical Thinking, students must be able to think critically about psychological claims, determine whether a source is objective (free of bias) and credible, and distinguish between real science and *pseudoscience* (APA, 2013a, 2016). To understand the meaning of pseudoscience, let's revisit the story unfolding in Northern Thailand.

**10 DAYS LATER**  Deep inside the Tham Luang Nang Non cave, British divers Rick Stanton and John Volanthen scaled rocks and swam through dark, fast-moving water in search of the Wild Boars soccer team. "I said from the outset, if anybody is going to find these kids, it will be these two divers, who are arguably the best in the world," remarked a spokesperson for the British Caving Association (Adam, 2018, para. 8). After a 6-hour journey through the cave's serpentine tunnels and crevices, Stanton and Volanthen came upon the soccer team (Paddock et al., 2018). The men captured the remarkable moment on camera. In their video, the boys are clustered together on a ledge, looking gaunt and weak after 10 days with no food. "Thank you," one of them can be heard saying, his voice cracking. A few more "thank you's" emerge from the darkness, and the divers ask how many are in the group. "Thirteen," one of the boys offers up (Thai NavySEAL, 2018). It was a miracle: Everyone was alive and well.

**Discovered Alive**
On July 2, 2018, divers from Great Britain found the soccer team sitting on a ledge deep within the cave. The boys asked how long they had been trapped and when they could get out. "You have been here 10 days. You are very strong," said one of the cave divers (Thai NavySEAL, 2018, July 2, 0:54). They promised help was on the way. "Many people are coming" (0:32).

## Think Critically

### WAS IT WRITTEN IN THE STARS?

How do you explain this extraordinary situation? To make sense of events, many people turn to the mystical explanations of astrology (Stierwalt, 2020). Using a chart of the heavens called a horoscope, astrologists "predict" everything from romantic relationships to the weather. If we look at a Cancer horoscope for the day the soccer team was discovered, for example, we come across this statement: "Unexpected meetings take place this evening" (Gat, 2018). Cancer is the zodiac sign for four of the trapped boys (Ellentube, 2018), so does this mean their encounter with the cave divers was written in the stars? We seriously doubt it.

**PSEUDOSCIENCE VERSUS TRUE SCIENCE**

In your everyday life, you will encounter many examples of belief systems that present themselves as "psychological science" but lack scientific backing. As you will learn in Chapter 1, the scientific method involves systematic measurement, manipulation, and observation of variables. It also involves a lot of critical thinking. Belief systems that falsely claim to be science fall into the category of *pseudoscience*. For example, *pseudopsychology* is an approach to explaining and predicting behavior and events that appears to be psychology but is not supported by scientific evidence. Surprisingly, many people have difficulty distinguishing between pseudosciences like astrology and true sciences like astronomy and psychology, even after earning a college degree (Impey et al., 2012; Schmaltz & Lilienfeld, 2014).

How then does astrology often seem to be accurate in its descriptions and predictions? Consider this excerpt from a monthly Aquarius horoscope: "The more you can accept responsibility for circumstances—past, present, and future—the more you can be empowered to rise to the occasion" ("Monthly Aquarius Horoscope," 2020). When you think about it, this statement could apply to just about any human being on the planet. We can all benefit from taking greater responsibility for what's going

Image Source/Getty Images.

**Bogus Fortune?**
What do you think about the message delivered in this fortune cookie? Because the statement is sufficiently vague and complimentary, it could apply to just about any person on the planet—and therefore, many people fall for it. We call this phenomenon the *Barnum effect*.

on in our lives. How could you possibly prove such a statement wrong? You couldn't. This is one of the many reasons astrology is not science. A telltale feature of a pseudopsychology, like any pseudoscience, is its tendency to make assertions so broad and vague that they cannot be refuted (Stanovich, 2019). Astrology, numerology, tarot readings, and other forms of pseudopsychology do not rest on a solid foundation of critical thinking. 

You have now learned that psychology is neither common sense nor pseudoscience, but a true science driven by critical thinking. We will soon explore how psychology can help you achieve your education and career goals. But first, let's discover the fate of the Thai soccer team. Did the boys ever make it out of the cave, and how did the ordeal impact their psychological health?

# Why Psychology Is Important

**A RISKY PLAN**   Once the soccer team had been located, a small group of Thai Navy SEALs came to their underground refuge and began to provide medical assistance (Paddock & Ives, 2018). After 10 days of consuming nothing but water

LILLIAN SUWANRUMPHA/Getty Images.

**Heroic Effort**
Rescuers work outside the Tham Luang Nang Non cave on July 8, 2018, about two weeks after the soccer team became trapped inside. By this point, over 10,000 people were involved in the rescue effort, helping with everything from transportation to supplying hot soup and coffee to rescuers (Mahtani & Wutwanich, 2018).

trickling down the cave walls, the boys were now eating (Bacon, 2018). Most of them could not swim, yet their escape would require passing through tunnels filled with water as dark as "black coffee," and navigating spaces so narrow that only a single body could squeeze through. It was a dangerous proposition, even for the world's most experienced cave divers. One rescuer had already died while stocking the cave with air tanks, most likely the result of hypothermia or insufficient oxygen levels (Beech et al., 2018; Paddock et al., 2018; Sutton, 2018).

Ultimately, officials decided the safest approach was to pull the boys out, one by one, on stretchers. They would be given facemasks to deliver oxygen and anti-anxiety drugs to keep them from panicking (Beech et al., 2018). The operation began on July 8 and was led by elite cave divers from six different countries (Mahtani & Wutwanich, 2018). On July 10, Thai Navy SEALs posted the following message on Facebook: "We are not sure if this is a miracle, a science, or what. All the thirteen Wild Boars are now out of the cave" (Thai NavySEAL, n.d.).

The soccer players and their coach were immediately transported to a hospital. It was clear they would recover physically, but there were many questions about their psychological health (Wongcha-um & Pearson, 2018). Would the trauma of being trapped in the cave haunt the boys once they had resumed a normal life, causing nightmares, anxiety, or perhaps even posttraumatic stress disorder (PTSD)? In Chapter 13, you will learn about the symptoms of PTSD and the types of traumas that can trigger this disorder. Would the boys prove to be resilient and bounce back from the ordeal (Keating, 2018)? Chapter 12 explores how people experience stress in different ways. How would being stuck in a dark cave impact the boys' circadian rhythms and sleeping patterns (Howard, 2018)? You can learn about that in Chapter 4. The questions go on and on, and many answers may be found in the chapters to come.

## What's in It for You?

The story of the Wild Boars soccer team, and all the stories in this book, illustrate the most important lesson we hope to impart in the chapters ahead: Psychology matters to all of us. It matters to a Thai soccer team trapped underground, a world-famous dog expert, a young man with narcolepsy, a blind triathlete, an ER nurse caring for people with COVID-19, and the warden of America's biggest single-site jail.

**TABLE 0.3   21st-Century Skills**

| 21st-Century Skill | What It Means | How to Develop It |
|---|---|---|
| Higher education | In order to support a family or enjoy a middle-class existence, you may need an education beyond high school—a minimum of college or technical training. | Well done! You have already taken care of this by choosing to attend college. |
| Basic competencies | You still need to master the basics of traditional education—math, science, language, and the arts. Even in today's culture of text messaging and emojis, students still need to know how to correspond in a professional manner—for example, writing an e-mail without grammar and punctuation errors. | To assist you in achieving this mastery, the key resources are your instructors and the assigned texts, plus all the resources your college has available for you (library, tutoring, social aspects, etc.). |
| Application of knowledge | Memorizing and repeating information is not enough. You must be able to retain and apply the knowledge to real-world scenarios. | Your instructor will be essential in this regard, helping you see how psychology relates to real life. To complement your instructor's efforts, each chapter features several Put Your Heads Together exercises prompting you and your classmates to apply material and generate ideas in small groups. |
| Critical thinking | Your ability to succeed hinges on certain competencies, among them "the ability to think critically about information, solve novel problems" and "communicate and collaborate" (Jerald, 2009, p. 23). | Your instructor will provide many opportunities for critical thinking. The text reinforces this effort with the following features: Think Critically, Put Your Heads Together, and Try This. |
| Understanding the context | The ideal way to learn competencies like critical thinking is by integrating them into the larger curriculum; for effective learning, you need context. | Throughout the course, your instructor will point out conceptual relationships among different content areas. The *Connections* appearing in the margins do the same, highlighting relationships between topics presented in different chapters. *Connections* illuminate some of the "big picture" themes in psychology. |

To thrive in today's world, you need what educational experts refer to as "21st-century skills." The five skills listed here, summarized from Jerald (2009), will help you thrive in an increasingly "complex, competitive, knowledge-based, information-age, technology-driven economy and society" (Hidden Curriculum, 2015, para. 3). Taking an introductory psychology course will help you cultivate these essential skills.

(This is just a sampling of the real-life stories woven into the chapters of this book.) Most importantly, psychology matters to you, a college student trying to thrive in the 21st century (TABLE **0.3**). What you learn in the upcoming chapters can help you become a more successful student, professional, friend, partner, parent, brother, or sister—a better citizen of the world. Now let's take a minute and zero in on that first category: How can knowledge of psychology empower you as a student?

**LO 4** Explain how psychological research findings can help you achieve your academic goals.

**CAN PSYCHOLOGY HELP YOU BECOME A BETTER STUDENT** Psychological research has taught us quite a lot about learning, helping to identify which study strategies are most effective. Consider, for example, the idea that testing enhances learning (often referred to as the "testing effect"). Research shows that we remember material better *after* we have been tested on it (Batsell et al., 2017; Yang et al., 2020). Ideally, tests should be given often. Students generally perform better in a course, and specifically on the final exam, when given ample opportunities to check for understanding and practice retrieving information (Foss & Pirozzolo, 2017; Welch, 2019). For this reason, we recommend you test yourself with the end-of-section Show What You Know and end-of-chapter Test Prep questions. Answers can be found at the back of the book in the Check Your Answers section. For more examples of how psychological research directs us toward effective study tools, see INFOGRAPHICS **0.2** and **0.3** on the next pages. (You may notice the Apply This! designation on these Infographics. When you see this label here and elsewhere in the book, it means the material may be useful in your everyday life.)

# Common Study Strategies: When Do They Work?

Some of us highlight; others make elaborate outlines or reread sections of text we find difficult. We all have our favorite study methods, but are we using them to our advantage? Summarized below are four of the most popular strategies among students and evidence-based guidelines on how to use them effectively (Miyatsu et al., 2018).

## REREADING

### Effective when you . . .

- have a comprehensive exam in a couple of days; if this is the case, make sure you space out your reading sessions.
- have a test coming up very soon; here, it's less important to space out the first and second readings.
- are prepping for a test that involves a lot of memorization.
- quiz yourself between the first and second readings.

### Ineffective when you . . .

- are cramming for a comprehensive exam.
- are studying for a test that asks you to make inferences and integrate knowledge.

## HIGHLIGHTING (OR UNDERLINING)

### Effective when you . . .

- highlight/underline important information and main ideas.
- mark up the text during your *second* read-through.
- think carefully about what should be marked.

### Ineffective when you . . .

- mark up the text during your first read-through.
- assume that reviewing your mark-up will lead to high performance on an exam.

## NOTE-TAKING

### Effective when you . . .

- review your notes.
- use this approach to retain material you have read in the text or heard in a lecture.
- take notes by hand.
- summarize, paraphrase, and outline as opposed to simply recording everything verbatim.

### Ineffective when you . . .

- type notes on a computer, as you are more likely to copy word-for-word rather than use your own words.
- have no opportunity to review the notes.

## OUTLINING

### Effective when you . . .

- fill in an incomplete, or "skeletal," outline during class.
- use an outline created by your instructor, especially if it is before you have read the material.
- organize your outline by identifying the key points of the reading.
- use your outline to test yourself; for example, looking at each main heading and trying to recall the supporting information.

### Ineffective when you . . .

- have not received any instruction on how to outline successfully; if you are uncertain about your outlining skills, ask your instructor for guidance.

# You've Got the Power

Looking at the page to the left should give you a sense of which study strategies work (and which don't). Now it's time to devise a course of action. Psychologists recommend that you take stock of all available resources and then map out a study plan (Chen et al., 2017). It's one thing to know what resources are available, but it is just as important to decide how and when you will use them.

## What's Your Plan?

To succeed in college, you must identify a set of valuable study strategies. Which of the following tools will help you learn the material and prepare for exams? Check all that apply:

☐ Attend classes.  ☐ Read assigned material before class. ← *Record questions to bring to class.*

☐ Ask questions in class and actively participate in learning activities.  ☐ Review the syllabus regularly.

☐ Plan ahead for assignments. ← *e.g., create a schedule for your study plan, use instructor-provided templates*

☐ Take notes on key points discussed in class.  ☐ Write summaries of major sections.

☐ Complete **Show What You Know** questions.  ☐ Discuss material with other students. ← *e.g., in-class activities, study groups*

☐ Use chapter learning objectives to test your understanding.  ☐ Do the **Try This** exercises on your own.

☐ Read the **Connections** to review how the new material relates to previous material.

☐ Meet with instructor.  ☐ Use resources provided by instructor. ← *e.g., PowerPoints, LaunchPad, LearningCurve, study guides*

☐ Use internet resources to complement material. ← *e.g., APA Style guides, instructor-recommended websites*

☐ Complete **Test Prep** questions.  ☐ Review **Infographics.**

☐ Review lecture notes.  ☐ Make a concept map.

☐ Use college-wide resources. ← *e.g., reference librarians, tutoring centers*

☐ Take breaks.  ☐ Get enough sleep.  ☐ Eat a balanced diet.

## Planning Pays Off

Introductory statistics students were asked to think about which resources they would find useful and how they would employ them prior to exam time. The blue bars in the graph represent students who did not complete the exercise (control group), while the red bars represent those who did (experimental group). Throughout the semester, students in the experimental group reflected more on their learning; they reported using resources more successfully; and their course grades were higher by about 3.5–4.5%, or one third of a letter grade (Chen et al., 2017).

Graph data from Chen, P., Chavez, O., Ong, D. C., & Gunderson, B. (2017). Strategic resource use for learning: A self-administered intervention that guides self-reflection on effective resource use enhances academic performance. *Psychological Science, 28,* 774–785.

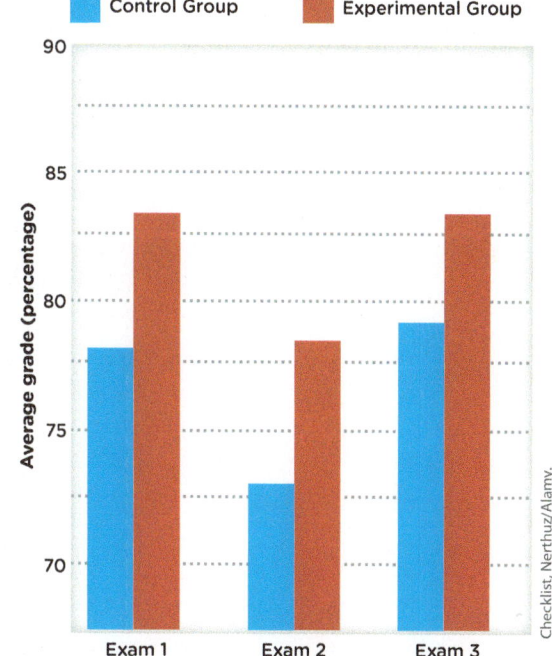

Control Group ■ Experimental Group ■

Average grade (percentage)

Exam 1   Exam 2   Exam 3

Research also suggests that students learn and remember material better when they see how it applies to personal experience, world events, and cultural phenomena (Hartwell & Kaplan, 2018; Kember et al., 2008; Roberson, 2013). For example, you might be more interested in learning about depression if you could see how it relates to a familiar everyday activity, like using social media (Ellis et al., 2020; Forchuk et al., 2020). Does frequent use of Instagram, TikTok, and Facebook increase the risk of suffering from depression? Psychology research is likely to provide some answers, or at least clues about whether a relationship exists, and you might pay more attention to the findings if you saw how they could apply to your life.

Another insight from psychological research is that active-learning exercises in the classroom increase students' understanding and retention of material (Deslauriers et al., 2019; Parril, 2020). The Put Your Heads Together features appearing in every chapter prompt you to apply material and generate new ideas in small groups. (Note, these activities will only be fully useful if you have read the material beforehand.) You can also take advantage of the Try This exercises scattered throughout the chapters, which ask you to apply key concepts by performing simple activities. These are typically fast, easy to do, and designed to reinforce chapter content.

## Put Your Heads Together

 Working in groups, **A)** identify resources in your textbook, class, and college that will help you learn and be successful. **B)** List the resources you plan to use. **C)** Discuss how you would create a chart to keep track of assignment due dates, plan your work schedule, and monitor your progress in the course.

**HOW CAN WE HELP YOU?**    It goes without saying, keep up with your assigned reading; your experience in class will be richer and more rewarding. As you make your way through each chapter, pay attention to the learning objectives (LOs), which serve as benchmarks for gauging your understanding of each section. You can also use learning objectives to pace yourself as a reader. In other words, read from one learning objective to the next, instead of trying to read the entire chapter in one sitting. For added reinforcement, we have tied the learning objectives to the end-of-chapter Summary and Show What You Know and Test Prep questions. Beginning in Chapter 1, you will see **Connections** features strategically placed in the margins. These brief summaries complement what many instructors do in the classroom—point out relationships between topics presented in the current chapter and those presented in earlier chapters. Every chapter also features an Online Video Profile to provide a more personal connection with the people featured in the chapter stories. Both components of the video profile, "In Their Own Words" and "You Asked, They Answered," are available online in your Achieve course.

**What Is a CONNECTION?**

*Connections* point out conceptual links between chapters. For example, while reading Chapter 1, you will see several Connections in the margins explaining how the current discussion relates to concepts introduced in Chapter 0. Further into the book, you will come across Connections linking back to more and more chapters.

## Getting Your Bang for the Buck

**LO 5**  Describe how an understanding of psychology can foster career success.

More than a million students enroll in introductory psychology courses every year (Franz, 2020; Gurung et al., 2016). Some will pursue psychology careers, but most will explore other academic disciplines or technical fields. Whatever path you choose, we guarantee that the material presented in this class will have some relevance (Hard et al., 2019). Throughout the book, we have included Career Connections, which point out how psychology relates to various career areas. We also encourage the development of skills required to succeed in a competitive, technology-driven world (Jerald, 2009; Strawser & McCormick, 2017). If you are skeptical about the utility of these skills, consider this study: Pollsters asked over 1,300 recruiters from more than 600 companies what qualifications they seek in college grads. They found strategic thinking, creative problem solving, leadership, and communication to be among the most desired skills across various careers (Levy & Rodkin, 2015). Whether you are interested in nursing, business, art, computer science, or agriculture, keep reading . . . this book is designed to help you.

We are almost ready to take off on our larger psychology adventure through Chapters 1–14, but first let's find out what happened to the Thai soccer team.

John Peters/Getty Images.

**Global Celebrities**
The Wild Boars pose with Gary Pallister, who used to play for Manchester United, one of the best soccer teams in Europe. Following their dramatic rescue, the boys were thrust into the international spotlight, attending events and making media appearances in various countries (Carlson, 2018). What kind of long-term psychological effects— both positive and negative—might the boys experience as a result of their ordeal?

**STRONGER TOGETHER**    After release from the hospital, the 12 boys and their coach were reported to be doing well, both mentally and physically. At a press conference, the hospital director indicated that they had been cleared to go home and were no longer "showing signs of mental trauma" (CBS/AP, 2018, para. 33). We can't be sure how the experience will impact the group in the long term, but their ability to survive the initial ordeal with such grace and dignity is remarkable. Why were there no reports of mental breakdowns, angry outbursts, or conflicts inside the cave? Perhaps it has something to do with the meditation the boys used. Evidence suggests that mindfulness meditation and similar techniques could potentially ease anxiety and depression, though the methodology of some meditation studies has been criticized (Dossett et al., 2020; Van Dam et al., 2018; Wielgosz et al., 2019). Maybe the boys were able to hold it together because they shared a strong sense of friendship and camaraderie. The team was described as a "tight-knit group" (Vejpongsa & Peck, 2018, para 12). Indeed, research suggests that the support of friends can help adolescents be more resilient (van Harmelen et al., 2017). A study of teenagers who survived a different type of trauma (an earthquake) provides some evidence of a link between social support and positive changes occurring after a trauma; that is, teens with greater social support still seemed able to "focus on the positive" following a harrowing event (Zhou et al., 2017, p. 6). This idea of human resiliency will resurface in the upcoming chapters, through the stories of people who have persevered and flourished in the face of great challenges.

## Here We Go

With this introduction, you should have a general sense of what psychology is (and isn't), why the discipline matters to all of us, and how to get the most out of this course. Are you ready to begin your journey through *Scientific American: Presenting Psychology?* Open your mind, and it could be a life-changing ride. Let's do this!

# 1

Dustin Franz/Barcroft USA via Getty Images.

# Introduction to the Science of Psychology

## What Is Psychology and How Did It Begin?

**PARALLEL LIVES**   December 15, 2012: It was a cold and rainy day in London, England. Twenty-five-year-old Anaïs (Ahn-a-YEES) Bordier was in a fabric shop, browsing materials for her upcoming fashion show. Born and raised in the suburbs of Paris, France, Anaïs had come to London to study fashion design at the prestigious arts and design college Central Saint Martins.

"Bzzzt, bzzzt!" Thoughts of design portfolios and fabric swatches were suddenly interrupted by Anaïs' cell phone. One of her friends had posted an image on her Facebook wall. Anaïs caught a glimpse of the post, which appeared to be a photo of her own face, but she couldn't figure out where it came from because the internet connection was slow. "[For] 30–35 minutes, I couldn't look at what was happening on my phone, and I could see people commenting on it," Anaïs recalls. "It was driving me crazy."

Left: *Twinsters* (2015). Small Package Films. Right: Anais Bordier.

**"I Was Like Whaaaa???"**

The original wall post by Anaïs' friend shows her American look-alike in a YouTube video (left). For comparison, see the profile photo of Anaïs to the right.

When Anaïs finally got home, she made a beeline for her laptop. The Facebook post generating so much buzz was a screen grab from a YouTube video—a close-up of a young woman looking over her shoulder and smiling coyly. She looked EXACTLY like Anaïs. Heart racing, Anaïs clicked on the video link, which led to a short comedy piece called "High School Virgin" produced by an American actor popularly known as KevJumba. The young woman in the video was a mirror image of Anaïs, and with the exception of her American accent, she sounded identical, too.

Anaïs felt her blood pressure drop. Could this American be a long-lost identical twin? Impossible. According to Anaïs' birth records, she was a single baby born to an unwed mother in Busan, South Korea, and adopted by a French couple, Jacques and Patricia Bordier. If the American look-alike wasn't a twin, perhaps she could be a cousin, a younger sister, a half-sister?

A couple of months (and many internet searches) later, Anaïs and her friends discovered the mystery woman in another online video: the trailer for a major Hollywood production called *21 & Over*. Anaïs immediately searched the online list of cast members, spotted her look-alike, and clicked on her profile. The young woman's name was Samantha Futerman, and she was born on November 19, 1987 . . . the same date as Anaïs.

## This Is Psychology

On a superficial level, the young actress Samantha Futerman appeared to be Anaïs' identical twin. Her facial features, voice, and physique were virtually the same. Of course, there is much more to a person than a physical body. Anaïs wondered if her look-alike shared similar attitudes, preferences, and behaviors. Did Samantha Futerman have the same offbeat sense of humor and explosive, rolling laugh? Did she surround herself with the same type of smart and creative friends, and was she a

*Note:* The story of Anaïs Bordier and Samantha Futerman is based on personal communications with them, as well as the book they coauthored with Lisa Pulitzer, *Separated@Birth*, and the documentary film *Twinsters*. Unless otherwise specified, quotations attributed to Anaïs Bordier, Samantha Futerman, and Dr. Nancy L. Segal are personal communications.

glutton for fried chicken and afternoon naps? When it came to Samantha's psychological characteristics—those related to her behavior and mental processes—Anaïs was totally in the dark.

## LO1  Describe the scope of psychology.

By now, you probably realize that psychology has something to do with how people think and act, but let's establish a more precise definition: **Psychology** is the scientific study of behavior and mental processes. Gasping, smiling, and laughing are observable behaviors Anaïs might have displayed when she first saw Samantha on YouTube. Anaïs' mental processes included thoughts (*Where was Samantha born? Was she adopted as well?*) and emotions (apprehension or excitement about discovering a long-lost twin). Underlying these behaviors and mental processes are biological activities, such as increased heart rate, changes in hormone secretion, and communication among neurons in the brain. All of these phenomena—behavior, mental processes, and the attendant biological processes—are potential research topics in psychology.

Psychology is a broad field that includes many perspectives and subfields. As mentioned in Chapter 0, the American Psychological Association (APA) has over 50 divisions representing various subdisciplines and areas of interest (APA, n.d.-d), and the Association for Psychological Science (APS) recognizes over 100 different societies, organizations, and agencies with some affiliation to the field of psychology (APS, n.d.-b). Each chapter in this textbook covers a broad subtopic representing one of psychology's primary subfields.

As scientists, **psychologists** can conduct two major types of research, *basic* and *applied*. Basic research, which often occurs in university laboratories, focuses on collecting data to support (or refute) theories. The goal of basic research is not to find solutions to specific problems, but rather to gather knowledge for the sake of knowledge. General explorations of human memory, sensory abilities, and responses to trauma are examples of basic research. Applied research, on the other hand, focuses on changing behaviors and outcomes, and often leads to real-world applications, such as specific behavioral interventions for children with autism spectrum disorder, or innovative keyboard layouts that improve typing performance. Applied research may incorporate findings from basic research, but it is often conducted in natural settings outside the laboratory.

## What's Our Aim?

The answer to this question varies according to subfield, but there are four main goals: to describe, explain, predict, and change behavior. These goals lay the foundation for the scientific approach and the research designs used to carry out experiments in psychology. Let's take a closer look at each one.

## LO2  Summarize the goals of psychology.

**DESCRIBE**  The first goal is to describe what we observe. Before we can understand behaviors or situations, we need to systematically examine them. Observation can be the starting point for a new research program, and sometimes it is the only way to explore a rare occurrence. Imagine you are a psychologist who wants to describe how mindfulness meditation might be used to reduce anxiety among school children. Once you have identified a group of students that are beginning a new meditation program at their school, you might assess and describe the students' academic performance, social adjustment, anxiety levels,

**psychology** The scientific study of behavior and mental processes.

**psychologists** Scientists who study behavior and mental processes.

and physical health. Then, after the meditation program is under way, you could monitor the participants over time, conducting assessments at various stages. Your goal would be to collect information in a systematic, unbiased way, and to create a snapshot of the phenomenon.

**EXPLAIN**    Another goal of psychology is to organize and make sense of research findings. Suppose you find that students report lower anxiety after the mindfulness meditation program is implemented; this observation may prompt you to explore other factors that could influence anxiety levels. Searching the scientific literature for clues, you might come across studies suggesting that a combination of yoga and meditation can reduce symptoms of anxiety through an increase in coping skills (Bazzano et al., 2018). If you determine that the reductions in anxiety are associated with improved coping skills, this could help explain why the students are feeling less anxious. However, you still would have to conduct a controlled experiment to determine whether meditation causes these effects (more on the experimental method later in the chapter).

**"Let's Meditate, Class"**
Children meditate with their teacher. Could this activity improve their mental health? A small, preliminary study of sixth graders found that students who practiced mindfulness meditation in school "reported greater improvement in emotional wellbeing" than those who did not engage in meditation. Female students seemed to benefit more than male students (Kang et al., 2018, p. 163).

**PREDICT**    If an explanation is valid, it can be used to predict behaviors or outcomes, another important goal of psychology. Suppose you determine that the decrease in anxious behaviors results from improved coping skills learned through mindfulness meditation. Then you could predict that meditation might lead to the same outcome among students at other schools, and perhaps in other groups of people as well (patients dealing with chronic pain, for instance). Indeed, researchers report that mindfulness meditation can help patients struggling with pain to direct their focus to "quiet the mind" and create calmness (Darnall, 2019).

**CHANGE**    An additional goal of psychology is to change or control behavior. This refers to how we can apply the findings of psychological research to direct behaviors in a beneficial way. In this example, you could use the findings to help schools implement meditation in their curricula (Semple et al., 2017).

**CONNECTION ESTABLISHED**    February 21, 2013: Samantha Futerman was in Los Angeles getting ready for the red-carpet premiere of *21 & Over*. A Twitter notification appeared on her phone: "Hey Sam, my friend Anaïs sent you a message on FB, check it out ☺ (it might be in the spam box)" (Bordier et al., 2014, p. 17). Sam did not recognize the sender of this message, nor did she know anyone named Anaïs. She opened Facebook and found a friend request from Anaïs Bordier, a 25-year-old woman living in London whose face appeared to be an exact duplicate of her own. A knot tightening in her stomach, Sam accepted Anaïs' friend request and opened up her message:

> Hey, my name is Anaïs, I am French and live in London. About 2 months ago, my friend was watching one of your videos with KevJumba on YouTube, and he saw you and thought we looked really similar . . . like VERY REALLY SIMILAR. . . . I checked more of your videos (which are hilarious) and then came upon the "how it feels to be adopted" . . . and discovered you were adopted too. (Bordier et al., 2014, p. 13)

### Love at First Skype

Six days after making contact on Facebook, Sam (left) and Anaïs had their first face-to-face conversation on Skype. They began at about 12:30 a.m. Paris time and continued until almost 4:00 a.m. "Speaking to Anaïs on Skype was unreal. I mean we had to be twins," Sam recalls in the book she coauthored with Anaïs, *Separated@ Birth* (Bordier et al., 2014, p. 102). "There was no reason to be scared anymore," Anaïs writes. "Even though I didn't have absolute proof, I had found my sister" (p. 100).

*Twinsters* (2015). Small Package Films.

Sam stared at her phone, mystified. Anaïs Bordier, a complete stranger living halfway around the world, had begun to dismantle her life story with a single Facebook message. According to Sam's papers, she was a single baby born to a mother in Busan, South Korea, and adopted a few months later by Judd and Jackie Futerman of New Jersey.

Scouring Anaïs' Facebook photos, Sam discovered more parallels: Anaïs had freckles on her nose (uncommon among Koreans); she wore the same kind of goofy animal costumes for Halloween; and comments from friends hinted that she had some of the same personality quirks. The physical resemblance was breathtaking. "I thought she could be my reflection in a mirror," Sam recalls. "It was beyond comprehension" (Bordier et al., 2014, p. 32).

It would take three months for Sam and Anaïs to finally meet in person, but thanks to Facebook, Skype, and WhatsApp, they would already be extremely close. Communicating daily, Sam and Anaïs began to uncover a mountain of shared characteristics—more evidence that they were twins.

## Think Critically

### NATURE AND NURTURE

Let's suppose Sam and Anaïs are indeed identical twins. This means that their genes (the units of heredity passed from parents to children) were identical at conception, making them virtually equivalent in their **nature** (Abdellaoui et al., 2015; McRae et al., 2015). But growing up in separate households means they have experienced distinct sets of environmental forces, making them different in their **nurture.** Any similarities observed between the two women are likely influenced by their common nature, whereas differences are presumably linked to their unique upbringing and life experiences, or nurture. Studying identical and fraternal twins (those raised together and those raised apart) helps psychologists learn how nature and nurture interact to produce a variety of characteristics, from personality traits to brain function (Polderman et al., 2015; Segal, 2017). For example, researchers have found that identical twins—even those raised apart—tend to be very close on measures of personality (Bouchard et al., 1990; Segal, 2012). This suggests that genes (nature) can play a major role in shaping

**TWIN RESEARCH MATTERS TO ALL OF US.**

**nature** The inherited biological factors that shape behaviors, personality, and other characteristics.

**nurture** The environmental factors that shape behaviors, personality, and other characteristics.

personality traits, an idea supported by genetic research (van der Linden et al., 2018; Vukasović & Bratko, 2015).

Twin research is not just important to twins; it has implications for parents and children all over the world. Consider autism spectrum disorder, a neurodevelopmental disorder characterized by differences in social communication and interactions. Research suggests that autism has a strong genetic component, though environment plays a role (Chapter 13; Yoon et al., 2020). Suppose one identical twin develops autism spectrum disorder but the other twin does not. That means some factor(s) in the environment (perhaps even those present during embryonic and fetal development) could have triggered the development of the disorder (de Zeeuw et al., 2017). If we can identify the triggers, which may be numerous and complex, then we can benefit from that knowledge (Segal, 1999). Studies of identical twins and fraternal twins (who, like non-twin siblings, share approximately 50% of their genes) have helped psychologists untangle the roles of nature and nurture in a variety of areas, including intelligence (Chapter 7), sexual orientation (Chapter 9), aspects of personality (Chapter 10), and psychological disorders (Chapter 13). 🦜

Courtesy Fred Nighout, Duke University, North Carolina, USA.

**Same Species, Really?**
Would you believe that these two butterflies belong to the same species? The wing markings and color differ because they were born in different seasons and therefore exposed to distinct environmental pressures (Hey, 2009). A testament to the power of nurture.

## What Are Psychology's Roots?

You have now learned some key lessons about psychology—areas of inquiry, goals of research, and the ever-important roles of nature and nurture. Soon, you will explore the basics of psychological research: how psychologists use a scientific approach, the many types of studies they conduct, and the ethical standards that guide them through the process. But first, let's take a trip back in time and meet the people whose philosophies, insights, and research findings molded psychology into the vibrant science it is today. Who planted the seeds of psychology?

**LO 3** Identify some of the people who laid the foundation for psychology, or helped establish it as a discipline; specify their contributions.

**ANCIENT AND MEDIEVAL SCHOLARS** The origins of psychology lie in fields as diverse as philosophy and physiology. In ancient Greece, the great philosopher Plato (427–347 BCE) believed that truth and knowledge exist in the soul before birth; that is, humans are born with some degree of innate knowledge. Plato raised an important issue that psychologists still contemplate: the contribution of *nature* in the human capacity for thinking.

One of Plato's renowned students, Aristotle (384–322 BCE), went on to challenge his mentor's basic teachings. Aristotle believed that we know reality through our perceptions, and we learn through our sensory experiences. This approach is now commonly referred to as *empiricism,* and it is how scientists acquire knowledge through their observations and experiments (Ludden, 2021). The **empirical method** is an invaluable tool for psychological research. Aristotle has been credited with laying the foundation for an objective approach to answering questions, including those pertaining to psychological concepts such as emotion, sensation, and perception (Slife, 1990; Thorne & Henley, 2005).

This notion that experience, or *nurture,* plays an all-important role in how we acquire knowledge contradicts Plato's belief that it is inborn, or in our *nature.*

**empirical method** A process that uses objective observation to measure and collect data.

**A Scientific Mindset**

Medieval mathematician Ibn al-Haytham rejected the once-common belief that the eyes emit light, enabling us to see things. He proposed that vision is made possible by light coming from objects—an idea we now know to be correct (Chapter 3).

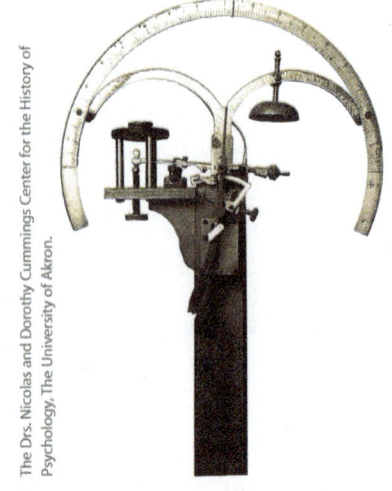

**Wundt Measures the Mind**

In 1861 Wilhelm Wundt conducted an experiment on reaction time, which was a turning point in the field of psychology. Using a pendulum that hit a bell upon reaching its outer limits, Wundt demonstrated a 10th of a second delay between a person hearing the bell and noting the position of the pendulum (and vice versa). It was during this very brief period that a mental process occurred. Finally, activities of the mind could be measured (Thorne & Henley, 2005).

**introspection**  The examination of one's own conscious activities.

**structuralism**  An early school of psychology that used introspection to determine the structure and most basic elements of the mind.

Today, psychologists agree that both nature *and* nurture, that is, inherited biological factors and forces in the environment, are important. Current research explores the contribution of each through studies of heredity and environmental factors.

Like Aristotle, the medieval mathematician Ibn al-Haytham (IB-un-el-HIGHthum; 965–1039 CE) embraced empiricism. Through "systematically arranged experiments and geometrical proofs," al-Haytham created a theory of vision that had a lasting impact on the fields of physics and medicine (Daneshfard et al., 2016; Sabra, 2003, para. 6). In addition to being "the father of optics," this Islamic scholar espoused a way of thinking that foreshadowed today's version of the scientific method, used by psychologists and other scientists. He appreciated the importance of publishing and replicating results (Daneshfard et al., 2016, p. 228), and was skeptical of commonly accepted "truths," which he believed to be "immersed in uncertainties" (Sabra, 2003, para. 7).

**DESCARTES**   Another influential skeptic was French philosopher René Descartes (day-KART; 1596–1650). Famous for saying, "I think, therefore, I am," Descartes believed that most everything else was uncertain, including what he saw with his own eyes. He proposed that the body is like a tangible machine, whereas the mind has no physical substance. The body and mind interact as two separate entities, a view known as *dualism,* and Descartes (along with many others) wondered how they were connected. Descartes' work allowed for a more scientific approach to examining thoughts, emotions, and other topics previously believed to be beyond the scope of study.

## Psychology Is Born

Thus far, the only people in our presentation of psychology's history have been a mathematician, a physicist, and various philosophers. *Where are all the psychologists?* you may be wondering. The answer is simple: There were none. It wasn't until the 19th century that psychology emerged as a scientific discipline. In 1879 Wilhelm Wundt (VILL-helm Vundt; 1832–1920) founded the first psychology laboratory, at the University of Leipzig in Germany, and for this he generally is considered the "father of psychology." Equipped with its own laboratory, research team, and meticulous accounts of experiments, psychology finally became a discipline in its own right (Landrum, 2016).

The overall aim of Wundt's early experiments was to measure psychological processes through **introspection,** a method for examining one's own conscious activities. For Wundt, introspection involved effortful reflection on the sensations, feelings, and images experienced in response to a stimulus, followed by reports that were *objective,* meaning free of opinions, beliefs, expectations, and values. In order to ensure reliable data, Wundt required all his participants to complete 10,000 "introspective observations" prior to starting data collection. His participants were asked to make quantitative judgments about physical stimuli—how strong they were, how long they lasted, and so on (Boring, 1953; Schultz & Schultz, 2016).

**STRUCTURALISM**   British-born psychologist Edward Titchener (TITCH-e-ner; 1867–1927), who was a student of Wundt, developed a movement in psychology known as **structuralism.** In 1893 Titchener set up a laboratory at Cornell University in Ithaca, New York, where he conducted introspection experiments aimed at determining the structure and most basic elements of the mind. Titchener's participants, also extremely well trained, were asked to describe the elements of their current consciousness. In contrast to Wundt's focus on objective, quantitative reports of conscious experiences, Titchener's participants provided detailed reports of their subjective (unique or personal) experiences (Hothersall, 2004; Ludden, 2021). So instead of providing labels for objects, participants would describe them; an egg would be referred to as a "white orb with a textured outer layer," but not an "egg." Structuralism did not last past Titchener's lifetime. Nevertheless, Titchener demonstrated that psychological studies could be conducted through observation and measurement. Many psychologists are still interested in exploring subjective experiences and structures of the brain (now observable with scanning technologies; Chapter 2).

**FUNCTIONALISM**   In the late 1870s, William James (1842–1910) offered the first psychology classes in the United States, at Harvard University. Eleven years later, James received a $300 grant for laboratory equipment. Wundt was given a small research grant that same year, an indication that both these founding psychologists were being recognized by their institutions (Harper, 1950). James had little interest in pursuing the experimental psychology practiced by Wundt and other Europeans (Gundlach, 2018); instead, he was inspired by the work of British naturalist Charles Darwin (1809–1882). Studying the elements of introspection was not a worthwhile endeavor, James believed, because consciousness is an ever-changing "stream" of thoughts. Consciousness cannot be studied by looking for fixed or static elements, because they don't exist, or so he reasoned. But James did believe that consciousness serves a function, and that it's important to study how thoughts, feelings, and behaviors help us adapt to the environment. This focus on purpose and adaptation in psychological research is the overarching theme of **functionalism.**

Students often confuse "functionalism" with "structuralism," perhaps because the terms sound similar, but they are very different. The focus of structuralism was to uncover the structure of the mind, whereas functionalism aimed to identify the adaptive function of thoughts, feelings, and behaviors. Although it didn't endure as a separate field of psychology, functionalism made an impact by influencing educational psychology, studies of emotion, and comparative studies of animal behavior (Benjamin, 2007; Schultz & Schultz, 2016).

**THOSE WHO BROKE BARRIERS**   Like most sciences, psychology began as a "White men's club," with Caucasian males earning the degrees, teaching the classes, and running the labs. Although some progress has been made, sexism and racism are still pervasive in psychology and other academic fields.

Before the 1970s, it was very difficult for people of color and women of all backgrounds to gain admission into psychology graduate programs (Alvarez et al., 2020). One of William James' students, Mary Whiton Calkins (1863–1930), completed all the requirements for a PhD at Harvard, but was not allowed to graduate from the then all-male college because she was a woman. Nonetheless, she persevered with her work on memory and personality and established her own laboratory at Wellesley College, eventually becoming the first female president of the American Psychological Association (APA) in 1905 (Milar, 2016).

The first African American psychologist to earn a PhD was Francis Sumner (1895–1954). After earning his doctorate from Clark University in 1920, Sumner went on to become a founder of Howard University's Psychology Department. He carried out his research and published articles—even when funding sources denied him financial support because he was Black. Sumner's research interests included racial bias, which continues to be a highly relevant topic in contemporary psychology (APA et al., 2019; APA, 2012; Scott et al., 2020; Todd et al., 2020).

Barriers to higher education may have been highest for women of color. Sumner (mentioned above) earned his PhD in 1920, which was 13 years before a female Black psychologist, Inez Beverly Prosser (1897–1934), reached the same milestone. The gender gap was also apparent among Latinx psychologists: The first Latino psychologist to earn

*Macmillan Learning*

**Breaking Ground**
Margaret Floy Washburn (1871–1939) is perhaps most famous for becoming the first woman psychologist to earn a PhD (in 1894 from Cornell University), but her scholarly contributions must not be underestimated. Her book *The Animal Mind: A Textbook of Comparative Psychology* (1908), which drew on her extensive research with animals, had an enduring impact on the field (APA, 2013b; Washburn, 2010).

**functionalism** An early school of psychology that focused on the function of thoughts, feelings, and behaviors and how they help us adapt to the environment.

**For the Children**
The work of Mamie Phipps Clark (left) raised awareness about the unique psychological issues affecting African American and other minority children. She and her husband founded Harlem's Northside Center for Child Development, an organization that continues to provide psychological and educational support to more than 4,000 children every year ("Northside Center," n.d.).

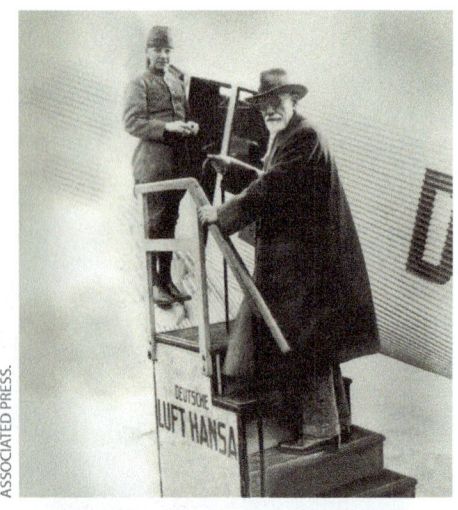

**Freud Takes Off**
Psychology's most famous icon boards his first airplane in 1928, years after psychoanalysis had gotten off the ground in Europe and the United States. Freudian ideas are still alive and well, though people often overestimate their importance in psychology. About 90% of APA members do not practice psychoanalysis, and most science-minded psychologists have distanced themselves from Freudian notions because they are not supported by solid experimental data (Hobson, 2006; Stanovich, 2019).

**psychoanalytic perspective** An approach developed by Freud suggesting that behavior and personality are shaped by unconscious conflicts.

**behaviorism** The scientific study of observable behavior.

his PhD was George Sanchez (1906–1972), in 1934, but 28 years would pass before a Latina psychologist, Martha Bernal (1931–2001), received hers (Alvarez et al., 2020).

Mamie Phipps Clark (1917–1983) was the first Black woman to be awarded a PhD in psychology from Columbia University. Her work, which she conducted with her husband Kenneth Bancroft Clark, examined the impact of prejudice and discrimination on child development. Their research played an important role in the 1954 Supreme Court decision declaring segregation in public schools unlawful (Milar, 2016). Although Clark's husband held a faculty position at City University of New York, she was never allowed to teach there. Instead, she found a job analyzing research data and eventually became executive director of the Northside Center for Child Development in upper Manhattan (Pickren & Burchett, 2014).

Nowadays, the field of psychology is more diverse, but still not an adequate reflection of demographic groups in the United States. As of 2016, 84% of working psychologists were White. Meanwhile, 5% were Hispanic, 4% Black, 4% Asian, 0.3% American Indian/Alaska Native, and 1.5% multiracial (APA, 2018). Since 2009, the number of women earning doctorates in psychology and social sciences has increased by almost 37%. Women comprise approximately 59% of students earning these advanced degrees (National Science Foundation, 2019). For more information on occupations in psychology, see the online appendix Careers in Psychology.

## Perspectives In Psychology

Some of the early schools of thought surrounding psychology had a lasting impact, while others seemed to fade. Nevertheless, they all contributed to the growth of the young science. (See the **Psychology's Roots** infographic in the online appendix Careers in Psychology.) Now let's explore the major perspectives in psychology, all of which shed light on the complex nature of human behavior.

**LO4** Summarize the major perspectives in psychology.

**PSYCHOANALYTIC**  Toward the end of the 19th century, while many early psychologists were busy investigating the "normal" functioning of the mind (in experimental psychology), Austrian physician Sigmund Freud (1856–1939) focused much of his attention on the "abnormal" aspects. Freud believed that behavior and personality are influenced by conflicts between one's inner desires (often sexual and aggressive in nature) and the expectations of society—clashes that primarily occur unconsciously or outside of awareness (Gay, 1988; Chapter 10). This **psychoanalytic perspective** suggests that personality development is heavily influenced by processes that are set into motion early in life and result from interactions with caregivers. Freud also pioneered *psychoanalysis,* an approach to psychotherapy, or "talk therapy" (Chapter 14). Psychoanalysis laid the foundation for an updated and more modern approach to treatment known as *psychodynamic therapy.* Although Freud's name is famous, few people understand that his theories lack solid scientific support, a phenomenon termed the "Freud Problem" (Griggs & Christopher, 2016; Stanovich, 2019).

**BEHAVIORAL**  As Freud worked on his new theories of the unconscious mind, Russian physiologist Ivan Pavlov (1849–1936) was busy studying canine digestion. During the course of his research, Pavlov got sidetracked by an intriguing phenomenon. The dogs in his study had learned to salivate in response to stimuli or events in the environment, a type of learning that eventually became known as *classical conditioning* (Chapter 5). Building on Pavlov's conditioning experiments, American psychologist John B. Watson (1878–1958) established **behaviorism,** which viewed psychology as the scientific study of behaviors that could be seen and/or measured. Consciousness, sensations, feelings, and unconscious processes were not suitable topics of study, according to Watson.

Carrying on the behaviorist approach to psychology, American psychologist B. F. Skinner (1904–1990) studied the relationship between behaviors and their consequences. Skinner's research focused on *operant conditioning,* a type of learning that occurs when behaviors are rewarded or punished (Chapter 5). Skinner acknowledged that mental processes such as memory and emotion might exist, but did not consider them topics for psychological research. To ensure that psychology was a science, he insisted on studying behaviors that could be observed and documented.

The **behavioral perspective** promoted by Watson and Skinner suggests that behaviors and personality are primarily determined by learning. People tend to repeat behaviors that lead to desirable consequences and discontinue behaviors with undesirable consequences. According to this view, personalities are largely shaped by forces in the environment—that is, *nurture.* But twin studies, as noted above, suggest that *nature* also plays a pivotal role; the genes we inherit from our biological parents can substantially influence the people we become (Polderman et al., 2015).

**HUMANISTIC**    American psychologists such as Carl Rogers (1902–1987) and Abraham Maslow (1908–1970) took psychology in yet another direction. These founders of **humanistic psychology** were critical of the way psychoanalysis and behaviorism suggested that people have little control over their lives. The humanistic perspective proposes that human nature is essentially positive, and that people are naturally inclined to grow and change for the better (Chapter 10) (Maslow, 1943; Rogers, 1961). Humanism challenged the thinking and practice of researchers and clinicians who had been "raised" on Watson and Skinner. The rise of humanism was, in some ways, a rebellion against the rigidity of psychoanalysis and behaviorism and the notion that humans seem to have little control of their behaviors. Humanism paved the way for the field of *positive psychology,* which focuses on the positive aspects of human nature (more on this shortly).

**COGNITIVE**    During the prime of behaviorism, many psychologists focused their research on observable behavior. Yet prior to behaviorism, psychologists had emphasized the study of thoughts and emotions. In the 1950s, a new force in psychology brought these unobservable elements back into focus. This renewed interest in the study of mental processes drove the development of *cognitive psychology* (Wertheimer, 2012), and American George Miller's (1920–2012) research on memory is considered an important catalyst for this cognitive revolution (Chapter 6). The **cognitive perspective** examines mental processes that direct behavior, focusing on concepts such as thinking, memory, and language. The *cognitive neuroscience* perspective, in particular, explores physiological explanations for mental processes, searching for connections between behavior and the human nervous system, especially the brain. With the development of brain-scanning technologies, cognitive neuroscience has flourished, interfacing with fields such as medicine and computer science.

**EVOLUTIONARY**    According to the **evolutionary perspective,** behaviors and mental processes are shaped by the forces of evolution. This perspective is based on Charles Darwin's theory of evolution by **natural selection.** Darwin observed great variability in the characteristics of humans and other organisms. He believed these traits were shaped by natural selection, the process through which inherited traits in a given population either increase in frequency because they are adaptive or decrease in frequency because they are maladaptive. Humans have many adaptive traits and behaviors that appear to have evolved through natural selection. David Buss, currently a professor of psychology at the University of Texas at Austin, is one of the founders of evolutionary psychology. He and others have

**Evolution of "Superbugs"**

Looking for an everyday example of evolution? Disease-causing bacteria like this *methicillin-resistant staphylococcus aureus (MRSA)* have evolved to outsmart the antibiotics we use to kill them. When exposed to the right antibiotic, a population of bacteria typically dies or becomes weakened. However, if some of those bacteria have traits that protect them against the antibiotic, they will survive and reproduce. This can lead to the proliferation of "superbugs" that cannot be killed with medicine. "Antibiotic resistance is one of the greatest public health challenges of our time" (Centers for Disease Control and Prevention [CDC], 2020, para. 1).

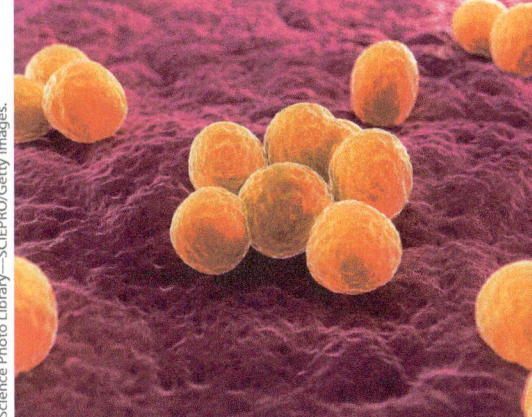

Science Photo Library—SCIEPRO/Getty Images.

**behavioral perspective**  An approach suggesting that behavior is primarily learned through associations, reinforcers, and observation.

**humanistic psychology**  An approach suggesting that human nature is by and large positive, and the human direction is toward growth.

**cognitive perspective**  An approach examining the mental processes that direct behavior.

**evolutionary perspective**  An approach that uses knowledge about evolutionary forces, such as natural selection, to understand behavior.

**natural selection**  The process through which inherited traits in a given population either increase in frequency because they are adaptive, or decrease in frequency because they are maladaptive.

used the evolutionary perspective to explain intelligence, infidelity in relationships, a variety of personality traits, and behaviors like risk-taking (Buss, 2018; Buss & Penke, 2015; Schultz & Schultz, 2016).

**BIOLOGICAL**   The **biological perspective** uses knowledge about underlying physiology to explain behavior and mental processes. Psychologists who take this approach explore how biological factors, such as hormones, genes, and brain activity, influence behavior and cognition. The focus of their research is varied, ranging from the genetic basis of physical fitness to the brain activity of infants and adults as they interact (Piazza et al., 2020; Schutte et al., 2016). Chapter 2 provides a foundation for understanding this perspective and introduces the field of *neuroscience,* which is the study of the brain and other parts of the nervous system.

Franz Marc Frei/Getty Images.

**Culture Matters**
Women shop for spices at the Khan el-Khalili Bazaar in Cairo, Egypt. In many African and Asian markets, the customer is expected to bargain with the seller. How does this compare to shopping in the United States, where prices are preestablished? When it comes to studying human thoughts and behavior, understanding cultural context is key.

**SOCIOCULTURAL**   The **sociocultural perspective** emphasizes the importance of social and cultural factors. Russian psychologist Lev Vygotsky (1896–1934) proposed that we should examine how these forces impact the cognitive development of children (Chapter 8), asserting that parents, teachers, and peers play a critical role in how a child gains knowledge and skills (Hagan, 2016). In light of this realization, researchers such as Mamie Phipps Clark have studied how prejudice, segregation, and discrimination impact the development of the person (Pickren & Burchett, 2014).

In the past, researchers often assumed that the findings of their studies applied to people of all ethnic and cultural backgrounds. Then in the 1980s, cross-cultural research began to reveal that Western research participants are not always representative of people from other cultures. Even groups within a culture can influence behavior and mental processes; thus, we need to take into account these various settings and subcultures. While some progress has been made, psychology research continues to focus on "Western, educated, industrialized, rich, and democratic" (aka "WEIRD") cultures. Many in the field are working hard to change this (Kupferschmidt, 2019; Muthukrishna et al., 2020).

**BIOPSYCHOSOCIAL**   Psychologists often use the **biopsychosocial perspective** to explain behavior; in other words, they examine the biological, psychological, and sociocultural influences involved (Beauchamp & Anderson, 2010). Take, for example, generalized anxiety disorder (GAD), discussed in Chapter 13. People with GAD may believe that the world is full of risks, and take steps to avoid uncertain situations. These thoughts and behaviors are *psychological,* but they may be learned from parents, and thus transmitted through *social* avenues (Aktar et al., 2017). Parents may also pass along genes that predispose their children to having thoughts and behaviors characteristic of GAD, an example of *biological* transmission (Gottschalk & Domschke, 2017). These factors do not exist in isolation but are constantly interacting to shape behaviors and mental processes. The biopsychosocial perspective is used by scientists in many fields, from psychologists studying chronic pain disorders (Yaghmaian & Miller, 2019) to physicians treating patients with sickle cell disease (Crosby et al., 2015).

**COMBINING THE PERSPECTIVES**   You can see that the field of psychology is extremely broad (Braat et al., 2020). With so many perspectives (**TABLE 1.1**), how do we know which one is the most useful for accomplishing psychology's goals? Human behavior is complex and requires an integrated approach—using the findings of multiple perspectives—to explain its origins. Many psychologists pick and choose among

**biological perspective** An approach that uses knowledge about underlying physiology to explain behavior and mental processes.

**sociocultural perspective** An approach examining how social interactions and culture influence behavior and mental processes.

**biopsychosocial perspective** Explains behavior through the interaction of biological, psychological, and sociocultural factors.

**TABLE 1.1** Current Perspectives in Psychology

| Perspective | Main Idea | Questions Psychologists Ask |
|---|---|---|
| Psychoanalytic | Underlying conflicts influence behavior. | How do unconscious conflicts affect decisions and behavior? |
| Behavioral | Behavior is learned primarily through associations, reinforcers, and observation. | How does learning shape behavior? |
| Humanistic | Humans are naturally inclined to grow in a positive direction. | How do choice and self-determination influence behavior? |
| Cognitive | Behavior is driven by cognitive processes. | How do thinking, memory, and language direct behavior? |
| Evolutionary | Humans have evolved characteristics that help them adapt to the environment, increasing their chances of surviving and reproducing. | How has natural selection influenced thoughts, emotions, and behaviors? |
| Biological | Behavior and mental processes arise from physiological activity. | How do biological factors, such as hormones, genes, and brain anatomy, influence behavior and mental processes? |
| Sociocultural | Other people, as well as the broader cultural context, influence behavior and mental processes. | How do social interactions and culture shape thoughts, emotions, and behaviors? |
| Biopsychosocial | Behavior and mental processes are shaped by a complex interplay of biological, psychological, and sociocultural factors. | How do the interactions of biology, psychology, and culture influence thoughts, emotions, and behaviors? |

Psychologists draw on a variety of theories in their research and practice. Listed here are the dominant theoretical perspectives, all of which reappear many times in this textbook. Human behaviors are often best understood when viewed through more than one lens.

the various approaches to explain and understand a given phenomenon. In some cases, creating a theoretical model helps clarify a complex set of observations. Models may draw from one or more perspectives and often enable us to form mental pictures of what we seek to understand.

## Put Your Heads Together

 **A)** Identify a movie or show that is familiar to all members of your group. **B)** Pick a scene that shows a character exhibiting inappropriate or risky behavior. **C)** Try to explain the behavior using at least two of the psychological perspectives outlined above.

Now let's shift our focus away from abstract concepts and onto practical matters. It's time to learn about one of the most trusted approaches for acquiring knowledge: *the scientific method.*

## ▶▶▶ SHOW WHAT YOU KNOW

1. The goal of _____ is to gather knowledge for the sake of knowledge, whereas the goal of _____ is to change behaviors and outcomes.

2. A college dean wants to increase student retention by instituting more formal study groups. She contacts members of the psychology department, who design a program to encourage students to study together. This program falls under which of the main goals of psychology?
   A. describe
   B. explain
   C. predict
   D. change

3. William James suggested that it is important to study the purpose of thoughts, feelings, and behaviors and how they help us adapt to the environment. This focus on purpose and adaptation in psychological research is the theme of:
   A. natural selection.
   B. functionalism.
   C. structuralism.
   D. psychology.

4. We have presented eight perspectives in this section. Describe how two of them are similar. Pick two other perspectives and explain how they differ.

   ✓ CHECK YOUR ANSWERS AT THE BACK OF THE BOOK.

# How Do Psychologists Do Research?

## The Scientific Method

**LO5** Describe how psychologists use the scientific method.

Like all scientists, psychologists conduct research using the **scientific method,** a process for gathering empirical evidence, or data from systematic observations or experiments (**INFOGRAPHIC 1.1**). This evidence is often used to support or refute a **hypothesis** (hi-POTH-uh-sis), which is a statement used to test a prediction about the outcome of a study. The scientific method is used in all types of *experiments,* which we will discuss at length later in the chapter. An **experiment** is a controlled procedure involving scientific observations and/or manipulations by the researcher to influence participants' thinking, emotions, or behaviors. Observations must be objective, or outside the influence of personal opinions and expectations. Humans are prone to errors in thinking, but the scientific method helps to minimize their impact. Let's examine the five basic steps.

**STEP 1: DEVELOP A QUESTION**   The scientific method typically begins when a researcher observes something interesting in the environment and comes up with a research question. For example, twin researcher Dr. Nancy L. Segal got the idea for her first twin study at a child's birthday party. She noticed a pair of fraternal twins working on a puzzle together and fighting over it like mad. This led her to wonder, would identical twins cooperate better than fraternal twins? Her curiosity also stemmed from years of studying behavioral genetics and evolutionary theory—the work of scientists who had come before her. Reading books and articles written by scientists is an excellent way to generate ideas for new studies. The infographic **How to Read a Scientific Article** (see Infographic 0.1 on page 0-4) explains how to find and read a journal article—skills that will help you in psychology and many other classes. It also shows you how to cite a journal article using the APA style established by the American Psychological Association (see APA, 2020).

## Put Your Heads Together

In your group, **A)** brainstorm areas of research that might involve twins. **B)** Choose one of these areas and write down questions you would like to explore. **C)** If you were to search for journal articles in a database, list several key terms and phrases you would use.

**STEP 2: DEVELOP A HYPOTHESIS**   Once a research question has been developed, the next step is to formulate a hypothesis, the statement used to test predictions about the study's outcome. Data collected by the experimenter will either support or refute the hypothesis. Dr. Segal's hypothesis was essentially the following: *When given a joint task, identical twins will cooperate more and compete less than fraternal twins.* Hypotheses can be difficult to generate for studies on new and unexplored topics, because researchers may not have fully developed expectations for the outcome; in these situations, a general prediction may take the place of a formal hypothesis. Researchers cannot just guess when they develop their hypotheses. They must carefully review research and consider relevant psychological perspectives. What perspective do you think influenced Dr. Segal's hypothesis?

While developing research questions and hypotheses, researchers should always be on the lookout for information that could offer explanations for the phenomenon they are studying. Dr. Segal based her hypothesis on behavioral genetics and evolutionary theory. A **theory** synthesizes observations in order to explain phenomena, and it can be used to make predictions that can be tested through research. Many

**scientific method** The process scientists use to conduct research, which includes a continuing cycle of exploration, critical thinking, and systematic observation.

**hypothesis** A statement that can be used to test a prediction.

**experiment** A controlled procedure that involves careful examination through the use of scientific observation and/or manipulation of variables (measurable characteristics).

**theory** Synthesizes observations in order to explain phenomena and guide predictions to be tested through research.

# The Scientific Method

Psychologists use the scientific method to conduct research. The scientific method allows researchers to collect empirical (objective) evidence by following a sequence of carefully executed steps. In this infographic, you can follow the steps of the scientific method using a real research example. The study outlined below explores how increases in happiness might impact physical health (Kushlev et al., 2020). Notice that the process is cyclical in nature. Answering one research question often leads researchers to develop additional questions, and the process begins again.

The researchers read articles suggesting that subjective well-being is associated with better immunity. They think about their own study and wonder:

**ASK NEW QUESTIONS**

*Do interventions that boost happiness lead to improvements in immune function?*

To develop a question, researchers will:
- observe the world around them;
- identify an interesting topic; and
- review scientific literature on this topic.

To develop a hypothesis (a testable prediction), researchers will:
- look for existing theories about the topic; and
- establish operational definitions to specify variables being studied.

**STEP 1: DEVELOP A QUESTION**

*"Happier people are healthier, but does becoming happier lead to better health?" (p. 807).*

**STEP 2: DEVELOP A HYPOTHESIS**

HYPOTHESIS: Participating in a program designed to increase happiness, or "subjective well-being," will lead to improvements in physical health.

**STEP 5: SHARE THE FINDINGS**

The researchers write a description of the study and submit it to an academic journal, where it will be peer-reviewed and, if approved, published for other researchers to read and use in their own research.

The researchers write an article titled "Does Happiness Improve Health? Evidence from a Randomized Controlled Trial." It is published in the journal *Psychological Science*.

**STEP 4: ANALYZE THE DATA**

The findings indicate that participants who completed the 10-week program felt progressively happier compared to the wait-list group. This group also reported having fewer sick days than the wait-list group. Despite feeling healthier, these participants did not experience significant changes in blood pressure and weight.

**STEP 3: DESIGN STUDY & COLLECT DATA**

**1 2 3** Participants were divvied up into two groups: one that engaged in a 10-week program designed to boost happiness, and another that was placed on a waiting list. Participants in both groups completed weekly surveys about their subjective well-being and health. They also received periodic blood pressure and weight checkups.

The researchers organize and analyze the data to determine whether the hypothesis is supported.

The researchers plan a well-controlled study. Data are collected using controlled measurement techniques.

people believe scientific theories are nothing more than unverified guesses, but they are mistaken (Stanovich, 2019). A theory is a well-established body of principles that often rests on a sturdy foundation of scientific evidence. Evolution is a prime example of a theory that has been mistaken for an ongoing scientific controversy. Thanks to inaccurate portrayals in the media, frequently involving opinions by non-scientists, many people believe evolution is an active area of "debate." In reality, evolution is a theory supported by the overwhelming majority of scientists, including psychologists.

**STEP 3: DESIGN STUDY AND COLLECT DATA**    Once a hypothesis has been developed, the researcher designs a study to test it and then collects the data. Dr. Segal's study involved videotaping sets of identical and fraternal twin children working together on a puzzle. Once the instructions were given ("Complete the puzzle together"), the pairs of twin children were free to solve the puzzle as they wished (Segal, 1984, p. 94). Later, looking at the videos, Dr. Segal and her colleagues rated the twins using a variety of "indices of cooperative behavior." For example, the researchers observed if the twins were equally involved, how often they handed each other puzzle pieces, whether they physically leaned on one another, pushed, or hit. They even tallied up the number of facial expressions each twin displayed (for example, sadness, surprise, and pride).

To study cooperative behavior and other characteristics, researchers must establish **operational definitions** that specify the precise manner in which they are observed and measured. Operational definitions are different from dictionary definitions, which tend to be very similar across dictionaries. For example, there are probably only a handful of ways that dictionaries define the word "cooperation." But because constructs like cooperation can be measured in a variety of ways, researchers need to establish objective, precise definitions for them. A good operational definition helps others understand how to perform an observation or take a measurement. In the example above, Dr. Segal operationally defined cooperative behavior based on how often twins worked together, accepted each other's help, or smiled at each other. If you were studying intoxication in college students, your operational definition of "drunkenness" might be based on a physiological measure, such as a blood alcohol level (BAC) of 0.8 or higher. What problems would result if researchers didn't operationally define the characteristics they are measuring?

Gathering data must be done in a very controlled fashion to minimize errors, which could arise from recording problems or from unknown environmental factors. Suppose you are studying how identical twins react to frustrating situations. You could collect information by talking with them for several hours, but your impressions may differ from those of another researcher facing the same task. To reduce bias, interviewers should follow a consistent questioning format, or coding scheme, and employ operational definitions. An even more objective approach would be to administer an assessment with a standard set of questions (true/false, multiple choice, circle the number) and an automated scoring system. The results of such a test do not depend on the researchers' biases or expectations, and should be the same no matter who administers it.

**STEP 4: ANALYZE THE DATA**    Now that the data are collected, they need to be analyzed, or organized in a meaningful way. As FIGURE **1.1** demonstrates, rows and columns of numbers are just that, numbers. In order to make sense of all the "raw" data, one must employ statistical methods. *Descriptive statistics* are used to organize

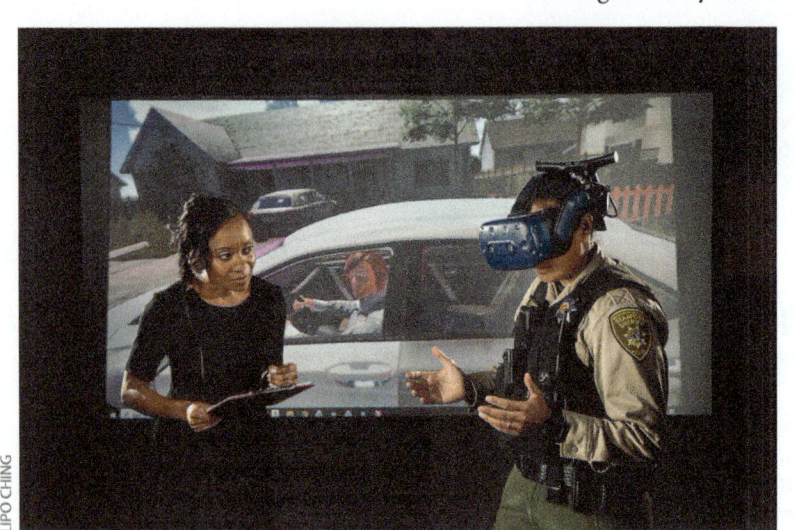

LIPO CHING

**Big Data Uncovers Big Bias**
Working with the Oakland Police Department, psychologist Jennifer Eberhardt collected data on 28,119 interactions between police and people in the community. The trove of data, derived from police reports, neighborhood surveys, and footage from body cameras, revealed that officers behaved differently toward people of different races (Parker, 2016). Black drivers were more likely than White drivers to be pulled over for "minor violations and indistinct reasons" and almost three times more likely to be handcuffed or searched (Starr, 2020, para. 27). With guidance from Eberhardt, the Oakland Police Department has implemented training programs to combat unconscious biases and promote fair police practices (Starr, 2020).

**operational definitions** The precise manner in which variables of interest are defined and measured.

and present data, often through tables, graphs, and charts. *Inferential statistics,* on the other hand, go beyond simply describing the data set, allowing researchers to make inferences and determine the probability of events occurring in the future. (We take a closer look at descriptive and inferential statistics in the Introduction to Statistics Appendix found in the e-book in your Achieve course.)

Following the data analysis, the researcher must ask several questions: Did the results support the hypothesis? Were the predictions met? In Dr. Segal's case, the results did support her hypothesis: "The identical twins were more cooperative on almost every index that I used," she says. "My conclusion was that yes, identical genes do contribute to the greater cooperation observed between partners." Even if results support a hypothesis, the researcher will reevaluate her hypotheses in light of the findings. For example, she might ask herself if the results are consistent with previous studies, or whether they increase support for a particular theory.

**STEP 5: SHARE THE FINDINGS**   Once the data have been analyzed and the hypothesis tested, it's time to share the findings with other researchers who might be able to build on the work. This typically involves conference presentations, online discussions, and written documentation. One of the best ways to disseminate information is to write a scientific article and submit it to a scholarly, peer-reviewed journal. Journal editors send these submitted manuscripts to subject-matter experts, or peer reviewers, who carefully read them and make recommendations for publishing, revising, or rejecting the articles altogether.

The peer-review process is notoriously meticulous, and it helps provide us with more certainty that research findings can be trusted. When looking for research to support your presentations or papers, try to use a search engine that allows you to narrow your search to studies that have been peer-reviewed. Although the internet is an amazing tool for gathering information, a search engine like Google Scholar casts a wide net, and some of the articles it lists are of questionable **origin and quality**.

Unfortunately, the peer-review method is not flawless. For example, editorial boards may show favoritism toward certain authors. One study found that articles are more likely to be accepted by prestigious journals when the authors have already published work there (Callier, 2018; Sekara et al., 2018). What's more, there have been cases of fabricated data slipping past the scrutiny of peer reviewers. About 4 in 10,000 published articles end up being retracted, the result of not only errors but also plagiarism, data meddling, and other forms of inappropriate behavior (Brainard & You, 2018). Such misconduct can have serious consequences for society. Case in point: the spread of misinformation about the safety of childhood vaccines, which has stirred a movement among a small subset of U.S. parents. In the late 1990s, researchers published a study suggesting that vaccination against infectious diseases caused "autism" (Wakefield et al., 1998). The findings sparked panic among parents, some of whom shunned the shots, putting their children at risk for life-threatening infections such as measles. The study turned out to be fraudulent and the reported findings were deceptive, but it took 12 years for journal editors to retract the article (Editors of *The Lancet,* 2010). One reason for this long delay was that researchers had to investigate all the accusations of wrongdoing and data fabrication (Godlee et al., 2011). The investigation included interviews with the parents of the children discussed in the study, which ultimately led to the conclusion that the information in the published account was inaccurate (Deer, 2011).

Since the publication of that deceptive research, several high-quality studies have found no credible support for the autism–vaccine hypothesis (Honda et al., 2005; Jain et al., 2015; Madsen et al., 2002). Still, the publicity given to the original article continues to cast a shadow: Some parents refuse vaccines for their children, with serious consequences for the community. Measles outbreaks involving

| Variable | Record Number | Columns | Format |
|----------|---------------|---------|--------|
| FAMILYID | 1 | 3–7 | Numeric |
| FROMWHO | 1 | 9–12 | Numeric |
| WHICHATT | 1 | 14–17 | Numeric |
| INT_T_ | 1 | 19–24 | Numeric |
| INT_S_ | 1 | 26–31 | Numeric |
| CON_T_ | 1 | 33–38 | Numeric |
| CON_S_ | 1 | 40–46 | Numeric |
| PERS | 1 | 48–52 | Numeric |
| GLOB | 1 | 54–58 | Numeric |
| STA_C_ | 1 | 60–64 | Numeric |
| STA_O_ | 1 | 66–70 | Numeric |
| BARR | 1 | 72–76 | Numeric |
| BREW | 2 | 1–5 | Numeric |

**FIGURE 1.1**
**Raw Data**
The information in this figure comes from a data file. Until the researcher analyzes the data, these numbers will have little meaning.

**CONNECTIONS**

In **Chapter 0**, we discussed the importance of considering the source and quality of information before accepting it as valid. This is an important component of critical thinking. Connections like this are scattered throughout the textbook, helping you see the relationships between topics discussed in the current chapter and those presented in earlier ones.

Chris Maddaloni/Newscom/CQ/Roll Call/Washington, DC, USA.

**Misguided Marchers?**
People gather in front of the Capitol building to protest the use of mercury-containing vaccines. Childhood vaccinations do carry a risk of mild side effects and serious (but very unusual) allergic reactions, but studies have repeatedly shown there is no link between vaccines and autism spectrum disorder (Centers for Disease Control and Prevention [CDC], n.d.). There is now some concern that the antivaccine movement could interfere with the fight against COVID-19. If people refuse to take an effective vaccine, controlling the disease will be more challenging (Ball, 2020).

unvaccinated people continue to occur in the United States and other parts of the world, putting those affected at risk for death and lasting disabilities (World Health Organization [WHO], 2019; Zucker et al., 2020).

Publishing an article is a crucial step in the scientific process because it allows other researchers to **replicate** an experiment, which might mean repeating it with other participants or altering some of the procedures. This repetition is necessary to ensure that the initial findings were not just a fluke or the result of a poorly designed experiment. The more a study is replicated and produces similar findings, the more confidence we can have in those findings. Some studies have proven difficult to replicate, but that doesn't necessarily mean the research should be cast aside. In some cases, difficulty with replication occurs because the topic of study is "more complex or nuanced" than assumed, or because methods of data analysis have changed since the original study was published (Morling & Calin-Jageman, 2020, p. 169).

In the case of Wakefield's fraudulent autism study, other researchers tried to replicate the research for over 10 years, but could never establish a relationship between autism and vaccines (Godlee et al., 2011). This fact alone made the Wakefield findings highly suspect.

**ASK NEW QUESTIONS**    Although the goal is to increase our knowledge, most studies generate more questions than they answer, and here lies the beauty of the scientific process. The results of one scientific study raise a host of new questions, and those questions lead to new hypotheses, new studies, and yet another collection of questions. New results also prompt researchers to rethink theories, as even the most established theories can be scrutinized and re-explored. You can see the cyclical nature of the scientific method illustrated in Infographic 1.1.

**CRITICAL THINKING**    This continuing cycle of exploration uses *critical thinking* at every step. **Critical thinking** is the process of weighing various pieces of evidence, synthesizing them, and evaluating the contributions of each; it is a type of thinking that is disciplined, clear, rational, and open to the consideration of new ideas. A critical thinker places importance on "the rules of logic and science," rather than popular beliefs that may or may not have scientific backing (Lamont, 2020, p. 244). For a review of critical thinking, revisit Chapter 0 and see INFOGRAPHIC **1.2**.

## Research Basics

**ENTER THE PSYCHOLOGIST**    Soon after making contact, Sam and Anaïs began contemplating the idea of creating a movie to capture their extraordinary story and share it with others. They knew the constant presence of a film crew would be a complete invasion of privacy, but it seemed worth the sacrifice. Their documentary film would be titled *Twinsters* ("twin" + "sisters"). Sam would be a producer, and the other crewmembers would be her trusted friends and colleagues from the film industry. The team immediately began preparing for what would become the film's climax: the first tangible, human-to-human meeting of Sam and Anaïs. It would take place in London, on May 14, two days before Anaïs' spring fashion show.

To raise money for the movie, Sam and her friends posted a proposal on the funding platform Kickstarter. Through Kickstarter, they caught the attention of twin expert Dr. Nancy L. Segal (introduced on p. 30). When Dr. Segal learned

**replicate** To repeat an experiment, generally with a new sample and/or other changes to the procedures, the goal of which is to provide further support for the findings of the first study.

**critical thinking** The process of weighing pieces of evidence, synthesizing them, and evaluating the contributions of each; disciplined thinking that is clear, rational, open-minded, and informed by evidence.

# Critical Thinking

What is critical thinking and why is it important? Being a critical thinker means carefully evaluating pieces of evidence, synthesizing them, and determining how they fit into the "big picture." Critical thinkers maintain a healthy dose of skepticism, but they are also able to adjust their thinking if presented with contradictory evidence. Consider the issue of global warming: Do you think it's real, and are human beings causing it?

At least **97%** of the world's leading climate scientists believe that greenhouse gas emissions generated by human activities, such as burning gasoline and coal, are most likely driving the warming trend (Herring & Scott, 2020).

"We have no time to lose if we are to avert climate catastrophe" (Guterres, 2020, para. 8).

## Yet some people still are not too worried about global warming, perhaps because they don't grasp the severity of the problem:
(Funk & Kennedy, 2020).

Global warming and other climate change events are not caused by humans.

Where is this information coming from?

What kind of evidence supports it?

### A critical thinker . . .

. . . is skeptical
. . . thinks deeply
. . . evaluates claims using existing knowledge
. . . asks questions
. . . considers alternative explanations
. . . reflects on own emotional reactions
. . . tolerates uncertainty
. . . is open-minded

CRITICAL THINKING *IN ACTION*

Although you will develop your critical-thinking skills in psychology class, they can be used in other contexts, from resolving everyday dilemmas, such as, "Why did I get such a mediocre grade after studying so hard?" to understanding global crises such as climate change.

### GO TO THE SOURCE: ASK CRITICAL QUESTIONS

**Who wrote the article?**
• What is the professional background of the author(s)?

**Where was it published?**
• Is it peer-reviewed, open-source, or popular press?

**What are the study's findings?**
• Do the findings support the hypothesis?
• Are there limitations cited?
• What other variables might have influenced the outcome?

**What were the methods used to conduct the study?**
• How big was the sample?
• How did researchers collect data?

**Has the study been replicated?**
• Have other studies reported the same results?
• Have other studies tried different samples?

**Where is money coming from?**
• What individuals or organizations provided funding for the study, and did they have an agenda in doing so?

Credits: Thermometer, dencg/Shutterstock; Globe, adike/Shutterstock

**Proof Is in the DNA**
Sam (left) and Anaïs on Skype, collecting DNA samples with cheek swabs. DNA (deoxyribonucleic acid) is the genetic material we inherit from our parents, and identical twins have almost the same DNA sequences ("almost" because, although identical twins have the same DNA at conception, small genetic changes can occur throughout life). After collecting the samples, Sam and Anaïs sent them to a laboratory, and the results of the analysis confirmed that they are indeed identical twins!

*Twinsters (2015). Small Package Films.*

about Sam and Anaïs, she immediately wondered if they had taken a DNA test to prove they were identical twins. "When I found out that they had not done that, I was very worried," Dr. Segal explains. Even though Sam and Anaïs had the same birthdates and shared many physical characteristics and behaviors, there was still the remote possibility that they were unrelated look-alikes. Dr. Segal had seen similar cases end in profound disappointment. As she puts it, "You need the biological proof."

Dr. Segal reached out to Sam and Anaïs, who agreed to participate in research. They took DNA tests, which affirmed what they already knew in their hearts . . . they were indeed identical twins! Sam and Anaïs also underwent a variety of tests organized by Dr. Segal and her colleagues at California State University, Fullerton. These tests focused on physical characteristics like height, weight, and hand preference, and psychological factors such as job satisfaction, self-esteem, personality traits, and cognitive abilities—all *variables* commonly studied by psychologists.

**VARIABLES**    Measurable characteristics that can vary, or change, over time or across individuals are called **variables.** In psychological experiments, researchers study a variety of characteristics relating to humans and other organisms. Examples of variables include personality characteristics (shyness or friendliness), cognitive characteristics (memory), number of siblings in a family, gender, and socioeconomic status.

The study of Sam and Anaïs revealed "striking similarities" across a variety of variables, including measures of job satisfaction, and certain mental abilities and personality traits. It also unearthed fascinating differences; for example, Anaïs scored higher on most of the tests measuring visual-spatial skills—not a surprise to Dr. Segal and her colleague Franchesca Cortez, who say this finding is "consistent with the idea that fashion designers benefit from good visual skills" (Segal & Cortez, 2014, p. 103). Meanwhile, Sam did better on some tests measuring memory, which could be a result of her experience memorizing lines for acting roles and waiting tables (Segal & Cortez, 2014). "It really would stress me out," says Sam, recalling her days running between tables. "I would have nightmares . . . I would wake up and be like, 'I didn't bring his ketchup!'"

**LO 6**    Explain the importance of a representative sample.

**POPULATION AND SAMPLE**    The findings described above focus on just two individuals—Sam and Anaïs. How do researchers decide who should participate in their studies? It depends on the **population,** or overall group the researcher wants to examine. If the population is large (all college students in the United States, for example), then the researcher selects a subset of that population called a **sample.**

There are many methods for choosing a sample. In an effort to ensure that the sample accurately reflects the larger population, a researcher may use a **random sample.** With a random sample, all members of the population have an equal chance of being invited to participate in the study. A researcher forming a random sample of high school seniors planning to go to college might try to gain access to SAT or ACT databases and then randomly select students from lists compiled by those test companies.

Think about the problems that may crop up if a sample is not random. Suppose a researcher is trying to assess attitudes about undocumented workers living in

**variables** Measurable characteristics that can vary over time or across people.

**population** All members of an identified group about which a researcher is interested.

**sample** A subset of a population chosen for inclusion in an experiment.

**random sample** A subset of the population chosen through a procedure that ensures all members of the population have an equal chance of being selected to participate in the study.

**representative sample** A subgroup of a population selected so that its members have characteristics similar to those of the population of interest.

the United States, but the only place she recruits participants is New York City, which (along with Los Angeles and Miami) has the biggest population of immigrants (Budiman, 2020). How might this bias her findings? A study of people in New York would certainly offer valuable insights about residents of that city, but it would not necessarily provide a complete picture of attitudes across the United States. New York residents do not constitute a **representative sample,** or group of people with characteristics similar to those of the population of interest (in this case, the entire U.S. population). **FIGURE 1.2** provides a visual illustration of the concept.

It is important for researchers to choose representative samples, because this allows them to generalize their findings, or apply information from a sample to the population at large. Let's say that 44% of the respondents in the study on attitudes toward undocumented workers believe current immigration laws are acceptable. If the sample is sufficiently similar to the overall U.S. population, then the researcher may be able to infer that this finding from the sample is representative: "Approximately 44% of people in the United States believe that current immigration laws are acceptable."

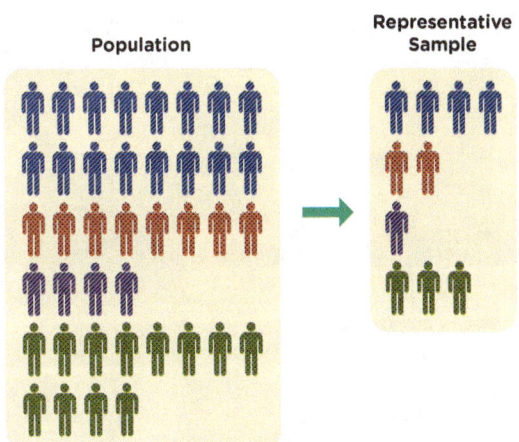

**Population**   **Representative Sample**

## FIGURE 1.2

**Representative Sample**

Researchers usually do not have the option to enlist an entire population in their studies. But they can strive for the next best thing—a representative sample of the population. A representative sample captures the diversity of a population, including relevant characteristics in the same proportions. For example, if half of the population is female, half of the sample should be female; if 10% of the population is Asian, 10% of the sample should be Asian, and so on.

## Put Your Heads Together

In your group, **A)** identify a population for a study examining attitudes toward undocumented workers. **B)** How could you get a sample that would be representative of the population? **C)** How could you get a sample that would not be representative of the population? **D)** How might the findings from these two approaches be different?

The topics we have explored thus far—the scientific method, variables, operational definitions, and samples—apply to psychology research in general. You will see how these concepts are relevant to studies presented in the upcoming sections when we explore three major categories of research methods: descriptive, correlational, and experimental.

 **SHOW WHAT YOU KNOW**

1. A research group is interested in studying college students' attitudes about the legalization of marijuana. The group randomly selects students from across the nation, trying to pick a _____ that closely reflects the characteristics of American college students.

   **A.** variable
   **B.** hypothesis
   **C.** representative sample
   **D.** representative population

2. The scientific method is a process for gathering empirical evidence. This evidence is often used to support or refute a(n) _____, a statement used to test a prediction about the outcome of a study.

3. Why might it be problematic to make inferences from small samples to large populations?

✓ CHECK YOUR ANSWERS AT THE BACK OF THE BOOK.

# Descriptive and Correlational Methods

Sam and Anaïs share many attributes, but they are not exact copies of one another. Obvious physical differences include height (Anaïs is a bit taller) and skin color (Sam is tanner from surfing in the California sun). As for psychological disparities, the twins seem to differ in their experience of emotional stress. "Depending on what it is, I can just shake it off, but it will kind of live with [Anaïs] a little bit more," says Sam, who attributes this coping style to her experience growing up with two older brothers. When Sam felt stressed or upset, her brothers would often tell her to "get over it" and find something to do. Anaïs was an only child, so she did not "benefit" from this type of sibling interaction. Given that these women started life genetically identical, you begin to wonder about the sources of their differences. When did these disparities emerge, and what environmental factors

**Power of Nurture**

(left to right) Sam's brother Andrew, Sam, Sam's brother Matt, and Anaïs. Personality assessments suggest that Sam is more extroverted than her twin sister (Segal & Cortez, 2014). Is this because Sam grew up with two older brothers, while Anaïs was an only child?

**Please Wash Your Hands**

Studies suggest that women are more conscientious than men about washing their hands in restrooms (Humphreys et al., 2015). In one naturalistic observation study, researchers sat quietly inside bathroom stalls on a university campus, using stopwatches to measure how long people spent using the facilities (as determined by the flushing sounds of toilets and urinals) and washing their hands. They found that most men and women washed their hands after using the toilet, but almost half of the men failed to clean their hands after using urinals (Berry et al., 2015). Do you think more men would have washed their hands if they knew they were being observed?

(apart from tough older brothers) shaped them? It would be fascinating to travel back in time and observe Sam and Anaïs as little girls playing with friends, interacting with family, and studying at school. If only time travel were possible, there would be endless opportunities for a psychologist to study their differing childhoods using *descriptive research methods*.

Remember that one of the main goals of psychology is to describe what we observe. **Descriptive research** is a type of investigation psychologists use to explore a phenomenon. It is primarily concerned with describing, and is useful for studying new or unexplored topics when researchers might not have specific expectations about outcomes. But there are certain things descriptive research cannot achieve. This approach helps us develop hypotheses about the causes of behaviors, yet it *cannot* reveal cause-and-effect relationships, a point we will revisit later in the chapter. Now let's get familiar with various descriptive research methods.

**LO 7** Recognize several forms of descriptive research.

## Naturalistic Observation

**Naturalistic observation** refers to the systematic observation of participants in their natural environments. And when we say "natural environments," we don't necessarily mean the "wild." It could be an office, a preschool, or even a dorm room. In one naturalistic study, researchers observed the behaviors of Starbucks patrons in cities across China and Hong Kong. The goal was to determine if people from different regions have distinct preferences for being physically close to others. Here's what the researchers observed: People in regions with a history of wheat-growing (where farmers work more independently) were more likely to sit alone. Meanwhile, those from areas with a tradition of rice-growing (where farmers often work together) were more inclined to sit with others. In this naturalistic study, we see how culture may play a role in shaping everyday behavior (Talhelm et al., 2018).

**NATURALLY, IT'S A CHALLENGE** As with any type of research, naturalistic observation centers around variables, and those variables must be pinned down with operational definitions. Suppose you are studying conscientiousness among toddlers. This is an intriguing topic, as research suggests that aspects of conscientiousness, such as self-control and compliance with parents, can present themselves early in life (Kim & Kochanska, 2019). At the beginning of the study, you would need to create an operational definition for conscientiousness, including detailed descriptions of specific behaviors that illustrate it. Then you might create a checklist of conscientious behaviors, such as waiting to eat a snack, choosing only one prize from a toy box, and whispering when it's time to be quiet, as well as a coding system to help keep track of them.

Naturalistic observation allows psychologists to observe participants going about their business in their normal environments, without the disruptions of artificial laboratory settings. Perhaps the most important requirement of naturalistic observation is that researchers must not disturb the participants or their environment. That way, participants won't change their normal behaviors, particularly those that the researchers wish to observe. Some problems arise with this arrangement, however. Natural environments may contain variables that the researchers are not interested in studying, but removing them can disrupt the natural setting they are striving to maintain. And because the variables in natural environments are so difficult to control, researchers may have trouble replicating findings. Suppose your study involved observing toddlers play with LEGOs at day care. In this natural setting, you would not be able to control who played and when; whoever showed up at the LEGO table would become a participant in your study.

**OBSERVER BIAS** How can we be sure observers will do a good job recording behaviors? If you haven't spent time around toddlers, you might pay attention to very different aspects of play behaviors than a researcher who has raised six children. One way to avoid such problems is to include multiple observers and then determine how similarly they record the behaviors. If the observers don't execute this task in the same way, **observer bias** may exist. This refers to errors introduced as a result of an observer's value system, expectations, attitudes, or personal characteristics.

## Case Study

Another descriptive research method is the **case study,** a detailed examination of an individual or small group. Case studies typically involve collecting a vast amount of data, often using multiple avenues to gather information. The process might include in-depth interviews with the person being studied and their friends, family, and coworkers, as well as questionnaires about medical history, career, and mental health. The goal of a case study is to provide a wealth of information from a variety of resources. Case studies are invaluable for studying rare events, like the reunion of identical twins born in South Korea and reared on different continents. They may offer valuable information we can't get anywhere else. This research method also helps guide the design of studies on relatively underexplored topics (Stanovich, 2019), such as the health and behavior of an astronaut on a space mission compared to his identical twin back on Earth (Garrett-Bakelman et al., 2019). Unlike naturalistic observation, where the researcher assumes the role of detached spectator, the case study may require immersion in the participant's environment. How do you think this might impact the researcher's observations and the conclusions of the study?

One of the most fascinating case studies in the history of twin research is that of the "Jim Twins." Identical twins Jim Springer and Jim Lewis were separated shortly after birth and reunited at age 39. When the Jims finally met, they discovered some jaw-dropping similarities: Both were named "James" by their adoptive parents and gravitated toward math and carpentry as kids. Each man had a dog named "Toy," a first wife named "Linda," and a second wife named "Betty." They even smoked the same cigarettes (Salems), drove the same type of blue Chevy, and traveled to the same vacation spot in Florida (Leo, 1987; Minnesota Center for Twin and Family Research, 2016; Segal, 2012).

No matter how colorful or thought-provoking a case study may be, it cannot provide definitive support for a hypothesis (Stanovich, 2019). Hypothesis testing involves evaluating different conditions, and because the subject of a case study represents a sample of one (consisting of an individual or a single group), comparisons are impossible. Like other types of descriptive research, this method is useful for furthering the development of theories, but it cannot identify the causes of behaviors and events.

Case studies are very specific examples, so they should not be used to make generalizations. In other words, we shouldn't draw broad conclusions from a specific instance. Suppose you are trying to examine how parent–child interactions at home might relate to preschoolers' transitions during morning drop-off. What would happen if you limited your research to a case study of a family with two working parents and 10 children? The dynamics of this family may not be representative of those in other families. We should not make sweeping generalizations based on our observations of a single person or group.

**So Many Twins!**
Every year, twins, triplets, and other multiples from around the world gather in Twinsburg, Ohio, for the Twins Days Festival. In addition to participating in talent shows, watching fireworks, and marching in the "Double Take Parade," attendees have the opportunity to meet the many scientists who flock to the festival in search of study participants (Dawidziak, 2018; Richards, 2018).

Dustin Franz/Barcroft USA via Getty Images.

**descriptive research** Research methods that describe and explore behaviors, but whose findings cannot definitively state cause-and-effect relationships.

**naturalistic observation** A type of descriptive research that studies participants in their natural environment through systematic observation.

**observer bias** Errors in the recording of observations, which result from the researcher's value system, expectations, or attitudes.

**case study** A type of descriptive research that closely examines an individual or small group.

## Survey Method

One of the fastest ways to collect data is the **survey method,** which relies on questionnaires or interviews. A survey is basically a series of questions that can be administered on paper, in face-to-face interviews, or via smartphone, tablet, and other digital devices. Your college might send out surveys to gauge student attitudes about new online classes and e-books (using questions such as, "How often do you encounter technical difficulties with your online courses?" or "How would you rate your overall satisfaction with the assigned e-book?"). The benefit of the survey method is that you can gather data from numerous people in a short period of time. Surveys can be used alone or in conjunction with other research methods.

**WORDING AND HONESTY**   Like any research design, the survey method has its limitations. The wording of survey questions can lead to biases in responses. For an example, see **FIGURE 1.3.** A question with a positive or negative spin may sway a participant's response one way or the other: Do you prefer a half-full glass of soda or a half-empty glass of soda?

More importantly, participants are not always forthright in their responses, particularly when the survey touches on sensitive issues. In short, people lie to make themselves look good. It's not always easy for researchers to determine whether this tendency to strive for *social desirability* has influenced the results. In one study, male and female college students were asked questions about cheating in relationships. When participants were led to believe their responses were being analyzed by a lie detector, men and women were equally likely to admit to cheating behaviors. But when they believed their self-reports were anonymous, the men were more likely to confess than the women (Fisher & Brunell, 2014). Researchers in the field recommend collecting information anonymously if possible, noting the irony that infidelity "is rooted in deceit and thus inimical [contrary] to the truth that science seeks to illuminate" (Fincham & May, 2017, p. 73).

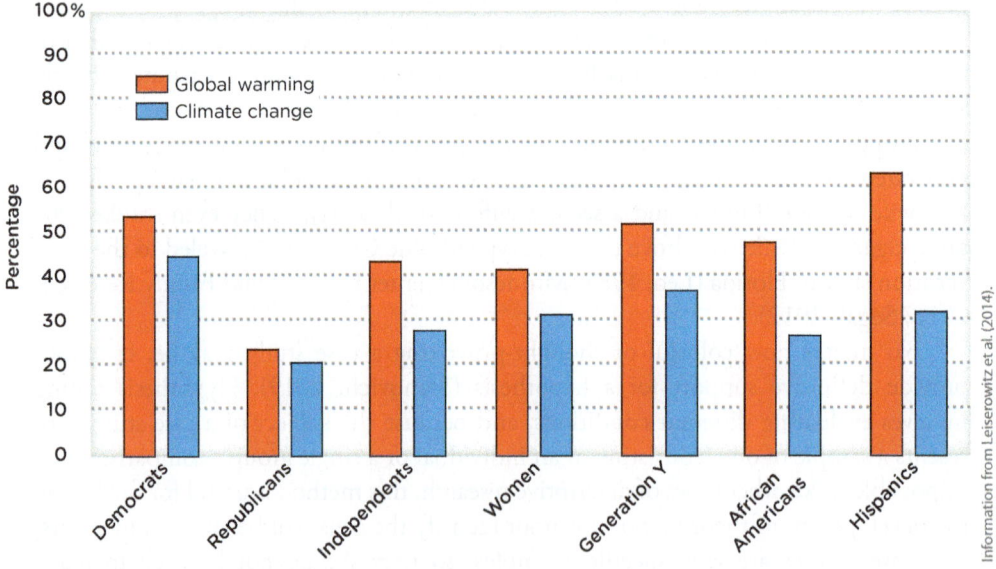

Percentage of respondents who say that global warming or climate change will "harm their family"

Information from Leiserowitz et al. (2014).

## FIGURE 1.3
**It Depends How You Ask**

What do *global warming* and *climate change* mean to you? To compare the impact of these two phrases, researchers surveyed a representative sample of U.S. adults. About half of the participants answered a series of questions about *global warming*, while the other half answered the exact same questions about *climate change*. In the example here, we can see how differently people reacted to these variations in wording: "how much do you think *global warming* will harm your family?" versus "how much do you think *climate change* will harm your family?" (Leiserowitz et al., 2014, p. 18). Apparently, global warming sets off more alarm bells than climate change, and this influences the way people answer questions about the issue.

**survey method** A type of descriptive research that uses questionnaires or interviews to gather data.

**SKIMMING THE SURFACE**    Another disadvantage of the survey method is that it tends to skim the surface of people's beliefs or attitudes, failing to uncover *why* people respond the way they do. Ask 1,000 people if they *intend* to exercise regularly, and you might get a substantial number of affirmative responses. But "yes" might mean something quite different from one person to the next ("Yes, it crosses my mind, but I can never go through with it" versus "Yes, I have a specific plan, and I have been able to follow through"). To obtain more precise responses, researchers conducting surveys often ask people to respond to statements using a scale indicating the degree to which they agree or disagree (for example, a 5-point scale ranging from *strongly agree* to *strongly disagree*), or the degree to which they have had an experience (a 5-point scale ranging from *never* to *almost always*).

**A SAMPLING PROBLEM**    Another common challenge is obtaining a representative sample. Many surveys fail to do so because their *response rates* fall short of ideal. If a researcher sends out 100 surveys to potential participants and only 20 people return them, how can we be sure that the answers of the 20 responders reflect those of the entire group? Or what if the survey is only sent to subscribers of *Teen Vogue*—is that a representative sample of all teenagers in the United States? Without a representative sample, we cannot generalize survey findings to the larger population. How can researchers get more people to respond to their surveys? Paying participants a small sum (about $3.00, in one study) may increase the response rate (Robb et al., 2017).

Surveys can inform our understanding about a broad range of issues. Have you ever been put off by an unpleasant email from a coworker? *Scientific American* explores this topic with the help of survey data from various time points.

# THE PSYCHOLOGICAL TOLL OF RUDE E-MAILS

From the **SCIENTIFIC** pages of **AMERICAN**

Research reveals the subtle ways that impolite electronic communication at work brings you down.

Imagine waking up on Monday morning to an e-mail in your inbox that was written entirely in capital letters—an e-mail that jolts you awake far quicker than the cup of coffee in your hand: "IS THIS A JOKE??? ARE YOU KIDDING ME?!" With the caps lock key and the stroke of an exclamation point, your co-worker has just done the equivalent of shouting at you across the office. Yet these days this kind of encounter is almost commonplace. Whether they come in all caps, exclamation marks, silence or snark, rude e-mails are on the rise.

For a civilized society, we're not always so civil. In fact, rudeness is a pervasive problem. In a 2002 report on a study conducted with a large representative sample of 2,013 adults, 88 percent of the general public indicated they had come across rude and disrespectful people on a daily basis. And the workplace is no escape. As the sheer volume of electronic communications has skyrocketed, the problem of "nasty e-mail" is becoming nonnegligible. In fact, more than 90 percent of professionals surveyed in a 2009 study said that they had experienced disrespectful e-mail exchanges at work. [. . .]

And being on the receiving end of such impoliteness can have a lasting effect. Studies have shown that dealing with rude e-mails at work can create lingering stress and take a toll on the recipient's well-being. In a simulated work experiment, participants who received such a message from their boss experienced more negative emotions, found it harder to stay engaged in work tasks and answered fewer questions correctly than the control group. The stress associated with e-mail rudeness can creep into family life as well. A diary study that surveyed employees twice a day over five workdays found that when employees received impolite messages during a workday, they were likely to report more stress symptoms both in the evening and the following morning. [. . .]

But it's not just derogatory or condescending remarks that create stress. Another culprit is a subtler form of aggression: avoidance. Unlike active e-mail rudeness, in which the content contains the insult, passive e-mail rudeness happens when a person does not reply to a request, essentially giving others the "silent treatment."

In a study[*] conducted on the nature of e-mail rudeness, we surveyed 233 people in the U.S. about their experiences with such messages at work. The collected data supported the idea of two distinct forms of impolite e-mails: active rudeness was empirically distinguishable from passive rudeness. As part of the study, we asked participants to either upload or describe a rude e-mail encounter they had experienced recently and to report their reactions to it. Based on the content/description of the exchange, we classified it as demonstrating either active or passive incivility. Interestingly, participants regarded active rudeness as emotionally charged, while they reported a great deal of ambiguity and uncertainty about passive rudeness. Derogatory remarks—that is, active rudeness—may get someone worked up because of their offensive nature. In contrast, the "silent treatment"—that is, passive rudeness—leaves people hanging and struggling with uncertainty. [. . .]

For employees, one effective way to cope is through psychological detachment. The best option is to unplug from work after-hours. Enjoy your family dinner or time with friends instead of perseverating over a work e-mail during your time off. For those working from home, this mental separation becomes even more important.

And no matter your level of stress, remember the rules of netiquette. How do you do that? Spend some time crafting your e-mail. Acknowledge when you have received a request. Reread your message for potentially inconsiderate expressions. If you are too busy, let your co-workers know you will get back to them within a reasonable time frame. Simply put, do unto others as you would have them do unto you—and perhaps keep caps lock off. Zhenyu Yuan & YoungAh Park. Reproduced with permission.

**Salary Isn't Everything**
Working as a research assistant can be highly satisfying, even though you might not bring home a huge paycheck (Griswold, 2013). An analysis of 92 studies found a correlation coefficient (*r*) of .14 between salary and job satisfaction (Judge et al., 2010). Remember, the closer *r* is to .00, the weaker the relationship.

sanjeri/Getty Images.

**correlational method** A type of research examining relationships among variables.
**correlation** An association or relationship between two (or more) variables.

## Correlations: Is There a Relationship?

**LO 8** Describe the correlational method and identify its limitations.

When researchers collect data on many variables, it can be useful to determine if these variables are associated in some way. The **correlational method** examines relationships among variables and assists researchers in making predictions. A **correlation** represents a relationship or link between variables (**INFOGRAPHIC 1.3** on page 44). For example, there is a correlation between the amount of time parents spend reading books to their children and the number of vocabulary words the children know. The more the parents read, the more words their children learn (Logan et al., 2019; Pace et al., 2017). This is an example of a positive correlation. As one variable increases, so does the other. Positive correlations also work the opposite way: As one variable decreases, so does the other. The less time parents spend reading, the fewer vocabulary words their children know. Even though values of both variables are decreasing, this still represents a positive relationship. On the other hand, a negative correlation represents an inverse relationship, which means as one variable goes up, the other goes down. An example might be the quantity of time students spend using their smartphones and their performance in school. As phone usage increases, academic performance decreases (Domoff et al., 2020; Samaha & Hawi, 2016). You have probably noticed correlations between variables in your own life. The longer you leave the lights on, the higher your electric bill will be (a positive correlation). The more you go shopping, the less money you have in the bank (a negative correlation). Other links may be less obvious. For example, did you know that there is a correlation between social connectedness and physical health?

*For more information on this study about e-mail rudeness, please see Yuan et al., 2020.

# Relationships

## IS YOUR SOCIAL LIFE AFFECTING YOUR HEALTH?

"The tighter someone is embedded in a network of friends, the less likely they are to become ill" (Bzdok & Dunbar, 2020, p. 717). Here we have an example of a negative correlation: As social connectedness goes up, the frequency of illness goes down. Why would this be the case? We can look to other correlations for clues. Studies suggests that immune responses may be stronger in people who are socially connected—a positive correlation (Bzdok & Dunbar, 2020). For example, one study found that college students with larger social networks (consisting of 13–20 people as opposed to 4–12) produced more of a specific disease-fighting antibody after getting a flu vaccine (Pressman et al., 2005). Feeling supported by others has also been linked to lower levels of C-reactive protein (CRP) in some people (a negative correlation). CRP is an indicator of chronic inflammation, which is a risk factor for heart disease, cancer, and other illnesses (Lee & Way, 2019; Uchino et al., 2016). These and other correlations do not equate to cause and effect, but they do suggest that the body and mind are linked.

**THESE LINKS MAY SURPRISE YOU.**

**CORRELATION COEFFICIENT**    Some variables are tightly linked, others weakly associated, and still others not related at all. Lucky for researchers, there is one number that indicates both the strength and direction (positive or negative) of the relationship: a statistical measure called the **correlation coefficient,** symbolized as $r$. Correlation coefficients range from to +1.00 to −1.00, with positive numbers indicating a positive relationship between variables and negative numbers indicating a negative (inverse) relationship between variables. The closer $r$ is to +1.00 or to −1.00, the stronger the relationship. The closer $r$ is to .00, the weaker the relationship. When the correlation coefficient is very close to zero, there may be no relationship between the variables. For example, consider the variables of shoe size and creativity. Are adults with bigger (or smaller) feet more creative? Probably not; there would be no link between these two variables, so the correlation coefficient between them (the $r$ value) is around zero. Take a look at FIGURE 1.4 and Infographic 1.3 to see how correlation coefficients are portrayed on graphs called *scatterplots*.

**DIRECTIONALITY**    Now let's consider the direction of the relationship between variables. Some researchers have reported a positive relationship between exposure to violence in media and aggressive behavior (Coyne et al., 2018; Teng et al., 2019). Since there appears to be a positive correlation, you might assume that media exposure leads to aggression. The more time spent playing violent video games, the more aggressive the child is. But could it be that aggressive children are more likely to be attracted to violent video games in the first place? If this is the case, then aggressive tendencies influence the amount of time spent using violent media, not the other way around. The direction of the relationship—*directionality*—matters. If we are talking about the relationship between aggression and exposure to violent media, the causal relationship could potentially go in both directions (Coyne, 2016).

**THIRD VARIABLE**    Even if there is a very strong correlation between two variables, this does not indicate a causal link exists between them. No matter how high the $r$ value is or how logical the relationship seems, a correlation is not equivalent to a cause-and-effect connection. Getting back to the positive relationship between exposure to violence in media and aggressive behavior, it's easy to jump to the conclusion that the exposure causes the aggression. But maybe some **third variable,** or unaccounted for characteristic of the participants or their environment, can explain the relationship. Can you think of any additional variables that might "cause" increases or decreases in aggression? One possibility is parenting behaviors; parents who limit and monitor

**correlation coefficient** The statistical measure (symbolized as $r$) that indicates the strength and direction of the relationship between two variables.

**third variable** An unaccounted for characteristic of participants or the environment that explains changes in the variables of interest.

# The Correlation Coefficient: What's in a Number?

A correlation indicates a relationship between two variables, such as the amount of time you spend studying and the grade you get on a test. This relationship is often indicated using a correlation coefficient, symbolized as *r*. To interpret the relationship using a correlation coefficient (*r*), ask yourself two questions:

(1) What is the *direction* of the relationship?

(2) What is the *strength* of the relationship?

A *scatterplot* helps us see what the relationship looks like.

And remember, a correlation between two variables does not necessarily mean that one variable caused the change in the other variable.

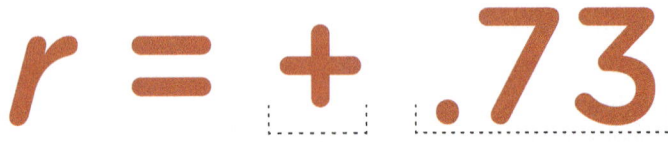

$$r = + .73$$

## ↕ What Is the **Direction** of the Correlation?

- *positive (+) correlation* as one variable increases, the other also increases

- *negative (−) correlation* as one variable increases, the other decreases (an inverse relationship)

**Example: +.73** is a positive number, showing a **positive correlation.** As hours spent studying increase, test grades also increase.

## 🏋 What Is the **Strength** of the Correlation?

**strength ranges from +1.00 to −1.00**

- a value close to +1.00 or −1.00 is a **strong** correlation

- a value close to .00 is a **weak** correlation

**Example: +.73** is close to 1.00. This shows a **strong correlation** between hours spent studying and test grades.

⚠️ **BEWARE** of the potential **Third Variable**

Correlation does not indicate that one variable *causes* a change in the other. A **third variable** may have influenced the results.

**Example:** Although time spent studying and exam grades are strongly and positively correlated, attendance is another variable. Students who attend classes regularly tend to spend more hours studying. Likewise, students who attend classes regularly know what to expect on the test and are therefore likely to get better grades.

## 👁 What does the correlation **look** like?

Using a scatterplot, we can express the relationship between two variables. One variable is labeled on the horizontal axis, and the second variable is labeled on the vertical axis. Each dot represents one participant's scores on the two variables. Notice how the shape of the graph changes depending on the direction and strength of the relationship between the variables.

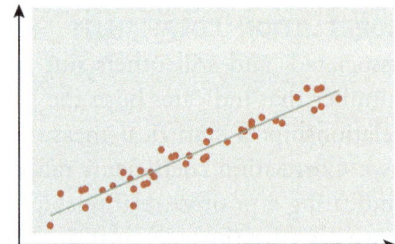

strong positive correlation (+.73)

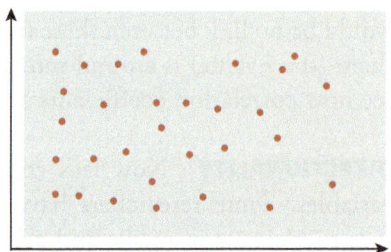

no relationship (.00)

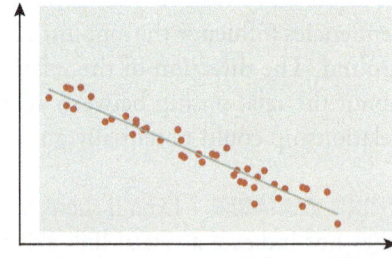

strong negative correlation (−.73)

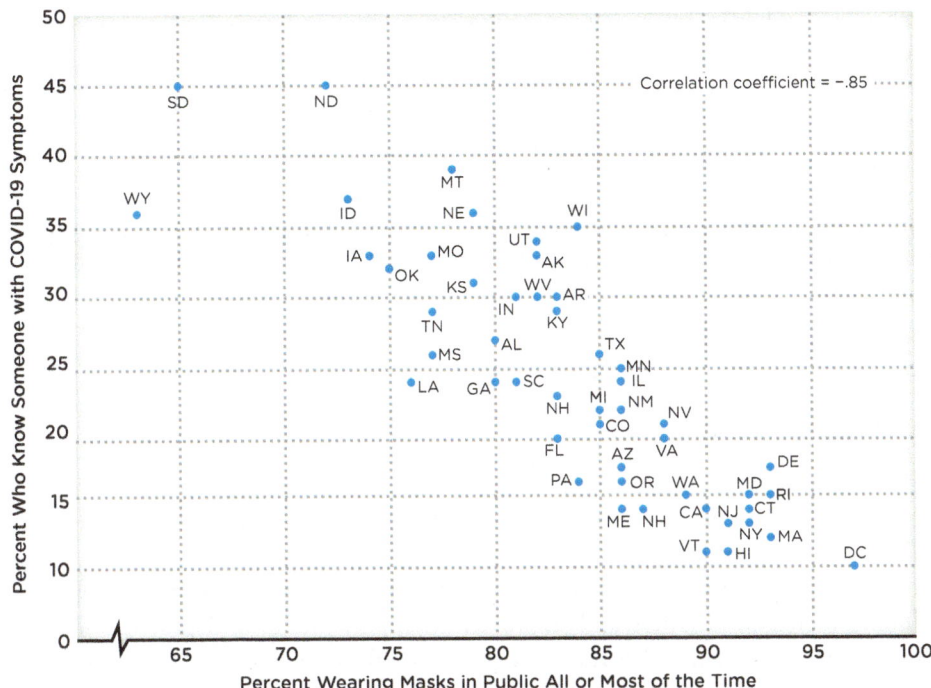

## FIGURE 1.4
### Real-World Correlations

The scatterplot to the left indicates a correlation between mask use and COVID-19 symptoms across U.S. states in October, 2020. The horizontal (*x*) axis shows the percentage of people in the state saying they usually wear masks in public. The vertical (*y*) axis shows the percentage of people in the state acquainted with someone experiencing COVID-19 symptoms. This is an example of a negative correlation: "As mask use increases, the frequency of observed COVID-19 symptoms decreases: More masks, less COVID-19" (Ingraham, 2020, para. 5).

Data from: Carnegie Mellon's COVIDCast (https://covidcast.cmu.edu).

exposure to violent media seem to have children who exhibit less aggressive behavior (Bushman et al., 2016). Perhaps some other quality of these parents (apart from their tendency to limit media exposure) causes their children to be less aggressive. Parenting style therefore would be considered a third variable because it influences both exposure to violence and aggressive behaviors. When you observe strong links between variables, consider other factors that could be related to both.

 **SHOW WHAT YOU KNOW**

1. Descriptive research is primarily useful for studying:
   A. operational definitions.
   B. observer bias.
   C. new or unexplored topics.
   D. visual-spatial skills.

2. If a researcher finds a positive correlation between smartphone use and absenteeism from work, why can't she claim that phone use causes absenteeism?

3. A researcher studying parent behavior during preschool drop-off trains teachers to record how long it takes caregivers to enter and leave the classroom. This approach to collecting data is referred to as _____.

✓ CHECK YOUR ANSWERS AT THE BACK OF THE BOOK.

# The Experimental Method

**TOGETHER AT LAST**   May 14, 2013, would be the most important day in the lives of Samantha Futerman and Anaïs Bordier. These young women, who shared a womb and came into the world together, would finally be reunited after 25 years of living on separate continents. The meeting would be captured on camera and become one of the most dramatic moments of their documentary film, *Twinsters*.

Sam and the movie crew landed at London's Heathrow Airport, collected their luggage, and headed straight to the apartment they had rented for the reunion. Shortly after they arrived, a few of Anaïs' friends came over, and the wait for Anaïs began. Sam, surging with adrenaline, did not know what to do with herself; she was excited and scared, wanting to hide. Then she heard it: a laugh coming from behind the door. It sounded just like her own, but it was Anaïs.

"I entered the room, and there was Sam," Anaïs recalls. "Neither of us knew what to do next, so we just stood in the middle of the room, staring at each other, like two tiny dogs sniffing each other out" (Bordier et al., 2014, p. 151). The twins

Twinsters (2015). Small Package Films.

**The First Meeting**
Sam and Anaïs' first meeting was both happy and stressful. Although this photo doesn't show them, several of their close friends were also there to witness the momentous event. As Anaïs recalls, "It felt like a big family, so it was really comforting."

watched each other in amazement, averting eye contact and periodically erupting in nervous laughter. At one point, Anaïs reached over to poke Sam, as if to see if she was real. "You don't know the person but you know her very well because you can read her perfectly," Anaïs explains. "It's the strangest thing."

After about 45 minutes, the whole group was emotionally exhausted and hungry. As they made their way toward a restaurant, Sam and Anaïs caught a glimpse of their reflection in a storefront window. "We both kind of stopped and were like, 'that is so weird,'" Sam recalls. "I'll never forget that moment." Following lunch, the twins returned to the apartment and took a nap together. Was it awkward crawling into bed and falling asleep with a person they had just met? "Not awkward at all," says Anaïs. "It took like two seconds."

## Control Is the Goal

Napping is what Sam and Anaïs do when they feel overwhelmed. It helps them reset and recharge. Many people use caffeine to achieve the same effect; they rely on soda, coffee, or energy drinks to clear away the mental fog that descends on them every afternoon. Research has linked low to moderate caffeine intake with various benefits, including increased alertness and improved attention, mood, and problem solving skills (Wilhelmus et al., 2017; Zabelina & Silvia, 2020). Suppose you are interested in researching how caffeine impacts one of these variables—let's say increased attention. How could you isolate the effects of caffeine when so many other factors could potentially affect attention, such as nutrition, sleep habits, and physical health? There is a research method that allows you to monitor these possible sources of interference: the *experimental method*.

**LO 9** Explain how the experimental method can establish cause and effect.

Unlike the descriptive and correlational methods discussed earlier, the **experimental method** can tell us about cause and effect, as it aims to ensure that every variable except those being manipulated by the researcher is held constant or controlled (see INFOGRAPHIC 1.4 on page 48).

So how does the experimental method allow us to control variables? The researchers randomly assign participants to two or more groups that they try to make equivalent with respect to all variables, with one key exception: the treatment or manipulation being studied. If the groups differ on the variable of interest following this treatment or manipulation, we can say with confidence that the experimental manipulation caused that change. In this way, the experimental method allows researchers to observe the variable of interest without interference from other variables.

If you are having trouble understanding what it means to control variables, consider this analogy: You are outside a football stadium, desperately trying to follow a friend lost in a swarm of people. Everyone is moving in different directions, making it exceedingly difficult to pinpoint your friend's location and direction of movement. But what if everyone in the crowd except your friend froze for a moment? Would it be easier to observe him now that he is the only one moving? This is similar to what researchers try to do with variables—hold everything steady except the variables they are examining.

How might you design a study using the experimental method? Suppose you want to investigate how caffeine impacts attention. Your hypothesis is the following: *Participants given a moderate dose of caffeine will perform better on a task that requires increased attention compared to participants given a sugar pill.* To test this hypothesis, you need to put together a group of participants who are very similar in age, educational background, physical health, and other variables that might affect their ability to stay attentive. Next, you divide the participants into two groups: one that

**experimental method** A type of research that manipulates a variable of interest (independent variable) to uncover cause-and-effect relationships.

receives caffeine supplements and another that gets sugar pills. After participants take the treatment or sugar pill for a designated amount of time, you compare the two groups' performance on standard attention tasks. If the group receiving the caffeine supplements performs better, then you can attribute that difference to caffeine. This may sound straightforward, but there are still some critical concepts you need to understand.

**RANDOM ASSIGNMENT**    Assigning participants to groups is a crucial step in the experimental method. Fail to divide participants in the correct way and your whole study is compromised. For this reason, researchers use **random assignment** to ensure that participants have an equal chance of being assigned to any of the groups. Randomly choosing which treatment the participants receive reduces the possibility that some other variable (a characteristic of the participants, such as age or sensitivity to caffeine) will influence the findings. You can flip a coin, roll dice, or use a computer to generate numbers, but the goal of random assignment is always the same: to ensure that the groups are roughly equal on all characteristics. If the groups are lopsided with respect to some variable, the results may be affected. Getting back to your caffeine study, imagine you assigned all the teenage participants to one group and all the middle-age participants to the other. Might age influence the results of a task measuring attention? Perhaps. Random assignment helps reduce some of the interference resulting from such characteristics.

You may have noticed some similarities between *random assignment* and *random sample* introduced earlier in the chapter. Here's the difference: Random sampling is used at the onset of a study to gather participants from a larger population. Random assignment comes into play later, when you are assigning participants to different groups.

**EXPERIMENTAL AND CONTROL GROUPS**    Returning to your study on caffeine supplements and attention, let's assume you did use random assignment to divvy your participants into two groups. One group receives the treatment (a daily dose of caffeine), and the other gets no treatment at all. (They are handed a sugar pill that looks identical to the caffeine supplement, or they are given nothing.) Those who get the treatment (caffeine supplements) comprise the **experimental group,** and those who get no treatment (a sugar pill or nothing at all) are members of the **control group.** You need a control group for the purpose of comparison: To determine the effects of the treatment, you must compare it to the effects of no treatment.

"Well, I guess we're the control group."

Loren Fishman/Cartoonstock.

**INDEPENDENT AND DEPENDENT VARIABLES**    Let's restate a point we made earlier in the section, this time using some new vocabulary terms: The only difference between the experimental and control groups should be the variable researchers are manipulating—in this case, caffeine intake. The different treatment given to the two groups is called the **independent variable (IV),** because it is the one variable the researchers are deliberately changing. (In this case, some participants get caffeine, others a sugar pill or nothing at all.) This is a critical point, and it's worth restating: In the experimental method, the independent variable is the variable researchers are manipulating. Because of the complex nature of human behavior, there may be more than one independent variable in a given experiment.

The **dependent variable (DV)** refers to the characteristic or response researchers are observing or measuring. As with the independent variable, there may be more than one dependent variable in a given study. In our hypothetical experiment, the dependent variable is the participants' performance on various attention tasks. Just remember, the independent variable is what the researchers are manipulating, and the dependent variable is what they are measuring as a result of that manipulation.

**random assignment** The process of appointing study participants to experimental or control groups, ensuring that every person has an equal chance of being assigned to either.

**experimental group** The participants in an experiment who are exposed to the treatment variable or manipulation by the researcher; represents the treatment group.

**control group** The participants in an experiment who are not exposed to the treatment variable; this is the comparison group.

**independent variable (IV)** In the experimental method, the variable manipulated by the researcher to determine its effect on the dependent variable.

**dependent variable (DV)** In the experimental method, the characteristic or response that is measured to determine the effect of the researcher's manipulation.

# The Experimental Method: Are You in Control?

The experimental method is the type of research that can tell us about causes and effects. It is different from descriptive and correlational studies in that key aspects of the experiment—participants, variables, and study implementation—are tightly controlled. The experiment typically includes at least two groups—an experimental group and a control group. This allows the researcher to isolate the effects of manipulating a single variable, called the independent variable.

Imagine you want to know if laws that ban texting while driving are worthwhile. Does texting really *cause* more accidents? Perhaps texting is merely correlated with higher accident rates in certain populations, such as college students, because college students are both more likely to text and more likely to have accidents. In order to find out, you have to perform an experiment.

## VARIABLES

### INDEPENDENT VARIABLE

The variable that researchers deliberately manipulate.

**Example:** The independent variable is texting while driving.

- **Experimental group** drives through obstacle course while texting.
- **Control group** drives through obstacle course without texting.

### DEPENDENT VARIABLE

The variable measured as an outcome of manipulation of the independent variable.

**Example:** The dependent variable is the number of accidents (objects hit in obstacle course).

### EXTRANEOUS VARIABLE

An unforeseen factor or characteristic that could interfere with the outcome.

**Example:** Some participants have more driving experience than others. Without controlling the amount of driving experience, we can't be certain the independent variable caused more accidents.

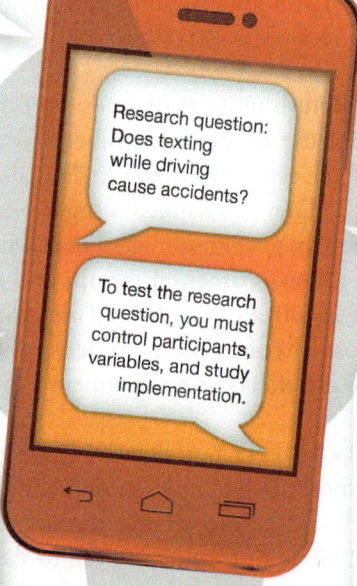

Research question: Does texting while driving cause accidents?

To test the research question, you must control participants, variables, and study implementation.

## STUDY IMPLEMENTATION

## PARTICIPANTS

### REPRESENTATIVE SAMPLE

Subset of the population chosen to reflect population of interest.

**Example:** Participants must be college students. Other groups might be affected differently by the independent variable.

### RANDOM SAMPLE

Method used to ensure participants do not introduce unexpected bias.

**Example:** Researchers recruit participants by randomly selecting students from the college directory.

### RANDOM ASSIGNMENT

Process by which researcher randomly assigns participants to experimental or control group.

**Example:** Experimenter flips coin to determine participant's group.

### EXPERIMENTER BIAS

Researchers' expectations and unintentional behaviors can unwittingly change the outcome of a study.

**Example:** Without thinking, researcher says "good luck" to one group. This might unintentionally cause them to try harder.

When possible, researchers control for these effects by using a double-blind study in which neither researcher nor participant knows what group participants are assigned to.

In other words, researchers are trying to determine whether the dependent variable (in this case, performance on the attention tasks) "depends" on the independent variable (caffeine supplement or sugar pill).

**EXTRANEOUS VARIABLES**   When planning experiments, researchers must take steps to ensure that *extraneous variables* do not interfere with their measures. **Extraneous variables** are characteristics of the environment or participants that could potentially affect the outcome of the research. While conducting your study of caffeine supplements, you discover that three of the participants are particularly sensitive to caffeine; even small doses make it very difficult for them to sleep at night. Their resulting sleep deprivation can definitely influence performance on attention tasks. Unfortunately, you failed to consider this very important variable in your research design, and thus it is an extraneous variable. Researchers must contemplate the many different kinds of variables that could influence the dependent variable.

In some cases, extraneous variables can *confound* the results of an experiment. A **confounding variable** is a type of extraneous variable that changes in sync with the independent variable, making it very difficult to discern which variable—the independent variable or the confounding variable—is causing changes in the dependent variable. Remember how we discussed *third variables* in correlational studies? Just as third variables can muddle the results of correlational studies, confounding variables can interfere with the outcomes of experimental studies.

Let's explore this concept of confounding variables further, returning to our hypothetical caffeine study. Imagine the lab is not big enough to accommodate all participants at once, so you collect data from the experimental group in the morning and the control group in the evening. But when you compare the two groups' performance on attention tasks, how can you be sure their differences result from the caffeine supplements, and not the time of day the data were collected? Participants may be more alert in the morning, so the time of day—and not just the caffeine supplement—could be driving changes in attentional capacity. And perhaps the behavior of the lab assistants changes as the day wears on, which, in turn, could influence the behavior of participants. Do you see how the time of day, and certain variables associated with it, could be confounding variables?

The good news is that we can take steps to minimize the influence of extraneous variables. That is, we can control variables. Earlier, we explained how researchers control variables with the help of random assignment. In the caffeine study, that would help to ensure that both groups have approximately the same number of participants who are sensitive to caffeine (meaning they don't sleep well after using it). Another way to control the impact of caffeine sensitivity is to remove the caffeine-sensitive participants from your sample and not include their information in your statistical analyses. Finally, you can minimize the influence of extraneous variables by treating the experimental and control groups exactly the same; for example, giving them attention tasks at the same time and location.

If you succeed in holding all variables constant except the independent variable, then you can make a statement about cause and effect. Getting back to your study on caffeine and attention, let's say the participants who took caffeine supplements perform better on attention tasks than those in the placebo group. It is relatively safe to attribute that disparity to the independent variable. In other words, you can presume that the caffeine supplements caused the superior performance of the experimental group.

**DOUBLE-BLIND STUDY**   When using the experimental method (or any type of research design), researchers use different methods to help control for extraneous variables. In a *single-blind study,* for example, participants do not know what treatment

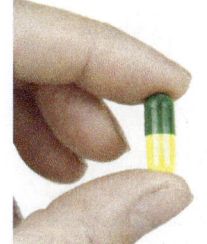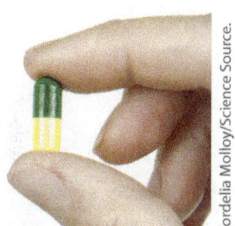

Cordelia Molloy/Science Source.

**Looks Real**
One of these pills contains an active ingredient; the other is a placebo. People taking placebos often experience benefits that are similar to those reported by participants receiving the actual drug. They can even experience similar side effects (Colloca, 2017).

**extraneous variable** A characteristic of participants or the environment that could unexpectedly influence the outcome of a study.
**confounding variable** A type of extraneous variable that changes in sync with the independent variable, making it difficult to discern which one is causing changes in the dependent variable.

they are receiving. With a **double-blind study,** both the participants and the researchers working directly with those participants are unaware who is getting the real treatment and who is getting the pretend treatment. In your caffeine study, this would mean that the people administering the pills and the attention tasks would not know who was receiving the caffeine supplement and who was receiving the sugar pill. Nor would the participants be privy to this information. Keeping participants in the dark is relatively easy; just make sure the treatment and sugar pill appear identical. Concealing details from the researchers is a little trickier but can be accomplished with the help of clever assistants who make it appear that all participants are getting the same treatment. Why is the double-blind study such a strong experimental design? It has to do with what's going on inside the minds of both participants and researchers.

**THINKING IS BELIEVING**    Prior research tells us that the expectations of participants can influence results. If someone hands you a cup of decaf coffee and says it is regular, you may feel energized after drinking it because you *think* it is caffeinated. Similarly, if someone gives you a sugar pill but tells you it is real medicine, you might end up feeling better simply because this is what you expect. Apparently, thinking is believing. When people are given a fake pill or other inactive "treatment," known as a **placebo** (pluh-SEE-bo), they often get better even though the contents of the pill are inert. Remarkably, this effect occurs even when participants are told they are receiving a placebo (Leibowitz et al., 2019). The placebo effect has been shown to ease pain, anxiety, depression, and even symptoms of Parkinson's disease. And although placebos are not able to reduce the size of tumors, they can help with some of the side effects of cancer treatment, such as pain, fatigue, and nausea (Kaptchuk & Miller, 2015). Researchers believe the placebo effect arises through both conscious expectations and unconscious associations between treatment cues and healing, and these psychological processes may influence what happens on a physiological level. In other words, expectations can influence what's going on in the body.

**EXPERIMENTER BIAS**    We've discussed the rationale for keeping participants in the dark, but why is it necessary to keep the researchers clueless as well? Researchers' expectations can influence the outcome of a study, a phenomenon known as **experimenter bias.** A researcher may unwittingly color a study's outcome through subtle verbal and/or nonverbal communication with the participants, conveying hopes or beliefs about the experiment's results (Nichols & Edlund, 2015). Saying something like "I really have high hopes for this medicine" might influence participants' reactions to the treatment. The researcher's value system may also impact the results in barely noticeable but very important ways. Beliefs and attitudes can shape the way a researcher frames questions, tests hypotheses, or interprets findings (Rosenthal, 1966, 2002; Stanley et al., 2018).

**RELIABILITY AND VALIDITY**    When evaluating a study, we should consider two important qualities of the measures used to collect data: reliability and validity. *Reliability* refers to the consistency or stability of a measure. A reliable test is one that yields consistent results across time. For example, if you take a personality test today and one week from now, the results should be very similar. The other important quality is the *validity* of measures used in a study. Do they measure what they intend to measure? In the example above, the personality test should measure personality characteristics, not some other variables. When examining an entire study, we should consider both its internal validity and external validity. If an experiment has *internal validity*, its design allows it to measure what it intends to measure (Campbell & Stanley, 1963). When an experiment has *external validity*, that means its findings can be generalized to the population of interest. Studies that use representative samples

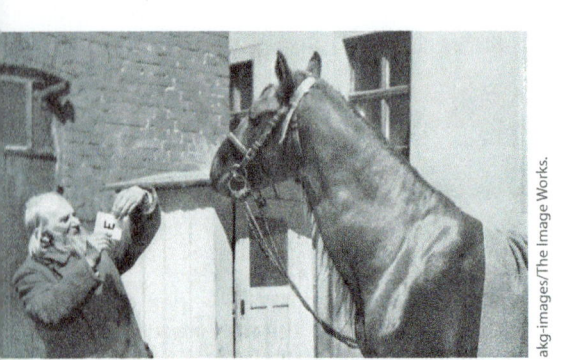

akg-images/The Image Works.

**Smart Horse, or Biased Humans?**
"Clever Hans," pictured here with his trainer Wilhelm von Osten, was a horse that appeared to be capable of counting, solving math problems, and a host of other cognitive tasks. When prompted with a question, Hans would signal the right answer by tapping his hooves. But as it turned out, Hans was just a brilliant reader of human behavior: By looking at the person asking the questions, Hans could tell when he was about to answer correctly. If Hans was wearing blinders, his amazing problem-solving ability vanished (Pfungst, 1911; Samhita & Gross, 2013). The case of "Clever Hans" illustrates experimenter bias, or the tendency for the experimenter's views or expectations to color the results of a study (Rosenthal, 1965).

**double-blind study** Type of study in which neither the participants nor the researchers administering the independent variable know which participants are receiving the treatment and which are getting the placebo.

**placebo** An inert substance or fake treatment given to members of the control group.

**experimenter bias** Researcher expectations that influence the outcome of a study.

**TABLE 1.2    Research Methods: Pros and Cons**

| Research Method | Advantages | Disadvantages |
|---|---|---|
| Descriptive | Good for tackling new research questions and studying phenomena in natural environments. | Very little control; increased experimenter/participant bias; cannot determine cause and effect. |
| Correlational | Shows whether two variables are related; useful when an experimental method is not possible. | Directionality and third-variable problems; cannot determine cause and effect. |
| Experimental | Can determine cause and effect; increased control over variables. | Results may not generalize beyond lab setting; potential for extraneous variables. |

How does a researcher choose which method to use? It depends on the research question. Each approach has advantages and disadvantages.

are more likely to have external validity; the results can be generalized from samples to populations.

**NOTHING IS PERFECT**    You have now learned the nuts and bolts of the experimental method, one of psychology's greatest myth-debunking, knowledge-gathering tools. The experimental method is also distinguished by its ability to establish cause and effect. But like any scientific approach, it does have some drawbacks. Laboratory settings are inherently unnatural and therefore cannot always paint an accurate picture of behaviors that would occur in natural settings. When people know they are being observed, their behavior changes; researchers call this the *Hawthorne effect* (Goodwin et al., 2017; Olson et al., 2004). Other weaknesses of the experimental method include cost (it's expensive to maintain a laboratory) and time (collecting data in a laboratory setting can be much slower than, say, sending out a survey). Finally, there are instances when it is not possible (or ethical) to manipulate certain variables. **TABLE 1.2** gives an overview of some of the advantages and disadvantages of the research methods we have described.

Before we move on, let's test our understanding of the experimental method with the help of a sprightly yellow square named SpongeBob.

## Didn't See That Coming

### SPONGEBOB ON THE BRAIN

⚡ A little television won't hurt a child, will it? Kids' programs are interspersed with lessons on colors, words, and numbers, and only run for periods of 20 to 30 minutes. It seems reasonable to assume that little snippets of TV can't possibly have any measurable effect.

**TURNING YOUNG BRAINS TO "SPONGE"?**

When it comes to the rapidly developing juvenile brain, it's probably not safe to assume anything. Consider the following experiment examining the cognitive changes observed in preschool children after just 9 minutes of exposure to a talking yellow sponge zipping across a television screen.

The research participants were sixty 4-year-olds, most of whom came from White, upper-middle-class households. Researchers randomly assigned the children to one of three conditions: watching the extremely fast-paced cartoon *SpongeBob SquarePants,* viewing an educational program, or drawing with crayons and markers. Following 9 minutes of the assigned activities, the children took a series of four commonly used tests to assess their executive function—the collection of brain processes involved in self-control, decision making, problem solving, and other higher-level functions. The results were shocking: Children in the SpongeBob group performed considerably worse than those in the other groups (Lillard & Peterson, 2011). Just 9 minutes of SpongeBob produced a temporary lapse in cognitive function.

HANDOUT/KRT/Newscom.

**Sponge Brain**
No one expects cartoons to make kids smarter, but can they hurt them? One study suggests that preschool children watching just 9 minutes of the high-energy, ultra-stimulating kids' show *SpongeBob SquarePants* experience a temporary dip in cognitive function.

How do we know that this was not the result of a different variable, such as some children's preexisting attentional issues or television-watching habits at home? Those factors were accounted for in the study. In the experimental method, researchers hold nearly all variables constant except the one they want to manipulate—the 9-minute activity, in this case. This is the independent variable (IV). In this way, the researchers can be somewhat confident that changes in the IV are driving changes in the dependent variable (DV)—performance on the cognitive tests.

What aspect of the cartoon caused this effect? The researchers hypothesized it had something to do with the show's "fantastical events and fast pacing" (Lillard & Peterson, 2011, p. 648), and a subsequent study suggests that the fantastical content may be the problem. Shows that are highly fantastical, or involve "physically impossible events" (for example, cartoon characters that magically change shape or disappear in poofs of smoke), seem to compromise short-term executive function in a way that non-fantastical shows do not. The negative impact of fantasy is even apparent with slow-paced programs like *Little Einsteins* and "educational" shows such as *Martha Speaks* (Lillard et al., 2015). Skeptics point out that findings from the original SpongeBob study have been difficult to replicate and that children are exposed to fantastical content elsewhere, even in classic storybooks such as *Where the Wild Things Are* by Maurice Sendak (Scarf & Hinten, 2018). And who could argue that imaginative storybooks are bad for children? In fact, research suggests that exposure to fantastical content in books has cognitive benefits, such as increased vocabulary development (Weisberg et al., 2015).

Many questions remain, but parents would be wise to impose limits, as greater amounts of screen time have been linked to slower development in young children. The relationship is not so surprising: "When young children are observing screens, they may be missing important opportunities to practice and master interpersonal, motor, and communication skills" (Madigan et al., 2019, p. E5). ⊕

## Is the Research Ethical?

**LO 10** Demonstrate an understanding of research ethics.

Conducting psychological research carries an enormous ethical responsibility. Psychologists do not examine dinosaur fossils or atomic particles. They study humans and other living creatures who experience pain, fear, and other complex feelings, and it is their professional duty to treat them with dignity and respect.

In Chapter 11, you will learn about some of the most famous and ethically questionable studies in the history of psychology. These studies would never be approved today, as psychologists have established specific guidelines to help ensure ethical behavior in their field. Professional organizations such as the American Psychological Association (APA) and the Association for Psychological Science (APS) provide written guidelines their members agree to follow. These guidelines attempt to ensure the ethical treatment of research participants, both human and nonhuman. (Keep in mind that notions of "ethical treatment" are highly variable; not everyone agrees with the codes established by these organizations.) The guidelines encourage psychologists to do no harm; safeguard the welfare of living beings in their research; know their responsibilities to society and community; maintain accuracy in research, teaching, and practice; and respect human dignity, among other best practices (APA, 2017a).

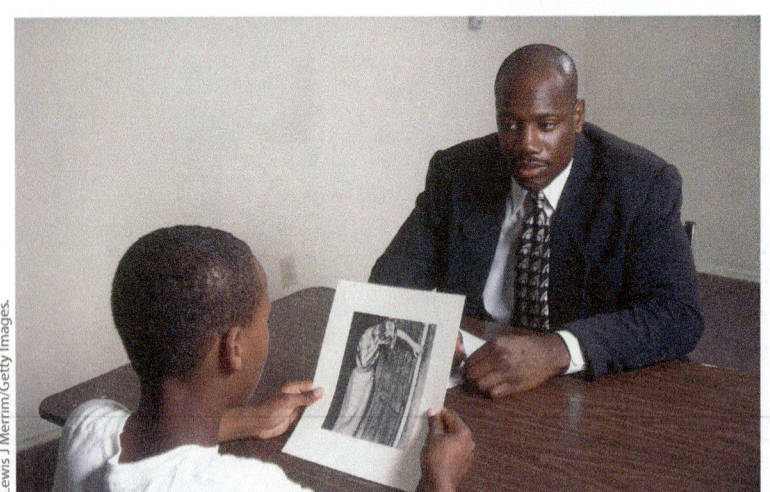

Lewis J Merrim/Getty Images.

**A Lofty Responsibility**
A psychologist administers the Thematic Apperception Test to a child. (You will learn about this projective personality test in Chapter 10.) Conducting research on minors involves additional ethical considerations, and informed consent must be obtained from parents or legal guardians.

**WHOSE WORDS ARE THESE?**   As mentioned earlier, psychologists disseminate information by publishing articles in scientific journals. Along with this comes an ethical responsibility to give credit where credit is due. Using the activity below, explore how APA (2020) style supports the fair use of other people's work.

## Put Your Heads Together

In your group, **A)** Pick any two sentences in this chapter and copy them, word for word, at the top of a piece of paper. **B)** Copy the sentences again, but this time include quotation marks at its beginning and end, and use APA style to cite the authors' last names, year of publication, and page number from the textbook. **C)** Paraphrase the content in your own words, and use APA style to cite the authors' last names and year of publication. **D)** Which of the above constitutes plagiarism and which does not? Why is it important to cite other people's work, and how do the APA guidelines make it obvious whose words are being used?

**CONFIDENTIALITY**   An important component of ethical treatment is confidentiality. Researchers must take steps to protect research data from misuse or theft. Psychologists who offer therapy services are obligated to keep client and therapy session information confidential; in fact, they are required to safeguard this information in their offices. Confidentiality enables clients to speak freely about deeply personal issues. It ensures that research participants feel protected when they share sensitive information (about sexual or controversial matters, for example), because they may rest assured researchers will keep it safe.

There are some occasions when psychologists are legally required to break confidentiality: for example, when a client is a danger to self or others (including the psychologist); in cases of abuse, neglect, or domestic violence; or when the psychologist receives a court order (APA, n.d.-c). At the client's request, psychologists may also share confidential information with an organization, physician, or legally authorized individual. Additionally, psychologists may share a limited amount of information in order to receive payment for services, but only the "minimum that is necessary" (APA, 2017a, para. 4.05).

**INFORMED CONSENT**   Ethical treatment also involves sharing information. Researchers have a duty to tell participants as much as they can about a study's purpose and procedures; they do this through *informed consent* and *debriefing*. Suppose you want to study a certain population—college seniors in the United States, for example. You have identified your sample, but before enlisting these people as participants and collecting data, you must make certain they are comfortable with their involvement. Through **informed consent,** the students in your study acknowledge that they understand what their participation will entail, including any possible harm that could result. Informed consent is a critical part of Dr. Segal's twin studies. "You prepare a letter, and you have to keep a copy yourself, and give [the participants] a signed copy as well," she explains. "It lays out everything they will be doing, what some of their benefits are, what some of the risks might be, and that you will ensure them confidentiality. You don't give away hypotheses, but you speak about the research in a more general way because you don't want to bias the findings. It's kind of like your contract with them, and they're also free to withdraw from the study or refuse to do something at any point." Informed consent is a participant's way of saying, *I understand my role in this study, and I am okay with it.* It's also the researcher's way of ensuring that participants know what they are getting into.

**DEBRIEFING**   Following a study, there is a second step of disclosure called **debriefing.** In a debriefing session, researchers provide participants with useful information about the study; in some cases, this means revealing any deception or manipulation used—information that couldn't be shared beforehand. Remember that concealing information

**informed consent** Acknowledgment from study participants that they understand what their participation will entail.

**debriefing** Sharing information with participants after their involvement in a study has ended, including the purpose of the research and any deception used.

is a key part of the double-blind study. Other types of psychological research require withholding information as well. In this book, you will learn about experiments in which participants were initially unaware of the study's purpose. In some cases, researchers purposely lied to participants, either because it was part of the manipulation, or because they needed to conceal the study's objective until the debriefing phase. It is important to note that no one is or should ever be forced to become a research participant. Involvement is completely voluntary, and participants can drop out at any time. And finally, all experiments on humans and animals must be approved by an **Institutional Review Board (IRB)** to ensure the highest ethical standards. An IRB is a committee that reviews research proposals to protect the rights and welfare of all participants.

## Apply This ⬇

### DON'T BELIEVE EVERYTHING YOU READ

As you venture deeper into the study of psychology, you may find yourself becoming increasingly skeptical of media reports on research relating to psychological phenomena. We encourage a healthy dose of skepticism. Although many news stories on scientific findings are accurate and balanced, others are distorted and exaggerated. Look at these headlines about a 2020 study investigating the relationship between food and psychological health:

**CORRELATION OR CAUSATION?**

> **"Study claims eating meat can help improve mental health"** (Cortes, 2020)
>
> **"Eating meat may IMPROVE mental health and one in three vegetarians are depressed, study suggests"** (Pinkstone, 2020)

It sounds as if meat-based diets are *causing* better mental health, while vegetarian diets create psychological problems. We must have a cause-and-effect relationship, right? Wrong. The following is a rough description of the research, which was actually a review of many studies published in the journal *Critical Reviews in Food Science and Nutrition*: Researchers combed through the scientific literature, looking for studies examining links between meat consumption (or meat avoidance) and variables related to mental health. Eighteen studies met the researchers' criteria for inclusion. Taken together, the results point to an association between meat avoidance and higher levels of anxiety and depression (Dobersek et al., 2020).

Provocative as these findings may be, they do not allow us to conclude that eating meat causes less anxiety and depression. In fact, the authors are careful to point this out: "Across all studies, there was no evidence to support a causal relation between the consumption or avoidance of meat and any psychological outcomes" (Dobersek et al., 2020, p. 9).

Isn't it possible that some third variable is at work, driving both eating behaviors and mental health symptoms? For example, research suggests that many people choose to become vegetarian for health reasons (Hopwood et al., 2020). Could it be that concerns about health are driving both anxiety and decisions to eliminate meat? Another factor to consider is the direction of causation. When we see headlines like those above, we tend to assume that cutting out meat *leads* to mental health issues. But what if the reverse is true, that is, experiencing anxiety or depression makes people more inclined to stop eating meat (Dobersek et al., 2020)? The take-home message: If a news report claims that *X causes Y*, **don't automatically assume** that the media has it right. In this case, the research has only demonstrated a correlation between variables, not a cause-and-effect relationship.

**Hyped Up Associations?**
Does eating meat *cause* people to experience better mental health outcomes . . . or does evidence suggest a *correlation* between these two variables? If you see a headline claiming "x causes y," immediately turn on your critical-thinking skills. Media reports sometimes suggest causation when the findings are based only on correlations.

mdphoto16/Getty Images.

## CONNECTIONS

In **Chapter 0,** we explained that psychology is driven by critical thinking, a process that involves synthesizing evidence, thinking beyond definitions, and being open-minded but skeptical at the same time. Here, we emphasize the importance of thinking critically about media reports of research findings; news stories can sometimes be misleading or inaccurate.

**Institutional Review Board (IRB)** A committee that reviews research proposals to protect the rights and welfare of all participants.

## CAREER CONNECTIONS

### COMMUNICATING WITH THE PUBLIC

 Given the previous example, you can see how important it is for journalists to understand the difference between correlation and causation. The same goes for public relations (PR) specialists, who act as liaisons between institutions (universities, companies, etc.) and the outside world.

Imagine you are a PR specialist for a university, and your job is to share research developments with the media and the general public. You write a press release describing the results of a study on herbal supplements intended to ease depression. If you exaggerate or misrepresent the results ("The supplement worked better than approved antidepressants!"), the public may get the wrong idea. What might happen if people with symptoms of depression suddenly stopped taking their regular medications and begin using an herbal supplement with questionable scientific backing?

Another tip for journalists, PR specialists, and anyone who shares complex information with the general public: Avoid using fancy words. Nonexperts have trouble processing information when they are presented with scientific jargon, even if definitions are provided. This may cause them to lose interest in the subject matter and feel less engaged with the scientific community (Shulman et al., 2020).

Scientists debate whether humans are causing global warming

**False Balance in the Media**

If 97% of climate scientists agree that humans are causing global warming, and only 3% disagree, why do news outlets sometimes present this issue as a "debate" between two individuals? By giving equal attention to the two viewpoints, the media promotes the misconception that scientists are split 50–50 on the issue. We call this "false balance."

## ▶▶▶ SHOW WHAT YOU KNOW

1. The experimental method can provide findings on the _____ of variables.
   A. experimenter bias
   B. confounding
   C. random assignment
   D. cause-and-effect relationship

2. Following a study involving a double-blind procedure with a treatment and a placebo, a researcher met with each participant individually to discuss important information about the study. This is known as a(n) _____.

3. What safeguards are in place to protect research participants from harm?

 CHECK YOUR ANSWERS AT THE BACK OF THE BOOK.

**"ANYTHING IS POSSIBLE"**    The momentous meeting of Sam and Anaïs marked the beginning of a new journey for the twins and their families. Sam's parents embraced Anaïs as a second daughter, and Anaïs' parents did the same with Sam. As Anaïs says, "We really see our family as one huge one living in America and one in France."

When Sam imagines what life would be like if she never connected with Anaïs, she sees a version of herself that is more self-absorbed. "I would have been so focused on my career, acting, and pushing myself . . . and it would have been all about me," she says. "Now I have this amazing human across the world that I'm always thinking about and always worrying about." For Anaïs, finding Sam has made her feel complete in a way she never did before. "I definitely was missing something. I don't know if it was from being adopted or from being separated from Sam," says Anaïs. "I feel complete now." When Anaïs looks at Sam, it's almost like observing herself from the outside.

Twinsters (2015). Small Package Films.

**Sister Love**

Sam and Anaïs on their trip to South Korea, where they attended a conference of the International Korean Adoptee Associations. Now that the twins have found each other, they want to help others. Sam and fellow actress Jenna Ushkowitz (also a Korean adoptee) founded Kindred, a nonprofit foundation that provides support and resources for adoptees and their families (Kindred, n.d.). Anaïs, now a designer for the fine leather company Jean Rousseau, hopes to create an educational foundation for orphans and adopted children in Korea, Cambodia, or other countries.

**positive psychology** An approach that focuses on human flourishing and the positive aspects of human nature, seeking to understand the roots of happiness, creativity, humor, and other strengths.

She sees a smart, funny, and charismatic young woman. Appreciating Sam's beautiful qualities has given her newfound confidence: "I feel like now anything is possible, thanks to Sam."

## Didn't See That Coming

INTRODUCING POSITIVE PSYCHOLOGY

Sam and Anaïs are wonderful examples of people who opt to see the brighter side of life. Instead of lamenting the fact that they spent 25 years apart, they rejoice in being united, anticipate good things to come, and want to help other twins and adoptees.

The twin's viewpoint seems to align with the **positive psychology** movement in the study of human behaviors and mental processes. A relatively new approach in the field, positive psychology explores human flourishing and the positive aspects of human nature—happiness, love, courage, hope, and all that is best about people (Seligman & Csikszentmihalyi, 2000). Historically, psychologists have tended to focus on the abnormal and maladaptive patterns of human behavior. Positive psychology does not deny the existence of these darker elements; it just directs the spotlight elsewhere. Positive psychologists explore the upside of personal experiences, traits, and institutions. They believe that humans "strive to lead meaningful, happy, and good lives" (Donaldson et al., 2015, p. 185). In this sense, positive psychology is similar to the humanistic perspective. In fact, the early work of the humanists helped set the stage for the current field of positive psychology (Friedman, 2014; Robbins, 2008).

**"MEANINGFUL, HAPPY, AND GOOD LIVES"**

Many positive psychology studies have focused on well-being and optimal functioning (Donaldson et al., 2015), producing results with immediate relevance to everyday life. For example, evidence suggests that people who have a positive outlook tend to have better mental and physical health than their less optimistic peers (Catalino & Fredrickson, 2011; Fredrickson & Joiner, 2018; Huffman et al., 2016).

Throughout this book, you will read about people whose lives seem to exemplify the power of this optimistic approach. Each chapter introduces you to one or more individuals who have faced challenges with courage and positivity, keeping their heads high when all hope seemed to be lost. Learning about these men and women has been a humbling experience for the authors. Their stories inspire us to be more thoughtful, compassionate, and fearless in our own lives. We hope they move you in the same way. As you proceed through these chapters, look for the positive messages that can be found in all types of psychological research. Open your mind and keep reading!

## Summary of Concepts

**LO 1**  Describe the scope of psychology. (p. 2)

Psychology is the scientific study of behavior and mental processes. Psychologists work in a variety of fields, and many conduct research. The two major types of research are basic and applied. Basic research focuses on collecting data to support or refute theories, gathering knowledge for the sake of knowledge.

Applied research focuses on changing behaviors and outcomes, often leading to real-world applications.

**LO 2**  Summarize the goals of psychology. (p. 2)

The goals of psychology are to describe, explain, predict, and change behavior. These goals lay the foundation for the scientific approach and the research designs used by psychologists.

**LO 3** Identify some of the people who laid the foundation for psychology, or helped establish it as a discipline; specify their contributions. (p. 5)

The roots of psychology lie in disciplines as diverse as philosophy and physiology. Early philosophers established the foundation for some of the longstanding debates in psychology (nature and nurture) and embraced scientific ways of thinking. In 1879 psychology was officially founded when Wundt created the first psychology laboratory. Titchener established structuralism to study the elements of the mind. James developed functionalism and offered the first psychology class in the United States.

**LO 4** Summarize the major perspectives in psychology. (p. 8)

Psychologists use different perspectives to understand and study topics in the field. Each perspective provides a different vantage point for uncovering the complex nature of human behavior. See Table 1.1 (p. 11) for a summary.

**LO 5** Describe how psychologists use the scientific method. (p. 12)

Psychologists use the scientific method to produce empirical evidence based on systematic observation or experiments. The scientific method includes five basic steps: develop a question, formulate a hypothesis, collect data, analyze data, and share the findings. A continuing cycle of exploration, the scientific method uses critical thinking at each step in the process and asks new questions along the way.

**LO 6** Explain the importance of a representative sample. (p. 18)

A population includes all members of a group a researcher is interested in exploring. If the population is large, then the researcher will select a subset, called a sample. With a random sample, all members of a population have an equal chance of being selected to participate in a study. Random sampling increases the likelihood of achieving a representative sample, or one that accurately reflects the population of interest. It is important for researchers to choose representative samples, because this allows them to generalize their findings, or apply information from a sample to the population at large.

**LO 7** Recognize several forms of descriptive research. (p. 20)

Descriptive research is a type of investigation used to describe and explore a phenomenon. It is especially useful for studying new or unexplored topics, when researchers might not have specific expectations about outcomes. Descriptive research methods include naturalistic observation, case studies, and the survey method.

**LO 8** Describe the correlational method and identify its limitations. (p. 24)

The correlational method examines relationships among variables. Variables can be positively correlated (as one variable goes up, the other goes up), negatively correlated (as one variable goes up, the other goes down), or not at all related. While useful for illuminating links between variables and helping researchers make predictions, the correlational method cannot determine cause and effect. Even a very strong correlation between two variables does not indicate a causal link, as a third variable might be influencing both.

**LO 9** Explain how the experimental method can establish cause and effect. (p. 28)

The experimental method is a type of research that can uncover cause-and-effect relationships between independent and dependent variables. A well-designed experiment holds everything constant except for the variables being manipulated by the researcher. If the groups of participants differ on the measure of interest, we can say with confidence that the experimental manipulation caused that change.

**LO 10** Demonstrate an understanding of research ethics. (p. 34)

Researchers must follow guidelines to ensure the ethical treatment of research participants. These guidelines encourage psychologists to do no harm; safeguard the welfare of living beings in their research; know their responsibilities to society and community; maintain accuracy in research, teaching, and practice; and respect human dignity.

# Key Terms

**behaviorism**, p. 8
**behavioral perspective**, p. 9
**biological perspective**, p. 10
**biopsychosocial perspective**, p. 10
**case study**, p. 21
**cognitive perspective**, p. 9

**confounding variable**, p. 31
**control group**, p. 29
**correlation**, p. 24
**correlation coefficient**, p. 25
**correlational method**, p. 24
**critical thinking**, p. 16
**debriefing**, p. 35

**dependent variable (DV)**, p. 29
**descriptive research**, p. 20
**double-blind study**, p. 32
**empirical method**, p. 5
**evolutionary perspective**, p. 9
**experiment**, p. 12

**experimental group**, p. 29
**experimental method**, p. 28
**experimenter bias**, p. 32
**extraneous variable**, p. 31
**functionalism**, p. 7
**humanistic psychology**, p. 9
**hypothesis**, p. 12

# Test Prep Are You Ready?

1. Experts at a large university were asked to devise and evaluate a campaign to reduce binge drinking. Using findings from prior research, they created a program to curb binge drinking among students. This is an example of:
   A. basic research.
   B. applied research.
   C. naturalistic observation.
   D. case studies.

2. An instructor in the psychology department assigns a project requiring students to read several journal articles on a controversial topic. They are then required to weigh various pieces of evidence from the articles, synthesize the information, and determine how the various findings contribute to understanding the topic. This process is known as:
   A. empiricism.
   B. critical thinking.
   C. basic research.
   D. applied research.

3. The Greek philosopher Plato believed that truth and knowledge exist in the soul before birth and that humans have innate knowledge. This position supports:
   A. empiricism.
   B. the nurture side of the nature–nurture issue.
   C. the nature side of the nature–nurture issue.
   D. dualism.

4. Positive psychology explores human flourishing and other positive aspects of human nature. This focus is most clearly aligned with which perspective?
   A. psychoanalytic
   B. psychodynamic
   C. biopsychosocial
   D. humanistic

5. The goal of _____ is to provide empirical evidence or data based on systematic observation or experimentation.
   A. operational definitions
   B. critical thinking
   C. the scientific method
   D. a hypothesis

6. A psychologist studying identical twins was interested in their leadership qualities and educational backgrounds. These characteristics are generally referred to as:
   A. operational definitions.
   B. hypotheses.
   C. variables.
   D. empiricism.

7. The less time students spend studying, the lower their grades will be. This is an example of a(n):
   A. positive correlation.
   B. negative correlation.
   C. confounding variable.
   D. extraneous variable.

8. A researcher interested in learning more about identical twins raised in separate households might use Sam and Anaïs as a(n) _____ , which is a type of descriptive research invaluable for studying rare events.
   A. experiment
   B. case study
   C. naturalistic observation
   D. correlational study

9. With a(n) _____ study, neither the researchers nor the participants know who is getting the treatment or who is getting the placebo.
   A. double-blind
   B. experimental
   C. correlational
   D. blind

10. A researcher forming a(n) _____ of high school seniors might select participants using a comprehensive database of all seniors in the United States, as all members of the population would have an equal chance of being selected for the study.
    A. control group
    B. experimental group
    C. natural selection
    D. random sample

11. Describe the goals of psychology and give an example of each.

12. A group of researchers is planning to conduct a study on aggression and exposure to media violence. What can they do to ensure the ethical treatment of the children in their study?

13. Use the perspectives of psychology to explain the similarities between Sam and Anaïs

14. Find an article in the popular media that presents the findings of a correlational study but portrays a cause-and-effect relationship between variables. Looking at the article, can you tell whether the researchers were using a representative sample?

15. Reread the feature on the SpongeBob study. How does it establish a cause-and-effect relationship between watching the cartoon and changes in cognitive function? If you were to replicate the study, what would you do to change or improve it?

✓ CHECK YOUR ANSWERS AT THE BACK OF BOOK.

# Biology and Behavior

## Introducing the Brain

**IN THE LINE OF FIRE**    It was November 9, 2004, and U.S. Marine Brandon Burns was surrounded on all sides by gunfire. The enemy was everywhere, in the buildings, streets, and alleyways of Fallujah. "I was in the deepest part of the city [and] there was chaos," remembers Brandon. At age 19, Brandon was on the front lines in the Iraq War, fighting in the battle of Fallujah.

"I was on top of the Humvee automatic grenade launcher shooting round after round," Brandon recalls. Suddenly, there was darkness. A bullet from an enemy sniper had pierced Brandon's helmet and skull, and ricocheted through the back left side of his brain. Bleeding and unconscious, Brandon was rushed from Fallujah to Baghdad. Medics had to resuscitate him on five separate occasions during that ambulance ride. As Brandon explains, "Five times I died."

From Baghdad, Brandon was transferred to a hospital in Germany. Doctors concluded that some parts of his brain were no longer viable. "They removed part of my skull and dug out the injured part of my brain," and now, Brandon says, "one third of my brain is gone."

*Note:* Quotations attributed to Brandon Burns, Laura Burns, and Christina Santhouse are personal communications.

**Sent to the Front Lines**

Brandon Burns poses for a photo at the Marine Corps Recruit Depot in Parris Island, South Carolina, in the fall of 2003 (left). The following year, he found himself engaged in some of the most rigorous urban combat of the Iraq War (Filkins, 2004).

## A Complex Communication Network

Imagine you were Brandon and lost a sizable chunk of your brain. How would it impact your life? Would you be the same person as before? Your brain houses your thoughts, emotions, and personality, and orchestrates your behavior. It files away all your memories and dark secrets, and is involved in your every move, from the beat of your heart to the blink of your eye.

As scientists have noted, "the human brain can be viewed as a system of unparalleled complexity" (Rietman et al., 2020, p. 1). This squishy, pinkish organ is definitely the most important component of your *nervous system*—a communication network that uses electrical and chemical processes to convey messages throughout your body. In this chapter, you will learn all about the human nervous system, which includes the brain, spinal cord, and nerves.

The building blocks of the nervous system are **neurons,** specialized cells that communicate with each other through electrical and chemical signals. The brain is home to approximately 100 billion neurons (Huang & Luo, 2015; Lake et al., 2018). And since a typical neuron can communicate with thousands of others, the total number of links among them could be about 100 trillion ($10^{14}$), or perhaps even a quadrillion ($10^{15}$) (Ascoli, 2015; Huang & Luo, 2015). This intricate, ever-adapting web of neural connections gives us the power to think and feel in ways that are different from—and vastly more complex than—the thinking and feeling capacities of most other organisms.

Consider the many tasks your brain is juggling at this very moment. As you scan the words on this page, your brain helps control the tiny muscles moving your eyes back and forth as well as the larger muscles in your neck and torso that keep you sitting upright. Light-sensitive cells in the back of your eyes relay signals to various brain regions that transform the black marks on this page into words, sentences, and ideas for you to remember. And all the while, your brain is processing sounds and smells, and working with other nerve cells in your body to make sure your heart keeps pumping, your lungs keep breathing, and your glands and organs keep releasing hormones properly.

**neurons** Specialized cells of the nervous system that transmit electrical and chemical signals in the body.

# From Bumps to Brain Scans

**LO 1**  Define neuroscience and biological psychology and explain how they contribute to our understanding of behavior.

Brandon's injury resulted in a significant loss of his brain tissue. Remarkably, not only did he survive, but he can still talk about what occurred, think about the events, and feel emotions associated with the experience. How exactly does his brain orchestrate all these complex functions, especially after severe trauma? And how does a noninjured brain carry out these processes? Scientists have developed a decent understanding of how individual brain cells communicate with each other, but they have yet to provide definitive answers to "big questions" involving the brain and other parts of the nervous system, such as "What is consciousness?" and "How are memories stored?" This is why the brain may be regarded as the "last frontier of scientific inquiry" (Huang & Luo, 2015, p. 44). **Neuroscience,** the study of the brain and other parts of the nervous system, draws upon disciplines as diverse as medicine, engineering, computer science, and our personal favorite—psychology. The subfield of psychology concerned with understanding how the brain and other biological systems influence human behavior is called **biological psychology,** which brings us to the goal of this chapter: to examine how biology influences our behavior.

**LO 2**  Compare and contrast tools scientists use to study the brain.

Brandon underwent many brain scans before and after his surgeries, which allowed doctors to get a detailed look inside his head without lifting a scalpel. But had Brandon lived in a different era, brain scans would not have been an option.

Before there were technologies to study the brain, people could only speculate about what was going on beneath the skull of a living person. One theory was that bumps on the skull revealed a person's characteristics. Judging the topography of the head was a core part of **phrenology,** the now discredited **brain "science"** that achieved enormous popularity at the beginning of the 19th century through its

**CONNECTIONS**

If phrenology were practiced today, we would consider it a pseudoscience, or an activity that resembles science but is not supported by objective evidence. See **Chapter 0** to learn more about pseudoscience and critical thinking.

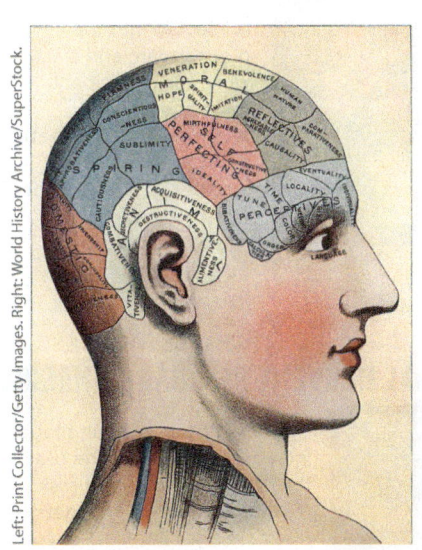

**All in Your Head**
Are you a secretive person? How high is your self-esteem? The answers to these questions lie on the surface of the skull, or so claimed 19th-century phrenologists, such as the one depicted in this 1886 illustration (right). The phrenological map (left) shows the locations of brain "organs" thought to be responsible for various psychological traits.

**neuroscience** The study of the brain and other parts of the nervous system.

**biological psychology** The branch of psychology that focuses on how the brain and other biological systems influence human behavior.

**phrenology** An early approach to explaining the functions of the brain by trying to link the physical structure of the skull with a variety of characteristics.

# Ways to Study the Living Brain

In the past, scientists were limited in their ability to study the brain. Most of what they learned came from performing surgeries, often on cadavers. Today, imaging and recording technologies enable us to investigate the structure and function of the living brain. CAT and MRI techniques provide static pictures of brain structures, while functional imaging and recording techniques allow us to see the relationship between brain activity and specific mental functions. Functional technologies can also be used to diagnose injuries and diseases earlier than techniques that look at structure.

New technologies are continually being developed, allowing us to study the brain in ways we couldn't imagine just a few years ago.

## Looking at Brain STRUCTURE

### COMPUTERIZED AXIAL TOMOGRAPHY — CAT

Using X-rays, a scanner creates multiple cross-sectional images of the brain. Here, we see the brain from the top at the level of the ventricles, which form the butterfly-shaped dark spaces in the center.

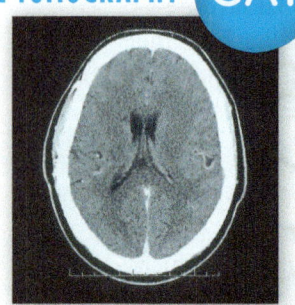

### MAGNETIC RESONANCE IMAGING — MRI

An MRI machine's powerful magnets create a magnetic field that passes through the brain. A computer analyzes the electromagnetic response, creating cross-sectional images similar to those produced by CAT, but with superior detail.

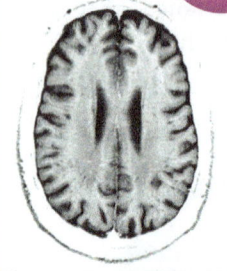

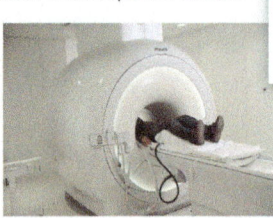

### What's Next?
### Making Connections

New technologies like diffusion spectrum imaging (DSI), which tracks the diffusion of water molecules through brain tissue, are being used to map neural connections. The resulting images show a complex information superhighway, with different colors indicating directions of travel.

## Watching Brain FUNCTION

### EEG — ELECTROENCEPHALOGRAM

Electrodes placed on the scalp record electrical activity from the area directly below. When the recorded traces are lined up, as in the computer readout seen here, we can see the scope of functional response across the brain's outer layer.

### PET — POSITRON EMISSION TOMOGRAPHY

A radioactively labeled substance called a tracer is injected into the bloodstream and tracked while the participant performs a task. A computer then creates 3-D images showing degrees of brain activity. Areas with the most activity appear in red.

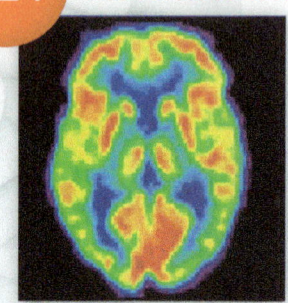

### fMRI — FUNCTIONAL MAGNETIC RESONANCE IMAGING

The flow of oxygen-rich blood increases to areas of the brain that are active during a task. fMRI uses powerful magnets to track changes in blood-oxygen levels. Like PET, this produces measurements of activity throughout the brain.

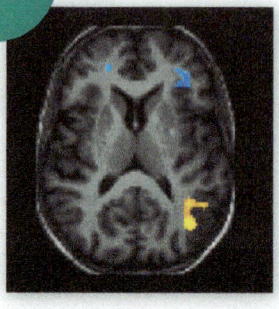

founder, German neuroanatomist Franz Joseph Gall (1757–1828). Another early approach to studying the brain was through *ablation,* a technique used by French physiologist Pierre Flourens (1794–1867). Ablation involved destroying parts of a living animal's brain and then determining whether some functioning was lost thereafter. Scientists also learned about the brain by studying people with existing brain damage. Despite their limitations, these early methodologies advanced the idea that areas of the brain might have particular functions (Eling & Finger, 2019; Wickens, 2015). The notion that specific brain regions are in charge of certain activities is known as *localization of function.*

Brain research has come a long way since the days of Gall and Flourens. Recent decades have witnessed an explosion of technologies for studying the nervous system (see INFOGRAPHIC 2.1). Such advances have made it possible to observe the brain as it solves problems, sleeps, listens to stories—virtually any activity you can imagine (Becker et al., 2020a; Demiral et al., 2019; Shain et al., 2020). With emerging technologies such as *optogenetics,* researchers can activate or deactivate individual neurons or groups of neurons and see how it affects animals' behavior (Deisseroth, 2015; Gutzeit et al., 2020; Chapter 4). Technology has even been used to test the claims of phrenologists, finding "no evidence" supporting the notion that the shape of the skull can be used to pinpoint mental abilities (Jones et al., 2018).

Now that we have learned how scientists study the brain, let's familiarize ourselves with some basic knowledge they have acquired.

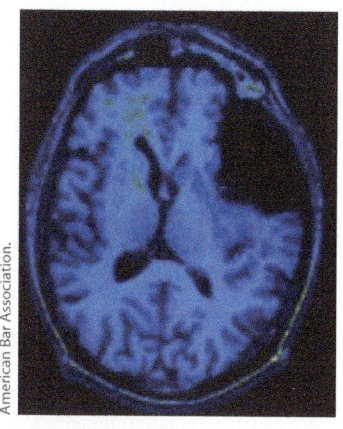

American Bar Association.

**Admissible in Court?**

This scan shows a large cyst in the brain of a man who was convicted of murder. His lawyer argued that the presence of the cyst impaired his client's ability to control his emotions and behaviors (Davis, 2012). A growing number of attorneys are submitting brain scans as legal evidence, but judges have been reluctant to accept them (Davis, 2015; Maron, 2018). As some experts note, neuroscience is not "ready for the courtroom" (Davis, 2020, para. 61).

### ► ► ► SHOW WHAT YOU KNOW

1. Match the technology on the left with its characteristic on the right:

   **A.** Positron emission tomography

   **B.** Electroencephalogram

   **C.** Magnetic resonance imaging

   **D.** Computerized axial tomography

   **E.** Functional magnetic resonance imaging

   _____ creates cross-sectional images using X-rays

   _____ records electrical activity from the brain

   _____ tracks changes of radioactive substances

   _____ tracks changes in blood oxygen levels

   _____ creates cross-sectional images with the help of magnetic fields

2. A researcher studying the impact of Brandon's brain injury might work in the field of _____, or the study of the brain and other parts of the nervous system.

✓ CHECK YOUR ANSWERS AT THE BACK OF BOOK.

# Neurons and Neural Communication

**THE AWAKENING** Two weeks after the shooting, Brandon finally awoke from his coma. He could not move or feel the right side of his body, and he had lost the ability to use language. There were so many things he wanted to say to his family, but when he opened his mouth, the only sound that came out was "ugh." Weeks went by before Brandon uttered his first word: "no." That was all he could say for months, even when he really wanted to say "yes."

Apart from the paralysis to his right side and his difficulty with language, Brandon's other faculties appeared to be intact. He could remember people, places, and objects, and he reported no trouble hearing, smelling, or tasting. And although Brandon was not as outgoing and self-assured as before, he hadn't changed much overall. What was occurring in Brandon's nervous system that enabled him to function after such a serious injury? The same process that makes it possible for you to pick up your textbook, read these words, and decipher their meaning: communication between neurons.

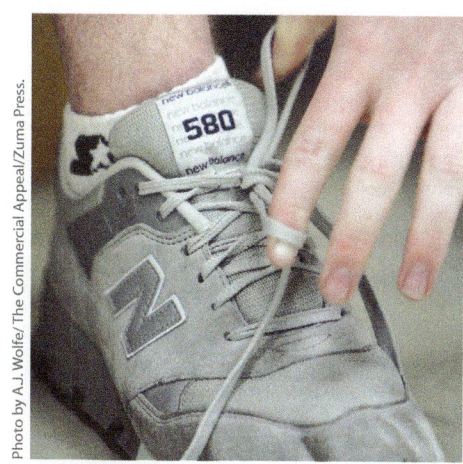

Photo by A.J. Wolfe/The Commercial Appeal/Zuma Press.

**One-Handed**

Brandon ties his shoelaces with his left hand. His traumatic brain injury occurred on the left side of his brain, causing paralysis and loss of sensation on the right side of his body.

## FIGURE 2.1
### The Neuron

The neuron, the basic building block of the nervous system, has three main components: (1) a cell body that contains vital cellular structures; (2) bushy dendrites that receive messages from neighboring neurons; and (3) a long, thin axon that sends messages to other neurons through its branchlike terminals.

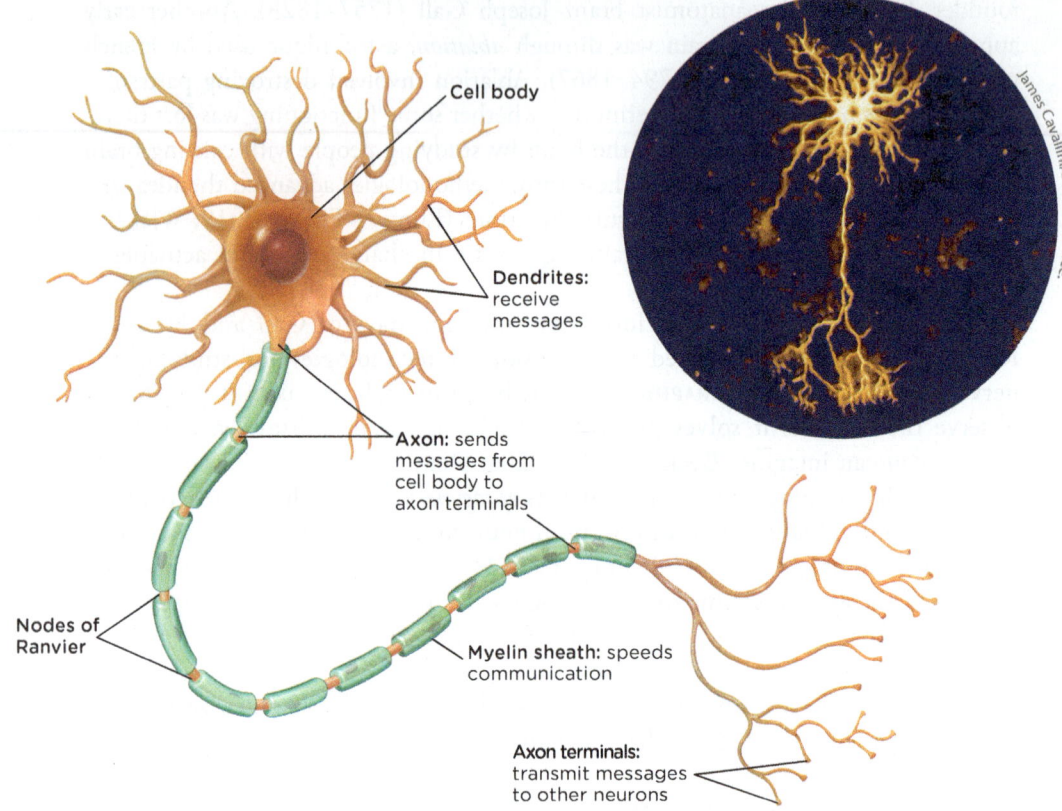

Cell body

Dendrites: receive messages

Axon: sends messages from cell body to axon terminals

Nodes of Ranvier

Myelin sheath: speeds communication

Axon terminals: transmit messages to other neurons

## What Do You Really Need to Know About Neurons?

**LO3** Label the parts of a neuron and describe an action potential.

**THE STRUCTURE OF A TYPICAL NEURON** A typical neuron has three basic parts: a cell body, dendrites, and an axon (**FIGURE 2.1**). The **cell body** of a neuron contains the standard components found in most human cells, including structures that nourish the cell and a nucleus containing **genetic material** (for more on genes, see Chapter 8 on human development). Extending from the cell body are many **dendrites** (DEN-drites), which are tiny, branchlike fibers that receive messages from sending neurons. Also projecting from the cell body is a long, skinny, tube-like structure called an **axon,** which sends signals away from the cell body. A neuron usually has one axon with branches ending in *axon terminals*. It is through these axon terminals that messages are sent to other neurons. Many axons are surrounded by a **myelin sheath** (MY-el-in sheath), a fatty substance that insulates the activities occurring within, speeding the transmission of neural messages down the axon. In such cases the axon is not entirely enclosed, but rather, covered in segments of myelin. The breaks between the myelin segments are called *nodes of Ranvier*. The **synapse** (SIN-aps) is where the axon terminal of a sending neuron meets a dendrite of a neuron or other type of cell receiving its signal (**INFOGRAPHIC 2.2** on page 48). The tiny space separating them is called the *synaptic gap,* and it is only about 0.000127 millimeters (mm) wide. For comparison, a single sheet of printer paper is 0.1 mm thick (the equivalent of about 788 synaptic gaps combined).

**HOLDING IT TOGETHER: GLIAL CELLS** Neurons transmit information up and down the body, and they need a little support and nurturing to get the job done. This is where the **glial cells** (GLEE-ul) come into play. Glial cells hold neurons together and maintain the structure of the nervous system. (*Glia* means "glue" in Greek.) Some researchers believe glial cells far outnumber neurons (Jäkel & Dimou, 2017), while

### CONNECTIONS

In **Chapter 1,** we discussed deoxyribonucleic acid (DNA), which is the genetic material we inherit from our parents. Here, we note that DNA is present in the cell body of a neuron.

**cell body** The region of the neuron that includes structures that nourish the cell, and a nucleus containing DNA.

**dendrites** Tiny, branchlike fibers extending from the cell body that receive messages from other neurons and send information in the direction of the cell body.

**axon** Skinny tube-like structure of a neuron that extends from the cell body and sends messages to other neurons through its terminals.

**myelin sheath** A fatty substance that insulates the axon and speeds the transmission of neural messages.

**synapse** The place where the axon terminal of a sending neuron meets the dendrite of a neighboring neuron or other type of cell receiving its signal; junction between neurons where communication occurs.

**glial cells** Cells of the nervous system that support, nourish, and protect neurons.

others estimate their numbers to be approximately the same (Allen & Lyons, 2018). More research is needed to clear up this controversy.

For many years, scientists believed that glial cells simply kept things together, but we now know they do much more (Allen & Lyons, 2018; Cserép et al., 2020). For example, after Brandon's injury, *microglia cells* defended his brain from infection and inflammation (Jäkel & Dimou, 2017; Streit, 2000), and *astrocyte cells* restored the barrier between brain and blood (Burda et al., 2016; Gruber, 2009). Astrocytes also support communication between neurons (Batiuk et al., 2020; Dutta et al., 2018). Other types of glial cells (*oligodendrocytes* and *Schwann cells*) provide the myelin sheath enveloping the axons of some neurons (Purves et al., 2018).

Thomas Deerinck, NCMIR/Science Source

**Not Just "Glue"**
A scanning electron micrograph shows neurons (green) and glia (orange). Glial cells serve as the "glue" of the nervous system, providing cohesion and support for the neurons. But glial cells may do much more, serving as "active participants in the information processing capabilities of neural circuits" (Deemyad et al., 2018, para. 1).

## What Language Do Neurons Speak?

Neurons are activated in response to other neurons, which can be stimulated by receptors attached to your skin, muscles, and other organs. The ongoing communication that occurs among groups of neurons underlies your every sensation, thought, emotion, and behavior. Neurons have unique properties that allow them to communicate with other cells. But what information do they convey? In essence, the message is simple: "I have been activated."

A neuron is surrounded by and filled with fluid containing *ions,* or particles that have an electrical charge (Infographic 2.2). Some ions have a negative charge (protein ions); others are positively charged (sodium and potassium ions). Two processes direct the flow of positive (+) and negative (−) ions into and out of the cell: diffusion and electrostatic pressure. *Diffusion* is the natural tendency of ions to spread out or disperse. *Electrostatic pressure* causes similarly charged ions to spread apart and oppositely charged ions to move toward each other (like magnets). The concentrations of positively and negatively charged ions inside and outside of the cell determine the potential difference (voltage) between the inside and outside of most neurons. Imagine a long building, with people standing inside and outside, all of them holding either a positive or negative sign. If we were to count up the total number of positives inside and outside the building, and do the same for the negatives, we could determine the overall difference. The difference in the "sum" of the positive and negative charges inside and outside of the neuron determines the voltage.

A neuron is encased in a membrane that is *selectively permeable,* allowing only some of the ions to pass in and out of its channels. The membrane is impermeable to positive sodium ions and negative protein ions (it does not allow these ions to enter or exit). Although there are some positive ions inside the neuron, the concentration of sodium ions (+) outside the cell is much greater than that inside. As a result, sodium ions on the outside are attracted to the membrane (because of diffusion and electrostatic pressure). Positive sodium ions approach the membrane from the outside, and negative protein ions approach the membrane from the inside; they move because the opposite charges are attracted to each other.

**RESTING POTENTIAL**    To summarize, here's what is going on when the neuron is not active: The negative protein ions are only on the inside of the cell, but they are attracted to the excess positive charge outside and move toward the membrane. Because the protein ions (−) are too big to get through the membrane, the inside of the neuron is negatively charged (Infographic 2.2). An electrical potential is created

# Communication Within Neurons

Neural communication involves different processes *within* and *between* neurons. In this infographic, we follow the electrical action that conveys messages *within* the neuron, from one end to the other.

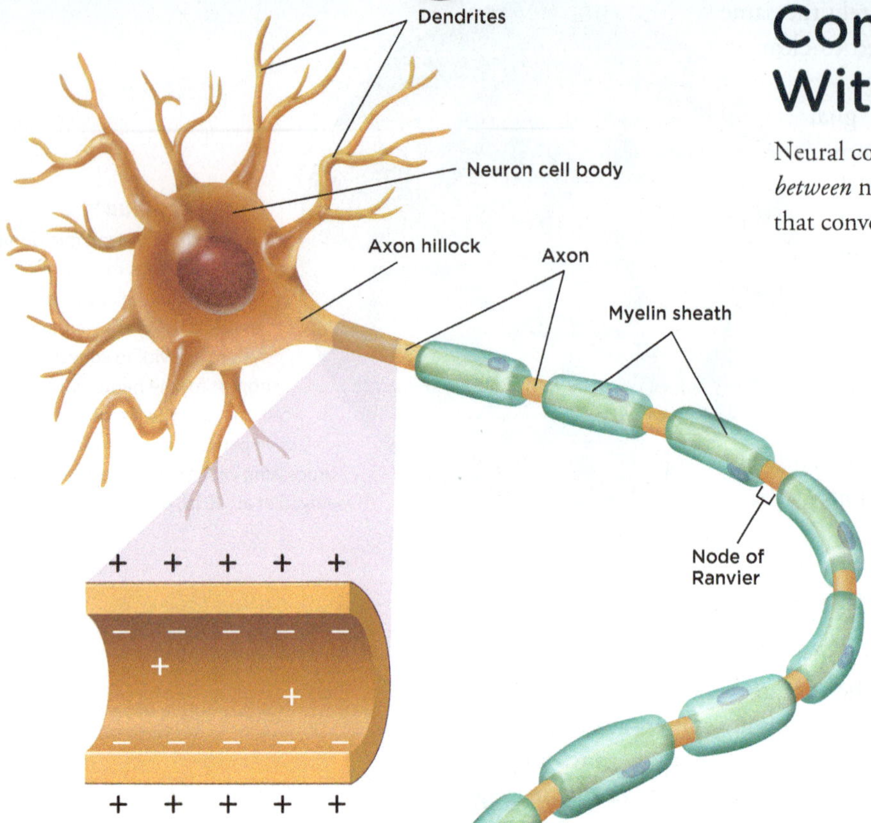

Dendrites

Neuron cell body

Axon hillock

Axon

Myelin sheath

Node of Ranvier

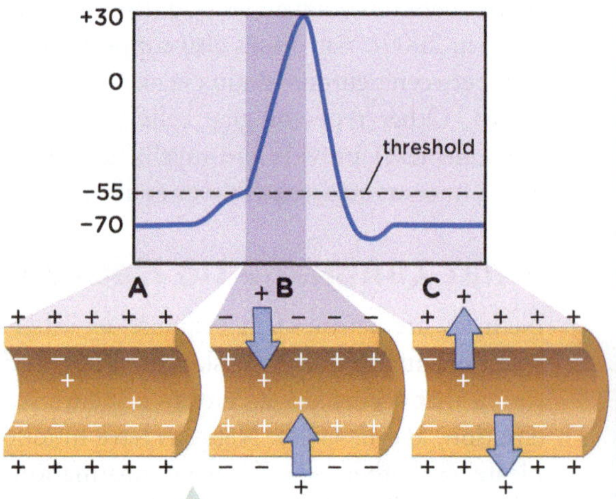

+ + + + +

## 1. THE NEURON AT REST

Before communication begins, the neuron is "at rest." Closed channels in the cell membrane prevent some positive ions from entering the cell, and the voltage inside of the cell is slightly more negative than the voltage outside. At –70 mV, the cell is at its resting potential.

+30
0
threshold
–55
–70

A        + B        C +

## 2. THE ACTION POTENTIAL

This graph shows the characteristic electrical trace of the action potential. When the neuron is stimulated, positive ions enter the cell, making the axon less negative (A). When the charge reaches the threshold (–55 mV), an action potential is triggered. Positive ions flood the cell, quickly reversing the charge from negative to positive (B). Afterward, the cell is restored to resting potential (C).

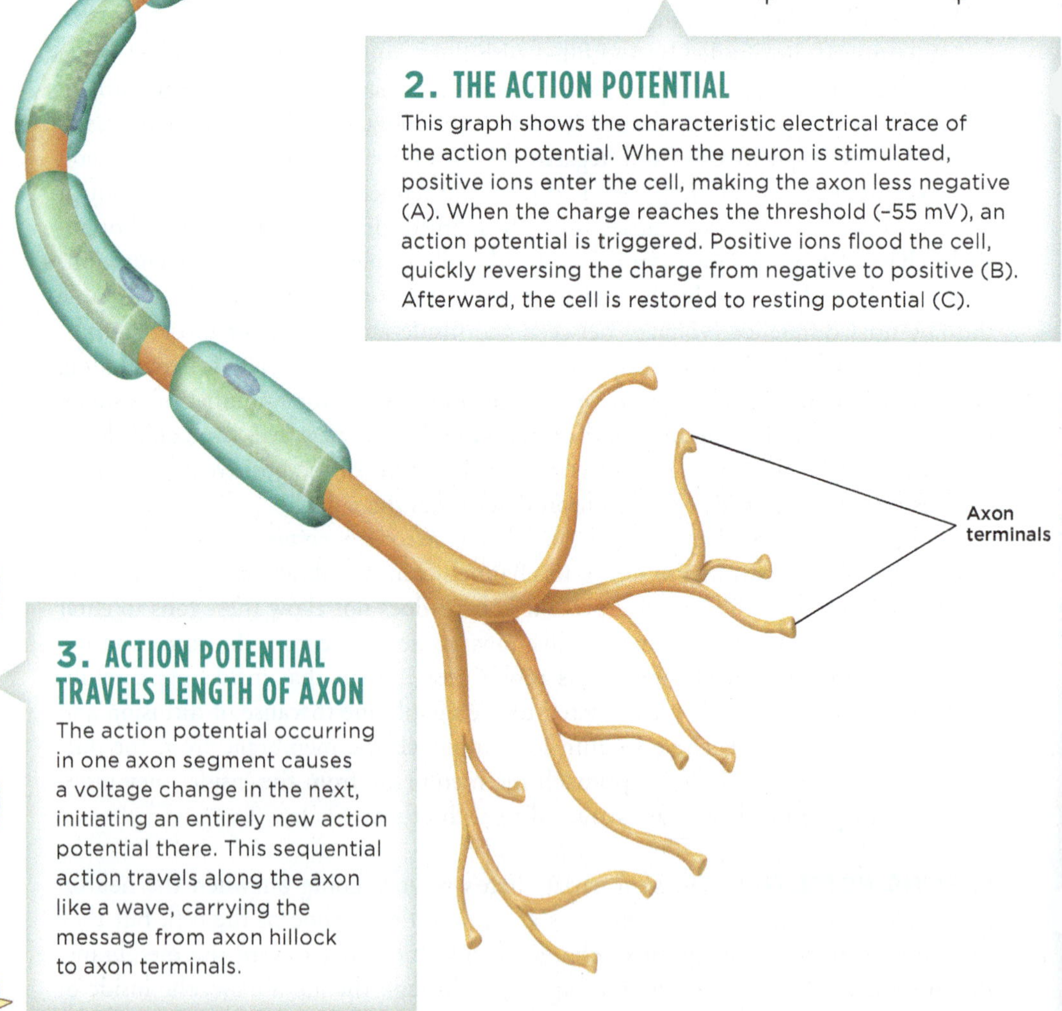

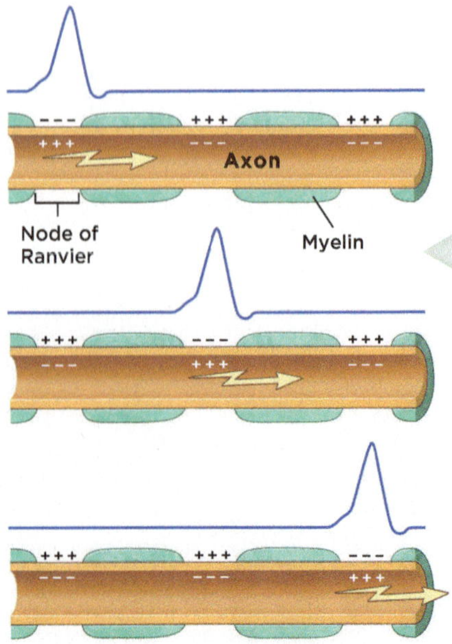

Axon

Node of Ranvier

Myelin

Axon terminals

## 3. ACTION POTENTIAL TRAVELS LENGTH OF AXON

The action potential occurring in one axon segment causes a voltage change in the next, initiating an entirely new action potential there. This sequential action travels along the axon like a wave, carrying the message from axon hillock to axon terminals.

by the difference in charge between the outside and the inside of the neuron. **Resting potential** represents the *electrical potential* of a neuron "at rest," and its value is −70 millivolts (mV). For comparison, the voltage of a AA battery is 1,500 mV. But what does this have to do with neurons transmitting information? Let's look at what happens when a neuron stops "resting" and goes into "action."

**ACTION POTENTIAL**    Remember, when a neuron is in its resting state, particles on the outside of the cell are being pulled toward the membrane and cannot move inside. If the neuron is stimulated by neighboring cells, channels in its membrane begin to open up, starting at the dendrites. An influx of positive sodium ions at the beginning of the axon, known as the *axon hillock,* causes a change in the voltage, going from −70 mV to the *threshold potential* −55 mV. This triggers the channels to open in that first segment of the axon, allowing an influx of more positive sodium ions. The voltage there rises rapidly, increasing from −55 mV to +30 mV. This spike in voltage, which passes through the axon of a neuron, is called an **action potential.**

What happens after this sudden jump in voltage? Resting potential is reestablished in order to return the neuron to its "natural" state. This is partly accomplished by the activity of a protein pump that restores the concentrations of ions in and outside the cell. The neuron must "reset"; solutions inside and outside this segment of the axon return to balance so that it is ready to do more work. We call this time the *refractory period.*

**MOVING DOWN THE AXON**    The spike in voltage, followed by the return to resting potential, begins at the axon hillock and travels along the axon, like a row of dominoes tumbling down. The action potential only travels in one direction—from axon hillock to axon terminals. Each action potential takes about 1 millisecond to complete, and a typical neuron can fire several hundred times per second. It's hard to comprehend, but the action potentials constantly occurring in billions of neurons are the basis for all of our thoughts, feelings, and behaviors.

**EXCITATORY AND INHIBITORY SIGNALS**    What triggers a neuron to fire an action potential? Neighboring cells deliver chemical messages, prompting channels in the dendrites to open up and allow sodium ions into the cell. These sending cells can be neurons or other types of cells that communicate with neurons, but we will assume they are neurons for the sake of simplicity. If enough sending neurons signal the receiving neuron to pass along the message, their combined signal becomes *excitatory* and the neuron fires. However, not all neighboring neurons send an excitatory signal. Some deliver an *inhibitory* signal, instructing the neuron not to fire. For an action potential to occur, excitatory signals must exceed inhibitory signals, and the difference between them has to meet the threshold potential of −55 mV. If enough positively charged ions enter the cell, the potential of the neuron reaches its threshold, or trigger point, and the cell "fires."

**ALL-OR-NONE**    Action potentials are **all-or-none:** They either happen or they don't, and their strength remains the same regardless of the conditions. So how does a neuron convey the strength of a stimulus? By (1) firing more often and (2) delivering its message to more neurons. Consider a loud scream and a quiet whisper. The loud scream is a stronger stimulus, so it causes more neurons to fire than the quiet whisper. The loud scream also prompts each neuron to fire more often. In summary, there is no such thing as a partial action potential, or a strong or weak action potential.

**ROLE OF THE MYELIN SHEATH**    The firing of a neuron is facilitated by the myelin sheath, which insulates and protects the tiny voltage changes occurring inside the axon. Myelin is a good insulator, but the axon is not covered with myelin at the

**resting potential** The electrical potential of a cell "at rest"; the state of a cell when it is not activated.

**action potential** The spike in voltage that passes through the axon of a neuron, the result of which is to convey information.

**all-or-none** A neuron either fires or does not fire; action potentials are always the same strength.

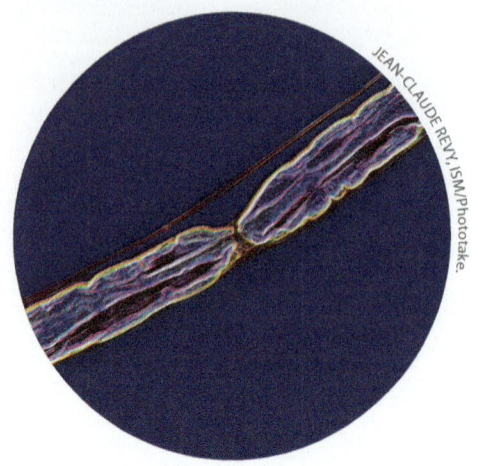

**So Fast**

Action potentials may travel as fast as 268 miles per hour through a myelinated axon (Purves et al., 2018). Myelin is a fatty substance that envelops and insulates the axon, facilitating faster transmission. The action potential "skips" over the segments of myelin, hopping from one node of Ranvier to the next (see small space in the center), instead of traversing the entire length of the axon.

From the **SCIENTIFIC** pages of **AMERICAN**

nodes of Ranvier (you can see this in the photograph to the left). The action potential appears to "jump" from node to node, as opposed to traversing the entire axon in one continuous movement, and this accelerates the transmission of the signal. Unmyelinated axons have slower transmission speeds because the signal must make its way down the entire length of the axon. The speed of the action potential in an unmyelinated axon is approximately 1.1 to 4.5 miles per hour (mph), while that in a myelinated neuron can reach 268 mph—"faster than a Formula 1 racing car" (Purves et al., 2018, p. 59). Myelination of axons starts early in life and relates to the development of a variety of cognitive abilities and motor skills (Krogsrud et al., 2018; Lebel & Deoni, 2018). As the human body grows, neural messages must travel greater distances, and myelination helps increase the efficiency of this communication.

Because of their light color, axons wrapped in myelin are referred to as "white matter," and destruction of this brain tissue can have serious consequences; for example, the symptoms of Alzheimer's disease are associated with white matter damage (Levit et al., 2020). (The brain also contains "gray matter" consisting of neuron cell bodies, glial cells, and other components.) Myelination damage from diseases such as multiple sclerosis can lead to many symptoms, including fatigue, weakness, and problems with vision and muscle coordination (Brownlee et al., 2017; Crouch et al., 2020). Head injuries have also been linked to white matter deterioration, but the effects may differ for males and females—and the magnitude of the disparity is surprising.

## HEADING OFF INJURY

### Female soccer players are more vulnerable to brain damage than males are.

Repeatedly heading a soccer ball exacts a toll on an athlete's brain. But this cost—measured by the volume of brain cells damaged—is five times greater for women than for men, new research suggests.

The study provides a biological explanation for why women report more severe symptoms and longer recovery times than men following brain injuries in sports. Previously some researchers had dismissed female players' complaints because there was little physiological evidence for the disparity, says Michael Lipton, a neuroscientist at the Albert Einstein College of Medicine and a coauthor of the paper.

Lipton's team used magnetic resonance imaging to peer into the skulls of 98 adult amateur soccer players—half of them female and half male—who headed the ball with varying frequency during the prior year. For women, eight of the brain's signal-carrying white matter regions showed structural deterioration, compared with just three such regions in men (damage increased with the number of reported headers). Furthermore, female athletes in the study suffered damage to an average of about 2,100 cubic millimeters of brain tissue, compared with an average of just 400 cubic millimeters in the male athletes.

Lipton does not yet know the cause of these sex differences, but he notes two possibilities. Women may suffer stronger whiplash from a cranial blow because they generally have less muscle mass than men to stabilize the neck and skull. Alternatively, a dip in progesterone, a hormone that protects against swelling in the brain, could heighten women's vulnerability to brain injury during certain phases of their menstrual cycle.

Thomas Kaminski, a sports physiologist at the University of Delaware, who was not involved in the work, calls it "truly groundbreaking." The research is unique in highlighting the cumulative effect of repetitive knocks on the skull, as opposed to major traumatic injuries, he says. "Very few of these subjects had a history of concussion."

Researchers are now eager to determine if these white matter changes carry long-term cognitive consequences. Until more is known, Kaminski advocates a proactive approach to limiting the damage caused by headers. [. . . and] met with U.S. Soccer Federation officials to craft science-based guidelines for practicing the move in youth leagues. [. . . ] **Daniel Ackerman. Reproduced with permission. Copyright © 2018 Scientific American, a division of Nature America, Inc. All rights reserved.**

**LO 4** Illustrate how neurons communicate with each other.

**COMMUNICATION BETWEEN NEURONS**    Neurons communicate with each other via chemicals called **neurotransmitters** (INFOGRAPHIC **2.3** on page 53). An action potential moves down the axon, eventually reaching the axon terminals. The action potential causes *vesicles* (small fluid-filled sacs) in the axon terminals to unload neurotransmitters into the synaptic gap. The majority of these neurotransmitters drift across the gap and come into contact with **receptor sites** of the receiving neuron's dendrites. Just as it takes the right key to unlock a door, the neurotransmitter must fit a corresponding receptor site to convey its message. And because there are many different neurotransmitters, there are also a variety of receptor sites. When the neurotransmitters latch onto the receptors, gates in the receiving neuron's membrane fly open, ushering in positively charged ions and thus restarting the cycle of the action potential (if the threshold is met).

What happens to the neurotransmitters once they have conveyed their message? Neurotransmitters that latched onto receptors may be reabsorbed by the sending axon terminal in a process known as **reuptake.** Those that are not reabsorbed may drift out of the synapse through diffusion. This is how the synapse is cleared of neurotransmitters in preparation for the next release of chemical messengers.

## How Do Neurotransmitters Influence Our Behavior?

**LO 5** Identify specific neurotransmitters and summarize how their activity affects human behavior.

Researchers have identified approximately 100 different types of neurotransmitters, with many more yet to be discovered. Neurotransmitters secreted by one neuron may influence the activity of neighboring neurons, which can affect the activity of muscles and organs, as well as the regulation of mood, appetite, arousal, and a variety of other functions (TABLE **2.1** on the next page). Scientists have been studying neurotransmitters since the late 1800s (Wickens, 2015), trying to understand how these chemicals influence bodily functions and behaviors. Keep in mind, however, that there is no one-to-one correspondence between the secretion of a neurotransmitter and a specific behavior. Let's take a closer look at some specific neurotransmitters, starting with the first one discovered, *acetylcholine.*

**ACETYLCHOLINE**    Acetylcholine is a neurotransmitter that relays messages from neurons to muscles, thus enabling movement. Any time you move some part of your body, whether dancing your fingers across a keypad or bouncing your head to a favorite song, you have, in part, acetylcholine to thank. Too much acetylcholine leads to muscle spasms; too little causes paralysis. Acetylcholine is also involved in memory. Low levels in the brain have been linked to Alzheimer's disease, which can lead to problems with memory, language, and thinking (Johannsson et al., 2015; Sabri et al., 2018). Normal acetylcholine activity can be disrupted by snake and black widow spider bites, as well as food poisoning (Duregotti et al., 2015).

**neurotransmitters** Chemical messengers that neurons use to communicate at the synapse.

**receptor sites** Locations on the receiving neuron's dendrites where neurotransmitters attach.

**reuptake** A process by which neurotransmitters are reabsorbed by the sending axon terminal.

**TABLE 2.1**   Neurotransmitters: You May Be Surprised About These FIVE

| Neurotransmitter | Function | Did You Know? |
|---|---|---|
| Acetylcholine | Muscle movement, memory, arousal, attention | The anti-wrinkle treatment Botox paralyzes the facial muscles by preventing activity of acetylcholine, which would normally enable muscle movement (Nichols, 2020). |
| Dopamine | Coordination of muscle movement, attention, pleasure | The same dopamine circuits involved in drug addiction may also be implicated in overeating and food addiction (Hauck et al., 2017). |
| GABA | Inhibits communication between neurons | Anti-anxiety drugs, such as Valium and Xanax, work by enhancing the effects of GABA (Drexler et al., 2013; Masiulis et al., 2019). |
| Glutamate | Promotes communication between neurons | Glutamate is a close chemical relative to the savory food additive monosodium glutamate, or MSG. Some people believe that consuming MSG causes brain damage, but such claims are not supported by solid scientific data (Hamzelou, 2015). |
| Serotonin | Mood, appetite, aggression, sleep | Physical exercise may boost serotonin activity in the brain, leading to improved mood and decreased symptoms of depression (Heijnen et al., 2015; Wipfli et al., 2011). |

Every thought, behavior, and emotion you have ever experienced can be traced to neurotransmitter activity in the nervous system. Listed here are some surprising facts about common neurotransmitters.

**GLUTAMATE AND GABA**   Much of the communication within the nervous system involves two neurotransmitters: *glutamate* and *GABA* (short for gamma-aminobutyric acid). Glutamate is an excitatory neurotransmitter, so its main job is to kick neurons into action (make them fire), whereas GABA is inhibitory (it puts the brakes on firing). Glutamate influences most cells in the brain. "It is absolutely critical for everything we do," so glutamate dysfunction can have a variety of effects (Dulka, 2020, para. 1). For example, overactivity of this neurotransmitter is associated with strokes (Campos et al., 2011; Khanna et al., 2015), while underactivity is theorized to be involved in some of the symptoms of schizophrenia (Catts et al., 2016; Madeira et al., 2018). As an inhibitory neurotransmitter, GABA plays a role in controlling sleep and wakefulness (Vanini et al., 2012) as well as behaviors associated with fear and anxiety (Botta et al., 2015; Füzesi & Bains, 2015).

**NOREPINEPHRINE**   *Norepinephrine* has a variety of effects, but one of its most important functions is to help prepare the body for stressful situations. In the brain, norepinephrine is involved in regulating arousal and sleep (Mitchell & Weinshenker, 2010; Moore & Depue, 2016). This neurotransmitter plays an important role in maintaining attention, but in some situations, high levels could lead to overarousal and hypervigilance, which could dramatically interfere with thinking and attention (Moore & Depue, 2016).

**SEROTONIN**   Serotonin helps control appetite, aggression, and mood, and regulates sleep and breathing. Abnormal serotonin activity is thought to be one of the factors driving depression (Moore & Depue, 2016). Antidepressants called selective serotonin reuptake inhibitors (SSRIs), including Prozac and Zoloft, boost the effects of this neurotransmitter (Chapter 14). Normally, neurotransmitters that do not connect with receptor sites can be reabsorbed by the sending axon terminal in the reuptake process. SSRIs work to prevent this reabsorption. The longer serotonin is in the synapse, the more time it has to attach to a receptor and exert its effects.

**ENDORPHINS**   *Endorphins* are a group of naturally produced opioids (see Chapter 4 for more information on opioid drugs) that regulate the secretion of other neurotransmitters. The term "endorphin" is derived from the words "endogenous,"

# Communication Between Neurons

Messages travel within a neuron via electrical signals. But communication *between* neurons depends on the movement of chemicals—neurotransmitters. Though they all work in the same way, there are many different types of neurotransmitters, each linked to unique effects on behavior. However, drugs and other substances, known as *agonists* and *antagonists,* can alter this process of communication between neurons by boosting or blocking normal neurotransmitter activity.

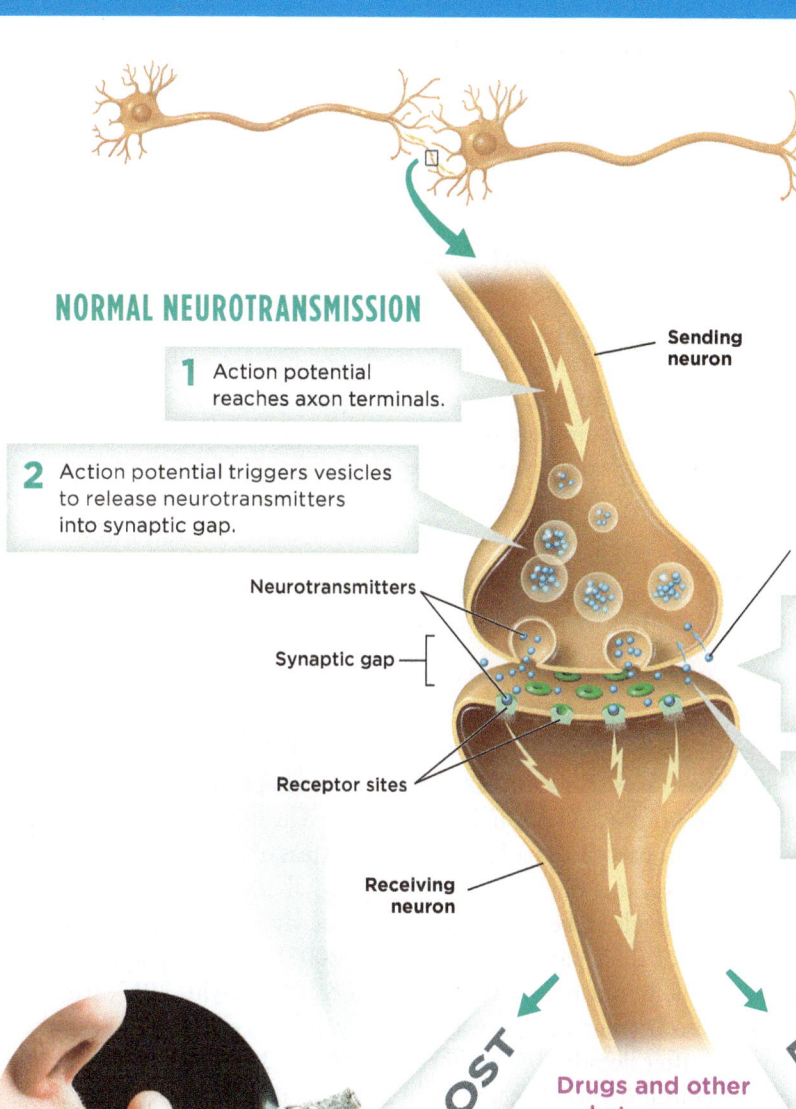

## NORMAL NEUROTRANSMISSION

**1** Action potential reaches axon terminals.

**2** Action potential triggers vesicles to release neurotransmitters into synaptic gap.

**3** Neurotransmitters bind to their matching receptor sites on receiving neuron's dendrite, causing positively charged particles to enter cell.

**4** After binding, neurotransmitters are reabsorbed or diffuse out of synaptic gap.

Sending neuron

Excess neurotransmitter being reabsorbed by the sending neuron

Neurotransmitters

Synaptic gap

Receptor sites

Receiving neuron

**BOOST**

**BLOCK**

**Drugs and other substances can alter normal neurotransmission.**

## AGONIST

Agonists boost normal neurotransmitter activity. Nicotine mimics acetylcholine and causes this same activation. More receptors are activated, and more messages are sent.

Agonists

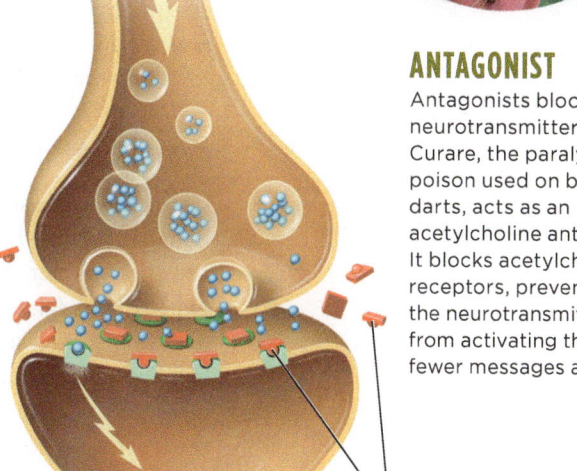

## ANTAGONIST

Antagonists block normal neurotransmitter activity. Curare, the paralyzing poison used on blowgun darts, acts as an acetylcholine antagonist. It blocks acetylcholine receptors, preventing the neurotransmitter from activating them, so fewer messages are sent.

Antagonists

**Dopamine and Parkinson's Disease**
Actor Michael J. Fox (left) and boxing legend Muhammad Ali greet each other at a red-carpet event. Fox and Ali (who passed away in 2016) are perhaps the most famous people to be diagnosed with Parkinson's disease, an incurable disorder that causes shaking ("resting tremor") and slow and stiff movements. Parkinson's disease is linked to deterioration of neurons that produce dopamine (Parmar et al., 2020).

KMazur/Getty Images.

meaning created within, and "morphine." Released in response to pain, endorphins block pain receptor sites. Brisk exercise increases their production, reducing the experience of pain and elevating mood (Harvard Health, 2020).

**DOPAMINE**    *Dopamine* plays a key role in attention, learning through rewards, and regulation of body movements. This neurotransmitter has been implicated in the abuse of certain substances, including stimulants like cocaine and amphetamines (Nutt et al., 2015; Siciliano et al., 2018). Repeated use of some drugs overstimulates and impairs functioning of the neurons in the brain's "pleasure" circuit, theoretically making it more difficult to enjoy non-drug-related activities. Given dopamine's important role in pleasure, perhaps it is no surprise that this neurotransmitter has been associated with romantic love.

## Relationships

### YOUR ROMANTIC BRAIN

The early stages of love tend to be intense. You feel energized and elated as the relationship develops, and then crestfallen if something goes wrong. Thoughts of your loved one occupy your mind, perhaps to the point of obsession, and you may fail to notice red flags (Fisher et al., 2006). What's happening in the brain as you ride this rollercoaster of love? Neuroimaging research tells us that dopamine plays an important part (Takahashi et al., 2015). Areas of the brain where dopamine is active, including the ventral tegmental area (VTA) and parts of the caudate nucleus, become excited when newly in-love individuals look at pictures of their partners (Aron et al., 2005). These regions play "an essential role in our reward pathway" (Xu & Tart-Zelvin, 2017, para. 2), and their activity has also been associated with romantic love in couples that say they are still "madly in love" after decades (Acevedo et al., 2012, p. 146).

**WHAT'S LOVE GOT TO DO WITH . . . DOPAMINE?**

Another brain chemical involved in the early stages of romantic love, and social bonding in general, is oxytocin (Ulmer-Yaniv et al., 2016). Oxytocin can behave as both a neurotransmitter and a hormone, and its activity has been associated with "complex romantic bonds" and feelings of love (Algoe et al., 2017; Quintana & Guastella, 2020, p. 519; Wu, 2020). In the first months of a relationship, oxytocin levels are high, and during times of bonding, oxytocin seems to increase alongside chemicals involved in experiences of reward and stress. Perhaps this is no surprise, as "the euphoria experienced during the period of falling in love goes hand in hand with increased stress reflecting the risk for the loss of the relationship" (Ulmer-Yaniv et al., 2016, p. 136).

## Agonists and Antagonists

Drugs and other substances influence behavior by interfering at the level of the synapse (Chapters 4 and 14). Certain substances mimic neurotransmitters, while others block neurotransmitter action. *Agonists* increase the normal activity of a neurotransmitter (whether its signal is excitatory or inhibitory), and *antagonists* reduce the effects of a neurotransmitter or block its release (Infographic 2.3). For example, muscarine (found in poisonous mushrooms) increases the secretion of acetylcholine, causing sweating, pupil constriction, nausea, and respiratory distress. Because these substances amplify the normal activity of acetylcholine, they are agonists. On the other hand, the popular anti-wrinkle treatment Botox is an antagonist because it blocks the release of acetylcholine, paralyzing the facial muscles so they can no longer wrinkle the overlying skin (Nichols, 2020). If you're searching for another example of an antagonist, look no further than your nearest coffee shop. . . .

## Think Critically

### WHERE'S MY MORNING ANTAGONIST?

 Did you jump-start your day with a cup of coffee, an energy drink, or a matcha latte? Caffeine perks you up at the crack of dawn or jolts you from a midafternoon daze by manipulating your nervous system. One way caffeine works is by blocking the receptors for a neurotransmitter called *adenosine;* it is an adenosine antagonist. When adenosine latches onto receptors, it slows down their activity (making neurons less likely to fire), and this tends to make you feel drowsy. Caffeine resembles adenosine enough that it can dock onto the same receptors ("posing" as adenosine). With caffeine occupying its receptors, adenosine can no longer "exert a sleep-inducing effect" (Advokat et al., 2019, p. 186; Clark & Landolt, 2017). The result: More neurons fire and you feel full of energy.

**CAFFEINE MANIPULATES YOUR NERVOUS SYSTEM. . . .**

Given the effects of caffeine, it's no wonder that the vast majority of college students—92%, according to one study—consume it (Mahoney et al., 2019). The right dose of caffeine can help maintain reaction time, attentiveness, and reasoning skills, even after several days of reduced sleep (Kamimori et al., 2015). This drug may even boost your ability to form long-term memories (Borota et al., 2014). The effects of caffeine do not stop at the brain. As anyone who has enjoyed a double espresso can testify, caffeine kicks the body into high gear; some research suggests it may enhance stamina in endurance exercise (Hodgson et al., 2013). And for coffee drinkers, in particular, the good news keeps coming. Drinking this beverage has been associated with decreased risk of type 2 diabetes, Parkinson's disease, and certain types of cancer, and lower overall mortality. However, these effects may be attributed to other compounds found in coffee—not necessarily the caffeine (Grosso et al., 2017; Loftfield et al., 2018).

As stimulating as these findings may be, they only depict part of a complex picture. Caffeine may also have undesirable effects. According to a review of 58 studies, using caffeine can make it harder to fall asleep, reduce total sleep time, and interfere with the deep stages of sleep that help you feel refreshed in the morning (Clark & Landolt, 2017). Yet, trying to cut back may lead to withdrawal symptoms such as headaches, sleepiness, and decreased concentration (Chawla, 2018; Chapter 4). For some people (pregnant women, children, and those with certain health conditions), caffeine use should be limited or avoided entirely (Advokat et al., 2019; Wikoff et al., 2017).

amenic181/Getty Images.

## Put Your Heads Together

Discuss the following scenario as a group: You need to stay up late preparing for an exam, so you head to the local coffee shop. **A)** How does the caffeine in your drink affect the adenosine receptors in your neurons? **B)** How does this translate to you staying awake? **C)** What are the potential problems with using this method to burn the midnight oil?

Now sit back, relax, and sip on a beverage, caffeinated or not. It's time to examine the nervous system running through your arms, legs, fingers, toes—and everywhere else.

## SHOW WHAT YOU KNOW

1. _____ are released into the _____ when an action potential reaches the axon terminal.
   A. Sodium ions; synaptic gap
   B. Neurotransmitters; synaptic gap
   C. Potassium ions; cell membrane
   D. Neurotransmitters; sodium gates

2. Many axons are surrounded by a _____ , which is a fatty substance that insulates the axon.

3. Describe how three neurotransmitters impact your daily behavior.

 CHECK YOUR ANSWERS AT THE BACK OF BOOK.

# The Brain Can't Do It Alone

Like any complex system, the brain needs a supporting infrastructure to carry out its directives and relay essential information from the outside world. Running up and down your spine and branching throughout your body are neurons that provide connections between your brain and the rest of you. As FIGURE 2.2 illustrates, the **central nervous system (CNS)** consists of the brain and spinal cord, while the **peripheral nervous system (PNS)** comprises all the neurons that are not in the central nervous system. The peripheral nervous system connects the central nervous system with the body's muscles, glands, and organs, and it can be divided into two branches: the *somatic nervous system* and the *autonomic nervous system.*

## The Spinal Cord and Simple Reflexes

Brandon suffered a devastating brain injury that temporarily immobilized half of his body. The paralysis could have affected his entire body if the bullet had pierced his **spinal cord.** This bundle of neurons allows communication between the brain and

**FIGURE 2.2**

**Overview of the Nervous System**
The nervous system is made up of the central nervous system (CNS), which includes the brain and spinal cord, and the peripheral nervous system (PNS), which connects the central nervous system to the rest of the body.

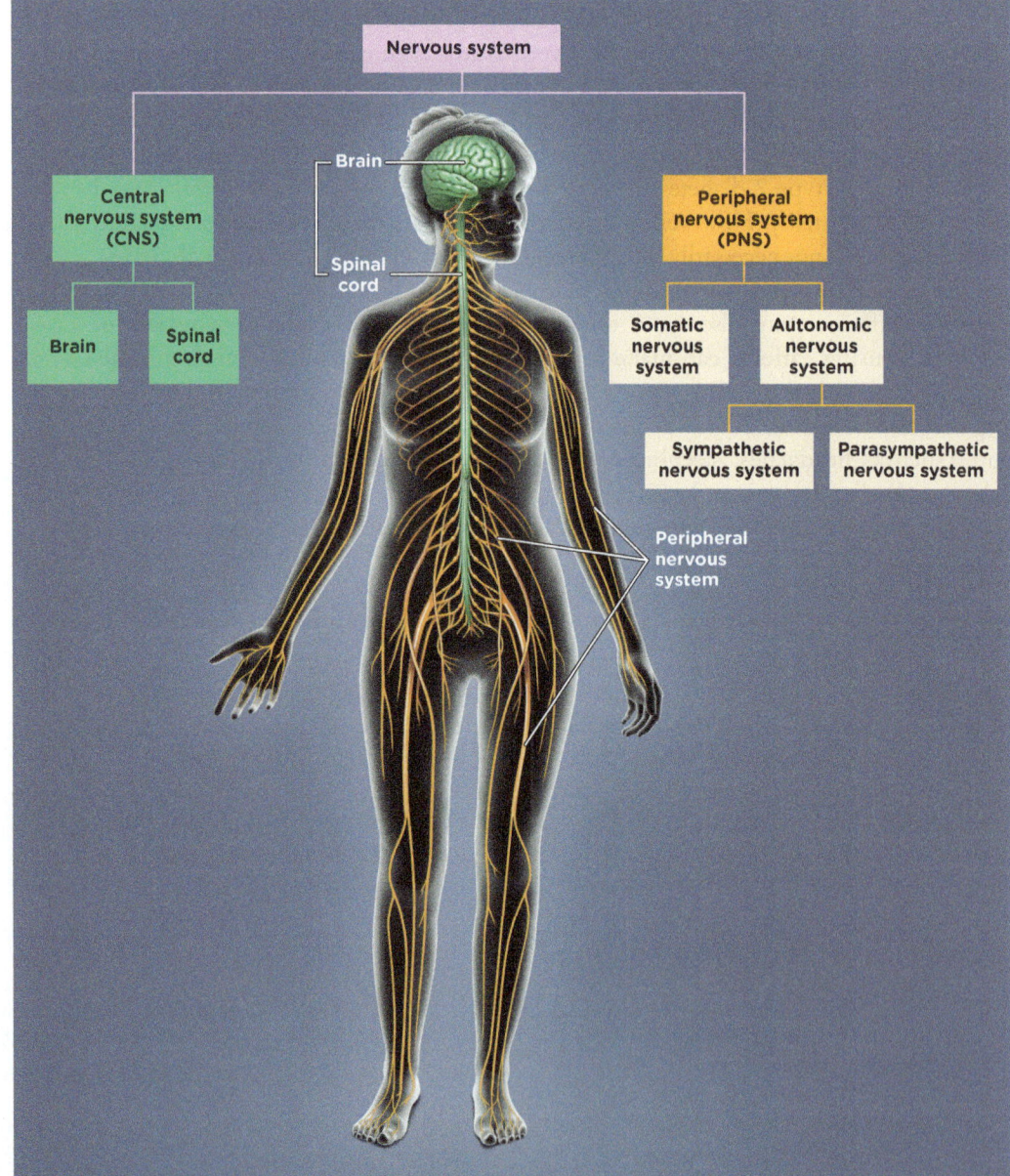

**central nervous system (CNS)** A major component of the human nervous system; includes the brain and spinal cord.

**peripheral nervous system (PNS)** The part of the nervous system that connects the central nervous system to the rest of the body.

**spinal cord** The bundle of neurons that allows communication between the brain and the peripheral nervous system.

the peripheral nervous system. The spinal cord has two major responsibilities: (1) receiving information from the body and sending it to the brain; and (2) taking information from the brain and delivering it throughout the body. If this pathway is blocked, commands from the brain cannot reach the muscles responsible for making you walk, talk, and pour yourself a glass of orange juice. Likewise, the skin and other parts of the body have no pathway for communicating sensory information to the brain, like "Ooh, that burner is hot," or "Oh, this massage feels good."

**LO 6** Explain how the central and peripheral nervous systems connect.

**TYPES OF NEURONS** How do the brain and spinal cord, which make up the *central nervous system,* communicate with the rest of the body through the *peripheral nervous system?* In essence, there are three types of neurons participating in this back-and-forth chatter. **Sensory neurons** receive information about the environment from the sensory systems and send it to the brain for processing. **Motor neurons** carry information from the central nervous system to various parts of the body, causing muscles to contract and glands to release chemicals. **Interneurons,** which reside exclusively in the brain and spinal cord, act as bridges connecting sensory and motor neurons. By gathering and processing sensory input from multiple neurons, interneurons facilitate the nervous system's most complex operations, from solving equations to creating lifelong memories. They are also involved in a relatively simple operation: the reflex.

**THE REFLEX ARC** Have you ever touched a burning hot pan? You probably withdrew your hand before you even had a chance to think about it. This ultrafast response to a painful stimulus is known as a reflex (**FIGURE 2.3**). Touching the hot

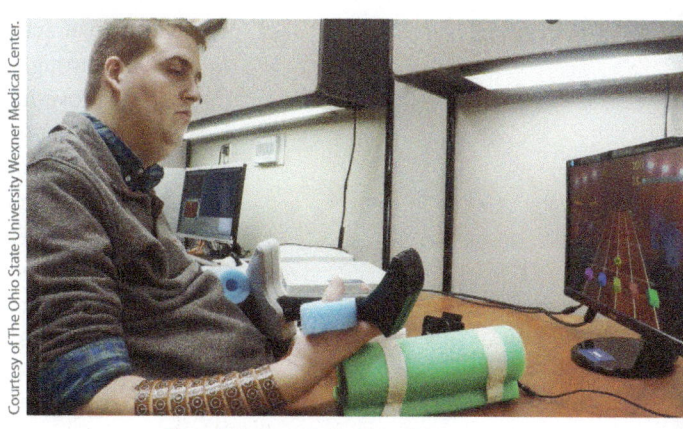

Courtesy of The Ohio State University Wexner Medical Center.

**Breakthrough Technology**
A tragic diving accident left Ian Burkhart with paralysis in all four limbs, but thanks to a groundbreaking technology developed at The Ohio State University, he can now manipulate objects with his fingers and wrists. The "brain–computer interface" essentially reads his thoughts about hand movements and turns those thoughts into action by electrically stimulating his arm. Here, Ian uses the interface to play Guitar Hero. The technology acts as a simplified version of the spinal cord, receiving commands from the brain and conveying those messages to muscles in the body (Bouton et al., 2016). The ultimate goal is to take the technology out of the lab and into homes and workplaces, allowing people with paralysis to achieve a new form of independence.

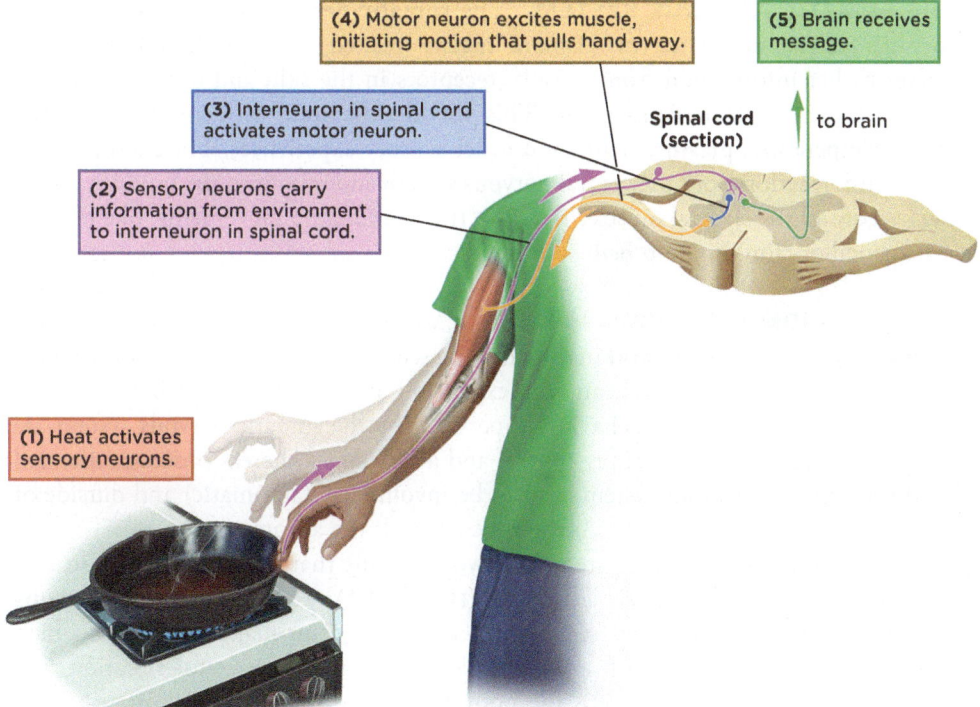

**(4)** Motor neuron excites muscle, initiating motion that pulls hand away.

**(5)** Brain receives message.

**(3)** Interneuron in spinal cord activates motor neuron.

Spinal cord (section)

to brain

**(2)** Sensory neurons carry information from environment to interneuron in spinal cord.

**(1)** Heat activates sensory neurons.

**FIGURE 2.3**
**The Reflex Arc**
Without any input from the brain, neurons in the spinal cord are capable of carrying out a simple reflex. While this reflex is occurring, sensory neurons also send messages to the brain, letting it know what has happened.

**sensory neurons** Neurons that receive information from the sensory systems and convey it to the brain for further processing.

**motor neurons** Neurons that transmit information from the central nervous system to the muscles and glands.

**interneurons** Neurons that reside exclusively in the brain and spinal cord; act as a bridge connecting sensory and motor neurons.

pan activates a communication pathway that begins with the sensory neurons, travels through interneurons in the spinal cord, and ends with motor neurons that cause movement. Amazingly, the brain is not involved in this initial reaction.

A sensory neuron has a rendezvous with an interneuron in the spinal cord, which then commands a motor neuron to react—no brain required. We refer to this process, in which a stimulus causes an involuntary response, as a **reflex arc.**

Eventually, your brain does process the event; otherwise, you would have no clue it happened. You become consciously aware of your reaction *after* it has occurred. (*My hand just pulled back; that pan was hot!*) Although many sensory and motor neurons are involved in this reaction, it happens very quickly, hopefully in time to reduce injury in cases when the reflex arc involves pain. Why do you think the reflex arc evolved? In other words, how might this behavior promote human survival over evolutionary time?

## The Peripheral Nervous System

**LO 7**  Describe the organization and function of the peripheral nervous system.

The peripheral nervous system (PNS) includes all the neurons that are not in the central nervous system (see Figure 2.2). These neurons are bundled together and act like electrical cables carrying signals from place to place. We call these collections of neurons **nerves.** Nerves of the peripheral nervous system inform the central nervous system about the body's environment—both the exterior (for example, sights, sounds, and tastes) and the interior (for example, heart rate, blood pressure, and temperature). The central nervous system, in turn, makes sense of all this information and then responds by dispatching orders to the muscles, glands, and other tissues through the nerves of the peripheral nervous system. As mentioned earlier, the PNS has two functional branches: the *somatic nervous system* and the *autonomic nervous system.*

**THE SOMATIC NERVOUS SYSTEM**    The **somatic nervous system** includes sensory nerves and motor nerves. (*Somatic* means "related to the body.") The sensory nerves gather information from sensory receptors in the skin and other tissues and send it to the central nervous system. This provides the brain with constant feedback about temperature, pressure, pain, and other sensory experiences. The motor nerves receive information from the central nervous system and relay it to the muscles. These nerves control the skeletal muscles that give rise to *voluntary* movements, like picking up a pencil or climbing into bed.

**THE AUTONOMIC NERVOUS SYSTEM**    Meanwhile, the **autonomic nervous system** (au-te-NOM-ic) is working behind the scenes, regulating *involuntary* activity, such as the pumping of the heart, the expansion and contraction of blood vessels, and digestion. Most of the behaviors supervised by the somatic nervous system are voluntary (within your conscious control and awareness), whereas processes directed by the autonomic nervous system tend to be involuntary (automatic) and outside of your awareness. Just remember: Autonomic controls the automatic.

The autonomic nervous system has two divisions that help us respond to and recover from stressful or crisis situations (FIGURE **2.4**). The **sympathetic nervous system** initiates what is often referred to as the "fight-or-flight" response, which prepares the body to deal with a crisis. When faced with a stressful situation, the sympathetic nervous system preps the body for action by increasing heart rate and respiration, and by slowing digestion and other maintenance functions. Earlier, we mentioned that caffeine makes you feel physically energized. This is because it activates the fight-or-flight response (Flueck et al., 2016).

**reflex arc** An automatic response to a sensory stimulus, using a simple pathway of communication from sensory neurons through interneurons in the spinal cord and back out through motor neurons.

**nerves** Bundles of neurons that carry information to and from the central nervous system; enable communication between the central nervous system and the muscles, glands, and sensory receptors.

**somatic nervous system** The branch of the peripheral nervous system that includes sensory nerves and motor nerves; gathers information from sensory receptors and controls the skeletal muscles responsible for voluntary movement.

**autonomic nervous system** The branch of the peripheral nervous system that controls involuntary processes within the body, such as contractions in the digestive tract and activity of glands.

**sympathetic nervous system** The division of the autonomic nervous system that mobilizes the "fight-or-flight" response to stressful or crisis situations.

**parasympathetic nervous system** The division of the autonomic nervous system that orchestrates the "rest-and-digest" response to bring the body back to a noncrisis mode.

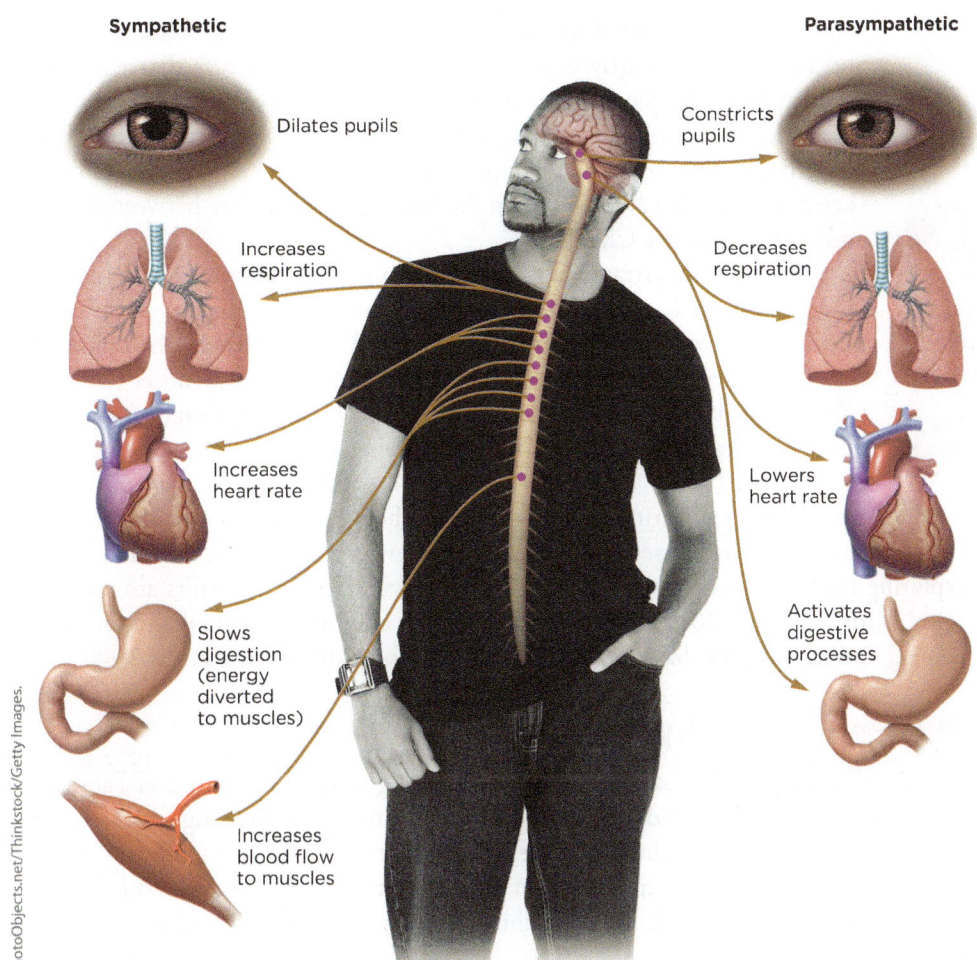

**Sympathetic**

Dilates pupils

Increases respiration

Increases heart rate

Slows digestion (energy diverted to muscles)

Increases blood flow to muscles

**Parasympathetic**

Constricts pupils

Decreases respiration

Lowers heart rate

Activates digestive processes

PhotoObjects.net/Thinkstock/Getty Images.

**FIGURE 2.4**
**The Sympathetic and Parasympathetic Nervous Systems**
The autonomic nervous system has two divisions: the sympathetic and parasympathetic nervous systems. In a stressful situation, the sympathetic nervous system initiates the "fight-or-flight" response. The parasympathetic nervous system calms the body when the stressful situation has passed.

The fight-or-flight response would certainly come in handy if fleeing predators were part of your day-to-day life (as it may have been for our primitive ancestors), but you probably are not chased by wild animals very often. You may, however, notice your heart race and your breathing rate increase during other types of anxiety-producing situations—going on a first date, taking a test, or speaking in front of an audience. For these effects, you have your sympathetic nervous system to thank (Chapter 12).

The **parasympathetic nervous system,** on the other hand, oversees the "rest-and-digest" process, which basically works to bring the body back to a noncrisis mode. When a crisis has ended, the parasympathetic system reverses the activity initiated by the sympathetic system (for example, lowering heart rate and respiration, increasing digestion). The two systems work together, balancing the activities of these primarily involuntary processes. The parasympathetic and sympathetic systems allow us to fight if we need to, flee when necessary, and calm down when danger has passed.

## Think Critically

### TEND AND BEFRIEND

Fighting and running are not the only ways we respond to stress. Humans also have an inclination to "tend and befriend" in response to threatening situations—that is, direct energy toward nurturing offspring and forging social bonds (von Dawans et al., 2019; von Dawans et al., 2012). Historically, the tend-and-befriend reaction has been associated with females (Taylor et al., 2000). Research suggests that women are generally

**DO MEN AND WOMEN REACT DIFFERENTLY?**

**Men Who Tend and Befriend**
Rescuers help a baby arriving on the Greek island Lésbos in a refugee boat. During times of stress, both women and men may demonstrate the "tend and befriend" response; that is, direct their energy toward nurturing offspring and developing social relationships.

BULENT KILIC/Getty Images.

more inclined than men to display this response (Taylor & Master, 2011), and this could be partly explained by differences in *nature*. For example, men have the *SRY* gene, which drives the development of male sex characteristics. SRY is also expressed in brain and body tissues where stress hormones are active, and it may work to amplify the "fight-or-flight" response in males (Lee & Harley, 2012; for more on the biological differences between female and male brains, see Chapter 7).

Biology is important, but we must also remember that stress responses (and all human behaviors) result from a complex interplay of nature *and* nurture. Can you think of any environmental factors that might influence the way males deal with stress? In the United States and other Western cultures, teenage boys may feel the need to develop "a 'tough' masculine image (e.g., alpha male) out of fear of being coined weak or being seen as inferior" (Kirby & Kirby, 2017, p. 74). Young men may withhold compassion and caring behaviors to avoid being rejected by peers. But we as a society have the power to resist this traditional view of masculinity. Researchers are exploring interventions aimed at increasing compassion, and the results are encouraging (Kirby & Kirby, 2017). What actions can you as an individual take to promote helping and nurturing behaviors among the men (and women) in your life? 🧠

## The Endocrine System

Imagine that you are 19-year-old Brandon Burns fighting in the battle of Fallujah, one of the bloodiest battles of the Iraq War. The sound of gunfire rings through the air. Bullets zip past your helmet. People are dying around you. Your life could end at any moment. Unless you have been in a similar situation, it would be difficult to fathom how you would feel. But one thing seems certain: You would be feeling a great deal of stress.

When faced with imminent danger, the sympathetic nervous system responds almost instantaneously. Activity in the brain triggers the release of neurotransmitters that cause increases in heart rate, breathing rate, and metabolism—changes that will come in handy if you need to flee or defend yourself. But the nervous system does not act alone. The *endocrine system* is also hard at work, releasing stress hormones such as *cortisol*, which prompt similar physiological changes.

**LO 8** Summarize how the endocrine system influences behavior and physiological processes.

**endocrine system** The communication system that uses glands to convey messages by releasing hormones into the bloodstream.

**hormones** Chemical messengers released into the bloodstream that influence mood, cognition, appetite, and many other processes and behaviors.

**pituitary gland** The small endocrine gland located in the center of the brain just under the hypothalamus; known as the master gland.

**thyroid gland** The endocrine gland that regulates the rate of metabolism by secreting thyroxin.

**adrenal glands** Endocrine glands involved in responses to stress and the regulation of salt balance.

The **endocrine system** (EN-doe-krin) is a communication system that uses glands, rather than neurons, to send messages (**FIGURE 2.5**). These messages are conveyed by **hormones,** chemicals produced by the glands and released into the bloodstream. There are many types of hormones. Some promote aggression and mood swings; others influence growth, alertness, cognition, and appetite. Like neurotransmitters, hormones are chemical messengers that affect many processes and behaviors. In fact, some chemicals, such as norepinephrine, can act as both neurotransmitters and hormones depending on where they are released. Neurotransmitters are unloaded into the synaptic gap between neurons, whereas hormones are secreted into the bloodstream by endocrine glands stationed around the body.

When neurotransmitters are released into a synaptic gap, their effects can be almost instantaneous. Hormones usually make long voyages to far-away targets by way of the bloodstream, creating a relatively delayed but usually longer-lasting impact. A neural impulse can travel over 250 mph, much faster than messages sent via hormones, which take minutes (if not longer) to arrive where they are going. However, the messages sent via hormones are more widely spread because they are disseminated through the bloodstream.

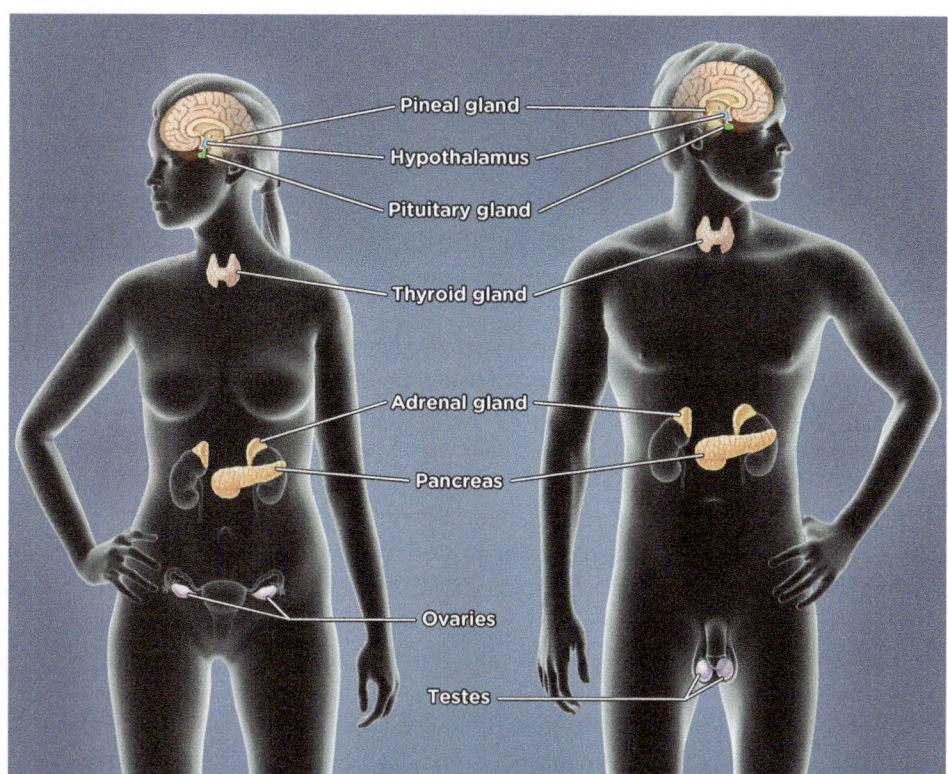

FIGURE 2.5
**The Endocrine System**
This system of glands secretes hormones directly into the bloodstream.

If the endocrine system had a chief executive officer, it would be the **pituitary gland,** a gland about the size of a pencil eraser located in the center of the brain, just under the *hypothalamus* (a structure we will explore later). Controlled by the hypothalamus, the pituitary gland, also known as the master gland, influences all the other glands and promotes growth through the secretion of its own hormones.

The **thyroid gland** regulates the rate of metabolism by secreting thyroxin, and the **adrenal glands** (uh-DREEN-ul) are involved in stress responses and maintenance of salt balance. Other endocrine glands and organs directed by the pituitary include the pineal gland, which secretes melatonin (controls sleep–wake cycles); the pancreas, which secretes insulin (regulates blood sugar); and the ovaries and testes, which secrete sex hormones (cause differences in male and female development). Together, these glands and organs can impact: (1) growth and sex characteristics, (2) regulation of some basic body processes, and (3) responses to emergencies. Just as our behaviors are influenced by neurotransmitters we can't see and action potentials we can't feel, the hormones secreted by the endocrine system are also hard at work behind the scenes.

Now that we have discovered how information moves through the body via electrical and chemical signals, let's turn our attention toward the part of the nervous system that integrates this activity, creating a unified and meaningful experience. Time to explore the brain.

## ⯈⯈⯈ SHOW WHAT YOU KNOW

1. The _____ regulates involuntary activity, such as the pumping of the heart, the expansion and contraction of blood vessels, and digestion.
   A. reflex arc
   B. spinal cord
   C. autonomic nervous system
   D. somatic nervous system

2. The _____ gland, located in the center of the brain, just under the hypothalamus, is in charge of the endocrine system.

3. As you recall, Brandon's brain injury led to paralysis on the right side of his body. What do you think would happen if a doctor tapped on his right knee—would he experience a reflex?

✓ CHECK YOUR ANSWERS AT THE BACK OF BOOK.

# The Amazing Brain

**THE GIRL WITH HALF A BRAIN**    As Brandon Burns began his long journey to recovery, a 17-year-old girl in Bristol, Pennsylvania, was enjoying a particularly successful senior year of high school. Christina Santhouse was an honor roll student for the fourth year in a row, and she had been named captain of the varsity bowling team. But these accomplishments did not come so easily. It took Christina twice as much time as classmates to do homework assignments because her brain needed extra time to process information. She had to invent a new bowling technique because the left side of her body was partially paralyzed, and she was constantly aware of being "different" from the other kids at school. Christina wasn't simply different from her classmates, however. She was extraordinary because she managed to do everything they did (and more) with nearly half of her brain missing.

Christina's remarkable story began when she was 7 years old. She was a vibrant, healthy child who loved soccer and playing outside with her friends. Barring an occasional ear infection, she basically never got sick—that is, until the day she suffered her first seizure. It was the summer of 1995 and Christina's family was vacationing on the Jersey Shore. While playing in a swimming pool with her cousins, Christina hopped onto the deck to chase a ball and noticed that something wasn't quite right. She looked down and saw her left ankle twitching uncontrollably. Her life was about to change dramatically.

As the days and weeks wore on, the tremors in Christina's ankle moved up her left side and eventually spread throughout her body. In time, she was having seizures every 3 to 5 minutes. Doctors suspected she had Rasmussen's encephalitis, a rare disease that causes severe swelling in one side of the brain, impairing movement and thinking and causing seizures that come as often as every few minutes (Varadkar et al., 2014).

Christina and her mother decided to seek treatment at The Johns Hopkins Hospital in Baltimore, the premiere center for treating children with seizure disorders. They met with Dr. John Freeman, a pediatric neurologist and an expert in *hemispherectomy,* a surgery to remove nearly half of the brain. A rare and last-resort operation, the hemispherectomy is only performed on patients suffering from severe seizures that can't be controlled in other ways. After examining Christina, Dr. Freeman made the same diagnosis—Rasmussen's encephalitis—and indicated that the seizures would get worse, and they would get worse fast. He recommended a hemispherectomy and told Christina (and her mother) to let him know when she had reached her limit with the seizures. Then they would go ahead with the operation.

Why did Dr. Freeman recommend this drastic surgery to remove nearly half of Christina's brain? And what side of the brain did he suggest removing? Before addressing these important questions, we need to develop a general sense of the brain's geography.

## The Two Hemispheres

**LO 9**  Describe the two brain hemispheres and how they communicate.

If you look at a photo or an illustration of the brain, you will see a walnut-shaped wrinkled structure—this is the **cerebrum** (Latin for "brain"), the largest and

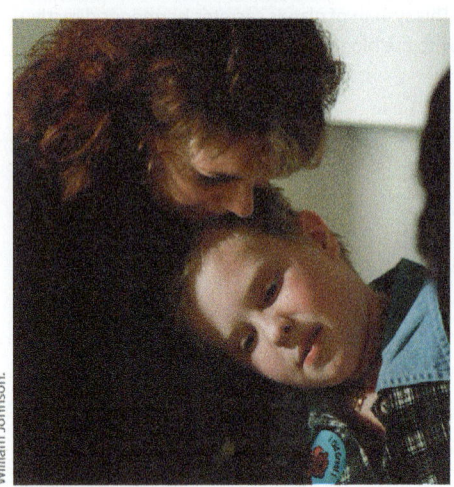

William Johnson.

**Staying Strong**
Christina Santhouse relaxes with her mother at Johns Hopkins, where she had a dramatic brain surgery known as a hemispherectomy. Prior to the operation, Christina experienced hundreds of seizures a day.

**cerebrum**  The largest area of the brain, includes virtually all parts of the brain except brainstem structures; has two distinct hemispheres.

**corpus callosum**  The thick band of nerve fibers connecting the right and left cerebral hemispheres; principal structure for information sharing between the two hemispheres.

**split-brain operation**  A rare procedure used to disconnect the right and left hemispheres; involves cutting the corpus callosum.

most conspicuous part of the brain. The cerebrum includes virtually all parts of the brain except the brainstem structures and the cerebellum, which you will learn about later. Like a walnut, the cerebrum has two distinct halves, or *hemispheres.* Looking at the brain from above, you can see a deep groove running from the front of the head to the back, dividing it into the right cerebral hemisphere and the left cerebral hemisphere. The hemispheres may look like mirror images of one another, with similar structures on the left and right, but they are not perfectly symmetrical, and they don't have identical jobs. Linking the two hemispheres is a bundle of axons (nerve fibers) known as the **corpus callosum** (KOR-pus kuh-LOW-sum). Through the corpus callosum, the left and right sides of the brain communicate and work together to process information. Generally speaking, the right hemisphere controls and processes sensations from the left side of the body, and the left hemisphere does the same for the right side of the body. This explains why Brandon, who was shot on the *left* side of his head, suffered paralysis and loss of sensation on the *right* half of his body. Christina's situation is roughly the opposite. Rasmussen's encephalitis struck the *right* side of her brain, which explains why her *left* ankle started twitching at the pool and why all her subsequent seizures affected the left side of her body. This is why Dr. Freeman recommended the removal of her right hemisphere.

**CHRISTINA MAKES THE DECISION**    Within 2 months, Christina's seizures were occurring every 3 minutes, hundreds of times a day. She was unable to play soccer or go outside during school recess, and she sat on a beanbag chair in class so she wouldn't hurt herself during a seizure. "I couldn't do anything anymore," Christina says. "I wasn't enjoying my life."

In February 1996, the doctors at Johns Hopkins removed the right hemisphere of Christina's brain. The operation lasted some 14 hours. When Christina emerged from the marathon surgery, her head was pounding with pain. "I remember screaming and asking for medicine," she recalls. The migraines persisted for months but eventually tapered off, and ultimately the surgery served its purpose: Christina no longer experienced debilitating seizures.

## Extreme Surgeries

Removing nearly half of a brain may sound barbaric, but hemispherectomies have proven to be effective for eliminating seizures, with success rates from multiple studies ranging from 54% to 90% (Lew, 2014). In a study from the Cleveland Clinic, 83% of hemispherectomy patients could walk independently nearly 13 years after surgery. Meanwhile, 70% possessed good spoken language skills, and 42% were able to read satisfactorily (Moosa et al., 2013).

Hemispherectomies are only used for cases that do not respond to drugs and other interventions, and are characterized by seizures originating in one hemisphere (Young et al., 2020). Another less extreme, last-resort surgery for drug-resistant seizures is the **split-brain operation,** which essentially disconnects the right and left hemispheres. Normally, the two hemispheres communicate through the corpus callosum. But this same band of nerve fibers can also serve as a passageway for the electrical storms responsible for seizures. With the split-brain operation, the corpus callosum is severed so that these storms can no longer pass freely between the hemispheres (Wolman, 2012).

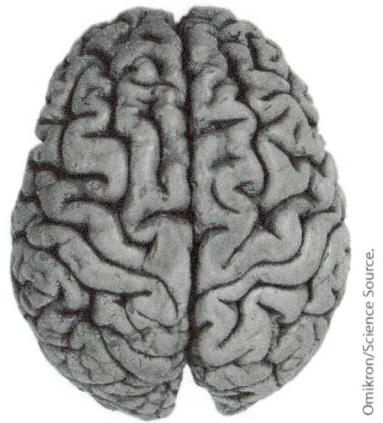

**Two Hemispheres**
The cerebrum looks like a walnut with its two wrinkled halves.

Omikron/Science Source.

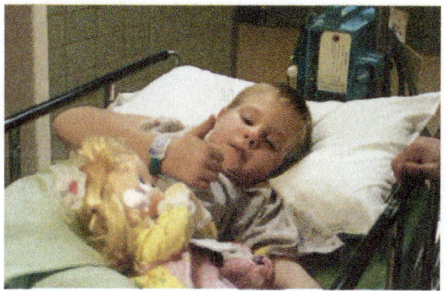

**Pre-Op**
Christina is wheeled into the operating room for her 14-hour hemispherectomy. She had a seizure in the elevator on the way to the surgery.

William Johnson.

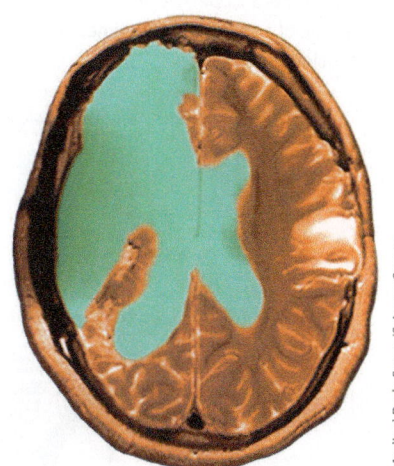

**Hemispherectomy**
This scan shows the brain of a person who has undergone a hemispherectomy. The green area, once occupied by the removed hemisphere, is now filled with cerebrospinal fluid.

Medical Body Scans/Science Source.

**LO 10** Define lateralization and explain what the split-brain experiments reveal about the right and left hemispheres.

**STUDYING THE SPLIT BRAIN**    In addition to helping many patients with severe, drug-resistant epilepsy, split-brain operations have provided researchers with an excellent opportunity to explore the specialization of the hemispheres (de Haan et al., 2020). Before we start to look at this research, you need to understand how visual information is processed. Each eye receives visual sensations, but that information is sent to the opposite hemisphere, and shared between the hemispheres via the corpus callosum. Specifically, information presented in the right visual field is processed in the left hemisphere, and information presented in the left visual field is processed in the right hemisphere.

Equipped with this knowledge, American neuropsychologist Roger Sperry and his student Michael Gazzaniga conducted groundbreaking research on epilepsy patients who had undergone split-brain operations to alleviate their seizures. Not only did Sperry and Gazzaniga's "split-brain" participants experience fewer seizures, they had surprisingly normal cognitive abilities and showed no obvious changes in "temperament, personality, or general intelligence" as a result of their surgeries (Gazzaniga, 1967, p. 24). But under certain circumstances, the researchers observed, they behaved as though they had two separate brains (Gazzaniga, 1967, 1998, 2005; FIGURE **2.6**).

Because the hemispheres are disconnected through the surgery, researchers can study each hemisphere separately to explore its unique capabilities (or specializations). Imagine that researchers flashed an image (let's say an apple) on the right side of a screen, ensuring that it would be processed by the brain's *left* hemisphere. The split-brain participant could articulate what they had seen (*I saw an apple*). If, however, the apple appeared on the left side of the screen (processed by the *right* hemisphere), they would claim they saw nothing. But when asked to identify the image in a nonverbal way (pointing or touching with their left hand), they could do this without a problem. This proved they could actually "see" the apple; they just couldn't put it into words (Gazzaniga, 1967, 1998).

**FIGURE 2.6**

**The Split-Brain Experiment**

An example of a split-brain experiment is shown below.

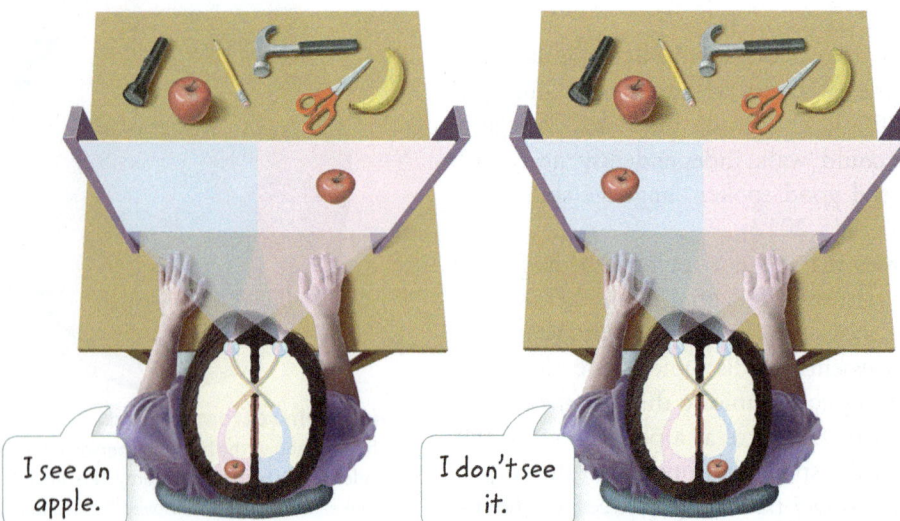
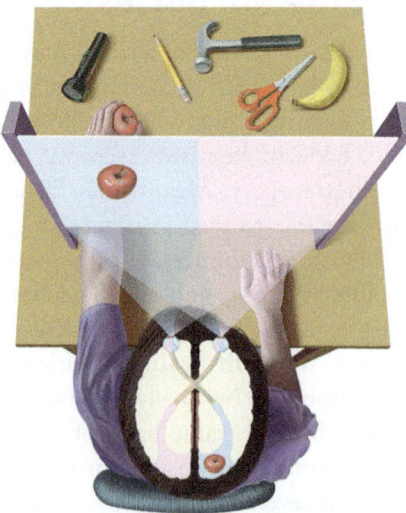

Touch the object matching the image on the screen.

I see an apple.

I don't see it.

Information presented in right visual field is sent to the left hemisphere where language processing occurs. Participant can speak the answer.

Information presented in left visual field is sent to the right hemisphere. Participant can't use language to say what they were shown.

The participant can touch the correct object even if they can't say what has been projected in their left visual field. The participant uses their left hand, which is controlled by the right hemisphere, where the visual information has been processed.

**LATERALIZATION**    The split-brain experiments offered an elegant demonstration of **lateralization**, the tendency for the left and right hemispheres to excel in certain activities. When images are flashed in the right visual field, the information is sent to the left side of the brain, which excels in language processing. This explains why the split-brain participants were able to articulate the image they had seen on the right side of the screen. Images appearing in the left visual field are sent to the right side of the brain, which excels at visual-spatial tasks but is generally not responsible for processing language. Thus, the participants were tongue-tied when asked to report what they had seen on the left side of the screen. They could, however, reach out and point to it using their left hand, which is controlled by the right hemisphere (Gazzaniga, 1998; Gazzaniga et al., 1965).

The split-brain studies revealed that the left hemisphere plays a crucial role in language processing and the right hemisphere in managing visual-spatial tasks. These are only generalizations, however. While there are clear differences in the way the hemispheres process information (and the speed at which they do it), they can also process the same types of information. In a split-brain individual, communication between the hemispheres is limited. This is *not* the case for someone with an intact corpus callosum. The hemispheres are constantly integrating and sharing all types of information (Lilienfeld et al., 2010; Pinto et al., 2017). Next time you hear someone claim that certain personality and cognitive characteristics are associated with being "left-brained" or "right-brained," ask them to identify research to back it up (Nielsen et al., 2013; Schmerling, 2017). There is no evidence for this strict dividing line between right- and left-brain activities. Similarly, beware of catchy sales pitches for products designed to increase your "logical and analytical" left-brain reasoning or to help you tap into your "creative" right brain (Staub, 2016). This way of thinking is oversimplified. Keep this in mind while reading the upcoming sections on specialization in the left and right sides of the brain. The two hemispheres may have certain areas of expertise, but they work as a team to create your experience of the world.

## Roles of the Left and the Right

Armed with this new knowledge of the split-brain experiments, let's return our focus to Brandon. His injury occurred on the left side of the brain, devastating his ability to use language. Before the battle of Fallujah, Brandon had breezed through Western novels at breakneck speeds. After his injury, even the simplest sentence baffled him. Words on a page looked like nothing more than black lines and curls. Brandon remembers, "It was like a puzzle that I couldn't figure out." Brandon's difficulties with language are fairly typical for someone with an injury to the left hemisphere, because regions on the left side of the brain tend to predominate in language. This is not true for everyone, however. The left hemisphere handles language processing in around 95% to 99% of people who are right-handed, but only in about 70% of those who are left-handed (Corballis, 2014). About 1 in 10 people are strongly left-handed, and these people are less likely to have language dominance in the left hemisphere (Papadatou-Pastou et al., 2020).

**LO 11**    Identify areas in the brain responsible for language production and comprehension.

**LANGUAGE PRODUCTION AND COMPREHENSION**    Evidence for the "language on the left" notion came from studying patients with *aphasia,* or language problems stemming from brain damage. As early as 1861, a French surgeon by the name of Pierre Paul Broca (1824–1880) encountered two patients who had, for all practical purposes, lost the ability to talk. One of the patients could only say the word "tan," and the other had an oral vocabulary of five words. Later, when Broca performed

A.J. Wolfe/The Commercial Appeal/Zuma Press.

**Speak Again**
Brandon works on his pronunciation in front of a mirror during a speech therapy session at the Memphis VA hospital. You can see the extent of his injury on the left side of his head. Upon awaking from his coma, Brandon could not articulate a single word. Today, he can hold his own in complex conversations.

**lateralization** The idea that each cerebral hemisphere processes certain types of information and excels in certain activities.

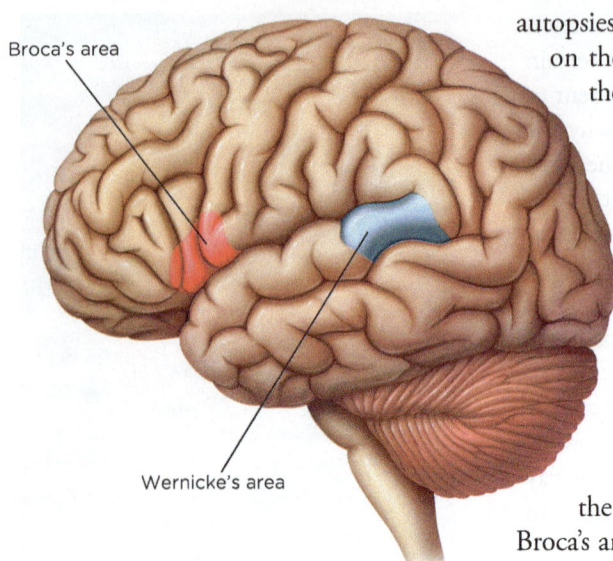

Broca's area

Wernicke's area

**FIGURE 2.7**
**Language Areas of the Brain**
For most people, the left hemisphere controls language. Broca's area plays a critical role in language production, and Wernicke's area in language comprehension.

autopsies on the men, he found that both had sustained damage to the same area on the side of the left frontal lobe (right around the temple; FIGURE **2.7**). Over the years, Broca identified several other speech-impaired patients with damage to the same area, a region now called **Broca's area** (BRO-kuz), which is involved in speech production (Wickens, 2015).

Around the same time Broca was doing his research, a German doctor named Karl Wernicke (1848–1905) pinpointed a different place in the left hemisphere that seemed to control speech comprehension. Wernicke noticed that patients suffering damage to a small tract of tissue in the left temporal lobe, now called **Wernicke's area** (VAIR-nick-uhz), struggled to make sense of what others were saying. Wernicke's area is the brain's headquarters for language comprehension (Wickens, 2015).

The work of Broca, Wernicke, and other early researchers highlighted the left hemisphere's critical role in language. Scientists initially suspected that Broca's area was responsible for speech creation and Wernicke's area for comprehension, but it is now clear that the use of language is far more complicated (Berwick et al., 2013; Friedrich et al., 2019). These areas may perform additional functions, such as processing music and interpreting hand gestures (Schlaug, 2015; Xu et al., 2009), and they cooperate with multiple brain regions to allow us to produce and understand language (Tate et al., 2014). Furthermore, a certain degree of speech processing appears to occur in the right hemisphere, and some researchers propose that other parts of the brain may also be involved in generating speech (Alexandrou et al., 2017; Tate et al., 2014).

**THE ROLE OF THE RIGHT**   We know that the left hemisphere tends to dominate in language processing, but where does the right hemisphere excel? Research suggests that the right hemisphere surpasses the left when it comes to identifying mirror images and spatial relationships, and mentally rotating images (Gazzaniga, 2005). This hemisphere also plays a key role in controlling where we direct attention in our immediate environments (Spagna et al., 2020). It is also involved in processing emotions and recognizing facial expressions (Burt & Hausmann, 2019; Gainotti, 2019; Moeck et al., 2020). A condition called prosopagnosia, or "face blindness," appears to result from abnormalities in the right fusiform gyrus. Someone with prosopagnosia may not be able to recognize the face of a family member, or distinguish between the faces of friends and complete strangers (National Institute of Neurological Disorders and Stroke [NINDS], 2019b).

**CHRISTINA WAKES UP**   When Christina was wheeled out of surgery, her mother approached, grabbed hold of her right hand, and asked her to squeeze. Christina squeezed, demonstrating that she could understand and respond to language. Remember, she still had her left hemisphere.

Losing the right side of her brain did come at a cost, however. We know that Christina suffers partial paralysis on the left side of her body; this makes sense, because the right hemisphere controls movement and sensation on the left. We also know that it took Christina extra time to do her schoolwork. But if you ask Christina whether she has significant difficulty with any of the "right-brain" tasks described earlier, her answer will be no.

In addition to making the honor roll and leading the bowling team, Christina managed to get her driver's license (even though some of her doctors said she never would), and graduate from high school and college. These accomplishments are the result of Christina's steadfast determination, but also a testament to the brain's amazing ability to heal and regenerate.

**Broca's area**   A region of the cortex that is critical for speech production.

**Wernicke's area**   A region of the cortex that plays a pivotal role in language comprehension.

# Neuroplasticity

**LO 12**  Define neuroplasticity and recognize when it is evident in the brain.

The brain undergoes constant alteration in response to experiences and is capable of some degree of physical adaptation and repair. Its ability to heal, grow new connections, and make do with what is available is a characteristic we refer to as **neuroplasticity.** New connections are constantly forming between neurons, and unused ones are fading away. Vast networks of neurons have the ability to reorganize in order to adapt to the environment and an organism's ever-changing needs, a quality particularly evident in the young. After brain injuries, younger children have better outcomes than do adults; their brains show more plasticity, although this depends somewhat on the type of injury (Johnston, 2009; Su et al., 2016).

In one study, researchers **removed the eyes** of newborn opossums and found that brain tissues normally destined to become visual processing centers took a developmental turn. Instead, they became areas that specialized in processing other types of sensory stimuli, such as sounds and touch (Karlen et al., 2006). The same appears to happen in humans. Brain scans reveal that when visually impaired individuals learn to read braille early in life, a region of the brain that normally specializes in handling visual information becomes activated. This suggests that visual processing centers are being used for another purpose—processing touch sensations (Burton, 2003; Lazzouni & Lepore, 2014; Liu et al., 2007).

The plasticity of young brains is also evident among hemispherectomy patients (Kliemann et al., 2019). After losing an entire left hemisphere (the primary location for language processing), speech is less severely compromised in young patients, though some impact is inevitable. The younger the person, the less disability in speech, but factors such as language delays prior to surgery and ongoing seizures after surgery can impact further language development (Choi, 2008; Moosa et al., 2013).

## CONNECTIONS

In **Chapter 1,** we described the guidelines psychologists use to ensure the ethical treatment of humans and animals. In order to conduct the experiment described here, the researchers had to get pre-approval from an ethics board. The board determined that the animals would be treated humanely and that the proposed research necessitated this surgery.

FatCamera/Getty Images.

stellalevi/Getty Images.

**Brain Boosters**

Both physical exercise and musical training support neuroplasticity, the brain's ability to change and adapt in response to experience. To maximize the brain benefits of exercise, some research suggests it is better to choose an activity that provides a cognitive challenge, not just a physical one (Raichlen & Alexander, 2020). For example, learning a Zumba routine might provide more cognitive stimulation than running on a treadmill. As for music, you don't have to perform on a stage to reap the benefits; learning and practicing an instrument at home is enough. "What is unique about music training is its capacity to induce neuroplastic changes in *all* areas of the brain" (Izbicki, 2020, para. 2).

**neuroplasticity** The brain's ability to heal, grow new connections, and reorganize in order to adapt to the environment.

## Put Your Heads Together

 In your groups, discuss the following: **A)** How is a split-brain operation different from a hemispherectomy? **B)** If you had to undergo a hemispherectomy, which half of your brain would you choose to have removed and why? **C)** What functions might you lose as a result? **D)** How might neuroplasticity impact your ability to regain these functions over time?

**STEM CELLS**   Scientists once thought that people were born with all the neurons they would ever have. Brain cells might die, but no new ones would crop up to replace them. Thanks to research beginning in the 1990s, that dismal notion has been turned on its head (Sailor et al., 2017). In the last several decades, studies with animals and humans have shown that some areas of the brain are capable of generating new neurons, a process known as **neurogenesis** (Eriksson et al., 1998; Gould et al., 1999). This formation of new neurons might be tied to learning and creating memories (Jurkowski et al., 2020). Evidence suggests that neurogenesis occurs in the hippocampus during childhood (Sorrells et al., 2018) and into adulthood (Moreno-Jiménez et al., 2019; Tobin et al., 2019).

The cells responsible for churning out new neurons are known as **stem cells,** and they are quite a hot topic in biomedical research. Scientists hope to harness these little cell factories to repair tissue that has been damaged or destroyed. Imagine you could use stem cells to bring back all the neurons Brandon lost from his injury, or replace those Christina lost to surgery. Researchers have been exploring stem cell therapies for survivors of traumatic brain injury, but large randomized controlled trials are needed to better understand which treatments are safest and most effective (Zhou et al., 2019). Repairing brain tissue is just one potential application of stem cell science. These cellular cure-alls might also be used to alleviate the symptoms of Parkinson's disease, or replenish neurons of the spine, enabling people with spinal cord injuries to regain movement. Both have already been accomplished in rodents, and clinical trials are underway for similar therapies in humans (Keirstead et al., 2005; Parmar et al., 2020; Tsuji et al., 2019; Wernig et al., 2008). Various types of stem cells are being investigated as treatments targeting the nervous system. Among these are neural stem cells, which generate new neurons; embryonic stem cells, which can give rise to virtually any type of cell found in the body; and induced pluripotent stem cells, which are engineered to behave like embryonic stem cells (Cyranoski, 2018; Song et al., 2018).

## The Cortex: A Peek Beneath the Skull

Imagine you were one of the surgeons performing Christina's hemispherectomy. What exactly would you see when you peeled away the scalp and cut an opening into the skull? Before encountering the brain, you would come upon a layer of three thin membranes, the *meninges,* which envelop and protect the brain and spinal cord (**INFOGRAPHIC 2.4** on page 70). Perhaps you have heard of meningitis, a potentially life-threatening condition in which the meninges become inflamed as a result of an infection. The meninges are bathed in a clear watery substance called cerebrospinal fluid, which offers additional cushioning and facilitates the transport of nutrients and waste into and out of the brain and the spinal cord. Once you peeled back the meninges, you would behold the pink cerebrum.

As Christina's surgeon, your main task would be to remove part of the cerebrum's outermost layer, the **cerebral cortex** (suh-REE-brul). The cerebral cortex is responsible for higher mental functions, such as decision making, language, and processing visual information. Remember our earlier comment that the cerebrum looks like a wrinkled walnut? This is because the cortex, which surrounds nearly all the other brain structures, is scrunched up and folded onto itself to fit inside a small space (the skull).

**neurogenesis** The generation of new neurons in the brain.

**stem cells** Cells responsible for producing new neurons.

**cerebral cortex** The wrinkled outermost layer of the cerebrum, responsible for higher mental functions, such as decision making, language, and processing visual information.

**LO 13** Identify the lobes of the cortex and explain their functions.

The cortex overlying each hemisphere is separated into different sections, or lobes (Infographic 2.4). The **frontal lobes** direct higher-level cognitive activities, such as language, emotions, control of social behavior, and decision making. The **parietal lobes** (puh-RYE-uh-tul) receive and process sensory information like touch, pressure, temperature, and spatial orientation. Visual information goes to the **occipital lobes** (ok-SIP-i-tul) for processing, and hearing and language comprehension are largely handled by the **temporal lobes.** We'll have more to say about the lobes as we discuss each in turn below (Table 2.2 on page 73).

## The Lobes: Up Close and Personal

Prior to her hemispherectomy, Christina was extroverted, easygoing, and full of energy. "I had absolutely no worries," she says, recalling her pre-Rasmussen's days. After her operation, Christina became more introverted and passive. She felt more emotionally unsettled. "You go into surgery one person," she says, "and you come out another."

The transformation of Christina's personality may be a result of many factors, including the stress of dealing with a serious disease, undergoing a major surgery, and readjusting to life with disabilities. But it could also have something to do with the fact that she lost a considerable amount of brain tissue, including her right frontal lobe. Networks of neurons in the frontal lobes are involved in processing emotions, making plans, controlling impulses, and carrying out a vast array of mental tasks that each person does in a unique way (Alexander & Brown, 2018; Miller & Cummings, 2018). The frontal lobes play a key role in the development of personality and many of its characteristics (Forbes et al., 2014; Stuss & Alexander, 2000; Williams et al., 2010). A striking illustration of this phenomenon involves an unlucky railroad foreman, Phineas Gage.

**PHINEAS GAGE AND THE FRONTAL LOBES**  The year was 1848, and Phineas Gage was working on the railroad. An accidental explosion sent a 3-foot-long iron tamping rod clear through his frontal lobe (Infographic 2.4). The rod, about as thick as a broom handle, drove straight into Gage's left cheek, through his brain, and out the top of his skull (Macmillan, 2000). What's peculiar about Gage's accident (besides the fact that he was walking and talking just hours later) is the extreme transformation it caused. Before the accident, Gage was a well-balanced, diligent worker whom supervisors referred to as their "most efficient and capable foreman" (Harlow, 1848, as cited in Neylan, 1999, p. 280). After the accident, he was unreliable, unpleasant, and downright vulgar. His character was so altered that people acquainted with him before and after the accident claimed he was "no longer Gage" (Harlow, 1848, as cited in Neylan, 1999, p. 280). However, there is evidence that Gage recovered to some degree, another illustration of the brain's remarkable neuroplasticity (Griggs, 2015a). After the accident, he spent years working as a horse caretaker and stagecoach driver in Chile (Harlow, 1868, 1869, as cited in Macmillan, 2000), where his colleague observed "no impairment of mental faculties" (Benjamin et al., 2018, p. 280). Gage died 12.5 years after the accident, apparently from a seizure (Benjamin et al., 2018).

Modern scientists have revisited Gage's case, using measurements from his fractured skull and brain-imaging data to estimate exactly where the damage occurred. Their studies suggest that the metal rod caused destruction in both the left and right frontal lobes (Damasio et al., 1994), although later researchers believe the rod did not pierce the right hemisphere (Ratiu et al., 2004; Van Horn et al., 2012). The only good thing about Gage's horrible accident, it seems, is that it

William Johnson.

**Enjoying Life**
Christina, as a teenager, walking her dog. The left side of her body is partially paralyzed, but her gait is quite natural. She wears a device on her left leg that activates her nerves, causing her muscles to contract at the appropriate time.

**frontal lobes** The area of the cortex that directs higher-level cognitive activities, such as language, emotions, control of social behavior, and decision making.

**parietal lobes** The area of the cortex that receives and processes sensory information such as touch, pressure, temperature, and spatial orientation.

**occipital lobes** The area of the cortex in the back of the head that processes visual information.

**temporal lobes** The area of the cortex that processes auditory stimuli and language.

# Getting Into the Brain

## Finding Personality in the Brain

In 1848 an accidental blast drove a 3-foot iron bar through the head of railroad worker Phineas Gage. He survived, but his personality was markedly changed. Previously described as having a "well-balanced" mind, post-injury Gage was prone to angry outbursts and profanity (Harlow, 1868, 1869, as cited in Macmillan, 2000).

Phineas Gage holding the iron bar that injured him.

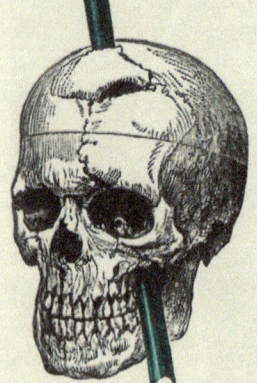

Using measurements from his fractured skull, scientists have been able to estimate where the damage occurred (Ratiu et al., 2004; Van Horn et al., 2012). Cases like this have helped psychologists understand the role of different structures in the brain.

## Getting TO the Brain

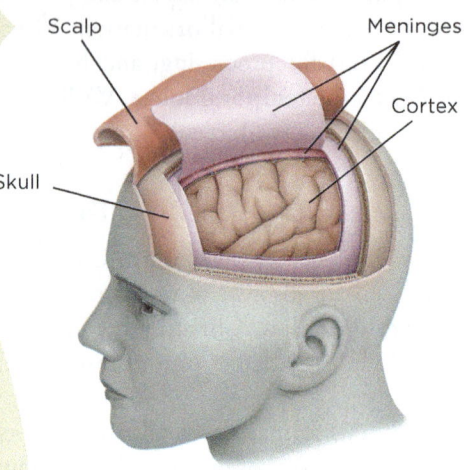

Scalp · Meninges · Cortex · Skull

In order to study the brain, we must get to it first. Peel away the scalp and cut away the bony skull, and you will find still more layers of protection. Three thin membranes—the meninges—provide a barrier to both physical injury and infection. Bypass them, and the outermost layer of the brain, the cortex, is revealed.

**Frontal lobe**
higher-level cognitive activities like language, emotions, and decision making

**Parietal lobe**
integration of sensory information like touch and temperature

**Occipital lobe**
processing of visual formation

**Temporal lobe**
hearing and language comprehension

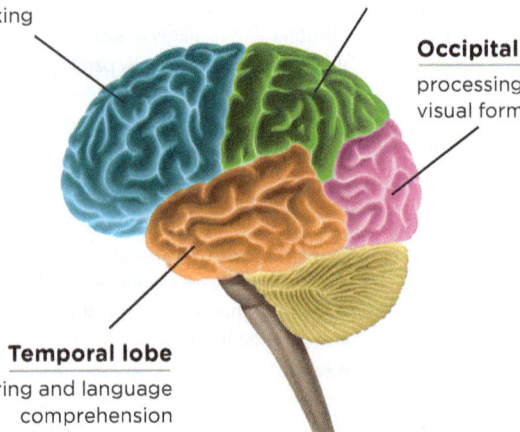

### Lobes of the Brain

This drawing shows the left hemisphere of the brain. Each hemisphere is divided into lobes, which are associated with certain functions.

**Motor cortex**
commands the body's movements

**Somatosensory cortex**
receives sensory information from the body

**Wernicke's area**
language comprehension

**Broca's area**
language production

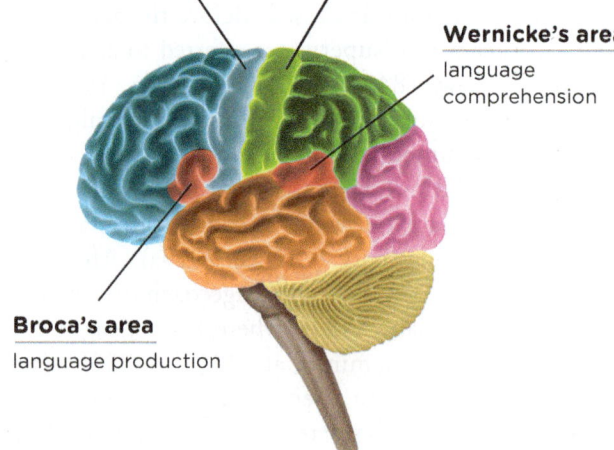

### Specialized Areas of the Brain

Unlike the lobes, which are associated with many functions, some areas of the brain have one specialized function.

illuminated the importance of the frontal lobes in defining personality characteristics. It also highlighted how adults can survive serious injury to their frontal lobes (Benjamin et al., 2018).

**DOGS, CARTOONS, AND THE MOTOR CORTEX**    Toward the rear of the frontal lobes is a strip of the brain known as the **motor cortex,** which works with other areas to plan and execute voluntary movements (Infographic 2.4). Evidence for this region's involvement in muscle movement first came from a study of dogs by Gustav Fritsch (1838–1927) and Edvard Hitzig (1838–1907). Working from a makeshift lab, these two German doctors discovered they could make the animals move by electrically stimulating their brains (Gross, 2007). A mild shock to the right side of the cortex might cause a twitch in the left forepaw or the left side of the face, whereas stimulating the left would spur movement on the right (Finger, 2001; Wickens, 2015).

North American neurosurgeon Wilder Penfield (1891–1976) conducted research on the brains of humans. Using a method similar to that of Fritsch and Hitzig, he created a map showing which points along the motor cortex correspond to the various parts of the body (Penfield & Boldrey, 1937). Penfield's map is often represented by the "homunculus" (huh-MUN-kyuh-lus; Latin for "little man") cartoon, a distorted image of a human being with huge lips and hands and a tiny torso (**FIGURE 2.8**). The size of each body part in the figure roughly reflects the amount of cortex devoted to it. This explains why parts requiring extremely fine-tuned motor control (the mouth and hands) are gigantic in comparison to other body parts.

### FIGURE 2.8
**The Motor and Somatosensory Cortex**
This illustration shows how areas on the motor and somatosensory cortex correspond to the various regions of the body. Parts of the body that are shown larger, such as the face and hands, indicate areas of greater motor control or sensitivity. The size of each body part reflects the amount of cortex allocated to it.

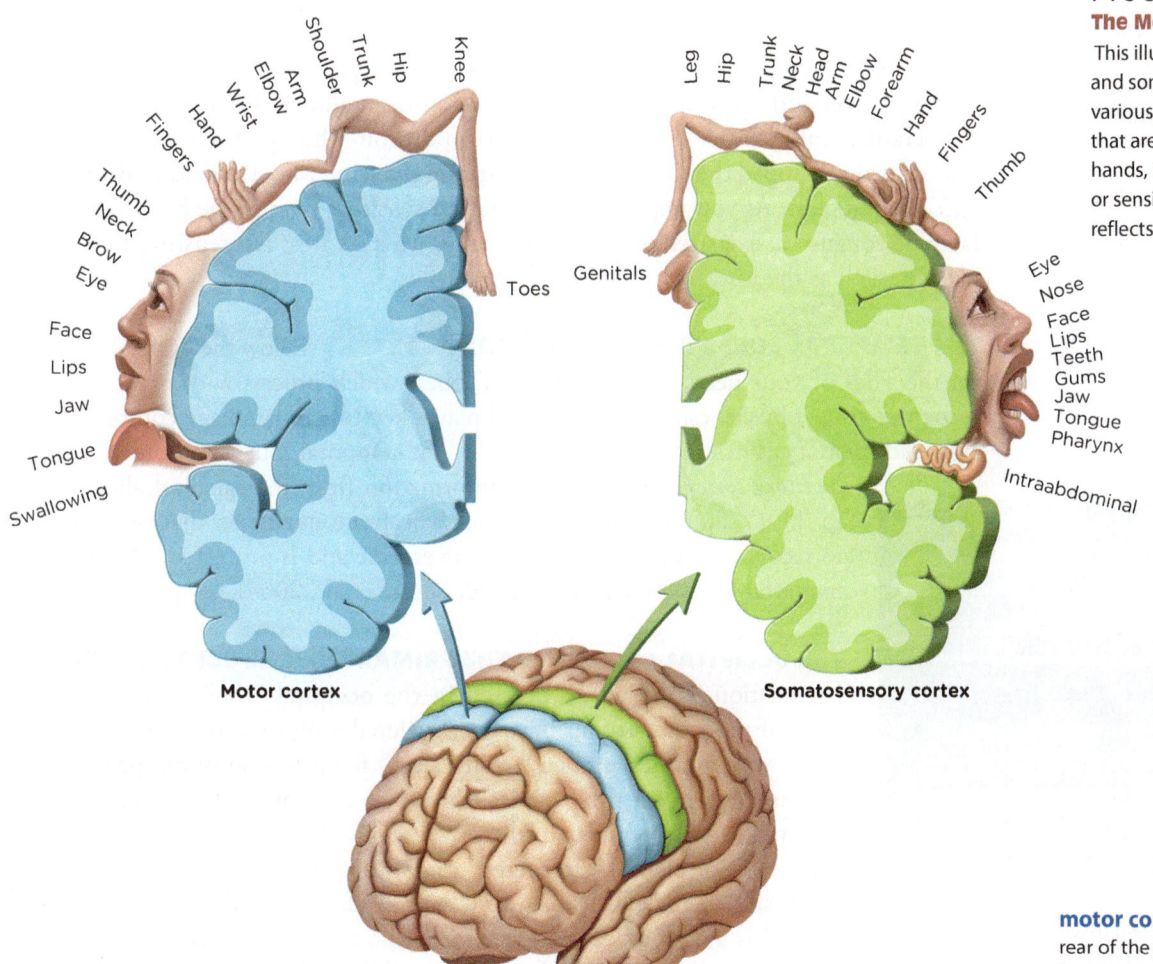

**motor cortex** A strip of brain tissue toward the rear of the frontal lobes that works with other brain regions to plan and execute voluntary movements.

### Research
## CONNECTIONS

In **Chapter 1**, we discussed the importance of having a representative sample and the potential problems with using case studies to make generalizations about the population. Comparing Einstein (a single participant) to the control group could be considered a type of case study, and may be problematic.

Keystone/Getty Images.

#### Superbrain

Irregularities in Albert Einstein's parietal lobes may explain some of his spectacular mathematical and visual-spatial abilities (Falk et al., 2013; Witelson et al., 1999). Could it be that Einstein's mathematical activities caused changes to his parietal lobes?

#### Seeing Stars

If you have ever been struck or fallen on the back of the head, you may recall perceiving bright blobs or dots floating by. The occipital lobes at the rear of the brain are home to the visual processing centers.

peepo/Getty Images.

**somatosensory cortex** A strip of brain tissue running parallel to the motor cortex that receives and integrates sensory information from all over the body.

**ALBERT EINSTEIN AND THE PARIETAL LOBES**    Directly behind the frontal lobes on the crown of your head are the parietal lobes (Infographic 2.4). The parietal lobes help orient the body in space, are involved in tactile processing (for example, interpreting sensations related to touch, such as pain and pressure), and may play a role in mathematical reasoning associated with spatial cognition (Desco et al., 2011; Grabner et al., 2007; Wolpert et al., 1998). One study compared the brain of **Albert Einstein** to a control group of 35 brain specimens from men who had donated their bodies for use in research. Prior to their deaths, these men had normal cognitive functioning, average intelligence, and no mental health issues.

The researchers reported that Einstein's brain did not exceed the average brain weight of the control group, but a region of his parietal lobe believed to be important for visual-spatial processing was 15% larger. They proposed that the differences in that specific region of Einstein's parietal lobe may have been linked to his "exceptional intellect" in areas of visual-spatial cognition and mathematical thinking (Witelson et al., 1999). Of course, the link between the size of Einstein's parietal region and his "exceptional intellect" is correlational, so we should be cautious in our interpretations. Did Einstein's unusual brain structure lead to his exceptional math abilities, or did all of his math-related thinking cause differences in his brain? We are also left to wonder how Einstein's other experiences molded the structure of his brain; for example, his long history playing the violin may have contributed to a "large 'knob'-shaped fold" in the part of his cortex responsible for movement of his left hand (Chen et al., 2014).

**PENFIELD AND THE SOMATOSENSORY CORTEX**    The parietal lobes are home to the **somatosensory cortex,** a strip of brain running parallel to the motor cortex, which receives and integrates sensory information from all over the body (pain and temperature, for example). Penfield, the neurosurgeon who collected data on the motor cortex, mapped the somatosensory cortex in the same way (Penfield & Boldrey, 1937; Figure 2.8). As you might expect, the most sensitive areas of the body like the face and tongue are oversized on the homunculus, whereas areas less sensitive to stimulation, such as the forearm and the calf, are smaller.

**THE TEMPORAL LOBES AND THE AUDITORY CORTEX**    Below the parietal lobes, on the sides of your head, are the temporal lobes, which process auditory stimuli; recognize visual objects, especially faces; and play a key role in language comprehension and memory (Hickok & Poeppel, 2000). The temporal lobes are home to the *auditory cortex,* which receives information from the ears and allows us to "hear" sounds. Studies of primate vocalizations suggest that the ability to recognize language has evolved over time and is processed within the temporal lobes (Scott, et al., 2000; Squire et al., 2004).

**THE OCCIPITAL LOBES AND THE PRIMARY VISUAL CORTEX**    Visual information is initially processed in the occipital lobes, in the lower back of the head. If you have ever suffered a blow to the rear of your head, you may remember "seeing stars" for a few seconds, probably because activity in the occipital lobes was disrupted. It is here, where the optic nerve connects to the *primary visual cortex,* that visual information is received, interpreted, and processed (for example, about color, shape, and motion). (See Chapter 3 for more on the visual process.) Damage to this area may cause severe visual impairment—even in a person with healthy eyes. Yet, such an individual would still be able to "see" vivid *mental images* (Bridge et al., 2012).

**LO 14** Describe the association areas and identify their functions.

**THE ASSOCIATION AREAS**    In addition to the different lobes described above, the cortex contains **association areas** whose role is to integrate information from all over the brain. The association areas are located in all four lobes; however, they are much harder to pinpoint than the motor and sensory areas. These areas allow us to learn (just as you're doing now), to have abstract thoughts (for example, 2 + 2 = 4), and to carry out complex behaviors like texting and tweeting. The language-processing hubs we learned about earlier, *Broca's area* and *Wernicke's area,* are association areas that play a role in the production and comprehension of speech. In humans, the vast majority of the brain's cortex is dedicated to the association areas (TABLE **2.2**).

**TABLE 2.2**   Regions of the Cortex

| Structure | Function and Importance |
|---|---|
| Association areas | Integrate information from all over the brain; allow us to learn, have abstract thoughts, and carry out complex behaviors. |
| Broca's area | Involved in speech production; helps us generate speech. |
| Corpus callosum | Connects the hemispheres; allows the left and right sides of the brain to communicate and work together to process information. |
| Frontal lobes | Process higher-level cognitive activities, such as language, emotions, control of social behavior, and decision making. |
| Left cerebral hemisphere | Controls the right side of the body; excels in language processing. |
| Motor cortex | Plans and executes voluntary movements; allows us to move our body. |
| Occipital lobes | Process visual information; help us see. |
| Parietal lobes | Receive and process sensory information; orient the body in space. |
| Primary visual cortex | Receives and interprets visual information; allows us to "see" vivid mental images. |
| Right cerebral hemisphere | Controls the left side of the body; excels in visual-spatial tasks. |
| Somatosensory cortex | Receives and integrates sensory information from the body; for example, helps us determine if touch is pleasurable or painful. |
| Temporal lobes | Play a key role in hearing, language comprehension, and memory; process auditory stimuli; recognize visual objects. |
| Wernicke's area | Plays a key role in language comprehension; enables us to make sense of what is being said. |

The cortex, or outermost layer of the brain, can be divided into functionally significant areas. This table summarizes the areas of the cortex and their importance.

# SOCIAL MEDIA AND PSYCHOLOGY

A MAGICAL NUMBER 150?

A major theme of this chapter is localization of function, the idea that certain areas of the brain tend to specialize in performing certain tasks. When we say "tasks," we mean just about any activity you can imagine, from riding a bicycle to managing friend networks on Facebook.

**HOW MANY FRIENDS DO YOU REALLY HAVE?**

Whether you're on social media or interacting in person, making connections and empathizing with other people rely on a system of neurons some refer to as a "social brain network" (Falk & Platt, 2018). One study even found a correlation between the number of Facebook friends and the density of gray matter in areas of the brain important for social interaction (Kanai et al., 2012). But how many meaningful social ties can your brain actually sustain? Facebook allows you to have thousands of friends, but it would be difficult, if not impossible, for anyone to keep track of so many connections.

**association areas** Regions of the cortex that integrate information from all over the brain, allowing us to learn, think in abstract terms, and carry out complex behaviors.

According to the "social brain hypothesis," humans can handle a maximum of about 150 "coherent personal relationships" at any point in time (Zhou et al., 2005, p. 439). This upper limit was originally meant to capture the number of offline relationships, but it seems to apply to online relationships as well (Bzdok & Dunbar, 2020; Dunbar, 1993). To summarize, you can only have about 150 real friends at a time—on social media or in person. Beyond that number, your "friends" are more like acquaintances.

## SHOW WHAT YOU KNOW

1. The left hemisphere excels in language and the right hemisphere excels in visual-spatial tasks. This specialization of the two hemispheres is known as:

   A. split-brain.
   B. homunculus.
   C. hemispherectomy.
   D. lateralization.

2. A man involved in a car accident suffered severe brain trauma. Following the accident, he had difficulty producing speech, even though he could understand what people were saying. It is very likely he had suffered damage to the left frontal lobe in a part of the brain referred to as:

   A. Wernicke's area.
   B. Broca's area.
   C. the visual field.
   D. the corpus callosum.

3. The brain is constantly undergoing alterations in response to experiences and is capable of a certain degree of physical adaptation and repair. This ability is known as:

   A. neuroplasticity.
   B. phrenology.
   C. ablation.
   D. lateralization.

4. How do the two brain hemispheres communicate? How does this change after a split-brain operation?

5. The _____ are regions of the cortex that integrate information from all over the brain, allowing us to learn, have abstract thoughts, and carry out complex behaviors.

6. Briefly describe the lobes of the cortex and their associated functions.

✓ CHECK YOUR ANSWERS AT THE BACK OF BOOK.

## Let's Dig a Little Deeper

Now that we have surveyed the brain's outer terrain, identifying some of the hotspots for language and other higher cognitive functions, let's dig deeper and examine some of its inner structures.

### Drama Central: The Limbic System

**LO 15** Distinguish the structures and functions of the limbic system.

Buried beneath the cortex is the **limbic system,** a group of interconnected structures that play an important role in our experiences of emotion, motivation, and memory. It also fuels our most basic drives, such as hunger, sex, and aggression. The limbic system includes the *thalamus, hypothalamus, amygdala,* and *hippocampus* (FIGURE **2.9**).

**THALAMUS**    Seated at the center of the limbic system is the **thalamus** (THAL-uh-muss), whose job is to process and relay sensory information to the appropriate parts of the cortex (visual information to the visual cortex, for example). The great majority of data picked up by all the sensory systems, except olfaction (sense of smell), pass through the thalamus before moving on to the cortex for processing (Mitchell et al., 2014). You might think of the thalamus as an air traffic control tower guiding incoming aircraft; when pilots communicate with the tower, the controllers direct their routes or tell them what runway to use.

**HYPOTHALAMUS**    Just below the thalamus is the **hypothalamus** (hi-po-THAL-uh-muss; *hypo* means "under" in Greek), which keeps the body's systems in a steady state, making sure variables like blood pressure, body temperature, and fluid/electrolyte balance remain within a healthy range. During emergencies, the hypothalamus and endocrine

**limbic system** A collection of structures that regulates emotions and basic drives such as hunger, and aids in the creation of memories.

**thalamus** A structure in the limbic system that processes and relays sensory information to the appropriate areas of the cortex.

**hypothalamus** A small structure located below the thalamus that maintains the internal environment within a healthy range; helps regulate sleep–wake cycles, sexual behavior, and appetite.

system work together to help us cope with perceived threats (Chapter 12). The hypothalamus is also involved in regulating sleep–wake cycles (Saper et al., 2005; Xu et al., 2015), sexual arousal, and appetite (Hurley & Johnson, 2014). For example, neurons from the digestive system send signals to the hypothalamus ("stomach is empty"), which then sends signals to higher regions of the brain ("it's time to eat"). But deciding what and when to eat does not always come down to being hungry or full. Other brain areas are involved in eating decisions and can override the hypothalamus, driving you to polish off the french fries or scarf down that chocolate bar even when you are not that hungry.

**AMYGDALA**    Another structure of the limbic system is the **amygdala** (uh-MIG-duh-la), which processes aggression and basic emotions such as fear, along with the memories associated with them (Janak & Tye, 2015; Kluver & Bucy, 1939). Having spent many months in a war zone, Brandon encountered more than his fair share of fear-provoking experiences. On one occasion, he was riding at nearly 60 mph in a Humvee that spun out of control and almost flipped over. "My heart was beating faster than ever before," Brandon recalls. In dangerous situations like this, the amygdala is activated and the nervous system orchestrates a whole-body response (racing heart, sweaty palms, and the like), as well as an emotional reaction (fear).

Life-threatening situations arise not only in war; they occasionally occur in every-day life. When faced with a potentially dangerous scenario, the brain must determine whether a real threat exists. In such cases, the amygdala shares information with areas in the frontal lobes to make this assessment (Likhtik et al., 2014; Sangha et al., 2020). Once a situation is deemed safe, the frontal lobes give the amygdala an "all clear" signal and fear diminishes. Like many parts of the nervous system, the amygdala has structural divisions that seem to play different roles; in assessing the threat of a situation, some structures come into play immediately (resulting in reflexive behavior), while others react slightly later as attention is focused on the threat (resulting in voluntary behavior). The speed of our fear reactions depends on these types of "dual routes" (de Gelder et al., 2012; also see Chapter 9). The amygdala also helps us to perceive and experience a wide range of positive emotions, with processing speed depending on the intensity of the emotion (Bonnet et al., 2015).

**HIPPOCAMPUS**    Right near the amygdala is a pair of seahorse-shaped structures called the hippocampus. The **hippocampus** is primarily responsible for processing and forming new memories from experiences, but it may not be where memories are permanently stored (see Chapter 6 on memory; Aly, 2020; Eichenbaum, 2004). Given its key role in memory, it may come as no surprise that the hippocampus is one of the brain areas affected by Alzheimer's disease (Hsu et al., 2015; Moreno-Jiménez et al., 2019). On the brighter side of things, the hippocampus is also one of the few places in the brain known to generate new neurons (Eriksson et al., 1998; Tate et al., 2014). However, some research questions the extent to which this neurogenesis occurs in adulthood and how it impacts behavior (Kempermann et al., 2018).

Given the special role of the hippocampus, you would be wise to take good care of it—but how? One simple way might be changing your diet. According to one study, eating large amounts of simple carbs and sugar may be associated with reduced

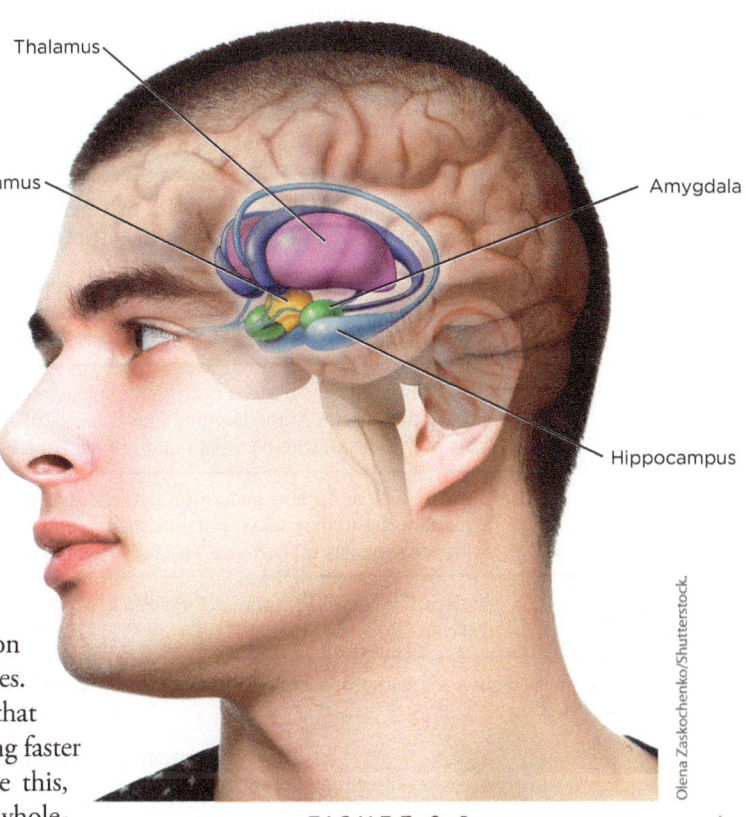

Thalamus

Hypothalamus

Amygdala

Hippocampus

Olena Zaskochenko/Shutterstock.

**FIGURE 2.9**
**The Limbic System**
The limbic system, which includes the hippocampus, amygdala, thalamus, and hypothalamus, fuels basic drives and processes emotions and memories.

**amygdala** A pair of almond-shaped structures in the limbic system that processes aggression and basic emotions such as fear, as well as associated memories.

**hippocampus** A pair of sea-horse shaped structures located in the limbic system; primarily responsible for creating new memories.

*Apply This* ⬇

**TABLE 2.3**   Food for Thought?

| Food | Potential Benefits |
|------|--------------------|
| Walnuts | Walnuts contain chemical compounds that may reduce inflammation in the brain (Ros et al., 2018). Eating walnuts has been associated with enhanced verbal reasoning, and better learning, recall, and processing speed (Arab & Ang, 2015; Pribis et al., 2012). |
| Berries | Like many fruits and vegetables, berries contain chemicals that reduce inflammation and limit the activity of cell-damaging free radicals (Stix, 2020; Whyte et al., 2019). Eating blueberries, strawberries, and other berries has been linked to better cognitive function (Devore et al., 2012; Whyte et al., 2019). |
| Dark chocolate and cocoa | Like many plant foods, cocoa beans contain *flavonoids,* which may have "neuroprotective effects" in areas of the brain important to memory and learning (Socci et al., 2017). Cocoa flavonoids appear to promote blood flow in the *dentate gyrus* (part of the hippocampus), which may enhance memory (Lamport et al., 2020; Socci et al., 2017). |
| Oily fish | Oily fish, such as salmon, lake trout, sardines, and albacore tuna, are packed with *omega-3 fatty acids,* which may play "an important role in maintaining brain structure and function with advancing age" (Pottala et al., 2014, p. 435). Preliminary evidence suggests that omega-3 Intake may help prevent cognitive decline in people at risk for dementia (Vemuri et al., 2019). |
| Broccoli | Broccoli is an excellent source of vitamin K, choline, and folic acid, all of which appear to have a positive impact on cognition (Ferland, 2013; Poly et al., 2011; Presse et al., 2013). |

Here are just a handful of the many foods that may promote brain health. If you have an allergy or any other medical condition, check with your doctor before adding new foods to your diet.

hippocampal size and decreased memory function (Reas, 2014). The brain seems to benefit from a diet that is highly plant-based, or rich in fruits, vegetables, nuts, whole grains, and legumes (such as peas, lentils, and beans), and low in saturated fat and red meat. This "Mediterranean diet," which also features olive oil and fish, has been correlated with lower rates of cognitive deterioration and decreased Alzheimer's risk (Hardman et al., 2016; Keenan et al., 2020; National Institutes of Health, 2020). For specific foods linked to better brain health, see **TABLE 2.3.**

## What Roles Do the Brainstem and Cerebellum Play?

The brain contains structures responsible for complex processes such as rebuilding a car's engine and selecting the right classes for a degree program. But delve deep, and you will find areas associated with more basic functions.

**LO 16**  Distinguish the structures and functions of the brainstem and cerebellum.

**COMPONENTS OF THE BRAINSTEM**   The brain's core consists of a stalklike trio of structures called the *brainstem* (**FIGURE 2.10**). The brainstem, which includes the midbrain, pons, and medulla, extends from the spinal cord to the **forebrain.** The forebrain is the largest part of the brain and includes the structures we have already discussed, including the cerebrum and the limbic system (NINDS, 2020).

The top portion of the brainstem is known as the **midbrain,** and although there is some disagreement about which brain structures belong to the midbrain, most agree it plays a role in arousal. The midbrain is also home to neurons that help generate movement patterns in response to sensory input (Stein et al., 2009). For example, if someone shouted "Look out!," neurons in your midbrain would play a role when you flinched. Also located in the midbrain is part of the **reticular formation,** an intricate web of neurons that is responsible for levels of arousal—whether you are awake, dozing off, or somewhere in between. The reticular formation also helps you selectively attend to important information and ignore what's irrelevant, by sifting through sensory data on its way to the cortex. Imagine how overwhelmed you would feel by all the sights, sounds, tastes, smells, and physical sensations in your

**forebrain**  The largest part of the brain; includes the cerebrum and the limbic system.

**midbrain**  The part of the brainstem involved in levels of arousal; responsible for generating movement patterns in response to sensory input.

**reticular formation**  A network of neurons running through the midbrain that controls levels of arousal and quickly analyzes sensory information on its way to the cortex.

environment if you didn't have a reticular formation to help you discriminate between information that is important (the sound of a honking car horn) and that which is trivial (the sound of a dog barking in the distance).

The **hindbrain** includes the pons, medulla, and cerebellum—areas of the brain responsible for fundamental life-sustaining processes. The **pons** helps regulate respiration and sleep–wake cycles and coordinates movement between the right and left sides of the body. It sits atop the **medulla** (muh-DUL-uh), a structure that oversees some of the body's most vital functions, including breathing and heart rate maintenance (Broadbelt et al., 2010). Behind the brainstem, just above the nape of the neck, sits the orange-sized **cerebellum** (sehr-uh-BELL-um). (Latin for "little brain," the cerebellum looks like a mini-version of the whole brain.) Centuries ago, scientists found that removing parts of the cerebellum from animals caused them to stagger, fall, and act clumsy. Although the cerebellum is best known for its importance in muscle coordination and balance, researchers are exploring how this "little brain" influences higher cognitive processes in the "big brain," such as controlling emotions and processing language (Kwon, 2019; Mariën et al., 2014). People with damaged cerebellums struggle with certain fine distinctions, such as telling the difference between words that sound somewhat alike (for example, "pause" versus "paws") or producing emotional reactions that are appropriate for a given situation (Bower & Parsons, 2003; Lupo et al., 2015). The cerebellum and other structures located below the cortex are summarized in TABLE **2.4.**

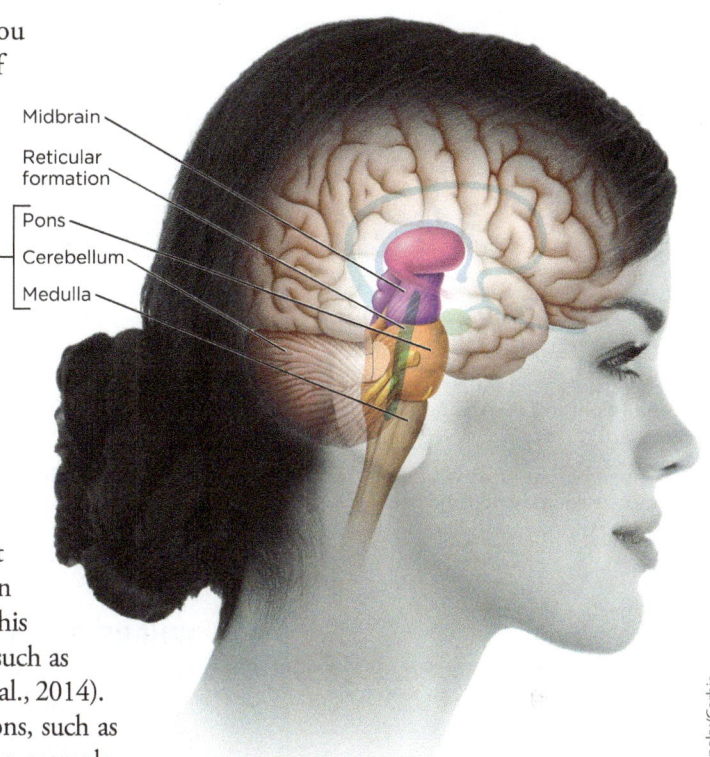

Onoky/Corbis.

**FIGURE 2.10**

**The Brainstem and Cerebellum**

Located beneath the structures of the limbic system, the brainstem includes the midbrain, pons, and medulla. These structures are involved in arousal, movement, and life-sustaining processes. The cerebellum is important for muscle coordination and balance and, when paired with the pons and medulla, makes up the hindbrain.

**TABLE 2.4**   Below the Cortex: Structures to Know

| Structure | Function and Importance |
|---|---|
| Limbic system | Group of interconnected structures that play a role in our experiences of emotion, motivation, and memory; fuels basic drives, such as hunger, sex, and aggression. |
| Thalamus | Processes and relays sensory information to the cortex. |
| Hypothalamus | Keeps the body's systems in a steady state. |
| Amygdala | Processes aggression and basic emotions like fear, along with the memories associated with them. |
| Hippocampus | Primarily responsible for processing and forming new memories from experiences. |
| Midbrain | Plays a role in levels of arousal; home to neurons that help generate movement patterns in response to sensory input. |
| Reticular formation | Responsible for levels of arousal and our ability to selectively attend to important incoming sensory data. |
| Hindbrain | Responsible for fundamental life-sustaining processes. |
| Pons | Helps regulate sleep–wake cycles and coordinates movement between the right and left sides of the body. |
| Medulla | Oversees functions such as breathing and heart rate. |
| Cerebellum | Involved in muscle coordination and balance. |

Tucked below the cortex are brain structures with a variety of different functions. Make sure you are familiar with these key regions.

**hindbrain** Includes areas of the brain responsible for fundamental life-sustaining processes.

**pons** A hindbrain structure that helps regulate sleep–wake cycles and coordinate movement between the right and left sides of the body.

**medulla** A hindbrain structure that oversees vital functions, including breathing, digestion, and heart rate.

**cerebellum** A hindbrain structure located behind the brainstem that is responsible for muscle coordination and balance; Latin for "little brain."

## Put Your Heads Together

At this point, you understand how hard your brain works 24/7, often in ways beyond your awareness. In your group, **A)** choose an important activity that you would like to examine (for example, giving a presentation in class, going on a first date) and discuss how specific structures of the **B)** limbic system, **C)** brainstem, and **D)** cerebellum may be involved.

## ▶▶▶ SHOW WHAT YOU KNOW

1. The specific brain structure that processes aggression and basic emotions like fear, along with memories associated with them, is the _____.

2. The structure located behind the brainstem that is responsible for muscle coordination and balance is the _____.

3. The primary role of the thalamus is to:
   **A.** relay sensory information.
   **B.** keep the body's systems in a steady state.
   **C.** generate movement patterns in response to sensory input.
   **D.** regulate sleep–wake cycles.

✓ CHECK YOUR ANSWERS AT THE BACK OF BOOK.

**WHERE ARE THEY NOW?**   You may be wondering what became of Brandon Burns and Christina Santhouse. Three years after returning from Iraq, Brandon married a woman named Laura who has witnessed his dramatic recovery. When Laura first met Brandon, he had a lot of trouble communicating his thoughts. His sentences were choppy; he often omitted words and spoke in a flat and emotionless tone. "His speech was very delayed, very slow," Laura recalls. Now he is able to use more humor and emotion, articulate his thoughts in lengthy, complex sentences, and read books. In addition to raising his children, Brandon has worked in a church ministry and in that capacity has traveled to numerous countries, including Haiti, Kenya, and Honduras.

As for Christina, she continues to reach for the stars—and grab them. After studying speech–language pathology at Misericordia University in Dallas, Pennsylvania, for 5 years (and making the dean's list nearly every semester), Christina graduated with both a bachelor's and a master's degree. But those years

**Life Is Good**
Three years after his traumatic brain injury, Brandon celebrated his marriage to Laura.

Laura Burns.

**Hard at Work**
For over a decade, Christina has been working as a speech–language pathologist in Buck's County, Pennsylvania, helping children overcome speech difficulties.

Matt Stanley/Bucks County Courier Times/Gatehouse Media LLC.

were not smooth sailing. Christina remembers the department chairman telling her that she wouldn't be able to handle the rigors of the program. According to Christina, on graduation day, that same chairman presented her with the department's Outstanding Achievement Award. "People often don't expect too much from people with disabilities," she says.

Today, Christina is married with two daughters and works as a speech–language pathologist, helping schoolchildren overcome their difficulties with stuttering, articulation, and other speech problems. "Hopefully, I have opened some doors for other people with disabilities," Christina offers. "There were never doors open for me; I've had to bang them down."

**LET THEIR STORIES INSPIRE YOU** Brandon and Christina provide breathtaking illustrations of neuroplasticity—the brain's ability to heal, grow new connections, and make do with what is available. These amazing changes can occur under a variety of circumstances—after a stroke, in the face of blindness, and even in response to a regular exercise routine (Convento et al., 2016; El-Sayes et al., 2019; Hasson et al., 2016). Your brain can change, too. Every time you acquire knowledge or learn a new skill, whether it's cooking pad thai or plucking out melodies on a guitar, new networks of communication are sprouting between your neurons (Barss et al., 2016; Vaquero et al., 2016). Expose yourself to new information and activities, and your brain will continue to develop and adapt. There is no limit to what you can learn!

The recoveries of Brandon and Christina also highlight the importance of maintaining hope, even in the face daunting obstacles (Abel et al., 2016; Brady et al., 2016). There were many times Brandon and Christina could have given up and wallowed in self-pity, but instead they decided to fight. So, too, did the neuropsychologists, physical therapists, occupational therapists, speech pathologists, and other professionals who assisted in their rehabilitation. The triumphs of Brandon and Christina bear testimony to the awesome tenacity of the human spirit.

# Summary of Concepts

**LO 1** Define neuroscience and biological psychology and explain how they contribute to our understanding of behavior. (p. 43)

Neuroscience is the study of the brain and other parts of the nervous system, and it overlaps with a variety of disciplines and research areas. Biological psychology is a subfield of psychology focusing on how the brain and other biological systems influence behavior.

**LO 2** Compare and contrast tools scientists use to study the brain. (p. 43)

Researchers use a variety of technologies to study the brain. An electroencephalogram (EEG) detects electrical impulses in the brain. Computerized axial tomography (CAT) uses X-rays to create many cross-sectional images of the brain. Magnetic resonance imaging (MRI) produces more detailed cross-sectional images with the help of magnetic fields;

both MRI and CAT scans only reveal the structure of the brain. Positron emission tomography (PET) uses radioactivity to track glucose consumption to construct an image of the brain. Functional magnetic resonance imaging (fMRI) captures changes in brain activity by tracking patterns of blood flow.

**LO 3** Label the parts of a neuron and describe an action potential. (p. 46)

A typical neuron has three basic parts: a cell body, dendrites, and an axon. The dendrites receive messages from other neurons, and branches at the end of the axon (axon terminals) deliver messages to neighboring neurons. These messages are electrical and chemical in nature. An action potential is the electrical signal that moves down the axon, causing a neuron to send chemical messages across the synapse. Action potentials are all-or-none, meaning they either occur or don't occur.

**LO 4**   Illustrate how neurons communicate with each other. (p. 51)

Neurons communicate with each other via chemicals called neurotransmitters. An action potential moves down the axon to the axon terminal, where neurotransmitters are released. Most of the neurotransmitters released into the synapse drift across the gap and come into contact with receptor sites of the receiving neuron's dendrites.

**LO 5**   Identify specific neurotransmitters and summarize how their activity affects human behavior. (p. 51)

Neurotransmitters are chemical messengers that neurons use to communicate. There are many types of neurotransmitters, including acetylcholine, glutamate, GABA, norepinephrine, serotonin, dopamine, and endorphins, and each has its own type of receptor site. Neurotransmitters can influence mood, cognition, behavior, and many other processes.

**LO 6**   Explain how the central and peripheral nervous systems connect. (p. 57)

The brain and spinal cord make up the central nervous system (CNS), which communicates with the rest of the body through the peripheral nervous system (PNS). There are three types of neurons participating in this back-and-forth communication: Motor neurons carry information from the CNS to various parts of the body, including muscles and glands; sensory neurons relay data from the sensory systems (for example, eyes and ears) to the CNS for processing; and interneurons, which reside exclusively in the CNS, act as bridges connecting sensory and motor neurons. Interneurons mediate the nervous system's most complex operations.

**LO 7**   Describe the organization and function of the peripheral nervous system. (p. 58)

The peripheral nervous system is divided into two branches: the somatic nervous system and the autonomic nervous system. The somatic nervous system controls the skeletal muscles that enable voluntary movement. The autonomic nervous system regulates the body's involuntary processes and has two divisions: the sympathetic nervous system, which initiates the fight-or-flight response, and the parasympathetic nervous system, which oversees the rest-and-digest processes.

**LO 8**   Summarize how the endocrine system influences behavior and physiological processes. (p. 60)

Closely connected with the nervous system, the endocrine system uses glands to send messages throughout the body. These messages are conveyed by hormones—chemicals released into the bloodstream that can cause aggression and mood swings, and influence growth and alertness, among other things.

**LO 9**   Describe the two brain hemispheres and how they communicate. (p. 62)

The cerebrum includes virtually all parts of the brain except for the brainstem structures. It is divided into two hemispheres: the right cerebral hemisphere and the left cerebral hemisphere. The left hemisphere controls most of the movement and sensation on the right side of the body. The right hemisphere controls most of the movement and sensation on the left side of the body. Connecting the two hemispheres is the corpus callosum, a band of nerve fibers that enables them to communicate.

**LO 10**   Define lateralization and explain what the split-brain experiments reveal about the right and left hemispheres. (p. 64)

Researchers have gleaned valuable knowledge about the brain hemispheres from experiments on split-brain patients—people whose hemispheres have been surgically disconnected. Under certain experimental conditions, people who have had the split-brain operation act as if they have two separate brains. By observing the brain hemispheres operating independently of one another, researchers have discovered that each hemisphere excels in certain activities, a phenomenon known as lateralization. Generally, the left hemisphere excels in language and the right hemisphere excels in visual-spatial tasks.

**LO 11**   Identify areas in the brain responsible for language production and comprehension. (p. 65)

Several areas in the brain are responsible for language processing. Located on the side of the left frontal lobe is Broca's area, which is primarily responsible for speech production. Located in the left temporal lobe is Wernicke's area, which is primarily responsible for language comprehension.

**LO 12**   Define neuroplasticity and recognize when it is evident in the brain. (p. 67)

Neuroplasticity is the ability of the brain to form new connections between neurons and adapt to changing circumstances. Networks of neurons, particularly in the young, can reorganize to adapt to the environment and an organism's ever-changing needs.

**LO 13**   Identify the lobes of the cortex and explain their functions. (p. 69)

The outermost layer of the cerebrum is the cerebral cortex. The cortex is separated into different sections called lobes. The frontal lobes are responsible for higher-level cognitive functions, such as language, emotions, control of social behavior, and decision making. The parietal lobes receive and process sensory information such as touch, pressure, temperature, and spatial orientation. Visual information goes to the occipital lobes for processing. The temporal lobes are primarily responsible for hearing and language comprehension.

**LO 14** Describe the association areas and identify their functions. (p. 73)

The association areas in the lobes integrate information from all over the brain, allowing us to learn, have abstract thoughts, and carry out complex behaviors.

**LO 15** Distinguish the structures and functions of the limbic system. (p. 74)

The limbic system is a group of interconnected structures that play an important role in our emotions and memories. The limbic system includes the hippocampus, amygdala, thalamus, and hypothalamus. In addition to processing emotions and

memories, the limbic system fuels the most basic drives, such as hunger, sex, and aggression.

**LO 16** Distinguish the structures and functions of the brainstem and cerebellum. (p. 76)

The brain's core consists of a stalklike trio of structures called the brainstem, which includes the midbrain, pons, and medulla. The brainstem extends from the spinal cord to the forebrain, which is the largest part of the brain and includes the cerebral cortex and the limbic system. Located at the top of the brainstem is the midbrain, which most agree plays a role in arousal levels. The hindbrain includes areas responsible for fundamental life-sustaining processes. Behind the brainstem is the cerebellum, which is responsible for muscle coordination and balance.

## Key Terms

action potential, p. 49
adrenal glands, p. 61
all-or-none, p. 49
amygdala, p. 75
association areas, p. 73
autonomic nervous system, p. 58
axon, p. 46
biological psychology, p. 43
Broca's area, p. 66
cell body, p. 46
central nervous system (CNS), p. 56
cerebellum, p. 77
cerebral cortex, p. 68
cerebrum, p. 62
corpus callosum, p. 63

dendrites, p. 46
endocrine system, p. 60
forebrain, p. 76
frontal lobes, p. 69
glial cells, p. 46
hindbrain, p. 77
hippocampus, p. 75
hormones, p. 60
hypothalamus, p. 74
interneurons, p. 57
lateralization, p. 65
limbic system, p. 74
medulla, p. 77
midbrain, p. 76
motor cortex, p. 71
motor neurons, p. 57

myelin sheath, p. 46
nerves, p. 58
neurogenesis, p. 68
neurons, p. 42
neuroplasticity, p. 67
neuroscience, p. 43
neurotransmitters, p. 51
occipital lobes, p. 69
parasympathetic nervous system, p. 59
parietal lobes, p. 69
peripheral nervous system (PNS), p. 56
phrenology, p. 43
pituitary gland, p. 61
pons, p. 77
receptor sites, p. 51

reflex arc, p. 57
resting potential, p. 49
reticular formation, p. 76
reuptake, p. 51
sensory neurons, p. 57
somatic nervous system, p. 58
somatosensory cortex, p. 72
spinal cord, p. 56
split-brain operation, p. 63
stem cells, p. 68
sympathetic nervous system, p. 58
synapse, p. 46
temporal lobes, p. 69
thalamus, p. 74
thyroid gland, p. 61
Wernicke's area, p. 66

## Test Prep Are You Ready?

1. _____ communicate with each other through electrical and chemical signals.
   A. Neurotransmitters
   B. The hemispheres
   C. Neurons
   D. Hormones

2. When positive ions at the axon hillock raise the internal cell voltage to the threshold potential, the neuron becomes activated. This spike in voltage causes _____ to occur.
   A. an action potential
   B. reuptake
   C. a reflex arc
   D. lateralization

3. Match the neurotransmitter on the left with its primary role(s) on the right.
   _____ 1. acetylcholine
   _____ 2. GABA
   _____ 3. endorphins
   _____ 4. serotonin

   A. reduction of pain
   B. sleep and wakefulness
   C. movement
   D. mood, aggression, appetite

4. A neuroscientist studying the brain and the spinal cord would describe her general area of interest as the:

   A. central nervous system.   C. autonomic nervous system.

   B. peripheral nervous system.   D. neurons.

5. A serious diving accident can result in damage to the _____, which is responsible for receiving information from the body and sending it to the brain, and for transmitting information from the brain to the body.

   A. corpus callosum   C. reflex arc

   B. spinal cord   D. somatic nervous system

6. Bzzt! You have a text. That sound is received by your auditory system, and information is sent via sensory neurons to your brain. Here, we can see how the _____ provides a communication link between the central nervous system and the rest of the body.

   A. endocrine system   C. corpus callosum

   B. cerebrum   D. peripheral nervous system

7. Lately, your friend has been prone to mood swings and aggressive behavior. The doctor has pinpointed a problem in his _____, which is a communication system that uses _____ to convey messages via hormones.

   A. endocrine system; action potentials

   B. endocrine system; glands

   C. central nervous system; glands

   D. central nervous system; peripheral nervous system

8. Broca's area is involved in speech production, and _____ is critical for language comprehension.

   A. the corpus callosum

   B. the right hemisphere

   C. neurogenesis

   D. Wernicke's area

9. Which of the following statements is correct regarding the function of the right hemisphere in comparison to the left hemisphere?

   A. The right hemisphere is less competent handling visual-spatial tasks.

   B. The right hemisphere is more competent handling visual-spatial tasks.

   C. The left hemisphere is more competent when it comes to recognizing faces.

   D. The right hemisphere is more competent with speech production.

10. Match the structures on the left with their principal functions on the right.

    _____ 1. association areas        A. protection of the brain

    _____ 2. temporal lobes          B. integration of information
                                         from all over brain
    _____ 3. meninges
                                      C. hearing and language
    _____ 4. occipital lobes            comprehension

    _____ 5. parietal lobes          D. receive sensory information,
                                         such as touch

                                      E. process visual information

11. What is neuroplasticity? Give an example of when it is evident.

12. Compare and contrast the body's two major chemical messengers.

13. Describe how the structures of the limbic system, brainstem, and cerebellum are involved in one of your daily activities.

14. The research conducted by Sperry and Gazzaniga examined the effects of surgeries that severed the corpus callosum. Describe what these split-brain experiments tell us about the lateralization and communication between brain hemispheres.

15. In Infographic 2.1, we described a handful of tools scientists use to study the brain. Compare their functions.

✓ CHECK YOUR ANSWERS AT THE BACK OF THE BOOK.

jasonfang/Getty Images.

# Sensation and Perception

Macmillan Learning.

**Music That Touches the Soul**
At least half of the music Mandy Harvey performs is original material; the other half consists of rearranged jazz numbers, 1960s music, and an occasional pop song like Cold Play's "Yellow." Her favorite songs tend to be those with poetic lyrics and "genuine emotion."

## 3

## An Introduction to Sensation and Perception

**THE JAZZ SINGER** A warm spotlight shines upon jazz singer Mandy Harvey. She begins strumming her ukulele, fingers moving with delicate confidence, head bobbing to the beat. A piano joins in, and Mandy begins to sing. Her voice is clear and sweet perfection, and her lyrics tell the story of an internal struggle. The song, "Try," is about accepting yourself and not being afraid to try, that is, take chances, perhaps fall on your face, and get up and move forward. As Mandy explained at one of her concerts, "Try" is about believing "what's within me is stronger than what's in my way" (No Barriers, 2015, 2:02). No one exemplifies this mantra better than Mandy herself.

Mandy has been deaf since her freshman year of college. That was more than a decade ago, and today she is living a dream most would consider inconceivable. With four albums to her name and a repertoire of original songs, Mandy is living proof that music can still be created and enjoyed after hearing loss. On a broader level, she shows all of us that good things come to those who dream big and confront their fears of failure. You can see this message resonating with her audience; look closely and you will likely observe a few lips trembling and eyes watering.

Mandy's band performs at all types of venues, from cozy jazz lounges to grand settings like the Kennedy Center in Washington, D.C. While singing, Mandy translates her lyrics into sign language, but this is the only clue that she is deaf. Her pitch, timing, and execution are virtually flawless. How does she do it?

## Where Does Sensation End and Perception Begin?

**LO 1**   Define sensation and perception and explain how they are different.

Mandy has had hearing problems since she was a baby, but she didn't face profound hearing loss until the age of 18, and thus has two decades of musical memories to draw upon. The sound of middle C still rings in her brain, and she knows how it feels to move up and down the scale, or change keys. "I remember music that I sang when I was four," Mandy says, "so once I learn a song, it's very difficult for me to forget it." But memories alone are not enough to stay in sync with a band of musicians. For this, Mandy relies on other *sensations*—what she sees and feels—to compensate for what she cannot hear.

**SENSATION VERSUS PERCEPTION**   The subject of this chapter is sensation and perception, the absorbing and deciphering of information from the environment. **Sensation** is the process by which receptors in our sensory organs (the eyes, ears, nose, mouth, skin, and other tissues) receive and detect stimuli. **Perception** is the process through which information about these stimuli is organized, interpreted, and transformed into something meaningful. Sensation is seeing a red burner on the stove; perception is thinking *hot.* Sensation is hearing a loud, shrill tone; perception is recognizing it as the warning sound of a fire alarm. Together sensation and perception provide a coherent experience of the world around and inside you, and they often occur without your effort or awareness.

Psychologists frequently characterize the processing of sensory information as *bottom-up* or *top-down*. **Bottom-up processing** occurs when the brain collects basic information about incoming stimuli and prepares it for further interpretation. Often occurring simultaneously is **top-down processing.** With top-down processing, the brain draws upon past experiences and knowledge to decipher and interpret sensory information (Riener, 2019). Bottom-up processing is what cameras and video recorders do best—collect data without any expectations. Top-down processing is where humans excel. Suppose your cell phone signal momentarily breaks up and you can't hear every word the other person is saying. Thanks to top-down processing, you can often fill in the gaps and make sense of what you are hearing. For another example of top-down processing, just look at the cover of this book. The title consists of

**sensation**  The process by which receptors in the sensory organs (the eyes, ears, nose, mouth, skin, and other tissues) receive and detect stimuli.

**perception**  The organization and interpretation of sensory stimuli by the brain.

**bottom-up processing**  Taking basic information about incoming sensory stimuli and processing it for further interpretation.

**top-down processing**  Drawing on past experiences and knowledge to decipher and interpret sensory information.

*Note:* Quotations attributed to Mandy Harvey are personal communications.

incomplete letters, but your brain is able to put the pieces together and make out the word "psychology."

Using bottom-up and top-down processing, the brain constructs a representation of the world based on what we have learned and experienced in the past. This representation is not always accurate, however. For an illustration of this phenomenon, look no farther than the "blue dress" and many other internet memes.

# A PAIR OF CROCS TO MATCH THE DRESS

New research casts light on viral illusions.

From the SCIENTIFIC pages of AMERICAN

In 2015, the picture of a white-and-gold dress (or was it black-and-blue?) divided humankind in two irreconcilable factions while revolutionizing scientists' understanding of color perception. It was a brand-new category of illusion, in which different people perceived the same image in diametrically opposing ways. The two sections were locked in their respective perceptions. Try as they might, neither blue/black nor white/gold adherents could make themselves see the garment as the other side did.

Similarly baffling Internet sensations followed: a dresser that people saw as either white/pink or blue/gray, a sneaker that looked pink/white or green/gray to different observers, and an Adidas jacket that was either blue/white or brown/black depending on whom you asked.

Despite their differences, a common feature of these described images is that they were flukes, revealed by happenstance. The serendipity of their discoveries raised the question of whether scientists had a true understanding of how the newfound illusions might come about.

Pascal Wallisch, a neuroscientist at New York University, believes that the key to the puzzle is observers' previous knowledge of lighting sources and materials such as fabrics—what psychology researchers call "priors." To prove it, Wallisch and his New York University collaborator Michael Karlovich devised a method of creating color illusions that are just as confounding as those previously found by chance. The Crocs and socks photograph at the beginning of this article is one example. To create the image, Wallisch and Karlovich started with an object that looks pink under white light (a pair of "Ballerina Pink Classic Crocs") and instead illuminated it with green light, equalizing its appearance to gray. Then, they made the background pitch-black, removing any contextual color cues that the visual system might utilize. As a result, the Crocs might be any color or at least any of the 28 different hues that you might find at your favorite Crocs retailer.

Depending on your past familiarity with white tube socks (your prior), your visual system may correctly conclude that the socks are truly white but illuminated by green lighting. If so, you may be able to retrieve the Crocs' original pink color in your perception. Observers who lack the white sock prior may instead perceive the Crocs as grayish.

People believe that they see things "how they really are," Wallisch says. "But does this mean the colors of the pixels in isolation or of the whole shoe in context? Those two [interpretations] can be different for different people." Susana Martinez-Conde and Stephen L. Macknik. Reproduced with permission. Copyright © 2020. Scientific American, a division of Nature America, Inc. All rights reserved.

We know our visual experiences are influenced by expectations from past experience (Leptourgos et al., 2020), like the "priors" noted in the *Scientific American* article above. Consider how this type of top-down processing impacts doctors' interpretations of ambiguous test results in the following Put Your Heads Together.

## Put Your Heads Together

In your groups, **A)** identify medical professionals who use visual stimuli to diagnose disease (for example, radiologists who look for tumors in CAT scans, or dermatologists who look for signs of cancer during skin checks). **B)** How might top-down processing help these professionals recognize signs of disease? **C)** How might it contribute to missed diagnoses?

Now it's time to learn how your sensory systems collect information from inside and outside your body and transform it into your impressions of the world. How are beams of light turned into an image of a fiery orange sunrise, and chemical sensations converted into the taste of a sweet strawberry? It all depends on *transduction*.

**LO 2** Define transduction and explain how it relates to sensation.

**CONNECTIONS**

In **Chapter 2,** we described how neurons work together to shape our experiences. Information moves through the body via electrical and chemical processes—action potentials traveling along the neuron's axon and neurotransmitters released at the synapse. Here, we see how this activity underlies sensation and perception.

**TRANSDUCTION** Sensation begins when your sensory systems receive input from your internal and external environment. Each sensory system is designed to respond to stimuli of a certain kind. Light waves and sound waves accost your eyes and ears, heat waves bathe your skin, molecules of different chemical compositions float into your nostrils and swim through your mouth, and physical objects press against your body. But none of these stimuli can have an impact on your brain unless they are translated into a language it understands: **electrical and chemical signals.** This is the job of the specialized sensory cells located in the back of your eyes, the caverns of your ears and nose, the spongy surface of your tongue and within your skin, muscle, and other tissues. The process of transforming stimuli into the electrical and chemical signals of neurons is called **transduction,** and it is the first step of sensation. The neural signals are then processed by the central nervous system (consisting of the brain and spinal cord), resulting in what we consciously experience as sensations (*seeing* a person's face or *smelling* smoke).

For sensations to be useful, we must assign meaning to them: "That face belongs to my girlfriend," or "I smell smoke; there must be a fire." And even though we may describe sensation and perception as two distinct events, there is no physical boundary in the brain marking the end of sensation and the beginning of perception. The processing of stimuli into sensations and perceptions happens quickly and automatically.

How do these concepts figure into *psychology,* the scientific study of behavior and mental processes? Sensation and perception are the starting points for every psychological process you can imagine, from learning psychology concepts to creating snaps on Snapchat. Through careful and systematic observation, psychologists are continually discovering ways that sensation and perception affect our thoughts, emotions, and behaviors.

## Sensation: It Just Depends

Studying sensation means studying human beings, who are complex and variable. Not everyone is born with the same collection of stimulus-detecting equipment. Some people have eyes that see 20/20; others have been wearing glasses since they were toddlers. There is even variation within a given individual. The ability to detect faint stimuli, for instance, depends on your state of mind and body (how preoccupied, bored, or stressed you happen to be, or whether you've had your morning cup of coffee, for example).

Such fluctuations in sensing ability can have profound consequences. Think about lifeguards and the enormous responsibility they take on, for example. Lifeguards are expected to prevent drownings and injuries at beaches and pools, yet they must contend with visual challenges like glare, interpret ambiguous behaviors (*are those joyous yelps or terrified screams?*), and maintain constant attention even when they are hot, tired, or bored (Lanagan-Leitzel et al., 2015; Laxton & Crundall, 2018).

**transduction** The process of transforming stimuli into neural signals.

**LO 3** Describe and differentiate between absolute thresholds and difference thresholds.

**ABSOLUTE THRESHOLDS**  Our sensory systems are prone to interferences from outside and within. This tendency makes it challenging for psychologists to measure sensory abilities, though they have been successful in many respects. For example, researchers have established various types of *sensory thresholds,* which are the lowest levels of stimulation people can detect. Of particular interest are **absolute thresholds,** defined as the weakest stimuli that can be detected 50% of the time. The absolute threshold commonly cited for vision, for instance, is the equivalent of being able to see the flame of one candle, in the dark of night, 30 miles away 50% of the time (**FIGURE 3.1;** Galanter, 1962). Absolute thresholds are important because they give us a sense of how strong a stimulus must be for our sensory systems to detect its presence. But there is more to sensation than identifying whether something is there. It's also critical to detect *changes* in stimuli.

**SENSORY ADAPTATION**  Have you ever put on deodorant or cologne and wondered if its scent was too strong, but within a few minutes you no longer notice it? Or perhaps you have jumped into an ice-cold swimming pool, and after 10 minutes you are oblivious to the frigid temperature. Our sensory receptors become less sensitive to constant stimuli through **sensory adaptation,** which leads to decreased awareness of unchanging conditions. This process allows us to focus instead on changes in our environment—a skill that has proven invaluable for **survival.**

**DIFFERENCE THRESHOLDS**  Suppose a friend asks you to turn down the volume of your music. How much does the sound level need to drop in order for them to notice? There is a certain *change in volume* that will catch their attention, but what is it, and does that value also apply to increases in sound level? Early psychologists asked similar questions; they wanted to know *how different* stimuli must be in order for someone to notice their difference. Through careful experimentation, they established various **difference thresholds,** or the minimum differences between two stimuli noticed 50% of the time.

Let's say you are blindfolded, holding 20 sheets of paper weighing 100 grams, and somebody places a strip of paper on top (the strip weighs 0.5 grams, which means

Henrik Sørensen/Getty Images.

**The Chill Wears Off**
The water may feel frigid when you first jump in, but after a while, you become accustomed to the temperature. If a stimulus is ongoing and steady, we tend to become less aware of it.

**CONNECTIONS**

In **Chapter 1,** we presented the evolutionary perspective, which may shed light on how sensory adaptation evolved. Being able to ignore unchanging stimuli makes it easier to detect changes in the environment, including those that signal danger. This ability may have helped our primitive ancestors survive, and thus reproduce and pass along their genes.

| Touch | Hearing | Smell |
|---|---|---|
| a bee's wing falling on your cheek | the tick of a clock at 20 feet | one drop of perfume throughout a six-room apartment |

| Vision | Taste |
|---|---|
| candle flame seen from 30 miles away on a clear dark night | 1 teaspoon of sugar in 2 gallons of water |

**FIGURE 3.1**
**Absolute Thresholds**
Absolute thresholds are the weakest stimuli that can be detected 50% of the time. Listed here are absolute thresholds for various senses. Information from Galanter (1962).

**absolute thresholds** The weakest stimuli that can be detected 50% of the time.

**sensory adaptation** The process through which sensory receptors become less sensitive to constant stimuli.

**difference threshold** The minimum difference between two stimuli that can be noticed 50% of the time.

David Hedges/SWNS.com.

**Could You Tell the Difference?**
Cadbury chocolate bars used to be 49 grams, but (much to the dismay of chocolate lovers) the company reduced the bars to 45 grams in 2012 (Poulter, 2012). Did consumers notice? The answer lies in the Weber ratio for weight: In order for a difference to be detected, the weight of objects lifted must differ by 2%. A loss of 4 grams represents an 8% decrease in weight, so the change would be noticeable.

**CONNECTIONS**

In **Chapters 0** and **1,** we discussed critical thinking. The claim that subliminal advertising can make us buy unwanted items is an example of "misinformation" about human behavior. With critical thinking, we determine if there is scientific evidence to support claims, including those conveyed by urban myths.

**Weber's law** States that each of the senses has its own constant ratio determining difference thresholds.

**signal detection theory** Explains how internal and external factors influence our ability to detect weak signals in the environment.

you're adding 0.5% of the weight of the stack of paper). Do you think you'd notice the added weight of that strip? Probably not. But if someone added an entire sheet (which weighs 5 grams, or 5% of the stack's weight), then you would almost definitely notice the change, right? Somewhere in between that strip of paper and full sheet of paper is the difference threshold.

In fact, the *just noticeable difference* for detecting changes in weight is 2%; that is, the proportion of added weight needed for you to feel the difference 50% of the time. We owe this knowledge, in part, to German physiologist Ernst Weber (1795–1878), who studied difference thresholds in the 1800s. **Weber's law** states that ratios, not raw number values, determine these difference thresholds, and each sense has its own constant Weber ratio. For humans to detect a difference between two stimuli 50% of the time, the intensity of two lights must differ by 8%; the weight of objects lifted must differ by 2%; the intensity of sounds must differ by 4%; the taste of salt must differ by 8%; and the strength of electric shocks must differ by 1% (Poulton, 1967; Teghtsoonian, 1971).

## Apply This ⬇

### HOW POWERFUL ARE SUBLIMINAL INFLUENCES?

The absolute and difference thresholds discussed above pertain to stimuli that we can detect 50% of the time. What about stimuli below these thresholds? Do *subliminal* stimuli, which are well beneath our absolute thresholds (lights too dim to see or sounds too faint to hear, for example), have an impact on us? Perhaps you have heard of "subliminal advertising," or stealthy attempts by marketers to woo you into buying products. Here's an example: You're watching a trailer for a movie and suddenly the words "buy this film!" flash across the screen, but only for a few milliseconds. Your sensory receptors may detect this fleeting stimulus, but it's so brief that you don't notice it. According to **urban myth**, subliminal marketing can make you purchase movies, food, personal products, or whatever items happen to be advertised. The truth is that subliminal marketing cannot affect behavior in this way. Subliminal messages cannot manipulate you to purchase something you had not planned on buying, or to quit smoking, for example (Karremans et al., 2006).

That being said, the brain does register information presented at an unconscious or nonconscious level. Studies show that neural activity is triggered by the "subliminal presentation" of stimuli (Axelrod et al., 2014). For example, brain activity changes when hungry people are presented with subliminal food images (Ilse et al., 2020). These subliminal messages may be able to influence fleeting moods without our awareness. In one study, researchers primed participants with subliminal images that were sexual in nature. After being exposed to these erotic images, participants seemed to experience an increase in positive emotions (Gillath & Collins, 2016). As you will learn throughout this textbook, we are often unaware of how events and people in our environments (initially experienced as sensations and perceptions) influence our thoughts, emotions, and behaviors.

Thus far, we have focused on the stimulus itself. But what about other environmental factors, such as background stimuli competing for the observer's attention, or internal factors like the observer's state of mind—how do these variables affect one's sensing capacity?

**SIGNAL DETECTION THEORY**    As previously noted, our ability to detect weak stimuli in the environment is based on many factors, including the intensity of the stimulus, the presence of interfering stimuli, and our psychological state. The theory that draws all these facets together is called **signal detection theory,** which is based on the idea that "noise" from our internal and external environments can interfere with sensation. Signal detection theory is relevant to any activity that involves interpreting potentially ambiguous sensory stimuli, from forecasting the weather to diagnosing disease, so its

Alistair Berg/Getty Images.

**Zoom and Gloom?**
Do you ever feel empty and unsatisfied after a Zoom or Skype call? It might have something to do with the artificial perceptual experience created by digital technologies. Screen freezes, blurry images, time lags, and other glitches may confuse our perceptual systems: "Our brains strain to fill in the gaps and make sense of the disorder, which makes us feel vaguely disturbed, uneasy and tired without quite knowing why" (Murphy, 2020, para. 3).

applications are extremely broad (Wixted, 2020). Suppose a physician is evaluating a patient for potential lung cancer. The doctor must make important decisions (like whether to refer a patient for cancer treatment) amid the **"noise" of variables** related to their years of experience and workplace standards (Kostopoulou et al., 2019). In a health-care context, the ability to sense and perceive may have life or death implications.

How might signal detection theory apply to your everyday life? Imagine your phone rings as you stand on a busy street corner. Whether you hear the ringtone depends on many external factors, such as competing sounds from traffic and nearby voices. It also depends on internal factors, including how tired or alert you may be. Have you ever "heard" your ringtone when no one is calling? Signal detection theory can help explain that, too. Neurons in our sensory systems sometimes fire spontaneously, even in the absence of sensory stimuli. If we are "highly attuned to detecting an extremely weak sensory signal," we might interpret that random neural activity as a true sensation (Wixted, 2020, p. 211). So, if you're anxiously awaiting a call and straining to detect any hint of a ring, you may perceive a ringtone when your phone didn't make a peep. Phantom Phone Signals (PPS), or "perception[s] of a mobile phone ringing, vibrating and blinking when in fact it did not," appear to be very common among both adult and child cell phone users (Pisano et al., 2019, p. 1; Tanis et al., 2015).

Now that we have discussed factors that influence our ability to sense stimuli, let's explore the process itself. What are the characteristics of sensory stimuli, and how does each sense collect and process this information? We'll start by exploring the sense that is generally considered most dominant: vision.

*Research*
**CONNECTIONS**

Here, the "noise" of variables relates to the potential bias of the doctor, and how that bias might impact their decisions related to patient care. In **Chapter 1,** we discussed how bias can change the outcome of experiments. Expectations, attitudes, and value systems can influence a person's observations (observer bias). Researcher expectations can also impact results, but this experimenter bias often can be controlled with double-blind studies.

## SHOW WHAT YOU KNOW

1. Information received by sensory receptors is organized, interpreted, and assigned meaning through the process of:
   A. perception.
   B. transduction.
   C. sensation.
   D. signal detection.

2. Identify some stimuli in your current surroundings that are being transformed (through transduction) into neural signals you experience as sensations.

3. A woman standing next to you at the supermarket has some very strong-smelling cheese in her basket. You notice the odor immediately, but within a matter of minutes you can barely detect it. This reduced sensitivity to a constant smell results from the process of:
   A. sensation.
   B. transduction.
   C. perception.
   D. sensory adaptation.

✓ CHECK YOUR ANSWERS AT THE BACK OF BOOK.

Courtesy Mandy Harvey.

**Showing Their Love**

Mandy's fans shower her in "deaf applause," the visual equivalent of clapping.

# Vision

**HOW DOES SHE DO IT?**    Mandy has near perfect pitch, a stunning ability given that she cannot hear the notes coming out of her mouth. As she explains, "certain areas of your throat, you can tell if you're hitting [a note] or not." But every once in a while, Mandy finds herself slightly off key. "If I'm singing not quite right, in my brain I'm like, this doesn't feel right. I'm not sure exactly where I'm wrong, but I know that I'm not right."

In these situations, Mandy may rely on her fellow musicians to adjust their key to match hers. "It's the benefit of having really great musicians back you up," Mandy says. "So you never really fall flat on your face." Other times, Mandy changes her key to match the band's. If she's singing a quarter step too low, for example, the pianist might use his hands to signal, "move up." Throughout the performance, Mandy and the other musicians continue communicating with visual cues, bobbing their heads to maintain rhythm and using eye contact to signal transitions. "Every musician looks at me when it's my turn to go in and sing . . . and I look at them when they're about to solo," Mandy says. At the end of the show, the crowd claps and cheers, and some show their appreciation with "deaf applause," raising their hands and shaking them.

The silent communication occurring between Mandy, her musicians, and the fans is made possible by a remarkable communication system running from the eyes to the brain. How does the visual system work? To tackle this question, we must have a basic understanding of light and color.

## Light and Color

**LO 4** Summarize the properties of light and color, and describe the structure and function of the eye.

When Mandy sees fans erupt in deaf applause, she is not seeing their actual hands; she is sensing light waves bouncing off those hands and entering her eyes. The eyes do not sense faces, objects, or scenery. They detect light. Remember: *If you don't have light, you don't have sight.* But what exactly *is* light? Light is an electromagnetic wave, composed of fluctuating electric and magnetic fields zooming from place to place at a very fast rate. And when we say "fast," we mean from Atlanta to Los Angeles in a tenth of a second. Electromagnetic waves are everywhere all the time, zipping past your head, and bouncing off your nose. As you can see in **FIGURE 3.2,** light that is visible to humans falls along a spectrum, or range, of electromagnetic energy.

**wavelength** The distance between wave peaks (or troughs).

**hue** The color of an object, determined by the wavelength of light it reflects.

**amplitude** The height of a wave; distance from midpoint to peak, or from midpoint to trough.

**saturation** Color purity.

**WAVELENGTH**    The various types of electromagnetic energy can be distinguished by their **wavelength,** which is the distance from one wave hump to the next (like the distance between the crests of waves rolling in the ocean; Figure 3.2). Gamma waves have short wavelengths and are located on the far left of the spectrum. At the opposite extreme (far right of the spectrum) are the long radio waves. In between these two extremes is the light humans can see,

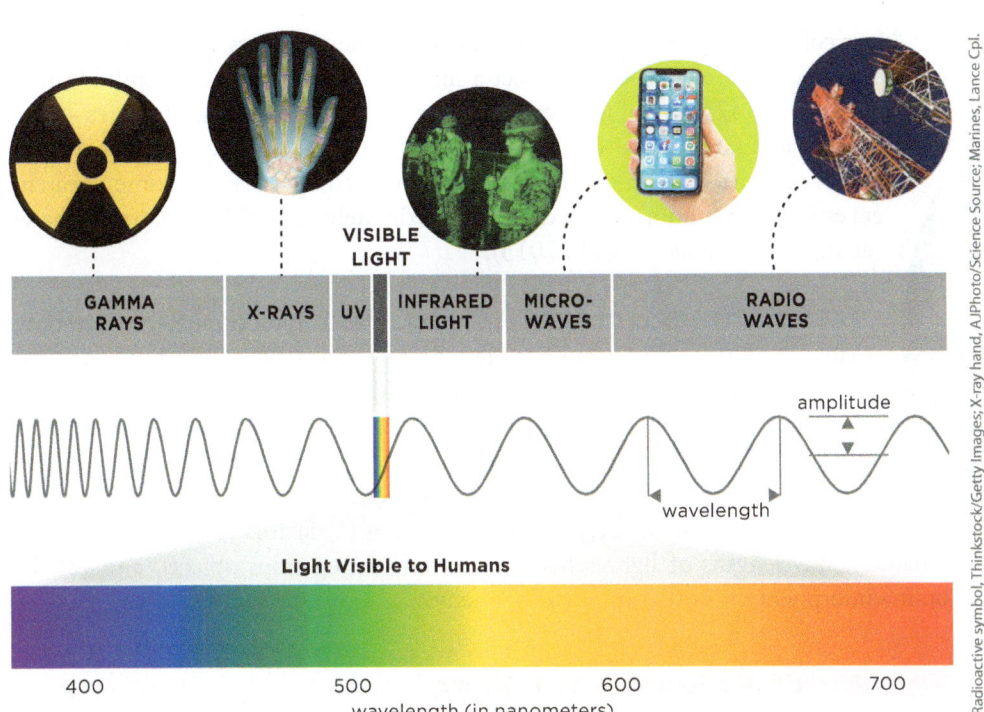

Radioactive symbol, Thinkstock/Getty Images; X-ray hand, A.JPhoto/Science Source; Marines, Lance Cpl. Tucker S. Wolf, U.S. Marine Corps; Hand holding cell phone: neirfy/Getty Images; Radio Tower, TERADAT SANTIVIVUT/Getty Images.

### FIGURE 3.2
**Visible Light and the Electromagnetic Spectrum**
Only a small part of the electromagnetic spectrum can be detected by the human visual system. Visible light wavelengths range from approximately 400 to 700 nanometers. We use electromagnetic energy for a variety of purposes, from warming our dinners to carrying on digital conversations.

measuring between 400 and 700 nanometers (nm) or billionths of a meter (Brown & Wald, 1964). Wavelength plays an important role in determining the colors humans and animals can detect.

**THE COLORS WE SEE**   Although dogs only see the world in blues, yellows, and grays, humans and other primates can detect a wider spectrum of colors, including reds and oranges (Pongrácz et al., 2017). This ability to see reds and oranges may be an adaptation to spot ripe fruits against the green backdrop of tree leaves, and to facilitate memorization and recognition of objects (Hofmann & Palczewski, 2015; Melin et al., 2014). Other creatures see "colors" that we can't. Snakes can detect infrared waves radiating off the bodies of their prey, and birds evaluate potential mates by sensing ultraviolet (UV) waves reflected by their feathers (Bennett et al., 1996; Gracheva et al., 2010; Lind & Delhey, 2015).

**FEATURES OF COLOR**   Every color can be described according to three features: hue, brightness, and saturation. The first feature, **hue,** is what we commonly refer to as "color." (Green grass reflects light with a green hue.) Hue is determined by wavelength: Violet has the shortest wavelength in the visible spectrum (400 nm), and red has the longest (700 nm). The *brightness* of a color represents a continuum from intense to dim. Brightness depends on wave height, or **amplitude,** the distance from midpoint to peak (or from midpoint to trough; Figure 3.2). Just remember: *The taller the height, the brighter the light.* **Saturation,** or color purity, is determined by uniformity of wavelength. Saturated colors are made up of the same wavelengths. Objects we see as pure violet, for instance, are reflecting only 400-nm light waves. We can "pollute" the violet light by mixing it with other wavelengths, resulting in a less saturated, pale lavender.

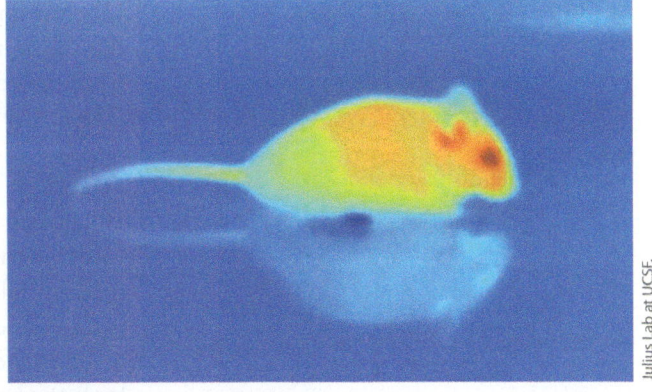

Julius Lab at UCSF.

**I "See" You**
This is what you might perceive if you were a snake searching for dinner in the dark. The western diamondback rattlesnake has facial sensors that detect infrared radiation from warm-blooded prey. Scientists have yet to determine exactly how the heat waves are transduced into neural signals, but the process depends on specialized channels in nerve fibers of the snake's face (Gracheva et al., 2010).

Most colors in the environment are not pure. The pigments in the blue lipstick of Lupita Nyong'o (left) probably reflect a mixture of wavelengths around 475 nm, rather than pure 475-nm blue. Combinations of these three basic features—hue, brightness, and saturation—can produce an infinite number of colors; our eyes are just not sensitive enough to tell them all apart. Findings vary, but some researchers estimate that humans can detect approximately 2.3 million colors (Linhares et al., 2008; Masaoka et al., 2013).

**PERCEPTION OF COLORS**     And now, the 2.3 million-dollar question: Most of us agree that stop signs are red and lemons are yellow, but can we be sure that one person's *perception* of color is identical to another's? Is it possible that your "red" may be someone else's "yellow"? Without getting inside the mind of another person and perceiving the world as they do, this question may be impossible to answer. The colors we perceive do not actually exist in the world around us. Rather, they are the product of (1) factors in the environment, namely, wavelengths of light reflecting and emanating from objects, and (2) the brain's interpretation of that light (neural activity).

## You Won't Believe Your Eyes

The eyes take light energy and transform it into neural code for the brain to interpret. The exquisite specificity of this code allows us to differentiate between patterns, textures, different shades of gray, and a multitude of colors. How does the process work? To answer this question, we must understand the eye's remarkable biology (see **INFOGRAPHIC 3.1** on page 94). When you look in the mirror, you see only a fraction of each ping-pong-sized eyeball; the rest is hidden inside your head. Let's explore this biological wonder, starting from the outside and working our way toward the brain.

**THE CORNEA**     The surface of the eye looks wet and glassy. This clear outer layer over the colored portion of the eye is called the **cornea,** and it has two important jobs: (1) shielding the eye from damage by dust, bacteria, or even a poke, and (2) focusing incoming light waves. About 65–75% of the focusing ability of the eye comes from the cornea, which is why imperfections in its shape can lead to blurred vision (University of Maryland Medical Center, n.d.).

**THE IRIS AND PUPIL**     Directly behind the cornea is the donut-shaped **iris.** When you say someone has velvety brown eyes, you are really talking about the color of their irises. The black hole in the center of the iris is called the *pupil.* In dim lighting, the iris muscle relaxes, enlarging the pupil to allow more light inside the eye. In bright sunlight, the iris muscle squeezes, constricting the pupil to limit the amount of light. Interestingly, the pupils also constrict when people look at photographs of the sun or think about bright objects (Binda et al., 2013; Hustá et al., 2019).

**THE LENS AND ACCOMMODATION**     Behind the pupil is the lens, a tough, transparent structure with dimensions similar to an "M&M's candy" (Mayo Clinic, 2017). Like the cornea, the lens specializes in focusing incoming light, but it can also change shape in order to adjust to objects near and far, a process called **accommodation.** If you take your eyes off this page and look across the room, faraway objects immediately come into focus because your lens changes shape. As we age, the lens begins to stiffen, impairing our ability to see things up-close, like the words you are reading right now.

Zak Hussein/Getty Images

**Very Blue**
Lupita Nyong'o sported intensely blue lipstick at the premiere of *Star Wars: The Force Awakens* in London. Her lipstick may appear to be a pure blue, but the color is most likely a blend of various blue wavelengths. Most colors we encounter in the real world are a mix of different wavelengths.

**cornea**  The clear, outer layer of the eye that shields it from damage and focuses incoming light waves.

**iris**  The part of the eye responsible for changing the size of the pupil.

**accommodation**  The process by which the lens changes shape in order to focus on objects near and far.

# The Retina

After passing through the cornea, pupil, and lens, light waves travel through the eyeball's jellylike filling and land on the **retina,** a carpet of neurons covering the back wall of the eye. The retina is responsible for the transduction of light energy into neural activity; that is, sensing light and relaying a message to the brain. Without the retina, vision is impossible.

**LO 5** Describe the functions of rods and cones.

**PHOTORECEPTORS AND OTHER NEURONS**   The retina is home to millions of specialized neurons called **photoreceptors,** which absorb light energy and turn it into electrical and chemical signals for the **brain to process.** Two types of photoreceptors are located in the retina: *rods* and *cones,* which get their names from their characteristic shapes. **Rods** are extremely sensitive, firing in response to even a single *photon,* the smallest possible packet of light. This doesn't mean we can *see* a single photon, however; the absolute threshold for detection of light through rods is 50 photons (Hofmann & Palczewski, 2015; Rieke & Baylor, 1998). If rods were all we had, the world would look something like an old black-and-white movie. **Cones** enable us to enjoy a visual experience more akin to Ultra HD TV (except for those of us with *color deficiencies,* discussed later). In addition to providing color vision, cones allow us to see fine details, such as the small print on the back of a gift card.

Rods and cones are just the first step in a complex neural signaling cascade that ultimately leads to a visual experience in the brain (see Infographic 3.1). When rods and cones are stimulated by light energy, they communicate with other specialized neurons called *bipolar cells.* These, in turn, convey their signal to *ganglion cells,* yet another type of neuron, located toward the front of the retina. Axons of the ganglion cells bundle together in the **optic nerve,** which is like an electrical cable (one extending from each eye) hooking the retina to the brain. The optic nerve exits the retina at the *optic disc,* causing a **blind spot,** since this area lacks rods and cones. You can find your blind spot by following the instructions in the Try This, below.

  **Try This**   Holding your book at arm's length, close your right eye and stare at the orange with your left eye. Slowly move the page closer to your face. The apple on the left will disappear when light from that picture falls on your blind spot.

**THE FOVEA**   The retina in each eye is home to approximately 120 million rods and 6 million cones (Amesbury & Schallhorn, 2003; Luo & da Cruz, 2014). Rods are found everywhere in the retina, except in the optic disc (mentioned earlier) and a tiny central spot called the *fovea.* Cones are packed most densely in the fovea, but are also sprinkled through the rest of the retina. When you need to study something in precise detail (like the tiny serial number on the bottom of a laptop), hold it under a bright light and stare at it straight-on. The cones in the fovea excel at sensing detail and operate best in ample light. If, however, you want to get a look at something in dim light, focus your gaze slightly to its side, stimulating the super-light-sensitive rods outside the fovea.

**CONNECTIONS**

In **Chapter 2,** we noted that neurons are activated in response to sensations. In the case of vision, sensation occurs when photoreceptors in the retina transduce light into neural signals. This causes a chain reaction in neurons of the visual pathway, which convey the message to the brain.

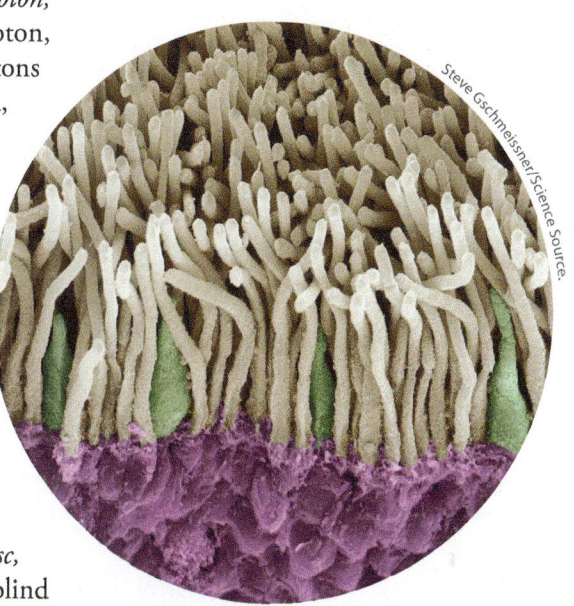

Steve Gschmeissner/Science Source.

**Rods and Cones**
You can see why the light-sensing neurons in the back of the eye are called rods (tan) and cones (green).

**retina**  The layer of the eye containing photoreceptor cells, which transduce light energy into neural activity.

**photoreceptors**  Specialized cells in the retina that absorb light energy and turn it into electrical and chemical signals for the brain to process.

**rods**  Photoreceptors that enable us to see in dim lighting; not sensitive to color, but useful for night vision.

**cones**  Photoreceptors that enable us to sense color and details.

**optic nerve**  The bundle of axons from ganglion cells leading to the visual cortex.

**blind spot**  A hole in the visual field caused by the optic disc (the location where the optic nerve exits the retina).

# Seeing

"Seeing" involves more than simply looking at an object. Vision is a complex process in which light waves entering the eye are directed toward the retina, where they are transduced into messages the brain can understand.

Within the retina are the photoreceptors (rods and cones), bipolar cells, and ganglion cells—all of which play a key role in conveying information from the eyes to the brain.

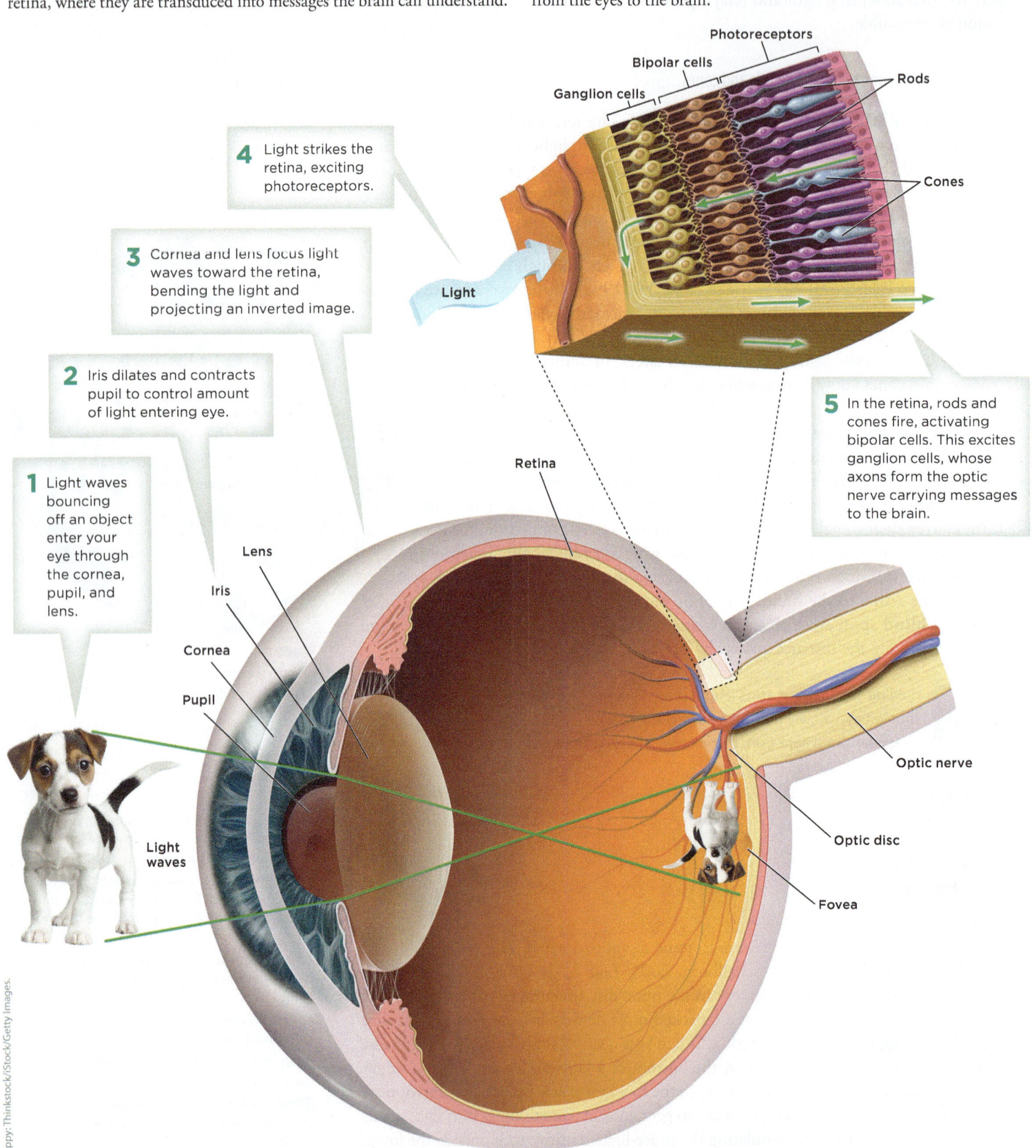

**4** Light strikes the retina, exciting photoreceptors.

**3** Cornea and lens focus light waves toward the retina, bending the light and projecting an inverted image.

**2** Iris dilates and contracts pupil to control amount of light entering eye.

**1** Light waves bouncing off an object enter your eye through the cornea, pupil, and lens.

**5** In the retina, rods and cones fire, activating bipolar cells. This excites ganglion cells, whose axons form the optic nerve carrying messages to the brain.

Photoreceptors

Bipolar cells

Ganglion cells

Rods

Cones

Light

Retina

Lens

Iris

Cornea

Pupil

Light waves

Optic nerve

Optic disc

Fovea

**DARK AND LIGHT ADAPTATION** The eye has an amazing ability to adjust to drastic fluctuations in light levels. This process starts with the pupil, which rapidly shrinks and expands in response to light changes, and then continues with the rods and cones, which need more time to adjust. When you walk into a dark movie theater, you can't see too well. Soon, your eyes start adjusting to the dark in a process called **dark adaptation,** which takes about 8 minutes for cones and 30 minutes for rods (Hecht & Mandelbaum, 1938; Klaver et al., 1998; Wolfe & Ali, 2015). When you leave the dark theater and return to the blinding light of day, the eyes also adjust. With **light adaptation,** the pupil constricts to reduce the amount of light flooding the retina, and the rods and cones become less sensitive to light. Light adaptation occurs relatively quickly, lasting at most 10 minutes (Ludel, 1978).

## Is That Oprah Over There?

Let's stop for a moment and examine how information flows through the visual pathway (Infographic 3.1). Suppose you are looking at Oprah Winfrey's face. Remember, you're actually seeing the light that her face reflects. Normally, light rays bouncing off Oprah would continue moving along a straight-line path, but they encounter the bulging curvature of the cornea covering your pupil, which bends them. (The light is further bent by the lens, but to a lesser extent.) Rays entering the top of the cornea bend downward and those striking the base bend upward. The result is an inverted, or flip-flopped, image projected on your retina. It's like your eye is a movie theater, the retina is its screen, and the feature film being played is *Your World, Turned Upside Down* (Kornheiser, 1976; Ramachandran & Rogers-Ramachandran, 2008; Stratton, 1896). The photoreceptors in the retina respond to the stimulus, sending signals to the bipolar cells, which then communicate with the ganglion cells that bundle into the optic nerves.

The optic nerves (one from each eye) intersect at a place in the brain called the *optic chiasm* (see Figure 4.2 on page 133). From there, information coming from each eye is split, with about half traveling to the same-side thalamus and half going to the opposite-side thalamus. **Interneurons** then shuttle the data to the *visual cortex,* located in the occipital lobes in the back of your head. Neurons in the visual cortex called **feature detectors** specialize in detecting specific features of your visual experience, such as angles, lines, and movements. How these features are pieced together into a unified visual experience (*I see Oprah!*) is complex. Researchers David Hubel (1926–2013) and Torsten Wiesel proposed that visual processing begins in the visual cortex, where teams of cells respond to specifically oriented lines (as opposed to just pixel-like spots of light), and then continues in other parts of the cortex, where information from both eyes is integrated (Hubel & Wiesel, 1979). More recent research on nonhuman primates suggests that different groups of neurons in the visual cortex process information about color, shape, or both (Garg et al., 2019).

## What Color Do You See?

Earlier, we discussed various features of color, but we have yet to explain how waves of electromagnetic energy relate to the colors we see. How does the brain know red from maroon, green from turquoise, yellow from amber? Two main theories explain human color vision—the *trichromatic theory* and the *opponent-process theory*—and you need to understand both because they address different aspects of the phenomenon.

**CONNECTIONS**

In **Chapter 2,** we explained how interneurons of the central nervous system (the brain and spinal cord) receive and process signals from sensory neurons. Here we discuss how interneurons facilitate the processing of visual information.

**dark adaptation** Process by which the eyes adjust to dark after exposure to bright light.

**light adaptation** Process by which the eyes adjust to light after being in the dark.

**feature detectors** Neurons in the visual cortex specialized in detecting specific features of the visual experience, such as angles, lines, and movements.

Peter Hermes Furian/Shutterstock.

### All Together It Makes White

When red, blue, and green light wavelengths are combined in equal proportions, they produce white light. This may seem counterintuitive, because most of us have learned that mixing different-colored paints yields brown (not white). The rules of light mixing differ from those of paints and other pigmented substances.

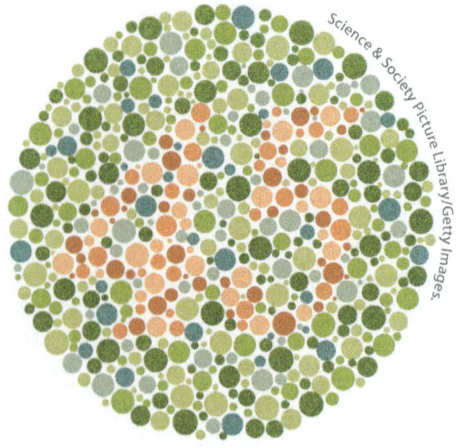

Science & Society picture Library/Getty Images.

### See It?

If you cannot make out the number 45 in this Ishihara color plate, then you might have a red–green color deficiency, the most common variation of "color blindness." Red–green deficiency results from a problem with the red or green cones.

**trichromatic theory** Suggests that perception of color results from the activation of three cone types, which are sensitive to wavelengths in the red, green, and blue spectrums.

**LO 6** Explain how the trichromatic theory and the opponent-process theory help us understand color vision.

**THE TRICHROMATIC THEORY**    Proposed in the 1800s by English physician-scientist Thomas Young and expanded upon decades later by Prussian physicist Hermann von Helmholtz, the **trichromatic theory** (try-kroh-MAT-ic) suggests that we have three types of cones. Red cones are excited by electromagnetic energy with wavelengths in the red range (about 620–700 nm); green cones fire in response to electromagnetic energy with wavelengths in the green realm (500–575 nm); and blue cones are activated by electromagnetic energy with wavelengths corresponding to blues (about 450–490 nm; Mollon, 1982). The primary colors of light are also red, green, and blue, and when mixed together in equal proportions, they appear as white light (see image to the left).

So, how is it that we can detect millions of colors when our cones are only sensitive to red, green, and blue? According to the trichromatic theory, the brain identifies a precise hue by calculating patterns of excitement among the three cone populations. When you look at a yellow banana, for example, both the red and green cones fire, but not the blue ones. The brain interprets this pattern of red and green activation as "yellow." And because white light is actually a mixture of all the wavelengths in the visible spectrum, it excites all three cone types, creating a sensation of "white" in the mind's eye. Thus, the brain makes its color calculations based on the relative activity of the three cone types.

**COLOR DEFICIENCY AND COLOR BLINDNESS**    Loss or damage to one or more of the cone types leads to *color deficiency,* more commonly known as "color blindness." These terms are often used interchangeably, but true color blindness is extremely rare. Most people with color deficiencies have trouble distinguishing between red and green because there is a problem with the red or green cones (Prieto et al., 2021). Yet, some of these individuals actually excel at certain visual tasks, such as detecting images that are camouflaged (Doron et al., 2019). If you can't see the number shown in the Ishihara color plate to the left, then you may have a red–green deficiency (Wong, 2011). This condition affects about 8% of men and 0.4% of women of European ancestry. And although estimates for other groups are variable, some research suggests that about 4–7% of men of Chinese and Japanese ancestry and 6–7% of African American men have difficulty distinguishing red and green (Birch, 2012; Deeb, 2005). If you have (or suspect you have) a color deficiency, don't hesitate to get your eyes checked. And keep in mind, there are steps instructors can take to make learning materials and activities more accessible to students who have trouble differentiating between colors (Prieto et al., 2021).

## Put Your Heads Together

This photo on the right illustrates what a traffic light might look like to someone with a red–green color deficiency. In your groups, discuss the following: **A)** How might traffic lights be designed to make it easier for people to discriminate between the three signals (stop, go, and slow down)? **B)** What other situations might create difficulties for people with this common color deficiency?

Jon Licht

Ample research backs up the trichromatic theory, but there are some color-related phenomena it cannot explain. A prime example is the *afterimage effect*. An **afterimage** is an *image* that appears to linger in your visual field *after* its stimulus, or source, is gone. See for yourself in the following Try This.

**Try This** Fix your eyes on the black cross in the center of the image below. After 30 seconds, shift your gaze to the blank white area to the left. What colors do you see now?

Jacquelyn S. Wong.

**OPPONENT-PROCESS THEORY** German physiologist Ewald Hering (1834–1918) realized that the trichromatic theory could not explain the afterimage effect and thus developed the **opponent-process theory** of color vision. Hering proposed that, in addition to the color-sensitive cones, there are special systems that respond to opponent colors—pairs of colors such as red–green and blue–yellow that cannot be perceived simultaneously. (We don't see objects as reddish-green or bluish-yellow.) For example, one neuron fires when you look at red but is inactive when you see green. Meanwhile, another neuron gets excited by green but not by red. If you spend enough time staring at the red and blue picture in the Try This above, the neurons excited by these colors become exhausted and stop responding. When you shift your gaze to the white surface (white reflects all colors), neurons that get excited by the opposite colors (green and yellow) fire. The result? You end up seeing a green and yellow afterimage. Research offers support for the opponent-process theory, identifying particular types of neurons in a region of the thalamus (DeValois & DeValois, 1975; Jameson & Hurvich, 1989).

As it turns out, we need both the trichromatic and the opponent-process theory to explain different aspects of color vision. Color perception occurs both in the light-sensing cones in the retina and in the opponent cells serving the brain. Remember, the ability to perceive color is not based on processing at a single point along the visual pathway, or even one area of the brain (Brogaard & Gatzia, 2017; Rentzeperis et al., 2014; Solomon & Lennie, 2007).

## ACROSS THE WORLD

### COLORS AND CULTURE

To complicate matters further, interpretations of color may be influenced by environmental factors. For example, people in cold, rainy areas are more likely to view yellow as a joyful color than those living in dry climates near the equator (Frederick, 2019; Jonauskaite, Abdel-Khalek et al., 2019). Why is this so? Researchers hypothesize that "yellow is reminiscent of life-sustaining sunshine and pleasant weather," and "this association should be especially strong in countries where sunny weather is a rare occurrence" (Jonauskaite, Abdel-Khalek et al., 2019, p. 2).

Social and cultural factors may also influence how we respond to colors. Blue is the most popular "favorite color" in the world, but it carries different meanings for various groups: sanctity in the Jewish religion, warmth for the Dutch, and the god Krishna for Hindus (Akcay et al., 2011; Sable & Akcay, 2011; Taylor et al., 2013). How might such associations develop? If a color is repeatedly presented in a certain

**Is Red the Color of Dominance?**
Red is the most popular color choice for national flags. In most cases, countries use this color to symbolize concepts related to aggression, such as "blood," "bravery," and "struggle" (Zhang et al., 2018, p. 117).

TommL/Getty Images.

**afterimage** An image that appears to linger in the visual field after its stimulus, or source, is removed.

**opponent-process theory** Suggests that perception of color derives from a special group of neurons that respond to opponent colors (red–green, blue–yellow).

context (black clothes at a funeral, pink clothes on a girl), mental associations begin to take hold (black is for grieving; pink is for girls). This type of learning may also explain how gender-specific color preferences evolve (Jonauskaite, Dael et al., 2019; Sorokowski et al., 2014).

As you can see, vision is a highly complex sensory system. The same could be said of hearing, the subject of the next section. Are you ready to find out how the auditory system takes sound waves and translates them into clapping thunder, chirping crickets, and trickling streams?

## ⟫⟫⟫ SHOW WHAT YOU KNOW

1. It's dark outside, and you are struggling to read a flyer posted outside the library. If you turn your gaze slightly to the side, you can make out the words. The ability to see them is due to your:

   **A.** difference threshold.      **C.** cones.

   **B.** optic disk.      **D.** rods.

2. Hue is determined by the _____ of the light reflecting off an object.

3. Explain the two major theories of color vision.

 Check your answers at the back of book.

# Hearing

**WHEN FEAR BECOMES REALITY**   In the fall of 2006, Mandy began to pursue her lifelong dream of becoming a musician. She enrolled at Colorado State University and started working toward a degree in vocal music education. But a few weeks into the semester, the voices of her professors began to sound faint and distant, and she had trouble discerning musical pitches and tones. Within 9 months, her world had fallen silent. "To describe it really as anything other than watching myself die, I don't feel has enough weight to it," Mandy recalled in an interview with the BBC (BBC News, 2017, 0:48). Up until then, Mandy's life had revolved around music. She spent her childhood listening to soulful songs of the 1960s and 1970s, singing in choirs, and dreaming of becoming a choir director. "I wanted to be able to direct voices and [create] cool stories, and make people feel things," says Mandy. Now that seemed impossible.

*Courtesy Mandy Harvey*

After about a year of pain and mourning, something miraculous happened. It was an ordinary day, and Mandy's dad asked her to jam with him on the guitar. They played for a while, and then he asked her to learn a new song—a request she found ridiculous but she decided to humor him anyway. Using a guitar tuner to teach herself the notes, Mandy spent 8 hours learning One Republic's "Come Home." When she performed it for her father, she nailed every note.

Eventually, Mandy tried singing at a local jazz club's open mic night. The idea of giving a solo performance was beyond nerve-racking (Mandy describes herself as "extremely introverted" and "shy"), but she summoned the courage. "I realized after losing my hearing, which was my biggest fear my entire life, what's the worst that can happen?" Mandy says. "I've already survived that, so I can survive this. If they don't like it, they don't like it." The next week Mandy came back and sang more songs; the following week, she did a longer set; and soon the club was a weekly gig. "Then I started having my own concerts at other venues, and then I made my first album," Mandy says. These days, fans can't get enough of Mandy Harvey. In 2017 Mandy captivated viewers with her performances on *America's Got Talent;* in 2018 she embarked on a national tour; and today she continues dazzling fans around the world.

**A Time of Mourning**

"I've had hearing issues my entire life," says Mandy, whose early auditory problems stemmed from deformed Eustachian tubes. These tubes, which run from the middle ear to the throat, normally regulate pressure in the middle ear. Mandy's were shaped in a way that allowed extreme pressure buildup, often leading to very painful eardrum ruptures. But the problems associated with her Eustachian tubes were just the beginning. "My main, deep hearing loss was when I was 18, 19 years old."

# Listen, Hear

**LO 7** Summarize how sound waves are converted into the sensation of hearing.

To understand how Mandy lost her sense of hearing, or **audition,** we need to learn how the ears receive sound waves from the environment and translate them into the electrical and chemical language of neurons. And to get a handle on that process, we need to know a little something about *sound waves:* rhythmic vibrations of molecules that travel through air and other materials.

**SOUND WAVES**    Every sound wave begins with a vibration. That could mean a pulsating loudspeaker, a quivering guitar string, or vocal cords fluttering in your throat. When an object vibrates, it sends a pressure disturbance through the molecules of the surrounding medium (usually air, but it can also be water, metal, wood, and other materials). Imagine a very quiet environment, such as the inside of a parked car, where the air molecules are fairly evenly distributed. Now turn on the radio, and the membrane of the amplified speaker immediately bulges outward, pushing air molecules out of its way. This creates a zone where the particles are tightly packed and the pressure is high. The particles directly in front of the speaker will hit the particles right in front of them, and so on throughout the interior of your car. As the speaker retracts, or pulls back, it gives the air particles ample room to move, creating a zone where particles are spread out and pressure is low. As the speaker rhythmically pushes back and forth, it sends *cycles* of high-pressure waves (with particles "bunched up") and low-pressure waves (with particles "spread out") rippling through the air (Ludel, 1978). It's important to note that molecules are not being transmitted from the car speaker to your ears; only the sound wave travels over that distance.

Now that we have established what sound waves are—alternating zones of high and low pressure moving through the environment—let's address the immense variation in sound quality. Why are some noises loud and others soft, some shrill like a siren and others deep like a bullfrog? The sounds we hear can be differentiated by three main qualities: *loudness, pitch,* and *timbre.*

**LOUDNESS**    Loudness is determined by the amplitude, or height, of a sound wave. A kitten purring generates low-amplitude sound waves; a NASCAR engine generates high-amplitude sound waves. The intensity of a sound stimulus is measured in decibels (dB), with 0 dB being the absolute threshold for human hearing. Meanwhile, normal conversation is around 60 dB. Noises at 140 dB can be instantly detrimental to hearing (Liberman, 2015), but you needn't stand next to a 140-dB jet engine to sustain hearing loss. Prolonged exposure to moderately loud sounds such as gas-powered lawn mowers and music at concerts or clubs can also cause damage (more on this to come).

**PITCH**    The **pitch** describes how high or low a sound is. An example of a high-pitched sound is a flute at its highest notes; a low-pitched sound is a tuba at its lowest notes. Pitch is based on wave **frequency.** We measure frequency with a unit called the *hertz* (Hz), which indicates the number of wave peaks passing a given point in 1 second. If you are hearing a 200-Hz sound wave, then theoretically 200 waves enter your ear per second. A higher-pitched sound has a higher wave frequency; the time between the "bunched up" particles and the "spread out" particles is less than that for a lower-pitched sound. Humans can detect frequencies ranging from about 20 Hz to 20,000 Hz, but we tend to lose the higher frequencies as we get older. For comparison, bats have an exquisite sense of hearing and can detect sound frequencies from 2,000 Hz to 110,000 Hz, well beyond the range of human hearing. Beluga whales

*Courtesy Mandy Harvey.*

**She Blew Them Away**
Mandy performs in the 2017 finals of NBC's reality show *America's Got Talent.* In her first performance on the show, the crowd was already on its feet clapping and giving deaf applause midway through the song. Even the notoriously surly judge Simon Cowell was beside himself. Following the performance, he walked on stage, hugged Mandy, and said: "I've done this a long time. That was one of the most amazing things I've ever seen and heard" (America's Got Talent, 2017, 4:43).

**audition**  The sense of hearing.

**pitch**  The degree to which a sound is high or low, determined by the frequency of its sound wave.

**frequency**  The number of sound waves passing a given point per unit of time; higher frequency is perceived as higher pitch, and lower frequency is perceived as lower pitch.

## FIGURE 3.3
### Sound Qualities

A tuning fork produces a pure tone (single frequency), while a flute and a human voice produce frequencies in addition to the dominant one. These additional frequencies, and the way they fluctuate across time, contribute to timbre, or sound "texture" (Lee & Müllensiefen, 2020; Patil et al., 2012). The ability to distinguish between different timbres varies from person to person (Lee & Müllensiefen, 2020).

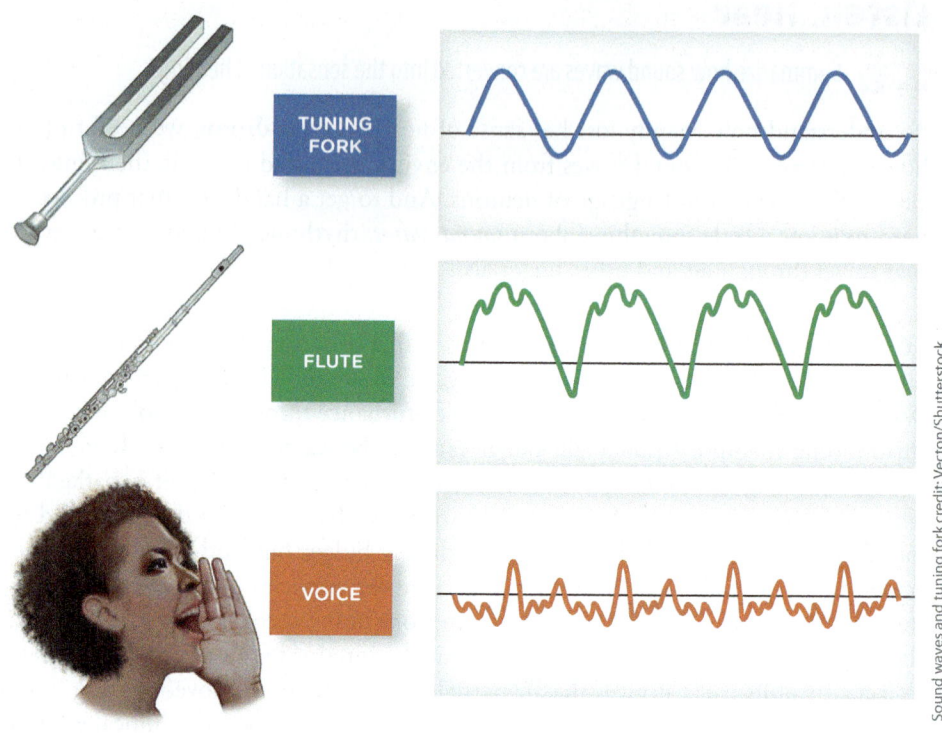

TUNING FORK

FLUTE

VOICE

Sound waves and tuning fork credit: Vecton/Shutterstock.

can sense frequencies from about 100 Hz to 123,000 Hz and mice from 1,000 Hz to 91,000 Hz (Strain, 2003).

**TIMBRE**   How is it possible that two sounds with similar loudness and pitch (Mandy Harvey and Beyoncé belting the same note at the same volume) can sound so different to us? The answer to this question lies in their *timbre* (TAM-ber), or sound "texture" (Lee & Müllensiefen, 2020). Most everyday sounds—people's voices, traffic noises, humming air conditioners—consist of various wave frequencies. A sound typically has one dominant frequency, which we perceive as pitch. Let's say Mandy sings a middle C note, which has a frequency of 282 Hz. As she hits that note, her vocal chords also produce softer accompanying frequencies, which may be higher or lower than 282 Hz. These additional frequencies, and the way they fluctuate across time, contribute to a sound's timbre (Patil et al., 2012). Timbre is the multifaceted quality that makes Mandy's voice sound different from that of Beyoncé, or any person, singing the same note at the same volume (Lee & Müllensiefen, 2020). Thanks to the brain's interpretation of timbre, we can identify a person without seeing who it is! For a visual description of timbre, see **FIGURE 3.3**.

## All Ears

We have outlined the basic properties of sound. Now let's learn how the ears transform sound waves into the language of the brain. As you will see, your ears are extraordinarily efficient at what they do—transducing the physical motion of sound waves into the electrical and chemical signals of the nervous system (see **INFOGRAPHIC 3.2** on page 102).

**FROM SOUND WAVE TO BONE MOVEMENTS**   What happens when a sound wave reaches your ear? First, it is ushered inside by the ear's funnel-like structure.

Then it sweeps down the auditory canal, a tunnel leading to a delicate membrane called the eardrum, which separates the outer ear from the middle ear. The impact of the sound wave bouncing against the eardrum sets off a chain reaction through the three tiny bones in the middle ear: the malleus (hammer), incus (anvil), and stapes (stirrup). The chain reaction of these tiny bones moving each other amplifies the sound wave, turning it into a physical motion with great strength. The malleus pushes the incus; the incus moves the stapes; and the stapes presses on a membrane called the *oval window* leading to the ear's deepest cavern, the inner ear (Luers & Hüttenbrink, 2016). It is in this cavern that transduction occurs.

**FROM MOVING BONES TO MOVING FLUID**   The primary component of the inner ear is the **cochlea** (KOHK-lee-uh), a snail-shaped structure filled with liquid. The entire length of the cochlea is lined with the *basilar membrane,* which contains about 16,000 hair cells. These hair cells are the receptor cells for sound waves that have been transformed into liquid waves. Recall that the sound waves enter your ear from the outside world, causing the eardrum to vibrate, which sets off a chain reaction in the middle ear bones. When the last bone in this chain (the stapes) pushes on the oval window, the fluid inside the cochlea vibrates, causing the hair cells to bend. Below the base of the hair cells are dendrites of neurons whose axons form the *auditory nerve* (Ludel, 1978). If a vibration is strong enough in the cochlear fluid, the bending of the hair cells causes the nearby neurons to fire. Signals from the auditory nerve pass through various processing hubs in the brain, including the thalamus, and eventually wind up in the auditory cortex, where sounds are given meaning. Let's summarize this process: (1) Sound waves hit the eardrum, (2) the tiny bones in the middle ear begin to vibrate, (3) this causes the fluid in the cochlea to vibrate, (4) the hair cells bend in response, initiating a neural cascade that eventually leads to the sensation of sound.

If any part of this pathway is compromised, hearing problems may arise. Mandy says that the profound hearing loss she experienced in college resulted from deterioration of the auditory nerve. In her case, this damage is associated with a connective tissue disorder called Ehlers–Danlos syndrome, Type III. According to one study, hearing loss is not uncommon among people with Ehlers–Danlos syndrome (Weir et al., 2016). Mandy suffers from a variety of other symptoms as well, including chronic pain and hypermobile joints. "All of my joints pop out of socket. . . . I dislocate my shoulders and my fingers all the time," says Mandy. "Your body is in a constant state of pain. You just kind of deal with it."

**CAN HEARING BE RECOVERED?**   For some people with hearing loss, medical technologies can help restore hearing. You are probably familiar with *hearing aids,* devices worn on the ears that increase the amplitude of incoming sound waves (making them louder) so the hair cells in the inner ear can better detect the vibrations. If the hair cells are no longer functioning, a hearing aid won't help. The cochlea is an extremely delicate structure: Damaged or destroyed hair cells will not regrow like blades of grass (at least in humans and other mammals). And, without functional hair cells, the inner ear cannot pass along messages to the brain. Scientists are trying to develop drug treatments to regenerate hair cells, and they have produced promising results in studies of nonhuman mammals (McLean et al., 2017).

Another way to address the problem of damaged hair cells is by using cochlear implants. These "bionic ears" pick up sound waves from the environment with a microphone and turn them into electrical impulses that stimulate the auditory nerve, much as the cochlea would do were it functioning properly (**FIGURE 3.4**). From there, the auditory nerve transmits electrical signals to the brain, where they are "heard," or

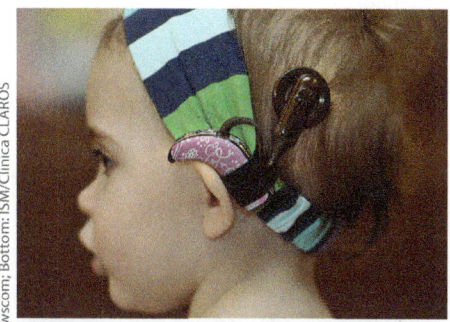
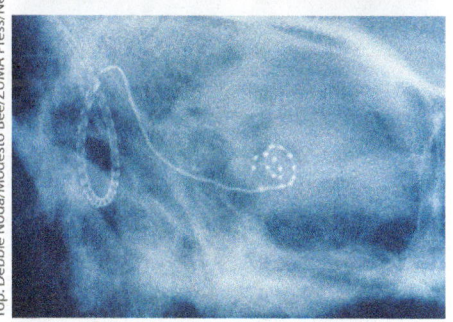

*Top: Debbie Noda/Modesto Bee/ZUMA Press/Newscom; Bottom: ISM/Clinica CLAROS*

**FIGURE 3.4**
**Cochlear Implants**
Cochlear implants enable hearing by circumventing damaged parts of the inner ear. An external microphone gathers sound, which is organized by a speech processor. Internally, an implanted receiver converts this signal into electrical impulses that directly stimulate the auditory nerve. The X-ray on the bottom shows the cochlear implant's electrode array coiling into the cochlea, directly reaching nerve fibers leading to the auditory nerve.

**cochlea** Fluid-filled, snail-shaped organ of the inner ear that is lined with the basilar membrane.

**INFOGRAPHIC 3.2**

# Can You Hear Me Now?

Hearing is a process in which stimuli (sound waves) are mechanically converted to vibrations that are transduced to neural messages. If one part of this complicated system is compromised, hearing loss results.

**1** The pinna funnels sound waves into the auditory canal, focusing them toward the eardrum.

**2** Vibrations of the eardrum cause malleus to push incus, which moves stapes, which presses on oval window, amplifying waves.

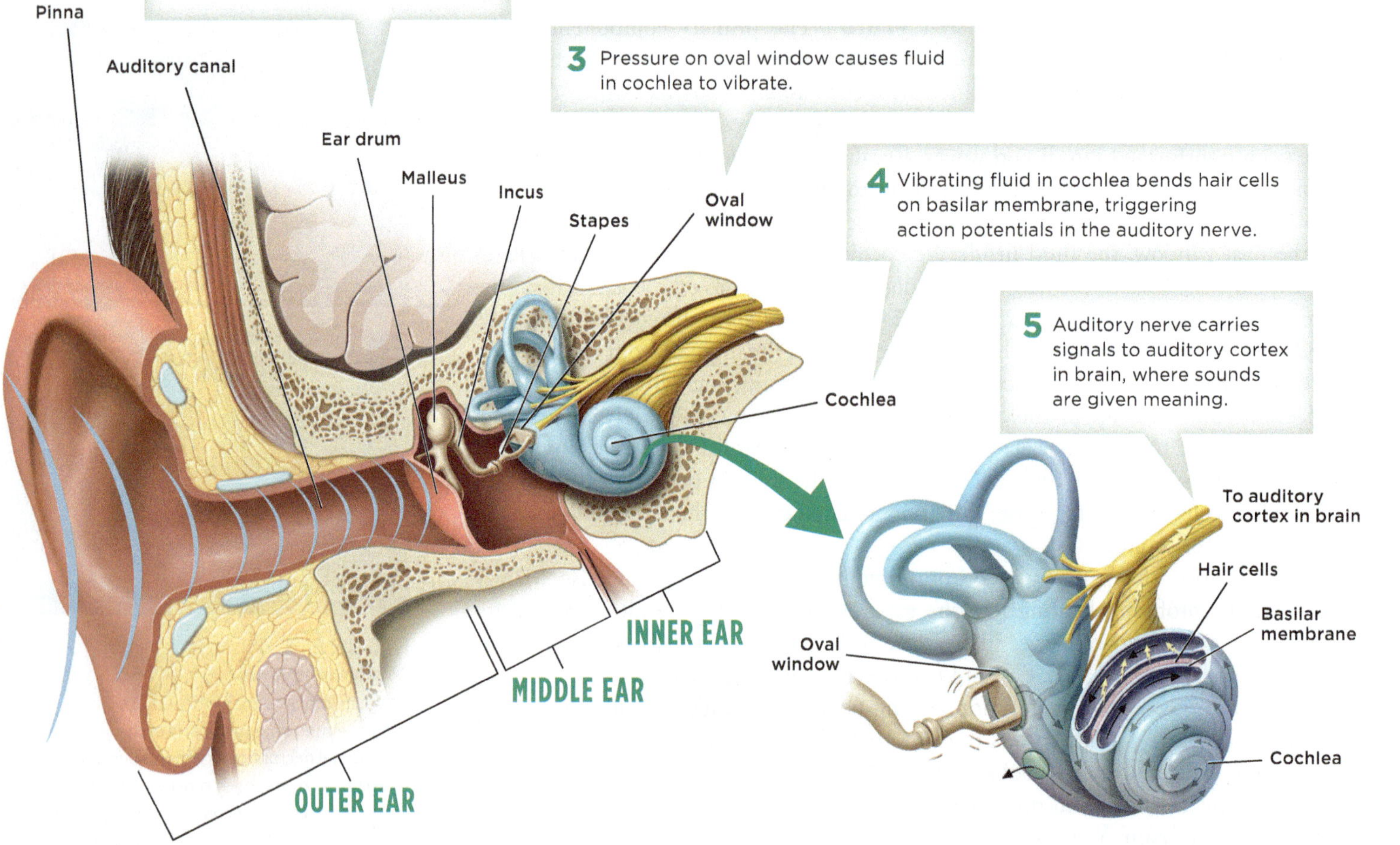

Pinna
Auditory canal
Ear drum
Malleus
Incus
Stapes
Oval window
3 Pressure on oval window causes fluid in cochlea to vibrate.
4 Vibrating fluid in cochlea bends hair cells on basilar membrane, triggering action potentials in the auditory nerve.
5 Auditory nerve carries signals to auditory cortex in brain, where sounds are given meaning.
Cochlea
To auditory cortex in brain
Hair cells
Basilar membrane
Oval window
Cochlea
INNER EAR
MIDDLE EAR
OUTER EAR


## Decibels and Damage

The intensity of a sound stimulus is measured in decibels (dB). The absolute threshold for human hearing—the softest sound a human can hear—is 0 dB. Loud noises, such as the 140 dB produced by a jet engine, cause immediate damage that leads to hearing loss. Chronic exposure to moderately loud noise, such as traffic or an MP3 player near maximum volume, can also cause damage (Carroll et al., 2017; Keith et al., 2008).

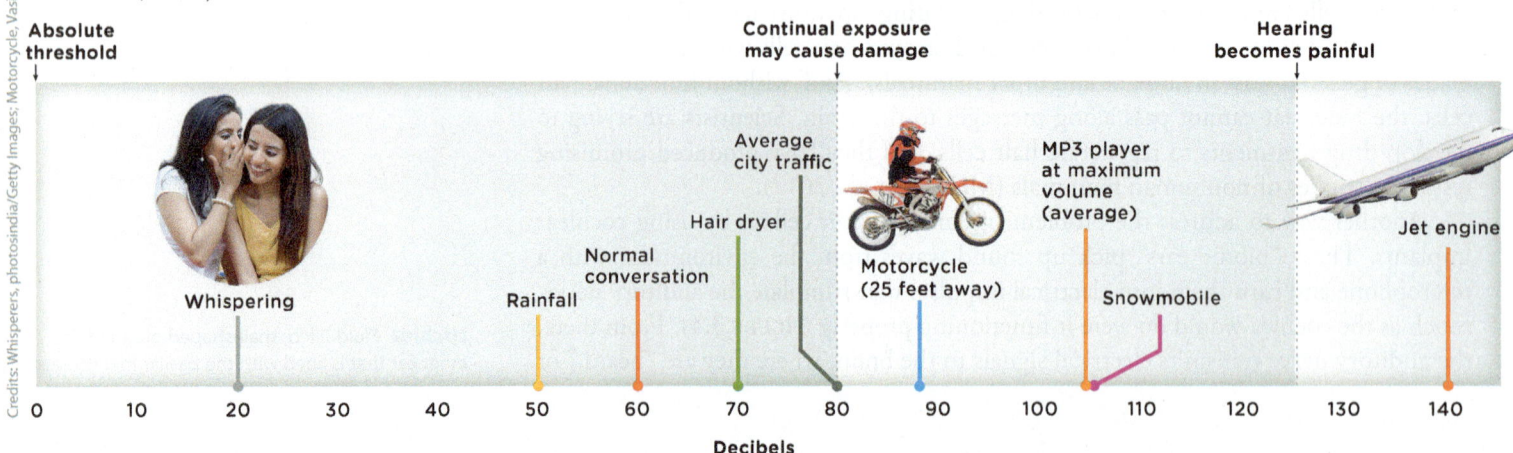

Absolute threshold
Continual exposure may cause damage
Hearing becomes painful
Whispering
Rainfall
Normal conversation
Hair dryer
Average city traffic
Motorcycle (25 feet away)
MP3 player at maximum volume (average)
Snowmobile
Jet engine
0
10
20
30
40
50
60
70
80
90
100
110
120
130
140
Decibels


Credits: Whisperers, photosindia/Getty Images; Motorcycle, Vasiliy Vishnevskiy/Alamy; Airplane, istockphoto/Thinkstock/Getty Images.

interpreted as human voices, hip-hop beats, and dog barks. But note that "hearing" with a cochlear implant is not exactly the same as hearing with two ears. Voices have been described as sounding like Mickey Mouse or the "Munchkins" from the *Wizard of Oz* movie (Dorman et al., 2019), but over time people can learn to understand these speech sounds (Mayo Clinic, n.d.).

## How Is Pitch Processed?

We know how sound waves are transformed into auditory sensations, but there are many types of sounds. How does the brain know the difference between the yap of a Chihuahua and the deep bark of a Rottweiler, or the whine of a dentist's drill and the hum of a fan? In other words, how do we distinguish between sound waves of high and low frequencies? There are two complementary theories that explain how the brain processes pitch.

**LO 8** Illustrate how we sense different pitches of sound.

**PLACE THEORY**    According to **place theory,** the location of neural activity along the cochlea allows us to sense the different pitches of high-frequency sounds. Hair cells toward the oval-window end of the basilar membrane vibrate more when exposed to higher-frequency sounds, while those toward the opposite end of the basilar membrane vibrate more in response to lower-frequency sounds. The brain determines the pitch by judging where along the basilar membrane neural signals originate. Place theory works well for explaining higher-pitch sounds (4,000–20,000 Hz), but not so well for lower-pitch sounds—specifically those with frequencies below 4,000 Hz. This is because lower-frequency sounds produce vibrations that are more dispersed along the basilar membrane, with less precise locations of movement.

**FREQUENCY THEORY**    To understand how humans perceive lower pitches, we can use the **frequency theory,** which suggests it is not where along the cochlea hair cells are vibrating, but how frequently they are firing (the number of neural impulses per second). The entire basilar membrane vibrates at the same frequency as a sound wave, also causing the hair cells to be activated at that frequency. The nearby neurons fire at the same rate as the vibrations, sending signals through the auditory nerve at this rate. If the sound wave has a frequency of 200 Hz, then the basilar membrane vibrates at 200 Hz, and the neurons in the auditory nerve fire at this rate as well.

Neurons, however, can only fire so fast, the maximum rate being about 1,000 times per second. How does the frequency theory explain how we hear sounds higher than 1,000 Hz? According to the **volley principle,** neurons can work together so that their combined firing exceeds 1,000 times per second. Imagine a hockey team practicing for a tournament. The coach challenges the players to fire shots on the goal at the fastest rate possible. The team members get together and decide to work in small groups, alternating shots on the goal. The first group skates and shoots, and as they skate away and return to the back of the line, the next group takes their shots. Each time a group is finished shooting on the goal, the next group is ready to shoot. Groups of neurons work in a similar way, firing together in *volleys;* as one group finishes firing and is "**recovering**," the next group fires. The frequency of the combined firing of all neuron groups results in our perception of pitch.

We have now examined what occurs in a hearing system working at an optimal level. But many of us have auditory functioning that is far from perfect.

---

**CONNECTIONS**

In **Chapter 2,** we described how neurons must return to resting potential following an action potential. During this process, they cannot fire; that is, they are "recovering." Without the ability to volley, the range of human hearing would be greatly reduced.

**place theory**  States that pitch corresponds to the location of the vibrating hair cells along the cochlea.

**frequency theory**  States that pitch is determined by the vibrating frequency of the sound wave, basilar membrane, and associated neural impulses.

**volley principle**  States that neurons work together so their combined firing reaches frequencies higher than one neuron can achieve alone.

jasonfang/Getty Images.

**Not Too Loud**

Long-term exposure to loud music can cause auditory damage, and not just in adults. A study of over 3,000 Dutch children (ages 9–11) found that 14.2% had already experienced hearing loss. There was a correlation between high-frequency hearing loss and use of portable media devices such as smartphones and tablets, which are often used with headphones (le Clercq et al., 2018).

## I Can't Hear You

In the United States, nearly half of people over age 65 and a quarter of those between 55 and 64 have hearing problems (Williams, 2018). At the onset of hearing loss, high frequencies become hard to hear, making it difficult to understand certain consonant sounds such as the "th" in thumb (Harvard Health Publishing, 2016). Everyone experiences some degree of hearing loss as they age, primarily resulting from normal wear and tear of the delicate hair cells. Damage to the hair cells or the auditory nerve leads to *sensorineural deafness*. In contrast, *conduction hearing impairment* results from damage to the eardrum or the middle-ear bones that transmit sound waves to the cochlea.

Older adults are not the only ones who ought to be concerned about hearing loss. One large study found that 15–20% of American teenagers suffers from some degree of hearing impairment (Barret & White, 2017). Worldwide, some 1.1 billion young people are vulnerable to hearing damage caused by "noise in recreational settings" (World Health Organization [WHO], 2018, para. 5). Keep in mind (and remind your friends) that hearing loss often occurs gradually and goes unnoticed for some time. But the damage is permanent, and its impact on communication and relationships can be life-changing (Portnuff, 2016).

### ▶▶▶ SHOW WHAT YOU KNOW

1. The pitch of a sound is based on the _____ of its waves.
   A. frequency
   B. timbre
   C. amplitude
   D. purity

2. A researcher studying the location of neural activity in the cochlea finds that hair cells nearest the oval window vibrate more to high-frequency sounds. This supports the _____ theory of pitch perception.

3. When a sound wave hits the eardrum, it causes vibrations in the bones of the middle ear, making the fluid in the cochlea vibrate. Hair cells on the basilar membrane bend in response to the motion, causing nerve cells to fire. This process is known as:
   A. the volley principle.
   B. transduction.
   C. the frequency theory.
   D. audition.

✓ Check your answers at the back of book.

# Smell, Taste, Touch

When Mandy lost her hearing, she began to rely more on her other senses to gather information from the environment. "I think everything else heightened a bit," Mandy explains. "I definitely taste things stronger and smell things stronger, but I've been purposely paying more attention." Mandy's enhanced smell and taste are likely the result of **changes in her brain**. After losing one sensory system, the brain reorganizes itself to adapt (Reichert & Schöpf, 2018). "If one sense is lost, the areas of the brain normally devoted to handling that sensory information do not go unused—they get rewired and put to work processing other senses" (Bates, 2012, para. 2).

**CONNECTIONS**

In **Chapter 2,** we introduced the concept of neuroplasticity, the ability of the brain to heal, grow new connections, and make do with what's available. Here, we suggest that Mandy's increased use of other senses is made possible by the plasticity of her nervous system.

## Smell: Nosing Around

**LO 9** Describe the process of olfaction.

Many people take **olfaction** (ohl-FAK-shun)—the sense of smell—for granted. But such individuals might think twice if they actually understood how losing olfaction would affect their lives. People with the rare condition of *anosmia* are unable to perceive odors. They cannot smell smoke in a burning building or a gas leak from a stove. They cannot tell whether the fish they are about to eat is spoiled. Nor can they savor the complex palates of pesto, curry, chocolate, coffee, or prime rib. Because, without smell, food doesn't taste as good.

**olfaction** The sense of smell.

**CHEMICAL SENSE**    Olfaction and taste are called chemical senses because they involve sensing chemicals in the environment. For olfaction, those chemicals are odor molecules dispersed through the air. For taste, they are flavor molecules surfing on waves of saliva. Odor molecules, which are emitted by a variety of sources (for example, spices, fruits, flowers, bacteria, and skin), make their way into the nose by hitchhiking on currents of air flowing into the nostrils or through the mouth. About 3 inches into the nostrils is a patch of tissue called the *olfactory epithelium*. Around the size of a typical postage stamp, the olfactory epithelium is home to millions of olfactory receptor neurons that provide tiny docking sites, or receptors, for odor molecules (much as a lock acts as a docking site for a key; **FIGURE 3.5**). When enough odor molecules attach to an olfactory receptor neuron, it fires, causing an **action potential**; this is how transduction occurs in the chemical sense of olfaction.

**WHAT'S UP WITH THAT SMELL?**    Olfactory receptor neurons project into a part of the brain called the *olfactory bulb,* where they converge in clusters called *glomeruli* (Figure 3.5). From there, signals are passed along to higher brain centers, including the hippocampus, amygdala, and olfactory cortex (Firestein, 2001; Seubert et al., 2013). The other sensory systems relay information through the thalamus before it goes to higher brain centers. But the wiring of the olfactory system is unique; olfaction is on a fast track to structures in the limbic system, where emotions like fear and anger are processed (Watanabe et al., 2018). This may be the reason that odor-induced memories are "more emotional, [and] associated with stronger feelings of being brought back in time" (Larsson & Willander, 2009, p. 318). Can you think of any smells that transport you to a time long ago—the "hot-lunch" smell of your elementary school cafeteria, or perhaps the musty scent of a closet where you once played hide-and-seek?

## CONNECTIONS

In **Chapter 2,** we discussed the properties that allow neurons to communicate. When enough sending neurons signal a receiving neuron to pass along its message, the neuron fires. Similarly, if enough odor molecules bind to an olfactory receptor neuron, an action potential occurs.

## FIGURE 3.5
**Olfaction**

When enough odor molecules attach to an olfactory receptor neuron, it fires, sending a message to the olfactory bulb in the brain. From there, the signal is sent to higher brain centers.

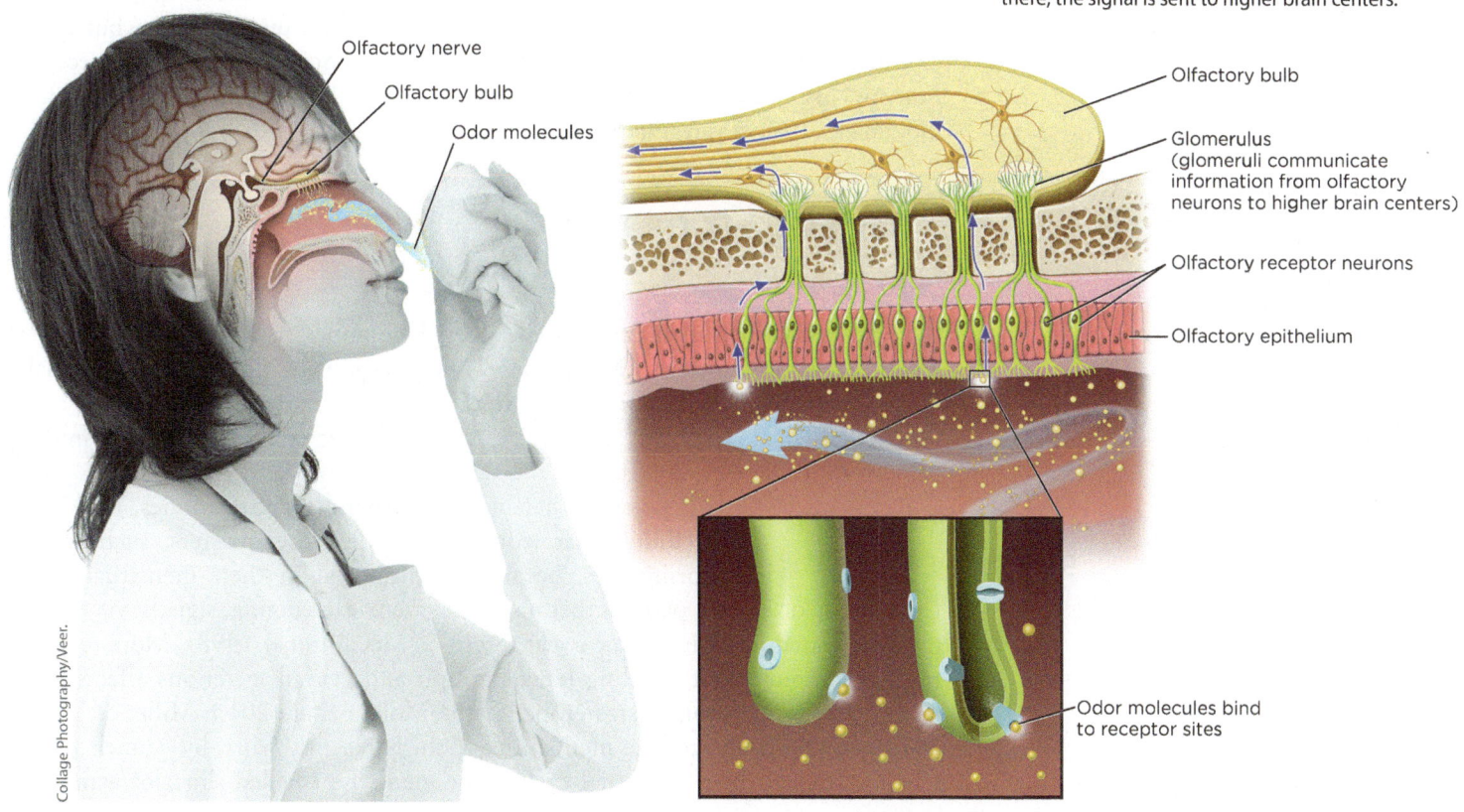

Olfactory nerve

Olfactory bulb

Odor molecules

Olfactory bulb

Glomerulus (glomeruli communicate information from olfactory neurons to higher brain centers)

Olfactory receptor neurons

Olfactory epithelium

Odor molecules bind to receptor sites

Collage Photography/Veer.

ALEJANDR PAGN/Getty Images.

**Why Does Coronavirus Impair Smell?**
A woman receives an "olfactory test" as part of a coronavirus monitoring program in La Plata, Argentina. Loss of smell and taste are commonly reported COVID symptoms, with studies showing olfactory dysfunction in 33.9–68% of cases (Meng et al., 2020; Menni et al., 2020). Evidence suggests that SARS-CoV-2 achieves this effect by infecting cells that support the olfactory neurons—not the olfactory neurons themselves (Brann et al., 2020).

Some researchers estimate that humans can distinguish over 1 trillion smells, while others take issue with the methods used to calculate this number (Bushdid et al., 2014; Gerkin & Castro, 2015). What we do know is that humans have about 400 different *types* of odor receptors (Trimmer et al., 2019). Each receptor type recognizes several odors, and each odor activates several receptors; a given scent creates a telltale pattern of neural activity that the brain recognizes as lemon, garlic, or smelly feet (Firestein, 2001). Remember that these odor receptors are found on olfactory neurons, which converge in glomeruli in the brain. Which glomeruli are activated, and the order in which they are activated, play an important role in identifying a smell (Chong et al., 2020; Stetka, 2020). Not surprisingly, we are much better at picking up on faint human odor "footprints" (the unique scents of people) than smells coming from inanimate objects (Pazzaglia, 2015).

**THE POWER OF SMELL**   Scents have a powerful influence on behaviors and mental processes. Minutes after birth, a baby uses the scent of their mother's breast to guide them toward the nipple, and they quickly learn to discriminate Mom's milk from someone else's. Within two days, they can recognize the odors of their mother's axillary areas (armpits) (Makin & Porter, 1989; Marin et al., 2015; Porter & Winberg, 1999). For adults, scents can trigger emotions (both positive and negative) and measurable physiological reactions (McGann, 2017). Odors of burning and vomit bring about disgust (Glass et al., 2015), while the scent of rose oil seems to dampen the body's stress response, perhaps by interfering with activity in the hypothalamic–pituitary–adrenal (HPA) system (Chapter 12; Fukada et al., 2012).

The relationship between olfaction and sexual behavior has long intrigued researchers, and evidence suggests that scent plays an important role in romantic attraction (Gangestad & Haselton, 2015; Griskevicius et al., 2015; Pazzaglia, 2015). Unpleasant body odors can be a turn-off, while "clean smells" (artificial fragrances from soap and toothpaste, for example) are generally considered more agreeable (Karandashev et al., 2020). These smells usually capture our attention, but do we also detect and respond to scents without realizing it? Some researchers suspect that humans, like animals, communicate via odor molecules called *pheromones* (Tan & Goldman, 2015; Wyatt, 2015).

## ...BELIEVE... IT OR NOT

### SEXY SMELLS?

Animals of all different kinds use pheromones to influence members of the same species. Male house mice—especially those that are socially dominant—release pheromones that attract "sexually receptive females" (Thoß et al., 2019), and female elephants invite males to mate by secreting a pheromone in their urine (Tirindelli et al., 2009).

**THEIR ARMPITS SMELLED ENTICING.**

Is it possible that humans respond to pheromones, too? Early studies found that women living in close quarters, such as college dormitories, became synchronized in their menstrual cycles (McClintock, 1971), perhaps because they were exchanging signals via pheromones released in their armpit sweat (Stern & McClintock, 1998). More recently, researchers found that smelling female armpit and genital secretions affects levels of the male sex hormone testosterone (Cerda-Molina et al., 2013; Miller & Maner, 2010). In one study, college men sniffed T-shirts recently worn by women in different phases of their menstrual cycles. The men who smelled shirts of women in their most fertile phase (around the time of ovulation) experienced higher levels of testosterone than those who sniffed shirts worn by women in their nonfertile phase, or shirts that had been worn by no one. What's more, they preferred the odors of ovulating women (Miller & Maner, 2010). A more recent study found that men are more attracted to the armpit odors of sexually aroused women (Wisman & Shrira, 2020). These results suggest that something in the women's armpit secretions—perhaps a pheromone—may trigger hormonal changes in men and make them more inclined to pursue sexual relationships with women whose bodies are primed for reproduction.

Such findings have sparked great excitement in the media and popular culture. (Perhaps you have heard of "pheromone parties," where people try to find the perfect mates by smelling their sweaty T-shirts.) Yet, research on chemicals suspected of acting as pheromones, namely androstadienone and estratetraenol, suggest they do not influence people's perceptions of potential sexual partners (Hare et al., 2017). To complicate matters, experts do not always agree which chemicals are the best human pheromone candidates, and how those substances should be investigated (Liberles, 2015; Wyatt, 2015). For now, the question of whether humans communicate through pheromones remains unsettled (Kupferschmidt, 2019; Pennisi, 2020).

**Love Smells?**
A small study of heterosexual women found that females prefer the body odors of their romantic partners over that of strangers. It is not yet clear whether these preferences have something to do with mate selection (being attracted to those who smell "good"), or simply liking smells that have become familiar (Mahmut et al., 2019).

## Put Your Heads Together

 The study by Miller and Maner (2010) used the experimental method to explore whether men could smell the difference between women who were in their most fertile phase and those in their nonfertile phase. In your group, **A)** identify the hypothesis, independent variable, dependent variable, and control group in the study. **B)** Use the evolutionary perspective to explain how communication through pheromones might have promoted the survival of our species.

## Taste: Just Eat It

Eating is more of an olfactory experience than many people realize. Just think back to the last time your nose was clogged from a really bad cold. How did your meals taste? When you chew, odors from food float up into your nose, creating a flavor that you perceive as "taste," when it's actually smell. If this mouth–nose connection is blocked, there is no difference between apples and onions, Sprite and Coke, or wine and cooled coffee (Herz, 2007). Don't believe us? Then do the Try This experiment.

**Try This** | Tie on a blindfold, squeeze your nostrils, and ask a friend to hand you a wedge of apple and a wedge of onion, both on toothpicks so that you can't feel their texture. Now bite into both. Without your sense of smell, you probably can't tell the difference (Rosenblum, 2010).

**LO 10** Discuss the structures involved in taste and describe how they work.

**TASTY CHEMICALS**   If the nose is so crucial for flavor appreciation, then what role does the mouth play? Receptors in the mouth are sensitive to five basic but very important tastes: *sweet, salty, sour, bitter,* and *umami.* You've probably heard of all these tastes, except perhaps umami, which is a savory taste found in seaweed, aged cheeses, protein-rich foods, mushrooms, and monosodium glutamate (MSG; Ando, 2020; Gaillard & Kinnamon, 2019). We call the ability to detect these stimuli our sense of taste, or **gustation** (guh-STAY-shun; FIGURE **3.6** on the next page).

Stick out your tongue, and what do you see in the mirror? All those little bumps are called *papillae,* and they are home to some 2,000 to 4,000 taste buds (PubMed Health, 2016). Jutting from each of these buds are 50 to 100 taste

**gustation** The sense of taste.

## FIGURE 3.6

### Tasting

Within the tongue's papillae are taste buds containing receptor cells. When stimulated by chemicals from food and drink, these receptor cells communicate signals to the brain, leading to the sensation of taste.

**Surface of tongue (magnified)**

Omikron/Science Source.

**Cross-section of papilla**

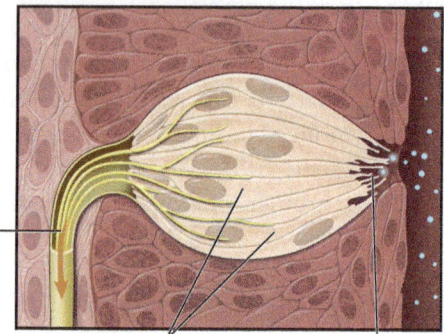

Taste bud

**Taste bud**

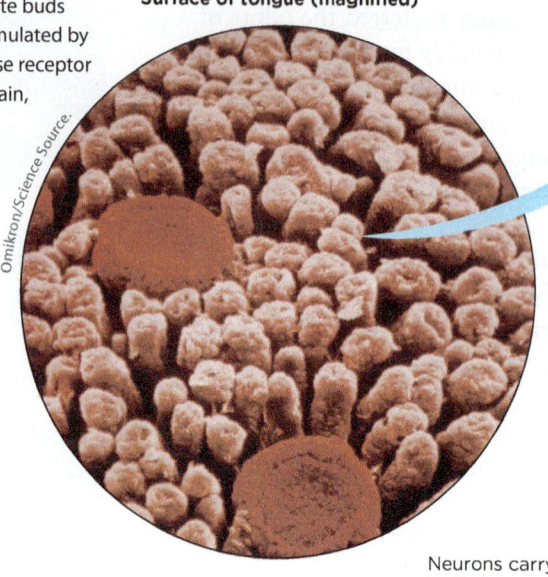

Neurons carry signal to thalamus

Taste receptor cells

Receptor sites

---

### CONNECTIONS

In **Chapter 2,** we explained that sensory neurons receive information from the sensory systems and send it to the brain. With gustation, the sensory neurons send information about taste. Once processed in the brain, information is sent back through motor neurons signaling you to take another bite!

receptor cells where food molecules bind (similar to the lock-and-key mechanism of an odor molecule binding to a receptor in the nose). These taste receptor cells are found in taste buds in the tongue's papillae, the roof of the mouth, and the lining of the cheeks.

As you bite into a juicy orange and begin to chew, chemicals from the orange (sour acid and sweet sugar) are released into your saliva, where they dissolve and bathe the taste buds throughout your mouth. These chemicals find their way to matching receptors and latch on, sparking action potentials in sensory neurons, another example of transduction. Signals are sent through **sensory neurons** to the thalamus, and then on to higher brain centers for processing.

Receptors for taste are constantly being replenished, but their life span is only about 8 to 12 days (Feng et al., 2013). If they didn't regenerate, you would be in trouble every time you burned your tongue sipping hot coffee or soup. Even so, by age 20, you have already lost half of the taste receptors you had at birth. And as the years go by, their turnover rate gets slower and slower, making it harder to appreciate the basic taste sensations, although not necessarily reducing eating pleasure or appetite (Arganini & Sinesio, 2015; Feng et al., 2013; Kaneda et al., 2000). Drinking alcohol and smoking worsen the problem by impairing the ability of receptors to receive taste molecules. Losing taste is unfortunate, and it may take away from life's simple pleasures, but it's probably not going to kill you—at least not if you are a modern human. We can't be so sure about our primitive ancestors.

### A Sixth Taste?

Scientists have long suspected there was a sixth taste in addition to the five already identified (sweet, salty, sour, bitter, and umami). Now strong evidence is available that this sixth taste exists (Gaillard & Kinnamon, 2019). Researchers call it *oleogustus,* or "the unique taste of fat" (Running et al., 2015, p. 507).

Rusty Hill/Getty Images.

**WHERE DID YOU GET THAT TASTE?**    The ability to taste has been essential to the survival of our species. Tastes push us toward foods we need and away from those that could harm us. We gravitate toward sweet, calorie-rich foods for their life-sustaining energy—an adaptive trait if you are a primitive human foraging in trees and bushes, not so adaptive if you are a modern human looking for something to eat in a vending machine. We are also drawn to salty foods, which tend to contain valuable minerals, and to umami, which signals the presence of proteins essential for cellular health and growth. Bitter and sour tastes we tend to avoid, on the other hand. This also gives us an evolutionary edge because poisonous plants or rancid foods are often bitter or sour. Our *absolute threshold* for bitter is lower than the threshold for sweet. Can you see how this is advantageous? Some people, known as "supertasters," are extremely sensitive to bitterness and other tastes and thus can be characterized as "picky eaters" (Hayes & Keast, 2011; Rupp, 2014).

Every person experiences taste in a unique way. You like cilantro; your friend thinks it tastes like bath soap. Taste preferences may begin developing before birth, as flavors consumed by a pregnant woman pass into amniotic fluid and are swallowed by the fetus. For example, babies who were exposed to carrot or garlic flavors in the womb (through their mothers' consumption of carrot juice or garlic pills) seem more tolerant of those flavors in their food and breast milk (Mennella et al., 2001; Underwood, 2014). As children mature, their eating choices are shaped by both genetic predispositions and environmental factors (DeJesus et al., 2019; Ragelienė & Grønhøj, 2020; Robino et al., 2019). One of those environmental factors is the people in their lives. Peers tend to have a negative impact, acting as "facilitators towards eating more snacks and junk foods," but more research is needed in this area (Ragelienė & Grønhøj, 2020, p. 15). Food preferences can also be influenced by families and culture (Daniels, 2019).

We have made some major headway in this chapter, examining four of the sensory systems: vision, hearing, smell, and taste. Now it is time to get a feel for a fifth sense: touch.

## Touch: Can You Feel It?

If you sat down with Mandy at a jazz club, coffee house, or anywhere that has music playing in the background, you might be surprised to see her bobbing her head or tapping her fingers. How does she move in time with music she can't hear? Mandy is constantly aware of vibrations; she feels them in the floor, table, whatever she may be touching. This ability is essential when it comes to staying in sync with fellow musicians. "I perform with my shoes off so I can feel the drum through the floor," Mandy explains. "You designate different parts of your body to paying attention to different things." To feel the instruments in specific parts of her body, Mandy relies on touch receptors, many of which dwell in the skin.

Take a moment to appreciate your vast *epidermis,* the skin's outermost layer. Weighing around 6 pounds on the average adult, the skin is the body's biggest organ and the barrier that protects our insides from cruel elements of the environment (bacteria, viruses, and physical objects) and distinguishes us from others (fingerprints, birthmarks). It also shields us from the cold, sweats to cool us down, and makes vitamin D (Bikle, 2004; Grigalavicius et al., 2015). And perhaps most importantly, skin is a data collector. Every moment of the day, receptors in our skin gather information about the environment. Among them are *thermoreceptors* that sense hot or cold, *Pacinian corpuscles* that detect vibrations,

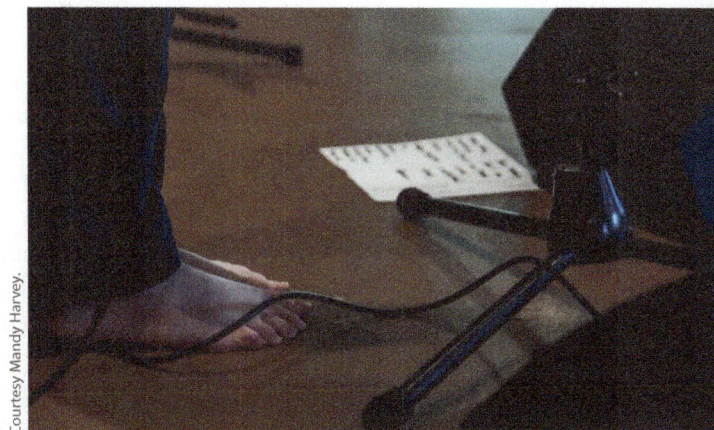

Courtesy Mandy Harvey.

**Good Vibrations**
Mandy stands on the stage barefoot so she can feel the rhythm of the other instruments coming through the floor. She also uses her sense of touch to gauge how loud she is singing, placing her foot on a monitor that produces vibrations in response to her voice. "I can put my foot on it, and feel that I'm making a rumble, and then I can judge, based off of how loud that rumble is . . . how loud I'm singing," Mandy explains.

**FIGURE 3.7**
**Touch**
The sensation of touch begins with our skin, which houses a variety of receptors including those shown here.

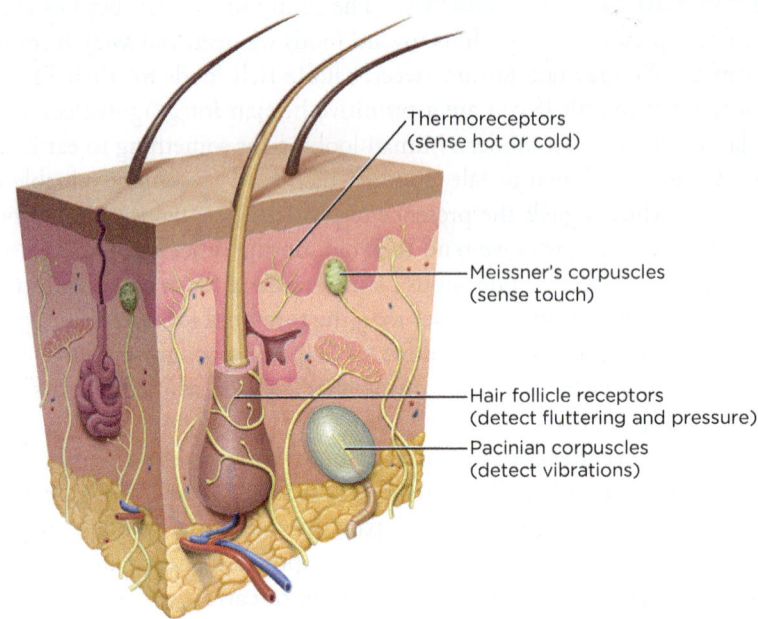

Thermoreceptors
(sense hot or cold)

Meissner's corpuscles
(sense touch)

Hair follicle receptors
(detect fluttering and pressure)

Pacinian corpuscles
(detect vibrations)

and *Meissner's corpuscles* sensitive to the slightest touch, like a snowflake landing on your nose (Bandell et al., 2007; Zimmerman et al., 2014; FIGURE **3.7**).

## Pain: It Hurts

Not all touch sensations are as pleasant as the tickle of a snowflake. Touch receptors can also communicate signals that are interpreted as pain. *Nociceptive pain* is caused by heat, cold, chemicals, and pressure. *Nociceptors* that respond to these stimuli are primarily housed in the skin, but they also may be found in muscles and internal organs.

In very rare cases, a baby is born without the ability to feel pain. Children with this type of genetic disorder face a greater risk of serious injury (Genetics Home Reference, 2020a). When scrapes and cuts are not felt, they may not receive the necessary protection and treatment. The "ouch" that results from the stub of a toe or the prick of a needle tells us to stop what we are doing and tend to our wounds. Let's find out how this protective mechanism works.

**CONNECTIONS**

In **Chapter 2,** we explained how a myelin sheath insulates the axon and speeds the transmission of neural messages. The myelin covering the fast nerve fibers allows them to convey pain information more rapidly than the slow, unmyelinated nerve fibers.

**TWO PATHWAYS FOR PAIN**    Thanks to the elaborate system of nerves running up and down our bodies, we are able to experience unpleasant, yet very necessary, sensations of pain. *Fast nerve fibers,* made up of large, **myelinated neurons,** are responsible for quickly conveying information about pain in the skin and muscles, generally experienced as a stinging feeling in a specific location. If you stub your toe, your fast nerve fibers enable you to sense a painful sting where the impact occurred. *Slow nerve fibers,* made up of smaller, unmyelinated neurons, are responsible for conveying information about dull aching pain that is not necessarily concentrated in a specific region. The diffuse pain that follows the initial sting of the stubbed toe results from activity in the slow nerve fibers.

The axons of the fast and slow nerve fibers band into nerves on their way to the spinal cord and brain (FIGURE **3.8**). The fast nerve pathway alerts the brain's reticular formation that something important has happened. The sensory information then goes to the thalamus and on to the somatosensory cortex, where it is processed further (for example, indicating where it hurts most). The slow nerve pathway starts out in the same direction, with processing occurring in the brainstem, hypothalamus, thalamus, and limbic system.

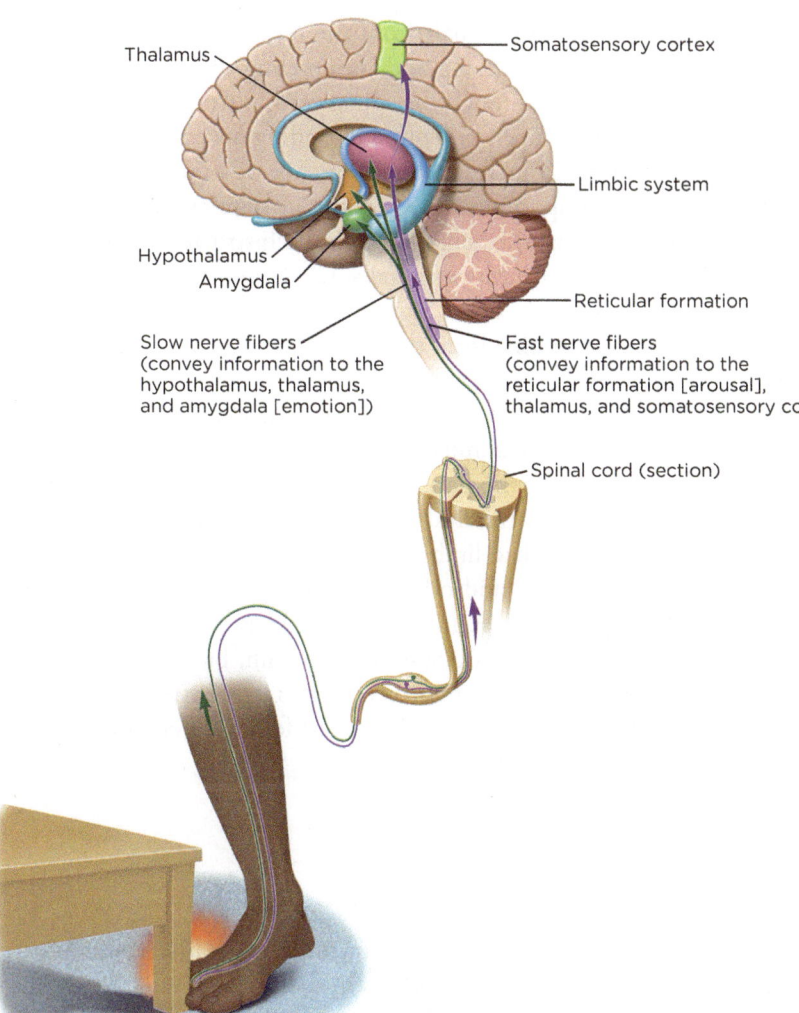

Thalamus

Somatosensory cortex

Limbic system

Hypothalamus
Amygdala

Reticular formation

Slow nerve fibers
(convey information to the
hypothalamus, thalamus,
and amygdala [emotion])

Fast nerve fibers
(convey information to the
reticular formation [arousal],
thalamus, and somatosensory cortex)

Spinal cord (section)

**FIGURE 3.8**

**Fast and Slow Pain Pathways**

When you stub your toe, two kinds of pain messages can be communicated to your brain. Your first perception of pain may be a sharp, clear feeling where the impact occurred. The message quickly travels through your spinal cord to your brain, signaling arousal and alerting you to react. Slow nerve fibers also travel through your spinal cord to carry messages about the pain that lingers after the initial injury, often generating an emotional response.

**LO 11**  Explain how the biopsychosocial perspective helps us understand pain.

**IT'S COMPLICATED**    Understanding the **mechanisms of pain** at the neural level is important, but biology alone cannot explain how we perceive pain and why people experience it so differently. How can the same flu shot cause intense pain in one person but mere discomfort in another? As with most complex topics in psychology, pain is best understood using a multilevel approach, such as the biopsychosocial perspective. Chronic pain, for example, can be explained by biological factors (the neurological pathways involved), psychological factors (distress, thoughts), and social factors (social support, or lack thereof; Sutherland, 2017). Prior experiences, environmental factors, and cultural expectations all influence how pain is processed (Gatchel et al., 2013; Gatchel & Maddrey, 2004). Even within the same individual, pain sensitivity can ebb and flow, and this is partly due to psychological factors (Gatchel et al., 2013; Rethorn et al., 2020). Negative feelings such as fear and anxiety can amplify pain, whereas laughter and distraction may soften it by redirecting attention.

To understand how psychological and social factors influence the experience of pain, we turn to the *gate-control theory.*

**OPEN THE GATES . . . NO, CLOSE THE GATES!**    According to the **gate-control theory,** a collection of *gates* is involved in shuttling information about pain between the brain and the rest of the body. The opening and closing of these gates depend on an interaction of biopsychosocial factors (Melzack & Wall, 1965). Returning to

**CONNECTIONS**

In **Chapter 2,** we discussed the reflex arc, which occurs when we automatically respond to painful stimuli before becoming conscious of them. Here, we describe pain that has entered our conscious awareness.

**gate-control theory**  Suggests that the perception of pain will either increase or decrease through the interaction of biopsychosocial factors; signals are sent to open or close "gates" that control the neurological pathways for pain.

your stubbed toe, recall that pain signals from the injury area travel up your spinal cord and to your brain. After receiving and interpreting the pain information, the brain sends a signal back down through the spinal cord, instructing the "gates" in the neurological pain pathways to open or close. Depending on psychological and social factors, the gates may open to increase the experience of pain, or close to decrease it. In situations where it's important to keep going in spite of an injury (athletes in competitions, soldiers in danger), the gates might be instructed to close. But when feeling intense pain has value (during an illness, when your body needs to rest), the gates may be instructed to remain open. Signals to shut the gates do not always come from the brain; they can also come from the body (Melzack, 1993, 2008).

**PHANTOM LIMB PAIN**    Pain is a complex psychological phenomenon, dependent on many factors beyond the initial stimulus—so complex that a stimulus may not even be necessary. Sometimes people who have had an arm or leg amputated feel like they are experiencing intense pain in the limb they have lost. *Phantom limb pain* occurs in 50–80% of people who have had limbs amputated. They may experience burning, tingling, intense pain, cramping, and other sensations that seem to come from the missing limb (Collins et al., 2018; Ramchandran & Hauser, 2010). Researchers are still trying to determine what causes phantom limb pain, but they have proposed a variety of plausible mechanisms, ranging from changes in the structure of neurons to reorganization of the brain in response to sensations felt in different locations in the body (Flor et al., 2006; Makin et al., 2015).

## Relationships

### KNOW SOMEONE WITH CHRONIC PAIN?

Another pain phenomenon that continues to baffle researchers is the *chronic* variety. About 20% of adults in the United States report that they suffer from *chronic pain,* or "pain on most days or every day in the past 6 months" (Dahlhamer et al., 2018, p. 1002). In some cases, this gnawing pain has a clear cause or activating event, like an injury or a neurological condition. Other times, there is no identifiable trigger (National Institute of Neurological Disorders and Stroke, 2019a).

As you might imagine, chronic pain can have a significant impact on relationships. In the words of one anonymous source, it makes you feel "like a turtle pulling into its shell." Dealing with pain can sap your energy and make you less inclined to reach out to friends and relatives. The experience may worsen if those loved ones are not empathetic: "Feeling like one's family members are demanding or criticizing is associated with greater depression and anxiety which is, in turn, associated with worse global health and pain interference" (Signs & Woods, 2020, p. 46). So if you're dealing with someone who struggles with chronic pain, remember that empathy goes a long way.

## Your Body in Space

**LO 12**    Illustrate how we sense the position and movement of our bodies.

You may have thought "touch" was the fifth and final sense, but there is more to sensation and perception than the traditional five categories. Closely related to touch is the sense of **kinesthesia** (kin-ehs-THEE-zhuh), which provides feedback about body position and movement. Kinesthesia endows us with the coordination we need to walk gracefully, perform the latest dance on TikTok, and put on our clothes without looking in the mirror. This knowledge of body location and orientation is

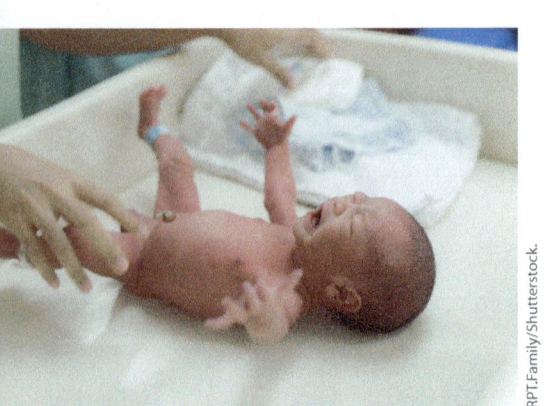

**Babies Feel It, Too**
Until the 1980s, doctors thought newborns were incapable of feeling pain, and these tiny babies were given no painkilling drugs for unpleasant procedures such as circumcision and needle pricks (Bellieni et al., 2013; Eccleston et al., 2020). With the help of functional magnetic resonance imaging (fMRI), researchers have demonstrated that the brain activity associated with pain is "extremely similar" for infants and adults, suggesting babies do indeed suffer just like other people (Goksan et al., 2015).

RPT.Family/Shutterstock.

**kinesthesia** Sensory system that conveys information about body position and movement.

made possible by specialized nerve endings called **proprioceptors** (PRO-pree-oh-sep-turz), which are primarily located in the muscles and joints. Proprioceptors monitor changes in the position of body parts and the tension in muscles. When proprioception is impaired, our ability to perform physical tasks like holding a book or opening a door is compromised.

The **vestibular sense** (veh-STIB-u-ler) helps the body maintain balance as it deals with the effects of gravity, movement, and position. Astronauts often become nauseated during their first days in space because their vestibular systems are confused. The vestibular system is comprised of fluid-filled organs in the inner ear: the *semicircular canals* and the nearby *vestibular sacs*. When the head tilts, fluid moves the hairlike receptors in these structures, causing neurons to fire (transduction once again), initiating a signal that travels to the cerebellum. According to *sensory conflict theory*, motion sickness (which many people experience on boats and roller coasters) results when signals from the vestibular system conflict with those coming from the visual system (Lackner, 2014; Nooij et al., 2017).

TIMOTHY A. CLARY/Getty Images.

**How Is It Possible?**
Without a sense of kinesthesia, these performers from the Alvin Ailey American Dance Theater could not have performed this stunning pose. Kinesthesia enables us to know our body position and movement.

## Put Your Heads Together

 Take a moment to appreciate the sensory systems that allow you to know and adapt to the surrounding world. In your group, discuss **A)** how you would function without vision, hearing, smell, taste, and touch, and **B)** what steps you can take to preserve them (**TABLE 3.1**).

## *Apply This* ⬇

**TABLE 3.1**   Protecting Your Senses

| Sense | Simple Steps to Guard Against Damage |
|---|---|
| Vision | Don't smoke. Wear sunglasses and a hat in the sun. Both smoking and sun exposure heighten your risk of developing cataracts and other eye diseases. Put on protective eye gear when doing work or playing sports that could endanger your eyes (mowing the lawn or playing baseball, for example); 90% of eye injuries can be avoided by wearing the right eye gear (Boyd, 2020; Turbert, 2019, 2020). |
| Hearing | Listen to media players at or below half volume. Wear earplugs or earmuffs when using leaf-blowers, power tools, and other loud devices (American Speech-Language-Hearing Association, n.d.). If the sound level seems too high at your workplace, talk to your employer; you are legally entitled to a working environment that is safe for your ears (Occupational Safety & Health Administration, n.d.). |
| Smell | Two of the leading causes of olfactory loss are head trauma and upper respiratory tract infections like the common cold (Holbrook & Leopold, 2020; Keller & Malaspina, 2013). Avoid head injuries by buckling your seatbelt, wearing a bike helmet, and using protective headgear for contact sports. Minimize your exposure to respiratory viruses with regular hand washing. |
| Taste | Don't smoke. Nicotine may change the structure and function of the tongue's papillae, which could explain why most smokers have decreased sensitivity to taste (Pavlos et al., 2009). Smoking also impairs olfaction (Holbrook & Leopold, 2020) and therefore dampens the appreciation of flavors. |
| Touch | Touch receptors are located in the skin and throughout the body, so protecting your sense of touch means taking good care of your body in general. Spinal cord or brain injuries can lead to widespread loss of sensation, so take commonsense precautions like buckling your seatbelt and wearing protective headgear for biking, football, construction work, and so on. |

Here are just a few tips for protecting your senses. These measures should be considered in addition to regular medical checkups, such as annual eye exams and physicals.

**proprioceptors** Specialized nerve endings primarily located in the muscles and joints that provide information about body location and orientation.

**vestibular sense** The sense of balance and equilibrium.

## SHOW WHAT YOU KNOW

1. The chemical sense called _____ provides the sensation of smell.

2. Chemicals from food are released in saliva, where they dissolve and bathe the taste buds. The chemicals find matching receptors and latch on, sparking action potentials. This is an example of:

   **A.** olfaction.              **C.** sensory adaptation.

   **B.** transduction.          **D.** thermoreceptors.

3. List five things you are currently doing that involve the sense of kinesthesia.

4. Maya notices that her severe back pain seems to diminish when she laughs and enjoys the company of friends. This observation is consistent with _____ , which suggests a variety of biopsychosocial factors can interact to amplify or diminish pain perception.

   **A.** the theory of evolution

   **B.** an absolute threshold

   **C.** the gate-control theory

   **D.** proprioception

✔ CHECK YOUR ANSWERS AT THE BACK OF BOOK.

**Did He Have Synesthesia?**
A self-portrait by Vincent Van Gogh. When the Dutch painter took up piano in his early thirties, he began to associate musical notes with particular colors. The piano teacher thought something was wrong with Van Gogh, but his ability to associate musical notes with colors may have been a manifestation of synesthesia (Safran & Sanda, 2015). "Synesthesia is a rare nonpathological phenomenon where stimulation of one sense automatically provokes a secondary perception in another" (Tilot et al., 2018, p. 3168).

*Imagno/Getty Images.*

# Perception: Is It All in Your Head?

We have learned how the sensory systems absorb information and transform it into the electrical and chemical language of neurons. Now let's look more closely at *perception,* which draws from experience to organize and interpret sensory information, turning it into something meaningful.

Before moving forward, let's establish one fundamental principle: Perceptions are rife with bias and, often, inaccuracies. If you don't believe us, consider the following experiment: Researchers asked a group of people, about half of whom were wine experts, to describe the odor and flavor of different wine types. The participants were given three different glasses containing the following: a white wine, a rosé, and a fake rosé (the white wine dyed pink). When it came time to evaluate the aromas and flavors of the wines, the participants—particularly the wine experts—used red fruit adjectives (most notably, "strawberry") to describe *both* the real rosé and the fake rosé. Remember, the fake rosé was actually a white wine colored pink, and the amount of dye used had no perceptible effect on the odor or taste (Spence, 2020; Wang & Spence, 2019). Apparently, the wine experts had been tricked by their eyes! When they looked at the fake rosé wine, they believed they were seeing a real rosé, so they *perceived* rosé aromas and flavors. *Perception* is essential to our functioning, but as the wine-tasting example illustrates, it is sometimes misleading.

## Perception Deception

One of the best ways to reveal distortions in perceptual processes is by studying *illusions.* An **illusion** is a perception that is incongruent with actual sensory data, conveying an inaccurate representation of reality (**INFOGRAPHIC 3.3**). When perception is working "incorrectly," we can examine top-down processing, which draws on past experience to make sense of incoming information (Carbon, 2014). Illusions help us understand how top-down processing works (Brogaard & Gatzia, 2017). Let's examine one.

Look at the Müller–Lyer illusion in **FIGURE 3.9.** Lines (b) and (d) appear to be longer, but, in fact, all four lines (a–d) are equal in length. Why does this illusion

## FIGURE 3.9

**The Müller–Lyer Illusion**
Which line looks longer? All are, in fact, the same length. Visual depth cues cause you to perceive that (b) and (d) are longer because they appear farther away.

**illusion** A perception that is inconsistent with sensory data.

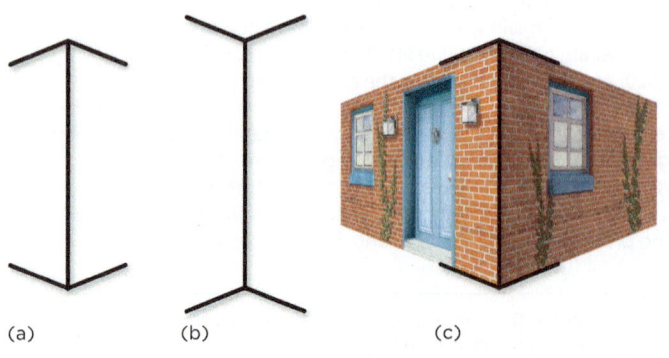

(a)          (b)          (c)          (d)

# Perceptual Illusions

What we see, hear, taste, touch, smell, and feel may seem very real, but perceptions are not always accurate representations of reality. The brain's perceptual systems are prone to errors and distortions. Studying illusions, like those shown here, we can detect and better understand the brain's misinterpretations of visual input.

## Moon illusion

Have you ever noticed that the moon can appear much larger when it's on the horizon versus high in the sky? Don't let perceptual errors trump logic: You know the moon does not change size! Researchers have yet to agree upon a definitive explanation for this illusion, but many suspect it has something to do with the surrounding environment (Weidner et al., 2014). Seeing the moon along with trees and other objects at different distances may influence our perception of the moon's size.

## Ponzo illusion

Which of the two orange bars is longer? Neither! They are identical. When you see two lines converging in the distance, your brain perceives them as getting farther away. Line A appears farther away. It seems longer because the images of the two lines projected onto the retina are the same size, but we interpret the farther line as being bigger. The Ponzo illusion demonstrates how we judge an object's size based on its context.

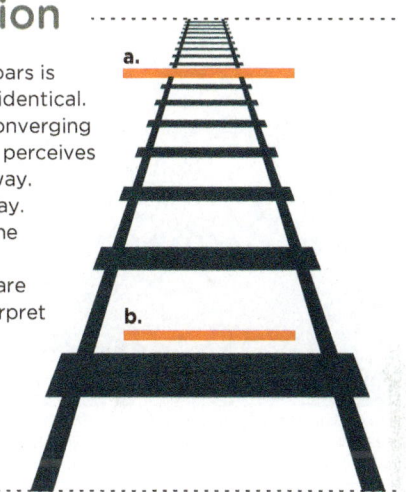

## Ames room illusion

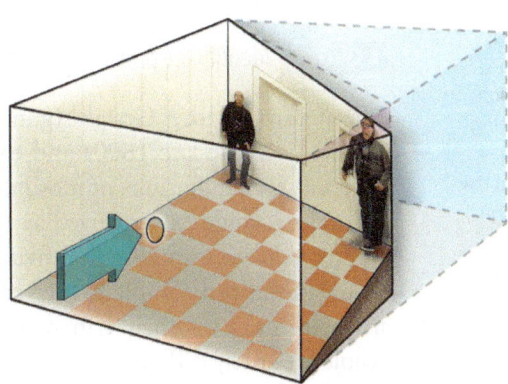

Would you believe that the two people in this room (photo far left) are approximately the same height? The woman on the right appears about twice as big, because the room isn't rectangular! The Ames room is actually trapezoidal (see diagram), but, as the photo shows, this is not apparent when it is viewed through a peephole with one eye.

## The Shepard Tables illusion

Look carefully at these two tables. Is one longer than the other? If you compare their measurements with your fingers or a piece of paper, you will see that both the length and width are identical.

The brain sees table (a) and thinks the back edge is farther away than table (b), and thus table (a) appears narrower and longer than table (b).

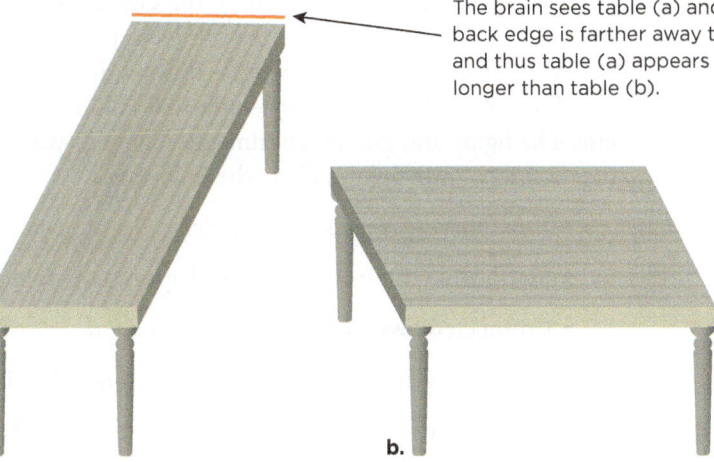

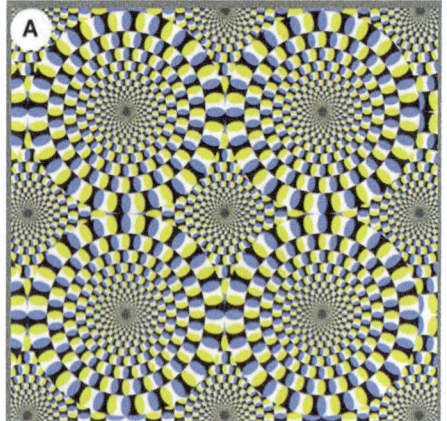

Regaiolli B., Rizzo A., Ottolini G., Miletto Petrazzini M.E., Spiezio C., and Agrillo C. (2019). Motion Illusions as Environmental Enrichment for Zoo Animals: A Preliminary Investigation on Lions (Panthera leo). *Front. Psychol.* 10:2220. doi: 10.3389/fpsyg.2019.02220. Creative Commons Attribution License (CC BY).

**Lions Fall for It, Too?**
A small study suggests that lions may be susceptible to some of the same visual illusions as humans. A group of researchers went to an Italian zoo and placed various images in the lion enclosure. One of those images was the "rotating snake" illusion (pictured in the bottom photo), which humans perceive as moving. Two out of the three lionesses in the study paid more attention to the rotating snake than the control images, suggesting "the intriguing possibility that they were attracted by the illusory motion" (Martinez-Conde, 2019; Regaiolli et al., 2019, para. 1).

**gestalt** The natural tendency for the brain to organize stimuli into a whole, rather than perceiving the parts and pieces.

**figure-ground** A central principle of Gestalt psychology, involving the shifting of focus; as attention is focused on one object, all other features drop or recede into the background.

occur? Our experience looking at buildings tells us that the corner presented in line (c) is nearer because it is jutting toward us. The corner presented in line (d) seems to be farther away because it is jutting away. Two objects of the same size but different distances from the eye will not project identical images on the retina; the farther object will project a smaller image. Through experience, the brain comes to expect this disparity. People living in "carpentered worlds" (that is, surrounded by structures constructed with corners, angles, and straight lines, as opposed to living in more "traditional" settings) are more likely to be tricked by this illusion because of their experience seeing manufactured structures. People in more traditional settings, without all the hard edges and straight lines, are less likely to fall prey to such an illusion (Masuda et al., 2020; Segall et al., 1968). However, other research suggests that the "processing mechanisms" involved in illusions may be hardwired (Gandhi et al., 2015). In what started as a humanitarian effort to help Indian children who were blind, neuroscientist Pawan Sinha and colleagues found that illusions were perceived by children and adolescents immediately following surgery to restore their sight (Chatterjee, 2015). This suggests that their vulnerability to illusions was not dependent on their environments.

Another visual illusion is *stroboscopic motion,* the appearance of motion produced when a sequence of still images is shown in rapid succession. (Think of drawing stick figures on the edges of book pages and then flipping the pages to see your figure "move.") Even infants appear to perceive this kind of motion (Valenza et al., 2006). Although illusions provide clues about how perception works, they cannot explain everything. Let's take a look at some universal principles of perceptual organization.

## The Whole Is Greater

**LO 13**   Identify the principles of perceptual organization.

Many turn to the Gestalt (guh-SHTAHLT) psychologists, who were active in Germany in the late 1800s and early 1900s, to understand how perception works. After observing illusions of motion, the Gestalt psychologists wondered how stationary objects could be perceived as moving and attempted to explain how the human mind organizes stimuli in the environment. Observing the tendency for perception to be organized and complete, they concluded that the brain naturally processes stimuli in their entirety rather than perceiving the parts and pieces. In other words, "the whole is entirely different from a mere sum; it is prior to its parts" (Wertheimer, 2014, p. 131). **Gestalt** means "whole" or "form" in German. The Gestalt psychologists, and others who followed, studied principles that explain how the brain perceives objects in the environment as wholes or groups (INFOGRAPHIC **3.4**).

One central idea illuminated by the Gestalt psychologists is the **figure-ground** principle (Fowlkes et al., 2007). As you focus your attention on a figure (for example, the vase in Infographic 3.4), all other features drop into the background. If, however, you direct your gaze onto the faces, the vase falls into the background with everything else. The figure and ground continually change as you shift your focus. Other gestalt organizational principles include the following:

- **Proximity**—Objects close to each other are perceived as a group.

- **Similarity**—Objects similar in shape or color are perceived as a group.

- **Connectedness**—Connected objects are perceived as a group.

- **Closure**—Gaps tend to be filled in if something isn't complete.

- **Continuity**—Parts tend to be perceived as members of a group if they head in the same direction.

# Gestalt Organizing Principles: The Whole Is Greater

The Gestalt psychologists identified principles that explain how the brain naturally organizes sensory information into meaningful wholes rather than distinct parts and pieces. These principles help you navigate the world by allowing you to see, for example, that the path you are walking on continues on the other side of an intersection. Gestalt principles also help you make sense of the information presented in your textbooks. Let's look at how this works.

## figure-ground

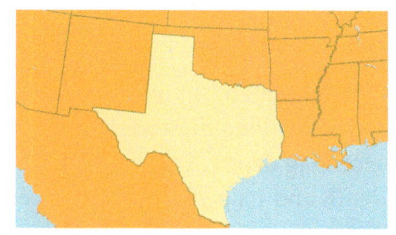

We tend to perceive visual stimuli as figures existing on a background. On this map, one area becomes the focus, while the rest functions as background.

Some stimuli, such as this classic figure–ground vase, are *reversible figures*. You see something different depending on whether you focus on the yellow or the black portion.

## LAW OF proximity

We tend to perceive objects that are near each other as a unit. This set of dots is perceived as three groups rather than six separate columns or 36 individual dots.

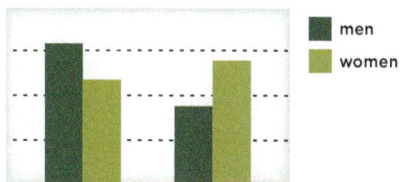

- men
- women

Proximity helps us read graphs like this one. We understand that bars close together should be compared.

## LAW OF similarity

We see objects as a group if they share features such as color or shape. In this example, we perceive eight vertical columns rather than four rows of alternating squares and dots.

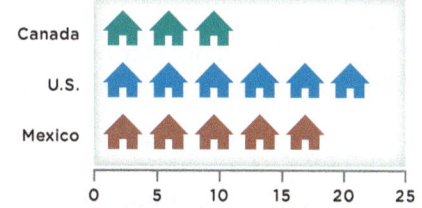

Canada
U.S.
Mexico

0   5   10   15   20   25

Similarity helps us read color-coded charts and graphs. We understand the graph above as having horizontal bars because we naturally group the similarly colored icons.

## LAW OF connectedness

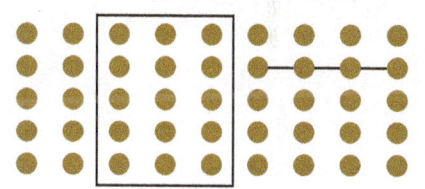

We tend to see objects as a group if there is something that connects them. In this group of dots, the ones enclosed in or connected by lines appear related even though all dots are the same.

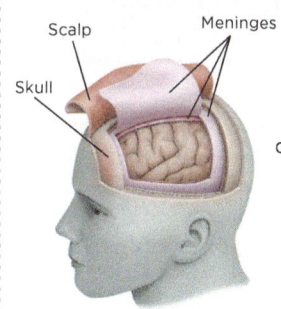

Scalp
Meninges
Skull

In a textbook figure, connectedness helps us understand what is being labeled.

## LAW OF closure

We tend to fill in incomplete parts of a line or figure. In this example, we perceive a circle even when the line is broken.

Closure allows us to read letters and images that are interrupted. We can read this letter even though it is made up of unconnected lines.

## LAW OF continuity

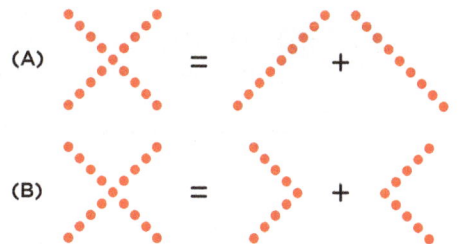

(A)
(B)

We perceive groups where objects appear to be going in the same direction. In this example, we perceive the figure as made up of two continuous lines that intersect (A) rather than two angles that are brought together (B).

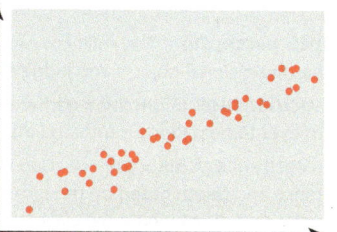

Continuity helps us read graphs like this scatterplot, where we perceive the overall pattern.

Although these organizational principles have been demonstrated for vision, it is important to note that they apply to the other senses as well (Barwich, 2019; Molloy et al., 2019). Imagine a father who can discern his child's voice amid the clamor of a busy playground: His child's voice is the figure and the other noises are the ground.

## Depth Perception

**LO 14** Describe some of the visual cues used in depth perception.

That same father can tell that the slide extends from the front of the jungle gym, thanks to his brain's ability to pick up on cues about depth. How can a two-dimensional image projected on the retina be perceived in three dimensions? There appear to be inborn abilities and learned cues for perceiving depth and distance. Let's start by examining the inborn ability to recognize depth and its potential for danger. Watch out, baby!

**Whoa, Baby**

A baby appears distressed when he encounters the visual cliff, a supportive glass surface positioned over a drop-off, or "cliff." Most babies will not proceed, even when coaxed by a trusted caregiver. This finding suggests that depth perception is already in place by the time a child is crawling (Gibson & Walk, 1960).

*Mark Richards/Photo Edit.*

**VISUAL CLIFF** In order to determine whether **depth perception** is innate or learned, researchers studied the behavior of babies approaching a "visual cliff" (see photo), a flat glass surface with a checkered tablecloth–like pattern directly underneath that gives the illusion of a drop-off (Gibson & Walk, 1960). The researchers placed infants ages 6 to 14 months at the edge of the glass. At the other end of the glass were the babies' mothers, coaxing them to crawl over. For the most part, the children refused to move toward what they perceived to be a drop-off, suggesting that the perception of depth was innate. Without ever having explored the edge of an actual abyss, these infants seemed instinctively to know it should be avoided. Interestingly, the original research included a series of studies with a variety of nonhuman animals, starting with rats, and then one-day-old chicks, newborn kids and lambs—and all of them avoided the visual cliff (Rodkey, 2015).

**BINOCULAR CUES** Some cues for perceiving depth are the result of information gathered by both eyes. **Binocular cues** provide information from the right and left eyes to help judge depth and distance. For example, **convergence** is the brain's interpretation of the tension (or lack thereof) in the eye muscles that direct where both eyes focus. If an object is close, there is more muscular tension (as the muscles turn our eyes inward toward our nose), and the object is perceived as near. This perception of distance is based on experience; throughout life, we have learned that muscular tension correlates with the proximity of the object: The more tension we experience, the closer the object. Take a moment to feel that tension.

**Try This** Point your finger up to the ceiling, arm straight, with both eyes open. Now slowly bring your finger close to your nose. Can you feel tension and strain in your eye muscles? Your brain uses this type of convergence cue to determine distance.

**depth perception** The ability to perceive three-dimensional objects and judge distances.

**binocular cues** Information gathered from both eyes to help judge depth and distance.

**convergence** A binocular cue used to judge distance and depth based on the tension of the muscles that direct where the eyes are focusing.

**retinal disparity** A binocular cue used to determine the distance of objects; the difference between the images seen by the right and left eyes.

Another binocular cue is **retinal disparity,** which is the difference between the images seen by the right and left eyes. The greater the difference, the closer the object. The more similar the two images, the farther the object. With experience, our brains begin using these image disparities to judge distance. The following Try This provides an example of retinal disparity.

 **Try This** Hold your index finger about 4 inches in front of your face pointing up to the ceiling. Quickly open your right eye as you are closing your left eye, alternating this activity for a few seconds; it should appear as if your finger is jumping back and forth. Repeat the procedure with your finger out at arm's length. Does the image seem to jump as much?

**MONOCULAR CUES**    Judgments about depth and distance can also be informed by **monocular cues**, which do not necessitate the use of both eyes. An artist who paints pictures can transform a white canvas into a three-dimensional perceptual experience by using techniques that take advantage of monocular cues. The monocular cues include (but are not limited to) the following:

- **Relative size**—If two objects are similar in actual size, but one is farther away, it appears to be smaller. We interpret the larger object as being closer.

- **Linear perspective**—When two lines start off parallel, then come together, where they converge appears farther away than where they are parallel.

- **Interposition**—When one object is in front of another, it partially blocks the view of the other object, and this partially blocked object appears more distant.

- **Texture gradient**—When objects are closer, it is easier to see their texture. As they get farther away, the texture becomes less visible. The more apparent the texture, the closer the object appears.

## Put Your Heads Together

 **A)** Write down the six gestalt organizational principles and four monocular cues on a sheet of paper. **B)** Find examples of each in the photos of this textbook. **C)** Team up with a classmate and compare your lists.

## CAREER CONNECTIONS

### IS ART IN YOUR FUTURE?

Understanding perceptual principles is essential for anyone pursuing a career in graphic design, animation, architecture, and other artistic fields. Suppose you are designing an online banner or a pop-up ad. People will be viewing the images you create on a two-dimensional computer screen, but you can simulate a three-dimensional experience using texture gradient, motion parallax, and other perceptual cues (Liao et al., 2018). If you're an architect drawing up blueprints, you can use depth cues and lighting tricks to make spaces appear larger than they actually are (Tai, 2015). Or suppose you are designing a virtual reality environment for a video game. The user will be wearing a head-mounted display with a screen positioned just inches from the eyes, so you will need to use retinal disparity to create a sense of depth (Turnbull & Phillips, 2017).

## Is That What I Think It Is?

All these perceptual skills are great—if you are standing still—but the world is constantly moving. How do our perceptual systems adapt to changes? We possess the ability to perceive objects as having stable properties even though our environments are always changing. **Perceptual constancy** refers to the tendency to perceive objects as maintaining their shape, size, and color even when the angle, lighting, and distance change. A door is shaped like a rectangle, but when it opens, the image

PATRICK KOVARIK/Getty Images.

**Monocular Cues**
You can gauge the distance and depth in this photo with at least four types of monocular cues: (1) People who are farther away look smaller (relative size). (2) The two sides of the street start out parallel but converge as distance increases (linear perspective). (3) The trees in the front block those that are behind (interposition). (4) Textures are more apparent for closer objects (texture gradient).

Image Source/Getty Images.

**Shape Constancy**
How do you know that all these doors are the same size and shape? The images projected onto your retina suggest that the opened doors are narrower, nonrectangular shapes. Your brain, however, knows from experience that all the opened doors are identical rectangles.

**monocular cues** Depth and distance cues that require the use of only one eye.

**perceptual constancy** The tendency to perceive objects in our environment as stable in terms of shape, size, and color, regardless of changes in the sensory data received.

### What Color Are They?

Believe it or not, there are no red pixels in this image, just gray and green hues (Kircher, 2017). The strawberries look red as a result of color constancy; we see the world in stable colors, even when the sensory data arriving at our photoreceptors are variable.

Akiyoshi Kitaoka.

### Letters or Numbers?

Look in the green square. What do you see? That depends on whether you viewed the symbol as belonging to a row of letters (A B C) or a column of numbers (12 13 14). Perceptions are shaped by the context in which a stimulus occurs, and our expectations about that stimulus.

**shape constancy** An object is perceived as maintaining its shape, regardless of the image projected on the retina.

**size constancy** An object is perceived as maintaining its size, regardless of the image projected on the retina.

**color constancy** Objects are perceived as maintaining their color, even with changing sensory data.

**perceptual set** The tendency to perceive stimuli in a specific manner based on past experiences and expectations.

projected on our retina is not a rectangle. Yet, we still perceive the door as having a rectangular shape. This is called **shape constancy,** and sometimes it can be misleading. When people are shown pictures of windows from a variety of perspectives, and then asked to match those images with outlines of shapes, they often have a difficult time choosing an outline that matches the angle of the window. More often than not, shape constancy takes over and participants pick shapes that look more like rectangles than the actual shape of the window images they saw (Cohen & Jones, 2008). Interestingly, artists don't seem to be any better at making these types of matches than nonartists (Ostrofsky et al., 2012).

As you gaze down at cars and trucks from the window of an airplane, they may look like bugs scurrying around, but you know some are as big as elephants because your perceptual toolkit also includes **size constancy.** Through experience, we get to know the size of everyday objects and perceive them accordingly, regardless of whether they are far or near. Similarly, **color constancy** allows us to see the world in stable colors, even when the sensory data arriving at our photoreceptors change. A bright red backpack appears bright red outside in the sunshine or inside a house. The light waves bouncing off the backpack have changed, but your understanding of the color has not been altered.

Although examples of these organizational tendencies occur with robust regularity, some of them are not universal. Certain studies suggest that children *learn* to perceive size constancy. For example, their ability to estimate the size of distant objects improves by around 9 years old, in step with cognitive developments such as improved reasoning (Granrud, 2009; Kavšek & Granrud, 2012).

Learning also plays a role in the phenomenon of **perceptual set**—the tendency to perceive stimuli in a specific manner based on past experiences and expectations. If someone handed you a picture of two women and said, "This is a mother with her daughter," you would be more likely to rate them as looking alike than if you had been given the exact same picture and told, "These women are unrelated." Indeed, research shows that people who believe they are looking at parent–child pairs are more likely to rate the pairs as similar than those who believe the members of the pairs are not related (even though they are looking at the same adult–child pairs; Oda et al., 2005). In short, we tend to see what we are looking for.

Perceptual sets are molded by the context of the moment, including the words you are hearing (Forder & Lupyan 2019). For example, if a news reporter uses the word "sects" in a story about feuding religious groups, you are unlikely to think they are saying "sex" even though "sects" and "sex" sound almost the same. Similarly, if you see a baby swaddled in a blue blanket, you are probably more likely to assume it's a boy than a girl. Such expectancies apply to crying babies as well—higher-pitched cries are assumed to be those of female infants, even though there are no measurable sex differences in the pitch of their cries. In one study, adults not only wrongly assumed they could attribute "sex and gender-related traits to crying babies," they were often misguided in their "assessment of the babies' discomfort" (Reby et al., 2016, p. 7). Think about how perceptual sets might lead to unfair treatment—not only of boys and girls, but also of people belonging to various races, religions, and cultures.

## NOTHING STANDS IN HER WAY

Looking back on her life, Mandy is thankful for everything that happened—even the devastating loss of her hearing. "The whole experience itself has changed who I am," Mandy says. "As a musician, I would adore being able to listen to music again, but I wouldn't trade the experience, and everything that I've learned, for any of it. . . . I've grown so much as a person." As for the future, Mandy wants to continue making music, performing, and spreading her message. You can learn more about her music, tours, and other projects by visiting mandyharveymusic.com, or by reading her book, *Sensing the Rhythm: Finding My Voice in a World Without Sound.*

Al Pereira/Getty Images.

**Shining Star**
Mandy performs the National Anthem at a New York Giants game at MetLife Stadium in 2018.

 **SHOW WHAT YOU KNOW**

1. One binocular cue called _____ is based on the brain's interpretation of the tension in muscles of the eyes.
   A. convergence
   B. retinal disparity
   C. interposition
   D. relative size

2. _____ means the "whole" or "form" in German.

✓ CHECK YOUR ANSWERS AT THE BACK OF BOOK.

# Summary of Concepts

**LO 1** Define sensation and perception and explain how they are different. (p. 84)

Sensation is the process by which receptors in our sensory organs receive and detect stimuli. Perception is the process of giving meaning to sensations. Bottom-up processing describes how the brain takes in basic sensory information and processes it. Top-down processing uses past experiences and knowledge in order to understand sensory information.

**LO 2** Define transduction and explain how it relates to sensation. (p. 86)

Sensory organs receive stimuli from the environment (for example, sound waves, light waves). Transduction is the transformation of stimuli into electrical and chemical signals. The neural signals are then processed by the central nervous system, resulting in what we consciously experience as sensations.

**LO 3** Describe and differentiate between absolute thresholds and difference thresholds. (p. 87)

One of the important goals of studying sensation and perception is to determine absolute thresholds, the weakest stimuli that can be detected 50% of the time. Difference thresholds indicate the minimum difference between two stimuli noticed 50% of the time. According to Weber's law, certain ratios

determine these difference thresholds. The ability to detect weak signals in the environment depends on many factors.

**LO 4** Summarize the properties of light and color, and describe the structure and function of the eye. (p. 90)

The eyes do not sense faces, objects, or scenery; they detect light, which is a form of electromagnetic energy. Visible light comprises one small portion of the electromagnetic spectrum, which also includes gamma rays, X-rays, ultraviolet light, infrared light, microwaves, and radio waves. The color, or hue, of visible light is determined by its wavelength. Apart from their hue, colors can be characterized by brightness (intensity) and saturation (purity). When light first enters the eye, it passes through a glassy outer layer known as the cornea. Then it travels through a hole called the pupil, followed by the lens. Both the cornea and the lens focus the incoming light waves, and the lens can change shape in order to adjust to objects near and far. Finally, the light travels through the eye's jellylike center and reaches the retina, where it is transduced into neural activity.

**LO 5** Describe the functions of rods and cones. (p. 93)

There are two types of photoreceptors in the retina: rods and cones. Rods are extremely sensitive to light; they enable vision in dim lighting but do not provide the sensation of color. Cones enable us to sense color and discern details, but they are not used when ambient light is low. Rods are found throughout the retina, but not in the fovea; this is where the cones are concentrated. Neither rods nor cones are found in the optic disc.

**LO 6** Explain how the trichromatic theory and the opponent-process theory help us understand color vision. (p. 96)

The trichromatic theory of color vision suggests there are three types of cones: red, green, and blue. The three types of cones fire in response to different electromagnetic wavelengths. The opponent-process theory of color vision suggests that in addition to the color-sensitive cones, we also have neurons that respond differently to opponent colors. These colors cannot be viewed simultaneously (for example, red–green, blue–yellow).

**LO 7** Summarize how sound waves are converted into the sensation of hearing. (p. 99)

Audition is the term used for the sense of hearing. Sound waves enter the ear, causing the eardrum to vibrate, which initiates a chain reaction in the tiny bones of the middle ear. The oval window vibrates, moving fluid in the cochlea (a fluid-filled, snail-shaped organ of the inner ear). The cochlea is lined with the basilar membrane, which contains hair cells that bend in response to the moving fluid, causing nearby nerve cells to fire. Neural messages are sent through the auditory nerve to the auditory cortex via the thalamus.

**LO 8** Illustrate how we sense different pitches of sound. (p. 103)

Place theory suggests that the location of neural activity along the cochlea allows us to sense different pitches of high-frequency sounds. With a high-frequency sound, vibrations occur closer to the end of the basilar membrane near the oval window. Frequency theory suggests that the frequency of the neural impulses determines the experience of pitch. The entire basilar membrane vibrates at the same rate as the sound wave, triggering neural impulses at this same rate. Place theory explains how we perceive pitches from 4,000 Hz to 20,000 Hz. Frequency theory explains how we perceive lower pitches. The volley principle explains how the frequency theory applies to sound frequencies that exceed neuron firing capacity. Essentially, neurons work together so their combined firing reaches frequencies higher than one neuron can achieve alone.

**LO 9** Describe the process of olfaction. (p. 104)

Olfaction (sense of smell) is called a chemical sense because it involves sensing chemicals in the environment. Molecules from odor-emitting objects in our environments make their way into our nostrils up through the nose or mouth. The olfactory epithelium is home to millions of olfactory receptor neurons, which provide receptors for odor molecules. When enough odor molecules bind to the receptor neuron, a signal is sent to the brain.

**LO 10** Discuss the structures involved in taste and describe how they work. (p. 107)

Gustation (sense of taste) is also a chemical sense. The receptor cells for taste are located in the taste buds, which are embedded in the tongue's papillae, the roof of the mouth, and the lining of the cheeks. Each taste bud contains 50 to 100 taste receptor cells, which provide binding sites for taste molecules. Taste is essential for survival, pushing organisms toward needed foods and away from harmful ones.

**LO 11** Explain how the biopsychosocial perspective helps us understand pain. (p. 111)

The biopsychosocial perspective explains the perception of pain by exploring biological, psychological, and social factors. According to the gate-control theory, a person's perception of pain can increase or decrease depending on how the brain interprets pain signals. Neural activity makes its way to the brain, where it is processed. The brain can block pain by sending a message via the spinal cord to "close the gates" so the pain won't be felt.

**LO 12** Illustrate how we sense the position and movement of our bodies. (p. 112)

Kinesthesia is the sense of position and movement of the body. We know how our body parts are oriented in space because of specialized nerve endings called proprioceptors, which are primarily located in the muscles and joints. Our proprioceptors monitor changes in the position of body parts and the tension in our muscles. The vestibular sense helps us deal with the effects of gravity, movement, and body position in order to keep us balanced.

**LO 13** Identify the principles of perceptual organization. (p. 116)

Gestalt psychologists sought to explain how the human mind organizes stimuli from the environment. They realized that the brain naturally organizes stimuli in their entirety rather than perceiving the parts and pieces. Gestalt indicates a tendency for human perception to be organized and complete. The organizational principles include proximity, similarity, connectedness, closure, and continuity.

**LO 14** Describe some of the visual cues used in depth perception. (p. 118)

Depth perception appears partially to be an innate ability. Babies in the visual cliff experiment, for example, refused to move toward what they perceived to be a drop-off. Binocular cues are the result of information gathered from both eyes, and they help us judge depth and distance. Monocular cues can be used by either eye alone and also help judge depth and distance.

# Key Terms

absolute thresholds, p. 87
accommodation, p. 92
afterimage, p. 97
amplitude, p. 91
audition, p. 99
binocular cues, p. 118
blind spot, p. 93
bottom-up processing, p. 84
cochlea, p. 101
color constancy, p. 120
cones, p. 93
convergence, p. 118
cornea, p. 92
dark adaptation, p. 95

depth perception, p. 118
difference threshold, p. 87
feature detectors, p. 95
figure-ground, p. 116
frequency, p. 99
frequency theory, p. 103
gate-control theory, p. 111
gestalt, p. 116
gustation, p. 107
hue, p. 91
illusion, p. 114
iris, p. 92
kinesthesia, p. 112
light adaptation, p. 95

monocular cues, p. 119
olfaction, p. 104
opponent-process theory, p. 97
optic nerve, p. 93
perception, p. 84
perceptual constancy, p. 119
perceptual set, p. 120
photoreceptors, p. 93
pitch, p. 99
place theory, p. 103
proprioceptors, p. 113
retina, p. 93
retinal disparity, p. 118

rods, p. 93
saturation, p. 91
sensation, p. 84
sensory adaptation, p. 87
shape constancy, p. 120
signal detection theory, p. 88
size constancy, p. 120
top-down processing, p. 84
transduction, p. 86
trichromatic theory, p. 96
vestibular sense, p. 113
volley principle, p. 103
wavelength, p. 90
Weber's law, p. 88

# Test Prep Are You Ready?

1. Stimuli are detected through the process called:
   A. perception.
   B. interposition.
   C. sensation.
   D. top-down processing.

2. You're listening to your favorite playlist. The sound waves transmitted through your earbuds lead to vibrations in the fluid in your cochlea. This activity causes the hair cells to bend, which causes nearby nerve cells to fire. This process of transforming stimuli into electrical and chemical signals of neurons is:
   A. transduction.       C. top-down processing.
   B. perception.         D. convergence.

3. While riding your bike, you get something in your eye. As the day goes on, your eye still feels irritated. It is possible you've scratched your _____, which is the transparent outer layer that protects the eye and bends light to help focus light waves.
   A. lens
   B. retina
   C. iris
   D. cornea

4. The various types of electromagnetic energy can be distinguished by their _____, only some of which can be detected by the human eye.
   A. binocular cues
   B. wavelengths
   C. proprioceptors
   D. feature detectors

5. In color vision, the opponent-process theory was developed to explain the _____, which could not be explained by the _____ theory.
   A. afterimage effect; trichromatic
   B. blind spot; place
   C. feature detectors; trichromatic
   D. color deficiencies; frequency

6. Frequency theory of pitch perception suggests it is the number of _____ that allows us to perceive differences in pitch.
   A. hair cells
   B. feature detectors
   C. neural impulses firing
   D. monocular cues

7. The wiring of the olfactory system is unique. Other sensory systems relay information through the _____ before it is passed along to higher brain centers, but this is not the case for olfaction.
   A. thalamus
   B. corpus callosum
   C. reticular formation
   D. basilar membrane

8. We are aware of our body position in space because of specialized nerve endings called _____, which are primarily located in joints and muscles.
   A. proprioceptors
   B. Meissner's corpuscles
   C. Pacinian corpuscles
   D. nociceptors

9. Hector is staring at the small print on the back of his credit card. Which of the following would be a binocular cue indicating how close the credit card is to his face?
   A. tension of the muscles focusing the eyes
   B. relative size of two similar objects
   C. feature detectors
   D. interposition

10. One of the gestalt organizational principles suggests that objects close to each other are perceived as a group. This is known as:
    A. continuity.        C. similarity.
    B. closure.           D. proximity.

11. Use the evolutionary perspective to explain the importance of any two aspects of human taste.

12. What are the different functions of the rods and cones? Give examples illustrating when your rods would be important for seeing something, and when your cones would be important.

13. The transformation of a sound wave into the experience of hearing follows a complicated path. To better understand the process, draw a diagram starting with a stimulus in the environment and ending with the sound heard by an individual.

14. Describe the biological activity underlying the pain you feel after stubbing your toe—both the sharp immediate pain and the dull pain that lingers several minutes afterward.

15. Describe the difference between absolute threshold and difference threshold.

✔ CHECK YOUR ANSWERS AT THE BACK OF THE BOOK.

Boy_Anupong/Getty Images.

# Consciousness

## An Introduction to Consciousness

**FRONT-ROW SEAT TO CONSCIOUSNESS**   Every day that Dr. Divya Chander walks through the doors of the hospital, she assumes a tremendous responsibility: keeping people alive and comfortable as they are sliced, prodded, and stitched back together by surgeons. Dr. Chander is an anesthesiologist, a medical doctor whose primary responsibility is to oversee a patient's vital functions and manage pain before, during, and after surgery. Using powerful drugs that manipulate the nervous system, she makes sure a patient's heart rate, blood pressure, and other critical processes remain in a safe range. She also administers drugs that block pain, paralyze muscles, and prevent memory formation (temporarily, of course). "I am very, very privileged that, as an anesthesiologist, I have access to these drugs that I use on a regular basis in order to make [patients'] lives better, to make surgery possible for them,"

Macmillan Learning, photo by Norbert von der Groeben.

**Exploring Inner Space**

As a child, Dr. Divya Chander dreamed of becoming a neuroscientist and an astronaut. She went on to earn both an MD and a PhD in neuroscience and now practices anesthesiology. As for the astronaut dream, it nearly became reality when she made it to the final round of NASA's astronaut selection. Dr. Chander still aspires to become a space explorer, but for now her exploration centers on what you might call "inner space"—uncovering the mysteries of consciousness.

Dr. Chander explains. Working as an anesthesiologist also affords Dr. Chander a unique opportunity to observe the brain as it falls into a deeper-than-sleep state, unaware of the outside world, and then emerges from the darkness, awake and alert. In other words, she has the ability to study human brains as they pass through various levels of *consciousness.*

## What Is Consciousness?

**LO 1**  Define consciousness.

The concept of *consciousness* can be difficult to pinpoint. Psychologist G. William Farthing offers a good starting point: **Consciousness** is "the subjective state of being currently aware of something either within oneself or outside of oneself" (1992, p. 6). Thus, consciousness might be conceived as a state of being aware of oneself, one's thoughts, and/or the environment. According to this definition of subjective awareness, one can be asleep and still be aware (Farthing, 1992).

We might also conceptualize consciousness as "the feeling of what it is like" to be someone (Klein, 2020, p. 2). What is it like to be you? This is your conscious experience, and only you are privy to it. Yet another conceptualization suggests that consciousness consists of two categories: (1) information in the brain, and (2) a "more mysterious, extra, experiential essence that people claim accompanies the informational content," but which is actually just our attempt to make sense of the information (Graziano et al., 2020, p. 156).

While such descriptions are useful, we should note that there is no universally agreed upon explanation of consciousness (Doerig et al., 2020). As scholars point out, "there are dozens of very different [theories of consciousness] and there is no clear, largely accepted 'winner'" (Doerig et al., 2020, p. 2). Scientists may not agree upon the exact definition of consciousness, but that doesn't mean they can't study it (Klein, 2020; Koch, 2018). This is a vibrant area of research, with accumulating evidence revealing how and where consciousness emerges in the brain (de Haan et al., 2020; Koch, 2018).

As we try to understand consciousness, we should consider two important concepts: (1) the *content of consciousness,* and (2) *states of consciousness.* The content of consciousness refers to what it holds, both within and outside our awareness. Suppose you are on a Zoom call with your classmates. The face of the person being spotlighted, what they are saying, and the items in their background may escape your awareness but nevertheless register (artwork on the wall, a coffee mug on the desk). All these things form the content of your consciousness at this moment. States of consciousness include conscious experiences (being awake) and unconscious experiences (being under anesthesia). During your Zoom call, you are awake and alert (we hope). But later in the day, you may doze off and enter a different state of consciousness (Doerig et al., 2020).

"Sometimes people think that when you lose consciousness, or you go to sleep, that your brain is less active," explains Dr. Chander. "In some dimensions it is less active," she notes, "[but] a better characterization might be that it's less functionally connected to itself." In other words, there is less communication occurring between different parts of the brain. As a person lies on the operating table, in a "less conscious" state, the brain also seems to be doing fewer calculations, processing less information. "When I say 'less conscious,' I do literally mean that because I do think it's an entire spectrum," Dr. Chander explains. "There isn't just 'unconscious' and 'conscious.' There are varied depths of consciousness."

**consciousness**  The state of being aware of oneself, one's thoughts, and/or the environment.

*Note:* Quotations attributed to Dr. Divya Chander and Matt Utesch are personal communications.

**A DELICATE BALANCE**    For a patient undergoing major surgery, the goal is to decrease the level of consciousness to a point where pain is no longer felt and awareness of the outside world dissipates. But the anesthesiologist must be careful; giving too much anesthetic can suppress vital functions and kill a person. To reduce consciousness and keep patients safe, the anesthesiologist must give just the right combination, and proper dosage, of anesthetic drugs. To keep her patients in this safe zone, Dr. Chander constantly monitors their brain activity with an electroencephalogram (EEG), which picks up electrical signals from the brain's surface (the cortex) and displays this information on a screen. Looking at the EEG monitor, Dr. Chander can determine a patient's depth of anesthesia, or the degree to which the drugs have induced a "hypnotic state," or changed their level of consciousness. Changes in wave frequency tell her when a patient is becoming "light" (getting close to waking up), "deep" (in a profound slumber, deeper than sleep), and even when they are receiving a particular drug.

Dr. Chander is unusual in this respect; most anesthesiologists are not trained to read an EEG with this level of precision (in addition to her medical degree, Dr. Chander has a PhD in neuroscience). Instead, they rely on other, less direct, indicators of consciousness, such as **blood pressure** and heart rate. This approach actually works very well because the amount of anesthetic needed to suppress blood pressure, heart rate, and movement is greater than that required to suppress consciousness (Aranake et al., 2013). But Dr. Chander's ability to read raw EEG data and her deep knowledge of neuroscience put her in an ideal position to track her patients' levels of consciousness.

## Studying Consciousness

Without modern technologies such as EEG, early psychologists were very limited in their ability to conduct research on consciousness. But that didn't stop them from trying. **Wilhelm Wundt and his student Edward Titchener** founded psychology as a science based on exploring consciousness and its contents. Another early psychologist, William James, believed consciousness serves a functional purpose. As one scholar points out, our "ordinary, waking state of consciousness" may help us survive in the world, while other states of consciousness such as meditation and dreaming could provide insights we may not glean from our normal waking experience (Cardeña, 2020). James regarded consciousness as a "stream" that provides a sense of day-to-day continuity (James, 1890/1983). Think about how this "stream" of thoughts is constantly rushing through your head. An e-mail from an old friend appears in your inbox, jogging your memory of the birthday party she threw last month, and that reminds you that tomorrow is your mother's birthday (better not forget that one). You notice your shoe is untied, think about school starting tomorrow, and remember the credit card bill you need to pay, all within a matter of seconds. Thoughts interweave and overtake each other like currents of flowing water; sometimes they are connected by topic, emotion, events, but other times they don't seem to be connected by anything other than your stream of consciousness.

Although psychology started with the introspective study of consciousness (Graiver, 2019), American psychologists John B. Watson, B. F. Skinner, and other behaviorists promoted the idea that psychology should restrict itself to the study of observable behaviors. The field broadened to include behaviorism and other perspectives during the 1930s, but the study of cognition was never abandoned. Then, in the 1950s, psychology experienced what has been called a *cognitive revolution,* or *cognitive turn,* as

Macmillan Learning, photo by Norbert von der Groeben.

**See It in the EEG**

Dr. Chander and a colleague review an electroencephalogram (EEG), the technology she uses to monitor her patients' level of consciousness. By observing the changes in wave frequency, she can tell if the patient is in a deep unconscious state, approaching wakefulness, or somewhere in between.

**CONNECTIONS**

Anesthetic drugs can lower blood pressure and heart rate by suppressing the sympathetic nervous system. In **Chapter 2,** we discussed how the sympathetic nervous system orchestrates the "fight-or-flight" response, prepping the body to respond to stressful situations. Surgery would certainly qualify as a stressful situation.

**CONNECTIONS**

In **Chapter 1,** we discussed the contributions of these early psychologists. Wundt founded the first psychology laboratory, edited the first psychology journal, and used experimentation to measure psychological processes. Titchener aimed to determine the structure and most basic elements of the mind.

### Are Animals Conscious?

The question is not *if* animals possess consciousness (evidence suggests many of them do), but rather what type of consciousness they experience (Birch et al., 2020). Chimpanzees, elephants, dolphins, and even some birds and fish have passed the mirror-mark test, "a classic test for self-awareness in animals" (Kohda et al., 2019, p. 2). To conduct the test, researchers put a mark on the animal's body and place it in front of a mirror. Then they watch for behaviors indicating the animal understands it is looking at its own body—scratching at the mark, for example (Birch et al., 2020).

### CONNECTIONS

In **Chapter 1,** we presented the concept of objective reports, which are free of opinions, beliefs, expectations, and values. Here, we note that descriptions of consciousness are subjective (unique or personal) and do not lend themselves to objective reporting.

psychologists began using new technologies and theoretical approaches to probe the mind (Braat et al., 2020). **Cognitive psychology,** the scientific study of conscious and unconscious mental processes such as thinking, problem solving, and language, emerged as a major subfield. Today, understanding consciousness is an important goal of psychology, and many believe science can be used to investigate its mysteries, although researchers don't always agree on which approaches should be used (Albertazzi, 2020).

In her neuroscience research, Dr. Chander has employed a cutting-edge technology called *optogenetics* that uses genetics and light sources to control the activities of individual neurons (Zhao, 2017). With optogenetics, researchers can activate or deactivate neurons or groups of neurons and see how these changes affect animals' behavior (Chong et al., 2020; Deisseroth, 2015). This technology helps Dr. Chander search for groups of neurons that may act as "on" or "off" switches for different states of consciousness (asleep versus awake, for example).

Technologies like optogenetics and functional magnetic resonance imaging (fMRI) have added to our growing knowledge base (Song & Knöpfel, 2016; Winter et al., 2020), yet barriers to studying consciousness remain. One is that consciousness is **subjective**, pertaining only to the individual who experiences it. Thus, some have argued it is impossible to *objectively* study another's conscious experience (Blackmore, 2005; Farthing, 1992). Then there is the mind–body conundrum: How does tangible physical matter (firing neurons) give rise to perceptions, thoughts, and emotions that seem so intangible (Blackmore, 2018; FIGURE **4.1**)? To make matters more complicated, one's conscious experience changes from moment to moment. In spite of these challenges, researchers around the world are inching closer to understanding

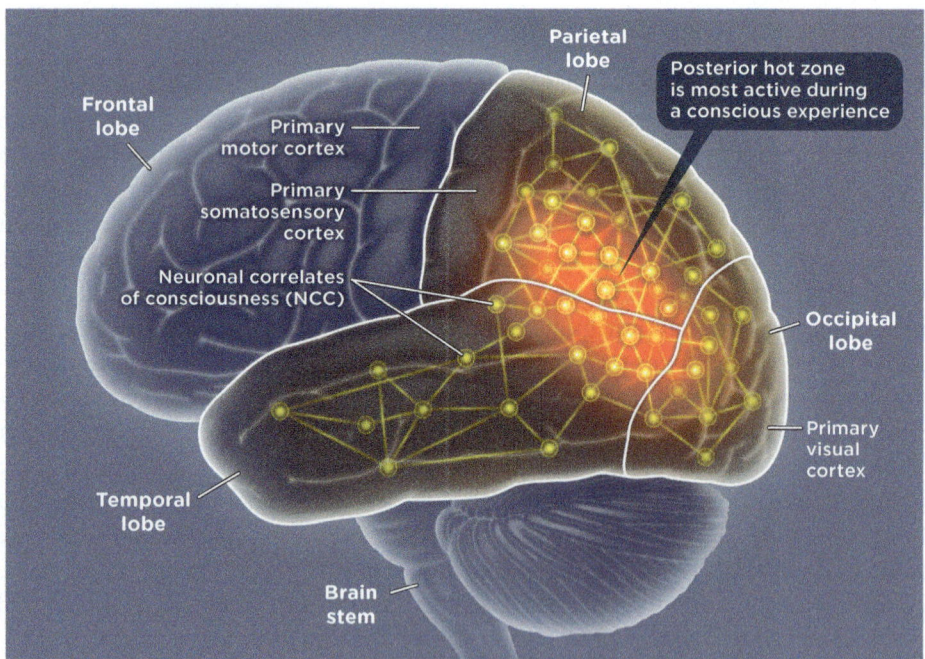

## FIGURE 4.1
### Where Does Consciousness Dwell?

Conscious experiences, or so-called qualia, are accompanied by activity in the brain's *posterior hot zone* (illuminated area), which includes parts of the occipital, parietal, and temporal lobes. Whether you are enjoying your favorite Netflix series, smelling sautéed garlic, or picking the perfect emoji to text your friend, this area of the brain is sure to be active. As neuroscientist Christof Koch explains, "It appears that the sights, sounds and other sensations of life as we experience it are generated by regions within the posterior cortex. As far as we can tell, almost all conscious experiences have their origin there." Research from Koch, 2018, para 15.

**cognitive psychology**  The scientific study of mental processes such as thinking, problem solving, and language.

consciousness by studying it from many perspectives (Frewen et al., 2020; Maraldi, & Krippner, 2019; Oluwole, 2019). Welcome to the world of consciousness and its many shades of gray.

## Are You Paying Attention?

There are many elements of conscious experience, including desire, thought, language, knowledge of self, and emotion. Memory is also involved, as conscious experiences usually involve the retrieval of memories (Chapter 6). Essentially, any cognitive process is potentially a part of your conscious experience (Chapter 7). Let's look at what this means, for example, when you go shopping on the internet. Your ability to navigate a store website hinges on your recognition of visual images (*There are 6 items in my shopping cart*), language aptitude (for reading), and motor skills (for typing and clicking). While browsing products, you access various memories (which link you just clicked, the shoes you saw last week, and so on)—all of this is part of your consciousness, your stream of thought. While carrying out this purchase, you are probably paying *attention* to what you are doing, or perhaps your attention is divided between this task and something else, like a text message exchange you are having at the same time. The precise relationship between consciousness and attention is disputed (Pitts et al., 2018), but where we direct our attention plays a key role in our conscious experience. Let's explore attention a little further.

**LO 2**  Explain how automatic processing relates to consciousness.

**AUTOMATIC PROCESSING**    Stop reading and listen. Do you hear background sounds you didn't notice before—a soft breeze rustling through the curtains, a clock ticking? You may not have been paying attention to these sounds, but your brain was monitoring them all along. In describing consciousness, psychologists often distinguish between cognitive processes that occur *automatically* (without effort, awareness, or control) and those that require us to focus on specific sensory input (with effort and awareness, we choose where and when to direct our attention). Our **sensory systems** detect an enormous amount of information, and the brain must sift through these data and determine what is important and needs immediate attention, what can be ignored, and what can be processed and stored for later use. This **automatic processing** allows us to attend to information with little or no conscious effort or awareness (Chapter 6; Hasher & Zacks, 1979, 1984). Without automatic processing, we would be overwhelmed with data.

Automatic processing can also refer to the involuntary cognitive activity guiding some behaviors. Some behaviors seem to occur without intentional awareness and without getting in the way of our other activities (Hassin et al., 2009). Do you remember the last time you walked a familiar route, talking on the phone and sending texts the entire time? Somehow you arrived at your destination without noticing much about your surroundings. You were conscious enough to complete complex tasks, but not enough to realize that you were doing so. This type of multitasking is commonplace, though research suggests only around 2.5% of people might be able to do it flawlessly. The rest of us have trouble handling the "cognitive overload" associated with juggling multiple tasks (Medeiros-Ward et al., 2015; Watson & Strayer, 2010). We should note that "multitasking" is actually a misnomer. The human brain simply does not have the attentional capacity to conduct two different cognitive tasks simultaneously. So, when it feels like you are texting and listening to an e-reader simultaneously, your attention is really just switching between the two tasks at a fast rate (Denning et al., 2018). See TABLE **4.1** on the next page for solutions to some multitasking problems.

### CONNECTIONS

In **Chapter 3,** we introduced the concept of sensory adaptation, the process by which our sensory receptors become less sensitive to constant stimuli (causing us to become less aware of unchanging conditions). This better prepares us to detect environmental changes that may require our attention. Here, we see how this can occur with automatic processing.

**automatic processing**  Attending to information with little or no conscious effort or awareness.

**TABLE 4.1    Be Smart About Multitasking**

| Problem | Solution |
|---|---|
| You think you can drive safely while using your phone, because Bluetooth allows you to keep your eyes on the road. | If your attention is divided, you are not being safe. Distracted driving, or "any activity that diverts attention from driving," leads to thousands of deaths per year in the United States (National Highway Traffic Safety Administration [NHTSA], n.d., para 2). |
| Sometimes you can't resist checking Instagram during study sessions. | Intersperse study sessions with "media breaks." For example, allow yourself 5 minutes of screen time for every 1 hour of studying. This is better than constantly switching your focus between studying and media, because every little adjustment requires time (Carrier et al., 2015). |
| You know you shouldn't text during class, but you must respond to a time-sensitive message before the lecture is over. | If you must text during class, and you know your instructor will permit this, choose a strategic time. Wait until your instructor has finished expressing a thought or explaining a concept (Carrier et al., 2015). |
| You have laundry to fold and lectures to listen to. | According to one study, folding laundry is almost as distracting as texting in an online learning situation (Blasiman et al., 2018). Try folding laundry while doing something less important, like watching TV. |
| You know it's rude, but you can't help glancing at your phone during conversations. | Put away your phone or turn down the volume during face-to-face conversations. Snubbing someone with your phone ("phubbing") can have a negative impact on both personal and professional relationships (Roberts & David, 2017, 2020). |

Multitasking with technology has become a part of everyday life, but it leads to divided attention (Chua et al., 2017). With strategies like these, you can avoid some of the safety issues and other negative effects associated with media multitasking.

## Put Your Heads Together

The link between consciousness and attention is not fully understood, but we do know that our attentional capacity—and therefore our ability to multitask effectively—is limited. In your group, discuss and record examples of **A)** when multitasking is advantageous to you and **B)** when multitasking could be risky or problematic. **C)** Decide if the benefits outweigh the risks.

**LO 3**  Describe how we narrow our focus through selective attention.

**SELECTIVE ATTENTION**    Although we have access to a vast amount of information in our internal and external environments, we can only focus our attention on a small portion at one time. This narrow focus on specific stimuli is known as **selective attention.** Talking to someone in a crowded room, you are able to block out surrounding chatter and noise and immerse yourself in the conversation. This efficient use of selective attention is known as the *cocktail-party effect,* and it occurs when the brain is responsive to some "speech streams" while ignoring others (Golumbic et al., 2013; Koch et al., 2011). Do you think you would hear someone saying your name in this type of scenario? Researchers have found that only around one third of people are able to do this (Röer & Cowan, 2020). Studies suggest selective attention can be influenced by emotions. Anger, for example, increases our ability to selectively attend to something or someone (Finucane, 2011). Personality characteristics may also impact our capacity to focus attention and avoid mind wandering (Welhaf et al., 2020). For example, people with higher levels of *grit,* or commitment to achieving long-term goals, seem to be particularly good at maintaining focus as they work to accomplish something (Smith et al., 2020). This tendency to focus on specific stimuli does not mean we fail to detect everything else; remember, the brain is constantly gathering data through automatic processing.

With so much data competing for our attention, what determines where we direct our focus? Humans are highly sensitive to abrupt, unexpected **changes in the environment**, and to stimuli that are unfamiliar, rewarding, or especially strong (Bourgeois et al., 2016; Daffner et al., 2007; Parmentier & Andrés, 2010). We are also sensitive to stimuli we find disgusting or frightening (Perone et al., 2020). Meanwhile, we tend to ignore continuous input, like unimportant background stimuli. Imagine you are studying in a busy coffee shop. You are aware the environment is bustling with activity, but you fail to pay attention to every person—until something

**CONNECTIONS**

In **Chapter 2,** we described the reticular formation, an intricate web of neurons responsible for levels of arousal. It also plays a role in selectively attending to important information by sifting through sensory data, picking out what's relevant and ignoring the rest. Here, we see how the brain pays attention to unexpected changes in the environment.

**selective attention**  The ability to focus awareness on a small segment of information that is available through our sensory systems.

changes (someone laughs very loudly, for example). Then your attention might be directed to that specific event.

**INATTENTIONAL BLINDNESS**     Selective attention is great if you need to study for a psychology test as people around you play video games, but it can also be dangerous. Suppose a friend sends you a hilarious text message while you are walking toward a busy intersection. Thinking about the text can momentarily steal your attention away from signs of danger, like a car turning right on red without stopping. While distracted by the text message, you might step into the intersection—without seeing the car turning in your path. This "looking without seeing" is referred to as *inattentional blindness* (Mack, 2003). Our example focuses on the distracted pedestrian, but drivers (particularly younger and older ones) are also susceptible to inattentional blindness. As you might suspect, drivers who fail to notice objects and other environmental circumstances may be more susceptible to errors and collisions (Saryazdi et al., 2019).

Ulric Neisser illustrated just how blind we can be to objects directly in our line of vision. In one of his studies, participants were instructed to watch a video of men passing a basketball from one person to another (Neisser, 1979; Neisser & Becklen, 1975). As the participants diligently followed the basketball with their eyes, counting each pass, a partially transparent woman holding an umbrella was superimposed walking across the basketball court. Only 21% of the participants even noticed the woman (Most et al., 2001; Simons, 2010); the others had been too fixated on counting the basketball passes to see her (Mack, 2003). It turns out even experts can fall prey to this phenomenon. In one study, researchers embedded an image of a gorilla on a CAT scan of a lung (see photo to the right). Twenty out of 24 expert radiologists failed to detect the gorilla (Drew et al., 2013). This phenomenon may not be limited to vision; research suggests we can also be "blind" to other sensory stimuli, including smells (Forster & Spence, 2018).

**LEVELS OF CONSCIOUSNESS**     People often equate consciousness with being awake and alert, and unconsciousness with being passed out or comatose. But as Dr. Chander suggested earlier, the distinction is not so clear. There are different *levels of consciousness,* such as those associated with wakefulness, sleepiness, and dreaming, as well as drug-induced, hypnotic, and meditative states. One way to define these levels of consciousness is to determine how much control you have over your awareness. When focusing intently on a task (using a sharp knife), you have great control over your awareness, but that control diminishes as you daydream. Sometimes we can identify what causes a change in the level of consciousness—the sound of a ringtone interrupting your dozing, for example. Psychologists typically delineate between *waking consciousness* and *altered states of consciousness* that may result from drugs, alcohol, or hypnosis—all topics covered in this chapter.

Wherever your attention is focused at this moment, that is your conscious experience—but there are times when attention essentially shuts down. What's going on when we lie in bed motionless, lost in a peaceful slumber? Sleep, fascinating sleep, is the subject of our next section.

**What Umbrella?**
In an elegant demonstration of inattentional blindness, researchers asked a group of participants to watch a video of men passing around a basketball. As the participants kept careful tabs on the players' passes, a semi-transparent image of a woman with an umbrella appeared among them. Only 21% of the participants (1 out of 5) even noticed (Most et al., 2001).

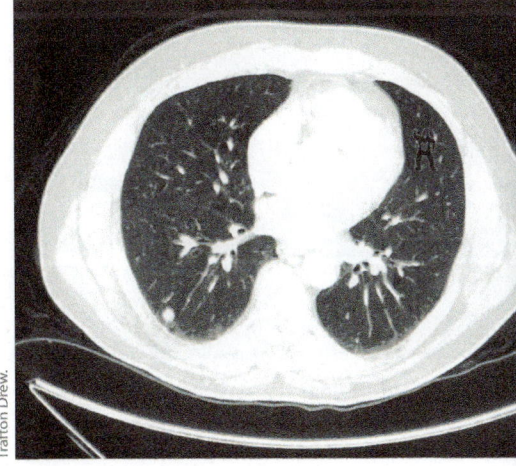

Trafton Drew.

**Is That a Gorilla in My Lung?**
Do you see a gorilla on the upper right side of this lung scan? Researchers showed this image to a group of radiologists, medical professionals who specialize in reading computerized axial tomography (CAT) scans like this. A whopping 83% did not notice the gorilla, even though it was 48 times bigger than the lung nodules they identify on a regular basis (Drew et al., 2013). A beautiful illustration of inattentional blindness.

 **SHOW WHAT YOU KNOW**

1. _____ is the state of being aware of oneself, one's thoughts, and/or the environment.
   **A.** Consciousness
   **B.** Automatic processing
   **C.** Cognitive psychology
   **D.** Inattentional blindness

2. Inattentional blindness is the tendency to "look without seeing." Given what you know about selective attention, how would you advise someone to avoid inattentional blindness?

3. While studying for an exam, your sensory systems absorb an inordinate amount of information from your surroundings, most of which escapes your awareness. Because of _____, you generally do not get overwhelmed with incoming sensory data.

 CHECK YOUR ANSWERS AT THE BACK OF THE BOOK.

# Sleep

**ASLEEP AT THE WHEEL**    Growing up, Matt Utesch had a lot of energy. He played basketball, ran cross-country, and competed in one of the nation's top-ranking private soccer leagues. But everything changed during Matt's sophomore year of high school. At first it seemed like nothing serious, just a little nap here and there. But eventually, Matt was dozing off in every class except physical education. Most of his teachers assumed he was exhausted from late-night partying. Nobody, not even Matt's doctor, suspected he had a serious medical condition—until the accident happened.

The summer before junior year, Matt was driving his truck home from work. One moment he was rolling along the street at a safe distance from other cars, and the next he was ramming into a brown Saturn that had slowed to make a left turn. What had transpired in the interim? Matt had fallen asleep. He slammed on the brake pedal, but it was too late; the two vehicles collided. Unharmed, Matt leaped out of his truck and ran to check on the other driver—a woman who, as he remembers, "was totally out of it." Her backrest had broken, and her back had nearly broken along with it. A few weeks after the accident, Matt went to the woman's home to bring her flowers. She invited him inside, and they sat down and began to chat. Then, right in the midst of their conversation, Matt fell asleep.

## We've Got Rhythm

Worms, monkeys, kangaroos. They all do it. "Virtually all animals, including insects, nematodes, scorpions, spiders, and vertebrates, show some form of sleep, or at least sleep-like states" (Libourel & Herrel, 2016, p. 836). There are animals that require plenty of sleep—bats and opossums sleep 18 to 20 hours a day—and those that need barely any—elephants and giraffes get by on 3 or 4 hours (Siegel, 2005). Sleep needs vary greatly among people, but the National Sleep Foundation recommends adults get between 7 and 9 hours per night (Hirshkowitz et al., 2015; Suni, 2020). Do the math and that translates to about a third of the day, and therefore a third of your *life*. Clearly, sleep serves some important function, but what is it? How can we study it? And how does it relate to consciousness? Before tackling these questions, let's get a handle on the basics.

**LO 4**  Identify how circadian rhythm relates to sleep.

**CIRCADIAN RHYTHM**    Have you ever noticed that you often get sleepy in the middle of the afternoon? Even if you had a good sleep the night before, you inevitably begin feeling tired around 2:00 or 3:00 P.M.; it's like clockwork. That's because it is clockwork. Many things your body does, including sleep, are regulated by a biological clock. Body temperature rises during the day, reaching its maximum in the early evening. Growth hormone is released at night, and the stress hormone cortisol soars in the morning, reaching levels 10 to 20 times higher than at night (Wright, 2002). These are just a few of the body functions that follow predictable daily patterns, affecting our behaviors, alertness, and activity levels. Such patterns in our physiological functioning roughly follow the 24-hour cycle of daylight and darkness; they follow a **circadian rhythm** (ser-KAY-dee-an).

In the circadian rhythm for sleep and wakefulness, there are two times when the desire for sleep hits hardest. The first is between 2:00 and 6:00 A.M., the same window of time when most car accidents caused by sleepiness occur (Caldwell et al., 2019; Horne, 2006). The second, less intense desire for sleep strikes midafternoon, between 2:00 and 4:00 P.M. (Lohr, 2015), when many college students seem to have trouble keeping their eyes open in class. This is a time when many people nap.

Not all biological rhythms are circadian. Some occur over longer time intervals (monthly menstruation), and others cycle much faster (90-minute sleep cycles, to be discussed shortly). Many animals migrate or hibernate during certain seasons and mate

John Gibbens/Getty Images.

**Sleeping Seal**
A Northern fur seal naps on a rocky beach. In the water, this animal engages in *unihemispheric* sleep, meaning one brain hemisphere sleeps while the other remains awake. The eye opposite the sleeping hemisphere is closed, while the other eye stays open (Lyamin et al., 2018). How might this form of sleep help the seal survive?

**circadian rhythm**  The daily patterns roughly following the 24-hour cycle of daylight and darkness; a 24-hour cycle of physiological and behavioral functioning.

according to a yearly pattern. Even when deprived of cues like changing levels of sunlight, some animals continue to follow these cycles. Birds caged indoors, for example, exhibit mood and behavioral changes at the times of year when they would normally be migrating. Biological clocks are everywhere in nature, acting as day planners for organisms as basic as bacteria and slime mold (Summa & Turek, 2015; Wright, 2002).

**SUPRACHIASMATIC NUCLEUS** Where in the human body do these inner clocks and calendars dwell? Miniclocks are found in cells all over your body, but a master clock is nestled deep within the hypothalamus, a brain structure that plays a central role in maintaining homeostasis, or balance, in the body's systems (regulating daily patterns of hunger and body temperature, for example). This master of clocks, known as the *suprachiasmatic nucleus (SCN),* consists of two clusters, each no bigger than an ant, totaling around 20,000 neurons (Bedrosian et al., 2016; Green, 2019). The SCN plays a role in our circadian rhythm by communicating with other areas of the hypothalamus and the reticular formation, which regulates alertness and sleepiness (**FIGURE 4.2**).

Although tucked away in the recesses of the brain, the SCN knows the difference between day and night because it receives signals from light-sensing cells in the eye called *retinal ganglion cells.* The SCN indirectly communicates with the **pineal gland**, a part of the endocrine system, to regulate the release of *melatonin,* a hormone that

**CONNECTIONS**

In **Chapter 2,** we presented the endocrine system, a communication system that uses glands to convey messages within the body. The messages are delivered by hormones, which are chemicals released in the bloodstream. The pineal gland, a part of the endocrine system, secretes melatonin, a hormone that is involved in sleep–wake cycles.

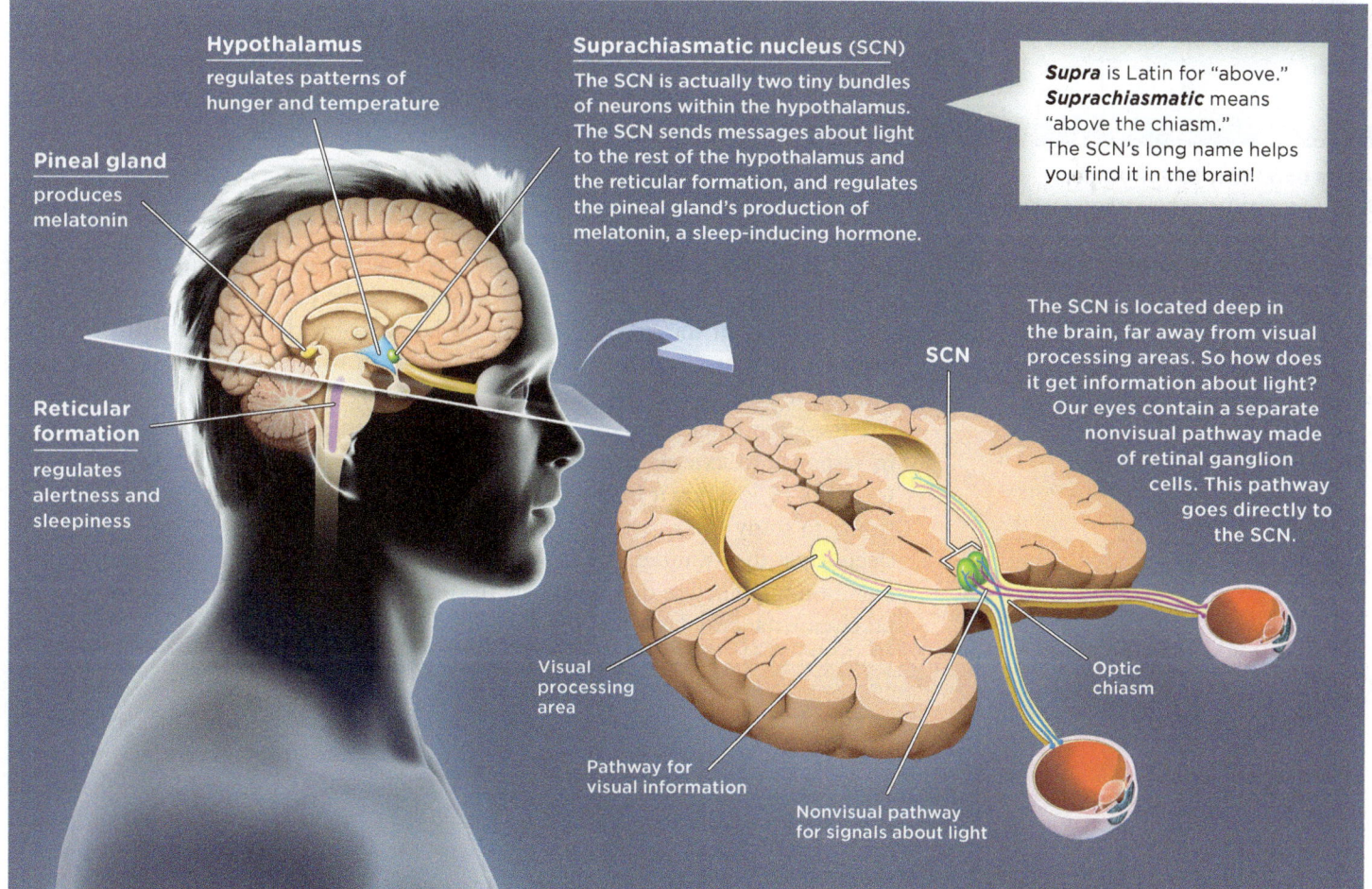

**FIGURE 4.2**
**The Suprachiasmatic Nucleus**
The suprachiasmatic nucleus (SCN) of the hypothalamus is the body's internal master clock, playing a role in regulating our circadian rhythms. These rhythms roughly follow the 24-hour cycle of daylight and darkness. But one doesn't have to consciously perceive light for the SCN to function properly; there is a dedicated, nonvisual pathway that carries light information from the eyes to the SCN.

promotes sleep (Bedrosian et al., 2016). In dark conditions, the clock commands the pineal gland to produce melatonin, making it easier to sleep. When light hits the eye, melatonin secretion slows down. So if you want to sleep, turn down the lights, and let the melatonin get to work. And when we say "lights," we are referring to all sources, including the screens of your favorite devices.

## Didn't See That Coming

### ARE SCREENS RUINING YOUR RHYTHM?

**PROTECT YOUR CLOCK.** Many Americans (as many as 90% of adults) use smartphones, tablets, and computers within 1 hour of bedtime, often to the detriment of their sleep (Bedrosian et al., 2016). In addition to providing stimulation when you are trying to relax (just think how you feel when you see an upsetting or riveting post right before going to bed), these devices emit blue light, which interferes with the release of melatonin (Bowler & Bourke, 2019; National Sleep Foundation, 2020, July 28). (Remember that melatonin promotes sleep, so suppressing it might have a negative impact on sleep.) Because of its effect on melatonin, blue light has gotten a "bad rap," but evidence from animal research suggests yellow light may be problematic as well (Mouland et al., 2019).

Given these findings, what practical steps can we take to protect our sleep? The National Sleep Foundation (n.d.) suggests removing electronics from the bedroom a minimum of 1 hour before sleep. If you must look at your devices right before bed, reduce your overall exposure to light by turning down the brightness (Ducharme, 2020).

Thanasis Zovoilis/Getty Images.

**Not a Good Way to Fall Asleep**
Most children and teens have at least one digital device in their bedrooms, and the majority of those kids make a habit of looking at their screens within an hour of going to sleep. Yet presleep screen time has been associated with going to bed later, lower-quality sleep, and less sleep overall—not a trivial issue, as sleep problems in childhood have been linked to obesity and behavioral issues (Hale et al., 2018; Williamson et al., 2020).

**LARKS AND OWLS**    Everyone has their own unique clock, which helps explain why some of us are "morning people" or so-called larks, and others are "night owls." If you are a lark, you roll out of bed feeling energized and alert, get more accomplished early in the day, yet grow weary as the day drags on (Ferrante et al., 2015). Owls, on the other hand, get up late and hit the sack late. But being an owl often means your energy level builds later in the day (Ferrante et al., 2015), making it easy to stay up late posting on Instagram or reading your textbook. Are these tendencies toward "lark" and "owl" predetermined, or can they change in response to external pressures, like work schedules and social activities? The COVID-19 lockdown in the spring of 2020 gave researchers an excellent opportunity to study this question. People were stuck at home and had more freedom to sleep when they wanted. A study of nearly 4,000 of these individuals uncovered a common tendency to drift into new sleep schedules, suggesting that environmental circumstances play a major role in determining what type of "bird" a person is (Roitblat et al., 2020).

**JET LAG**    Whether you are a lark or an owl, your biological clock is likely to become confused when you travel across time zones. Your clock does not automatically reset to match the new time. The physical and mental consequences of this delayed adjustment, known as "jet lag," may include gastrointestinal distress, headaches, and a noticeable decrease in the efficiency of brain activity (Zhang et al., 2020). Fortunately, the biological clock can readjust by about 1 or 2 hours each day, eventually falling into step with the new environmental schedule (Cunha & Stöppler, 2016).

## CAREER CONNECTIONS

### THE CHALLENGES OF SHIFT WORK

Now imagine plodding through life with a case of jet lag you just can't shake. This is the tough reality for some of the world's shift workers—firefighters, nurses, miners, military service members, and other professionals who work while the rest of the world snuggles under the covers. Shift workers represent about 20% of the workforce in the United States and other developed countries, or 1 in 5 people who are employed (Di Lorenzo et al., 2003; Wright et al., 2013). Some work rotating shifts, which means they are constantly going to bed and waking up at different times; others consistently work the overnight shift, so their sleep–wake cycles are permanently out-of-step with the light and dark cycles of the Earth. Constantly fighting the clock takes a heavy toll on the mind and body, causing drowsiness that could potentially lead to workplace accidents (Pilcher & Morris, 2020). Irregular sleep schedules may also cause changes in metabolism that could lead to weight gain and increased risk for diabetes (James et al., 2017). Finally, shift workers face a greater risk for high blood pressure, heart disease, and chronic inflammation, which could potentially set the stage for the development of cancer (Good et al., 2020; James et al., 2017).

How can shift workers minimize circadian disturbances? Remember that light is the master clock's most important external cue. Maximizing light exposure during work time and steering clear of it close to bedtime can help (Bedrosian et al., 2016). Some night shifters don sunglasses on their way home, to block the morning sun, and head straight to bed in a quiet, dark room (Epstein & Mardon, 2007). Establishing consistent schedules for both eating and sleeping, and avoiding alcohol within 3 hours of bedtime can help, too (Caldwell et al., 2019; UCLA Health, n.d.). Many people use over-the-counter melatonin supplements in hope of improving their sleep, but there are questions about the quality of these products and their efficacy for different people (Erland & Saxena, 2017; National Sleep Foundation, 2020, August 6).

**"CONSTANTLY FIGHTING THE CLOCK TAKES A HEAVY TOLL ON THE MIND AND BODY . . ."**

**Night Shift**
Construction workers are among the many professionals who work during the night. Trying to sleep after a night shift can be difficult for various reasons, including disruptions to circadian rhythms and the stress associated with working atypical hours (Cheng et al., 2018).

## The Stages of Sleep

**LO 5** Summarize the stages of sleep.

Have you ever watched someone sleeping? The person looks blissfully tranquil: body still, face relaxed, chest rising and falling like a lazy ocean wave. Don't be fooled. Underneath the body's quiet front is a very active brain, as revealed by an electroencephalogram (EEG). If you could look at an EEG trace of your brain right at this moment, you would probably see a series of tiny, short spikes in rapid-fire succession. These high-frequency brain waves are called **beta waves,** and they appear when you are solving a math problem, reading a book, or any time you are alert (see **INFOGRAPHIC 4.1** on page 137). Researchers call this state of consciousness Stage W, indicating a "waking state," and it can range from being fully alert to slightly drowsy (Berry et al., 2016). Now let's say you climb into bed, close your eyes, and relax. As you become more and more drowsy, the EEG would likely begin showing **alpha waves,** which are lower in frequency than beta waves (Cantero et al., 1999; Silber et al., 2007). At some point, you drift into a different state of consciousness known as sleep.

**beta waves** Brain waves that indicate an alert, awake state.

**alpha waves** Brain waves that indicate a relaxed, drowsy state.

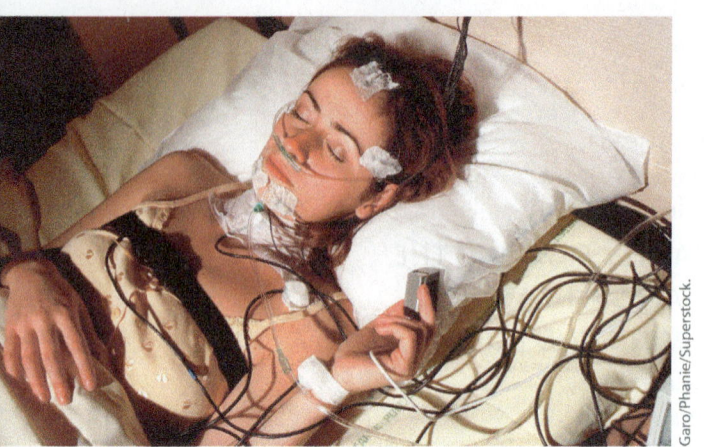

Garo/Phanie/Superstock.

**Sleep Waves**

A sleep study participant undergoes an EEG test. Electrodes attached to her head pick up electrical activity from her brain, which is transformed into a series of spikes on a computer screen. Through careful study of EEG data, researchers have come to understand the various stages of sleep.

**non-rapid eye movement (non-REM or NREM)** The nondreaming sleep that occurs during sleep Stages N1 to N3.

**theta waves** Brain waves that indicate light sleep.

**delta waves** Brain waves that indicate a deep sleep.

**rapid eye movement (REM)** The stage of sleep associated with dreaming; sleep characterized by bursts of eye movements, with brain activity similar to that of a waking state, but with a lack of muscle tone.

**NON-REM SLEEP**    A normal sleeper begins the night in **non-rapid eye movement (non-REM or NREM)**, or nondreaming, sleep, which has three stages (Berry et al., 2016; Infographic 4.1). The first and lightest is Stage N1 (NREM 1 sleep), also known as "light sleep." During Stage N1, muscles go limp and body temperature starts to fall. The eyeballs may move gently beneath the lids. If you looked at an EEG of a person in Stage N1, you would likely see **theta waves,** which are lower in frequency than both alpha and beta waves. This is the type of sleep many people deny having. Example: Your friend begins to snooze while watching TV, so you poke them in the ribs and say, "Wake up!" but they swear they weren't asleep. It is also during this initial phase of sleep that *hallucinations,* or imaginary sensations, can occur. Do you ever see blotches of color or bizarre floating images as you drift off to sleep? Or perhaps you have felt a sensation of falling or swinging and then jerked your arms or legs in response? False perceptions that occur during the limbo between wakefulness and sleep are called *hypnagogic* (hip-nuh-GOJ-ik) *hallucinations,* and they are no cause for concern—in most cases. More on this when we return to Matt's story.

After a few minutes in Stage N1, the sleeper moves on to the next phase of non-REM sleep, called Stage N2 (NREM 2 sleep), which is slightly deeper than Stage N1. It is now harder to awaken them. Theta waves continue showing up on the EEG, along with little bursts of electrical activity called *sleep spindles* and large waves called *K-complexes* appearing every 2 minutes or so. Researchers suspect sleep spindles are associated with memory consolidation and intelligence (Fogel & Smith, 2011; van Schalkwijk et al., 2020). Studies suggest K-complexes are involved in processes as diverse as forming memories, preparing the brain for arousal, and regulating the cardiovascular system (Caporro et al., 2012; de Zambotti et al., 2016; Latreille et al., 2020).

After passing through Stages N1 and N2, the sleeper descends into Stage N3 (NREM 3 sleep). Stage N3 is considered slow-wave sleep, and it has a higher proportion of tall, low-frequency **delta waves** than prior stages (Berry & Wagner, 2015). Waking a person from slow-wave sleep is not easy. Most of us feel groggy, disoriented, and downright irritated when jarred from a slow-wave slumber. This is also the peak time for the secretion of growth hormone, which helps build tissue and promotes growth in children, making them taller and stronger (Backeljauw & Hwa, 2016).

**REM SLEEP**    Deep sleep doesn't last too long, however. After about 40 minutes of Stage N3 sleep, the sleeper works their way back to Stage N2. Then, instead of waking up, they enter Stage R, or **rapid eye movement (REM)** sleep. During REM sleep, the eyes often dart around, even though they are closed (hence the name "rapid eye movement" sleep). The brain is very active, with EEG recordings showing faster and shorter waves similar to those of someone who is wide awake. Pulse and breathing rate fluctuate, and blood flow to the genitals increases, which explains why people frequently wake up in a state of sexual arousal. Another name for REM sleep is *paradoxical sleep,* because the sleeper appears to be quiet and resting but the brain is full of electrical activity. Most dreaming takes place during REM sleep, and REM dreams tend to be jam-packed with rich sensory details and narrative. (Dreams also occur during non-REM sleep, but they are less frequently reported; Siclari et al., 2017.) People roused from REM sleep often report having vivid, illogical dreams—thankfully, there is a mechanism to prevent us from acting them out. During REM sleep, certain neurons in the brainstem control the voluntary muscles, keeping most of the body still.

What would happen if the neurons responsible for disabling the muscles during REM sleep were destroyed or damaged? Researchers led by Michel Jouvet

# Sleep

Looking in on a sleep study, you'll see that the brain is actually very active during sleep, cycling through non-REM stages and ending in REM sleep approximately five times during the night. Transitions between stages are clearly visible as shifts in EEG patterns.

Graphs illustrating the human sleep cycle typically present an 8-hour time span, as shown below. But this doesn't tell the whole story of sleep. The amount of time spent sleeping and the content of our sleep change across the life span. Only two thirds of U.S. adults get the recommended minimum of 7 hours per night (Liu et al., 2016).

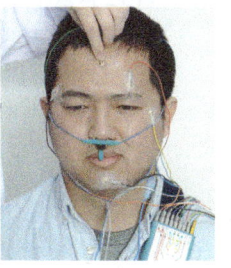
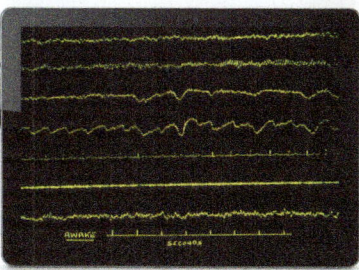

This sleep study participant wears electrodes that will measure his brain waves and body movements during sleep.

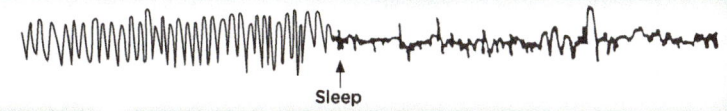

Sleep

Looking at brain waves allows us to trace a person's stage of sleep. Here, we can see a clear shift from waking to sleeping patterns. (Data from Dement & Vaughan, 1999.)

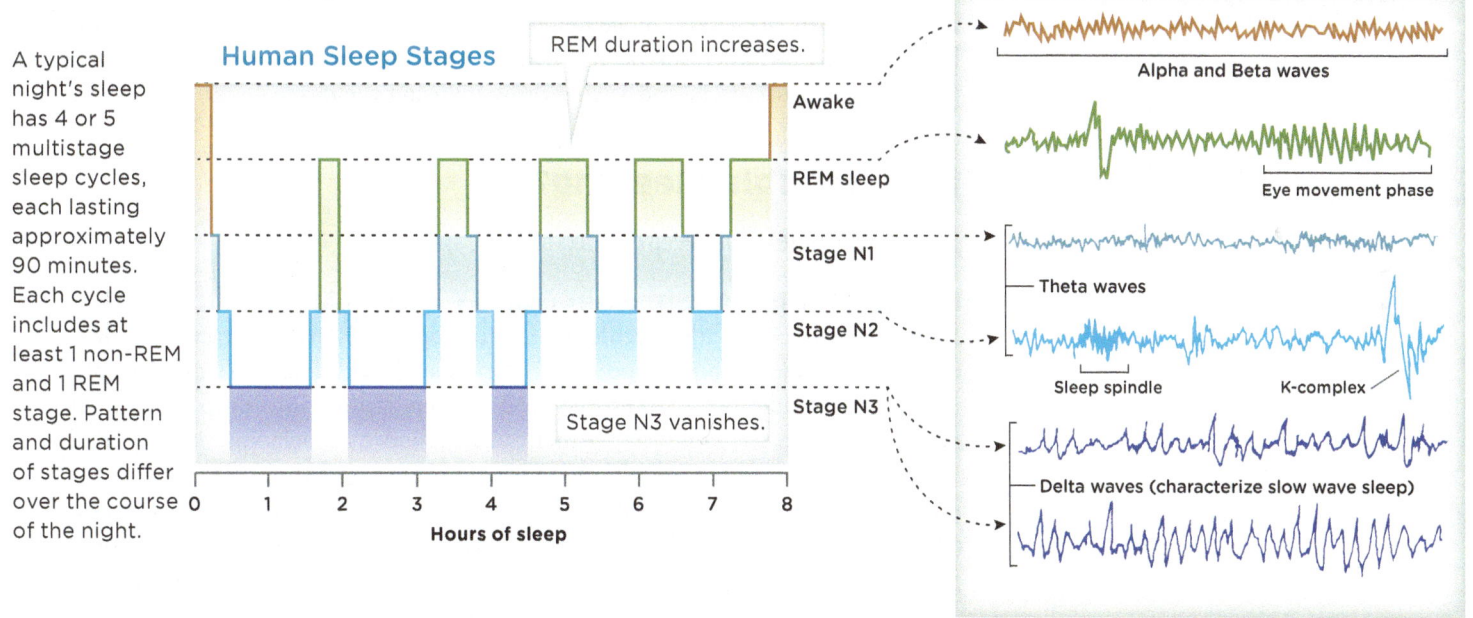

## Human Sleep Stages

A typical night's sleep has 4 or 5 multistage sleep cycles, each lasting approximately 90 minutes. Each cycle includes at least 1 non-REM and 1 REM stage. Pattern and duration of stages differ over the course of the night.

REM duration increases.

Awake

REM sleep

Stage N1

Stage N2

Stage N3

Stage N3 vanishes.

Hours of sleep

Alpha and Beta waves

Eye movement phase

Theta waves

Sleep spindle    K-complex

Delta waves (characterize slow wave sleep)

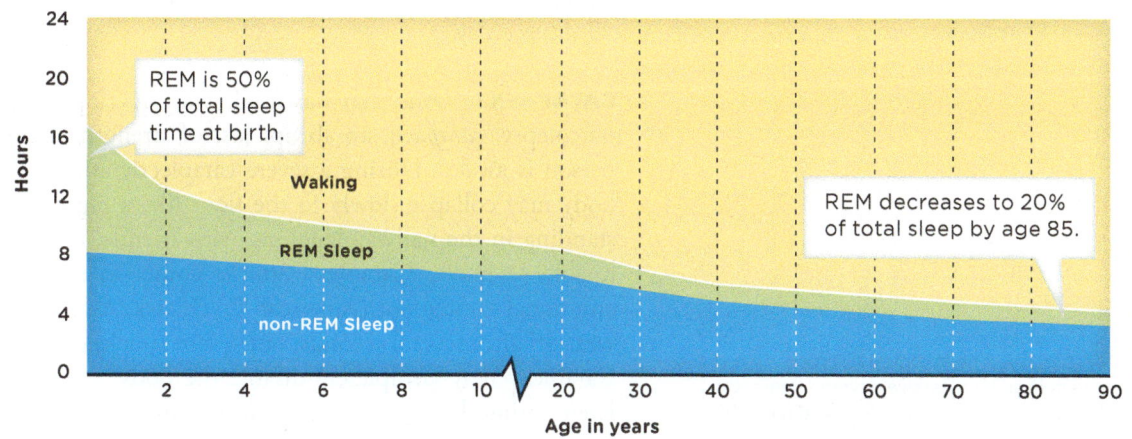

As we age, we need fewer hours of sleep, and the proportion of time spent in REM diminishes.

REM is 50% of total sleep time at birth.

Waking

REM Sleep

non-REM Sleep

REM decreases to 20% of total sleep by age 85.

Hours

Age in years

(1925–2017) in France and Adrian Morrison in the United States determined the answer to that question in the 1960s and 1970s. Both teams showed that severing these neurons in the brains of cats caused them to act out their kitty dreams. Not only did the sleeping felines stand up; they arched their backs in fury, groomed and licked themselves, and hunted imaginary mice (Jouvet, 1979; Sastre & Jouvet, 1979).

**SLEEP ARCHITECTURE**    Congratulations. You have just completed one sleep cycle, working your way through Stages N1, N2, and N3 of non-REM sleep and ending with a dream-packed episode of REM. Each of these cycles lasts about 90 minutes, and the average adult sleeper loops through five of them per night. The composition of these 90-minute sleep cycles changes as the hours pass. During the first two cycles, a considerable amount of time is devoted to the deep sleep Stage N3. Halfway through the night, however, Stage N3 vanishes. Meanwhile, the REM periods become progressively longer, with the first REM episode lasting only 5 to 10 minutes, and the final one lasting nearly a half-hour (Siegel, 2005). Therefore, we pack in most of our non-REM sleep early in the night and most of the dreaming toward the end; and the sleep stage we spend the most time in—nearly half the night—is Stage N2 (Epstein & Mardon, 2007).

The makeup of our sleep cycles, or *sleep architecture,* changes throughout life. Infants spend almost half of their sleep in REM (Skeldon et al., 2016). Older people spend far less time in REM sleep and the deeply refreshing stage of N3 sleep. Instead, they experience longer periods of light sleep (Stages N1 and N2), which can be interrupted easily by noises and movements (Cirelli, 2012; Ohayon et al., 2004; Scullin & Bliwise, 2015). Could this be the reason some older people complain of sleeping poorly, waking up often, and feeling drowsy during the day?

## Have Trouble Sleeping?

**LO 6**  Recognize various sleep disorders and their symptoms.

**PROBLEM IDENTIFIED: NARCOLEPSY**    Shortly after the car accident, Matt was diagnosed with **narcolepsy,** a neurological disorder characterized by excessive daytime sleepiness and other sleep-related disturbances. Symptoms of narcolepsy include the "irrepressible need to sleep, lapsing into sleep, or napping occurring within the same day" (American Psychiatric Association, 2013, p. 372). "Sleep attacks" are measured in seconds or minutes, and they often progress into longer naps (Genetics Home Reference, 2020b). They can strike anytime, anywhere—during a job interview, while riding a bicycle, or in the midst of a passionate kiss. One time Matt fell asleep while making a sandwich. When he awoke, he was still holding a slice of meat in his hand. By the time Matt was a junior in high school, his uncontrollable naps were striking upward of 20 to 30 times a day.

**CATAPLEXY**    And that wasn't all. Matt developed another debilitating symptom of narcolepsy: *cataplexy,* an abrupt loss of strength or muscle tone that occurs when a person is awake. During a severe cataplectic attack, some muscles go limp, and the body may collapse slowly to the floor like a rag doll. One moment Matt would be standing in the hallway laughing with friends; the next he was splayed on the floor unable to move. Cataplexy attacks come on suddenly, usually during periods of emotional excitement (American Psychiatric Association, 2013). The effects typically wear off after several seconds, but severe attacks can immobilize a person for minutes. Cataplexy may completely disable the body, but it produces no loss in awareness. Even during the worst attack, Matt remained completely aware. He could hear people

Boy_Anupong/Getty Images.

**Coronavirus, Sleep, and Anxiety**
Sleep loss can increase anxiety, and anxiety can cause sleep loss, potentially "creating a negative feed-back cycle wherein sleep disruption and escalating anxiety become self-reinforcing" (Simon et al., 2020, p. 107). The coronavirus pandemic appears to have exacerbated these and other mental health problems across the world (Sher, 2020). To mitigate the psychological effects of future disease outbreaks, we should create systems to monitor mental health and swiftly respond with interventions (Huang & Zhao, 2020).

**narcolepsy** A neurological disorder characterized by excessive daytime sleepiness, which includes lapses into sleep and napping.

talking about him; sometimes they snickered in amusement. "Kids can be cruel," Matt says. By junior year, Matt was having 60 to 100 cataplexy attacks a day.

**SLEEP PARALYSIS AND HYPNAGOGIC HALLUCINATIONS**    Matt also developed two other common narcolepsy symptoms: sleep paralysis and hypnagogic hallucinations. *Sleep paralysis* is a temporary paralysis that strikes just before falling asleep or upon waking (American Psychiatric Association, 2013). Recall that the body becomes paralyzed during REM sleep, but sometimes this paralysis sets in prematurely or fails to turn off on time. Picture yourself lying in bed, awake and fully aware yet unable to roll over, climb out of bed, or even wiggle a toe. You want to scream for help, but your lips won't budge. Sleep paralysis is a common symptom of narcolepsy, but it can also strike ordinary sleepers. About 8% of people in the general population and 28% of college students have experienced sleep paralysis at least once in their lives (Jalal & Ramachandran, 2014; Jalal et al., 2014; Sharpless & Barber, 2011). Episodes usually last a few seconds, but some go on for several minutes—a terrifying experience for most people.

Sleep paralysis may seem scary, but now imagine seeing bloodthirsty vampires standing at the foot of your bed just as you are about to fall asleep. Earlier we discussed the *hypnagogic hallucinations* people can experience during Stage N1 sleep (seeing strange images, for example). But not all hypnagogic hallucinations involve harmless blobs. They can also be realistic visions of axe murderers or space aliens trying to abduct you (McNally & Clancy, 2005). Matt had a recurring hallucination of a man with a butcher knife racing through his doorway, jumping onto his bed, and stabbing him in the chest. Upon awakening, Matt would often quiz his mother with questions like, "When is my birthday?" or "What is your license plate number?" He wanted to verify she was real, not just another character in his dream. Like sleep paralysis, vivid hypnagogic hallucinations can occur in people without narcolepsy, too. Shift work, insomnia, and sleeping face-up are all factors that appear to heighten one's risk (Cheyne, 2002; McNally & Clancy, 2005).

**LIVING WITH NARCOLEPSY**    Throughout junior year, Matt took various medications to control his narcolepsy, but his symptoms persisted. Narcolepsy was beginning to interfere with virtually every aspect of his life. At the beginning of high school, Matt had a 4.0 grade point average; now he was working twice as hard and earning lower grades. Playing sports had become a major health hazard because his cataplexy struck wherever and whenever, without notice. If he collapsed while sprinting down the soccer field or diving for a basketball, he might twist an ankle, break an arm, or worse. It was during this time that Matt realized who his true friends were. "The people that stuck with me [then] are still my close friends now," he says. Matt's loyal buddies learned to recognize the warning signs of his cataplexy (for example, when he suddenly stands still and closes his eyes) and did everything possible to keep him safe, grabbing hold of his body and slowly lowering him to the ground. His buddies had his back—literally.

Narcolepsy is rare, affecting far less than 1% of the U.S. population (National Institute of Neurological Disorders and Stroke, 2020). Although several medications are available to help control symptoms, there is no known cure. The disorder is believed to result from the loss of a specific type of neuron that helps regulate sleep–wake patterns (Lecendreux et al., 2017). Normally, the boundaries separating sleep and wakefulness are relatively clear—you are awake, in REM sleep, or in non-REM sleep. With narcolepsy, the lines separating these different realms of consciousness fade, allowing sleep to spill into periods of wakefulness. The loss of muscle tone during cataplexy, sleep paralysis, and dreamlike hypnagogic hallucinations may be explained by occurrences of REM sleep in the midst

**Did She Have Narcolepsy?**
Harriet Tubman is famous for helping hundreds of people escape slavery through the Underground Railroad. But few people know that Tubman suffered from symptoms of narcolepsy. Her sleep problems began after an incident that occurred when she was still a slave: She was struck on the head as punishment for protesting the beating of a fellow slave (Michals, 2015; Poole, 2016).

**TABLE 4.2**   Sleep Disturbances

| Sleep Disturbance | Definition | Defining Characteristics |
|---|---|---|
| Narcolepsy | Neurological disorder characterized by excessive daytime sleepiness, which includes lapses into sleep and napping. | Irrepressible need to sleep; daytime napping; cataplexy; sleep paralysis; hypnagogic hallucinations. |
| REM sleep behavior disorder | A sleep disturbance in which the mechanism responsible for paralyzing the body during REM sleep is not functioning, resulting in the acting out of dreams. | Dreamers vocalize and act out dreams, which may be action-packed and violent; upon awakening, they remember the dream; presents risk of injury to self and sleeping partners. |
| Obstructive sleep apnea hypopnea | Serious disturbance characterized by a complete absence of air flow (apnea) or reduced air flow (hypopnea). | Upper throat muscles go limp; airway closes; breathing stops for 10 seconds or longer; sleeper awakens, gasping for air. |
| Insomnia | Inability to fall asleep or stay asleep. | Poor sleep quantity or quality; tendency to wake up too early; the sleeper has trouble falling back asleep and does not feel refreshed in the morning. |
| Sleepwalking | Disturbance of non-REM sleep characterized by complex behavior during sleep. | Expressionless face; open eyes; may sit up in bed, walk around, or speak gibberish; upon awakening, has limited recall. |
| Sleep terrors | Disturbance of non-REM sleep generally occurring in children. | Screaming, inconsolable child; usually, no memory of the episode the next day. |

Problems can arise during both REM and non-REM sleep. This table outlines some of the most common sleep disturbances and their defining characteristics.

of wakefulness (Attarian et al., 2000). In other words, REM sleep occurs in the wrong place, at the wrong time (see a summary of this and other sleep disturbances in **TABLE 4.2**).

**REM SLEEP BEHAVIOR DISORDER**   Problems with REM regulation can also lead to other sleep disturbances, including **REM sleep behavior disorder.** The defining characteristics of this disorder include "repeated episodes of arousal often associated with vocalizations and/or complex motor behaviors arising from REM sleep" (American Psychiatric Association, 2013, p. 408). People with REM sleep behavior disorder are much like the cats in Morrison's and Jouvet's experiments; something has gone awry with the brainstem mechanism responsible for paralyzing their bodies during REM sleep, so they are able to move around and act out their dreams (Hu, 2020; Schenck & Mahowald, 2002). This is not a good thing, since the dreams of people with REM sleep behavior disorder tend to be unusually violent and action-packed, involving fights with wild animals and other attackers (Fantini et al., 2005; Hu, 2020). According to some research, up to 65% of REM sleep behavior disorder sufferers have injured either themselves or their bedmates at one point or another. Scrapes, cuts, and bruises are common, and traumatic brain injuries have also been reported (American Psychiatric Association, 2013; Aurora et al., 2010). REM sleep behavior disorder primarily affects older men (age 50 and up) and frequently foreshadows the development of serious neurodegenerative disorders—conditions such as Parkinson's disease and dementia that are associated with the gradual decline and death of neurons (Hu, 2020; Peever et al., 2014; Postuma et al., 2009).

**REM sleep behavior disorder**  A sleep disturbance in which the mechanism responsible for paralyzing the body during REM sleep is not functioning, resulting in the acting out of dreams.

**obstructive sleep apnea hypopnea**
A serious disturbance of non-REM sleep characterized by complete absence of air flow (apnea) or reduced air flow (hypopnea).

**BREATHING-RELATED SLEEP DISORDERS**   Obstructive sleep apnea hypopnea (hi-POP-nee-uh) is relatively common, affecting about 1 in 5 adults, according to a review of research spanning two decades (Franklin & Lindberg, 2015). As the name indicates, this condition is characterized by a complete absence of air flow (apnea) or reduced air flow (hypopnea). During normal sleep, the airway remains open, allowing air to flow in and out of the lungs. With obstructive sleep apnea hypopnea, the upper throat muscles go limp, allowing the upper airway to close (American

Psychiatric Association, 2013). Breathing stops for 10 seconds or more, causing blood oxygen levels to drop (Chung & Elsaid, 2009; Teodorescu et al., 2015). The brain responds by commanding the body to *wake up and breathe!* The sleeper awakes and gasps for air, sometimes with a noisy nasal sound, and then drifts back to sleep. This process can repeat itself several hundred times per night, preventing a person from experiencing the deep stages of sleep crucial for feeling reenergized in the morning. Most people have no memory of the repeated awakenings and wonder why they feel so exhausted during the day; they are completely unaware that they suffer from this serious sleep disturbance.

Obstructive sleep apnea hypopnea is more common among men than women and is more prevalent in the obese, and in women after menopause. This condition is linked to increased risk of death in the elderly, traffic accidents, and reduced quality of life, as well as elevated blood pressure, which increases the risk of cardiovascular disease (American Psychiatric Association, 2013).

**INSOMNIA**   The most prevalent sleep disturbance is **insomnia,** characterized by an inability to fall asleep or stay asleep. People with insomnia may complain of waking up in the middle of the night or arising too early, and not being able to fall back asleep. This poor-quality sleep can lead to daytime sleepiness and difficulty with cognitive tasks (American Psychiatric Association, 2013). About a third of adults experience some symptoms of insomnia, and 6–10% meet diagnostic criteria for *insomnia disorder* (American Psychiatric Association, 2013; Mai & Buysse, 2008; Roth, 2007). Evidence suggests that more than 25% of college students experience sleep disturbances, and close to 8% qualify as having insomnia (Bravo et al., 2018; Friedrich & Schlarb, 2018). As you probably know, many aspects of college life can interfere with sleep, including loud roommates and worries about school assignments, work, and finances. Insomnia is, to a certain degree, inherited (Song et al., 2020; Van Someren et al., 2015), but its symptoms can be triggered by many factors, including the stress of a new job, depression, anxiety, jet lag, aging, drug use, and chronic pain.

**OTHER SLEEP DISTURBANCES**   Have you ever found yourself feeling around in the dark of night, wondering where you are and how you got there? This scenario may sound familiar to those who have experienced *sleepwalking,* a common disturbance that occurs during non-REM sleep (typically Stage N3). A quarter of all children will experience at least one sleepwalking incident, and it seems to run in families (Licis et al., 2011; Petit et al., 2015). Sleepwalkers may be spotted sitting up in bed, walking around with their eyes wide open, and speaking gibberish. (Note that this garbled speech is different from *sleep talking,* which can occur in either REM or non-REM sleep, and is not considered a sleep disturbance.) Sleepwalkers can accomplish a variety of tasks, such as opening doors, going to the bathroom, and getting dressed, all of which they are likely to forget by morning. Most sleepwalking episodes are not related to dreaming, and contrary to urban myth, awakening a sleepwalker will not cause sudden death or injury. What's dangerous is leaving the front door unlocked and the car keys in the ignition, as sleepwalkers have been known to wander into the street and even attempt driving (American Psychiatric Association, 2013).

**Sleep terrors** are non-REM sleep disturbances primarily affecting children. A child experiencing a sleep terror may sit up in bed, stare fearfully at nothing, and scream. Parents may find the child crying hysterically, breathing rapidly, and sweating. No matter what the parents say or do, the child remains inconsolable. Fortunately, sleep terrors only last a few minutes, and most children outgrow them. Children generally do not remember the episode the next day (American Psychiatric Association, 2013).

Mike Marsland/Wireimage/Getty Images.

**When Apnea Turns Tragic**
About a year after the release of *Star Wars: The Force Awakens,* actor Carrie Fisher ("Princess Leia") died of "sleep apnea and other undetermined factors" (County of Los Angeles, Department of Medical Examiner-Coroner, 2017, p. 4). The coroner found evidence of cocaine, heroin, and ecstasy (MDMA) in Fisher's body, but it remains unclear if and how these drugs might have contributed to her death.

**insomnia**  Sleep disturbance characterized by an inability to fall asleep or stay asleep, impacting both the quality and quantity of sleep.

**sleep terrors**  A disturbance of non-REM sleep, generally occurring in children; characterized by screaming, staring fearfully, and usually no memory of the episode the following morning.

**Nightmares** are frightening dreams that occur in REM sleep. Nightmare disorder affects approximately 4% of the population (Aurora et al., 2010). And unlike sleep terrors, nightmares can often be recalled in vivid detail. Because nightmares usually occur during REM sleep, they are generally not acted out (American Psychiatric Association, 2013). Research suggests that people who frequently experience nightmares are "more susceptible to daily stressors" and may suffer from other problems like depression and insomnia (Hochard et al., 2016, p. 47; Nadorff et al., 2015). In some cases, nightmares do not have an apparent cause; in other cases, they may be related to issues such as posttraumatic stress disorder (PTSD; see Chapter 13), substance abuse, and anxiety. Approximately 80% of people with PTSD report having nightmares (Aurora et al., 2010).

## Losing Sleep?

Matt's worst struggle with narcolepsy stretched through the last 2 years of high school. During this time, he was averaging 20 to 30 naps a day. You might think that someone who falls asleep so often would at least feel well rested while awake. Not the case. Matt had trouble sleeping at night, and it was taking a heavy toll on his ability to think clearly. He remembers nodding off at the wheel a few times but continuing to drive, reassuring himself that everything was fine. He forgot about homework assignments and couldn't recall simple things people told him. Matt was experiencing two of the most common symptoms of sleep deprivation: impaired judgment and lapses in memory (Goel et al., 2009).

Let's face it. No one can function optimally without a good night's sleep. But the expression "good night's sleep" can mean something quite different from one person to the next. Newborns need anywhere from 14 to 17 hours of sleep per day, toddlers 11 to 14 hours, school-aged children 9 to 11 hours, and teens 8 to 10 hours (National Sleep Foundation, 2020, July 31). The American Academy of Sleep Medicine and the Sleep Research Society recommend that adults (ages 18–60) get a minimum of 7 hours of sleep every night (Watson et al., 2015), yet 1 in 3 Americans fails to achieve this goal (Liu et al., 2016).

**SHORT-TERM SLEEP DEPRIVATION**    What happens to living things when they don't sleep at all? Laboratory studies show that sleep deprivation kills rats faster than starvation (Rechtschaffen & Bergmann, 1995; Siegel, 2005). Curtailing sleep in humans leads to rapid deterioration of mental and physical well-being. Stay up for a full 48 hours and you can expect your memory, attention, reaction time, and decision making to suffer noticeably (Goel et al., 2009; Van Someren et al., 2015). Sleepy people find it especially challenging to accomplish tasks that are monotonous and boring; they may have trouble focusing on a single activity, like keeping their eyes on the road while driving (Lim & Dinges, 2010). Using driving simulators and tests to measure alertness, hand–eye coordination, and other factors, researchers report that getting behind the wheel while sleepy is similar to driving drunk. Staying awake for just 17 to 19 consecutive hours (which many of us do regularly) produces the same effect as having a blood alcohol content (BAC) of 0.05%, the legal limit in many countries. Driving under these circumstances is dangerous (Watson et al., 2015; Williamson & Feyer, 2000). Sleep loss also makes you more prone to *microsleeps,* or uncontrollable mininaps lasting several seconds—enough time to miss a traffic light turning red. Staying awake for several days at a time (11 days is the current world record, based on experimental data; Gillin, 2002) produces a host of disabling effects, including fragmented speech, cognitive deficits, mood swings, and hallucinations (Gulevich et al., 1966).

**Tired Teen**
Matt's battle with narcolepsy climaxed during his junior year of high school. In addition to falling asleep 20 to 30 times a day, he was experiencing frequent bouts of cataplexy, an abrupt loss of muscle tone that occurs while one is awake.

*Courtesy Matthew Utesch.*

**nightmares**    Frightening dreams that occur during REM sleep.

**REM rebound**    An increased amount of time spent in REM after sleep deprivation.

**LONG-TERM SLEEP DEPRIVATION** A more chronic form of sleep deprivation results from insufficient sleep night-upon-night for weeks, months, or years. People in this category are less likely than their well-rested peers to exercise, eat healthy foods, have sex, and attend family events (National Sleep Foundation, 2009). They also face a greater risk for heart disease, diabetes, cancer, and weight gain (Luyster et al., 2012), and have decreased immune system responses and slower reaction times (Besedovsky et al., 2012; Orzeł-Gryglewska, 2010). Many researchers suspect the obesity epidemic currently plaguing industrialized countries like the United States is partially linked to chronic sleep deprivation. Skimping on sleep appears to disrupt appetite-regulating hormones, which may lead to excessive hunger and overeating (Lin et al., 2020).

**REM DEPRIVATION** So far we have only covered sleep loss in general. What happens if REM sleep is compromised? Some research suggests depriving people of REM sleep can cause emotional overreactions to threatening situations (Rosales-Lagarde et al., 2012). REM deprivation can also lead to **REM rebound,** an increased amount of time spent in REM sleep when one finally gets an opportunity to sleep in peace. Researchers report that sleep disturbances following surgery, for example, often result in REM sleep rebound (Chouchou et al., 2014).

**WHY DO WE SLEEP?** The purpose of sleep has yet to be conclusively identified (Assefa et al., 2015). Drawing from sleep deprivation studies and other types of experiments, researchers have constructed various theories to explain *why* we spend so much time sleeping. TABLE **4.3** describes some of the main theories.

Whatever the purpose of sleep, there is no denying its importance. After a couple of sleepless nights, we are grumpy, clumsy, and unable to think straight. Although we may appreciate the value of sleep, we don't always practice the best bedtime habits—or know what they are. Read on to discover some behaviors and assumptions to avoid.

**Record-Breaking Randy**
A half-century ago, 17-year-old Randy Gardner set the record for the longest documented period of self-imposed sleep deprivation. With the help of two friends, and no caffeine or stimulants of any sort, the young man went 11 consecutive days without snoozing (Gulevich et al., 1966).

**TABLE 4.3** Theories of Sleep

| Theory | Description | A Closer Look |
|---|---|---|
| Restorative | Sleep allows for growth and repair of the body and brain. | Growth hormone is secreted during non-REM sleep, and protein production ramps up in the brain during REM. Sleep is a time for rest and replenishment of neurotransmitters, especially those important for attention and memory (Borbély et al., 2016; Hobson, 1989). |
| Evolutionary | Sleep serves adaptive function; evolved as it helped survival. | Dark environments were unsafe for our primitive ancestors; humans have poor night vision compared to animals hunting at night, so it was adaptive to avoid moving around. The development of circadian rhythms driving nighttime sleep served an important evolutionary purpose (Barton & Capellini, 2016). |
| Consolidation | Sleep aids in the consolidation or formation of memories and learning (Tononi & Cirelli, 2014). | The exact role of sleep is still being investigated, but evidence suggests that good sleep makes for better processing of memories (Cordi & Rasch, 2021; Rasch & Born, 2013; Sawangjit et al., 2018). |

We spend approximately a third of our lives sleeping, yet the precise purpose of sleep is still to be established. Listed here are three of the dominant theories.

**Good for Your Brain?**
During the day, your brain produces a lot of waste, and sleep appears to be an important time for clearing it away (Stoica, 2019; Xie et al., 2013). Research in animals suggests that this process of "cleaning house" is most efficient when the body is positioned sideways (Lee et al., 2015). So if you want to facilitate this detox process, sleeping sideways may be your best bet.

## Think Critically

### 6 SLEEP MYTHS

**HAVE YOU FALLEN FOR ANY OF THEM?**

- **Drinking alcohol before bed helps you sleep better:** Alcohol helps you fall asleep, but it undermines sleep quality and may cause you to awaken in the night (American Psychological Association, 2020; Caldwell et al., 2019).
- **Yawning means you are exhausted:** It likely means you are hot. Yawning appears to be related to temperature and functions to help cool the brain (Massen et al., 2014).
- **Everyone needs 8 hours of sleep each night:** Experts recommend that we get more than 7 hours of sleep each night (Watson et al., 2015), but sleep needs can range greatly from person to person. Some people do fine with 6 hours; others genuinely need 9 or 10 (Schoenborn et al., 2013).
- **Losing sleep during the week is no big deal, as long as you catch up on the weekend:** Sleep deprivation is associated with metabolic changes that can lead to weight gain, and "weekend recovery sleep" does not appear to cancel these effects (Depner et al., 2019).
- **Pressing snooze is a good way to catch a few more minutes of rest:** Because we need more than a few minutes of sleep to feel rested, hitting snooze is a good indication that you are not getting enough sleep (Oexman, 2013).
- **Sleep aids are totally safe:** When taken according to prescription, sleep aids are relatively safe and effective, although they do not guarantee a normal night of sleep. That being said, research has linked some of these medications to serious health problems (DeKosky & Williamson, 2020; Kripke et al., 2012), as well as an increased risk of sleep eating, sleep sex, and "driving while not fully awake" (U.S. Food and Drug Administration, n.d., para. 5).

Now that we have busted some sleep-related myths, you may be wondering how you can improve your nightly shut-eye. For some helpful hints, see **TABLE 4.4**.

**TABLE 4.4**   How to Get a Good Night's Sleep

| To Get Good Sleep | Reasoning |
| --- | --- |
| Get on a schedule. | The body operates according to daily cycles, or circadian rhythms. Putting your body and brain on a regular schedule—going to bed and waking up at roughly the same time every day—is critical. |
| Set the stage for sleep. | Turn down the lights, turn off your phone, and slip into soft pajamas. Do everything possible to create a quiet, dark, and comfortable sleeping environment. |
| Watch your eating, drinking, and smoking. | Don't eat too much before going to bed, and avoid excessive use of alcohol, caffeine, and nicotine (known enemies of sleep), especially late in the day. |
| Move it or lose it. | Exercise on a regular basis. |

Do you wake up feeling groggy and unrestored? Here are a few simple measures that can improve the quality of your sleep. Information from American Academy of Sleep Medicine (2017).

### ▶▶▶ SHOW WHAT YOU KNOW

1. The suprachiasmatic nucleus obtains its information about day and night from:
   A. circadian rhythms.
   B. beta waves.
   C. K-complexes.
   D. retinal ganglion cells.

2. Narcolepsy is a neurological disorder characterized by excessive daytime sleepiness and other sleep-related disturbances such as _____, which refers to an abrupt loss of muscle tone that occurs when a person is awake.

3. In which of the following stages of sleep do adults spend the most time at night?
   A. Stage N1
   B. Stage N2
   C. Stage N3
   D. Stage W

4. Make a drawing of the 90-minute sleep cycle. Label each stage with its associated brain wave(s).

 CHECK YOUR ANSWERS AT THE BACK OF THE BOOK.

# Dreams

REM is a particularly active sleep stage, characterized by brain waves that are fast and irregular. During REM, anything is possible. We can soar through the clouds, swim in molasses, and ride roller coasters with frogs. Time to explore the weird world of dreaming.

**SLEEP, SLEEP, GO AWAY**    Just 2 months before graduating from high school, Matt began taking a new medication that vastly improved the quality of his nighttime sleep. He also began strategic power napping, setting aside time in his schedule to go somewhere peaceful and fall asleep for 15 to 30 minutes. "Power naps are probably the greatest thing a person with narcolepsy can do," Matt insists. The naps helped eliminate the daytime sleepiness, effectively preempting all those unplanned naps that had fragmented his days. Matt also worked diligently to create structure in his life, setting a predictable rhythm of going to bed, taking medication, going to bed again, waking up in the morning, attending class, taking a nap, and so on.

Now a college graduate and working professional, Matt manages his narcolepsy quite successfully. All of his major symptoms—the spontaneous naps, cataplexy, sleep paralysis, and hypnagogic hallucinations—have faded. "Now if I fall asleep, it's because I choose to," Matt says. "Most people don't even know I have narcolepsy."

When Matt goes to sleep at night, he no longer imagines people coming to murder him. In dreams, he soars through the skies like Superman, barreling into outer space to visit the planets. "All my dreams are now pleasant," says Matt, "[and] it's a lot nicer being able to fly than being stabbed by a butcher knife." Onward and upward, like Superman.

*Courtesy Mathew Utesch.*

**Under Control**
After a few very challenging years, Matt developed effective strategies for managing his narcolepsy. In addition to using a medication that helps him sleep more soundly at night, Matt takes strategic power naps and sticks to a regular bedtime and wake-up schedule.

## What Are Dreams?

**LO 7**  Summarize theories explaining why we dream.

What are dreams, and why do we have them? People have contemplated the significance of dreams for millennia, and scholars have developed many intriguing theories to explain them.

**PSYCHOANALYSIS AND DREAMS**    The first comprehensive theory of dreaming was developed by the founder of psychoanalysis, Sigmund Freud. In 1900 Freud laid out his theory in the now-classic *The Interpretation of Dreams,* proposing that dreams are a form of "wish fulfillment," or a playing out of unconscious desires. As Freud saw it, many of the desires expressed in dreams are forbidden and would produce great anxiety in a dreamer if they were aware of them. In dreams, these desires are disguised so they can be experienced without danger of discovery. Freud believed dreams have two levels of content: *manifest* and *latent.* **Manifest content,** the apparent meaning of a dream, is the actual story line of the dream—what you remember when you wake up. **Latent content** is the hidden meaning of a dream, and can provide a window into unconscious conflicts and desires. During therapy sessions, psychoanalysts look deeper than the actual story line of a dream, using its latent content to uncover what's occurring unconsciously. Critics of Freud's approach to dream analysis would note that it is not grounded in scientific evidence (Domhoff, 2017b). What's more, there are an infinite number of ways to interpret any dream, all of which are impossible to prove wrong.

**manifest content**  The apparent meaning of a dream; the remembered story line of a dream.

**latent content**  The hidden meaning of a dream, often concealed by the manifest content of the dream.

**ACTIVATION–SYNTHESIS MODEL**    In contrast to Freud's theory, the **activation–synthesis model** suggests that dreams have no meaning whatsoever (Hobson & McCarley, 1977). During REM sleep, the areas of the brain that control movement are inhibited (remember, the body is paralyzed), but sensory areas of the brain hum with a great deal of neural activity. According to the activation–synthesis model, we create meaning in response to this activity, even though this sensory excitement is only random chatter among neurons (Hobson & Pace-Schott, 2002). Our creative minds make up stories to match this activity, and these stories are our dreams. During REM sleep, the brain is also trying to make sense of neural activity in the **vestibular system**. If the vestibular system is active while we are lying still, then the brain may interpret this as floating or flying—both common experiences reported by dreamers. Not only do we create meaning in response to the neural activity, but our recent waking experiences influence our dreams as well (Hobson, 2009; Hobson & Friston, 2012).

## CONNECTIONS

In **Chapter 3**, we noted that the vestibular system helps the body maintain balance as it deals with the effects of gravity, movement, and position. If there is activity in the neural networks that process vestibular information during sleep, the brain may interpret this as movement sensations normally felt during times of wakefulness.

**NEUROCOGNITIVE THEORY OF DREAMS**    The neurocognitive theory of dreams proposes there is a high degree of similarity between thinking when we are awake and the cognitive activity of dreaming. In fact, most dream content resembles "waking thought" in terms of "personal concerns" and how we view ourselves and others (Domhoff, 2017a). Stated differently, "Both of these states [being awake and dreaming] are dealing with the same psychological issues to a large extent" (Domhoff, 2001, p. 26).

According to the neurocognitive theory, there is a network of neurons essential for dreaming (and perhaps daydreaming, too) in areas of the limbic system and forebrain (Domhoff, 2001; Domhoff & Fox, 2015). People with damage to these brain areas either do not have dreams, or their dreams are not normal (they lack visual imagery, for example). This finding provides support for the neurocognitive theory of dreams. Another line of supporting evidence comes from studies of children. Before about 13 to 15 years of age, children report dreams that are less vivid and story-oriented than those of adults. Certain brain developments must occur before a child experiences the cognitive activities that allow them to dream like an adult.

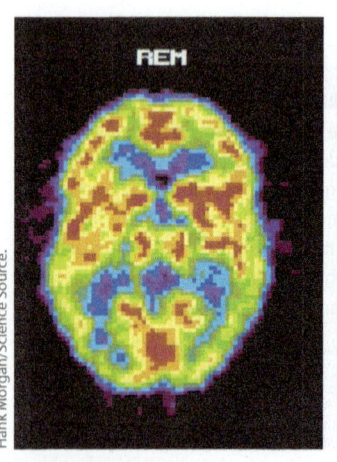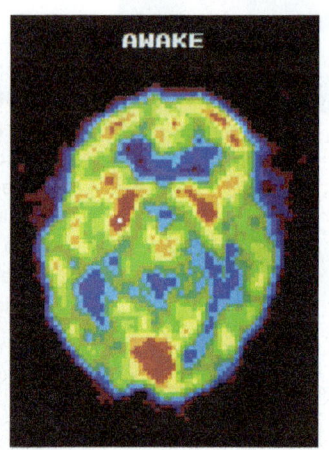

Hank Morgan/Science Source.

**Dreaming Brain**
PET scans reveal the high levels of brain activity during REM sleep (left) and wakefulness (right). During REM, the brain is abuzz with excitement. (This is especially true of the sensory areas.) According to the activation–synthesis model, dreams may result when the brain tries to make sense of all this neural activity.

Unlike Freud, who proposed that the content of dreams has special meaning, neurocognitive theorists suggest that dreams result from the same type of cognition we experience when awake. In fact, dreams may be a "by-product" of evolution; over time, the human brain has evolved increasingly sophisticated cognitive abilities, and dreams are just a consequence of that process (Domhoff, 2018). Dreams may also result from another cognitive process: memory consolidation. Studies suggest that sleep facilitates the formation of memories (Murkar et al., 2014).

## Put Your Heads Together

 Team up and discuss the three theories of dreaming. Now consider the following dream: You walk outside and spot a UFO in the sky. Suddenly, it shoots out an eerie green light and starts to "beam you up." Explain this dream using one of the three theories. Write down your responses.

## Dream a Little Dream

Most dreams feature ordinary, everyday scenarios like driving a car or sitting in class. The content of dreams tends to be repetitive and is frequently in line with our activities, emotions, and thoughts during wakeful hours. Life experiences that get incorporated into our dreams tend to be emotional (Malinowski & Horton, 2014). The content of dreams is relatively consistent across cultures. For example, dreams about teachers, school, flying, being chased, sexual experiences, and eating delicious foods

**activation–synthesis model**    A theory proposing that humans respond to random neural activity while in REM sleep as if it has meaning.

were the most frequent themes for both Chinese and German participants across dream studies (Mathes et al., 2014; Yu, 2015). Dreams are more likely to include sad events than happy ones and, contrary to popular assumption, less than 12% of dream time is devoted to sexual activity (Yu & Fu, 2011). Have you ever noticed that dreams are different when you have a fever? To pinpoint these differences, researchers asked people to fill out a survey about their recent dreams. The participants described "fever dreams" as being more bizarre and negative than ordinary dreams, and more likely to include themes of health and temperature (Schredl & Erlacher, 2020).

Some people believe they don't dream at all, but they probably just don't remember their dreams. Typically, the ability to recall dreams is dependent on the length of time since they occurred. For example, you are more likely to recall a dream if someone wakes you up during the dream as opposed to asking you to remember it hours later.

The average person starts dreaming about 90 minutes into sleep, and then goes on to have about four to six dreams during the night. The total time dreaming is about 1 to 2 hours per night. An interesting feature of dreams is that they happen in real time. In one early study investigating this phenomenon, researchers roused a small number of sleepers after they had been in a 5-minute REM cycle and again after a 15-minute REM cycle, asking them how long they had been dreaming (5 or 15 minutes). Eighty percent of the participants gave the right answer (Dement & Kleitman, 1957).

Have you ever realized that you are in the middle of a dream? A *lucid dream* is one that you are aware of having, and research suggests that about half of us have had one (Gackenbach & LaBerge, 1988). There are two parts to a lucid dream: the dream itself and the awareness that you are dreaming. This awareness seems to have different triggers, including intense emotions (feeling frightened by the dream, for example) and the realization that what's happening is abnormal or dreamlike ("this doesn't make sense" or "this just feels like a dream") (Adams & Bourke, 2020). Some suggest lucid dreaming is actually a way to direct the content of dreams (Gavie & Revonsuo, 2010), but this is a potentially contentious claim because dreams cannot be experienced by an outsider, making them challenging to "verify objectively" (LaBerge, 2014). However, researchers have had some recent success inducing lucid dreaming in a lab setting (Carr et al., 2020).

Fantastical, funny, or frightening, dreams are a distinct state of consciousness—a fluid, ever-changing entity. Now it's time to explore how consciousness transforms when chemicals are introduced into our bodies, or when we undergo hypnosis. On to the *altered states*.

## ▶▶▶ SHOW WHAT YOU KNOW

1. According to the _____, dreams have no meaning whatsoever. Instead, the brain is responding to random neural activity as if it has meaning.

   **A.** psychoanalytic perspective   **C.** activation–synthesis model
   **B.** neurocognitive theory        **D.** evolutionary perspective

2. Freud believed dreams have two levels. The _____ refers to the apparent meaning of the dream, whereas the _____ refers to its hidden meaning.

3. What occurs in the brain when you dream?

   ✓ CHECK YOUR ANSWERS AT THE BACK OF THE BOOK.

# What Are Altered States?

**UNDER THE KNIFE**   You wake in the morning with a dull pain around your belly button. By the time you get to your 10:00 A.M. class, the pain is sharper and has migrated to your lower right abdomen, so you head to the local emergency room. Doctors diagnose you with appendicitis, an inflammation of the appendix often caused by infection (and potentially fatal if allowed to progress too far). You need an emergency

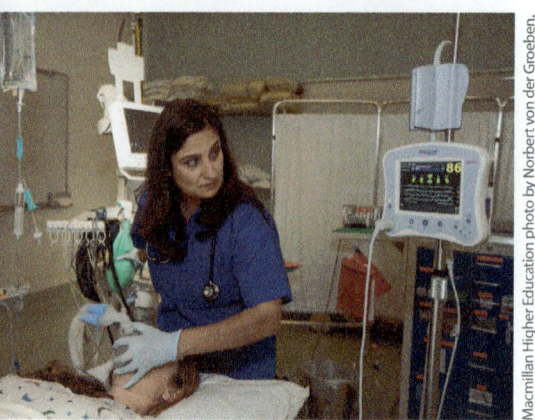

Macmillan Higher Education photo by Norbert von der Groeben.

**Going Under**
Dr. Chander uses various drugs to lull her surgical patients into a deeper-than-sleep state. She may administer a gas, such as nitrous oxide, or a volatile liquid, such as sevoflurane, through a mask (as demonstrated here). In other instances, she delivers drugs through injection.

**CONNECTIONS**

In **Chapter 2,** we described neurotransmitters and their role in the nervous system. Acetylcholine is a neurotransmitter that relays messages from motor neurons to muscles, enabling movement. Here, we see how drugs can block the normal activity of acetylcholine, causing the paralysis that is useful during surgery.

**psychoactive drugs** Substances that can cause changes in psychological activities such as sensation, perception, attention, judgment, memory, self-control, emotion, thinking, and behavior; substances that cause changes in conscious experiences.

operation to remove your appendix. You've never had surgery, and the prospect of "going under" is making you very nervous: *I hate needles—do I have to have an IV? What if I wake up in excruciating pain? What if I never wake up?*

Dr. Chander, introduced at the start of the chapter, is your anesthesiologist. She is there to keep you safe and comfortable throughout the process; she also may be able to ease your anxiety by connecting with you on a human level. "The most important thing, in addition to assessing what their surgical and anesthetic risk is, is to form that quick bond, and rapport with that patient," Dr. Chander explains. "If you're an anesthesiologist that can really connect to humans . . . you can really make a difference in someone's life," she adds. "I think you can impact their entire healing process by taking away a lot of their fear in the beginning."

After taking notes on your medical history and examining your heart, lungs, and airways, Dr. Chander explains the procedure you are about to undergo. When you're ready, she starts an IV, delivering a drug such as Versed (midazolam) to ease your anxiety and interfere with your ability to form new memories for the next 20 minutes or so. Why the need for this temporary memory block? The moments before surgery are terrifying; some patients tremble and cry in anticipation. But everyone is different. A small number of Dr. Chander's patients refuse the Versed because they want to remember their presurgery experience.

The Versed kicks in; you start to feel relaxed and sleepy; and before you know it, you're in the operating room, hooked up to all sorts of tubes and monitors. Dr. Chander lulls you into unconsciousness with a drug called propofol, and blunts your perception of pain with a powerful narcotic such as fentanyl. She also paralyzes your muscles with drugs such as rocuronium or vecuronium, whose effects are readily reversible. These drugs are modern derivatives of curare, an arrowhead poison used by South American natives. Curare works by blocking the activity of the neurotransmitter **acetylcholine**, which stimulates muscle contractions in the body. But curare does not cross into the brain, and therefore it does not have the power to transport you to another level of consciousness (Czarnowski et al., 2007).

A few minutes ago, you were awake, sensing, perceiving, thinking, and talking. Now you see nothing, hear nothing, feel nothing. It's like you are gone. The anesthetics Dr. Chander used to produce these effects are called *psychoactive drugs*.

## Psychoactive Drugs: From Caffeine to Heroin

**LO 8** Define psychoactive drugs.

**Psychoactive drugs** cause changes in psychological activities such as sensation, perception, attention, judgment, memory, self-control, emotion, thinking, and behavior—all of which are associated with our conscious experiences. You don't have to visit a hospital to have a psychoactive drug experience. Mind-altering drugs are everywhere—in the coffee shop around the corner, at the liquor store down the street, and probably in your own kitchen. About 90% of U.S. adults ingest caffeine through coffee, tea, and other products—mostly in the morning when they tend to be less alert (Lieberman et al., 2019). Trailing close behind caffeine are *alcohol* (found in beer, wine, and liquor) and *nicotine* (in cigarettes, e-cigarettes, and other tobacco products), two substances that present serious health risks. Another huge category of psychoactive drugs is prescription medications—drugs for pain relief, depression, insomnia, and just about any ailment you can imagine. Don't forget the illicit, or illegal, drugs like LSD and Ecstasy. Thirteen percent of Americans aged 12 and older report having used illegal drugs within the past month (Substance Abuse and Mental Health Services Administration [SAMHSA], 2020). It's important to note that both legal and illegal drugs can be misused. Later in the chapter, we will discuss "substance use disorder," the continued use of a drug despite significant problems associated with "cognitive, behavioral, and physiological symptoms" (American Psychiatric Association, 2013, p. 483).

Psychoactive drugs alter consciousness in an untold number of ways. They can rev you up, slow you down, reduce your inhibitions, and convince you that the universe is on the verge of collapse. We will discuss the three major categories of psychoactive drugs—depressants, stimulants, and hallucinogens—but keep in mind that some drugs fall into more than one group.

# Depressants

**LO 9** Identify several depressants and stimulants and know their effects.

In the operating room, Dr. Chander relies heavily on a group of psychoactive drugs that *suppress* certain kinds of activity in the central nervous system (CNS), or slow things down. They are known as sedative-hypnotics or, more broadly, **depressants.** In the example above, you learned how she used Versed to ease anxiety. Versed is a *benzodiazepine*—a type of depressant that has a calming, sleep-inducing effect. Other examples of benzodiazepines are Valium (diazepam) and Xanax (alprazolam), used to treat anxiety disorders. A growing number of Americans have been overusing and misusing benzodiazepines in recent years, but because so much attention has been focused on the opioid epidemic (soon to be discussed), this problem has been somewhat ignored (Lembke et al., 2018). To warn the public about the danger for abuse, addiction, and other adverse effects, the U.S. Food and Drug Administration (FDA) has issued a black box warning for prescription benzodiazepines (U.S. FDA, 2020).

"The date-rape drug" Rohypnol (flunitrazepam), also known as "roofies," is a benzodiazepine legally manufactured in other countries but not approved in the United States (Drug Enforcement Administration [DEA], 2020a). Sex predators have been known to slip Rohypnol pills, which are flavorless and sometimes colorless, into their victims' alcoholic drinks—a potentially deadly combination. Rohypnol can cause confusion, amnesia, physical weakness, and sometimes loss of consciousness, preventing victims from defending themselves or remembering the details of a sexual assault (DEA, 2020a).

**BARBITURATES**    Once a patient is in the operating room and ready for surgery, Dr. Chander puts them "to sleep," a process called *induction*. In the past, anesthesiologists might have induced patients with a type of depressant called a **barbiturate** (bar-BICH-er-it), which has a calming or sleep-inducing effect. In low doses, barbiturates cause many of the same effects as alcohol—relaxation, "emotional depression," or alternatively, aggression (Advokat et al., 2019)—and they have become popular among recreational users. But these substances are addictive and extremely dangerous when taken in excess or mixed with other drugs. If barbiturates are taken with alcohol, for example, the muscles of the diaphragm may relax to the point of suffocation (INFOGRAPHIC **4.2** on the next page).

**OPIOIDS**    Putting a patient to sleep is not enough to prepare them for a major surgery; they also need drugs that combat pain. Even when a patient is out cold on the operating table, the brain receives pain impulses, and pain during surgery can lead to greater pain during recovery. "When the surgeon is cutting, it causes trauma to the body whether or not you're consciously perceiving it," explains Dr. Chander. "If you don't block pain receptors up front, you could have significant pain afterwards, sometimes lasting well beyond the period of healing from the surgery. We call this conversion from acute to chronic pain." With this in mind, Dr. Chander may use an *opioid*, a drug

**depressants** A class of psychoactive drugs that depress or slow down activity in the central nervous system.

**barbiturates** Depressant drugs that decrease neural activity and reduce anxiety; a type of sedative.

# The Dangers of Drugs in Combination

Taking multiple drugs simultaneously can have unintended and potentially fatal consequences because of how they work in the brain. Drugs can modify neurotransmission by increasing or decreasing the chemical activity. When two drugs work on the same system, their effects can be additive, greatly increasing the risk of overdose. For example, alcohol and barbiturates both bind to GABA receptors. GABA's inhibitory action has a sedating effect, which is a good thing when you need to relax. But too much GABA will relax physiological processes to the point where unconscious, life-sustaining activities shut down, causing you to stop breathing and die.

In the United States, alcohol use leads to nearly 5 million emergency room visits per year. Combined use of alcohol and other drugs is more likely to result in hospital admissions (White et al., 2018).

## NORMAL GABA ACTIVITY

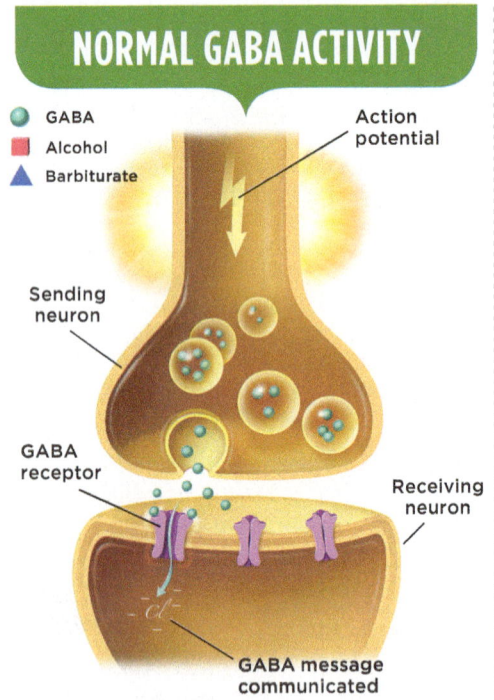

- ● GABA
- ■ Alcohol
- ▲ Barbiturate

Action potential

Sending neuron

GABA receptor

Receiving neuron

GABA message communicated

GABA activation, which calms nervous system activity, is essential for proper functioning of the central nervous system. Without GABA, nerve cells fire too frequently.

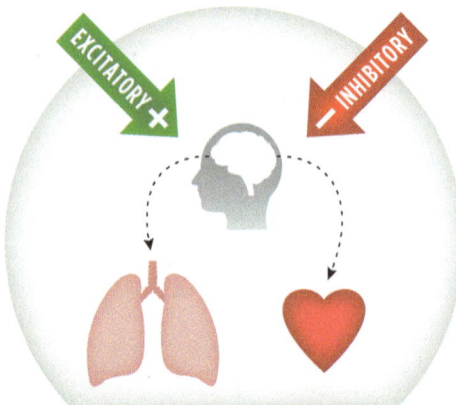

EXCITATORY + / INHIBITORY −

When systems are functioning normally, GABA's inhibitory signals perfectly balance excitatory signals in the central nervous system (CNS). This results in regular breathing and heart rate.

## ALCOHOL

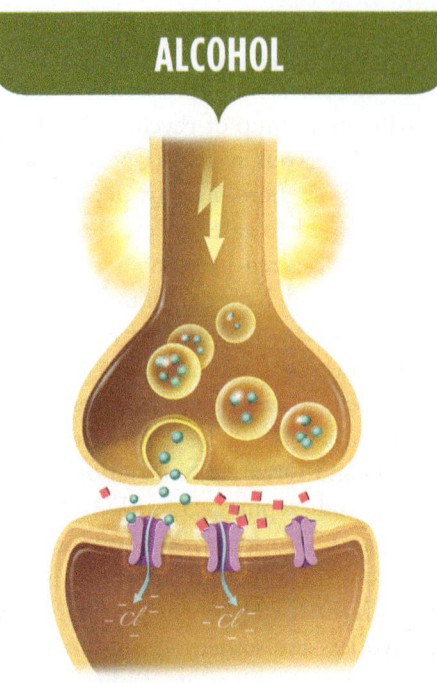

Alcohol activates the same receptors, increasing GABA's activity.

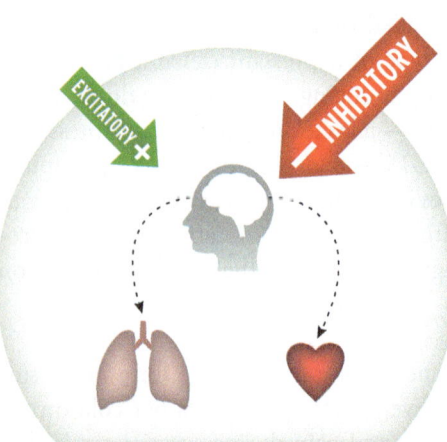

EXCITATORY + / INHIBITORY −

When alcohol increases GABA's inhibitory signals, excitatory and inhibitory signals in the CNS are out of balance. Along with increased relaxation, heart and breathing rates decrease. Increasing levels of alcohol could eventually lead to stupor and coma.

## ALCOHOL + BARBITURATE

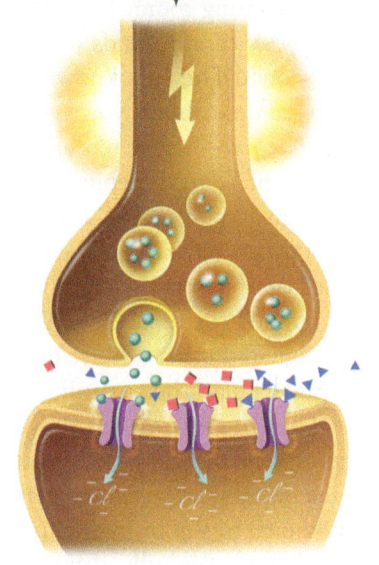

Barbiturates bind to and activate GABA receptors too, creating even more GABA-related inhibition.

EXCITATORY + / INHIBITORY −

Together, alcohol and barbiturates further unbalance excitatory and inhibitory signals, suppressing heart rate and the impulse to breathe.

that minimizes the brain's perception of pain, induces drowsiness and euphoria, and slows breathing (Advokat et al., 2019). "Opioid" is an umbrella term for a large group of similarly acting drugs, some found in nature and others synthesized by humans. There are two types of naturally occurring opioids: endorphins produced by your body, and **opiates** found in the opium poppy. Morphine, which is derived from the opium poppy, is used to alleviate pain in medical settings; it also serves as the raw material for making heroin, which enters the brain more quickly and has 3 times the strength (Advokat et al., 2019). Human-made opioids include methadone, fentanyl, and other drugs used in medical settings. There are also a host of illegally made opioids, many of which are chemical variations of fentanyl (DEA, 2020b).

## Think Critically

### AMERICA'S OPIOID EPIDEMIC

On an average day in the United States, approximately 185 people die from drug overdoses, and more than two thirds of these cases involve opioids (Centers for Disease Control and Prevention [CDC], 2020, March 19). To put this in perspective, more Americans are dying from drug overdoses than gun murders and car crashes together. And the situation is not poised to improve; researchers estimate that the number of overdose deaths will reach 81,700 per year by 2025; that's a 147% increase from 2015 (Chen et al., 2019). As *New York Times* reporter Josh Katz has observed, "It's the worst drug overdose epidemic in American history" (Katz, 2017, para. 5). The crisis has been magnified by the misuse of fentanyl, a powerful anesthetic drug that should only be administered in a medical setting. When fentanyl is illegally manufactured and packaged with other drugs like heroin and cocaine, its effects can be deadly (Scholl et al., 2019). What can be done to stem the disaster?

First, health-care professionals need to be extremely careful about prescribing opioids. For their part, patients should think carefully when it comes to using these potentially addictive painkillers. The medical community has already taken steps to curb unnecessary prescriptions and provide patients in need with naloxone, a drug that acts as an opioid antagonist and may prevent fatal overdoses (American Medical Association [AMA], 2018). There has also been a push for increasing access to buprenorphine, a drug used to treat opioid dependence, though barriers remain (Cooper et al., 2020; Wakeman & Barnett, 2018).

At the community level, people need to understand that opioid abuse can signal a "disease" that needs treatment—it is not a sign of personal weakness or failure. As the American College of Physicians (ACP) recommends, "Substance use disorder is a chronic medical condition and should be managed as such" (Crowley et al., 2017, p. 734). Finally, we all need to be on heightened alert for signs of trouble (**FIGURE 4.3**).

MIKE BELLEME/The New York Times/Redux.

**Children Learn to Reverse Overdoses**
Opioid overdoses are so common in some parts of the United States that children (beginning at age 6) are being taught how to deliver the lifesaving drug Narcan. After taking a class at their local library, these children in Elizabethton, Tennessee, will go home with two doses of Narcan and an understanding of how to use it (Levin, 2020).

**FIGURE 4.3**
**You Might Save a Life**

> ## Do you know someone who might have a problem with opioids or other drugs?
> Do something before the situation spirals into tragedy. Help is available 24-7 through the **National Health Helpline: 1-800-662-HELP (4357)**. You can also find a nearby treatment facility through SAMHSA's Behavioral Health Treatment Services Locator: https://findtreatment.samhsa.gov.

**opiates** A class of psychoactive drugs that cause a sense of euphoria; drugs that imitate the endorphins naturally produced in the brain.

Do you know what an opioid overdose looks like? If you have the slightest suspicion that someone is suffering from a drug overdose, call 911 immediately. Look for three signs in particular: (1) pinpoint pupils (unusually small pupils), (2) unconsciousness, and (3) difficulty breathing (World Health Organization, 2020).

## Alcohol: The Most Commonly Used Depressant

We end our coverage of depressants with alcohol, which, like other drugs in its class, has played a central role in the history of anesthesia. The ancient Greek doctor Dioscorides gave his surgical patients a special concoction of wine and mandrake plant (Keys, 1945), and 19th-century Europeans used an alcohol-opium mixture called *laudanum* for anesthetic purposes (Barash et al., 2009). These days, you won't find anesthesiologists knocking out patients with alcohol, but you will encounter plenty of people intoxicating themselves.

**BINGE DRINKING**    Alcohol is the most commonly used depressant in the United States. About 18% of U.S. adults report binge drinking (consuming four or more drinks for women and five or more for men, on one occasion) in the last 30 days. In recent years, binge drinkers have become more extreme, consuming larger amounts of alcohol as time goes by (Kanny et al., 2020). Many people think binge drinking is fun, but they might change their minds if they reviewed the research. Studies have linked binge drinking to poor grades, low self-esteem, and behavior problems in adolescents (Patrick & Schulenberg, 2014). Even worse, binge drinking may lead to death by accidental injury: "Of the nearly 90,000 people who die from alcohol each year, more than half, or 50,000, die from injuries and overdoses associated with high blood alcohol levels," noted George F. Koob, director of the National Institute on Alcohol Abuse and Alcoholism (National Institutes of Health, 2017, para 2). Think getting wasted is sexy? Consider this: Too much alcohol impairs sexual performance, particularly for men, who may have trouble obtaining and sustaining an erection.

You don't have to binge drink in order to have an alcohol problem. Some people cannot get through the day without a midday drink; others need alcohol to unwind or fall asleep. The point is there are many forms of alcohol misuse. About 12.7% of the adult population in the United States (1 in 8 people) have alcohol use disorder in a given year (American Psychiatric Association, 2013; Grant et al., 2017).

**ALCOHOL AND THE BODY**    Let's stop for a minute and examine how alcohol influences consciousness (**FIGURE 4.4**). People sometimes say they feel "high" when they drink. How can such a statement be true when alcohol is a *depressant,* a drug that slows down activity in the central nervous system? Alcohol boosts the activity of GABA, a neurotransmitter that dampens activity in certain neural networks, including those that regulate social inhibition—a type of self-restraint that keeps you from doing things you will regret the next morning. This release of social inhibition can lead to feelings of euphoria. Drinking affects other conscious processes, such as reaction time, balance, attention span, memory, speech, and involuntary life-sustaining activities like breathing (Howland et al., 2010; McKinney & Coyle, 2006). Drink enough, and these vital functions will shut down entirely, leading to coma and even death (Infographic 4.2).

The female body is less efficient at breaking down (metabolizing) alcohol. Women achieve higher blood alcohol levels (and thus a significantly stronger "buzz") than men who have consumed equal amounts. Why? Some research suggests that men have more of an alcohol-metabolizing enzyme in their stomachs, which means they start to break down alcohol almost immediately after ingestion (Baraona et al., 2001). However, it is still not entirely clear why men and women metabolize alcohol differently; it may be related to hormonal differences (Erol & Karphyak, 2015).

South_agency/Getty Images.

**Drinking Through the Pandemic?**
Alcohol sales increased significantly at the onset of the COVID-19 pandemic, a concerning trend given that alcohol tends to weaken the immune system, making people less able to fight off the coronavirus and other pathogens (Macmillan, 2020).

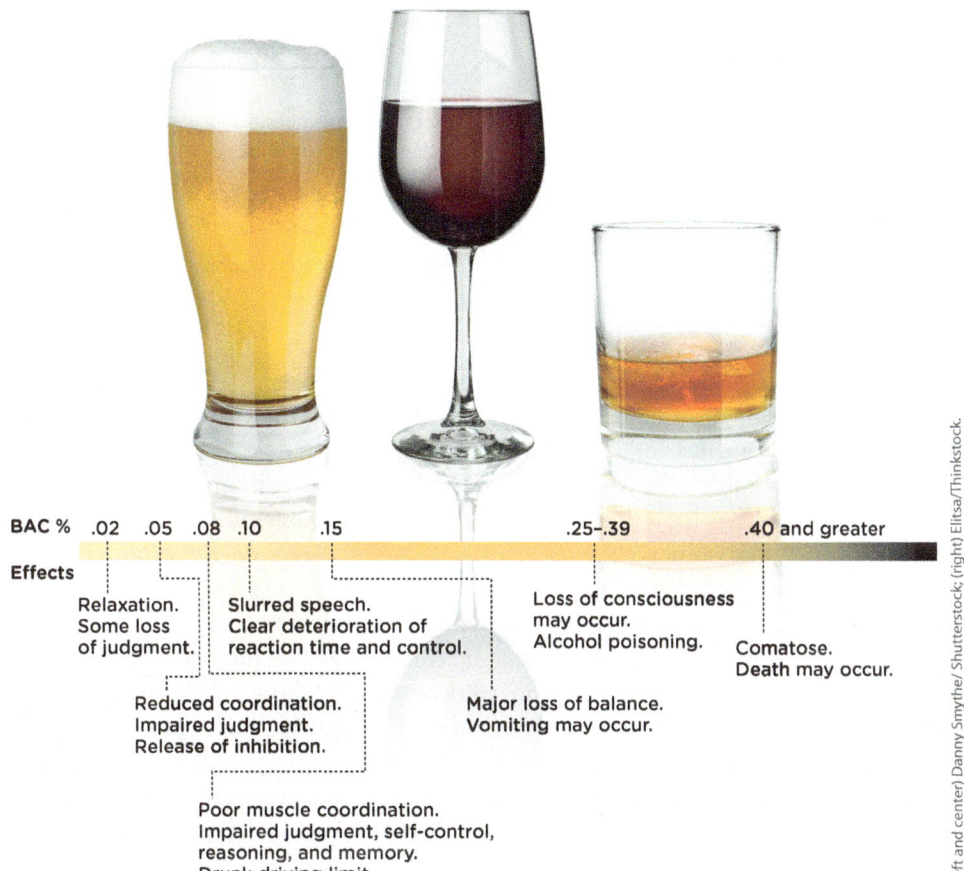

(left and center) Danny Smythe/ Shutterstock; (right) Elitsa/Thinkstock.

### FIGURE 4.4
**Blood Alcohol Concentration (BAC)**
The effects of one drink—a 12-oz bottle of beer, 4-oz glass of wine, or 1-oz shot of hard liquor—vary depending on a person's weight, ethnicity, gender, and other factors. Across most of the United States, a BAC of .08 is the legal limit for driving. But even at lower levels, our coordination and focus may be impaired. Information from: CDC (2017); University of Notre Dame (n.d.).

## Relationships

### SEE THAT WOMAN HOLDING A BEER?

There is another way in which men and women differ with respect to alcohol, and that is in others' *perceptions* of them. In one study, researchers asked participants to describe the characteristics of men and women in photos. Some of the photos showed people holding beers, while others showed them holding water bottles. When looking at a woman with a beer in hand, both male and female participants were more likely to "dehumanize" her (Riemer et al., 2019), that is, view her more like an animal, machine, or something other than human (Haslam, 2006). Meanwhile, "the presence of alcohol compared to water had no impact on dehumanization of men" (Riemer et al., 2019, p. 617). Why were beer-toting females dehumanized? Participants seemed to think that alcohol-drinking women were more "sexually disinhibited," or relaxed about sex (Riemer et al., 2019). We know that alcohol induces changes in consciousness, but obviously such changes do not make people less human. How can we make sense of such findings?

### Put Your Heads Together

The study described above highlights a double standard. In other words, different principles are being applied to men and women. In your groups, discuss the following: **A)** Why do you think men and women were perceived differently? **B)** When people make assumptions about women's sexual availability and interest, how might this impact the safety of those women?

**HERE'S TO YOUR HEALTH?** Light alcohol consumption by adults—one to two drinks a day—has been linked to better cardiovascular health. But correlation does not prove causation. People who have a glass or two of red wine with dinner may

- Having your friends or relatives express concern
- Being annoyed when people criticize your drinking behavior
- Feeling guilty about your drinking behavior
- Thinking you should drink less but being unable to do so
- Needing a morning drink as an "eye-opener" or to relieve a hangover
- Not fulfilling responsibilities at work, home, or school because of drinking
- Engaging in dangerous behavior (like driving under the influence)
- Having legal or social problems due to drinking

**FIGURE 4.5**

**Warning Signs of Problematic Drinking**
The presence of one or more warning signs listed to the right could indicate a developing problem with alcohol. Information from: APA (2012); National Institute on Alcohol Abuse and Alcoholism (n.d.).

also be eating heart healthy foods (American Heart Association News, 2019). Could dietary factors be a third variable influencing heart health?

While the health effects of moderate drinking are still under investigation, excessive drinking has been linked to a host of medical problems. Overuse of alcohol can lead to malnourishment, cirrhosis of the liver, and *Wernicke–Korsakoff syndrome,* whose symptoms include confusion and memory problems. Heavy alcohol use has also been linked to heart disease, various types of cancer, tens of thousands of yearly traffic deaths, and *fetal-alcohol syndrome* in children whose mothers drank during pregnancy. Would you believe that 1 in 10 deaths of "working-age" Americans (ages 20 to 64) results from overuse of alcohol (Stahre et al., 2014)? Every year, over 95,000 Americans die of alcohol-related causes; that's 261 people per day (CDC, 2020, October 1). Looking at the overall impact of alcohol consumption across the world, the risks outweigh the benefits (Rehm et al., 2016). Take a look at the warning signs of problematic drinking presented in **FIGURE 4.5**.

## Stimulants

Not all drugs used in anesthesia are depressants. Did you know that some doctors use cocaine as a local anesthetic for nose and throat surgeries (Dwyer et al., 2016)? Cocaine is a **stimulant**—a drug that increases neural activity in the sympathetic nervous system, producing heightened alertness, energy, elevated mood, and other effects (Advokat et al., 2019). When applied topically, cocaine blocks sensation in the peripheral nerves and thereby numbs the area.

**History of Coca**
A man in Peru chews coca leaves, which contain less than 1% cocaine. For thousands of years, people in South America's Andean regions have been chewing coca leaves to increase energy, reduce hunger, and fight altitude sickness (Morales Ayma, 2009). In the late 1850s a German chemist named Albert Niemann extracted an active part of the coca leaf and dubbed it "cocaine" (Advokat et al., 2019; Keys, 1945). Within a few decades, doctors were using cocaine for anesthesia, Sigmund Freud was giving it to patients (and himself), and Coca-Cola was putting it in soda (Keys, 1945; Musto, 1991).

**stimulants** A class of drugs that increase neural activity in the central nervous system.

**COCAINE** Cocaine is illegal in the United States and most other countries, but it has been a popular recreational drug for many decades. Depending on the form in which it is prepared (powder, rocks, and so on), it can be snorted, injected, or smoked. The sense of energy, euphoria, and other alterations of consciousness that cocaine induces after entering the bloodstream and infiltrating the brain last anywhere from a few minutes to an hour, depending on how it is delivered. Cocaine produces a rush of enjoyment and excitement by amplifying the effects of the neurotransmitter dopamine. This high comes at a steep price. People who use cocaine risk suffering a seizure, stroke, or heart attack, even if they are young and healthy (National Institute on Drug Abuse [NIDA], 2018, July). It is also extremely addictive. Many users find they can never quite duplicate the high they experienced the first time, so they take increasingly higher doses, developing a physical need for the drug and increasing their risk for anxiety, insomnia, schizophrenia-like psychosis, and other effects (Advokat et al., 2019).

Cocaine use grew rampant in the 1980s. That was the decade *crack*—an ultra-potent (and ultra-cheap) crystalline form of cocaine—began to ravage America's urban areas. Although cocaine is still a major problem, another stimulant—methamphetamine—has come to rival it.

**AMPHETAMINES** *Methamphetamine* belongs to a family of stimulants called the **amphetamines** (am-FET-uh-meens). In the 1930s and 1940s, doctors used amphetamines to treat medical conditions as diverse as excessive hiccups and hypotension (unusually low blood pressure; Advokat et al., 2019). During World War II, soldiers and factory workers used methamphetamine to increase energy and boost performance (Lineberry & Bostwick, 2006). Nonprescription use of methamphetamine is illegal, but people have learned how to brew this drug in their own laboratories, using ingredients from ordinary household products such as drain cleaner, battery acid, and over-the-counter cough medicines. "Cooking meth" is a dangerous enterprise. The flammable ingredients, combined with the reckless mentality of "tweaking" cookers, make for toxic fumes and accidental explosions (Lineberry & Bostwick, 2006; Melnikova et al., 2011). Despite the enormous risk, many people continue to cook meth at home, endangering and sometimes killing their own children.

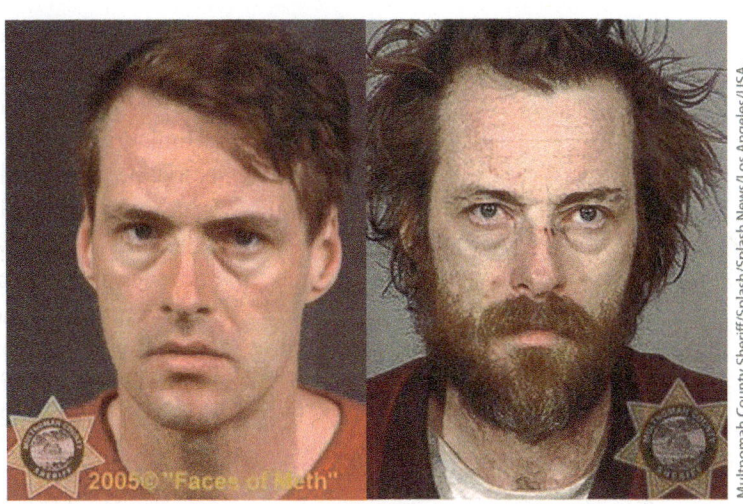

**This Is Your Face on Meth**
Are you shocked by this dramatic physical transformation? Methamphetamine ravages the body, the brain, and one's overall appearance. Imagine experiencing horrific tactile hallucinations that cause you to believe bugs have invaded your skin and are crawling underneath it, and that in response you tear your skin to the bone in order to kill them.

Methamphetamine stimulates the release of the neurotransmitter dopamine, causing a surge in energy and alertness similar to a cocaine high. Users often "binge and crash" repeatedly after the high has worn off (NIDA, 2018, June). This drug has "toxic effects" on the brain, damaging the frontal lobes and other areas. Irregular neural activity may help explain some of the attentional problems observed in meth users (Chen et al., 2020). Chronic meth use causes harm at the neuronal level. This damage is "greater and more widespread" in the brains of teenagers and has been linked to cognitive problems (Lyoo et al., 2015). Other consequences of meth use include severe weight loss, tooth decay ("meth mouth"), frequent skin scratching (causing skin lesions), paranoia, and violent behavior (NIDA, 2018, June).

**CAFFEINE** Most people have not experimented with illegal stimulants like cocaine and meth, but many are regular users of caffeine. We usually associate caffeine with beverages like coffee, but this pick-me-up drug also lurks in places you wouldn't expect, such as over-the-counter cough medicines, chocolate, and energy bars. Caffeine acts as an antagonist of adenosine, a neurotransmitter that normally exerts a calming effect by blocking the activity of other neurotransmitters (McLellan et al., 2016). Caffeine resembles adenosine enough that it can dock onto the same receptors ("posing" as adenosine). With caffeine occupying its receptors, adenosine can no longer exert its calming, sleep-inducing effect (Advokat et al., 2019; Clark & Landolt, 2017). Thus, caffeine makes you feel physically and mentally wired.

Moderate caffeine use (up to four cups of coffee per day) has been associated with increased alertness, enhanced recall ability, elevated mood, and greater endurance during physical exercise (McLellan et al., 2016). Some studies have also linked moderate long-term consumption with lower rates of depression and suicide, and reduced cognitive decline with aging (Lara, 2010; Rosso et al., 2008). But just because researchers find a **link** between caffeine and positive health outcomes, we should not necessarily conclude that caffeine is responsible for it. We need to remember that correlation does not prove causation. What's more, too much caffeine can make your heart race, your hands tremble, and your mood turn irritable. It takes several hours for your body to metabolize caffeine, so a late afternoon mocha latte may still be present in your system as you lie in bed at midnight counting sheep—with no luck.

 *Research*
**CONNECTIONS**

In **Chapter 1,** we emphasized that correlation does not prove causation. Here, we need to be cautious about making too strong a statement about coffee causing positive health outcomes, because third variables could be driving both increased caffeine consumption and better health.

**amphetamines** Stimulant drugs; methamphetamine falls in this class of drugs.

One final note of warning: Be wary of energy drinks, some of which contain three times as much caffeine as soda (Marczinski et al., 2017). Although they might help you get through a long night of studying, the high level of caffeine, sugar, and other stimulants can lead to a variety of problems like "rapid heartbeat, insomnia, increased blood pressure and even death" (Kim & Anagondahalli, 2017, p. 898). Perhaps even more concerning is the combination of alcohol and energy drinks, particularly when driving is involved. People who consume beverages containing both alcohol and energy drinks are more likely to think they are sufficiently sober to drive than those who drink the same amount of alcohol without the mixer. This bears repeating: "Alcohol consumers should be warned that the use of energy drink mixers with alcohol could lead to a false sense of security in one's ability to drive after drinking" (Marczinski et al., 2018, p. 147).

**TOBACCO**    Prior to the COVID-19 pandemic, what do you think was the number one cause of premature death—AIDS, illegal drugs, traffic accidents, murder . . . suicide? None of the above. In the United States, tobacco causes more deaths than any of these other factors combined—a total of 480,000 each year (CDC, 2017, 2020, April 28). This is because smoking is associated with a variety of ailments, including cancer (many types, not just lung cancer), heart disease, stroke, lung disease, and others you might not expect, such as kidney failure (Carter et al., 2015).

Despite these harrowing statistics, about 14% of adults in the United States continue to light up (CDC, 2020, May 21). They say it makes them feel relaxed yet more alert, less hungry, and more tolerant of pain. And those who try to kick the habit find it exceedingly difficult. Cigarettes and other tobacco products contain a highly addictive stimulant called *nicotine,* which sparks the release of epinephrine and norepinephrine. Nicotine use appears to be associated with activity in the same brain area activated by cocaine, another drug that is extremely difficult to give up (Pich et al., 1997; Zhang et al., 2012). Around 90% of quitters relapse within 6 months (Nonnemaker et al., 2011), suggesting that relapse is a normal experience when quitting, not a sign of failure.

Smoking is not just a problem for the smoker. It is a problem for spouses, children, friends, and anyone who is exposed to the *secondhand smoke.* Secondhand smoke is particularly dangerous for children, whose developing tissues are highly vulnerable (Chapter 8). By smoking, parents increase their children's risk for sudden infant death syndrome (SIDS), respiratory infections, asthma, and bronchitis (CDC, 2020, February 27). Secondhand smoke contributes to 41,000 deaths in nonsmokers and 400 infant deaths every year in the United States (Homa et al., 2015), and according to the Centers for Disease Control and Prevention (2020, February 27), "There is no risk-free level of exposure" (para. 3).

Use of traditional cigarettes has recently decreased among teens, while electronic nicotine delivery systems, such as "e-cigarettes," "vape pens," and "pod mods," have gained popularity (Barrington-Trimis & Leventhal, 2018; U.S. Food and Drug Administration, 2019). In addition to delivering a whopping dose of nicotine—more than traditional cigarettes—many of these products are infused with potentially hazardous chemicals (Barrington-Trimis & Leventhal, 2018). Electronic nicotine delivery systems like e-cigarettes might be appropriate for adults who are trying to quit traditional cigarettes (Eisenberg et al., 2020). However, vaping carries many risks. In addition to serving as a gateway to regular smoking, vaping has been linked to serious—and sometimes fatal—lung disease in thousands of people (NIDA, 2020, January; **FIGURE 4.6**).

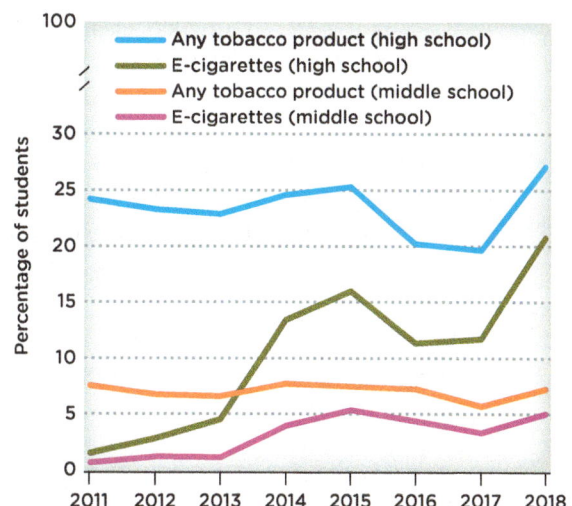

FIGURE 4.6
**The Rise of Vaping**
In 2011 nicotine vaping had a "near-zero prevalence" among adolescents (Miech et al., 2019, p. 192). By 2018, about 21% of high school students and 5% of middle school students were vaping (Cullen et al., 2018). This graph shows how the use of various tobacco products has changed among middle and high school students since 2011. Note the increasing use of e-cigarettes among high school students. Information from Cullen et al., 2018.

## Hallucinogens, Club Drugs, and Marijuana

**LO 10** Discuss how hallucinogens alter consciousness.

We have learned how various depressants and stimulants are used in anesthesia. Believe it or not, there is also a place for **hallucinogens** (huh-LOO-suh-nuh-gens)—drugs that produce hallucinations (sights, sounds, odors, or other sensations of things that are not actually present), altered moods, and distorted perception and thought. Phencyclidine (PCP or *angel dust*) and ketamine (*Special K*) were developed to block pain in surgical patients during the 1950s and 1960s (Advokat et al., 2019). PCP is highly addictive and extremely dangerous. Because users cannot feel normal pain signals, they run the risk of unintentionally harming or killing themselves. Long-term use can lead to depression and memory impairment. Doctors stopped giving PCP to patients long ago; its effect was just too erratic.

Ketamine, on the other hand, continues to be used in hospitals across the country. Unlike many of the depressants used in anesthesia, which can reduce respiratory drive to the point of death (hence the need for the breathing tube and ventilator), ketamine causes less interference with breathing and respiratory reflexes. "Ketamine is an amazing drug for preventing pain," Dr. Chander says. "It's great to use in trauma. You can give it in the muscle, especially if somebody can't start an IV . . . and help them go to sleep that way," she adds. "But used in medicinal ways, or even for recreational purposes, it can have long-lasting effects, much like LSD, a structurally analogous drug, which can cause later flashbacks. Ketamine can in fact induce lasting plastic changes in the brain. Some of these changes can be positive. Interestingly, researchers are finding that ketamine may contribute antidepressant effects through different brain networks than the ones that provide analgesia (pain relief). The drug is being investigated further for this."

**LSD** The most well-known hallucinogen is probably **lysergic acid diethylamide (LSD)** (lih-SER-jic A-sid die-eth-ul-AM-ide)—the odorless, tasteless, and colorless substance that produces extreme changes in sensation and perception. People using LSD may report seeing wild colors and visions of spirals and other geometric forms. Some experience a crossover of sensations, such as "tasting sound" or "hearing colors." Emotions run wild and bleed into one another; a person "tripping" can quickly flip between depression and joy, excitement and terror

**hallucinogens** A group of psychoactive drugs that can produce hallucinations, distorted sensory experiences, alterations of mood, and distorted thinking.

**lysergic acid diethylamide (LSD)** A synthetically produced, odorless, tasteless, and colorless hallucinogen that is very potent; produces extreme changes in sensations and perceptions.

**LSD Sheets**

Lysergic acid diethylamide, or LSD, is usually taken by mouth, administered through candy, sugar cubes, or blotter sheets like the one pictured here. DEA/Science Source.

**CONNECTIONS**

In **Chapter 2,** we reported that serotonin is critical for the regulation of mood, appetite, aggression, and automatic behaviors like sleep. Here, we see how the use of Ecstasy can alter levels of this neurotransmitter.

**methylenedioxymethamphetamine (MDMA)** A synthetic drug that produces a combination of stimulant and hallucinogenic effects.

(Advokat et al., 2019). Trapped on this sensory and emotional roller coaster, some people panic and injure themselves. Others believe that LSD opens their minds, offers new insights, and expands their consciousness. The outcome of a trip depends a great deal on the environment and people who are there. The popularity of LSD increased between 2015 and 2018, perhaps because users were attempting "to find relief from depression, anxiety and general stress over the state of the world" (Nuwer, 2020, para. 1). Still, use of this drug remains rare, with less than 1% of U.S. adults reporting they have tripped in the past year (Nuwer, 2020). Long-term use of LSD may be associated with depression and other psychological problems, including flashbacks that can occur weeks, months, or years after taking the drug. These flashbacks may be triggered by fatigue, stress, and illness (Centre for Addiction and Mental Health, 2010; Friedman, 2017).

**MDMA**    In addition to the traditional hallucinogens, there are quite a few "club drugs," or synthetic "designer drugs." Among the most popular is **methylenedioxymethamphetamine (MDMA)** (meth-ul-een-die-ox-ee-meth-am-FET-uh-meen), commonly known as *Ecstasy* (NIDA, 2020, January). Ecstasy produces a combination of stimulant and hallucinogenic effects (NIDA, 2020a, June). A trip might bring on feelings of euphoria, love, openness, heightened energy, and floating sensations. This drug also seems to have "unusual sociability-enhancing effects," meaning it seems to increase behaviors that benefit others. Some researchers are exploring the potential therapeutic use of MDMA for people dealing with trauma (Kamilar-Britt & Bedi, 2015). But Ecstasy can also cause a host of troubling changes in the body and brain, including nausea, lockjaw, blurred vision, and heightened anxiety. If taken in large amounts, this drug can cause a dangerous increase in body temperature that can lead to organ failure and, in some cases, even death (NIDA, 2020a, June).

Ecstasy triggers a sudden general unloading of **serotonin** in the brain, after which serotonin activity is temporarily depleted until its levels are restored (Klugman & Gruzelier, 2003; Roberts et al., 2016). Studies of animals have shown that even short-term exposure to MDMA can result in long-term, perhaps even permanent, damage to the brain's serotonin pathways, and there is evidence that a similar type of damage affecting reuptake from the synapse and storage of serotonin occurs in humans as well (Campbell & Rosner, 2008; Reneman et al., 2001). The growing consensus is that even light to moderate Ecstasy use can handicap the brain's memory system, and heavy use may impair higher-level cortical functions, such as planning for the future and shifting attention (Klugman & Gruzelier, 2003; Parrott, 2015; Roberts et al., 2016). Studies also suggest that Ecstasy users are more likely to experience symptoms of depression (Guillot, 2007; Parrott, 2015).

**MARIJUANA**    Weed, herb, reefer, chronic, 420—call it what you will. After alcohol, *marijuana* is the most widely used drug in the United States (**INFOGRAPHIC 4.3**; NIDA, 2020, April 8). The U.S. government has marijuana listed as a Schedule I drug, indicating that it has "no currently accepted medical use and a high potential for abuse" (DEA, n.d., para. 3), but the majority of states have now passed laws permitting its use for medical purposes, and 15 states allow its recreational use (Mercado, 2020).

Marijuana comes from the hemp plant, *Cannabis sativa,* which has long been used as—surprise—an anesthetic (Keys, 1945). These days, doctors prescribe cannabis and

# Marijuana in the United States

Marijuana is a psychoactive drug with a complex history and an ever-evolving status. Here, we explore three major categories of change: how people feel about marijuana, the drug's dynamic legal status, and developments in research.

## Attitudes are changing . . .

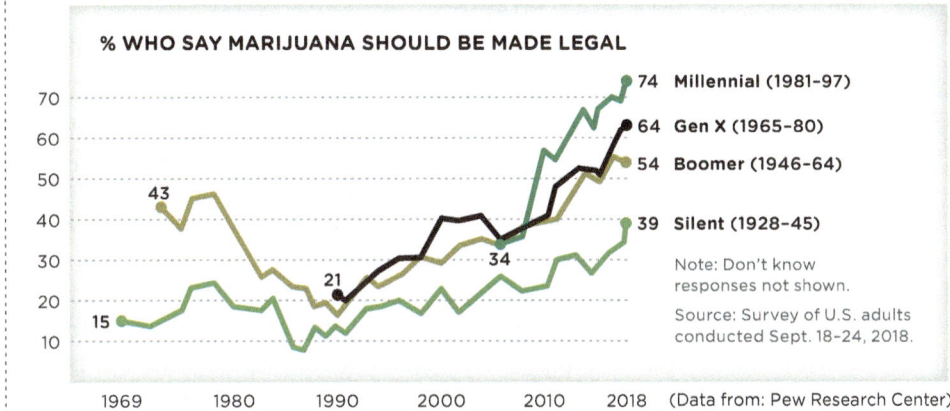

**% WHO SAY MARIJUANA SHOULD BE MADE LEGAL**

- 74 **Millennial (1981–97)**
- 64 **Gen X (1965–80)**
- 54 **Boomer (1946–64)**
- 39 **Silent (1928–45)**

Note: Don't know responses not shown.

Source: Survey of U.S. adults conducted Sept. 18–24, 2018.

(Data from: Pew Research Center)

### SUPPORT FOR LEGALIZATION

The graph to the left shows how Americans' attitudes about marijuana have changed over the last 5 decades. You can see that attitudes differ by generation, but overall the trend is toward legalizing marijuana.

### 6 OUT OF 10

**Americans support the legalization of marijuana**

(Hartig & Geiger, 2018)

## Laws are changing . . .

### STATES WHERE MARIJUANA IS LEGAL

- No broad laws legalizing marijuana
- Medical marijuana broadly legalized
- Marijuana legalized for recreational use

(Lozano, 2020; NIDA, 2019)

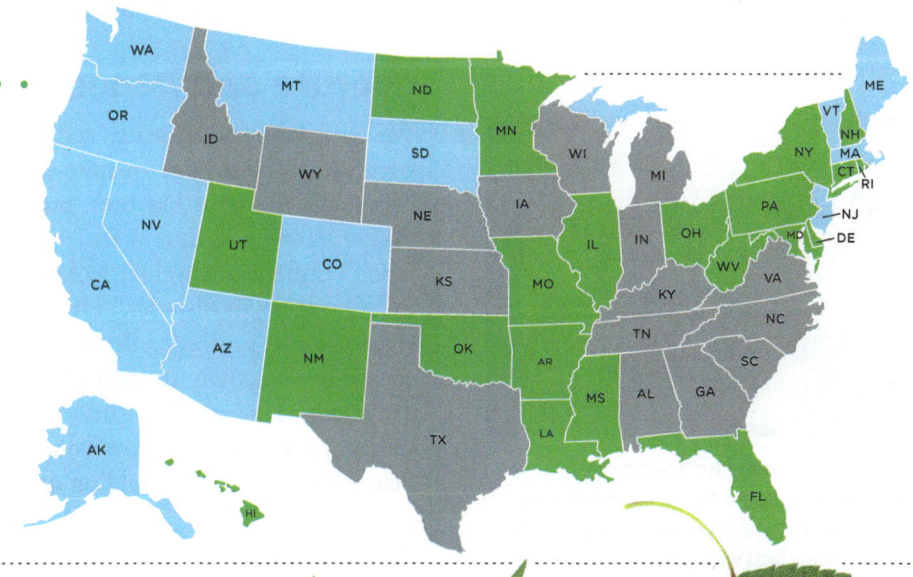

## And the research is evolving . . .

- Studies suggest marijuana compounds may be effective for treating chronic pain, muscle spasms, nausea from chemotherapy, and symptoms of multiple sclerosis (National Academies of Sciences, Engineering, and Medicine, 2017; Whiting et al., 2015; Wilkie et al., 2016).

- Clinical trials have paved the way for the first FDA-approved drug created from marijuana. In 2018, the FDA signed off on Epidiolex (cannabidiol) for the treatment of seizures in patients with certain types of epilepsy (U.S. FDA, 2018).

- Collision insurance data reveal that Colorado, Nevada, Oregon, and Washington experienced a 6% increase in car accidents following the legalization of recreational marijuana. This combined average is in comparison to four nearby states that did not enact such laws (Insurance Institute for Highway Safety, Highway Loss Data Institute, 2018).

- More studies are needed, but there is reason to believe that marijuana may not be good for young brains (Wallis, 2017). Long-term cannabis use, especially that which begins in adolescence, has been associated with lasting cognitive impairments (Meier et al., 2012). What's more, researchers have discovered a link between teen cannabis use and an increased risk for depression and suicidal tendencies later in life (Gobbi et al., 2019).

Matthew Staver/ZUMA Wire/Alamy Live News.

**4-20 Linked to Car Accidents?**
Revelers in Denver, Colorado, celebrate "4-20."
Every year on April 20, people around the world
join together to celebrate marijuana. The occasion
is followed by an uptick in fatal car accidents
(Sifferlin, 2018). Perhaps this is not surprising,
since marijuana impairs reaction time, attentional
capacity, and other abilities required for staying
safe on the road (Compton, 2017; Das et al., 2021).

Photo 12/Alamy Stock Photo.

**Uncertain About "Heisenberg"**
How accurately did the AMC series *Breaking Bad*
portray the methamphetamine underworld? The
show got some facts wrong; for example, there is
no such thing as pure blue meth (Wickman, 2013).
But as far as representing the horrors of drug
trafficking, *Breaking Bad* comes uncomfortably
close to the truth (Keefe, 2012).

**RESEARCH HAS HIGHLIGHTED
THE "ADDICTIVE POTENTIAL"
OF SOCIAL MEDIA.**

**tetrahydrocannabinol (THC)** The
psychoactive ingredient in marijuana.

its chemical derivatives to treat chronic pain, nausea from chemotherapy, and some symptoms of multiple sclerosis, and there is "conclusive or substantial evidence" that such treatments are effective (National Academies of Sciences, Engineering, and Medicine, 2017, para. 4). Outside of a medical context, marijuana use poses significant risks, especially for teenagers. It may harm the brain's neurons, and this damage may be linked to increased impulsivity (acting without thinking), particularly among adolescents (Gruber et al., 2014; Weir, 2015).

Marijuana contains **tetrahydrocannabinol (THC)** (te-truh-high-druh-kuh-NAB-uh-nawl), which toys with consciousness in a variety of ways, making it hard to classify the drug into a single category (for example, stimulant, depressant, or hallucinogen). In addition to altering pain perception, THC can induce mild euphoria and create intense sensory experiences and distortions of time. At higher doses, THC may cause hallucinations and delusions (Murray et al., 2007). It's important to recognize that not all products called "marijuana" contain THC. A relatively new group of psychoactive drugs collectively known as "synthetic marijuana" target the same receptors as THC, but they do not come from the hemp plant. Instead, they are prepared with synthetic chemicals and can be smoked, vaped, or inhaled (NIDA, 2020b, June).

Now that we have discussed the major categories of drugs (INFOGRAPHIC **4.4**), let's explore what it means to become dependent on them.

## Overuse and Dependence

We often joke about being "addicted" to our coffee or soda, but do we understand what this really means? In spite of frequent references to *addiction* in everyday conversations, the term has been omitted from the American Psychiatric Association's diagnostic manual due to its "uncertain definition and potentially negative connotation" (American Psychiatric Association, 2013, p. 485). Instead, the manual refers to "substance use disorder." Historically, the term addiction has been used (both by laypeople and professionals) to refer to the urges people experience to use a drug or engage in an activity to such an extent that it interferes with their functioning or is dangerous. This could mean a gambling habit that depletes your bank account, a sexual appetite that destroys your marriage, or perhaps even a social media fixation that prevents you from holding down a job.

## Social Media and Psychology

### CAN'T GET ENOUGH

Is it difficult for you to sit through a movie without checking your Twitter "Mentions"? Are you constantly looking at Instagram stories in between work e-mails? Do you sleep with your iPhone? If you answered "yes" to any of the above, you are not alone. People around the world, from Hong Kong to the United States, are getting hooked on social media—so hooked in some cases that they are getting evaluated and treated for social media or internet "addiction" (Kessler, 2016; Leung et al., 2020; Saikia, 2017). Indeed, research has highlighted the "addictive potential" of social media for certain individuals (Müller et al., 2016), and some scholars have examined ways to understand and diagnose the problem (van den Eijnden et al., 2016; van Rooij et al., 2017). However, the latest edition of the American Psychiatric Association's (2013) diagnostic manual does not include any such thing as a social media disorder. Will this diagnosis appear in a future edition? Stay tuned. . . .

# Psychoactive Drugs

Recreational use of psychoactive drugs is not only dangerous; it can have disastrous personal and financial consequences for users, families, and society as a whole. Summarized below are some common effects and negative outcomes seen with drugs belonging to three broad categories: depressants, stimulants, and hallucinogens. Note that responses can vary from person to person.

## What are some possible consequences?

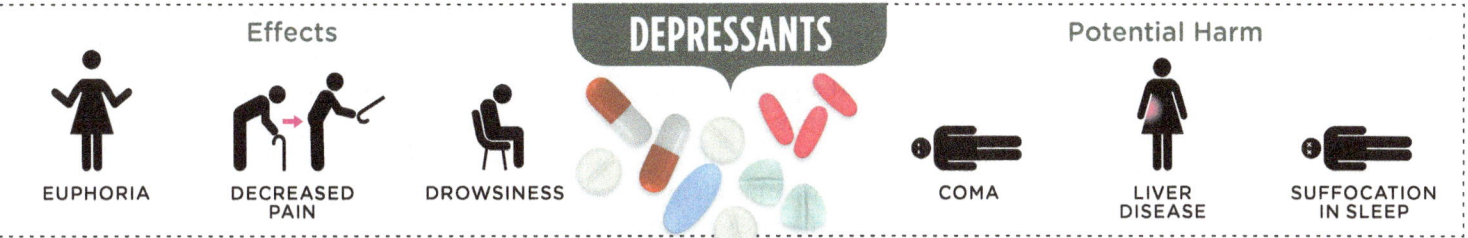

### DEPRESSANTS

**Effects**
- EUPHORIA
- DECREASED PAIN
- DROWSINESS

**Potential Harm**
- COMA
- LIVER DISEASE
- SUFFOCATION IN SLEEP

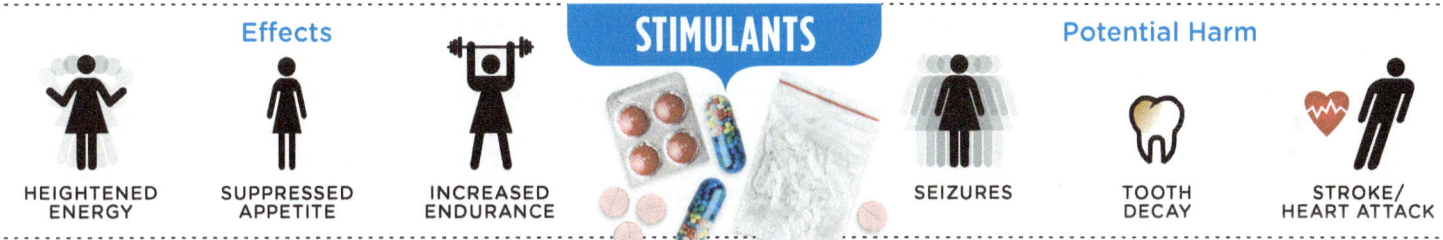

### STIMULANTS

**Effects**
- HEIGHTENED ENERGY
- SUPPRESSED APPETITE
- INCREASED ENDURANCE

**Potential Harm**
- SEIZURES
- TOOTH DECAY
- STROKE/ HEART ATTACK

     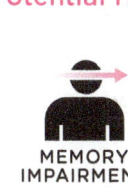 

### HALLUCINOGENS

**Effects**
- EMOTIONAL ROLLER COASTER
- DISTORTION OF TIME
- HALLUCINATIONS

**Potential Harm**
- LONG-TERM FLASHBACKS
- MEMORY IMPAIRMENT
- DEPRESSION

## A Country in Crisis: The Opioid Epidemic

The United States is experiencing an unprecedented epidemic of opioid misuse.
LEFT Various government statistics on the opioid epidemic.
RIGHT Number of deaths by type of opioid and altogether.

### The Opioid Epidemic in the U.S. in 2018/2019

**10.3 million** people misused prescription opioids

**2 million** people misused prescription opioids for the first time

**47,600** people died from overdosing on opioids

**2 million** people had opioid use disorder

**808,000** people used heroin

**32,656** deaths attributed to overdosing on nonmethadone synthetic opioids

**81,000** people used heroin for the first time

**15,349** deaths attributed to overdosing on heroin

Data from U.S. Department of Health and Human Services, 2019.

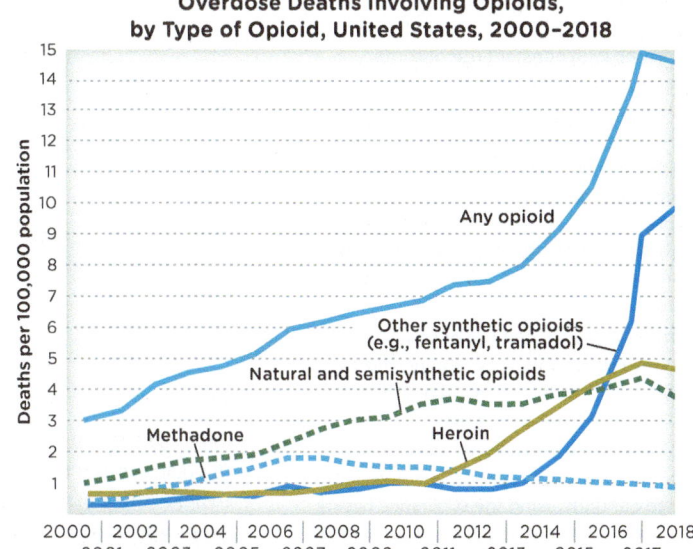

**Overdose Deaths Involving Opioids, by Type of Opioid, United States, 2000–2018**

Deaths per 100,000 population

- Any opioid
- Other synthetic opioids (e.g., fentanyl, tramadol)
- Natural and semisynthetic opioids
- Methadone
- Heroin

Data from: Hedegaard, Miniño, & Warner (2020).

**LO 11**   Explain how physiological and psychological dependence differ.

**WHAT IS DEPENDENCE?**    Substance use can be fueled by both *physiological* and *psychological* dependence. **Physiological dependence** means the body no longer functions normally without the drug (see FIGURE 4.7). Want to know if you are physiologically dependent on your morning cup of Joe? Try removing it from your routine for a few days and see if you get a headache or feel fatigued. If your answers are yes and yes, odds are that you have experienced *withdrawal,* a sign of physiological dependence. **Withdrawal** is the constellation of symptoms that surface when a drug is removed or withheld from the body, and it's not always as mild as a headache and fatigue. If a person who is physiologically dependent on alcohol suddenly stops drinking, they may suffer from **delirium tremens (DTs),** withdrawal symptoms that include sweating, restlessness, hallucinations, severe tremors, seizures, and even death. Withdrawal symptoms disappear when they take the drug again, and this of course makes them more likely to continue using it. (The removal of the unpleasant symptoms acts as negative reinforcement for taking the drug, a process you will learn about in Chapter 5.) In this way, withdrawal powers the overuse cycle.

Another sign of physiological dependence is **tolerance.** Persistent use of alcohol and other drugs alters the chemistry of the brain and body. Over time, your system adapts to the drug and therefore needs more and more to re-create its original effect. If it once took you 2 beers to unwind, but now it takes you 4, then tolerance has probably set in. Tolerance increases the risk for accidental overdose, because more of the drug is needed to obtain the desired effect.

**Psychological dependence** is indicated by a host of problematic symptoms distinct from tolerance and withdrawal. It is a strong urge or craving, not a physical need to continue using the substance. Individuals with psychological dependence believe, for example, they need the drug because it will increase their emotional or

**physiological dependence** With constant use of some psychoactive drugs, the body no longer functions normally without the drug.

**withdrawal** With constant use of some psychoactive drugs, the body becomes dependent and then reacts when the drug is withheld; a sign of physiological dependence.

**delirium tremens (DTs)** Withdrawal symptoms that can occur when a person who is physiologically dependent on alcohol suddenly stops drinking; can include sweating, restlessness, hallucinations, severe tremors, and seizures.

**tolerance** With constant use of some psychoactive drugs, the body requires more and more of the drug to create the original effect; a sign of physiological dependence.

**psychological dependence** With constant use of some psychoactive drugs, a strong desire or need to continue using the substance occurs without the evidence of tolerance or withdrawal symptoms.

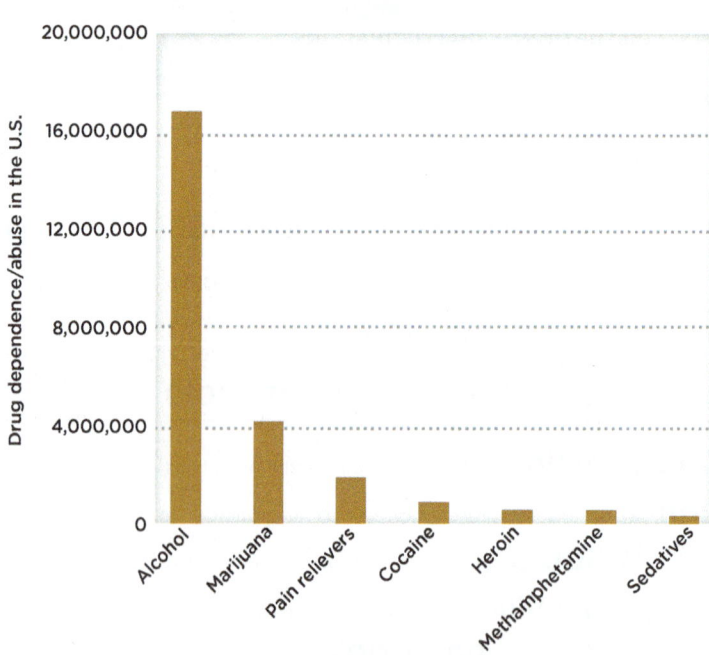

**FIGURE 4.7**

**Rates of Drug Dependence in the United States**

This graph depicts the rates of drug dependence/abuse in the United States. As you can see, alcohol tops the list, followed by marijuana, and then pain relievers such as Vicodin and OxyContin. The sedatives category includes benzodiazepines and barbiturates, which are powerful depressants. Data from: National Institute on Drug Abuse (2012); Center for Behavioral Health Statistics and Quality (2015).

mental well-being. The "pleasant" effects of a drug can act as positive reinforcement for taking the drug (Chapter 5). In some cases, environmental cues can facilitate psychological dependence. Suppose a smoker develops a habit of smoking while talking on the phone. If the phone rings, they immediately reach for their cigarettes and lighter. Their smoking behavior has become linked to cues associated with using the phone (Bold et al., 2013).

Psychologists and psychiatrists use specific criteria for drawing the line between use and overuse of drugs. Overuse is maladaptive and causes significant impairment or distress to the user and/or their family: problems at work or school, neglect of children or household duties, physically dangerous behaviors, and so forth. In addition, the behavior has to be sustained for a certain period of time (that is, over a 12-month period). The American Psychiatric Association (2013) has established these criteria to help professionals distinguish between drug use and substance use disorder.

Making a diagnosis is one thing, but getting a person into treatment is quite another. Some people avoid getting help because the stigma surrounding substance use disorder causes debilitating shame. Nora D. Volkow, the director of the National Institute on Drug Abuse explains in the following piece from *Scientific American:*

# THE STIGMA OF ADDICTION

When health care providers demonize people addicted to drugs or alcohol, it just makes the problem worse.

From the SCIENTIFIC
pages of AMERICAN

Untreated drug and alcohol use contributes to tens of thousands of deaths every year and affects the lives of many more people. We have effective treatments, including medications for opioid and alcohol use disorders, that could prevent a significant number of these deaths, but they are not being utilized widely enough, and people who could benefit often do not even seek them out. One important reason is the stigma around those with addiction.

Stigma is a problem for people with health conditions ranging from cancer and HIV to a variety of mental illnesses, but it is especially powerful in the context of substance use disorders. Even though medicine long ago reached the consensus that addiction is a complex brain disorder, those with addiction continue to be blamed for their condition. The public, as well as many people working in health care and in the justice system, continues to view addiction as a result of moral weakness and flawed character.

Stigma on the part of health care providers who see patients' drug or alcohol problems as their own fault can lead to substandard care or even to the rejection of individuals seeking treatment. Staff in emergency departments, for instance, may be dismissive of addicted people because they do not view treating drug problems as part of their job. As a result, those showing signs of acute intoxication or withdrawal symptoms are sometimes expelled from the ER by staff who are fearful of their behavior or who assume they are only seeking drugs. People with addiction can internalize this stigma, feeling shame and refusing to seek treatment. [. . .]

Beyond just impeding the provision or seeking of care, stigma may actually drive addicted people to continue using drugs. Research by Marco Venniro of the National Institute on Drug Abuse has shown that drug-dependent rodents choose social interaction over the drug when given the choice, but when the social choice is punished, the animals revert to drug use. Humans, too, are social beings, and some of us respond to both social and physical punishments by turning to substances to alleviate our pain. The humiliating rejection experienced by those who are stigmatized for their drug use acts as a powerful social punishment, driving them to continue and perhaps intensify their drug taking. [. . .]

There must be wider recognition that susceptibility to the brain changes in addiction is substantially influenced by factors outside an individual's control, such as genetics and the environment in which one is born and raised, and that medical care is often necessary to facilitate recovery as well as to avert the worst outcomes, such as overdose. When people with addiction are stigmatized and rejected, especially by those in health care, it only contributes to the vicious cycle that makes their disease so entrenched. **Nora D. Volkow. Reproduced with permission. Copyright © 2020. Scientific American, a division of Nature America, Inc. All rights reserved.**

Depressants, stimulants, hallucinogens, marijuana—every drug we have discussed, and every drug imaginable—must gain entrance to the body in order to access the brain. Some are inhaled, others snorted or injected directly into the veins, but they all alter the user's state of consciousness (**TABLE 4.5**). Is it possible to enter an altered state of consciousness without using a substance? Time to explore hypnosis.

**TABLE 4.5**   Psychoactive Drugs

| Drug | Classification | Effects | Potential Harm |
|---|---|---|---|
| Alcohol | Depressant | Disinhibition, feeling "high" | Coma, death |
| Barbiturates | Depressant | Decreases neural activity, relaxation, possible aggression | Loss of consciousness, coma, death |
| Caffeine | Stimulant | Alertness, enhanced recall, elevated mood, endurance | Heart racing, trembling, insomnia |
| Cocaine | Stimulant | Energy, euphoria, rush of pleasure | Heart attack, stroke, anxiety, psychosis |
| Heroin | Depressant | Induces pleasure, reduces pain, rush of euphoria and relaxation | Boils on the skin, hepatitis, liver disease, spontaneous abortion |
| LSD | Hallucinogen | Extreme changes in sensation and perception, emotional roller coaster | Depression, long-term flashbacks, other psychological problems |
| Marijuana | Hallucinogen | Stimulates appetite, suppresses nausea, relaxation, mild euphoria, distortion of time, intense sensory experiences | Respiratory problems, immune system suppression, cancer, memory impairment, deficits in attention and learning |
| MDMA | Stimulant; hallucinogen | Euphoria, heightened energy, and anxiety | Blurred vision, dizziness, rapid heart rate, dehydration, heat stroke, seizures, cardiac arrest, death |
| Methamphetamine | Stimulant | Energy, alertness, increases sex drive, suppresses appetite | Lasting memory and movement problems, severe weight loss, tooth decay, psychosis, sudden death |
| Opioids | Depressant | Blocks pain, induces drowsiness, euphoria, slows down breathing | Respiratory problems during sleep, falls, constipation, sexual problems, overdose |
| Tobacco | Stimulant | Relaxation, alertness, increased pain tolerance | Cancer, emphysema, heart disease, stroke, reduction in life span |

Most drugs can be classified under one of the major categories listed above, but there are substances, such as MDMA, that fall into more than one class. Psychoactive drugs carry serious risks.

## Hypnosis

**LO 12**   Describe hypnosis and explain how it works.

The term *hypnosis* was taken from the Greek root word for "sleep," but hypnosis is not the equivalent of sleep. Most would agree **hypnosis** is an altered state of consciousness in which changes in perceptions and behaviors result from suggestions made by a hypnotist. "Changes in perceptions and behaviors" can mean a lot of things, of course, and there is some uncertainty about what hypnosis is and how it is achieved (Dienes et al., 2020). Before going any further, let's be clear about what hypnosis *is not*.

**hypnosis** An altered state of consciousness allowing for changes in perceptions and behaviors, which result from suggestions made by a hypnotist.

# ...BELIEVE IT...OR NOT

## FALSE CLAIMS ABOUT HYPNOSIS

 Popular conceptions of hypnosis often clash with scientists' understanding of the phenomenon. Let's take a look at some examples.

- **People can be hypnotized without consent:** You cannot force someone to be hypnotized; they must be willing.

- **Hypnotized people will act against their own will:** Stage hypnotists seem to make people walk like chickens or miscount their fingers, but these are things they would likely be willing to do when not hypnotized.

- **Hypnotized people can exhibit "superhuman" strength:** Hypnotized or not, people have the same capabilities (Druckman & Bjork, 1994). Stage hypnotists often choose feats that their hypnotized performers could achieve under normal circumstances.

- **Hypnosis helps people retrieve lost memories:** Studies find that hypnosis may actually promote the formation of false memories and one's confidence in those memories (Kihlstrom, 1985, 2014).

- **Hypnotized people experience age regression. In other words, they act childlike:** Hypnotized people may indeed act immaturely, but the underlying cognitive activity is that of an adult (Nash, 2001).

- **Hypnosis induces long-term amnesia:** Hypnosis cannot make you forget your first day of kindergarten or your wedding. Short-term amnesia is possible if the hypnotist specifically suggests that something will be forgotten after the hypnosis wears off.

**NO ONE CAN FORCE YOU TO BECOME HYPNOTIZED.**

Now that some misconceptions about hypnosis have been cleared up, let's focus on what we know. Researchers propose the following characteristics are evident in a hypnotized person: (1) ability to focus intently, ignoring all extraneous stimuli; (2) heightened imagination; (3) an unresisting and receptive attitude; (4) decreased pain awareness; and (5) high responsivity to suggestions (Hoeft et al., 2012; Kosslyn et al., 2000; Silva & Kirsch, 1992).

Does this process have any application to real life? With some limited success, hypnosis has been used therapeutically to treat phobias and commercially to help people change lifestyle habits (Green, 1999; Kraft, 2012). Hypnotherapy may help some people confront fears of visiting the dentist (Butler, 2015). Hypnosis has also been used on children to alleviate chronic pain, insomnia, and anxiety related to routine medical procedures (Adinolfi & Gava, 2013). And researchers have demonstrated the benefits of hypnosis in conjunction with traditional therapies for the treatment of chronic issues such as tension headaches (Shahkhase et al., 2014). While more clinical trials are needed, "hypnotic intervention can deliver meaningful pain relief for most people and therefore may be an elective and safe alternative to pharmaceutical intervention" (Thompson et al., 2019, p. 298).

**HYPNOSIS AND THE MIND** People in hypnotic states sometimes report having sensory experiences that deviate from reality; they may, for example, see or hear things that are not there. In a classic experiment, participants were asked to place one hand in ice-cold water. If they felt pain, they were supposed to press a button with the other hand. Because these participants were hypnotized to believe that they wouldn't experience pain, they did not report any pain. Yet they did press the button (Hilgard et al., 1975). This suggests a "divided consciousness," that is, part of our consciousness is always aware, even when hypnotized and instructed to feel no pain.

Jean-Loup Charmet/Science Source.

**Mesmerizing**
A 19th-century doctor attempts to heal a patient using the hypnotic techniques created by Franz Mesmer in the 1770s. Mesmer believed that every person was surrounded by a magnetic field, or "animal magnetism," that could be summoned for therapeutic purposes (Wobst, 2007). The word "mesmerize" derives from Mesmer's surname.

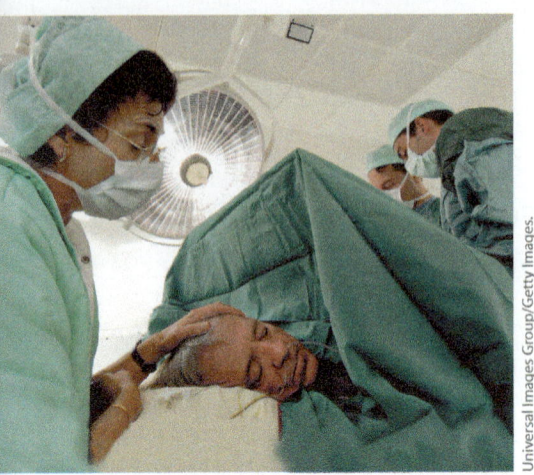

Universal Images Group/Getty Images.

**Hypnosis for Pain**
A doctor in Belgium performs hypnosis on a patient undergoing a painful procedure. For those who are receptive to hypnosis, this approach may complement the use of anesthesia by reducing pain and anxiety (Häuser et al., 2016; Thompson et al., 2019).

With the help of PET scans, some researchers have found evidence that hypnosis induces changes in the brain that might explain this diminished pain perception (Faymonville et al., 2000; Rainville et al., 1997). Various regions of the brain appear to be involved, including those associated with the processing of sensory stimuli (Thompson et al., 2019).

Another state of consciousness that can influence pain perception is mindfulness, "a form of non-reactive awareness of one's present-moment experience" (Grant & Zeidan, 2019, p. 193). Earlier in the chapter we described consciousness as being aware of oneself, one's thoughts, and/or the environment. We can think of mindfulness as being aware of the current moment without reacting to it. Depending on a person's degree of training, mindfulness meditation can allay pain through different pathways in the nervous system (Grant & Zeidan, 2019).

## Fade to Black

It is almost time to conclude our discussion of consciousness, so let's run through some of the big picture concepts you should take away from this chapter. There is no universally agreed upon definition of consciousness, but it seems to involve a state of awareness—awareness of self and things outside of self—that has many gradations and dimensions. Sleep has many stages, but the two main forms are non-REM and REM. Dreams may serve a purpose, but they may also be nothing more than your brain's interpretation of neurons signaling in the night. You learned from Dr. Chander that anesthetic drugs can profoundly alter consciousness. The same is true of drugs used outside of medical supervision; legal or not, many drugs can lead to dependence, health problems, and death. And although somewhat controversial and misunderstood, hypnosis appears to induce an altered state of consciousness and may have useful applications.

 **SHOW WHAT YOU KNOW**

1. Match the drug in the left column with an outcome on the right:

    ___ I. depressant            **A.** blocks pain

    ___ II. opioid               **B.** slows down activity in the CNS

    ___ III. alcohol             **C.** increases activity in the CNS

    ___ IV. cocaine              **D.** cirrhosis of the liver

2. People often describe dangerous or risky behaviors as being addictive. You might hear a character in a movie say that he is addicted to driving fast, for example. Given what you have learned about physiological and psychological dependence, how would you determine if behaviors are problematic?

3. An acquaintance described an odorless, tasteless, and colorless substance he took many years ago. He discussed a variety of changes to his sensations and perceptions, including seeing colors and spirals. It is likely he had taken which of the following hallucinogens?

    **A.** alcohol

    **B.** nicotine

    **C.** LSD

    **D.** cocaine

4. Dr. Chander uses a range of _____ to inhibit memories of surgery and change levels of consciousness.

✓ CHECK YOUR ANSWERS AT THE BACK OF THE BOOK.

## Summary of Concepts

**LO 1**  **Define consciousness. (p. 126)**

Consciousness might be conceived as the state of being aware of oneself, one's thoughts, and/or the environment. As we try to understand consciousness, we should consider both the content of consciousness and states of consciousness. The content of consciousness refers to what it holds, both within and outside our awareness. States of consciousness include conscious experiences (being awake) and unconscious experiences (being under anesthesia).

**LO 2**  **Explain how automatic processing relates to consciousness. (p. 129)**

Our sensory systems absorb large amounts of information—so much that we cannot be aware of it all. Without our awareness, the brain determines what is important, what requires immediate attention, and what can be processed and stored for later use if necessary.

**LO 3** Describe how we narrow our focus through selective attention. (p. 130)

We can only direct our attention toward a small portion of the information that is available to us. This narrow focus on specific stimuli is referred to as selective attention. Humans are highly sensitive to abrupt, unexpected changes in the environment, and to stimuli that are unfamiliar, rewarding, or especially strong.

**LO 4** Identify how circadian rhythm relates to sleep. (p. 132)

Predictable daily patterns influence our behaviors, alertness, and activity levels in a cyclical fashion. These circadian rhythms in our physiological functioning roughly follow the 24-hour cycle of daylight and darkness. In the circadian rhythm for sleep and wakefulness, there are two times when the desire for sleep hits hardest. The first occurs in the early hours of the morning, between about 2:00 and 6:00 A.M., and the second, less intense desire for sleep, strikes midafternoon, around 2:00 or 3:00 P.M.

**LO 5** Summarize the stages of sleep. (p. 135)

Sleep begins in non-rapid eye movement (non-REM), or non-dreaming sleep, which has three stages. The lightest is Stage N1; this is the time when imaginary sensations can occur. Stage N1 lasts only a few minutes, and then Stage N2 begins. At this point, it is more difficult to rouse the sleeper before they drift even further into Stage N3, also known as slow-wave sleep. The sleeper then works their way back up to Stage N2. And instead of waking up, they enter the R Stage, known as rapid eye movement (REM) sleep. During this stage, closed eyes dart around, and brain activity changes. People awakened from REM sleep often report having vivid dreams. Each cycle, from Stage N1 through REM, lasts about 90 minutes, and the average adult loops through five complete cycles per night. The composition of these cycles changes as the night progresses.

**LO 6** Recognize various sleep disorders and their symptoms. (p. 138)

Narcolepsy is a neurological disorder characterized by excessive daytime sleepiness and other sleep-related disturbances. REM sleep behavior disorder occurs when the mechanism responsible for paralyzing the body during REM sleep does not function properly. As a result, the individual is able to move around and act out dreams. Obstructive sleep apnea hypopnea is a serious disturbance of non-REM sleep characterized by periodic blockage of breathing. Insomnia is the inability to fall asleep or stay asleep. People with insomnia report poor quantity or quality of sleep, and some may complain about waking up too early and being unable to fall back to sleep.

**LO 7** Summarize theories explaining why we dream. (p. 145)

Freud believed dreams have two levels of content. Manifest content, the apparent meaning of the dream, is the actual story line of the dream. Latent content is the hidden meaning of the dream, consisting of unconscious conflicts and desires.

The activation–synthesis model suggests that dreams have no meaning whatsoever: We respond to random neural activity of the sleeping brain as if it has meaning. Neurocognitive theory suggests there is a network of neurons in the brain necessary for dreaming to occur, and that dreams result from the same type of cognition we experience when awake.

**LO 8** Define psychoactive drugs. (p. 148)

Psychoactive drugs can cause changes in psychological activities such as sensation, perception, attention, judgment, memory, self-control, emotion, thinking, and behavior. These drugs alter consciousness in an untold number of ways. They can, for example, depress activity in the central nervous system, produce hallucinations, or cause a sense of euphoria.

**LO 9** Identify several depressants and stimulants and know their effects. (p. 149)

Depressants decrease activity in the central nervous system. These include barbiturates, opioids, and alcohol. Stimulants increase activity in the central nervous system, producing effects such as heightened alertness, energy, and mood. These include cocaine, methamphetamine, caffeine, and nicotine.

**LO 10** Discuss how hallucinogens alter consciousness. (p. 157)

Hallucinogens produce hallucinations, altered moods, and distorted perception and thought. The most well-known is lysergic acid diethylamide (LSD). This odorless, tasteless, and colorless substance often produces extreme changes in sensation and perception. Others are the "club drugs," or synthetic "designer drugs." Of these, the most popular is methylenedioxymethamphetamine (MDMA), which produces a combination of stimulant and hallucinogenic effects. After alcohol, marijuana is the most widely used drug in the United States. At high doses, tetrahydrocannabinol (THC) can induce mild euphoria and create intense sensory experiences.

**LO 11** Explain how physiological and psychological dependence differ. (p. 162)

With continued use of some psychoactive drugs, the body may become dependent. Signs of this physiological dependence include tolerance and withdrawal. Psychological dependence is indicated by a host of problematic symptoms distinct from tolerance and withdrawal. It is an urge or craving, not a physical need. People with psychological dependence believe they need the drug because it increases their emotional or mental well-being.

**LO 12** Describe hypnosis and explain how it works. (p. 164)

Hypnosis is an altered state of consciousness that can create changes in perceptions and behaviors, usually resulting from suggestions made by a hypnotist. For some people, hypnosis can mitigate the experience of pain and reduce the need for painkillers.

# Key Terms

activation–synthesis model,
  p. 146
alpha waves, p. 135
amphetamines, p. 155
automatic processing,
  p. 129
barbiturates, p. 149
beta waves, p. 135
circadian rhythm, p. 132
cognitive psychology, p. 128
consciousness, p. 126
delirium tremens (DTs),
  p. 162

delta waves, p. 136
depressants, p. 149
hallucinogens, p. 157
hypnosis, p. 164
insomnia, p. 141
latent content, p. 145
lysergic acid diethylamide
  (LSD), p. 157
manifest content, p. 145
methylenedioxy-
  methamphetamine
  (MDMA), p. 158
narcolepsy, p. 138

nightmares, p. 142
non-rapid eye movement
  (non-REM or NREM),
  p. 136
obstructive sleep apnea
  hypopnea, p. 140
opiates, p. 151
physiological dependence,
  p. 162
psychoactive drugs,
  p. 148
psychological dependence,
  p. 162

rapid eye movement (REM),
  p. 136
REM rebound, p. 143
REM sleep behavior disorder,
  p. 140
selective attention, p. 130
sleep terrors, p. 141
stimulants, p. 154
tetrahydrocannabinol (THC),
  p. 160
theta waves, p. 136
tolerance, p. 162
withdrawal, p. 162

# Test Prep Are You Ready?

1. A great deal of information is available in our internal and external environments, but we can only focus on a small portion of it. This narrow focus on specific stimuli is known as:
   A. stream of consciousness.
   B. selective attention.
   C. waking consciousness.
   D. creating memories.

2. The daily patterns of our physiological functioning, such as changes in body temperature, roughly follow the 24-hour cycle of daylight and darkness. These patterns are driven by our:
   A. psychological dependence.
   B. need for sleep.
   C. narcolepsy.
   D. circadian rhythm.

3. Shift workers may experience problems with their sleep–wake cycles, sometimes resulting in _____, which refers to difficulty falling asleep and sleeping soundly.
   A. insomnia
   B. cataplexy
   C. narcolepsy
   D. hypnagogic hallucinations

4. Lysergic acid diethylamide (LSD) is classified as a _____ as it can produce altered moods and distorted perceptions and thoughts.
   A. depressant
   B. hallucinogen
   C. microsleep
   D. circadian rhythm

5. The fourth stage of sleep is known as _____, when brain activity looks similar to that of someone who is wide awake.
   A. sleep paralysis
   B. cataplexy
   C. non-REM sleep
   D. REM sleep

6. Depriving people of REM sleep can result in:
   A. REM rebound.
   B. insomnia.
   C. more beta waves while they sleep.
   D. increased energy levels.

7. According to Sigmund Freud's theory, dreams are a form of:
   A. REM rebound.
   B. wish fulfillment.
   C. microsleep.
   D. sleep terror.

8. _____ such as caffeine, alcohol, and hallucinogens can cause changes in psychological activities, such as sensation, perception, attention, and judgment.
   A. Tranquilizers
   B. Depressants
   C. Psychoactive drugs
   D. Stimulants

9. Methamphetamine stimulates the release of the neurotransmitter _____, causing a surge in energy and alertness.
   A. dopamine
   B. serotonin
   C. acetylcholine
   D. adenosine

10. _____ dependence means the body no longer functions normally without a drug. One sign of such dependence is _____, as indicated by the symptoms that occur when the drug is withheld.
    A. Psychological; tolerance
    B. Physiological; substance abuse
    C. Physiological; withdrawal
    D. Psychological; withdrawal

11. Give an example showing that you still can be aware of your environment even when you are asleep.

12. Describe automatic processing, and give two reasons why it is important.

13. Interns and residents in hospitals sometimes work 48-hour shifts. Why wouldn't you want a doctor keeping such a schedule to care for you at the end of their shift?

14. Name four different sleep disturbances. Differentiate them by describing their characteristics.

15. Give four examples of legal drugs that people use on a daily basis.

✔ CHECK YOUR ANSWERS AT THE BACK OF THE BOOK.

Independent birds/Shutterstock.

# Learning

## An Introduction to Learning

**BEFORE HE WAS THE DOG WHISPERER**
December 23, 1990: Cesar Millan had made up his mind; it was time to leave Mexico and start a new life in America. He was 21 years old, spoke no English, and had exactly $100 in his pocket. Since the age of 13, Cesar had dreamed of becoming the greatest dog trainer in the world. Now he was ready to pursue that goal, even if it meant saying goodbye to everything he knew and cherished—his family, his homeland, and his culture (Millan & Peltier, 2006).

From his home in Mazatlán, Cesar traveled to the border city of Tijuana, where he met a human smuggler who said he would get him into the United States for a fee of—you guessed it—$100. Trudging over muddy terrain, darting across a busy freeway, and hiding in a frigid trench of water, Cesar stuck with the smuggler. When he finally reached San Diego, he was "dripping wet, filthy, thirsty, [and] hungry." But, as Cesar recalls in his book *Cesar's Way*, "I was the happiest man in the world" (Millan & Peltier, 2006, p. 39).

Courtesy of Cesar's Way Inc.

**No Dream Is Too Big**
Young Cesar Millan works with a dog on a treadmill. Early on, Cesar knew he wanted to devote his life to dogs. He remembers himself as a 13-year-old asking his mother, "Mom, you think I can be the best dog trainer in the world?" She responded, "You can do whatever you want" (NPR, 2014).

Gregg Cobarr/WireImage/Getty Images.

**Dog's Best Friend**
Young Cesar walks a pack of large and powerful dogs. Cesar doesn't train dogs—he trains people. "I'm training humans to understand how dogs react, how dogs behave, what is their communication, and what makes them happy," Cesar explains. It's all about bringing balance to dogs' lives and promoting more fulfilling relationships between dogs and their owners.

For more than a month, Cesar slept under a freeway and lived on hotdogs from 7-Eleven (Partisan Pictures, 2012). Technically, he was "homeless," but he didn't feel like a drifter. "I never felt lost," Cesar recalls, "I always knew what I wanted." Cesar got a job at a pet-grooming parlor in San Diego and eventually moved to Los Angeles, where he worked as a kennel boy, a limousine washer, and a self-employed dog trainer. His dog-training business was based in Inglewood, a city just south of Los Angeles with a strong gang presence and many dogs trained to protect and fight (Fine, 2013; Lopez, 2012; Millan & Peltier, 2006). Capable of pacifying even the fiercest of dogs, Cesar could be seen strolling through the city with a pack of Rottweilers and pit bulls—off leash (Millan, n.d.)! Word spread about the "Mexican guy who has a magical way with dogs" (Millan & Peltier, 2006, p. 50), and Cesar accumulated more and more clients. The *Los Angeles Times* got wind of Cesar's work and profiled him in 2002, sparking the interest of several television producers (Levine, 2002).

Fast-forward to 2021. Cesar Millan is now a U.S. citizen and perhaps the most famous dog expert on the planet. His résumé includes nine seasons of the Emmy-nominated reality television series *Dog Whisperer with Cesar Millan* (broadcast in more than 100 countries), along with other TV series such as *Cesar 911* and *Cesar Millan's Dog Nation.* A best-selling author, Cesar travels the world, giving seminars in auditoriums packed with thousands of eager listeners. Fans flood his website with comments, some of them desperate ("HEY Cesar! I really need HELP! I have a 10 month old pit mix. . . ."), others adoring ("Dear Cesar, keep doing what you're doing. . . . You've got a believer in me and millions of others"; Millan, n.d.).

How do you explain Cesar's rise from poverty to superstardom? Clearly, he is hardworking, motivated, and has an innate gift for understanding dogs. But Cesar's life, and the lives of countless dogs and their owners, have also been shaped by *learning.*

## What Is Learning?

**LO 1**   Define learning.

Psychologists define **learning** as a relatively enduring change in behavior or thinking that results from our experiences. These modifications of behavior and thinking are sometimes, but not always, permanent. Studies suggest that learning can begin before we are even born—fetuses can hear voices and learn basic speech sounds from inside the womb (Lang et al., 2020). This becomes apparent immediately following birth when they are able to discriminate among vowel sounds and distinguish different ways of speaking (Háden et al., 2020; Moon et al., 2013; Partanen et al., 2013). Learning occurs every day and may continue until our dying breath. Underlying this process are changes in the brain, including alterations to individual **neurons** and their networks. Although learning has a huge impact on who we are and how we act, it is not responsible for all changes in behavior and thinking. For example, infants begin holding their heads up at about 3–4 months (Medline Plus, n.d.). This results from the development of neck muscles, which is a normal part of maturation (not learning).

The ability to learn is not unique to humans. Dogs can learn to do backflips and jump rope (Tomanney, 2019), and crows can be trained to drop pebbles into tubes of water (Hennefield et al., 2018). Female elk are so good at learning to elude people with rifles and bows that they are "almost invulnerable to human hunters" after reaching 9 or 10 years of age (Thurfjell et al., 2017, p. 1).

*Note:* Unless otherwise specified, quotations attributed to Cesar Millan are personal communications.

**CONNECTIONS**

In **Chapter 2,** we discussed some of the brain processes involved in learning. For example, dopamine activity plays an important role in learning through rewards. Neurogenesis (the generation of new neurons) is also thought to be associated with learning.

**learning**  A relatively enduring change in behavior or thinking that results from experiences.

One basic form of learning is **habituation.** Habituation is evident when an organism **reduces its response** to a recurring *stimulus* (Hall & Rodríguez, 2020). (A **stimulus** is an event or object that generally leads to a change in behavior). Initially, an animal might respond to a stimulus, but that response may diminish with repeated exposures (assuming the stimulus is not threatening). For example, when 3-day-old chicks are exposed to a loud sound, they automatically freeze. But if the loud sound is repeated, even just five times, the newborn chicks become habituated to it and carry on with what they were doing (Chiandetti & Turatto, 2017). Essentially, they learn about the stimulus and become less responsive to it. This type of learning is apparent in a wide range of living beings, from chickens to humans to sea slugs.

Researchers have used a variety of animals to study learning. The history of psychology is full of stories about scientists who began studying animal *biology*, but then switched their focus to animal *behavior* as unexpected events unfolded in the laboratory. These scientists were often excited to see the connections between biology and experience that became evident as they explored the principles of learning.

Animals can be excellent models for studying and understanding human behavior, including learning. Conducting animal research sidesteps many of the ethical dilemmas that arise with human research. It's generally considered okay to keep rats, cats, and birds in cages to ensure control over experimental variables (as long as they are otherwise treated humanely), but locking up people in laboratories would obviously be unacceptable.

This chapter focuses on three major types of learning: classical conditioning, operant conditioning, and observational learning. As you make your way through the pages discussing each, you will begin to realize that learning is very much about creating associations. Through *classical conditioning*, we associate two different stimuli: for example, the sound of a buzzer and the arrival of food. In *operant conditioning*, we make connections between our behaviors and their consequences: for example, through rewards and punishments. With *observational learning*, we learn by watching and imitating other people, establishing a closer link between our behavior and the behavior of others.

Learning can occur in predictable or unexpected ways. It allows us to grow and change, and it is a key to achieving goals. Let's see how learning has shaped the life and work of Cesar Millan.

## CONNECTIONS

In **Chapter 3,** we discussed sensory adaptation, the process by which our sensory receptors become less sensitive to constant stimuli. Habituation refers to changes in behavior: If we are repeatedly exposed to a stimulus, we become less responsive to it. Becoming habituated to sensory input keeps us alert to changes in the environment.

### ▶▶▶ SHOW WHAT YOU KNOW

1. Learning is often described as the creation of associations—for example, associations between behaviors and their consequences. List some associations you have made this week.

2. Learning is a relatively enduring change in _____ that results from our _____.

✓ CHECK YOUR ANSWERS AT THE BACK OF THE BOOK.

# Classical Conditioning

**PATRIOT WITH A PROBLEM** Every year around July 4th, animal shelters around the country report a surge in the number of runaway dogs and other pets (Santa Cruz, 2020). The banging and popping of fireworks are so terrifying to some dogs, they flee their homes to escape the sounds. A dog that fears fireworks or thunder is nothing out of the ordinary. But what if the animal went into panic mode every time they heard the beep of a microwave, cell phone, or elevator? This was the sad reality for Gavin, a sweet Labrador retriever who had worked as a bomb-sniffing dog for the Bureau of Alcohol, Tobacco, Firearms and Explosives (ATF).

**habituation** A basic form of learning evident when an organism does not respond as strongly or as often to an event following multiple exposures to it.

**stimulus** An event or object that generally leads to a response.

AP Photo/Wilfredo Lee.

**Serving His Country**

Special Agent L. A. Bykowsky works with Gavin in an explosives-detecting exercise. During his 5 years with the Bureau of Alcohol, Tobacco, Firearms and Explosives (ATF), Gavin helped ensure the safety of people attending Super Bowls and NASCAR races; then he went on a mission in Iraq, where his problems with noises seemed to begin (Millan & Peltier, 2010).

**CONNECTIONS**

In **Chapter 1,** we discussed the ethical guidelines psychologists follow when conducting research on living creatures. These guidelines encourage psychologists to do no harm and safeguard the welfare of living research subjects, be they humans, chimpanzees, cats, mice, dogs, or any living thing. Pavlov's massive laboratory, which employed some 100 lab assistants, was far from an exemplar of ethical treatment. Many dogs died and suffered under Pavlov's oversight, and he displayed little concern for their well-being (Adams, 2020; Todes, 2014).

**CONNECTIONS**

A dog naturally begins to salivate when exposed to the smell of food, even before tasting it. This is an involuntary response of the autonomic nervous system, which we explored in **Chapter 2.** A dog does not normally salivate at the sound of footsteps, however. This response is a *learned* behavior, as the dog begins to salivate without tasting or smelling food.

When Cesar first met Gavin, the yellow Lab had already retired from the ATF, but he couldn't relax and enjoy his golden years because he was so traumatized by events from the past. While on a tour in the Iraq War, Gavin had witnessed several loud explosions. Whenever an explosion occurred, "he quivered and shook," but then was able to carry on with his duties, according to his handler, Special Agent L. A. Bykowsky (Millan & Peltier, 2010, p. 58). Gavin may have been able to hold it together in Iraq, but the experience had a profound impact on him. Shortly after returning to his home in Florida, Gavin lived through two consecutive hurricanes (Millan & Peltier, 2010), which "just took him [through] the roof," according to Cesar. As a result of these experiences, Gavin became hypersensitive to many different sounds. Any beeping noise would trigger his fear response: The sound of a voicemail notification might cause uncontrollable shaking.

How did Gavin come to associate harmless everyday sounds with danger, and what did Cesar do to rehabilitate him? To answer these questions, we need to travel back in time and visit the laboratory of an aspiring Russian scientist: Ivan Pavlov.

**LO 2** Explain what Pavlov's studies teach us about classical conditioning.

The son of a village priest, Ivan Pavlov had planned to devote his life to the church. He changed his mind at a young age, however, due to a combination of the changing political times in Russia and the readings that challenged his worldview (Todes, 2014). His primary interest was physiology, a branch of biology that investigates the physical and chemical mechanisms underlying life's processes. Although he won a Nobel Prize in 1904 for his research on the physiology of digestion, Pavlov's most enduring legacy was his trailblazing research on learning (Fancher & Rutherford, 2012).

Pavlov spent the 1890s studying the digestive system of dogs at Russia's Imperial Institute of Experimental Medicine (Todes, 2014; Watson, 1968). His treatment of the dogs was **inhumane and cruel**, but this "darker and more complex" side of his research has been somewhat ignored (Adams, 2020, p. 127). However, his findings did have a transformative effect on the field of psychology, so it is important to cover them in introductory courses. Many of Pavlov's early experiments involved measuring how much dogs salivate in response to food. Initially, the dogs salivated as expected, but as the experiment progressed, they began salivating in response to other stimuli as well. After repeated trials with an assistant giving food and then measuring saliva output, Pavlov realized that instead of **salivating** the moment food was served, the dogs began to salivate at the mere sight or sound of the lab assistant arriving to feed them. The assistant's footsteps, for example, might act like a trigger (*stimulus*) for the dogs to start salivating (*response*). Pavlov realized that the dogs' "psyche," or personality, and their "thoughts about food" were interfering with the collection of objective data on their digestion (Todes, 2014, p. 158). In other words, the dogs' psychological activities were affecting their physiology, making it difficult for the researchers to study digestion as an isolated phenomenon. Pavlov had discovered that associations develop through a process of learning we now call *conditioning*. The dogs were associating the sound of footsteps or the sight of the bowl with the arrival of food; they had been *conditioned* to link certain sights and sounds with eating. Intrigued by his discovery, Pavlov began to shift the focus of his research and investigate the dogs' salivation (which he termed "psychic secretions") in such scenarios, as well as other dog behaviors (Adams, 2020, June 1; Fancher & Rutherford, 2012; Todes, 2014).

## Mouth-Watering Science

Pavlov followed up on his observations about psychic secretions with numerous studies starting in the early 1900s, examining the link between stimulus (for example, the sound of human footsteps) and response (how much the dog salivates). The type of behavior Pavlov was studying (salivating) is involuntary, or reflexive (Pavlov, 1906). The connection between food and salivating is innate and universal (occurs in all members of the species), whereas the link between the sound of footsteps and salivating is learned. Learning has occurred whenever a new, nonuniversal link between stimulus (footsteps) and response (salivation) is established.

Many of Pavlov's studies had the same basic format (see INFOGRAPHIC 5.1 on the next page). Prior to the experiment, the dog had a tube surgically inserted into its cheek so researchers could determine exactly how much saliva it was producing. Once the dog had recovered from the surgery, it was placed alone in a soundproof room and outfitted with equipment to keep it from moving around. Because Pavlov was interested in exploring the link between a stimulus and the dog's response, he had to pick a stimulus that was **more controlled** than the sound of someone walking into a room. Pavlov used a variety of stimuli, including flashing lights and sounds produced by metronomes and buzzers, which under normal circumstances have nothing to do with food or salivation. In other words, they are *neutral* stimuli in relation to feeding and responses to food.

On numerous occasions during an experimental trial, Pavlov and his assistants presented a dog with a chosen stimulus—the sound of a buzzer, for instance—and then moments later gave the dog a piece of meat. Each time the buzzer was sounded, the assistant would wait a couple of seconds and then offer the dog meat. All the while, its drops of saliva were being measured. After repeated pairings, the dog began to link the buzzer with the meat; it would salivate in response to the sound alone, with *no* meat present, evidence that learning had occurred. The dog had *learned* to associate the sound with food. Remember, we call this type of learning *conditioning*.

## What Do You Need to Know?

**LO 3**  Identify the differences between the US, UR, CS, and CR.

Now that you know Pavlov's basic research procedure, it is important to learn the specific terminology psychologists use to describe what is happening (Infographic 5.1). Before the experiment begins, the sound of the buzzer is a **neutral stimulus (NS)**—something in the environment that does not normally cause a relevant automatic response. In this case, that automatic response is salivation; dogs do not normally salivate when they hear a buzzer. But through experience, they learn to link this neutral stimulus (the buzzer sound) with another stimulus (food) that normally prompts salivation. This type of learning is called **classical conditioning,** and it is evident when an originally neutral stimulus (NS) triggers an involuntary response, such as salivation, eye blinks, and other types of reflexive behaviors.

**US, UR, CS, AND CR**   At the start of a trial, before a dog is conditioned or has learned anything about the neutral stimulus (NS), it salivates when it smells or receives food, in this case meat. The meat is considered an **unconditioned stimulus (US)** because it triggers an automatic response. Salivating in response to food is an **unconditioned response (UR)** because it doesn't require any learning; the dog just does it involuntarily. To reiterate, the smell or taste of meat (US) elicits the automatic response of salivation (UR). After conditioning has occurred, the dog responds to the

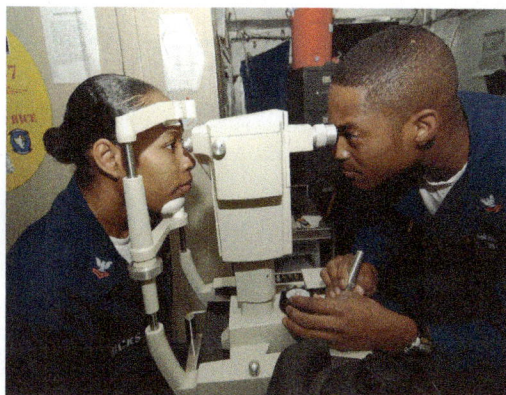

PJF Military Collection/Alamy.

**Here Comes the Puff!**
If you've ever had a visual exam, you may remember the eye doctor giving you an air puff test to check the pressure inside your eye. The sudden puff of air hitting the eye causes you to blink reflexively. If you have taken the test before, you may blink in anticipation—before the air puff even reaches your eye. Through classical conditioning, you have learned to associate the stimuli associated with the procedure with the sensation of the air puff.

### CONNECTIONS

In **Chapter 1,** we discussed the importance of control in the experimental method. If Pavlov were to use the sound of footsteps as his stimulus, he would need to *control* the number of steps taken and the type of shoes worn to ensure the sound was identical across trials. Otherwise, he would be introducing extraneous variables, or characteristics that interfere with the research outcome, making it difficult to determine what caused the dog to salivate.

**neutral stimulus (NS)**  A stimulus that does not cause a relevant automatic or reflexive response.

**classical conditioning**  A learning process in which two stimuli become associated with each other; when an originally neutral stimulus is conditioned to elicit an involuntary response.

**unconditioned stimulus (US)**  A stimulus that automatically triggers an involuntary response without any learning needed.

**unconditioned response (UR)**  A reflexive, involuntary response to an unconditioned stimulus.

# Learning Through Classical Conditioning

During his experiments with dogs, Ivan Pavlov noticed them salivating before food was even presented. Somehow the dogs had learned to associate the lab assistant's approaching footsteps with eating. This observation led to Pavlov's discovery of classical conditioning, in which we learn to associate a neutral stimulus with an unconditioned stimulus that produces an automatic, natural response. The crucial stage of this process involves repeated pairings of the two stimuli.

## HAVE **YOU** BEEN CONDITIONED?

**Before conditioning**

Neutral stimulus          No response

Unconditioned stimulus → Unconditioned response (mouth waters)

**During conditioning**

Neutral stimulus    +    Unconditioned stimulus

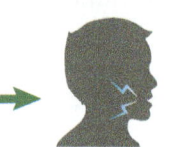 →

repeated over time

Unconditioned response (mouth waters)

**After conditioning**

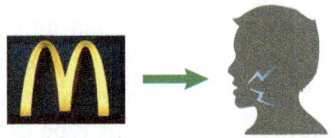

Conditioned stimulus → Conditioned response (mouth waters)

## PAVLOV'S EXPERIMENT

**Before conditioning**

**Dog salivates automatically when food is presented.**

Unconditioned stimulus → Unconditioned response (salivate)

**Buzzer means nothing to dog, so there is no response.**

Neutral stimulus (buzzer sound)          No response

**During conditioning**

**In the process of conditioning, buzzer is repeatedly sounded right before dog receives food. Over time, dog learns that buzzer signals arrival of food.**

 +  →

Neutral stimulus (buzzer sound)  +  Unconditioned stimulus  =  Unconditioned response (salivates)

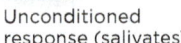

repeated over time

**After conditioning**

**Dog has now learned to associate buzzer with food and will begin salivating when buzzer sounds.**

 →

Conditioned stimulus (buzzer sound)          Conditioned response (salivates)

Classical conditioning is an involuntary form of learning that happens every day. Does your mouth water when you see the McDonald's "golden arches"? Just like Pavlov's dogs, we learn through repeated pairings to associate neutral stimuli (the golden arches) with food (french fries). Once this association is formed, the sight of the golden arches can be enough to get our mouths watering.

buzzer almost as if it were food. The buzzer, previously a neutral stimulus (NS), has now become a **conditioned stimulus (CS)** because it prompts the dog to salivate. When salivation occurs in response to the buzzer, it is a learned behavior, and thus we call it a **conditioned response (CR).** If you're trying to figure out the proper label for the response, think about what caused it: Was it the food or the buzzer? Knowing this will help you determine whether it is conditioned (learned) or unconditioned (not learned).

**THE ACQUISITION PHASE**    The pairings of the neutral stimulus (the buzzer) with the unconditioned stimulus (meat) occur during the initial learning phase, called **acquisition.** Some points to remember:

- The meat is always an unconditioned stimulus (US)—the dog never has to learn how to respond to it.
- The dog's salivating is initially an unconditioned response (UR) to the meat, but eventually becomes a conditioned response (CR) as well; it occurs when the buzzer is sounded (without the sight or smell of meat).
- The unconditioned stimulus (US) is always different from the conditioned stimulus (CS); the US automatically triggers the response, while the CS elicits a response that has been *learned* by the organism.

Pavlov's work paved the way for a new generation of psychologists who considered behavior to be a topic of **objective**, scientific study. Like many scientists who would follow, he focused on the objective recording of measurable behaviors, in this case counting the exact number of saliva drops produced by the dogs. His work transformed our understanding of learning and our approach to psychological research.

## Nuts and Bolts of Classical Conditioning

We have discussed classical conditioning in Pavlov's dogs, defining terms along the way. Now it's time to take our learning (about learning!) to the next level and examine some of the principles guiding the process.

**LO 4**    Recognize and give examples of stimulus generalization and stimulus discrimination.

**GENERALIZATION AND DISCRIMINATION**    What would happen if a dog in one of Pavlov's experiments heard a sound with slightly different qualities? For example, suppose the dog was conditioned to salivate in response to the sound of a ticking metronome. Would the dog still salivate if presented with a metronome that ticked faster or slower than the original? Pavlov (1927/1960) asked this same question and found that a stimulus similar to the conditioned stimulus (CS) did indeed cause the dogs to salivate. This is an example of **stimulus generalization.** Once an association is forged between a conditioned stimulus (CS) and a conditioned response (CR), the learner often responds to similar stimuli as if they were the original CS. When Pavlov's dogs learned to salivate in response to a metronome ticking at 90 beats per minute, they also salivated when the metronome ticked a little more quickly (100 beats per minute) or slowly (80 beats per minute; Hothersall, 2004). Their response was *generalized* to metronome speeds ranging from 80 to 100 beats per minute. Perhaps you have been classically conditioned to salivate at the sight of a tall glass of lemonade. Stimulus generalization predicts you would now salivate when seeing a shorter glass of lemonade, or even a mug, if you knew it contained your favorite drink.

What would happen if Pavlov's dogs were presented with two stimuli that differed significantly? Let's say the dogs have learned to associate the meat with a high-pitched sound; they salivate whenever they hear it. Expose these same dogs to lower-pitched sounds, and they may not salivate. If so, they are demonstrating

**CONNECTIONS**

In **Chapter 1,** we described the scientific method and its dependence on *objective* observation. This approach requires us to observe and record without letting personal opinion or expectations interfere. We are all prone to biases, but the scientific method helps minimize their effects. Pavlov was among the first to insist that behavior be studied objectively.

**conditioned stimulus (CS)** A previously neutral stimulus that an organism learns to associate with an unconditioned stimulus.

**conditioned response (CR)** A learned response to a conditioned stimulus.

**acquisition** The initial learning phase in both classical and operant conditioning.

**stimulus generalization** The tendency for stimuli similar to the conditioned stimulus to elicit the conditioned response.

NBC/Photofest.

**Office Pranks**

In Season 3 of NBC's *The Office*, "Jim" played by John Krasinski (right) plays a classical conditioning trick on his coworker "Dwight" played by Rainn Wilson (left). Every time Jim's computer makes the reboot sound, Jim hands Dwight an Altoids breath mint. After several pairings of the reboot sound and the mint, Dwight automatically reaches out his hand in anticipation of the mint. "What are you doing?" asks Jim. Looking confused, Dwight replies, "My mouth tastes so bad all of the sudden" (Williams & Whittingham, 2007, 0:53–1:03).

**stimulus discrimination** The ability to differentiate between a conditioned stimulus and other stimuli sufficiently different from it.

**extinction** In classical conditioning, the process by which the conditioned response decreases after repeated exposure to the conditioned stimulus in the absence of the unconditioned stimulus; in operant conditioning, the disappearance of a learned behavior through the removal of its reinforcer.

**spontaneous recovery** The reappearance of a conditioned response following its extinction.

**higher order conditioning** With repeated pairings of a conditioned stimulus and a second neutral stimulus, that second neutral stimulus becomes a conditioned stimulus as well.

**stimulus discrimination,** the ability to distinguish between a particular conditioned stimulus (CS) and other stimuli **sufficiently different** from it. Someone who's been stung by a bee might only have an involuntary fear response to the sight of bees (and not flies) because they have learned to discriminate among various flying insects. They have only been conditioned to fear bees.

**EXTINCTION**    Once the dogs in a classical conditioning experiment associate the buzzer sound with meat, can they ever listen to the sound without salivating? The answer is yes—if they are repeatedly exposed to the buzzer *without* the meat. Present the conditioned stimulus (CS) without the unconditioned stimulus (US), over and over, and the association may fade. The conditioned response (CR) decreases and eventually disappears in a process called **extinction**. In general, if dogs are repeatedly exposed to a conditioned stimulus (for example, a metronome or buzzer) without any tasty treats to follow, they produce progressively less saliva in response to the stimulus and, eventually, none at all (Watson, 1968).

**SPONTANEOUS RECOVERY**    But take note: Even with extinction, the connection is not necessarily gone forever. After conditioning a dog to associate the sound of a buzzer with meat, Pavlov (1927/1960) repeatedly sounded the buzzer *without* presenting meat, and the association was eventually extinguished. (The dog no longer salivated in response to the sound.) However, 2 hours following this extinction, Pavlov presented the sound again and the dog salivated. This reappearance of the conditioned response (CR) following its extinction is called **spontaneous recovery.** With the presentation of a conditioned stimulus (CS) after a period of rest, the conditioned response (CR) reappears. The dog had not "forgotten" the association when the pairing was extinguished. Rather, the conditioned response (CR) was suppressed when the dog was not being exposed to the unconditioned stimulus (US). The link between the sound and the food had remained, simply simmering beneath the surface. Let's return to that tall refreshing glass of lemonade—a summer drink you may not consume for 9 months out of the year. Your conditioned response (CR) of salivating may be suppressed by extinction from September to the end of May when you see the unused lemonade glass in your cupboard. However, when June rolls around (marking the return of lemonade season), spontaneous recovery may occur: You find yourself salivating at the sight of that lemonade glass again (the conditioned stimulus).

**HIGHER ORDER CONDITIONING**    Is it possible to add another layer to the conditioning process? Absolutely. Suppose the buzzer sound has become a conditioned stimulus (CS) for the dog. Now the researcher adds a new neutral stimulus (NS), such as a flashing light, every time the dog hears the buzzer. After pairing the buzzer and the flashing light (without the meat anywhere in sight or smell), the light becomes associated with the sound and the dog will begin to salivate in response to seeing the light alone. This is called **higher order conditioning** (FIGURE 5.1). With repeated pairings of the conditioned stimulus (buzzer tone) and a new neutral stimulus (flashing light), the second neutral stimulus becomes a conditioned stimulus (CS) as well. When all is said and done, both stimuli (buzzer and flashing light) have gone from being neutral stimuli (NS) to conditioned stimuli (CS), and either of them can elicit the conditioned response (CR) of salivation. Note that in higher order conditioning, the second neutral stimulus (NS) is paired with a conditioned stimulus (CS) instead of being paired with the original unconditioned stimulus (US) (Pavlov, 1927/1960). In our example, the flashing light is associated with the buzzer sound, not with the food directly.

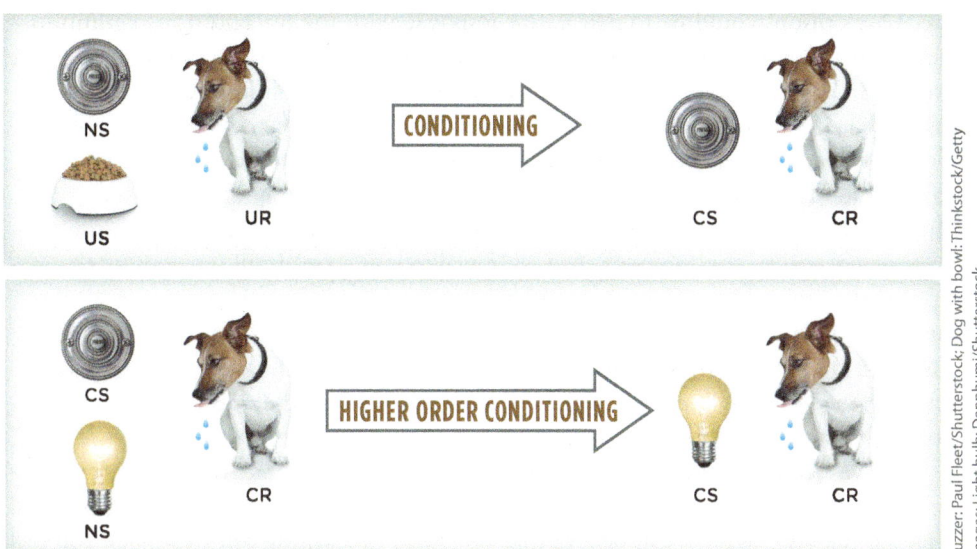

Buzzer: Paul Fleet/Shutterstock; Dog with bowl: Thinkstock/Getty Images; Light bulb: Denphumi/Shutterstock.

**FIGURE 5.1**
**Higher Order Conditioning**
Once an association has been made through classical conditioning, the conditioned stimulus (CS) can be used to learn new associations. When a conditioned stimulus (CS), such as a buzzer that now triggers salivation, is repeatedly paired with a neutral stimulus (NS), such as a flashing light, the dog will learn to salivate in response to the light—without food ever being present! These multiple layers of learning help us understand how humans form associations between many different stimuli.

**CLASSICAL CONDITIONING IN YOUR LIFE**   Classical conditioning is not limited to salivation. It affects you in ways you may not even realize. Just think of what happens to your heart rate when you walk into a room where you have had a bad experience, or when you come face to face with a person (perhaps a boss) who has caused you great anxiety. The same learning process that makes you anxious around your boss can make you excited (in a good way) when presented with stimuli that have romantic significance. Perhaps there is a song you have come to associate with someone you find really attractive. When you hear that song, you feel a change in your body (your heart rate increases, and maybe your cheeks start to flush). That physiological arousal is a classically conditioned response.

We launched the discussion of classical conditioning with the story of Gavin, the ATF dog who became fearful of everyday sounds after serving in the Iraq War. Let's apply our newfound knowledge of classical conditioning to conjecture how Gavin's unusual behaviors developed, and discover how Cesar helped this yellow Lab overcome his fear.

**FROM IVAN PAVLOV TO CESAR MILLAN**   An explosion is an alarming event. Think of the sound it emits as an unconditioned stimulus (US) that can elicit a physiological fear response of shaking (the unconditioned response; UR). Somewhere along the line, Gavin likely heard another sound paired with explosions—perhaps the faint popping sound of faraway artillery fire. (It doesn't seem too farfetched that one would hear artillery fire and explosions in the same general location.) After repeated pairings of the distant artillery fire (the neutral stimulus; NS) and the nearby explosion sound (the unconditioned stimulus; US), Gavin came to associate these two stimuli. During this acquisition phase, the sound of distant artillery fire became a conditioned stimulus (CS) that could elicit the conditioned response (CR) of shaking. In other words, the sound of artillery fire came to evoke the same physiological response (shaking) as an explosion.

So, what does all this have to do with Gavin's fear of beeping microwaves, cell phones, and elevators? We can only speculate because we weren't there to observe Gavin. But supposing he was conditioned to fear the sound of distant artillery fire, then it's possible that this fear became generalized to other rhythmic, mechanical sounds, such as beeping cell phones and elevators. Through *stimulus generalization,* these nondangerous sounds began to evoke a conditioned response (CR) as well. How could this seemingly classically conditioned response be extinguished?

Courtesy Cesar's Way Inc.

**Calm in the Water**

According to Cesar, being in the water brings out the instinctual side of most dogs, connecting them with nature and making them feel calm. To help Gavin the ATF dog overcome his fear of everyday noises (the conditioned stimulus), Cesar paired the disturbing sounds with activities that were relaxing and pleasurable for Gavin.

One option would be to pair a new response with the unconditioned stimulus (US) or the conditioned stimulus (CS). Cesar took this approach, and it worked wonders. To help Gavin overcome his fear of everyday loud noises (conditioned stimulus), Cesar combined those sounds with something relaxing or pleasurable. For example, he would create a loud noise just as he presented Gavin with his favorite food (carrots). To reduce Gavin's fear of truly frightening sounds like thunder, fireworks, and explosions (unconditioned stimulus), Cesar placed him in a virtual reality environment. As Gavin walked on a treadmill (an activity that appeared to relax him), Cesar exposed him to the sounds he feared most (not all at once, but in small steps). Eventually, Gavin's fear response diminished and he could visit a firing range without "shutting down" and shaking (Millan & Peltier, 2010). In Chapter 14, we will present similar techniques used by therapists to help clients struggling with anxiety and fear.

We've learned how classical conditioning can cause a variety of reflexive responses, including salivation (Pavlov's dogs), increased heart rate (humans), and shaking (Gavin). Would you believe that this form of learning can also make you feel nauseous?

## Yuck: Conditioned Taste Aversion

**LO 5**  Summarize how classical conditioning is dependent on the biology of the organism.

Have you ever experienced food poisoning? After falling ill from something you ate, whether it was bad fish, uncooked chicken, or tainted peanut butter, you probably steered clear of that particular food for a while. This is an example of **conditioned taste aversion,** a powerful form of classical conditioning that occurs when an organism learns to associate a particular food or drink with illness. Often, it only takes a single pairing between a food and a bad feeling—that is, one-trial learning—for an organism to change its behavior. Imagine a grizzly bear that avoids poisonous berries after it vomits from eating them. In this case, the unconditioned stimulus (US) is the poison in the berries; the unconditioned response (UR) is the vomiting. After acquisition, the conditioned stimulus (CS) would be the sight of the berries, and the conditioned response (CR) would be a nauseous feeling. In all likelihood, the bear would avoid the berries in the future.

Avoiding foods that induce sickness has **adaptive value,** meaning it helps organisms survive, upping the odds they will reproduce and pass their genes along to the next generation. According to the **evolutionary perspective,** humans and other animals have a powerful drive to ensure that they and their offspring reach reproductive age, so it's critical to steer clear of tastes that have been associated with illness.

How might conditioned taste aversion play out in your life? Suppose you eat a hot dog a few hours before coming down with a stomach virus that's coincidentally spreading throughout your college campus. The hot dog isn't responsible for your illness—and you may be aware of this—but thereafter, the slightest taste of one, or the thought of eating one, can make you feel sick even after you have recovered. Physical experiences like this can sometimes be so strong that they override our knowledge of the facts.

**CONNECTIONS**

In **Chapter 1,** we introduced the evolutionary perspective, which suggests that behaviors and traits are shaped by natural selection. Here, this perspective helps clarify why some types of learning are so powerful. In the case of conditioned taste aversion, species gain an evolutionary advantage through quick and efficient learning about poisonous foods.

**conditioned taste aversion**  A form of classical conditioning that occurs when an organism learns to associate the taste of a particular food or drink with illness.

**adaptive value**  The degree to which a trait or behavior helps an organism survive.

**biological preparedness**  The tendency for animals to be predisposed or inclined to form certain kinds of associations through classical conditioning.

 **Try This**  Identify the neutral stimulus (NS), the unconditioned stimulus (US), the unconditioned response (UR), the conditioned stimulus (CS), and the conditioned response (CR) in the hot dog scenario.

✓ CHECK YOUR ANSWERS AT THE BACK OF THE BOOK.

**RATS WITH BELLYACHES** American psychologist John Garcia (1917–2012) and his colleagues demonstrated conditioned taste aversion in their well-known studies with laboratory rats (Garcia et al., 1966). They designed a series of experiments to explore how rats would respond to eating and drinking foods that became associated with sickness. In one study, Garcia and his colleagues provided the animals with flavored water followed by injections of a drug that upset their stomachs. The animals rejected that flavored drink thereafter.

The rats in Garcia's studies seemed naturally inclined to link their "internal malaise" (sick feeling) to tastes and smells and less likely to associate their nausea with things they heard or saw (Garcia et al., 1966). This is clearly adaptive, because nausea often results from ingesting food that is poisonous or spoiled. In order to survive, an animal must be able to recognize and shun the tastes of dangerous substances. Garcia's research highlights the importance of **biological preparedness,** the predisposition or inclination of animals (and people) to form certain kinds of associations through classical conditioning. Conditioned taste aversion is a powerful form of learning. Would you believe it can be used to **save endangered species**?

### Didn't See That Coming

RESCUING ANIMALS WITH CLASSICAL CONDITIONING

An animal is in trouble in Australia: A large lizard called the "floodplain goanna" is threatened by a nonnative "cane toad" that is invading its tropical habitat. Cane toads may look delicious (at least to the goannas), but they pack a lethal dose of poison, killing the unlucky lizards that try to feast on them. Cane toads are "extraordinarily difficult to control" (Indigo et al., 2018, p. 592). In areas where they have invaded, goanna populations have plummeted, with death estimates exceeding 90% (Ujvari & Madsen, 2009; Ward-Fear et al., 2016).

**ATTACK OF THE KILLER TOADS!**

How could you use conditioned taste aversion to protect these lizards from looming toad invasions? Remember that conditioned taste aversion occurs when an organism rejects a food or drink after consuming it and becoming very sick. To encourage the goannas to avoid the toxic toads, you must teach them to associate the

> **CONNECTIONS**
>
> In **Chapter 1,** we introduced two types of research: basic and applied. Basic research is focused on gathering knowledge for the sake of knowledge. Applied research focuses on changing behaviors and outcomes, often leading to real-world applications. Here, we see how classical conditioning principles are *applied* to protect wildlife.

**Learning to the Rescue**

Australia's large lizard species, the floodplain goanna (held by University of Sydney researcher Dr. Georgia Ward-Fear) is threatened by the introduction of an invasive species known as the cane toad (right). The goannas eat the toads, which carry a lethal dose of poison, but they can learn to avoid this toxic prey through conditioned taste aversion (Ward-Fear et al., 2017).

Courtesy Dr. David Pearson;

Chris Mattison/FLPA/Science Source.

little amphibians with nausea. You could do this by feeding them baby cane toads. Unlike their parents, these youngsters pack a "sublethal" dose of poison—enough to induce nausea, but not enough to cause death. After an unpleasant training with the baby toads, the goannas should avoid eating the more dangerous adult toads. Researchers from the University of Sydney used such an approach, and the results were promising. Goannas subjected to conditioned taste aversion prior to a toad invasion were less likely than their unconditioned comrades to eat the killer toads and die (Ward-Fear et al., 2016; Ward-Fear et al., 2017).

Similar approaches have been tried with other wildlife in Australia, and in animals across the world (Indigo et al., 2018). In Africa, ranchers often kill lions for preying upon cattle (Platt, 2015). But researchers have shown that the big cats can learn to avoid beef through conditioned taste aversion (Platt, 2011). A recent study in India demonstrated that this approach may also be effective on monkeys that steal human crops (Pebsworth & Radhakrishna, 2020). As you can see, lessons learned by psychologists working in labs can have far-reaching applications. ⚡

## Lessons from Little Albert

**LO 6** Describe the Little Albert study and explain how fear can be learned.

So far, we have focused chiefly on the classical conditioning of physical responses, like salivation, shaking, and nausea. Now let's take a closer look at how classical conditioning can influence emotions. A **conditioned emotional response** occurs when a neutral stimulus (NS) is paired with a stimulus that creates an emotional reaction.

The classic case study of "Little Albert," conducted by John B. Watson (1878–1958) and Rosalie Rayner (1898–1935), provides a famous illustration of a conditioned emotional response (Watson & Rayner, 1920). Little Albert was around 9 months old when first assessed by Watson and Rayner (Griggs, 2015b; Powell et al., 2014). Initially, he had no fear of rats; in fact, he was rather intrigued by the white critters and sometimes reached out to touch them. But all this changed when Albert was about 11 months old; that's when the researchers began banging a hammer against a steel bar (an unconditioned stimulus for a fear response in younger children) whenever he reached for the rat (Harris, 1979). After seven pairings of the loud noise and the appearance of the rat, Albert began to fear rats and generalized this fear to other furry objects, including a sealskin coat and a rabbit (Harris, 1979). The sight of the rat went from being a neutral stimulus (NS) to a conditioned stimulus (CS), and Albert's fear of the rat became a conditioned response (CR).

Nobody knows exactly what happened to Little Albert after he participated in Watson and Rayner's research. Scholars have attempted to determine his fate, but their efforts have been criticized for potential bias and flaws in logic (Digdon, 2020; Harris, 2020). Some believe Little Albert's true identity is still unknown (Powell, 2010; Reese, 2010). Others have proposed Little Albert was Douglas Merritte, who had a neurological condition called hydrocephalus and died at age 6 (Beck et al., 2009; Fridlund et al., 2012, 2020). Still others suggest Little Albert was a healthy baby named William Albert Barger (later known as William Albert Martin), who lived until 2007 and reportedly had an "aversion to dogs" (Bartlett, 2014; Digdon et al., 2014; Powell et al., 2014). Did Barger's distaste for dogs and other animals stem from his supposed participation in Watson and Rayner's experiment, his dislike of messiness, or was it the result of seeing a childhood pet killed in an accident (Powell et al., 2014)? Researchers cannot be sure, and we may never know the true identity of Little Albert or the long-term effects of his conditioning through this unethical study. Although Watson and Rayner (1920) discussed how they might have reduced Little

The Drs. Nicholas and Dorothy Cummings Center for the History of Psychology, The University of Akron.

**Poor Albert**

"Little Albert" was a baby who developed a fear of rats through his participation in an ethically questionable experiment conducted by John B. Watson and Rosalie Rayner. Watson and Rayner repeatedly showed the child a rat while terrifying him with a loud banging sound (Watson & Rayner, 1920). Albert quickly learned to associate the sight of the rat with the scary noise; his resulting fear of rats was a conditioned emotional response.

**conditioned emotional response** An emotional reaction acquired through classical conditioning; process by which an emotional reaction becomes associated with a previously neutral stimulus.

Albert's fear (for example, giving him candy while presenting the rat), they did not provide him with such treatment (Griggs, 2014b).

The Little Albert study would never happen today; at least, we hope it wouldn't. Contemporary psychologists conduct research according to stringent ethical guidelines, and instilling terror in a baby would not be considered acceptable. Nor would such a study be allowed at research institutions.

## Do You Buy It?

Classical conditioning affects you in ways you may not realize (TABLE **5.1**). Advertisements can instill emotions and attitudes toward product brands, and these classically conditioned responses may linger as long as 3 weeks (Grossman & Till, 1998). Are you more likely to buy a product if it is endorsed by a celebrity? Maybelline makeup looks pretty appealing on the face of Gigi Hadid, and who can resist Adidas gear worn by Yankees slugger Aaron Judge? Celebrity endorsements can promote more positive attitudes toward products—especially when the celebrity is male and is well-matched with the item (a basketball player endorsing basketball shoes, for example) (Knoll & Matthes, 2017). Although celebrities tend to make a big impression, social media influencers may have more clout when it comes to advertising. This may be because "influencers are deemed more trustworthy than celebrities, and . . . people feel more similar to influencers and identify more with them than celebrities" (Schouten et al., 2019, p. 276).

This does not mean that classical conditioning can force you to go out and spend money on items you otherwise would not buy. If it did lead to changes in purchasing behavior, the implications could be far-reaching. Imagine, for example, that consumers made decisions based on medical advice offered by celebrities, as opposed to health professionals (Hoffman & Tan, 2013).

The time has come to wrap up our discussion of classical conditioning. Remember, this type of learning is associated with automatic (or involuntary) behaviors. In the next section, we'll shift our focus to voluntary behaviors. How do we learn to get things we want and avert unpleasant events? Read on.

Grzegorz Czapski/Alamy Stock Photo.

**Does Sexy Sell?**
Beyoncé appears in an ad campaign for "Heat," a fragrance for women. Advertisements may evoke emotions and instill attitudes toward brands through classical conditioning (Chen et al., 2013; Grossman & Till, 1998; Poels & Dewitte, 2019), but how do these psychological changes affect sales? Now, that is a question worth researching.

**TABLE 5.1**  Real-Life Examples of Classical Conditioning

| Type | NS and US | Expected Response |
|---|---|---|
| Advertising | Repeated pairing of products such as cars (NS) with celebrities (US) | Automatic response to celebrity may include sexual desire and arousal, or increased heart rate (UR); pairing leads to a similar response (CR) to the product (CS). |
| Fears | Pairing of a dog lunging (US) at you, and the street where the dog lives (NS) | Automatic response to the dog lunging at you is fear (UR); pairing leads to a similar response of fear (CR) to the street (CS) where the dog lives. |
| Fetishes | Repeated pairings of originally nonsexual objects like shoes (NS) and sexual activity (US) | Automatic response to sexual activity is sexual arousal (UR); pairing leads to sexual arousal (CR) in response to the objects (CS). |
| Romance | Repeated pairings of a cologne (NS) with your romantic partner (US) | Automatic response to your feelings for your partner is sexual arousal (UR); pairing leads to sexual arousal (CR) in response to the cologne (CS). |
| Pet behavior | Repeated pairings of an electric can opener sound (NS) and the serving of food (US) | Automatic response to food is the dog/cat's salivation (UR); pairing leads to salivation (CR) in response to the sound of the can opener (CS). |
| Startle reaction | Repeated pairings of seeing someone squeeze a balloon (NS) with the sudden "pop" of the balloon breaking (US) | Automatic response to the "pop" sound is flinching (UR); pairing causes the person to flinch (CR) in response to the sight of someone squeezing the balloon (CS). |

The implications of classical conditioning extend far beyond salivating dogs. Here are just a few examples illustrating its widespread relevance.

## SHOW WHAT YOU KNOW

1. _____ is a learning process in which two stimuli become associated.

2. Because of _____ , animals and people are predisposed to form associations that increase their chances of survival.

3. Watson and Rayner used classical conditioning to instill fear in Little Albert. Create a diagram of the NS, US, UR, CS, and CR in their experiment. In what way did Little Albert exhibit stimulus generalization?

4. Hamburgers were once your favorite food, but ever since you ate a burger tainted with salmonella (a common cause of food poisoning), you cannot smell or taste one without feeling nauseous. Which of the following is the unconditioned stimulus?

   A. salmonella
   B. nausea
   C. hamburgers
   D. the hamburger vendor

 CHECK YOUR ANSWERS AT THE BACK OF THE BOOK.

# Operant Conditioning

**WE'VE GOT DOG PROBLEMS**    Cesar spent much of his early life on his grandfather's cattle ranch in Ixpalino, a small town in Sinaloa, Mexico. He loved being around the ranch animals, especially the dogs. They lived in a pack of about five to seven members, slept outside, and hunted wild animals. Cesar's family depended on the dogs to herd cattle and guard the property, but also gave them plenty of "free time" to splash around in the creek and play. The ranch dogs organized their activities as a pack, as wolves do in nature, and their needs for daily exercise were satisfied (Fine, 2013; Millan & Peltier, 2006).

When Cesar arrived in the United States, he encountered quite a different type of dog. In America, dogs dined on gourmet biscuits, slept on memory foam mattresses, and got their hair blown dry at doggie salons. Cesar began to realize that many American owners didn't understand their dogs or know how to communicate with them. The dogs were suffering from an untold number of "issues," including anxiety, aggression, and hyperactivity (Millan & Peltier, 2006). In order to "fix" the dogs' misbehaviors, Cesar would have to teach their human owners a few things. As Cesar often says, "I rehabilitate dogs, and I train people" (Millan, 2013, March 26, para. 3).

So how exactly does Cesar train humans? We can't possibly cover the myriad approaches he employs, but we can explore how *operant conditioning* impacts his work.

## Consequences Matter

Whether pleasant or unpleasant, the effects of our behaviors influence what we do in the future. Think about the many consequences of Cesar's hard work. Helping people understand and connect with their dogs is one positive consequence: "When I show them how the brain of a dog works, when I show them what makes a dog happy, when I show them how dogs communicate, and how we can communicate with [dogs]," Cesar explains, "then [I] see people understanding and making sense of what's happening." This is a rewarding experience for Cesar, one that makes him more likely to continue his work in the future. Imagine what would happen if all of Cesar's human clients ignored his advice and continued with their bad habits. How do you think this consequence would influence Cesar's future behaviors—would he be more or less likely to continue his work rehabilitating dogs and training people?

**LO 7**  Describe Thorndike's law of effect.

**THORNDIKE AND HIS CATS**    One of the first scientists to objectively study how consequences affect behavior was American psychologist Edward Thorndike (1874–1949). Thorndike's early research focused on chicks and other animals, which he sometimes kept in his apartment. But after an incubator almost caught fire, his

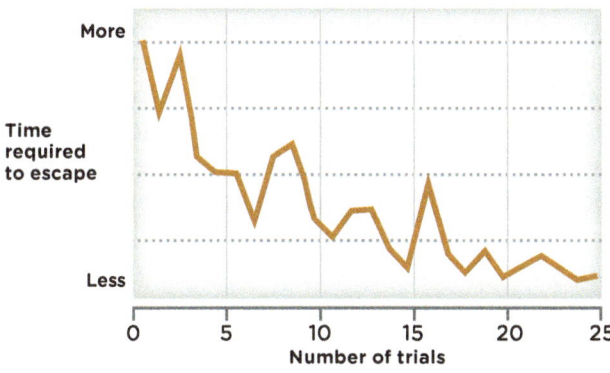

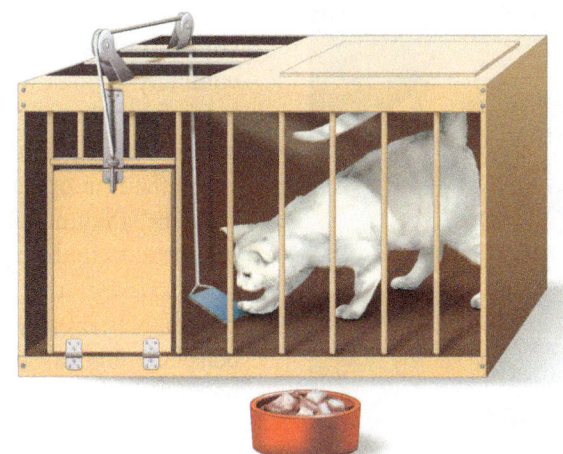

## FIGURE 5.2
**Puzzle Box**

Early psychologist Edward Thorndike conducted his well-known cat experiments using "puzzle boxes" like the one shown here. At the start of the experiment, Thorndike's cats pawed around haphazardly until they managed to unlatch the door and then eat the fish treats placed outside. As the trials wore on, the felines learned to free themselves more quickly. After several trials, the amount of time needed to escape the box dropped significantly (see the graph above). Thorndike attributed this phenomenon to the *law of effect,* which essentially states that behaviors are more likely to reoccur if they are followed by pleasurable outcomes.

landlady insisted he get rid of the chicks (Hothersall, 2004). Thorndike was assisted by William James, whose "habitual kindness and devotion to underdogs" led him to house the chickens in his basement for a time (Thorndike, 1936, p. 264).

Researching the chicks was only a starting point, as Thorndike's most famous studies involved cats. One of his experimental setups involved putting a cat in a latched cage called a "puzzle box" and planting enticing pieces of fish outside the door. When first placed in the box, the cat would scratch and paw around randomly, but after a while, just by chance, it would pop the latch, causing the door to release. The cat would then escape the cage to devour the fish (**FIGURE 5.2**). The next time the cat was put in the box, it would repeat this random activity, scratching and pawing with no particular direction. And again, just by chance, the cat would pop the latch that released the door and freed it to eat the fish. Each time the cat was returned to the box, the number of random activities decreased until eventually it was able to break free almost immediately (Thorndike, 1898).

The cats' behavior, Thorndike reasoned, could be explained by the **law of effect,** which says that a behavior (opening the latch) is more likely to happen again when followed by a pleasurable outcome (delicious fish). Behaviors that lead to pleasurable results will be repeated, while behaviors that don't lead to pleasurable results (or are followed by something unpleasant) will not be repeated. The law of effect is not limited to cats. When was the last time your behavior changed as a result of a pleasurable outcome?

Most contemporary psychologists would call the fish in Thorndike's experiments **reinforcers,** because these treats increased the likelihood that the preceding behavior (escaping the cage) would occur again. Reinforcers are consequences that follow behaviors, and our daily lives abound with them. A dog praised for sitting is more likely to obey the "sit" command in the future. An Instagram user who is reinforced with a lot of "likes" is more apt to post photos and videos in the future. Praise, hugs, good grades, enjoyable food, and attention can all act as reinforcers, increasing the probability that the behaviors they follow will be repeated. Through the process of **reinforcement,** target behaviors become more frequent.

**law of effect** Thorndike's principle stating that behaviors are more likely to be repeated when followed by pleasurable outcomes, and less likely to be repeated when followed by unpleasant outcomes.

**reinforcers** Events, stimuli, and other consequences that increase the likelihood of a behavior recurring.

**reinforcement** Process of increasing the frequency of behaviors with consequences.

**Radical Behaviorist**
American psychologist Burrhus Frederic Skinner, or simply B. F. Skinner, is one of the most influential psychologists of all time. Skinner believed that all thoughts, emotions, and behaviors (basically all things psychological) are shaped by factors in the environment. Using animal chambers known as "Skinner boxes," he conducted carefully controlled experiments on animal behavior.

**operant conditioning** Learning that occurs when voluntary actions become associated with their consequences.

**positive reinforcement** The process by which reinforcers are added or presented following a target behavior, increasing the likelihood of it occurring again.

**SKINNER AND BEHAVIORISM**    Reinforcement is a key component of **operant conditioning,** a type of learning whereby people or animals come to associate their voluntary actions with consequences. B. F. Skinner coined the term, and its meaning is fairly simple. The term *operant* "emphasizes the fact that the behavior *operates* on the environment to generate consequences" and in "operant conditioning we 'strengthen' an operant in the sense of making a response more probable . . . or more frequent" (Skinner, 1953, p. 65). Some of the earliest and most influential research on operant conditioning came from Skinner's lab. His work followed the principles of *behaviorism,* the scientific study of observable behavior. Behaviorists believe that psychology can only be considered a "true science" if it restricts itself to the study of behaviors that can be seen and documented. And although mental processes such as memory and emotion may not be directly observable, Skinner and other behaviorists have proposed that all behaviors, thoughts, and emotions are shaped by factors in the external environment. In other words, they are learned.

## Types of Reinforcement

Like most people who have achieved a high level of success and fame, Cesar has accumulated a fair number of critics. They question his "antiquated view of dominance hierarchies," suggesting that his discipline-before-affection approach is misguided (Derr, 2016, para. 2), and contend that his self-taught approach "ignores 80 years of research in animal behavior" (Breeden, n.d., para. 35). Some claim he is too physical with the animals, forcing them into submission with foot taps to the area above the hind leg and vibrating collars (Barber, 2012; Grossman, 2012). Cesar has defended himself by saying he reserves these techniques for "red zone" dogs—those that pose a threat to other animals and/or people and therefore may be at risk for being euthanized. "My mission has always been to save dogs—especially troubled and abandoned dogs," he said in an interview with the *Daily Mail.* "I've dedicated my life to this" (Barber, 2012, para. 4).

We are not interested in taking sides here; our goal is to examine the role of learning in Cesar's life and work. Watch him closely, and you'll see that he employs quite a bit of *positive reinforcement.*

**LO 8**  Explain how positive and negative reinforcement differ.

**POSITIVE REINFORCEMENT**    Earlier, we explained that a reinforcer is a consequence that increases the likelihood of a behavior being repeated. *Any* stimulus, good or bad, is considered a reinforcer if it eventually leads to an increase in the behavior that immediately precedes it. What we haven't addressed is that a reinforcer can be something added or something taken away. In the process of **positive reinforcement,** reinforcers are presented (added) following the target behavior, and they are generally pleasant. The fish treats that Thorndike's cats received for escaping the puzzle box were positive reinforcers. They were pleasurable; they were added following the desired behavior; and they increased the frequency of that desired behavior.

What reinforcers does Cesar employ in dog rehabilitation? Sometimes it's not as obvious as a biscuit or bone. Before giving reinforcement, Cesar explains, you have to help your dog feel calm and happy, and that requires exercise and mental stimulation. Once the dog reaches that relaxed state, you can reinforce it with affection. It's important to remember that the definition of "positive reinforcer" depends entirely on the organism receiving it (Skinner, 1953). For some dogs, playtime is a powerful positive reinforcer. Remember Gavin, the ATF agent with the classically conditioned response to certain noises? After Gavin completed his sessions in the virtual reality environment, Cesar would reinforce the Lab's good work with "a vigorous play period," which often meant a dip in the pool (Millan & Peltier, 2010, p. 63).

Dogs offer positive reinforcement to humans as well; you just have to be perceptive enough to notice. Consider this example from Cesar: "Your dog wants to go outside and pee. He sits by the door. You open the door. The dog walks out, but as he passes by you, he looks up at you for a moment and makes eye contact. He just rewarded you" (Millan & Peltier, 2010, p. 121). Why is eye contact reinforcing? When you gaze into your dog's eyes, both you and the dog release the hormone *oxytocin,* which plays an important role in social bonding. Oxytocin increases "social reward" and enhances attachment between infants and their mothers, and between **sexual partners**. Eye contact is just one of the ways dogs and humans have established mutually reinforcing relationships during the course of evolution (MacLean & Hare, 2015; Nagasawa et al., 2015).

But take note: Not all positive reinforcers are pleasant. When we refer to *positive* reinforcement, we just mean that something (either pleasant or unpleasant) has been *added*. For example, if a child is starved for attention, then any kind of attention (including a reprimand) might act as a positive reinforcer. Every time the child misbehaves, they get reprimanded, and reprimanding is a form of attention, which the child craves. The scolding reinforces the misbehavior.

One other interesting fact about positive reinforcement—it can lead to superstitious behavior. Have you ever known someone who wears a "good luck" piece of clothing? For example, your friend wears a special baseball cap every time the Red Sox are playing, because the first time they wore it the Red Sox won. That win, and every subsequent win, has nothing to do with your friend's hat, but the hat-wearing behavior is nevertheless reinforced (Hayashi & Modico, 2019).

**NEGATIVE REINFORCEMENT**   We have established that behaviors can be increased or strengthened by the addition of a stimulus. But it is also possible to increase a behavior by taking something away. Behaviors increase in response to **negative reinforcement,** through the process of *taking away* (or subtracting) something unpleasant. Skinner demonstrated how negative reinforcement could be used to influence the behavior of rats. He placed them in special cages with floors that delivered a continuous mild electric current—except when they pushed on a lever. At the start of the experiment, the animals would scamper around the floors to escape the electric current, but every once in a while, they would accidentally hit the lever and turn off the electric current. Eventually, they learned to associate pushing the lever with the removal of the unpleasant stimulus (a mild shock). After several trials, the rats would push the lever immediately, reducing the amount of time they were exposed to the current.

Think about some examples of negative reinforcement in your own life. Have you ever started driving before putting on your seat belt? If so, you likely heard an annoying beeping sound. In order to stop the beeping (an unpleasant stimulus), you buckle up (the desired behavior). Automakers have cleverly used negative reinforcement to increase seat belt use. We are more inclined to buckle up right away (an increase in the desired behavior) because we have learned that it stops the beeping. For another example, think about a dog that constantly begs for treats. The begging (an unpleasant stimulus) stops the moment the dog is given a treat, a pattern that increases *your* treat-giving behavior. (Meanwhile, the dog's begging behavior is being strengthened through positive reinforcement; the dog has learned that the more it begs, the more treats it receives.) The previous two examples involved stopping unwanted stimuli in the present moment. But sometimes we learn to avoid unpleasant stimuli that may happen in the future. Do you get regular dental checkups? If so, it's probably not because you have painful dental issues right now, but because you want to avoid

**CONNECTIONS**

In **Chapter 2,** we introduced oxytocin, a chemical that can behave as both a neurotransmitter and a hormone. Oxytocin levels rise during the early stages of a romantic relationship, and its activity may be associated with feelings of love.

**negative reinforcement** The removal of an unpleasant stimulus following a target behavior, which increases the likelihood of that behavior occurring again.

them in the future. Through experience, you have learned you can avoid tooth pain through routine care. Remember that with negative reinforcement, desired behaviors increase in order to avoid or escape an unwanted stimulus.

## Put Your Heads Together

Before COVID-19, it was rare to see Americans wearing face masks in public. The pandemic led to widespread mask use, but many people chose not to wear masks against the advice of public health officials. Could this have something to do with rewards, or lack thereof (Svoboda, 2020)? In your groups, discuss how reinforcement might have influenced these behaviors. **A)** What reinforcers drive people to wear masks? **B)** What reinforcers drive people to forgo masks?

**LO 9** Distinguish between primary and secondary reinforcers.

**PRIMARY AND SECONDARY REINFORCERS** There are two major categories of reinforcers: primary and secondary. The fish Thorndike gave his cats is considered a **primary reinforcer,** because it satisfies a biological need. Food, water, and physical contact are considered primary reinforcers (for both animals and people) because they meet essential requirements. **Secondary reinforcers** do not satisfy biological needs, but often derive their power from their connection with primary reinforcers. Money is not a primary reinforcer, but we know from experience that it gives us access to primary reinforcers, such as food, a safe place to live, and perhaps even the ability to attract desirable mates. Thus, money is a secondary reinforcer. Good grades and extra credit assignments might also be considered secondary reinforcers (Whittington, 2019), because doing well in school leads to job opportunities, which provide money to pay for food and other basic needs.

Secondary reinforcers influence your everyday social interactions. Think about how your behaviors change in response to praise from a boss, a pat on the back from a coworker, or even a nod of approval from a friend on social media.

Rana Faure/Getty Images.

**"Trophy Culture"?**

In decades past, trophies and medals were only awarded to top teams and players. These days, children often receive such rewards for simply participating. Some claim that "participation trophies" fail to prepare kids for a competitive world; others value the idea of reinforcing children (especially younger ones) for making an effort, regardless of their skill or success (Dickinsin, 2019). Research suggests we should encourage children to focus on their own improvement ("Am I doing better than last year?") rather than comparing themselves to others (Gürel & Brummelman, 2020).

## Social Media and Psychology

### TAPPING INTO THE BRAIN'S "REWARD CIRCUITRY"

**A "DOPAMINE GOLD MINE"?**

Why do you keep glancing at TikTok, and what compels you to check your phone 10 times an hour? All those little updates you receive can serve as reinforcers. Getting re-tweeted or seeing your photos and videos "liked" makes you more likely to post content in the future. The lure of digital technology is powerful; as one study found, college students find their phones "more reinforcing than food" (O'Donnell & Epstein, 2019, p. 130). Underlying this process of social media reinforcement are patterns of brain activity scientists are just beginning to understand.

In one small study, researchers used fMRI to observe the brains of teenagers as they looked at social media posts with varying numbers of "likes." When the teens looked at heavily "liked" photos (particularly ones they had posted themselves), activity increased in a brain area called the nucleus accumbens, which is "an important hub of the brain's reward circuitry" (Sherman et al., 2016, p. 1033). The nucleus accumbens has also been implicated in drug-seeking behaviors and overeating. Studies in animals show that dopamine-secreting neurons in this area and other parts of the brain play an important role in reinforcement (Chen et al., 2018; Lafferty et al., 2020; Volkow et al., 2017). Marketers are well aware of the

**primary reinforcer** A reinforcer that satisfies a biological need; innate reinforcer.

**secondary reinforcer** A reinforcer that does not satisfy a biological need but often gains power through its association with a primary reinforcer.

"dopamine gold mine" offered by social media, and they may use it to promote brands (Parkin, 2018; Soat, 2015, p. 20). Remember this the next time you share commercial content through social media. In doing so, you are airing someone else's message—and you may be fueling an ad campaign. ▣

Now that we have explored some ways that reinforcement impacts your daily life, let's venture back into the lab and see how this process can produce some astonishing animal behaviors.

## Shaping and Successive Approximations

**LO 10** Explain shaping and the method of successive approximations.

Building on Thorndike's law of effect and Watson's approach to research, Skinner demonstrated, among other things, that rats can learn to push levers and pigeons can learn to bowl (Peterson, 2004). Animals cannot immediately perform such complex tasks, but they can learn through **successive approximations,** the use of reinforcers to change behaviors through small steps toward a desired behavior (see INFOGRAPHIC **5.2** on the next page). Skinner placed animals in chambers, or *Skinner boxes,* outfitted with food dispensers the animals could activate (by pecking a target or pushing on a lever, for instance) and recording equipment to monitor these behaviors (see photo on page 184). Such boxes allowed Skinner to conduct carefully controlled experiments, measuring activity with precision and advancing the scientific and systematic study of behavior.

Some of Skinner's most incredible results occurred through **shaping,** a process in which a person observes the behaviors of another organism (an animal, for example) and provides reinforcers if the organism performs at a required level. Through shaping by successive approximations, Skinner taught a rat to "play basketball" (dropping a marble through a hole) and pigeons to "bowl" (nudging a ball down a miniature alley; Goddard, 2018; Peterson, 2000).

Let's nail down this concept using the bowling pigeons example. Skinner's first task was to break the bowling lessons into activities the birds could accomplish. Next, he introduced reinforcers (usually food) as a reward for behaviors that came closer and closer to achieving the desired goal—bowling a strike! Choosing the right increments for the behaviors was crucial. If his expectations started too high, the pigeons would never receive any reinforcers. If his expectations were too low, the pigeons would get reinforcers for most everything they did. Either way, they would be unable to make the critical connection between desired behavior and the reward. Every time the animals did something that brought them a step closer to completing the desired behavior, they would get a reinforcer. The first reward might be given for simply looking at the ball; the second, for bending down and touching it; and the third, for nudging the ball with their beaks. By the end of the experiment, the pigeons were driving balls down miniature alleys, knocking down pins with a swipe of the beak (Peterson, 2004).

Shaping by successive approximations can also be used with humans, who are sometimes unwilling or unable to change problematic behaviors overnight. For example, psychologists have employed this approach to change truancy behavior in adolescents (Enea & Dafinoiu, 2009). The truant teens were provided reinforcers for consistent attendance, but with small steps requiring increasingly more days in school.

It is amazing that the principles of animal training can also be harnessed to keep teenagers in school. Is there anything operant conditioning *can't* accomplish?

**successive approximations** A method that uses reinforcers to condition a series of small steps that gradually approach the target behavior.

**shaping** A process by which a person observes the behaviors of another organism, providing reinforcers if the organism performs at a required level.

# Learning Through Operant Conditioning

Operant conditioning is a type of learning in which we associate our voluntary actions with the consequences of those actions. For example, a pigeon naturally pecks things. But if every time the pigeon pecks a ball, it is given a *reinforcer,* the pigeon will soon learn to peck the ball more frequently.

B. F. Skinner showed that operant conditioning could do more than elicit simple, isolated actions. He taught pigeons to "bowl" and play "tennis" with the help of *shaping;* that is, he observed their behaviors and provided reinforcers when they performed at a required level. Today, shaping is used routinely by parents, teachers, coaches, and employers to change behaviors.

## SKINNER'S EXPERIMENT: TRAIN A PIGEON TO PLAY TENNIS

Pigeon is rewarded with seeds for pecking the ball.

peck **REINFORCEMENT**

*reinforcement with seeds*

Ball-pecking behavior increases.

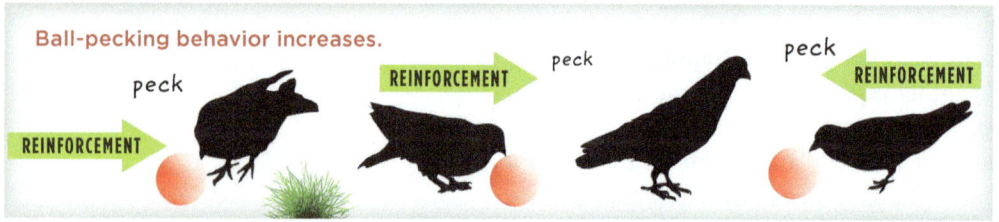

**REINFORCEMENT** peck **REINFORCEMENT** peck peck **REINFORCEMENT**

Now only the next step toward "tennis" is rewarded.

peck peck pushing the ball **REINFORCEMENT**

*reinforcement with seeds*

Ball-pushing behavior increases.

pushing the ball **REINFORCEMENT** pushing the ball **REINFORCEMENT** pushing the ball **REINFORCEMENT**

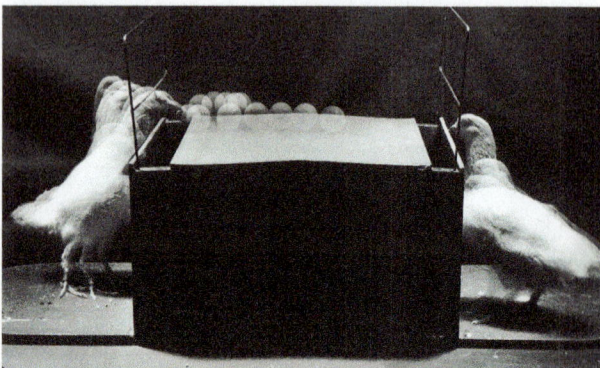

After behavior has been shaped through reinforcement, the pigeon has learned to play tennis.

## HAVE YOU BEEN TRAINED?

Not every child is born loving the healthy foods their parent offers. But shaping can help a child learn to eat their vegetables. Over a period of time, reinforcement is given for behaviors that are closer and closer to this goal. Can you think of anything that would be a reward for eating vegetables? Praise or the excitement of a contest may work in this way.

**1** Child refuses to eat vegetables.

**2** YES! Reinforced for touching fork

**3** GOOD JOB! Now, reinforced for touching vegetables

**4** After behavior has been shaped through reinforcement, the child has learned to eat their vegetables.

## Think Critically

### CHICKENS CAN'T PLAY BASEBALL

Rats can be conditioned to press levers; pigeons can be trained to bowl; and—believe it or not—chickens can learn to dance and play the piano (Breland & Breland, 1951). Keller and Marian Breland (1915–1965, 1920–2001), a pair of Skinner's students, managed to train 6,000 animals not only to dance but also to vacuum, dine at a table, and play sports and musical instruments (Breland & Breland, 1961). But as hard as they tried, the Brelands could not coax a chicken to play baseball.

Here's a rundown of what happened: The Brelands placed a chicken in a cage adjacent to a scaled down "baseball field," where it had access to a loop attached to a baseball bat. If the chicken managed to swing the bat hard enough to send the ball into the outfield, a food reward was delivered at the other end of the cage. Off the bird would go, running toward its meal dispenser like a baseball player sprinting to first base—or so the routine was supposed to go. But as soon as the Brelands took away the cage, the chicken behaved nothing like a baseball player; instead, it madly chased and pecked at the ball (Breland & Breland, 1961).

How did the Brelands explain the chickens' behavior? They believed that the birds were demonstrating **instinctive drift,** the tendency for instinct to undermine conditioned behaviors. A chicken's pecking, for example, is an instinctive food-getting behavior. Although it's useful for opening seeds and killing insects (Breland & Breland, 1961), pecking won't help the bird get to first base. Animal behavior can be shaped by forces in the environment (nurture), but instinct (nature) may interfere with the process.

**Musical Bunny**

Keller and Marian Breland observe one of their animal performers at the IQ Zoo in Hot Springs, Arkansas, circa 1960. Using the operant conditioning concepts they learned from B. F. Skinner, the Brelands trained ducks to play guitars, raccoons to shoot basketballs, and chickens to tell fortunes. But their animal "students" did not always cooperate; sometimes their instincts interfered with the conditioning process (Bihm et al., 2010).

## Continuous or Partial?

Now that we have a basic understanding of what reinforcement can—and cannot—accomplish, let's explore the various ways it may be delivered.

**LO 11**   Describe continuous reinforcement and partial reinforcement.

**CONTINUOUS REINFORCEMENT**   When it comes to teaching new behaviors to dogs, children, and other organisms, most psychologists would agree that positive reinforcement is extremely effective. Let's say you are teaching your puppy to "sit." You begin the process by giving them a treat every time they obey the "sit" command. Rewarding the pup in this manner is called **continuous reinforcement,** because the reinforcer is presented every time the desired behavior occurs. Continuous reinforcement can be used in a variety of settings: a child getting praise every time they do the dishes; a salesperson receiving a bonus every time they make a sale. You get the commonality: reinforcement every time the behavior occurs.

**PARTIAL REINFORCEMENT**   Continuous reinforcement is ideal for establishing new behaviors during the initial learning phase, but delivering reinforcers intermittently generally works better for maintaining behaviors. We call this approach **partial reinforcement.**

Returning to the examples of continuous reinforcement, we can also imagine applying partial reinforcement: The child gets praise *almost* every time they do the dishes; a salesperson gets a bonus for *every third* sale they make. The reinforcer is not given every time the behavior is observed, only on some occasions.

The amazing thing about partial reinforcement is that it happens to all of us, in an infinite number of settings, and we might never know how many times we have

**instinctive drift**   The tendency for animals to revert to instinctual behaviors after a behavior pattern has been learned.

**continuous reinforcement**   A schedule of reinforcement in which every target behavior is reinforced.

**partial reinforcement**   A schedule of reinforcement in which target behaviors are reinforced intermittently, not continuously.

been partially reinforced for any particular behavior. Common to all these partial reinforcement situations is that the target behavior is exhibited, but the reinforcer is not supplied each time it occurs.

**PARTIAL REINFORCEMENT EFFECT**    Skinner used partial reinforcement to train his pigeons to peck at a target. Once the behavior had been learned, they would continue to peck at the target up to 10,000 times with no further reinforcers given (Skinner, 1953). According to Skinner, "Nothing of this sort is ever obtained after continuous reinforcement" (p. 99). The same seems to be true with humans. In one study from the mid-1950s, researchers observed college students playing slot machines. Some of the slot machines provided continuous reinforcement, delivering pretend coins every time students pulled their levers. Other slot machines provided partial reinforcement, dispensing coins only some of the time. After the students played eight rounds, all the machines stopped giving coins. Without any coins to reinforce them, the students stopped pulling the levers—but not at the same time. Those who had received coins with every lever pull gave up more quickly than those rewarded intermittently. In other words, lever-pulling behavior took longer to extinguish when established through partial reinforcement (Lewis & Duncan, 1956). Psychologists call this phenomenon the **partial reinforcement effect:** Behaviors take longer to disappear (through the process of *extinction*) when they have been acquired or maintained through partial, rather than continuous, reinforcement. Some people, in particular those who gamble frequently, seem to be especially responsive to partial reinforcement, though it's not clear whether this tendency is a precursor to gambling or the result of it (Horsley et al., 2012; Ramnerö et al., 2019).

Remember, partial reinforcement works very well for maintaining behaviors, but not necessarily for establishing behaviors. Imagine how long it would take Skinner's pigeons to accomplish the first step in learning how to bowl if they were rewarded for looking at the ball only every fifth time. The birds learn fastest when reinforced every time, but their behavior will persist longer if they are given partial reinforcement thereafter.

## Timing Is Everything: Reinforcement Schedules

**LO 12**    Name the schedules of reinforcement and give examples of each.

Skinner identified various ways to administer partial reinforcement, or *partial reinforcement schedules*. As often occurs in scientific research, he stumbled on the idea by chance. Late one Friday afternoon, Skinner realized he was running low on the food pellets he used as reinforcers for his laboratory animals. If he continued to reward the animals on a continuous basis, the pellets would run out before the end of the weekend. With this in mind, he decided to reinforce only some of the desired behaviors (Skinner, 1956, 1976). The new strategy worked like a charm. The animals kept performing the desired behaviors, even though they weren't given reinforcers every time.

Clearly, partial reinforcement is effective, but how exactly should it be delivered? Four different reinforcement schedules can be used: fixed-ratio, variable-ratio, fixed-interval, and variable-interval (see **INFOGRAPHIC 5.3**).

**FIXED-RATIO SCHEDULE**    If reinforcement is delivered in a **fixed-ratio schedule,** the subject must exhibit a preset number of desired responses or behaviors before a reinforcer is given. A pigeon in a Skinner box, for example, must peck a spot five times in order to score a delicious pellet. Generally, the fixed-ratio schedule produces a high

QUIQUE GARCIA/Getty Images.

**Uber Reinforcement**
Why do so many Uber drivers work painfully long shifts? Partial reinforcement may be driving their behavior. With fares constantly fluctuating, drivers can never be certain when they are going to meet their earnings goals. Eventually, they will reach a certain target; it's just not clear when (Shahani, 2017).

**partial reinforcement effect** The tendency for behaviors acquired through intermittent reinforcement to be more resistant to extinction than those acquired through continuous reinforcement.

**fixed-ratio schedule** A schedule in which the subject must exhibit a predetermined number of desired behaviors before a reinforcer is given.

# Schedules of Reinforcement

Continuous reinforcement is ideal for establishing new behaviors. But once learned, a behavior is best maintained through partial reinforcement. Partial reinforcement can be delivered according to four schedules: fixed-ratio, variable-ratio, fixed-interval, and variable-interval.

## TIMING IS EVERYTHING

### Fixed-Ratio

peck peck peck peck peck — *reinforcement with food pellet on 5th peck* — REINFORCEMENT

**Fixed-Ratio**
Subject must exhibit a predetermined number of desired responses before a reinforcer is given.

### Variable-Ratio

peck peck peck — *reinforcement with food pellet on 3rd peck* — REINFORCEMENT

peck peck peck peck peck peck peck peck — *reinforcement with food pellet on 8th peck* — REINFORCEMENT

peck peck peck peck — *reinforcement with food pellet on 4th peck* — REINFORCEMENT

**Variable-Ratio**
Reinforcement is unpredictable; that is, the number of desired responses that must occur before a reinforcer is given changes across trials.

### Fixed-Interval

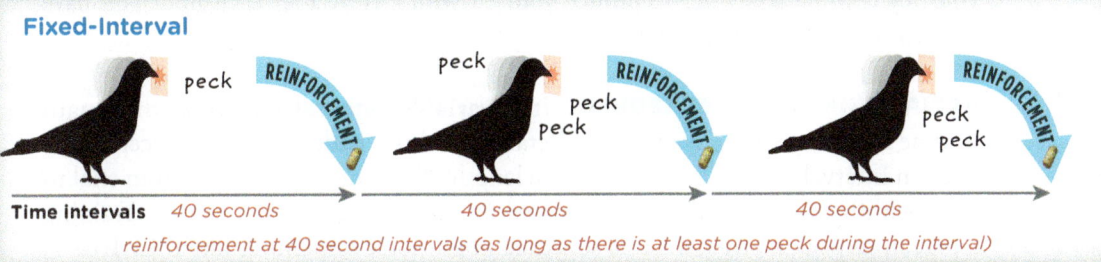

peck — REINFORCEMENT

peck peck peck — REINFORCEMENT

peck peck — REINFORCEMENT

**Time intervals** *40 seconds* *40 seconds* *40 seconds*

*reinforcement at 40 second intervals (as long as there is at least one peck during the interval)*

**Fixed-Interval**
The reinforcer comes after a preestablished interval of time; the target response is only reinforced after the given time period is over.

### Variable-Interval

peck peck — REINFORCEMENT

peck peck — REINFORCEMENT

peck peck — REINFORCEMENT

**Time intervals** *41 seconds* *43 seconds* *40 seconds*

*reinforcement at variable intervals (as long as there is at least one peck during the interval)*

**Variable-Interval**
Reinforcement follows the first target response after the time interval has elapsed. The length of the time interval changes from trial to trial.

**test yourself**

Which schedule of reinforcement matches each of the following examples? Choose from **fixed-ratio, variable-ratio, fixed-interval,** and **variable-interval.**

1. Checking the clock more frequently as the time for your favorite television show approaches is an example of _____.

2. You listen intently to your favorite radio show because its producers will randomly select times throughout the day for listeners to call in to win free tickets to a concert. This is an example of _____.

3. Finding it difficult to walk away from the slot machine because you think the next pull will be a winner is an example of _____.

4. You consistently submit your chapter summaries to your instructor because you can earn 5 points for every 4 summaries submitted. This is an example of _____.

**Answers** 1. fixed-interval, 2. variable-interval, 3. variable-ratio, 4. fixed-ratio

response rate, but with a characteristic dip immediately following the reinforcement. Pigeons rest briefly before pecking away at the target again. Some instructors use the fixed-ratio schedule to reinforce attendance. For example, extra points are given when all students show up on time for three classes in a row.

**VARIABLE-RATIO SCHEDULE**   In a **variable-ratio schedule,** the subject must exhibit a specific number of desired responses or behaviors before a reinforcer is given, but the number changes across trials (fluctuating around a precalculated average). If the goal is to train a pigeon to peck a spot on a target, a variable-ratio schedule can be used as follows: Trial 1, the pigeon gets a pellet after pecking the spot twice; Trial 2, the pigeon gets a pellet after pecking the spot once; Trial 3, the pigeon gets a pellet after pecking the spot three times; and so on. Here's another example: To encourage on-time attendance, an instructor provides extra points after several classes in a row, but students don't know if this will happen on the third class, the second class, or the fifth class. Because of its unpredictability, the variable-ratio schedule tends to produce a high response rate and behaviors that are difficult to extinguish.

**FIXED-INTERVAL SCHEDULE**   Sometimes it's important to focus on the interval of time between reinforcers, rather than the number of desired responses. In a **fixed-interval schedule,** a reinforcer is given for the first target behavior occurring after a specific time interval. If a pigeon is on a fixed-interval schedule of 30 seconds, it can peck away at the target once the interval starts, but it will only get a reinforcer following its first response after the 30 seconds have ended. With this schedule, the target behavior tends to increase as each time interval comes to an end. The pigeon pecks the spot more often when the time nears 30 seconds. Do you want to increase your focus while studying? Reinforce yourself with a treat after each hour you have worked without digital distractions.

**VARIABLE-INTERVAL SCHEDULE**   In a **variable-interval schedule,** the length of time between reinforcers is unpredictable. In this schedule, the reinforcer comes after an interval of time goes by, but the length of the interval changes from trial to trial (within a predetermined range based on an average interval length). Training a pigeon to peck a target on this schedule might look something like this: Trial 1, the pigeon gets a pellet after 41 seconds; Trial 2, the pigeon gets a pellet after 43 seconds; Trial 3, the pigeon gets a pellet after 40 seconds; and so on. As with the fixed-interval schedule, the pigeon is rewarded for the first response it makes after the interval of time has passed (but in this case, the interval length varies from trial to trial). The variable-interval schedule tends to encourage steady patterns of behavior. The pigeon tries its luck pecking a target once every 40 seconds or so. Want to increase your study group's focus? Reinforce them with a break following 45 minutes of steady work, and then after their next 30 minutes of work. Keep them guessing!

## Put Your Heads Together

Imagine you are teaching math to third-grade students. In your groups, **A)** explain how you would use each of the four reinforcement schedules to increase the amount of time students study for math quizzes; **B)** describe how each schedule might affect student behavior; and **C)** predict the problems that could arise with each schedule.

So far, we have learned about increasing behaviors through reinforcement, but sometimes we need to decrease behaviors. Let's turn our attention to techniques used for this purpose.

---

**variable-ratio schedule** A schedule in which the number of desired behaviors that must occur before a reinforcer is given changes across trials and is based on an average number of behaviors to be reinforced.

**fixed-interval schedule** A schedule in which the reinforcer comes after a preestablished interval of time; the behavior is only reinforced after the given interval is over.

**variable-interval schedule** A schedule in which the reinforcer comes after an interval of time, but the length of the interval changes from trial to trial.

**punishment** The application of a consequence that decreases the likelihood of a behavior recurring.

**positive punishment** The addition of something unpleasant following an unwanted behavior, with the intention of decreasing that behavior.

**negative punishment** The removal of something desirable following an unwanted behavior, with the intention of decreasing that behavior.

# In the Doghouse: Punishment

In contrast to reinforcement, which makes a behavior more likely to recur, the goal of **punishment** is to decrease or stop a behavior (see INFOGRAPHIC **5.4** on the next page). Punishment accomplishes this by instilling an association between a behavior and some unwanted consequence (for example, between stealing and going to jail, or between misbehaving and loss of screen time). Punishment isn't always effective, as people are sometimes willing to accept unpleasant consequences to get something they really want.

**WHAT KIND OF PUNISHMENT?**    There are two major categories of punishment: *positive* and *negative.* With **positive punishment,** something aversive or disagreeable is applied following a target behavior. When children misbehave, some parents try to stop the undesirable behavior by spanking, or "striking a child on the bottom with an open hand" (Gershoff et al., 2018, p. 626). Spanking is a controversial form of positive punishment. While spanking may provide a "quick fix" for bad behavior, many researchers contend that it leads to *more* behavior problems in the long run (Gershoff et al., 2018). Other psychologists contend there is not adequate data to conclude a causal relationship exists (Larzelere et al., 2019). Survey data indicate that "overwhelmingly, psychologists are opposed to parental use of spanking" (Miller-Perrin & Rush, 2018, p. 405). An alternative discipline strategy is to use "time out from positive reinforcement." This approach is effective for addressing problematic behaviors that are within the child's control, as long as parents behave in a way that is consistent and fair, and take steps to ensure the child feels secure and loved (Dadds & Tully, 2019).

   **Negative punishment** also aims to reduce behaviors, but it involves *taking away* something pleasant or valuable. People who drive drunk run the risk of negative punishment, as their driver's license may be taken away. Show up late for class, and you may suffer the negative punishment of missing that day's lecture altogether, as your instructor may lock the door at the beginning of class. Their goal is to decrease the unwanted behavior of arriving late.

**LO 13**   Explain how punishment differs from negative reinforcement.

**PUNISHMENT VERSUS NEGATIVE REINFORCEMENT**    Punishment and negative reinforcement are two concepts that students often find difficult to distinguish (TABLE **5.2**; also see Infographic 5.4). Remember that punishment (positive or negative) is designed to *decrease* the behavior that it follows, whereas reinforcement (positive or negative) aims to *increase* the behavior.

**Honking Drivers Get Punished**
Police in Mumbai, India, came up with a creative way to discourage excessive honking during red lights. (Yes, you read that correctly: Traffic is so bad in Mumbai that people routinely honk during red lights.) As the tweet above explains, they installed technology that measured the collective honking noise from cars waiting at intersections. Every time the sound level reached 85 decibels, the red light would reset, making drivers wait all over again (Ellis-Petersen, 2020). The purpose was to reduce an unwanted behavior (honking) through positive punishment (the addition of more wait time).

**TABLE 5.2**   Reinforcement Versus Punishment

| Term | Defined | Goal | Example |
|---|---|---|---|
| Positive reinforcement | Addition of a stimulus (usually pleasant) following a target behavior | Increase desired behavior | Students who complete an online course 15 days before the end of semester receive 10 points of extra credit. |
| Negative reinforcement | Removal of an unpleasant stimulus following a target behavior | Increase desired behavior | Students with perfect attendance do not have to take weekly quizzes. |
| Positive punishment | Addition of something unpleasant following an unwanted behavior | Decrease undesired behavior | Students who are late to class more than two times have to write an extra paper. |
| Negative punishment | Removal of something pleasant following an unwanted behavior | Decrease undesired behavior | Students late to class on exam day are not allowed to use their notes when taking the exam. |

The positive and negative forms of reinforcement and punishment are easy to confuse. Above are some concrete definitions, goals, and examples to help you sort them out.

# Learning: Reinforcement and Punishment

## Behavior: *Driving Fast*

### Do you want to increase this behavior?

**YES!**
It's NASCAR! You have to drive faster than anyone else to win.
We will apply a reinforcer to **increase** the behavior.

**NO!**
We're not at the racetrack! Speeding is dangerous and against the law.
We will apply a punishment to **decrease** the behavior.

**REINFORCEMENT**

**PUNISHMENT**

SPEED LIMIT 25

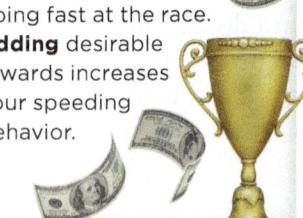

### Negative Reinforcement

You don't like working in the family auto-body shop. Your family says you can work fewer hours if you win the next race. **Taking away** unwanted work increases the speeding behavior.

### Positive Reinforcement

You win a trophy and a cash prize for going fast at the race. **Adding** desirable rewards increases your speeding behavior.

### Negative Punishment

Your license is suspended. **Taking away** something desirable decreases your speeding behavior.

### Positive Punishment

The police officer gives you a citation. **Adding** something undesirable decreases your speeding behavior.

---

**test yourself**

Which process matches each of the following examples?
Choose from **positive reinforcement**, **negative reinforcement**, **positive punishment**, and **negative punishment**.

1. Carlos' parents grounded him the last time he stayed out past his curfew, so tonight he came home right on time.

2. Jinhee spent an entire week helping an elderly neighbor clean out their basement after a flood. The local newspaper caught wind of the story and ran it as an inspiring front-page headline. Jinhee enjoyed the attention and decided to organize a neighborhood work group.

3. The trash stinks, so Sheri takes it out.

4. Gabriel's assistant had a bad habit of showing up late for work, so Gabriel docked his pay.

5. During food drives, the basketball team offers to wash your car for free if you donate six items or more to the local homeless shelter.

6. Claire received a stern lecture for texting in class. She doesn't want to hear that again, so now she turns off her phone when she enters the classroom.

**Answers** 1. negative punishment, 2. positive reinforcement, 3. negative reinforcement, 4. negative punishment, 5. negative reinforcement, 6. positive punishment.

If all the positives and negatives are confusing you, just think in terms of math: Positive always means adding something, and negative means taking it away. Punishment can be positive, which means the addition of something viewed as unpleasant ("Because you made a mess of your room, you have to clean the toilets!"), or negative, which involves the removal of something viewed as pleasant or valuable ("Because you made a mess of your room, no ice cream for you!").

## CAREER CONNECTIONS

### REINFORCEMENT IS GOLDEN

Reinforcement is one of the most effective ways to change behaviors, but many people fail to take full advantage of its power. Would you believe that 37% of business managers report that they never offer positive reinforcement? Yet this type of input is key to maintaining good work relationships. Managers who offer positive reinforcement are actually perceived as more effective than those who provide mere criticism (Zenger & Folkman, 2017). What's more, workers tend to be more engaged when supervisors emphasize their strengths rather than homing in on their weaknesses (Fessler, 2017; Harter & Adkinds, 2015).

### Put Your Heads Together

Team up and brainstorm some of the ways you could use operant conditioning to modify behaviors in the workplace. Discuss these specific questions: **A)** Imagine you run a clothing store, and you have just created a rewards program to encourage customer loyalty. What schedule of reinforcement would you use to keep customers buying merchandise? **B)** What schedule of reinforcement might you use to get sales representatives *selling* more merchandise? **C)** Now suppose you are working as an animal trainer. Your job is to teach a service dog to pick up and bring various objects to a person with limited mobility. What specific approach would you use?

*Hint for part C:* Remember, continuous reinforcement is most effective for establishing behaviors, but a variable schedule (that is, giving reinforcers intermittently) is a good bet if you want to make the behavior stick. You are also more likely to succeed if you take things "one step at a time," that is, use successive approximations.

As you can see, operant conditioning has far-ranging applications. Whether we are aware of it or not, our behaviors are constantly being shaped by reinforcement and punishment. In Chapter 14, we will discuss some of the ways therapists use operant conditioning to help clients develop healthier behaviors. We call this treatment approach *behavior modification*. As you may recall from Chapter 1, the four main goals of psychology are to describe, explain, predict, and change behavior. Can you see how behavior modification helps us achieve that fourth goal—to *change* behavior?

## Let's Compare

Both operant and classical conditioning are forms of learning, and they share many common principles (TABLE **5.3** on page 196). As with classical conditioning, behaviors learned through operant conditioning go through an *acquisition* phase. It takes a certain number of practice sessions for a dog to learn a new command, such as "stay" or "down." Similarly, the cats in Thorndike's experiments learned how to escape their puzzle boxes after a series of trials. In both cases, the acquisition stage occurs gradually. Behaviors learned through operant conditioning are also subject to *extinction*— that is, they may fade in the absence of reinforcers. A rat in a Skinner box eventually gives up pushing on a lever if there is no longer a reinforcer awaiting. But that same lever-pushing behavior can make a sudden comeback through *spontaneous recovery*. After a rest period, the rat returns to his box and reverts to his old lever-pushing ways.

Stimulus generalization and discrimination also occur in operant conditioning. If a rat is conditioned to push a particular type of lever, it may push a variety of other

**TABLE 5.3**   Conditioning Basics

| Concept | Classical Conditioning | Operant Conditioning |
|---|---|---|
| The association | Links different stimuli, often through repeated pairings | Links behaviors with consequences, often through repeated pairings |
| Response | Involuntary behavior | Voluntary behavior |
| Acquisition | The initial learning phase | The initial learning phase |
| Extinction | The disappearance of a conditioned response after repeated exposure to the conditioned stimulus in the absence of the unconditioned stimulus | The disappearance of a learned behavior through the removal of its reinforcer |
| Spontaneous recovery | The reappearance of the conditioned response following its extinction | The reappearance of a learned behavior following its extinction |

These fundamental learning concepts apply to both classical and operant conditioning.

lever types similar in shape, size, and color (*stimulus generalization*). But that same rat may not push a button; it can differentiate between a button and a lever (*stimulus discrimination*). Reptiles behave in the same way (Szabo et al., 2020). For example, turtles can learn to discriminate among black, white, and gray paddles when given positive reinforcers (morsels of meat) (Leighty et al., 2013).

## Let's Contrast

Students sometimes have trouble differentiating between classical and operant conditioning (**FIGURE 5.3**). After all, both forms of conditioning—classical and operant—involve forming associations. In classical conditioning, the learner links different *stimuli;* in operant conditioning, the learner connects their behavior to its *consequences* (reinforcement and punishment). But there are many key differences between classical and operant conditioning. In classical conditioning, the learned behaviors are involuntary, or reflexive. Gavin the ATF agent could not directly control his shaking any more than Pavlov's dogs could decide when to salivate. Operant conditioning, on the other hand, concerns voluntary behavior. Cesar had power over his decision to work with problem dogs, just as Skinner's pigeons had control over swatting bowling balls with their beaks. In short, classical conditioning is an involuntary form of learning, whereas operant conditioning requires active effort.

Another important distinction is the way in which behaviors are strengthened. In classical conditioning, behaviors become more established with repeated pairings of stimuli. The more often the sight of the "golden arches" is paired with the taste of french fries, the tighter the association between these stimuli (recall the mouth-watering example from Infographic 5.1). With operant conditioning, behaviors are also strengthened by repeated pairings, but the connection is between a behavior and its consequences. Reinforcers strengthen the behavior; punishment weakens it. The more benefits (reinforcers) Cesar accrues by working with people and dogs, the greater the likelihood he will continue cultivating his career.

In some cases, classical conditioning and operant conditioning occur simultaneously (Kim & Anderson, 2020). Babies learn that they get fed when they cry; getting formula or breast milk reinforces the crying behavior (operant conditioning). Babies also learn to associate formula or breast milk with the appearance of the bottle or breast; the moment they see either, they begin salivating in anticipation of being fed (classical conditioning).

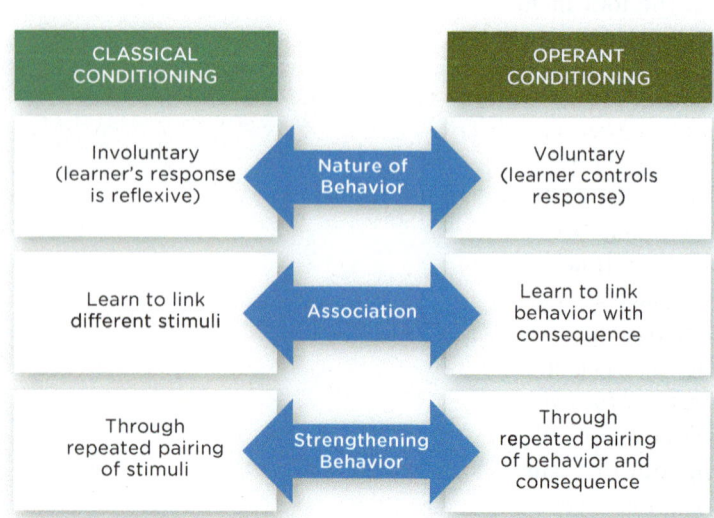

**FIGURE 5.3**

**Differences Between Classical and Operant Conditioning**

Classical and operant conditioning are not the only ways we learn. There is another major category of learning we have yet to cover. Use this hint to guess what it might be: How did you learn to cut an apple, brush your teeth, or throw a Frisbee?

## SHOW WHAT YOU KNOW

1. A third-grade teacher gives her students prizes for passing math tests. Not only do the students improve their math scores, they also begin studying harder for spelling tests as a result of this reinforcement schedule. Their increased studying of spelling is an example of:

   **A.** classical conditioning.

   **B.** an unconditioned response.

   **C.** an unconditioned stimulus.

   **D.** stimulus generalization.

2. Think about a behavior you would like to change (either yours or someone else's). Devise a plan using positive and negative reinforcement to change that behavior. Also contemplate how you might use successive approximations. What primary and secondary reinforcers would you use?

3. According to Thorndike's _____, behaviors are more likely to be repeated when they are followed by pleasurable outcomes.

4. A child disrupts class and the teacher writes their name on the board. For the rest of the week, the child does not act up. The teacher used _____ to decrease the child's disruptive behaviors.

   **A.** positive punishment

   **B.** negative punishment

   **C.** positive reinforcement

   **D.** negative reinforcement

5. How do continuous and partial reinforcement differ?

✓ CHECK YOUR ANSWERS AT THE BACK OF THE BOOK.

# Observational Learning and Cognition

**CESAR'S ROLE MODELS**  Growing up in Mexico, Cesar loved watching reruns of the dog shows *Lassie* and *The Adventures of Rin Tin Tin* from the 1950s and 1960s. The dogs in these shows performed incredible physical and intellectual feats—behaviors young Cesar imagined were typical of all American dogs. Once in the United States, Cesar began searching for someone who could teach him the art of American dog training. "You have to look for somebody with wisdom," Cesar says. "That's what kept me going."

But Cesar would eventually discover that his most important teachers were back in Mexico, and he had already learned from them. His grandfather Teodoro had taught him what it means to be a pack leader, and how to interact effectively with dogs. He didn't talk much, but he demonstrated behaviors that Cesar could observe and imitate. "Never work against Mother Nature," Teodoro would say, or "you have to be calm." Then, after stating these tenets, Teodoro would execute them, and the dogs would trot after him and perform desired behaviors.

The ranch dogs also served as role models for young Cesar. "From the time I was very little, I found joy in dogs simply by observing them" (Millan & Peltier, 2006, p. 25). Cesar spent hours studying how the dogs interacted, and adopted some of these behaviors himself. If you watch Cesar meet a dog for the first time, you'll see he demonstrates "no talk, no touch, no eye contact" (Millan & Peltier, 2006, p. 46). This is exactly how dogs greet one another with respect.

Cesar's grandfather and the ranch dogs served as **models,** demonstrating behaviors that could be observed and imitated. Learning by watching and mimicking others is called **observational learning.** According to Bandura (1986), observational learning is more likely to occur when learners: (1) pay attention to the model; (2) remember what they observed (Bahrick et al., 2002); (3) are capable of performing the observed behavior; and (4) are motivated to demonstrate the behavior.

What specific skills have you developed through observational learning? If you have ever used a "how to" video on YouTube or TikTok (for example, "how to unclog a drain" or "how to get six-pack abs"), you were probably watching and imitating a model. Or, perhaps someone has shown you how to change a flat tire, prepare an omelet, or perform CPR. All these skills can be acquired with the help of observational learning. What about table manners—remember how you learned those?

Courtesy Cesar's Way Inc.

**On the Ranch**

Left to right: Cesar's mother, grandmother, sister, cousin, grandfather, and Cesar on the family farm in Ixpalino. Many of the behaviors Cesar learned in childhood came from observing role models on the family farm.

**model**  An individual or character whose behavior is being imitated.

**observational learning**  Learning that occurs as a result of watching the behavior of others.

## Across the World

MIND YOUR MANNERS

**LOOK BEFORE YOU EAT.**

Travelers, be advised: Eating etiquette can greatly differ from one culture to the next. Something as simple as eating with your left hand, which is commonplace in the United States, is considered unsanitary in India and the Middle East (Boscamp, 2013). In Afghanistan and Korea, people sit down on the floor to eat a meal (Leontovich, 2016), but this is rarely done in France or Italy. Slurping noodles, generally viewed as ill-mannered in the United States, is interpreted as a sign of contentment in Japan (Japan-guide.com, 2020). Mexicans often eat with their hands, while Chileans use utensils for almost everything, including french fries (Boscamp, 2013)!

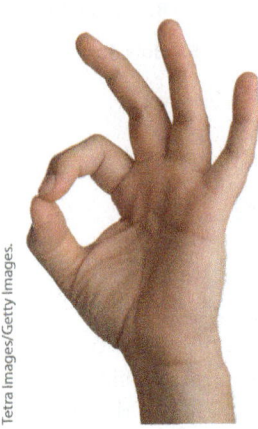

Tetra Images/Getty Images.

Table manners are, to some degree, acquired through observational learning. Children observe family members using utensils, sipping from cups, and wiping their mouths with napkins, and then imitate these behaviors. Operant conditioning plays a role as well. You can imagine a child being reprimanded (punishment) for resting their feet on the table or shouting in a restaurant, or praised (reinforcement) for sitting up straight and saying "please" and "thank you." Think about the manners you acquired growing up. How did you learn them and what role did your culture play?

**Not "Okay" Everywhere**
If you grew up in the United States, you probably picked up the "okay" hand gesture by watching and imitating others (observational learning). If you grew up in Brazil, you likely learned not to use this gesture because it is considered rude and obscene.

## Monkey See, Monkey Do

**LO 14** Summarize what Bandura's classic Bobo doll study teaches us about learning.

Just as observational learning can lead to positive outcomes (Cesar adopting the ways of his grandfather, or children learning manners), it can also breed undesirable behaviors. The classic Bobo doll experiment by American psychologist Albert Bandura and his colleagues reveals just how fast children can adopt aggressive ways they see modeled by adults, as well as exhibit their own novel aggressive responses (Bandura et al., 1961). In one of Bandura's studies, 76 preschool children were placed in a room one at a time with an adult. Some of the children were paired with adults who acted aggressively toward a 5-foot-tall inflatable Bobo doll—punching it in the nose, hitting its head with a mallet, kicking it around the room, and yelling phrases such as "Sock him in the nose" and "Pow!" The other children in the study were paired with adults who played with toys peacefully (Bandura et al., 1961).

At the end of the experiment, all the children were allowed to play with a Bobo doll themselves. Those who had observed adults attacking and shouting were much more likely to do the same. Boys were more likely than girls to mimic physical aggression, especially if they had observed it modeled by men. And boys and girls were about equally likely to imitate verbal aggression (Bandura et al., 1961).

**Try This**  Identify the independent variable and dependent variable in the experiment by Bandura and colleagues. What might you change if you were to replicate this experiment?

✓ CHECK YOUR ANSWERS AT THE BACK OF THE BOOK.

Dr. Albert Bandura.

**Bobo Doll**

Preschool children in Albert Bandura's famous Bobo doll experiment performed shocking displays of aggression after seeing such behaviors modeled by adults. The children were more likely to copy models who were rewarded for their aggressive behavior and less likely to mimic those who were punished (Bandura, 1986).

## ...BELIEVE IT...OR NOT

### DO KIDS LEARN AGGRESSION FROM MEDIA?

Psychologists have followed up on Bandura's research with studies investigating how children and adults are influenced by violence they see in the media. Much of the focus has been on violent video games, whose use has been **associated with**  decreases in helping behaviors and increases in problematic behaviors, including aggression (Coyne et al., 2018; Prescott et al., 2018). A comprehensive literature review and meta-analysis by the American Psychological Association (APA) Task Force on Violent Media arrived at this conclusion: "The use of violent video games results in increases in overall aggression as well as increases in the individual variables of aggressive behaviors, aggressive cognitions, aggressive affect, desensitization, physiological arousal, and decreases in empathy" (Calvert et al., 2017, p. 142). These findings apply to older kids, teens, and young adults, as studies of children younger than 10 are lacking. It is also worth noting that the APA task force did not uncover a link between exposure to violent video games and criminal activities (Calvert et al., 2017).

Some scholars are not convinced there is a cause-and-effect relationship between violent video games and aggression. They contend many studies on the topic are methodologically flawed and provide evidence indicating that the links between these variables are negligible (Ferguson, 2015a; Ferguson et al., 2020; Przybylski et al., 2019). Confusing matters further, the results of different meta-analyses appear to contradict one other. (A *meta-analysis* is a statistical approach researchers use to combine the results of different studies and draw general conclusions.) Searching for some area of agreement in the "meta-analysis wars," one group of researchers reanalyzed the data from three notable studies and reported the following: "Despite seemingly conflicting results . . ., all of the meta-analyses do in fact point to the conclusion that, in the vast majority of settings, violent video games do increase aggressive behavior but that these effects are almost always quite small" (Mathur et al., 2019, p. 705).

**MOVING BEYOND THE "META-ANALYSIS WARS"**

The research on video games and aggression is ongoing, and we should follow it closely. As we do, it is important to keep in mind that media violence is one of many

*Research* **CONNECTIONS**

In **Chapter 1,** we discussed some of the limitations of correlational research. Studies may uncover correlations between media violence and aggression, but that doesn't prove a cause-and-effect relationship. There could be a third variable influencing both media exposure and aggression. Perhaps parents who allow their children to see violent media are also more likely to model aggressive behaviors their children might imitate.

variables that might play a role in the development of aggression (Anderson et al., 2017). Other environmental factors, such as abuse and exposure to trauma, are also established risk factors. We must consider the role of heredity, too. Childhood aggression is partly explained by genes, with heritability estimates ranging from 50–68% (Lubke et al., 2018; Provençal et al., 2015). In other words, aggressive behavior may run in families. Like any psychological phenomenon, aggression is shaped by a complex and ongoing interaction of nature and nurture.

Given what we do (and don't) know about violent media and aggression, what practical steps should parents and caregivers take to promote children's well-being? First, they should consider the positive impact of sending children outdoors to play—it improves their sleep, health, and social well-being (Xu et al., 2016; Yogman et al., 2018). When kids do consume electronic media, adults can set time limits. The American Academy of Pediatrics recommends minimal screen time for children under the age of 2, no more than 1 hour per day for preschoolers, and parental supervision for all age groups (American Academy of Pediatrics, 2016a, 2016b). Unfortunately, children and their parents have not followed these guidelines. The average American child spends 7 hours per day watching TV and using tablets, cell phones, and other electronic media (American Academy of Pediatrics, n.d.). In addition to setting limits on screen time, parents and caregivers should consider media content. Not all media are violent, and some confer psychological benefits. For example, "action video games" that require 3-D navigation, quick shifts in attention, and other skills may improve perceptual abilities (Green & Bavelier, 2015), while some TV shows and mobile apps encourage *prosocial behaviors* (Christakis et al., 2013; Rasmussen et al., 2019).

**Let Them Play**
One of the best ways for children to learn prosocial behaviors is by playing. When children play, they learn how to work together, negotiate rules, and resolve conflict. "Social skills, which are part of playful learning, enable children to listen to directions, pay attention, solve disputes with words, and focus on tasks without constant supervision," all of which are critical for success in school and beyond (Yogman et al., 2018, p. 2).

**prosocial behaviors** Actions that are kind, generous, and beneficial to others.

**LEARNING TO BE NICE**    **Prosocial behaviors** are actions that are kind, generous, and beneficial to others, and people can pick them up by observing models (Jung et al., 2020). Some mobile apps and TV shows like *Sesame Street* can encourage prosocial behaviors in children (Cole et al., 2008; Flynn et al., 2019). In fact, *Sesame Street* is the only show specifically mentioned in the American Academy of Pediatrics (2016a) policy statement on Media and Young Minds: "Well-designed television programs, such as Sesame Street, can improve cognitive, literacy, and social outcomes for children 3 to 5 years of age" (p. 2).

In one study, researchers had parents change the television shows their preschoolers were viewing, substituting "aggression-laden programming" with "high quality prosocial and educational programming" (Christakis et al., 2013, p. 431). When assessed 6 and 12 months after the intervention, the children who had switched to prosocial/educational programming showed more behavioral improvement than those in the control group. This effect was pronounced for boys from low-income households (Christakis et al., 2013). Perhaps the prosocial messages of shows like *Dora the Explorer* and *Super Why* had made a difference.

Environmental forces can push adults to adopt prosocial behaviors as well. Consider the example of wearing facemasks, which have been shown to reduce the transmission of the novel coronavirus and therefore save lives (Chu et al., 2020; Eikenberry et al., 2020). *Scientific American* reports on the major social transformation that occurred in 2020:

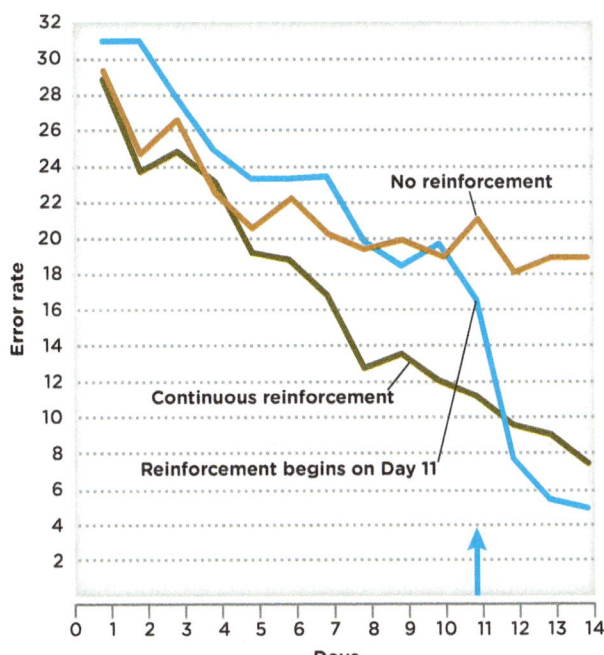

### FIGURE 5.4
**Latent Learning**

In a classic experiment, groups of rats learned how to navigate a maze at remarkably different rates. Rats in a group receiving reinforcement from Day 1 (the green line on the graph) initially had the lowest rate of errors and were able to work their way through the maze more quickly than the other groups. But when a group began to receive reinforcement for the first time on Day 11 (the blue line), their error rate dropped immediately. This shows that the rats were learning the basic structure of the maze even when they weren't being reinforced. Information from Tolman (1948).

experiment, when they, too, received food after finding the goal box. As you might expect, rats getting the treats from the onset solved the mazes more quickly as the days wore on. Meanwhile, their unrewarded compatriots wandered through the twists and turns. But on Day 11 when the researchers started to give treats to the third group of rats, their behavior changed markedly. After just one round of treats, the rats were scurrying through the mazes and scooping up the food as if they had been rewarded throughout the experiment (Tolman & Honzik, 1930). They had apparently been learning, even when there was no reinforcement for doing so—or in simpler terms, learning just for the sake of learning.

**A MAP THAT CANNOT BE SEEN** Like Tolman's rats, we remember locations, objects, and details of our surroundings without realizing it, and bring this information together in a mental layout (Lynch, 1960). This latent learning is evident in our ability to form **cognitive maps,** or mental representations of the physical surroundings. Research suggests that visually impaired people forge cognitive maps without the use of visual information. Instead, they use "compensatory sensorial channels" (hearing and sense of touch, for example) to gather information about their environments (Lahav & Mioduser, 2008). The brain processes that enable cognitive map-making may help us form "social maps," too. Social maps help us understand where people fit into hierarchies and how close they are to others (good friends versus acquaintances, for example; Shafer & Schiller, 2020).

Studies on latent learning and cognitive maps focus on the cognitive processes underlying behavior, and their findings suggest that learning can occur in the absence of reinforcement. This emphasis on cognition conflicts with the strict form of behaviorism endorsed by Skinner and some other 20th-century psychologists.

Many other studies have challenged the behaviorist notion that all behaviors and mental processes are determined by forces in the environment. For example, German psychologist Wolfgang Köhler (1887–1967) found evidence that chimpanzees are capable of thinking through a problem before taking action. Köhler designed an experiment in which chimps were presented with out-of-reach bananas and showed that the animals were able to plan a variety of banana-fetching strategies, including stacking crates to climb on (1925). The chimps were displaying *insight,* a sudden

Independent birds/Getty Images.

**Bats Form Cognitive Maps, Too**
Egyptian fruit bats travel through areas as large as 1,000 square kilometers, or 386 square miles, to forage from fruit trees. The movement of these animals does not appear to be random. They make goal-directed trips and often take shortcuts—evidence that they form cognitive maps of their territories (Toledo et al., 2020).

**cognitive map** A mental representation of physical space.

coming together of awareness of a situation, leading to the solution of a problem (Chapter 7). Like latent learning, insight can occur in the absence of reinforcement.

Today, most psychologists agree that both observable, measurable behaviors and internal cognitive processes such as insight are necessary and complementary elements of learning. Environmental factors have a powerful influence on behavior, as Pavlov, Skinner, and others discovered, but every action can be traced to activity in the brain. Understanding how cognitive processes translate to behaviors remains one of the great challenges facing psychologists.

**YOU ARE A VALUABLE MEMBER OF THE PACK** The time has come to wrap up this chapter on learning, but first let's take one more opportunity to learn something from Cesar Millan. Imagine you could sit down and talk with Cesar. What advice might he offer about lifelong learning and career goals?

Each of us plays a unique and important role in society, or the "human pack," as Cesar might describe it. "I see that we're all part of a pack," Cesar explains. "You have to find your place in the pack. And once you find your place in the pack, you serve a big purpose." Some of us are leaders, others are not, but every pack member has equal value.

What would Cesar say to those of us still struggling to find our place in the pack, or purpose in life? It may sound like a platitude, but find your passion, figure out what makes you happy, and pursue a path that allows you to nurture it. "Once you find your passion, you don't think you're working," Cesar says. Indeed, research suggests that people who are satisfied at work often feel more satisfied in their personal lives (Allen & McCarthy, 2016). If you ever find yourself lost, focus your energy on learning. "I think the listening is more powerful than anything else," Cesar explains. "When you're lost, when you're sad, you have to ask questions." In other words, learning should be a continuous, lifelong activity.

**Sharing His Love**
Cesar presents to an audience in Berlin, Germany. It has now been more than three decades since this celebrated dog expert illegally crossed the border into the United States. And although he became a U.S. citizen in 2009, Cesar really views himself as a citizen of the world. "I belong to a worldwide community of people who love dogs," he writes. "This is my pack" (Millan, 2013, p. 12).

Frank Hoensch/Getty Images.

## SHOW WHAT YOU KNOW

1. Bandura's Bobo doll study shows us that observational learning results in a wide variety of learned behaviors. Describe several types of behaviors you have learned by observing others.

2. You want to learn how to play basketball, so you watch videos of Stephen Curry executing plays. If your game improves as a result, this would be considered an example of:
   **A.** observational learning.
   **B.** association.
   **C.** prosocial behavior.
   **D.** your cognitive map.

3. Although Skinner believed that reinforcement is the cause of learning, there is robust evidence that reinforcement is not always necessary. This comes from experiments studying:
   **A.** positive reinforcement.
   **B.** negative reinforcement.
   **C.** latent learning.
   **D.** stimulus generalization.

✓ CHECK YOUR ANSWERS AT THE BACK OF THE BOOK.

# Summary of Concepts

**LO 1** Define learning. (p. 170)

Learning is a relatively enduring change in behavior or thinking that results from experiences. Organisms as simple as sea slugs and as complex as humans have the ability to learn. Learning is about creating associations. Sometimes we associate two different stimuli (classical conditioning). Other times we make connections between our behaviors and their consequences (operant conditioning). We can also learn by watching and imitating others (observational learning), creating a link between our behavior and the behavior of others.

**LO 2** Explain what Pavlov's studies teach us about classical conditioning. (p. 172)

The dogs in Pavlov's studies learned to link various stimuli with the arrival of food, which caused them to salivate when the stimuli were introduced. He discovered that associations develop through a learning process now referred to as classical conditioning. With classical conditioning, two stimuli become associated; once this association has been established, an originally neutral stimulus elicits an involuntary response.

**LO 3** Identify the differences between the US, UR, CS, and CR. (p. 173)

In classical conditioning, a neutral stimulus (NS) is something in the environment that does not normally cause a relevant automatic or reflexive response. This neutral stimulus (NS) is repeatedly paired with an unconditioned stimulus (US) that triggers an unconditioned response (UR). During this process of acquisition, the neutral stimulus (NS) becomes a conditioned stimulus (CS) that elicits a conditioned response (CR). In Pavlov's experiments with dogs, the neutral stimulus (NS) might have been the sound of a buzzer; the unconditioned stimulus (US) was the meat; and the unconditioned response (UR) was the dog's salivation. After repeated pairings with the meat, the buzzer (originally a neutral stimulus) became a conditioned stimulus (CS), eliciting the conditioned response (CR) of salivation, a learned behavior.

**LO 4** Recognize and give examples of stimulus generalization and stimulus discrimination. (p. 175)

Once conditioning has occurred, and the conditioned stimulus (CS) elicits the conditioned response (CR), the learner may respond to similar stimuli as if they were the original CS. This is called stimulus generalization. For example, someone who has been bitten by a small dog and reacts with fear to all dogs, big and small, demonstrates stimulus generalization. Stimulus discrimination is the ability to differentiate between a conditioned stimulus (CS) and other stimuli sufficiently different from it. Someone who was bitten by a small dog may have a fear reaction to small dogs, but not large dogs, thus demonstrating stimulus discrimination.

**LO 5** Summarize how classical conditioning is dependent on the biology of the organism. (p. 178)

Animals and people show biological preparedness, meaning they are predisposed to learn associations that have adaptive value. For example, conditioned taste aversion is a form of classical conditioning that occurs when an organism learns to associate the taste of a particular food or drink with illness. Avoiding foods that induce sickness increases the odds the organism will survive and reproduce, passing its genes along to the next generation.

**LO 6** Describe the Little Albert study and explain how fear can be learned. (p. 180)

The case study of Little Albert illustrates the conditioned emotional response, an emotional reaction (fear in Little Albert's case) acquired via classical conditioning. When Little Albert heard a loud bang (an unconditioned stimulus), he exhibited a fear response (unconditioned response). Through conditioning, the sight of a rat became paired with the loud noise and went from being a neutral stimulus to a conditioned stimulus (CS). Little Albert's fear of the rat was a conditioned response (CR).

**LO 7** Describe Thorndike's law of effect. (p. 182)

Thorndike's law of effect was important to the study of operant conditioning, a type of learning in which people or animals come to associate their voluntary actions with consequences. The law of effect states that if a behavior is followed by a pleasurable outcome, that behavior is more likely to recur. Thorndike's cats learned that if they escaped the puzzle box, they would get to eat fish; this increased the speed with which they opened the puzzle box.

**LO 8** Explain how positive and negative reinforcement differ. (p. 184)

Positive reinforcement is a process by which reinforcers are presented following a target behavior. The addition of these reinforcers, which generally are pleasant stimuli, increases the likelihood of the behavior recurring. The fish treats Thorndike gave his cats are examples of positive reinforcers. (They increased the likelihood of the cats opening the latch.) Behaviors can also increase in response to negative reinforcement, or the removal of something unpleasant. Putting on a seat belt to stop an annoying beep is an example of negative reinforcement. (It increases the likelihood of wearing a seat belt.) Both positive and negative reinforcement increase desired behaviors.

**LO 9** Distinguish between primary and secondary reinforcers. (p. 186)

Primary reinforcers satisfy biological needs. Food, water, and physical contact are considered primary reinforcers. Secondary reinforcers do not satisfy biological needs, but often derive their power from their connection with primary reinforcers. Money is an example of a secondary reinforcer; we know from experience that it gives us access to primary reinforcers, such as food, a safe place to live, and perhaps even the ability to attract desirable mates.

**LO 10** Explain shaping and the method of successive approximations. (p. 187)

Building on Thorndike's law of effect and Watson's behaviorism, Skinner used shaping through successive approximations (small steps leading to a desired behavior) to mold the behavior of animals. With shaping, a person observes the behaviors of animals, providing reinforcers when they perform at a required level. Animal behavior can be shaped using successive approximations, but instinct can interfere with the process. Instinctive drift is the tendency for animals to revert to instinctual behaviors after a behavior pattern has been learned.

**LO 11** Describe continuous reinforcement and partial reinforcement. (p. 189)

Reinforcers can be delivered on a constant basis (continuous reinforcement) or intermittently (partial reinforcement). Continuous reinforcement is generally more effective for establishing a behavior, whereas learning through partial reinforcement is more resistant to extinction (the partial reinforcement effect).

**LO 12** Name the schedules of reinforcement and give examples of each. (p. 190)

In a fixed-ratio schedule, reinforcement follows a preset number of desired responses or behaviors. In a variable-ratio schedule, reinforcement follows a certain number of desired responses or behaviors, but the number changes across trials (fluctuating around a precalculated average). In a fixed-interval schedule, reinforcement comes after a preestablished interval of time; the response or behavior is only reinforced after the interval passes. In a variable-interval schedule, reinforcement comes after an interval of time passes, but the length of the interval changes from trial to trial.

**LO 13** Explain how punishment differs from negative reinforcement. (p. 193)

In contrast to reinforcement, which makes a behavior more likely to recur, the goal of punishment is to decrease a behavior. Negative reinforcement strengthens a behavior that it follows by removing something aversive or disagreeable. Punishment decreases a behavior by instilling an association between a behavior and some unwanted consequence (for example, between stealing and going to jail, or between misbehaving and loss of screen time).

**LO 14** Summarize what Bandura's classic Bobo doll study teaches us about learning. (p. 198)

Observational learning can occur when we watch a model demonstrate a behavior. Albert Bandura's classic Bobo doll experiment showed that children readily imitate aggression when they see it modeled by adults. Studies suggest that children and adults may be inclined to mimic aggressive behaviors portrayed in the media. Observation of prosocial behaviors, on the other hand, can encourage kindness, generosity, and additional forms of behavior that benefit others.

**LO 15** Describe latent learning and explain how cognition is involved in learning. (p. 202)

Learning can occur without reinforcement. Edward Tolman showed that rats could learn to navigate mazes even when given no rewards. Their learning only became apparent when it was needed (latent learning). The rats were learning without reinforcement, just for the sake of learning. To fully understand learning, we must study both measurable behaviors and cognitive processes.

## Key Terms

**acquisition**, p. 175
**adaptive value**, p. 178
**biological preparedness**, p. 179
**classical conditioning**, p. 173
**cognitive map**, p. 203
**conditioned emotional response**, p. 180
**conditioned response (CR)**, p. 175
**conditioned stimulus (CS)**, p. 175
**conditioned taste aversion**, p. 178
**continuous reinforcement**, p. 189

**extinction**, p. 176
**fixed-interval schedule**, p. 192
**fixed-ratio schedule**, p. 190
**habituation**, p. 171
**higher order conditioning**, p. 176
**instinctive drift**, p. 189
**latent learning**, p. 202
**law of effect**, p. 183
**learning**, p. 170
**model**, p. 197
**negative punishment**, p. 193
**negative reinforcement**, p. 185
**neutral stimulus (NS)**, p. 173

**observational learning**, p. 197
**operant conditioning**, p. 184
**partial reinforcement**, p. 189
**partial reinforcement effect**, p. 190
**positive punishment**, p. 193
**positive reinforcement**, p. 184
**primary reinforcer**, p. 186
**prosocial behaviors**, p. 200
**punishment**, p. 193
**reinforcement**, p. 183
**reinforcers**, p. 183
**secondary reinforcer**, p. 186
**shaping**, p. 187

**spontaneous recovery**, p. 176
**stimulus**, p. 171
**stimulus discrimination**, p. 176
**stimulus generalization**, p. 175
**successive approximations**, p. 187
**unconditioned response (UR)**, p. 173
**unconditioned stimulus (US)**, p. 173
**variable-interval schedule**, p. 192
**variable-ratio schedule**, p. 192

## Test Prep Are You Ready?

1. One basic form of learning occurs during the process of _____, which is evident when an organism does not respond as strongly or as often to an event following multiple exposures to it.
   A. insight
   B. habituation
   C. classical conditioning
   D. operant conditioning

2. Turtles can learn through operant conditioning, as evidenced by their:
   A. innate urge to get food.
   B. reaction to an unconditioned stimulus.
   C. ability to learn through positive reinforcement.
   D. reactions to predators.

3. The behaviors learned with classical conditioning are _____, whereas those learned with operant conditioning are _____.
   A. involuntary; voluntary
   B. voluntary; involuntary
   C. voluntary; innate
   D. involuntary; innate

4. Every time you open the pantry where dog food is stored, your dog starts to salivate. His salivating is a(n):
   A. unconditioned response.
   B. conditioned response.
   C. stimulus discrimination.
   D. reaction based on observational learning.

5. Little Albert was a baby who originally had no fear of rats. In an experiment conducted by Watson and Rayner, he was classically conditioned to fear white rats through the pairing of a loud noise with exposure to a rat. His resulting fear is an example of:
   A. an unconditioned stimulus.
   B. operant conditioning.
   C. a conditioned emotional response.
   D. biological preparedness.

6. _____ indicates that if a behavior is followed by a pleasurable outcome, it likely will be repeated.
   A. Latent learning
   B. Classical conditioning
   C. Biological preparedness
   D. The law of effect

7. Which of the following is an example of negative reinforcement?
   A. working hard to get an A on a paper
   B. a child getting more computer time when they finish their homework
   C. a dog whining in the morning, which prompts the owner to wake up and take it outside
   D. getting a speeding ticket and then not exceeding the speed limit in the future

8. A child is reprimanded for misbehaving, but then seems to misbehave even more! This indicates that reprimanding the child was:
   A. negative punishment.
   B. positive reinforcement.
   C. positive punishment.
   D. an unconditioned response.

9. In Bandura's Bobo doll study, children who saw an adult attacking and shouting at the doll:
   A. were more likely to display aggressive behavior.
   B. were less likely to display aggressive behavior.
   C. did not play with the Bobo doll at all.
   D. began to cry when they saw the adult acting aggressively.

10. In a classic experiment, rats were allowed to explore a maze without getting reinforcers until the 11th day. From that point on, the rats scurried through the mazes as if they had been rewarded throughout the experiment. Their behavior is evidence of:
    A. latent learning.
    B. observational learning.
    C. classical conditioning.
    D. operant conditioning.

11. What is the difference between stimulus generalization and stimulus discrimination?

12. Give an example showing how you have used shaping and partial reinforcement to change your behavior. Which schedule of reinforcement do you think you were using?

13. What is the difference between primary reinforcers and secondary reinforcers? Give an example of each and explain how they might be used to change a behavior.

14. How are punishment and negative reinforcement different? Give examples of negative reinforcement, positive punishment, and negative punishment and explain how they aim to change behavior.

15. Describe conditioned taste aversion and provide an example. Label each of the components using the terminology of classical conditioning.

✔ CHECK YOUR ANSWERS AT THE BACK OF THE BOOK.

Monica Rodriguez/Getty Images.

# 6

# Memory

## What Is Memory?

**MEMORY BREAKDOWN: THE CASE OF CLIVE WEARING**   Monday, March 25, 1985: Deborah Wearing awoke in a sweat-soaked bed. Her husband, Clive, had been up all night perspiring, vomiting, and with a high fever. He said that he had a "constant, terrible" headache, like a "band" of pain tightening around his head (Wearing, 2005, p. 27). The symptoms worsened over the next few days, but the two doctors caring for Clive reassured Deborah that it was just a bad case of the flu. By Wednesday, Clive had spent three nights awake with the pain. Confused and disoriented, he turned to Deborah and said, "Er, er, darling. . . . I can't . . . think of your name" (p. 31).

The doctor arrived a couple of hours later, reassured Deborah that her husband's confusion was merely the result of sleep deprivation, and

Ros Drinkwater/Alamy.

**The Conductor**
In 1985 conductor Clive Wearing (pictured here with his wife, Deborah) developed a brain infection—viral encephalitis—that nearly took his life. Clive recovered physically, but his memory was never the same.

prescribed sleeping pills. Deborah came home later that day, expecting to find her husband in bed. But no Clive. She shouted out his name. No answer, just a heap of pajamas. After the police had conducted an extensive search, Clive was found when a taxi driver dropped him off at a local police station; he had gotten into the cab and couldn't remember his address (Wearing, 2005). Clive returned to his flat (which he did not recognize as home), rested, and took in fluids. His fever dropped, and it appeared that he was improving. But when he awoke Friday morning, his confusion was so severe he could not identify the toilet among the various items in his bathroom. As Deborah placed urgent calls to the doctor, Clive began to drift away. He lost consciousness and was rushed to the hospital in an ambulance (Wearing, 2005; Wilson & Wearing, 1995).

Prior to this illness, Clive Wearing had enjoyed a fabulous career in music. As the director of the London Lassus Ensemble, he spent his days leading singers and instrumentalists through the emotionally complex music of his favorite composer, Orlande de Lassus. A renowned expert on Renaissance music, Clive produced music for the prestigious British Broadcasting Corporation (BBC), including that which aired on the wedding day of Prince Charles and Lady Diana Spencer (Sacks, 2007; Wilson et al., 1995; Wilson et al., 2008). But Clive's work—and his whole life—tumbled into chaos when a virus that normally causes blisters on the mouth invaded his brain.

Millions of people carry herpes simplex virus type 1 (HSV-1). Usually, it causes unsightly cold sores on the mouth and face. (There is also HSV-2, more commonly associated with genital herpes.) But for a small minority of the adult population— as few as 1 in 500,000 annually—the virus invades the central nervous system and causes a life-threatening infection called *encephalitis* (Anderson, 2017). Left untreated, herpes encephalitis causes death in over 70% of its victims. Most who survive have lasting neurological deficits (Bradshaw & Venkatesan, 2016).

Although Deborah saw to it that Clive received early medical attention, having two doctors visit the house day and night for nearly a week, these physicians mistook his condition for the flu with meningitis-like symptoms (Wilson & Wearing, 1995). Diagnosing herpes encephalitis is difficult (even to this day), as its symptoms resemble those of other conditions, including stroke, cancer, and different types of infection (Bradshaw & Venkatesan, 2016). When Clive and Deborah arrived at the hospital on the sixth day of his illness, they waited another 11 hours just to get a proper diagnosis (Wearing, 2005; Wilson & Wearing, 1995).

Clive survived, but the damage to his brain was extensive and profound; the virus had destroyed a substantial amount of neural tissue. And though Clive could still sing and play the keyboard (and spent much of the day doing so), he was unable to continue working as a conductor and music producer (D. Wearing, personal communication, June 18, 2013; Wilson & Wearing, 1995). In fact, he could barely get through day-to-day life. In the early stages of recovery, simple activities like eating baffled him. He ate the menu and attempted to spread cottage cheese on his bread, apparently mistaking it for butter. He confused basic concepts such as "scarf" and "umbrella," and shaved his eyebrows and nose (Wearing, 2005; Wilson & Wearing, 1995).

In the months following his illness, Clive was overcome with the feeling of just awakening. His senses were functioning properly, but every sight, sound, odor, taste, and feeling registered for just a moment, and then vanished. As Deborah described it, Clive saw the world anew with every blink of his eye (Wearing, 2005). Desperate to make sense of it all, Clive would pose the same questions time and again: "How long have I been ill?" he would ask Deborah and the hospital staff members looking after him. "How long's it been?" (Wearing, 2005, p. 181). For much of the first decade following his illness, Clive repeated the same few phrases almost continuously in his conversations with people. "I haven't heard anything, seen anything, touched anything, smelled anything," he would say. "It's just like being dead" (p. 160).

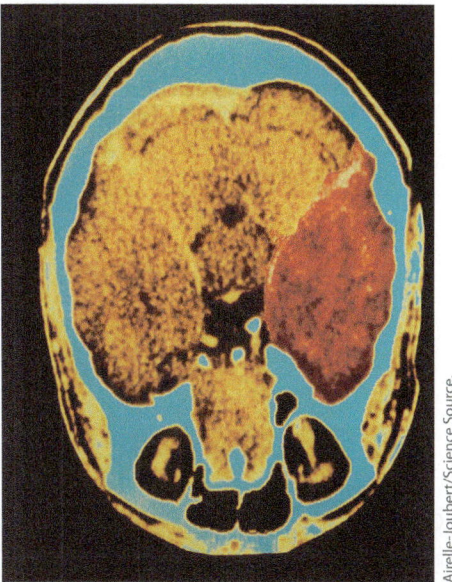

Airelle-Joubert/Science Source.

**Encephalitis**

The red area in this computerized axial tomography (CAT) scan reveals inflammation in the temporal lobe. The cause of this swelling is herpes simplex virus, the same virus responsible for Clive Wearing's illness. Many people carry this virus (it causes cold sores), but herpes encephalitis is rare, affecting approximately 1 in 500,000 people annually (Anderson, 2017). Often patients do not get timely treatment, and this increases the risk for negative outcomes (Tyler, 2018).

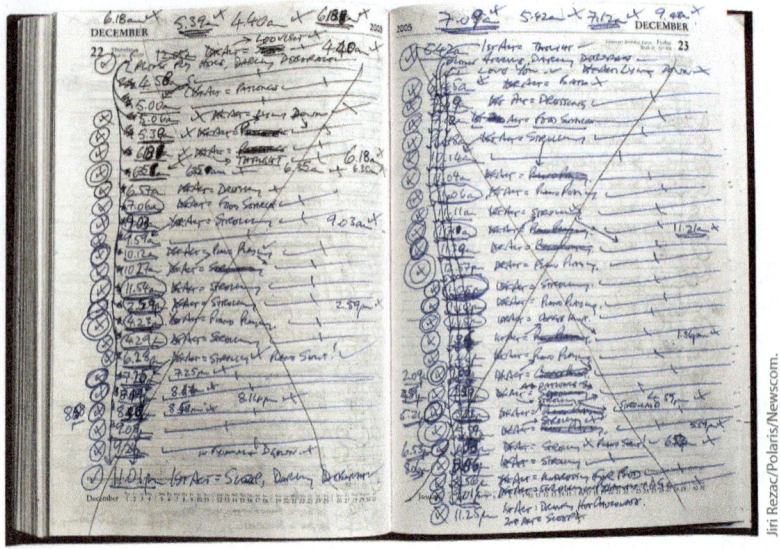

Jiri Rezac/Polaris/Newscom.

**The Diary**

Looking at a page from Clive Wearing's diary, you can see the fragmented nature of his thought process. He writes an entry, forgets it within seconds, and then returns to the page to start over, often writing the same thing. Encephalitis destroyed areas of Clive's brain that are crucial for learning and memory, so he can no longer recall what is happening from moment to moment.

The depth of Clive's impairment is revealed in his diary, where he wrote essentially the same entries all day long. On August 25, 1985, he wrote, "I woke at 8:50 A.M. and baught [sic] a copy of *The Observer*," which is then crossed out and followed by "I woke at 9:00 A.M. I had already bought a copy of *The Observer*," The next line reads, "This (officially) confirms that I awoke at 9:05 A.M. this morning" (Wearing, 2005, p. 182). Having forgotten all previous entries, Clive reported throughout the day that he had just become conscious. His recollection of writing in his journal—along with every experience in his life—came and went in a flash. The herpes virus had ravaged his memory system.

The story of Clive Wearing launches our journey through *memory*. You may be wondering why we chose to start this chapter with the story of a person whose memory system failed. When it comes to understanding complex cognitive processes, sometimes it helps to examine what happens when elements of the system are not working properly. And when we say "working properly," we do not mean working perfectly. Unlike a smartphone camera, which captures, stores, and reproduces events with high fidelity, the human memory system is vulnerable to errors, distortions, and sometimes manipulation (Brewin et al., 2020). By the time you finish this chapter, you may find yourself questioning some of the memories you once considered absolute truths.

## Encoding, Storage, and Retrieval

**LO1** Define memory.

In everyday conversations, "memory" refers to anything remembered ("I remember my 14th birthday" or "I recall our trip to the beach"). In psychology, **memory** refers to the processes involved in the encoding (collection), storage, and retrieval of information. Scientists have proposed many theories and models to explain how the brain processes, or works on, data en route to becoming memories. As you learn about some of these theories and models, keep in mind that none are perfect. Rather than labeling one as right and another as wrong, most psychologists embrace a combination of approaches, considering their strengths and weaknesses. We don't completely understand how a functioning memory system works, but there is basic agreement on its general processes, particularly *encoding, storage,* and *retrieval.*

**LO2** Describe the processes of encoding, storage, and retrieval.

**ENCODING**   During the course of a day, we are bombarded with information coming from all of our senses and internal data in the form of thoughts and emotions. Some of this information we will remember, but the majority of it will not be retained for long. What is the difference between what is preserved and what is not? Most psychologists agree that it all starts with **encoding,** the process through which information enters our memory system. Imagine you are getting your hair cut. Sitting in the chair, you smell hair products, feel a comb running over your scalp, and hear the sounds of voices and snipping scissors. The stimuli associated with this event are taken in by your senses and then **converted to neural activity** that travels to the brain. The information is processed, and from this point it can take one of two paths: Either it enters the memory system (it is encoded to be stored for a longer period of time) or it slips away. For Clive Wearing, much of this information slips away.

**CONNECTIONS**

In **Chapters 2** and **3,** we described how sensory information is taken in by sensory receptors and transduced; that is, transformed into neural activity. Here, we explore what happens *after* transduction, when information is processed in the memory system.

**memory**  The processes involved in the encoding, storage, and retrieval of information.

**encoding**  The process through which information enters our memory system.

**STORAGE** For information that is successfully encoded, the next step is **storage.** Storage is exactly what it sounds like: preserving information for possible recollection in the future. Before Clive Wearing fell ill, his memory was excellent. His brain was able to encode and store a variety of events and learned abilities. Following his bout with encephalitis, his ability to create new long-term memories was destroyed—he could no longer store new information for more than seconds at a time.

**RETRIEVAL** After information is stored, how do we access it? Perhaps you still have a memory of your first-grade teacher's face, but can you remember their name? This process of recovering stored information (*Ms. Nautiyal! Mr. Kopitz!*) is called **retrieval.** Sometimes information is encoded and stored in memory but cannot be accessed, or retrieved. Have you ever felt that a person's name or a certain vocabulary word was just sitting "on the tip of your tongue"? Chances are you were struggling from a retrieval failure, which we will discuss later in this chapter.

## How Deep Are Your Memories?

Now that we understand the three major processes involved in memory—encoding, storage, and retrieval—let's focus on how deeply information is processed. To what degree does incoming data get worked on, and how does that affect a memory's staying power? According to the *levels of processing* framework, there is a "hierarchy of processing stages" corresponding to different depths of information processing (Craik, 2020; Craik & Lockhart, 1972). Thus, processing can occur along a continuum from shallow to deep (**FIGURE 6.1**). Shallow-level processing is primarily concerned with physical (structural) features, such as the brightness or shape of an object, or the number of letters in a word, and generally results in short-lived memories. Deeper-level processing relies on characteristics related to patterns, like rhymes (phonemic processing) and meaning (semantic processing), and generally results in longer-lasting and easier-to-retrieve memories. So when you don't pay much **attention to data entering your sensory systems**, shallow processing occurs, resulting in more transient memories. If you really contemplate incoming information and relate it to memories you already have, deeper processing occurs, and the new memories are more likely to persist (Craik & Tulving, 1975; Francis & Gutiérrez, 2012; Newell & Andrews, 2004).

Fergus Craik and Endel Tulving explored levels of processing in their classic 1975 study. After presenting college students with various words, the researchers asked them yes or no questions, prompting them to think about and encode the words at three different levels: shallow, intermediate, and deep. The shallow questions required the students to study the appearance of the word: "Is the word in capital letters?" The intermediate-level questions related to the sound of the word: "Does the word rhyme with 'weight'?" And finally, the deep questions challenged students to consider the word's meaning: "Is the word a type of fish?" When the researchers surprised the students with a test to see which words they remembered without any cues or clues, the students were best able to recall words whose meaning they had thought about (Craik & Tulving, 1975). The take-home message: Deep thinking helps create stronger memories (Dunlosky et al., 2013; Foos & Goolkasian, 2008).

The levels of processing model helps explain why testing, which often requires you to connect new and old information, can improve memory and help you succeed in school. Research strongly supports the idea that testing improves learning

**FIGURE 6.1**
**The Levels of Processing Framework**
Information can be processed along a continuum from shallow to deep, affecting the probability of recall. Shallow processing, in which only certain details like the physical appearance of a word might be noticed, results in brief memories that may not be recalled later. We are better able to recall information we process at a deep level, thinking about meaning and tying it to memories we already have.

Shallow: notice some physical features

Intermediate: notice patterns and a little more detail

Deep: think about meaning

PROCESSING

FISH fish fish
fish
fish/dish

Fish: Gunnar Pippel/Shutterstock.

**CONNECTIONS**

In **Chapter 4,** we discussed the limited capacity of attention. The brain simply does not have the attentional capacity to conduct two different cognitive tasks simultaneously. If you want to remember something, give it your full attention and try to engage in deep processing.

**storage** The process of preserving information for possible recollection in the future.

**retrieval** The process of accessing information encoded and stored in memory.

among students of differing abilities, as long as the stakes are low (Batsell et al., 2017; Dunlosky et al., 2013; Jonsson et al., 2020). The Show What You Know and Test Prep resources in this textbook are designed with this in mind. Repeated testing results in a variety of benefits: better information retention, identification of areas needing more study, and increased self-motivated studying (Roediger et al., 2011; Welch, 2019; Yang et al., 2020). We call this the *testing effect*. Speaking of testing, why not take a moment and show what you know?

 **SHOW WHAT YOU KNOW**

1. A good friend claims she cannot remember you coming to her birthday dinner last year. You had a conversation with her that night, so the fact that you were there must have entered her memory system. Which of the following might explain her inability to remember you were there?

   **A.** Retrieval failure
   **B.** Deeper-level processing
   **C.** Loss of consciousness
   **D.** Sleep deprivation

2. _____ refers to the processes involved in the collection, storage, and retrieval of information.

3. How might you illustrate shallow processing versus deep processing as it relates to studying?

✓ CHECK YOUR ANSWERS AT THE BACK OF THE BOOK.

# Stages of Memory

**CONNECTIONS** ————————————
In **Chapter 1,** we described the importance of using theoretical models to organize and conceptualize observations. In this chapter, we present several of these to explain the human memory system.

Psychologists use numerous **models** to explain how the memory system works (Malmberg et al., 2019). Among the most influential is the *information-processing model*, first developed by Richard Atkinson and Richard Shiffrin. This model conceptualizes memory as a flow of information through a series of stages: *sensory memory, short-term memory,* and *long-term memory* (**FIGURE 6.2**) (Atkinson & Shiffrin, 1968; Baddeley et al., 2019; Wood & Pennington, 1973).

## The Information-Processing Model

**LO3**   Identify the stages of memory described by the information-processing model.

According to the information-processing model, each stage of memory has a certain type of storage with distinct capabilities: **Sensory memory** can hold vast amounts of sensory stimuli for a sliver of time, **short-term memory** can temporarily maintain and process limited information for longer periods (about 30 seconds, if there are no distractions), and **long-term memory** has almost unlimited capacity and can hold onto information indefinitely. In the sections that follow, we will flesh out these stages, which are incorporated in most memory models.

**CONNECTIONS** ————————————
In **Chapter 3,** we defined sensation as the process by which receptors receive and detect stimuli. Perception is the process through which sensory information is organized, interpreted, and transformed into something meaningful. Some critics of the information-processing model suggest that sensory memory is an important component of perception, not a stage of memory.

The information-processing model is a valuable tool for learning about and researching memory, but like any scientific model, it has flaws. Some contend that *sensory memory* is really a primary component of **perception** (Craik, 2020). Others doubt that a clear boundary exists between *short-term* and *long-term* memory

**sensory memory** A stage of memory that captures near-exact copies of vast amounts of sensory stimuli for a very brief period of time.

**short-term memory** A stage of memory that temporarily maintains and processes a limited amount of information.

**long-term memory** A stage of memory with essentially unlimited capacity and the ability to store information indefinitely.

**FIGURE 6.2**
**The Information-Processing Model**

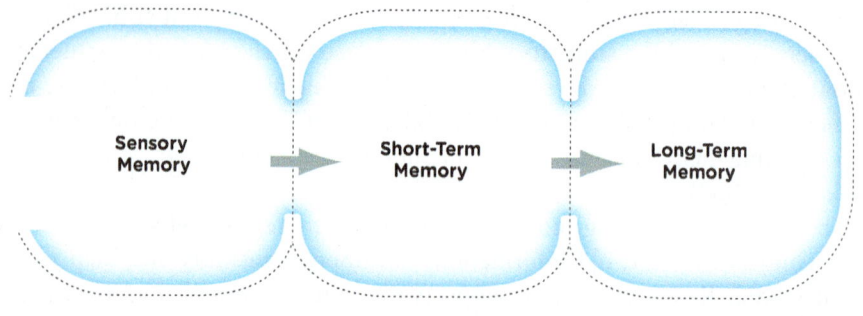

Sensory Memory → Short-Term Memory → Long-Term Memory

(Baddeley, 1995). Still others argue that this "pipeline" model is a simplistic representation because information does not necessarily flow through the memory system in a straight-line path (Cowan, 1988). Despite its weaknesses, the information-processing model remains an essential tool for explaining how memory works. As you read about Clive Wearing in the pages to come, you will see how both his short- and long-term memory are severely impaired.

## Sensory Memory

**LO4** Describe sensory memory.

Think of all the information streaming through your sensory channels at this very moment. Your eyes may be focused on this sentence, but you are also collecting data through your peripheral vision. You may be hearing noises (voices in the distance), smelling odors (the scent of lotion or deodorant you applied earlier today), tasting foods (if you are snacking), and even feeling things (shoes gently squeezing your feet). Many of these sensory stimuli never catch your attention, but some are being registered in your sensory memory, the first stage of the information-processing model. The bulk of information entering sensory memory comes and goes like images flitting by in a movie. A few things catch your attention—the beautiful eyes of Priyanka Chopra, the sound of her voice, and perhaps the color of her shirt—but not much more before the frame switches and you're looking at another image. Information floods our sensory memory through multiple channels—what we see enters through one channel, what we taste through another, and so on.

**"MORE IS SEEN THAN CAN BE REMEMBERED"**    The visual impressions in our sensory memory, also known as **iconic memory,** are photograph-like in their accuracy but dissolve in less than a second. To explore how the brain processes data entering the visual channel, Harvard graduate student George Sperling (1960) set up a screen that flashed multiple rows of letters for one-twentieth of a second, and then asked participants to report what they saw. When an array of letters (for example, three rows of four letters) was flashed briefly, he found that, on average, the participants only reported four letters. Were the participants able to store only one row at a time, or did they store all the rows, but just not long enough to recite them before they were forgotten?

Sperling suspected that "more is seen than can be remembered" (1960, p. 1), so he repeated the procedure—briefly flashing the array of letters with all rows visible. But instead of having the participants report what they remembered from all the rows, he asked them to report what they remembered from just one row at a time (**FIGURE 6.3**). In this version of the study, the participants doubled their

**Lion of a Memory**
Saroo Brierley at the Berlin premiere of *Lion,* the Oscar-nominated film that tells his amazing story. Brierley was just 5 years old when he lost contact with his family in India. After being separated from his older brother at a train station, Brierley boarded a train to Kolkata (previously Calcutta), 1,000 miles from home. He survived on the streets for weeks, ended up in an orphanage, and was adopted by a couple in Tasmania, Australia. Two decades later, Brierley used Google Earth and his memory of landmarks to find his way back home, where he reunited with his biological family (Dunlop, 2017; NPR Staff, 2014).

Letters flash on screen, then disappear.

A tone sounds. Participants report only the row associated with that tone.

Participants can report the assigned row. All rows initially registered in their sensory memory, but the iconic memory dissolves before more letters can be reported.

**FIGURE 6.3**
**How Fast It Fades**
Participants in Sperling's (1960) study were shown an array of letters and asked to recall one row corresponding to a particular tone. For example, a high tone told them to report the top row, a medium tone told them to report the middle row, and so on. They performed well recalling the assigned row but couldn't recall letters from the other rows: Their sensory memory had faded.

**iconic memory** Visual impressions that are photograph-like in their accuracy but dissolve in less than a second; a form of sensory memory.

**Almost Photographic**
After one helicopter flight over Mexico City, artist/architect Stephen Wiltshire is able to produce this cityscape from memory. "Wiltshire's drawings are so accurate that even small details, such as the number of columns or windows on individual buildings are faithfully reproduced in images that encompass many city blocks, even whole cities" (Martin, 2013, pp. R732–R733). Wiltshire appears to possess eidetic imagery.

performance, recalling approximately 76% of the letters regardless of which row they were assigned (Sperling, 1960). Sperling's research suggests that the visual impressions in our sensory memory dissolve quickly, and subsequent findings have confirmed this (Pratte, 2018). Given the short duration of iconic memory, can you predict what would happen if there were a delay before participants had to report what they saw?

**EIDETIC IMAGERY**  Perhaps you have heard friends talk about someone who claims to have a "photographic memory" that can record and store images with the accuracy of a camera: "My cousin Dexter can look at a textbook page, remember exactly what it says in a few seconds, and then recall the information days later, seeing the pages exactly as they were." That may be what Dexter claims, but there is no solid scientific evidence that this type of photographic memory exists (Gordon, 2013; MacLeod et al., 2013; Patihis et al., 2019).

According to some reports, however, there is a phenomenon that comes fairly close to photographic memory. It's called *eidetic imagery* (ahy-DET-ik), and the rare "handful" who possess this ability can "see" an image or object sometimes long after it has been removed from sight, describing its parts with amazing specificity. However, the details they "see" are not always accurate, and thus their memories are not quite photographic. This ability seems to occur primarily in children and may be lost as a child's brain grows and develops (Ko, 2015; Searleman, 2007).

 Stare at the photo below for about 10 seconds, and then shut your eyes. Does an image of the dancer linger in your mind's eye? How long do you think this iconic memory lasts?

**ECHOIC MEMORY**  Exact copies of the sounds we hear linger longer than visual impressions; **echoic memory** (eh-KOH-ik) can last from about 1 to 10 seconds (Lu et al., 1992; Peterson et al., 1970) and capture very subtle changes in sound. Research has shown that the introduction of a **single tone** played for 300 milliseconds initiates changes in brain activity (Inui et al., 2010). Even if you are not aware of it, your auditory system is picking up slight changes in stimuli and storing them in echoic memory for a brief moment. In this way, you don't have to pay attention to every incoming sound. Perhaps you have had the following experience: During class, your instructor notices a classmate daydreaming and tries to bring her back to reality: "Olivia, could you please restate the question for us?" Her mind was indeed wandering, but amazingly she can recall the instructor's last sentence, responding, "You asked us if brain scans should be allowed as evidence in courtrooms." For this, Olivia can thank her echoic memory.

**CONNECTIONS**

In **Chapter 3,** we described sensory adaptation, the process by which our sensory receptors become less sensitive to constant stimuli. This allows us to focus on the slightest changes in our environment, an ability that promotes survival. Echoic memory allows us to store and follow changes in sounds.

**echoic memory** Exact copies of the sounds we hear; a form of sensory memory.

Although brief, sensory memory is critical to the creation of memories. Without it, how would information enter the memory system in the first place? The bulk of research has focused on iconic memory and echoic memory, which register sights and sounds, but memories can also be rich in smells, tastes, and touch. Data received from all the senses are held momentarily in sensory memory. Most of this information disappears in a flash, but items that capture your attention can move to short-term memory, the second stage of the information-processing model (Atkinson & Shiffrin, 1968; Baddeley et al., 2019).

## Short-Term Memory

**LO 5**  Summarize short-term memory.

The amount of time information is maintained and processed in short-term memory depends on how much you are distracted by other cognitive activities, but the duration can be about 30 seconds (Atkinson & Shiffrin, 1968). You can stretch short-term memory further with **maintenance rehearsal,** a technique of repeating what you want to remember over and over in your mind. Using maintenance rehearsal, you can theoretically hold onto information as long as you desire. This strategy comes in handy if you use rote memorization for learning, or if you need to remember a series of numbers or letters (for example, phone numbers or zip codes). Imagine the following: While strolling down the street, you witness a hit-and-run accident. A truck runs a red light, smashes into a car, and then speeds away. As the truck zooms off, you manage to catch a glimpse of the license plate number, but how will you remember it long enough before reaching the 911 operator? If you're like most people, you will say the plate number to yourself over and over, either aloud or in your mind, using maintenance rehearsal.

But maintenance rehearsal does not work so well if you are distracted. In a classic study examining the duration of short-term memory, most participants were unable to recall three-letter combinations beyond 18 seconds while performing another task (Peterson & Peterson, 1959; **FIGURE 6.4**). The task (counting backward by 3s) interfered with their natural inclination to mentally repeat the letter combinations; in other words, they were limited in their ability to use maintenance rehearsal. What this study reveals is that short-term memory has a limited capacity. Remember this next time you text during class or watch Netflix while studying; if your goal is to remember the material, don't clutter your short-term memory with competing information. (See Chapter 4 for more on multitasking.)

**LO 6**  Give examples of how we can use chunking to expand our short-term memory.

With maintenance rehearsal, you try to remember numbers, letters, or other items by repeating them over and over in your mind. But how many items can we realistically hold in our short-term memory at one time? Using a task called the Digit Span Test (**FIGURE 6.5**), cognitive psychologist George Miller (1956) determined that most people can retain only five to nine digits: He called this the "magical number seven, plus or minus two." Indeed, researchers following up on this discovery have found that most people can only attend to about five to nine *items* at one time (Cowan et al., 2004; Norris et al., 2020), although there is some disagreement about the lower and upper bounds of this range (Barrouillet et al., 2020; Cowan, 2001). But what exactly constitutes an item? Must it be a single-digit number? Not necessarily; we can expand short-term memory by packing more information into the items to be remembered.

Consider this example: Your friend has just gotten a new phone number, which they rattle off as the elevator door closes between you. How are you going to

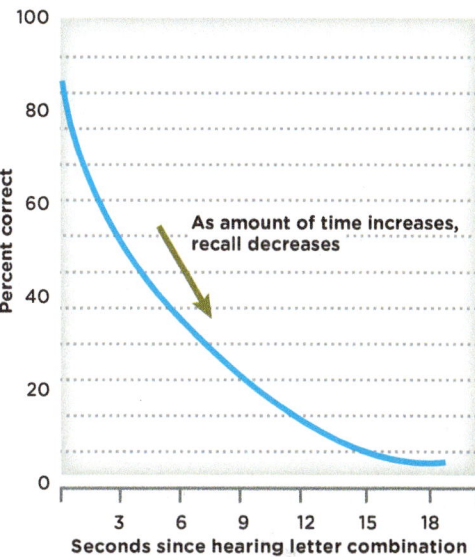

**FIGURE 6.4**
**Duration of Short-Term Memory**
Distraction can reduce the amount of time information remains in short-term memory. When performing a distracting cognitive task, most people were unable to recall a letter combination beyond 18 seconds. Information from Peterson and Peterson (1959), Figure 3, p. 195.

As amount of time increases, recall decreases

2390
45791
340982
0128957
93781256
501298347

**FIGURE 6.5**
**Digit Span Test**
The Digit Span Test is a simple way to assess memory. Participants are asked to listen to a string of numbers and then repeat them. The string of numbers grows longer as the test progresses. Ask a friend to give you this test and see how many numbers you can remember. For a real challenge, you can even try to recite the list backward!

**maintenance rehearsal** Technique of repeating information to be remembered, increasing the length of time it can be held in short-term memory.

remember their number long enough to create a new entry in your cell phone? You could try memorizing all 10 digits in a row (8935550172), but a better strategy is to break the number into more manageable pieces (893-555-0172). Here, you are using **chunking,** Miller's (1956) name for grouping numbers, letters, or other types of information into meaningful "chunks," or units (Cowan, 2015).

### Put Your Heads Together

 Short-term memory can only hold so much, but we can push the limit by chunking. In your group, **A)** discuss what chunking is, and **B)** describe some ways you use chunking in everyday life (like when you study, or try to remember items on a list). Write down at least three examples your group identifies.

The fact that we can expand short-term memory by chunking suggests that this stage of memory is more than just a temporary holding place for information. Indeed, many psychologists believe that short-term memory has an active processing component.

## Working Memory

**LO7** Describe working memory and its relationship to short-term memory.

Updated versions of the information-processing model include a concept known as **working memory** (Baddeley, 2012; Baddeley & Hitch, 1974; Baddeley et al., 2019), which refers to what is *going on* in short-term memory. Working memory is the active processing through which we maintain and manipulate information in the memory system. Let's use an analogy of a "bakery" and the activities happening inside. Short-term memory is the bakery, that is, the place that hosts your current thoughts and whatever your brain is working on at this very moment. Working memory is what's going on inside the bakery—making bread, cakes, and pastries—or in the case of the brain, processing information. Some psychologists use the terms short-term and working memory interchangeably. For our purposes, we will identify *short-term memory* as a stage in the original information-processing model as well as the "location" where information is temporarily held, and *working memory* as the activities and processing occurring within.

According to the model of working memory originally proposed by psychologists Alan Baddeley and Graham Hitch (1974; Baddeley, 2012), the purpose of working memory is to actively maintain information and thus enable complex cognitive tasks. Those "complex cognitive tasks" include anything from solving math equations to following directions (Chen & Bailey, 2021; Covre et al., 2019). Working memory may even help you negotiate relationship problems.

## Relationships

### WHAT'S LOVE GOT TO DO WITH WORKING MEMORY?

 Sometimes the best way to resolve a problem is by talking it through. You tell someone what's bothering you ("I feel sad when you ditch me at parties" or "I feel like you criticize me a lot"), and then perhaps they will make behavioral changes to address the issue. Whether these conversations are fruitful or futile may depend on working memory function.

**GET YOUR RELATIONSHIP WORKING WITH WORKING MEMORY.**

To find out how working memory influences problem solving between romantic partners, researchers studied 101 newlywed pairs, both heterosexual and same-sex couples. After giving the participants working memory assessments, the researchers observed the couples talking through their relationship problems. Then they separated the pairs and had each

**chunking** Grouping numbers, letters, or other items into recognizable subsets as a strategy for increasing the quantity of information that can be maintained in short-term memory.

**working memory** The active processing of information in short-term memory; the maintenance and manipulation of information in the memory system.

member recount what their partner had said. Four and 8 months later, the researchers checked in with the couples to see whether the problems they had discussed had diminished to some degree (Baker et al., 2020).

Here's what the study revealed: Talking about problems led to **better outcomes** when partners had a solid working memory capacity, or the "ability to actively maintain information during ongoing processing and despite distractions" (Baker et al., 2020, p. 580). Presumably, a good working memory capacity enabled them to focus on one another's statements, even while dealing with their own thoughts, emotions, and distractions in the environment. This likely helped them create long-term memories of the conversation and therefore make behavioral changes to allay the problem (Baker et al., 2020).

How can these findings help you? Talk about relationship problems when you have the ability to focus your attention on the issue, not when you are tired, distracted, or drinking alcohol (Hambrick & Katsumata, 2020). Make a point to listen, truly listen, to what your partner is saying so that information can be transferred into your long-term memory. 🔴

Now that we have established the importance of working memory, let's take a closer look at how it functions. Working memory has four components: the phonological loop, visuospatial sketchpad, central executive, and episodic buffer (Baddeley, 2002; Baddeley & Hitch, 2019; FIGURE **6.6**).

**PHONOLOGICAL LOOP**    The *phonological loop* is responsible for working with verbal information for brief periods of time; when exposed to verbal stimuli, we "hear" an immediate corollary in our mind. This component of working memory is what we use when reading our textbook or trying to remember what a friend told us yesterday.

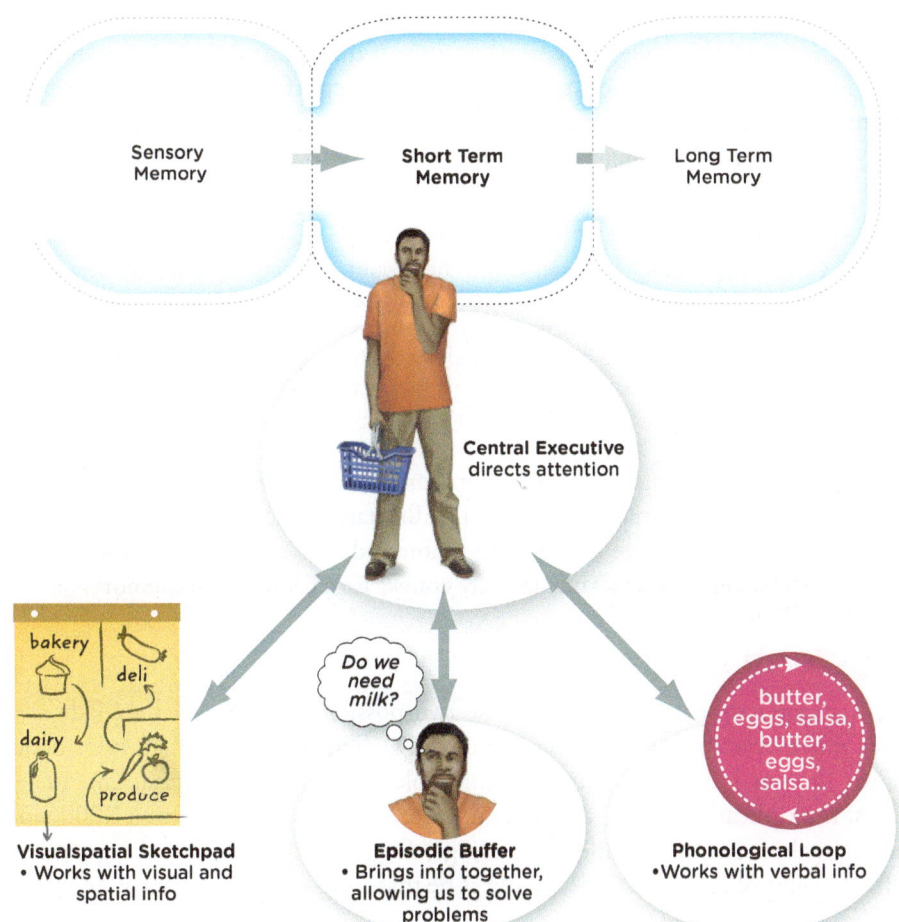

**FIGURE 6.6**
**Working Memory**
Working memory represents the active processing occurring in short-term memory. Overseeing the big picture is the central executive, which directs attention and integrates processing among three subsystems: the phonological loop, visuospatial sketchpad, and episodic buffer. To see how this model works, imagine you have stopped by the supermarket to pick up groceries. You rehearse the shopping list with your phonological loop, produce a mental layout of the store with your visuospatial sketchpad, and use the episodic buffer to access long-term memories and determine whether you need any additional items. Tying together all these activities is the central executive.

**VISUOSPATIAL SKETCHPAD**    The *visuospatial sketchpad* is where visual and spatial data are briefly stored and manipulated, including information about your surroundings and where things are in relation to each other and you. This working memory component allows you to close your eyes and reach for the coffee mug you just set down (Baddeley, 1999, 2006).

**CENTRAL EXECUTIVE**    The *central executive* has responsibilities similar to those of the chief executive in any organization—it directs attention, makes plans, and coordinates activities (Baddeley, 2002). Part of its role is to determine what information is important, and to help organize and manipulate awareness. Why is it that we cannot actually text, eat, and safely drive all at once? Like a juggler, the central executive can only catch and toss one ball at a time. We may think we are doing all three tasks at once, but we are really just swapping the alternatives in and out at a fast pace.

**EPISODIC BUFFER**    The *episodic buffer* is the part of working memory where information from the phonological loop, visuospatial sketchpad, and long-term memory can be brought together temporarily, under the direction of the central executive (Baddeley, 2000). The episodic buffer forms the bridge between memory and conscious awareness. It enables us to assign meaning to past events, solve problems, and make plans for the future.

**LET'S WORK IT OUT**    Here's an everyday example to help you flesh out these concepts: Imagine you are shopping for a unique gift on Etsy. You need your password to login, so you retrieve it from long-term memory and then "hear" the letters and numbers in your *phonological loop*. Now you need your credit card, so you think back to the last place you saw it—the kitchen counter—and bring forth a mental image of how your kitchen is laid out in your *visuospatial sketchpad*. The *episodic buffer* allows memories of your password and credit card location to come into your awareness, and then fade away. All the while, the *central executive* is directing your attention from one place to the next, enabling you to complete every step of the purchase. Remember, the central executive can only handle one task at a time. Keep this in mind next time you try to complete a reading assignment.

Golden Productions/Getty Images.

**Are You Cyber-Slacking?**
One would hope this tech savvy "Net Generation" would use digital technologies to study and work more efficiently, but unfortunately this is not always the case. Many college students "cyber-slack," or use electronic media to socialize and entertain themselves during lectures and study sessions. Instructors can reduce cyber-slacking by engaging students with active learning exercises (which tend to reduce boredom), using student devices as learning tools in class, establishing and enforcing classroom policies about media use, and helping students understand how those policies can improve the learning process (Flanigan & Kiewra, 2018).

## Put Your Heads Together

With a partner, **A)** choose an activity that requires your attention (for example, texting each other the names of your favorite movie characters; taking turns naming books you have read). **B)** As you perform this task, try to memorize the 41 key terms listed at the end of the chapter. **C)** After 5 minutes, close your textbook and write the key terms (in order) on a blank sheet of paper. **D)** Discuss how multitasking affected your maintenance rehearsal of the key terms.

Both short-term memory and working memory are limited in their capacity and duration. So how do we maintain so much information over the years? What aspect of memory makes it possible to memorize thousands of vocabulary words, scores of names and facts, and lyrics to your favorite songs? Enter long-term memory.

## Long-Term Memory

Items that enter short-term memory have two possible fates: Either they fade away or they move into *long-term memory* (FIGURE **6.7**). Think of how much information is stored in your long-term memory: funny jokes, important conversations, images of faces, multiplication tables, and so many words—around 10,000 to 11,000 word families (such as "smile," "smiled," "smiling") for English-speaking college students (Treffers-Daller & Milton, 2013). Could it be that long-term memory has an endless

FIGURE 6.7
**Long-Term Memory**

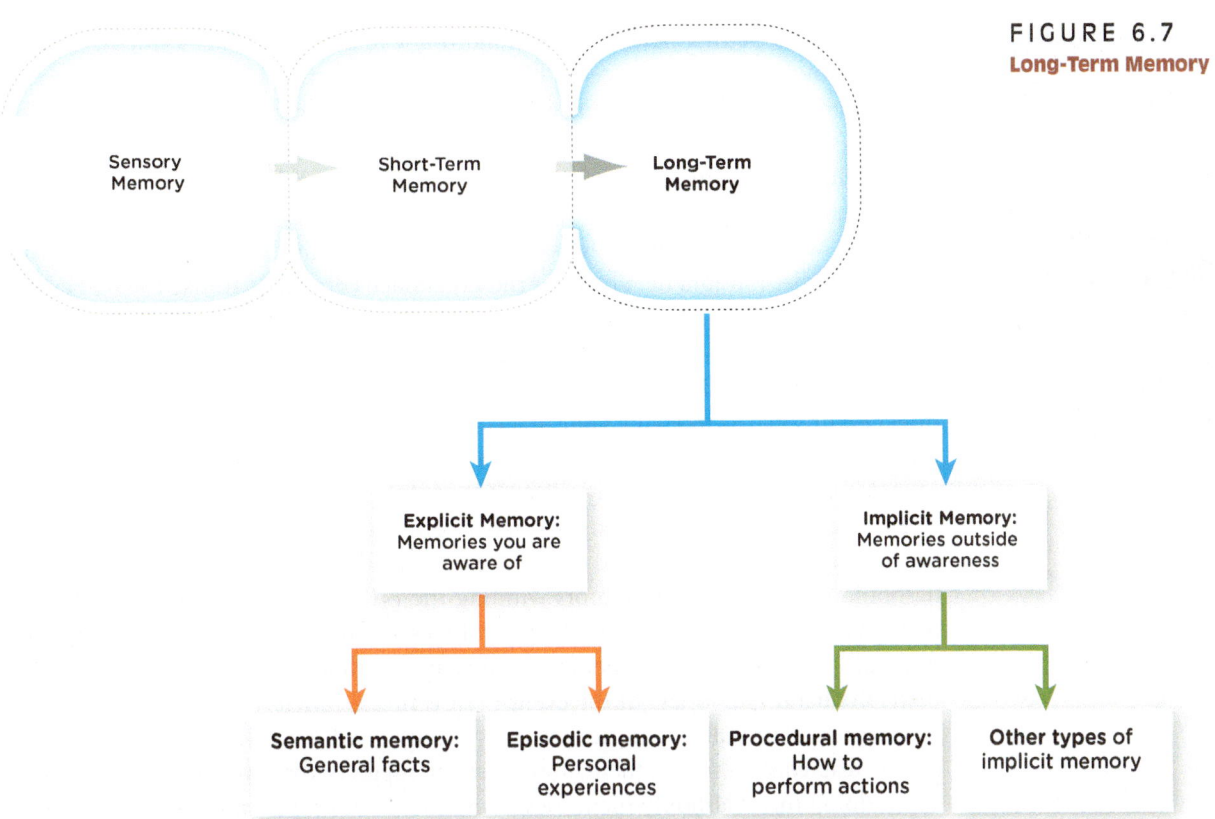

holding capacity? It may be impossible to answer this question, but for all practical purposes our long-term memory has no limits. Some memories stored there, such as street names from your childhood, may even last a lifetime (Schmidt et al., 2000; Smolen et al., 2019).

**LO 8** Describe long-term memory.

Long-term memory can be described in a variety of ways, but psychologists often distinguish between two categories: explicit and implicit. **Explicit memory** is the type of memory you are aware of having and can consciously express in words or declare: *Roses are red; guacamole is made with avocados; I wore my favorite jeans yesterday.* **Implicit memory** is a memory of something you know or know how to do, which may be automatic, unconscious, and difficult to bring to awareness and express: braiding hair, typing, salivating at the sight of french fries.

**EXPLICIT MEMORY**    Endel Tulving (1972) proposed that there are two forms of explicit memory: semantic and episodic. **Semantic memory** pertains to general facts about the world (*the Earth is located in the Milky Way; the United States holds presidential elections every 4 years; the brain has two hemispheres*). But there is also a type of memory you can call your own. Your first experience riding a bike, the time you got lost in the supermarket, the sandwich you ate yesterday—all of these personal memories are part of your **episodic memory** (ep-uh-SOD-ik). You can think of episodic memory as the record of memorable experiences, or "episodes," in your life, including when and where they occurred (Tulving, 1985). One could say that semantic memories are verifiable, while episodic memories may not be.

Often, our most vivid episodic memories are associated with intense emotion. Think about an emotionally charged experience from your past: learning about a

**explicit memory** A type of memory you are aware of having and can consciously express in words or declare, including memories of facts and experiences.

**implicit memory** A memory of something you know or know how to do, which may be automatic, unconscious, and difficult to bring to awareness and express.

**semantic memory** The memory of information theoretically available to anyone, which pertains to general facts about the world; a type of explicit memory.

**episodic memory** The record of memorable experiences or "episodes" including when and where they occurred; a type of explicit memory.

**Effortless**
Following his bout with encephalitis in 1985, Clive Wearing could still read music and play the piano, demonstrating that his procedural memory was not destroyed. Researchers documented a similar phenomenon in a professional cello player who battled herpes encephalitis in 2005 (Vennard, 2011).

terrorist attack, getting news that someone you love has been in an accident, or hearing that your favorite sports team has won a historic championship. If recollecting these moments feels like watching a 4-D movie, you might be experiencing what psychologists call a **flashbulb memory,** a detailed account of circumstances surrounding an emotionally significant or shocking, sometimes historic, event. With flashbulb memories, you frequently recall the precise moment you learned of an event—where you were, who or what source relayed the news, how it made you feel, what you did next, and other random details about the experience (Brown & Kulik, 1977). Perhaps you have a flashbulb memory of learning that Joe Biden won the 2020 presidential election; you recall whom you were with, what you were drinking and eating, what music was playing. Or maybe you have a flashbulb memory of a more private, emotional event, such as receiving your first college acceptance letter or witnessing a crime (Lanciano et al., 2018). Flashbulb memories are experienced across cultures, but the content of those memories may differ (Gandolphe & El Haj, 2017; Talarico et al., 2019). For example, people in Chicago might have a vivid memory of the Cubs finally winning the 2016 World Series. Meanwhile, those in Toronto are likely to have flashbulb memories of the Raptors winning the NBA Championship in 2019. Note that a flashbulb memory is a specific type of episodic memory. In some cases, we have flashbulb memories of the experiences associated with *learning about* an event rather than "firsthand memories" of the event itself (Hirst & Phelps, 2016).

Because flashbulb memories seem so strong, vivid, and rich in detail, we often place great confidence in them, but research suggests that we should be cautious about doing this. Flashbulb memories sometimes include inaccuracies or lack specific details (Hirst et al., 2015; Neisser, 1991).

**CONNECTIONS**

In **Chapter 4,** we described automatic processing, involuntary cognitive activity that guides many everyday behaviors. When you mindlessly type your passcode into your phone or walk a familiar route without thinking about where to turn, you are using automatic processing. This automatic processing relies on implicit memory.

**IMPLICIT MEMORY**    Unlike explicit memory, which can easily flow into conscious thought, implicit memory is difficult to bring into awareness and express. It is a memory for something you know or know how to do, but which might be **automatic** or unconscious. Many of the physical activities we take for granted, such as playing an instrument, driving a car, and dribbling a basketball, use a special type of implicit memory called **procedural memory,** that is, the memory of how to carry out an activity without conscious control or attention. After his illness, Clive Wearing could still pick up a piece of music and play it on the piano. He had no recollection of learning to sight-read or play, yet he could execute these skills like the professional he had always been (Vennard, 2011). Therefore, Clive's procedural memory was still working.

**CONNECTIONS**

In **Chapter 5,** we introduced the concept of classical conditioning, which is evident when an originally neutral stimulus elicits an involuntary response, such as salivation, eye blinks, and other types of reflex reactions. Here, we can see how closely linked learning and memory are.

Memories acquired through classical conditioning are also implicit. Let's say you enjoy eating food at McDonald's and the very sight of the golden arches makes you salivate like one of **Pavlov's dogs.** Somewhere along the line, you formed a memory linking the appearance of that restaurant to juicy hamburgers and creamy shakes, but the association does not require your conscious awareness (Cowan, 1988). It is implicit.

## What's the Best Way to Make Memories?

How does the process of moving data into the memory system lead to the creation of long-term memories? Some strategies work well for keeping information in short-term memory (maintenance rehearsal, for example). Others involve moving information from short-term memory to long-term memory. Here, we will describe some evidence-based approaches for improving your memory. (If you're wondering if we recommend online "brain training" programs, the answer is probably not; brain training does not appear to have a measurable effect on memory or other cognitive abilities; Stojanoski et al., 2020.)

**flashbulb memory** A detailed account of circumstances surrounding an emotionally significant or shocking, sometimes historic, event.

**procedural memory** The unconscious memory of how to carry out a variety of skills and activities; a type of implicit memory.

**USE MNEMONICS**    Have you ever relied on the *first-letter technique* to remember the order of operations in math (Please Excuse My Dear Aunt Sally)? Or, perhaps you have used an *acronym,* such as ROY G BIV, to remember the colors of the rainbow (**FIGURE 6.8**)? These are **mnemonic** (nih-MON-ik) devices, or techniques for improving memory. Chunking, which we discussed earlier, is another mnemonic device. So, too, is the *method of loci* (LOH-sahy, meaning "places"), which involves placing items to be remembered along a mental journey. Just pick a familiar route—through your favorite restaurant, college campus, or your body—and mentally place things you need to remember at points along the way. Suppose you need to pick up five items at the grocery: *olive oil, cherries, tomatoes, bananas,* and *bread.* To remember these items, you could visually connect them to a journey along your body (O'Brien, 2013). For example, your hair is slicked back in *olive oil; cherries* dangle from your ears like earrings; your heart is a beating red *tomato;* your arms hang down like *bananas;* and your legs are two solid loaves of *bread.* The method of loci works very well for memorizing lists, especially if you practice often. For additional mnemonics and strategies to help you retain material learned in class, see **INFOGRAPHIC 6.1** on the next page.

**CREATE HIERARCHIES**    Another way to boost your memory is to arrange the material you are trying to memorize into a hierarchy, or a system of meaningful categories and subcategories. In one classic study, researchers presented some participants with a list of words arranged in a hierarchical structure and other participants with the same words not organized in any meaningful way. Those presented with words in a hierarchy had an easier time recalling them. In fact, the participants who had learned the words using the hierarchy were able to recall three times as many words as the other group (Bower et al., 1969).

**PUT SOME EFFORT INTO IT**    Earlier we noted that stronger memories result when you think about information on a deep level. This requires **effortful processing.** As the name implies, effortful processing is not only intentional but also requires "cognitive effort," which broadly refers to the "degree of engagement with demanding tasks" (Westbrook & Braver, 2015, p. 396). In other words, how much you are willing to buckle down and put your mind to a task. Some types of effortful processing, such as maintenance rehearsal, are useful for extending the amount of time you can hold information in short-term memory. Others employ patterns and meaning to encode information for longer storage.

What can a student do to facilitate effortful processing? Here are a few things that may help: sit at the front of the classroom, study in a quiet room with cell phones and TVs out of sight, and keep your eye on a clock so you can use your time wisely (Duckworth et al., 2016).

**ELABORATE AND VISUALIZE**    Effortful processing is evident in **elaborative rehearsal,** the method of connecting incoming information to knowledge in long-term memory. Here, the *level of processing* occurs at a deep level, and therefore the encoding of information is likely to be more successful. Earlier we described how you might remember your grocery list by mentally placing the items-to-be-bought along different parts of your body (olive oil in your hair, cherries dangling from your ears, and so on). This method of loci employs elaborative rehearsal and *visualization,* another effective encoding strategy. People tend to remember verbal information better when it's accompanied by vivid imagery.

**SPACE IT OUT**    You've probably heard this before, but you should avoid cramming when studying. Psychologists refer to cramming as **massed practice,** meaning that learning sessions generally occur within the same day, "back-to-back or in relatively

**FIGURE 6.8**

**Mnemonics**

Mnemonics enable us to translate information into a form that is easier to remember. For example, the common acronym ROY G BIV helps us remember the order of the seven colors in the rainbow. And when music students have trouble remembering the notes on the lines of the treble clef (EGBDF), they often rely on the first-letter technique, creating a sentence out of words beginning with these letters: *Every Good Boy Deserves Fudge.*

**mnemonic** Techniques to improve memory.

**effortful processing** The encoding and storage of information with conscious effort, or awareness.

**elaborative rehearsal** The method of connecting incoming information to knowledge in long-term memory; a deep level of encoding.

**massed practice** Studying for long periods of time without breaks.

# Study Smarter: Methods of Improving Your Memory

As a college student, you must be able to remember many details when taking an exam. Lucky for you, research has identified several memory strategies and study techniques that can help you retain information.

*start studying*

## Recall details

**Mnemonics** translate information into a more easily remembered form.

**ROYGBIV**

**Acronyms and first-letter technique**
It's easier to remember a short phrase than a string of information.

**Chunking**
It's easier to remember a few chunks than a long string.

8935550172
893-555-0172

**Method of loci**
It's easier to remember information when you deliberately link it to locations along a familiar route.

## Organize information

**Hierarchical structures** organize information into a meaningful system. The process of organizing aids encoding and, once encoded, the information is easier to recall.

furniture

fruit

flowers

## Make connections

**Elaborative rehearsal** is deep processing that boosts transfer to long-term memory by connecting new information to older memories.

## Give yourself time

**Distributed practice** creates better memory than study crammed into a single session.

## Get some rest

**Sleep**, or even wakeful resting after study, allows newly learned material to be encoded better.

NOVEMBER 13
NOVEMBER 15
NOVEMBER 18
NOVEMBER 21

↰ *study* ↱

NOVEMBER 23 ↰ *test*

ZZZ

A+ test

close succession" (Dunlosky et al., 2013, p. 36). A better approach is **distributed practice,** or spreading study sessions over the course of many days. Research starting as early as the 1800s resoundingly shows that distributed practice is much more effective for learning material than cramming sessions at the last minute (Dunlosky et al., 2013; Ebbinghaus, 1885/1913; Rohrer & Taylor, 2006). When researchers asked students to learn a new mathematical skill, they found that participants who practiced the new skill in two sessions (separated by a week) did better on a practice test 4 weeks later than those who spent the same amount of time practicing in one session (Pashler et al., 2007). Similarly, students who reviewed material from a natural science class 8 days after the original lectures did better on final exams than those who reviewed the material 1 day after the lectures (Kapler et al., 2015). If we extend that time frame to a year, the difference between massed and distributed practice becomes less clear (Burns & Gurung, 2020), but there is no doubt that spacing out your study sessions is a smart way to prepare for your next test.

## Put Your Heads Together

 In groups, **A)** create a weekly calendar showing your study schedule for this class, indicating the time and duration of each study session. **B)** Are you using massed practice or distributed practice? **C)** Explain how you could adjust your schedule to take full advantage of distributed practice.

**EXERCISE AND SLEEP**    We have touched on many strategies for boosting memory, from chunking to visualization to distributed practice (TABLE **6.1**). If we could leave you with one final piece of advice, it would be to prioritize your physical health.

**TABLE 6.1**    Study Smart (and Often)

| Technique | What to Do |
|---|---|
| Survey | Skim the material to determine what may be useful to you: Review questions, learning objectives, chapter summaries. Identify main ideas and concepts. |
| Question | Note any questions that arise after your survey. Create an outline to help organize your study based on the questions you generate. |
| Read | Read through your chapter, ask questions, and take notes on the content. Remember, studying is not the same as reading. |
| Recall | Go over the material you have read in your mind. Identify key facts and concepts. |
| Review | Reread the material and generate your own examples to illustrate the content. "Teach" the material to someone else. |
| Individualize the process | Break down the reading into small sections you can read, recall, and review effectively. |
| Space your study | Build in breaks and spread the study sessions over time. |
| Minimize distractions | Focus on the task at hand; multitasking while studying diverts attention, making your learning slower. |
| Test frequently | Test yourself frequently. Low-stakes feedback provides an opportunity to learn the material and retain it longer. Work together—collaborative study can be quite effective. |
| Sleep | Get enough rest. Good sleep helps us learn new material and retain it. |

Listed here are some practical tips for more effective studying and learning. Information from Al Firdaus (2012); Cordi and Rasch (2021); Roediger et al. (2011); Rohrer and Taylor (2006).

**distributed practice** Spreading out study sessions over time with breaks in between.

**CONNECTIONS**

In **Chapter 4,** we discussed how sleep and dreams relate to memory. For example, researchers suspect that sleep spindles are associated with memory consolidation, and some theorists emphasize the importance of REM sleep in this process.

A growing body of evidence suggests that physical exercise benefits the brain, including structures involved in memory. Exercise increases blood flow to the brain and promotes the activity of proteins called growth factors that are important for memory and learning (Armstrong, 2020; El Hayek et al., 2019; Steventon et al., 2020). Getting rest is critical, too. The exact role of **sleep** is still being investigated, but evidence suggests that good sleep makes for better processing of memories (Cordi & Rasch, 2021; Rasch & Born, 2013; Sawangjit et al., 2018). Even periods of "wakeful resting" can be of benefit (Schlichting & Bäuml, 2017). In one study, participants who experienced a 15-minute period of wakeful resting (sitting in a dark quiet room) displayed better retention of newly learned material than those who played a game for 15 minutes. Wakeful resting seems to allow newly learned material to be encoded better and thus retained in memory longer (Dewar et al., 2012).

"Wow, that's a lot to remember," you may be saying. Hopefully, you can retain it with the help of some of the mnemonic devices we have presented. You might also take a wakeful resting break in preparation for the next section, which focuses on the topic of memory retrieval.

## Put Your Heads Together

In your group, describe three strategies you could use to memorize the definitions of the key terms listed at the end of this chapter. (*Hint:* Refer to the section "What's the Best Way to Make Memories?")

### SHOW WHAT YOU KNOW

1. According to the information-processing model, short-term memory can hold onto information for up to about _____ if we are not distracted by something else.

   **A.** 10 seconds      **C.** 45 seconds

   **B.** 30 seconds      **D.** 60 seconds

2. As you enter the airport, you try to remember the location of the baggage claim area. You remember the last time you picked up your friend at this airport and, using your visuospatial sketchpad, realize the area is to your left. This ability demonstrates the use of your:

   **A.** sensory memory.      **C.** phonological loop.

   **B.** working memory.      **D.** flashbulb memory.

3. If you are trying to memorize a long password, you could use _____, grouping the numbers and symbols into meaningful units of information.

4. Develop a mnemonic device to help you memorize the following terms from this section: sensory memory, long-term memory, explicit memory, semantic memory, episodic memory, flashbulb memory, implicit memory, and procedural memory.

5. When people talk about "short-term memory," they typically are referring to something that happened a few hours or days ago. Is this definition accurate from a psychological perspective? Explain.

✓ CHECK YOUR ANSWERS AT THE BACK OF THE BOOK.

**Friends Forever**
Elephants Jenny and Shirley remembered each other after being separated for 23 years. Reunited at the Elephant Sanctuary in Hohenwald, Tennessee, they examined one another's trunks and hollered with joy (Ritchie, 2009).

Courtesy of Carolyn Buckley, www.carolbuckley.com.

# Retrieval and Forgetting

Have you ever heard the saying "An elephant never forgets?" Granted, this might be somewhat of an overstatement, but as far as animals go, elephants do have remarkable memories. Consider the story of two elephants that briefly worked together in the circus and then were separated for 23 years. When they re-encountered one another at an elephant sanctuary in Tennessee, the two animals started to inspect each other's trunk scars and "bellowed" in excitement: The long-lost friends had recognized one another (Ritchie, 2009)! An elephant's memory—and yours, too—is only as good as its ability to retrieve stored memories.

## What Can You Retrieve?

Anything that jogs your memory, be it a post-it note or a cell phone alarm, is called a **retrieval cue**—a stimulus that helps you retrieve stored information that is difficult to access (Tulving & Osler, 1968). Let's say you are trying to remember the name of the researcher who coined the phrase, "the magical number seven, plus or minus two." If we gave you the first letter of his last name, *M,* would that help you retrieve the information? If your mind jumps to "Miller" (the correct answer), then *M* serves as your retrieval cue. You probably create your own retrieval cues to memorize important information. When you take notes, for example, you don't copy everything you are reading; you write down enough information (the cue) to help you later retrieve what you are trying to learn. Or when you save a photo on your computer, the name of the file ("SanFran2018" or "NOLA2020") might serve as a retrieval cue to help you recall where and when it was taken. "The ability of a learner to remember target information may fade over time; a good external cue can sustain memory retrieval in the face of considerable forgetting" (Tullis & Benjamin, 2015, p. 922).

Even Clive Wearing, who could not remember what was happening from one moment to the next, showed evidence of using retrieval cues. For instance, Clive spent 7 years of his life at St. Mary's Hospital in Paddington, London, yet had no conscious memory of living there. And, according to his wife, Deborah, Clive was "completely devoid" of knowledge of his own location; the hospital name was not at all connected with his sense of location (D. Wearing, personal communication, June 25, 2013). But if Deborah prompted him with the words "St. Mary's," he would chime back, "Paddington," oblivious to its connection (Wearing, 2005, p. 188). In this instance, the *retrieval cue* in Clive's environment (the sound of the word "St. Mary's") was **priming** his memory of the hospital name.

But how can priming occur in a person with severe amnesia? Priming is made possible by *implicit memory* (discussed earlier), which is often unconscious and difficult to express (Schacter, 2019). Although Clive's conscious, *explicit* memory is diminished, his *implicit* memory still functions. He could not articulate, or "declare," the name of the hospital, but that does not mean the previously known word combination had vanished from his memory system.

**RECALL AND RECOGNITION**    Unfortunately, we don't always have retrieval cues to help us. Sometimes we must rely on pure **recall,** the process of retrieving information held in long-term memory without the help of retrieval cues. Recall is what you depend on when you answer fill-in-the-blank or short-answer essay questions on exams. Say you are given the following prompt: "What are the three processes involved in memory?" In this situation, you must come up with the answer from scratch: "The three processes are *encoding, storage,* and *retrieval.*"

Now let's say you are faced with a multiple-choice question: "One proven way to help you retain information is: (a) distributed practice, (b) massed practice, or (c) eidetic imagery." Answering this question relies on **recognition,** the process of matching incoming data to information stored in long-term memory. Recognition is generally a lot easier than recall because the information is right before your eyes; you just have to identify it (*Hey, I've seen that before*). Recall, on the other hand, requires you to come up with information on your own. Most of us find it easier to recognize the correct answer from a list of possible answers in a multiple-choice question than to recall the same correct answer for a fill-in-the-blank question.

**SERIAL POSITION EFFECT**    Recall and recognition come into play outside of school as well. Just think about the last time someone asked you to pick up several things at the drugstore. In order to find the requested goods, you had to recognize them (*There's the dental floss*), but even before that you had to recall them—a much harder task if they are not written down. The ability to recall items from a list depends on where they fall in the list, a phenomenon psychologists call the **serial position effect** (FIGURE 6.9 on the next page). When given a list of words to memorize, research participants are better able to remember items at the beginning of the list, which is known as the **primacy effect,** as well as items at the end, which is called the **recency effect** (Deese & Kaufman, 1957; Kelley et al., 2015; Murdock, 1962).

Mat Hayward/Getty Images.

**Can Bieber Retrieve?**
Like all of us, singer/songwriter Justin Bieber is vulnerable to occasional retrieval failures. He famously forgot the lyrics to his own song "Despacito" while performing at a New York nightclub in 2016. "I don't know the words, so I say Dorito," he reportedly sang in place of the Spanish lyrics (Izadi, 2017, para. 31).

**retrieval cues**  Stimuli that help in the retrieval of stored information that is difficult to access.

**priming**  The stimulation of memories as a result of retrieval cues in the environment.

**recall**  The process of retrieving information held in long-term memory without the help of explicit retrieval cues.

**recognition**  The process of matching incoming data to information stored in long-term memory.

**serial position effect**  The ability to recall items in a list depends on where they are in the series.

**primacy effect**  The tendency to remember items at the beginning of a list.

**recency effect**  The tendency to remember items at the end of a list.

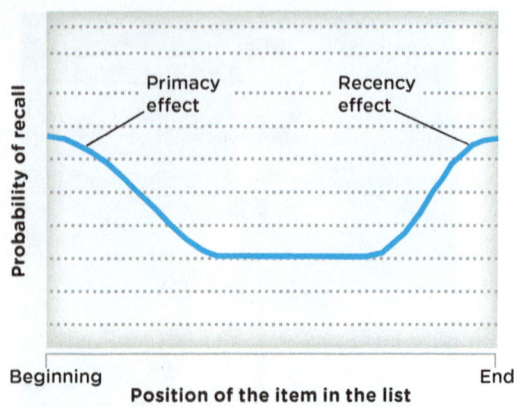

**FIGURE 6.9**

**The Serial Position Effect**

People are more likely to recall items at the beginning of a list and items at the end of a list; we call this the serial position effect.

Imagine you are on your way to the store to buy supplies for a dinner party, but your cell phone battery is about to die. Your housemate calls asking you to pick up the following items: napkins, paper towels, dish soap, butter, laundry soap, paper plates, sparkling water, ice cream, plastic spoons, bread, pickles, and flowers. Without any way to write down this list, you are at the mercy of the serial position effect. In all likelihood (and if you don't use mnemonics), you will return home with napkins, paper towels, and a bottle of dish soap (due to the primacy effect), as well as bread, pickles, and flowers (due to the recency effect); the items in the middle will more likely be forgotten. The serial position effect also seems to influence which items are ordered from restaurant menus. Foods tend to be more "popular" when listed at the beginning or end of a menu, as opposed to the middle; presumably, they pop into your head more easily when you are ordering your meal (Bar-Hillel, 2015).

## ACROSS THE WORLD

### MEMORY AND CULTURE

**MEMORIES OF WE, OR MEMORIES OF ME?**

Culture is another factor that may influence what types of information are available for retrieval (Wang, 2019). For example, if you ask people from the United States and China to recount some life memories, you may detect some interesting cultural themes in their reports. Research suggests that Chinese people are more likely than North Americans to remember social and historical occurrences and focus their memories on other people. Americans, on the other hand, tend to recall events as they relate to their individual actions and emotions (Schmidt & Qiao, 2020; Wang, 2016; Wang & Conway, 2004). Why is this so?

It may have something to do with the fact that China—like many countries in Asia, Africa, and Latin America—has a *collectivist* culture, whereas the United States is more *individualistic*. People in collectivist societies tend to prioritize the needs of family and community over those of the individual. Individualistic cultures are more "me" oriented, or focused on autonomy and independence. It thus makes sense that people from the collectivist culture of China would have more community-oriented memories than their U.S. counterparts. Keep in mind this is just a general trend—not a rule that applies to every person from China and the United States. Within any society, there is substantial variation with regard to individualism and collectivism, and this may relate to levels of urbanization. For example, a study conducted in Turkey (a collectivist society) found that country-dwelling children were more likely than urban children to have memories involving social interactions, and this could be related to the more collectivistic orientation of rural communities (Göz et al., 2017). What are some of your most important memories, and do you think culture helped shape them?

## The Encoding Specificity Principle

Now that we have touched on how cultural context might influence memory, let's explore context in a more general sense. How does your environment—both internal and external—impact your ability to retrieve memories?

**LO 9**  Illustrate how encoding specificity relates to retrieval cues.

**CONTEXT IS EVERYTHING**    In a classic study, participants learned lists of words under two conditions: while underwater (using scuba gear) and on dry land (Godden & Baddeley, 1975). Then they were tested for recall in both conditions: If they learned

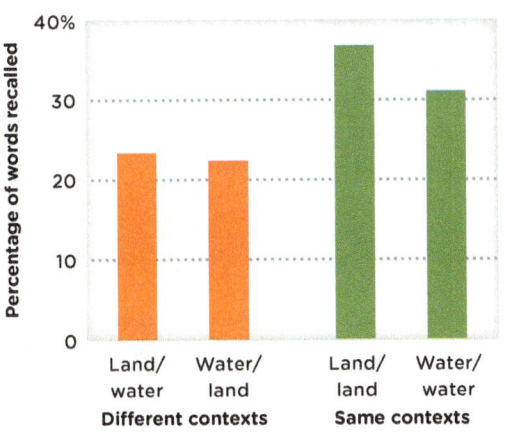

Sergey Dubrow/Shutterstock

**FIGURE 6.10**

**Diving into Memory Research**

Researchers asked participants to learn a list of words in two contexts, underwater and on dry land. The participants had an easier time recalling words when learning and recall happened in the same setting: learning underwater and recalling underwater, or learning on dry land and recalling on dry land. Information from Godden and Baddeley (1975).

the list underwater, they were tested underwater and on dry ground; if they learned the list on dry ground, they were tested on dry ground and underwater. The participants were better able to retrieve words when the learning and recall occurred in the same location (FIGURE **6.10**). If they learned the words underwater, they had an easier time recalling them underwater. Similarly, words learned on land were easier to recall on land. Here, we have an example of *context-dependent memory;* memories are easier to access when the encoding and retrieval occur in similar contexts.

Context-dependent memory is part of a broader phenomenon conveyed by the **encoding specificity principle,** which states that memories are more easily recalled when the context and cues at the time of encoding are similar to those at the time of retrieval (Smith et al., 1978; Tulving & Thomson, 1973). There is even evidence that summoning a memory for an event reactivates the same brain areas that became excited during the event itself (Craik, 2020). This suggests that the activity in your brain at the time of encoding is similar to that at retrieval.

**IT ALL COMES FLOODING BACK**    In your own life, you may have noticed that old memories tend to emerge from the woodwork when you return to the places where they were created. Dining at a restaurant you once frequented with an ex-boyfriend or ex-girlfriend probably sparks memories of romantic moments (or perhaps a bitter argument) you had there. Going to a high school reunion might bring back memories of football games, dances, and classrooms not recalled in years. How does returning to the birthplace of a memory help bring it to mind? Places where memories are created often abound with retrieval cues—sights, sounds, tastes, smells, and feelings present at the time of encoding. These retrieval cues help awaken stored memories.

**MOODS, INTERNAL STATES, AND MEMORY**    The encoding specificity principle does not merely apply to the external context. Remembering things is also easier when physiological and psychological conditions, including moods and emotions, are similar at the time of encoding and retrieval. We call this *state-dependent memory.* One morning, you awake to see a red cardinal on your window ledge. You forget about the cardinal for the rest of the day—even when you pass the very same window. But come tomorrow morning when you are once again half-awake and groggy, memories of the red bird return. Here, your ability to recall the cardinal is dependent on your internal or physiological state being the same as it was at the time of encoding.

Album/Alamy Stock Photo.

**Retrieval Cues**

The characters Jules (left, played by Hunter Schafer) and Rue (Zendaya) as they appeared in the 1st season of HBO's *Euphoria.* Suppose you enjoyed a bowl of microwave popcorn the last time you watched a *Euphoria* episode. The smell and taste of the popcorn, and all the sensory experiences you enjoyed at the time, become entwined with your memory of the show, and therefore can serve as retrieval cues now and in the future. So, next time you smell buttery popcorn, don't be surprised if an image of Rue pops into your head.

**encoding specificity principle** States that memories are more easily recalled when the context and cues at the time of encoding are similar to those at the time of retrieval.

Retrieval is also easier when the content of a memory corresponds to our present emotional state, a phenomenon known as *mood congruence* (Bower et al., 1981; Drace et al., 2010). If you are in a happy mood, you are more likely to recollect a happy-go-lucky character from a book, but if you are in a sour mood, you are more inclined to remember the character whose bad mood matches yours.

## Memory Savings: Easier the Second Time Around

Retrieval is clearly at work in recall and recognition, the two processes we compared earlier. But there is another, less obvious form of retrieval that occurs in the process of **relearning.** Perhaps you've noticed that you learn material much faster a second time around (Mazza et al., 2016; Storm et al., 2008). Math equations, vocabulary, and grammar rules seem to make more sense if you've been exposed to them before.

**CONNECTIONS**

As we noted in **Chapter 1,** case studies often have only one participant. Here, we see that the researcher (Ebbinghaus) was the sole participant. It is important to consider this when interpreting the findings, especially as we try to generalize them to the population.

**HERMANN EBBINGHAUS**   The first person to quantify the effect of relearning was Hermann Ebbinghaus (1850–1909), a German psychologist and pioneering researcher of human memory. Ebbinghaus was the **sole participant** in his experiments, so his research actually shed light on *his* memory, although the trends he uncovered in himself seem to apply to human memory in general (Murre & Dros, 2015).

Thorough scientist that he was, Ebbinghaus spent hour upon hour, day after day memorizing lists of "nonsense syllables"—meaningless combinations of vowels and consonants such as DAZ and MIB. Once Ebbinghaus had successfully remembered a list, meaning he could recite it smoothly and confidently, he would put it aside. Later, he would memorize it all over again and calculate how much time he had saved in Round 2, a measure called the "savings score" (Ebbinghaus, 1885/1913). In a study that supports Ebbinghaus' findings, participants who were asked to memorize number–word pairs (for example, 17-snake, 23-crown) showed significant savings in the amount of time needed to relearn them 6 weeks later (Marmurek & Grant, 1990).

Since no one spends all day memorizing nonsense syllables, you may wonder how Ebbinghaus' research and the "savings score" apply to real life. At some point in school, maybe you had to memorize a famous speech like Dr. Martin Luther King's "I Have a Dream." Let's say it took you 100 practice sessions to recite the speech flawlessly. Then, a month later, you tried memorizing it again and it only took 50 attempts. Because you cut your learning time in half (from 100 practice sessions to 50), your savings score would be 50%.

**A FOREIGN LANGUAGE?**   Learning is a lot like blazing a trail through freshly fallen snow. Your first attempt plowing through the powder is hard work and slow going, but the second time (relearning) is easier and faster because the snow is packed and the tracks already laid down. This also seems to be true for relearning a forgotten childhood language. One small study focused on native English speakers who as children had been exposed to either Hindi or Zulu to varying degrees. Although none of the adults in the study had any *explicit* memories of the languages, those who were under 40 could still distinguish sounds from their childhood languages better than members of a control group with no exposure to these languages (Bowers et al., 2009). The implication is that people who have some knowledge of a language (even if they don't realize it) benefit from this memory, as they show a "memory savings" if they try to learn the language again. They are a step ahead of other adults learning that language for the first time.

**relearning**  Material learned previously is acquired more quickly in subsequent exposures.

# Why Do We Forget?

**LO 10** Identify some of the reasons why we forget.

In addition to demonstrating the effects of relearning, Ebbinghaus was the first to illustrate just how rapidly memories vanish. Through his experiments with nonsense syllables, Ebbinghaus (1885/1913) found that the bulk of forgetting occurs immediately after learning. If you look at his *curve of forgetting* (FIGURE **6.11**), you will see his memory of word lists plunging downward the hour following learning, then leveling off thereafter. Think about how the curve of forgetting applies to you. Some of what you hear in a psychology lecture may disappear from memory as soon as you walk out the door, but what you remember a week later will probably not differ much from what you recall in a month.

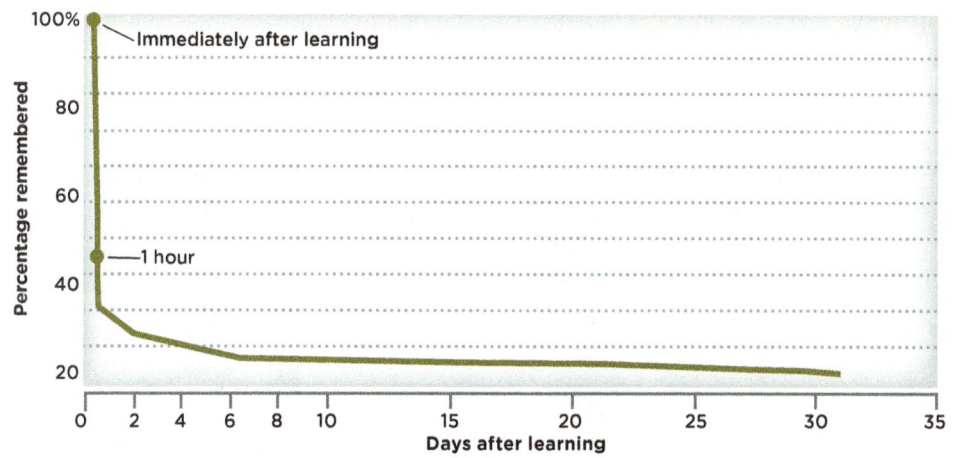

FIGURE 6.11
**Ebbinghaus' Curve of Forgetting**
Ebbinghaus discovered that most forgetting occurs within 1 hour of learning and then levels off. Data from Ebbinghaus (1885/1913).

**ENCODING FAILURE**    What exactly causes us to forget? That may depend on the stage of memory processing—encoding, storage, or retrieval—at which a given instance of memory failure occurs. Sometimes details and events we think we have forgotten were actually never encoded in the first place. Take this example: After a long and stressful day, you stop at the supermarket to pick up some blackberries and dark chocolate. While fumbling through your bag in search of your wallet, you put your keys on the cashier's counter, but because your attention is focused on finding your wallet, you don't even notice where you've placed the keys. Then you pay and walk out the door, only to get to your car wondering where you left your keys! This is an example of *encoding failure* because the data never entered your memory system. You didn't register putting your keys on the counter in the first place, so how can you expect to remember where you left them? For a demonstration of encoding failure, take a look at the four images appearing in the Try This. You've looked at the Apple logo countless times, so it should be easy to tell if you're looking at one that's phony, right?

If you're like most people, you identified one of the wrong logos as correct (the real Apple logo is not shown), perhaps because there is no "functional reason" for you to *encode* the logo's visual elements. Or, maybe you have been exposed to the logo so many times that you no longer attend to its details (Blake et al., 2015).

**STORAGE FAILURE**    Memory lapses can also result from *storage failure.* Take a moment and try to remember your high school locker combination. At one point, you knew these numbers by heart, but they have slipped your mind because you no longer use them. You cannot access this information because it is no longer

Are any of these the correct Apple logo?

Research from Adam B. Blake and Alan D. Castel, 2015.

in your memory system. Memories may decay over time, but there is plenty of evidence that we can store a vast fund of information, sometimes for very long periods (Smolen et al., 2019). Such memories might include the name of the street where you grew up (Schmidt et al., 2000), grades in college (Bahrick et al., 2008), and factual knowledge from college courses (Conway et al., 1991). However, such memories are subject to a variety of inaccuracies and distortions, and tapping into them is not always easy.

**RETRIEVAL FAILURE**    Sometimes we know that we have knowledge of something but just can't pull it out of storage, or retrieve it. The name of that college classmate or that new blockbuster movie, it's just sitting on the tip of your tongue but it won't slide off! This simple *retrieval failure* is called the *tip-of-the-tongue phenomenon.* Most of us have this feeling about once a week, but luckily we are able to retrieve the elusive phrase approximately 50% of the time (James & Burke, 2000; Schwartz, 2012). Often, we can correctly guess the first letter of the word or how many syllables it has (Hanley & Chapman, 2008). Studies suggest that the tip-of-the-tongue phenomenon becomes more common with age (Brown & Nix, 1996).

Steve Granitz/Getty Images.    David Livingston/Getty Images.    Steve Granitz/Getty Images.

**Can You Name Them All?**
Sometimes a name we are trying to remember feels so close, yet we cannot quite pull it out of storage. This feeling of near-retrieval is known as the tip-of-the-tongue phenomenon, and it happens frequently when we try to recall the names of celebrities.

Retrieval can be influenced, or even blocked, by information we learn before and after a memory is made, a phenomenon we call *interference* (Waugh & Norman, 1965). If you have studied more than one foreign language, you have probably experienced interference. Suppose you take Spanish in middle school and then begin studying Italian in college. As you try to learn Italian, you may find Spanish words creeping into your mind and confusing you; this is an example of **proactive interference,** the tendency for information learned in the past to interfere with the retrieval of new material. People who learn to play a second musical instrument experience the same problem; the fingering of the old instrument interferes with the retrieval of new fingering.

Now let's say you are going on a trip to Mexico and need to use the Spanish you learned back in middle school. As you approach a vendor in an outdoor market in Costa Maya, you may become frustrated when the only words that come to mind are *ciao bello* and *buongiorno* (Italian for "hello handsome" and "good day"), when you really are searching for phrases with the same meaning in Español. Here, recently learned information interferes with the retrieval of things learned in the past. We call this **retroactive interference.** This type of interference can also impact the musician; when they switch back to the original instrument, the fingering techniques they use to play the new instrument interfere with the old

**proactive interference** The tendency for information learned in the past to interfere with the retrieval of new material.

**retroactive interference** The tendency for recently learned information to interfere with the retrieval of things learned in the past.

FIGURE 6.12
**Proactive and Retroactive Interference**

**Proactive Interference:**
Old information interferes with newly learned information

Interference

SPANISH → ITALIAN → Italian Test F

Time

**Retroactive Interference:**
New information interferes with information learned in the past

Interference

SPANISH → ITALIAN → Spanish Test F

techniques. To summarize, proactive interference results from knowledge acquired in the past and retroactive interference is caused by information learned recently (**FIGURE 6.12**).

Now that we have discussed the many ways you can forget, let's turn our attention in the opposite direction. What would happen if you couldn't forget—that is, you remembered almost everything?

## Didn't See That Coming

### HIGHLY SUPERIOR AUTOBIOGRAPHICAL MEMORY

About two decades ago, researchers became aware of a rare form of super memory, which has come to be called *highly superior autobiographical memory*, or HSAM (McGaugh & LePort, 2014). People with HSAM have "an uncanny ability to recollect an abundance of detail pertaining to autobiographical experiences" (Palombo et al., 2018, p. 583), and this is associated with unique patterns of brain activity (Santangelo et al., 2020). If you ever encounter someone with HSAM (unlikely, as there are only about 60 documented cases in the world; McRobbie, 2017), pick a date—let's say March 14, 2018. Right away, they will know it was a Wednesday, and they will probably remember this was the day that students and teachers across the United States staged a walkout to protest gun violence. They also may recall that physicist Stephen Hawking died on this day. Additionally, several autobiographic details will come to mind—the extra shot of espresso they got in their latte that morning, the motivational quote they saw on Instagram, and the rerun of *Modern Family* they watched before bed.

People with HSAM can remember almost every day of their lives, often beginning at some point in middle childhood (Patihis, 2016). For 27-year-old Markie Pasternak, it began on February 13, 2005, when she was in fifth grade. "I can literally remember everything since this one day," recalls Markie, whose HSAM has been confirmed by researchers at the University of California, Irvine, where the phenomenon was first identified (M. Pasternak, personal communication, March 6, 2017). Markie feels blessed to have memory superpowers, but she notes there are some drawbacks. For example, the tendency to get lost in intense recollection can interfere with other cognitive activities. If presented with a retrieval cue

**"I CAN LITERALLY REMEMBER EVERYTHING...."**

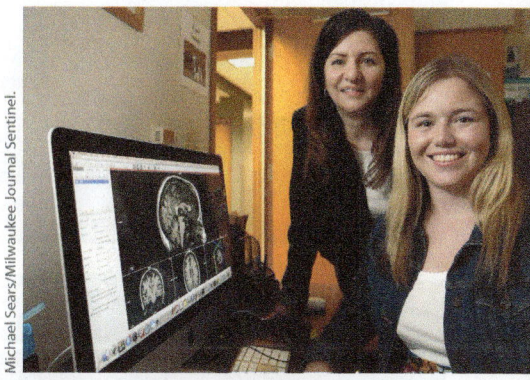

Michael Sears/Milwaukee Journal Sentinel.

**Super Memory Revealed**
Growing up, Markie Pasternak knew there was something unusual about her memory; she could remember every day of her life in astounding detail beginning at age 11. But it wasn't until college that Markie discovered her gift had a scientific name: highly superior autobiographical memory (HSAM). Here, Markie (right) appears with her psychology professor from Marquette University, Dr. Kristy Nielson, who helped identify her remarkable ability.

(an odor, for instance), Markie may fall into an episode of "hardcore reminiscing" that feels like another state of consciousness, similar to hypnosis. Just one whiff of the perfume "Sensual Amber" by Bath & Body Works can transport her back to the ninth grade and awaken thoughts and emotions she had at specific moments. "I can picture all my classes," says Markie. "I can picture my friends, I can even feel my heart flutter for the guy that I liked at that time" (M. Pasternak, personal communication, March 6, 2017). Snapping out of a deep memory can take a minute or two, so you can imagine how it might get in the way of academic and professional endeavors—even for a highly successful individual like Markie. Could there be some advantages to forgetting? The research certainly suggests there are. Forgetting allows you to focus on items that need your attention, and it clears the way for new memories (Williams et al., 2013; Wimber et al., 2015). ⚡

## Can Memories Be Trusted?

Interestingly, people with HSAM can remember what they had for lunch a decade ago, but when asked to remember a word list, they make a similar number of errors as members of a control group (Patihis et al., 2013). Like the rest of us, these individuals can suffer from "memory distortions." You see, memories are not reliable records of reality. They are *malleable* (that is, capable of being changed or reshaped by various influences) and constantly updated and revised, like a wiki. We can see how this occurs with a little help from Elizabeth Loftus.

**LO 11**   Explain how the malleability of memory influences the recall of events.

A renowned psychologist and law professor, Loftus has been studying memory and its reliability for close to five decades. During the course of her career, she has been an expert witness in over 200 trials. The main focus of her work is a problem you have probably pondered at some point in life: If two people have different memories of an event, who do we believe?

**MEMORY RECONSTRUCTED**   Loftus suggests that we should not expect our accounts of the past to be identical to those of other people. Nor should we assume that our own memories remain unchanged over time. Instead, she and others propose a *reconstructionist* model of memory "in which memories are understood as creative blendings of fact and fiction" (Loftus & Ketcham, 1994, p. 5). Over the course of time, memories can fade, and because they are permeable, they become more vulnerable to the invasion of new information. In other words, your memory of some event might include revisions to what really happened, based on knowledge, opinions, and information you have acquired since the event occurred.

Suppose you watch a debate between two political candidates on live television. A few days later, you see that same debate parodied on *Saturday Night Live*. Then a few weeks later, you try to remember the details of the actual debate—the topics discussed, the phrases used by the candidates, the clothes they wore. In your effort to recall the real event, you may very well incorporate some elements of the *Saturday Night Live* skit (words or expressions used by the candidates, for example).

**Comedy or Reality?**

Maya Rudolph and Beck Bennett (top) impersonated then-vice presidential candidate Kamala Harris and vice president Mike Pence on *Saturday Night Live* (photo from actual Harris/Pence debate below). Did Kamala Harris really discuss toilet paper shortages during the debate, or was that just part of the *SNL skit*? Sometimes we unknowingly edit our memories, incorporating bits and pieces of information learned after the fact.

The memories we make are **not precise depictions of reality**, but representations of the world as we perceive it. With the passage of time, we lose bits and pieces of a memory and unknowingly replace them with new information.

**THE MISINFORMATION EFFECT** If you witnessed a car accident, how accurately would you remember it? Elizabeth Loftus and John Palmer (1974) tested the reliability of people's memories for such an event in a classic experiment. After showing participants a short film clip of a multiple-car accident, Loftus and Palmer quizzed them about what they had seen. They asked some participants, "About how fast were the cars going when they smashed into each other?" Replacing the word "smashed" with "hit," they asked others, "About how fast were the cars going when they hit each other?" Can you guess which version resulted in the highest estimates of speed? If you guessed "smashed," you are correct.

One week later, the researchers asked the participants to recall the details of the accident, including whether they had seen any broken glass in the film. Although no broken glass appears in the film, the researchers nevertheless predicted there would be some "yes" answers from participants who had initially been asked about the speed of the cars that "smashed" into each other. Their predictions were correct. Participants who had heard the word "smashed" apparently incorporated a faster speed in their memories and were more likely to report having seen broken glass. Participants who had not heard the word "smashed" seemed to have a more accurate memory of the filmed car collision. The researchers concluded that memories can change in response to new information, and specifically that the participants' recollections were altered by the wording of a questionnaire (Loftus & Palmer, 1974). This research suggests that eyewitness accounts of accidents, crimes, and other important events might be modified by factors that come into play *after* the event occurs. Because memories are malleable, the wording of questions can change the way events are recalled, and care must be taken when questioning people about the past, whether it's in a therapist's office, a social service agency, or a police station.

Researchers have since conducted numerous studies on the **misinformation effect,** or the tendency for new and misleading information to distort one's memory of an incident. Studies with a variety of participants have resulted in their "remembering" a stop sign that was really a yield sign, a screwdriver that was really a hammer, and a barn that did not actually exist (Loftus, 2005).

**EYEWITNESS ACCOUNTS** Knowing that memories are malleable, how can prosecutors, police officers, and other interviewers reduce the likelihood of obtaining flawed information from eyewitnesses? Experts have offered many evidence-based recommendations, including the practice of using open-ended, rather than suggestive, questions (Wells et al., 2020). For example, it would be better to say "describe everything you saw" as opposed to "the suspect was wearing a baseball cap, right?" Another good policy is to ask questions immediately. People who witness crimes are often asked to rate their confidence in identifying a suspect. This "eyewitness confidence" is linked to accuracy—but only when the confidence level is assessed "at the time of the initial identification," that is, when suspects are viewed in a lineup (Wixted et al., 2015, p. 515). Simply stated, if the eyewitness has a high level of confidence in identifying a suspect *shortly after the crime,* their identification is more accurate (Brewin et al., 2020; Wixted & Mickes, 2017). Believe it or not, this may be true even when the witness has had a few drinks.

**CONNECTIONS**

In **Chapter 1,** we introduced the concepts of expectations and bias, noting that these can produce inaccuracies in thinking and research. Here, we describe the ways in which our memories can fail. As accurate as our thoughts and memories may seem, we must be aware that they are vulnerable to error.

Amy Stocklein Images/Getty Images.

**What If the Witness Is a Child?**
Obtaining an accurate eyewitness account from a child can be challenging, in part because children are vulnerable to suggestion (Wells et al., 2020). To minimize inaccuracies, interviewers should be as neutral as possible. They should not show approval or disapproval of the child's statements—smiling and saying "good," or frowning and saying "that's not right," for example (Sparling et al., 2011, p. 588). Asking children to close their eyes increases the accuracy of the testimony (Vredeveldt et al., 2014).

**misinformation effect** The tendency for new and misleading information obtained after an incident to distort one's memory of it.

# DRUNK WITNESSES REMEMBER A SURPRISING AMOUNT

Interviewing an inebriated person at the scene may be more accurate than waiting until he or she is sober.

Police officers investigating a crime may hesitate to interview drunk witnesses. But waiting until they sober up may not be the best strategy; people remember more while they are still inebriated than they do a week later, a new study finds.

Malin Hildebrand Karlén, a senior psychology lecturer at Sweden's University of Gothenburg, and her colleagues recruited 136 people and gave half of them vodka mixed with orange juice. The others drank only juice. In 15 minutes women in the alcohol group consumed 0.75 gram of alcohol per kilogram of body weight, and men drank 0.8 gram (that is equivalent to 3.75 glasses of wine for a 70-kilogram woman or four glasses for a man of the same weight, Hildebrand Karlén says). All participants then watched a short film depicting a verbal and physical altercation between a man and a woman. The researchers next asked half the people in each group to freely recall what they remembered from the film. The remaining participants were sent home and interviewed a week later.

The investigators found that both the inebriated and sober people who were interviewed immediately demonstrated better recollection of the film events than their drunk or sober counterparts who were questioned later. The effect held even for people with blood alcohol concentrations of 0.08 or higher—the legal limit for driving in most of the U.S. (Intoxication levels varied because different people metabolize alcohol at different speeds.) The results suggest that intoxicated witnesses should be interviewed sooner rather than later, according to the study, which was published online [. . .] in *Psychology, Crime & Law*.

The findings are in line with previous research, says Jacqueline Evans, an assistant professor of psychology at Florida International University, who was not involved in the new work. Evans co-authored and published a 2017 study in *Law and Human Behavior* that found similar results for moderately drunk witnesses. "Any effect of intoxication is not as big as the effect of waiting a week to question somebody," she says.

The new study also found that some aspects of the drunk people's recollections were not that different from those of the sober participants. For instance, both groups seemed particularly attuned to the details of the physical aggression portrayed in the film. "This research should at least make us more interested in what intoxicated witnesses have to say," Hildebrand Karlén says, "and perhaps take them a bit more seriously." **Agata Boxe. Reproduced with permission. Copyright 2019 Scientific American, a division of Nature America, Inc. All rights reserved.**

Prosecutors often tell people who have witnessed crimes not to speak to each other, and with good reason. Information provided by one witness can "contaminate" the memory of another (Wells et al., 2020). Suppose two people see an elderly woman being robbed. One witness remembers a bearded man wearing a blue jacket swipe the woman's purse. The other noticed the blue jacket but *not* the beard. If, however, the two witnesses exchange stories of what they saw, the second witness may unknowingly incorporate the beard into their "memory." Information learned after the event (that is, the "fact" that the thief had a beard) can get mixed up with memories of that event (Loftus, 2005; Loftus et al., 1978). If we can instill this type of "false" information into a "true" memory, do you suppose it is possible to give people memories for events that never happened? Indeed, it is.

# Can Memories Be . . . Fake?

**LO 12** Describe the meaning of rich false memories.

Elizabeth Loftus knows firsthand what it is like to have a memory implanted. Tragically, her mother drowned when she was 14 years old. For 30 years, she believed that someone else had found her mother's body in a swimming pool. But then her uncle, in the middle of his 90th birthday party, said that she, Elizabeth, had found her mother's body. Loftus initially denied any memory of this horrifying experience, but as the days passed, she began to "recall" the event, including images of the pool, her mother's body, and numerous police cars arriving at the scene. These images continued to build for several days, until she received a phone call from her brother informing her that her uncle had been wrong, and that all her other relatives agreed Elizabeth was not the one who found her mother. According to Loftus, "All it took was a suggestion, casually planted" (Loftus & Ketcham, 1994, p. 40), and she was able to create a memory of an event she never witnessed. Following this experience, Loftus began to study **rich false memories,** that is, "wholly false memories" characterized by "the subjective feeling that one is experiencing a genuine recollection, replete with sensory details, and even expressed with confidence and emotion, even though the event never happened" (Loftus & Bernstein, 2005, p. 101).

Would you believe that about a quarter of participants in rich false memory studies are able to "remember" an event that never happened? Using the "lost in the mall" technique, Loftus and Pickrell (1995) showed just how these imaginary memories take form. The researchers recruited pairs of family members (for example, two siblings or a parent and child) and then told them they would be participating in a study on memory. With the help of one member from each pair, the researchers recorded three *true* events from the pair's shared past and one *fabricated* but plausible story of a trip to a shopping mall. Then they asked the other member of the pair, whom we will refer to as the participant, to recall as many details as possible about each of the four events (remember, only three of the events were real), which were presented in a book provided by the researchers. If the participant could not remember any details from an event, they were instructed to write, "I do not remember this." In the "lost in the mall" story, the participant was told they had been separated from the family in a shopping mall around the age of 5. According to the story, the participant began to cry but was eventually helped by an elderly woman and reunited with their family. Mind you, the "lost in the mall" episode was pure fiction, but it was made to seem real through the help of the participant's family member (who was working with the researchers). Following a series of interviews, the researchers concluded that 29% of the participants were able to "recall" either part or all of the fabricated "lost in the mall" experience (Loftus & Pickrell, 1995). These findings may seem shocking (they certainly caused a great uproar in the field), but keep in mind that a large majority of the participants did not "remember" the fabricated event (Hyman et al., 1995; Loftus & Pickrell, 1995). Still, this research highlights the importance of "educating people about the malleability of memory" (Scoboria et al., 2017, p. 160).

If you're not convinced, consider these findings: Following a series of interviews using suggestive memory-retrieval methods, 70% of the young adults participating in one study generated rich false memories of criminal behavior they had not committed during adolescence. They recalled incidents involving theft and assault, including interactions with the police that never happened (Shaw & Porter, 2015)! These participants were videotaped describing both true emotional memories and the false memories that had been implanted during the study. Later, researchers showed this footage to another group of participants, whose ability to identify false memories

*Mike Sonnenberg/Getty Images.*

**False Memories**
Would you believe that looking at photoshopped pictures can lead to the creation of false memories? In one study, researchers discovered that participants could "remember" hot air balloon rides they never took after looking at doctored photos of themselves as children on balloon rides. The researchers speculate that a photo "helps subjects to imagine details about the event that they later confuse with reality" (Garry & Gerrie, 2005, p. 321).

**rich false memories** Detailed recollections of events that never occurred, which are expressed with emotions and confidence.

Gregg Vigliotti/The New York Times/Redux.

**Innocent**

Huwe Burton (center) served 19 years in prison after detectives manipulated him into giving a false confession at age 16. During the investigation, detectives grilled young Burton for hours and indicated that he would be off the hook for statutory rape (sex with his 13-year-old girlfriend) if he confessed to killing his mother. Burton's murder conviction was finally vacated in 2019, when a Bronx judge recognized that police officers had used "psychologically coercive interrogation techniques" to elicit a false confession (Ransom, 2019, para. 6).

**CONNECTIONS**

In **Chapter 4,** we described an altered state of consciousness called hypnosis that allows for changes in perceptions and behavior, resulting from suggestions made by a hypnotist. Here, we discuss the use of hypnosis in a therapeutic setting; the hypnotist is a therapist trying to help a client "remember" an abuse that the therapist believes has been repressed.

was "no better than chance" (Shaw, 2020, p. 5). What does this tell us? Not only do false memories feel real to the people experiencing them; their accounts of these "memories" appear real to observers (Shaw, 2020). These findings have implications in legal situations. Suggestive interrogation techniques could potentially result in the false recall of crimes that were not committed. A person could believe they committed a crime that never happened, falsely confess to it, and then be wrongly convicted (Starr, 2019).

## Repressed Memories?

Given what you have learned thus far, do you think it's possible that false memories can be planted during psychotherapy? Imagine a clinical psychologist or psychiatrist who firmly believes that their client was sexually abused as a child. The client has no memory of abuse, but the therapist is convinced that the abuse occurred and that the traumatic memory for it has been *repressed,* or unconsciously pushed below the threshold of awareness (see Chapter 10). Using methods such as **hypnosis** and dream analysis, the therapist helps the client resurrect a "memory" of the abuse (that may not have occurred). Angry and hurt, the client then confronts the "abuser," who may be a close relative, and forever damages the relationship. Believe it or not, this scenario is very plausible (Patihis & Pendergrast, 2019). Consider these true stories picked from a long list:

- With the help of a psychiatrist, Nadean Cool came to believe that she was a victim of sexual abuse, a former member of a satanic cult, and a baby killer. She later claimed these to be false memories brought about in therapy (Loftus, 1997).
- Under the influence of prescription drugs and persuasive therapists, Lynn Price Gondolf became convinced that her parents molested her during childhood. Three years after accusing her parents of such abuse, she concluded the accusation was a mistake (Loftus & Ketcham, 1994).
- Laura Pasley "walked into her Texas therapist's office with one problem, bulimia, and walked out with another, incest" (Loftus, 1994, p. 44).

In the history of psychology, few topics have stirred up as much controversy as repressed memories (Brewin, 2020; Patihis, Ho, et al., 2014; Patihis, Lilienfeld, et al., 2014). Some psychologists believe that painful memories can indeed be repressed and recovered years or decades later, but others are skeptical (Otgaar et al., 2019; Patihis et al., 2019). Although childhood sexual abuse is shockingly common, with approximately 18% of girls and 8% of boys affected worldwide (Stoltenborgh et al., 2015), there is not solid evidence that these traumas are repressed. Even if they were, many believe retrieved memories of them would likely be inaccurate (Patihis, Ho, et al., 2014; Roediger & Bergman, 1998). Trauma survivors often face quite a different challenge—letting go of painful memories that continue to haunt them. (See Posttraumatic Stress Disorder in Chapter 13.)

The American Psychological Association (APA) and other authoritative mental health organizations have investigated the repressed memory issue at length. In 1998 the APA issued a statement offering its main conclusions, summarized below:

- Sexual abuse of children is very common and often unrecognized, and the repressed memory debate should not detract attention from this important issue.
- Most victims of sexual abuse have at least some memory of the abuse.
- Memories of past abuses can be forgotten and remembered at a later time.
- People sometimes do create false memories of experiences they never had.
- We still do not completely understand how accurate and flawed memories of childhood abuse are formed.

Keep these points in mind next time you hear the term "repressed memory" tossed around in talk shows, internet posts, or casual conversations (Otgaar et al., 2020). You are now equipped with scientific knowledge to evaluate claims about repressed memories, so weigh all the evidence and ask critical questions. If you or someone you know is dealing with issues related to abuse, seek help from a licensed psychotherapist (APA, n.d.-o).

Before you read on, take a minute and allow the words of Elizabeth Loftus to sink in: "Think of your mind as a bowl filled with clear water. Now imagine each memory as a teaspoon of milk stirred into the water. Every adult mind holds thousands of these murky memories. . . . Who among us would dare to disentangle the water from the milk?" (Loftus & Ketcham, 1994, pp. 3–4). What is the basis for all this murkiness? Time to explore the biological roots of memory.

## SHOW WHAT YOU KNOW

1. A friend remarks that their scores are better when they study at Starbucks and then take their online quiz there, as opposed to studying at Starbucks and taking the quiz at home. Your friend is exhibiting:
   A. context-dependent memory.
   B. proactive interference.
   C. retroactive interference.
   D. mood-congruent memory.

2. Ebbinghaus reported that his memory of word lists plunged the first hour after he learned them; he displayed this phenomenon in his:
   A. encoding-specificity principle.
   B. curve of forgetting.
   C. recency effect.
   D. serial position effect.

3. Your uncle claims he attended a school play in which you played the "Cowardly Lion." He describes the costume you wore, the lines you mixed up, and even the flowers he gave you. At first you can't remember the play, but eventually the memory seems to come back. Your mother insists you were never in that school play, and your uncle wasn't in the country that year, so he couldn't have attended the performance at all. Instead, you have experienced a:
   A. curve of forgetting.
   B. state-dependent memory.
   C. savings score.
   D. rich false memory.

4. The _____ refers to the tendency for new and misleading information to distort memories.

✓ CHECK YOUR ANSWERS AT THE BACK OF THE BOOK.

# The Biology of Memory

What did you do today? Did you have breakfast, brush your teeth, put your clothes on, drive your car, read an assignment, text a friend? Whatever you did, we are sure of one thing: It required a whole lot of memory. You could not send a text message without knowing how to spell, read, and use a phone—all things you had to learn and remember. Likewise, you could not drive without remembering how to unlock your car, start the engine, and use the pedals. Memory is involved in virtually everything you do.

If memory is behind all your daily activities, important processes must be occurring in the brain to make this happen: both on the macro (large) and micro (small) scale. But as we learned from Clive's example, these processes are fragile and vulnerable to disruption. Exploring the causes of memory failure can help us understand the biological basis of memory.

## Amnesia

**THE AFTERMATH** In the months and years following Clive's illness, researchers administered many tests to assess his cognitive functioning. They found his IQ to be within an average range but his ability to remember past events deeply impaired. When prompted to name as many musical composers as possible in 1 minute, Clive—a man who had devoted his career to the study of music—could only produce four: Mozart, Beethoven, Bach, and Haydn. He denied that dragonflies have wings and claimed he had never heard of John F. Kennedy (Wilson et al., 1995).

**Love Triumphs**
Clive forgot many things, but not the love he has for his wife. Every time Deborah came to visit, he recognized her but could not recall their last meeting, even if it had happened just minutes before. Hugging, kissing, and sometimes twirling Deborah in the air, he would ask how much time had passed (Wearing, 2005).

Clive was even more disabled when it came to developing new memories. Initially, he could not hold onto incoming information for more than a blink of an eye. If his wife Deborah left the room, even for a short trip to the restroom, he would welcome her back as if she had been away for years—embracing, celebrating, sometimes weeping. "How long have I been ill?" he would ask, forgetting the answer and repeating himself within seconds (Wearing, 2005, p. 181).

**LO 13**  Compare and contrast anterograde and retrograde amnesia.

Amnesia, or memory loss, can result from either a physical or a psychological condition. There are different types and degrees of amnesia, ranging from extreme (losing decades of episodic memories) to mild (temporarily forgetting people's names after a concussion).

**ANTEROGRADE AMNESIA**    According to researchers, Clive suffers from "a more severe anterograde amnesia than any other patient previously reported" (Wilson et al., 1995, p. 680). **Anterograde amnesia** (ANT-er-oh-grade) is the inability to "lay down" or create new long-term memories (**FIGURE 6.13**), and it is generally caused by damage to the brain resulting from surgery, alcohol, head trauma, or illness. Someone with anterograde amnesia cannot form memories of events and experiences that occur following the brain damage; as you can imagine, this inability to lay down new memories makes it hard to remember routine tasks and function in the world. For Clive, his short-term memory still functioned to a certain extent, but he could only absorb and process information for several seconds before it was lost. From his perspective, every experience was fresh, and every person (with the exception of some he knew well from the past) a total stranger.

**RETROGRADE AMNESIA**    A second type of memory loss is **retrograde amnesia,** an inability to access memories created before damage to the brain occurred (Brandt & Benedict, 1993; Figure 6.13). With retrograde amnesia, a person has difficulty retrieving old memories, though how "old" depends on the extent of trauma to the

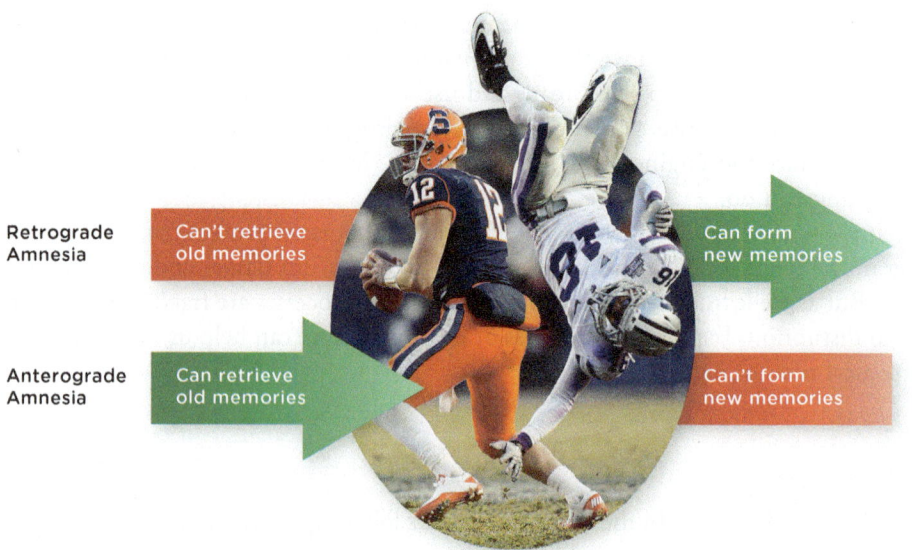

Retrograde
Amnesia — Can't retrieve old memories / Can form new memories

Anterograde
Amnesia — Can retrieve old memories / Can't form new memories

Chris McGrath/Getty Images.

**FIGURE 6.13**
**Retrograde and Anterograde Amnesia**
*Retro* means "before," so retrograde amnesia is the inability to retrieve memories for events that occurred *before* an amnesia-causing injury. *Antero* means "after," so anterograde amnesia is the inability to form memories for events that occur *after* an injury.

**anterograde amnesia**  A type of memory loss; an inability to create new memories following damage to the brain.

**retrograde amnesia**  A type of memory loss; an inability to access memories formed prior to damage to the brain.

brain. People with retrograde amnesia generally remember who they are and the most important events of their earlier lives (Manns et al., 2003; Squire & Wixted, 2011). Remember that *retrograde* refers to an inability to access old memories (think of "retro," meaning in the past, to help you distinguish between the terms), and *anterograde* refers to an inability to create new memories.

Clive suffered from retrograde amnesia in addition to his anterograde amnesia. While he appeared to retain a vague outline of his past (hazy information about his childhood, the fact that he had been a choral scholar at Clare College, Cambridge, and so on), he could not retrieve the names of his children unless prompted. And although Clive's children were all adults when he developed encephalitis, he came out of the illness thinking they were young children. The retrograde amnesia has improved, but only minimally. In 2005, for example, Clive asked his 40-something son what subjects he was studying in grammar school (equivalent to American high school). Nowadays when inquiring about his children, Clive simply asks, "What are they doing?" (D. Wearing, personal communication, June 18 and 25, July 11, 2013).

In spite of the severe retrograde and anterograde amnesia, some of Clive's memory functions continued to operate quite well. At one point, Deborah arranged for Clive to be reunited with the singers from the London Lassus Ensemble, a group he had conducted for more than a decade before his illness. At first, Clive paused and looked at the musicians with uncertainty, but then he raised his hands and began conducting, leading them through the music with precision and grace. Remembering the piece (which he had edited himself), Clive mouthed its words in Latin and employed the same tempo and conducting style he had used in the past (D. Wearing, personal communication, July 11, 2013). After the performance, the musicians left and Clive sat in the empty chapel wondering what had gone on there earlier (Wearing, 2005). When shown a video of himself leading the chorus, he remarked, "I wasn't conscious then" (Wilson et al., 2008, p. 534). Clive's explicit memory of the event vanished in seconds, but his implicit memory—knowing how to conduct—was intact.

How is it possible that some of Clive's long-term memories were blotted out, while others, such as how to conduct music, remained fairly clear? Evidence suggests that different types of long-term memories have distinct processing routes in the brain. Thus, damage to one area of the brain may impair some types of memory but not others. Let's take a closer look at where memories appear to be stored.

## Memories in the Brain: A Macro Perspective

**LO 14** Identify the brain structures involved in memory.

A few years after the onset of Clive's illness, doctors evaluated his brain using an MRI scan. A troubling picture emerged; the virus had destroyed many parts of his brain, notably the **hippocampus**, which plays a vital role in the creation of new memories (Wilson et al., 2008).

Only in the last 60 years or so have scientists come to appreciate the role of the hippocampus in memory (**INFOGRAPHIC 6.2** on page 241). Back in the 1920s, psychologist Karl Lashley (1890–1958) set out to find a **memory trace:** the physical spot where memories are etched in the brain, also called an *engram*. Lashley selected a group of rats that had learned the layout of specific mazes, and then made large cuts at different places in their cortices to see how this affected their memory of the mazes. No matter where Lashley sliced, the rats still managed to maneuver their way through the mazes (Costandi, 2009; Lashley, 1950). These findings led Lashley and other scientists to believe that memory is spread throughout the brain rather than localized in a particular region (Costandi, 2009; Kandel & Pittenger, 1999). *Connectionism* is a model that suggests our memories are distributed throughout the brain in a network of

**CONNECTIONS**

In **Chapter 2,** we described the hippocampus as a pair of seahorse-shaped structures located in the limbic system. The hippocampus is primarily responsible for processing and making new memories, but is not where memories are permanently stored. It is also one of the brain areas where neurogenesis occurs, that is, where new neurons are generated.

**memory trace** The physical spot where memories are etched in the brain, also called an *engram*.

interlinked neurons. Lashley spent over 30 years looking for an engram, and researchers continue to carry on this search (Josselyn & Tonegawa, 2020).

**THE CASE OF H.M.**    Henry Molaison (better known as "H.M.") forced scientists to completely reevaluate their understanding of the brain's memory system. From the onset of his amnesia in 1953 until his death in 2008, H.M. served as a research participant for some 100 scientists (Corkin, 2002), making him the most thoroughly studied person in the history of neuroscience (Benjamin et al., 2018).

H.M.'s brain troubles began at the age of 10, a year or so after being knocked unconscious in a bicycle accident. He began to experience seizures, which worsened with age and eventually became so debilitating that he could no longer hold a steady job. Anti-seizure medications were unsuccessful in controlling his seizures, so at the age of 27, H.M. opted for an experimental surgery to remove parts of his brain: the temporal lobes (just beneath the temples), including the hippocampus (Scoville & Milner, 1957).

H.M.'s surgery succeeded in reining in his epilepsy but left his memory in shambles. Upon waking from the operation, he could no longer find his way to the bathroom or recognize the hospital workers caring for him. He played with the same jigsaw puzzles and read the same magazines day after day as if he were seeing them for the first time (Scoville & Milner, 1957). Like Clive, H.M. suffered from profound *anterograde amnesia,* the inability to encode new long-term memories, and a milder form of *retrograde amnesia,* trouble retrieving existing memories from storage. Although H.M. had difficulty recalling what occurred during the few years leading up to his surgery (Scoville & Milner, 1957), he did remember events from the more distant past, for example, the 1929 stock market crash and the events of World War II (Carey, 2008).

However, H.M. maintained a working implicit memory, which he demonstrated in an experiment involving the complex task of tracing a pattern reflected in a mirror. With repeated practice sessions (none of which he remembered), H.M. improved his performance on the drawing task, learning it as well as someone without amnesia (Gabrieli et al., 1993). Clive can also acquire new implicit memories, but his ability is very limited. According to Deborah, it took years for Clive to learn how to get to his bedroom in the small community residence where he moved after leaving the hospital (Wearing, 2005).

**THE ROLE OF THE HIPPOCAMPUS**    Imagine you are a scientist trying to figure out exactly what role the hippocampus plays in memory. Consider the facts you know about H.M.: (1) He has virtually no hippocampus; (2) he has lost the ability to make new *explicit* memories yet can create *implicit* memories; and (3) he can still tap into memories of the distant past. What do you think the hippocampus does? Evidence suggests that the hippocampus is essential for creating new explicit memories but *not* necessarily implicit memories. (This is in addition to other functions, such as decision making [Biderman et al., 2020].) Researchers have also shown that explicit memories are processed and stored in other parts of the brain, including areas of the frontal cortex (García-Lázaro et al., 2012).

As in H.M.'s case, Clive's ability to form explicit memories is profoundly compromised, largely a result of the destruction of his hippocampus. Yet Clive also struggles with the creation of implicit memories—not surprising given the extensive damage to other regions of his brain (Wilson et al., 2008). Studies have zeroed in on certain areas, such as the cerebellum and amygdala, as processing hubs for implicit memory (Thompson & Kim, 1996; Thompson & Steinmetz, 2009). The amygdala also plays a central role in the processing of emotional memories (García-Lázaro et al., 2012). See Infographic 6.2 for more information about memory processing in the brain.

Meera Paleja, PhD.

**"One of the Giants of Our Time"**
Neuropsychologist Brenda Milner studied patient H.M. over the course of 5 decades (Squire, 2009). The work of Milner and her colleagues transformed our understanding of memory. As Nobel Laureate Eric Kandel remarked, "Brenda Milner is one of the giants of our time. Her delineation of memory dysfunction after lesions of the hippocampus has provided the basis for modern understanding of memory and for the divisions of memory storage mechanisms into explicit and implicit forms" (Tin, 2004, para. 3).

# Tracking Memory in the Brain

Whether with lab rats or case studies, psychologists have spent decades tracking the location of memory in the brain. Their findings point to a complex system involving multiple brain regions. Memory is formed, processed, and stored throughout the brain, and different types of memory have different paths. So it helps to know your way around the brain's structures. Remembering the amygdala's role in processing basic emotion, for instance, can help you understand its role in processing the emotional content of memories.

## Learning from H.M.

Henry Molaison, or "H.M." (1926–2008), may be the "best known single patient in the history of neuroscience" (Squire, 2009, p. 6). Following the surgical removal of his hippocampus, H.M. lost the ability to form new explicit memories, but he could still create certain types of implicit memories. This suggests that the hippocampus plays a key role in the creation of explicit—but not necessarily implicit—memories.

After his death, H.M.'s brain was cut into over 2,000 slices that were preserved and digitized for research.

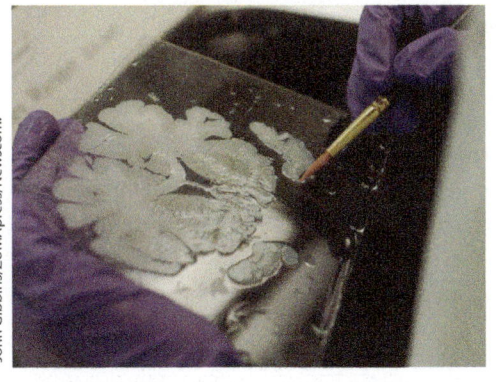

John Gibbins/ZUMApress/Newscom.

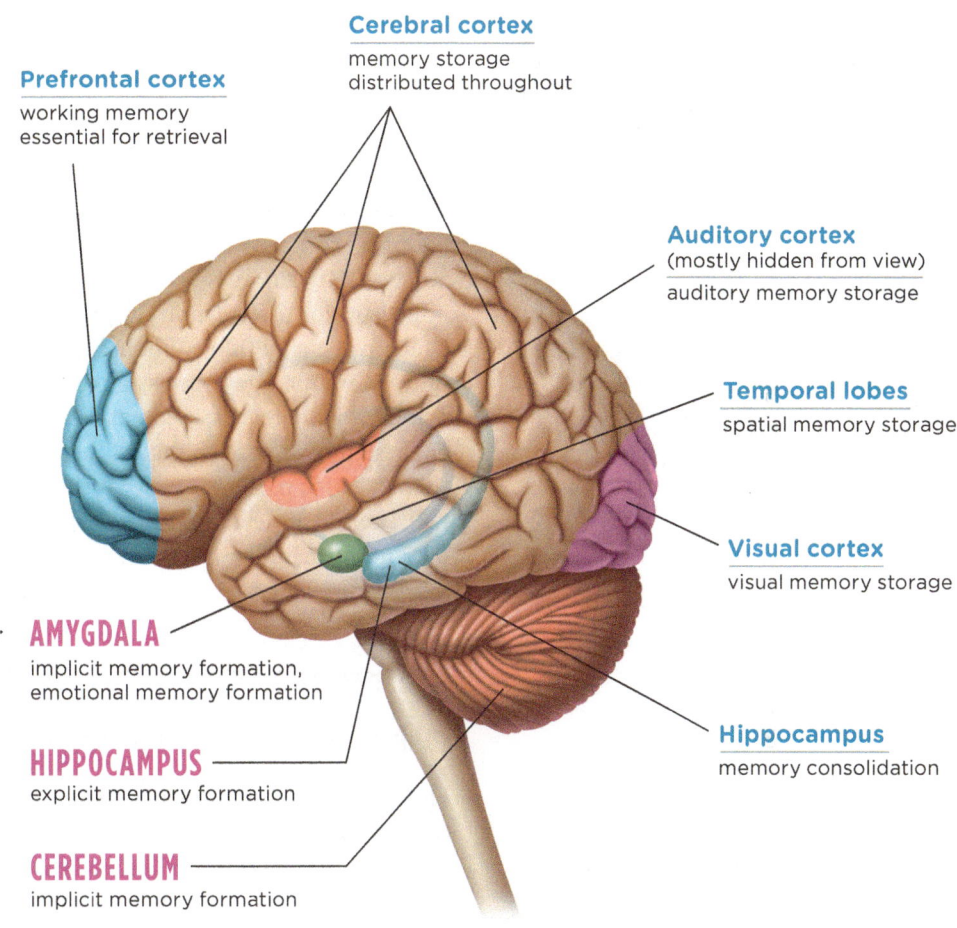

**Prefrontal cortex**
working memory
essential for retrieval

**Cerebral cortex**
memory storage
distributed throughout

**Auditory cortex**
(mostly hidden from view)
auditory memory storage

**Temporal lobes**
spatial memory storage

**Visual cortex**
visual memory storage

**Hippocampus**
memory consolidation

**AMYGDALA**
implicit memory formation,
emotional memory formation

**HIPPOCAMPUS**
explicit memory formation

**CEREBELLUM**
implicit memory formation

## Lashley's Quest

Through his experiments with rats, Karl Lashley tried to find the physical location of memories in the brain. He would train the rats to navigate mazes, make slices in various parts of their cortices, and then observe how their memories of the mazes were affected. In many cases, these slices had minimal impact on the rats' ability to navigate the mazes. With the help of modern technologies, researchers have discovered that memory activities occur in many areas of the brain (Shen, 2018). In a process called *memory consolidation,* which is thought to occur in the hippocampus and cortex, information is moved into long-term storage (Genzel et al., 2017).

Lashley kept a careful record of the sizes and locations of lesions made in each rat as part of his experiments.

L. E. Wiley, Copyrn_ _.933 The Wistar Institute of Anatomy and Biology.

Rogdy Espinoza Photography/Moment Open/Getty Images.

**Do Forgotten Memories Matter?**
By the time this child is an adult, he will have long forgotten his first birthday celebration, so why go to the trouble of throwing a party? The memory of the event may disappear, but something more important sticks for life. As psychologist Dima Amso explains, "Specific memories may be forgotten, but because those memories form the fabric of our identities, knowledge and experiences, they are never truly or completely gone" (Amso, 2017, p. 73).

Although the hippocampus is important for laying down new memories, it may not always serve as their ultimate destination. There is some evidence that memory formation may be occurring simultaneously in both the hippocampus and the cortex, but little is known about the specific processes (Kitamura et al., 2017). Researchers have yet to fully understand how and where memories are stored: "The representation of memory in the brain is one of the unresolved questions in neuroscience" (Assaf, 2018, p. 995). We do know that memories start out "fragile" but may eventually stabilize through memory consolidation (Alberini & Kandel, 2015). As for retrieval, the hippocampus appears to be in charge of accessing young memories, but then passes on that responsibility to other brain regions as memories grow older (Smith & Squire, 2009).

This idea that the hippocampus is essential for creating explicit memories (as opposed to implicit memories) is supported by what we know about *infantile amnesia,* that is, the inability to remember events from our earliest years. Most adults cannot remember events before the age of 3, and memories from age 1 or 2 are most likely fictional (Akhtar et al., 2018). Simply stated, young children do not construct complete episodic memories of their experiences (Bauer & Larkina, 2014). Some researchers suggest this is because the hippocampus and frontal cortex, both important for the creation of long-term explicit memories, are not fully developed in children (Bauer, 2006; Willoughby et al., 2012). We are less likely to forget memories starting around age 7 because the memories we begin generating are more elaborate and personally relevant. The efficiency of neural processes underlying the formation of these memories also makes them "more impervious to the ravages of forgetting" (Bauer, 2015, p. 225).

The macro-level perspective presented in this section allows us to see the "big picture" of memory, but what's going on microscopically? Next, we will focus on the important changes occurring in and between neurons.

## Memories in the Brain: A Micro Perspective

**LO 15** Describe long-term potentiation and its relationship to memory.

How does your brain change when you learn a new driving route to school? If we could peer into your skull, we might see a change in your hippocampus. Now imagine what might happen in the brain of a taxicab driver in London, who must memorize the 25,000 streets in the city, including their businesses and landmarks. As one study found, London taxicab drivers with more time spent on the job experienced structural changes in some regions of their hippocampus, particularly to an area that processes "spatial knowledge" (Maguire et al., 2006; Rosen, 2014). Zooming in for a closer look, we might actually see changes at the level of the neuron. If you are looking for a memory imprint, the best place to look is the **synapse**. "In an adult brain, synapses can change their strength and size within minutes or hours in response to new experience and learning" (Cirelli & Tononi, 2019, p. 189).

**CONNECTIONS**

In **Chapter 2,** we introduced the synapse, the junction between two neurons. Neurons communicate with each other via chemicals called neurotransmitters, which are released into the synapse. Here, we see how the activities at the neural level are related to the formation and maintenance of memories.

**LONG-TERM POTENTIATION**    The more neurons communicate with each other, the stronger the connections between them. **Long-term potentiation** occurs when sending neurons release neurotransmitters more effectively, and receiving neurons become more sensitive, boosting synaptic strength for days or even weeks (Lynch, 2002; Malenka & Nicoll, 1999; Whitlock et al., 2006). In other words, long-term potentiation refers to the increased efficiency of neural communication over time, resulting in the formation of memories. Researchers suggest long-term potentiation may be the biological basis for many kinds of learning. As you learn a new skill, for example, the neurons involved in performing that skill communicate more with each

**long-term potentiation** The increased efficiency of neural communication over time, resulting in learning and the formation of memories.

other. It might start with a somewhat random firing of neurons, but eventually the neurons responsible for the new skill develop pathways through which they communicate more efficiently.

Having trouble visualizing the process? Imagine this scenario: Your college has opened a new campus with an array of brand-new buildings, but it has yet to construct the sidewalks connecting them. In order to go from one class to the next, students have to wade through tall grass and weeds. All the trampling eventually gives way to a system of paths linking the buildings. Long-term potentiation occurs in a similar fashion: Over time, the communication among neurons improves and strengthens, allowing for the skill to develop and become more natural (Whitlock et al., 2006). These paths represent how a skill, whether tying your shoes or texting, is learned and thus becomes a memory.

**IF A SEA SLUG CAN, SO CAN YOU!**    Amazingly, we have learned much about long-term potentiation from the sea slug *Aplysia,* which has only about 20,000 neurons (Kandel, 2009)—a little easier to work with than the billions of neurons in a human brain. In addition to having a small number of neurons, the sea slug's synapses are relatively easy to examine at an individual level. Studies on sea slugs indicate that long-term potentiation, or increases in synaptic strength, is associated with learning and memory. What can a sea slug learn? They can be classically conditioned to retract their gills in response to being squirted with water, resulting in structural changes to both presynaptic and postsynaptic cells (Kandel, 2009)—evidence of long-term potentiation. So never, ever complain that you cannot learn: If a sea slug can do it, so can you!

**ALZHEIMER'S DISEASE**    On a less positive note, disruptions in long-term potentiation appear to be at work in *Alzheimer's disease,* a progressive, devastating brain illness that causes cognitive decline, including memory, language, and thinking problems.

Alzheimer's affects upward of 5 million Americans (National Institute on Aging, n.d.). The disease was first discovered by Alois Alzheimer (1864–1915), a German neuropathologist, in the early 1900s. He had a patient with severe memory problems whose autopsy revealed that neurons in her brain had become tangled. These *neurofibrillary tangles,* as they came to be called, were eventually shown to result from twisted protein fibers accumulating inside brain cells. In addition to the tangles, the other distinctive sign of Alzheimer's is the presence of *amyloid plaques,* protein clumps that build up between neurons (Fymat, 2018).

**Smart Slug**
Studying the neurons of sea slugs, researchers have observed the synaptic changes that underlie memory. Long-term potentiation enables a sea slug to retract its gills in anticipation of being squirted with water.

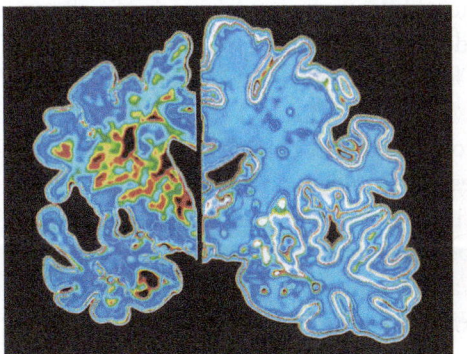
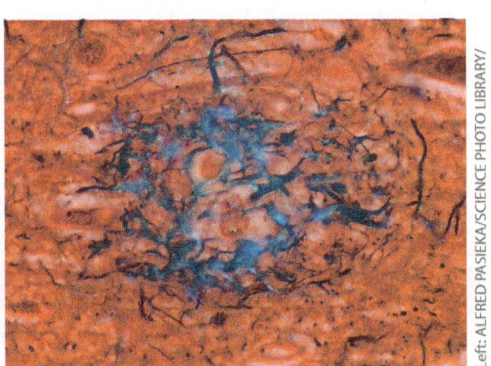

**Inside Alzheimer's**
Computer-generated images show the cross section of a brain affected by Alzheimer's (left portion of the blue image) compared to a healthy brain (right portion). The diseased specimen shows a substantial loss of brain volume. Pictured on the far right are amyloid plaques that have accumulated in the brain of an Alzheimer's patient. Both amyloid plaques and neurofibrillary tangles are telltale characteristics of Alzheimer's, but researchers are still trying to understand the exact roles they play in the disease process (He et al., 2018; Kuznetsov & Kuznetsov, 2018).

Although we still don't have a solid understanding of what causes Alzheimer's, we know some forms of the disease are inherited. People who have a first-degree relative (a parent, sibling, or child) with Alzheimer's are more likely to be affected. Researchers have zeroed in on a certain gene, APOEε4, that seems to increase the risk of developing Alzheimer's, particularly among women (Nebel, 2018). We also know that factors such as diet and exercise can influence the development and progression of the disease (Sohn, 2018). Being obese and sedentary can heighten one's risk; in fact, studies suggest that the standard U.S. diet (one that is high in sugar, fats, and processed food, and low in fruits, vegetables, and whole grains) can cause "nutrient deficiency and inflammation that could impact cognition directly" (Graham et al., 2016, p. 2). Even the air we breathe may play a role, as long-term exposure to air pollution has been linked to increased rates of Alzheimer's disease and other forms of dementia in populations around the world (Chen el at., 2017; Oudin et al., 2016; Shell, 2020)

There is no cure for Alzheimer's at this time, and current treatments focus on reducing the severity of symptoms rather than correcting the brain damage responsible. But there is also reason to be hopeful. Clinical trials for new drugs are underway (Servick, 2019), and a growing body of evidence suggests that simple lifestyle changes, like becoming more physically active, eating healthy foods, and pursuing intellectually and socially stimulating activities, may actually decrease the speed and severity of cognitive decline (Grinstein, 2018; Ko et al., 2018; Lourida et al., 2019; Morris et al., 2015).

**CHRONIC TRAUMATIC ENCEPHALOPATHY**    Similar in some ways to Alzheimer's disease, **chronic traumatic encephalopathy (CTE)** also impairs memory (Fesharaki-Zadeh, 2019). CTE is a neurodegenerative disease that leads to atypical deposits of tau protein throughout various regions in the brain. This disease results from repeated hits to the head or, in some cases, perhaps even a single traumatic brain injury (Smith et al., 2019). CTE affects football players, soccer players, wrestlers, rugby players, boxers, hockey players, lacrosse players, combat war veterans, and many other people who have suffered head trauma (Maroon et al., 2015; McKee et al., 2016). Symptoms include significant memory issues, impulsivity, aggression, and depression. CTE is progressive; its symptoms may not appear for months to years following the trauma; and it can only be diagnosed after death (McKee et al., 2013; Stern et al., 2019). Who's at risk and what are some of the more obvious symptoms of CTE? Discover the answers in INFOGRAPHIC **6.3.**

As we continue to learn more about CTE, parents must make difficult decisions about the type of sports they encourage their children to participate in. Studies on football players, in particular, have produced alarming results. One group of researchers examined the brains of 202 deceased football players with experience ranging from high school to the NFL; they found evidence of CTE in 177, or 87%, of those brains (Mez et al., 2017). Another group concluded that playing football before the age of 12 may lead to greater risk of depression, problems regulating behavior, and other "clinically meaningful impairments" in adulthood. As the researchers pointed out, the brain undergoes critical changes between ages 9 and 12, so the impact of head trauma may have special significance at this stage in life (Alosco et al., 2017). To better understand the impact of this disease, read the story of NFL Hall of Famer Harry Carson in Chapter 7.

Like many topics psychologists study, the biological mechanisms that give rise to memory remain somewhat mysterious. We know we have memories, we know they are formed in the brain, and we know the brain is a physical entity; yet we still don't know exactly how we go from arrays of firing neurons to vivid recollections that create the stories of our lives. Studies attempting to test the various theories of memory formation are inconclusive, often generating more questions than answers. But one thing seems certain: Memory researchers face plenty of important work ahead.

**chronic traumatic encephalopathy (CTE)** A neurodegenerative disease that leads to atypical deposits of tau protein throughout various regions in the brain as a result of traumatic brain injury.

# Chronic Traumatic Encephalopathy

Chronic traumatic encephalopathy (CTE) is a progressive neurodegenerative disease caused by one or more blows to the head. CTE affects athletes of many types, combat war veterans, and others who experience head trauma (McKee et al., 2016; Smith et al., 2019). The symptoms, which may not appear for months or years after the injury, include changes to memory, emotions, thinking, and personality. CTE is somewhat similar to other neurodegenerative diseases like Alzheimer's and Parkinson's in that it can impair memory, movement, and the ability to plan and carry out everyday tasks (McKee et al., 2013).

In 2012, after 20 seasons as an NFL player, **Junior Seau** committed suicide at age 43. In the years leading to his death, Seau's family noticed a change in his thinking, personality, and enthusiasm for the game. Impulsive gambling, alcoholism, and violence became the new conversation around the man once known as a beloved philanthropist (Fainaru-Wada, 2013). Upon his death, his brain showed the hallmarks of CTE (National Institute of Neurological Disorders and Stroke).

Retired soccer star **Brandi Chastain** has announced she will donate her brain to research. Chastain believes this will be a bigger legacy than her game-winning shot in the 1999 World Cup. Like many soccer players, Chastain advocates the banning of headers in youth soccer (Branch, 2016).

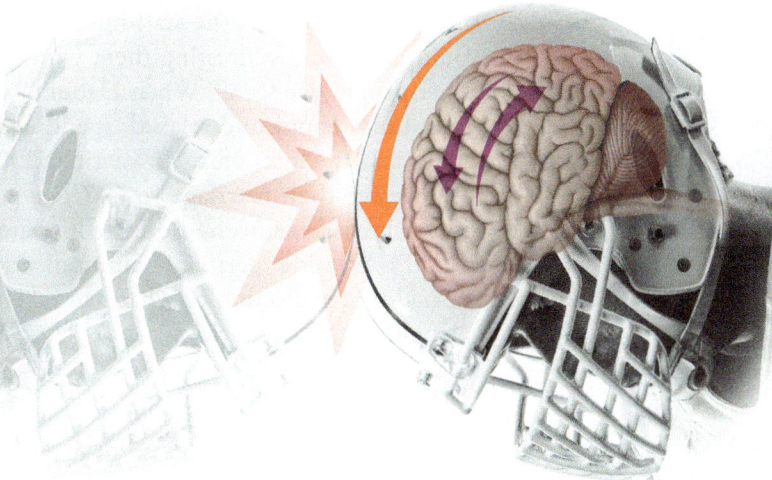

## THE PROGRESSION OF CTE

### Stage 1

Tau protein accumulates locally in the cortex.

**Symptoms:** headaches, and difficulty maintaining focus.

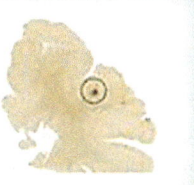

### Stage 2

The damage spreads to surrounding areas.

**Symptoms:** short-term memory impairment, mood swings, depression, explosive temper, and continued headaches and trouble focusing.

### Stage 3

Damage continues to spread, reaching areas such as the hippocampus, amygdala, and brainstem.

**Symptoms:** memory loss, difficulty planning and carrying out tasks, "visuospatial abnormalities," and ongoing difficulties with mood and attention.

### Stage 4

Widespread damage across many regions of the brain, including the medial temporal lobe, hypothalamus, and thalamus.

**Symptoms:** worsening of existing symptoms, along with language difficulties and paranoia. Severe memory loss.

How does CTE differ from other neurodegenerative diseases such as Alzheimer's? Symptoms associated with CTE typically present around age 40, while those of Alzheimer's generally appear around 60. Changes in thinking, cognition, and personality are common symptoms of CTE, while Alzheimer's is typically associated with memory problems (Frequently Asked Questions, n.d.). However, emerging evidence suggests there is some overlap in the brain changes and symptoms of these two diseases (Elsawaf et al., 2019; LoBue et al., 2020).

## >>> SHOW WHAT YOU KNOW

1. _____ is the inability to lay down new long-term memories, generally resulting from damage to the brain.
   A. Anterograde amnesia
   B. Retrograde amnesia
   C. Infantile amnesia
   D. Long-term potentiation

2. The _____ is a pair of curved structures in the brain that play a central role in memory.
   A. engram
   B. temporal lobe
   C. hippocampus
   D. aplysia

3. _____ occurs when sending neurons release neurotransmitters more effectively, and receiving neurons become more sensitive.
   A. Long-term potentiation
   B. Memory consolidation
   C. Priming
   D. The memory trace

4. Infantile amnesia makes it difficult for people to remember events that occurred before the age of 3. What is your earliest memory, and how old were you when that event occurred?

 CHECK YOUR ANSWERS AT THE BACK OF THE BOOK.

**Onward**
Nearly two decades after falling ill, Clive renewed his wedding vows with Deborah. Now in his eighties, Clive lives in a country residence for people suffering from brain injuries (Vennard, 2011).

**A PEACEFUL LIFE**   At this point, you may be wondering what became of Clive Wearing. After living in the hospital for 7 years, Clive moved to a country residence specially designed for people suffering from brain injuries. As he left the hospital, some of the staff members offered him a farewell and said they would miss him. Addressing them with a polite bow, Clive exclaimed, "You're the first people I've seen!" When Deborah would visit Clive in his new home, she found him happy and relaxed, spending much of his time on walks through gardens and the local village (Wearing, 2005, p. 293). In 2002 Clive and Deborah renewed their marriage vows. Clive participated fully in the service, reciting scripture he had memorized during his career as a professional singer decades before (D. Wearing, personal communication, June 10, 2013). After the ceremony, he had no recollection of what had taken place but nevertheless was very happy, laughing and devouring sponge cake (Wearing, 2005).

# Summary of Concepts

**LO 1** Define memory. (p. 210)

Memory refers to the processes involved in the encoding (collection), storage, and retrieval of information. Exactly how the brain absorbs information from the outside world and files it for later use is still not completely understood. However, scientists have proposed many theories and constructed various models to help explain how the brain processes, or works on, data on their way to becoming memories.

**LO 2** Describe the processes of encoding, storage, and retrieval. (p. 210)

Encoding is the process through which new information enters our memory system. Information is taken in by our senses and converted into neural activity that travels to the brain, and if successfully encoded, it is stored. Storage preserves the information for possible recollection in the future. Retrieval is the process of accessing information stored in memory.

**LO 3** Identify the stages of memory described by the information-processing model. (p. 212)

The information-processing model conceptualizes memory as a flow of information through a series of stages: sensory memory, short-term memory, and long-term memory. Each

of these stages has a certain type of storage with distinct capabilities.

**LO 4** Describe sensory memory. (p. 213)

Data picked up by the senses enter sensory memory, where almost exact copies of our sensations are processed for a very brief moment. Information from the outside world floods our sensory memory through multiple channels. Although this stage of memory is fleeting, it is critical to the creation of memories.

**LO 5** Summarize short-term memory. (p. 215)

Short-term memory is the second stage of the original information-processing model. This is where information is temporarily maintained and processed before moving on to long-term memory or leaving the memory system. Short-term memory is limited; its capacity and duration depend on how much we are distracted by other cognitive activities. Through maintenance rehearsal, we can prolong short-term memory.

**LO 6** Give examples of how we can use chunking to expand our short-term memory. (p. 215)

Grouping numbers, letters, or other items into meaningful subsets, or "chunks," is an effective strategy for increasing the amount of information in short-term memory. Chunking can also help nudge information into long-term memory.

### LO 7  Describe working memory and its relationship to short-term memory. (p. 216)

Working memory is the active processing component of short-term memory, and it has four important parts. The phonological loop is responsible for working with verbal information for brief periods of time. The visuospatial sketchpad is where visual and spatial data are briefly stored and manipulated. The central executive directs attention, makes plans, coordinates activities, and determines what information should be ignored. The episodic buffer is where information from the phonological loop, visuospatial sketchpad, and long-term memory can all be brought together temporarily, as directed by the central executive.

### LO 8  Describe long-term memory. (p. 219)

Long-term memory is a stage of memory with essentially unlimited capacity. Long-term memories may be explicit or implicit. Explicit memory is the type of memory you are aware of having and can consciously express; it may be further divided into semantic and episodic memory. Semantic memory pertains to general facts about the world, whereas episodic memory is your record of the memorable experiences in your life. Implicit memory is a memory of something you know or know how to do, which might be automatic or unconscious, and therefore difficult to articulate.

### LO 9  Illustrate how encoding specificity relates to retrieval cues. (p. 226)

Retrieval cues are stimuli that help you retrieve stored information that is difficult to access. The encoding specificity principle states that memories are more easily recalled when the context (external and internal) and cues at the time of encoding are similar to those at the time of retrieval. Priming, recall, and recognition also play a role in the retrieval of stored information.

### LO 10  Identify some of the reasons why we forget. (p. 229)

Memory failure may occur during any of the three stages of memory processing: encoding, storage, and retrieval. Encoding failure occurs when data fails to enter the memory system in the first place; storage failure occurs when information held in the memory system decays over time; and retrieval failure occurs when the information is in the memory system but cannot be accessed.

### LO 11  Explain how the malleability of memory influences the recall of events. (p. 232)

Memories can change over time: We lose bits and pieces and unknowingly replace them with new information, which can lead to inaccurate recall of events. The tendency for new and misleading information to distort one's memory of an incident is called the misinformation effect. Eyewitness accounts are not always reliable because people's memories are imperfect.

### LO 12  Describe the meaning of rich false memories. (p. 235)

Rich false memories are detailed recollections of events that never occurred, which are expressed with emotions and confidence. Some researchers have managed to implant false memories in the minds of participants.

### LO 13  Compare and contrast anterograde and retrograde amnesia. (p. 238)

Amnesia, or memory loss, can result from either a physical or a psychological condition. Anterograde amnesia is the inability to create new long-term memories, and is generally caused by damage to the brain resulting from surgery, alcohol, head trauma, or illness. Retrograde amnesia is an inability to access memories created before damage to the brain occurred.

### LO 14  Identify the brain structures involved in memory. (p. 239)

Researchers have identified several brain structures involved in the processing and storage of memory. The hippocampus and frontal cortex are important for creating new explicit memories. Other areas, such as the cerebellum and amygdala, are integral in the processing of implicit memories.

### LO 15  Describe long-term potentiation and its relationship to memory. (p. 242)

Long-term potentiation refers to the increased efficiency of neural communication over time, resulting in learning and the formation of memories. The communication among neurons improves and strengthens, allowing for new skills to develop and become more natural. These new pathways explain how a skill like tying your shoes or texting is learned and thus becomes a memory.

## Key Terms

anterograde amnesia, p. 238
chronic traumatic encephalopathy (CTE), p. 244
chunking, p. 216

distributed practice, p. 223
echoic memory, p. 214
effortful processing, p. 221
elaborative rehearsal, p. 221
encoding, p. 210

encoding specificity principle, p. 227
episodic memory, p. 219
explicit memory, p. 219
flashbulb memory, p. 220

iconic memory, p. 213
implicit memory, p. 219
long-term memory, p. 212
long-term potentiation, p. 242
maintenance rehearsal, p. 215

# Test Prep Are You Ready?

1. You are struggling to recall the name of a movie you watched last year. When you do finally remember the film was *Hillbilly Elegy,* which memory process were you using?

   **A.** short-term memory

   **B.** sensory memory

   **C.** encoding

   **D.** retrieval

2. In a classic experiment, Sperling (1960) showed that participants could recall 76% of the letters briefly flashed on a screen. The findings from this study indicate the capabilities of:

   **A.** eidetic imagery.

   **B.** depth of processing.

   **C.** iconic memory.

   **D.** the phonological loop.

3. Miller (1956) reviewed findings from the Digit Span Test and found that short-term memory capacity is limited to between five and nine numbers, that is, the "magical number seven, plus or minus two." However, through the use of _____, we can improve the span of our short-term memory.

   **A.** echoic memory

   **B.** iconic memory

   **C.** multitasking

   **D.** chunking

4. Baddeley and colleagues proposed that the purpose of _____ is to actively maintain information while the mind is performing complex tasks. The phonological loop, visuospatial sketchpad, central executive, and episodic buffer all play a role in this process.

   **A.** eidetic imagery

   **B.** working memory

   **C.** short-term memory

   **D.** semantic memory

5. In a classic study, Godden and Baddeley (1975) asked participants to learn lists of words under two conditions: while underwater and while on dry land. Participants were better able to recall the information in the same context in which it was encoded. This finding supports:

   **A.** the encoding specificity principle.

   **B.** Baddeley's working memory model.

   **C.** the serial position effect.

   **D.** the information-processing model of memory.

6. _____ causes problems with the retrieval of memories because of information you learned in the past, and _____ causes problems with retrieval due to recently learned information.

   **A.** The recency effect; the primacy effect

   **B.** The primacy effect; the recency effect

   **C.** Proactive interference; retroactive interference

   **D.** Retroactive interference; proactive interference

7. In studies by Loftus and colleagues, around 25% of participants were able to "remember" an event that never happened. This type of _____ shows us how the malleability of memory can influence recall.

   **A.** flashbulb memory

   **B.** rich false memory

   **C.** proactive interference

   **D.** serial position effect

8. Retrograde amnesia is generally caused by some sort of trauma to the brain. People with retrograde amnesia generally cannot:

   **A.** form memories of events that occur following the trauma.

   **B.** access memories of events created before the trauma.

   **C.** form semantic memories following the trauma.

   **D.** use procedural memories.

9. _____ refers to the increased efficiency of neural communication over time, resulting in learning and the formation of memories.

   **A.** Memory consolidation

   **B.** Long-term potentiation

   **C.** Memory trace

   **D.** Priming

10. The _____ is essential for creating new explicit memories, but not necessarily implicit memories.

    **A.** parietal lobe

    **B.** amygdala

    **C.** cerebellum

    **D.** hippocampus

11. A friend says, "My grandmother has terrible short-term memory. She can't remember anything from a couple of hours ago." This statement represents a very common mistake people make when discussing memory. How would you explain this confusion about short-term versus long-term memory?

12. How are iconic memory and echoic memory different from each other?

13. How does working memory differ from short-term memory?

14. Create a mnemonic to help you remember the processes of encoding, storage, and retrieval.

15. Imagine you are a teacher creating a list of classroom rules in case of an emergency. If you were expecting your students to remember these rules after reading through them only once, where in the list would you position the most important rules? Why?

✓ CHECK YOUR ANSWERS AT THE BACK OF THE BOOK.

Lawren/Getty Images.

# Cognition, Language, and Intelligence

## What Is Cognition?

AJ Mast/The New York Times/Redux.

**BLEEDING BRAIN**  December 10, 1996, was the day a blood vessel in Dr. Jill Bolte Taylor's brain began to bleed. At approximately 7:00 A.M., Dr. Taylor awoke to a pain behind her left eye, a stabbing sensation she found similar to the "brain freeze" felt after a hasty gulp of ice cream. It seemed strange for a healthy 37-year-old woman to experience such a terrible headache, but Dr. Taylor was not the type to lounge in bed all day. Pushing through the pain, she got up and climbed onto her cardio-glider. But as soon as she began moving her limbs back and forth, a weird out-of-body sensation took hold. "I felt as though I was observing myself in motion, as in the playback of a memory," Dr. Taylor writes

**The Brain Scientist**
An accomplished neuroanatomist, Dr. Jill Bolte Taylor had devoted her career to studying the brains of others. But one winter morning in 1996, she was given the frightening opportunity to observe her own brain in the midst of a meltdown.

in her book *My Stroke of Insight*. "My fingers, as they grasped onto the handrail, looked like primitive claws" (Taylor, 2006, p. 37).

The pain, meanwhile, kept hammering away at the left side of her head. She stepped off the cardio-glider and headed toward the bathroom, but her steps seemed plodding, and maintaining balance demanded intense concentration. Finally reaching the shower, Dr. Taylor propped herself against the wall and turned on the faucet, but the sound of the water splashing against the tub was like an earsplitting roar. Her brain was no longer processing sound normally. For the first time that morning, she began to wonder if her brain was in serious trouble (Taylor, 2006).

"What is going on?" she thought. "What is happening in my brain?" (Taylor, 2006, p. 41). If anyone was poised to answer these questions, it was Dr. Taylor herself. A devoted neuroanatomist, she spent her days studying neurons at a laboratory affiliated with Harvard Medical School. Wading in a dreamlike fog, Dr. Taylor managed to shower and put on clothes. Then, just as she began visualizing the journey to work, her right arm fell limp like a dead fish. It was paralyzed. At that moment she knew: "Oh my gosh, I'm having a stroke! I'm having a stroke!" (p. 44). Then: "Wow this is so cool! . . . How many scientists have the opportunity to study their own brain function and mental deterioration from the inside out?" (p. 44).

Dr. Taylor was indeed having a rare form of stroke caused by a defective linkage between blood vessels in the brain. Having a backstage pass to her own stroke was a once-in-a-lifetime learning opportunity for a neuroanatomist, but it was also a serious condition requiring immediate medical attention. Aware of this urgency, Dr. Taylor took a seat by the phone, racking her brain for ideas of how to get help. The usual strategies like calling 911 or knocking on a neighbor's door simply did not cross her mind. As she gazed at the phone keypad, a string of digits materialized in her brain: the phone number of her mother in Indiana. But Dr. Taylor did not want to worry her mom, so she sat and waited, hoping another phone number would come to mind (Taylor, 2006).

Finally, the digits of her work number flickered by. She scrawled them down as fast as she could, but her writing looked like cryptic lines and curves. Fortunately, those lines and curves matched the figures she saw on the phone keypad. Dr. Taylor picked up the receiver and dialed (Taylor, 2006). Her coworker and friend Dr. Stephen Vincent answered immediately, but his words were incomprehensible to Dr. Taylor. "Oh my gosh, he sounds like a golden retriever!" she thought. Mustering all her mental might, she opened her mouth and said, "This is Jill, I need help!" But her own voice sounded like a golden retriever as well (Taylor, 2006, p. 56, 2008). Luckily, Dr. Vincent recognized that the murmurs and cries belonged to his friend Jill, and before long he was driving her to the hospital (Taylor, 2006).

As blood hemorrhaged into Dr. Taylor's brain, she struggled to process sensory information, tap into memories, and use language. As she later reflected: "In the course of four hours, I watched my brain completely deteriorate in its ability to process all information" (Taylor, 2008, 2:05–2:12). The bleeding was limiting her capacity for cognition.

*Cognition.* You've probably heard the word tossed around in conversation, and perhaps you know it has something to do with thinking. But what exactly do we mean by cognition, and where does it figure in the vast landscape of psychology?

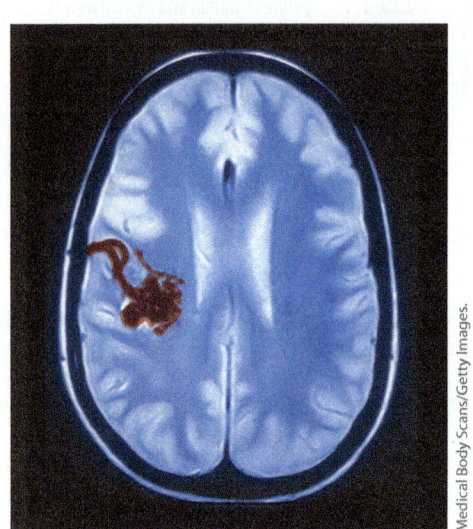

Medical Body Scans/Getty Images.

**A Dangerous Knot**
This MRI scan shows a tangled intersection of arteries and veins called an arteriovenous malformation (AVM), the anatomical abnormality that led to Dr. Taylor's stroke. An AVM is essentially a clump of blood vessels that results when there are no capillaries linking arteries to veins. Sometimes the vessels of an AVM burst under pressure, allowing blood to pool in the brain; this is called a hemorrhagic stroke (National Institute of Neurological Disorders and Stroke, 2019).

*Note:* Story and quotations from *My Stroke of Insight,* by Jill Bolte Taylor, © 2006 by Jill Bolte Taylor. Used by permission of Viking Penguin, a division of Penguin Group (USA) Inc. Unless otherwise stated, quotations attributed to Harry Carson are personal communications.

# Cognition and Thinking

The study of cognition is deeply rooted in the history of psychology. Early psychologists focused on understanding the mysterious workings of the mind, often using **introspection** (examination of one's own conscious activities) in their studies (Graiver, 2019). With the rise of behaviorism in the 1930s, the field broadened and some psychologists redirected their studies toward the exploration of observable behaviors. Then, in the 1950s, researchers began using new technologies and theoretical approaches to probe the mind. Psychology experienced what has been called a *cognitive revolution,* or *cognitive turn,* as researchers began to develop "new methods, approaches, and frameworks to study 'mental' processes in a strictly empirical fashion" (Braat et al., 2020, p. 255). Research on thinking and other aspects of cognition has flourished ever since.

**LO 1** Define cognition and explain how it relates to thinking.

**Cognition** is the mental activity associated with obtaining, converting, and using knowledge. But how is this different from *thinking?* Thinking is a specific type of cognition that requires us to "go beyond" or manipulate information to reach a goal. **Thinking** involves transforming information to make a decision, reach a solution, or form a belief (Farmer & Matlin, 2019). This activity is not just "in your head." As some scholars point out, thinking may be influenced by an interaction of processes associated with perception, the body, and the surrounding environment (Barsalou, 2020). To summarize, cognition is a broad term that describes mental activity, and **thinking** is a subset of cognition. Dr. Taylor was clearly experiencing significant impairments in both cognition and thinking on the morning of her stroke.

**THE HOSPITAL**   At Mount Auburn Hospital, Dr. Taylor had a computerized axial tomography (CAT) scan, which revealed a giant hemorrhage in the left side of her brain. "My left hemisphere was swimming in a pool of blood and my entire brain was swollen in response to the trauma," she recalls (Taylor, 2006, p. 68). Dr. Taylor was rushed by ambulance to Massachusetts General Hospital, which has a neurological intensive care unit.

The following day, Dr. Taylor was told that her mother, who went by the name of "G.G.," was on her way. She found the news perplexing (Taylor, 2006). What on Earth was a *mother,* and who or what was a *G.G.?* "Initially, I didn't understand the significance of G.G.—as I had lost the *concept* of what a mother was," she writes (p. 88). When G.G. arrived, she walked over to her daughter's bed and climbed in alongside her. As Dr. Taylor recalls, "She immediately wrapped me up in her arms and I melted into the familiarity of her snuggle" (p. 90).

# Can You Grasp This Concept?

**LO 2** Demonstrate an understanding of concepts and how they are organized.

Although the touch of G.G. felt familiar, the *concept* of her had slipped away, at least temporarily. What exactly is a concept? We can define **concepts** as mental representations of categories. These categories include objects, situations, and ideas that belong together based on their central features (characteristics). The concept of *superhero,* for example, includes a variety of recognizable characteristics, such as supernatural powers, bravery, and a strong desire to protect the innocent. Concepts are a central ingredient of cognitive activity, playing an important role in memory, learning, and language (Bowman & Zeithamova, 2020; Bruett et al., 2020; Yee, 2019).

**CONNECTIONS**

In **Chapter 1,** we described how Wundt used introspection to examine psychological responses to stimuli. Titchener also used introspection—to explore the structure and most basic elements of the mind. These early psychologists paved the way for cognitive psychology, the study of mental processes, and cognitive neuroscience, the study of biological activities underlying mental processes.

**CONNECTIONS**

In **Chapters 0** and **1,** we discussed critical thinking, which drives the cycle of scientific exploration. The process involves weighing and synthesizing evidence—thinking clearly, rationally, and with an open mind. Here, we explore thinking more broadly.

**cognition** The mental activity associated with obtaining, converting, and using knowledge.

**thinking** Mental activity associated with coming to a decision, reaching a solution, or forming a belief.

**concepts** Mental representations of categories of objects, situations, and ideas that belong together based on their central features or characteristics.

### Cool Clouds

You may not know the scientific names of these clouds: cumulus (left), altocumulus (center), and cirrus (right). However, you immediately know they are clouds because you have developed a "cloud" concept, which specifies the defining features of these water and ice formations that float in the sky.

Without concepts, we would have a hard time communicating and organizing our thoughts. For example, we all know what a *cloud* is. But if the concept *cloud* did not exist, we would have to describe many of the characteristics we associate with clouds whenever one comes up in conversation: "I see a white mass in the sky—you know, a collection of frozen or liquid water particles floating in the atmosphere?" Thanks to our *cloud* concept, we can simply use the word "cloud" as shorthand ("There is a cloud in the sky"). Even if you encounter a cloud that doesn't look typical (for example, a cirrus cloud, which looks more like white streaks than balls of fluff), you still know it's a cloud. Your cloud concept may be slightly different from that of the next person, but it is useful nevertheless. Concepts allow us to organize and synthesize information, and to draw conclusions about specific objects, situations, and ideas that we have never encountered before (Bruett et al., 2020; Yee & Thompson-Schill, 2016). Imagine how exhausting thinking and talking would be if we did not have concepts to fall back on.

**ORGANIZING FURNITURE?**   One way to understand concepts is to consider how they can be organized in *hierarchies,* or rankings. Generally, psychologists use a three-level concept hierarchy to categorize information. At the top of the hierarchy are *superordinate* concepts. This is the broadest category, encompassing all objects belonging to a concept. In INFOGRAPHIC **7.1** on the next page, we see the superordinate concept of furniture, a broad group that includes everything from couches to nightstands, at the top of the hierarchy. If we limit our focus to couches only, we are looking at the *midlevel* or basic level of the hierarchy. Narrowing our focus further brings us to the *subordinate level,* which includes specific types or instances of couches, such as a loveseat, a La-Z-Boy, or that family couch with crumbs between the cushions.

We typically use the midlevel category to identify objects in our everyday experience ("That's a nice couch"). Most children learn the midlevel concepts first, followed by the superordinate and subordinate concepts (Mandler, 2008; Rosch et al., 1976). Although a child might grasp the meaning of *couch,* they may not understand *furniture* (the superordinate level) or *chaise lounge* (the subordinate level). Children become familiar with concepts like "luck" and "happiness" early in life, but it can take many years for them to understand the complexities of these ideas (Woolley & Kelley, 2020; Yang et al., 2021).

Relearning concept hierarchies was a formidable task for Dr. Taylor, because so many of their layers had been washed away by the hemorrhage. With hard work, optimism, and the help of G.G., she slowly reconstructed concepts as diverse as *alphabet letters* and *tuna salad.* Using children's books, G.G. helped her daughter retrain her brain to read, and by putting together puzzles, Dr. Taylor was able to re-create concepts such as *right side up* and *edge* (Taylor, 2006).

**LO 3**   Differentiate between natural concepts and formal concepts.

**LOGICAL OR PERSONAL?**   Concepts can be divided into two major categories: *natural* and *formal.* **Natural concepts** are defined by general characteristics and are acquired during the course of our daily lives (Rosch, 1973; Yee & Thompson-Schill, 2016).

### Forest Bathing?

If you were born in Japan, you may be familiar with the concept of *shinrin-yoku,* which means to bathe in the relaxing environment of a forest, experiencing all its sensory stimuli (Li, 2018). But this natural concept may not be familiar if you were raised in the United States. Concept formation is shaped by culture and individual experiences.

**natural concepts** The mental representations of categories developed through everyday experiences.

Examples we have already discussed include *furniture* and *superhero*. Like all natural concepts, these are mental representations of categories formed through each person's unique experience and culture. Your concept of superhero, for example, is likely based on stories you've heard, books you've read, and movies you've seen. There are no universal or fixed rules for what constitutes a superhero, as they are "constantly changing and are inextricably linked to their contexts" (Yee & Thompson-Schill, 2016, p. 1015). Identifying objects that fall into natural concept categories is difficult because their boundaries are imprecise and hard to define. They don't have rigid rules for identification (Hampton, 1998).

**Formal concepts,** on the other hand, are based on rigid and logical rules (or "features" of a concept). When children learn that 5 is an odd number because, like all other odd numbers, it cannot be divided evenly by 2 without a remainder, they are developing a simple formal concept. An object, idea, or situation must explicitly adhere to strict criteria in order to meet the definition of a particular formal concept. Science uses formal concepts to develop laws, theorems, and rules.

In Chapter 1, we introduced operational definitions, which specify the precise manner in which variables are defined and measured. Creating operational definitions for formal concepts is relatively straightforward, because they are already defined by rigid and logical rules. Natural concepts are more challenging, as experts do not always agree on how to define or measure them. Sometimes psychologists create operational definitions with the help of *prototypes* (Luo et al., 2020).

**PROTOTYPES—THE BEST EXAMPLES?**   **Prototypes** are the ideal or most representative examples of natural concepts (Mervis & Rosch, 1981). A prototype is the image or definition that quickly comes to mind when you consider a concept. If asked to give an example of a fruit, you would most likely say apple or orange—and *not* rambutan, unless you happen to be from Indonesia, where this sweet fruit is eaten regularly. Infographic 7.1 presents a list of fruits organized from the most frequently suggested prototype (orange) to the least frequently suggested prototype (olive) among a group of American college students (Rosch & Mervis, 1975).

Prototypes help us identify objects and ideas as members of a concept. This process is much easier when the items presented closely resemble our prototypes. If shown an image of a papaya, many people in the United States would take longer to identify it as belonging to the fruit category than if they were shown an image of a peach (which is more similar to the common prototypes of apples and oranges). It would likely take them even longer to identify a durian or rambutan, fruits that are relatively unusual in our part of the world. Now let's consider the concept of *hero* (scaling back from superheroes), the subject of much research over the years. The natural concept of hero can be defined by its "most prototypical features," including bravery, moral integrity, conviction, self-sacrifice, honesty, altruism, and determination (Kinsella et al., 2015).

## Put Your Heads Together

Research suggests that we form prototypes of people with certain illnesses (Houlihan, 2019). For example, when we think of a person with type 2 diabetes, certain characteristics may automatically come to mind. In your group, discuss **A)** how "patient prototypes" might affect individuals who have medical conditions, and **B)** how these prototypes could influence the behavior of health care providers.

We now know that the brain organizes information into meaningful categories, or concepts. But how is that information represented inside our heads, especially for concepts related to people, places, and things that aren't present? With the help of *mental imagery,* we can imagine how they look, sound, smell, taste, and feel.

**Unfamiliar Fruits**
If we asked you to classify a durian (top) or a rambutan (bottom), you might pause before saying the word "fruit"! This is because durians and rambutans do not closely resemble our typical fruit prototypes, apples and oranges. If we showed you a peach, however, your response might be faster because peaches are more similar to apples and oranges.

**formal concepts** The mental representations of categories that are created through rigid and logical rules, or features.

**prototype** The ideal or most representative example of a natural concept; helps us categorize or identify specific members of a concept.

# Concepts and Prototypes

*Concepts* are used to organize information in a manner that helps us understand things even when we are encountering them for the first time. *Formal concepts*, like "circle," allow us to categorize objects and ideas in a very precise way—something either meets the criteria to be included in that category, or it doesn't. *Natural concepts* develop as a result of our everyday encounters, and vary according to our culture and individual experiences. We tend to use *prototypes*, ideal representations with features we associate most with a category, to identify natural concepts.

## formal
### CONCEPT
Defined by rigid, precise rules

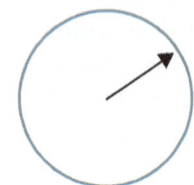

*A circle is a two-dimensional shape in which all points are the same distance from its center.*

## natural
### CONCEPT
Defined by general characteristics established through everyday encounters

*A couch is a large piece of furniture used for sitting.*

Concepts can be organized into **HIERARCHIES**

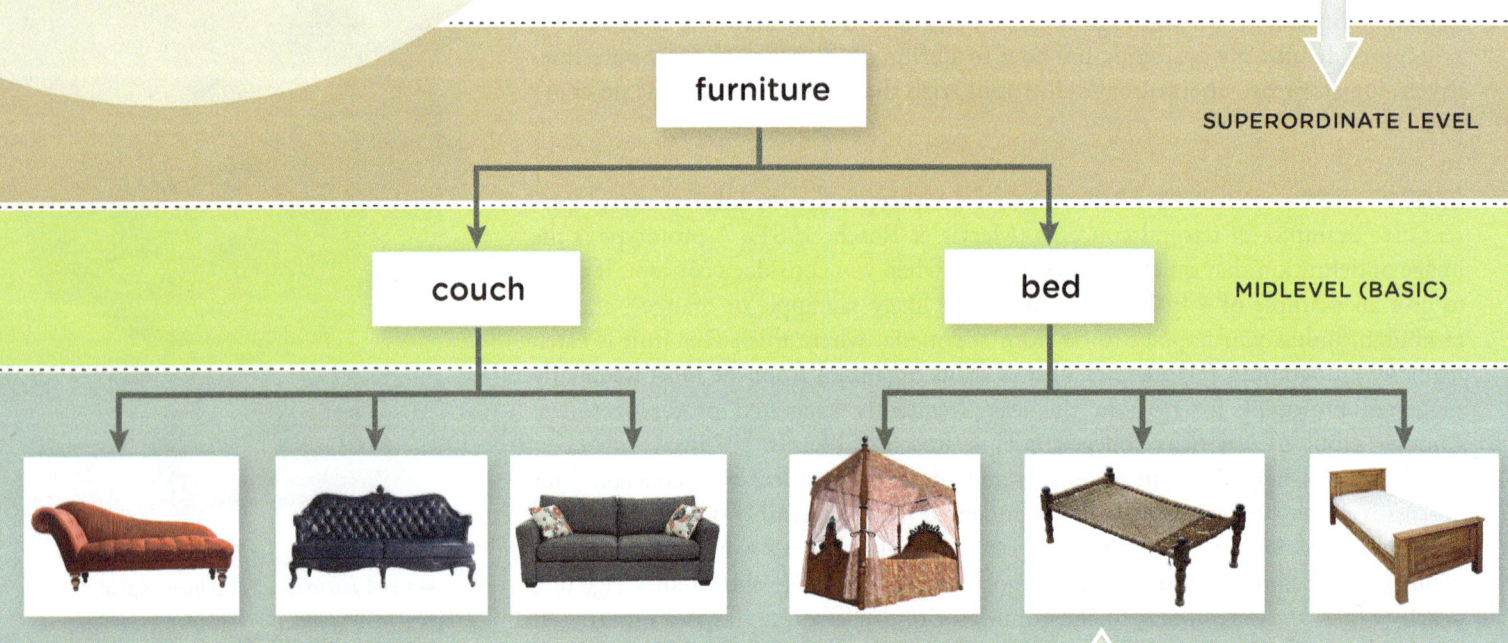

**furniture** — SUPERORDINATE LEVEL

**couch** | **bed** — MIDLEVEL (BASIC)

SUBORDINATE LEVEL

**Did you think of this?** Maybe not. But if you're from India, the traditional charpai may be your prototype—the first image that comes to mind when someone says "bed." What comes to mind when you think of the concept "fruit"? Researchers studying the development of categories organized a group of items from the most prototypical to the least prototypical (Rosch & Mervis, 1975). How long would it take you to think of an olive?

most prototypical

least prototypical

orange · apple · banana · strawberry · pineapple · lemon · date · coconut · tomato · olive

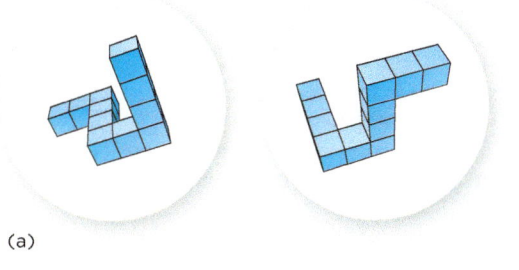

(a)

(b)

## FIGURE 7.1
### Manipulating Mental Images
Can you tell which object pair is congruent? In order to determine this, you must hold images of these figures in your mind and mentally manipulate them. (The answer appears below.*) Generally speaking, males tend to outperform females in mental rotation tasks, and this disparity may become apparent as early as infancy. Information from Johnson and Moore, 2020.

## Picture This

Where is your phone right now? Did a picture of your beloved mobile device suddenly materialize in your "mind's eye"? If so, you have just created a *mental image*. Whether you're wondering where your phone is or daydreaming about celebrities, your brain is constantly whipping up vivid pictures. This cognitive activity often involves manipulating objects in three dimensions.

Let's consider what happens when we first examine a new object. Typically, we hold the object in our hands (assuming it's not too heavy) and rotate it to get a better view. If the object is too large to hold, we often walk around it to see how it looks from various angles. Do we mentally behave this way as well? To answer this question, researchers have spent a great deal of time studying mental imagery and, specifically, mental rotation tasks.

**IMAGINING OBJECTS**   In one of the earliest studies on this topic, researchers had eight participants look at 1,600 pairs of object drawings like those displayed in **FIGURE 7.1** and then asked them to mentally rotate one of the objects in the pair to determine if they were identical. The amount of time it took participants to rotate the object (their reaction time) depended on the degree of difference between the orientations of the two objects. The greater the rotation, the longer it took participants to decide if the objects were identical (Shepard & Metzler, 1971). In the last 50 years, research has indicated that "cognitive processes involved with mental rotation are analogous to rotating actual objects physically" (Stieff et al., 2018, p. 1161). In fact, imagery and perception appear to share many of the same neural mechanisms (Ganis et al., 2004; Lisman, 2015). Neurons often display similar patterns of activity when a person imagines something or sees it in real life (Lisman, 2015).

The ability to mentally rotate objects can be extremely useful. Remember the last time you tried to fit a large piece of furniture through a doorway or cram a dirty bowl into an overcrowded dishwasher? In each case, you probably relied on some type of mental rotation in planning how to maneuver these objects. Teachers use mental rotation activities to help students understand three-dimensional structures (Chamberlain et al., 2019; Stieff et al., 2018). In organic chemistry, for example, students learn by manipulating concrete and virtual models of molecules. This makes it possible to "internalize a mental model of these transformations," which helps them use more accurate mental rotation when the models are not physically present (Stull & Hegarty, 2016, p. 521). These types of hands-on activities are also good for younger children, who generally benefit more from in-person (as opposed to online) learning (Pappas, 2020).

For an additional example of research on mental imagery, see **FIGURE 7.2.** And take note: Imagery is not always visual. Have you ever imagined the smell of freshly baked banana bread? Or, perhaps you have "heard" a song in your head. We use all types of sensory experiences to construct imagery in our minds.

*Answer: a

## FIGURE 7.2
### Scanning Mental Images
In a study on mental imagery, participants were instructed to study a map of a small fictional island. They closed their eyes and imagined the map, first picturing one object (the hut) and then scanning across their mental image until they "arrived" at a second object (the rock). As with the scanning of real objects, it takes longer to "find" objects on a mental image when they are far apart. Information from Kosslyn, Ball, and Reiser (1978).

## SHOW WHAT YOU KNOW

1. _____ is the mental activity associated with obtaining, converting, and using knowledge.

2. If you were to define the _____ of *hero*, you might include characteristics such as bravery, moral integrity, self-sacrifice, honesty, and determination.
   - **A.** cognition
   - **B.** concept
   - **C.** hierarchy
   - **D.** mental imagery

3. Your instructor explains that the pitch of a sound is defined by the frequency of the sound wave. They are describing a _____, which is based on rigid rules or features.
   - **A.** prototype
   - **B.** natural concept
   - **C.** formal concept
   - **D.** cognition

 CHECK YOUR ANSWERS AT THE BACK OF THE BOOK.

# Problem Solving and Decision Making

**THE BIG DILEMMA**    On Day 3 at the hospital, a team of doctors arrived at Dr. Taylor's bedside to discuss the possibility of performing surgery. One of the doctors informed Dr. Taylor that there was a blood clot as big as a "golf ball" on the left side of her brain. Both the clot and the remainder of the blood vessel malformation needed to be extracted; otherwise, she risked suffering another stroke (Taylor, 2006). But brain surgery carries its own set of risks. Dr. Taylor had a very big *problem* on her hands, and a very important *decision* to make: Would she undergo the operation?

## What's the Problem?

Have you ever considered the many problems you encounter and solve every day? Problems crop up when something gets in the way of a goal, like a computer crashing when you are racing to finish a project. They range from mundane (*the vending machine stole my dollar*) to potentially overwhelming (*I have a life-threatening brain bleed*). **Problem solving** refers to the variety of approaches we can use to achieve our goals.

One early model suggests that problem solving proceeds from an initial state (the situation at the start of a problem) to a goal state (the situation when the problem is solved; Farmer & Matlin, 2019; Newell et al., 1958). How might this model apply to Dr. Taylor? Her *initial state* included a massive blood clot and a troublesome clump of vessels in her left hemisphere. The *goal state* was maximizing her health, both physically and cognitively.

A crucial component of problem solving is recognizing obstacles that block the paths to a solution (Farmer & Matlin, 2019). Think about a problem you want to solve and identify the initial state, the goal state, and the obstacles in your way. If your initial state is unfinished homework and your goal state is timely completion, the obstacles might include competing responsibilities like having to go to work, or something more internal like sleepiness.

## How Do We Solve It?

The first step in problem solving is understanding the problem (see **INFOGRAPHIC 7.2** on page 259). If you can't identify or label a problem, then solving it is going to be difficult. Once you grasp the problem, you must choose one of many available approaches or strategies to tackle it. Which strategy you settle on—and the speed, accuracy, and success of your solution—will depend on many factors, including your reservoir of knowledge and the amount of time you spend assessing the problem (Ericsson, 2003; Goldstein, 2011). Let's look at some strategies.

**problem solving** The variety of approaches that can be used to achieve a goal.

**LO 4** Explain how trial and error and algorithms can be used to solve problems.

**TRIAL AND ERROR**    One common approach to problem solving is **trial and error,** the process of finding a solution through a series of attempts. Mistakes are likely, but you can simply eliminate options that don't work. Let's say you have a HUGE set of keys, but you don't know which one, if any, fits the lock you are trying to open. Using trial and error, you would try the keys, one by one, until you find the right one (assuming the correct key is on the ring). But this approach is only useful in certain circumstances and should be avoided when the stakes are high. Imagine if Dr. Taylor's physicians had used trial and error to choose the procedure she needed. *Let's try this surgery first. If it doesn't work, we'll try a different one next week, and then another the following week.* Trial and error is also not recommended for problems with too many possible solutions. If you have 50 keys, you probably don't want to spend your time trying every single one of them. Besides, there is no guarantee you will arrive at a solution.

**ALGORITHMS**    If you're looking for a problem-solving approach that is more of a sure thing, an *algorithm* is probably your best bet. **Algorithms** (AL-guh-rith-umz) use formulas or sets of rules to solve problems. Unlike trial and error, algorithms ensure a solution, as long as you choose the right one and follow all its steps. Have you ever assembled furniture using a manual, followed the instructions on a food package, or installed software with a series of drags and clicks? If so, you were using an algorithm. Sometimes the steps of an algorithm are not written; you just have to remember them. Suppose you need to calculate a 20% tip. Here's an algorithm that can help: Take the total amount of your bill, move the decimal to the left one space, and multiply by 2. Voilà: You've just calculated 20% of the bill.

**LO 5** Explain how heuristics help us solve problems.

**HEURISTICS**    When it comes to solving everyday problems, algorithms may be impractical, time-consuming, or simply unavailable. In these cases, we may turn to **heuristics** (hyoo-RISS-tiks). A heuristic is a problem-solving shortcut that employs a "rule of thumb," guideline, or strategy for finding a solution. These heuristics do not always work, but they help us identify and evaluate possible solutions to our problems. Suppose you find yourself in the midst of a thunderstorm. To determine how far you are from lightning, a good rule of thumb is to count the number of seconds between the burst of lightning and the sound of thunder, then divide by 5. This will tell you the approximate number of miles between you and the lightning bolt (Palermo, 2013). But unlike algorithms, which use formulas and sets of rules, there is no guarantee a heuristic will yield a correct solution.

The advantage of heuristics is that they help shrink the number of possible solutions to a size that is manageable. Once that is accomplished, trial and error may be useful for identifying the best solution. Suppose a hacker is trying to break into an online bank account with Wells Fargo. They use a heuristic that combines a commonly used password (123456, password, football) and something from the domain itself (WF), producing passwords such as 123456WF, passwordWF, and footballWF. From there, the hacker uses trial and error to break into the account.

## Put Your Heads Together

You are running late for an appointment, and traffic is really bad. You need to find the fastest route to your destination. With your group, solve this problem using the following approaches: **A)** trial and error, **B)** an algorithm, and **C)** heuristics. **D)** Decide which approach would work best in this situation.

**64,000 Combos**
Forgot your lock combination? Trying to figure it out by trial and error is not an effective strategy, as there are 64,000 possible solutions. Better buy a new lock.

**trial and error** An approach to problem solving that involves finding a solution through a series of attempts and eliminating those that do not work.

**algorithm** An approach to problem solving using a formula or set of rules that, if followed, ensures a solution.

**heuristics** Problem-solving shortcuts that incorporate a rule of thumb, guideline, or strategy.

**I Want a Banana**

In a classic study, Gestalt psychologist Wolfgang Köhler provided chimpanzees with some out-of-reach bananas and materials that could potentially be used to fetch them. Resourceful chimps they were, building towers of crates and poking at the fruit with sticks. Rather than using trial and error to solve the problem, they seemed to rely on intelligence and insight. Research from Köhler, 1925.

**CONNECTIONS**

In **Chapter 3,** we described perceptual set, which is the tendency to perceive stimuli in a specific manner based on past experiences and expectations. With functional fixedness, we can only imagine using objects in their usual way.

**Think Outside the Box**

Who knew that money can be hidden in an empty lip balm tube, and that a cell phone camera could be used as a mirror? Sometimes it's hard to imagine using things for unconventional purposes. Our resistance to using familiar objects in new ways is known as functional fixedness, and it can get in the way of problem solving.

**insight** An understanding or solution that occurs in a sudden stroke of clarity (the "aha!" feeling).

**functional fixedness** A barrier to problem solving that occurs when familiar objects can only be imagined to function in their usual way.

**INSIGHT** Problems can also be solved through **insight,** an understanding that occurs in a sudden stroke of clarity (that oh-so-satisfying "aha!" or "eureka!" moment). Insight can stem from experience solving previous problems, or it can be totally new. Often, insight comes as a pleasant surprise because we are not aware of the mental "work" we did to achieve it. Many of the products and services you use every day were conceived in a sudden flash of insight by a scientist or entrepreneur. Have you heard of the furniture company IKEA? The founder of IKEA reportedly got his idea for selling "flat-packed" furniture while watching one of his employees take the legs off a table so it could be moved more easily (Wilson, 2018). Were it not for this lightbulb moment, IKEA might not be the multibillion-dollar company it is today.

Sometimes insight happens so suddenly that we find ourselves wondering, *Why did it take me so long to figure that out? The answer seems so obvious now.* Without our conscious awareness, the mind is busy reorganizing the way the problem is represented, and this allows us suddenly and inexplicably to see things in a new light (Sio & Ormerod, 2009). A unique pattern of neural activity appears to accompany insight (as opposed to problem-solving without the aha! experience; Becker et al., 2020b). Immediately preceding a moment of insight, we see increased activation in the frontal and temporal lobes (Kounios & Beeman, 2009). Flashes of insight are also accompanied by activity in dopamine "reward networks" beneath the cortex, which might help explain why these experiences are so satisfying (Tik et al., 2018).

When faced with a tricky problem, sometimes the best thing to do is step away and allow your brain to work behind the scenes; the solution may pop into your head unexpectedly (Sio & Ormerod, 2009). Evidence also suggests that fatigue, moderate alcohol consumption, and letting go of complex problem-solving approaches can potentially increase "insight problem solving" (DeCaro et al., 2016).

## We've Hit a Roadblock

With the capacity for insight, humans can be masterful problem solvers. Still, barriers do arise (Infographic 7.2). One such barrier is **functional fixedness,** which occurs when we can only imagine using familiar objects in their **usual way**. This *fixation* can stop us from finding new, creative uses for objects. Suppose the hem of your pants catches on something and tears. A roll of tape and a stapler are on your desk, and both could be used to fix your wardrobe malfunction. But because of functional fixedness, you only view these items in their usual capacities. Functional fixedness may be less apparent when people flip into "survival mode." When the mind is focused on meeting basic needs (finding food and avoiding predators in unfamiliar territory), it may be easier to "think outside the box" and find unconventional uses for things in the environment (Kroneisen et al., 2021). Children have less trouble with functional

Coco Ballantyne.

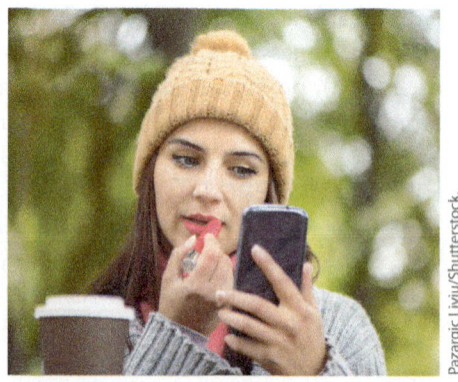

Pazargic Liviu/Shutterstock.

# Problem Solving

When you're trying to solve a problem, it helps to identify an initial state and a goal state (Newell et al., 1958). The strategy you choose and your ability to develop a solution will depend on many factors, including your reservoir of knowledge and the amount of time you spend assessing the problem (Ericsson, 2003; Goldstein, 2011). Sometimes, obstacles derive from the problem itself—for example, you must register for classes by a certain date. Other times, the barriers exist in your mind, preventing you from identifying different approaches.

## Understand the Problem

**IDENTIFY *INITIAL STATE*:**
What do you know about the problem situation? What is the *goal state*?

PROBLEM:

*I need to register for classes, but I don't know what to take.*

*My major has requirements. Not every class is offered this semester. Some classes have prerequisites.*

(obstacles)

## Choose an Approach

**TRIAL AND ERROR:** Try every option.
**ALGORITHMS:** Follow step-by-step procedure to guaranteed solution.
**HEURISTICS:** Use general strategies that provide shortcuts.

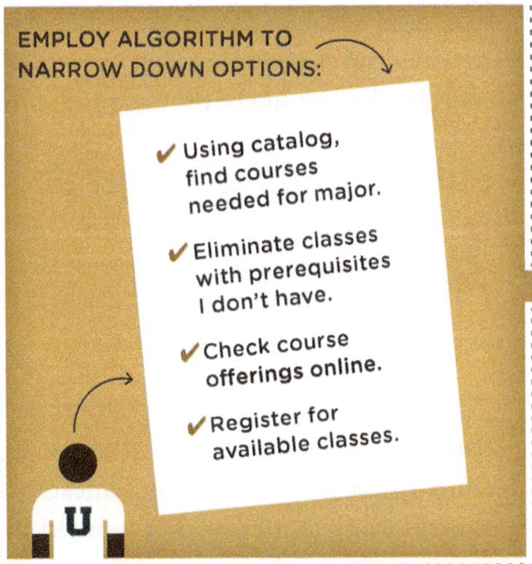

EMPLOY ALGORITHM TO NARROW DOWN OPTIONS:

✓ Using catalog, find courses needed for major.

✓ Eliminate classes with prerequisites I don't have.

✓ Check course offerings online.

✓ Register for available classes.

## Evaluate

**PROBLEM SOLVED?**
If not, try again.

*No, I can't take Biology. It's only offered at 4:30pm, when I have to be at work.*

## Barriers to Problem Solving

Being stuck in a certain way of thinking about a problem can limit what we see as available approaches. For example, our student registering for classes may assume that "classes" must be in-person with an instructor on campus. This assumption prevents the student from investigating more flexible online classes, hybrid classes, or classes that could be transferred from another college.

Sticking with our usual solution strategies is called a *mental set*. To see if you can overcome your mental set, try solving this problem:

Without lifting your pencil, can you connect all nine dots using only four straight lines and without crossing any dot more than once? *(Solution on page 260.)*

*Functional fixedness* is another barrier in which we can only imagine using familiar objects in their usual way. Say you need to tie two ropes together, but you can't reach them both at the same time. The only tool you have is a small shovel. Will functional fixedness keep you from solving this problem? *(Solution on page 260.)*

## FIGURE 7.3

**(A) Solution to the Dot Problem in Infographic 7.2**

Did your mental set cause you to assume the square implied boundaries? If so, it may not have occurred to you that lines could be drawn extending outside the square.

**(B) Solution to the Two-Rope Problem in Infographic 7.2**

Using a shovel to create a pendulum will allow you to swing the second rope. When it swings near you, you can grab it and hold both ropes at the same time. People get stuck on this problem because they can't think of alternative ways to use the shovel (functional fixedness).

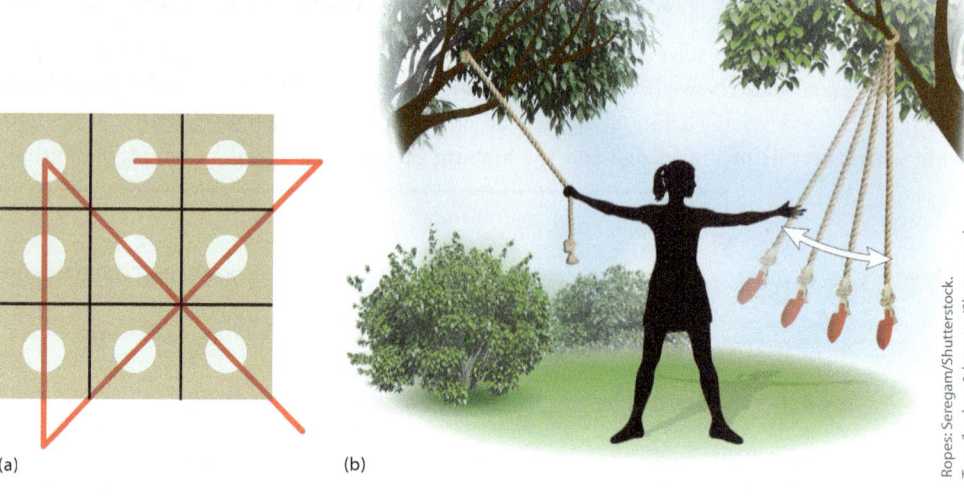

(a)                    (b)

Ropes: Seregam/Shutterstock. Trees/bushes: 3dmentor/Shutterstock.

fixedness because they have not become accustomed to using common objects in specified ways (German & Defeyter, 2000). Yet, the more they observe others using objects, the less likely they are to be innovative.

## Put Your Heads Together

In your group, **A)** list the conventional uses of paper clips and pencils and then **B)** brainstorm creative uses for them. **C)** Discuss the ways that functional fixedness has interfered with your ability to solve problems in the past. **D)** What are other examples of familiar objects that can be used in unconventional ways?

*Mental sets* are another barrier to problem solving. People tend to fall back on strategies they have always used—even if they don't work so well. For example, students often start their first semester of college believing they can succeed in their courses using strategies that worked in high school. But these old methods are often incompatible with the requirements and expectations of college. High school students might get away with finishing assignments during class, but college students? No way! Mental sets can prevent us from seeing other solutions—like starting on assignments as soon as they are given.

Emotional barriers can also get in the way of problem solving. If you are trying to figure out how to fix a dripping faucet and someone is peering over your shoulder saying, "Hurry up! What's taking you so long?," you may feel rushed, anxious, and annoyed. These negative emotions affect your ability to think clearly and creatively. Positive emotions, on the other hand, are thought to promote a "flexible" way of thinking, one that enables quick shifts in attention and strategy in response to changing conditions (Isen, 2008). Keep this in mind next time you help someone solve a problem.

## Decisions, Decisions

**UNDER THE KNIFE**   With the help of her mother's gentle coaxing, Dr. Taylor made the decision to go through with surgery. On the afternoon of December 27, 1996, she awoke in the recovery room with the left side of her head shaved clean and a 9-inch wound in the shape of a horseshoe (Taylor, 2006). Dr. Taylor had survived the operation, and she didn't feel drained and confused, as you might expect: "Upon awakening, I realized that I felt different now. There was brightness in my spirit again and I felt happy" (p. 112).

© My Stroke of Insight, Inc. Photo by Kip May.

**Brightness in Her Spirit**

Dr. Taylor poses with her mother, G.G., who played an instrumental role in the recovery process.

"Say something!" demanded G.G. as she approached her daughter's bedside (Taylor, 2006, p. 113). G.G. needed to know that her daughter could still use language. Surgeons had just spent hours poking around her left hemisphere, home to the language-processing regions of Broca's and Wernicke's areas. The surgeons might have inadvertently damaged one of these key regions, compromising her ability to understand or produce words. Dr. Taylor opened her mouth and responded, and she and G.G. both became teary-eyed. The operation appeared to have gone well; Dr. Taylor, it seemed, had made the right decision (Taylor, 2006).

**LO 6** Describe the process of decision making and how heuristics can lead us astray.

If problem solving refers to the variety of approaches you can use to achieve a goal, how is it different from decision making? **Decision making** is the cognitive process of choosing from these approaches. Thus, problem solving and decision making can occur together.

Often, decision making involves predicting the future: What is the likelihood that Event A will occur under these circumstances? How about Event B? Some situations lend themselves to accurate guesses: If the Weather Channel predicts a 99% chance of thunderstorms today, you can probably assume it's going to rain. Better bring your umbrella. Other times, predicting the future is like rolling dice—you have almost no way of knowing the outcome. Suppose you're looking for a used car on Facebook Marketplace. With no prior knowledge of the cars or their owners (apart from the information they have chosen to post and a few clues you have gathered from your own research), all you can do is hope that you don't end up with a lemon. Choices that hinge on unknowns can be risky, and sometimes we make bad decisions.

## Why Do We Make Bad Decisions?

Predicting the future can be easier with heuristics, but these problem-solving shortcuts can also lead us astray. Israeli American psychologists Daniel Kahneman and Amos Tversky (1937–1996) were among the first to systematically research the errors caused by heuristics. They found that people tend to ignore important information while using these shortcuts (Kahneman & Tversky, 1996). This is particularly true for the *availability heuristic* and the *representativeness heuristic*.

**THE AVAILABILITY HEURISTIC**  With the **availability heuristic,** we predict the probability of something happening in the future based on how easily we can recall a similar type of event from the past. The availability heuristic is essentially a decision-making strategy that relies on memory. If we can easily recall a certain event, then we tend to base our decisions on the assumption that it can happen again. Many factors make an event more available for recall, including its **recency**, frequency, familiarity, and vividness. Let's take a look at each of these qualities.

Imagine you have just seen a series of news reports about a major airplane crash. Every time you look at the news, you learn new details about the tragedy. Because of the *recency* of the reports, you may be vulnerable to the availability heuristic and decide that flying is a dangerous form of travel. Yet, the odds of dying in a plane crash are extremely low—lower than losing your life in a car, motorcycle, or bicycle accident. In fact, you are more likely to die from a dog attack than an airplane accident (National Safety Council, n.d.). But the recency of the plane crash (and the resulting media storm) makes it easier to recall. Thus you are more inclined to overestimate the likelihood of it happening again—and perhaps decide that driving is safer.

The *frequency* of an event also makes it more available for recall. Suppose you work at the campus bookstore, and you need to order software that is compatible

**CONNECTIONS**

In **Chapter 6,** we described the recency effect, the tendency to remember items more accurately when they appear at the end of a list or series. Here, we discuss the tendency to overestimate the probability of an event occurring if a similar event has occurred recently.

**decision making** The cognitive process of choosing from alternatives that might be used to reach a goal.

**availability heuristic** A decision-making strategy that predicts the likelihood of something happening based on how easily a similar type of event from the past can be recalled.

**Back When I Was a Kid . . .**
"I never wore a bicycle helmet when I was growing up, and I turned out okay." People often use this argument to defend certain parenting behaviors, but it is critically flawed, as psychologist Justin Coulson pointed out in *The New York Times*. Personal memories are readily available in our minds, so we may over-rely on them when making decisions. Sometimes this means ignoring "well-substantiated, scientific evidence" (Coulson, 2018, para. 18). This cognitive error is known as the availability heuristic.

**representativeness heuristic** A decision-making strategy that evaluates the degree to which the primary characteristics of a person or situation are similar to our prototype of that kind of person or situation.

**confirmation bias** The tendency to look for evidence that upholds our beliefs and to overlook evidence that runs counter to them.

with students' computers. Before deciding what to buy, you need to figure out the rough proportion of students using Macs and PCs. You may base your estimate on the number of students you have seen using these computers in the halls, classrooms, and library; the frequency of occurrence influences your estimate. If you only focus on the art department, you will probably see a higher representation of Macs. (Macs tend to be popular among art students.) Limiting your observations to this department, or any single department, makes for a sample that is not representative of the entire college. The availability heuristic can only lead you to the correct decision if you consider the right information.

Now consider the *familiarity* of an event. If you and your friends are all avid PC users, you may overestimate the extent to which others use PCs. The more familiar you are with a situation, the more likely you will predict a similar occurrence in the future—and base your decisions on this faulty estimate.

Finally, the *vividness* of an event can make it more available for recall. Try to conjure up an image of someone winning big at a casino. The prizewinner jumps joyfully in the air, hollering at the top of their lungs, with onlookers clapping in approval. This type of dramatic display never occurs when people lose money; the details of a losing bet would be far more difficult to recall. Because the winning image is more vivid, we are more likely to recall it and thus overestimate the likelihood of a win occurring in our own lives (and perhaps decide to spend money at the casino). Memorable imagery leads us to believe that such wins happen all the time, when, in fact, they are very rare. If an event has made a striking impression, you will be more likely to overestimate the probability of it happening again (Tversky & Kahneman, 1982).

**THE REPRESENTATIVENESS HEURISTIC** Often, we make decisions based on our evaluation of a situation or person. With the **representativeness heuristic,** we make quick, effortless judgments about how closely a person or situation fits our preconceived prototype (Lerner et al., 2015; Shah & Oppenheimer, 2008). (As mentioned earlier, a prototype is the ideal or most representative example of a natural concept.)

Let's examine how the representativeness heuristic works in practice. Peter is a middle-aged man. He is conservative, an eloquent speaker, thoughtful, and well read. He lives alone in an apartment in the city. Is Peter a truck driver or a poet? Using the representativeness heuristic, most people would decide that Peter is a poet because his description better matches their prototype of a poet. But this approach fails to consider the *base rate,* or prevalence, of these occupations. There are far more truck drivers than poets, suggesting that Peter is more likely a truck driver. The representativeness heuristic can be useful for decision making, but not when our prototypes ignore base rates and draw on simplistic stereotypes. As you will learn in Chapter 11, stereotypes are the conclusions or inferences we make about people who are different from us, based on their group membership.

**CONFIRMATION BIAS** We can also miss important information through the **confirmation bias,** when we unintentionally look for evidence that upholds our beliefs, and overlook or discount evidence that runs counter to them. For example, suppose you've tried vaping and you really like it, so you look online to research its health effects. One of the sites you come across claims that vaping is relatively safe, and you notice friends on social media are saying it's not as bad as smoking cigarettes. Focusing on this information (and ignoring all evidence that might not be compatible with it), you decide to continue using e-cigarettes. What you fail to recognize is that highly regarded scientific sources are saying that vaping carries significant health risks, including fatal lung disease (Christiani, 2020; Stanbrook & Drazen, 2020). Because of the confirmation bias, we tend to focus on information that supports desired outcomes (Dobbs et al., 2020; Krizan & Windschitl, 2007; Scherer et al., 2012). Confirmation bias is one of the reasons we are vulnerable to misinformation spread through the internet (American Psychological Association, 2018).

## Social Media and Psychology

### CONFIRMATION BIAS AND FAKE NEWS

Did you read the tweet about Joe Biden arranging to have Navy SEALs murdered, or the one about Trump's presidential campaign ordering MAGA hats from China? (Fichera, 2020; Fichera & Spencer, 2020)? These are just a few examples of *fake news,* or "fabricated information that mimics news media content in form but not in organizational process or intent" (Lazer et al., 2018, p. 1094)—in other words, false information that is not produced by established news outlets that use fact-checking, editorial oversight, and other safeguards to ensure accuracy.

**HOW CAN WE FIGHT IT?**

Social media is an excellent environment for breeding and propagating fake news because most any adult can open an account and share information. It also provides a way for people to consume information that reinforces their own belief systems. In a sense, "a Facebook or Twitter newsfeed is just confirmation bias backed with computer power: What you see when you look at the top of the feed is determined algorithmically by what you and your friends like. Any discordant information gets pushed further and further down the queue, creating an insidious echo chamber" (Waldrop, 2017, p. 12633).

How can we combat fake news? Social media companies are trying various strategies to address the problem; for example, Twitter has limited the sharing options for Tweets that contain false information about COVID-19 (Lyons, 2020; Scheufele & Krause, 2019). But we can take action as individuals, too. Be aware of confirmation bias and take steps to minimize its impact. If you see a story that reinforces opinions or beliefs you already have, don't automatically accept it as truth and share it with your friends (Waldrop, 2017). Ask critical questions: Was the content created by a trusted news source? What evidence is provided to support the claims in this report? Does the author have certain political or ideological motivations? Perhaps more importantly, force yourself to consume content that challenges your long-held opinions and beliefs. If we take the time to understand other perspectives, we are able to have more constructive conversations (American Psychological Association, 2018; Waldrop, 2017).

**HINDSIGHT BIAS**    The **hindsight bias,** or "I knew it all along" feeling, leads us to believe that we could have predicted the outcome of an event. It may seem obvious in retrospect, but that doesn't mean we could have foreseen it. Examples of hindsight bias abound in everyday life. Suppose your instructor returns an exam, and you are surprised to learn that you got a certain question wrong. Now that you're staring at the correct answer, it seems so obvious. But if you really knew it all along, why did you give the wrong answer (Tauer, 2009)? Even practicing physicians fall victim to hindsight bias. When doctors hear the details of an autopsy and learn about the cause of death, they often believe they could have easily predicted it (Arkes, 2013). In these scenarios, hindsight bias can get in the way of learning and decision making. How do you learn from your mistakes if you cannot identify gaps in your knowledge (Arkes, 2013; Tauer, 2009)?

**Nothing to Do with Climate Change?**
California's 2020 wildfire season was the worst on record (Krishnakumar & Kannan, 2020). Scientists say the problem is linked to rising temperatures: "Climate change plays an undeniable role in the unprecedented wildfires of recent years" (Miller et al., 2020, para. 4; Union of Concerned Scientists, 2020). Yet, many people continue to believe that wildfires have nothing to do with rising temperatures associated with human-caused climate change, and they consume media that reinforces their view. This is an example of confirmation bias: We tend to look for information that supports our beliefs (and overlook information that contradicts them). JOSH EDELSON/Getty Images.

**hindsight bias** The mistaken belief that an outcome could have been predicted easily; the "I knew it all along" feeling.

## The Problem with the Problem

We have spent a great deal of time discussing factors that impede the decision maker. But in many situations, some aspect of the problem is to blame.

The *framing effect* demonstrates how the presentation or context of a problem can influence our decision making, often in ways beyond our awareness. Consider the following study: Researchers instructed participants to imagine they had purchased a $10 ticket to attend a show, but lost their ticket on the way to the theater. Each participant was then asked whether they would be willing to pay $10 for another ticket. Only 46% of participants indicated that they would spend another $10 for a new ticket. Participants were next instructed to imagine another situation: This time, they planned to buy a $10 ticket to attend a show, but once they got in the ticket line, they suddenly realized they had lost one of their $10 bills. Faced with this second scenario, 88% of the participants were willing to fork over the $10. In each case, the participants considered the idea of spending an additional and unexpected $10, but they tended to make different decisions. The circumstances framing these hypothetical scenarios influenced the decisions made, even though the outcomes would have been identical—a net loss of $10 (Kahneman & Tversky, 1984; Tversky & Kahneman, 1981).

The framing effect also **applies to wording**. One study found that people are more likely to prefer ground beef if it is described as "80% lean," as opposed to "20% fat." Although 80% lean and 20% fat describe the exact same product, these phrases evoke very different responses (Johnson, 1987). Another study demonstrated how the wording of a question can influence people's descriptions of themselves. Researchers prompted college students to describe themselves using one of two questions: "Please take five minutes and write what you *think* about yourself," or "Please take five minutes and write what you *feel* about yourself." The group assigned to the "feel" condition evaluated themselves in a more negative way than the group assigned to the "think" condition. This may be because those in the "feel" condition were focusing on emotions, and the English language has more words to describe negative emotions than positive emotions (Holtgraves, 2015).

Jill Bolte Taylor's story has helped us understand how quickly cognitive functions can deteriorate. But not all changes in cognition and behavior stem from catastrophic events like strokes. Brain injuries may also occur in small increments, accumulating over time. Imagine you spent 21 years playing a game that required slamming your body against 200- to 300-pound men. How would the rapid changes in speed and direction, and the constant banging of your skull, affect the delicate brain inside? Football Hall of Famer Harry Carson is here to tell you.

**CONNECTIONS**

In **Chapter 1,** we presented the survey method, a form of descriptive research that relies on questionnaires and interviews. Here, we see that the wording of questions can influence the way people respond.

## SHOW WHAT YOU KNOW

1. It's the first day of the semester, but you forgot to write down where your psychology class is being held. You decide to stick your head in a random number of rooms until you see the assigned psychology textbook on someone's desk. This problem-solving approach is called:

   **A.** functional fixedness.

   **B.** an algorithm.

   **C.** trial and error.

   **D.** heuristics.

2. A(n) _____ is a problem-solving approach that employs a "rule of thumb."

3. We often predict the probability of an event happening in the future based on how easily we can recall a similar type of event from the past. This is known as the:

   **A.** framing effect.

   **B.** confirmation bias.

   **C.** representativeness heuristic.

   **D.** availability heuristic.

4. A good friend is terrified of flying. How would you use your knowledge of heuristics to make your friend feel less afraid?

CHECK YOUR ANSWERS AT THE BACK OF THE BOOK.

# The Power of Language

**"I SAW STARS"**    Harry Carson was 14 years old when he first stepped onto the football field. It was August in Florence, South Carolina; the air was warm, moist, and steeped in the scent of freshly cut grass. Wearing 20 pounds of football equipment was uncomfortable, but Harry felt proud having it on, especially the imposing shoulder pads and helmet (Carson, 2011).

During that first practice at Wilson High School, the coaches assigned the players to a man-on-man blocking drill. Young Harry was pitted against "Bubble Gum," a bigger, more experienced player. "He must have blocked me three or four times, and with each block I felt like a rag doll being chewed up by a pit bull," Harry recalls in his memoir *Captain for Life* (Carson, 2011, p. 12). Colliding with Bubble Gum was not only painful; it jarred Harry's brain, causing immediate changes in perception. "I was conscious," Harry recalls, "[but] I saw little stars twinkling before my eyes." Like most players of his time, Harry didn't realize that "seeing stars" or momentarily "blacking out" was a sign of concussion, a brain injury that is not fatal but can have life-changing consequences.

After playing football in high school, Harry went on to become a star lineman and team captain at South Carolina State. Then he achieved what many American boys only dream about—he was drafted into the National Football League (NFL). During his 13-year career with the New York Giants, Harry established himself as one of the greatest middle linebackers in the history of professional football. Eventually, he was inducted into the Pro Football Hall of Fame. But becoming a football legend came at a price.

About halfway through his professional career, Harry starting having migraines, unexplained mood swings, and suicidal thoughts. He also had difficulties with language. During media interviews, he sometimes had trouble processing and responding to reporters' questions. Maybe no one else noticed the problem because Harry did a good job filling in the gaps with expressions like "um" and "you know." But he knew something was wrong.

It was not until his retirement from pro football that Harry began to connect his symptoms with the repeated brain trauma he had sustained on the field. In 1990, two years after he left the NFL, a neuropsychologist diagnosed him with *post-concussion syndrome,* a collection of physical and psychological symptoms that linger after a concussion occurs (Mayo Clinic, 2020). "I came to realize that all of this stuff that I was experiencing was a result of the dings, the bell-ringers, the concussions that I sustained as a player," says Harry, who began sharing his story at conferences and in media interviews. "There were people who probably thought I was crazy for even talking about it," he says. "Football players are very proud individuals, and they do not go around talking about being brain damaged."

**Hard-Hitting Legend**
The football career of Harry Carson (#53) spanned 21 years. How many blows to the head do you think he sustained during that time? Using data from a study of collegiate players, which found the number of head impacts per season to be as high as 1,444 (Crisco et al., 2010), we estimate that Harry took as many as 30,000 hits to the head.

*Jonathan Daniel/Getty Images.*

## Chronic Traumatic Encephalopathy (CTE)

In 2005, many years after Harry began raising awareness about sports-related brain injuries, a groundbreaking scientific report came out in the journal *Neurosurgery.* The study, led by pathologist Dr. Bennet Omalu, detailed the extensive brain damage of deceased NFL player Mike Webster (Omalu et al., 2005). It was the first time a retired pro football player had been diagnosed with **chronic traumatic encephalopathy (CTE),** a neurodegenerative disease caused by repeated head trauma. Since then, researchers have studied the brains of many more football players; an analysis led by neuropathologist Dr. Ann McKee found evidence of CTE in 110 out of 111, or 99%, of the NFL players studied (Mez et al., 2017).

**CONNECTIONS**

In **Chapter 6,** we describe the stages and symptoms of CTE and its impact on memory. Here, we explore the history that led to the discovery of this neurodegenerative disease and its effect on cognition.

### "Extreme Case" of CTE

Dr. Anne McKee (left) presents brain images of the late NFL player Aaron Hernandez (right). The advanced case of CTE that can be observed in Hernandez' brain is something "we've never seen . . . in our 468 brains, except for individuals very much older," noted McKee, director of Boston University's Chronic Traumatic Encephalopathy Center (Barlow, 2017, para. 2). Hernandez was only 27 when he committed suicide in prison. Before his death, he was serving time for one murder and had been accused and acquitted of two additional murders (Barlow, 2017). Did his tragic behaviors result from the cumulative brain damage he sustained as a football player?

One of the telltale signs of CTE is abnormal accumulation of *tau,* a protein also implicated in Alzheimer's disease (Falcon et al., 2019). The symptoms of CTE may include anxiety, depression, explosive anger, suicidal tendencies, and a host of cognitive problems (Fesharaki-Zadeh, 2019; McKee et al., 2013; Mez et al., 2017). Advanced cases have been associated with "severe memory loss with dementia" (McKee et al., 2013, p. 59).

The discovery of CTE in professional football players came as no surprise to Harry Carson. In fact, he is relatively confident he suffers from CTE as well: "I don't really worry about it, because I think that, with the information that has already been presented, we all probably have it." The damage Harry sustained cannot be undone, but he doesn't seem bitter or hardened. Instead, he focuses on managing his life in a positive way—eating healthy foods, exercising, and educating others about sports-related brain injuries.

**SEE THE WORDS**    When Harry gets a headache, it often starts on the left side (Kirk & Carson, 2013). Perhaps it's no coincidence that his pain originates in the brain hemisphere where language processing occurs. As you may recall, Harry periodically struggled with media interviews, taking extra time to digest journalists' questions and articulate his responses. These language roadblocks continued popping up when Harry left the NFL and began a career as a sports commentator. "Once football was over, I went into broadcasting," he says, "and that was something that I failed at horribly because I would lose my train of thought live on the air." There are still times that Harry has difficulty expressing thoughts, but he has developed a cognitive strategy for dealing with it: "Sometimes when I am trying to make the points that I want to make . . . I have to visualize each word that I want to use in my brain before I allow it to leave my lips."

## Let's Get Down to Basics

Until something goes wrong, it's easy to take language for granted. Words are so much a part of our daily routines that it's difficult to imagine life without them. How would we conduct Google searches, rant on Twitter, or read this book if we didn't have words? There would be no such thing as the U.S. Constitution or the Bill of Rights. No Bible, Torah, or Qur'an. You wouldn't be able to say, "I love you" or "What are you thinking about?" Language allows us to explicitly convey complex thoughts and feelings. Some might say it is the "window into human nature" (Pinker, 2007, p. 27).

**LO 7** Define language and give examples of its basic elements.

**Language** can be defined as a system for using symbols (words, gestures, and sounds) to think and communicate. These symbols can be spoken, written, and signed. The average English-speaking college student is familiar with around 10,000 to 11,000 word families (groups of related words such as "smile," "smiled," "smiling"; Treffers-Daller & Milton, 2013). What's more, humans are always finding new meanings for old words or inventing new ones. Have you ever heard of a "squib kick," a "pooch punt," or a "flea flicker" (Kostora, 2012)? All these were created to describe kicks and plays in football.

**PHONEMES**   At the core of all spoken words are **phonemes** (FOH-neemz), the units of sound that serve as basic building blocks for all words (INFOGRAPHIC **7.3** on the next page). Examples of English phonemes include the sounds made by the letter *t* in the word "tail" and the letter *s* in "sail." Some letters correspond to more than one phoneme. For example, the letter *i* can represent two clearly different phonemes, as in the words "bit" and "bite."

Infants between 6 and 8 months can recognize all phonemes from all languages, but this ability begins to diminish at about 10 months. At this point, babies show the first signs of being "culture-bound listeners" (Kuhl, 2015, p. 67). That is, they have a harder time distinguishing between phonemes of unfamiliar languages (de Boysson-Bardies et al., 1989; Werker & Tees, 1984). This is why older children and adults have difficulty learning to speak foreign languages without the accent of their birth language.

**MORPHEMES**   Representing the next level of language are **morphemes** (MOR-feemz). Morphemes consist of one or more phonemes, and they bring meaning to a language. For example, the word "unimaginable" has three morphemes: *un, imagine,* and *able.* Each morpheme communicates something. Remove just one, and the word takes on a whole new significance. Clipping off *un,* for example, produces the word "imaginable," which means the exact opposite of "unimaginable."

**GRAMMAR**   **Grammar** refers to the rules associated with both word and sentence structure (Evans & Green, 2006). It tells us how words are made from sounds, how sentences are formed with words, where to place punctuation, and which word tenses to use. It combines syntax and semantics.

**Syntax** refers to the collection of rules dictating where words and phrases should be placed. It guides both word choice and word order, providing consistency in sentence organization (Brandone et al., 2006). We say, "I love you," not "Love you I," because English syntax demands that the words appear in this order. Different languages have different syntaxes. In German, some verbs come at the end of sentences, which is striking to native English speakers learning German.

**Semantics** represents the rules used to bring meaning to words and sentences. Here are two sentences with different word order (syntax), but the same meaning (semantics): "Jane kicked the ball." "The ball was kicked by Jane." Now, here are two sentences with the same syntax, but slightly different semantics: "Some people enjoy cooking, their families, and their dogs." "Some people enjoy cooking their families and their dogs" (Oxford Royale Academy, 2014, para. 3). Semantics also refers to the context in which words appear. Consider the meaning of "snap" based on the context of the following sentences: Can you *snap* your fingers? He got the job done in a *snap*. Don't *snap* at me! Oh, *Snap!*

**PRAGMATICS**   Language is used in social interactions, which are governed by certain norms and expectations. **Pragmatics** are the social rules that help organize this activity. We have to learn how to take turns in a conversation, what gestures to use and when, and how to address people according to social standing (Steiner, 2012; Yule, 1996). When addressing the Queen of Denmark, you would say, "Good day, Your Majesty," but to a friend you might say, "Hey there."

Lifestyle pictures/Alamy.

**Yoda Syntax**
Moments before his death in *Return of the Jedi*, Yoda says to Luke Skywalker, "When gone am I, the last of the Jedi you will be" (Lucasfilm & Marquand, 1983, 43:46). Yoda's syntax is atypical, as most people would order the words like this: "When I am gone, you will be the last Jedi."

**language** A system for using symbols to think and communicate.

**phonemes** The basic building blocks of spoken language.

**morphemes** The fundamental units that bring meaning to language.

**grammar** The rules associated with word and sentence structure.

**syntax** The collection of rules concerning where to place words or phrases.

**semantics** The rules used to bring meaning to words and sentences.

**pragmatics** The social rules that help to organize language.

# The Building Blocks of Language

Language is made up of a collection of units and rules. These build upon each other to help us think and communicate. At the base are phonemes, which combine to make morphemes, the smallest units of language that carry meaning. At the top is displacement, which is the human ability to refer to things that are abstract or hypothetical.

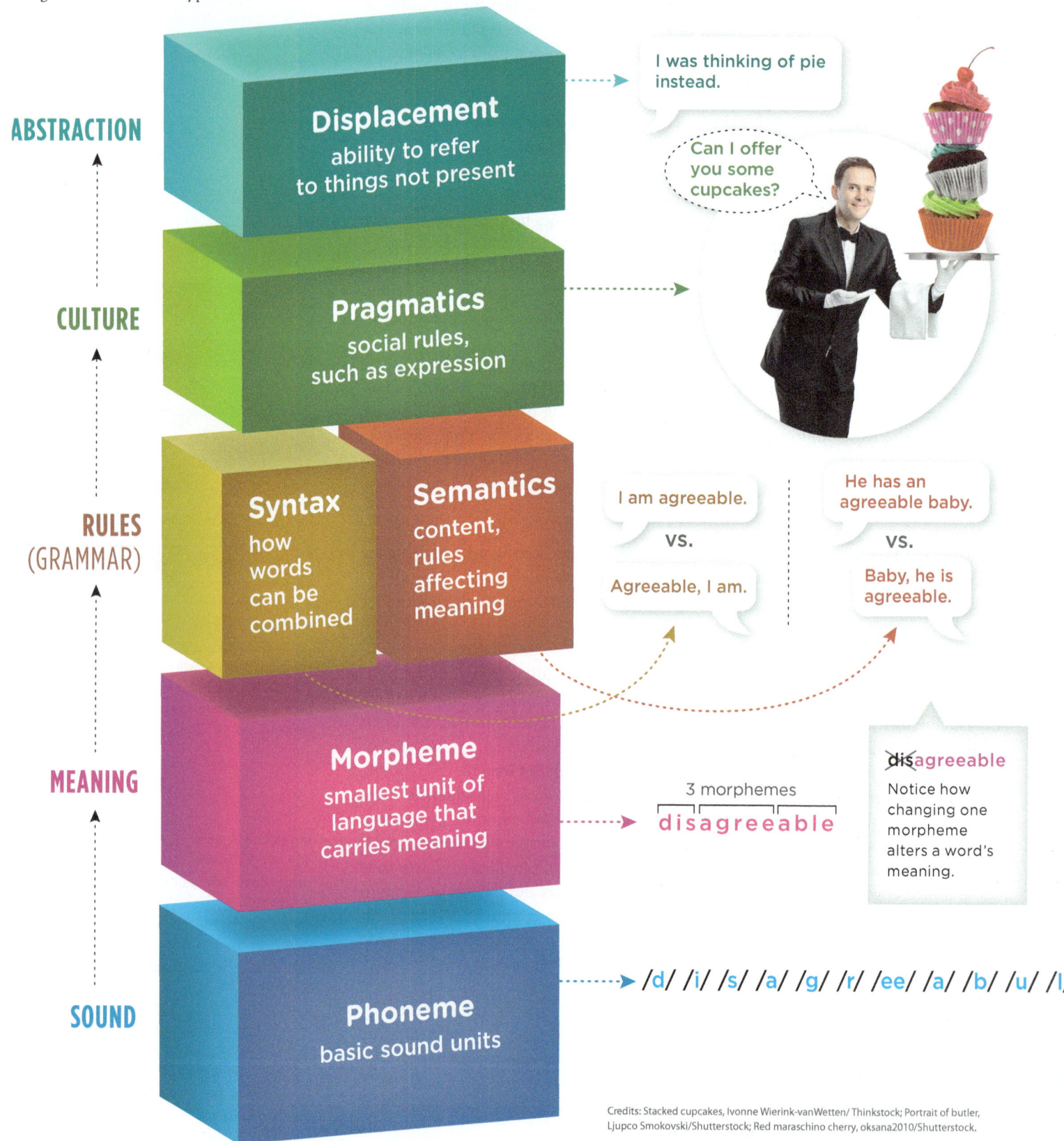

**ABSTRACTION**

**Displacement**
ability to refer
to things not present

I was thinking of pie instead.

Can I offer you some cupcakes?

**CULTURE**

**Pragmatics**
social rules,
such as expression

**RULES (GRAMMAR)**

**Syntax**
how words can be combined

**Semantics**
content, rules affecting meaning

I am agreeable.

vs.

Agreeable, I am.

He has an agreeable baby.

vs.

Baby, he is agreeable.

**MEANING**

**Morpheme**
smallest unit of language that carries meaning

3 morphemes
disagreeable

~~dis~~agreeable
Notice how changing one morpheme alters a word's meaning.

**SOUND**

**Phoneme**
basic sound units

/d/ /i/ /s/ /a/ /g/ /r/ /ee/ /a/ /b/ /u/ /l/

Credits: Stacked cupcakes, Ivonne Wierink-vanWetten/ Thinkstock; Portrait of butler, Ljupco Smokovski/Shutterstock; Red maraschino cherry, oksana2010/Shutterstock.

**IS IT HARDWIRED?**    How do we "know" these rules for language? Learning theorists propose that children learn language just like they learn other behaviors, through processes such as reinforcement and modeling (Bandura, 1977; Skinner, 1957). In contrast, linguist Noam Chomsky suggests that humans are born with inherent language capabilities. Children needn't be taught the basics of language, according to Chomsky (2000); language develops like other organs in the body. Chomsky's position is based on the observation that children possess a much deeper knowledge of language than would be expected if they only learned through experience. This knowledge is not simply the result of hearing and imitating; it is hardwired within the brain. A built-in *language acquisition device* (LAD) accounts for the universality of language development. In fact, researchers have observed this capacity for language across cultures and in nonhearing children (Chomsky, 2000; Petitto & Marentette, 1991).

**IS IT UNIQUE?**    Many scientists argue that language, more than any other human ability, truly sets us apart from other species. Animals have evolved complex systems of communication, but some features of human language appear to be unique. One such feature is *displacement*—the ability to talk and think about things that are not present at the moment. "I wonder if my instructor is going to give a pop quiz today," you might say to a friend. This statement demonstrates displacement, because it refers to a hypothetical event. Displacement allows us to communicate about the future and the past, and to fantasize about things that may or may not exist.

## Thinking What We Say?

**LO 8** Explain how language influences thought.

For many years, psychologists have tried to understand the relationship between language and thought. According to the *linguistic relativity hypothesis* developed by Benjamin Lee Whorf (1897–1941), the language people speak has an impact on their thinking and perception (1956). For example, the Inuit and other Indigenous Peoples of Alaska have many terms that refer to "snow" (in contrast to the single word used in English). This may lead them to perceive and think about snow differently than English speakers. Whorf's hypothesis is not universally accepted, however. Critics suggest that he exaggerated the number of words Indigenous Peoples of Alaska have for "snow" and underestimated the number of words in English (Pullum, 1991).

Although language might not *determine* how we perceive and think about the world, it certainly has an influence (Athanasopoulos et al., 2015; Kersten et al., 2010). Consider how languages such as English and Swedish often use "he" and "his" when gender is unspecified; this use of masculine pronouns often results in people focusing on males when forming mental images (Gastil, 1990; Hegarty & Buechel, 2006; Lindqvist et al., 2019). Perhaps you can predict the potential downside of this tendency. Narrowing the focus to male images inevitably promotes gender bias and stereotyping. In one study, researchers exposed Dutch and German schoolchildren to job titles in plural form (an English example being "firefighters") or pairs of the titles in female and male forms ("fireman" and "firewoman"). Children who were exposed to both male and female forms were more confident about their ability to be successful in traditionally male jobs (Vervecken & Hannover, 2015).

### ▶▶▶ SHOW WHAT YOU KNOW

1. According to the linguistic relativity hypothesis, language has distinct effects on:

   **A.** phonemes.

   **B.** thinking and perception.

   **C.** the language acquisition device.

   **D.** displacement.

2. _____ are the basic building blocks of spoken language.

 CHECK YOUR ANSWERS AT THE BACK OF THE BOOK.

**Play It Smart**

A play diagram illustrates the positions and movements of football players on the field. A defense playbook may contain as many as 300 plays, and members of the defense are expected to learn all of them, according to Harry. Memorizing plays and mentally adjusting when things don't go as planned require a certain level of intelligence.

**"Bird Brains" Are Pretty Intelligent**

Meet the kea, a very clever parrot from the mountain regions of New Zealand. Not only is this bird extremely adept with its beak (it has been known to pry wipers from car windshields); the kea displays evidence of complex decision making. Scientists once thought only humans and great apes could predict future events by observing the relative numbers of items in the environment (for example, knowing that you will get more red jellybeans if you reach into a jar containing 70% red and 30% green jellybeans). But now there is evidence that keas can make these types of predictions, too (Bastos & Taylor, 2020; Morell, 2020).

**intelligence** Innate ability to solve problems, adapt to the environment, and learn from experiences.

**general intelligence (g-factor)** A singular underlying aptitude or intellectual ability that drives capabilities in many areas, including verbal, spatial, and reasoning competencies.

# Intelligence

**INTELLIGENT ATHLETES**   In high school and college, Harry was a defensive lineman, one of the guys who tries to disrupt the opposing team's offense before they can execute their play. When drafted by the Giants, Harry was challenged to learn a new position: middle linebacker. "It was a position that basically, I had to become the leader, the quarterback of the defense," says Harry, who spent many hours taking cognitive tests and meeting with the team psychologist. It was the psychologist's job to determine whether Harry was cognitively fit to play the demanding position of middle linebacker. As history shows, Harry was more than qualified. A fast-thinking problem solver, he proved he could multitask and make sound judgments on the fly. For any given play, he was able to remember what every defensive player was supposed to be doing, and he learned from past experiences, rarely making the same mistake twice. Harry demonstrated a high level of *intelligence*.

## What Is Intelligence?

**LO 9** Distinguish among various theories of intelligence.

Generally speaking, **intelligence** is one's innate ability to solve problems, adapt to the environment, and learn from experiences. Intelligence relates to a broad array of psychological processes, including memory, learning, perception, and language, and how it is defined may depend on the variable being measured.

In the United States, intelligence is often associated with "book smarts." Many of us think "intelligent" people are those who score high on tests measuring academic abilities. But intelligence is more complicated than that—so complicated, in fact, that psychologists have yet to agree on its precise parameters. It is not even clear whether intelligence is a single unified entity, or a collection of capabilities.

We do know that intelligence is, to a certain degree, a cultural construct. So although people in the United States tend to equate intelligence with school smarts, this is not the case everywhere in the world. Children living in a village in Kenya, for example, grow up using herbal medicine to treat parasitic diseases in themselves and others. Identifying illness and developing treatment strategies are a regular part of life. These children would score much higher on intelligence tests relating to practical knowledge than on those assessing vocabulary (Sternberg, 2004). Even within a single culture, the meaning of intelligence changes across time. Intelligence for modern Kenyans may differ from that of their 14th-century ancestors.

As we explore the theories of intelligence, please keep in mind that intelligence does not always go hand in hand with *intelligent behavior*. People can score high on intelligence measures but exhibit poor judgment. Perhaps you know a straight-A student who is somewhat lacking in common sense?

**THE G-FACTOR**   How can we explain differences in intelligence? English psychologist and statistician Charles Spearman (1863–1945) speculated that humans have a **general intelligence** (or **g-factor**). This g-factor is a singular underlying aptitude or intellectual ability that drives capabilities in many areas, including verbal, spatial, and reasoning competencies. Simply stated, the g-factor is the common link.

**MANY TYPES OF INTELLIGENCE?**   American psychologist Howard Gardner suggests that people have *multiple intelligences* (Gardner, 1999, 2011, 2020). He proposed various types of intelligences or "frames of mind": linguistic (verbal),

**TABLE 7.1**  Gardner's Multiple Intelligences

| Intelligences | Core Competencies | Occupational or Avocational Matches |
|---|---|---|
| Linguistic | Verbal abilities, including speech, reading, writing, communication of meaning; aware of sound dynamics and goals of language | Poet, journalist, lawyer, storyteller, public relations professional |
| Logical-Mathematical | Complex math and reasoning abilities; aware of numerical patterns | Scientist, mathematician, accountant, computer analyst, stockbroker |
| Musical | A range of musical abilities including sensitivity to pitch, rhythm, and sound quality, and an understanding of the emotional meaning of music | Composer, musical performer, music critic, music fan |
| Spatial | Spatial cognition abilities; skilled in visual arts, adept in 3-D navigation and mental rotation tasks | Architect, pilot, sculptor, chess master, landscape designer, graphic designer |
| Bodily-Kinesthetic | Body awareness; body control; dexterity; competence with handling objects | Dancer, athlete, craftsperson, surgeon, laboratory worker, fitness instructor |
| Interpersonal | Social perception; interpersonal understanding, such as responding to other's moods, personality characteristics, wishes; competent leadership | Therapist, salesperson, spirtual or religious leader, teacher |
| Intrapersonal | Self-awareness; self-regulation; self-other management; knowledge of own weaknesses, wishes, competencies | Therapist |
| Naturalist | Pattern cognition (classifying objects), understanding living entities, animals, and plant life | Scientist, veterinarian, zoologist, arborist |

Summarized here are Gardner's multiple intelligences, all of which are associated with certain strengths and capabilities. Information from Gardner, 2003, 2020; Gardner and Hatch, 1989; Shearer, 2020; Visser et al., 2006.

logical-mathematical, spatial, bodily-kinesthetic, musical, intrapersonal, interpersonal, and naturalist. Take a look at **TABLE 7.1** and consider how various occupations might be better suited for people with strengths in different intelligences.

According to Gardner (2011), partial evidence for multiple intelligences comes from studying people with brain damage. Some mental capabilities are lost, whereas others remain intact, suggesting that they are actually distinct categories. Further evidence for multiple intelligences (as opposed to just a *g*-factor) comes from observing people with *savant syndrome*. Individuals with savant syndrome have some area of extreme singular ability (calendar calculations, art, mental arithmetic, and so on; Treffert, 2015). The late Kim Peek, for example, was able to simultaneously read two pages of a book—one with each eye—and memorize nearly all the information it contained. Like the movie character he inspired ("Raymond Babbitt" in the film *Rain Man*), Peek had extraordinary intellectual abilities (Brogaard & Marlow, 2012; Treffert, 2015).

**THREE KINDS OF INTELLIGENCE?**   American psychologist Robert Sternberg proposed three kinds of intelligence. Sternberg's (1988) **triarchic theory of intelligence** (trahy-AHR-kik) suggests that humans have varying degrees of analytical, creative, and practical competencies (**FIGURE 7.4**). *Analytic intelligence* refers to our capacity to solve problems; *creative intelligence* represents the knowledge and skills we use to handle new situations; and *practical intelligence* includes our ability to adjust to different environments.

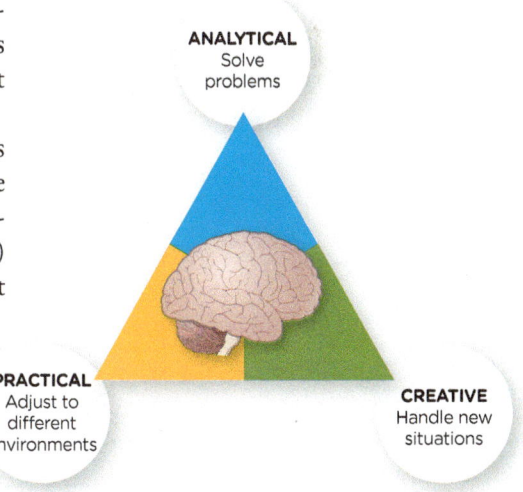

**FIGURE 7.4**
**Sternberg's Triarchic Theory of Intelligence**

**triarchic theory of intelligence** Theory suggesting that humans have varying degrees of analytical, creative, and practical abilities.

**TABLE 7.2    Theories of Intelligence**

| Theory | Summary | Further Questions |
|---|---|---|
| **Spearman's general intelligence (*g*-factor):** There is a general intelligence driving abilities in many areas. | A connection exists among different abilities, such as verbal, spatial, and reasoning competencies. | Given the complexity of the mind, can intelligence really be explained by a single general factor? |
| **Gardner's multiple intelligences:** There are eight types of intelligences, each associated with certain strengths and capabilities. | Different "frames of mind" allow humans to succeed. | What differentiates intelligence from skills? |
| **Sternberg's triarchic theory:** Humans have varying degrees of analytical, creative, and practical competencies. | Analytic intelligence is the capacity to solve problems; creative intelligence is the knowledge and skills used to handle new situations; and practical intelligence is the ability to adjust to different environments. | Are each of these areas separate, or do they share something in common (like a *g*-factor)? |

Summarized here are the main theories of intelligence and some of the questions they raise.

Critics contend Sternberg's triarchic theory of intelligence and Gardner's multiple intelligence theory lack scientific support (Gardner, 2020; Shearer & Karanian, 2017; Waterhouse, 2006). There are many ways to understand intelligence (TABLE 7.2), and it's important to remember that none are categorically "right" or "wrong."

## Measuring Intelligence

**LO 10** Describe how intelligence is measured and identify the important characteristics of assessment.

The development of the theories described above was to some degree aided by tests of intelligence. What are these tests, and what exactly do they aim to measure?

Tests of intelligence ("IQ tests") generally aim to measure **aptitude,** or a person's potential for future learning. On the other hand, measures of **achievement** (tests such as the SAT and ACT) are designed to assess acquired knowledge; that is, what a person has previously learned. The line between aptitude and achievement tests can be blurry, as tests are not always one or the other. For example, the SAT is considered an achievement test because it measures knowledge, but acquiring knowledge is somewhat contingent on innate ability. Therefore, the SAT might also qualify as an indirect measure of aptitude. Likewise, aptitude tests may incorporate some level of achievement, or learned content. For example, intelligence tests can be biased in favor of groups of people who have had certain life experiences (exposure to high-quality schools, for example). More on this to come.

**HOW DID INTELLIGENCE TESTING BEGIN?**    Intelligence testing is more than a century old. In 1904 psychologist Alfred Binet (1857–1911) joined a commission of the French government that was looking for a way to predict the performance of schoolchildren (Fancher & Rutherford, 2012; Watson, 1968). Working with one of his students, Théodore Simon (1872–1961), Binet constructed an intelligence assessment consisting of 30 items (Ludden, 2021). These items were designed to be of increasing difficulty, starting with a simple test instructing the child to follow the movement of a lit match, and later asking them to explain how paper and cardboard are different, and to create rhymes with words, among other things (Fancher & Rutherford, 2012).

Binet and Simon assumed that children generally follow the same path of intellectual development. By comparing a child's mental ability with the mental abilities of other children in the same age group, they could determine the child's **mental age (MA).** For example, a 10-year-old child with average intellectual abilities would

**aptitude** An individual's potential for learning.

**achievement** Acquired knowledge, or what has been learned.

**mental age (MA)** A score representing the mental abilities of an individual in relation to others of a similar chronological age.

perform similarly to other 10-year-old children and thus would have a *mental age* of 10. An intelligent 10-year-old child would perform better than other 10-year-old children and thus have a mental age that was higher than their chronological age (for example, 12). Similarly, a child who was intellectually delayed would have a mental age that was lower than their chronological age.

Although Binet and Simon's intelligence measure was groundbreaking at the time, it had limitations. Perhaps most importantly, it could not be used to compare intelligence levels *across* age groups. You can't use mental age to compare the intelligence levels of an 8-year-old child and a 12-year-old child, for example. German psychologist William Stern (1871–1938) solved this problem by devising the **intelligence quotient (IQ).** To calculate an IQ score, simply divide a child's mental age by their chronological age and multiply by 100. For example, a 10-year-old with a mental age of 8 would have an IQ score of $(8 \div 10) \times 100 = 80$. When mental age and chronological age are the same, the IQ score is 100. The IQ score allows you to compare a child with children of all different ages.

The IQ calculation does not work with adults, however. It wouldn't make sense to give a 60-year-old individual who scores the same as a 30-year-old individual an IQ score of 50 (that is, $(30 \div 60) \times 100 = 50$). Modern intelligence tests still assign a numerical score (which we continue to refer to as "IQ"), but they no longer use the actual quotient.

### THE STANFORD–BINET TEST

American psychologist Lewis Terman (1877–1956) revised Stern's work so that Binet's test could be used in the United States, where it came to be known as the Stanford–Binet. Terman (1916) changed some items, added items, developed standards based on American children, and extended the test to include teens and adults. *The Stanford–Binet Intelligence Scales,* now in its fifth edition (Roid, 2003), includes the assessment of verbal and nonverbal abilities (for instance, defining words, tracing paths in a maze). This test generates an overall score for general intelligence as well as scores associated with more specific abilities, such as knowledge, reasoning, visual processing, and working memory (Becker, 2003).

### THE WECHSLER TESTS

In the late 1930s, American psychologist David Wechsler (1896–1981) began creating intelligence tests for adults (Anastasi & Urbina, 1997). At the time, adults were often given the Stanford–Binet, which was really geared to the daily experiences of school-aged children. The Wechsler Adult Intelligence Scale (WAIS) was published in 1955 and has since been revised numerous times (1981, 1997, 2008). As of this printing, the newest version (WAIS-5) has not yet been released. In addition to creating assessments for adults, Wechsler also developed scales for older children (Wechsler Intelligence Scale for Children, WISC–V) and younger children (Wechsler Preschool and Primary Scale of Intelligence, WPPSI–IV).

The Wechsler assessments consist of subtests designed to measure different aspects of intellectual ability (Gibbons & Warne, 2019). For example, the 10 subtests on the WAIS (adult version of the test) target four domains of intellectual performance: verbal abilities, perceptual reasoning, working memory, and processing speed. If you take the WAIS–IV, you will receive scores for these four domains, as well as an overall intelligence quotient (IQ) score. Psychologists look for consistency among the domain and subtest scores, as opposed to focusing only on the overall IQ score. A substantial inconsistency could be a sign of a problem, such as a reading or language disability. In the United States, Wechsler tests are now used more frequently than the Stanford–Binet.

### IQ TESTS AND SCIENTIFIC RACISM

As we discuss the history of intelligence testing, we cannot ignore the fact that some assessments, including those developed by Binet, were used to produce evidence that perpetuated harmful racial stereotypes.

**What's Your IQ?**
French psychologist Alfred Binet (pictured above) collaborated with one of his students, Théodore Simon, to create a systematic assessment of intelligence. The materials pictured here come from Lewis Terman and Maude Merrill's 1937 version of Binet and Simon's test. Using these materials, the test administrator prompts the test taker with statements such as "Point to the doll's foot," or "What advantages does an airplane have over a car?" (Sattler, 1990).

**intelligence quotient (IQ)** A score from an intelligence assessment; originally based on mental age divided by chronological age, multiplied by 100.

In the early 1900s, researchers comparing children of different ethnicities concluded that Black children were adept at rote memory but didn't measure up to White children in intellectual activities such as reasoning, use of words, and logical memory (Belgrave & Allison, 2019). But such conclusions are based on evidence from tests that were fundamentally biased in favor of White children. As some scholars have pointed out, "early standardized testing quite clearly operated as a technology to support supposedly 'scientific' basis for claims of white superiority" (Knoester & Au, 2017, p. 6). To illustrate how intelligence tests are slanted in favor of the White majority, researchers have created tests biased toward minority cultural groups. For example, the *Dove Counterbalance General Intelligence Test,* also known as the *Chitling Test,* shows how children of color from urban backgrounds can surpass White, middle-class children on measures of knowledge generally not included in standard IQ tests (Kaplan & Saccuzzo, 2018).

## Let's Test the Intelligence Tests

How do you know if an intelligence test is effective? Psychologists focus on three important characteristics: validity, reliability, and standardization (INFOGRAPHIC 7.4 on page 276).

ATTA KENARE/AFP/Getty Images.

**Cognitive Smog**
We usually associate smog with lung disease, but did you know that air pollution also has a toxic effect on the brain (Maher et al., 2016)? One group of researchers looked at the cognitive test scores of a large Chinese sample at two points in time: 2010 and 2014. They matched the scores to air quality data corresponding to "the exact time and geographic locations of the cognitive tests" (Zhang et al., 2018, p. 9193). The findings were alarming: Exposure to air pollution was associated with impairments in cognitive performance, especially on verbal assessments, and particularly among aging men (Zhang et al., 2018).

**HOW VALID IS IT?**   **Validity** is the degree to which an assessment measures what it intends to measure. A valid intelligence test measures intelligence, not something else. We can assess the validity of a measure by comparing its results to those of other assessments that measure the factor of interest. We can also determine whether the test predicts future performance on other assessments (a concept known as *predictive validity*). Valid intelligence tests generate scores that are consistent with those of other intelligence tests, and they can predict future performance on tasks related to intellectual ability.

**HOW RELIABLE IS IT?**   Another important characteristic of assessment is **reliability,** the ability of a test to provide consistent, reproducible results. If given repeatedly, a reliable test will continue producing similar scores. Suppose you take an intelligence test today, next month, and 5 years from now; if the test is reliable, your scores should be consistent. Another way to gauge reliability is by splitting the test in half and then determining whether the findings of the first and second halves agree with each other; we call this *split-half reliability.*

Is it possible for a test to be reliable, but not valid? Absolutely. For this reason, we always have to determine *both* reliability and validity. Imagine a psychologist is using a test that claims to measure intelligence. The test is reliable because it produces similar scores when people are retested, but it's not valid because it actually measures reading level instead of intelligence. In other words, the test reliably measures reading level (achievement), but it does not measure intelligence (aptitude).

**IS IT STANDARDIZED?**   In addition to being valid and reliable, a good intelligence test provides *standardization.* Perhaps you have taken a test that measured your achievement in a particular area (for example, an ACT or SAT), or an aptitude test to measure your innate abilities (an IQ test). Upon receiving your scores, you may have wondered how you performed in comparison to other people in your class, college, or state. Most aptitude and achievement tests allow you to make these judgments through **standardization.** Test developers achieve standardization by administering a test to a large sample of people and then publishing the average scores, or *norms,* for specified groups. This allows you to compare your score (often as a percentile) with people of the same age, socioeconomic status, or geographic region.

**validity** The degree to which an assessment measures what it intends to measure.

**reliability** The ability of an assessment to provide consistent, reproducible results.

**standardization** Occurs when test developers administer a test to a large sample and then publish the average scores for specified groups.

Standardization is also achieved through the use of **standard procedures**, which ensure that no one is given an unfair advantage. Intelligence tests are subject to tight control. The public does not have access to the questions or answers, and all testing must be administered by a professional. Perhaps you have come across IQ tests on the internet? We don't recommend them, in part because they lack standardization, and they aren't necessarily reliable or valid.

**THE NORMAL CURVE**    Have you ever wondered how many people in the population are really smart? Or perhaps how many people have average intelligence? With results from aptitude tests like the Wechsler and Stanford–Binet, we can graph a **normal curve,** which shows us how scores on intelligence tests are distributed (Infographic 7.4). The normal curve is symmetrical and shaped like a bell. The highest point on the graph represents the average score.

The normal curve shown in Infographic 7.4 portrays the distribution of scores for the Wechsler tests. As you can see, the *mean* or average score is 100. As you follow the horizontal axis, notice that the higher and lower scores occur less and less frequently in the population. A score of 145 or 70 is far less common than a score of 100, for example. The normal curve can be used to make predictions about a variety of traits, including IQ, height, weight, and personality characteristics. (See Chapter 1 and the Introduction to Statistics Appendix found in the e-book in your Achieve course for more information about the normal curve and other statistical concepts.)

**BUT ARE THEY FAIR?**    As we discussed earlier, one major concern with intelligence assessments is fairness. Are these tests biased in favor of people of a certain gender, ethnicity, or socioeconomic class? The evidence suggests they are. For example, researchers have reported disparities among groups within the United States (Ceci & Williams, 2009; Cottrell et al., 2015; Dickens & Flynn, 2006; Warne et al., 2018). Additionally, a review from over a decade ago found average test score differences among groups with origins in various parts of the world (Asia, Africa, Europe, Latin America, and so on; Rushton & Jensen, 2010).

Although researchers disagree about what causes these gaps in IQ scores, they generally agree that there is no evidence to support a "genetic hypothesis" across races (Nisbett et al., 2012). As you will learn in Chapter 11, race is just a cultural construct, not a meaningful biological category. IQ scores are shaped by a variety of environmental factors, including income level, education, and maternal verbal abilities (Cottrell et al., 2015). Socioeconomic status (SES) appears to play a key role (von Stumm et al., 2020). A disproportionate number of children of color grow up in lower SES households (Noël, 2018), and therefore are exposed to environmental factors that may be linked to performance on tests of intelligence. For example, children raised in homes with lower SES are more likely to witness violence, which may impair certain aspects of **memory** (Rosen et al., 2019). They may also have more exposure to TV, caregivers who are not available to read to them, and less access to books, technology, and quality schools (Hanscombe et al., 2012).

Stress is another factor that may contribute to the IQ score gap. Research suggests that low-income children are more likely to experience chronic stress caused by frequent exposure to "frightening or threatening events" (Morsy & Rothstein, 2019, p. 1). Chronic stress can have a negative impact on the function of the brain, particularly those areas responsible for attention and memory (short-term, long-term, and working memory) (McEwen, 2000).

When discussing sensitive topics like IQ scores, it is important to remember that IQ tests were developed in a society that is plagued by systemic racism, and all the individuals taking these tests were raised under the influence of systemic racism. It's

*Research* **CONNECTIONS**

In **Chapter 1,** we discussed the importance of operational definitions, which specify the precise manner in which variables are defined and measured. Operational definitions help ensure standardization across experiments. Here, we note that standard procedures are important when administering assessments as well. Data must be collected in a controlled fashion to ensure errors don't arise from unknown environmental factors.

**CONNECTIONS**

In **Chapter 6,** we discussed the biology of memory, exploring areas of the brain responsible for memory processing (hippocampus, cerebellum, and amygdala) as well as changes at the level of the neuron (long-term potentiation). Here, we note that environments can impact the functioning of the memory system.

**normal curve** Depicts the frequency of values of a variable along a continuum; bell-shaped symmetrical distribution, with the highest point reflecting the average score.

# How Smart Are Intelligence Tests?

Tests that claim to measure intelligence are everywhere—online, in your favorite magazine, at job interviews, and in many elementary and secondary schools. But can all of these tests be trusted? The results of an intelligence test aren't meaningful unless the test is *valid*, *reliable*, and *fair*. But what do those concepts mean, and how can we be sure whether a test is valid, reliable, or fair—let alone all three? Let's take a look.

## validity DOES THE TEST MEASURE WHAT IT INTENDS TO MEASURE?

Is a bathroom scale valid for measuring height?

How about a ruler missing its first inch?

A shortened ruler would not be a valid measure because it would provide different results than other rulers.

A valid intelligence test will provide results that:

✔ agree with the results of other valid intelligence tests
✔ predict performance in an area related to intelligence, such as academic achievement

## reliability WILL YOUR SCORE BE CONSISTENT EVERY TIME YOU TAKE THE TEST?

A shortened ruler isn't valid, but it is *reliable* because it will give the same result every time it's used.

A reliable intelligence test will provide results that:

✔ are reproducible (produces a similar score if taken a second time)
✔ show the first and second halves of the test are consistent with each other

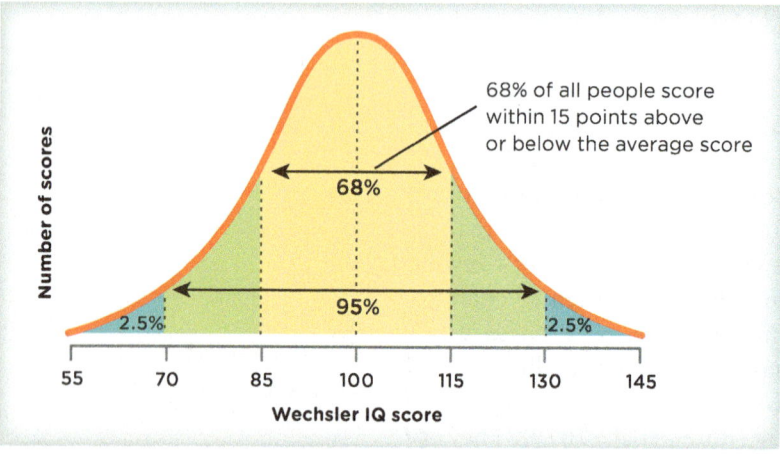

68% of all people score within 15 points above or below the average score

68%

95%

2.5%        2.5%

55    70    85    100    115    130    145

**Wechsler IQ score**

*Number of scores*

Because most intelligence tests are *standardized*, you can determine how well you have performed in comparison to others. Test scores tend to form a bell-shaped curve—called the normal curve—around the average score. Most people (68%) score within 15 points above or below the average. If the test is reliable, each person's score should stay around the same place on the curve across multiple testings.

## fairness IS THE TEST VALID FOR THE GROUP?

An animal weighing 2 stone is likely to be a:
(a) sparrow        (c) mature lion
(b) small dog      (d) blue whale

Unless you live in the United Kingdom, where the imperial system of weights is used, you probably wouldn't know that a stone is approximately 14 pounds, and therefore the correct answer is B. Does this mean that you are less intelligent, or that the test is biased against people without a specific background? A test that is culture-fair is designed to minimize the bias of cultural background.

3 inches        2.286 Chinese Imperial cùn        .1667 cubits

also important to establish some "ground rules" for these discussions. Here are a few we think are particularly important (Burton & Warne, 2020, p. 137):

- "Even though mean differences exist across groups, there is still a lot of overlap across groups."
- "All possible explanations for causes of mean group differences should be explored."
- "Mean group differences do not justify discriminatory behavior."

**CAN WE LEVEL THE PLAYING FIELD?**    We have discussed some environmental factors that might lead to disparities in IQ scores (maternal qualities, SES, and stressful living conditions). We have also noted that the gaps in test scores could result from biases of the tests themselves. Early versions of IQ tests exhibited some bias against individuals from rural areas, people of lower socioeconomic status, and Black Americans. Bias may result from language, dialect, or the culture of those who have created the tests (Sattler, 1990; Sternberg, 2004).

Psychologists have tried to create **culture-fair intelligence tests,** which aim to measure intelligence without putting people at a disadvantage because of their cultural backgrounds. One way to avoid bias is to create questions that are familiar to people from a variety of cultures. Another approach is to use nonverbal questions. (See the sample item in **FIGURE 7.5**.) Since intelligence is defined within a culture, and tests are created within a culture, it may be impossible to develop assessments that are truly culture-fair or culture-free (Sternberg, 2004).

Despite their limitations, IQ tests are useful in certain contexts. For example, they can be used to predict academic success. IQ scores, particularly those in the higher and lower ranges, are strongly correlated with performance on SATs, ACTs, and Graduate Record Examinations (GREs), although some researchers have found that self-discipline may be a better predictor of success (Duckworth & Seligman, 2005). Intelligence tests are also helpful for identifying delays in intellectual functioning, or *intellectual disability.*

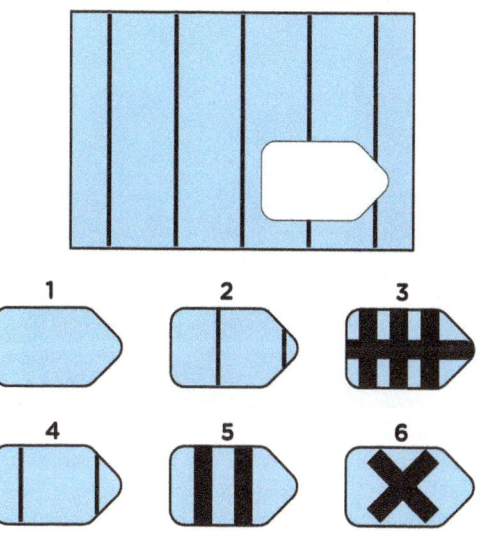

**FIGURE 7.5**
**Nonverbal Intelligence**
The Raven's Progressive Matrices test is used to assess components of nonverbal intelligence. For the sample question pictured here, the test taker chooses the item that completes the matrix pattern (correct answer is #2). Such assessments are generally considered culturally fair, meaning they do not favor certain cultural groups over others. Sample item is similar to those found in the Raven's Progressive Matrices (Coloured, Parallel, Sets A, AB, B) (CPM). Copyright © 1998 NCS Pearson, Inc. Reproduced with permission. All rights reserved. "Ravens" and "Raven's Progressive Matrices" are trademarks, in the U.S. and/or other countries, of Pearson Education, Inc. or its affiliates(s).

# The Diversity of Human Intelligence

Intellectual disability consists of delays in thinking, intelligence, and social and practical skills that are evident before age 18. This condition is indicated by low IQ scores (below approximately 70 on the Wechsler tests) and adaptive functioning deficits (difficulty living independently and understanding number concepts, money, and hygiene, for example; American Psychiatric Association, 2013). Although intellectual disability is the preferred term, prior to October 5, 2010, references to "mental retardation" existed in many laws and policies (Schalock et al., 2010). On that special day in 2010, President Barack Obama signed Rosa's Law declaring that all earlier references to this phrase be removed from federal, health, education, and labor laws (Ford et al., 2013).

There are many causes of intellectual disability, but we cannot always pinpoint them. According to the American Association on Intellectual and Developmental Disabilities (AAIDD), nearly half of intellectual disability cases have unidentifiable causes (Schalock et al., 2010). Known causes include Down syndrome (when there is an extra chromosome in what would normally be the 21st pair), fetal alcohol syndrome (the result of in utero exposure to alcohol), and fragile X syndrome (a defect in a gene on the X chromosome leading to reductions in protein needed for development of the brain). There are also

Syracuse University InclusiveU.

**"Disability = Diversity"**
Students gather for a photo at Syracuse University (SU), home to the "InclusiveU" program that serves students with intellectual disabilities. Students in InclusiveU take regular college classes, pursue internships, and participate in athletics. "At SU, we celebrate disability because it makes our campus stronger, more diverse, and much more interesting" (Syracuse University, n.d., para. 3).

**culture-fair intelligence tests** Assessments designed to minimize cultural bias.

**Equal Opportunity?**
An SAT prep class in Connecticut. Tests such as the SAT and ACT are supposed to be reliable, valid, and standardized (and thus fair), but do they really level the playing field? Some families can pay for SAT prep classes and private tutors, while others can afford only test prep books, or nothing at all. As Dylan Hernandez of Flint, Michigan, wrote in *The New York Times*, "The majority of low- and middle-income 11th graders I know in Michigan didn't even sit for the preliminary exams. Most took the SAT cold." What they didn't know, Hernandez points out, is that "one must train for standardized tests with the intensity of an athlete" in order to gain admission to America's elite colleges (Hernandez, 2017, para. 7).

known environmental factors that contribute to intellectual disability, including lead and mercury poisoning, lack of oxygen at birth, various diseases, and exposure to drugs during fetal development.

At the other end of the intelligence spectrum are the intellectually **gifted,** those who have IQ scores of 130 or above. With a score above 140, one is considered a "genius." As you might imagine, very few people—about 2% of the population—are classified as gifted. An even smaller proportion falls in the genius range: only 1% of the population (Simonton, 2012).

**THE "TERMITES"** Lewis Terman (mentioned earlier) was curious to know how gifted children function in adulthood. His work led to the longest-running longitudinal study on genius and giftedness (Warne, 2019). This study, formerly referred to as the Genetic Studies of Genius, is now called the Terman Study of the Gifted. Terman (1925) monitored 857 boys and 671 girls with IQ scores ranging from 130 to 200. These children (known as "Termites") were well adjusted socially, showed leadership skills, and were physically healthy and conventionally attractive (Terman & Oden, 1947). They also had lower rates of mental illness (Ludden, 2021). Following the participants into adulthood, the study found that they earned a greater number of academic degrees and achieved more financial success than their nongifted peers (Fancher & Rutherford, 2012; Holahan & Sears, 1995; Ludden, 2021). Compelling as these findings may be, they do not necessarily indicate that high IQ scores guarantee success in all areas of life. As *Scientific American* reports, perceptions of highly intelligent people are not categorically positive.

# INEFFECTIVE GENIUSES?

### People with very high IQs can be perceived as worse leaders.

Intelligence makes for better leaders—from undergraduates to executives to presidents—according to multiple studies. It certainly makes sense that handling a market shift or legislative logjam requires cognitive oomph. But new research on leadership suggests that, at a certain point, having a higher IQ can be viewed as harmful.

Although previous research has shown that groups with smarter leaders perform better by objective measures, some studies have hinted that followers might subjectively view leaders with stratospheric intellect as less effective. Decades ago Dean Simonton, a psychologist at the University of California, Davis, proposed that brilliant leaders' words may simply go over people's heads, their solutions could be more complicated to implement and followers might find it harder to relate to them. Now Simonton and two colleagues have finally tested that idea, publishing their results in the July 2017 issue of the *Journal of Applied Psychology*.

The researchers looked at 379 male and female business leaders in 30 countries, across fields that included banking, retail and technology. The managers took IQ tests (an imperfect but robust predictor of performance in many areas), and each was rated on leadership style and effectiveness by an average of eight co-workers. IQ positively correlated with ratings of leader effectiveness, strategy formation, vision and several other characteristics—up to a point. The ratings peaked at an IQ of around 120, which is higher than roughly 80 percent of office workers. Beyond that, the ratings declined. The researchers suggest the "ideal" IQ could be higher or lower in various fields, depending on whether technical versus social skills are more valued in a given work culture.

"It's an interesting and thoughtful paper," says Paul Sackett, a psychology professor at the University of Minnesota, who was not involved in the research. "To me, the right interpretation of the work would be that it highlights a need to understand what high-IQ leaders do that leads to lower perceptions by followers. The wrong interpretation would be, 'Don't hire high-IQ leaders.'" [. . .] **Matthew Hutson. Reproduced with permission. Copyright 2018 Scientific American, a division of Nature America, Inc. All rights reserved.**

**gifted** Highly intelligent; defined as having an IQ score of 130 or above.

**LIFE SMARTS** So what makes an ideal leader? One important component is a high level of *emotional intelligence* (Grunberg et al., 2020). **Emotional intelligence** is the capacity to perceive, understand, regulate, and use emotions to adapt to social situations (Goleman, 1995). People with emotional intelligence are empathetic and use information about their emotions to direct their behavior in an efficient and creative way (Salovey et al., 2002). They are self-aware and can properly judge how to behave in social situations. A high level of emotional intelligence is indicated by self-control—the ability to manage anger, impulsiveness, and anxiety. As you might predict, emotional intelligence is related to performance on the job and at school (Joseph et al., 2015; MacCann et al., 2011). It sounds like a wonderful gift, something you don't want to stifle. If this is a priority for you, read on . . .

## Relationships

LITTLE LIES, BIG PROBLEMS?

Have you ever told a little lie (e.g., "Sorry I am late; I got stuck in traffic!"), stretched a story to impress friends, or cheated in a card game? These little lapses in morality may seem relatively benign, but research suggests they can erode aspects of your emotional intelligence (Lee et al., 2020). "Specifically . . . dishonest conduct can reduce one's generalized empathic accuracy—the ability to accurately read other people's emotional states" (Lee et al., 2019, p. 1557).

**DO LIES HAVE CONSEQUENCES?**

Why would it be important to read the emotional states of others? Understanding other people's feelings can help you address their needs, negotiate and work through problems, and develop tighter bonds (Lee et al., 2019). If you act dishonestly, you are compromising this ability, and this may occur because you are becoming increasingly detached. As researchers explain, "once we engage in dishonest behavior, we may also distance ourselves from other people by regarding them as less human, which allows us to continue down a path of subsequent, repeated unethical behavior" (Lee et al., 2020, p. 22).

As you may have observed in your own life, people display varying degrees of emotional intelligence. From where does this diversity in emotional intelligence—or any facet of intelligence—arise? Like most topics in psychology, it comes down to nature and nurture.

## Is Intelligence Genetic?

Researching identical and fraternal twins is an excellent way to evaluate the contributions of nature and nurture for virtually any psychological trait. The Minnesota Study of Twins Reared Apart (MISTRA) indicates there are strong correlations between the IQ scores of identical twins—stronger than those between fraternal twins or other siblings. In other words, the closer the genetic relationship (identical twins have identical genes at conception), the greater similarity in IQ scores (Johnson & Bouchard, 2011; McGue et al., 1993; Shakeshaft et al., 2015). In fact, identical twins' IQ scores have correlations as high as .86. (Remember that the closer $r$ is to +1.00 or to −1.00, the stronger the relationship; **FIGURE 7.6** on the next page.) This suggests that genes play a major role in determining scores on intelligence tests. In other words, performance on IQ tests appears to be highly *heritable*.

**Heritability** refers to the degree to which heredity is responsible for a particular characteristic or trait in the population. Many traits, such as eye color and height, are highly heritable. Others, such as manners, are largely determined by the environments in which we are raised (Dickens & Flynn, 2001). Results from twin and adoption studies suggest that heritability for "general cognitive abilities" is about

**emotional intelligence** The capacity to perceive, understand, regulate, and use emotions to adapt to social situations.

**heritability** The degree to which hereditary factors (genes) are responsible for a particular characteristic observed within a population.

## FIGURE 7.6
**Nature, Nurture, and Intelligence**
The most genetically similar people, identical twins, exhibit the strongest correlation between their scores on IQ tests. This suggests that genes play a major role in determining intelligence. But if identical twins are raised in different environments, the correlation is slightly lower, showing some environmental effect. Information from McGue et al. (1993).

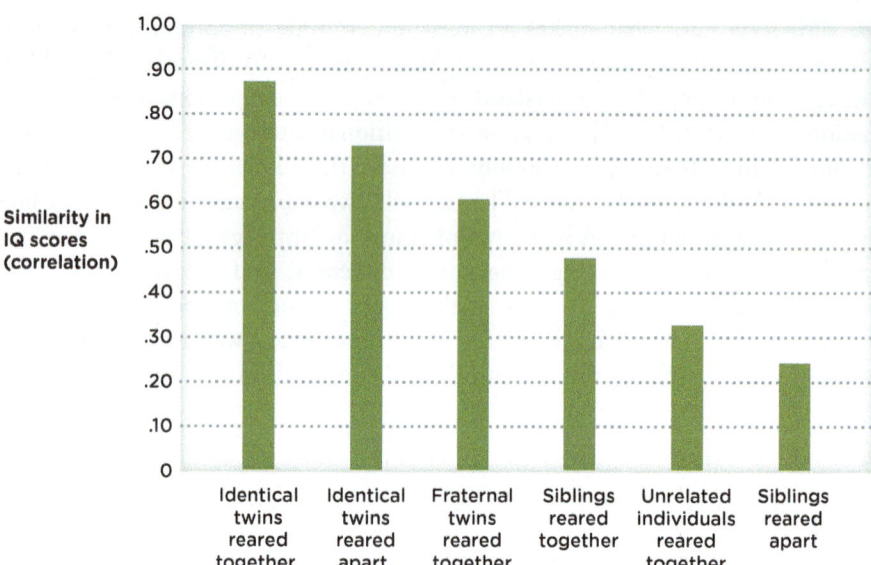

50% (Plomin & DeFries, 1998; Plomin et al., 2013). In other words, about half of the variation in intellectual or cognitive ability can be attributed to genetic make-up, and the other half to environment. But heritability estimates of cognitive abilities can be misleading. As scholars point out, "intelligence seems to be quite malleable, and changes in the environment can, by *interacting* with genes, explain a great deal of differences in IQ across families, life span, socioeconomic status, and generations" (Sauce & Matzel, 2018, p. 27).

We should close this discussion with a few important points to remember: (1) Heritability applies to groups of people, not individuals. We cannot say, for example, that an individual's intelligence level is 40% due to genes and 60% the result of environment. We can only make general predictions about groups and how they are influenced by genetic factors (Dickens & Flynn, 2001; Sauce & Matzel, 2018). (2) Although we see gaps in cognitive test results across groups of people, these differences are not thought to result from genetics. They most likely result from environmental factors, including those relating to socioeconomic status (Cottrell et al., 2015). (3) Cognitive abilities run in families, with approximately 40–50% of variation due to genes (Davies et al., 2011).

Given the complex relationship among genes, environment, and cognitive abilities, you may be wondering how sex and gender figure into this equation. Are male and female brains different?

## CONNECTIONS

In **Chapter 2,** we described gray matter and white matter in the brain. Gray matter consists largely of neuron cell bodies and glial cells. White matter is made up of axons wrapped in myelin. Here we note some differences between women and men in regard to their gray and white matter.

**MALES AND FEMALES ARE MORE ALIKE THAN DIFFERENT.**

## Think Critically

### HIS AND HER BRAIN DIFFERENCES—DO THEY MATTER?

Over the years, researchers have uncovered some intriguing differences between the brains of men and women. For example, women tend to have more **gray matter** volume in some parts of the frontal lobes, including an area important for emotional awareness and emotional processing in working memory (Lotze et al., 2019; Smith et al., 2018). Meanwhile, men tend to have more gray matter volume in some areas beneath the cortex, including the amygdala and hippocampus (Lotze et al., 2019). Male brains also may differ in their degree of connectivity. A study of children and young adults found that males had stronger connections within hemispheres, whereas females had stronger connections between hemispheres (Ingalhalikar et al., 2014; Jahanshad & Thompson, 2017).

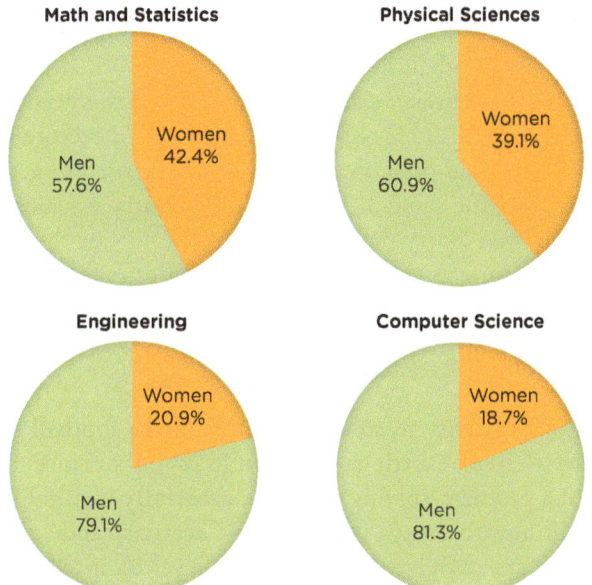

**Math and Statistics**

Men 57.6%
Women 42.4%

**Physical Sciences**

Men 60.9%
Women 39.1%

**Engineering**

Women 20.9%
Men 79.1%

**Computer Science**

Women 18.7%
Men 81.3%

FIGURE 7.7

**Bachelor's Degrees Awarded in the United States**

Women earned the majority (57.3%) of all bachelor's degrees awarded in the United States in 2016. But when it comes to degrees awarded in science, technology, engineering, and math (STEM), the numbers look very different. Why do so many fewer women receive degrees in STEM fields? Information from National Science Foundation, 2019.

While researchers may agree about some of the structural inconsistencies between male and female brains, it is not entirely clear how these disparities relate to behaviors and cognitive abilities (Grabowska, 2017; Lonsdorf, 2017). For example, do differences in brain structure influence the educational and career choices of the sexes? Men outnumber women in some science, technology, engineering, and mathematics (STEM) fields, namely computer science, physics, and engineering (Cimpian et al., 2020; National Science Foundation, 2019; FIGURE 7.7). Meanwhile, women are overrepresented in accounting, writing, and K–12 education (Rocheleau, 2017). They also earn more degrees in psychology—though we should mention that female psychologists earn lower salaries and are less likely than their male counterparts to get their research published in high-impact journals (Gruber et al., 2020). Do these trends occur because men and women are "hardwired" differently? Or, are they **socially conditioned** to develop certain interests and skills? Remember, the brain can change in response to experience, a phenomenon called neuroplasticity.

Whatever the cause, sex differences have been observed in certain cognitive domains. For example, studies suggest that females outperform males in tests of verbal ability while males perform better in mental rotation tasks (Heil et al., 2018; Stoet & Geary, 2013). But such propensities are small and apply to populations, not necessarily individuals. And while it's important to study this topic, we should be wary of research discoveries being "used to legitimize false stereotypes and provide fuel for those determined to convince the world of the inferiority of females" (Halpern, 2014, p. 92). Perhaps the most important thing to remember is that the brains of males and females are more alike than different, in terms of both structure and function (Joel et al., 2018). "There is no evidence for a smarter sex" (Halpern, 2014, p. 91).

**CONNECTIONS**

In **Chapter 1,** we presented the nature and nurture theme and discussed its importance in the field of psychology. Here, we can see how both nature and nurture could potentially explain the gender imbalance in career choices. Researchers continue to evaluate the relative influence of nature and nurture in female and male behavior patterns.

## Put Your Heads Together

In your group discuss the following: **A)** What occupations are commonly thought to be more suitable for women? **B)** For men? **C)** Are these beliefs based on stereotypes or scientific evidence? Use information from the textbook to back up your claims. **D)** How might such beliefs about gender impact education and career choices?

We have explored the concept of intelligence and various approaches to assess it. Now let's shift our focus to a quality that is associated with intelligence but far more difficult to measure: *creativity*.

## Let's Get Creative

Harry never approached football in a conventional way. When he was learning the ropes in his new middle linebacker position with the Giants, the coach provided specific instructions to accomplish his objectives. Harry would execute the task, but not always the way the coach had prescribed. "Everything he tried to get me to do, I did it [backwards], but I got the same or better results," Harry explains. Eventually, the coach gave up and allowed Harry the freedom to think outside the box. He threw up his hands and said, "As long as you get the job done, I can't fault you!"

**LO 11**    Define creativity and its associated characteristics.

Harry was using creativity to solve problems on the football field, just as you might use creativity to resolve a tricky situation in school or spice up a bland recipe in your kitchen. In a problem-solving scenario, **creativity** is the ability to construct valuable results in innovative ways (**TABLE 7.3**). Creativity and intelligence are not equivalent, but they are correlated, and a basic level of intelligence is necessary for creativity to flow (Jaarsveld et al., 2015). For example, you need to have a certain level of intelligence to generate original ideas, as opposed to just more ideas (Benedek et al., 2012; Nusbaum & Silvia, 2011).

**TABLE 7.3    Characteristics of Creativity**

| Characteristic | Meaning |
|---|---|
| **Originality** | The ability to come up with unique solutions when trying to solve a problem |
| **Fluency** | The ability to create many potential solutions |
| **Flexibility** | The ability to use a variety of problem-solving tactics to arrive at solutions |
| **Knowledge** | A sufficient base of ideas and information |
| **Thinking** | The ability to see things in new ways, make connections, see patterns |
| **Personality** | Characteristics of a risk taker, someone who perseveres and tolerates ambiguity |
| **Intrinsic motivation** | Influenced by internal rewards, motivated by the pleasure and challenge of work |

Creativity is difficult to measure because it doesn't present itself in a singular or uniform manner. However, these basic characteristics are generally associated with creativity (Baer, 1993; Sternberg, 2006a, 2006b).

**DIVERGENT AND CONVERGENT THINKING**    An important component of creativity is **divergent thinking,** or the ability to devise many solutions to a problem (Baer, 1993; Kerr & Stull, 2019). A classic measure of divergent thinking is the *unusual uses test* (Guilford, 1967; Guilford et al., 1960; **FIGURE 7.8**). A typical prompt would ask a test taker to come up with as many uses for a brick as the test taker can imagine. (What ideas do you have? Paperweight? Shot put? Stepstool?) Remember that we often have difficulty thinking about how to use familiar objects in atypical ways, a result of functional fixedness.

In contrast to divergent thinking, **convergent thinking** focuses on finding a single best solution by converging on the correct answer. Here, we fall back on previous experience and knowledge. This conventional approach to problem solving leads to one solution, but, as we have noted, problems often have multiple solutions.

**creativity** In problem solving, the ability to construct valuable results in innovative ways; the ability to generate original ideas.

**divergent thinking** The ability to devise many solutions to a problem; a component of creativity.

**convergent thinking** A conventional approach to problem solving that focuses on finding a single best solution to a problem by using previous experience and knowledge.

Creativity comes with many benefits. People with this ability tend to have a broader range of knowledge and interests. They are open to new experiences and often less inhibited in their thoughts and behaviors (Feist, 2004; Simonton, 2000). The good news is that we can become more creative by practicing divergent thinking, taking risks, and looking for unusual connections between ideas (Baer, 1993).

**HAPPY ENDINGS**    This chapter may be coming to an end, but the stories of Dr. Taylor and Harry Carson continue full speed ahead. It took Dr. Taylor 8 years to recuperate from what she now calls her "stroke of insight." Regaining her physical and cognitive strength required steadfast determination and painstaking effort. "Recovery was a decision I had to make a million times a day," she wrote (Taylor, 2006, p. 115). She also had many people cheering her on—family and friends who had faith in her brain's plasticity, or ability to repair and rewire (Taylor, 2006). Today, Dr. Taylor is busy writing a new book and working on various projects aimed at increasing awareness and understanding of the brain, and supporting those recovering from neurological damage (drjilltaylor.com, n.d.).

In 2006 Harry Carson was inducted into the Pro Football Hall of Fame, but he was not in the mood for celebrating. Harry used his enshrinement speech to advocate on behalf of his fellow players: "I would hope that the leaders of the NFL, the future commissioner, and the player[s] association do a much better job of looking out for those individuals. . . . If we made the league what it is, you have to take better care of your own" (Pro Football Hall of Fame, n.d.).

It would take another decade for the NFL to finally admit that head injuries sustained in football are associated with CTE (Fainaru, 2016). Although this represents a positive shift in the discussion about football-related brain injuries, Harry's work is far from done. One of his main goals is to help other NFL retirees understand that they are not alone in their struggles with mood swings, cognitive impairment, and other symptoms of traumatic brain injury—and that these challenges can become manageable. Another of his major objectives is to educate parents about the neurological consequences of contact sports in general. Brain injuries may happen in a variety of sports, including soccer, lacrosse, hockey, and horseback riding. As Harry says, "There needs to be a warning to parents to understand that in signing [their] kids up to play ice hockey or football or some other sport where their child might sustain neurological damage, that young person might not be the same after they've been concussed."

In this test, you will be asked to consider some common objects. Each object has a common use, which will be stated. You are to list as many as six other uses for which the object or parts of the object could serve.

**Example:**

Given: A NEWSPAPER (used for reading). You might think of the following other uses for a newspaper.

a. *Start a fire*
b. *Wrap garbage*
c. *Swat flies*
d. *Stuffing to pack boxes*
e. *Line drawers or shelves*
f. *Make a kidnap note*

Notice that all of the uses listed are different from each other and different from the primary use of a newspaper. Each acceptable use must be different from others and from the common use.

**FIGURE 7.8**

**Guilford's Alternate Uses Task**

The sample question above is from Guilford's Alternate Uses Task, a revised version of the unusual uses test, which is designed to gauge creativity. Reproduced by special permission of the publisher, MIND GARDEN, Inc., www.mindgarden.com from the Alternate Uses by J. P. Guilford, Paul R. Christensen, Philip R. Merrifield, & Robert C. Wilson. Copyright 1960 by Sheridan Supply Co. Further reproduction is prohibited without the publisher's written consent.

**Dr. Jill Bolte Taylor**

**Harry Carson**

## SHOW WHAT YOU KNOW

1. Sternberg believed that intelligence is made up of three types of competencies, including:
   A. linguistic, spatial, musical.
   B. intrapersonal, interpersonal, existential.
   C. analytic, creative, practical.
   D. achievement, triarchic, prototype.

2. Define intelligence quotient (IQ). How was the original IQ score derived?

3. Tests of intelligence are designed to measure _____, or a person's potential for learning, and other tests are used to assess _____, or acquired knowledge.

4. An artist friend of yours easily comes up with many unique solutions when trying to solve problems. This _____ is one of the defining characteristics of creativity, and it can be measured with the *unusual uses test*.

✓ CHECK YOUR ANSWERS AT THE BACK OF THE BOOK.

## Summary of Concepts

**LO 1** Define cognition and explain how it relates to thinking. (p. 251)

Cognition is the mental activity associated with obtaining, converting, and using knowledge. Thinking is a specific type of cognition, which involves coming to a decision, reaching a solution, forming a belief, or developing an attitude. Cognition is a broad term that describes mental activity, and thinking is a subset of cognition.

**LO 2** Demonstrate an understanding of concepts and how they are organized. (p. 251)

Concepts are mental representations of categories of objects, situations, and ideas that belong together based on their central features (characteristics). Psychologists often use a three-level hierarchy to categorize objects. At the top of the hierarchy is the superordinate category, which encompasses all objects belonging to a concept. Below is the more specific midlevel category, often used to identify objects. At the bottom of the hierarchy is the subordinate level, or most specific category.

**LO 3** Differentiate between natural concepts and formal concepts. (p. 252)

Formal concepts are created through rigid and logical rules (or features of a concept). Natural concepts, on the other hand, are acquired through everyday experience. Natural concepts don't have the same types of rigid rules for identification that formal concepts do, and this makes them harder to outline. We organize our worlds with the help of prototypes, the ideal or most representative examples of particular natural concepts.

**LO 4** Explain how trial and error and algorithms can be used to solve problems. (p. 257)

Problem solving refers to the variety of approaches used to achieve goals. One approach to problem solving is trial and error, which involves finding a solution through a series of attempts. Algorithms provide a virtually guaranteed solution to a problem by using formulas or sets of rules. Unlike trial and error, algorithms ensure that you will reach a solution if you follow all the steps correctly.

**LO 5** Explain how heuristics help us solve problems. (p. 257)

Heuristics are problem-solving approaches that incorporate a rule of thumb or broad application of a strategy. Although they help us identify and evaluate possible solutions to our problems, these shortcuts do not guarantee solutions.

**LO 6** Describe the process of decision making and how heuristics can lead us astray. (p. 261)

Decision making generally refers to the cognitive process of choosing among various approaches to reach a goal. Using the availability heuristic, we predict the probability of something happening based on how easily we can recall a similar event from the past. If this recall occurs easily, we judge the event as being more likely to occur. With the representativeness heuristic, we evaluate the degree to which the primary characteristics of a person or situation are similar to our prototype.

**LO 7** Define language and give examples of its basic elements. (p. 267)

Language is a system for using symbols to think and communicate. These symbols are words, gestures, or sounds, and there are specific rules for putting them together. Phonemes are the basic building blocks of spoken language. Morphemes consist of one or more phonemes and represent the fundamental units of meaning. Grammar refers to the rules associated with word and sentence structures. It includes both syntax and semantics. Syntax is the collection of rules guiding word choice and word order. Semantics refers to rules used to bring meaning to words and sentences. Pragmatics refers to the social rules for using language.

**LO 8** Explain how language influences thought. (p. 269)

The linguistic relativity hypothesis proposes that language differences lead to disparities in thinking and perception. Most psychologists agree that, although language might not determine thinking and perception, it certainly can influence it.

**LO 9**  Distinguish among various theories of intelligence. (p. 270)

Charles Spearman speculated that intelligence consists of a general intelligence (or *g*-factor), which refers to a singular underlying aptitude or intellectual ability. Howard Gardner suggested we have multiple intelligences, proposing eight different types of intelligences or "frames of mind": linguistic (verbal), logical-mathematical, spatial, bodily-kinesthetic, musical, intrapersonal, interpersonal, and naturalist. Robert Sternberg proposed three kinds of intelligences. His triarchic theory of intelligence suggests that humans have varying degrees of analytical, creative, and practical abilities.

**LO 10**  Describe how intelligence is measured and identify the important characteristics of assessment. (p. 272)

Some tests of intelligence aim to measure aptitude, or a person's potential for learning. Measures of achievement are designed to assess acquired knowledge (what a person has learned). Psychologists must ensure the accurate assessment of intelligence by determining validity, that is, the degree to which the test measures what it intends to measure. Another important characteristic is reliability, the ability of a test to provide consistent, reproducible results. A reliable test, given repeatedly, will result in similar scores. Another important quality, standardization, is achieved when test developers administer a test to a large sample and then publish the average scores for specified groups.

**LO 11**  Define creativity and its associated characteristics. (p. 282)

Creativity is the ability to construct valuable results in innovative ways. Basic components of creativity include divergent thinking, originality, fluency, and flexibility.

## Key Terms

achievement, p. 272
algorithm, p. 257
aptitude, p. 272
availability heuristic, p. 261
cognition, p. 251
concepts, p. 251
confirmation bias, p. 262
convergent thinking, p. 282
creativity, p. 282
culture-fair intelligence test, p. 277
decision making, p. 261

divergent thinking, p. 282
emotional intelligence, p. 279
formal concepts, p. 253
functional fixedness, p. 258
general intelligence (*g*-factor), p. 270
gifted, p. 278
grammar, p. 267
heritability, p. 279
heuristics, p. 257
hindsight bias, p. 263

insight, p. 258
intelligence, p. 270
intelligence quotient (IQ), p. 273
language, p. 267
mental age (MA), p. 272
morphemes, p. 267
natural concepts, p. 252
normal curve, p. 275
phonemes, p. 267
pragmatics, p. 267
problem solving, p. 256

prototypes, p. 253
reliability, p. 274
representativeness heuristic, p. 262
semantics, p. 267
standardization, p. 274
syntax, p. 267
thinking, p. 251
trial and error, p. 257
triarchic theory of intelligence, p. 271
validity, p. 274

## Test Prep Are You Ready?

1. _____ is a mental activity associated with obtaining, converting, and using knowledge, and _____ means coming to a decision, reaching a solution, or forming a belief.
   A. Thinking; formal concept
   B. Cognition; superordinate concept
   C. Thinking; cognition
   D. Cognition; thinking

2. _____ are the mental representations of categories of objects, situations, and ideas that share central features or characteristics.
   A. Concepts
   B. Prototypes
   C. Algorithms
   D. Heuristics

3. The boundaries of _____ are imprecise and hard to define; they do not have rigid rules for identification.
   A. algorithms
   B. heuristics
   C. natural concepts
   D. formal concepts

4. After eating at a restaurant, you try to calculate a 20% tip for the server. Your friend suggests that you take the amount of the bill, move the decimal to the left one space, and multiply by 2. Your friend is using _____ to solve the problem.
   A. prototypes
   B. a heuristic
   C. trial and error
   D. an algorithm

5. The _____ suggests that language can affect thinking and perception.

   A. confirmation bias

   B. *g*-factor

   C. triarchic theory

   D. linguistic relativity hypothesis

6. A(n) _____ is a problem-solving strategy that employs a "rule of thumb," such as using 2 cups of water for every cup of rice.

   A. aptitude

   B. heuristic

   C. normal curve

   D. confirmation bias

7. Sometimes we do not gather important information when making decisions because we are only looking for evidence that upholds our beliefs. This is known as the:

   A. availability heuristic.

   B. framing effect.

   C. hindsight bias.

   D. confirmation bias.

8. The wording of a question can influence the outcome of a decision. People are more likely to prefer ground beef if it is described as 80% lean as opposed to 20% fat. This is an example of:

   A. insight.

   B. the confirmation bias.

   C. the framing effect.

   D. the vividness of an event.

9. Infants can recognize and distinguish among all _____ from all languages until about 10 months of age. This is why older children and adults have more difficulty learning to speak a foreign language without the accent of their birth language.

   A. morphemes

   B. phonemes

   C. words

   D. semantics

10. To determine the _____ of an intelligence test, you could give the assessment to a sample of participants and then compare the results with another assessment of intelligence to make sure the test is measuring what it intends to measure.

    A. reliability

    B. validity

    C. standardization

    D. norms

11. How are formal and natural concepts different? Give examples of each.

12. Compare the theories of intelligence presented in this chapter.

13. Many people live in the path of hurricanes. Some choose not to leave their homes when told to evacuate. These people may give the following reason: When they returned home after the last hurricane, they found no significant damage, so there is no need to evacuate this time. What heuristic do you think they used?

14. Why are reliability and validity important in test construction? What are the risks associated with an unreliable IQ test? Can you think of any negative consequence of using an IQ test that is not valid?

15. How many uses can you think of for a hammer? Use divergent thinking.

✓ CHECK YOUR ANSWERS AT THE BACK OF THE BOOK.

YOSHIKAZU TSUNO/Getty Images.

# Human Development

## Why Study Human Development?

**COLLEGE DOWN THE DRAIN?** Joan Brown was 18 years old when she became pregnant for the first time. From that point on, she put her personal ambitions on hold and focused on taking care of her family. Joan worked as a waitress, took a job at Kmart, and spent several years caring for her three kids at home. When her middle child Ericka began preschool, Joan went along with her. She never intended to accompany her daughter to preschool 6 hours a day for the entire year, but if this eased Ericka's anxiety, Joan was willing to do it.

By the time Ericka was 16, the insecurity of her preschool days had vanished. Ericka was now a strong and independent young woman with the ability to accomplish most anything she wanted. "She was very smart, and I saw potential in her," Joan says. "And I knew that she was going to be better than I was, and that's what I always wanted."

Courtesy Ericka Harley.

**Girl with Potential**
Ericka Harley was an honor roll student with a promising future. Her mother, Joan, had high hopes for Ericka's academic and professional endeavors.

But Joan's expectations were shattered one summer day at the doctor's office. Ericka had not been feeling well, though she couldn't quite articulate what was wrong, so Joan took her in for a checkup. When the doctor emerged from the examination room and said, "Ericka wants me to tell you something," Joan knew immediately: "What, she's pregnant?"

The car ride home was very quiet. Joan didn't say much of anything, and she remained withdrawn for a couple days. "I was furious because, you know, you have that talk so many times," Joan recalls. "I figured no college; [it's] gone down the drain."

Joan had reason to be concerned, as the statistics were not in Ericka's favor. Half of all teenage moms don't graduate from high school by the age of 22. By comparison, 90% of women who don't have babies in their teenage years earn high school diplomas (Centers for Disease Control and Prevention [CDC], n.d.-a).

Ericka had reached a crossroads, both in her relationship with her mom and in her life. How would she face the challenge of teen pregnancy? What kinds of physical, mental, and social changes would she experience in the months and years ahead? In other words, how would this major life event affect Ericka's *development?*

## Three Categories of Change

**LO 1** Define human development.

Mel Yates/Getty Images.

**We Can Sit!**
Most babies begin sitting up on their own around 6 months (CDC, n.d.-d). Sitting upright is one of the milestones of physical development. Although it appears to be learned, this behavior is biologically driven. Maturation tends to follow a predictable pattern, regardless of ethnicity or culture.

When psychologists use the word "development," they are referring to the age-related changes that occur in our bodies, minds, and social functioning from conception to death. The goal of **developmental psychology** is to examine these changes. Research in developmental psychology helps us understand the struggles and triumphs of everyday people like Ericka and Joan as they journey through life. Psychologists often focus their studies on "typical" people, as it helps them uncover common themes and variations across the life span.

This chapter homes in on three major categories of developmental change: physical, cognitive, and socioemotional. *Physical development* begins the moment a sperm unites with an egg, and it continues until we take our final breath. The physical growth experienced by children and teens is referred to as **maturation.** For the most part, the changes associated with maturation progress in a predictable pattern that is biologically driven and universal across cultures and ethnicities. After maturation, physical changes continue, but not necessarily in a positive or growth direction. Some people, for example, experience vision loss as they age—this is psychologically challenging and requires adjustments to everyday activities and goals (Maaswinkel et al., 2020; Schilling et al., 2016). Changes in memory, problem solving, decision making, language, and intelligence all fall under the umbrella of *cognitive development.* *Socioemotional development* refers to social behaviors, emotions, and changes people experience with respect to their relationships and overall disposition.

In this chapter, we draw on the biopsychosocial perspective, which recognizes a variety of forces shaping human development. We consider the intricate interplay of heredity, neural activity, and hormones (biological factors); learning and personality traits (psychological factors); and family, culture, and media (social factors).

**developmental psychology** A field of psychology that examines age-related physical, cognitive, and socioemotional changes across the life span.

**maturation** Physical growth beginning with conception and ending when the body stops growing.

*Note:* Quotations attributed to Ericka Harley and Joan Brown are personal communications.

Psychologists use the biopsychosocial perspective to understand a range of events occurring across the life span. Some study the psychological impact of childbirth; others examine changes to health and well-being associated with threats like COVID-19. Just about any phenomenon related to human development can be explored using this approach (Diamond et al., 2020; Melchert, 2015; Saxbe, 2017).

## Three Debates

**LO 2** Outline the three longstanding discussions in developmental psychology.

Science is, at its core, a work in progress, full of unresolved questions and areas of disagreement. In developmental psychology, longstanding debates and discussions tend to cluster around three major themes: nature and nurture, stages and continuity, and stability and change.

**NATURE AND NURTURE** Psychologists debate the degree to which heredity (nature) and environment (nurture) influence behavior and development, but few would dispute the important contributions of both (Kaufman, 2019; Moore, 2013). Researchers can study a trait like impulsivity (the tendency to act before thinking) to determine how much it results from hereditary factors and environment. In this particular case, **nature and nurture** both appear to play a substantial role (Anokhin et al., 2015; Gustavson et al., 2020).

**CONNECTIONS**

In **Chapter 1,** we introduced the concepts of nature and nurture in our discussion of the ancient philosophers. In **Chapter 7,** we introduced the concept of heritability, or the degree to which heredity (nature) is responsible for a particular characteristic in a population. Here, we examine how nature and nurture influence human development.

**STAGES AND CONTINUITY** Some aspects of development occur in stages with clear beginning and end points, and others through a steady, continuous process. Examples of physical changes that may occur in stages include learning to walk and talk, or developing the physical characteristics of a sexually mature adult.

One line of evidence supporting the existence of discrete developmental stages comes to us indirectly through the animal kingdom. Konrad Lorenz (1937) documented the *imprinting* phenomenon, showing that when baby geese hatch, they become attached to the first "moving and sound-emitting object" they see, whether it's their mother or a nearby human (p. 269). Lorenz made sure he was the first moving creature several goslings saw. As a result, the young geese became permanently attached and followed him as soon as they could stand up and walk. But there appeared to be a limited time frame during which this behavioral change (imprinting) occurred. During a **critical period** of development, experiences can lead to new behavior patterns and "irreversible changes" in brain function (Knudsen, 2004; Nelson & Gabard-Durnam, 2020). Unlike baby geese, humans do not exhibit dramatic behavioral changes resulting from experiences that occur during critical periods. However, some researchers hypothesize that there are critical periods for the normal development of vision, attachment, and language (Hensch, 2004; Myers, 1987/2014).

While some developmental changes occur in steps, others happen gradually, without clear beginning and end points (McAdams & Olson, 2010). In other words, they are continuous. Observing a toddler transition into early childhood, you probably won't be able to pinpoint the shift from the "terrible twos" to the more emotionally self-controlled young child. Similarly, you may not notice the gradual growth of a child you see on a regular basis. The child is getting taller all the time, perhaps even passing through "spurts," or periods of accelerated growth, but the process is relatively continuous.

Nina Leen/The LIFE Picture Collection/Getty Images.

**He Must Be My Mother**
A brood of baby geese follows scientist Konrad Lorenz. The goslings treated Lorenz like a mother because he was the first "moving and sound-emitting" object with whom they had contact (Lorenz, 1937, p. 269). As Lorenz discovered, there appears to be a critical period during which this behavioral change called imprinting occurs.

**critical period** Specific time frame in which an organism is sensitive to environmental factors, and certain behaviors and abilities are readily shaped or altered by events or experiences.

**STABILITY AND CHANGE**   Yet another debate centers on the degree to which characteristics change across the life span. For example, how stable is personality over time and across situations? Some researchers suggest that personality traits identified early in life can be used to predict behaviors across the life span (Tang et al., 2020; Wagner et al., 2020). Others report that personality characteristics change as a result of relationships and other experiences. The way we adapt to aging may also influence personality development (Kandler et al., 2015; Specht et al., 2011).

## Three Designs

Developmental psychologists use a variety of research designs to study differences across age groups and time periods (INFOGRAPHIC **8.1**).

**LO 3**  Identify several research methods used in the study of human development.

**A SNAPSHOT IN TIME**   With the **cross-sectional method,** we can examine people of different ages at a given point in time. For example, researchers used the cross-sectional method to investigate maladaptive personality traits, by dividing their participants into groups according to age and then comparing the presence of these traits across the life span (Ruiz et al., 2020). One advantage of the cross-sectional method is that it can provide a great deal of information quickly; by studying differences across age groups, we don't have to wait for people to get older. However, this approach doesn't tell us whether differences across age groups result from actual developmental changes or from common experiences within groups, a phenomenon known as the **cohort effect.** Members of each age group, or **cohort,** have lived through similar historical and cultural eras, and these common experiences may be responsible for some disparities across groups. For example, people from "Generation X" grew up before the internet really took off, while those in "Generation Y" (aka the "millennials") were raised in the era of smartphones, tablets, and other digital technologies. These different environmental exposures may influence how they think and relate to others.

**FOLLOWING PEOPLE OVER TIME**   Researchers can avoid the cohort effect by using the **longitudinal method,** which follows one group of individuals over a period of time. Curious to find out how decision-making abilities change with age, one team of researchers studied older people (spanning ages 60 to 85) over 5 years. After comparing participants' performance at the beginning and end of this period, the researchers concluded that, overall, "a high level of competence can be preserved in healthy old adulthood" (Del Missier et al., 2020, p. 559). But longitudinal studies are difficult to conduct because they require a great deal of money, time, and participant investment. Common challenges include attrition (people dropping out of the study) and practice effects (people performing better on measures as they get more "practice").

**BEST OF BOTH WORLDS?**   The **cross-sequential method,** also used by developmental psychologists, is a mixture of the longitudinal and cross-sectional methods. Participants are divided into groups and followed over time, so researchers can observe changes in individuals as they age *and* identify differences across age groups. Researchers used this approach to explore cognitive decline, assigning participants to 5-year age groups, and then following them for as long as 28 years (Sabia et al., 2017; Singh-Manoux et al., 2012). This method has its own set of drawbacks, however. It is costly and requires many participants, some of whom may drop out before the study is complete.

---

**CONNECTIONS**

In **Chapter 1,** we described confounding variables as unaccounted factors that change in sync with the independent variable, making it very difficult to discern which is causing changes in the dependent variable. Here, we consider how a cohort can act as a confounding variable.

---

**cross-sectional method**  A research design that examines people of different ages at a single point in time.

**cohort effect**  The differences across groups that result from common experiences within the groups.

**longitudinal method**  A research design that examines one sample of people over a period of time to determine age-related changes.

**cross-sequential method**  A research design that examines groups of people of different ages, following them across time.

# Research Methods in Developmental Psychology

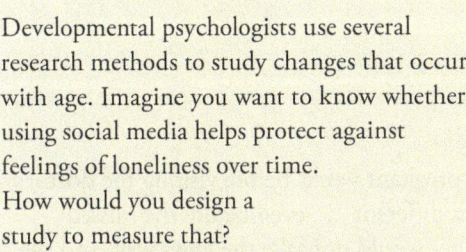

Developmental psychologists use several research methods to study changes that occur with age. Imagine you want to know whether using social media helps protect against feelings of loneliness over time. How would you design a study to measure that? Let's compare methods.

## Longitudinal

Measure a **single group** at **different points in time**

**Example:** Researchers follow a sample of participants, interviewing them every decade for a total of three measurements. As they age, participants report lower levels of loneliness than expected. But because the study is longitudinal, we can't eliminate the possibility that this particular group of participants is less lonely because of some historically specific effect.

GROUP 1

**2005** **2015** **2025**

**BENEFITS**
+ Can track age-related changes.

**PROBLEMS**
– Measured changes could be specific to the particular group of participants.
– Takes a long time, leading some participants to drop out before study is complete.

## Cross-sectional

Measure groups of people of **different ages** (for example, 20-, 40-, and 60-year-olds) at a **single point in time**

**Example:** Researchers interview participants in three different age groups: 20-, 40-, and 60-year-olds. The oldest group reports higher levels of loneliness. But because the study is cross-sectional, we can't be sure if this finding reflects a cohort effect, in which differences may be due to age or to common experiences within the group, as opposed to developmental changes in physical, cognitive, or socioemotional functioning.

GROUP 3
GROUP 2
GROUP 1

2005    **2015**    2025

**BENEFITS**
+ Allows comparison between age groups.
+ Can be completed relatively quickly.

**PROBLEMS**
– Susceptible to cohort effect.

## Cross-sequential

Measure groups of people of **different ages,** following them across **different points in time**

**Example:** Researchers interview participants from three age groups every decade for a total of three measurements. This results in data showing how social media use and loneliness change within each group as they age.

GROUP 3

GROUP 2

GROUP 1

**2005** **2015** **2025**

**BENEFITS**
+ Shows changes within individuals and between groups.
+ Better addresses cohort effect.

**PROBLEMS**
– Requires substantial resources and many participants.
– Takes a long time, leading some participants to drop out before study is complete.

>>> **SHOW WHAT YOU KNOW**

1. A 6-month-old infant sits upright without help, and the parents are delighted that their child has reached this physical milestone. Here we have an example of _____, as this change in behavior is biologically driven.

2. Explain the three longstanding debates in developmental psychology.

3. A researcher asks 300 participants to take a memory test and then compares the results across five different age groups. This researcher is using which of the following methods?
   **A.** cross-sequential
   **B.** longitudinal
   **C.** cross-sectional
   **D.** biopsychosocial

   ✓ CHECK YOUR ANSWERS AT THE BACK OF THE BOOK.

# Inside the Womb

**LIFE GOES ON**   Ericka suspected she was pregnant weeks before visiting the doctor's office with her mom. "I felt like something was different . . . even before the missed period," she recalls. Ericka feared that her mother would not take the news well, and she was right. Joan was indeed angry and disappointed in the beginning, but a talk with her own mother changed her outlook: "I remember having a conversation with my mom," Joan recalls, "and she said, '[Ericka is] not the first, and she won't be the last,' and something just clicked."

From that point on, Joan continued to do what she had always done as a mother—give Ericka unconditional emotional support. She also made it clear that Ericka would be taking full responsibility for herself and her child. Ericka was welcome to live at home, but there would be no complimentary babysitting or financial assistance.

As the pregnancy progressed, Ericka began to imagine the little person developing inside of her. "I wondered about everything," Ericka says. "Would she smile like me? Would she act like me? Would she love me back? . . . I found out at about 5 months that I was having a girl. My heart melted and I was even more in love."

The qualities Ericka imagined in her baby—the smile, the voice, the sex, and even to some degree the behaviors—would be influenced by the *genes* of the developing baby. Let's venture inside the cell and find out where those genes dwell.

## What Are Chromosomes and Genes?

**LO4** Examine the role genes play in our development.

With the exception of red blood cells, every cell in the human body has a nucleus at its center. Within this nucleus is material containing the blueprint, or plan, for building a complete person. This material is coiled tightly into 46 **chromosomes,** the threadlike structures we inherit from our biological parents (23 from our father and 23 from our mother). A chromosome contains one molecule of **deoxyribonucleic acid (DNA).** Looking at the DNA molecule in FIGURE **8.1,** you can see that a specific section along its length has been identified. This section corresponds to a **gene,** and each person has 20,000–25,000 of them (Medline Plus, 2020, September 17). Genes provide the instructions for making proteins that determine the texture of your hair, the color of your eyes, and some aspects of your personality. Genes influence nearly every dimension of the complex living system known as YOU.

As noted, your chromosomes, and all the genes they contain, come from your biological parents. In the moment of conception, your father's sperm united with your mother's egg to form a **zygote** (ZAHY-goht), a single cell that eventually gave rise to the trillions of cells that now make up your body (Sherwood, 2016).

**chromosomes** Inherited threadlike structures composed of deoxyribonucleic acid (DNA).

**deoxyribonucleic acid (DNA)** A molecule that provides instructions for the development of an organism.

**gene** Specified segment of a DNA molecule.

**zygote** a single cell formed by the union of a sperm and egg.

**monozygotic twins** Identical twins who develop from one egg inseminated at conception, which then splits into two separate zygotes.

**dizygotic twins** Fraternal twins who develop from two eggs inseminated by two sperm, and are as genetically similar as any sibling pair.

**androgens** The male hormones secreted by the testes in males and by the adrenal glands in both males and females.

**estrogens** The female hormones secreted primarily by the ovaries and by the adrenal glands in both males and females.

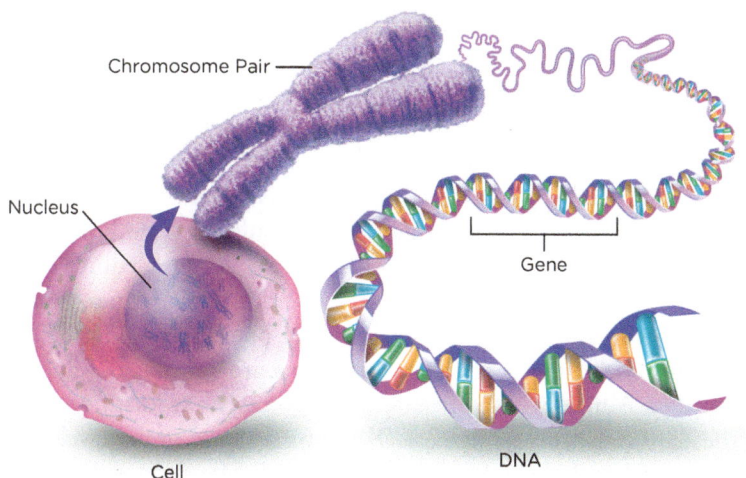

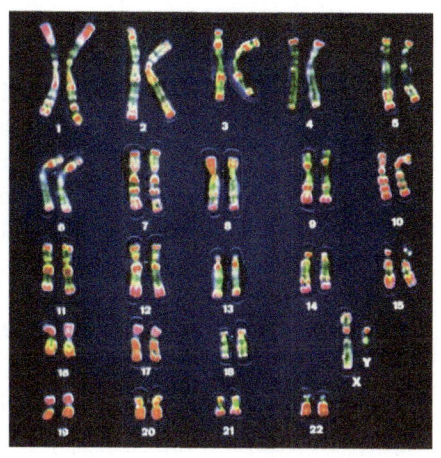

Chromosome Pair

Nucleus

Cell

Gene

DNA

CNRI/Science Source.

**FIGURE 8.1**

**Chromosomes, DNA, and Genes**

Every cell in your body, except red blood cells and sex cells (sperm or egg), contains a full set of chromosomes like that shown in the photo on the far right. These 23 chromosome pairs contain the full blueprint for you as a complete, unique person. The primary component of each chromosome is a single, tightly wound molecule of DNA. Your DNA contains 20,000–25,000 genes (Medline Plus, 2020, September 17), each determining specific traits such as hair texture and eye color. Note the sex chromosomes (*X* and *Y*) on the lower right, indicating that the sex is male.

**TWINS**   In some cases, conception leads to twins or multiples. Identical or **monozygotic twins** develop when one egg is fertilized by one sperm and then splits, forming two separate zygotes with identical sets of 46 chromosomes. (This means they share 100% of their genes at conception.) Eventually, these zygotes develop into identical twin infants who have the same sex and almost identical features. Fraternal or **dizygotic twins,** on the other hand, result when two eggs are fertilized by two different sperm, leading to two distinct zygotes. Twins and multiples resulting from distinct sperm–egg combinations (that is, not identical) are like other biological siblings; they share around 50% of their genes. The likelihood of a woman giving birth to twins, triplets, or other multiples has increased in recent decades because more people are using assisted reproductive technology (ART). Often ART involves transferring multiple embryos into the womb; if more than one of those embryos survives, the woman may give birth to multiples (Sunderam et al., 2019).

**SEX CHROMOSOMES**   Typically, both sperm and egg contain 23 chromosomes, so the resulting zygote has 23 *pairs* of chromosomes, or a total of 46. The 23rd pair of chromosomes, also referred to as the *sex chromosomes,* includes specific instructions for the zygote to develop into a male or female (*XX* for female, and *XY* for male). This genetic sex depends on the father's sperm, which can contribute either an *X* or a *Y* to the 23rd pair (the egg, on the other hand, can only contribute an *X*). If the sperm carries an *X,* the genetic sex is *XX,* and the zygote generally develops into a female. If the sperm carries a *Y,* the genetic sex is *XY,* and the zygote typically develops into a male. This designation of genetic sex is called *sex determination,* and it guides the activity of hormones directing the development of reproductive organs and structures (Ngun et al., 2011).

Genetic sex is established at conception and remains constant throughout life. In a genetic male, the presence of the *Y* chromosome causes the fetal sex glands (also known as *gonads*) to become testes. If the *Y* chromosome is not present, as in the case of a genetic female, then the gonads develop into ovaries (Koopman et al., 2016; Parivesh et al., 2019). Both the testes and ovaries secrete sex hormones that influence the development of reproductive organs: **Androgens** come from the testes and **estrogens** from the ovaries. *Testosterone,* for example, is an androgen that promotes the development of male genitalia (Kothandapani et al., 2020).

**DIVERSITY OF SEXUAL DEVELOPMENT**   In some cases, irregularities in genes or hormone activity can lead to differences of sex development (APA, 2015c; Parivesh et al. 2019; Topp, 2013). Differences of sexual development are caused by a variety of

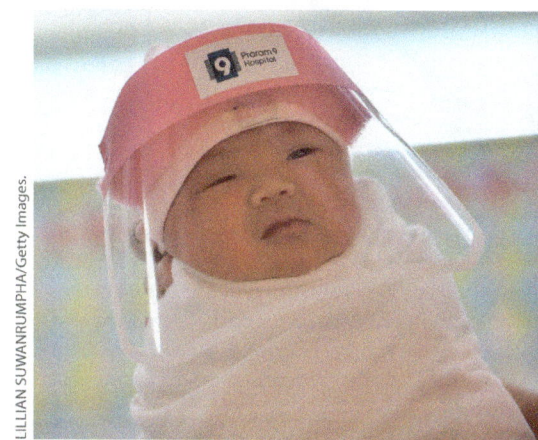

LILLIAN SUWANRUMPHA/Getty Images.

**Was There a COVID Baby Boom?**

Some people predicted that the U.S. birth rate would increase following the initial COVID-19 lockdowns in the spring of 2020 (Naftulin, 2020). Couples were stuck at home, so they would have more opportunities to have sex—or so the reasoning went. Actually, the pandemic appears to have created more of a "baby bust" than a "baby boom." Economic insecurity, concerns about health, and other pandemic-related factors led many women to hold off on having children (Dockterman, 2020; Kearney & Levine, 2020).

"congenital conditions in which development of chromosomal, gonadal, or anatomic sex is atypical" (Lee et al., 2006, p. e488). According to the American Psychiatric Association (2013, p. 451), **intersexual** refers to having "conflicting or ambiguous biological indicators" of male or female in sexual structures and organs. In some cases, intersexual development occurs as a result of atypical hormone activity. For example, an individual with *androgen insensitivity syndrome* is genetically male (*XY*) but is partly or completely insensitive to androgens. As a result, they are born with sex organs that are female-like or ambiguous (Gottlieb et al., 2014; Medline Plus, 2020, August 18). In other cases, intersex traits result from irregularities in sex chromosomes. A female with Turner's syndrome has only one *X* chromosome (as opposed to two *X* chromosomes), female genitals, ovaries that are not fully developed, and problems with fertility. A male with Klinefelter's syndrome has at least one extra *X* chromosome in the 23rd pair (for example, *XXY*) and may have underdeveloped sexual organs and secondary sex characteristics (Conway, 2014; Mandoki et al., 1991; Manning et al., 2013).

Intersex traits are commonly referred to as "disorders of sexual development," but this terminology has "pathologising implications"; in other words, it may suggest intersex traits are medical problems that need to be fixed (Schweizer et al., 2014). The word "hermaphrodite" is also problematic; in addition to being outdated, this term is derogatory and misleading because it refers to the impossible condition of being both fully male and fully female (Vilain, 2008). Research suggests that 0.13% of infants (or a little more than one per thousand) are born with intersex traits (Aydin et al., 2019).

**Have a Peak?**
Some traits are determined by the presence of a single, dominant gene. The "widow's peak," or V-shaped hairline, is thought to be one of them (Chiras, 2015). The person on the left must have at least one dominant widow's peak gene, while the one on the right has two recessive straight hairline genes.

**DOMINANT OR RECESSIVE?**    Genes are behind just about every human trait you can imagine—from height, to disease susceptibility, to behavior. But remember, you possess two versions of each chromosome (one from mom, one from dad), and therefore two of each gene. Sometimes the genes in a pair are identical (both encode dimples, for instance). Other times, the two genes differ, providing dissimilar instructions for development (one encodes dimples, while the other encodes no dimples). Often one gene variant has more influence than the other. This **dominant gene** governs the expression of the inherited characteristic, overpowering the recessive, or subordinate, gene in the pair. A **recessive gene** cannot overcome the influence of a dominant gene. For example, "dimples" are dominant, and "no dimples" are recessive. If one gene encodes for dimples and the other no dimples, then dimples will be expressed. If both genes encode for no dimples, no dimples will be expressed. This all sounds relatively straightforward, but it's not. Psychological traits—and the genetics behind them—are exceedingly complex. Characteristics like creativity and aggression, as well as disorders like autism spectrum disorder, are influenced by multiple genes (a phenomenon known as polygenic inheritance), and most of these genes have yet to be identified (Li et al., 2020; Quick et al., 2020; Ruisch et al., 2020).

**LO 5** Discuss how genotype and phenotype relate to development.

**GENOTYPE AND PHENOTYPE**    Remember, almost every cell in your body has 23 chromosome pairs (46 chromosomes total). These chromosomes contain all your genes, collectively known as your **genotype.** Genotypes do not change in response to the environment, but gene expression is influenced by environmental factors. Because so much variability exists in the surrounding world, the outcome of this interaction is not predetermined. The color and appearance of your skin, for example, result from an interplay between your genotype and a variety of environmental factors including sun and wind exposure, age, nutrition, and smoking—all of which can impact

**intersexual** Having ambiguous or inconsistent biological indicators of male or female in the sexual structures and organs.

**dominant gene** One of a pair of genes that has power over the expression of an inherited characteristic.

**recessive gene** One of a pair of genes that is overpowered by a dominant gene.

**genotype** An individual's complete collection of genes.

how your genes are expressed (Kolb et al., 2019; Rees, 2003). The product of this interaction is the **phenotype**—a person's observable characteristics. Your phenotype is apparent in your unique physical, cognitive, and socioemotional characteristics (Henrich & Muthukrishna, 2021; Plomin et al., 2016; Scarr & McCartney, 1983).

## Think Critically

### WHAT IS EPIGENETICS?

The field that examines the processes involved in the development of phenotypes is known as **epigenetics,** which literally means "on top of or in addition to genetics" (Kanherkar et al., 2014, p. 1). Your DNA is surrounded by chemical compounds, collectively known as the epigenome, that can control gene expression. Environmental factors, such as exposure to toxins, smoking, and nutrition, may trigger changes in the epigenome and thereby influence which genes are "turned on" or "turned off" (Kanherkar et al., 2014; Medline Plus, 2020, September 21). Sometimes these patterns of activation and deactivation can pave the way for diseases like cancer, or impact family environments—through parenting behaviors, for example (Hein et al., 2019; Medline Plus, 2020, September 21). Epigenetics serves as a "bridge" or "link" between nature and nurture (Tammen et al., 2013).

**A "BRIDGE" BETWEEN NATURE AND NURTURE?**

**HOW IS IT RELEVANT?**   You might be wondering what genotypes, phenotypes, and epigenetics have to do with psychology. The interaction of genes and environment influences our behavior, and psychologists want to learn how this occurs. Consider schizophrenia, a disabling psychological disorder with symptoms ranging from hallucinations to disorganized thinking (Chapter 13). A large body of evidence suggests that some people have genotypes that predispose them to schizophrenia, with **heritability estimates** between 60% and 80% (Baselmans et al., 2020; Cardno & Owen, 2014; Edwards et al., 2016). But the expression of the disorder results from a combination of genotype and experience, including diet, stress, toxins, and childhood adversity (Hameed & Lewis, 2016; Zhang & Meaney, 2010). Identical twins, who have the same genotype at conception, may display different phenotypes, including distinct expressions of schizophrenia if they both develop this disorder. Researchers have identified epigenetic characteristics associated with schizophrenia, although more research is needed to determine how they fit into the bigger picture (Hannon et al., 2016; Montano et al., 2016). We do know this: Schizophrenia and other psychological phenomena result from complex relationships between genes and the environment (Bolhuis et al., 2019; Kremen et al., 2016).

Now that we have a basic handle on genotypes and phenotypes, let's shift our attention toward the developmental changes that occur within the womb. How do we get from a single cell to a living breathing human with 10 little fingers and toes, fully functional organ systems, and a brain equipped with 100 billion neurons (Huang & Luo, 2015; Lake et al., 2018)? It's time to explore prenatal development, the 39–40 weeks between conception and the birth of a full-term baby (Spong, 2013).

## From Single Cell to Full-Fledged Person

**LO 6** Describe the progression of prenatal development.

Once the zygote is formed, it immediately begins to divide into two cells, then each of those cells divides, and so on. From conception to the end of the second week is the *germinal period,* which ends with the rapidly dividing mass of cells implanting in

**CONNECTIONS**

In **Chapter 7,** we described heritability as the degree to which heredity is responsible for a particular characteristic. Here, we see that around 60–80% of the population-wide variation in schizophrenia can be attributed to genetic make-up and 20–40% to the environment.

**phenotype** The observable expression or characteristics of one's genetic inheritance.

**epigenetics** A field of study that examines the processes involved in the development of phenotypes.

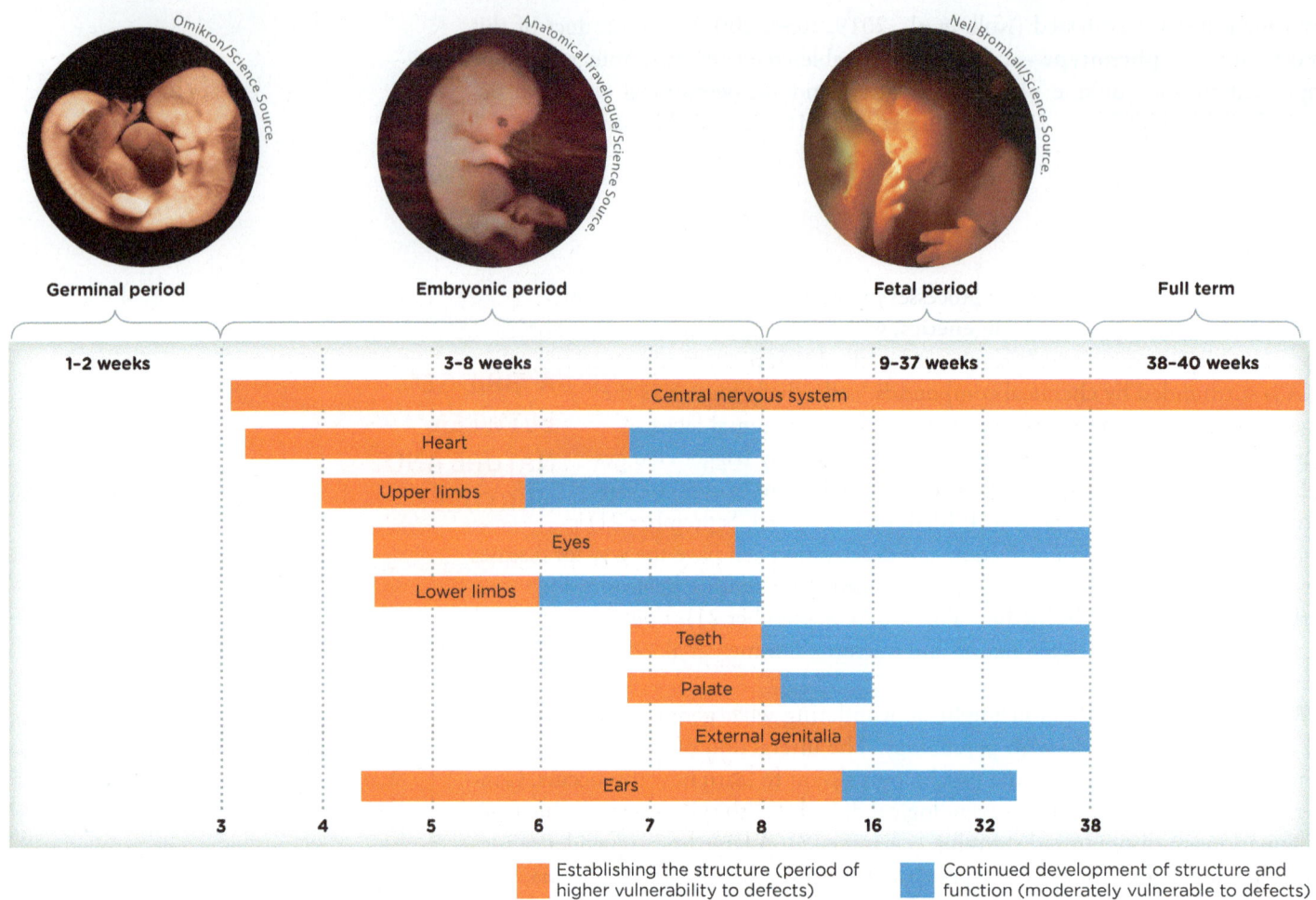

**FIGURE 8.2**

**Prenatal Development and Periods of Critical Growth**

During prenatal development, individual structures form and are fine-tuned at different times. As each structure is being established, it is particularly vulnerable to interference.

the uterine wall. Implantation is successful less than half the time, however (Gold, 2005). Of reported pregnancies, nearly 20% end in miscarriage (Rossen et al., 2017), many of which result from genetic abnormalities of the embryo (Velagaleti & Moore, 2011).

Between weeks 3 and 8, the growing mass of cells is called an **embryo.** The embryo develops in the *amniotic sac,* which is a "bag" of fluids that provides protection. An organ called the *placenta* supplies the embryo with oxygen and nourishment, disposes of waste, and prevents mixing of blood between mother and baby. The embryo is connected to the placenta by the *umbilical cord.* Unlike the germinal period, when all cells are identical, the *embryonic period* marks the time when cells differentiate and the major organs and systems begin to form (**FIGURE 8.2**). This differentiation allows for the heart to begin beating, the arms and legs to grow, and the spinal cord and intestinal system to develop.

**embryo** The unborn human from the beginning of the third week of pregnancy, lasting through the eighth week of prenatal development.

**teratogens** Environmental agents that can damage the growing embryo or fetus.

**fetal alcohol syndrome (FAS)** Delays in development that result from moderate to heavy alcohol use during pregnancy.

**THE WORLD CAN BE TOXIC**  The embryo may be safely nestled in the amniotic sac, but it is not protected from all dangers. **Teratogens** (tuh-RAT-uh-jenz) are environmental agents that can damage an embryo or fetus (**TABLE 8.1**). Radiation, viruses, bacteria, chemicals, and drugs are all considered teratogens. The damage depends on the agent, as well as the timing and duration of exposure, and can result in miscarriage, decreased birth weight, heart defects, long-term behavioral problems, and other adverse outcomes (Jamkhande et al., 2014).

**TABLE 8.1** Dangerous Environments

| Category | Teratogen | Potential Effects |
|---|---|---|
| **Drugs** | Acne medication (isotretinoin) | Heart defects; neurological, musculoskeletal, and liver issues |
| | Alcohol | Fetal alcohol syndrome: intellectual disability, poor growth, heart problems, growth delay |
| | Caffeine | High exposure associated with miscarriage |
| | Cocaine | Birth defects, miscarriage, placental abruption |
| | Marijuana | Low birth weight, small skull, tremors |
| | Nicotine | Malformations, low birth weight, cleft lip or palate, heart defects |
| **Environmental factors** | Lead | High exposure linked with miscarriage and stillbirth, intellectual disability |
| | Mercury | Cerebral palsy, intellectual disability, blindness |
| | Radiation exposure | Small skull, blindness, spina bifida, cleft palate |
| **Infections** | Rubella | Heart disease, small skull, liver issues |
| | Syphilis | Inflamed joints, rash, swollen liver and spleen |
| | Toxoplasmosis | Small skull, intellectual disability, malformations of the eye |
| **Maternal disease** | Diabetes | Abnormal tissue formation, birth defects |
| | Epilepsy (antiepileptic drugs and seizures) | Miscarriages, spina bifida, heart defects, small skull, cleft lip, cleft palate, developmental delays |

From conception until birth, the developing human is nestled deep inside a woman's body, but it remains vulnerable to threats. Listed here are some common teratogens and their effects. Remember, teratogens may include both legal and illegal drugs. Information from Brent (2004), Huizink (2014), and Jamkhande et al. (2014).

One well-known teratogen is alcohol, which can lead to fetal alcohol spectrum disorders (FASD). In particular, **fetal alcohol syndrome (FAS)** is the result of moderate to heavy alcohol use during pregnancy, which can cause delays in normal development, a small head, lower intelligence, and distinct facial characteristics (for example, wide-spaced eyes, flattened nose). Wondering how much alcohol is safe to drink during pregnancy? The answer is none (Dejong & Olyaei, 2019; Landgren, 2017; Vall et al., 2015). "Alcohol readily crosses the placenta with fetal blood alcohol levels approaching maternal levels within 2 hours of maternal intake" (Dejong et al., 2019, p. 144). For women who drink during pregnancy, the odds of delivering a baby with FAS are 1 in 67 (Popova et al., 2017). Alcohol consumption is something we can control, but this is not the case with all teratogens. Simply living near a farm that applies certain pesticides may increase a mother's risk of giving birth to a child with autism spectrum disorder, developmental delay, and abnormal brain development (Hertz-Picciotto et al., 2018; Rauh, 2018; Shelton et al., 2014).

**FROM PUMPKIN SEED TO WATERMELON** Between 2 months and birth, the growing human is called a fetus (Figure 8.2). During the *fetal period,* the developing person grows from the size of a pumpkin seed to a small watermelon, the average birth weight being approximately 7 pounds (by North American standards). It is also during this time that the developing person begins to

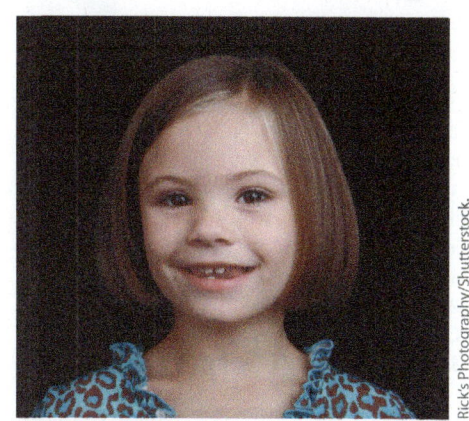

Rick's Photography/Shutterstock.

**Life with FAS**
This child has fetal alcohol syndrome (FAS). Children affected by FAS tend to have difficulty with physical activities that require coordination and other motor skills. They also may have attentional problems that interfere with their school performance. Having a secure, loving family that provides structure and predictability can help children with FAS thrive (National Organization on Fetal Alcohol Syndrome, n.d.).

demonstrate clear **sleep–wake cycles** (Suwanrath & Suntharasaj, 2010). By the end of the fetal period, most systems and structures are fully developed, and the baby is ready for the outside world.

If you step back and contemplate the baby-making phenomenon, it's really quite amazing. But many more exciting developments are in store. Are you ready for some shrieking, babbling, and a little game of peekaboo? Let's move on to infancy and childhood.

## CONNECTIONS

In **Chapter 4,** we noted that some physiological activities are driven by a *circadian* rhythm; that is, they roughly follow the 24-hour cycle of daylight and darkness. Here, we can see that daily sleep–wake cycles become evident before birth.

 **SHOW WHAT YOU KNOW**

1. _____ are threadlike structures we inherit from our biological mothers and fathers.
   A. Teratogens
   B. Zygotes
   C. Genes
   D. Chromosomes

2. _____ represents a complete collection of genes, and _____ represents the observed expression of inherited characteristics.

3. A coworker is in her 6th week of pregnancy. She is excited because during this _____, her baby is developing a spinal cord and its heart is beginning to beat.
   A. embryonic period
   B. phenotype
   C. germinal period
   D. genotype

 CHECK YOUR ANSWERS AT THE BACK OF THE BOOK.

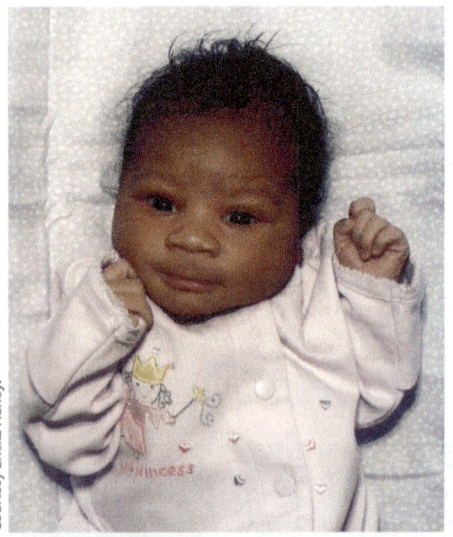

Courtesy Ericka Harley.

**Introducing . . . Aa'Niyah!**
Ericka's baby was full-term, but many newborns arrive before the typical 39–41 weeks. Without medical intervention, some of these premature infants would not survive. Thanks to scientific advances, the *age of viability* is now about 20–26 weeks in the United States (American College of Obstetricians and Gynecologists & Society for Maternal-Fetal Medicine, 2017).

# Infants and Children

**BABY'S COMING!**    April, 18, 2006: Ericka was already three days past her due date. Doctors were concerned the baby was growing too big, so they planned to induce labor (use medications to activate contractions of the uterus, and thereby start the birthing process). But just a few hours before Ericka was supposed to be induced, she began feeling strange sensations in her abdomen. Her little girl was coming. Twenty hours and many painful contractions later, Ericka was in the final stages of labor. As she strained to push the baby out, doctors asked if she wanted to feel the baby's head. "I don't want to feel her head. I just want it to be over!" Ericka remembers saying. Within minutes, she was looking into the eyes of her baby girl. "She was just perfect," Ericka recalls. "I couldn't believe how tiny her fingers were, and I counted them, and I touched all of them."

Ericka cried as she watched Joan take the baby in her arms. Then the baby's father held her, and he looked like he might cry, too. It was an emotional moment. After 9 months of anticipation, a new little person had arrived. They named her Aa'Niyah.

## Newborns

**LO 7** Summarize the physical changes that occur in infancy.

From the moment she was born, Aa'Niyah (affectionately called "Niyah") was intensely interested in people. She made a lot of eye contact, listened closely to voices, and responded with her own little noises. Babies come into the world equipped with keen sensory capabilities that seem to be designed for facilitating relationships (Makin, 2020).

## CONNECTIONS

In **Chapter 3,** we described specialized neurons called photoreceptors, which absorb light energy and turn it into electrical and chemical signals for the brain to process. A cone is a type of photoreceptor that enables us to see colors and details. Newborns have blurry eyesight, in part because their cones have not fully developed.

**NEWBORN SENSES**    Vision can be blurry for the first few months, one reason being that the **light-sensitive cones** in the eyes are still developing (Banks & Salapatek, 1978). Even so, newborns are drawn to people and prefer to look at human faces over geometric shapes (Salva et al., 2011; Simion & Di Giorgio, 2015). They tend to focus their gaze at about 8–10 inches away (American Optometric Association, n.d.), which happens to be the approximate distance between the baby's face and the face of the caregiver cradling them. Eye contact is thought to strengthen the relationship between infants and caregivers.

The auditory system is functioning before birth, but it takes time for fluids to dry up so the baby can hear clearly (Hall et al., 2004). Within hours of being born, newborns can discriminate their mother's voice from those of other women, and they show a preference for her voice (DeCasper & Fifer, 1980; Moon et al., 2015). This ability to recognize Mom's voice may begin developing in utero (Kisilevsky et al., 2003; Moon et al., 2015).

Smell and taste are also well developed in newborn infants, who can distinguish the scent of their mothers' breast milk from that of other women within days of birth (Marin et al., 2015; Schaal et al., 2020). Babies prefer sweet tastes, react strongly to sour tastes, and notice certain changes to their mothers' diets because those tastes are present in breast milk. If a mother has eaten something very sweet, for instance, the infant tends to breast-feed longer.

The sense of touch, and thus the ability to feel pain, are evident before birth (Marx & Nagy, 2015). It was once believed that newborns were incapable of experiencing pain, but research suggests otherwise. The brain activity infants and adults display in response to painful stimuli is "extremely similar," suggesting that babies suffer like the rest of us (Eccleston et al., 2020; Goksan et al., 2015).

**NEWBORN REFLEXES**    Newborns exhibit several *reflexes,* or automatic responses to stimuli. Some are necessary for survival, while others serve no obvious purpose. Reflexes may fade away in the first weeks and months of life, but many resurface as voluntary movements as the infant grows and develops motor control (Thelen & Fisher, 1982). TABLE **8.2** describes several reflexes seen in recently born babies.

**TABLE 8.2    Newborn Reflexes**

| Reflex | The Response | See It | Reflex | The Response | See It |
|---|---|---|---|---|---|
| Rooting | When cheek is touched, newborn turns head toward stimulus. | Christine Hanscomb/Science Source. | Babinski (toes curl) | When sole of newborn foot is stroked, big toe bends toward ankle and other toes fan out. | Ray Ellis/Science Source. |
| Sucking | Mouth area touched by object, then newborn sucks on object. | BSIP SA/Alamy Stock Photo. | Stepping | Newborn will take steps when feet are put on hard surface. | Picture Partners/Alamy. |
| Grasping | Newborn actively grasps when object is placed in palm of hand. | michellegibson/Getty Images. | Moro (startle) | Abrupt extension of head, arms, and legs after a sudden noise or movement. | ASTIER/age fotostock. |

Newborns exhibit various reflexes, or automatic responses to stimuli. Listed here are some of the reflexes first evident at birth. Information from Zafeiriou (2004).

A newborn spends most of the time eating, sleeping, and crying. But this stage soon gives way to a period that is far more interactive and features some of the most memorable milestones of human development, from waving "bye-bye" to taking first steps. INFOGRAPHIC **8.2** details some of the sensory and motor milestones of infancy, and the average ages at which they occur. Although the sequence and timing of these achievements are fairly universal, there can be significant variation from one infant to the next.

## What's Going On in the Brain?

**CONNECTIONS**

In **Chapter 2,** we described the structure of a typical neuron, which includes an axon projecting from the cell body. Many axons are surrounded by a myelin sheath, a fatty substance that insulates the activities occurring within, speeding the transmission of neural messages down the axon. Here, we see how myelination impacts motor development.

The speed of brain development in the womb and immediately after birth is astounding. There are times in fetal development when the brain is producing approximately 250,000 new neurons per minute (Kolb & Gibb, 2011)! At birth, a baby's brain has approximately 100 billion neurons (Toga et al., 2006)—roughly the same number as that of an adult. Meanwhile, **axons** are growing longer, and more neurons, particularly those involved in motor control, are developing a myelin sheath around their axons. The myelin sheath increases the efficiency of neural communication, which leads to better motor control, enabling a baby to wave and walk.

**MAKING—AND BREAKING—CONNECTIONS**  As young children interact with the environment, new connections sprout between neurons, but not uniformly throughout the brain. Between ages 3 and 6, for example, the greatest increase in neural connections occurs in the frontal lobes, the area of the brain involved in planning and attention (Thompson et al., 2000; Toga et al., 2006). As more links are established, more associations can be made between different stimuli, and between behavior and consequences. A young person needs to learn quickly, and this process makes it possible. The extraordinary growth in synaptic connections does not last forever, though, as the number of connections decreases by 40–50% by the time a child reaches puberty (Thompson et al., 2000; Webb et el., 2001). This decrease in synaptic connections occurs through a process called *synaptic pruning:* Unused synaptic connections are downsized or eliminated, and frequently used connections get stronger, which helps increase the efficiency of the brain (Chechik et al., 1998; Sakai, 2020; Spear, 2013; Vainchtein et al., 2018). The process is like trimming a rose bush: Getting rid of the thin, weak areas allows the stronger parts of the plant to flourish (Sakai, 2020).

**ENRICHMENT**  Many aspects of brain development are strongly influenced by experiences and input from the environment. In the 1960s and 1970s, Mark Rosenzweig and his colleagues at the University of California, Berkeley, studied this

**Environment Matters**
The children on the left appear to be immersed in an enriched environment, which offers opportunities for physical exercise, social interaction, and other types of stimulating activity that promote positive changes in the brain (Khan & Hillman, 2014; van Praag et al., 2000). Fewer signs of enrichment appear in the photo to the right, which shows children in a Romanian orphanage in the late 1990s.

# Infant Brain and Sensorimotor Development

As newborns grow, they progress at an astounding rate in seen and unseen ways. When witnessing babies' new skills, whether it be reaching for a rattle or pulling themselves into a standing position, it's easy to marvel at how far they have come. But what you can't see is the real action. These sensorimotor advancements are only possible because of the incredible brain development happening in the background.

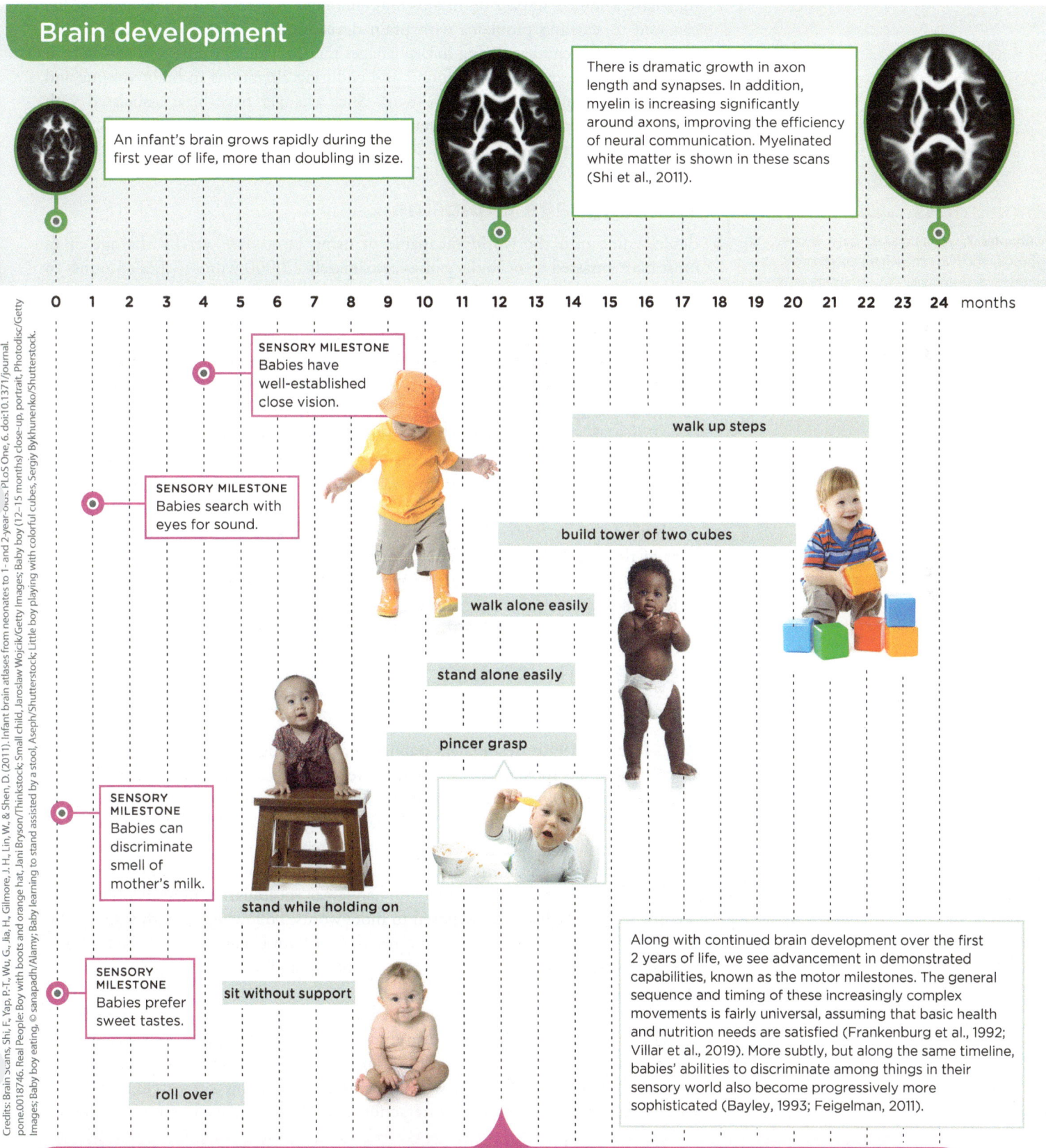

## Brain development

An infant's brain grows rapidly during the first year of life, more than doubling in size.

There is dramatic growth in axon length and synapses. In addition, myelin is increasing significantly around axons, improving the efficiency of neural communication. Myelinated white matter is shown in these scans (Shi et al., 2011).

0 1 2 3 4 5 6 7 8 9 10 11 12 13 14 15 16 17 18 19 20 21 22 23 24 months

**SENSORY MILESTONE**
Babies have well-established close vision.

**SENSORY MILESTONE**
Babies search with eyes for sound.

**SENSORY MILESTONE**
Babies can discriminate smell of mother's milk.

**SENSORY MILESTONE**
Babies prefer sweet tastes.

walk up steps

build tower of two cubes

walk alone easily

stand alone easily

pincer grasp

stand while holding on

sit without support

roll over

Along with continued brain development over the first 2 years of life, we see advancement in demonstrated capabilities, known as the motor milestones. The general sequence and timing of these increasingly complex movements is fairly universal, assuming that basic health and nutrition needs are satisfied (Frankenburg et al., 1992; Villar et al., 2019). More subtly, but along the same timeline, babies' abilities to discriminate among things in their sensory world also become progressively more sophisticated (Bayley, 1993; Feigelman, 2011).

## Motor and Sensory Development

phenomenon in rodents (Kolb & Whishaw, 1998). They found that rats placed in stimulating environments (furnished with opportunities for exploration and social interaction) experience greater increases in brain weight and synaptic connections than those put in nonstimulating environments (Barredo & Deeg, 2009; Kolb & Whishaw, 1998; Rosenzweig, 1984). Environmental stimulation (or lack thereof) may have a similar impact on infants and children. "Severe deprivation" early in life can lead to startling problems with brain development (Mackes et al., 2020). For example, young children living in orphanages that provide minimal care and human interaction may experience "profound and enduring alterations in brain volume and structure in young adulthood" (p. 644). Such changes have been associated with symptoms of attention-deficit/hyperactivity disorder (ADHD) and lower performance on intelligence tests (Mackes et al., 2020).

**CONNECTIONS**

In **Chapter 7,** we introduced basic elements of language, such as phonemes, morphemes, and semantics, and explored how language relates to thought. In this chapter, we discuss how language develops.

## The Language Explosion

Babies come into the world incapable of using **language**, yet by the age of 6, most have amassed a vocabulary of approximately 13,000 words—that amounts to about one new word every 2 hours awake (Pinker, 1994). One important component of this learning process is *infant-directed speech (IDS),* sometimes referred to as "motherese," which is often used by parents and other caregivers. High-pitched and repetitious, infant-directed speech is observed throughout the world (Singh et al., 2009). Can't you just hear Ericka saying to baby Niyah, "Who's my baby girl?" Infants as young as 5 months pay more attention to people who use infant-directed speech, which allows them to choose "appropriate social partners," or adults who are more likely to provide them with chances to learn and interact (Schachner & Hannon, 2011). When parents use IDS, infants listen (Golinkoff et al., 2015; Spinelli et al., 2017).

Infants benefit from a lot of interaction, and language is an important component of this interaction. But it's not entirely clear how language exposure impacts cognitive development, particularly when it comes to comparing children from different socioeconomic backgrounds.

### ...BELIEVE IT...OR NOT

IS THERE A "30-MILLION-WORD GAP"?

In the 1990s, researchers published a study suggesting that the amount of language spoken in the home correlates with socioeconomic status (SES) (Hart & Risley, 1992). The study drew upon 2.5 years of monthly observations of 42 families with varying income levels. By the age of 3, kids raised in families of higher SES had heard approximately 30 million more spoken words than those from lower SES households—or so the study concluded. The affluent children also had larger vocabularies, presumably because they had been exposed to more words. Following up with some of the families years later, the researchers found that kids who had already been ahead at age 3 performed better on vocabulary and reading comprehension tests at age 9–10 (Hart & Risley, 2003).

**THE AFFLUENT KIDS HAD LARGER VOCABULARIES....**

The research has been cited well over 8,000 times and is frequently referenced in the popular media, but it has also drawn criticism. One point of contention is that the study may not have captured families in environments that **were truly natural**. Perhaps some families were uncomfortable having a researcher sitting in their homes and recording their interactions, and thus displayed atypical behaviors

**Research CONNECTIONS**

In **Chapter 1,** we talked about the importance of not disrupting participants or natural environments during observational studies. In this case, the presence of the researcher in the family home may have created a disruption. Even if researchers are quiet and unobtrusive, their mere presence may cause study participants to behave unnaturally.

(Kamenetz, 2018). Some researchers have tried to get around this issue by using digital recording devices that can be worn by the study participants (d'Apice et al., 2019). Their findings suggest there is more day-to-day variation in the amount of adult speech within a given home than across different homes (not the same conclusion reached by the researchers who identified the 30-million-word gap). However, they did conclude that "the overall quantity of adult speech that children were exposed to was positively associated with their cognitive ability," and this is consistent with the original findings (d'Apice et al., 2019, p. 1422).

Yet another group of researchers tried to replicate the 30-million-word study and concluded that the "massive" word gap does not exist. They pointed out that the original study ignored background conversations in the children's homes (which could potentially contribute to language development), narrowing their focus on caregiver-to-child speech (Sperry et al., 2019). The replication attempt has been criticized, in turn, for neglecting to include "highly educated" families that would be comparable to the "professional" families used in the original study, among other factors (Golinkoff et al., 2019).

Many questions remain unresolved, but one thing seems clear: Early language development is critical for success in many academic areas. As one study concluded, language competence coming into elementary school is "the most consistent predictor of subsequent skill levels across academic and social domains" (Pace et al., 2019, p. 121).

**A UNIVERSAL SEQUENCE?**   No matter where children grow up, or who raises them, you can almost be certain they will follow the universal sequence of language development (Chomsky, 2000; TABLE **8.3**). A "vocabulary explosion" tends to occur at about 2 to 3 years of age (McMurray, 2007; FIGURE **8.3**); and as they mature, children begin using more complete sentences and increasingly complex grammar. By age 5 to 6, most are fluent in their native language, although their vocabulary does not match that of an adult. There are two important components of normal language acquisition: (1) physical development, particularly in the language-processing areas of the brain (Chapter 2); and (2) exposure to language. Children who do not observe people using language during the first several years of life fail to develop normal language skills. Evidence for this comes from case studies of people who were deprived of language in childhood (Goldin-Meadow, 1978).

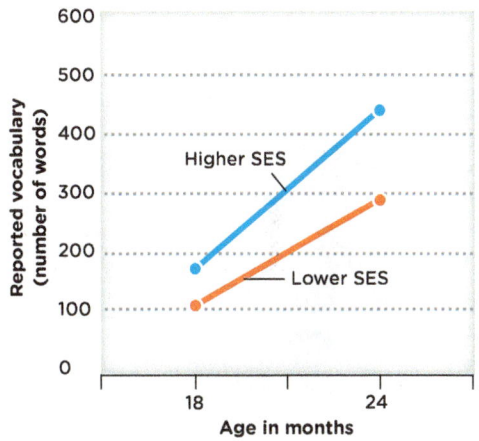

**FIGURE 8.3**
**Language Disparities**
During the first few years of life, a child's vocabulary increases dramatically. In one study, parents identified the words understood and spoken by their children (from a list of 680 items). As shown above, the vocabulary gap between children of higher and lower socioeconomic status (SES) widened between 18 and 24 months.
Information from Fernald, Marchman, and Weisleder (2014).

## TABLE 8.3   Sequence of Language Acquisition

| Language Milestone | Age | Defined | Examples |
|---|---|---|---|
| Cooing | 2 to 3 months | Vowel-like sounds | "oooo"; "ahhh" |
| Babbling | 4 to 6 months | Combining consonants; sounds are meaningless but resemble real language | "ma, ma, ma"; "da, da, da" |
| Holophrase | Around 12 months | Nouns used to convey an entire message | "juice!"; "up!" |
| Telegraphic speech | Around 18 months | Two-word phrases that include the most important words of a sentence | "baby crying"; "sock wet" |

The development of language occurs in stages that are relatively predictable and consistent across cultures.

**At Play with Piaget**
Developmental psychologist
Jean Piaget (center) works with
students in a New York City
classroom. Piaget's research
focused on school-age children,
including his own three, who
became participants in some of his
studies. Children think differently
from adults, Piaget proposed,
and they experience cognitive
development in distinct stages.

Bill Anderson/Science Source.

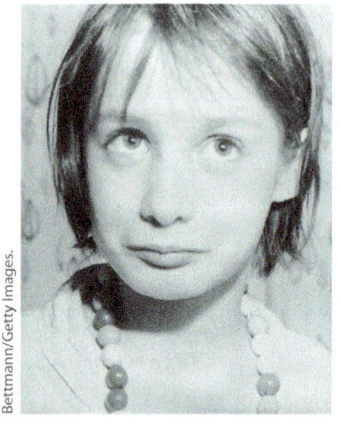

Bettmann/Getty Images.

**Deprived of Language**
What happens when a child has virtually no
exposure to language in the first decade of life?
The tragic case of "Genie" offers clues. Between the
ages of 20 months and 13 years, Genie was locked
away in a dark room, strapped to a potty chair or
confined in a cage-like crib. There she stayed for
12 years, alone in silence, deprived of physical
activity, sensory stimulation, and affection
(Curtiss et al., 1974). When Genie was taken from
her family at age 13, "there was little evidence
that she had acquired any language; she did
not speak" (Curtiss et al., 1974, p. 127). Although
Genie eventually did learn to speak in complete
sentences, there were certain linguistic skills she
never mastered (Goldin-Meadow, 1978).

**schema**  A collection of ideas that represents a
basic unit of understanding.

**assimilation**  Using existing knowledge and
ideas to understand new information and
experiences.

**A MISSED OPPORTUNITY?**   Some psychologists suggest there is a *critical period*
for language acquisition. Until a certain age, children are highly receptive to learning
language, but after that period ends, acquiring a first language that is age-appropriate
and "normal" is difficult (Friedmann & Rusou, 2015; Kuhl et al., 2005). Others
propose that language development occurs during *sensitive periods,* which are characterized by substantial, but not necessarily irreversible, changes in the brain (Knudsen,
2004). Perhaps *both* critical and sensitive periods come into play: "Language
acquisition is characterized by multiple critical and sensitive periods, with different
onsets and offsets and different dynamics" (Werker & Hensch, 2015, p. 175).

## Lessons from Piaget

**LO 8**  Discuss the key elements of Piaget's and Vygotsky's theories of cognitive development.

Language is just one domain of cognitive development. How do other processes like
memory and problem solving evolve through childhood? Swiss biologist and developmental psychologist Jean Piaget (pee-uh-ZHAY; 1896–1980) was among the first
to propose that infants have cognitive abilities.

One important component of cognition, according to Piaget (1936/1952), is the
**schema** (SKEE-muh), a collection of ideas that serves as a building block of understanding. Young children create schemas by learning about functional relationships.
The schema "toy," for example, might include any object used for play, such as a
doll, truck, or ball. As children mature, so do their schemas, which begin to organize
their thinking around more abstract categories, such as "love" (romantic love, love
for one's country, and so on). In other words, they expand their schemas in response
to experiences.

Piaget (1936/1952) believed humans are biologically driven to advance intellectually,
partly because they have an innate need to maintain *cognitive equilibrium,* or a feeling
of cognitive balance. Suppose a toddler's schema of house pets only includes small dogs
like their own, which they recognize as having fur, four legs, and a tail. When the child
sees a very large cat for the first time, they look to their father and say "puppy," because
they notice that it, too, has fur, four legs, and a tail. This is an example of **assimilation;**
the child attempts to understand new information (the sight of an unfamiliar small
animal) using their already existing knowledge base, or schema (the characteristics
of small animals familiar to them). Hearing the mistake, the child's father responds,
"That's a cat, and cats say 'meow.' 'Woof' is what puppies say." This shakes up the
child's notion of what a house pet is, causing an uncomfortable sense of *disequilibrium*
that motivates the child to restore cognitive balance. The new information about this
four-legged creature is confusing and it cannot be assimilated. Instead, the child must

use **accommodation,** the restructuring of old notions to make a place for new information. In this case, the child forms a new schema: *Small furry animals with four legs and a tail that say "meow" are cats.* Both assimilation and accommodation enable great strides in cognitive growth. We assimilate new information to fit into old ways of thinking, and we accommodate old ways of thinking to understand new information.

As noted earlier, psychologists do not always agree on whether development is continuous or occurs in steps. Piaget (1936/1952) proposed that cognitive development occurs in four stages with distinct beginnings and endings (INFOGRAPHIC **8.3** on page 307).

**SENSORIMOTOR STAGE**     From birth to about age 2 is what Piaget called the **sensorimotor stage.** Infants use their sensory and motor activities to explore the surrounding world—crawling around, reaching for things, and handling objects with their mouths, fingers, and toes. One significant milestone of the sensorimotor stage is **object permanence,** or an infant's realization that objects and people still exist when they are out of sight or touch. While playing with babies, Piaget observed how they react when a toy is hidden under a blanket. Those who had reached the object permanence milestone realized the toy still existed even though it was out of sight; they would actively look for it (Piaget, 1936/1952). Babies who had not reached this stage would continue playing as if nothing were missing.

**PREOPERATIONAL STAGE**     The next stage in Piaget's cognitive development theory is the **preoperational stage,** which occurs between ages 2 and 7. Rather than relying primarily on sensory and motor activities, children in this stage start using language to explore and understand their worlds. They ask questions and use symbolic thinking in their pretend and fantasy play. Dirt and sticks in a bowl might symbolize food for the baby doll. A toy truck becomes a real fire engine rushing to extinguish flames in a burning building. Children in the preoperational stage tend to be somewhat limited by their **egocentrism,** primarily imagining the world from their own perspective (see the Three Mountains task in Infographic 8.3). This egocentrism makes it hard to understand another person's point of view, but it does not necessarily mean children are selfish or spoiled. Egocentrism may dominate during this period, but a *theory of mind* is also developing: Children begin to understand that other people have thoughts, emotions, and perceptions of their own. For example, "an adult knows certain things that they, themselves, do not" (Atance & Caza, 2018, p. 862). Theory of mind develops parallel to empathy and is important for social interactions (Schurz et al., 2020). Some research even suggests that theory of mind promotes school readiness (Cavadel & Frye, 2017).

According to Piaget (1936/1952), children in the preoperational stage have not yet mastered *operations,* the logical reasoning processes older children and adults use to understand the world. For example, young children have a difficult time understanding the *reversibility* of some actions and events. They may have trouble comprehending that vanilla ice cream can be refrozen after it melts, but not turned back into sugar, milk, and vanilla. This difficulty with operations is also apparent in errors involving **conservation,** which refers to the unchanging properties of volume, mass, or amount in relation to appearance (FIGURE **8.4** on the next page). For example, if you take two masses of clay of the same shape and size, and then roll only one of them out into a hotdog shape, a child in this stage may think that the hotdog-shaped clay contains more clay than the undisturbed clump. Or, the child may see that the newly formed clump of clay is skinnier and therefore assume it is smaller. Children in the preoperational stage do not understand that an object stays fundamentally the same, even if it is manipulated or takes on a different appearance.

Courtesy Ericka Harley.

**Hello, Doctor**
During the preoperational stage (ages 2–7), many children relish imaginative play. In addition to pretending to be a "baker" in her kitchen, Niyah played the role of family "doctor," nursing the wounds of grandmothers, aunts, uncles, and, of course, her mom. "She would always fix my boo boos, even if I didn't have any," Ericka says. "She was very nurturing."

**accommodation**  A restructuring of old ideas to make a place for new information.

**sensorimotor stage**  Piaget's stage of cognitive development during which infants use their sensory capabilities and motor skills to learn about the surrounding world.

**object permanence**  A milestone of the sensorimotor stage of cognitive development; an infant's realization that objects and people still exist even when out of sight or touch.

**preoperational stage**  Piaget's stage of cognitive development during which children can start to use language to explore and understand their worlds.

**egocentrism**  When a person is only able to imagine the world from their own perspective.

**conservation**  Refers to the unchanging properties of volume, mass, or amount in relation to appearance.

**FIGURE 8.4**
**Conservation Tasks**
Children in the preoperational stage don't realize that properties like volume and mass stay constant when items are rearranged or reshaped. Tasks like these are used to gauge children's understanding of conservation.

| Type of Conservation Task | Original Presentation | Alteration | Question | Preoperational Child's Answer |
|---|---|---|---|---|
| Volume | Two equal beakers of liquid | Pour one into a taller, narrower beaker. | Does one beaker have more liquid? | The taller beaker has more liquid. |
| Mass | Two equal lumps of clay | Roll one lump into a long, hotdog shape. | Does one lump weigh more? | The original lump weighs more. |

Mohd Akhir/EyeEm/Getty Images.

**Little Scientist**
Piaget proposed that logic takes years to develop, but some research suggests that babies as young as 12 months are able to draw conclusions using the process of elimination. This may represent the beginning of logical reasoning (Cesana-Arlotti et al., 2018; Halberda, 2018).

**concrete operational stage**  Piaget's stage of cognitive development during which children begin to think more logically, but mainly in reference to concrete objects and circumstances.

**formal operational stage**  Piaget's stage of cognitive development during which children begin to think more logically and systematically.

**CONCRETE OPERATIONAL STAGE**    Around age 7, children enter what Piaget called the **concrete operational stage.** They begin to think more logically, but mainly in reference to concrete objects and circumstances: things that can be seen or touched, or are well defined by strict rules. Children in this stage tend to be less egocentric and can understand the concept of conservation. However, they still have trouble with abstract ideas and hypothetical thinking. For example, a 7-year-old may respond with a blank stare when asked a question such as, "What would you do if you could travel to the future?" Or, "If you had to choose between losing your eyebrows or your eyelashes, which would you give up?"

**FORMAL OPERATIONAL STAGE**    At age 11, children enter Piaget's **formal operational stage;** they begin to think more logically and systematically. For example, they can understand that objects weigh less on the moon because the moon's gravitational pull is weaker than that of earth. Children in this stage also can solve problems such as the Third Eye task (Infographic 8.3), which asks where they would put a third eye and why ("I'd put it in the back of my head so that I could see what is going on behind my back"). Such logical abilities do not necessarily develop overnight and are likely to advance in the pursuit of career interests and skills. Piaget suggested that not everyone reaches the stage of formal operations. But to succeed in most colleges, this type of logical thinking is essential; students need to use abstract ideas to solve problems.

**WHAT DO THE CRITICS SAY?**    Cognitive development may occur in stages with distinct characteristics, as Piaget suggested, but critics contend that transitions between stages are likely gradual and may not represent complete leaps from one type of thinking to the next. Some believe Piaget's theory underestimates children's cognitive abilities. For example, object permanence may occur sooner than Piaget suggested, depending on factors such as the length of time an object is out of sight (Baillargeon et al., 1985; Bremner et al., 2015). Others question Piaget's assertion that children reach the formal operational stage by 11 to 12 years of age, and that no further delineations can be made between the cognitive abilities of adolescents and adults of various ages.

## Lessons from Vygotsky

Another major criticism of Piaget's theory is that it overlooks the social interactions influencing child development. The work of Russian psychologist Lev Vygotsky (vie-GOT-skee) helps fill in some of these gaps. Vygotsky was particularly interested

# Piaget's Theory of Cognitive Development

Jean Piaget proposed that children's cognitive development occurs in stages characterized by particular cognitive abilities. These stages have distinct beginnings and endings.

### Formal Operational

Child is now able to think logically and systematically and is capable of hypothetical thinking.

### Concrete Operational

Child understands operations and thinks more logically in reference to concrete objects and circumstances.

### Preoperational

Child uses symbolic thinking to explore and understand the world. Children at this stage are known for magical thinking and egocentrism.

### Sensorimotor

Child uses sensory capabilities and motor activities to learn about the world; develops object permanence.

Piaget's four stages of cognitive development

**Sensorimotor** birth–2 yrs

**Preoperational** 2–7 yrs

**Concrete Operational** 7–11 yrs

**Formal Operational** 11 yrs and up

Credits: Child playing peekaboo, © Peter Polak/Fotolia.com; Child playing vet with Teddy bear, © Gina Sanders/Fotolia.com; Object permanence test, Doug Goodman/Science Source; Blocks, pavel siamionau/ Thinkstock; Teenage girl writing on chalkboard, Creatas/Thinkstock; Boy pouring oil into cake batter, AnnWorthy/ istockphoto/Thinkstock; Open hand, zweiger alexandre/istockphoto/Thinkstock; Piaget Conservation-Girl with milk glasses, Bianca Moscatelli/Worth Publishers; Eye featured in the hand, © Flashon Studio/Dreamstime.com.

## How do we assess a child's stage of cognitive development?

**Piaget developed techniques to test characteristic capabilities associated with each stage.**

**Object Permanence** test: Does the child realize objects continue to exist when they are hidden? Infants who have developed object permanence will search for an object.

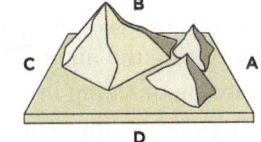

**Three Mountains** task tests egocentrism. Can the child imagine a perspective different from her own? "What would you see if you were standing at Point B?"

**Conservation of Volume** test assesses understanding of operations. Does a child understand that the amount of liquid remains constant when it is poured into a container with a different shape?

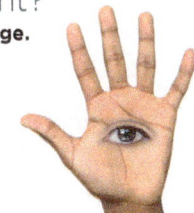

**Third Eye** task tests formal operational thought. "If you had a third eye, where would you put it?" Children at this stage come up with logical, innovative answers.

Photononstop/Superstock.

**Culture and Cognition**
A man and a boy thresh rice in the fields of Madagascar. What this child learns and how his cognitive development unfolds are shaped by the circumstances of his environment. Children reared in agricultural societies may acquire different cognitive skill sets than those raised in urban, industrialized settings.

**scaffolding** Pushing children to go just beyond what they are competent and comfortable doing, while providing help in a decreasing manner.

**zone of proximal development** The range of cognitive tasks that can be accomplished alone and those that require the guidance and help of others.

**temperament** Characteristic differences in behavioral patterns and emotional reactions that are evident from birth.

in how social and cultural factors affect a child's cognitive development (Vygotsky, 1934/1962). As he saw it, children are like apprentices to others who are more capable and experienced (Zaretskii, 2009), and those who receive help from older children and adults progress more quickly in their cognitive abilities.

One way to support children's cognitive development is through **scaffolding**: pushing them to go just beyond what they are competent and comfortable doing, but also providing help in a decreasing manner. A parent gives support when necessary, but allows the child to solve problems independently: "Successful scaffolding is like a wave, rising to offer help when needed and receding as the child regains control of the task" (Hammond et al., 2012, p. 275). Instructors often use scaffolding to challenge college students—for example, having them start with an outline, then requiring a rough draft, and adding complexity to an assignment as the semester progresses.

In order to scaffold effectively, we should consider not only what children know, but also where they are in their current development and what remains to be learned. In other words, we must consider their **zone of proximal development,** which includes cognitive tasks they can accomplish alone and those that require guidance and help from others. An ideal environment provides opportunities for both. Suppose a group of kindergarteners is learning to write. They are familiar with uppercase letters, but they are just learning lowercase letters. A teacher could take advantage of the students' zone of proximal development by creating an exercise that has them practice both what they know (uppercase letters) and what they are still learning (lowercase letters). Similarly, a college professor could instruct students to read their introductory-level textbooks, but also explain difficult concepts and challenge them with critical-thinking questions. If the instructor simply opened the textbook and read aloud to the class, they would not be working within the students' zone of proximal development—and therefore not be using effective scaffolding.

Vygotsky also emphasized that learning always occurs in a cultural context. Children across the world have different sets of expected learning outcomes, from raising sheep to completing a proof in geometry. We need to keep these cross-cultural differences in mind when exploring their cognitive development.

Until now, we have focused on physical and cognitive development, but recall we are also interested in *socioemotional* development.

## Temperament and Attachment

**"BEST BABY EVER"**    After Niyah was born, Ericka finished high school and began working full time. "She went to school, she worked, she took care of Niyah, and she took her to the babysitter," says Joan. "She lived in my house, but she took full responsibility for everything." Niyah spent only 2–3 days a month with her father, so Ericka was essentially a single parent. But it was manageable because Niyah was such a good-natured and happy baby. She was, according to Ericka, "the best baby ever."

Ericka was lucky, because not all babies are so easygoing. Niyah began sleeping solid 8-hour stretches when she was just 3 months old, but many newborns wake up crying every 2 hours during the night. They may cry for no obvious reason, or only fall asleep when nursing or riding in a car. Some babies experience *separation anxiety,* which typically peaks at approximately 13 months (Hertenstein & McCullough, 2005). "I don't ever remember there being a situation where she would just not stop crying," Ericka says. Apparently, Niyah was born with a calm and happy *temperament.*

**FROM LOW-KEY TO HIGH-STRUNG**    **Temperament,** which refers to a person's distinct patterns of emotional reactions and behaviors, is apparent across all developmental stages. We begin to see evidence of temperament in the first days of life. "High-reactive" infants exhibit a great deal of distress when exposed to unfamiliar stimuli, such as new sights, sounds, and smells. "Low-reactive" infants do not respond to new stimuli with great distress (Fox et al., 2015; Kagan, 2003). Classification as high- and low-reactive is based on measures of behavior, emotional response, and physiological factors, such as heart rate and blood pressure (Kagan, 1985, 2003).

**EASY, DIFFICULT, OR SLOW TO WARM UP?**    Another way to classify babies is to focus on how easy they are to care for. Researchers have found that the majority of infants can be categorized as having one of three fundamental temperaments (Thomas & Chess, 1986). Around 40% are considered "easy" babies; they are easy to care for because they follow regular eating and sleeping schedules. These happy babies can be soothed when upset and don't appear to get rattled by transitions or changes in their environments. Compared to their less happy peers, happy infants go on to score higher on tests of intelligence in childhood and reach greater academic achievement in young adulthood (Coffey, 2020). "Difficult" babies (around 10%) are more challenging because they don't seem to have a set schedule for eating and sleeping, nor do they deal well with transitions or changes in the environment. Often irritable and unhappy, these babies are far less responsive than their "easy" counterparts to the soothing attempts of caregivers. They also tend to be very active, kicking their legs on the changing table and wiggling around in their strollers. "Slow to warm up" babies (around 15%) are not as irritable or active as difficult babies, but they are not fond of change. Give them enough time, however, and they will adapt.

Although these temperament categories are useful, it's important to note that 35% of babies share the characteristics of more than one type and therefore are difficult to classify. And no matter what their temperament, babies are strongly influenced by the *attachments* they form with parents and other caregivers.

**Can Temperament Change?**
Characteristics associated with temperament seem to be innate, as they are apparent from birth (Plomin et al., 2013), but they can also be shaped by the environment (Briley & Tucker-Drob, 2014).

**ATTACHMENT**    **Attachment** is the degree to which an infant feels an emotional connection with primary caregivers. British psychiatrist John Bowlby (1907–1990) was the first to formulate a theory of attachment, proposing that infants naturally form an emotional bond with caregivers (Polat, 2017). Expanding on Bowlby's work, American Canadian psychologist Mary Ainsworth (1913–1999) studied the attachment styles of infants between 12 and 18 months using a research procedure called the *Strange Situation* (Ainsworth, 1979, 1985; Ainsworth & Bell, 1970; Ainsworth et al., 1978; Van Rosmalen et al., 2016). In one study, (1) a mother and child are in a room alone. (2) A stranger enters, and (3) the mother then exits the room, leaving the child in the unfamiliar environment with the stranger, who tries to interact with the child. (4) The mother returns to the room but leaves again, and then returns once more. At this point, (5) the stranger departs. During this observation, the researchers note the child's anxiety before and after the stranger arrives, willingness to explore the environment, and reaction to the mother's return. Here are three of the response patterns observed:

- **Secure attachment:** The majority of children in the study were mildly upset when their mothers left the room, but were easily soothed upon their return, quickly returning to play. These children seemed confident that their needs would be met and felt safe exploring their environment, using the caregiver as a *secure base*.

- **Avoidant attachment:** Some of the children displayed no distress when their mothers left, and no signs of wanting to interact with their mothers when they returned. They were happy to play in the room without looking at their mothers or the stranger.

- **Ambivalent:** Children in this group were quite upset and very focused on their mothers, showing signs of wanting to be held, but unable to be soothed. They were angry (often pushing away their mothers) and not interested in returning to play.

**Feeling Secure**
A child stays close to his father while taking in the surroundings. Children are more willing to explore their environments when they have caregivers who consistently meet their needs and provide a secure base. Attachments with children may be compromised when parents spend a great deal of time looking at their phones and computers (Courtney & Nowakowski-Sims, 2019).

**attachment** The degree to which an infant feels an emotional connection with primary caregivers.

A fourth category, known as *disorganized attachment,* was proposed after the original study and has been difficult to define. It was created to describe children who exhibit contradictory and unexpected behaviors like freezing and moving erratically—perhaps a result of feeling conflicted about their caregiver (Duschinsky & Solomon, 2017). Children who fall into this category may be at increased risk for subsequent psychological problems, including depression, anxiety, and behavioral issues (Ensink et al., 2020).

Ideally, parents and caregivers provide a secure base for infants, and are ready to help regulate emotions (soothe or calm) or meet other needs. This makes infants feel comfortable exploring their environments. Ainsworth and colleagues (1978) suggested that development, both physical and psychological, is greatly influenced by the quality of an infant's attachment to caregivers. More recent research indicates that attachment impacts cognition, as children with a secure base have more accurate memories of their experiences in settings like the Strange Situation (Chae et al., 2018).

Critics of the Strange Situation method suggest it creates an artificial environment and fails to provide good measures of how infant–mother pairs act naturally (Vicedo, 2017). Another drawback of the early research is that it focused on mothers in one cultural context. We should also examine attachment to fathers, close relatives, and other caregivers across cultures (Field, 1996; Rothbaum et al., 2000; Vicedo, 2017). Finally, some suggest that temperament, not just attachment, predisposes infants to react the way they do in this setting. Those prone to anxiety and uncertainty are more likely to respond negatively (Kagan, 1985).

Attachments are formed early in childhood, but they have implications for a lifetime (Høeg et al., 2018; Lopez et al., 2018; Simpson & Rholes, 2010). Some people who experienced ambivalent attachment as infants have been described as exhibiting an "insatiability for closeness" in their adult relationships. Meanwhile, those who had secure attachments are more likely to expect that they are lovable and that others are capable of love (Cassidy, 2001). Infant attachment may even have long-term health consequences. A longitudinal study spanning 32 years found that adults who had been insecurely attached as infants were more likely to report inflammation-based illnesses (for example, asthma, cardiovascular disease, and diabetes) than those with secure attachments (Puig et al., 2013).

A very important component of attachment is physical touch. If you don't believe us, consider the harrowing experiment described below.

**MONKEYS LIKE TO KEEP IN TOUCH**  Harry Harlow, Margaret Harlow, and their colleagues at the University of Wisconsin were among the first to explore the importance of physical touch in an experimental situation (Harlow et al., 1971). These researchers were initially interested in learning how infants and mothers develop attachments, and what role physical contact may play in the process. Realizing that **such a study** would be difficult to conduct with human infants, they turned to newborn macaque monkeys (Harlow, 1958).

Here's how the experiment worked: Infant monkeys were put in cages alone, each with two artificial "surrogate" mothers. One surrogate was outfitted with a soft cloth and heated with a bulb, and thus provided some degree of "contact comfort." The other surrogate mother did not provide such comfort, as she was made of wire mesh with no cloth covering. Both these surrogates could be set up to feed the infants. In one study, half of the infant monkeys received milk from the cloth surrogates and the other half got their milk from the wire surrogates. Regardless of which surrogate provided milk, the infant monkeys showed a strong preference for the cloth mother, holding and touching her 15 to 18 hours a day, as opposed to 1 to 2 hours for the wire mother.

**CONNECTIONS**

In **Chapter 1,** we discussed the importance of ensuring the ethical treatment of research participants (human and animal). Psychologists must do no harm and safeguard the welfare of participants. Obviously, the Harlows could not take human newborns from their parents to study the importance of physical contact. Many question the ethics of using newborn monkeys in this manner.

Harlow and colleagues also created situations in which they purposefully scared the infant monkeys with a moving toy bear. They found that the great majority of them (around 80%) ran to the cloth mother, regardless of whether she provided milk. In times of fear and uncertainty, these infant monkeys found more comfort in the soft, cloth mothers (Harlow, 1958; Harlow & Zimmerman, 1959). Do you think human children would do the same?

## Put Your Heads Together

In your group, **A)** list the characteristics of an effective caregiver or parent, and **B)** support this list using the lessons you learned from Vygotsky, Ainsworth, and the Harlow experiments.

## Erikson's Psychosocial Stages

**LO 9** Explain Erikson's theory of psychosocial development up until puberty.

One of the most influential theories of socioemotional development comes from German-born American psychologist Erik Erikson (1902–1994). According to Erikson, human development is marked by eight psychosocial stages, spanning infancy to old age (**INFOGRAPHIC 8.4** on the next page; Erikson & Erikson, 1997). Each of these stages is marked by a developmental task or an emotional crisis that must be handled successfully to allow for healthy psychological growth. The crises, according to Erikson, stem from conflicts between the needs of the individual and expectations of society (Erikson, 1993). Successful resolution of a stage makes it possible to approach the following stage with more tools, while unsuccessful resolution creates difficulties. Let's take a look at the stages associated with infancy and childhood.

- **Trust versus mistrust (birth to 1 year):** In order for infants to learn to trust, caregivers must attend to their needs. If caregivers are not responsive, infants will develop in the direction of mistrust, always expecting the worst of people and the environment.

- **Autonomy versus shame and doubt (1 to 3 years):** If caregivers provide freedom to explore, children learn how to be autonomous and independent. If exploration is restricted and children are punished, they may learn to feel shame and doubt.

- **Initiative versus guilt (3 to 6 years):** During this time, children have more opportunities to extend themselves socially. Often, they become more responsible and capable of creating and executing plans. If children do not have responsibilities or cannot handle them, they will develop feelings of guilt and anxiety. The reactions of caregivers are important at this stage. If a child spills milk, the caregiver may respond in a way that encourages initiative ("That's okay, mistakes happen to all of us") or in a way that fosters guilt ("You are so clumsy").

- **Industry versus inferiority (6 years to puberty):** Children in this stage frequently gauge their learning accomplishments by making comparisons with peers. When successful, they feel a sense of accomplishment, and their self-esteem increases. When unsuccessful, they feel a sense of inferiority or incompetence, which could theoretically lead to unstable work habits or unemployment later on.

Erikson's theory includes four additional stages (Infographic 8.4), all discussed in the upcoming sections on adolescence and adulthood. Before we delve into these later stages, let's explore some research that attempts to bridge the gap between childhood and adulthood. Can childhood behaviors be used to predict what will happen later

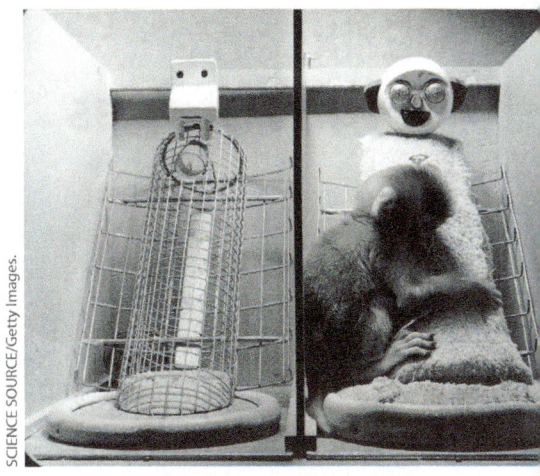

**Soft Like Mommy**
A baby monkey in a laboratory experiment clings to a furry mother surrogate. Research by Harry and Margaret Harlow and colleagues at the University of Wisconsin showed that physical comfort is important for the socioemotional development of these animals. When given the choice between a wire mesh "mother" that provided milk and a cloth-covered "mother" without milk, most of the monkeys opted to snuggle with the cuddly cloth-covered one (Harlow, 1958).

SCIENCE SOURCE/Getty Images.

# Erikson's Eight Stages

Psychologist Erik Erikson proposed that human development proceeds through eight psychosocial stages, outlined below. Each stage is marked by a developmental task or an emotional crisis that must be handled successfully to allow for healthy psychological growth (Erikson & Erikson, 1997). Critics contend that Erikson's theory does not rest on a solid foundation of scientific evidence, but it provides a useful model for conceptualizing the different phases of human life.

 **POSITIVE RESOLUTION**     **NEGATIVE RESOLUTION**

| **BIRTH to 1 YEAR)** | **Trust versus mistrust** | + Trusts others, has faith in others. |
| | | ✕ Mistrusts others, expects the worst of people. |

| **1 to 3 YEARS** | **Autonomy versus shame and doubt** | + Learns to be autonomous and independent. |
| | | ✕ Learns to feel shame and doubt when freedom to explore is restricted. |

| **3 to 6 YEARS** | **Initiative versus guilt** | + Becomes more responsible, shows the ability to follow through. |
| | | ✕ Develops guilt and anxiety when unable to handle responsibilities. |

| **6 YEARS to PUBERTY** | **Industry versus inferiority** | + Feels a sense of accomplishment and increased self-esteem. |
| | | ✕ Feels inferiority or incompetence, which can later lead to unstable work habits. |

| **PUBERTY to TWENTIES** | **Ego identity versus role confusion** | + Tries out roles and emerges with a strong sense of values, beliefs, and goals. |
| | | ✕ Lacks a solid identity, experiences withdrawal, isolation, or continued role confusion. |

| **YOUNG ADULTHOOD (20s to 40s)** | **Intimacy versus isolation** | + Creates meaningful, deep relationships. |
| | | ✕ Lives in isolation. |

| **MIDDLE ADULTHOOD (40s to mid-60s)** | **Generativity versus stagnation** | + Makes a positive impact on the next generation through parenting, community involvement, or work that is valuable and significant. |
| | | ✕ Experiences boredom, conceit, and selfishness. |

| **LATE ADULTHOOD (mid-60s and older)** | **Integrity versus despair** | + Feels a sense of accomplishment and satisfaction. |
| | | ✕ Feels regret and dissatisfaction. |

in life? Perhaps you've heard of the "marshmallow test." Research psychologist Francis Vergunst, who conducted a similar experiment, explains this classic study in a piece he wrote for *Scientific American.*

# A SIMPLE TEST PREDICTS WHAT KINDERGARTNERS WILL EARN AS ADULTS

### Psychologists zero in on the skills that predict future success.

From the pages of **SCIENTIFIC AMERICAN**

Chances are you have heard about the "marshmallow test." Put a marshmallow in front of a child and give them two choices: eat it now or wait 15 minutes and get two. According to a classic study, children able to delay gratification and wait for the second marshmallow have better academic, social and health outcomes years later. Since these early experiments, researchers have shown that a wide range of childhood traits from social and emotional skills to motivation and self-control can predict better life outcomes. These children go on to have more educational and occupational success and to live longer, healthier lives.

Now a new study I helped lead has found another link between behavior in childhood and success later in life. Published in the medical journal *JAMA Psychiatry*, my colleagues and I report that children who were rated as "inattentive" by kindergarten teachers had lower earnings at ages 33 to 35, and those rated as prosocial—such as being kind, helpful and considerate—earned more.

This study shows that inattention may be among the most powerful early behavioral predictors of future earnings. It also demonstrates that it is possible to identify children at risk of lower future earnings based on a single teacher assessment made in kindergarten, which has important practical implications. If these children can be identified, then it may be possible to intervene—for example, by flagging them for further assessment or by providing support or prevention programs—and thus improve their life chances. An important strength of the paper is that it examined a range of specific childhood behaviors and controlled for the children's IQ and family background (such as their parents' education level and occupational status), something not all previous investigations have done. [. . .]

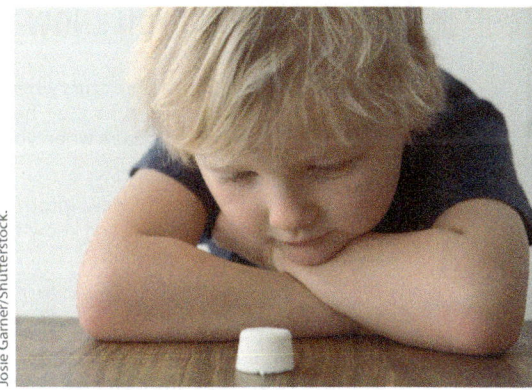

Josie Garner/Shutterstock.

My and my colleagues' new study was based on analysis of nearly 3,000 children living in Canada, who were rated by teachers for behaviors, including inattention, hyperactivity, aggression, opposition, anxiety and prosocial traits, when they were in kindergarten. The children were then followed up for 30 years, and the behavioral ratings were linked to their tax-return records in adulthood. For boys and girls, ratings of inattention at age six was more strongly linked with lower future earnings than any other behavior. Furthermore, for boys only, ratings of aggression and opposition were linked with lower earnings, and prosocial behaviors were linked with higher earnings. The study accounted for other childhood behaviors, including hyperactivity and anxiety, which were not associated with earnings. [. . .]

Inattention in childhood is known to be linked with poor peer relations, substance abuse and antisocial behavior in adolescence, all of which can harm educational attainment and diminish employment opportunities, consequently lowering earnings. Similarly, childhood aggression and opposition are linked with substance dependence, antisocial behavior and criminal convictions, which could undermine educational and employment opportunities and lead to lower earnings. The association between boys' prosocial behaviors and higher earnings may be more intuitive: prosocial children typically get on better with their peers, have fewer behavioral problems in adolescence and perform better at school, which should enhance employment opportunities, collegial relations and, consequently, earnings.

The next step is to figure out which of these mediating pathways are most important in explaining the link between childhood behavior and poor economic outcomes in adulthood so they can be tested in intervention programs. Another important question, which wasn't addressed in our study, is why the behaviors associated with future earnings appear to differ for males and females. The answer may, in turn, suggest different interventions.

While the ability to wait for a couple of marshmallows may not predict life success, other traits do seem to matter. Where earnings are concerned, kindergarteners' ability to pay attention—and boys' ability to be kind—appear particularly important. Fortunately, there are many good reasons to promote these traits. Francis Vergunst. Reproduced with permission.

## Put Your Heads Together

 At the start of the *Scientific American* article above, the author describes the classic "marshmallow test" study, which suggested that children with the self-control to delay gratification achieve greater success later in life. Subsequent research suggests that this interpretation is overly simplistic, and that environmental factors may influence the way children behave in this scenario (Michaelson & Munakata, 2020; Watts et al., 2018). In your group, discuss the following: **A)** How might a child's family environment influence their decision to wait for the second marshmallow? **B)** How might physiological needs like hunger play a role?

## SHOW WHAT YOU KNOW

1. The _____ reflex occurs when you stroke a baby's cheek; they open their mouth and turn their head toward your hand. The _____ reflex occurs when you touch the baby's lips; this reflex helps with feeding.

2. When we try to understand new information and experiences by incorporating them into our existing knowledge base, we are using what Piaget called:
   **A.** the rooting reflex.
   **B.** schemas.
   **C.** accommodation.
   **D.** assimilation.

3. What can new parents expect regarding the sequence of their child's language development, and how might they encourage it?

4. Erikson proposed that socioemotional development comprises eight psychosocial stages that include:
   **A.** scaffolding.
   **B.** physical maturation.
   **C.** developmental tasks or emotional crises.
   **D.** conservation.

5. Vygotsky recommended supporting children's cognitive development through _____, pushing them a little harder while gradually reducing the amount of help you give them.

✓ CHECK YOUR ANSWERS AT THE BACK OF THE BOOK.

# The Teenage Years

**WALKING ON PINS AND NEEDLES**   Ericka got pregnant with Niyah when she was 16 years old, and it was not something she had planned. Like many teenagers, she was probably living in the moment and not too worried about the long-term consequences of her decisions. The teen years were also a time of rebellion. Although Ericka kept up with her schoolwork and made the honor roll each semester, skipping school was one of her favorite escapes. (If only Joan had known her daughter was home watching TV during school hours!) Adolescence also brought out the emotional side of Ericka. Unable to predict what might trigger one of Ericka's angry outbursts, Joan often felt like she was "walking on pins and needles" in her own house. "I don't want to talk about it," Ericka would say defensively, or "I want to go to Grandma's."

Behaviors like these are stereotypical of teenagers, or *adolescents*. **Adolescence** refers to the transition period between late childhood and early adulthood, and it can be challenging for both parents and kids.

## A Time of Change

**LO 10**   Give examples of significant physical changes that occur during adolescence.

Adolescence is a time of dramatic physical growth, comparable to that which occurs during fetal development. The "growth spurt" includes rapid changes in height,

**adolescence** The transition period between late childhood and early adulthood.

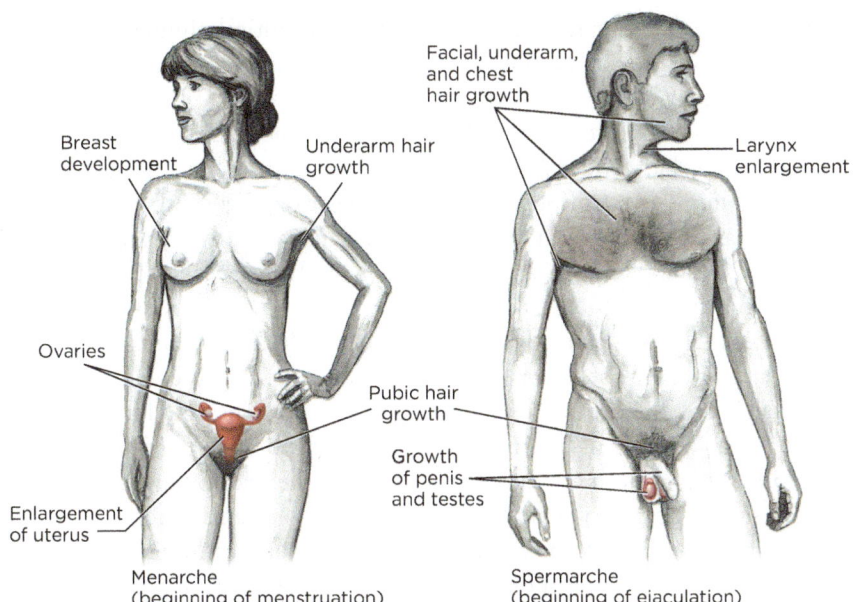

**FIGURE 8.5**
**Physical Changes at Puberty**
During puberty, the body changes and becomes sexually mature and able to reproduce. The primary sex characteristics (reproductive organs), including the ovaries, uterus, vagina, penis, scrotum, and testes, mature. Meanwhile, secondary sex characteristics, such as breasts and pubic hair, become more distinct.

weight, and bone growth, and usually begins between ages 9 and 10 for girls and ages 12 and 16 for boys. Sex hormones, which influence this growth and development, are at high levels.

**Puberty** is the period during which the body changes and becomes sexually mature and able to reproduce. During puberty, the **primary sex characteristics** (reproductive organs) mature; these include the ovaries, uterus, vagina, penis, scrotum, and testes. At the same time, the **secondary sex characteristics** (physical features not associated with reproduction) become more distinct; these include pubic, underarm, and body hair (FIGURE **8.5**).

During this time, girls experience **menarche** (meh-NAR-key), or the beginning of menstruation. Menarche can occur as early as age 9 or after age 14, but typical onset is around 12 (Martinez, 2020). Boys have their first ejaculation, **spermarche** (sper-MAR-key), during this time period, but when it occurs is more difficult to specify, as boys may be reluctant to talk about the event (Ladouceur, 2012; Mendle et al., 2010).

Not everyone goes through puberty at the same time. Researchers have linked the timing of puberty to diet, exercise, and exposure to chemicals such as pesticides (Seltenrich, 2015; Windham et al., 2015). Genetics also may play a role, as the age of puberty for both mother and father may be a "strong influence" on that of their children (Wohlfahrt-Veje et al., 2016, p. 2673).

Sexual interest peaks in adolescence, yet the brain is not fully developed; this combination of factors can set the stage for risky sexual behaviors. Over half of new *sexually transmitted infections* affect people ages 15–24, yet this group represents only 25% of the sexually active population (CDC, n.d.-e). Sexually transmitted infections are especially risky for adolescents because such infections often go untreated and can lead to a host of problems, including infertility.

**LO 11** Summarize Piaget's description of cognitive changes occurring in adolescence.

**WHAT ARE THEY THINKING?** Alongside the remarkable physical changes of adolescence are equally remarkable cognitive developments. As noted earlier, children in this age range are better able to understand abstract and hypothetical concepts. This ability indicates that a teenager has entered Piaget's formal operational stage, which begins in adolescence and continues into adulthood. Individuals in this stage begin

**puberty** The period of development during which the body changes and becomes sexually mature and capable of reproduction.

**primary sex characteristics** Organs associated with reproduction, including the ovaries, uterus, vagina, penis, scrotum, and testes.

**secondary sex characteristics** Body characteristics, such as pubic hair, underarm hair, and enlarged breasts, that develop in puberty but are not associated with reproduction.

**menarche** The point at which menstruation begins.

**spermarche** A boy's first ejaculation.

using deductive reasoning to draw conclusions and critical thinking to approach arguments. They can reason abstractly, classify ideas, use symbols, and think beyond the current moment.

A specific type of egocentrism emerges in adolescence. At a young age, children can only imagine the world from their own point of view, but during adolescence they start becoming aware of other people's perspectives. Egocentrism is still apparent, however, as adolescents believe that others share their preoccupations and ways of thinking. For example, a teenager who focuses on their appearance may think that others are focusing on it, too (Elkind, 1967).

This intense focus on the self may contribute to feelings of immortality, which can result in risk-taking behaviors (Elkind, 1967; Lin, 2016). Because adolescents have not had many life experiences, they may fail to consider the long-term consequences of behaviors such as unprotected sex or drug use. Their focus on the present (for example, having fun in the moment) outweighs their ability to assess the potential repercussions (pregnancy or addiction). To help adolescents avoid risky behaviors such as vaping, we might focus on short-term consequences like bad breath when kissing a partner, and long-term dangers such as lung cancer (Lin, 2016; Robbins & Bryan, 2004).

Richard Ross.

**Too Young**

Detainees line up at a juvenile detention facility in California. As a result of the 2005 *Roper v. Simmons* decision (Borra, 2005), defendants being tried for crimes committed before age 18 are no longer candidates for the death penalty. The U.S. Supreme Court arrived at this decision after carefully weighing evidence submitted by the American Psychological Association (APA) and others, which suggests that the juvenile mind is still developing and vulnerable to impulsivity and poor decision making (APA, 2013c).

**ACTING WITHOUT THINKING**    Characteristics of the adolescent brain are thought to contribute to risk taking. The limbic system, which is responsible for processing emotions and perceiving rewards and punishments, undergoes significant development during adolescence. Meanwhile, more axons are becoming myelinated in the prefrontal cortex, which strengthens connections between neural circuits involved in planning, weighing consequences, and multitasking (Steinberg, 2012). Because the prefrontal cortex develops more slowly than the limbic system, the adolescent may not foresee the possible consequences of reward-seeking activities. Activity in the limbic system overrides that in the prefrontal cortex, sometimes resulting in poor decisions. Changes to the structure of the brain continue through adolescence, resulting in a fully adult brain between ages 22 and 25, and a decline in risk-taking behaviors (Giedd et al., 2009; Steinberg, 2010, 2012). But take note: Studies on brain structure provide results for groups, so we cannot assume they apply to every individual (Bonnie & Scott, 2013; Bzdok et al., 2020).

## Social, Emotional Teens

Adolescence is a time of great socioemotional development. Conflicts may arise as teenagers search for their **identity,** or sense of self based on values, beliefs, and goals. Until this point in development, identity has been based primarily on the values and beliefs of parents and caregivers. Adolescents explore who they are by trying out different ideas in a variety of categories, including politics and religion. Then they begin to commit to a particular set of beliefs and attitudes, making decisions to engage in activities related to their evolving identity. However, their commitment may shift back and forth, sometimes on a day-to-day basis (Klimstra et al., 2010). The process of identity formation is, to some degree, influenced by genetics (Markovitch et al., 2017).

**LO 12**   Describe how Erikson explained changes in identity during adolescence.

**ERIKSON AND ADOLESCENCE**    Erikson's theory of development addresses this important issue of identity formation (Erikson & Erikson, 1997). From puberty to the twenties is the stage of *ego identity versus role confusion,* which leads to the creation of an adult identity. When teenagers fail to resolve the tasks and crises of the

**identity** A sense of self based on values, beliefs, and goals.

first four stages, they may enter this stage with distrust toward others, and feelings of shame, guilt, and inadequacy (see Infographic 8.4 on page 312). During this time, the developing person grapples with important life questions: *What career do I want to pursue? What religion (if any) is compatible with my beliefs?* This stage often involves "trying out" different roles. A person who fails to resolve this crisis will not have a solid sense of identity and may experience withdrawal, isolation, or continued role confusion. Resolution, on the other hand, leads to a stronger sense of values, beliefs, and goals.

**WHAT PART DO PARENTS PLAY?** Generally speaking, parent–adolescent relationships are positive (Paikoff & Brooks-Gunn, 1991), but conflict does increase during early adolescence (Van Doorn et al., 2011). Parent–teen struggles often relate to issues of control and parental authority and may revolve around everyday issues such as curfews and chores (Branje, 2018). Parents are routinely faced with decisions that impact the health, safety, and well-being of their children: *Should I allow my child to* **play a contact sport***? How much screen time should I permit each day? Is a midnight curfew too late?* Such dilemmas can spark disagreements between parents and teens, but the turmoil serves an important purpose; it gives teenagers practice dealing with conflict and negotiation in the context of the family (Moed et al., 2015). Fortunately, conflict tends to decline as both parties become more comfortable with the adolescent's growing sense of autonomy and self-reliance (Lichtwarck-Aschoff et al., 2009; Montemayor, 1983).

**FRIENDS MATTER** During adolescence, friends assume a new level of importance. Some parents express concern about the negative influence of peers, but the friendships formed by teens often support the types of behaviors and beliefs parents encouraged during childhood (McPherson et al., 2001). Adolescents tend to behave more impulsively around peers; their ability to "put the brakes on" may be inhibited by perceived social pressure (Albert et al., 2013). But peers can also have a positive influence, supporting prosocial behaviors like getting good grades and helping others (Roseth et al., 2008; Wentzel et al., 2004). With the use of smartphones and tablets, these negative and positive influences can be transmitted through digital space.

## SOCIAL MEDIA AND PSYCHOLOGY

### HAVE TEENS GONE OVERBOARD?

The average teenager in the United States spends 4–6 hours a day using digital technology, which includes texting, social media, and other online activities (Twenge et al., 2019). How does all this screen time affect their well-being? Let's start with the good news: Evidence suggests that social media can provide a safe medium for self-exploration, and may facilitate friendship building (Uhls et al., 2017). Interacting through touchscreens may also keep teenagers away from risky activities, like using drugs and alcohol. Researchers have yet to identify a causal relationship, but the rising availability of tablets and smartphones does correlate with a recent trend of decreasing alcohol and drug use (Richtel, 2017; Twenge & Park, 2019).

But here's the bad news: Overuse of digital technologies has been associated with mental health problems in young people (Flora, 2018; George et al., 2018). For example, one large study found that teens who spent 7 or more hours in front of screens (as opposed to 1 hour) per day were "more than twice as likely" to have received a diagnosis of depression at some point (Twenge & Campbell, 2018, p. 278). But how can

**CONNECTIONS**

In **Chapters 6** and **7,** we discussed chronic traumatic encephalopathy (CTE), a neurodegenerative disease caused by head trauma. Researchers have found that people who play contact sports are at a higher risk for CTE. Parents should consider the risks of CTE before allowing their children to play contact sports.

Westend61/Getty Images.

**"I'm Kind of a Big Deal"**
Narcissistic teenagers may be inclined to overuse social media, perhaps because these platforms offer a way to get the validation and attention they crave (Hawk et al., 2019). Narcissistic individuals "feel superior to others, fantasize about personal successes, and believe they deserve special treatment" (Brummelman et al., 2015, p. 3659). What makes young people narcissistic? Mom and Dad may be partly to blame. Some evidence suggests that narcissism is encouraged by parents who view their kids as "more special and more entitled than other children" (p. 3660).

**"Addicted" to Smartphones?**
Research suggests that most adolescents use social media in a healthy way. "However, for a small percentage of individuals, time spent on social media can become problematic, particularly when use sharply increases or fails to be regulated at any point during the course of adolescence" (Coyne et al., 2019, p. 905).

we know if screen time was causing those mental health outcomes? Studies have yet to identify definitive cause-and-effect relationships between media use, mental health, and other related variables like sleep deprivation (Flora, 2018). We should also note that social media use appears to impact people in different ways. In one study, researchers explored how teenagers feel after "passive use" of WhatsApp and Instagram—that is, looking at other people's stories, photos, and other content without directly communicating with them. They found that 46% of participants experienced an improvement in well-being, 10% experienced a decline in well-being, and the rest reported no change (Beyens et al., 2020). The bottom line is that we need more research to fully capture how social media (not just the amount of use, but also the type of activity) affects the mental health of adolescents with different characteristics.

## How Does Morality Develop?

**LO 13**  Examine Kohlberg's levels of moral development.

We cannot help but wonder how the constant presence of digital technology impacts morality, another important aspect of socioemotional growth. With so much communication occurring on screens, do we have sufficient real-world interactions to develop a sense of "right" and "wrong"? If only we could ask Lawrence Kohlberg (1927–1987). Kohlberg proposed that three levels of moral development occur sequentially over the life span (TABLE 8.4).

To assess the moral reasoning of his study participants, Kohlberg presented them with a variety of fictional stories. The *Heinz dilemma,* for example, is a story about a man named Heinz trying to save his critically ill wife. Heinz did not have enough money to buy a drug that could save her, so after trying unsuccessfully to borrow money, he finally decided to steal the drug. After learning about Heinz's situation, participants were presented with the following questions: "Should the husband have done that? Was it right or wrong?" (Kohlberg, 1981, p. 12). Kohlberg was not really interested in whether his participants thought Heinz should steal the drug; his goal was to determine the moral reasoning behind their answers.

**TABLE 8.4**    Kohlberg's Stages of Moral Development

| Level | Age of Emergence | Moral Understanding | What Should Heinz Do? |
|---|---|---|---|
| **Preconventional moral reasoning** | Young children | Right and wrong are determined by the consequences. | Heinz should not steal the drug because he may go to jail if caught. |
| **Conventional moral reasoning** | Around puberty | Right and wrong are informed by the expectations of society and important others, not simply personal consequences. Duty and obedience to authorities define what is right. | Because society says a husband must take care of his wife, Heinz should steal the drugs so that others won't think poorly of him. Or, Heinz should not steal because stealing is against the law. |
| **Postconventional moral reasoning** | Adulthood | Right and wrong are determined by the individual's beliefs about morality, which may be inconsistent with society's rules and regulations. Moral behavior is determined by universal principles of justice, equality, and respect for human life. | Heinz should steal the drug because the laws of society fail to consider his unique situation. Or, Heinz should thoughtfully consider all possible options, but ultimately decide that human life overrides societal laws. |

Kohlberg believed that people pass through different stages of moral development, described here. Information from Kohlberg & Hersh (1977).

Although Kohlberg described moral development as sequential and universal, he noted that environmental influences and interactions with others (particularly those at a higher level of moral reasoning) support its continued development. Additionally, not everyone progresses through all three levels; a person may get stuck at an early stage and remain there for life.

## Put Your Heads Together

 In your group, **A)** choose three people in the news whose behaviors exemplify one of Kohlberg's stages of moral development outlined in Table 8.4. **B)** Justify your selections with specific examples of those behaviors. **C)** Team up with another group and compare and contrast your results.

**NOT A PERFECT THEORY**   Kohlberg's theory of moral development has certain limitations. American psychologist Carol Gilligan leveled a number of serious critiques, suggesting that the theory did not represent the moral reasoning of women (1982). Gilligan asserted that Kohlberg discounted the importance of caring and responsibility, and that his initial use of all-male samples was partially to blame. Another issue with Kohlberg's theory is that it focuses on the moral reasoning of individuals and thus primarily applies to Western cultures; in more collectivist cultures, the focus is on the group (Endicott et al., 2003). Kohlberg's theory may be useful for examining and measuring moral reasoning, but not necessarily for making predictions. Research indicates that the ability to predict moral behavior is weak at best (Blasi, 1980; Krebs & Denton, 2005).

## What Role Does Gender Play?

**LO 14** Define gender and explain how culture plays a role in its development.

An important process that often occurs during childhood and adolescence is the development of gender identity. **Gender** refers to categories or dimensions of masculinity and femininity based on social, cultural, and psychological characteristics. Men are often expected to be masculine in their "attitudes, feelings, and behaviors," while women are expected to be more feminine (APA, 2015c). But concepts of masculine and feminine vary according to culture, social context, and the individual. You may be wondering how *gender* differs from *sex*: Sex is the classification of someone as male, female, or intersex based on biological characteristics. Gender is a social construct.

**NOT A SIMPLE DICHOTOMY**   Although society has traditionally embraced a "gender binary" system—that is, the notion that there are just two genders—not everyone identifies with these categories (APA, 2015b). Some people do not consider themselves male or female; their *gender identity* is "nonbinary" (Liszewski et al., 2018). A person's **gender identity** is a "deeply felt, inherent sense of being a girl, woman, or female; a boy, a man, or male; a blend of male or female; or an alternative gender" (APA, 2015b, p. 834). The American Psychological Association (APA, 2012b, 2014, 2020) recommends using the term "sex" when referring to biological status and "gender" for the cultural roles and expectations that distinguish females, males, and nonbinary people.

**LEARNING GENDER ROLES**   We learn how to behave in gender-conforming ways through the **gender roles** designated by our culture. This understanding of expected male and female behavior is generally demonstrated by age 2 or 3. So, too, is the ability to differentiate between boys and girls, and men and women (Zosuls et al., 2011). Let's explore how these gender roles are learned.

Instants/Getty Images.

**India's Hijra**
This dancer in Sabalpura belongs to the nonbinary hijra community. In precolonial India, the hijra were accepted, but the arrival of British colonists marked the beginning of "a mainstream discomfort in India with homosexuality, transgender people and hijras" (Gettleman, 2018, para. 23). Many other cultures, including Native American and Samoan groups, have a history of embracing nonbinary people (Burton, 2017).

**gender**  The dimension of masculinity and femininity based on social, cultural, and psychological characteristics.

**gender identity**  The feeling or sense of being male, female, or an alternative gender, and compatibility, contentment, and conformity with one's gender.

**gender roles**  The collection of actions, beliefs, and characteristics that a culture associates with masculinity and femininity.

**CONNECTIONS**

In **Chapter 5,** we described how people and animals learn by observing and imitating models. Here, we see how observational learning can shape the formation of gender roles.

**CONNECTIONS**

In **Chapter 5,** we discussed operant conditioning, or learning that results from consequences. Here, the positive reinforcer is encouragement, which leads to an increase in a desired behavior. The punishment is discouragement, which reduces the unwanted behavior.

The social-cognitive theory suggests that gender roles can be acquired through **observational learning** (Bussey & Bandura, 1999; Else-Quest et al., 2012; Tenenbaum & Leaper, 2002). We learn from our observations of people around us, particularly those of the same gender. Children also learn and model the behaviors represented in electronic media and books (Kingsbury & Coplan, 2012).

Operant conditioning is another way gender roles are established. Children often receive reinforcement for behaviors considered gender-typical, and punishment (or lack of attention) for those viewed as atypical. Parents, caregivers, relatives, and peers reinforce gender-typical behavior by smiling, laughing, or encouraging. But when children exhibit gender-atypical behavior (a boy playing with a doll, for example), the people in their lives might frown, get worried, or even put a stop to it. Through this combination of **encouragement and discouragement**, a child may learn to conform to society's expectations.

**THINKING ABOUT GENDER**    Children also seem to develop gender roles by actively processing information (Bem, 1981). In other words, they think about the behaviors they observe, including any differences between males and females. Often they watch their parents' behavior and follow suit (Tenenbaum & Leaper, 2002). Using the information they have gathered, children develop a variety of gender-specific rules they believe should be followed—for example, girls help around the house, and boys play with model cars (Martin & Cook, 2018; Yee & Brown, 1994). These rules provide a framework for **gender schemas,** the psychological or mental guidelines that dictate how to be masculine or feminine. Gender roles and gender schemas are easy to confuse. Gender roles are imposed from the outside (society's expectations) but they may shape the gender schemas (mental frameworks for understanding gender) in our minds.

**BIOLOGY AND GENDER**    Clearly, culture and learning influence the development of gender-specific behaviors and interests, but could biology play a role, too? Research on nonhuman primates suggests this is the case (Hines, 2011a). A growing body of literature points to a link between testosterone exposure *in utero* and specific play behaviors (Swan et al., 2010). For example, male and female infants as young as 3 to 8 months demonstrate gender-specific toy preferences that cannot be explained by mere socialization or learning (Hines, 2011b). Research using eye-tracking technology reveals that baby girls spend more time looking at dolls, while boys tend to focus on toy trucks (Alexander et al., 2009). Thus it seems, not all gender-specific behaviors can be attributed to culture and upbringing (Martin & Cook, 2018).

**Monkey Play**

A male vervet monkey rolls a toy car on the ground (left), and a female examines a doll (right). When provided with a variety of toys, male vervet monkeys spend more time playing with cars and balls, whereas females are drawn to dolls and cooking pots (Alexander & Hines, 2002). Similar behaviors have been observed in rhesus monkeys (Hassett et al., 2008). These studies suggest a biological basis for the gender-specific toy preferences often observed in human children.

**GENDER-ROLE STEREOTYPES**    Despite these findings, not all "girls" want to play with Barbies, and not all "boys" enjoy rolling around toy trucks. In other words, many children don't adhere to the *gender-role stereotypes* assigned to them. Gender-role stereotypes, which begin to take hold around age 3, are strong ideas about the nature of males and females—how they should dress, what kinds of games they should

**gender schemas** The psychological or mental guidelines that dictate how to be masculine and feminine.

like, and so on. Decisions about children's toys, in particular, follow strict gender-role stereotypes (boys play with trucks, girls play with dolls), and any crossing over risks ridicule from peers, sometimes even adults. Gender-role stereotypes are apparent in toy commercials, toy packaging, and pictures in coloring books (Auster & Mansbach, 2012; Fitzpatrick & McPherson, 2010; Kahlenberg & Hein, 2010; Owen & Padron, 2016; Spinner et al., 2018). They also manifest themselves in academic settings. For example, many girls have negative attitudes about math, which seem to be associated with parents' and teachers' expectations about gender differences in math competencies (Gunderson et al., 2012).

Children, especially boys, tend to cling to gender-role stereotypes. You are much more likely to see a girl playing with a "boy toy" than a boy playing with a "girl toy." Society, in turn, tends to be more tolerant of girls who go against gender stereotypes (Weisgram et al., 2014).

**ANDROGYNY**   Those who cross gender-role boundaries and engage in behaviors associated with different genders are said to exhibit **androgyny.** An androgynous person might be nurturing (generally considered a feminine quality) and assertive (generally considered a masculine quality), thereby demonstrating characteristics associated with different genders (Johnson et al., 2006; Wood & Eagly, 2015). But concepts of masculine and feminine—and therefore what constitutes androgyny—are not consistent across cultures. Children in the African nation of Swaziland are dressed androgynously, wearing any color of the rainbow (Bradley, 2011). Meanwhile, American parents frequently dress boy babies in blue and girl babies in pink.

**TRANSGENDER AND TRANSSEXUAL**   The development of gender identity and the acceptance of gender roles go relatively smoothly for most people. But sometimes societal expectations of being male or female differ from what an individual is feeling inwardly, leading to discontent. At birth, most infants are identified as "boy" or "girl"; this is referred to as a person's *natal gender,* or gender assignment. When natal gender does not feel right, an individual may have *transgender* experiences. According to the American Psychological Association, **transgender** refers to people "whose *gender identity, gender expression,* or behavior does not conform to that typically associated with the sex to which they were assigned at birth" (APA, 2014a, p. 1). This incongruence can be temporary or persistent (American Psychiatric Association, 2013). Almost a million individuals in the United States (around 0.4% of the population) consider themselves transgender (Meerwijk & Sevelius, 2017).

The American Psychological Association (APA, 2015d; Goldberg & Kuvalanka, 2018) notes that transitioning "from one gender to another" may involve medical treatments and changes to names, pronouns, hair, and clothing (APA, 2015d, p. 422; Goldberg & Kuvalanka, 2018). Although the term **transsexual** is not embraced by all, the American Psychiatric Association (2013) uses it to describe those who undergo "a social transition from male to female or female to male, which in many, but not all, cases also involves a somatic transition by cross-sex hormone treatment and genital surgery" (p. 451). Using medical treatments to make this type of transition is also termed *gender affirmation* (APA, 2014).

We have discussed the meaning of transgender and transsexual, both of which fall into the larger classification of trans. Generally speaking, *trans* refers to "all people whose gender identity, gender expression, or both, fall outside social norms" (Hendricks & Testa, 2012, p. 461). Because there is inconsistency in the labeling of trans people, we should be sensitive in our use of terminology and, when possible, ask people how they would like to be identified (Hendricks & Testa, 2012). Note that trans is included in the acronym LGBTQ+, an even larger category encompassing lesbian, gay, bisexual, transgender, queer/questioning, and other identities (Cherry, 2020).

Ron Sachs/ZUMA Press, Inc./Alamy Stock Photo.

**Breaking Barriers**
In November 2020, Sarah McBride became the first trans individual to be elected to a state senate. Following her victory, the senator-elect from Delaware tweeted, "I hope tonight shows an LGBTQ kid that our democracy is big enough for them, too" (Henley, 2020, para. 3)

**androgyny** The tendency to cross gender-role boundaries, exhibiting behaviors associated with different genders.

**transgender** Refers to people whose gender identity and expression do not match the sex assigned to them at birth.

**transsexual** Describes a person who undergoes a social transition from male to female or female to male, often by making changes to the body through surgery and/or medical treatment.

# When Do We Become Adults?

In the United States, the legal age of adulthood is 18 for some activities (voting, military enlistment) and 21 for others (drinking, financial responsibilities). These ages are not consistent across cultures; in some countries, for example, the legal drinking age is as young as 16. The transition into adulthood is often marked by ceremonies and rituals starting as early as age 12—Jewish *bar/bat mitzvahs,* Australian walkabouts, Christian confirmations, and Latin American *quinceañeras,* to name a few.

The line between adolescence and adulthood is becoming somewhat blurred in Western societies, where young people are depending on their families longer and marrying much later (Arnett, 2000; U.S. Census Bureau, 2019; FIGURE **8.6**). Psychologists propose a phase of **emerging adulthood,** which spans 18 to 25 years of age, and is characterized by exploration and opportunity. The emerging adult has neither the permanent responsibilities of adulthood nor the dependency of adolescence. By this time, most adolescent egocentrism has disappeared, which is apparent in intimate relationships and empathy (Elkind, 1967). One can seek out loving relationships, education, and new world views before settling into the relative permanency of family and career (Arnett, 2000).

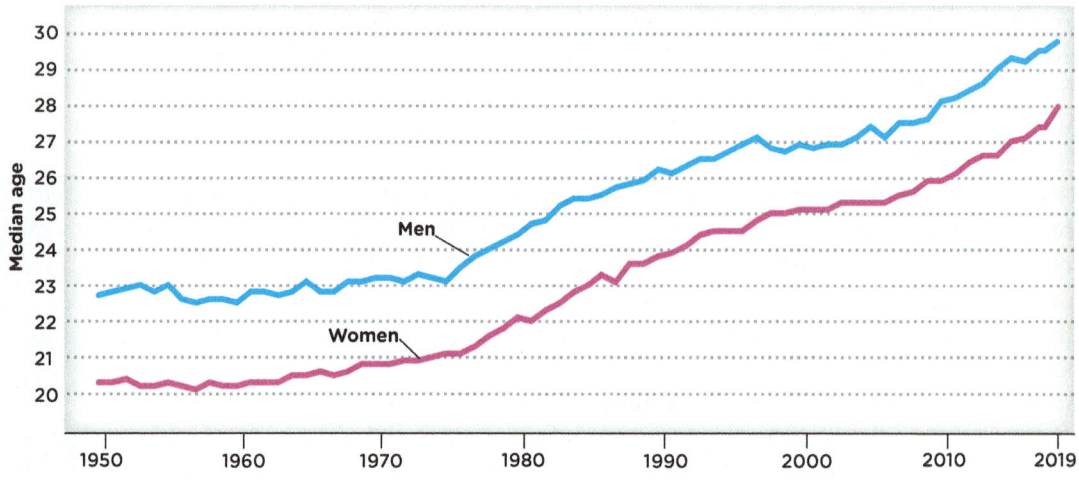

## FIGURE 8.6

**Age of First Marriage**

Many developmental psychologists consider marriage a marker of adulthood because it can represent the first time a person leaves the family home. Since the 1950s and 60s, the median age at which men and women marry for the first time has increased, a trend that appears likely to continue. Information from the U.S. Census Bureau (2019).

 **SHOW WHAT YOU KNOW**

1. A 14-year-old has begun to use deductive reasoning to draw conclusions and critical thinking to support their arguments. Their cognitive development is occurring in Piaget's:

   **A.** formal operational stage.

   **B.** concrete operational stage.

   **C.** ego identity versus role confusion stage.

   **D.** conservation task.

2. The physical features not associated with reproduction, but that become more distinct during adolescence, are known as:

   **A.** primary sex characteristics.

   **B.** secondary sex characteristics.

   **C.** menarche.

   **D.** puberty.

3. A sixth grader states that men are more assertive, logical, and in charge than women. The child has learned about this _____ from sources in their immediate environment and culture.

   **A.** gender identity            **C.** gender role

   **B.** observational learning      **D.** androgyny

4. "Helicopter" or "drone" parents pave the way for their children, troubleshooting problems for them and attempting to make certain they are always successful. How might this type of parenting impact an adolescent in Erikson's stage of ego identity versus role confusion?

5. _____ moral reasoning usually is seen in young children, and it focuses on the consequences of behaviors, both good and bad.

 CHECK YOUR ANSWERS AT THE BACK OF THE BOOK.

# Adulthood

**"SHE PROVED ME WRONG."** When Joan learned of Ericka's pregnancy, she assumed college was no longer an option. But today, Joan is proud to say, "She proved me wrong."

When Niyah was 3 years old, Ericka enrolled at Trinity Washington University in Washington, D.C. Juggling a full-time job and college was not easy, but Ericka "planned out every minute, every hour" to maximize her time with Niyah. In 2011 Ericka earned her associate's degree, and in 2014 she graduated cum laude with a bachelor's degree in business administration.

Ericka proved that she could do it all, and do it all well—motherhood, college, and career. Her accomplishments speak to her own hard work and resolve, and also to the dedicated support of three strong women: her mother Joan, her grandmother Katherine, and a PhD student named Aisha. Ericka met Aisha through her participation in Generation Hope, a nonprofit organization devoted to helping teen parents get through college. Like every Generation Hope scholar, Ericka was paired with a mentor (Aisha) who provided financial and emotional support during college.

Ericka is now married and immersed in young adulthood, a stage of life when many people are forging their identities and laying the groundwork for lifelong relationships. While others her age are still exploring the "Who am I?" type of questions that emerged in adolescence, Ericka already seems to know the answers. "I am pretty confident, and I believe what I believe," Ericka says.

Whatever you want from life, you are most likely to attain it during the developmental stage known as adulthood. Developmental psychologists have identified various stages of this long period, each corresponding to an approximate age group: *early adulthood* spans the twenties and thirties, *middle adulthood* the forties to mid-sixties, and *late adulthood* everything beyond.

*Courtesy Ericka Harley.*

**Support System**
(Left to right, and front) Joan, Ericka, Ericka's mentor Aisha, and Niyah. In addition to Ericka's grandmother, these are the people who helped keep Ericka motivated and inspired throughout college. Ericka considered withdrawing from college at one point, but then she discovered Generation Hope, a nonprofit organization devoted to supporting teen parents as they work toward college degrees. In addition to graduating cum laude, Ericka served as president of the Student Government Association and belonged to two honor societies.

## Aging Bodies

**LO 15** Name several of the most important physical changes that occur across adulthood.

The most obvious signs of aging tend to be physical in nature. Often you can estimate a person's age just by looking at their hands or facial lines. Understanding physical development is important because it impacts behavior and mental processes.

**EARLY ADULTHOOD** During early adulthood, we are at the height of our muscular and cardiovascular ability. Other systems have already begun their downhill journey, however. One example is hearing, which often starts to decline as a result of **noise-induced damage** beginning in early adolescence (Niskar et al., 2001; World Health Organization [WHO], 2018). The body is fairly resilient at this stage, but lifestyle choices can have profound health consequences. Heavy drinking, poor eating habits, obesity, lack of exercise, and smoking can make a person look, feel, and function like someone much older. All these factors have been associated with a high risk for cardiovascular disease and premature death in middle adulthood (Bakker et al., 2020; Hulsegge et al., 2016; Liu et al., 2012).

During this time, fertility-related changes occur for both men and women. Female fertility decreases by 6% in the late twenties, 14% in the early thirties, and 31% in the late thirties (Menken et al., 1986; Nelson et al., 2013). Men also experience a fertility dip, but it appears to be gradual and results from fewer and poorer-quality sperm (Sloter et al., 2006). It is not until age 50 that male fertility declines substantially (Kidd et al., 2001).

**MIDDLE ADULTHOOD** In middle adulthood, the skin wrinkles and sags due to loss of collagen and elastin, and skin spots may appear (Bulpitt et al., 2001). Hair starts to

**CONNECTIONS**

In **Chapter 3**, we described the causes of hearing impairment. Sensorineural deafness results from damage to the hair cells or auditory nerve. Conduction hearing impairment occurs when the eardrum or middle-ear bones are compromised. Exposure to loud sounds may play a role in hearing impairment that begins in adolescence.

**emerging adulthood** A phase of life between 18 and 25 years that includes exploration and opportunity.

turn gray and might fall out. Hearing loss continues and may be exacerbated by exposure to loud noises (Kujawa & Liberman, 2006). Eyesight may decline. The bones weaken, and osteoporosis can occur (Kaczmarek, 2015). Oh, and did we mention you might shrink? But do not despair. There are measures you can take to slow the aging process occurring in cells throughout your body. Cellular aging has been associated with the shortening of *telomeres*—DNA and protein structures found at the ends of chromosomes—and some research suggests you can combat telomere shrinkage with simple lifestyle choices. Getting exercise and good sleep, steering clear of cigarettes, and taking steps to reduce stress may help preserve the integrity of telomeres, possibly reducing your risk of age-related ailments (Lina et al., 2012; Ornish et al., 2013; Weintraub, 2017).

For women, middle adulthood is a time of major physical change. Estrogen production decreases, the uterus shrinks, and menstruation no longer follows a regular pattern. This marks the transition toward **menopause,** the time when ovulation and menstruation cease, and reproduction is no longer possible. Menopausal women can experience hot flashes, sweating, vaginal dryness, and sleep disruptions (Santoro et al., 2021). These symptoms may sound unpleasant, but many women report a sense of relief following the cessation of their menstrual periods, as well as increased interest in sexual activity (Etaugh, 2008).

Men experience their own constellation of midlife physical changes, sometimes referred to as male menopause or *andropause* (Kaczmarek, 2015). Some suggest calling it *androgen decline,* as there is a reduction in testosterone production, not an end to it (Morales et al., 2000). Men in middle adulthood may complain of depression, fatigue, and cognitive difficulties, which might be associated with lower testosterone. But research suggests this link between hormones and behavior is evident in only a tiny proportion of aging men (Pines, 2011).

**LATE ADULTHOOD**    Late adulthood, which begins around 65, is also characterized by the decline of many physical functions. Eye problems, such as cataracts and impaired night vision, are common. Hearing continues on a downhill course, and research suggests age-related hearing loss is linked to cognitive decline. However, the causal relationship between these two factors is unclear, and using hearing aids may help preserve some cognitive functions (Loughrey et al., 2018).

## Apply This ↓

### CAN YOU SLOW THE AGING PROCESS?

As the years go by, some degree of physical decline is inevitable. But with simple lifestyle changes, we may be able to slow some of the processes associated with aging (Distefano & Goodpaster, 2018; Duggal et al., 2018). One of the best strategies is to get your body moving. Resistance (strength) training is associated with a long list of health benefits, including increased muscle mass and strength, both of which are "predictors of longevity" (Fisher et al., 2017, p. 80). Strength training also helps prevent injuries from falls, which often pave the way for other health problems (Loudin, 2020). Meanwhile, aerobic exercise improves bone density and muscle strength, and lowers the risk for cardiovascular disease and obesity. It's good for your brain, too. According to one study, a single 15-minute workout (either walking on a treadmill or doing a high-intensity circuit training) provided a short-term boost in working memory in young adults (Wilke, 2020). The biological processes underlying these changes are still being investigated (Maass et al., 2016), but animal research suggests that exercise promotes the production of **new neurons** in the hippocampus, a brain structure that plays a

nensuria/Getty Images.

**What Do the Legs Reveal About Aging?**
Slow gait (walking speed) in middle age may be a sign of early aging, according to a study of more than 900 people in New Zealand. Participants who were slow walkers at age 45 also displayed signs of "deterioration of multiple organ systems" and "smaller total brain volume" (Hartmann Rasmussen et al., 2019, p. 10).

## CONNECTIONS

In **Chapter 2,** we discussed neurogenesis, the creation of new neurons that occurs in some areas of the brain. As we age, this production of new neurons seems to be supported by physical exercise.

**menopause**  The time when a woman no longer ovulates, her menstrual cycle stops, and she is no longer capable of reproduction.

central role in memory (Raichlen & Alexander, 2017; Weintraub, 2019; **FIGURE 8.7**). When you take good care of your body, you're also taking care of your mind.

## Aging Minds

What goes on in the brain as we pass through the stages of adulthood, and how do these changes affect our ability to function? Let's explore cognitive development in adulthood.

**LO 16** Identify the most significant cognitive changes that occur across adulthood.

**EARLY ADULTHOOD**   Measures of aptitude, such as intelligence tests, indicate that cognitive ability remains stable from early to middle adulthood (Larsen et al., 2008), though processing speed begins to decline (Schaie, 1993). Young adults are theoretically in Piaget's formal operational stage, which means they can think logically and systematically, but some estimate that only 50% of adults ever exhibit formal operational thinking (Arlin, 1975).

**MIDDLE AND LATE ADULTHOOD**   Good news for people in their forties and fifties: Cognitive function does not necessarily fade during this time of life. In fact, longitudinal studies indicate that decreases in cognitive abilities cannot be reliably measured before 60 (Gerstorf et al., 2011; Schaie, 1993, 2008). There are some exceptions, however. Midlife is a time when information processing and memory can decline, particularly long-term memory (Ren et al., 2013).

Now here's the good news: Older people may be getting sharper from one generation to the next. The Seattle Longitudinal Study has shown that the cognitive performance of today's 70-year-old participants is similar to the performance of 65-year-olds tested 30 years ago (Gerstorf et al., 2011; Schaie, 1993, 2008). What does this finding tell us? From a cognitive abilities perspective, turning 65 does not mean it is time to retire. Processing speed may slow with old age, but older adults are still capable of innovation and awe-inspiring accomplishments (Kennedy, 2017). Frank Lloyd Wright finished designing New York's Guggenheim Museum when he was 89 years old, and Nelson Mandela became president of South Africa when he was 76.

If you look at studies from the 20th century, you will see intelligence scores increasing over the generations and across the world, although some evidence suggests that these gains have not remained consistent (Flynn & Shayer, 2018). The differences are so impressive that many people taking IQ tests in the 1930s would be considered cognitively delayed by today's standards (Flynn, 2009). We call this global

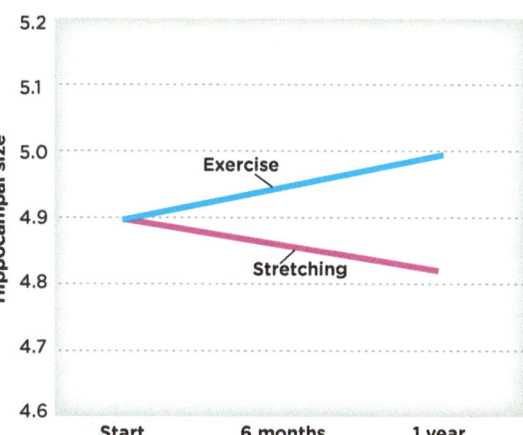

**FIGURE 8.7**
**Exercise to Build Bigger . . . Brains?**
To study the effects of exercise on the aging brain, researchers randomly assigned participants to two groups: One group engaged in a program of gentle stretching exercises, and the other began doing more aerobic activity. During the course of the yearlong study, the researchers found typical levels of age-related shrinkage in the hippocampi of the stretching group. However, in the group that exercised more vigorously, not only was age-related deterioration prevented, hippocampal volume actually increased, with corresponding improvements in memory (Erickson et al., 2011).
Information from Erickson et al. (2011).

**Golden Years**
Late adulthood can be a time of great intellectual, humanitarian, and physical achievement. Ingeborg Syllm-Rapoport (left) was 102 when she earned her doctorate degree; Nelson Mandela (middle) was 76 when he became the first Black president of South Africa; and Wang Deshun (right) was 79 when he strolled down this catwalk in China Fashion Week.

phenomenon the *Flynn effect* (Flynn, 2012). Does this mean that people of today are smarter than those from decades past? Researcher James Flynn (1934–2020) suggested this was not the case (2012). Intelligence scores are most likely increasing because we confront a larger spectrum of "cognitive problems" than those who came before us. In other words, we now seem to encounter more issues that require abstract thinking.

Earlier we mentioned that physical exercise provides a cognitive boost. The same appears to be true of mental exercises, such as those required for playing a musical instrument (Hanna-Pladdy & MacKay, 2011). That said, there does appear to be a lot of hype surrounding the "use it or lose it" mantra of aging. The declaration that exercising the brain will stop cognitive decline might be a slight overstatement (Salthouse, 2006). Although there are clear benefits to doing crossword puzzles and reading the newspaper, the evidence is not conclusive that the effects are unique to older adults. Perhaps the best advice for older people is to keep both their brain and body active. People who continue to work, both physically and mentally, and remain in good physical shape are less likely to experience **significant cognitive decline** (Hamm et al., 2020; Rohwedder & Willis, 2010). They may even live longer, as later retirement has been linked to longer survival (Wu et al., 2016). Thus, if your goal is to maintain a sharp mind as you age, don't just increase your Sudoku playing or reading time. You need to maintain a balanced approach that incorporates a broad range of activities, including those that provide social stimulation.

### Social, Emotional Adults

**LO 17**  Explain some of the socioemotional changes that occur across adulthood.

Earlier we described Erikson's approach to explaining socioemotional development from infancy through adolescence, noting that unsuccessful resolution of prior stages has implications for the stages that follow (see Infographic 8.4 on page 312). Here, we will look at the stages associated with adulthood.

- **Intimacy versus isolation (twenties to forties):** During young adulthood, people tend to focus on creating meaningful, deep relationships, and failing at this endeavor may lead to a life of isolation. The focus shifts away from fun-filled first experiences with sex and love to deeper connections. For many, the twenties represent a transition between the "here and now" type of relationships of adolescence to the serious, long-term partnerships of adulthood (Arnett, 2000).
- **Generativity versus stagnation (forties to mid-sixties):** Moving into middle adulthood, we begin to evaluate our lives. Positive resolution of this stage includes feeling like we have made a real impact on the next generation, through parenting, community involvement, or work that is valuable and significant. Those who cannot resolve this crisis face stagnation, characterized by boredom, conceit, and selfishness.
- **Integrity versus despair (mid-sixties and beyond):** In late adulthood, we look back on life and evaluate how we have done. If previous stages have resulted in positive resolutions, we feel a sense of accomplishment and satisfaction. If not, we feel regret and dissatisfaction.

Erikson's work has an important place in the field of developmental psychology, but it provides more of a framework than substantive research findings. His theory was based on case studies, with limited supporting evidence. Furthermore, the developmental tasks associated with the eight stages might not be limited to particular time frames. For example, creating an adult identity is not restricted to adolescence, as this stage may resurface at any point in adulthood (Schwartz, 2001).

**CONNECTIONS**

Here, we are reminded of an issue presented in **Chapter 1:** We must be careful not to equate correlation with causation. In this case, a decline in cognitive ability may lead to earlier retirement (not the other way around).

Now it's time to revisit a topic touched on in earlier sections—something that many people consider the most challenging, yet rewarding, aspect of adult life: parenthood.

## The Many Shades of Parenting

Earlier we described the different types of attachment that can form between children and parents. In most cases, these attachments are influenced by parenting approaches. American psychologist Diana Baumrind (1927–2018) studied parenting for over four decades, and she identified four parenting behavioral styles (1966, 1971, 2013). These styles seem to be stable across situations, and are distinguished by levels of warmth, responsiveness, and control (Baumrind, 2013; Maccoby & Martin, 1983).

Parents who insist on rigid boundaries, show little warmth, and want to control their children exhibit **authoritarian parenting.** They want things done in a certain way, "because I said so," no questions asked. Authoritarian parents are extremely strict and demonstrate poor communication skills with their children. Their kids, in turn, tend to have lower self-assurance and autonomy, and experience more problems in social settings (Baumrind, 1991). There may be exceptions to this rule, however. In situations where child safety is at risk, "authoritarian parenting is actually more adaptive" (Herzog et al., 2015, p. 121).

**Authoritative parenting** may sound similar to authoritarian parenting, but it is very different. Parents who practice authoritative parenting set high expectations, demonstrate a warm attitude, and are responsive to their children's needs. Being supported and respected, children of authoritative parents are responsive to their parents' expectations. They also tend to be self-assured, independent, responsible, and friendly (Baumrind, 1991). There appears to be a positive relationship between the authoritative style and parental education (Anton et al., 2015).

With **permissive parenting,** the parent demands little of the child and imposes few limitations. These parents are very warm but often make next to no effort to control their children. Ultimately, their children tend to lack self-control, act impulsively, and show little respect for boundaries.

Those who demonstrate **uninvolved parenting** seem indifferent to their children. Emotionally detached, these parents exhibit minimal warmth and devote little time to their kids, apart from taking care of basic needs. Children raised by uninvolved parents tend to exhibit behavioral problems, poor academic performance, and immaturity (Baumrind, 1991).

Keep in mind that the great majority of research on these parenting styles has been conducted in the United States, and that the impact of parenting styles may be mediated by cultural norms (Grusec et al., 2000; Lansford et al., 2018). For example, permissive parenting may have benefits that are specific to some Western European and Latin American cultures, perhaps because these societies place a high value on "affection and egalitarian relations" (Pinquart & Kauser, 2018, p. 84). Additional factors to consider include the home environment, the child's temperament and personality, and the unique parent–child relationship. Children with irritable and easygoing dispositions will not exhibit the same reactions to the restrictions imposed by authoritarian parents, for example (Grusec & Goodnow, 1994).

## Put Your Heads Together

In your group, **A)** discuss specific ways that the parenting styles outlined above could impact children's development. **B)** How might a child's behavior patterns influence parenting styles? **C)** How does cultural background influence parenting styles?

Palm Beach Post/Getty Images.

**Helicopter Parents**
They are overprotective, overbearing, and controlling. "Helicopter parents" try to organize the environment so that their kids won't get hurt or fail, but this approach may have unintended consequences. Researchers who studied hundreds of children over an 8-year period found that toddlers with "overcontrolling" mothers were more likely to have trouble regulating emotions and behaviors later in childhood (Perry et al., 2018, p. 1551).

**authoritarian parenting** A rigid parenting style characterized by strict rules and poor communication skills.

**authoritative parenting** A parenting style characterized by high expectations, strong support, and respect for children.

**permissive parenting** A parenting style characterized by low demands of children and few limitations.

**uninvolved parenting** A parenting style characterized by a parent's indifference to a child, including a lack of emotional involvement.

## Growing Old with Grace

When some people think of growing older, they imagine a disabled and frail person sitting in a bathrobe and staring out the window. This stereotype is simply not accurate. Less than 1% of the U.S. population lives in a nursing home or residential care community (National Center for Health Statistics, 2019). Most older adults enjoy active, healthy, independent lives. They are involved in their communities, faiths, and social networks, and contrary to popular belief—a large number have active sex lives (Lindau et al., 2007; Malani et al., 2018).

Americans are now living longer than ever, with the average life expectancy of women being 81.2 years and men 76.2 years (Xu et al., 2020). Many of us dread this "winter of life," but perhaps we should look forward to it; research suggests that happiness generally increases with age (Kieny et al., 2020). Positive emotions become more frequent than negative ones, and emotional stability increases, meaning that we experience fewer extreme mood swings (Carstensen et al., 2011). Sadness, fear, and anger tend to diminish with age, although the frequency of these emotions may depend somewhat on personality (Potter et al., 2020). Why might older people feel happy? Perhaps they no longer care about proving themselves, feel pleased with the outcome of their lives, or have developed a strong sense of emotional equilibrium (Jeste et al., 2013).

### Put Your Heads Together

Think of some older people you respect and want to emulate. In your group, **A)** describe some recent accomplishments of these older individuals. **B)** Discuss the factors that you think have led to their successful aging. **C)** How would you define successful aging? **D)** What would you say to someone who harbors negative stereotypes about older people?

**THE LIFE OF KAT WRIGHT**   "My grandmother passed away on September 5, 2011," Ericka says. "I really remember it like it was yesterday."

It was Labor Day weekend and the family was hoping to have a cookout at Grandma's house, just as they did every year. But Grandma wasn't feeling well and asked for a small family dinner instead. When Ericka and her relatives arrived, Grandma wanted to stay in bed—unusual for a woman who was the focal point of every family get-together. Eventually, she got up, but her breathing was abnormal. The family called 911, and medical workers came but did not find evidence of any major problem. Ericka wasn't too worried because Grandma had experienced health issues in the past, but she had always recovered.

"Okay Grandma, I'll see you tomorrow," Ericka said on her way out. "I love you." Grandmother told Ericka she loved her, too, and said "goodbye" (odd, because she usually said "see you later"). Later that night, Ericka awoke to the sound of her mom getting ready to go visit Grandma, now in the hospital. Assuming her grandmother would pull through as always, Ericka went back to bed, her mind spinning. She headed for the hospital around 2:00 A.M., but by the time she arrived, Grandma was already gone. "I couldn't like breathe, I couldn't say anything," Ericka recalls. "I knew that one day she would pass away, but I wasn't ready for it."

The death of Katherine Wright had a profound impact on Joan, Ericka, and the whole family. One of the hardest parts of grieving was the sudden loss of everyday contact—the daily phone calls, the frequent visits. Ericka's pregnancy had brought together four generations of women—Katherine, Joan, Ericka, and Niyah—and they were as close as ever. But now their leader was gone. "I remember the first couple months I was really angry at God," Ericka explains. "I felt like, if God loves us, why would he take her away?"

## Dying and Death

Ericka eventually came to the realization that having her grandmother for the first 22 years of life had been a great gift, but the anger she felt is relatively typical for a person in mourning. Those who are dying may also experience anger. As psychiatrist Elisabeth Kübler-Ross (2009) observed in the early 1960s, people often have similar reactions when confronted with the news they are dying: stages of denial, anger, bargaining, depression, and acceptance. These stages, Kübler-Ross suggested, are coping mechanisms for dealing with what is to come.

- **Denial:** In the denial stage, people may react to the news with shock and disbelief, perhaps even suggesting the doctors are wrong. Unable to accept the diagnosis, they may seek other medical advice.

- **Anger:** Dying people may feel anger toward others who are healthy, or toward the doctor who does not have the cure. *Why me?* they may wonder, projecting anger and irritability in a seemingly random fashion.

- **Bargaining:** This stage may involve negotiating with God, doctors, or other powerful figures for a way out. Usually, this involves some sort of time frame: *Let me live to see my firstborn get married*, or *Just give me one more month to get my finances in order.*

- **Depression:** There comes a point when dying people can no longer ignore the inevitable. Depression may be due to the symptoms of illness, but it can also result from the overwhelming sense of loss—the loss of the future.

- **Acceptance:** Eventually, dying people accept the finality of their predicament; death is inevitable, and it is coming soon. This stage can deeply impact family and close friends, who, in some respects, may need more support than the person who is dying. According to one oncologist, the timing of acceptance is quite variable. For some people, it occurs moments before death; for others, soon after they learn there is no chance of recovery from their illness (Lyckholm, 2004).

Kübler-Ross was instrumental in bringing attention to the importance of attending to the dying person (Charlton & Verghese, 2010; Kastenbaum & Costa, 1977). The stages she proposed provide a valuable framework for understanding death, but every person responds in a unique way. For some, the stages are overlapping; others don't even experience them (Schneidman, 1973). Also note that this theory has not been thoroughly investigated, and it arose in a Western cultural context. Evidence suggests that people from other cultures have very different perspectives on dying and death.

## ACROSS THE WORLD

### DEATH IN DIFFERENT CULTURES

What does death mean to you? Some of us believe death marks the beginning of a peaceful afterlife. Others see it as a crossing over from one life to another. Still others believe death is like turning off the lights; once you're gone, it's all over.

Views of death are very much related to religion and culture. A common belief among Indian Hindus, for example, is that one should spend a lifetime preparing for a "good death" (*su-mrtyu*). Often this means dying in old age, after conflicts have been put to rest, family matters settled, and farewells said. To prepare a loved one for a good death, relatives place the person on the floor at home (or on the banks of the Ganges River, if possible) and give them water from the hallowed Ganges. If these and other rituals are not carried out, the dead person's soul may become trapped and the family suffers the consequences: nightmares, infertility, and other forms of misfortune (Firth, 2005).

ALEJANDRO MEDINA/Getty Images.

**Celebrating the Dead**
Crowds in Yucatan, Mexico, parade the streets for the Dia de los Muertos, or "Day of the Dead" festival. During this holiday, people in Mexico and other parts of Latin America celebrate the lives of the deceased. Music is played, feasts are prepared, and graves are adorned with flowers to welcome back the spirits of relatives who have passed. In this cultural context, death is not something to be feared or dreaded, but rather a part of life that is embraced (National Geographic, 2015).

**Kat Wright Lives On**
Ericka's grandmother (left) suddenly passed away at the age of 72, leaving behind a huge family that loved and depended on her. Many years later, Kat Wright is still very much alive in the thoughts and memories of Joan, Ericka, and the rest of the family. She lives on through Niyah, who inherited many of her best qualities, including a seemingly endless capacity for love. As Joan puts it, "We love. We love hard."

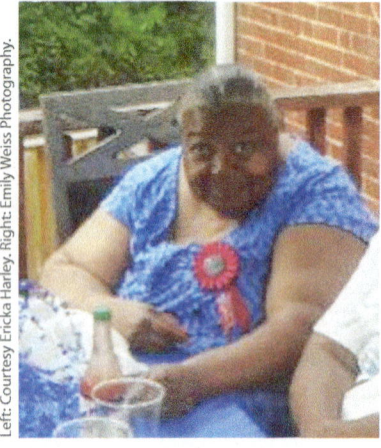

*Left: Courtesy Ericka Harley. Right: Emily Weiss Photography.*

In cultures heavily influenced by Confucianism, family members may care for parents at the end of their lives: "In Korea and Taiwan, dying and death is perceived not as a personal issue, but rather a family issue" (Cheng et al., 2015, p. 4). Meanwhile, in some Western cultures, elderly people may not plan for death or believe in an afterlife. One study found that nearly half of German centenarians did not believe in life after death (Boerner et al., 2018). Imagine a psychologist trying to assist grieving relatives without any knowledge of these beliefs and traditions, or the culture-specific ways people show sympathy and compassion for others (Koopmann-Holm & Tsai, 2014).

**RESILIENT MOTHERS**   Today, when Ericka reflects on her pregnancy with Niyah, she is nothing but grateful: "Even though it was really unexpected, I think it might have been one of the best things that ever happened." Ericka is in good company, as many young women demonstrate resiliency when faced with the stigma of teen pregnancy. How do these teenage moms achieve successful outcomes? Those who are resilient tend to resist stereotypes about teenage mothers and maintain a positive attitude; they are driven to reach educational goals and willing to put the needs of their children above their own. "Strong social support systems" and quality health care are also important (Solivan et al., 2015, p. 352). If we focus on resiliency, we start to see "what is 'right' instead of what is 'wrong'" (p. 354).

 **SHOW WHAT YOU KNOW**

1. Physical changes during middle adulthood include declines in hearing, eyesight, and height. Which of the following does research suggest can help limit the aging process?
   A. physical exercise
   B. elastin
   C. andropause
   D. collagen

2. An aging relative in their mid-seventies is looking back on their life and evaluating what they have accomplished. They feel satisfied with their work, family, and friends. Erikson would say that this relative has succeeded in solving the crisis of _____ versus _____.

3. What are some important cognitive changes that occur across adulthood?

 CHECK YOUR ANSWERS AT THE BACK OF THE BOOK.

# Summary of Concepts

**LO 1**   Define human development. (p. 288)

Development refers to the changes that occur in physical, cognitive, and socioemotional functioning over the course of the life span. The goal of developmental psychology is to examine these changes, which begin at conception and end at death.

**LO 2**   Outline the three longstanding discussions in developmental psychology. (p. 289)

In the field of developmental psychology, debates often center on three major themes: stages and continuity; nature and nurture; and stability and change. Each of these themes relates to a basic question: (1) Does development occur in separate or discrete stages, or is it a steady, continuous process? (2) What are the relative roles of heredity and environment in human development? (3) How stable is personality over a lifetime and across situations?

**LO 3**   Identify several research methods used in the study of human development. (p. 290)

Developmental psychologists use various methods to explore changes across the life span. The cross-sectional method examines people of different ages at one point in time, while the longitudinal method follows one sample of individuals over a certain period. In the cross-sequential method, participants are divided into age groups and followed over time, so researchers can examine developmental changes within individuals and across different age groups.

**LO 4** Examine the role genes play in our development. (p. 292)

All the cells in the human body (except for red blood cells) have a nucleus at their center. Inside this nucleus are chromosomes, which contain genes made of deoxyribonucleic acid (DNA). Genes provide the blueprint for physiological development (and to some degree, psychological development). At conception, the sperm and egg merge to form a zygote, a single cell that eventually gives rise to the trillions of cells that make up a human body. The 23rd pair of chromosomes, also referred to as the sex chromosomes, provides specific instructions for the individual to develop into a female or male. When both members of the 23rd pair are X chromosomes (XX), the zygote generally develops into a female. When one member is an X and the other a Y (XY), the zygote generally develops into a male.

**LO 5** Discuss how genotype and phenotype relate to development. (p. 294)

Genotype refers to an individual's unique collection of genes. These genes are found on the 23 pairs of chromosomes (46 chromosomes in all) located in the nucleus of most cells. Genotype does not change in response to the environment, but it does interact with the environment. The result of this interaction is one's phenotype, or unique set of physical and psychological characteristics.

**LO 6** Describe the progression of prenatal development. (p. 295)

At the moment of conception, the mother's egg and the father's sperm come together to form a zygote. The zygote immediately begins to divide into two cells, then each of those cells divides, and so on. During the germinal period (conception to the end of the second week), the rapidly dividing zygote implants in the uterine wall. Between the third and eighth weeks of development, the mass of cells is called an embryo. From 2 months to birth, the growing human is identified as a fetus. The amniotic sac serves as a protective barrier, but harmful environmental agents called teratogens can damage the growing embryo or fetus. Radiation, viruses, bacteria, chemicals, alcohol, and drugs are all considered teratogens.

**LO 7** Summarize the physical changes that occur in infancy. (p. 298)

As newborns grow, they experience astounding changes, both seen and unseen. We see advancement in demonstrated capabilities, known as the motor milestones, and an increasingly sophisticated ability to discriminate among sensory stimuli. These sensorimotor advances are made possible by dramatic developments in the brain. Neurons rapidly sprout new connections, and this synaptic growth is influenced by experiences and stimulation from the environment.

**LO 8** Discuss the key elements of Piaget's and Vygotsky's theories of cognitive development. (p. 304)

One important component of cognition, according to Piaget, is the schema, a collection of ideas that serves as a building block of understanding. Humans are driven to advance intellectually, partly as a result of an innate need to maintain cognitive equilibrium. With assimilation, we understand new information using an already existing schema. With accommodation, we restructure old notions to make a place for new information. Piaget proposed that cognitive development occurs in four stages: sensorimotor, preoperational, concrete operational, and formal operational. Vygotsky was interested in how social and cultural factors affect cognitive development. One way to help children's cognitive development is through scaffolding, pushing them to go just beyond what they are competent and comfortable doing, but also providing help when needed, in a decreasing manner.

**LO 9** Explain Erikson's theory of psychosocial development up until puberty. (p. 311)

According to Erikson, human development is marked by eight psychosocial stages, spanning infancy to old age. Each stage is marked by a developmental task or an emotional crisis that must be handled successfully to allow for healthy psychological growth. The stages from infancy to puberty are the following: trust versus mistrust, autonomy versus shame and doubt, initiative versus guilt, and industry versus inferiority.

**LO 10** Give examples of significant physical changes that occur during adolescence. (p. 314)

The "growth spurt" of adolescence includes rapid changes in height, weight, and bone growth. Sex hormones, which influence this growth and development, are at high levels during this time. Primary sex characteristics (features associated with reproductive organs) and secondary sex characteristics (features not associated with reproductive organs) mature in both boys and girls.

**LO 11** Summarize Piaget's description of cognitive changes occurring in adolescence. (p. 315)

During the formal operational stage of cognitive development, adolescents begin to use deductive reasoning and logic to draw conclusions. A specific type of egocentrism emerges, as adolescents tend to believe that others think the same way they do. Because they have not had many life experiences, teens may not consider the long-term consequences of their behaviors.

**LO 12** Describe how Erikson explained changes in identity during adolescence. (p. 316)

The stage of ego identity versus role confusion occurs during adolescence and is marked by the creation of an adult identity.

During this stage, adolescents try out different roles as they attempt to define their values, beliefs, and goals. Successful resolution of this stage results in stronger values, beliefs, and goals with a firmer sense of identity.

**LO 13** Examine Kohlberg's levels of moral development. (p. 318)

Kohlberg proposed there are three levels of moral development occurring sequentially over the life span. Preconventional moral reasoning usually applies to young children and focuses on the personal consequences of behaviors, both good and bad. At puberty, conventional moral reasoning is used, with the determination of right and wrong based on the expectations of society and important others. In postconventional moral reasoning, right and wrong are determined by the individual's beliefs about morality, which may not coincide with society's rules and regulations.

**LO 14** Define gender and explain how culture plays a role in its development. (p. 319)

Gender refers to the dimension of masculinity and femininity based on social, cultural, and psychological characteristics. It is often used in reference to the cultural roles that distinguish males and females, but not everyone fits into this gender binary system. We generally learn by observing other people's behavior and by internalizing cultural beliefs about what is appropriate for males and females.

**LO 15** Name several of the most important physical changes that occur across adulthood. (p. 323)

We typically reach our physical peak in early adulthood, and then decline as we approach late adulthood. Gradual changes occur, including hearing and vision loss, wrinkles, graying hair, reduced stamina, menopause for women, and reduced fertility for men. Lifestyle can have a significant impact on health. Heavy drinking, drug use, poor eating habits, and sleep deprivation can make one look, feel, and function like someone much older.

**LO 16** Identify the most significant cognitive changes that occur across adulthood. (p. 325)

Cognitive ability remains stable from early to middle adulthood, but midlife is a time when information processing and memory can decline, particularly long-term memory. Processing speed may slow with old age.

**LO 17** Explain some of the socioemotional changes that occur across adulthood. (p. 326)

According to Erikson, we face the crisis of intimacy versus isolation during young adulthood; failure to create meaningful, deep relationships may lead to a life of isolation. In middle adulthood, we face the crisis of generativity versus stagnation. Positive resolution of this stage includes feeling like we have made a valuable impact on the next generation. During the crisis of integrity versus despair (late adulthood), we look back on life and evaluate how we have done.

# Key Terms

accommodation, p. 305
adolescence, p. 314
androgens, p. 293
androgyny, p. 321
assimilation, p. 304
attachment, p. 309
authoritarian parenting, p. 327
authoritative parenting, p. 327
chromosomes, p. 292
cohort effect, p. 290
concrete operational stage, p. 306
conservation, p. 305
critical period, p. 289
cross-sectional method, p. 290
cross-sequential method, p. 290

deoxyribonucleic acid (DNA), p. 292
developmental psychology, p. 288
dizygotic twins, p. 293
dominant gene, p. 294
egocentrism, p. 305
embryo, p. 296
emerging adulthood, p. 322
epigenetics, p. 295
estrogens, p. 293
fetal alcohol syndrome (FAS), p. 297
formal operational stage, p. 306
gender, p. 319
gender identity, p. 319
gender roles, p. 319

gender schemas, p. 320
gene, p. 292
genotype, p. 294
identity, p. 316
intersexual, p. 294
longitudinal method, p. 290
maturation, p. 288
menarche, p. 315
menopause, p. 324
monozygotic twins, p. 293
object permanence, p. 305
permissive parenting, p. 327
phenotype, p. 295
preoperational stage, p. 305
primary sex characteristics, p. 315

puberty, p. 315
recessive gene, p. 294
scaffolding, p. 308
schema, p. 304
secondary sex characteristics, p. 315
sensorimotor stage, p. 305
spermarche, p. 315
temperament, p. 308
teratogens, p. 296
transgender, p. 321
transsexual, p. 321
uninvolved parenting, p. 327
zone of proximal development, p. 308
zygote, p. 292

# Test Prep Are You Ready?

1. A researcher is interested in studying changes in memory, problem solving, and language across the life span. They choose a large sample of college seniors and follow the participants for the next 30 years. This is an example of:
   A. socioemotional development.
   B. longitudinal research.
   C. cross-sectional research.
   D. epigenetics.

2. Ricardo's grandmother suffers from Alzheimer's disease. Ricardo wonders if he will experience a similar future because of his biological connection to her. This line of thinking relates to which of the following debates in developmental psychology?
   A. stability and change
   B. stages or continuity
   C. critical or sensitive period
   D. nature and nurture

3. DNA molecules include sections corresponding to _____, which encode proteins that determine the texture of hair, color of eyes, and some aspects of personality.
   A. phenotypes
   B. epigenetics
   C. zygotes
   D. genes

4. Your psychology instructor often discusses the environmental factors that can influence how genes are expressed. This topic is central to the field of:
   A. epigenetics.
   B. maturation.
   C. the cohort effect.
   D. prenatal development.

5. Human development is influenced by the interaction of many factors. Brain development, for example, is shaped by biological maturation and experiences in the environment. This is evident in _____, which occurs when unused synaptic connections are eliminated.
   A. myelin
   B. socioemotional development
   C. synaptic pruning
   D. the rooting reflex

6. According to Vygotsky, _____ is an approach that helps children learn, providing support when necessary but allowing them to problem solve as much as possible on their own.
   A. assimilation
   B. scaffolding
   C. phenotype
   D. schema

7. _____ are agents that can damage a growing embryo or fetus.
   A. Phenotypes
   B. Genotypes
   C. Zygotes
   D. Teratogens

8. _____ further develop during adolescence. These changes are associated with the maturation of reproductive organs, such as the ovaries, uterus, penis, and testes.
   A. Gender schemas
   B. Temperaments
   C. Primary sex characteristics
   D. Secondary sex characteristics

9. Adolescents begin thinking more logically and systematically, using deductive reasoning to draw conclusions. They have entered what Piaget referred to as the:
   A. formal operational stage.
   B. postconventional moral reasoning stage.
   C. industry versus inferiority stage.
   D. concrete operational stage.

10. A research team is following a large group of infants starting from birth. They observe that the majority of infants begin combining consonants and vowels at about 4 to 6 months. This is called the:
    A. babbling stage.
    B. rooting reflex.
    C. cohort effect.
    D. phenotype.

11. According to Erikson, one of the tasks of adolescence is searching for identity, that is, finding a sense of self based on values, beliefs, and goals. How is identity related to gender? How does culture influence identity?

12. Draw a diagram that outlines how Erikson's stages of psychosocial development, Piaget's stages of cognitive development, and Kohlberg's stages of moral development fit together on a developmental timeline.

13. What are the most important physical changes that can occur across adulthood?

14. Describe the types of crises that adults face using Erikson's stages of socioemotional development.

15. We have described how cognitive abilities tend to decline with age. What kinds of cognitive activities might actually improve with age?

 CHECK YOUR ANSWERS IN APPENDIX C.

# 9

G. John Schmidt/Courtesy Ivonne Mosquera-Schmidt.

# Motivation and Emotion

## Motivation

**RIO . . . AT LAST**  September 17, 2016: Ivonne Mosquera-Schmidt took her place at the starting line of the 1500-meter race for blind female athletes at the 2016 Paralympics. She had been dreaming of this moment since age 8, and the journey had been long and hard. Just 2 years before, Ivonne had been diagnosed with cancer for the third time in her life. Sitting in the doctor's office with tears streaming down her face, she vowed, "Whatever happens, I have to make it to Rio." Despite the shock, fear, and anger of facing cancer, Ivonne held onto the idea that she was a warrior—a small warrior at 88 pounds—but a warrior no less. "It's not about how big we are," says Ivonne. "It's about how strong we are."

Ivonne has been a fighter all her life. When she was 2 years old, doctors removed both of her eyes to stop the spread of an aggressive cancer. She is completely blind and has no memory of vision, but that hasn't stopped her from doing much of anything. Growing up in New York City, Ivonne used to ride her bicycle across the George Washington Bridge, her father running alongside. She went to school with sighted kids, climbed trees in the park, and studied ballet, tap, and jazz dance (Boccella, 2012; iminmotion.net, n.d.). A year after earning her undergraduate degree in mathematics from Stanford University, Ivonne took up running. With the help of trainers, guides, and her husband John, she has turned herself into a world-class runner and triathlete, racking up records and titles all over the globe. In Rio, Ivonne showed her warrior strength and did her country proud, earning 6th place in the 1500 meters.

But athletic accomplishments are only part of what makes Ivonne so phenomenal. Did we mention that she speaks four languages, climbs mountains, and has a graduate degree in business? Despite her blindness and repeated battles with cancer, Ivonne has garnered more achievements and life experiences than we can count. How does she do it?

There is little doubt that Ivonne is blessed with intelligence, athletic ability, and other remarkable gifts. But these are not the only ingredients in the recipe for outstanding achievement: Motivation is essential, too (Bardach et al., 2020; McCoach & Flake, 2018; Reifsteck et al., 2016).

## What Is Motivation?

**LO 1** Define motivation.

Psychologists propose that **motivation** is a stimulus or force that can direct the way we behave, think, and feel. A motivated behavior is guided (has a direction), energized, and persistent. When Ivonne is training, her behavior is *guided* because she sets goals like meeting certain running times, *energized* because she goes after those goals with zeal, and *persistent* because she sticks with her goals even when challenges arise. We exhibit behaviors all the time, but motivated behaviors are different from behaviors that are simply reactions to environmental stimuli.

In this chapter, you will learn about various forms of motivation and theories that attempt to explain them. Keep in mind that human behavior is complex and should be studied in the context of biology, culture, and other environmental factors. Every behavior is likely to have a multitude of causes (Maslow, 1943).

**DOES LEARNING PLAY A ROLE?** One way to explain motivated behavior is through learning theory. We know that people (not to mention dogs, chickens, and slugs) can *learn* behaviors through classical conditioning, operant conditioning, and observational learning (Chapter 5). Let's take a look at how operant conditioning can help us understand the relationship between learning and motivation. When a behavior is reinforced (**with positive or negative reinforcers**), an association is established. This association between a behavior and its consequence becomes the **incentive,** or reason you are motivated to repeat the behavior. Imagine you have been avoiding a particular term paper assignment. You decide to treat yourself to an hour of watching Netflix for every three pages you write. Adding a reinforcer (Netflix) increases your writing behavior; thus, we call it a *positive reinforcer.* The association between the behavior (writing) and the consequence (watching your favorite show) is the incentive. Before long, you begin to expect this break from work, which motivates you to write. Do you think Ivonne's running behavior was shaped by incentives?

**THE POWER OF CHOCOLATE** After graduating from college and moving back to New York City, Ivonne started looking for a new activity to get outside and moving. She came across the New York Road Runners Club, which connected her with an organization that supports and trains runners with all types of disabilities. Having no

*Note:* Quotations attributed to Ivonne Mosquera-Schmidt and Ibrahim Hashi are personal communications.

Lucas Uebel/Getty Images.

**Paralympian**
Ivonne Mosquera-Schmidt (right) and her guide Kyle Wardwell at the 2016 Paralympics in Rio. Representing the United States in the Paralympics is just one of Ivonne's extraordinary athletic feats. In addition to winning two gold medals in the Paratriathlon World Championships, she has won first place in the women's visually impaired category of the Boston Marathon on three occasions, and she holds three American records: in the 1500 meters, 3000 meters, and 5000 meters for totally blind women (iminmotion.net, n.d.).

**CONNECTIONS**

In **Chapter 5,** we introduced positive and negative reinforcers, which are stimuli that increase future occurrences of target behaviors. In both cases, the behavior becomes associated with the reinforcer. Here, we see how these associations become incentives.

**motivation** A stimulus that can direct behavior, thinking, and feeling.

**incentive** An association established between a behavior and its consequences, which then motivates that behavior.

running experience (apart from jogging on a treadmill), Ivonne showed up at a practice one Saturday morning in Central Park and ran 2 miles with one of the running club's guides. The next week she came back for more, and then the next, and the next. During these early practices, Ivonne's teammates promised to buy her hot chocolate whenever she increased her distance. "Every time they would try to get me to run further, they'd say, 'We'll have hot chocolate afterwards!'" Ivonne remembers. "They actually would follow through with their promise!"

**LO 2** Explain how extrinsic and intrinsic motivation impact behavior.

**EXTRINSIC MOTIVATION**   The idea of being rewarded with hot chocolate provided Ivonne with an incentive to return to practice again and again. When a learned behavior is motivated by the incentive of external reinforcers in the environment, there is **extrinsic motivation** to continue that behavior (Deci et al., 1999; Deci et al., 2017; Ryan & Deci, 2017, 2020). In other words, the motivation comes from consequences that exist outside of the person. Bagels and coffee might provide extrinsic motivation for people to attend a boring meeting, grades and diplomas for students to work hard in college. For most of us, money is a powerful form of extrinsic motivation. Even the avoidance of punishment can serve as extrinsic motivation (Ryan & Deci, 2017). The thought of late fees, traffic tickets, and reprimands from authority figures can motivate people to follow rules.

**INTRINSIC MOTIVATION**   Ivonne's motivation to run also originated from inside; she came to love the sense of freedom running gave her, the experience of being in nature, smelling the grass and feeling the breeze, and sharing it with others. When learned behaviors are driven by personal satisfaction, interest in a subject matter, and other variables that exist within a person, **intrinsic motivation** is at work (Deci et al., 1999; Rheinberg, 2020; Ryan & Deci, 2017). Is reading this textbook inherently interesting? Do you study it carefully because you enjoy the feeling that comes from mastering the material? If so, your reading behavior stems from intrinsic motivation. The reinforcers originate inside of you (learning feels good and brings you satisfaction), and not from the external environment.

**EXTRINSIC VERSUS INTRINSIC**   What compels you to offer your seat to someone on a bus? Is it because you've been praised for helping others (extrinsic motivation), or because it simply feels good to help someone (intrinsic motivation)? Many behaviors are inspired by a blend of extrinsic and intrinsic motivation. But there do appear to be potential disadvantages to extrinsic motivation, especially the type that focuses on external rewards and avoidance of punishment (Ryan & Deci, 2020). Researchers have found that using rewards, such as money and marshmallows, to reinforce already interesting activities (like doing puzzles, playing word games, and so on) can lead to a decrease in behaviors that were once intrinsically motivating (Ryan & Deci, 2017). "Tangible rewards—both material rewards, such as pizza parties for reading books, and symbolic rewards, such as good student awards—are widely advocated by many educators and are used in many classrooms, yet the evidence suggests that these rewards tend to undermine intrinsic motivation" (Deci et al., 2001, p. 15). Even athletic scholarships appear to undercut intrinsic motivation, and this effect may persist long after college, influencing athletes' feelings toward their sport (Moller & Sheldon, 2020). Yet, research suggests the link may not be that simple (Akin-Little & Little, 2019). Extrinsic motivators such as merit-based salary increases do not always erode intrinsic motivation, and the timing of the reward may determine the extent of its impact (Gerhart & Fang, 2015; Woolley & Fishbach, 2018).

Courtesy Ivonne Mosquera-Schmidt.

**For the Love of Running**
Ivonne competes in the 2008 New York City Triathlon. During her early running days, Ivonne's friends reinforced her efforts with hot chocolate. When the incentive to continue a behavior stems from external reinforcers (hot chocolate, in this case), the motivation is extrinsic. These days, Ivonne doesn't need sweet treats to keep her running. Her motivation is more intrinsic; she derives pleasure from the activity itself.

**extrinsic motivation** The drive or urge to continue a behavior because of external reinforcers.

**intrinsic motivation** The drive or urge to continue a behavior because of internal reinforcers.

## Put Your Heads Together

Imagine you are a psychology instructor and your goal is to motivate students to perform better on exams. Team up and discuss **A)** extrinsic motivation strategies you could implement, and **B)** ways to encourage intrinsic motivation. **C)** Which would be more effective in the long term?

We now have developed a basic understanding of what motivation is; we also have established that motivation may be influenced by learning. Let's take a look at some other theories of motivation, keeping in mind that each has its strengths and limitations.

## Do Humans Have Instincts?

*Instinct.* Surely, you've heard the word in everyday conversation: "Trust your instincts," people say. "That boxer has a killer instinct," a commentator remarks during a pay-per-view fight. But what exactly are instincts, and do humans really have them? **Instincts** are complex behaviors that are fixed, unlearned, and consistent within a species. Because of instinct, honeybees communicate through a "waggle dance," and baby sea turtles head to the ocean after hatching (Malkemus, 2015). No one teaches the bees to dance or the turtles to scurry to sea; through evolution, these behaviors appear to be etched into their genetic make-up.

Instincts form the basis of one of the earliest theories of motivation. Inspired in part by Charles Darwin's theory of evolution, early scholars proposed that a variety of instincts motivate human behavior (Krueger & Reckless, 1931; McDougall, 1912). Thousands of human "instincts" were named, among them curiosity, flight, and aggressiveness (Bernard, 1926; Kuo, 1921). Yet, there was little evidence they were true instincts—that is, complex behaviors that are fixed, unlearned, and consistent within a species. Only a handful of human activities, among them rooting behavior in newborn infants, might be considered instincts (Brimdyr et al., 2019; Chapter 8). But even these are more akin to reflexes than complex activities like honeybee waggle dancing. Although instinct theory faded, some of its themes are apparent in the **evolutionary perspective**, which suggests that evolutionary forces influence human behavior. For example, emotional responses, such as fear of snakes, heights, and spiders, may have evolved to protect us from danger (Langeslag & van Strien, 2018; Plomin et al., 2013).

Elena Tyapkina/Alamy.

**Turtles on a Mission**
Baby loggerhead sea turtles instinctually crawl toward the ocean after hatching. When the females reach adulthood, they return to the same beach to lay their own eggs, finding their way "home" with the help of the Earth's magnetic field (Brothers & Lohmann, 2018).

### CONNECTIONS

In **Chapter 1,** we presented the evolutionary perspective, which proposes that humans have evolved adaptive traits through natural selection. Behaviors that improve the chances of survival and reproduction are most likely to be passed along to offspring and therefore tend to increase in frequency. Meanwhile, less adaptive behaviors tend to decrease in frequency.

## Just Stayin' Alive

 **LO3** Describe drive-reduction theory and explain how it relates to motivation.

In order to survive, living things must maintain internal conditions, such as temperature and oxygen levels, at a baseline or constant state. **Homeostasis** refers to the way in which our bodies maintain these constant states through internal controls. The **drive-reduction theory** proposes that this biological balancing act (homeostasis) is the basis for motivation (Hull, 1952). In other words, behaviors are driven by the process of fulfilling basic **needs** for nutrients, fluids, oxygen, sleep, and so on (see **INFOGRAPHIC 9.1** on page 341). Eating, drinking, sleeping, and other behaviors help us meet these physiological needs. If a need is not fulfilled, this creates a **drive,** or state of tension, that pushes us (motivates our behaviors) to meet the need and restore equilibrium. Once a need is satisfied, the drive is reduced, but not forever. The need inevitably returns, and we feel driven to meet it once again. A good example is hunger. You wake up with an empty stomach, fill it with food, but then find yourself hungry at noon so you eat lunch, but the hunger returns in the evening, and the cycle continues.

**instincts** Complex behaviors that are fixed, unlearned, and consistent within a species.

**homeostasis** The tendency for bodies to maintain constant states through internal controls.

**drive-reduction theory** Suggests that homeostasis motivates us to meet biological needs.

**needs** Physiological or psychological requirements that must be maintained at some baseline or constant state.

**drive** A state of tension that pushes us (motivates our behaviors) to meet a need.

The drive-reduction theory helps us understand how physiological needs can be motivators, but it is less useful for explaining why we buy new clothes, go to college, or drive cars too fast.

**LEAPING INTO THE UNKNOWN**    Ivonne has never been afraid of new experiences. In fact, she has sought out novel and stimulating adventures all her life. "I remember even as a little kid wanting to be on roller skates," she says. "I was always ready to go down the slide, and I had no idea how long the slide was." At age 8, Ivonne was already using the New York City bus system to get from her elementary school to piano lessons. "I would walk over to 5th Avenue and wait for one of the buses," she explains. "I would count my steps from the corner of 81st Street toward 80th Street so that I knew where the bus stop was." To determine when it was safe to move into the crosswalk, Ivonne listened for the sound of cars moving in the same direction she wanted to go. Then she would put her cane out and venture forward.

**Adrenaline Rush**
Sensation seeking is most common in middle and late adolescence. During this period, the brain's self-regulatory mechanisms are immature, and they won't be fully developed until sometime in the mid-twenties. Some have compared it to "starting a car's engines before a well-functioning braking system is in place" (Steinberg et al., 2018, p. 2).

mikkelwilliam/Getty Images.

## Looking for Some Excitement?

New experiences can be frightening. They can also be delightfully exhilarating. Humans are fascinated by novelty, and you see evidence of this innate curiosity in the earliest stages of life. Babies grab, taste, and smell just about everything they can get their hands on; children fearlessly climb trees and playground structures; even adults seek out novel experiences, paying money to try out rock climbing, barre classes, or tae kwon do. Sometimes boredom motivates us to explore new things (Bench & Lench, 2019): Have you ever visited Wikipedia or YouTube just to learn about something unfamiliar?

Why engage in activities that have little, if anything, to do with satisfying basic biological needs? Humans are driven by other types of urges, including the apparent need for stimulation.

**LO 4**   Explain how arousal theory relates to motivation.

According to **arousal theory,** humans (and perhaps other primates) seek an optimal level of arousal, as not all motivation stems from physical needs. Arousal, or engagement in the world, can be a product of anxiety, surprise, excitement, interest, fear, and many other emotions. Have you ever had an unexplained urge to make simple changes to your daily routines, like taking the stairs instead of the elevator, eating eggs instead of cereal, or styling your hair differently? These behaviors may stem from your need to increase arousal. Optimal arousal is not the same for everyone (Infographic 9.1 on page 341). Evidence suggests that some people are *sensation seekers;* that is, they appear to seek activities that increase arousal (Zuckerman, 1979, 1994). The **heritability** of this trait appears to be quite high, ranging from 58% to 67% (Zuckerman, 2015). Popularly known as "adrenaline junkies," these individuals relish activities like cliff diving, racing motorcycles, and watching horror movies. A cross-cultural study involving more than 5,000 participants from Africa, North America, South America, Asia, and Europe found that sensation seeking generally rises during the teen years, reaches a maximum around age 19, and then diminishes in the twenties (Steinberg et al., 2018).

High sensation seeking is not necessarily a bad thing, as it may be associated with a greater tolerance for stressful events (Roberti, 2004). And according to some interpretations of the *Yerkes–Dodson law,* moderate levels of arousal can actually help performance in humans and other mammals (Teigen, 1994; Winton, 1987; Yerkes & Dodson, 1908). Suppose you are taking an exam. You don't want to be underaroused because you may fall asleep; nor do you want to be overaroused, as you might have trouble concentrating. You need just the right amount of arousal, somewhere in the moderate range.

**CONNECTIONS**

In **Chapter 7,** we discussed heritability, the degree to which heredity is responsible for a particular characteristic in a population. The heritability for sensation seeking is 58–67%. This means 58–67% of the population-wide variation in sensation seeking can be attributed to genes, and 33–42% to environmental influences.

**arousal theory**   Suggests that humans are motivated to seek an optimal level of arousal, or alertness and engagement in the world.

# Maslow's Hierarchy of Needs

**LO 5**  Outline Maslow's hierarchy of needs.

Have you ever been in a car accident, lived through a hurricane, or witnessed a violent crime? At the time, you probably were not thinking about what show you were going to watch on HBO that night. When physical safety is threatened, everything else tends to take a backseat. This idea that certain needs take priority over others is central to the **hierarchy of needs,** a theory of motivation proposed by Abraham Maslow, one of many leading figures in the **humanistic movement** (Henry, 2017). Maslow organized human needs into a hierarchy, often depicted as a pyramid (Infographic 9.1; Bridgman et al., 2019). These needs, which are both biological and psychological in nature, are considered universal and are ordered according to the strength of their associated drives.

**PHYSIOLOGICAL NEEDS**  The most critical needs are situated at the base of the hierarchy and generally take precedence over higher-level needs. These *physiological needs* include requirements for food, water, sleep, and an overall balance of bodily systems. If a life-sustaining need such as fluid intake goes unsatisfied, other needs are placed on hold and the person is motivated to satisfy it. Maslow suggested that the basic physiological needs of people from most societies are "relatively well gratified" (Maslow, 1943), but this is not always the case. One example is the widespread need for nutrition. In 2019, about 1 in 10 American households (10.5%) were "food insecure," meaning they "had difficulty at some time during the year providing enough food for all their members due to a lack of resources" (Coleman-Jensen et al., 2020, p. v). The COVID-19 pandemic has only served to magnify this problem (Center on Budget and Policy Priorities, 2021; Gundersen et al., 2020).

**SAFETY NEEDS**  If physiological needs are satisfied, human behavior is motivated by the next level in the hierarchy: *safety needs.* When Ivonne began cancer treatments as a baby, she had a safe place to stay in New Jersey, but traveling to New York City for chemotherapy and radiation was treacherous. "[My mother] would have to come from New Jersey by herself without knowing English and traipse through the snow, and take the buses and the trains to get down to the hospital with me," Ivonne says. During this period (the late 1970s), the city's dark subway tunnels were not the safest place for a mother and baby. In 1979, for example, the subway system saw over 250 felonies per week (Samaha, 2014).

For many people in the United States, safety is equated with the need for predictability and order: having a steady job, a home in a safe neighborhood, health insurance, and living in a country with a stable economy. What does safety mean for you, and how might it differ from that of someone living in Venezuela, Thailand, or Afghanistan?

**LOVE AND BELONGINGNESS NEEDS**  If safety needs are being met, then people will be motivated by *love and belongingness needs.* Maslow suggested this includes the need to avoid loneliness, to feel like part of a group, and to maintain affectionate relationships. As a blind child in the mainstream school system, Ivonne did not always have an easy time fitting in. Her parents could not afford all the material things other kids had, but they provided unconditional love, support, and a strong sense of cultural identity.

What happens when love and belongingness needs go unsatisfied? People who feel disconnected or excluded may demonstrate less prosocial behavior (Twenge et al., 2007) and act more aggressively and less cooperatively, which only tends to intensify their struggle for social acceptance (DeWall et al., 2008; Stenseng et al., 2014). Yet, this effect is reduced when the excluded people think about the future and consider

CONNECTIONS

In **Chapter 1,** we discussed Maslow and his involvement in humanistic psychology. The humanists suggest that people are inclined to grow and change for the better, and this perspective is apparent in the hierarchy of needs. Humans are motivated by the universal tendency to move up the hierarchy and meet needs toward the top.

SOPA Images/Getty Images.

**Food Security, Ripped Away**
Volunteers in the Orlando area deliver food aid a few days ahead of Thanksgiving, 2020. The COVID-19 pandemic, and the job losses it triggered, caused many Americans to become food insecure. People who previously had no worries about putting enough food on the table (and thus meeting the physiological needs tier in Maslow's hierarchy) found themselves waiting in line at food banks.

**hierarchy of needs**  A continuum of needs that are universal and ordered in terms of the strength of their associated drives.

**self-actualization**  The need to be one's best and strive for one's fullest potential.

Courtesy Ivonne Mosquera-Schmidt.

**She's Always Been Unstoppable**
Ivonne (center) with her family. Even in preschool, Ivonne appeared to be motivated by esteem needs. She was self-directed, confident, and commanded respect from others.

the long-term implications of their actions (Balliet & Ferris, 2013). The lockdowns associated with the COVID-19 pandemic thrust people across the world into social isolation, threatening their love and belongingness needs. Living under quarantine conditions can foster anxiety, insomnia, moodiness, and other symptoms of psychological disorders, even among people without preexisting mental health issues. For some, extended quarantine may serve as a "traumatic event," triggering symptoms associated with posttraumatic stress disorder, or PTSD (Chapter 13; Usher & Jackson, 2020).

**ESTEEM NEEDS**    If the first three levels of needs are being met, then the individual might be motivated by *esteem needs,* including the need to be respected by others, to achieve, and to have self-respect and feelings of independence. Fulfilling these needs fosters a sense of confidence and self-worth, both qualities that Ivonne possessed early in life. In preschool, she was determined to do everything her sighted peers did, from riding a tricycle to pouring her own juice. "I remember those little pitchers and cups like [it] was just yesterday," recalls Ivonne, who insisted on serving herself. "It's me, it's my juice, and I want to pour it!"

**SELF-ACTUALIZATION**    When the above-mentioned needs are being met, a person can be motivated by what Maslow (1943) called the need for **self-actualization:** "to become more and more what one is, to become everything that one is capable of becoming" (p. 382). This need to self-actualize, or reach one's fullest potential, is at the heart of the humanistic movement. It represents the human tendency toward growth and self-discovery (Chapter 10). For some, self-actualization means becoming the best possible parent; others aim to be outstanding designers or musicians. Ivonne is a prime example of a self-actualizer because she is always striving to learn and achieve new goals. "Some of my dreams have come true," she says. "I wanted to be in finance, so I found a way to go to business school . . . and I was a financial analyst." Then there are her many physical accomplishments, like climbing Tanzania's Mount Kilimanjaro and competing in over 25 triathlons. "There is always so much more to learn about myself and so much more to learn about the world," she says. "It's like I'm never done."

**SELF-TRANSCENDENCE**    Toward the end of his life, Maslow proposed an additional level in the hierarchy: the need for *self-transcendence.* This need motivates us to go beyond our own needs and feel outward connections through "peak experiences" of ecstasy and awe. Fulfilling this need might mean devoting oneself to a humanitarian cause or achieving spiritual enlightenment; there is no "right" or "wrong" path to self-transcendence (Kaufman, 2018). For Ivonne, it means bridging the gap between the able-bodied and disabled communities, bringing people together to pursue common passions, such as running and yoga.

Johan Spanner/Polaris.

**Breaking Fast**
Iraqi families gather for Iftar, the evening meal eaten after the daytime fast during Ramadan. "As defined in the Qur'an, fasting is a strict practice of deep personal worship in which Muslims seek the highest level of awareness of the Divine" (Ilias et al., 2016, p. 147). Basic needs (food and water) are put on hold for something more transcendent.

**EXCEPTIONS TO THE RULE**    Maslow's hierarchy suggests a certain order of needs, but this sequence is not set in stone. Sometimes we work toward meeting multiple needs simultaneously; other times, we abandon lower-level needs in favor of higher-level needs (Henry, 2017). For example, we may put off physiological requirements to meet a self-actualization need—going on a hunger strike or giving up material possessions, for example. The practice of fasting, which occurs in many faiths, including Islam, Christianity, Hinduism, and Judaism, illustrates how basic physiological needs (food and water) can be placed on hold for a spiritual purpose. Safety is another basic need often relegated in the pursuit of something more transcendent. Throughout history, soldiers have given their lives fighting for causes like freedom and social justice.

# Theories of Motivation

Motivational forces drive our behaviors, thoughts, and feelings. Psychologists have proposed different theories addressing the needs that create these drives within us. Let's look at the three most prominent theories of motivation. Some theories, like drive-reduction theory, best explain motivation related to physiological needs. Other theories focus on psychological needs, such as the need for an optimum level of stimulation, as described in arousal theory. In his hierarchy of needs, Abraham Maslow combined various drives and proposed that we are motivated to meet some needs before others.

## Drive-Reduction Theory

Homeostasis motivates us to meet physiological needs.

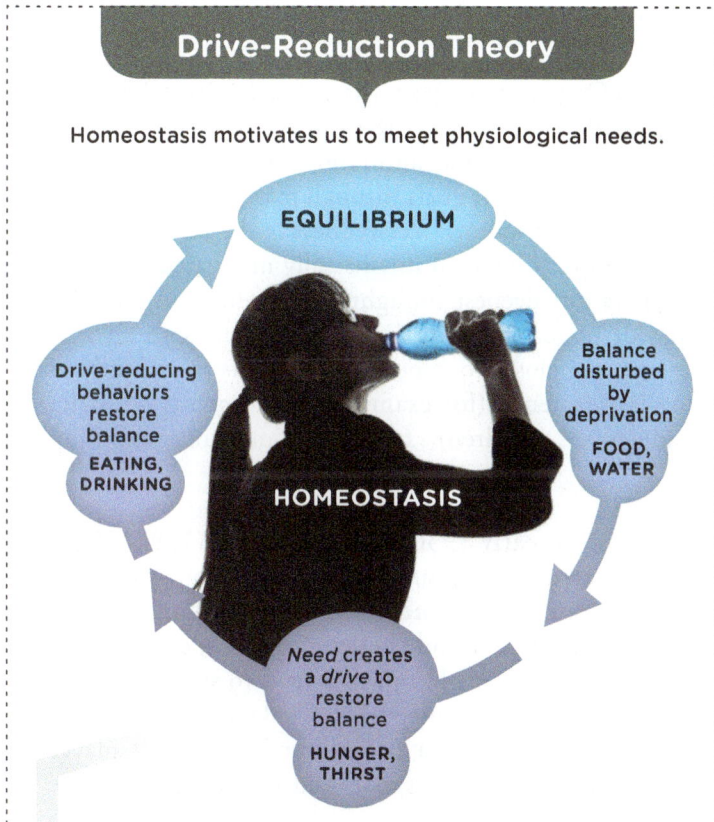

EQUILIBRIUM

Drive-reducing behaviors restore balance
**EATING, DRINKING**

Balance disturbed by deprivation
**FOOD, WATER**

HOMEOSTASIS

*Need* creates a *drive* to restore balance
**HUNGER, THIRST**

## Arousal Theory

Humans have an innate need to seek an optimal level of stimulation.

Boredom drives curiosity and activity-seeking behavior.

Feels like anxiety to some, but **sensation seekers** are comfortable here.

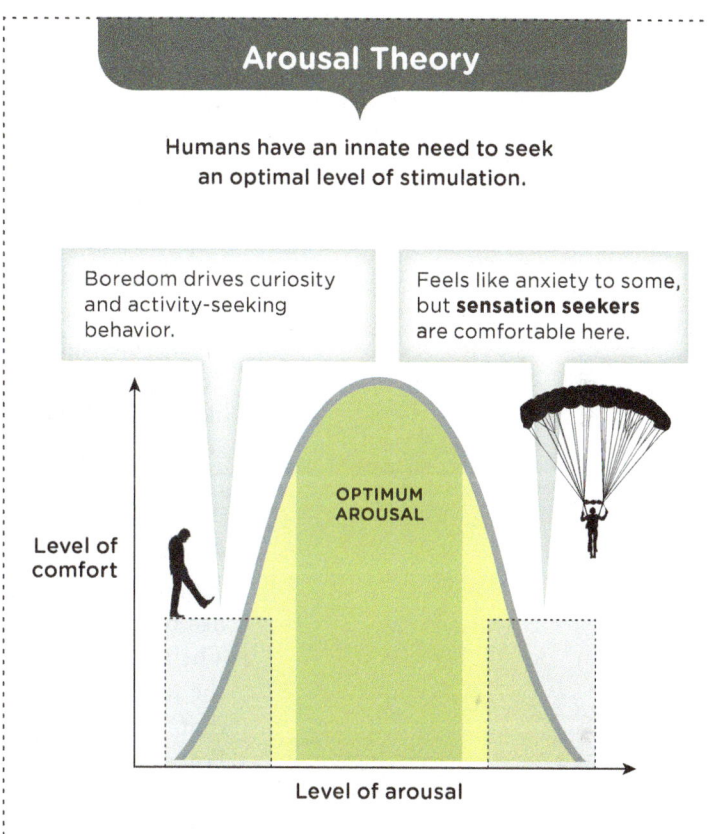

OPTIMUM AROUSAL

Level of comfort

Level of arousal

## Hierarchy of Needs

Abraham Maslow's theory combines physiological and psychological needs in a hierarchy, or sequence. We are motivated to meet higher-level needs when physiological needs at the base of the hierarchy have been met.

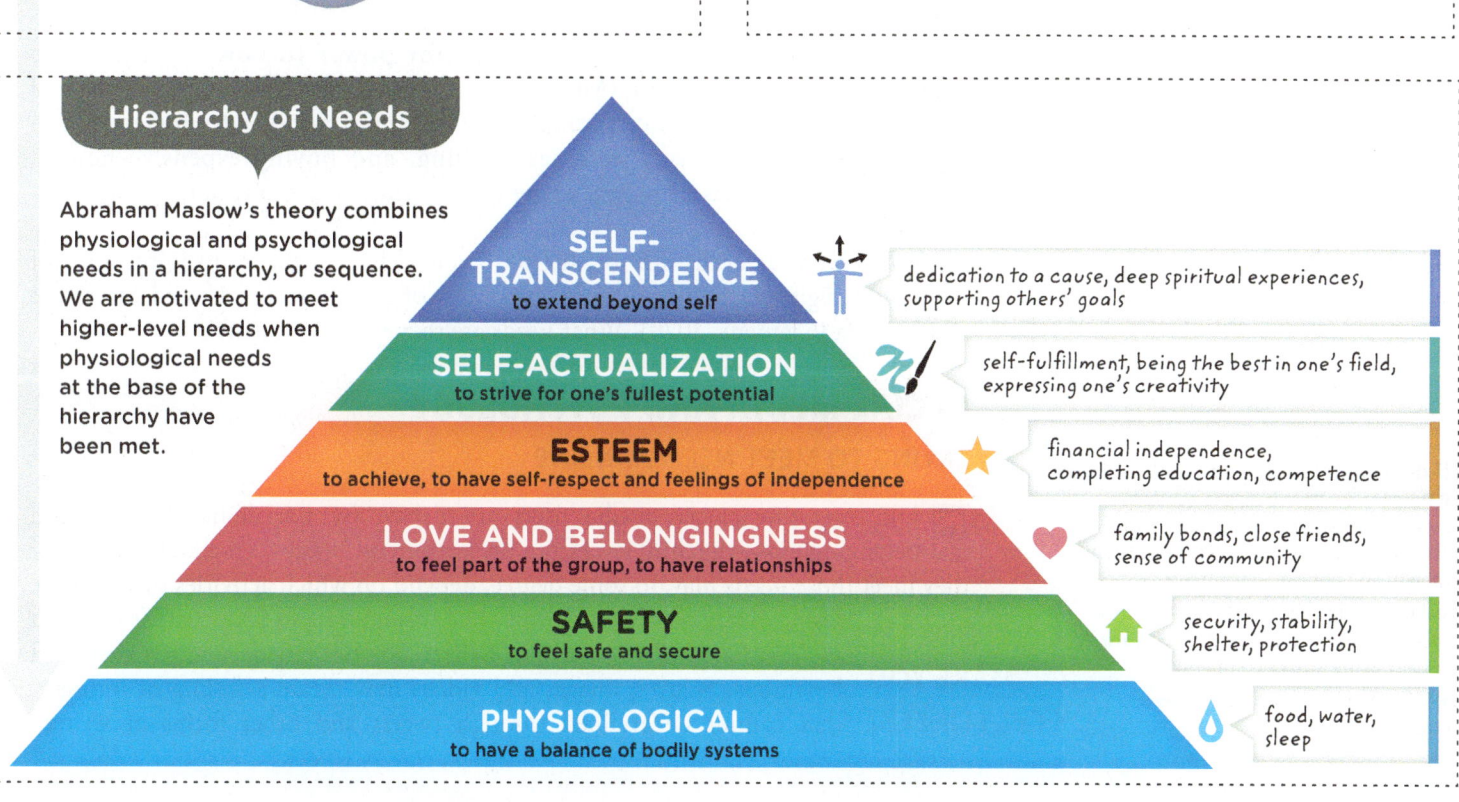

**SELF-TRANSCENDENCE**
to extend beyond self
*dedication to a cause, deep spiritual experiences, supporting others' goals*

**SELF-ACTUALIZATION**
to strive for one's fullest potential
*self-fulfillment, being the best in one's field, expressing one's creativity*

**ESTEEM**
to achieve, to have self-respect and feelings of independence
*financial independence, completing education, competence*

**LOVE AND BELONGINGNESS**
to feel part of the group, to have relationships
*family bonds, close friends, sense of community*

**SAFETY**
to feel safe and secure
*security, stability, shelter, protection*

**PHYSIOLOGICAL**
to have a balance of bodily systems
*food, water, sleep*

## Put Your Heads Together

Maslow's hierarchy of needs was developed more than 50 years ago. Do you think it still rings true? In your group, **A)** discuss possible problems with Maslow's hierarchy. **B)** What are some cross-cultural differences you might expect to encounter with respect to the levels? **C)** Modify Maslow's hierarchy or create a new one that you believe resonates more with today's college students.

## More Needs

**CONNECTIONS**

In **Chapter 8,** we introduced Erikson's theory of psychosocial development, which suggests that stages of development are marked by tasks or emotional crises. These crises often touch on issues of competence, relatedness, and autonomy.

**SELF-DETERMINATION THEORY** Building on the ideas of Maslow and **Erik Erikson**, researchers Edward Deci and Richard Ryan (2008) proposed the **self-determination theory (SDT),** which suggests that we are born with three universal, fundamental needs that are always driving us in the direction of optimal functioning: competence, relatedness, and autonomy (Stone et al., 2009). Competence represents the need to reach our goals through mastery of day-to-day responsibilities (passing an exam, for instance). Relatedness is the need to create meaningful and lasting relationships. We are all intrinsically motivated to establish bonds that allow us to share our deepest thoughts and feelings. Autonomy means managing one's behavior to reach personal goals. Meeting with an academic advisor as you move one step closer to choosing a career is an example of autonomy. When autonomy is threatened (for example, when parents are strict and controlling of their adolescent children), frustration may increase (Van Petegem et al., 2015).

**ACHIEVEMENT AND POWER** In the early 1930s, Henry Murray (1893–1988) proposed that humans are motivated by 20 fundamental needs, one of which has been the subject of extensive research: the **need for achievement (n-Ach).** The n-Ach creates a drive to reach attainable and challenging goals, especially in the face of competition. Researchers suggest that people tend to seek situations that provide opportunities for satisfying this need (McClelland et al., 1976). For example, a child who aspires to become a professional basketball player might practice every day, read books about the sport, and try out for selective basketball teams.

Some people are motivated by a **need for power (n-Pow),** or a drive to control and influence others (McClelland et al., 1976). People with this need may project their importance through outward appearances—driving around in luxury cars, wearing flashy designer clothing, and buying expensive houses. Those with high levels of n-Pow enjoy dominating others but hate being dominated themselves.

Whatever your needs may be, there is a good chance you try to fulfill some of them with digital technology. More than 70% of people in the United States use social media (Clement, 2020). What needs are they trying to satisfy?

## SOCIAL MEDIA AND PSYCHOLOGY

TRYING TO MEET NEEDS ONLINE

**self-determination theory (SDT)** Suggests that humans are born with the needs for competence, relatedness, and autonomy, which are always driving us in the direction of growth and optimal functioning.

**need for achievement (n-Ach)** A drive to reach attainable and challenging goals, especially in the face of competition.

**need for power (n-Pow)** A drive to control and influence others.

**DOES IT MAKE YOU FEEL LONELY?**

Like everyone, social media users are driven by the desire for love and belongingness—the third level from the bottom on Maslow's hierarchy. Whether they meet those needs may, to some degree, depend on which activities they choose. Using "image-based platforms" like Instagram and Snapchat, as opposed to "text-based platforms" like Twitter, has been associated with reduced loneliness. Sharing images and videos may create a feeling of intimacy that cannot be attained through tweets and other forms of written communication (Pittman & Reich, 2016). Additionally, research suggests that active use of social media (exchanging messages, sharing videos, and other tools) may be better for mental health than passive use (consuming content created by others) (Escobar-Viera et al., 2018). This latter activity, which includes viewing other people's photos and status updates, may lead to feelings of envy and thereby decrease "affective well-being" (Verduyn et al., 2015). In other words, it diminishes positive emotions. But this effect is not observed in all people. A study of teenagers found that only 10% felt worse after passively consuming social media—the rest felt either better or no change in well-being (Beyens et al., 2020). If ever you do feel a twinge of sadness when you see online "evidence" of the cool and exciting lives of friends, remember this: People often use social media to portray themselves in the most flattering ways. Perhaps more importantly, recognize that passively viewing other people's content may not satisfy your need for love and belongingness. Find a way to connect with friends more directly, online and offline. Comment on a post, send a message, or make plans to spend time together in person. #

We have now examined the theories of motivation and how they apply to real people, including Ivonne. Before we move on, let's explore a phenomenon that can have either a positive or negative impact on motivation—depending on how you respond to it.

**Posting in the Pandemic**
During the early months of the COVID-19 pandemic, use of social media reportedly increased by 61% (Holmes, 2020). Not only were people using these platforms to connect with others they could no longer see in person (fulfilling love and belongingness needs); they were making different decisions about what to share (Nabity-Grover et al., 2020). Prior to COVID-19, it was totally normal to post a group photo from inside a restaurant; in the pandemic era, posting images of maskless group gatherings might cause alarm and disapproval.

ViewApart/Getty Images.

## FAILING SUCCESSFULLY

Research reveals how to turn defeat to one's advantage.

From the **SCIENTIFIC** pages of **AMERICAN**

People often say that "failure is the mother of success." This cliché might have some truth to it, but it does not tell us how to actually turn a loss into a win, says Emmanuel Manalo, a professor of educational psychology at Kyoto University in Japan. As a result, he says, "we know we shouldn't give up when we fail—but in reality, we do."

Manalo and Manu Kapur, a professor of learning sciences at the Swiss Federal Institute of Technology Zurich, put together a special issue of the journal *Thinking Skills and Creativity* in 2018 on benefiting from failure. The issue's 15 studies provide teachers and educational researchers with a guide for achieving success. One study reported, for example, that the sooner and more often students fail at a task, such as building a robot, the sooner they can move forward and improve. Another confirmed that feedback on failures is most constructive when the giver comes across as caring, and the receiver is prepared to weather negative emotions.

Manalo and his co-authors also contributed their own study focused on overcoming one fundamental, everyday form of failure: not completing a task. They asked 131 undergraduates to write an essay about their school experiences. Half of the students received instructions for structuring their writing, and half were left to their own devices; all, however, were stopped prior to finishing. Afterward the researchers found that those in the structured group were more motivated to complete their essays, compared with those who lacked guidance—even if the latter were closer to being done. Knowing how to finish, in other words, was more important than being close to finishing.

The researchers dubbed this finding "the Hemingway effect," for the author's self-reported tendency to stop writing only when he knew what would happen next in the story—so as to avoid writer's block when he returned to the page. Manalo believes that learning how to fail temporarily can help people avoid becoming permanent failures at many tasks, such as completing a dissertation, learning a language or inventing a new technology.

Demystifying failure and teaching students not to fear it make goals more attainable, says Stephanie Couch, executive director of the Lemelson-MIT Program, a nonprofit organization dedicated to developing and supporting inventors. Couch, whose work was also featured in the special issue, adds that we "should really be thinking of failure as part of a process of iterating toward success." Rachel Nuwer. Reproduced with permission. Copyright © 2019 Scientific American, a division of Nature America, Inc. All rights reserved.

 **SHOW WHAT YOU KNOW**

1. _____ is a stimulus or force that directs the way we behave, think, and feel.

2. When behaviors are driven by internal factors such as interest and personal satisfaction, _____ is involved.

   **A.** extrinsic motivation      **C.** persistence

   **B.** intrinsic motivation      **D.** external consequences

3. According to Maslow, the biological and psychological needs motivating behavior are arranged in a _____.

4. How does drive-reduction theory of motivation differ from arousal theory?

 CHECK YOUR ANSWERS AT THE BACK OF THE BOOK.

# Sexuality

In the last section, we discussed various theories of motivation, including Maslow's hierarchy of needs. As we explored the various levels of the hierarchy, you may have wondered where sex fits in. Surely, humans are motivated to have sex, but why? "Sex may be studied as a purely physiological need," according to Maslow (1943), "[but] ordinarily sexual behavior is multi-determined" (p. 381). In other words, there are many forces motivating us to engage in sexual activity. These include the need for affection and love, and that means "both giving and receiving love" (p. 381). Every person is different, of course. There is tremendous variability in human **sexuality,** a dimension of human nature encompassing everything that makes us sexual beings: sexual activities, attitudes, and behaviors.

## The Birds and the Bees

 **LO 6** Describe the human sexual response as identified by Masters and Johnson.

To grasp the complexity of sexual experiences, we must understand the basic physiology of the sexual response. Enter William Masters (1915–2001) and Virginia Johnson (1925–2013) and their pioneering laboratory research, which included the study of approximately 10,000 distinct sexual responses of 312 male and 382 female participants (Masters & Johnson, 1966). These researchers were particularly interested in determining the physiological changes that occurred during sexual activities such as masturbation and intercourse. Using a variety of instruments to measure blood flow, body temperature, muscular changes, and heart rate, they discovered that most people experience a similar physiological sexual response, which can result from oral stimulation, manual stimulation, vaginal intercourse, or masturbation. Men and women tend to follow a similar cycle: *excitement, plateau, orgasm,* and *resolution* (**FIGURE 9.1**). These phases vary in duration for different people.

Sexual arousal begins during the *excitement phase,* when physical changes start to become evident. Muscles tense, the heartbeat quickens, breathing accelerates, blood pressure rises, and the nipples become firm. In men, the penis becomes erect, the scrotum constricts, and the testes pull up toward the body. In women, the vagina lubricates and the clitoris swells.

**Sexy Science**
In the mid-1950s, William Masters teamed with Virginia Johnson to study the bodily changes that occur during masturbation and sex. Their research was groundbreaking, and it upended many long-held misconceptions about sex. For example, Masters and Johnson found that the length of a man's penis does not determine his ability to give pleasure (Fox, 2013).

Bettmann/Getty Images.

**sexuality** A dimension of human nature encompassing everything that makes us sexual beings: sexual activities, attitudes, and behaviors.

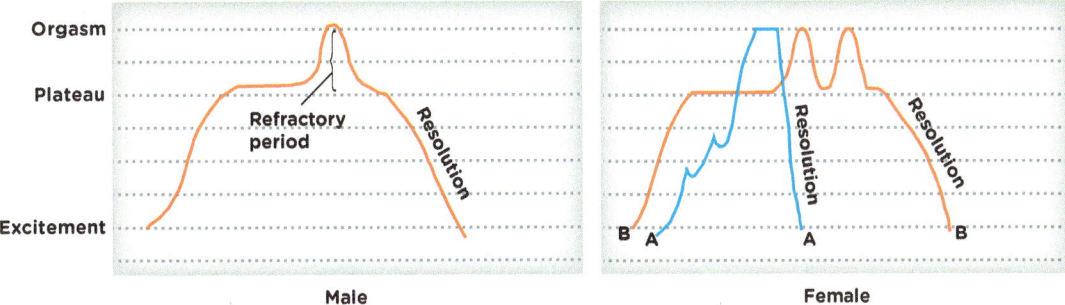

**FIGURE 9.1**

**Masters and Johnson's Human Sexual Response Cycle**

In the male sexual response (left), excitement is typically followed by a brief plateau, orgasm, and then a refractory period during which another orgasm is not possible. In the female sexual response (right), there is no refractory period. Orgasm is typically followed by resolution (A) or, if sexual stimulation continues, additional orgasms (B).

Next is the *plateau phase*, leading up to the orgasm. During this time, the muscles continue to tense, breathing and heart rate increase, and blood pressure rises. This phase is usually quite short-lived, lasting only a few seconds to minutes.

The shortest phase of the sexual response cycle is the *orgasm phase*. As the peak of sexual response is reached, an **orgasm** occurs, which is a powerful combination of extremely gratifying sensations and a series of rhythmic muscular contractions. When men and women are asked to describe their orgasmic experiences, it is very difficult to differentiate between them. Some studies using PET scans suggest that the brain activity of males and females is very similar during an orgasm (Georgiadis et al., 2009; Mah & Binik, 2001); other research indicates that certain patterns of brain activation may differ (Wise et al., 2017).

The final phase of the sexual response cycle, according to Masters and Johnson, is the *resolution phase*. This is when bodies return to a relaxed state. Without further sexual arousal, the blood flows out of the genitals, and blood pressure, heart rate, and breathing return to normal. Men lose their erections, the testes move down, and the skin of the scrotum loosens. They also experience a **refractory period,** an interval during which they cannot attain another orgasm. This can last from minutes to hours, and typically the older a man is, the longer the refractory period lasts. For women, the resolution phase is characterized by a decrease in clitoral swelling. Women do not experience a refractory period, and if sexual stimulation continues, some are capable of having multiple orgasms.

Now that we have explored the physiology of sex, let's move on to its underlying psychology. How are sexual activities shaped by learning, relationships, and the need to be loved and belong?

## Sexual Orientation: It's a Continuum

**LO 7**  Define sexual orientation and summarize how it develops.

**Sexual orientation** refers to "the **sex** of those to whom one is sexually and romantically attracted" (APA, 2015, p. 22). Some describe it as a continuum that includes many dimensions of our sexuality, including attraction, desire, emotions, and all the behaviors that result. Human beings can be "attracted to men, women, both, neither, or to people who are gender-queer, androgynous, or have other gender identities" (APA, 2015, p. 22; **FIGURE 9.2** on the next page). People attracted to members of the opposite sex are commonly referred to as **heterosexual;** those attracted to members

### CONNECTIONS

In **Chapter 8,** we outlined the difference between sex and gender. Sex is the classification of someone as male, female, or intersex based on biological characteristics. Gender is a social construct. Here, we discuss the complex nature of sexual attraction as it relates to sex and gender.

**orgasm**  A powerful combination of extremely gratifying sensations and a series of rhythmic muscular contractions.

**refractory period**  An interval of time during which a man cannot attain another orgasm.

**sexual orientation**  A person's enduring sexual attraction to others; a continuum that includes dimensions of sexuality, attraction, desire, and emotions.

**heterosexual**  Attraction to members of the opposite sex.

**FIGURE 9.2**

**The Sexual Orientation Continuum**

We can think of sexual orientation as a continuum rather than a set of discrete categories. This graph shows the range of orientations that might characterize a population (Epstein, 2016).

Information from Epstein (2016).

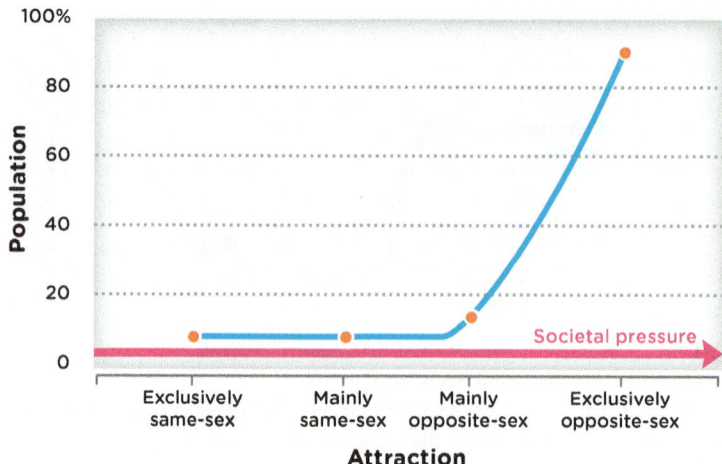

of the same sex were once classified as "**homosexual**" (a term that is antiquated and derogatory; GLAAD, n.d.); and those attracted to more than one sex or gender are called **bisexual.** But, as we noted earlier, sexual orientation does not necessarily fit into these neat categories: If sexual orientation is "more like height than eye color—why should we try to force it into a small number of categories?" (Epstein et al., 2012, p. 1377).

Those who do not feel sexually attracted to others are referred to as *asexual.* Lack of interest in sex does not necessarily prevent a person from maintaining relationships with spouses, partners, or friends. We can't be sure how many people consider themselves asexual, but estimates range from 0.6–5.5% of the population (Crooks & Baur, 2021).

There is a universe of labels for different sexual orientations. In America, commonly used adjectives for people attracted to same-sex partners include "lesbian" (women attracted to women) and "gay" (men attracted to men) (APA Style, 2019). Some people refer to themselves as "queer," thereby avoiding the "gender binaries of male and female or . . . the perceived restrictions imposed by lesbian, gay, and bisexual orientations" (APA, 2015, p. 22). In other words, such individuals choose not to be boxed into a certain category. There are many more labels for sexual orientation, some of which are mentioned in **TABLE 9.1**.

## How Does Sexual Orientation Develop?

We are not sure how sexual orientation develops, but most professionals in the field agree it is not a matter of choice. Consistent with this perspective, most people feel they do not have control over whom they find attractive. Research suggests sexual orientation results from an interaction of many biological and environmental factors—nature *and* nurture (Epstein, 2016; Xu et al., 2019).

### CONNECTIONS

In **Chapter 1,** we introduced twin studies, which are commonly used to examine the degree to which nature and nurture contribute to psychological traits. Because identical (monozygotic) twins share 100% of their genetic make-up at conception, they share more genetically influenced characteristics than fraternal (dizygotic) twins, who share about 50% of their genes. Since sexual orientation is influenced by genes, we would expect identical twins to be more similar in their orientations than fraternal twins.

**GENETICS AND SEXUAL ORIENTATION**　　To determine the influence of nature on sexual orientation, we turn to large-scale gene studies. After examining the genetic make-up of nearly half a million people, researchers concluded that many different genes—perhaps hundreds or thousands—play a role in determining our orientation (Ganna et al., 2019; Kaiser, 2019). But DNA is only part of the story. As **twin** studies have shown, environmental factors also contribute to the development of sexual orientation. In a large study of Swedish twins, researchers explored the impact of genes and environment on "same-sex sexual behavior" (among 2,320 identical twin pairs and 1,506 fraternal twin pairs). In their sample, the identical twins were moderately more likely than the fraternal twins to have the same sexual orientation. They also found that same-sex sexual behavior for identical twins had heritability estimates of

**homosexual**　An antiquated and derogatory term referring to those who are attracted to members of the same sex.

**bisexual**　Being attracted to more than one sex or gender.

**TABLE 9.1** Terms to Describe Gender Identity and Sexual Orientation

| Terms | Defined |
|---|---|
| AFAB/AMAB | Assigned female at birth/assigned male at birth (Webb et al., 2015). |
| Allies | People who support and advocate for those in the LGBTQ+ community (Gardner & Alanis, 2020). |
| Androgyny | Crossing gender-role boundaries, exhibiting behaviors associated with both genders. |
| Asexual | Not feeling sexually attracted to any person (Crooks & Baur, 2021). |
| Bisexual | Describes one who "experiences emotional, romantic and/or sexual attractions to, or engages in romantic or sexual relationships with, more than one sex or gender" (APA, 2017). |
| Cisgender | Describes a person whose gender identity aligns with the gender assigned at birth (Gold, 2019). |
| Gay | Attraction to the same sex. |
| Intersex | Having ambiguous or inconsistent biological indicators of male or female in sexual structures and organs (GLAAD, n.d.). |
| Lesbian | Refers to a woman who is attracted to other women. |
| LGBTQ+ | Inclusive ways to represent lesbian, gay, bisexual, transgender, queer/questioning, intersex, asexual/ally, and other identities (Cherry, 2020). |
| Natal gender | Gender, generally male/female, assigned at birth. |
| Nonbinary gender identity and/or genderqueer | "Terms used by some people who experience their gender identity and/or gender expression as falling outside the categories of man and woman" (GLAAD, n.d., p. 11). |
| Pansexual | Being sexually attracted to people irrespective of their sex and/or gender (BBC Newsbeat, 2015). |
| Questioning | Still exploring sexuality and/or gender identity (BBC Newsbeat, 2015). |
| Transsexual | A word to describe one who undergoes a social transition from male to female or female to male, often by making changes to the body through surgery and/or medical treatment (American Psychiatric Association, 2013). |
| Transgender/Trans | Describes a person whose gender identity and expression do not match the gender assigned at birth. |

Above is terminology commonly used to identify different gender identities and sexual orientations. It's important to note that these concepts are independent; knowing someone's gender identity does not necessarily tell you anything about their sexual orientation (Liszewski et al., 2018). Before using these terms to describe people, find out their preferred pronouns and how they identify.

around 34–39% for men and 18–19% for women (Långström et al., 2010). Others report heritability estimates ranging from 25% to 50% for men, and "substantially lower" percentages for women (Epstein, 2016). These findings highlight two important factors: Men and women differ in terms of the heritability of same-sex sexual behavior, and both genes and environment (nature and nurture) contribute to sexual orientation.

**THE BIOLOGY OF SEXUAL ORIENTATION** The development of sexual orientation may begin before birth. The fetal gonads secrete hormones (estrogen and androgens) that influence reproductive anatomy. The presence of androgens (secreted primarily by the male gonads) may steer the development of sexual orientation toward women. This could potentially lead to heterosexual orientation in men, but same-sex attraction in women (Breedlove, 2017). To explore this possibility, researchers have studied pregnant women with elevated hormone levels (the result of a genetic abnormality or medication). Evidence from these cases suggests that early in utero exposure to high levels of androgens may be associated with "male-typed" development and same-sex attraction in females (Berenbaum et al., 2011; Jordan-Young, 2012).

Axelle/Bauer-Griffin/Getty Images.

In an interview with *Rolling Stone,* singer-songwriter Janelle Monáe said that she identified with pansexuality, or being attracted to people irrespective of gender. "I want young girls, young boys, nonbinary, gay, straight, queer people who are having a hard time dealing with their sexuality, dealing with feeling ostracized or bullied for just being their unique selves, to know that I see you. . . . Be proud" (Spanos, 2018, para. 10).

Interestingly, having older brothers in the family seems to be associated with a higher probability of same-sex attraction in men, a phenomenon known as the *fraternal birth order effect* (Blanchard, 2008; Blanchard et al., 2020). One study found that males with one older brother were 38% more likely than those with no older brothers to be gay (Blanchard et al., 2020). Why would this be? According to the *maternal immunity hypothesis,* cells from a male fetus are introduced into the mother's circulatory system, triggering an immune response. The mother's immune system produces antibodies that influence the development of the next male fetus she carries, resulting in a variety of changes in neurons that direct the person to "later be attracted to men rather than to women" (Blanchard et al., 2020, p. 2). However, some researchers have had difficulty replicating the early maternal immunity hypothesis studies (Currin et al., 2015; Kishida & Rahman, 2015; Xu & Zheng, 2017).

Some scholars question efforts to uncover biological causes of same-sex attraction (Jacobs, 2012). Could this line of inquiry lead to discriminatory practices, like editing "gay genes" out of embryos? Given the biological complexity of sexual orientation, this scenario is highly unlikely. And as researchers point out, "bigotry needs no data." We should use our scientific knowledge "ethically and thoughtfully to arrive at a fuller understanding of who we are" (Phelps & Wedow, 2019, para 16).

**WHERE'S THE NURTURE?**   We have spent a great deal of time discussing the potential role of nature in sexual orientation. How does nurture fit into the picture? Earlier, we noted that sexual orientation might be understood as a continuum. At one end of the continuum are people who are strictly heterosexual, and at the other end are those who are undeniably gay or lesbian. Many people fall somewhere in the middle of these two extremes. These individuals have some flexibility in their orientation, particularly when they are young, and environmental factors (nurture) help determine where they fall on the continuum. Because we live in a *homomisic society*—one that strongly favors heterosexuality—most people in the middle will be pushed toward a heterosexual orientation. Those at either end of the continuum are less likely to be flexible in their orientation, in part due to the strong genetic component of sexual orientation (Epstein, 2016).

**A HISTORY OF UNFAIR TREATMENT**   Although differences in sexual orientation and gender identity are universal and have been evident throughout recorded history, individuals who identify as LGBTQ+ have been subjected to stereotyping, prejudice, and discrimination. LGBTQ+ people in the United States, for example, have been, and continue to be, subjected to harassment, violence, and unfair practices related to housing and employment. Many states are working to rectify these issues, and the federal government recently took a big step toward protecting the rights of LGBTQ+ people. In June 2020, the U.S. Supreme Court ruled that the 1964 Civil Rights Act shields "gay and transgender employees" from discrimination (Barnes, 2020, para. 2).

## "Normal" Is Relative

It is only natural for us to wonder if what we are doing between the sheets (or elsewhere) is normal or healthy. Is it normal to masturbate? Is it normal to fantasize about sex with strangers? The answers to these types of questions depend somewhat on cultural context. Most of us unknowingly learn *sexual scripts,* or cultural rules that tell us what types of activities are "appropriate" and don't interfere with healthy sexual intimacy. In some cultures, the sexual script suggests that women should have minimal, if any, sexual experience before marriage, but men are expected to explore their sexuality, or "sow their wild oats."

**GATHERING SEX DATA**   Alfred Kinsey (1894–1956) and colleagues were among the first to try to scientifically and objectively examine the sexual behavior of people in the United States (Kinsey et al., 1948; Kinsey et al., 1953). Using the survey method, Kinsey and his team collected data on the sexual behaviors of 5,300 White males and 5,940 White females. They found that both men and women masturbated and had experiences with premarital sex, adultery, and sexual activity with someone of the same sex.

The Kinsey study was groundbreaking in terms of its data content and methodology, which included accuracy checks and assurances of confidentiality. The data continue to serve as a valuable reference for researchers studying how sexual behaviors and attitudes have evolved over time. However, Kinsey's work was not without limitations. For example, Kinsey and colleagues (1948, 1953) failed to obtain a **representative sample** of the population. The sample lacked ethnic diversity, and there was an overrepresentation of well-educated Protestants (Potter, 2006; Wallin, 1949).

Subsequent research has been better designed, using samples that are more representative of the population (Herbenick et al., 2010; Michael et al., 1994). "As recently as 2002, the average adult American had sex approximately 64 times a year, but by 2014 that declined to about 53 times a year" (Twenge et al., 2017, p. 2391). As people get older, both masturbation and partnered sex become somewhat less frequent. Males may direct some of their energy away from "mating effort" and toward nurturing children and grandchildren (Gray et al., 2020). Single older people express less interest in hookups, multiple partners, and other sexual adventures. Interestingly, older single women tend to be more satisfied with their sex lives than younger single women (Gray et al., 2019).

**HOW DO MEN AND WOMEN DIFFER?**   As stereotypes suggest, men think about sex more often than women (Laumann et al., 1994), and they consistently report a higher frequency of masturbation (Peplau, 2003). Decades ago in the United States, men tended to be more tolerant than women about casual sex before marriage, and more permissive in their attitudes about extramarital sex (Laumann et al., 1994). But these differences are not apparent in heterosexual teenagers and young adults, as young men and women more commonly engage in "hookups," which were once called "one-night-stands" (Dajches & Terán, 2020). Hookups, which can be anything from kissing to sexual intercourse, reveal major shifts in the way people view sexual activity.

## Problems with Sex

**Sexual dysfunction** occurs when there is a "significant disturbance" in the ability to respond sexually or to gain pleasure from sex (American Psychiatric Association, 2013). Survey data suggest that 43% of women and 31% of men suffer from some sort of sexual dysfunction (Laumann et al., 1999). Temporary difficulties can result from everyday stressors or situational factors, while longer-term problems stem from a variety of issues, including health conditions, beliefs about sex, ignorance about sexual practices, and performance expectations. Let's explore the major categories of sexual dysfunction, keeping in mind that they sometimes overlap.

**DESIRE**   Illness, fatigue, relationship frustration, and other situational factors can lead to temporary problems with desire. In some cases, lack of desire is persistent and distressing. This is the most common sexual issue reported by women, but men may be affected, too (Brotto, 2010; Derogatis et al., 2020).

**AROUSAL**   Problems with arousal occur when the psychological desire to engage in sexual behavior is present, but the body does not cooperate. Men with *erectile disorder* may have trouble getting or maintaining an erection or experience a decrease in

**CONNECTIONS**

In **Chapter 1,** we emphasized that representative samples enable us to generalize findings to populations. Here, we see that inferences about sexual behaviors for groups other than White, well-educated Protestants could be problematic, as few members of these groups participated in the Kinsey study.

Wallace Kirkland/Getty Images.

**Radical Research**
Alfred Kinsey interviews a subject in his office at the Institute for Sex Research, now The Kinsey Institute. Kinsey began investigating human sexuality in the 1930s, when talking about sex was taboo. He started gathering data with surveys, but then switched to personal interviews, which he believed to be more effective. These interviews often went on for hours and included hundreds of questions (PBS, 2005).

**sexual dysfunction** A significant disturbance in the ability to respond sexually or to gain pleasure from sex.

rigidity (American Psychiatric Association, 2013). Up to 20% of all men report they have occasionally experienced problems with erections (Hock, 2016). Women can also struggle with arousal. *Female sexual interest/arousal disorder* is apparent in reduced interest in sex, lack of initiation of sexual activities, reduced excitement, or decreased genital sensations during sex (American Psychiatric Association, 2013).

**ORGASM**   Disorders related to orgasm are yet another category of dysfunction. *Female orgasmic disorder* is diagnosed when a woman is consistently unable to reach orgasm, has reduced orgasmic intensity, or does not reach orgasm quickly enough during sexual activity (American Psychiatric Association, 2013). Men who experience frequent delay or inability to ejaculate might have a condition known as *delayed ejaculation* (American Psychiatric Association, 2013; Segraves, 2010). With this disorder, the ability to achieve orgasm and ejaculate is inhibited or delayed during partnered sexual activity. Preliminary data suggest delayed ejaculation may be more common in men who habitually masturbate to pornography (Fog-Poulsen et al., 2020). Men who have trouble controlling when they ejaculate (particularly during vaginal sex) may suffer from *premature (early) ejaculation* (American Psychiatric Association, 2013).

**PAIN**   The final category of sexual dysfunction, painful intercourse, typically affects women. *Genito-pelvic pain/penetration disorder* refers to four types of co-occurring symptoms specific to women: difficulty having intercourse, pain in the genitals or pelvis, fear of pain or vaginal penetration, and tension of the pelvic floor muscles (American Psychiatric Association, 2013). Up to 15% of women in North America report frequent pain during intercourse, and issues related to pain are associated with reduced desire and arousal.

## Sexually Transmitted Infections

A growing number of people in the United States carry **sexually transmitted infections (STIs)**—diseases or illnesses passed on through sexual activity (Williamson & Chen, 2020; **TABLE 9.2**). STIs have many causes, but most are *bacterial* or *viral*.

**Standing Up to Sexual Violence**
Dr. Denis Mukwege (left) and Nadia Murad (right) shared the 2018 Nobel Peace Prize for "their efforts to end the use of sexual violence as a weapon of war and armed conflict" (Nobel Media, 2018, para. 1). Mukwege is a physician who has devoted much of his life to caring for victims of sexual assault in eastern Democratic Republic of the Congo, which has been dubbed "the rape capital of the world" (Sullivan, 2018, para. 4). Murad was kidnapped and forced into sexual slavery by ISIS in northern Iraq. She comes from the Yazidi community, where rape is shrouded in shame and secrecy, but she has fearlessly spoken out about the trauma she suffered (Sullivan, 2018).

**sexually transmitted infections (STIs)**
Diseases or illnesses transmitted through sexual activity.

Christian Lutz/AP Images.

**TABLE 9.2** Sexually Transmitted Infections (STIs)

| STI | Symptom | Annual Cases in the U.S. |
|---|---|---|
| Chlamydia | Women often have no symptoms; men can experience discharge from penis, burning when urinating, and pain/swelling of the testicles. | 1.8 million |
| Gonorrhea | No symptoms may be present in men or women. Men can experience burning when urinating, and white, yellow, or green discharge. Women can experience pain and burning when urinating, and vaginal discharge. | 583,405 |
| Syphilis | Firm, round sores that first appear where the infection enters the body and can then spread to other parts of the body. | 35,063 |
| Herpes (HSV-2) | Blisters on the genitals, rectum, or mouth; painful sores after blisters break; fever, body aches, and swollen glands can occur. | 11.9% of adults ages 14–49 |
| Human papillomavirus (HPV) | Genital warts; certain cancers; warts growing in the throat. | 42.5% of adults ages 18–59 |

Sexually transmitted infections (STIs) are extremely common in the United States. Listed here are the number of cases of chlamydia, gonorrhea, and syphilis reported in 2017, along with the percentage of adults infected with HSV-2 (the most common cause of genital herpes) and HPV. Information from CDC (2017, 2020).

Bacterial infections such as *syphilis, gonorrhea,* and *chlamydia* sometimes clear up with antibiotics, but many bacterial strains have become resistant to mainstay antibiotics (Williamson & Chen, 2020). Viral infections like *genital herpes* and *human papillomavirus (HPV)* have no cure, only treatments to reduce symptoms (World Health Organization [WHO], 2019).

### *Apply This* ⬇

#### PROTECT YOURSELF

The more sexual partners you have, the greater your risk of acquiring an STI. But you can lower your risk by communicating with your partner. People who know that their partners have had (or are having) sex with others face a lower risk of acquiring an STI than those who do not know. Why is this so? If you are aware of your partner's activities, you may be more likely to take preventative measures, such as using condoms. Of course, there is always the possibility that your sexual partner (or you) has a disease but doesn't know it. Some people with STIs are asymptomatic, meaning they have no symptoms. Others know they are infected but lie because they are ashamed, in denial, afraid of rejection, or for other reasons. Given all these unknowns, your best bet is to play it safe and use protection.

In the next section, we return our focus to the base of Maslow's pyramid, where life-sustaining drives are represented. We will explore hunger, one of the most powerful motivators of human behavior.

### ⟫⟫⟫ SHOW WHAT YOU KNOW

1. Masters and Johnson studied physiological changes that accompany sexual activity. Men and women experience a similar sexual response cycle, including the following ordered phases:
   A. excitement, plateau, orgasm, and resolution.
   B. plateau, excitement, orgasm, and relaxation.
   C. excitement, plateau, and orgasm.
   D. excitement, orgasm, and resolution.

2. Having older brothers seems to be associated with same-sex attraction in men, a phenomenon known as the _____.

 CHECK YOUR ANSWERS AT THE BACK OF THE BOOK.

# Hunger

Jahi Chikwendiu/The Washington Post via Getty Images.

**Serving His Country**
Ibrahim's motivation for joining the military came partly from his parents, who raised him with a strong sense of social responsibility: "You don't take anything for free," Ibrahim says. "For a country that has been so generous to my family and I, for me to just live here and not contribute or give back in any way was unacceptable" (Shams, 2016, 0:35).

**"I KNOW HUNGER"**    Ibrahim Hashi has had enough excitement, fear, and discomfort for a lifetime. While serving with the U.S. Marines, he was deployed on three combat missions—two in Iraq and one in Afghanistan. Those tours gave him a front row seat to the horrors of war. He has seen bodies of the dead, slept on floors littered with cow feces, and heard the screams of a friend who lost both legs to an improvised explosive device (IED). He also knows how it feels to be hungry, truly hungry. During his missions, there were times when food shipments never made it to his unit. "I remember one time we were supposed to get a resupply; the airplane that was going to drop it in got shot at, so they aborted the mission," Ibrahim says. "We just stayed hungry for almost a whole week." As you might imagine, everyone became irritable, and sleep was virtually impossible. "It felt like my stomach was in a knot; it was just empty," Ibrahim recalls. "If you're lucky enough to go to sleep, I guarantee you are going to be dreaming about food. . . . There was no reprieve from the hunger. It was constant."

## Hungry Brain, Hungry Body

Have you ever felt a knot in your stomach, as Ibrahim describes? Perhaps you have noticed your stomach contracting and growling when you haven't eaten for a while. What causes these rumblings, and are they a sign of hunger, or something else?

**LO 8**   Discuss how the stomach and the hypothalamus make us feel hunger.

**THE STOMACH AND BLOOD SUGAR**    In a classic study, Walter Cannon and A. L. Washburn (1912) sought to answer this question (**FIGURE 9.3**). Here's a brief synopsis of their experiment: Washburn swallowed an inflatable balloon that could be used to record his stomach contractions. Whenever Washburn felt "hunger pangs," he pushed a button. Using this procedure, the researchers found that stomach contractions and hunger pangs occurred at the same time.

Cannon and Washburn's experiment demonstrates that the stomach plays an important role in hunger, but evidence suggests this is just one piece of the puzzle. For example, cancer patients who have had their stomachs surgically removed consume normal amounts of food and experience typical levels of satiety, that is, the feeling of being full (Bergh et al., 2003; Karanicolas et al., 2013). We also must consider chemicals in the blood, such as glucose, or blood sugar. When glucose levels dip, the stomach and liver send signals to the brain that something must be done about this reduced energy situation. The brain, in turn, initiates a sense of hunger.

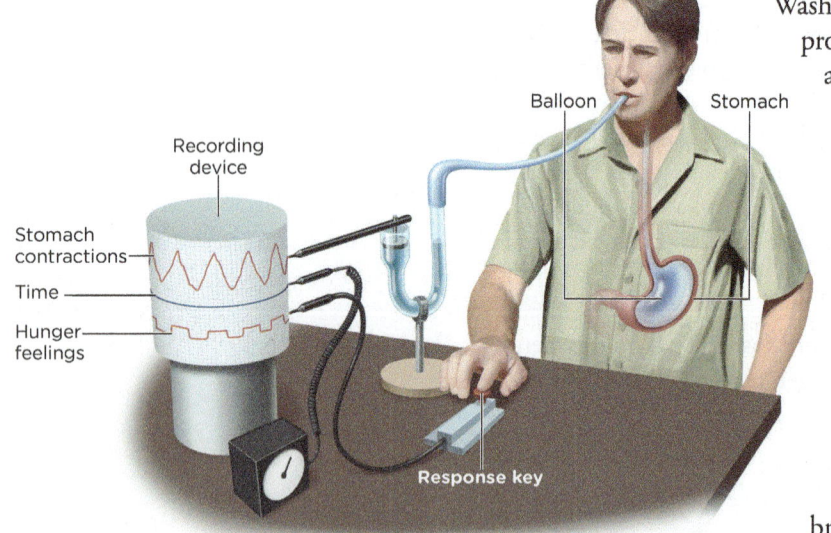

**FIGURE 9.3**
**Cannon and Washburn's Classic Study**
Washburn swallowed a special balloon attached to a device for monitoring stomach contractions. While the balloon was in place, he pressed a key every time he felt hungry. Comparing the record of key presses against the balloon measurements, Washburn showed that stomach contractions accompany feelings of hunger.

**THE HYPOTHALAMUS AND HUNGER**    A key player in hunger regulation is the hypothalamus, which can be divided into functionally distinct areas. When the *lateral hypothalamus* is activated, appetite increases. Even well-fed animals will experience a surge in appetite when researchers electrically stimulate this area of the brain. Destroy the lateral hypothalamus, and animals lose interest in food, even to the point of starvation. Because the lateral hypothalamus plays a role in motivating eating behavior, it helps preserve the balance between energy supply and demand (Leinninger, 2011; Stamatakis et al., 2016).

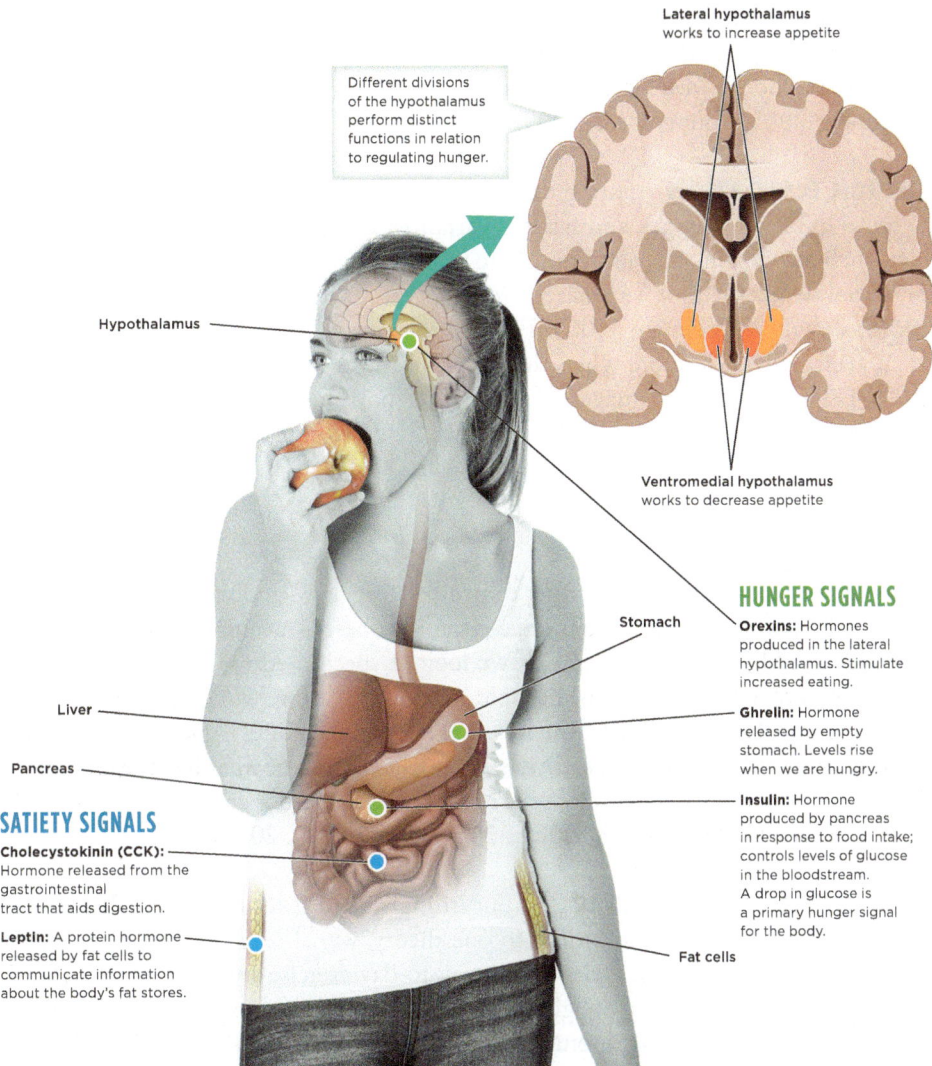

Different divisions of the hypothalamus perform distinct functions in relation to regulating hunger.

Lateral hypothalamus
works to increase appetite

Hypothalamus

Ventromedial hypothalamus
works to decrease appetite

Stomach

Liver

Pancreas

**HUNGER SIGNALS**

**Orexins:** Hormones produced in the lateral hypothalamus. Stimulate increased eating.

**Ghrelin:** Hormone released by empty stomach. Levels rise when we are hungry.

**Insulin:** Hormone produced by pancreas in response to food intake; controls levels of glucose in the bloodstream. A drop in glucose is a primary hunger signal for the body.

**SATIETY SIGNALS**

**Cholecystokinin (CCK):** Hormone released from the gastrointestinal tract that aids digestion.

**Leptin:** A protein hormone released by fat cells to communicate information about the body's fat stores.

Fat cells

**FIGURE 9.4**
**Hunger Regulation**
Feelings of hunger and satisfaction result from a complex communication system linking the brain and body. Hormones from the digestive organs communicate information about satiety and hunger to the hypothalamus, a part of the brain that plays an important role in maintaining homeostasis, or balance, in the body's systems. Separate areas of the hypothalamus then send signals to other parts of the brain, motivating us to increase or decrease eating. Photo: Piotr Marcinski/ AGE Fotostock.

If the *ventromedial hypothalamus* becomes activated, appetite declines, causing an animal to stop eating. Disable this region of the brain, and the animal will overeat to the point of obesity. The ventromedial hypothalamus receives information about levels of blood glucose and other feeding-related stimuli, as it, too, works to maintain the body's energy balance (Drougard et al., 2015; King, 2006).

The hypothalamus has a variety of sensors that react to information about hunger and food intake. This information is communicated via **hormones** in the bloodstream (**FIGURE 9.4**). One such hormone is *leptin,* which is secreted by fat cells and plays a role in suppressing hunger. Another is *insulin,* a pancreatic hormone involved in controlling levels of glucose in the bloodstream. With input from these and other hormones, the brain can monitor energy levels and respond accordingly. This complex system enables us to know when we are hungry, full, or somewhere in between.

**CONNECTIONS**

In **Chapter 2,** we described hormones as chemical messengers released into the bloodstream. Hormones do not act as quickly as neurotransmitters, but their messages are more widely spread throughout the body. Here, we see how hormones are involved in communicating information about hunger.

## Let's Have a Meal: Cultural and Social Context

Biology is not the only factor influencing eating habits. We must also consider the social and cultural context. In the United States, social activities, holidays, and work events often revolve around food. We frequently eat on the go, rushing to our next class or meeting, and don't take the time to experience the taste of food. We also tend to match our food intake to those around us, although we may not

## CONNECTIONS

In **Chapter 1,** we discussed naturalistic observation, the study of participants in their natural environments. When conducting this type of descriptive research, one must avoid disturbing participants or their environment. Here, we assume the researchers measured and recorded meals without interfering with participants' behaviors.

be aware of their influence (Herman et al., 2003; Vartanian et al., 2015). Gender plays a role in eating habits, too. Using **naturalistic observation**, researchers found that women choose lower-calorie meals or eat less when trying to impress others (Vartanian, 2015; Young et al., 2009).

**PORTION DISTORTION**   Eating decisions are driven by a variety of factors, including social influence, hunger, and satiety (Vartanian et al., 2016). But more subtle variables, such as portion size, also come into play. Serving sizes have increased over the last several decades (think "supersized" meals), and this may lead to greater consumption (Steenhuis & Poelman, 2017). For example, a meta-analysis found that people eat an average of 35% more when their food portions are doubled (Zlatevska et al., 2014). Being exposed to images of large food portions tends to "recalibrate perceptions of what is a 'normal' serving of that food" (Robinson et al., 2016, p. 32). Remember this the next time you order takeout.

## Obesity

Around the world, a growing number of people struggle with obesity. Approximately 42% of adults in the United States are considered obese—meaning they have a body mass index (BMI) that exceeds 30. If we look at specific ethnic groups, the lowest rates of obesity are among non-Hispanic Asian Americans, while the highest rates are among non-Hispanic Black Americans (Hales et al., 2020). The problem is not poised to improve, if childhood statistics are any indication of what lies ahead: One in five U.S. children is obese, and, if we narrow our focus to older children (ages 16–19), the prevalence of obesity is a shocking 42% (Skinner et al., 2018).

Radharc Images/Alamy.

**Is Processed Food to Blame?**
Americans get about 60% of their calories from processed food. This includes microwave dinners, canned goods, deli meats, hot dogs, chips, pretzels, and any foods that have been modified in some way—by adding sweeteners, colors, and preservatives, for instance (American Heart Association, n.d.-b). Researchers suspect processed foods are contributing to the obesity epidemic, and not just because they are high in calories. The chemicals they contain appear to "interact with the gut-brain [signaling] pathway," which "could promote overeating and metabolic dysfunction" (Small & DiFeliceantonio, 2019, p. 347).

**HOW MUCH CAN YOU CONTROL?**   Surprisingly, there is relatively little fluctuation in adult weight over time. According to one theory, we all tend to maintain a stable weight, or **set point,** despite variability in day-to-day exercise and food intake. If you cut back on calories and your weight falls below this set point, metabolism decreases, causing you to gain weight and return to your set point (deShazo et al., 2015). Exceed the set point and metabolism increases, once again moving you back toward your stable weight (deShazo et al., 2015; Keesey & Hirvonen, 1997). The set point acts like a thermostat, helping maintain a consistent weight despite changing conditions.

Some critics of the set point model suggest that it fails to appreciate the importance of social and environmental influences (Stroebe et al., 2013). These theorists suggest we should consider a *settling point,* which is less rigid and might explain how the "set" point can actually change based on the relative amounts of food consumed and energy used. A settling point may also help us understand how body weight can shift to a newly maintained weight, and why so many people are overweight as a result of environmental factors, such as bigger meal portions, calorie-dense foods, and eating during other activities like watching television. This brings us to an important point: If you always have dinner while watching TV or snack before going to sleep, these activities become associated with "hunger." Conditioning is also an important part of emotional eating, or eating because you feel depressed or upset (Bongers et al., 2015).

Whatever your settling point may be, it is partly a result of your genetic make-up. Studies suggest that the heritability of BMI is around 65% (Speakman et al., 2011). Researchers following participants for 25 years reported an even higher heritability (84%), and at least one study of monozygotic twins found heritability of fat mass to be as high as 90% (Albuquerque et al., 2015). These findings are striking, but they should be taken with a grain of salt because heritability may vary depending on the population being studied. For example, one group of researchers found that the heritability of BMI for children in "lower-risk" homes (where people tend to engage

**set point** The stable weight that is maintained despite variability in exercise and food intake.

in healthy behaviors like physical exercise) was 39%, compared to 86% for children from "higher-risk" homes (Schrempft et al., 2018).

We may be genetically predisposed to stay within a certain weight range, but that doesn't mean our BMI is written into our genes. Lifestyle choices and environmental factors play an important role, too.

**OVEREATING, SLEEP, AND SCREEN TIME**    Have you ever noticed how sleep deprivation affects your eating habits? Preliminary research suggests that inadequate sleep is linked to weight problems; in other words, there is a negative correlation between sleep and weight gain. Meanwhile, there is a positive correlation between screen time (that is, using a tablet, smartphone, computer, or television) and weight gain: As screen time goes up, weight increases. It seems that screen time interferes with making healthy eating choices and getting regular exercise (Buchanan et al., 2016; Elder et al., 2012; Elder et al., 2015).

**THE SECRET TO SLIMMING DOWN?**    To lose weight, a good strategy is to eat less and move more (**TABLE 9.3**); in other words, use more calories than you are taking in. Our ancestors didn't have to worry about this. Needing energy to sustain themselves, they had no choice but to choose foods rich in calories—an efficient means of survival for them, but not ideal for those of us living in a world of deep dish pizzas, curly fries, and supersized sodas. When experiencing a "famine" (a decrease in the body's habitual caloric intake), our metabolism naturally slows down; we require fewer calories and have a harder time losing weight.

We have now explored many facets of motivation, from basic drives like hunger to more abstract needs for achievement and power. As you may have guessed from the title of this chapter, motivation is intimately tied to emotion. In the sections to come, we will explore the complex world of human emotion.

**How Many Servings?**
A single serving of this snack mix contains 130 calories, but did you check how many servings are in the bag? If you eat the whole bag (a total of 8 servings), you are consuming 1040 calories! That's about half of the daily calories needed by a "moderately active" young woman and more than a third required by a "moderately active" young man (Office of Disease Prevention and Health Promotion, n.d.).

**TABLE 9.3    Weight Loss: Making It Fit**

| Strategies | Description |
|---|---|
| Set realistic goals. | Set goals and expectations that are specific, realistic, and flexible. For example, a reasonable goal would be to lose 1–2 pounds per week. |
| Get regular exercise. | Walking at a fast pace for 30 minutes every day (or almost every day) can help with weight loss. Add a variety of physical activities to your daily routines. |
| Eat regularly and track intake. | Avoid mindless eating; focus your attention on what you are consuming. Eat only when hungry, and write down what and how much you consume in a food diary. |
| Avoid nighttime eating. | Keep your metabolism going strong by eating every 3–4 hours throughout the day, rather than cramming in calories close to bedtime. |
| Drink water. | Eliminate sweetened beverages like soda. |
| Plan out your meals. | Go shopping for ingredients ahead of time and cook your own healthy meals. That way you don't have to order unhealthy takeout food at the last minute. |

Losing weight is not an easy task, but it doesn't have to be painful. Making basic lifestyle changes can have significant benefits. Information from Mayo Clinic Staff (2019) and Yale University (n.d.).

## SHOW WHAT YOU KNOW

1. Washburn swallowed a balloon to record his stomach contractions. He also pressed a button to record feelings of hunger. The findings indicated that whenever he felt hunger pangs, his:

   **A.** stomach was contracting.

   **B.** stomach was still.

   **C.** blood sugar went up.

   **D.** ventromedial hypothalamus was active.

2. Describe how the hypothalamus initiates hunger and influences eating behaviors.

✓ CHECK YOUR ANSWERS AT THE BACK OF THE BOOK.

Courtesy Ibrahim Hashi.

**Ibrahim Hashi**

# Emotion

**FOR HIS FAMILY**   At a very young age, Ibrahim knew he wanted to join the military. Like many people who enter the armed forces, he was motivated by a desire to serve his country. But after the terrorist attacks of September 11, 2001, he had another reason to enlist. Prejudice toward Muslims, or Islamophobia, reached record levels in the months following 9/11. According to the Federal Bureau of Investigation (FBI), there were 481 anti-Muslim hate crimes reported in 2001, a 1,600% increase from the previous year (FBI Uniform Crime Reports, n.d.; Serrano, 2002). Aware of this changing cultural climate, Ibrahim enlisted to protect his family from those who might perceive them as un-American. "I went into the military so people could not accuse my parents or any other family members of not having done anything for the United States," Ibrahim says. "I [could] be the example, and they could point to me and say, 'Look that's our son, and he served in the military.'"

Ibrahim's behavior could be understood from a motivational perspective. For example, you might argue that he was operating at one of the most basic levels in Maslow's hierarchy, trying to secure safety needs. But what else might have been driving his decision to join the Marines? Think about how you would *feel* as you watched news reports about murders, assaults, vandalism, and threats targeting your religious or ethnic group. (Perhaps you belong to a group that has been targeted in such a way.) How might *emotions* shape your behaviors?

## What Are Emotions?

Motivation and emotion are tightly intertwined. Emotions can motivate behaviors (helping others when you're feeling happy), and motivation can influence emotions (feeling disappointed when you are not motivated to complete an important task). In fact, the words "emotion" and "motive" have similar roots. Emotion can be traced to the Latin word *emovere,* which means to "move out, remove, agitate" (Emotion, n.d.), whereas motive is related to the Latin word *movere,* meaning "to move" (Motive, n.d.). But how do psychologists define emotions?

**LO 9**   Define emotions and explain how they differ from moods.

An **emotion** is a psychological state that includes a subjective or inner experience. In other words, emotion is intensely personal; we cannot actually feel each other's emotions firsthand. Emotion also has a physiological component; it is not only "in our heads." For example, anger can make you feel hot, anxiety might cause sweaty palms, and sadness may sap your physical energy. Finally, emotion entails a behavioral expression that is often apparent in the face. We scream and run when frightened, gag in disgust, and shed tears of sadness. Think about the last time you felt joyous. What was your inner experience of that joy, how did your body react, and what would someone notice about your behavior?

**emotion** A psychological state that includes a subjective or inner experience, physiological component, and behavioral expression.

We described emotion as a subjective psychological state that includes both physiological and behavioral components. But are these three elements—psychology, physiology, and behavior—equally important, and how do they interact? Such questions are being explored by people from many fields and perspectives (Davidson et al., 2002; Ekman, 2016). In fact, the very definition of emotion is still a subject of academic debate (Coan, 2010; Ekman, 2016).

Most psychologists agree that emotions are different from moods. Emotions tend to be strong, but they generally don't last as long as moods, and they are more likely to have an identifiable cause. An emotion is initiated by a stimulus, and it is more likely than a mood to motivate someone to action. Moods are longer-term emotional states that are less intense than emotions and do not appear to have distinct beginnings or ends (Farmer & Matlin, 2019; Kemeny & Shestyuk, 2008; Oatley et al., 2006). Here's an example to clarify: Imagine your mood is happy, but a car cuts you off on the highway, creating a negative emotional response like anger. Fortunately, this flash of anger is likely to vanish as quickly as it appeared, and your happy mood persists.

**LANGUAGE AND EMOTION**   Think about all the words you can use to communicate subtle differences in emotions. "I feel *angry* at you" conveys a slightly different meaning than "I feel *resentful* of you," or "I feel *annoyed* by you." Words not only facilitate communication; they also influence our perceptions of emotions and "perhaps even emotional experiences" (Lindquist et al., 2015, p. 99). Imagine that diamonds were called "doodleboogers"—do you think they would inspire the same emotions as "diamonds"? The English language includes about 200 words to describe emotions. But does that mean we are capable of feeling only 200 emotions? Probably not. While closely linked, words and emotions are not one and the same. Their relationship has captivated the interest of linguists from fields as different as psychology, anthropology, and evolutionary biology (Majid, 2012).

Rather than focusing on words or labels, scholars typically characterize emotions along different dimensions. American psychologist Carroll Izard (1923–2017) suggested we can describe emotions according to valence and arousal (Izard, 2007; FIGURE 9.5). The *valence* of an emotion refers to how pleasant or unpleasant it is. Happiness, joy, and satisfaction are on the pleasant end of the valence dimension; anger and disgust are on the unpleasant end. The *arousal level* of an emotion describes how active, excited, and involved a person is while experiencing the emotion, as opposed to how calm, uninvolved, or passive they may be. With valence and arousal level, we can compare and contrast emotions. Feeling relaxed has a low arousal level and a positive valence. Fear, on the other hand, is characterized by high arousal and negative valence. Let's explore this emotion with a little help from Ibrahim.

**"I DON'T EVEN KNOW IF I'M STILL ALIVE."**   Fortunately for Ibrahim, his first two deployments to Iraq were not extremely violent, as he spent much of the time working as an interpreter. His 7-month tour in Afghanistan was quite a different story. "My Afghan deployment, my last one, was the most violent," he says. "I definitely felt my life was in danger most of the [time]." It wasn't the combat that scared him: "Training kicks in," he explains. "You're almost a robot during the actual firefight." It was the aftermath that terrified him—seeing the injuries and deaths, and realizing just how close he had come to dying himself.

"I remember this one time, we were on top of a roof in Afghanistan. We were in a firefight all day, pretty much," he explains. "Towards the end of the day, we thought everything was over . . . we're coming down off the roof, we're ready to bed

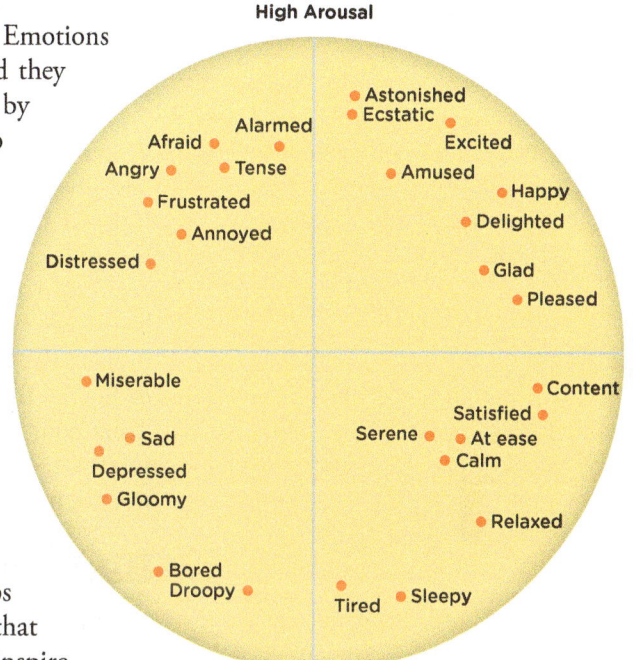

**FIGURE 9.5**
**Dimensions of Emotion**
Emotions can be compared and contrasted according to their valence (how pleasant or unpleasant they are) and their arousal level.
Copyright © 2005 by the American Psychological Association. Adapted with permission from Lyubomirsky, S., Sheldon, S.M., & Schkade, D. (2005). Pursuing happiness: The architecture of sustainable change. *Review of General Psychology, 9,* 111–131.

**A Dangerous Time**
Ibrahim Hashi during one of his deployments in the Middle East.

down for the night." As Ibrahim relaxed and sipped water, thinking he was safe, a group of Taliban fighters snuck up on the Marine compound, ready to ambush. Fortunately for Ibrahim, someone detected them: A fighter jet dropped from the sky and did a "gun-run," raining bullets on the enemy. "At this point, I don't even know if I'm still alive," Ibrahim says. "My body froze. I couldn't move. . . . I was breathing so fast, I was starting to get lightheaded, and . . . I could almost feel myself starting to black out."

## Feel It in Your Body?

**CONNECTIONS**

In **Chapter 2,** we explained how the sympathetic nervous system prepares the body to respond to an emergency, whereas the parasympathetic nervous system brings the body back to a noncrisis mode through the "rest-and-digest" process. Here, we see how the autonomic nervous system is involved in physiological experiences of emotion.

Five minutes later, when Ibrahim realized what had occurred (the fighter jet had saved them), his heart was still pounding and his hands were shaking. The **fight-or-flight** response had taken hold. When faced with a crisis situation, stress hormones are released into the blood; breathing rate increases; the heart pumps faster and harder; blood pressure rises; the liver releases extra glucose into the bloodstream; and blood surges into the large muscles. All these physical changes prepare the body for confronting or fleeing the threat; hence the expression "fight or flight." But fear is not the only emotion that involves dramatic physical changes. Tears pour from the eyes during intense sadness and joy. Anger is associated with sweating, elevated heart rate, and heightened blood flow to the hands, apparently in anticipation of a physical confrontation (Ekman, 2003).

**LO 10** List the major theories of emotion and describe how they differ.

Most psychologists agree that emotions and physiology are deeply intertwined, but they have not always agreed on the precise order of events. What happens first: body changes associated with an emotion, or the emotion itself? That's obvious, you may be thinking. Emotions occur first, and then the body responds. American psychologist William James would have begged to differ.

**JAMES–LANGE THEORY**   In the late 1800s, William James (1842–1910) and Danish physiologist Carl Lange (1834–1900) independently derived similar explanations for emotion (James, 1890/1983; Lange & James, 1922). The **James–Lange theory of emotion** suggests that a stimulus initiates a physiological reaction (for example, increased heart and breathing rates) and/or a behavioral reaction (crying or striking out) *before* we feel an emotion (INFOGRAPHIC **9.2** on page 360). Emotions do not cause physiological or behavioral reactions, as common sense might suggest. Instead, "we feel sorry because we cry, angry because we strike, afraid because we tremble" (James, 1890/1983, p. 1066). In other words, changes in the body and behavior pave the way for emotions. Our bodies automatically react to stimuli, and awareness of this physiological response leads to the subjective experience of emotion. As proponents of the James–Lange theory explain, "Feelings are the consequences, not the causes, of emotional behavior and bodily response" (Laird & Lacasse, 2014, p. 32).

How might the James–Lange theory apply to Ibrahim's experience? It all begins with a stimulus—in this case, the unexpected sound of a jet engine and machine guns overhead. Next occur the physiological reactions (increased heart rate, faster breathing, and so on) and the behavioral responses (freezing, in Ibrahim's case). Finally, the emotion registers: He feels fear. Imagine that, for some reason, Ibrahim had no physiological reaction to the sound. Would he still experience the same degree of terror? According to the James–Lange theory, no.

Critics contend that the James–Lange theory cannot fully explain emotions because (1) people who are incapable of feeling physiological reactions (as a result of surgery or spinal cord injuries, for example) can still experience emotions;

**James–Lange theory of emotion** Suggests that a stimulus initiates the experience of a physiological and/or behavioral reaction, and this reaction leads to the feeling of an emotion.

(2) the speed of an emotion is much faster than physiological changes; and (3) when physiological functioning is altered (through a hormone injection, for instance), emotions do not necessarily change (Bard, 1934; Cannon, 1927; Hilgard, 1987). In one experiment, researchers used surgery to stop animals from becoming physiologically aroused, yet the animals continued to exhibit behaviors associated with emotions, such as growling and posturing (Cannon, 1927).

**CANNON–BARD THEORY**    A prominent critic of the James-Lange theory was American physiologist Walter Cannon (1871–1945), whose research on hunger was mentioned earlier in the chapter. Cannon and his student Philip Bard (1898–1977) believed the James–Lange theory could not explain all emotions (Bard, 1934; Cannon, 1927). The **Cannon–Bard theory of emotion** suggests that we do not feel emotion as a result of physiological and behavioral reactions; instead, the emotions and the body responses occur *simultaneously* (Infographic 9.2). The starting point of this response is a stimulus in the environment.

Let's use our knowledge of the brain and the Cannon–Bard theory to understand what happened to Ibrahim. The sudden sound and appearance of the fighter jet activated sensory neurons in his ears, eyes, and perhaps his skin (through touch receptors detecting the engine's wind). This sensory information passed through the thalamus, where it was split in two directions—one to the cortex and the other to the limbic system. Activity in the cortex created Ibrahim's perception of the fighter jet, while his limbic system activated a physiological and behavioral response, causing his heart to race and his breathing to increase. As all this was happening, he experienced an emotion. The emotion and physiological reaction occurred simultaneously.

Critics of the Cannon–Bard theory suggest the thalamus might not be capable of carrying out this processing on its own, as other brain areas may contribute (Beebe-Center, 1951; Hunt, 1939). Emotions are processed in many areas of the brain, including the **limbic system** and prefrontal cortex (Kolb & Whishaw, 2015; Northoff et al., 2009).

## How Does Cognition Fit In?

American psychologists Stanley Schachter (1922–1997) and Jerome E. Singer (1934–2010) also took issue with the James–Lange theory, primarily because different emotions do not always have distinct and recognizable physiological responses (Schachter & Singer, 1962). They suggested there is a *general* pattern of physiological arousal caused by the sympathetic nervous system, and this pattern is common to a variety of emotions. The **Schachter–Singer theory of emotion** proposes that the experience of emotion is the result of two factors: (1) physiological arousal, *followed by* (2) a cognitive label for this physiological arousal. According to this theory, if you experience physiological arousal but don't know why it has occurred, you will label the arousal and explain your feelings based on your "knowledge" of the environment and previous experiences. "Depending on the cognitive aspects of the situation," you may label the physiological arousal as joy, fear, anxiety, fury, or jealousy (Schachter & Singer, 1962, p. 382; Infographic 9.2).

To test their theory, Schachter and Singer injected participants (male college students) with either epinephrine to mimic physiological reactions of the sympathetic nervous system (increased blood pressure, respiration, heart rate, and so on) or a placebo. The participants were left in a room with a "stooge," a confederate secretly working for the researchers, who was either euphoric or angry. When the confederate behaved euphorically, the participants who had been given no explanation for their physiological arousal were more likely to appear happy or report

Kyle Burgess via ViralHog.

**How Would You Feel?**

This is a screenshot of a video taken by a hiker in Utah. The charging mountain lion got extremely close but did not attack, perhaps because the hiker kept his cool, slowly backing away and talking loudly (Brito, 2020). If you were this person, what would you experience first: the emotion of fear, a physiological response (increased heart rate), or a behavioral reaction (flinching)? The Cannon–Bard theory of emotion suggests that all these events would occur simultaneously.

## CONNECTIONS

In **Chapter 2,** we introduced the limbic system, a group of interconnected structures that play an important role in emotion, motivation, and memory. It also fuels basic drives, such as hunger and sex. The limbic system includes the thalamus, hypothalamus, amygdala, and hippocampus.

**Cannon–Bard theory of emotion**   Suggests that environmental stimuli are the starting point for emotions, and physiological or behavioral responses occur at the same time emotions are felt.

**Schachter–Singer theory of emotion**   Suggests that the experience of emotion is the result of physiological arousal and a cognitive label for this physiological state.

# Theories of Emotion

Imagine you are swimming and you think you see a shark. Fear pierces your gut, sending your heart racing as you swim frantically to shore. Or is it actually your churning stomach and racing heart that cause you to feel so terrified? And what part, if any, do your thoughts play in this process?

Psychologists have long debated the order in which events lead to emotion. Let's compare four major theories, each proposing a different sequence of events.

| Body changes lead to emotions. | Body changes and emotions happen together. | Our thoughts about our body changes lead to emotions. | Our thoughts about our situation lead to emotions. |
| :---: | :---: | :---: | :---: |
| **James–Lange** | **Cannon–Bard** | **Schachter–Singer** | **Cognitive Appraisal** |

STIMULUS

PHYSIOLOGICAL RESPONSE

**FEAR**

EMOTION

STIMULUS

PHYSIOLOGICAL RESPONSE     **FEAR** EMOTION

STIMULUS

PHYSIOLOGICAL RESPONSE

*I'm scared.*

COGNITIVE LABELING

**FEAR**

EMOTION

STIMULUS

*I'm scared.*

COGNITIVE APPRAISAL

**FEAR**

EMOTION

---

 **STIMULUS:** external situation

 **PHYSIOLOGICAL RESPONSE:** physical changes (for fear, preparing body for threat: heart pounds, muscles contract, breathing changes)

**COGNITIVE ACTIVITY:** evaluation of the situation and/or labeling the physiological response

**FEAR** **EMOTION:** subjective experience (fear)

feeling happy. When the confederate behaved angrily, participants were more likely to appear angry or report feeling angry. It was clear that the participants who did not receive an explanation for their physiological arousal could be manipulated to feel either euphoria or anger, depending on the emotion displayed by the confederate. The participants who were accurately informed about side effects did not show signs or report feelings of euphoria or anger. Instead, they attributed their physiological arousal to the side effects clearly explained to them at the beginning of the study (Schachter & Singer, 1962).

Some have criticized the Schachter–Singer theory, suggesting that it overstates the link between physiological arousal and the experience of emotion (Reisenzein, 1983). What's more, studies have shown that people can experience an emotion without labeling it, especially if neural activity sidesteps the cortex and heads straight to the limbic system (Dimberg et al., 2000; Lazarus, 1991a). We will discuss this process in the upcoming section on fear.

**COGNITIVE APPRAISAL AND EMOTION**    Rejecting the notion that emotions result from cognitive labels of physiological arousal, American psychologist Richard Lazarus (1922–2002) suggested that emotion stems from the way people appraise or interpret the interactions they have (Lazarus, 1984, 1991a). It doesn't matter if we can label an emotion or not; we experience the emotion nonetheless. Emotions such as happiness, anxiety, and shame are universal, and we don't need an agreed upon label or word to experience them. Babies, for example, can feel emotions long before they are able to label them with words.

Lazarus also suggested emotions are adaptive because they help us cope with our surroundings. In a continuous feedback loop, our appraisals or interpretations of the environment change, causing changes in emotions (Folkman & Lazarus, 1985; Lazarus, 1991b). This is the foundation of the **cognitive appraisal approach** to emotion (Infographic 9.2), which suggests that the appraisal causes an emotional reaction. In contrast, the Schachter–Singer theory asserts the arousal comes first and then has to be labeled, leading to the experience of an emotion.

Responding to the cognitive appraisal approach, social psychologist Robert Zajonc (ZI-yunce; 1923–2008) suggested that thinking is not always involved when we experience an emotion. Emotions can precede thoughts and may even cause them (Zajonc, 1980, 1984). Zajonc also suggested we can experience emotions without interpreting environmental circumstances. Emotion can influence cognition, and cognition can influence emotion.

As you may have noticed, there is substantial disagreement about what role cognition plays in the experience of emotion. The relationship is complex and bidirectional, as thoughts can influence emotions, and emotions can impact memories, perceptions, interpersonal relationships, and physiology (Farb et al., 2013; Forgas, 2008).

 **Try This**    Think about a recent life event and choose two theories of emotion to explain your emotional experience. Which theory works best in this particular case?

Whew! You made it through the theories of emotion—not an easy topic. Now let's see how one of the concepts covered relates to real life. You learned that certain physiological changes are likely to occur when a person experiences emotion. By measuring these internal changes, can we "get inside" the mind of a human and determine if they are lying? This is the basic premise of the polygraph, "or lie detector" test.

**Hot Tempers**
A man scuffles with police on a summer day in Australia. Hot temperatures have been associated with increased aggression, both in laboratory and real-world settings, and researchers suspect that violent crime will increase as global warming continues (Plante & Anderson, 2017). If you find yourself angry on a hot day (or any day), take a moment and focus on your breathing. Researchers have shown that just a single meditation session can help reduce the physiological responses to anger (Fennell et al., 2016).

**cognitive appraisal approach**  Suggests that the appraisal or interpretation of interactions with surroundings causes an emotional reaction.

## ...BELIEVE IT...OR NOT

### JUST HOW ACCURATE ARE POLYGRAPH TESTS?

Since its introduction in the early 1900s, the polygraph has been used by government agencies for a variety of purposes, including job screening, crime investigation, and spy identification (Hart, 2020; Nelson, 2014). The polygraph machine works by measuring aspects of physiological arousal presumed to be associated with deceit. When people lie, they often experience changes in breathing rate, blood pressure, and other variables controlled by the autonomic nervous system (Nelson, 2014). By monitoring these variables, the polygraph can theoretically detect when a person is being deceitful.

But here's the problem: These biological changes do not always go hand-in-hand with deception. There are many other reasons one might experience them while taking a polygraph, among them "fear, anxiety, anger, and many medical or mental conditions" (Rosky, 2013, p. 260). Estimates of polygraph accuracy are sometimes as high as 90%. However, critics contend that studies often cited to justify polygraph use are riddled with methodological problems and have not been subjected to proper peer review (Kotsoglou, 2021; Nelson & Handler, 2013; Rosky, 2013). Some researchers have serious doubts about the **validity** of polygraph testing, noting its "weak scientific basis and unknown error rate" (Iacono & Ben-Shakhar, 2019, p. 86). One possible alternative is **fMRI** lie detection, but researchers have yet to identify patterns of brain activation that reliably distinguish truth-telling from deceit (Schaarschmidt, 2018).

## Relationships

### CAN YOU SPOT A LIAR?

Without accurate scientific tools, is there any surefire way to recognize dishonesty? Many people think they can intuit if someone is lying through simple observation, but research suggests they should not be so confident. "Research has shown that people, including trained police officers, only perform around chance level in detecting deception" (Bogaard et al., 2016, p. 1). In other words, our lie detection accuracy is not much better than 50% (Schaarschmidt, 2018). Why are we so bad at sniffing out dishonesty? One reason is that we over-rely on nonverbal cues like shifty eyes, changes in posture, and other body movements—behaviors that are generally *not* good indicators of deceit (Bogaard et al., 2016; DePaulo et al., 2003; Vrij et al., 2019).

Rather than focusing on the face and the body, we might have better luck examining the *content* of the message—that is, what the person is saying (Vrij et al., 2019). When judging the veracity of a claim, you might consider asking questions like this:

1. Does the information fit together logically? People who are lying "generally tell a less coherent story" (Bogaard et al., 2016, p. 2).
2. Does the person provide details suggestive of a real memory? Truth-tellers are more inclined to report sensory tidbits (*the café was dimly lit and smelled of croissants*) and information about the relative locations of people and objects in space (*Maricruz was sitting at the table to the right of the bathroom*; Bogaard et al., 2016).
3. Does the claim conflict with known facts? A good way to catch someone in a lie is to get them to say something verifiably untrue (Ormerod & Dondo, 2015). Suppose a person claims to have attended the University of Wisconsin (UW), but you have reason to believe this is false. Being familiar with the UW

### Research CONNECTIONS

In **Chapter 1,** we discussed the validity of psychological experiments and how it depends on the accuracy of the measures used. If these assessments are reliable and valid, they consistently measure what they intend to measure. Here, we discuss the polygraph, which measures physiological variables presumed to be associated with lying. These variables may not always be associated with deception, however.

### CONNECTIONS

In **Chapter 2,** we described how fMRI technology tracks the flow of oxygen-rich blood in the brain, revealing which areas are active. Here, we see how researchers are trying to use this technology to detect lying.

Kryssia Campos/Getty Images.

**Lying Eyes?**

A common misconception is that people look away when they aren't telling the truth. Actually, liars may be more inclined to engage in "deliberate eye contact" (Mann et al., 2012). Researchers say there are two reasons for this: (1) Liars want to come across as more believable and, apparently, they think looking a person in the eyes will do the trick; and (2) they want to gauge the response of the person listening to their lies (*Do they believe me?*) (Vrij et al., 2019).

campus, you know many students enjoy warm days at the union terrace where they can eat an unusual flavor of ice cream: orange custard chocolate chip. You could ask the person about popular student hangouts and unusual desserts sold at the student union.

What's the bottom line? Researchers continue to study ways that liars betray their dishonesty, but research to date seems to suggest that paying attention to verbal information—as opposed to nonverbal cues—may be the best strategy. 🪙

Recognizing dishonesty may not be our forte, but we are pros at identifying basic emotions like happiness, anger, and fear.

## Face Value

Think about the clues you rely on when trying to "read" other people's emotions. Where do you look for signs of anger, sadness, or surprise? It's written all over their face, of course.

**"SIR, SOMETHING BAD IS ABOUT TO HAPPEN."**    To stay safe in wartime, you need to be one step ahead of your enemy. That's why Ibrahim and his platoon mates often seized radios from defeated Taliban fighters and used the devices to eavesdrop on enemy communications. The Marines couldn't understand the Taliban's language, so they relied on allies in the Afghan army to interpret. But sometimes verbal translation wasn't even necessary. Ibrahim remembers a specific instance during a mission in the Musa Qala District in Helmand Province. His Afghan colleague heard something on the radio, and his face immediately transformed. Just by looking at the soldier's face, Ibrahim knew they were in trouble. "Sir, something bad is about to happen," the soldier said. Moments later, their platoon was ambushed.

**LO 11**    Discuss evidence supporting the idea that emotions are universal.

How did human beings become such experts in reading facial expressions? Writing in *The Expression of the Emotions in Man and Animals* (1872/2002), Charles Darwin suggested that this is not a learned ability, but rather an innate characteristic that evolved because it promotes survival. Sharing the same facial expressions allows us to communicate critical information, like the presence of danger. If facial expressions are truly innate and universal, then people from all cultures ought to interpret them in the same way. A "happy face" should look much the same all over the world, from the United States to the Pacific island of New Guinea.

**EKMAN'S FACES**    Some 5 decades ago, American psychologist Paul Ekman traveled to a remote mountain region of New Guinea to study an isolated group of indigenous people. Ekman and his colleagues were very careful in selecting their participants, choosing only those who were unfamiliar with *Western facial behaviors*—the signature facial expressions we equate with basic emotions like disgust and sadness. The participants didn't speak English, nor had they watched Western movies, worked for anyone with a "Caucasian" background, or lived among Westerners. The study went something like this: The researchers told the participants stories conveying emotions such as fear, happiness, and anger. In the story conveying fear, for example, a man is sitting alone in his house with no knife, axe, bow, or any weapon to defend himself. Suddenly, a wild pig appears in his doorway, and he becomes frightened that the pig will bite him. Next, the researchers asked the participants to match the emotion described in the story to a picture of a person's face (choosing from 6–12 sets of photographs). The results indicated that the same facial expressions represent the same

REUTERS/Dylan Martinez.

**Can You Guess How They Feel?**
Players from the German men's national soccer team display the same physical response during the match that led to their elimination from the 2018 World Cup. Why do athletes reflexively put their hands on their heads when they miss a shot? Some psychologists believe this behavior is a universal display of shame, a signal to others that "you know you messed up" (Gendelman, 2018, para. 6). Expressions of shame and pride are relatively consistent across cultures and observed in both blind and sighted individuals, suggesting that these displays may be innate (Tracy & Matsumoto, 2008).

### Universal Expressions

A smile in Kenya (top left) means the same thing as a smile in Lithuania (top middle) or India (top right). Facial expressions for other basic emotions such as sadness (middle row) and anger (bottom row) are also strikingly similar across cultures (Ekman & Friesen, 1971). Top row, left to right: M Lohmann/agefotostock; Wojtek Buss/agefotostock; Design Pics Inc /Alamy Stock Photo. Middle row, left to right: Rieko Honma/Getty Images; Giantstep Inc/Getty Images; Ravi Shekhar/Dinodia Photo /AGE Fotostock. Bottom row, left to right: khoa vu/Getty Images; Kerry Lorimer/Getty Images; Ezra Bailey/Getty Images.

basic emotions across cultures—and this finding has been replicated approximately 200 times (Ekman & Friesen, 1971; Ekman & Keltner, 2014).

And so it seems, a "happy face" really does look the same to people in the United States and New Guinea. Further evidence for the universal nature of facial expressions is apparent in children born blind; although they have never seen a human face demonstrating emotion, their smiles and frowns are similar to those of sighted children (Galati et al., 1997; Matsumoto & Willingham, 2009). Newer research based on artifacts from ancient Mesoamerica (a region reaching from Mexico to Central America) suggests that early people used emotional expressions easily recognizable to modern humans. For example, sculptures of people fighting in battles have "angry" faces, while war prisoners appear "sad" (Cowen & Keltner, 2020).

## Put Your Heads Together

In your groups, have everyone take out a piece of paper and sketch faces (or emojis) demonstrating happiness, sadness, disgust, anger, surprise, and fear. Compare your faces with others in your group. Describe the similarities. Are there any differences?

## ACROSS THE WORLD

### WHEN TO REVEAL, WHEN TO CONCEAL

**CAN YOU FEEL THE CULTURE?**

Although the expression of some basic emotions appears to be universal, culture acts like a filter, determining the appropriate contexts in which to exhibit them. A culture's **display rules** provide guidelines for when, how, and where an emotion is expressed. In North America, where individualism prevails, people tend to be fairly expressive. Showing emotion, particularly positive emotions, is socially acceptable. This is less the case in the collectivist (community-oriented) societies of East Asia, where concealing emotions is more the norm.

**display rules** Framework or guidelines for when, how, and where an emotion is expressed.

Display rules are taught early in life, as parents show approval or disapproval of children's emotional expressions (Scherr et al., 2019). For example, Korean and Asian American parents appear more inclined than European American parents to favor "modesty and suppression of children's emotions" (Louie et al., 2013, p. 429). Why do collectivist cultures tend to discourage emotional displays? Showing emotions, particularly anger, can threaten the social harmony that is highly valued by their societies (Louie et al., 2013).

However, we cannot attribute all variations in display rules to collectivism and individualism because there are key distinctions within these two categories. For example, the United States and Germany (both considered individualistic) appear to have different display rules for contempt and disgust, with Americans more inclined to reveal these emotions (Koopmann-Holm & Matsumoto, 2011). To understand the origins of display rules, we must explore how expressions of specific emotions (not emotions in general) are influenced by cultural values (Hareli et al., 2015; Koopmann-Holm & Matsumoto, 2011).

**DOES SMILING MAKE YOU HAPPY?**    As you've probably noticed, facial expressions can have a dramatic impact on social interactions. If you walk into class with an angry frown, people are unlikely to approach you and say "hi." A smile, on the other hand, tends to attract waves and "hellos." Did you ever think about how your facial expressions might affect *you?* Believe it or not, the simple act of smiling can make a person *feel* happier. According to the **facial feedback hypothesis,** facial expressions can impact the experience of emotions (Buck, 1980; Coles et al., 2019). If this hypothesis is correct, we should be able to manipulate our emotions with activities like the one described below.

**Try This**    Take a pen and put it between your teeth, keeping your mouth open for about 30 seconds. Consider how you are feeling. Next, hold the pen with your lips, but don't let it touch your teeth, for 30 seconds. Again, consider how you are feeling.

If you are like many participants, holding the pen in your teeth should result in your seeing objects and events in your environment as funnier than if you hold the pen with your lips (Marsh, et al., 2019; Strack et al., 1988). Why would that be? Take a look at the photo on the upper right and note how the person holding the pen in his teeth seems to be smiling—the feedback of those smiling muscles leads to a happier mood.

## Types of Emotions

Ibrahim witnessed disturbing sights and sounds in Iraq and Afghanistan, but violence was nothing new to a man who had spent some of his formative years in Somalia. After living in the United States until age 8 or 9, Ibrahim spent a few years in his family's homeland, which was mired in civil war. He remembers traveling through the city with his aunt when a firefight broke out between rival factions, just meters away. His aunt ran for her life, leaving Ibrahim to fend for himself as bullets whizzed by his head. Fortunately, Ibrahim escaped the situation unscathed, but how do you think he felt afterward? *Fear* is the emotion that immediately comes to mind, but there may be others, including *anger* toward his aunt, *disgust* at the sight of blood, *anxiety* about his future safety, and *gratitude* toward those who helped him.

Are such feelings common to all people? There may be a set of "basic emotions," including "fear, anger, happiness, sadness, and disgust or contempt," that are common to people of all cultures (Hofmann & Doan, 2018, p. 14). However, some who study facial expressions contend there are only four patterns of universally recognized emotions—happiness, sadness, surprise/fear, and disgust/anger (Jack et al., 2016).

Robert M. Errera.

Robert M. Errera.

**Facial Feedback**
Holding a pen between your teeth (top) will probably put you in a better mood than holding it with your lips closed (bottom). This is because the physical act of smiling, which occurs when you place the pen in your teeth, promotes feelings of happiness. So next time you're feeling low, don't be afraid to flex those smile muscles!

**facial feedback hypothesis** Suggests that the facial expression of an emotion can affect the experience of that emotion.

Such emotions are considered *basic* because people all over the world experience and express them in similar ways; they appear to be innate and have an underlying neural basis (Izard, 1992).

It is also noteworthy that unpleasant emotions (fear, anger, disgust, and sadness) have survived throughout our evolutionary history, and are more prevalent than positive emotions such as happiness, surprise, and interest (Ekman, 1992; Forgas, 2008; Izard, 2007). This suggests that negative emotions have "adaptive value"; in other words, they may be useful in dangerous situations, like those that demand a fight-or-flight response (Adolphs, 2013; Forgas, 2008; Friedman et al., 2014).

## The Biology of Fear

**LO 12**  Describe the amygdala's role in the experience of fear.

What's going on in your brain when you feel afraid? With the help of brain-scanning technologies, researchers have zeroed in on an almond-shaped structure in the limbic system (Cheng et al., 2006; Pape & Pare, 2010). This structure, known as the amygdala, is central to our experience of fear (Hariri et al., 2002; Méndez-Bértolo et al., 2016; Schaffner, 2020). If a person views threatening images, or even looks at an image of a frightened face, the amygdala is activated (Chiao et al., 2008; Laeng et al., 2010; Méndez-Bértolo et al., 2016).

**PATHWAYS TO FEAR**  Any time you are confronted with a fear-provoking situation, the amygdala enables an ultrafast, unconscious response. Researchers have constructed various models to explain how this occurs (Schaffner, 2020). According to one conceptualization, sensory information (sights, sounds) entering the thalamus can either go to the cortex for processing, or head straight for the amygdala without stopping at the cortex (LeDoux, 1996, 2000, 2012). The direct path going from the thalamus to the amygdala conveys raw information about the threat, enabling your brain and body to respond to danger without your awareness. Like a panic button, the amygdala issues an alert, summoning other parts of the brain that play a role in the experience of fear (for example, the hypothalamus and medulla), which then alert the sympathetic nervous system. A pathway also goes to the pituitary gland, resulting in the secretion of stress hormones (LeDoux, 2012).

Let's see how this immediate fear response might play out using the example of Ibrahim. Visual information about the gunfight went directly to his thalamus, and from there to his amygdala, triggering an alarm reaction. His heart and breathing rates increased, preparing him to flee the fight scene. Meanwhile, information sent to the sensory processing centers of his visual cortex resulted in a visual representation of the chaotic scene.

Now suppose it had all been a false alarm; the conflict between the rival factions never escalated to violence, and the fighters dispersed. In this case, Ibrahim's cortex would have alerted the amygdala: "False alarm. The scene is safe." The key fact to note is that it takes longer for neural information to go from the thalamus to the cortex than from the thalamus to the amygdala. This explains why you generally need a moment to calm down: The physiological reaction starts before the false alarm message from the cortex reaches the amygdala (INFOGRAPHIC **9.3**).

There appears to be an evolutionary advantage to having direct and indirect routes for processing information about potential threats (LeDoux, 2012). The direct route (thalamus to amygdala, causing physiological and emotional reactions) enables us to react quickly to threats for which we are biologically prepared (snakes, spiders, aggressive faces). The pathway to the cortex allows us to evaluate more complex threats (nuclear weapons, job layoffs), overriding the fast-response pathway when necessary.

# The Anatomy of Fear

You instantly recoil when you spot a snake—then sigh with relief just a moment later when it registers that the snake is a rubber toy. Have you ever wondered why you react with fear when a "threat" turns out to be nothing? Why does it take longer for you to process a threat than react to it? Sensory information (sight, sound) entering the brain travels to the thalamus and is then routed to the cortex for processing. Sensory information can also go directly to the amygdala. In the case of a threat, the amygdala alerts other areas of the brain and the endocrine system instantly without waiting for a conscious command. This enables a response to fear before you are even fully aware of what you are reacting to.

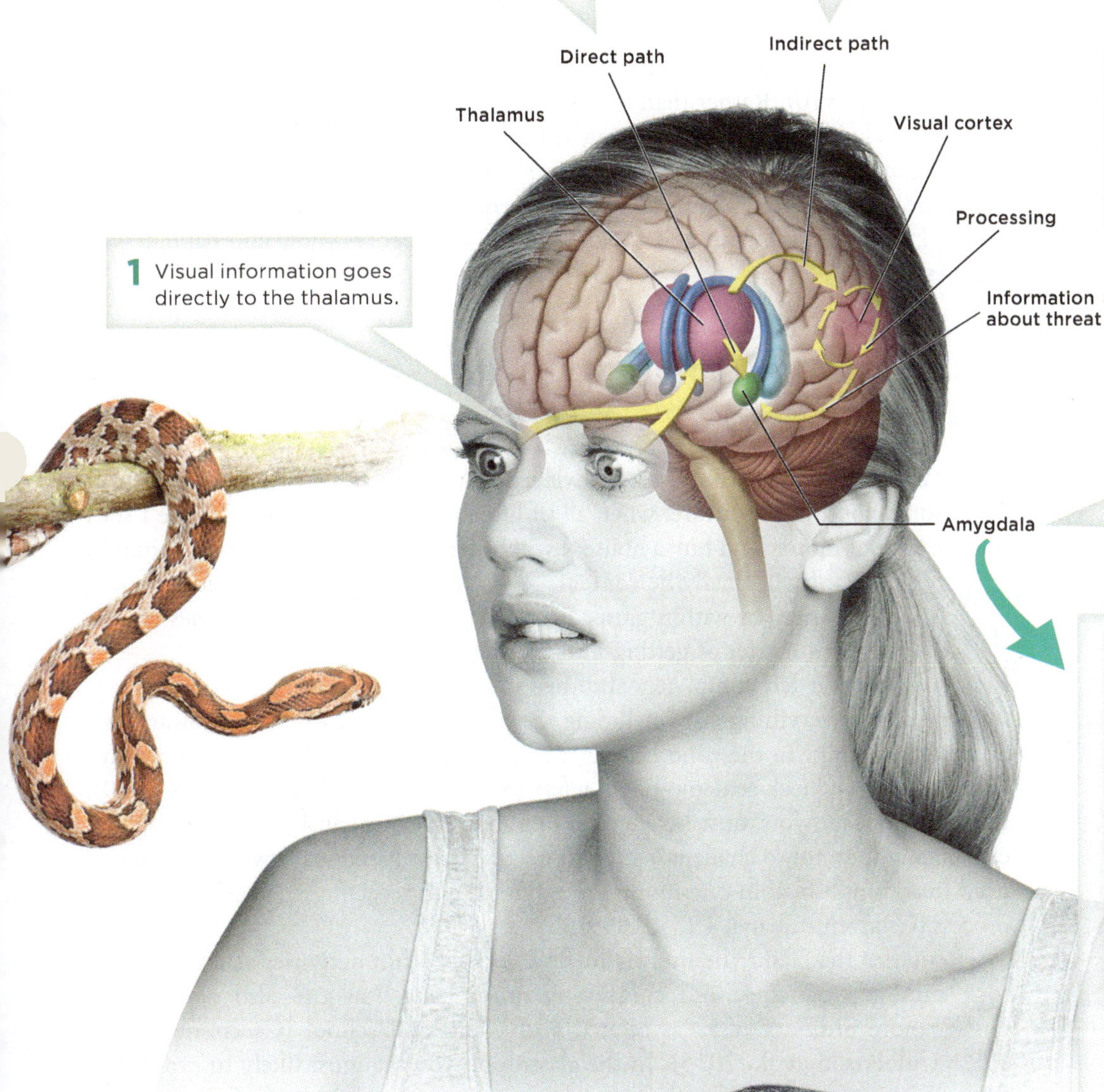

**2** Basic information about threat is conveyed directly to the amygdala, enabling rapid response.

**3** It takes longer for neural information to go to the visual cortex for processing.

**4** If it's been determined that the threat is a false alarm, this message will instruct the amygdala to inhibit the fear reaction.

**1** Visual information goes directly to the thalamus.

**5** After receiving information about threat, the amygdala:
- instructs hypothalamus and medulla to alert sympathetic nervous system;
- prompts pituitary gland to secrete stress hormones.

Direct path

Indirect path

Thalamus

Visual cortex

Processing

Information about threat

Amygdala

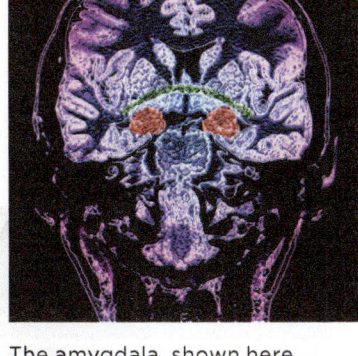

The amygdala, shown here in red, plays a pivotal role in experiencing fear. Information about threats prompts the amygdala to activate the physiological responses that characterize fear.

What happens when the amygdala doesn't work? Animals with amygdala damage may not exhibit any response to a threat. For example, the mouse in this picture is uncharacteristically comfortable with a predator. Similarly, one study found that people with amygdala damage demonstrated an absence of expected fear behaviors (Feinstein et al., 2011).

**Master of Flow?**
Psychologist Mihaly Csikszentmihalyi makes a funny face as his colleague Jeanne Nakamura laughs in the background. Csikszentmihalyi, who is a Distinguished Professor Emeritus of Psychology and Management at Claremont Graduate University in California, is famous for establishing the concept of flow and furthering our understanding of happiness.

Mel Melcon/Getty Images.

**HOW IMPORTANT IS THE AMYGDALA?**    What happens to these automatic responses when the amygdala is not working? Studies in animals suggest that damage to the amygdala impairs the fear response (Bliss-Moreau et al., 2011; Phillips & LeDoux, 1992). Similarly, people with damage to the amygdala exhibit weaker-than-normal responses to stimuli that inspire fear or disgust (Buchanan et al., 2004). They also have difficulty comprehending nonverbal behavior associated with emotion (Adolphs, 2008).

Now it is time to move on to brighter things. What makes you happy, and how might you become more content?

## Happiness

In Chapter 1 of this book, we introduced the field of positive psychology, "the study of positive emotions, positive character traits, and enabling institutions" (Seligman & Steen, 2005, p. 410). Rather than focusing on mental illness and abnormal behavior, positive psychology emphasizes human strengths and virtues. The goal is well-being and fulfillment, and that means "satisfaction" with the past, "hope and optimism" for the future, and "flow and happiness" at the current time (Seligman & Csikszentmihalyi, 2000). Let's take a moment and explore that third category—flow and happiness of the present.

### Didn't See That Coming

GOING WITH THE FLOW

People often make the mistake of viewing happiness as a goal they will attain at some point in the future, when all of life's pieces fall into place: "Once I start making a lot of money and buy a house, I will be happy," or, "If I just lose 10 pounds,

**IS IT THE SECRET TO ACHIEVING HAPPINESS?**

I will finally be content." What they don't realize is that happiness may be within grasp, right here and right now. Sometimes it's just a matter of getting into the "flow."

Have you ever felt completely absorbed in a challenging task, guided by a focus so intense that everything else, including the past and future, faded from awareness? Some call it being "in the zone"; Hungarian-born psychologist Mihaly Csikszentmihalyi (me-High Cheek-sent-me-hi-ee) refers to it as "flow" (Csikszentmihalyi, 1999). For flow to occur, you must be engaged in a task that is intrinsically rewarding and challenging (but not so challenging that it makes you feel anxious), aware of what you need to accomplish from one minute to the next, and receiving feedback during the process (Csikszentmihalyi, 1975, 1999).

Activities that lend themselves to flow include "fun activities" such as chess, rock climbing, dancing, and composing music, but flow can also be achieved during more ordinary tasks associated with work and school (Csikszentmihalyi, 1990; Culbertson et al., 2015). In the classroom, you are most likely to experience flow while performing tasks that afford you some control and require active participation, such as individual assignments and group work (Shernoff et al., 2003). So next time the opportunity arises, try to achieve flow by giving an activity your undivided attention and being fully present in the moment. You may become more interested in the material and enjoy the process. What's more, your positive experience may rub off on those around you, as flow appears to be somewhat contagious (Culbertson et al., 2015).

Flow is one of the secrets to achieving happiness, and it can be experienced by anyone. However, some of us seem more inclined toward happiness than others. Why is this so?

**LO 13** Summarize evidence pointing to the biological basis of happiness.

**THE BIOLOGY OF HAPPINESS**     To what degree do we inherit happiness? Heritability estimates are between 35% and 50%, and as high as 80% in longitudinal studies (Bartels, 2015; Nes et al., 2010). In other words, a sizable proportion of the population-wide variation in happiness, life satisfaction, and well-being can be explained by genetic make-up, as opposed to environmental factors.

Research suggests that happiness may have a biologically based "set point" similar to the set point for body weight (Bartels et al., 2010; Cummins et al., 2014; Lyubomirsky et al., 2005). Happiness tends to fluctuate around this fixed level, which is influenced by genes and related to **temperament**. But this is only a starting place and does not mean that we cannot increase our happiness.

Some researchers suggest that the set point theory fails to account for the variety of events that impact well-being over a lifetime. One such event is marriage. Research suggests that people who are married tend to have higher levels of life satisfaction, particularly those who consider their partners to be their "best friends" (Grover & Helliwell, 2019).

**INCREASING HAPPINESS**     That being said, the happiness brought about by positive life events does not seem to last forever (Diener et al., 2006; Mancini et al., 2011). We tend to become quickly **habituated** to events that make us feel happy. If you win the lottery, get a new job, or buy a beautiful house, you will likely experience an increased level of happiness for a while, but then go back to your baseline, or "set point," of happiness (Lyubomirsky et al., 2005). Circumstances that feel new and improved or life-changing quickly become mundane, suggesting that happiness will not be found in new possessions or shopping sprees. The implication is that we need to be careful when pursuing happiness as a goal in life, as we don't want to emphasize obtaining a specific outcome (like moving to a house near the ocean) or acquiring a desired object (Lyubomirsky et al., 2005). Rather than trying to become happier, we should be content with what we have (Lyubomirsky et al., 2011).

With this in mind, there are many steps you can take to maximize enjoyment of your life right now (**INFOGRAPHIC 9.4** on the next page). Engaging in physical exercise, cultivating close relationships with family and friends, and being generous with others have all been linked to greater happiness (Dunn et al., 2014; Helliwell et al., 2018; Lathia et al., 2017; Park et al., 2017). The same can be said for "counting your blessings" (Emmons et al., 2019; Krejtz et al., 2016). In one study, participants were asked to write in a diary each day, identifying what they were most grateful for. The researchers measured well-being and found that the participants in the diary group were better off than those who didn't count their blessings. Members of the diary group were also more likely to report they had helped or offered emotional support to another person (Emmons & McCullough, 2003). As this study shows, "Simple intentional changes in one's thoughts and behaviors can precipitate meaningful increases in happiness" (Lyubomirsky & Layous, 2013, p. 60). We should also repeat experiences we enjoyed the first time. Watching a movie, reading a book, playing a game, or visiting a museum can bring happiness time and time again (O'Brien, 2019).

**CONNECTIONS**

In **Chapter 8,** we described some of the temperaments exhibited by infants. About 40% can be classified as "easy" babies, meaning they are relatively happy and easy to soothe, follow regular schedules, and quickly adjust to changes in the environment. This early evidence of temperament lends support to the biological basis of happiness discussed here.

**CONNECTIONS**

In **Chapter 5,** we presented the concept of habituation, a basic form of learning wherein repeated exposure to an event generally results in a reduced response. Here, we see the same effect can occur with events resulting in happiness. With repeated exposure, we habituate to events that initially elicited happiness.

# Pathways to Happiness

When it comes to being happy, there is no "magic bullet," but the latest research suggests we may be able to cultivate positive emotions and well-being through a variety of activities, many of which do not involve spending money. That being said, money does play a role—and it's not so much about how much you have, but how you choose to use it.

## YES!
### Going to college

Higher levels of education have been linked to greater happiness (Assari, 2019).

## YES!
### Achieving "flow"

While studying, working, or pursuing an interest, allow yourself to become completely absorbed in challenging and rewarding tasks (Csikszentmihalyi, 1999; Culbertson et al., 2015).

## NO!
### Buying new stuff

Buying new things may provide temporary pleasure, but it is unlikely to increase long-term happiness (Donnelly et al., 2016; Lyubomirsky et al., 2005).

## YES!
### Prioritizing relationships

Cultivating deep and meaningful relationships with family and friends seems to bolster happiness (Helliwell et al., 2018).

## YES!
### "Buying time"

Paying for timesaving services, such as grocery delivery, is associated with "greater life satisfaction" (Whillans et al., 2017, p. 8523).

## NO!
### Becoming a millionaire

Salary increases may boost happiness, but "most data suggest that after basic needs have been met, additional income is not associated with increases in well-being" (Mogilner & Norton, 2016, p. 12).

## MAYBE
### Moving your body

Evidence suggests that college students feel "happier and less anxious" when they exercise more (Kroencke et al., 2019).

## YES!
### Counting your blessings

Being grateful for what you have may lead to less stress and greater well-being (Chopik et al., 2019; Krejtz et al., 2016).

## MAYBE
### Buying experiences

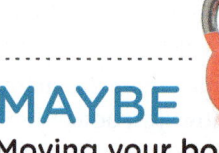

Investing in vacations, restaurant meals, and other activities is more likely to promote "enduring happiness" than purchasing material items (Gilovich & Kumar, 2015).

## YES!
### Being kind and generous

Whether you are buying a gift or donating to charity, spending money on others is likely to increase your happiness (Aknin et al., 2020; Dunn et al., 2014).

Top: Cap/diploma, Carolyn Franks/Alamy; Violin, Zoonar GmbH/Alamy; Gift bags, age fotostock/Alamy; Delivery van, Jakub Krechowicz/Alamy; Exercise Mat/kettle bells, Milic Djurovic/Alamy; Fruit, jean-paul chassenet/Alamy; Gift with bow, Milkos/Getty Images; Irrell/Alamy; Man wearing glasses, szefei/AGE Fotostock; Heart thank you note, stockcam/Getty Images; U.S. money, Concert tickets, Mir

## Put Your Heads Together

Can money buy happiness? Team up and discuss: **A)** How money influences happiness. **B)** How would your group spend $200 to increase the happiness of each member? **C)** How would you spend $2,000? **D)** Compare your answers with those of other groups.

**IN A GOOD PLACE**     You may be wondering how Ivonne Mosquera-Schmidt and Ibrahim Hashi are doing these days. Ivonne is in a good place, and she attributes that to her faith in God. "Because I have that trust and that sense of hope, I can have peace," she says. "I can be in the moment and I can learn what I need to learn from that moment." When does Ivonne feel happiest? While running, of course! The greatest runs are those that take her through the beautiful outdoors. "My breathing connects me to nature." She explains. "I breathe out, and that's what the plants and trees and everything else take in, and they breathe in and out, and it's kind of this exchange of energy that is so free and open when you're outside."

**Ivonne Mosquera-Schmidt**

**Ibrahim Hashi**

Ibrahim completed his service with the Marine Corps in 2011, enrolled in American University in Washington, D.C., in 2012, and graduated in 2016. Returning to civilian life was difficult, and it took him a long time to let go of the "super-vigilant, hyper-aware" mindset that once kept him alive in combat. Ibrahim isolated himself, avoiding interactions with people, even family members. During that readjustment period, his only lifeline was friendship with fellow Marines. "Whenever I needed help, I would call them, and if they needed help, they would call me." Like many of his platoon mates, Ibrahim was diagnosed with posttraumatic stress disorder (PTSD; Chapter 13). But eventually he began talking about his experiences, and this helped him heal. "It's not something I hide anymore, and honestly that's been the best thing for me," he says. "Now, within the past year or so, I'm very happy, I'm content with life. . . . What makes me happy is having a good solid network of relationships, of friends and family members and loved ones."

 ## SHOW WHAT YOU KNOW

1. On the way to a wedding, you get mud on your clothing. Describe how your mood and emotion might differ.

2. _____ of a culture provide a framework for when, how, and where an emotion is expressed.
   A. Beliefs
   B. Display rules
   C. Feedback loops
   D. Appraisals

3. Name two ways that the Cannon–Bard and Schachter–Singer theories of emotion differ.

4. What evidence suggests that emotions are universal?

5. When people view images that are threatening, or when they see faces of people who are afraid, the _____ becomes active.

6. "Happiness has heritability estimates as high as 80%." How would you explain this statement to a fellow student?

 CHECK YOUR ANSWERS AT THE BACK OF THE BOOK.

# Summary of Concepts

**LO 1** Define motivation. (p. 335)

Motivation is a stimulus that can direct the way we behave, think, and feel. A motivated behavior tends to be guided (has a direction), energized, and persistent. When a behavior is reinforced, an association is established between the behavior and this consequence. With motivated behavior, this association becomes the incentive, or reason, to repeat the behavior.

**LO 2** Explain how extrinsic and intrinsic motivation impact behavior. (p. 336)

When a learned behavior is motivated by the incentive of external reinforcers in the environment, there is an extrinsic motivation to continue that behavior. Intrinsic motivation occurs when a learned behavior is motivated by the prospect of internal reinforcers. Performing a behavior because it is inherently interesting or satisfying exemplifies intrinsic motivation; the reinforcers originate from within.

**LO 3** Describe drive-reduction theory and explain how it relates to motivation. (p. 337)

The drive-reduction theory of motivation suggests that human behaviors are driven by the need to maintain homeostasis—that is, to fulfill basic biological needs for nutrients, fluids, oxygen, and so on. If a need is not fulfilled, this creates a drive, or state of tension, that pushes us (motivates our behaviors) to meet it. Once a need is satisfied, the drive is reduced, but not forever. The need inevitably returns, and you feel driven to meet it once again.

**LO 4** Explain how arousal theory relates to motivation. (p. 339)

According to arousal theory, humans seek an optimal level of arousal, or alertness and engagement in the world. What constitutes an optimal level of arousal is variable, and depends on individual differences. Some people seem to be sensation seekers; that is, they seek activities that increase arousal.

**LO 5** Outline Maslow's hierarchy of needs. (p. 340)

The needs in Maslow's hierarchy, often depicted as a pyramid, are considered universal and are ordered according to the strength of their associated drives. At the base of the hierarchy are physiological needs, which include requirements for food, water, sleep, and overall balance of body systems. Moving up the pyramid are increasingly higher-level needs: safety, love and belongingness, esteem, self-actualization, and self-transcendence. Maslow suggested that basic needs must be met before higher-level needs motivate behavior. In some cases, people abandon their lower-level needs to meet higher-level needs.

**LO 6** Describe the human sexual response as identified by Masters and Johnson. (p. 344)

The human sexual response is the physiological pattern that occurs during sexual activity. Men and women tend to experience a similar cycle of excitement, plateau, orgasm, and resolution, but the duration of these phases varies from person to person.

**LO 7** Define sexual orientation and summarize how it develops. (p. 345)

Sexual orientation refers to the identity of those we feel attracted to; it is a continuum that includes dimensions of sexuality, attraction, desire, and emotions. Research has focused on the causes of sexual orientation, but there is no strong evidence pointing to any one factor or factors; it results from an interaction between nature and nurture.

**LO 8** Discuss how the stomach and the hypothalamus make us feel hunger. (p. 352)

In a classic experiment, researchers confirmed that events in the stomach accompany hunger. When glucose levels dip, the stomach and liver send signals to the hypothalamus. When the lateral hypothalamus is activated, appetite increases. When the ventromedial hypothalamus is activated, appetite declines.

**LO 9** Define emotions and explain how they differ from moods. (p. 356)

An emotion is a psychological state that includes a subjective or inner experience, a physiological component, and a behavioral expression. Emotions tend to be strong, but they generally don't last as long as moods. Emotions are more likely to have identifiable causes (as reactions to stimuli), and they are more likely to motivate a person to action. Moods are longer-term emotional states that are less intense, and do not appear to have distinct beginnings or ends.

**LO 10** List the major theories of emotion and describe how they differ. (p. 358)

The James–Lange theory of emotion suggests that a stimulus initiates a physiological and/or behavioral reaction, and this reaction leads to an emotion. The Cannon–Bard theory of emotion suggests that we do not feel emotion as a result of physiological and behavioral reactions; instead, all these experiences occur simultaneously. The Schachter–Singer theory of emotion suggests that there is a general pattern of physiological arousal caused by the sympathetic nervous system, and this pattern is common to a variety of emotions. The experience of emotion is the result of two factors:

(1) physiological arousal and (2) a cognitive label for this physiological arousal. The cognitive appraisal theory suggests that emotion stems from the way people appraise or interpret the interactions they have.

**LO 11** Discuss evidence supporting the idea that emotions are universal. (p. 363)

Darwin suggested that interpreting facial expressions is not something we learn, but rather an innate ability that evolved because it promotes survival. Sharing the same facial expressions allows for communication. Research on isolated indigenous peoples in New Guinea indicated that the same facial expressions represent the same basic emotions across cultures. In addition, children born blind have the same types of expressions of emotion (for example, happiness and anger), suggesting the universal nature of such displays.

**LO 12** Describe the amygdala's role in the experience of fear. (p. 366)

The amygdala is an almond-shaped structure found in the limbic system that appears to be central to our experience of fear. When people view threatening images, or even look at an image of a frightened face, the amygdala is activated. When confronted with a fear-provoking situation, the amygdala enables an ultrafast and unconscious response.

**LO 13** Summarize evidence pointing to the biological basis of happiness. (p. 369)

Happiness has heritability estimates between 35% and 50%, and as high as 80% in longitudinal studies. There may be a set point for happiness, or level around which our happiness tends to fluctuate. But this is only a starting place and does not mean that we cannot increase our happiness.

## Key Terms

arousal theory, p. 338
bisexual, p. 346
Cannon–Bard theory of emotion, p. 359
cognitive appraisal approach, p. 361
display rules, p. 364
drive, p. 337
drive-reduction theory, p. 337
emotion, p. 356

extrinsic motivation, p. 336
facial feedback hypothesis, p. 365
heterosexual, p. 345
hierarchy of needs, p. 339
homeostasis, p. 337
homosexual, p. 346
incentive, p. 335
instincts, p. 337

intrinsic motivation, p. 336
James–Lange theory of emotion, p. 358
motivation, p. 335
need for achievement (n-Ach), p. 342
need for power (n-Pow), p. 342
needs, p. 337
orgasm, p. 345
refractory period, p. 345

Schachter–Singer theory of emotion, p. 359
self-actualization, p. 340
self-determination theory (SDT), p. 342
set point, p. 354
sexual dysfunction, p. 349
sexual orientation, p. 345
sexuality, p. 344
sexually transmitted infections (STIs), p. 350

## Test Prep Are You Ready?

1. If a parent wants a child to practice math facts, they could allow the child to play games on a tablet after studying. Playing the games eventually will provide _____ for learning math facts.
   A. negative reinforcement
   B. intrinsic motivation
   C. satiety
   D. an incentive

2. The entire week before final exams, the resident advisor (RA) in your dorm provides delicious cookies for students who come to group study sessions in the common room. The RA seems to be using _____ to encourage students to study together.
   A. extrinsic motivation
   B. intrinsic motivation
   C. negative reinforcement
   D. instincts

3. Human behaviors are driven by the need to maintain homeostasis—that is, to fulfill basic biological needs. If a need is not fulfilled, this creates a state of tension that pushes us to meet it. This describes the _____ theory.
   A. self-actualization
   B. drive-reduction
   C. cognitive-appraisal
   D. Schachter–Singer

4. Arousal theory suggests that humans seek an optimal level of arousal, but "optimal" is different for each person. Some people are _____; they appear to seek out activities that increase arousal.
   A. sensation seekers
   B. externally motivated
   C. driven by extrinsic motivation
   D. sympathetic

5. According to Masters and Johnson, sexual arousal begins in the _____ phase, when physical changes begin to take place.
   A. excitement
   B. plateau
   C. resolution
   D. orgasm

6. Emotion is a psychological state that includes a subjective experience, a physiological component, and a(n):
   A. mood.
   B. drive.
   C. behavioral expression.
   D. incentive.

7. To study the universal nature of emotions, Paul Ekman traveled to New Guinea to explore interpretations of facial expressions. Although unfamiliar with Western facial behaviors, the participants in his study:
   A. could not identify the facial expressions in the photos he showed them.
   B. could identify the facial expressions common across the world.
   C. could understand English.
   D. had no display rules.

8. The Schachter–Singer theory suggests that the experience of emotion results from:
   A. physiological arousal.
   B. cognitive labeling.
   C. physiological arousal and cognitive labeling.
   D. an appraisal of the environment.

9. The _____ suggests emotion results from the way people appraise or interpret what is going on in the environment, and that emotion does not result from a cognitive label of physiological arousal.
   A. James–Lange theory
   B. cognitive-appraisal approach
   C. Schachter–Singer theory
   D. Cannon–Bard theory

10. A large proportion of population-wide variation in happiness can be explained by genes as opposed to environmental factors. Evidence comes from _____, which are reported to be between 35% and 50%, and as high as 80%.
    A. display rules
    B. heritability estimates
    C. instincts
    D. feedback loops

11. Explain how twin studies have been used to explore the development of sexual orientation.

12. Describe a situation in which someone's motivation did not follow the order outlined in Maslow's hierarchy of needs.

13. What role do the stomach and hypothalamus play in hunger? How do cultural and social factors influence our eating habits?

14. What role does the amygdala play in the experience of fear? Describe the two pathways that fear-related information can travel in the brain.

15. Explain how you might use set points for body weight or happiness to help someone struggling with weight and/or happiness.

✓ CHECK YOUR ANSWERS AT THE BACK OF THE BOOK.

MadamSaifa/Shutterstock.

# Personality

# 10

## An Introduction to Personality

**WHO IS SAIFA?**  Sometimes a simple question can change your life. For Sean Saifa Wall, the critical question came in 2007. He was 28 years old and appeared to have his life in order. A graduate of Williams College, Saifa had built an impressive résumé, acquired a desirable job, and amassed a large number of social contacts. But he was tormented on the inside. Unable to make sense of his thoughts, Saifa felt he was losing control, and he worried that something terrible would happen if he didn't seek help: "I was just like, either someone's going to kill me, or I'm going to kill myself."

In a move that may have saved his life, Saifa picked up the phone and made an appointment to talk with a psychotherapist. A few days later, he was sitting on the therapist's couch and beginning to unravel his complicated life story. Apparently, the therapist was perceptive, because during that first appointment, he posed a question that set Saifa's healing process in motion and changed the course of his life: "When did you realize love was not possible?" Saifa broke down and began weeping. "I don't know," he said in between tears. The weeping continued for many sessions.

For years leading to that moment, Saifa had wrestled with feelings of loneliness, isolation, and self-hatred. He tried to fill the void with new relationships and sex, but the emptiness persisted. "I thought that if I just had more sex, that I would

Courtesy Sean Saifa Wall.

**Eyes of Discontent**
Sean Saifa Wall was 26 years old when this picture was taken. Looking at this photo today, Saifa sees a young man who is "performing masculinity" to compensate for feelings of insecurity.

---

**CONNECTIONS**

In **Chapter 8,** we described various infant temperaments. Some of the attending characteristics of these temperaments seem to persist throughout life. Here, we introduce temperament in the context of personality development.

---

**personality** The unique, core set of characteristics that influence the way one thinks, acts, and feels, which are relatively consistent and enduring throughout the life span.

---

eventually be full," Saifa explains. "[But] the more sex I had from all sources (casual sex, relationship sex, pornography), the more miserable and lonely I felt." Saifa's focus on sex was a symptom of something much bigger. "For me, sexual addiction is not about sex," Saifa explains. "Sexual addiction is me dealing with something that is so, so visceral, and so deep. It's such a well of hurt and shame that some places I can't access."

This hurt and shame had prevented Saifa from loving himself, but he went to great lengths to attain approval from others. "I was trying to impress the women I dated," he explains. "I wanted all these material things that I thought would bring me happiness . . . that would bring me more self-esteem, but the more I got these things, the more I realized I wasn't really happy, 'cause I wasn't myself." Like a chameleon, Saifa changed according to the environment. He adjusted his behaviors and roles to please other people. "I could be whatever you wanted me to be," he says.

Who was the person beneath that chameleon-like exterior, and how did he fall into that crater of self-hatred? Perhaps most importantly, did he ever climb out? Let's start with the first question: Who is Sean Saifa Wall?

## What Is Personality?

**LO 1**    Define personality.

If you ask Saifa to describe himself, he will use words like "vivacious," "loud," "charismatic," "direct," and "empathetic." He might also mention that he has a strong sense of fairness, and always leans in the direction of justice. These attributes have been apparent for much of Saifa's life, and therefore would be considered facets of his *personality*. Generally speaking, **personality** refers to the unique, core set of characteristics that influence the way one thinks, acts, and feels—characteristics many psychologists believe are relatively consistent and enduring throughout the life span and in a variety of settings (Diehl & Wahl, 2020).

We should point out that personality is not the equivalent of *character*. When people discuss character, they often are referring to qualities of morality or culture-specific ideas about what makes a person "good" or "bad." People who are untrustworthy or make "poor" choices might be described as having a weak character, while those who stand up for what they believe might be said to have a strong character. You may hear that the guy with the blue mohawk or the woman with the multiple body piercings is a "real character." Psychologists try not to make such judgments; our goal is to describe behaviors and personality characteristics objectively. Unlike character, which is essentially a label based on superficial observations, personality is defined by a core set of characteristics that often become evident in infancy.

**TEMPERAMENT**    Certain aspects of adult personality appear to derive from **temperament**, the distinct patterns of emotional reactions and behaviors observed early in life (Soto & Tackett, 2015; Tang et al., 2020). Some infants are easy to calm, others cranky, sociable, or highly reactive. Because various temperaments are evident in infants, they appear to have a genetic basis (Plomin et al., 2013). Although behavioral patterns associated with temperament remain somewhat stable across the life span, they can be molded by the prenatal and postnatal

*Note:* Unless otherwise specified, quotations attributed to Sean Saifa Wall are personal communications.

**TABLE 10.1** Theoretical Perspectives on Personality

| Personality Theory | Main Points | Criticisms |
|---|---|---|
| Psychoanalytic | Personality develops early in life; we are greatly influenced by unconscious processes (internal conflicts, aggression, and sexual urges, for example). | Ignores the importance of current experiences; overemphasizes the role of sexuality and the unconscious. Theory is based on a biased, nonrepresentative sample; concepts are difficult to operationally define and empirically test. |
| Behavioral | Personality is shaped by interactions with the environment, specifically through learning (operant conditioning and observational learning). | Narrowly focuses on behavioral processes; ignores the influence of unconscious processes and emotional factors. |
| Humanistic | We are innately good and in control of our destinies; a force within moves us toward growth. | Concepts are difficult to operationally define and empirically test; ignores the negative aspects of human nature. |
| Social-cognitive | Focuses on social influences and mental processes that affect personality; emphasizes the interaction of environment, cognitive activity, and behavior. | Narrowly focuses on social-cognitive factors; ignores the influence of unconscious processes and emotional factors. |
| Biological | Emphasizes the physiological and genetic influences on personality development; explains the emergence of certain characteristics through gene–environment interactions. | Findings are inconsistent when it comes to the stability of personality dimensions; estimates of environmental influences are variable. |
| Trait | Looks at current traits to describe personality and predict behaviors. | Underestimates the environmental influences on personality; does not fully explain the foundations of personality. |

Psychology uses a variety of theoretical perspectives to explain the development of personality. Listed here are the major theories and some of their key limitations.

environment (Briley & Tucker-Drob, 2014; Caspi et al., 2005; Costa et al., 2019; Van den Bergh et al., 2020). For example, a child born with a calm, easygoing temperament may become more fearful and irritable if caregivers are neglectful. A child's behavior can shape parental responses, too (Van den Akker et al., 2014; Wittig & Rodriguez, 2019). You can imagine how an anxious or defiant child might cause a normally laid-back parent to become irritable. Although temperament shines through early in life, it takes time for adult personality to fully take shape. The exact timing of this process is debated, but we can think of temperament as an important, stable aspect of personality (Goldsmith et al., 1987; Soto & Tackett, 2015).

**LO2** Distinguish how the perspectives of psychology explain personality development.

**HOW CAN WE EXPLAIN PERSONALITY?** Psychologists use a variety of theoretical perspectives to explain the development and expression of personality (TABLE 10.1). None of them are perfect, but all provide valuable insights and contribute to our understanding of personality. These theoretical perspectives also help accomplish three of psychology's main goals: to describe, explain, and predict behavior. They have strong ties to their founders, all of whom were influenced by their life experiences and the historical period in which they lived. Sigmund Freud's emphasis on sexuality, for example, was partly a reaction to the prudish Victorian culture into which he was born.

In the next section, we will examine these theories of personality in greater depth, but first let's take a quick detour somewhere fun. How would you describe your sense of humor?

## Think Critically

### THE FUNNY THING ABOUT PERSONALITY

**WHERE DID YOU GET THAT SENSE OF HUMOR?**

Humor takes various forms, but it appears to be a "relatively stable personality trait" (Plessen et al., 2020, p. 1). Some of us rely on humor to connect with other people, cracking jokes and acting silly for their enjoyment. Others use it as a way to cope with challenges. (We must admit, it does feel good to let loose and laugh when we're feeling overwhelmed.) Both of these styles of humor are inversely correlated with anxiety and depression (Martin et al., 2003; Menéndez-Aller et al., 2020). This means that people who possess them are less likely to experience symptoms of anxiety and depression. There are also negative forms of humor, like ridiculing another person to make yourself look good, or poking fun at yourself in a way that is "excessively self-disparaging" (Martin & Kuiper, 2016, p. 505). When people are exposed to different humor styles, they experience distinct patterns of brain activation—further evidence that humor is a multifaceted phenomenon (Chan et al., 2018).

Where do humor styles originate? According to one large study conducted in Australia, identical twins (who have nearly identical genes) are more likely to share humor styles than fraternal (nonidentical) twins. In fact, the study suggests that 30–47% of the population-wide variation in humor styles can be attributed to genetics (Baughman et al., 2012), and some research indicates an even higher proportion (Martin & Kuiper, 2016; Vernon et al., 2008). But genes aren't everything; environmental factors, such as relationships, may also shape humor. For example, a study of 11- to 13-year-olds found that affiliative humor (the type that strengthens social bonds) can be reinforced by close friends (Hunter et al., 2016). Additional research suggests that couples in long-lasting marriages (those that have endured at least a decade) tend to share similar styles of humor; this could be a result of their humor becoming more alike with time (Tsai et al., 2019). What do these findings tell you about the roles of nature and nurture in the development of humor styles?

**Who Is Funnier?**
Amy Schumer appears on *Jimmy Kimmel Live*. Have you ever noticed that most famous comedians are men? Perhaps this has something to do with the commonly held—and mistaken—belief that men are funnier than women. In one study, researchers showed participants cartoon captions written by men and women. Participants unknowingly rated men's and women's captions to be equally funny, but they were more likely to credit the funniest captions to male authors (Hooper et al., 2016; Kennison, 2020).

Randy Holmes/© Walt Disney Television/ABC/Getty Images.

Nearly 8 billion human beings inhabit this planet, and no two of them have the same personality. Each individual's personality reflects a distinct interplay of inborn characteristics and life experiences. Consider this nature-and-nurture dynamic as you explore the theories of personality in the pages to come. We'll get this discussion going with the help of Saifa.

## Put Your Heads Together

In your group, **A)** pick a character from a fairy tale, TV show, or movie, and describe some aspects of their personality. **B)** Now consider the six theoretical perspectives presented in Table 10.1, and pick at least three of them to explain how these characteristics might have developed.

## SHOW WHAT YOU KNOW

1. A study concludes that the heritability of humor styles is 30–47%. Which perspective of psychology would you use to explain this finding, and why?

2. _____ is the unique, core set of characteristics that influence the way one thinks, acts, and feels.

 CHECK YOUR ANSWERS AT THE BACK OF THE BOOK.

# Psychoanalytic Theories

**BEFORE SAIFA, THERE WAS SUSANNE**   Saifa was born in 1978, at Columbia–Presbyterian Hospital in New York City. Unlike most babies, who are readily identified as "boy" or "girl," Saifa had ambiguous genitalia (not clearly male, not clearly female). Doctors assigned him female and instructed his mother to raise him as a girl, indicating that he would "function as such" (Wall, 2015, p. 118). During that era, many psychologists and medical professionals believed that human behaviors were primarily shaped by environmental input, or nurture (Schultz & Schultz, 2016; Segal, 2012). But as you will learn from Saifa's story, nature can sometimes overpower nurture.

Saifa was, and still is, genetically male (*XY*). He has an **intersex trait** called androgen insensitivity syndrome (AIS), characterized by reduced sensitivity to male hormones, or androgens. People with AIS are genetically male, but their bodies do not follow the typical "male" or "female" path of sexual development (Gottlieb & Trifiro, 2017; Singh & Ilyayeva, 2020). Some are designated "male" at birth, others "female." These gender assignments appear to work out for some people (about 75%, according to one study), but a substantial minority feel unsatisfied (Schweizer et al., 2014).

Saifa was raised as a female named "Susanne," but fulfilling society's gender expectations did not come naturally. He didn't like feminine clothes, and he certainly was not attracted to boys. "I knew from, like the age of five, that I liked girls," Saifa recalls. His parents accepted this nonconformist approach to girlhood, but within limits. One of Saifa's first memories is from the age of 4 or 5; he was getting ready to visit his grandmother and wanted to wear overalls. But his mom insisted he wear a sundress with spaghetti straps and put his hair in pigtails. Saifa protested and cried, but ended up complying—and feeling miserably out of his element: "I remember being on the train going downtown and just feeling so vulnerable."

Childhood presented other challenges. Saifa grew up in the Bronx during the 1980s, when crack cocaine was devastating urban communities and crime was rampant. He witnessed trauma and suffering not only in his neighborhood, but also within his family: "If we're talking about the most formative experiences I had, if we're talking about between the ages of 0 and 6," Saifa explains, "[it] was seeing my dad drunk, witnessing the domestic violence that took place in the home."

How did these early childhood experiences impact Saifa in the long term, and what role did they play in the development of his personality? If we could pose this question to Sigmund Freud, he would probably say they were critical. Freud believed that childhood is the prime time for personality development, the early years and basic drives being particularly important because they shape our thoughts, emotions, and behaviors in ways beyond our awareness. **Psychoanalysis** refers to Freud's theories about personality, discussed below, as well as his system of psychotherapy and tools for the exploration of the unconscious (see Chapter 14).

Before launching our discussion of Freud, we should point out that his approach is controversial and lacking in scientific support. Freud presented novel and groundbreaking insights on personality development, but his theories are mostly based on isolated case studies that may not be representative of the larger population. Despite these weaknesses, most psychology professors who teach courses in personality recognize the impact of Freud's legacy and teach students about his perspective (Posey & Cushing, 2019).

## Does the Mind Have Three Levels?

Sigmund Freud spent the majority of his life in Vienna, Austria. A smart, ambitious young man, Freud attended medical school and became a physician and researcher with a primary interest in physiology and later neurology. Freud loved research, but he soon came to realize that the anti-Semitic culture in which he lived would drastically interfere with his studies. (Freud was Jewish.) So, instead of pursuing the career he loved, he opened a medical practice in 1881, specializing in clinical neurology. Many of his patients had unexplained or unusual symptoms that seemed to be related to emotional problems. The basis of these problems, Freud and his colleagues hypothesized, appeared to be sexual in nature, though the patients weren't necessarily

**CONNECTIONS**

In **Chapter 8,** we discussed differences of sex development. People with intersex traits may have internal and external reproductive organs that are not clearly male or female.

Courtesy Sean Saifa Wall.

**Growing Up Susanne**

(Left) Five-year-old Susanne (now Saifa) with friends. "When I was growing up, I felt more connected to boyhood," Saifa explains. "Innately, I felt more masculine, more male [but] externally, what I was presenting to the world based on my body, based on my physical characteristics, was female."

**psychoanalysis** Freud's theories of personality as well as his system of psychotherapy and tools for the exploration of the unconscious.

aware of this (Freud, 1900/1953). Thus began Freud's lifelong journey to untangle the mysteries of the unconscious mind (Safran & Hunter, 2020a).

**LO 3**  Illustrate Freud's models for describing the mind.

Freud (1900/1953) proposed that the mind has three levels of consciousness—conscious, preconscious, and unconscious—and that mental processes occurring on these levels guide behaviors and shape personality. Everything you are aware of at this moment exists at the *conscious* level, including thoughts, emotions, sensations, and perceptions. At the *preconscious* level are mental activities **outside your current awareness**, which can easily drift into the conscious realm. The **unconscious** level is home to activities outside of your awareness. Unconscious feelings, memories, wishes, thoughts, and urges may be very difficult to bring to awareness without concerted effort and/or therapy. Freud did suggest, however, that some content of the unconscious can enter the conscious level through manipulated and distorted processes beyond a person's control or awareness (more on this shortly). To help patients understand the influence of their unconscious activities, Freud (1900/1953) used a variety of techniques, such as dream interpretation, hypnosis, and free association (Chapters 4 and 14; Safran & Hunter, 2020a).

This *topographical model* consisting of the conscious, preconscious, and unconscious was Freud's earliest attempt to explain the bustling activity occurring within the head (Westen et al., 2008). Freud was influenced by German physicist Gustav Fechner's (1801–1887) idea that the great majority of the mind is "hidden below the surface where it is influenced by unobservable forces" (Schultz & Schultz, 2016, p. 290). Many who describe Freud's model compare it to an iceberg: What we see on the surface is just the "tip of the iceberg" (the conscious level), small in comparison to the vast and influential unconscious mind (Schultz & Schultz, 2017; FIGURE 10.1).

**CONNECTIONS**

In **Chapter 6,** we presented a component of working memory called the episodic buffer, which allows information from long-term memory to reach conscious awareness. Although Freud did not refer to this buffer, the preconscious level includes activities similar to those of the episodic buffer.

**FIGURE 10.1**
**Psychoanalytic Description of the Mind**

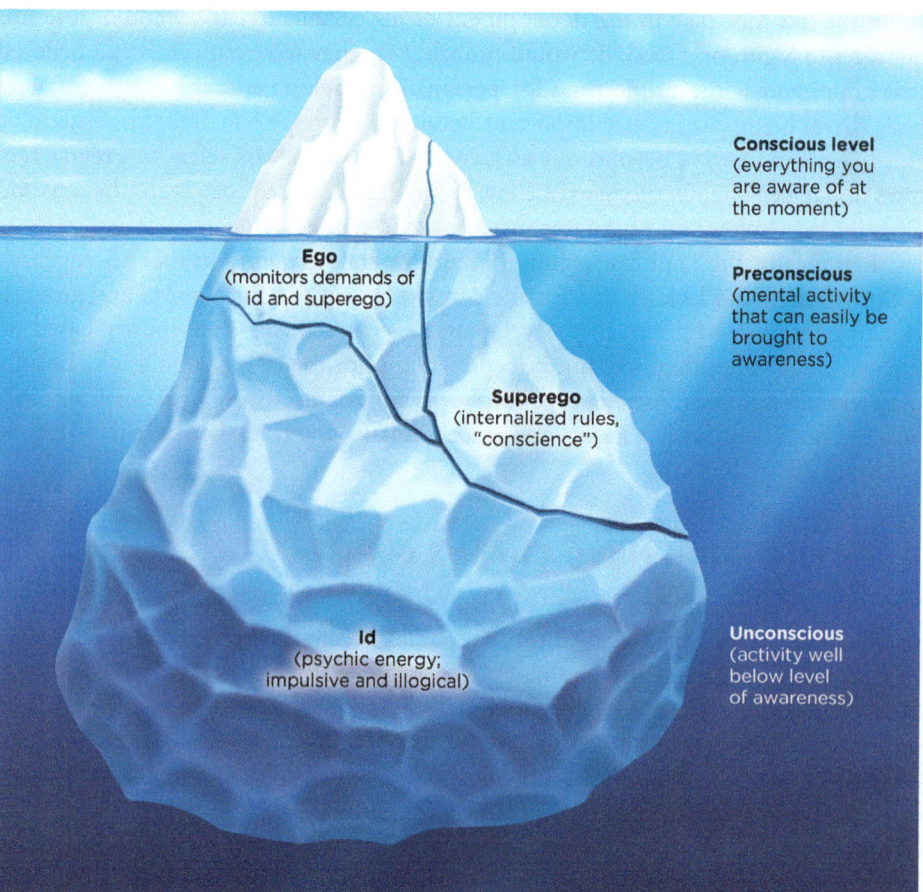

**Conscious level**
(everything you are aware of at the moment)

**Preconscious**
(mental activity that can easily be brought to awareness)

**Ego**
(monitors demands of id and superego)

**Superego**
(internalized rules, "conscience")

**Id**
(psychic energy; impulsive and illogical)

**Unconscious**
(activity well below level of awareness)

**unconscious**  According to Freud, the level of consciousness outside of awareness, which is difficult to access without effort or therapy.

# Id, Ego, and Superego

In addition to the topographical model, Freud proposed a *structural model* describing the mind's three structures: the *id, ego*, and *superego* (Westen et al., 2008). These structures serve as "psychic agencies" that direct the energy driving our behaviors (Safran & Hunter, 2020a). The battle among these components occurs unconsciously, influencing our thoughts, emotions, and behaviors, and forming our personality (Westen et al., 2008).

**THE ID**   The most primitive structure of the mind is the **id.** Present from birth, the id operates at the unconscious level and is responsible for the biological drives motivating behavior. It also fuels the impulsive, illogical, and infant-like aspects of our thoughts and personality. Freud proposed that the id represents the mind's primary pool of *psychic energy* (Freud, 1923/1961, 1933/1964). Included in that pool is sexual energy, which motivates much of our behavior. The primary goal of the id is to ensure that needs are being met, which helps maintain **homeostasis**. The id is not rational, and unfulfilled needs or urges compel it to insist on immediate action. It follows the **pleasure principle,** which guides behavior toward instant gratification—and away from contemplating consequences. The id seeks pleasure and avoids pain.

**THE EGO**   As an infant grows and starts to realize that the desires of the id cannot prevail in all situations, their **ego,** which is not present from birth, begins to develop from the id (Freud, 1933/1964, 1940/1949). The ego manipulates situations, creates plans, solves problems, and makes decisions to satisfy the needs of the id. The goal is to make sure that the id is not given free rein over behavior, as this would cause problems. Imagine what a busy supermarket would be like if everyone were ruled by their ids. People would ignore societal expectations to stand in line, speak politely, and pay for food; the store would be full of adults having toddler-like tantrums. To negotiate between the id and the environment, the ego follows the **reality principle,** adhering to the rules of the "real" world and delaying gratification as needed (Freud, 1923/1960). The reality principle works through an awareness of potential consequences; the ego can predict what will happen if we act on an urge. We are aware of the ego's activities, although some happen at the preconscious level, and even fewer at the unconscious level (Figure 10.1).

**THE SUPEREGO**   The **superego** is the structure of the mind that develops last, guiding behavior to follow the rules of society, parents, or other authority figures (Freud, 1923/1960). The superego begins to form as toddlers start moving about on their own, coming up against rules and expectations. (*No, you cannot hit your sister! You need to put your toys away.*) Children eventually incorporate the values of others, including ideas about right and wrong, often referred to as the *conscience*. Once the superego is rooted, it serves as a critical internal guide to the values of society so that children can make "good" choices without reminders from parents, caregivers, or religious leaders. Sometimes, the internal voice of the superego can be harsh and judgmental, and it may set unrealistic standards. For example, married people may feel guilty when their eyes (and imaginations) stray toward attractive individuals who are not their spouses. When this happens, their judgmental superego might say, *What's wrong with you? Are you a cheater?* Some activities of the superego are conscious, but the great majority occur at the preconscious and unconscious levels.

**CAUGHT IN THE MIDDLE**   The ego monitors the demands of the id and the superego, trying to satisfy both. Think of the energy of the id, pushing to get all desires met instantly. The ego must ensure the id's needs are met in a manner acceptable to the superego, reducing tension as much as possible (Safran & Hunter, 2020a). But not all urges and desires can be met (not instantly, perhaps not ever).

**CONNECTIONS**

In **Chapter 9,** we discussed the concept of drive reduction, which suggests that unmet needs create tension that motivates behavior. Fulfilling needs reduces tension and helps maintain homeostasis, or balance in the body's systems. Here, we discuss Freud's view that the id directs our behavior to meet these needs.

**id** According to Freud, the most primitive structure of the mind, the activities of which occur at the unconscious level and are guided by the pleasure principle.

**pleasure principle** A principle that guides the id, directing behavior toward instant gratification and away from contemplating consequences.

**ego** According to Freud, the structure of the mind that uses the reality principle to manipulate situations, plan for the future, solve problems, and make decisions to satisfy the needs of the id.

**reality principle** A principle that guides the ego as it negotiates between the id and the environment, directing behavior to follow society's rules.

**superego** According to Freud, the structure of the mind that guides behavior to follow the rules of society, parents, or other authority figures.

**It Can Happen to Anyone**
While speaking at a 2015 fundraiser, then-President Barack Obama reportedly said this: "We should be reforming our criminal justice system in such a way that we are not incarcerating nonviolent offenders in ways that renders them incapable of getting a job after they leave *office*" (Fabian, 2015, para. 3). Obama meant to say "after they leave *prison*," and he acknowledged his "Freudian slip" to a laughing audience (Fabian, 2015). A Freudian slip is an unintended word or phrase that accidentally slips off the tongue, shedding light on unconscious thoughts.

**CONNECTIONS**

In **Chapter 6,** we discussed the controversy over repressed memories of childhood abuse. Some psychologists believe that memories can be repressed and retrieved at a later time. Many others question the validity of research supporting the existence of such memories. Freud's case studies describing childhood sexual abuse have also been questioned.

**ego defense mechanisms** Unconscious processes the ego uses to distort perceptions and memories and thereby reduce anxiety created by the id–superego conflict.

How might this conflict between the id and superego play out in a real-world situation? Imagine you are about to leave for class and you get a text from a friend, inviting you to a movie. You are torn, because you know an exam is coming up and you should not skip today's class. Your id is demanding a movie, some popcorn, and freedom from work. Your superego demands that you go to class. Clearly, your ego cannot satisfy both of these demands. Freud (1923/1960) proposed that this sort of struggle is an everyday, recurring experience that the ego cannot always resolve. Sometimes the id triumphs, and the person acts in an infantile, perhaps even destructive, manner. (You give in to the pressures of your friend and your id, and happily decide to skip class.) Or perhaps the superego prevails, causing you to feel a great deal of remorse or guilt for not living up to some moral ideal. (You skip class, but you feel so guilty you can't enjoy the movie.) The anxiety associated with the id–superego conflict is generally unconscious, but sometimes it surfaces to the conscious level. The ego then must deal with this anxiety and make it more bearable (perhaps by suggesting that a day off will help you study, because you haven't had any free time all semester).

## Defense Mechanisms

If conflicts between the id and superego cannot be resolved and anxiety becomes overwhelming, the ego may turn to **ego defense mechanisms.** According to Freud, ego defense mechanisms distort perceptions and memories of the real world without our awareness. Most people unknowingly use defense mechanisms from time to time, but it's generally better to confront problems directly.

Freud proposed a variety of defense mechanisms, which were further developed by his daughter, psychoanalyst Anna Freud (1895–1982). As you learn about some of these defense mechanisms in INFOGRAPHIC **10.1**, remember two points: (1) We are often unaware of using them, even if they are brought to our attention; and (2) defense mechanisms are not necessarily a bad thing (Cramer, 2015; Vaillant, 2000). In some cases, distortions appear to be helpful because they can reduce anxiety (Zimmerman et al., 2019). But if we overuse defense mechanisms, behaviors may turn inappropriate or unhealthy (Cramer, 2000, 2008; Prunas et al., 2019; Tallandini & Caudek, 2010).

One of the more commonly known defense mechanisms is *repression*, which occurs when the ego moves uncomfortable thoughts, feelings, or **memories** from the conscious to unconscious level. With anxiety-provoking memories, the reality of an event can become distorted to such an extreme that you don't even remember it. The repressed memories do not cease to exist, however, and they may pop up in unexpected forms, influencing behaviors and decisions.

### Put Your Heads Together

It's Saturday morning and you have a paper due this week. You could spend the day at the library gathering research and writing the paper, but there is tail-gaiting to do, a football game to watch, and a post-game party to attend. Team up and explain how you might unconsciously justify your decision to avoid the library using at least four ego defense mechanisms outlined in Infographic 10.1.

### Stages of Development

**LO 4** Summarize Freud's use of psychosexual stages to explain personality.

In addition to his topographical and structural models of the mind, Freud (1905/1953) proposed a *developmental* model to explain how personality is formed through experiences in childhood, with a special emphasis on sexuality. According to Freud, the

# Ego Defense Mechanisms

At some point or another, we all experience socially unacceptable thoughts and feelings. What's going on with the id, ego, and superego when this happens? In the scenario described below (being attracted to someone who is "off limits"), we see how the dynamic might play out. The impulsive demands of the id conflict with the moralistic demands of the superego, resulting in anxiety. When that anxiety becomes excessive, the ego works to relieve this uncomfortable feeling through the use of defense mechanisms (Freud, 1923/1960). Defense mechanisms give us a way to "defend" against tension and anxiety, but they are not always adaptive, or helpful. The scale on the right shows how defense mechanisms can be categorized as ranging from less adaptive to more adaptive (Vaillant, 1992).

**EGO** relieves anxiety by employing a defense mechanism.

**EGO**

*I am physically attracted to my best friend's boyfriend.*

*How dare I? I am wrong to feel those impulses.*

anxiety

**ID**    **SUPEREGO**

✳ We may get better at dealing with stress and anxiety as we age. In a study comparing the use of defense mechanisms in different age groups, older participants were found to use fewer maladaptive defense mechanisms (Segal et al., 2007).

### SUBLIMATION
Redirecting unacceptable impulses into acceptable outlets.

*Example: Instead of worrying about wanting to date your best friend's boyfriend, you use a dating app to meet other singles.*

### IDENTIFICATION
Unconsciously modeling your feelings or actions on the behaviors of someone you admire.

*Example: Admiring your best friend, and adopting her mannerisms and characteristics.*

### DISPLACEMENT
Shifting negative feelings and impulses to an acceptable target.

*Example: Being rude to someone who's interested in you. "Sorry, I am busy tonight."*

### REPRESSION
Anxiety-producing information is pushed into the unconscious.

*Example: Unconsciously avoiding your friend and her boyfriend in social situations.*

### RATIONALIZATION
Creating an acceptable excuse for an uncomfortable situation.

*Example: "I am a human being. Of course I feel sexually attracted to other people."*

### PROJECTION
Attributing your own anxiety-provoking thoughts and impulses to someone else.

*Example: "What is wrong with Sara? She always seems to be checking out other people's boyfriends."*

### DENIAL
Refusing to recognize a distressing reality.

*Example: "I don't like him. He's just not my type."*

MORE ADAPTIVE

LESS ADAPTIVE

**TABLE 10.2**    Freud's Psychosexual Stages

| Stage | Age | Erogenous Zone | Focus | Type of Conflict | Results of Fixation |
|-------|-----|----------------|-------|------------------|---------------------|
| Oral | Birth–1½ years | Mouth | Sucking, chewing, and gumming | Weaning | Smoking, drinking, nail biting, excessive talking |
| Anal | 1½–3 years | Anus | Eliminating bodily waste and controlling bodily functions responsible for this process | Toilet training | Being rule-bound, stingy, chaotic, destructive |
| Phallic | 3–6 years | Genitals | Sexual feelings and awareness of self | Self-stimulation | Promiscuity, flirtation, vanity, or overdependence, and a focus on masturbation |
| Latency period | 6 years–puberty | Period during which children develop mentally, socially, and physically | | | |
| Genital | Puberty and beyond | Genitals | Reawakening of sexuality, with focus on relationships | Sexuality and aggression | Inability to thrive in adult experiences such as work and love |

According to Freud, psychological and sexual development proceeds through distinct stages. Each stage is characterized by a certain pleasure area, or "erogenous zone," and a conflict that must be resolved. If resolution is not achieved, the person may develop a problematic "fixation."

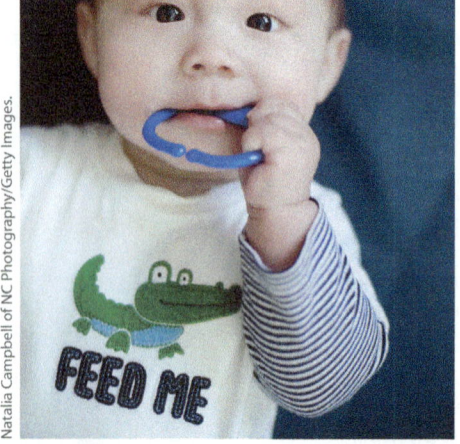

**Oral Fixation**
The average baby (birth to 18 months) spends 108 minutes per day sucking on a pacifier and another 33 minutes mouthing other objects (Juberg et al., 2001). Freud identified this phase of life with the oral stage of psychosexual development.

**psychosexual stages** According to Freud, the stages of development of sexuality and personality, from birth to adulthood, each of which has an erogenous zone and a conflict that must be dealt with.

**fixation** Being stuck in a particular psychosexual stage of development; occurs when one is unsuccessful at resolving the conflict associated with that stage.

development of sexuality and personality proceeds through **psychosexual stages,** which all children experience as they mature into adulthood (**TABLE 10.2**). Driving this development is the sexual energy of the id; children are sexual beings starting from birth, indicating there is a strong biological component to personality development. Each psychosexual stage is associated with a specific *erogenous zone*, or area of the body that provides more sexual pleasure than other areas.

Along with each psychosexual stage comes a conflict that the individual must resolve in order to become a well-adjusted adult. If these conflicts are not successfully addressed, one may suffer from a **fixation,** that is, get stuck in a particular stage and fail to progress smoothly through the remaining stages. Freud believed that fixation in a psychosexual stage during the first 5 to 6 years of life can last into adulthood, and this may have a dramatic impact on personality. Let's look at each stage, its erogenous zone and conflicts, and some consequences of fixation.

**ORAL STAGE**    The *oral stage* begins at birth and lasts until 1 to 1½ years old. As the name suggests, the erogenous zone for the oral stage is the mouth; infants derive their greatest pleasure from sucking, chewing, and gumming. According to Freud, the conflict during this stage generally centers on weaning. Infants must stop nursing or using a bottle or pacifier, and the caregiver often decides when it's time. Weaning too early or too late can have long-term consequences for personality development. Freud suggested that oral fixation is associated with certain personality traits and behavior patterns, which might include smoking, nail biting, excessive talking, and increased alcohol consumption.

**ANAL STAGE**    Following the oral stage is the *anal stage*, which lasts until about age 3. The erogenous zone is the anus, and pleasure is derived from eliminating bodily waste and learning to control the process. The conflict during this stage centers on toilet training: Parents want their child to use a toilet, but the child is not necessarily ready. Once again, how caregivers deal with this task may have long-term implications for personality. If a parent is too harsh (growing angry when there are accidents, forcing a child to sit on the toilet until they go) or too lenient (making excuses for accidents, not really encouraging the child to learn control), the child might grow up with an *anal-retentive* personality (rule-bound, stingy) or an *anal-expulsive* personality (chaotic, destructive).

**PHALLIC STAGE**    Ages 3 to 6 mark the *phallic stage* (*phallus* means "penis" in Latin). During this period, the erogenous zone is the genitals, and many children begin to discover that self-stimulation is pleasurable. Freud (1923/1960) assigned special importance to the conflict that occurs in the phallic stage.

During this time, little boys experience the **Oedipus complex** (ED-uh-puss): They develop a desire to replace their fathers—a normal feeling, according to Freud, but one that leads to jealously because the boy considers his father a rival for his mother's affection. When the boy becomes aware of his attraction to his mother, he realizes his father is a formidable adversary and feels anger toward him. He also begins to fear his powerful father, and worry that he might be punished. Specifically, he fears that his father will castrate him (Freud, 1917/1966). In order to reduce the tension, the boy must identify with and behave like his father, a process known as *identification*. This defense mechanism resolves the Oedipus complex, allowing the boy to take on or internalize the behaviors, mannerisms, morals, and standards of his father. The boy realizes that sexual affection should only be between his father and mother, and the incest taboo develops.

Freud (1923/1960) believed that little girls also experience conflict during this period. Feeling an attraction to their fathers, they become jealous and angry toward their mothers. They also realize that they do not have a penis, which leads to feelings of loss and jealousy, known as *penis envy*. The girl responds with anger, blaming her mother for her missing penis. Realizing she can't have her father, she begins to act like her mother through the process of *identification*. She takes on her mother's behaviors, mannerisms, morals, and standards. Some of Freud's followers labeled this conflict the *Electra complex* (Kilmartin & Dervin, 1997; Schultz & Schultz, 2017).

If children do not resolve the sexual conflicts of the phallic stage, they develop a fixation, which can lead to flirtation, vanity, overdependence, bravado, and an increased focus on masturbation.

**LATENCY PERIOD**    From age 6 to puberty, children go through a *latency period* (not a "stage" according to Freud's definition, as there is no erogenous zone, conflict, or fixation). During this time, psychosexual development slows and sexual energy is repressed: Although children develop mentally, socially, and physically, their sexual development is on hold.

**GENITAL STAGE**    Following the calm of the latency period, a child's psychosexual development regains speed. The *genital stage* begins at puberty and marks a reawakening of sexuality. The erogenous zone is once again the genitals, but now in association with relationships, as opposed to masturbation. The Oedipus or Electra complex is resolved, and the individual often becomes attracted to partners who resemble the opposite-sex parent (Freud, 1905/1953). Because of the ever-present demands of the *id*, unconscious conflicts persist, including the continual battle against hidden sexual and aggressive urges. If such conflicts are resolved, then it is possible to thrive in adult experiences such as work and love.

## Who Are the Neo-Freudians?

**A DARK PERIOD**    Young childhood was difficult for Saifa, who faced an ongoing conflict between his innate sense of gender and society's expectations for him as a "girl." But the early years were also a time of great freedom. "When I was like 5, 6, 7, I was

**Oedipus complex** According to Freud, the attraction a boy feels toward his mother, along with resentment or envy directed toward his father.

Courtesy Sean Saifa Wall.

Courtesy Sean Saifa Wall.

**What's Beneath That Smile?**
Saifa, 18, poses for his high school graduation photo (top) and a portrait with his older sister. After doctors removed his internal testes, Saifa fell into a deep depression. "I didn't comb my hair, I didn't brush my teeth, I didn't shower," Saifa explains. "It was so bad, I wouldn't even go outside."

the adult that I am now," Saifa says. "I was very uninhibited; I was very loud; I was very free; I was weird."

Life took a dramatic turn when police showed up at his building and took away his father. Saifa, 10 years old, observed the whole event. "That's the last time I saw him alive, [he] was being taken away in handcuffs." While Saifa's mother dealt with the aftermath, Saifa went to live with his sister in North Carolina, where he was relentlessly bullied at his new school. "I think living in North Carolina just really killed my fire as a child," Saifa says. "I was still that quirky, weird, loud kid, but then I was teased, I was bullied, my self-esteem was really low."

A year or two after moving to North Carolina, Saifa began to experience puberty. His voice deepened; he began growing facial hair; and his muscles became more defined—all changes associated with *male* puberty. But Saifa was still a "girl" at this point; recall that he had been assigned female at birth and raised as "Susanne." The masculinization of his body was fueled by testosterone from his undescended testes. (People with AIS may be born with internal, as opposed to descended, testes.) "I was experiencing this male puberty," Saifa says. "But it felt normal; it felt good."

The male puberty Saifa enjoyed came to an abrupt halt at age 13, when he moved back to New York City and doctors removed his testes. The purpose of the operation was to eliminate the pain he had been feeling in his groin, possibly the result of hernias in his testes. The other reason, doctors told Saifa's mother, was that the internal gonads would likely become cancerous. This procedure has since become a subject of controversy, as the risk of cells becoming cancerous, or even precancerous, is low among children and teens going through puberty (Dreuning et al., 2020).

Following the surgery, Saifa's doctor put him on female hormones, which feminized his face and body. "[The doctors] wanted to create this feminine body that was going against what my body was naturally doing. . . . I was developing with both male and female characteristics, and that's what makes my particular intersex trait so beautiful," Saifa says. "The right to my body was taken away from me."

According to Freud, personality is largely shaped by early childhood experiences and sexual impulses. Yet, some of the most transformative experiences in Saifa's life—the arrest of his father, the bullying at school, and the surgery to remove his testes—occurred later in life and had little to do with sexual urges. Some theorists would argue that such events are important factors in personality development. We now turn to the neo-Freudians, who agree with Freud on many points but depart from his intense emphasis on early childhood experiences, aggression, and sexuality.

**LO5** Explain how the neo-Freudians' theories of personality differ from Freud's.

**DRIFTING APART**    Freud's psychoanalytic theory was quite controversial, but he did have a following of students who adapted some central aspects of his theory. Erik Erikson, for example, considered himself a "loyal Freudian," yet he took Freud's ideas in a new direction (Schultz & Schultz, 2017). **Erikson** suggested that psychosocial development occurs throughout life and proceeds through eight stages, each marked by a conflict between the individual's needs and society's expectations. His approach was more positive than Freud's, drawing attention to "lifelong personal growth" in psychologically healthy people (Ludden, 2021). Erikson was not the only one to disagree with Freud on key points. Those who broke away and developed their own theories are often referred to as neo-Freudians (neo = "new").

**ALFRED ADLER**    One of the first followers to forge his own path was a fellow Austrian physician, Alfred Adler (1870–1937), whose theory conflicted with Freud's notions of child sexuality and male superiority. Adler believed some parts

**CONNECTIONS**

In **Chapter 8,** we discussed Erikson's psychosocial stages. Building on the views of Freud, Erikson suggested that every developmental stage is marked by a task or emotional crisis that must be handled successfully for healthy psychological growth.

of the mind exist outside of awareness—but not permanently, as they can be brought forth with guidance (Ludden, 2021). Humans are not just pleasure seekers, but conscious and intentional in their behaviors. We are motivated by the need to feel superior—to grow, overcome challenges, and strive for perfection. This drive originates during childhood, when we realize that we are dependent on and inferior to adults (Wertheimer & Puente, 2020). Whether imagined or real, our sense of inferiority pushes us to compensate, so we cultivate our special gifts and skills. This attempt to balance perceived weaknesses with strengths is not a sign of abnormality, but a natural response.

Adler's theory of *individual psychology* focuses on each person's unique struggle with feelings of inferiority. Unfortunately, not everyone is successful in overcoming this sense of helplessness and dependence. Those who fail may develop what is known as an *inferiority complex* (Adler, 1927/1994). People with an inferiority complex feel incompetent, vulnerable, and powerless, and cannot achieve their full potential.

Adler was also one of the first to theorize about the psychological repercussions of birth order—that is, how people are affected by their place in the family (first, middle, or youngest child). He believed that firstborn children experience different environmental pressures than youngest and middle children, and these pressures can set the stage for the development of certain personality traits (Ansbacher & Ansbacher, 1956; Hartmann & Goudarzi, 2019).

## ...BELIEVE IT...OR NOT

### HOW BIRTH ORDER MAY—OR MAY NOT—AFFECT YOUR PERSONALITY

Firstborns are conscientious and high achieving. They play by the rules, excel in school, and become leaders in the workforce. Youngest children are favored and coddled by their parents, and grow up to be gregarious and rebellious. Middle children tend to get lost in the shuffle, but they learn to be self-sufficient.

**DO MIDDLE CHILDREN GET LOST IN THE SHUFFLE?**

Have you heard these stereotypes about birth order and personality? How well do they match your personal experience, and do you think they are valid?

If you search the scientific literature, you will indeed find research supporting such claims. According to one analysis of 200 studies, firstborns (as well as only children) are often accomplished and successful; middle children are sociable but tend to lack a sense of belonging; and last-born children are agreeable and rebellious (Eckstein et al., 2010). Other research suggests that later-born children, particularly middle siblings, often go out of their way to help others (Salmon et al., 2016). These findings are intriguing and often seem consistent with our everyday observations, but many of them are correlational in nature. Remember, a correlation is just a relationship between variables—not an establishment of cause and effect. Like all research, birth order studies are vulnerable to **confounding variables**, and designing studies to circumvent them has proven difficult. When researchers have been able to control some of these variables, birth order does not strongly correlate to the presence of any specific personality characteristics (Botzet et al., 2021; Damian & Roberts, 2015; Rohrer et al., 2015). This means that we can't make broad generalizations about people based on where they fall in the family's birth order. As psychologist Frank Spinath explained in an interview with *Scientific American,* "It is quite possible that the position in the sibling sequence shapes the personality—but not in every family in the same way. . . . In other words, there may be an influence but not a systematic one" (Hartmann & Goudarzi, 2019, para. 9).

*Research* **CONNECTIONS**

In **Chapter 1,** we discussed what it means to have a confounding variable. A confounding variable is a type of extraneous variable that changes in sync with an independent variable (IV). This makes it difficult to discern which variable—the IV or the confounding variable—is causing changes in the dependent variable.

**Timeless Heroines?**
Scarlett Johansson (left) plays the role of Natasha Romanoff in the 2021 film *Black Widow*. Her strength, bravery, and charisma resemble those of 15th-century French heroine Joan of Arc, portrayed in the poster (right). These heroines have the qualities of a Jungian archetype; the thoughts and feelings they evoke are relatively consistent across time and culture.

**CARL GUSTAV JUNG**   Neo-Freudian Carl Gustav Jung (Yoong; 1875–1961) was a Swiss psychiatrist who emphasized growth, self-understanding, and the spiritual aspects of human nature. Jung claimed that Freud viewed the brain as "an appendage to the genital glands" (Westen et al., 2008, p. 66), and proposed that personality development is not limited to childhood, but evolves throughout life. His *analytic psychology* deemphasized biological urges (sex and aggression), and proposed that we are driven by psychological energy (not sexual energy) that promotes growth, insight, and balance (Jung, 1969).

According to Jung, personality is made up of the *personal conscious* that is within our awareness, as well a *personal unconscious* and a *collective unconscious* (Ludden, 2021). The personal unconscious is akin to Freud's notion of the preconscious and the unconscious mind; it contains material that is readily available (easy-to-retrieve memories) and material that is very difficult to access (repressed memories and other anxiety-provoking content). The **collective unconscious** holds the universal experiences of humankind passed from generation to generation—memories that are not easily retrieved without some degree of effort or interpretation. We inherit a variety of primal images, patterns of thought, and story lines. The themes of these **archetypes** (AHR-ki-types) may be found in art, literature, music, dreams, and religions across time, geography, and culture. Some of the consistent archetypes include the nurturing mother, powerful father, innocent child, and brave hero. Archetypes provide a blueprint for responding to objects, people, and situations (Jung, 1969). Jung also proposed that every personality has both feminine and masculine elements, respectively known as the *anima* and *animus*, and both should be acknowledged and appreciated.

**KAREN HORNEY**   Karen Horney (HOR-nahy; 1885–1952) was a German psychoanalyst who immigrated to the United States in the early 1930s. She agreed with Freud that the early years play an important role in shaping adult personality, and that conflict arises between individual desires and the needs of society (Schultz & Schultz, 2017; Tummala-Narra, 2016). But rather than focusing on erogenous zones and psychosexual stages, Horney emphasized the role of social environment, particularly the family. She believed that inadequate parenting can create feelings of

**collective unconscious** According to Jung, the universal experiences of humankind passed from generation to generation.

**archetypes** Primal images, patterns of thought, and story lines stored in the collective unconscious, with themes that may be found in art, literature, music, dreams, and religions.

**TABLE 10.3** "The Neo-Freudians"

**Alfred Adler**
- Rejected Freud's notion that personality is primarily shaped by unconscious processes.
- Adler's *individual psychology* suggests that personality is strongly influenced by the drive to conquer feelings of inferiority.
- Birth order plays a role in personality development.

**Carl Gustav Jung**
- Agreed with Freud that unconscious processes are critical to personality development, but did not share his focus on sexuality and aggression.
- Jung's *analytic psychology* emphasized the importance of growth, self-understanding, and spiritual development over the life span.
- Personality is made up of the personal conscious, the *personal unconscious*, and the *collective unconscious*.

**Karen Horney**
- Agreed with Freud that childhood is an important time for personality development, but dismissed his sexist approach.
- Relationships between children and caregivers are paramount, and poor parenting can lead to helplessness and isolation, or *basic anxiety*.
- Men envy women's ability to bear and breast-feed children.

Not all of Freud's students completely embraced his approach. Alfred Adler, Carl Gustav Jung, Karen Horney, and others branched off on their own theoretical paths. Photos (top to bottom): Imagno/Hulton Archive/Getty Images; World History Archive/Ann Ronan Collection/AGE Fotostock; Bettmann/Getty Images.

helplessness and isolation, or *basic anxiety* (Horney, 1945). Horney suggested that people deal with this anxiety using three strategies: moving toward people (looking for affection and acceptance), moving away from people (looking for isolation and self-sufficiency), or moving against people (looking to control others). A balance of these three strategies is important for psychological stability and healthy personality development (Kaufman, 2020). A strong critic of Freud's sexist view of the female psyche, Horney pointed out that women are not jealous of the penis itself, but rather what it represents in terms of power and status in society. Horney (1926/1967) also proposed that boys and men can envy women's ability to bear and breast-feed children (**TABLE 10.3**). In many respects, Horney was ahead of her time. Not only did she resist the sexist culture that dominated the field; she recognized that children need to feel secure in their relationships with caregivers—a key concept of attachment theory (Ludden, 2021).

## Freud's Legacy: It's Complicated

Freud's psychoanalytic theory was groundbreaking, and it led to a variety of extensions and permutations through neo-Freudians such as Erikson, Adler, Jung, and Horney. His work is considered among the most important in the field of personality development, but his legacy extends far beyond (Wertheimer & Puente, 2020). Although some of his ideas had already been expressed by others, Freud brought them together in a unified theory (Ludden, 2021). He called attention to the existence of infant sexuality at a time when sex was a forbidden topic of conversation, recognized the importance of infancy and early childhood in the unfolding of personality, and appreciated the universal stages of human development. Psychoanalysis helps us understand that the "self has depth; that the complexity of the psyche and of human existence are not an impediment to living a good life, but are the source of our identity" (Strenger, 2015, p. 304).

Despite these key contributions (and some evidence that Freud's system of psychotherapy works for certain people), many scientists consider Freud's work to be unscientific (Horgan, 2017). Freud's theories are virtually impossible to prove wrong and can be used to explain most any human behavior (Shea, n.d.), both characteristics of pseudoscience (Chapter 0; Stanovich, 2019). Had Freud's theories been more amenable to scientific study, perhaps they would have earned him a Nobel Prize in Physiology or Medicine. He was nominated 12 times, but never granted this high honor (Nobelprize.org, 2009; Shaw, 2016).

Critics also contend that Freudian theory fails to appreciate the importance of development beyond childhood, overemphasizes the role of sexuality, and places too much weight on the unconscious forces guiding behavior. His theory is based on a biased, **nonrepresentative sample** consisting of middle- and upper-class Viennese women and himself. Finally, Freud's theory is male-centered and assumes that women are inferior in their "character development" and should accept their "passive position in a world that is male-dominated" (Tummala-Narra, 2016, p. 18).

### CONNECTIONS

In **Chapter 1,** we introduced a form of descriptive research called the case study. Freud's case studies (and all case studies) are based on isolated cases rather than representative samples. Therefore, their findings cannot be generalized to the larger population.

## ▶▶▶ SHOW WHAT YOU KNOW

1. Freud's _____ includes three levels: conscious, preconscious, and unconscious.
   A. structural model of the mind
   B. developmental model
   C. individual psychology
   D. topographical model of the mind

2. According to Freud, all children go through _____ stages as they mature into adulthood. If conflicts are not resolved, a person may suffer from a _____.

3. How did the theories of the neo-Freudians differ from Freud's psychoanalytic theory with regard to personality development?

✓ CHECK YOUR ANSWERS AT THE BACK OF THE BOOK.

# Humanistic, Learning, and Trait Theories

**ON A POSITIVE PATH**    After Saifa's testes were removed and he began taking female hormones, doctors expected (or hoped) he would blossom into a lovely young woman. But as Saifa recalls, "I did not succumb to the pressure to be more feminine, but actually gravitated toward masculinity" (Wall, 2015, p. 118). He excelled in school and eventually became a leader at Williams College, spearheading campus demonstrations against police brutality and anti-gay hate crimes. A few years after graduating, Saifa decided to make the biological and social transition to manhood; he changed his name to Sean Saifa Wall, began taking testosterone, and underwent a double mastectomy.

Saifa had assumed control of his body and his life like never before, yet he could not shake the feelings of loneliness and self-hatred. To do this, he would need to confront a lifetime of trauma, which included the loss of his father—first to prison and then to AIDS—and life-changing medical interventions that occurred before he was old enough to give informed consent. Saifa courageously faced these traumas by going to psychotherapy and enrolling in a 12-step recovery program for sex addiction.

Since then, Saifa has been on a journey to heal himself and help others. Through his writing, public speaking, and work with Rooted in Research (a company he founded), Saifa has established himself as a leading intersex activist. In 2016 he cofounded the Intersex Justice Project (IJP), which "seeks the end of medically invasive and unnecessary surgeries in the United States that target intersex

Courtesy Sean Saifa Wall.

**Every Body Is Beautiful**
Saifa advocates for the legal rights of children with intersex traits. "Accepting myself as intersex and advocating for intersex people and children, I really put forward that our bodies are our mosaic," Saifa says. "There is no such thing as a 'normal body'. . . . This variation is what makes us, as a species, beautiful."

children and adolescents by empowering intersex people of color to advance that change" (IJP, n.d., para. 1). "We had our first protest in front of Lurie Children's Hospital in October 2017, and less than three years later, in July 2020, Lurie Children's Hospital was the first hospital in the United States to issue an apology for the harm that was caused to intersex people and declared a moratorium on intersex genital surgeries for six months," Saifa says. There were some caveats Saifa did not support, but he considers it a step in the right direction. "The victory was not perfect, but it was a start." Saifa currently lives in the United Kingdom, where he is examining the intersex policies of The Republic of Ireland and England as part of a fellowship sponsored by the European Commission. "I've definitely been on this journey," Saifa says, "looking outward about how I can change the world around me, but also this inward journey of how I can change the world within me."

Saifa is now in his 40s and seems to have reached a point of self-acceptance and love. "I still have more work to do and more growing to do, as we all do," he says, "but I can see that I have returned to that child of like 7 who is just in the world . . . totally free."

## The Brighter Side: Maslow and Rogers

A humanistic theorist might say that Saifa's drive to grow and improve is, and has always been, the main force shaping his personality. Leading humanists such as Abraham Maslow and Carl Rogers believed that people are innately good and in control of their destinies, and these positive aspects of human nature drive the development of personality. This perspective began gaining momentum in the 1960s and 1970s in response to the negative, **mechanistic view** of human nature apparent in the psychoanalytic and behaviorist theories. Thus, humanism is often referred to as the *Third Force* in psychology (Ludden, 2021).

**MASLOW AND PERSONALITY**    Some consider **Abraham Maslow** to be the "single person most responsible for creating humanistic psychology" (Moss, 2015, p. 13). As a humanist, Maslow believed that psychologists should study human creativity, growth, and healthy functioning, not just mental illness and maladaptive personality traits. He was particularly interested in *self-actualizers*, or people who are continually seeking to reach their fullest potential (Compton, 2018; TABLE **10.4**).

### CONNECTIONS

The behaviorists, presented in **Chapters 1** and **5,** were only interested in measuring observable behaviors. They suggested that our behaviors are shaped by input from the environment, and thus we are at the mercy of forces beyond our control. The humanists challenged this position.

### CONNECTIONS

In **Chapter 9,** we presented Maslow's hierarchy of needs. According to Maslow, behaviors are motivated by both physiological and psychological needs. These needs are considered universal and are ordered according to the strength of their associated drives. In addition to contributing to our understanding of motivation, Maslow helped propel psychology's humanistic movement.

**TABLE 10.4    Are You a Self-Actualizer?**

| Tendencies | Characteristics | Example |
|---|---|---|
| Realistic perceptions | Nonjudgmental, objective, and acutely aware of others | An individual who is empathetic and unbiased |
| Acceptance of self, others, and nature | Patient with weaknesses of self, others, and society | Someone who is accepting of others |
| Spontaneity and creativeness | Original, flexible, and willing to learn from mistakes | Someone who is self-sufficient, flexible, and spontaneous |
| Independent and private | Not reliant on others, able to enjoy time alone | A person with a strong sense of self, who doesn't need approval from others |
| Peak experiences | Has moments of ecstasy and transcendence | A highly spiritual individual who experiences intense happiness in day-to-day activities |
| Social interest and fellowship | Empathic and sympathetic toward others | A person who is devoted to helping others |
| Autonomous and resistant to enculturation | Independent and free from cultural pressures | An individual who is self-sufficient and resists social pressure |

According to Maslow, "self-actualizers" are people who continually strive to achieve their maximum potential. Listed here are common traits and examples of self-actualizers. Perhaps some of these qualities characterize you. Information from Schultz and Schultz (2017).

Photofest.

**Too Much of a Good Thing?**

*Schitt's Creek* character Moira Rose (played by Catherine O'Hara) may not be the most attentive mother, but she adores and showers praise on her son David (Dan Levy). Constant praise and other attempts to boost a child's self-esteem might foster narcissism, but researchers suggest this outcome can be avoided: "The development of self-esteem without narcissism can be cultivated through realistic feedback (rather than inflated praise), a focus on growth (rather than on outperforming others), and unconditional regard (rather than regard that is conditional)" (Brummelman & Sedikides, 2020, p. 83).

**LO 6**  Discuss Rogers' view of self-concept, ideal self, and unconditional positive regard.

**ROGERS AND PERSONALITY**    Like Maslow, Carl Rogers had great faith in the essential goodness of people and their ability to make sound choices (Rogers, 1979). Humanistic theory was espoused by many in Rogers' era, but he was able to synthesize its ideas into a coherent theory of personality and create a new client-centered approach to psychotherapy (Ludden, 2021). According to Rogers, we all have an innate urge to move toward situations and people that will help us grow and move away from those that could inhibit growth. This tendency toward self-enhancement begins in infancy and continues throughout life (Murphy & Joseph, 2016). We should trust our ability to find happiness and mental balance, that is, to be *fully functioning*, and strive to actively experience life, according to Rogers. At the same time, we must also be sensitive to the needs of others.

Rogers highlighted the importance of **self-concept,** which refers to knowledge of one's strengths, abilities, behavior patterns, and temperament. Problems arise when the self-concept is *incongruent* with, or does not correspond to, a person's experiences in the world (Rogers, 1959). If an individual believes they are kind and sociable but they fail to get along with most people in their life, this incongruence will produce tension and confusion. Rogers also proposed that people often develop an **ideal self,** which is the self-concept they fervently strive to achieve. As suggested above, problems emerge when the ideal self is unattainable or incongruent with the self-concept (Rogers, 1959). We will discuss this topic further in Chapter 14.

Like Freud and Horney, Rogers believed caregivers play a vital role in the development of personality. Ideally, caregivers show **unconditional positive regard,** or total acceptance of children regardless of their behavior. According to Rogers, people need to feel totally accepted and valued for who they are, not what they do. Caregivers who place too much emphasis on rules, morals, and values, ignoring children's innate goodness, can cause them to experience *conditions of worth*. In other words, children feel loved by their parents only if they act in accordance with their wishes. What happens if parents withhold interest and affection when kids misbehave?

## Relationships

I LOVE YOU . . . WHEN YOU DO WHAT I WANT

Researchers have explored the long-term impact of *parental conditional regard,* which "involves providing or withdrawing affection to motivate children to do what the parents want" (Moller et al., 2019, p. 35). This parenting approach might be conceived as the opposite of showing unconditional positive regard. Children who experience this kind of treatment tend to feel less securely attached to their parents, and these feelings may persist, contaminating their adult relationships. As one study found, college students who said their parents used this approach reported being less content in their current relationships. These students were inclined to believe their romantic partners were using the same type of conditional regard their parents had employed, and they felt less securely attached (Moller et al., 2019).

**HOW PARENTS CAN INFLUENCE THEIR CHILDREN'S FUTURE RELATIONSHIPS.**

If you are a parent or intend to become one, keep this in mind: When children feel their behaviors or emotions are being judged as bad or wrong, they feel unworthy and may try to hide or repress them. As caregivers, it is important to show children that we value them all the time, not just when they obey and act the way we want.

**self-concept**  The knowledge an individual has about their strengths, abilities, behavior patterns, and temperament.

**ideal self**  The self-concept a person strives for and fervently wishes to achieve.

**unconditional positive regard**  According to Rogers, the total acceptance or valuing of a person, regardless of behavior.

**HUMANISTIC THEORIES: WHAT'S THE TAKEAWAY?**    The humanistic perspective has led to a more positive and balanced view of human nature, influencing approaches to parenting, education, and research. Its legacy is alive and well in the emerging field of **positive psychology** (Seligman, 2019). From psychotherapy to research on human strengths and optimal functioning, we can see the "resurgence" of the humanists' work in the field (DeRobertis, 2016).

Despite its far-reaching and positive impact, the humanistic approach has limitations. For humanistic and psychoanalytic theories alike, creating operational definitions can be challenging. How can you use the experimental method to test a subjective approach whose concepts are open to interpretation (Schultz & Schultz, 2017)? Imagine submitting a research proposal that included two randomly assigned groups of children: one group whose parents were instructed to show them *unconditional positive regard* and another group whose parents were told to instill *conditions of worth*. The proposal would never amount to a real study, not only because it raises ethical issues, but also because it would be impossible to control the experimental conditions. And while it is important to recognize that humans have great potential to grow and move forward, we should not discount the developmental impact of early experiences. Finally, some have argued that the humanistic approach almost ignores the negative aspects of human nature evident in war, greed, abuse, and aggression (Burger, 2015). This may be partly true, but some humanistic psychologists are "inspired by the challenges" presented by humanity's darker side (Stern, 2016, p. xii).

Next, we will explore how personality is influenced by forces in the outside world. How do you think your interactions with the environment have shaped your personality?

## Can Personality Be Learned?

**NANA LIVES ON**    Many years have passed since Saifa's therapist asked him the crucial question: "When did you realize love was not possible?" Even today, these words strike Saifa in a deep and vulnerable place. But he no longer falls apart—perhaps because he knows that love is possible. There is no doubt he pours love into the world, advocating for the rights of intersex children and others who don't fit neatly into society's male and female gender categories. For those in his close circle, Saifa demonstrates love by cooking and hosting—making sure they are comfortable and happy. He learned these nurturing behaviors from his grandmother, who passed away in 2003.

"One of my role models was my Nana," Saifa says. "She didn't really talk much, she was kind of shy . . . . but she was an amazing cook." Preparing meals and cleaning were the ways she expressed her love. "To speak to her history, she was a domestic worker for most of her life, so that's what she knew," Saifa explains. "She showed her love by doing rather than saying."

**LO 7**  Use the behavioral perspective to explain personality development.

Saifa's caretaking behaviors have been shaped by years of observational learning—watching and following his role model, Nana. These same behaviors have been strengthened through operant conditioning. When Saifa's friends praise the meals he makes, this provides positive reinforcement for his cooking and nurturing. These learned behaviors follow a predictable pattern, and therefore constitute part of Saifa's personality. According to the behavioral perspective, personality is shaped by a lifetime of learning.

**CONNECTIONS**

In **Chapter 1,** we described positive psychology as a relatively new approach. The humanists' optimism struck the right chord with many psychologists, who wondered why the field was not focusing on human strengths and virtues.

As you may recall, personality is the core set of characteristics that influence the way one thinks, acts, and feels. The behaviorist perspective focuses on just one of those elements: the way a person acts. Behaviorists view personality as a collection of behaviors, all of which have been shaped through learning: Each person "develops under a different or unique set of stimulus conditions and consequently his resulting personality becomes uniquely his own" (Lundin, 1963, p. 265). This perspective offers valuable insights on personality development, but does it overstate the importance of behavior? Critics contend that behaviorism is too simplistic; it ignores everything that is not directly observable and assumes that humans are passive and unaware of what is going on in their internal and external environments.

**LO 8** Summarize Rotter's view of personality.

**LOOKING BEYOND BEHAVIOR**  U.S. psychologist Julian Rotter (1916–2014) was an early social learning theorist who examined the ongoing dynamic between humans and their surroundings. Rotter believed that "personality is the interaction between a person and his or her environment and is dependent on a particular individual's learning experiences and life history" (Strickland, 2014, p. 546). Rotter also suggested that some aspects of personality cannot be directly observed (Rotter, 1990). He proposed several cognitive aspects of personality, including *locus of control* and *expectancy*. Locus of control refers to a pattern of beliefs about where control or responsibility resides. People with an *internal* locus of control believe that the causes of life events generally reside within them, and that they have some control over those causes. Such individuals would be inclined to say that their career success depends on how hard they work, not on luck, for example (Rotter, 1966). Those with an *external* locus of control generally believe that causes of events reside outside of them; they assign great importance to luck, fate, and other features of the environment they cannot control. Getting a job occurs when circumstances are just right and luck is on their side (Rotter, 1966). A person's locus of control refers to beliefs about the self, not about others, and it may change in response to stressors (Nowicki et al., 2018).

Rotter also explored how personality is influenced by thoughts about the future. **Expectancy** refers to the predictions we make about the outcomes and consequences of our behaviors (INFOGRAPHIC **10.2** on page 396). Suppose you have a bad meal at a restaurant. Your decision to let it go or confront the manager is based on expectancy: Do you believe complaining will lead to a free meal, or do you expect to be treated like a scam artist who doesn't want to pay the bill? In these situations, there is an interaction among expectancies, behaviors, and environmental factors.

**LO 9** Discuss Bandura's social-cognitive perspective of personality.

**BELIEFS, BEHAVIOR, AND ENVIRONMENT**  Albert Bandura also challenged the behaviorist approach, rejecting the notion that psychologists should only focus on observable behavior (Bandura, 2006). His **social-cognitive perspective** suggests that personality results from reinforcement, relationships, and other environmental factors (social) and patterns of thinking (cognitive). Our personalities are shaped by experience, and our cognitive abilities and knowledge partly result from interactions with others (Bandura, 1977b, 2006).

Bandura also pointed to the importance of **self-efficacy,** which refers to beliefs about our ability and effectiveness in reaching goals (Bandura, 1977a, 2001). People who exhibit high self-efficacy often achieve greater success at work because they are more likely to be flexible and open to new ideas (Bandura, 2006). Those who demonstrate low self-efficacy generally believe they will not succeed in a particular

**expectancy** The predictions we make about the outcomes or consequences of our behaviors.

**social-cognitive perspective** Suggests that personality results from relationships and other environmental factors (social) and patterns of thinking (cognitive).

**self-efficacy** Beliefs about our ability and effectiveness in reaching goals.

situation, regardless of their abilities or experience. Beliefs about self-efficacy are influenced by experience and may change across situations. Generally speaking, people who believe they can change and progress are more likely to persevere in difficult situations—including those presented by college (Stajkovic et al., 2018). Self-efficacy tends to grow as we succeed in our endeavors (*I have tackled tough challenges before*) and witness similar others do the same (*If they can do it, so can I!*) (Bandura & Cherry, 2020).

Beliefs play a key role in our ability to make decisions, solve problems, and deal with life's challenges. The environment, in turn, responds to our behaviors. In essence, we have internal forces (beliefs, expectations) directing our behavior, external forces (reinforcers, punishments) responding to those behaviors, and the behaviors themselves influencing our beliefs and the environment. Beliefs, behavior, and environment form a complex system that determines our behavior patterns and personality (Infographic 10.2). Bandura (1978, 1986) refers to this multidirectional interaction as **reciprocal determinism.**

Let's look at an example showing how reciprocal determinism might work. A student harbors a certain belief about themselves (*I am going to graduate with honors*). This belief influences their behavior (they study hard and reach out to instructors), which affects their environment (instructors take note of their enthusiasm and offer support). Their ambition and determination result from an ongoing interaction among cognition, behaviors, and the environment.

**SOCIAL-COGNITIVE THEORIES: WHAT'S THE TAKEAWAY?**    The social-cognitive theorists were among the first to realize that we are not just products of our environment, but dynamic agents capable of altering the environment itself. Personality is shaped by an ongoing interplay of cognitive expectancies, behaviors, and the environment. The focus on research and testable hypotheses provides a clear advantage over the psychoanalytic and humanistic theories. Some argue that these approaches minimize the importance of unconscious processes and emotional influences (Schultz & Schultz, 2017; Westen, 1990), but overall, the inclusion of cognition and social factors offers valuable ways to study and understand personality.

# What Are Personality Traits?

Earlier in the chapter, we used some words to describe Saifa's personality— "vivacious," "loud," "charismatic," "direct," and "empathetic." All these might be considered examples of **traits,** the relatively stable properties that describe elements of personality. Unlike the theories presented thus far, which focus on how and why personality develops, the **trait theories** center on describing personality and predicting behaviors.

**LO 10**  Distinguish trait theories from other personality theories.

**ALLPORT IDENTIFIES 4,504 TRAITS**    One of the first trait theorists was U.S. psychologist Gordon Allport (1897–1967), who compiled a comprehensive list of traits to describe personality. The goal was to operationalize the terminology used in personality research, as researchers need to agree on definitions when studying the same topic. (Suppose two psychologists are investigating a trait called "vivacious"; they will have an easier time comparing results if they use the same definition.) Allport and his colleague carefully reviewed *Webster's New International Dictionary* (1925) and identified 17,953 words (among some 400,000 entries) that were "descriptive of personality or personal behavior"

**The Power of Self-Efficacy**
Fashion model Jillian Mercado appears at the 2018 Webby Awards in New York City. Mercado has muscular dystrophy, but she hasn't let her disability stand in the way of a modeling career. This young woman, who has appeared in ad campaigns for Diesel and Beyoncé, seems to have a high level of self-efficacy, or belief in her ability to reach goals. As she has said, "[Having a disability] doesn't stop me from doing anything. It's an honour and a privilege to show people that it's ok to be yourself and still do what you love" (United Nations, 2019, para. 3).

Gary Gershoff/Getty Images.

**reciprocal determinism** According to Bandura, multidirectional interactions among cognition, behaviors, and the environment.

**traits** The relatively stable properties that describe elements of personality.

**trait theories** Theories that focus on personality dimensions and their influence on behavior; can be used to predict behaviors.

# The Social-Cognitive Perspective on Personality

Social-cognitive theorists rejected behaviorists' exclusive focus on observable behavior. Acknowledging that personality may be shaped through learning, social-cognitive theorists such as Albert Bandura also emphasized the roles of cognition and environmental influences on behavior. Bandura's theory of reciprocal determinism shows how cognition, behaviors, and the environment all interact to determine our personality.

*"Good job!"* — Child is praised for reading quietly.

★★★ — Child receives attention for effort in school.

🎓 — Child is rewarded for school achievement.

Behaviorists believe personality is the compilation of behaviors shaped through a lifetime of learning. A child who receives reinforcement for studying and effort in school will repeat this behavior, eventually exhibiting the personality characteristic "studious."

## cognition

Thinking about behaviors and what they have led to in the past creates expectancies, predictions about what future outcomes will result from a behavior. When we recognize that past efforts to study usually resulted in good grades, we will expect that studying will lead to good grades in the future. Bandura calls this learned expectation of success *self-efficacy*.

*I succeed because I am a studious person.*

*I will apply to college because I can succeed there.*

*I get good grades when I study, so I will continue to do this.*

*I am in college, so I know I can handle a busy schedule like other college students.*

**EXPECTANCIES INFLUENCE BEHAVIOR.**

**EXPECTANCIES INFLUENCE THE ENVIRONMENT YOU SEEK OUT.**

**ENVIRONMENT INFLUENCES EXPECTANCIES.**

*When I study, I get good grades.*

**PRIOR EXPERIENCES CREATE EXPECTANCIES.**

## environment

*I'm a college student now, so I need to spend more time studying.*

## behavior

Reinforced behaviors become more consistent over time. When an instructor praises our participation in class, that reinforcement will lead us to participate again. We also learn by observing others' behaviors. If our classmates form a study group that helps them better understand the material, we may learn to adopt that technique.

**ENVIRONMENT INFLUENCES BEHAVIOR.**

**BEHAVIOR INFLUENCES ENVIRONMENT.**

The environment can include the college you choose, the major you select, the classes you enroll in, and also the culture where you are a student. For example, in Chinese classrooms, struggle is assumed to be part of the learning process. However, in Western classrooms, struggle is often seen as a sign of lower ability (Li, 2005; Schleppenbach et al., 2007). The culture you live in—your environment—can influence how you think about your own skills and behaviors, and how hard you work at something that is difficult for you.

*I study hard and am a successful student, so I've chosen to go to college.*

(Allport & Odbert, 1936, p. 24). The list contained terms considered personal traits (such as "acrobatical" and "zealous"), temporary states ("woozy" and "thrilled"), social evaluations ("swine" and "outlandish"), and words that were metaphorical and doubtful ("mortal" and "middle-aged"). Most relevant to personality were the personal traits, of which they identified 4,504—a little over 1% of all entries in the dictionary. Surely, this long list could be condensed, reduced, or classified to make it more manageable. Enter Raymond Cattell.

**CATTELL NARROWS THE LIST**    British-born psychologist Raymond Cattell (1905–1998) proposed grouping the long list of personality traits into two major categories: surface traits and source traits (Cattell, 1950). **Surface traits** are the easily observable personality characteristics commonly used to describe people: *Josie is quiet. Amir is friendly.* **Source traits** are the foundational qualities that give rise to surface traits. For example, "extraversion" is a source trait, and the surface traits it produces may include "warm," "gregarious," and "assertive." There are thousands of surface traits but only a few source traits. Cattell (1950) proposed that source traits are the product of both heredity and environment (nature and nurture), and surface traits are the "combined action of several source traits" (p. 34).

Cattell also condensed the list of surface traits into a much smaller set of 171. Realizing that some of these surface traits would be **correlated**, he used a statistical procedure known as *factor analysis* to group them into a smaller set of dimensions according to common underlying properties. With factor analysis, Cattell was able to produce a list of 16 personality factors, or dimensions. These 16 factors can be considered primary source traits (**FIGURE 10.2**).

**EYSENCK PROPOSES 3 TRAITS**    Hans Eysenck (AHY-sengk; 1916–1997), a German born psychologist, continued to develop our understanding of source traits, proposing three personality dimensions: introversion–extraversion (E), neuroticism (N), and psychoticism (P).

People high on the *extraversion* end of the introversion–extraversion (E) dimension tend to display a marked degree of sociability and are outgoing and active with others in their environment. Those on the *introversion* end tend to be quiet and careful and enjoy time alone. Having high *neuroticism* (N) typically goes hand-in-hand with being restless, moody, and excitable, while low neuroticism means being calm, reliable, and emotionally stable. People high on the *psychoticism* dimension tend to be cold, impersonal, and antisocial, while those at the opposite end of this dimension are warm, caring, and empathetic. (The psychoticism dimension is not related to psychosis, described in Chapter 13.)

In addition to identifying these dimensions, Eysenck worked diligently to unearth their biological basis. For example, he proposed a direct relationship between behaviors associated with the introversion–extraversion dimension and the reticular formation (Eysenck, 1967). According to Eysenck (1967, 1990), introverted people display higher reactivity in their **reticular formation**. Because they have higher arousal levels, introverts are more likely to react to stimuli, and thus develop certain coping patterns—being more careful or restrained, for example. An extravert has lower levels of arousal, and thus is less reactive to stimuli. Extraverts seek stimulation, so they tend to be more impulsive and outgoing.

Eysenck contributed a great deal to our understanding of personality, but he has been accused of serious scientific misconduct. Scholars have alleged he manipulated data, engaged in unethical collaboration with the tobacco industry, and "systematically and repeatedly published false science" (Marks, 2019, p. 409; Pelosi, 2019).

| 1. | Reserved | ⟷ | Outgoing |
| 2. | Concrete thinker | ⟷ | Abstract thinker |
| 3. | Affected by feelings | ⟷ | Emotionally stable |
| 4. | Submissive | ⟷ | Dominant |
| 5. | Serious | ⟷ | Happy-go-lucky |
| 6. | Expedient | ⟷ | Conscientious |
| 7. | Timid | ⟷ | Bold |
| 8. | Tough-minded | ⟷ | Sensitive |
| 9. | Trusting | ⟷ | Suspicious |
| 10. | Practical | ⟷ | Imaginative |
| 11. | Forthright | ⟷ | Shrewd |
| 12. | Self-assured | ⟷ | Insecure |
| 13. | Conservative | ⟷ | Experimenting |
| 14. | Group-dependent | ⟷ | Self-sufficient |
| 15. | Undisciplined | ⟷ | Controlled |
| 16. | Relaxed | ⟷ | Tense |

**FIGURE 10.2**

**Cattell's 16 Personality Factors**
Raymond Cattell produced personality profiles by measuring where people fell along each of these 16 dimensions, or personality factors. The ends of the dimensions represent polar extremes ("reserved" versus "outgoing," for example).
Information from Cattell (1973b) and Cattell et al. (1970).

**CONNECTIONS**

In **Chapter 1,** we described a correlation as a relationship between two variables. Here, we mention factor analysis, which examines the relationships among an entire set of variables.

**CONNECTIONS**

In **Chapter 2,** we described the reticular formation, a network of neurons responsible for levels of arousal. By sifting through sensory data headed toward the cortex, the reticular formation helps you selectively attend to important information and ignore what's irrelevant. Eysenck suggested that the reticular formation is also associated with the introversion–extraversion dimension of personality.

**surface traits**  Easily observable characteristics that derive from source traits.

**source traits**  Basic underlying or foundational characteristics of personality.

Some journals have retracted Eysenck's papers, others have issued statements conveying "concern," but his research continues to be cited (O'Grady, 2020). This controversy is ongoing and important to keep an eye on.

The theories of Allport, Cattell, and Eysenck paved the way for the trait theories commonly used today. Let's take a look at one of the most popular models.

**LO 11** Identify evidence supporting the biological basis of the five-factor model of personality.

**THE BIG FIVE** The **five-factor model of personality,** also known as the Big Five, is a current trait approach for explaining personality (McCrae & Costa, 1987; McCrae et al., 2013; Soto, 2019). This model, developed using factor analysis, indicates there are five factors, or dimensions, to describe personality. There is not complete consensus on the names for these factors, but trait theorists generally agree on the following labels: (1) openness to experience, (2) conscientiousness, (3) extraversion, (4) agreeableness, and (5) neuroticism (de Raad & Mlačić, 2017; McCrae et al., 2013; Soto, 2019). Openness is the degree to which a person is willing to try new experiences. Conscientiousness refers to one's organizational tendencies and attention to detail. The extraversion and neuroticism dimensions are similar to those proposed by Eysenck: Extraversion refers to degree of sociability and outgoingness, while neuroticism connotes emotional stability (the extent to which a person is calm, secure, and even-tempered). Agreeableness indicates how trusting and easygoing a person is. To remember these factors, students sometimes use the mnemonic OCEAN: Openness, Conscientiousness, Extraversion, Agreeableness, and Neuroticism (**FIGURE 10.3**).

Empirical support for this model has been established using cross-cultural testing, with people in more than 50 cultures exhibiting these five dimensions (Allik et al., 2017; McCrae et al., 2000, 2005; McCrae et al., 2010). The five-factor model of personality "appears to be a universal aspect of human nature" (McCrae et al., 2013, p. 17).

One possible explanation for these cross-cultural similarities is that the five dimensions are rooted in biology (Allik & McCrae, 2004; McCrae et al., 2000). That is, they are influenced by genes, brain structures, and other biological factors—not just culture and experience (Karwowski & Lebuda, 2016; Riccelli et al., 2017). In fact, three decades of **twin and adoption studies** point to a genetic basis for the five factors (Boomsma et al., 2018; McCrae et al., 2000; Yamagata et al., 2006), with openness to experience showing the greatest degree of heritability (McCrae et al., 2000; **TABLE 10.5**). Heritability is the degree to which heredity is responsible for a particular characteristic or trait in the population.

**CONNECTIONS**

**Chapter 7** describes twin studies, which indicate that genes play an important role in intelligence. Identical twins share 100% of their genes at conception, fraternal twins share about 50% of their genes, and adopted siblings are genetically very different. Comparing personality traits among these siblings can show the relative importance of genes and the environment.

**FIGURE 10.3**
**The Five-Factor Model of Personality**

The mnemonic OCEAN will help you remember these factors.

Information from McCrae and Costa (1990).

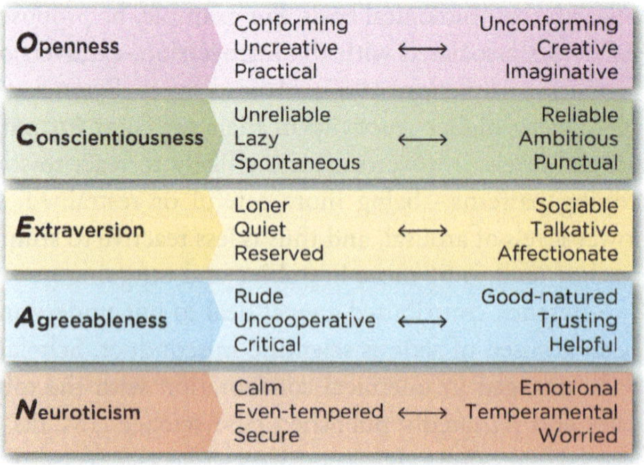

| **O**penness | Conforming Uncreative Practical | ⟷ | Unconforming Creative Imaginative |
|---|---|---|---|
| **C**onscientiousness | Unreliable Lazy Spontaneous | ⟷ | Reliable Ambitious Punctual |
| **E**xtraversion | Loner Quiet Reserved | ⟷ | Sociable Talkative Affectionate |
| **A**greeableness | Rude Uncooperative Critical | ⟷ | Good-natured Trusting Helpful |
| **N**euroticism | Calm Even-tempered Secure | ⟷ | Emotional Temperamental Worried |

**five-factor model of personality** A trait approach to explaining personality, including dimensions of openness to experience, conscientiousness, extraversion, agreeableness, and neuroticism; also known as the "Big Five."

**TABLE 10.5** Heritability and the Big Five

| Big Five Personality Dimensions | Heritability |
| --- | --- |
| Openness | .61 |
| Conscientiousness | .44 |
| Extraversion | .53 |
| Agreeableness | .41 |
| Neuroticism | .47 |

Listed here are heritability estimates for the Big Five personality characteristics. Heritability is the degree to which heredity is responsible for a particular characteristic in the population. Information from Boomsma et al. (2018) and Jang, Livesley, and Vernon (1996).

Further evidence for the biological basis of the five factors comes from longitudinal studies, which suggest that these characteristics are generally stable over time, for periods as long as 40 years (Kandler et al., 2010; McCrae et al., 2000, 2013; Terracciano et al., 2006). This implies that nature shapes personality more than nurture. The environment does play a role, however. This is evidenced by the fact that the five factors, and the characteristics associated with them, may change over the life span (Sakaki et al., 2018; Specht et al., 2011). As people age, they tend to score higher on conscientiousness (Diehl & Wahl, 2020). They also seem to become happier and more easygoing as the years go by, displaying more positive attitudes (Marsh et al., 2013).

Additional support for the biological underpinnings of the five factors comes from animal studies. For example, researchers have found that some squid respond to stimuli "boldly or aggressively," while others act more shyly (Sinn & Moltschaniwskyj, 2005, p. 105). Could this mean squid display different degrees of extraversion and introversion? Others suggest that dog personalities can be described using dimensions such as aggression and attention seeking, which appear to have a genetic basis (MacLean et al., 2019; Pennisi, 2019). A variety of animals seem to display personality characteristics that resemble those observed in humans (Sinn & Moltschaniwskyj, 2005; Weiss et al., 2017). *Scientific American* takes a closer look at this phenomenon below:

# KILLER WHALES AND CHIMPANZEES HAVE SIMILAR PERSONALITIES

Animals of both species can be assessed using many of the "big five" factors used to describe humans.

Anybody who has taken an undergraduate psychology course or filled out one of those online tests is probably familiar with the "big five" personality traits: openness, conscientiousness, extraversion, agreeableness, and neuroticism. For example, if you identify with the statement "I talk to a lot of different people at parties," you might score high on extraversion. An individual's personality is thought to be fairly stable by adulthood, and the idea that it can be measured by just a handful of factors goes back at least a century.

But humans are not the only species whose personalities can be quantified along these lines; caregivers in zoos, sanctuaries and other captive environments commonly assess the personalities of animals, based on months or years spent observing and

### Animals with Personality

There appears to be some overlap in the personality traits observed in humans, killer whales, and chimpanzees (Goldman, 2019). Some of these traits appear to be associated with longevity. For example, a study of chimpanzees found that males rated high in agreeableness—"the personality trait characterized by low aggression and positive social interactions such as cooperation"—tend to live longer than their less agreeable peers (Altschul et al., 2018, p. 2).

interacting with them. The specifics vary among species (for example, newts can be scored for their libidinousness and zebra finches and rhesus macaques for boldness), but the underlying notion that personality can be described by a small set of factors remains the same. Now research suggests that animals as widely divergent as chimpanzees and killer whales have surprisingly similar personality profiles.

A team of researchers led by University of Edinburgh primatologist Drew Altschul amassed a quarter-century of chimp personality surveys. After passing data from 538 individual chimpanzees through a statistical model, Altschul and his team found that chimpanzee personality can be reduced to the same five traits applied to humans—plus a sixth known as dominance, which reflects the apes' "competitive prowess [and] social competence," they write. The results were published online [. . .] in *eLife*.

That chimpanzees and humans have similar personality profiles makes some sense, given that the two species are so closely related. But what about our more distant cousins? Primatologist Yulán Úbeda of the University of Girona in Catalonia was recently busy preparing a lecture for staffers at the Loro Parque zoo in the Canary Islands. She decided to see if any personality research had been conducted with killer whales, one of the zoo's main attractions. "Not only were there no studies of personality in killer whales," but the only such cetacean studies she could find were limited to bottlenose dolphins, she says—and these did not utilize statistical techniques to reduce those personality metrics to a handful of factors. Úbeda asked trainers and researchers caring for 24 killer whales at three facilities in Spain and the U.S. to complete a survey originally designed to assess chimpanzee personality (though not the same survey Altschul used).

Killer whale personalities cluster into four traits, according to Úbeda's study, which was published [. . .] in the *Journal of Comparative Psychology*. The first three are extraversion, dominance, and carefulness; the fourth can be thought of as a combination of conscientiousness and agreeableness. When Úbeda compared these findings with the results of her own earlier research with chimpanzees, she found that the personality structures of the two species were quite similar (even though chimpanzee personality has six factors rather than four).

Given the differences in both habitat and neuroanatomy, not to mention the 94 million years that have passed since chimps and whales shared a common ancestor, Úbeda says she had not expected the two animals' personality traits to align so well with each other—or with those of humans. Still, "there's something about their social environment that has created this similarity in personality," says Justin Gregg, senior research associate at the Dolphin Communication Project, who was not involved in the study. Indeed, he explains, chimps and killer whales are both known for complex cognition, large brains relative to body size, and cultural learning—also features of our own species—and have similar societal structures as well. [. . .] Jason G. Goldman. **Reproduced**

## Put Your Heads Together

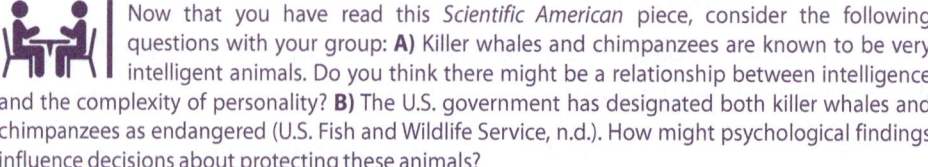 Now that you have read this *Scientific American* piece, consider the following questions with your group: **A)** Killer whales and chimpanzees are known to be very intelligent animals. Do you think there might be a relationship between intelligence and the complexity of personality? **B)** The U.S. government has designated both killer whales and chimpanzees as endangered (U.S. Fish and Wildlife Service, n.d.). How might psychological findings influence decisions about protecting these animals?

**TRAITS ARE US** Personality traits impact human life in ways you may find surprising. Would you believe that politicians with less agreeable personalities are more likely to prevail? As disheartening as it sounds, sometimes "nice guys finish last" (Joly et al., 2019). Another aspect of personality, conscientiousness, has been associated with certain measures of success, including income level and life satisfaction (Duckworth et al., 2012). Even the personality traits of the people in your life may impact you. One study suggests that marrying a conscientious person could benefit your career; conscientious spouses support their partners' professional lives by taking care of household chores and by modeling conscientious behaviors, for example (Solomon & Jackson, 2014). How might such information be useful in everyday life?

**HIS TRAITS, HER TRAITS?**    Men and women appear to differ with respect to the five factors, although there is not total agreement on how. A review of studies from 55 nations reported that, across cultures, women score higher on conscientiousness, extraversion, agreeableness, and neuroticism (Schmitt et al., 2008). Men, on the other hand, seem to demonstrate greater openness to experience. These disparities are not extreme, however; the variation within males and within females is greater than the differences between the sexes. Larger distinctions emerge when broad personality traits are broken down into sub traits, or "facets." For example, men and women are relatively close in their levels of extraversion, but we see greater contrast when we zero in on certain elements of extraversion: Men tend to be more "assertive" while women tend to be more "sociable and friendly" (Kaufman, 2019, para. 7).

Would you have predicted that women are, on average, more sociable and friendly? Research suggests that some gender stereotypes do indeed contain a kernel of truth (Costa et al., 2001; Kajonius & Johnson, 2018; Terracciano et al., 2005). Let's find out if this is the case for cultural stereotypes as well.

## ACROSS THE WORLD

### DOES CULTURE INFLUENCE PERSONALITY?

Have you heard the old joke about European stereotypes? It goes like this: In heaven, the chefs are French, the mechanics German, the lovers Italian, the police officers British, and the bankers Swiss. In hell, the cooks are British, the police officers German, the mechanics French, the lovers Swiss, and the bankers Italian (Mulvey, 2006). This joke plays upon what psychologists might call "national stereotypes," or preconceived notions about the personalities of people belonging to certain cultures. Are such stereotypes accurate?

**PLEASE LEAVE YOUR STEREOTYPES AT THE BORDER!**

To get to the bottom of this question, a group of researchers used personality tests to assess the Big Five traits of nearly 4,000 people from 49 cultures. When they compared the results of the personality tests to national stereotypes, they found no evidence that the stereotypes mirrored reality (Terracciano et al., 2005). Subsequent research supports this conclusion (McCrae et al., 2013), though some scholars contend that studies on national stereotypes have been methodologically flawed (Hřebíčková et al., 2018). The bottom line is that national stereotypes are potentially inaccurate, and the type of thinking that drives them may have "far-reaching political consequences" (Sierp & Karner, 2017, para. 3). How do you think these stereotypes might impact relationships between nations, or between host countries and their immigrant communities?

**TRAIT THEORIES: WHAT'S THE TAKEAWAY?**    As you can see from the example above, trait theories have facilitated research that sheds light on issues that might appear unrelated to psychology, like politics. Trait theory research can also lead to new insights on psychological phenomena, including psychological disorders. For example, we can understand personality traits as existing on a continuum, with "normal" traits at one end and those associated with disorders at the other (DeYoung et al., 2016). This approach may help combat the stigma associated with mental illness, because it reveals that we all share these traits to some extent.

**Mountains or Beach?**
When asked if they prefer the mountains or the beach, introverts tend to choose the mountains, while extroverts gravitate toward the beach. Mountains are perceived as quiet places to unwind, and beaches are associated with social activity (Oishi et al., 2015).

Like all perspectives in psychology, trait theories have limitations. One major criticism is that they fail to capture the nuances of personality. Suppose you have a group of people who are equivalent with respect to all five factors, yet each individual has a unique personality. The "nuanced variations" responsible for these distinctions are still being investigated (Mõttus et al., 2019). Trait theories may also be limited in their ability to explain the origins of personality. What aspects of personality are innate, and which are shaped by the environment? How do unconscious processes, motivations, and development influence personality? Another issue with trait theories is their tendency to underestimate environmental influences on personality. As Austrian-born U.S. psychologist Walter Mischel (1930–2018) pointed out, external circumstances can affect the way traits manifest themselves (Mischel & Shoda, 1995). An individual who is high on the openness factor may be nonconforming in college, but after they join the military, their nonconformity assumes a new form. Critics also contend that the samples used in some Big Five cross-cultural studies are not representative. If most of the study participants are college students, for instance, the sample is not necessarily representative of the larger population. Finally, there is some debate over whether the five-factor model applies to all nonindustrialized cultures (Gurven et al., 2013; van der Linden et al., 2018).

## Put Your Heads Together

In your group, **A)** discuss the personality traits presented in this section, and what it means when we say that a trait exists "on a continuum." **B)** Choose three of the traits and write a brief scenario involving a fictitious college student who possesses these traits. **C)** Team up with another group and see if you can determine the traits used in each other's case studies.

Time to wrap up our discussion of the trait theories and move on to the intriguing topic of personality assessment. How do psychologists evaluate personality, what do these tests reveal, and can we be confident in the results?

### ►►► SHOW WHAT YOU KNOW

1. Total acceptance of children regardless of their behavior is known as:
   - **A.** conditions of worth.
   - **B.** repression.
   - **C.** the real self.
   - **D.** unconditional positive regard.

2. According to _____, personality is a compilation of behaviors that have been shaped via reinforcement and other forms of learning.

3. Julian Rotter proposed several cognitive aspects of personality, including _____, or one's beliefs about where responsibility or control exists.
   - **A.** reinforcement
   - **B.** locus of control
   - **C.** expectancy
   - **D.** reinforcement value

4. Name the Big Five traits and give one piece of evidence for their biological basis.

5. The relatively stable properties that describe personality are:
   - **A.** traits.
   - **B.** expectancies.
   - **C.** reinforcement values.
   - **D.** ego defense mechanisms.

6. Reciprocal determinism refers to a complex multidirectional interaction among beliefs, behavior, and environment. Draw a diagram illustrating how reciprocal determinism explains one of your behavior patterns.

 ✓ CHECK YOUR ANSWERS AT THE BACK OF THE BOOK.

## Personality Tests

To assess personality, psychologists rely on both *subjective* and *objective* tests. Subjective assessments are based on intuition, clinical judgment, opinion, and interpretation of question responses, dreams, and other personal material. Objective assessments are less influenced by opinions, personal beliefs, expectations, and values because they are administered and evaluated using standardized procedures. Both approaches have strengths and limitations, which we will explore in the pages to come, but first let's get a handle on the qualities that render these tests effective—reliability and validity.

## Are They Reliable and Valid?

**LO 12** Explain why reliability and validity are important in personality assessment.

**Reliability** can refer to two aspects of an assessment. *Test–retest reliability* is how consistent results are when the same person takes the test more than once: Your scores should not change significantly from today to tomorrow on measures of personality. (We wouldn't expect aspects of your personality to change from day to day.) *Interrater reliability* refers to the degree of consistency across people scoring an assessment: With high interrater reliability, results are the same regardless of who scores the test. Validity is the other important quality of a personality test; a valid test is one that measures what it intends to measure. Let's say a psychologist develops an assessment for extraversion. In order for the test to be considered valid, it must yield results that are similar to already established and valid assessments of extraversion. If the test can predict future scores on other measures of extraversion, this would indicate it has *predictive validity*.

**CONNECTIONS**

In **Chapter 7,** we discussed ways to determine the reliability of intelligence tests. In addition to test–retest reliability, we can split a test in half to see if the findings of the two halves agree. This type of reliability can be determined with personality assessments as well.

## CAREER CONNECTIONS

### PERSONALITY TESTS AT WORK

Personality assessments are used in many contexts, with profound implications. Psychologists use them to get to know their clients and diagnose mental disorders. Companies and government entities may enlist psychologists to administer these tests to job applicants (Moyle & Hackston, 2018; Trent et al., 2020). *Does this person have what it takes to be a manager?* (For more information on the different roles psychologists play, see the online appendix Careers in Psychology.) Personality tests may also take place in legal settings—as one of many assessments used to evaluate the functioning of parents in custody disputes, for example (Benjamin & Kaslow, 2020; Neal et al., 2019). *Is the parent depressed? Can they care for this child?* Personality tests are not only used to describe personality; mental health professionals may use them to identify symptoms and behaviors related to psychological disorders (Chapter 13). Do you see why it's so important for these tests to be valid and reliable?

In the next section, we will explore the major types of personality assessments used by psychologists: interviews, projective personality tests, and objective personality tests. Many of these are aligned with specific perspectives (psychoanalytic or behavioral, for example), but most psychologists use an integrative approach, drawing on multiple perspectives.

## What Brings You Here Today?

Psychologists can gather a great deal of information about clients in face-to-face interviews. An unstructured, or open-ended, interview has no predetermined path, and may begin with a question such as "What brings you here today?" From there, the psychologist may gently direct the conversation in a way that helps uncover aspects of the client's personality. Semi-structured and structured **interviews**, on the other hand, employ specific paths of questioning that hinge on the respondent's answers. This format provides a more systematic means of comparing personality characteristics across individuals.

One advantage of the interview is that it allows a psychologist to see a client in a relatively natural, realistic setting. Talking with a client face-to-face, a psychologist can observe facial expressions and body language, which may offer clues about what's going on inside. There are drawbacks, however. Interview subjects may lie to the

Wavebreakmedia/Getty Images.

**Tell Me About Yourself**
Psychologists assess personality using a variety of tools, including personal interviews. These face-to-face sessions range from open-ended and exploratory to highly structured.

**CONNECTIONS**

When conducting interviews, psychologists must keep in mind that memories are malleable, a concept discussed in **Chapter 6.** They should avoid posing questions that might lead to the misinformation effect, or the tendency for new or misleading information to distort memories.

**CONNECTIONS**

In **Chapter 1,** we discussed a form of descriptive research known as the survey method. With the survey method, information is gathered using questionnaires or interviews administered on paper, in face-to-face interviews, or with digital technologies. The wording of survey questions may be biased, which can influence the way people respond. This same problem can arise with personality assessments.

interviewer (in some cases without even realizing it), spin the facts to misrepresent themselves, or share memories that are distorted or incomplete. Another possible source of error is the interviewer. Sometimes interviewers unknowingly lead the conversation in a particular direction or interpret responses in a way that reinforces their beliefs about personality. Clients can also be influenced by interviewers' nonverbal language. Finally, the **wording of questions** can have a profound influence on the answers obtained. For example, asking someone "Are you happy in your marriage?" versus "Are you unhappy in your marriage?" may not elicit the same response.

## What Do You See? Projective Tests

**LO 13**  Describe projective personality tests, and evaluate their strengths and limitations.

It's a hot summer day and you're lying in the park, gazing at the clouds. "What do you see?" you ask your friend. "I see the profile of a puppy," they reply. "That's funny," you say. "I see a clump of grapes."

How can two people look at the same image and come away with such different impressions? Some would argue that it has a lot to do with personality. The idea that personality influences perception is the premise of **projective personality tests,** which psychologists use to explore characteristics that might not be accessible through interview or observation (**INFOGRAPHIC 10.3**). A person taking a projective test is presented with an ambiguous stimulus and then *projects* meaning onto it. The assumption is that people harbor anxiety and unresolved conflicts, often unconsciously, that may come out in their responses. The test administrator takes the manifest content (what the person reports seeing) and tries to understand its underlying meaning. Because these tests attempt to gather information indirectly, they are less threatening than other methods and therefore provoke less resistance.

**THE RORSCHACH INKBLOTS**   The best-known projective personality test is the Rorschach, originally developed by Swiss psychiatrist Hermann Rorschach (1884–1922). Today's psychologists typically use Rorschach inkblots with a comprehensive coding system introduced in the 1970s (Exner, 1980, 1986).

Here is a rough description of how the test is administered: A psychologist hands you a series of cards covered in odd-looking blotches of ink—five black-and-white, five in color. Presenting the cards one by one, the psychologist asks you to report what you see. The images you describe and the details you report will be systematically compared to answers given by other test takers who have been identified as having certain personality characteristics and diagnoses. Do you see bears playing patty cake? Seeing animals in motion might be interpreted as a sign of rashness. Are you concentrating on the black areas? This could suggest a feeling of melancholy or sadness (Lilienfeld et al., 2005).

**THE THEMATIC APPERCEPTION TEST (TAT)**   Developed in the mid-1930s by Henry Murray and his colleagues, the Thematic Apperception Test (TAT) consists of 20 cards showing black-and-white illustrations of ambiguous scenes. Test takers are asked to tell a story about each card. These stories typically describe the people pictured, including their emotions and thoughts, an explanation of the events leading up to the scene, and a conclusion to the story. The TAT is based on the premise that test takers project underlying conflicts onto the ambiguous stimuli; the test administrator's job is to unearth those conflicts.

**PROJECTIVE PERSONALITY TESTS: WHAT'S THE TAKEAWAY?**   Perhaps the greatest strength of projective tests is their unstructured format, which allows test

**projective personality tests** Assessments used to explore characteristics that might not be accessible through interview or observation; the test taker is presented with ambiguous stimuli and then projects meaning onto them.

# Examining the Unconscious: Projective Personality Tests

The psychoanalytic perspective holds that some aspects of personality exist beneath conscious awareness. Projective personality tests seek to uncover these characteristics. Ideas and anxieties in the unconscious will appear in descriptions of ambiguous stimuli, revealing previously hidden conflicts that the test administrator can evaluate.

## Test Administration

The best-known projective tests, the Thematic Apperception Test (TAT) and the Rorschach Inkblot Test, are both conducted in the same way (Lilienfeld et al., 2005): The test administrator presents a series of picture cards, one at a time, then records the participant's responses. The administrator also notes behaviors such as gestures, tone of voice, and facial expressions.

The standard administration of the TAT presents a selection of 5 to 12 cards. The participant is asked to tell a story for each scene, including what the characters are feeling and how the story might end.

The Rorschach has 10 cards with symmetrical inkblots, 5 in color and 5 in black-and-white. The participant is prompted to give multiple responses for each image, identifying details.

## Test Interpretation

To help decrease bias in interpretation of projective tests, comprehensive systems have been developed to standardize scoring and interpretation of some tests. For the Rorschach Inkblot Test, responses are coded on dimensions such as location (whole inkblot or one detail), themes (unique or consistent), and thought processes (Erdberg, 1990). The use of a comprehensive system allows administrators to compare typical and atypical responses.

### PARTICIPANT RESPONSES

"Looks like two people."

"The people are fighting over something."

"Or they're carrying something heavy together."

"Maybe it's one person looking in a mirror."

"I also see a butterfly."

These sample responses are representative of this type of inkblot (Burstein & Loucks, 1989).

### EXAMINER RESPONSES

Participant mentions the typical response of two figures.

Suggestion that the people are fighting could indicate issues with aggression or an aggressive personality.

Focus on individuals working together could represent a need for social connection.

However, seeing one person alone could indicate social anxiety.

Now participant switches to a specific part of the image, which could also show that they are uncomfortable thinking about others, perhaps a result of their introversion.

**CONNECTIONS**

In **Chapters 0** and **7,** we noted that people are prone to the hindsight bias, or the "I knew it all along" feeling. The hindsight bias is just one type of bias that can interfere with personality assessment and other forms of data collection.

takers to speak openly, honestly, and freely. But these tests are time-consuming, and the process of scoring and interpreting their results is somewhat subjective. As noted in prior chapters, humans are prone to a **variety of biases** and cognitive errors that can interfere with their ability to accurately assess people and situations. Test administrators may score differently, and test takers may get inconsistent results when they take the test on different occasions. Thus, projective tests may lack both interrater and test–retest reliability. The comprehensive scoring system for the Rorschach inkblots has resolved some reliability concerns, but the issue of validity remains. Many critics suggest that projective tests are not valid because they do not measure what they claim to measure (Schultz & Schultz, 2017). For these reasons, projective tests should be used cautiously, especially in nonclinical situations such as job interviews.

You may not have Rorschach inkblots at your disposal, but surely you use other tools to size up the personalities of new people. Perhaps you observe the way they interact with others, or how much they tolerate uncertainty. Did it ever occur to you that social media might be a good place to look for clues?

## Social Media and Psychology

### A PICTURE IS WORTH A THOUSAND WORDS

What does your Instagram reveal about your personality? According to one study, people who frequently post images of pets tend to score low on a measure of sociability. Could this mean they "prefer to surround themselves by animals rather than people" (Cooper et al., 2020, p. 969)? Another study found that Instagram users with delicate self-esteem tend to post selfies that emphasize physical appearance (Barry et al., 2017), but this finding has been hard to replicate (Barry et al., 2019). Twitter can offer clues about personality, too. People who are high in conscientiousness tend to select Twitter profile photos that convey positive emotions (a picture of themselves smiling); meanwhile, extroverts seem to favor colorful pictures that project youth (photos that make them look younger, or show them with younger people); and those high on openness often skip the headshots and choose artistic photos with high "aesthetic quality" (Liu et al., 2016). There is still much research to be done, but early findings suggest that social media behaviors may provide some information about the personality traits of users (Azucar et al., 2018).

**WHAT DO YOUR PHOTOS SAY ABOUT YOU?**

## Objective Tests

**LO 14** Describe objective personality tests, and evaluate their strengths and limitations.

Unlike the projective tests, which tend to be open-ended and subjective, *objective personality tests* use a standard set of questions with answer choices (true/false, multiple choice, circle the number) and have clear scoring instructions that are identical for everyone taking the test. Often, the scores are calculated by a computer. These tests are called *objective* because the results are assessed in a standardized way and mostly free of personal bias. In addition to being convenient, objective tests have a solid base of evidence supporting their reliability and validity (Anastasi & Urbina, 1997). Some focus on a particular personality trait or characteristic such as locus of control; others assess a group of traits like the Big Five. For example, the Big Five Inventory-2 (BFI-2) is a short assessment that is self-administered and designed to be easily understood and completed quickly, reducing testing fatigue (Soto & John, 2017). For a more detailed examination of the Big Five traits, clinicians often use the NEO Personality Inventories (Bleidorn et al., 2020; Louie et al., 2018). These assessments divide the Big Five into smaller "facets" (Mõttus et al., 2019).

zeynep bogoclu/Getty Images.

**Are Selfie Enthusiasts Narcissistic?**
Some research suggests that frequent self-posting is associated with narcissism, which is "characterised by a highly inflated, grandiose, and positive but unrealistic self-concept"; however, the relationship may only apply to a those with a certain type of narcissism and low self-esteem (March & McBean, 2018, p. 108). So if you see a friend posting a lot of selfies, don't jump to the conclusion that they are vain and self-absorbed. This very common activity "is not necessarily indicative of narcissism" (Barry et al., 2019, p. 29).

**THE MMPI**    The most commonly used objective personality test is the Minnesota Multiphasic Personality Inventory (MMPI-2; Ben-Porath, 2012; Butcher & Rouse, 1996; Williams & Lally, 2017). This self-report questionnaire consists of 338 statements with three answer choices: "true," "false," or "cannot say." Examples of these statements include "I often wake up rested and ready to go" and "I want to work as a teacher." Since the original purpose of the MMPI was to identify disorders and abnormal behavior, it included 10 clinical scales (cynicism and antisocial behavior, for example). The assessment also has validity measures, including the Lie Scale and the Defensiveness Scale, to help determine whether test takers are trying to appear more disturbed or healthier than they really are. The MMPI is used in a variety of contexts, including custody disputes, but many feel its application outside of therapeutic settings is inappropriate.

**THE 16PF**    The Sixteen Personality Factor Questionnaire (16PF), originally created by Raymond Cattell and based on his trait theory, consists of 185 questions. The results are used to construct a profile indicating where the respondent falls along the continuum for each of the 16 dimensions (Cattell, 1973a). Looking at **FIGURE 10.4**, you can see how airline pilots and writers compare on these 16 factors.

**MYERS–BRIGGS**    One very popular objective personality assessment is the Myers–Briggs Type Indicator (MBTI) (Briggs & Myers, 1998). Katherine Briggs and her daughter Isabel Briggs-Myers created this assessment in the 1940s. It designates a personality "type" using these four dimensions: extraversion (E) versus introversion (I); sensing (S) versus intuiting (N); thinking (T) versus feeling (F); and judgment (J) versus perception (P). For example, someone characterized as ISTP would be introverted, rely on the senses (rather than intuition) to understand the environment, favor logic over emotion, and focus on using perception as opposed to judgment.

One problem with the MBTI is that it uses relatively vague descriptions of personality traits. Some would even liken it to the Barnum effect, which was named after P. T. Barnum (1810–1891), the U.S. showman and founder of the Barnum and Bailey Circus. Barnum was famous for his ability to convince people he could read minds. Essentially, he did this by making generally complimentary and vague statements that could be true about anyone. (*You are creative and work well with others and you sometimes procrastinate, but ultimately you get the job done.*) The MBTI is similar in this respect, providing personality type descriptions that are "generally flattering and sufficiently vague so that most people will accept the statements as true of themselves" (Pittenger, 1993, p. 51). Although the MBTI is quite popular, especially in the corporate world,

**Personality Tests in the Workplace**

In addition to running criminal background checks and credit scores, some employers use objective personality assessments to screen job applicants. For example, police departments use assessments such as the MMPI-2 to help predict performance on the job (Detrick & Chibnall, 2014; Kaul, 2017).

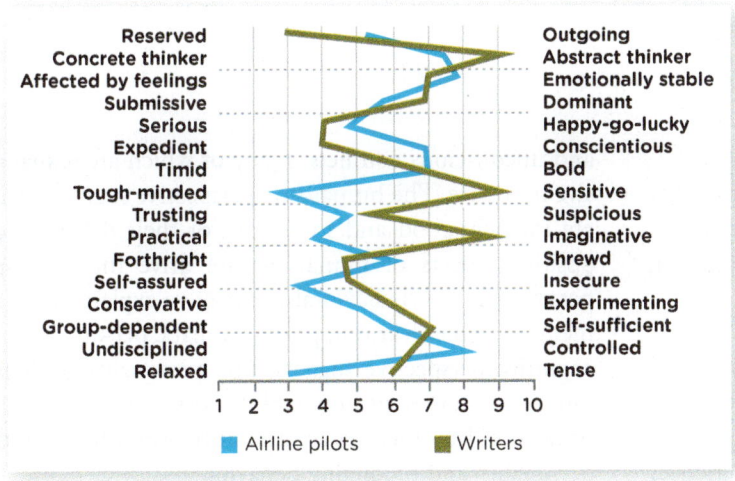

Airline pilots    Writers

**FIGURE 10.4**

**Example Profiles Generated by the 16PF**

On Cattell's 16PF, writers appear to be more reserved, sensitive, and imaginative than airline pilots. Pilots, on the other hand, tend to fall on the tough-minded end of the continuum. Are you surprised that they also appear to be more relaxed? Information from Cattell (1973b).

the supporting research is weak when it comes to job performance, career choices, and other professional matters (Chen, 2018; Lussier, 2018; Pittenger, 2005). Because test results don't always correlate with job success, the validity of the MBTI is questionable. This assessment can also fall short when it comes to test–retest reliability; a person may take the test twice and end up with different results (Hunsley et al., 2003; Pittenger, 2005). After weighing the evidence, one group of researchers arrived at the following conclusion: "Despite its popularity, the MBTI theory does not represent a suitable framework for understanding personality" (Stein & Swan, 2019, p. 8).

**OBJECTIVE PERSONALITY TESTS: WHAT'S THE TAKEAWAY?**    We have noted specific criticisms of the MMPI-2 and Myers–Briggs tests, but objective assessments have other, more general, drawbacks. Many of these tests include some sort of mechanism for checking the validity of the test taker's answers (Wetzel et al., 2021), but people still may lie, particularly when something personal is at stake like a job or child custody decision. Social desirability can also influence the results, as test takers may unintentionally answer questions in a way that makes them look better to others. Even if test takers try to be honest, self-reports are inevitably biased (can anyone truly see themselves objectively?). Finally, the standardization of these tests may come at a cost, as they have been criticized for lacking flexibility and failing to appreciate the diversity of individual experience. Despite many criticisms, tests like the MMPI-2 are the best tools we have for assessing personality.

**AUTHENTIC AND HONEST**    You may be wondering why we chose to feature the story of an intersex man in this chapter on personality. Wouldn't Sean Saifa Wall be a better fit for Chapter 8 or 9, which cover gender and sexuality? We don't believe that gender-non-conforming people should be confined to discussions of sex and gender. We chose to include Saifa's story here because we were captivated by him, and his rare ability to reflect on his personality development in an authentic and honest way.

**Sean Saifa Wall**
To learn more about Saifa—his activism, art, and other projects—visit https://www.seansaifa.com.

### SHOW WHAT YOU KNOW

1. _____ personality tests present ambiguous stimuli to the test taker. The administrator interprets the responses to uncover underlying personality characteristics.

   **A.** Objective          **C.** 16PF

   **B.** Projective         **D.** Myers–Briggs

2. A psychologist gives a client several personality tests to help them choose a career path. What might be the consequences if the tests are not valid? How would the client know if the tests were reliable?

3. Critics of objective personality tests report that the _____ of these tests does not allow for flexibility and fails to consider the diversity of individual experiences.

   **A.** standardization    **C.** neuroticism

   **B.** extraversion       **D.** factor analysis

 CHECK YOUR ANSWERS AT THE BACK OF THE BOOK.

## Summary of Concepts

**LO 1**  **Define personality. (p. 376)**

Personality refers to the unique, core set of characteristics that influence the way one thinks, acts, and feels—characteristics many psychologists would agree are consistent and enduring throughout the life span.

**LO 2**  **Distinguish how the perspectives of psychology explain personality development. (p. 377)**

The psychoanalytic perspective suggests that personality development is strongly influenced by early childhood experiences and unconscious conflicts, many of which are sexual or aggressive in nature. The humanistic perspective suggests that humans are innately good and in control of their destinies, and these positive aspects of human nature drive the development of personality. The behavioral perspective explains how reinforcement and other learning processes shape personality. The social-cognitive perspective suggests that personality is shaped by an interaction of environmental factors, cognitive activity, and behaviors. Trait theories are primarily concerned with describing personality and predicting behavior.

**LO 3** Illustrate Freud's models for describing the mind. (p. 380)

Psychoanalysis refers to Freud's theories of personality and his system of psychotherapy and tools for exploring the unconscious. According to his topographical model, our personalities and behaviors result from mental processes occurring at three levels: the conscious, preconscious, and unconscious. Freud's structural model describes the functions of the mind's components. The id is the most primitive component, and its activities occur at the unconscious level. As an infant grows, the ego develops from the id. The ego manipulates situations, creates plans, solves problems, and makes decisions to satisfy the needs of the id. The superego develops last and guides our behavior to follow the rules of society, parents, or other authority figures.

**LO 4** Summarize Freud's use of psychosexual stages to explain personality. (p. 382)

According to Freud, the development of sexuality and personality proceeds through psychosexual stages, which all children experience as they mature into adulthood. Each psychosexual stage is associated with an erogenous zone and a conflict that must be addressed. If the conflict is not successfully resolved, the child may suffer from a fixation and get "stuck" in that particular stage, unable to progress smoothly through the remaining stages. The progression includes the oral stage, anal stage, phallic stage, latency period, and genital stage.

**LO 5** Explain how the neo-Freudians' theories of personality differ from Freud's. (p. 386)

Some of Freud's followers disagreed with his intense emphasis on early childhood experiences, aggression, and sexuality, and developed their own theories. Adler proposed that humans are conscious and intentional in their behaviors. Jung suggested that we are driven by a psychological energy (as opposed to sexual energy) that encourages positive growth, self-understanding, and balance. Horney emphasized the role of relationships between children and their caregivers, not psychosexual stages and erogenous zones.

**LO 6** Discuss Rogers' view of self-concept, ideal self, and unconditional positive regard. (p. 392)

Rogers suggested that humans have an innate urge to move toward situations and people that provide opportunities for growth, and move away from those that inhibit growth. Self-concept is knowledge of one's strengths, abilities, behavior patterns, and temperament. Rogers believed that individuals develop an ideal self, or self-concept they fervently wish to achieve. Ideally, caregivers show unconditional positive regard, or total acceptance of children regardless of their behavior. People need to feel completely accepted and valued for who they are, not for what they do.

**LO 7** Use the behavioral perspective to explain personality development. (p. 393)

According to the behavioral perspective, personality is a collection of behaviors, all of which have been shaped through a lifetime of learning. Some behaviorists explain personality using learning principles, including those of operant conditioning and observational learning.

**LO 8** Summarize Rotter's view of personality. (p. 394)

Rotter suggested that some aspects of personality cannot be directly observed. He believed a key component of personality is locus of control, or a pattern of beliefs about where control or responsibility for outcomes resides. Rotter explored how these beliefs can influence behavior. Expectancy refers to the predictions we make about the consequences or outcomes of our behavior.

**LO 9** Discuss Bandura's social-cognitive perspective of personality. (p. 394)

Bandura rejected the notion that psychologists should focus solely on observable behavior; he realized behavior is determined by cognition as well as reinforcers and other environmental influences. The social-cognitive perspective suggests that personality results from reinforcement, relationships, and other environmental factors (social) and patterns of thinking (cognitive). Bandura refers to the multidirectional interaction among beliefs, behaviors, and the environment as reciprocal determinism.

**LO 10** Distinguish trait theories from other personality theories. (p. 395)

Traits are the relatively stable properties that describe elements of personality. The trait theories are different from other personality theories in that they focus less on explaining why and how personality develops, and more on describing personality and predicting behaviors. Allport created a comprehensive list of traits to help operationalize the terminology used in personality research. Cattell grouped the traits into two categories: surface traits and source traits. He used factor analysis to uncover the relationships among surface traits, resulting in 16 personality factors, and developed the Sixteen Personality Factor Questionnaire (16PF) to measure them. Eysenck proposed that personality can be described using three dimensions: introversion–extraversion, neuroticism, and psychoticism. He also worked to understand the biological basis of these dimensions.

**LO 11** Identify evidence supporting the biological basis of the five-factor model of personality. (p. 398)

The five-factor model of personality, also known as the Big Five, includes the following factors: openness to experience, conscientiousness, extraversion, agreeableness, and neuroticism. These characteristics are stable over time and are shaped by genes, brain structures, and other biological factors—not just culture and experience.

**LO 12** Explain why reliability and validity are important in personality assessment. (p. 403)

Reliability generally refers to two aspects of a personality assessment: test–retest reliability and interrater reliability. Test–retest reliability is consistency of results when the same person takes a test more than once. Interrater reliability refers to the consistency across people scoring an assessment. Validity is the degree to which an assessment measures what it is intended to measure. A valid test must yield results similar to established assessments.

**LO 13** Describe projective personality tests, and evaluate their strengths and limitations. (p. 404)

Projective tests are based on the premise that personality influences perceptions. The test taker is presented with an ambiguous stimulus and then prompted to project meaning onto it. The administrator takes the manifest content (what the person reports seeing) and tries to understand its underlying meaning. Because these tests attempt to gather information indirectly,

they are less threatening than other methods, and therefore provoke less resistance. Projective tests are time-consuming, and the process of scoring and interpreting their results is somewhat subjective, which can lead to problems with reliability and validity. Some of the best-known projective tests are the Rorschach Inkblot Test and Thematic Apperception Test (TAT).

**LO 14** Describe objective personality tests, and evaluate their strengths and limitations. (p. 406)

Objective personality tests comprise a standard set of questions with answer choices (true/false, multiple choice, circle the number). These tests are called objective because the results are assessed in a standardized way and mostly free of bias. But these assessments are not perfect. Test takers may be dishonest or unintentionally answer questions in a way that makes them look better (social desirability). Two commonly used objective personality tests are the Minnesota Multiphasic Personality Inventory (MMPI–2) and the Sixteen Personality Factor Questionnaire (16PF).

# Key Terms

**archetypes**, p. 388
**collective unconscious**, p. 388
**ego**, p. 381
**ego defense mechanisms**, p. 382
**expectancy**, p. 394
**five-factor model of personality**, p. 398

**fixation**, p. 384
**id**, p. 381
**ideal self**, p. 392
**Oedipus complex**, p. 385
**personality**, p. 376
**pleasure principle**, p. 381
**projective personality tests**, p. 404

**psychoanalysis**, p. 379
**psychosexual stages**, p. 384
**reality principle**, p. 381
**reciprocal determinism**, p. 395
**self-concept**, p. 392
**self-efficacy**, p. 394
**social-cognitive perspective**, p. 394

**source traits**, p. 397
**superego**, p. 381
**surface traits**, p. 397
**traits**, p. 395
**trait theories**, p. 395
**unconditional positive regard**, p. 392
**unconscious**, p. 380

# Test Prep Are You Ready?

1. The _____ perspective of personality suggests that personality is shaped by interactions with the environment, specifically through learning.
   A. trait
   B. humanistic
   C. biological
   D. behavioral

2. Freud's topographical model suggests our personalities and behaviors result from:
   A. beliefs, behaviors, and the environment.
   B. the reality principle.
   C. the pleasure principle.
   D. mental processes that occur at three levels of consciousness.

3. According to Freud, all children progress through _____ as they mature into adulthood, but if their progress is not smooth, they may suffer from a _____.
   A. psychosexual stages; fixation
   B. three levels of consciousness; superego
   C. defense mechanisms; locus of control
   D. erogenous zones; reciprocal determinism

4. Rogers believed that problems can develop when a person's self-concept is _____ with their experiences in the world.
   A. incongruent
   B. in harmony
   C. self-actualized
   D. conditioned

5. A person high in _____ strongly believes they will succeed in a particular situation even if they have experienced failure under similar circumstances.
   A. reciprocal determinism
   B. reinforcers
   C. self-efficacy
   D. source traits

6. _____ refers to the unique, core set of characteristics that influence how we think, act, and feel.
   A. Personality
   B. Ego defense mechanism
   C. Reciprocal determinism
   D. Expectancy

7. Cattell proposed there are 16 personality dimensions that can be considered primary _____ , and these are the product of both nature and nurture.
   A. source traits
   B. conditions of worth
   C. Big Five traits
   D. defense mechanisms

8. Evidence for the biological basis of the five-factor model includes:
   A. the instability of personality characteristics over time.
   B. the stability of personality characteristics over time.
   C. the fact that there are no gender differences in personality characteristics.
   D. the absence of heritability of personality characteristics.

9. _____ is apparent when someone takes the same personality assessment more than once and the results do not change.
   A. Heritability
   B. Effectiveness
   C. Reliability
   D. Validity

10. The neo-Freudians agree with Freud on many issues, but tend to disagree with which of the following?
    A. his belief in the positive aspects of human nature
    B. his belief in the importance of personality growth throughout life
    C. his intense emphasis on sex and aggression
    D. his notion that caregivers cannot shape personality

11. Think about a friend who is outgoing. How would a behaviorist explain the development of your friend's personality characteristic?

12. How do the humanistic and social-cognitive perspectives of personality differ?

13. Describe the Oedipus complex and Electra complex. How are they different?

14. Consider your current performance in your college courses. Name three causes for your successes that represent an internal locus of control. Name three causes for your successes that represent an external locus of control.

15. Describe the differences between objective and subjective personality assessments.

✓ CHECK YOUR ANSWERS AT THE BACK OF THE BOOK.

# 11

Diarmuid Greene/Getty Images.

# Social Psychology

## An Introduction to Social Psychology

**IS THE SWIPE RIGHT?**  It was an unusually hot evening in Escondido, California. Twenty-six-year-old Alexa Antoni was sweaty from playing kickball with some teenagers she worked with at San Pasqual Academy, a residential school for foster children. She was already running late for her first date with Dennis Conforti, a 30-year-old Marine she had met through the mobile dating app Tinder. "I almost cancelled because I was so gross and icky," Alexa recalls. Approaching the meeting place, Alexa suddenly felt unsure. It was a small restaurant tucked in between an abandoned car lot and a tire sales place: *Oh my gosh, he's going to kill me!*

Dennis was sitting in the back corner, sipping a drink and listening to the band. The first thing Alexa noticed was how relaxed and happy he appeared. "I remember he wasn't nervous," says Alexa. "It was almost like he was there enjoying it even without me being there, which was refreshing." Dennis dressed nicely, but not in a flashy way, and he had tranquil brown eyes.

The date went well. Alexa appreciated how Dennis was kind to the waitress without being a flirt. He was witty and attractive, and exuded a calm self-confidence. Alexa hoped to see Dennis again and learn more about him. But after a brief text exchange, things just "fizzled out." What was the story with Dennis?

Courtesy Alexa Antoni.

Courtesy Alexa Antoni.

**Dennis, 30**

less than a mile away

Interested in meeting new people to be friends or
whatever comes from it. I run, workout, ride, read
and usually up for anything adventurous.

Snap: kcco121

**165 Friends For Common Connections**

We compare your Facebook friends with
those of your matches to display any

**Alexa, 27**

Clinical Therapist
108 miles away

California grown
New York educated
Adventure seeker
Recently relocated
Pretty terrible at using tinder
Old fashioned kind of girl, not interested in
hookups :)

**The Profile Photos**
These are the Tinder profile pictures that helped bring
together Dennis (left) and Alexa (right, at left in photo).

# What Is Social Psychology?

As it turned out, Dennis was equally interested in Alexa. "She was smart, beautiful,"
he recalls. "I really liked her." But in between a full-time job in the Marine Corps,
classes at Palomar College, family obligations, and a 4-week-old puppy, Dennis barely
had any free time. Not knowing all these details, Alexa could only speculate about the
reasons Dennis hadn't reached out. Trying to understand people's actions, thoughts,
and feelings in response to others is something we all do on a regular basis. This is
also a major area of interest for those who study *social psychology.*

**LO 1**  Define social psychology and identify how it differs from sociology.

**Social psychology** is the study of human cognition, emotion, and behavior in
relation to others. Look carefully, and you can see connections to social psychology
in stories throughout this book. In Chapter 3, for example, we journeyed into the
world of Mandy Harvey, a jazz singer who is completely deaf. How might Mandy's
social interactions differ from those of a singer without hearing loss? Then there
was Clive Wearing from Chapter 6. How do you suppose Clive's devastating
memory loss affects his relationships? Social psychologists strive to answer these
types of questions.

Many times, we have emphasized the importance of the biopsycho*social*
perspective, which recognizes the biological, psychological, and social factors
underlying human behavior. This chapter focuses on the third aspect of that triad:
social forces.

**HOW IS IT DIFFERENT FROM SOCIOLOGY?**    Students often ask how social psychology
differs from the field of *sociology.* The answer is simple: Social psychology explores the
way individuals behave, think, and feel in relation to others and groups (Gollwitzer &
Bargh, 2018). Sociology centers on examining the groups themselves—their societies,
cultures, and institutions. A social psychologist studying religion might focus on the

damircudic/Getty Images.

**Craving Connection**
Social psychologists study how behaviors are
shaped by interactions with other people. These
interactions are fundamental to who we are as
humans. When deprived of social stimulation, the
brain may exhibit activity similar to that which is
seen during hunger (Tomova et al., 2020). "Positive
social interactions in and of themselves may be
basic human needs, analogous to other basic
needs like food consumption or sleep" (para. 3).

**social psychology** The study of human
cognition, emotion, and behavior in relation to
others.

*Note:* Quotations attributed to Julius Achon and Alexa and Dennis Conforti are personal communications.

relationship between individual congregants and their spiritual leaders. A sociologist would more likely investigate religious practices, rituals, and organizations.

**RESEARCH WITH A TWIST** Like all psychologists, social psychologists use a variety of research methods, including surveys, naturalistic observation, and the experimental method. But their studies sometimes have an added twist of deception. In some cases, deception is necessary because people do not always **behave naturally** when they know they are being observed (Lasser et al., 2020). Participants may try to conform to expectations, or do just the opposite—behave in ways they believe will contradict the researchers' predictions. Suppose researchers are studying the facial expressions of people drinking alcohol and listening to jokes (Fairbairn et al., 2020; Sayette et al., 2019). If participants know that every smile is being analyzed, they may feel self-conscious and display atypical facial expressions. Instead of revealing the real focus of their investigation, researchers might lead participants to believe they are studying something else, like reaction time. That way, they can examine the behavior of interest (facial expressions in social settings) more naturally.

Social psychology studies often involve *confederates,* or people secretly working for the researchers. Playing the role of participants, experimenters, or simply bystanders, confederates say what the researchers tell them to say and do what the researchers tell them to do. They are, unknown to the participants, just part of the researchers' experimental manipulation.

In most cases, the deception is not kept secret forever. Researchers debrief their participants at the end of a study, that is, review aspects of the research initially kept under wraps. Even after learning they were deceived, many participants say they would be willing to take part in subsequent psychology experiments (Blatchley & O'Brien, 2007). College students, who are frequently participants in research, "may be inclined to believe that the use of deception is justified" (Lasser et al., 2020, p. 20). Debriefing is also a time when researchers make sure that participants were not harmed or upset by their involvement in a study.

We should note that all psychology research affiliated with colleges and universities must be approved by an Institutional Review Board (IRB) to ensure that no harm will come from participation. Additionally, psychologists must follow ethical guidelines to safeguard the welfare of those involved in their research. These requirements are partly a reaction to early studies involving extreme deception and manipulation—studies that many viewed as dehumanizing and unethical. Psychologists agree that deception is only acceptable if there is no other way to study the topic of interest. We will describe many examples of such research in the upcoming pages, but first let's familiarize ourselves with some basic concepts in social psychology. We'll get started with a little help from Dennis and Alexa.

**DATE TWO: MAKE IT OR BREAK IT** About 2 weeks after their first date, Dennis finally texted Alexa, hoping she wouldn't think he was a total jerk for waiting so long. Alexa responded, but she had already been on another Tinder date with a different person and did not have high expectations for date #2 with Dennis. Their second meeting was a big success, though, and they soon began connecting on a deeper level. "We were able to kind of ask the tough questions," says Dennis, who told Alexa he had been married, and explained some of the reasons for his divorce. Alexa described her motivation for becoming a social worker and helping foster children. "She's just a very kind-hearted person," says Dennis, who was beginning to see the potential for a relationship. He asked Alexa for another dinner date, but this time at his house so she could meet his French bulldog puppy Brutus. This made Alexa feel a bit on edge: "Usually . . . if a guy invites you over they are expecting a lot."

**CONNECTIONS**

In **Chapter 1,** we described the Hawthorne effect: When research participants know they are being observed, their behavior changes. Here, we explain how deception is used to minimize the Hawthorne effect.

NurPhoto/Getty Images.

**Love in the Time of COVID-19**

Online dating was already popular before the pandemic, with nearly a third of U.S. adults having tried it (Anderson et al., 2020). Singles continued finding ways to connect during the COVID-19 lockdowns—meeting up with masks, sharing their favorite TikToks, and using pandemic pickup lines like "quarantine and chill?" (Tinder, 2020, para. 5). The dating app Tinder saw an increase in profile lines such as, "If you're not voting, don't even try" (para. 4) and "If you don't support BLM, we aren't gonna work" (para. 9), and the most popular emoji was this: 👎🤮👎 (Tinder, 2020).

# Why Do People Do the Things They Do?

**LO 2** Define social cognition and describe how we use attributions to explain behavior.

Alexa barely knew Dennis, but he seemed like a gentle soul—or perhaps a really good actor. On a conscious level, she was processing all sorts of information she had picked up by observing Dennis, namely through his words and behaviors. There was also some information processing occurring outside of her awareness. It is possible that Dennis reminded her of someone she knew—perhaps a family member—and that sense of familiarity made her more inclined to trust him. Ultimately, she accepted his invitation.

Alexa's decision relied on **social cognition**—the way one thinks about others, attends to social information, and uses this information in life, both consciously and unconsciously. You use social **cognition** all the time, whether you are trying to infer what another person is thinking by looking in their eyes or understand what they are feeling using cues in the social environment (Schurz et al., 2020). One critical component of social cognition is the process of making *attributions,* or explaining the behavior of others.

**WHAT ARE ATTRIBUTIONS?**   As you probably know, the "dating game" typically involves a lot of guesswork about other people's behavior: *Why did Dennis take so long to text? What did Alexa mean by that 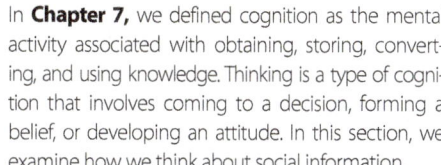 she included at the end of her message?* These kinds of questions are relevant to all human relationships, not just the romantic kind. Just think about how much time you spend wondering why people do the things they do. The "answers" you come up with are called **attributions.** *Why is my friend in such a bad mood?* you ask yourself. Your attribution might be, *Maybe he just got some bad news* or *Perhaps he is hungry.* Attributions are the beliefs we develop to explain human behaviors and characteristics, as well as situations. When psychologists characterize attributions, they use the term *observer* to identify the person making the attribution, and *actor* to identify the person exhibiting the behavior of interest. If Alexa is trying to figure out why Dennis took so long to text, then Alexa is the observer and Dennis is the actor.

**TYPES OF ATTRIBUTIONS**   Psychologists often describe attributions along three dimensions: controllable–uncontrollable, stable–unstable, and internal–external. Let's see how these might apply to attributions relating to Alexa and Dennis:

*Controllable–uncontrollable dimension:* Alexa was 15 minutes late to her first date with Dennis. If Dennis assumed it was because she got stuck in unavoidable traffic, we would say he was making an uncontrollable attribution. If he assumed that Alexa's lateness resulted from factors within her control, such as how fast she drove or what time she left work, then the attribution would be controllable.

*Stable–unstable dimension:* According to Alexa, Dennis turned out to be a "pretty good cook." If she inferred that his success in the kitchen stemmed from a longtime interest in cooking, the attribution would be stable—the cause is long-lasting. If she thought it resulted from a short-lived inspiration after watching an episode of *Ugly Delicious,* then her attribution would be unstable—the cause is temporary.

*Internal–external dimension:* Why did Alexa have bad luck on Tinder before she met Dennis? If Dennis thought it was because most guys on Tinder are creepy, this would be an external attribution, because the cause of the problem resides outside of Alexa. If he believed Alexa was unsuccessful because she was reluctant to explore new relationships, this would be an internal attribution—the cause lies within Alexa.

**CONNECTIONS**

In **Chapter 7,** we defined cognition as the mental activity associated with obtaining, storing, converting, and using knowledge. Thinking is a type of cognition that involves coming to a decision, forming a belief, or developing an attitude. In this section, we examine how we think about social information.

**social cognition** The way people think about others, attend to social information, and use this information in their lives, both consciously and unconsciously.

**attributions** Beliefs one develops to explain human behaviors and characteristics, as well as situations.

## Put Your Heads Together

Suppose your instructor assigns a group project. One of the students in your group contributes virtually nothing to the endeavor. Team up and explain this behavior using **A)** several attributions that are external, uncontrollable, and unstable, and **B)** several attributions that are internal, controllable, and stable. **C)** Consider how your emotional reactions might differ if you think the cause of your classmate's inactivity is **A)** versus **B)**.

Now that we have explored various types of attributions, let's see how they relate to your life online.

## SOCIAL MEDIA AND PSYCHOLOGY

### WHAT'S IN A SELFIE?

Think about the last time you posted a professional headshot on LinkedIn or a fun photo on Instagram. What was your motivation for doing so? For most of us, the primary goal is to make a good impression—to appear attractive, confident, and likable. To this end, you may take a self-portrait. With a selfie, you can control the angle of the shot to highlight your best features. You can also use filters and photo editing apps to smooth out your skin, whiten your teeth, and reshape your features. The problem is that most people viewing your selfie know that you may have manipulated the photo, and this may lead to unfavorable attributions. (For example, viewers assume you are a bit vain—an internal and stable attribution.) In fact, research shows that filtered selfies posted on Instagram receive fewer likes than natural selfies. That is, there is an inverse relationship between use of filters and number of likes. Meanwhile, there is a positive correlation between the presence of "social cues" and the number of likes. Social cues are pieces of information that reveal something about a person, in this case the selfie taker. For example, a fitness enthusiast might snap a selfie wearing exercise gear or showing workout equipment in the background. These types of cues offer a window into the person's life and "indicate eagerness to interact, a sentiment that can lead to higher audience interest and favorability" (Hong et al., 2020, p. 3). Overall, the findings suggest that you can make a good impression by posting selfies that reveal who you really are—not some idealized version of yourself.

**Easy on the Filters**
If you're trying to make a good impression, try posting a photo that shows your authentic self (photo on the left) as opposed to one that has been heavily filtered (right). A study of more than 2,000 Instagram posts found that filtered selfies received fewer likes than unfiltered ones. It all has to do with attributions: When people see an image with obvious enhancements, they tend to perceive this as "ingenuine behavior because it reflects the intent to only present the ideal depiction of self" (Hong et al., 2020, p. 5).

**LO 3**  Describe several common attribution errors.

Whether online or in person, making attributions about human behavior often involves some degree of speculation. This, of course, leaves plenty of room for error. Let's take a look at four of the most common mistakes (**INFOGRAPHIC 11.1** on page 419).

**FUNDAMENTAL ATTRIBUTION ERROR**   Suppose you are hosting a party tomorrow night. You e-mailed invitations a month ago, and everyone responded except your friend Julia. If you automatically assume Julia failed to reply because she is a little snooty and thinks she's too good for your party, rather than considering situational factors (like the fact that your invitation may have gone straight into her spam folder), then you might be falling prey to the **fundamental attribution error.** Here, the tendency is to use *dispositional attributions* rather than *situational attributions.* A **dispositional attribution** is a particular type of internal attribution wherein behaviors are assumed to result from traits or personality characteristics. These are deep-seated,

**fundamental attribution error**  The tendency to overestimate the degree to which the characteristics of an individual are the cause of an event, and to underestimate the involvement of situational factors.

**dispositional attribution**  A type of internal attribution where behaviors are assumed to result from traits or personality characteristics.

enduring characteristics, as opposed to more transient states, like feeling tired and cranky. A **situational attribution** is an external attribution wherein behaviors are assumed to result from situational factors.

The fundamental attribution error is common; we often assume people's behaviors are caused by personal characteristics (a dispositional attribution) rather than factors in the environment (a situational attribution) (Ross, 1977, 2018; Ross, Amabile, et al., 1977). For example, people sometimes assume that poverty results from personal characteristics—dispositional factors such as laziness and lack of motivation. But a closer look at economic variables seems to suggest that situational factors play a more important role (Engler et al., 2020). As of the printing of this book, the federal minimum wage is $7.25 per hour. If you work at this rate full-time (40 hours per week) without taking any weeks off, your annual salary is $15,080, which is close to the poverty threshold (Semega et al., 2020). "Since 1973, American productivity has increased by 77 percent, while hourly pay has grown by only 12 percent" (Desmond, 2018, para. 10). In an economy with this degree of wage growth, working hard may not be enough to escape the grip of poverty.

Imagine how dangerous the fundamental attribution error could be in a medical setting, when doctors and nurses need to make quick choices about treatment. Seeing a patient with slurred speech, difficulty walking, and aggressive behavior, a nurse might assume they are a drunk "alcoholic" and ignore situational factors, such as homelessness and severe dehydration (Levett-Jones et al., 2010). Similarly, a doctor might take one look at a patient and decide they are uncooperative and dirty, and simply write them off, when in fact the patient is on the verge of a diabetic coma (Groopman, 2008, p. 55). Doctors must avoid these automatic responses, and patients and their families should recognize that health-care workers are not immune to attribution errors. What other professionals make decisions that impact the well-being of others, and how might the fundamental attribution error lead to mistakes?

Why do we fall prey to the fundamental attribution error? Perhaps it has something to do with our "illusion of personal objectivity"; we deem our own perceptions to be accurate and unbiased, and assume people with opposing views are irrational and biased (Ross, 2018, p. 775). The good news is that we may be able to combat this way of thinking with training exercises. For example, one group of researchers put college students and social workers through a "poverty simulation" that helped them understand the day-to-day challenges faced by people who are poor. As a result of this intervention, the participants (especially the college students) began to focus less on dispositional characteristics and more on situational factors (Engler et al., 2020). Other researchers are exploring strategies to help medical professionals combat the fundamental attribution error, including the use of educational video games for medical students. For clinicians who want to reduce their cognitive biases, it may help to "slow down," consider "alternative diagnoses," and question hypotheses, among other things (O'Sullivan & Schofield, 2018).

**JUST-WORLD HYPOTHESIS**    Another attribution error associated with biased values and belief systems is the **just-world hypothesis,** which assumes that if people are suffering, they must have done something to deserve it (Rubin & Peplau, 1975). According to this view, the world is a fair place and "bad" things happen for a reason. Thus, when people are "bad," it should be no surprise when things don't go well for them (Riggio & Garcia, 2009). In one study, researchers told a group of participants about a man who was violent toward his wife, slapping and yelling at her. Another group heard about a loving man who gave his wife flowers and frequently made her dinner. Participants who heard about the "bad person" were more likely to predict a bad outcome for him (he will have a "terrible car accident") than

**Why Do We Blame Victims?**
Workers in South Korea show their support for the Me Too movement, the global fight against sexual harassment and assault. In some cases, people blame the victims of sexual assault instead of the perpetrators (Correia et al., 2015). Victims may even blame themselves, especially if they were using alcohol at the time of the assault (Peter-Hagene & Ullman, 2018). The tendency to assume that victims "had it coming," or did something to deserve abuse, is an example of the just-world hypothesis. Victim-blaming can deter people from speaking out and seeking justice.

Seung-il Ryu/NurPhoto/Getty Images.

**situational attribution**  A type of external attribution where behaviors are assumed to result from situational factors.

**just-world hypothesis**  The tendency to believe the world is a fair place and individuals generally get what they deserve.

those who heard about the "good person" (he will win a "hugely successful business contract"; Callan et al., 2013, p. 35). Why do people believe in the just-world hypothesis? Maybe because it helps them understand events and feel in control of their lives, even though much of what happens is unpredictable and beyond their control (Strelan, 2018).

**CONNECTIONS** ———————

In **Chapter 7,** we described the availability heuristic. With this heuristic, we predict the probability of something happening based on how easily we can recall a similar event from the past. The false consensus effect may result partly from using the availability heuristic. We rely on information about ourselves because it is easy to recall, and thus overestimate the degree to which other people think and act like we do.

**FALSE CONSENSUS EFFECT**    When trying to decipher the causes of other people's behaviors, we **over-rely on knowledge about ourselves**. This can lead to the **false consensus effect,** which is the tendency to overestimate the degree to which others think or act like we do (Ross, Greene, et al., 1977). For example, people tend to believe that their favorite celebrities are more popular than they really are: *I love Taylor Swift, as does everyone else!* (Collisson et al., 2021). The false consensus effect may also be apparent in beliefs about vaccines: *I think the flu shot is dangerous, and most of my friends agree* (Bruine de Bruin et al., 2020). We seem to make such mistakes because we have an overabundance of information about ourselves, and often limited information about others.

**CONNECTIONS** ———————

In **Chapter 10,** we discussed locus of control, or patterns of beliefs about where control resides. People with an internal locus of control believe they have control over their lives. Those who fall prey to the self-serving bias appear to have an internal locus of control when it comes to explaining the reasons for their successes.

**SELF-SERVING BIAS**    People who attribute their successes to **internal characteristics** and their failures to environmental factors may be prone to the **self-serving bias.** As research reveals, people exhibit "a generalized tendency to attribute positive outcomes to themselves and negative outcomes to others," and this can impact the way they learn and interpret events (Dorfman et al., 2019, p. 523).

One of the reasons Dennis was so drawn to Alexa was her apparent *lack* of self-serving bias. She was humble about her academic accomplishments, and she took responsibility for the failures of past relationships. Someone more vulnerable to the self-serving bias might have attributed their accomplishments to internal characteristics, such as intelligence and talent, and blamed their relationship woes on external circumstances, like the behavior of ex-boyfriends.

Now that we have a grasp of attributions (and the many errors associated with them), let's explore another facet of social cognition: attitudes.

## What's with the Attitude?

**"I AM TOTALLY CRAZY ABOUT THIS GUY"**    When Alexa arrived at Dennis' house for dinner, her worries evaporated. It was clear he just wanted to make a nice meal and help her relax after a stressful week. "After the third date . . . it kind of took off from there," Alexa recalls. About 2 months later, Dennis had to go into "the field," or train with the Marines for several days in a remote location. Being out of touch forced Alexa to recognize her feelings: *Oh my gosh, I am totally crazy about this guy.*

When Dennis came home, the couple went to the beach, watched the sun set over the ocean, and had a long talk. They discussed their values and beliefs about raising children, caring for aging parents, and handling finances. "We just ran the gamut of everything you could possibly run into if you continue a relationship," says Alexa. "We [were] either going to come out of this with a really positive future, or . . . break up." By the end of the conversation, Dennis was saying "I love you," and it was clear that they were highly compatible. Alexa and Dennis shared many of the same *attitudes*.

**false consensus effect** The tendency to overestimate the degree to which others think or act like we do.

**self-serving bias** The tendency to attribute our successes to personal characteristics and our failures to environmental factors.

**attitudes** The relatively stable thoughts, feelings, and responses one has toward people, situations, ideas, and things.

**WHAT ARE ATTITUDES?**    **Attitudes** are the relatively stable thoughts, feelings, and responses we have toward people, situations, ideas, and things (Ajzen, 2001; Wicker, 1969). Psychologists suggest that attitudes are composed of cognitive, affective, and

# Errors in Attribution

*Attributions* are beliefs we develop to explain human behaviors and characteristics, as well as situations. We can explain behaviors in many ways, but social psychologists often compare explanations based on traits or personality characteristics (dispositional attributions) to explanations based on external situations (situational attributions). But as we seek to explain events and behaviors, we tend to make predictable errors, making the wrong assumption about why someone is behaving in a certain way. Let's look at four of the most common types of errors in attribution.

## Fundamental attribution error

Observer tends to think actor's behavior is caused by internal characteristics, ignoring the role of the situation.

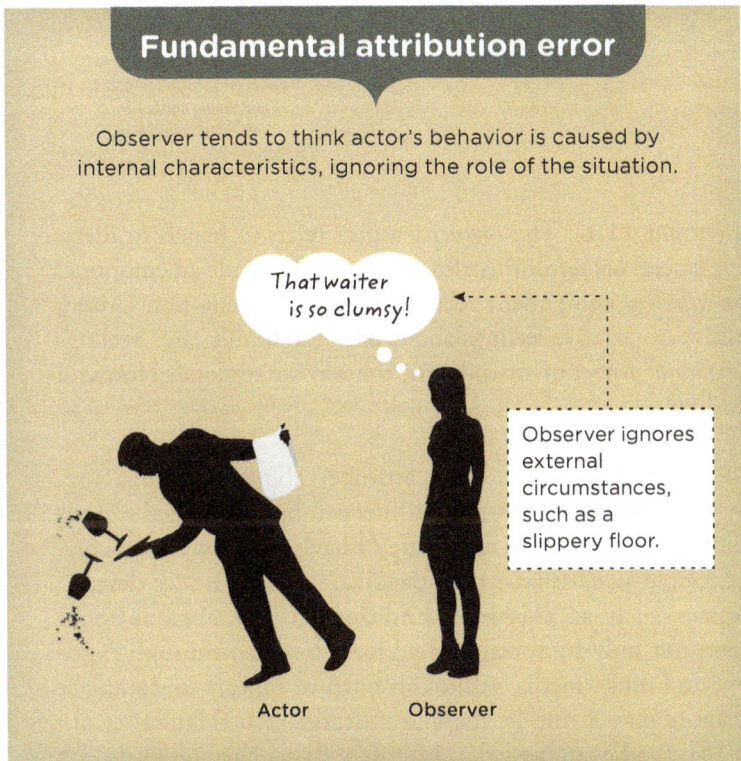

That waiter is so clumsy!

Observer ignores external circumstances, such as a slippery floor.

Actor          Observer

## Just-world hypothesis

Observer tends to think people get what they deserve.

YOU'RE FIRED!

Bad things happen to bad people. He had it coming.

Observer ignores other possible reasons, such as the manager's desire to hire a friend instead.

Actor          Observer

## Self-serving bias

We tend to attribute our successes to internal characteristics and our failures to external circumstances.

Success! I got a lot of tips tonight.

I'm an excellent waiter so I earn good tips.

TIPS

Failure! I hardly earned any tips.

Diners were really stingy tonight, so I wasn't tipped well.

TIPS

## False consensus effect

Observer tends to assume the actor is behaving similarly to how she would act in that situation.

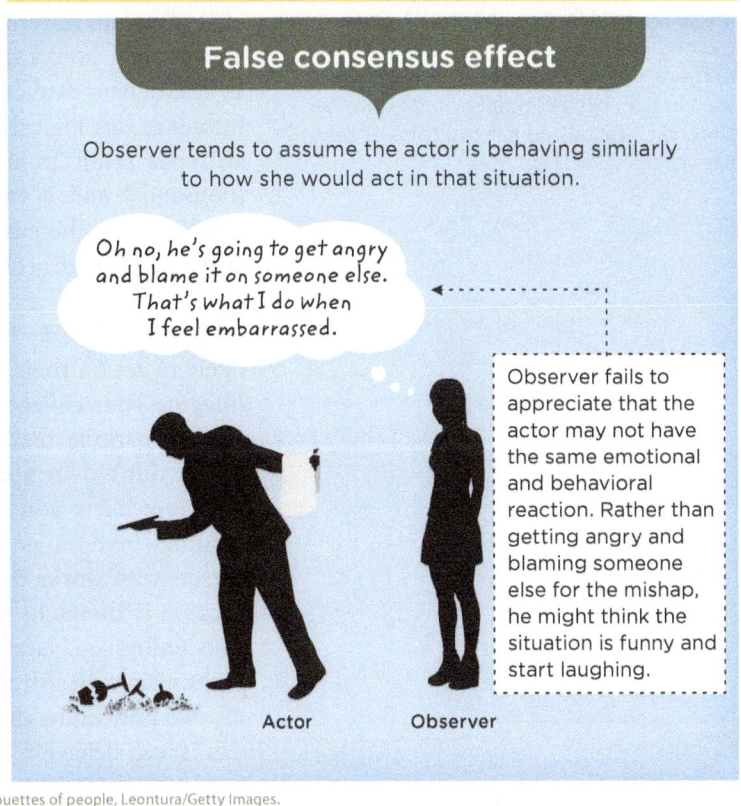

Oh no, he's going to get angry and blame it on someone else. That's what I do when I feel embarrassed.

Observer fails to appreciate that the actor may not have the same emotional and behavioral reaction. Rather than getting angry and blaming someone else for the mishap, he might think the situation is funny and start laughing.

Actor          Observer

**FIGURE 11.1**
**Attitudes**
Attitudes are composed of cognitive, affective, and behavioral components. Cognitive and affective components usually guide the behavioral aspect of an attitude.

behavioral components (**FIGURE 11.1**). The *cognitive* aspect refers to beliefs or ideas: What do you think about federal tax reform? Attitudes may also include an emotional evaluation, which is the *affective* component relating to mood or emotion (Ajzen, 2001). Do you have positive or negative feelings about universal health care? Feelings and beliefs guide the *behavioral* aspect of attitudes, or the way we respond. How will you vote in the next election?

**CONNECTIONS**

In **Chapter 5,** we described how classical conditioning might instill emotions and influence attitudes toward product brands. Attitudes may also develop through observational learning: We observe the attitudes of family members and friends, and sometimes take on those attitudes ourselves.

**CONNECTIONS**

In **Chapter 7,** we explored the heritability of intelligence. Heritability is the degree to which hereditary factors are responsible for differences in physical and psychological characteristics in the population. Heritability research often involves comparing identical and fraternal twins, as seen here with the study of attitudes.

**WHERE DO ATTITUDES COME FROM?**  Your attitudes about marijuana use, immigration, and many other issues are strongly influenced by your social experiences. This is even true of attitudes you are not aware of having—about sexual orientation and race, for example (Charlesworth & Banaji, 2019). Attitudes develop through learning processes such as **classical conditioning and observational learning**; they are shaped not only by social interactions, but also through exposure to books, television, and social media. Although nurture appears to dominate in this arena, genetic factors play a role in shaping attitudes, too (Hatemi et al., 2015; Hatemi et al., 2014). Studies suggest that **identical twins** have more similar attitudes than fraternal twins on topics such as politics, roller coasters, loud music, and reading books (Hufer et al., 2020; Olson et al., 2001; Verhulst, 2020). But, as researchers explain, "A single gene or small group of genes does not directly influence ideological preferences" (Hatemi et al., 2014, p. 292). In all probability, attitudes result from an interaction between a large number of genes (perhaps thousands) and a variety of environmental factors. Our genetic predispositions can influence the environments we create for ourselves, which in turn impact our attitudes (Hatemi et al., 2015).

**CAN ATTITUDES PREDICT BEHAVIOR?**  Not surprisingly, people are more likely to act on their attitudes when something important is at stake—like money. Imagine your college is holding a meeting to discuss the possibility of increasing student parking fees. What are the chances of your showing up to that meeting if you don't own a car? The greater personal investment you have in an issue, the more likely you are to act (Sivacek & Crano, 1982; Steindl & Jonas, 2015). Personal investment may also help explain antiscience attitudes. For example, a person who works in the coal or fossil fuel industry may dismiss climate science because it threatens their source of employment (Hornsey, 2020). Similarly, one who enjoys e-cigarettes might ignore medical evidence suggesting that vaping poses serious health risks.

We now know that attitudes can influence behaviors, but is the opposite true— that is, can behaviors shape attitudes? Read on.

## Think Critically

### SOMETHING DOESN'T FEEL RIGHT

Most would agree that cheating on a partner is not right. Even so, some people contradict their beliefs by seeking sexual gratification outside their primary relationships. How do you think cheating makes a person feel—relaxed and at peace? Probably not. The tension that results when a behavior (in this case, cheating) clashes with an attitude (*cheating is wrong*) is known as **cognitive dissonance** (Aronson & Festinger, 1958; Festinger, 1957). One way to reduce cognitive dissonance is to adjust the behavior (stop fooling around). Another approach is to change the attitude to better match the behavior: *Cheating is okay because my partner isn't nice to me; they deserve this* (Jeanfreau et al., 2016). Such attitude shifts often occur without our awareness.

**APPARENTLY, THE BIG BUCKS MADE IT EASIER TO JUSTIFY THEIR LIES.**

Imagine, for a moment, you are a participant in a classic study on cognitive dissonance (Festinger & Carlsmith, 1959). Researchers have assigned you to a very boring task—placing 12 objects on a tray and then putting them back on a shelf, over and over again for a half hour. Upon finishing, you spend an additional half hour twisting 48 pegs ever so slightly, one peg at a time, again and again and again. How would you feel at the end of the hour—pretty bored, right?

Regardless of how you may feel about these activities, you have been paid one dollar to convince someone else that they are a blast: "I had a lot of fun [doing] this task," you say. "It was intriguing, it was exciting . . ." (Festinger & Carlsmith, 1959, p. 205). Unless you like performing repetitive behaviors like a robot, we assume you would feel some degree of cognitive dissonance, or tension resulting from this mismatch between your attitude (*Ugh, this activity is so boring*) and your behavior (saying, "I had so much fun!"). What could you do to reduce the cognitive dissonance? If you're like participants in Festinger and Carlsmith's study, you would probably adjust your attitude to better fit your claims. In other words, you would rate the task as more interesting than it actually was.

Some of the participants in the study were paid $20 (as opposed to $1). These individuals were less inclined to change their attitudes to match their claim that the activity was fun—a sign that they felt less cognitive dissonance. Apparently, the big bucks made it easier to justify their lies. *I said I liked the boring task because I got paid $20, not because I actually liked it.*

And now, one more example to drive home the concept of cognitive dissonance. Imagine you are studying for an upcoming economics exam in the student cafe. A friend approaches and the two of you start talking. Your friend says they took the same economics class last year, and they know for a fact that the professor doesn't change the exam from year to year. Then they proceed to tell you about specific questions from last year's exam. You begin to feel uneasy because you know that your instructor would consider this a form of cheating. Your behavior (listening to details about the exam) conflicts with your attitude (*cheating is wrong*). Reducing the conflict between the attitude and behavior could be accomplished in one of two ways: by changing the attitude or by changing the behavior. Which path would you take?

**"I Really Should Be Studying"**
You know that studying ought to take priority over recreational activities, yet you just can't resist watching TikTok videos at the library. This may create some cognitive dissonance, which occurs when your behavior (watching videos) is inconsistent with your belief: *Studying hard leads to good grades.* You could reduce this cognitive dissonance in one of two ways: (1) by changing your behavior (putting down the phone and studying), or (2) by altering your belief: *I actually study harder when I give myself TikTok breaks.*

Sam Edwards/Getty Images.

We have learned about cognitive processes that form the foundation of our social existence. Attributions help us make sense of events and behaviors, and attitudes provide continuity in the way we think and feel about the surrounding world. Now it's time to explore the ways other people influence our behaviors. Are you ready to meet runner extraordinaire Julius Achon?

**cognitive dissonance** A state of tension that results when behaviors are inconsistent with attitudes.

## ▶▶▶ SHOW WHAT YOU KNOW

1. _____ is the study of individuals in relation to others and groups, whereas _____ is the study of the groups themselves, including cultures and societies.
   - **A.** Sociology; social psychology
   - **B.** Social psychology; sociology
   - **C.** Sociology; a confederate
   - **D.** A confederate; social psychology

2. _____ are beliefs used to explain human behaviors and characteristics, as well as situations.
   - **A.** Attributions
   - **B.** Confederates
   - **C.** Dispositions
   - **D.** Attitudes

3. Because of the fundamental attribution error, we tend to attribute causes of behaviors to the:
   - **A.** characteristics of the situation.
   - **B.** factors involved in the event.
   - **C.** length of the activity.
   - **D.** disposition of the person.

4. Social psychology research occasionally employs some form of deception involving confederates. How is this type of deception different from that used in a double-blind study?

✓ CHECK YOUR ANSWERS AT THE BACK OF THE BOOK.

# Social Influence

**11 ORPHANS**    In 1983, a 7-year-old boy in northern Uganda came down with the measles. The child was feverish and coughing. He appeared to be dying. In fact, he did die—or so the local villagers believed. They dug his grave, wrapped him in a burial cloth, and sang him a farewell song. Then, just as they were about to lower the body into the ground, someone heard a sneeze. A few moments later, another sneeze. Could it be? Hastily unwrapping the cloth, the mourners found the child frantically kicking and crying. It's a good thing the boy sneezed that day at his funeral, as the world is a much happier place because he survived. His name is Julius Achon.

Julius grew up in Awake, a village that had no electricity or running water. "Life in Uganda is very tough," says Julius, who spent his childhood sleeping between eight brothers and sisters on the floor of a one-room hut. At age 12, Julius was kidnapped by a government opposition group known as the Lord's Resistance Army (LRA) and forced to become a child soldier. Three months later, he escaped from the rebel camp and, running much of the distance, returned to his village some 100 miles away.

After coming home, Julius began to run competitively. He ran 42 miles barefoot to his first major track meet in the city of Lira. Hours after arriving, Julius was racing—and winning—the 800-, 1,500-, and 3,000-meter races. From that point on, it was one success after another: a stunning victory at the national championships, a scholarship from George Mason University in the United States, a collegiate record in 1996, and participation in the 1996 and 2000 Olympics (Kahn, 2018).

As awe-inspiring as these accomplishments may be, Julius' greatest achievement had little to do with running. In 2003, while training in Uganda, he came upon a bus station in Lira. "I stopped, and then I saw children lying under the bus," Julius says. One of them stood up and started to beg for money. Then more children emerged, 11 of them in all, some as young as 3. They were thin and dirty, and the little ones wore nothing more than long T-shirts and underwear. "Where are your parents?" Julius remembers asking. One of the children said their parents had been killed. "Can I walk you to my home, you know, to go eat?" Julius asked. The children eagerly agreed and followed him home for a meal of rice, beans, and porridge. What happened next may seem unbelievable, but Julius and his family are extraordinary people. Julius asked his father to shelter the 11 orphans, pledging to help with their living expenses (even though he was barely making ends meet himself). His father, who already had six people living in his one-room home, replied, "Ah, it's no problem." And just like that, Julius and his family adopted 11 children.

Charlie Shoemaker.

**Running Hero**
Julius runs by the Lira bus station where he discovered 11 orphans lying under a bus.

# Power of Others

Throughout the years Julius was trotting the globe and winning medals, he never forgot about Uganda. He thought of the people back home with empty stomachs and no access to lifesaving medicine, living in constant fear of the LRA. Julius was raised in a family that had always reached out to neighbors in need, and he felt blessed by all the support he had received from outside the family. "I feel I was so loved [by] others," says Julius, referring to the mentors and coaches who had provided him with places to stay, clothes to wear, and family away from home. So when Julius encountered those 11 orphans lying under the bus, he didn't think twice about coming to their rescue. His decision probably had something to do with the positive interactions he had experienced with people in his past.

**LO 4** Explain the meaning of social influence and recognize factors associated with persuasion.

Rarely a day goes by that we do not come into contact with other human beings. The interactions we have with friends, family, and even strangers impact us in ways we may not realize. Psychologists refer to this as **social influence**—how a person is affected by others as evidenced in behaviors, emotions, and cognition. We begin our discussion with a powerful, yet often unspoken, form of social influence: *expectations.*

Think back to your days in elementary school. What kind of student were you—an overachiever, a kid who struggled, or perhaps the class clown? The answer to this question may depend somewhat on the way your teachers perceived you. In a classic study, researchers administered a nonverbal intelligence test to students in a San Francisco elementary school (Rosenthal & Jacobson, 1966, 1968). Then all the teachers were provided with a list of students who were likely to "show surprising gains in intellectual competence" during the next year (Rosenthal, 2002a, p. 841). But the list was fake; these kids were just a group selected at random (a good example of how deception is used in social psychology research). About 8 months later, the students were given a second intelligence test. The "surprising gains" children showed greater test score increases than their classmates. Mind you, the only difference between these kids and the rest of the students was teacher expectations. The students who were expected to show superior improvement actually did. Why do you think this happened?

Here, we have a case in which teachers' expectations (based on false information) seemed to transform students' aptitudes and facilitate substantial gains. You might call this a *self-fulfilling prophecy:* "The behavior expected actually came to pass because the expecter expected it" (Rosenthal, 2002a, p. 847). What types of teacher behaviors might explain this self-fulfilling prophecy? The teachers may have inadvertently communicated expectations by demonstrating "warmer socioemotional" attitudes toward the "surprising gains" students, provided them with more material and opportunities, or given them more complex and personalized feedback (Rosenthal, 2002a, 2003). From the student's perspective, teacher behaviors can create a desire to work hard, or they can result in a decline in interest and confidence (Kassin et al., 2017).

Since this classic study was conducted some 50 years ago, researchers have studied expectations in a variety of classroom settings. Their results demonstrate that teacher expectations do not have the same effect or degree of impact on all students (Jussim & Harber, 2005). They appear to have greater influence on younger children (first and second graders) and those of lower socioeconomic status (Sorhagen, 2013). Children of color (particularly females) seem to be disproportionally affected by low teacher expectations. As one study found, teachers may predict greater math ability in students who are White as opposed to Black or Hispanic, and male as opposed to female. "This is especially important given that students' perceptions of their academic

Courtesy Elizabeth Farias.

**Expectations Pay Off**
Liz Farias graduates from Eastside College Preparatory School in East Palo Alto, California. Before the school was founded in 1996, high schoolers from East Palo Alto were bused to schools in other communities, and the majority dropped out before graduating. Eastside raised the expectations for these teenagers, putting every single one of them on a college track. These high expectations, combined with the hard work of students, families, faculty, and staff, have produced impressive results: "Over 99% of Eastside's graduates have been accepted to four-year colleges and universities" (Eastside College Preparatory School, n.d., para. 4).

**social influence** How a person is affected by others as evidenced in behaviors, emotions, and cognition.

ability are developed based on messages they receive from their social environment, especially those of their teachers and parents" (Copur-Gencturk et al., 2020, p. 37).

Expectations are powerful, but they are just one form of social influence. Let's return to the story of Julius and learn about more deliberate types of influence.

## Persuasion

When Julius asked his father to shelter and feed the 11 orphans, he was using a form of social influence called **persuasion.** With persuasion, one intentionally tries to make other people change their attitudes and beliefs, which may (or may not) lead to changes in their behaviors. The person doing the persuading does not necessarily have control over those they seek to persuade. Julius could not force his father to feel sympathy for the orphans.

**SOURCE, MESSAGE, AUDIENCE**    According to American psychologist Carl Hovland (1912–1961), persuasive power is determined by three factors: the source, the message, and the audience (Hovland et al., 1953).

> *The source:* People are more likely to be persuaded if the individual or organization sending the message is credible, and credibility may depend on perceived expertise and trustworthiness (Hovland & Weiss, 1951). The familiarity and closeness of the source can also play a role. When it comes to persuading people to get behind a cause on social media, friends and relatives seem to have more clout than organizations (Nekmat et al., 2019).

> *The message:* Persuasion is more likely if the delivery of the message is logical and to the point (Chaiken & Eagly, 1976). Fear-inducing information can increase persuasion, though it might backfire under certain circumstances (Meczkowski et al., 2016). Imagine someone using this message to encourage teeth-flossing: "If you don't floss daily, you can end up with infected gums, and that infection can spread to your eyes and create total blindness!" If the audience is overly frightened by a message (imagine small children being told to floss . . . or else!), the tension they feel may actually interfere with their ability to process the message (Janis & Feshbach, 1953).

> *The audience:* Many characteristics of the audience are important, among them age. Middle-age adults (40 to 60 years old) are unlikely to be persuaded, whereas children are relatively susceptible (Roberts & DelVecchio, 2000). Another factor is emotional state; when people are happy (and eating tasty food, interestingly enough), they are more likely to be persuaded (Aronson, 2018; Janis et al., 1965). Mental focus is also key: If your mind is elsewhere, you are less likely to be affected by message content (Petty & Cacioppo, 1986).

**ELABORATION LIKELIHOOD MODEL**    The *elaboration likelihood model* proposes that the way people process information can impact how persuadable they are. Those who think critically and focus on the content of a message process information using the *central route*. Meanwhile, those who pay more attention to "simple, issue-irrelevant cues," such as the credibility or attractiveness of the source, process information using the *peripheral route* (Li et al., 2017, p. 1076; Petty & Cacioppo, 1986). Think about a stereotypical beer commercial: Good-looking people are laughing and having fun with beers in hand. The ad has little to do with the quality of the beer, but many people are still persuaded to buy it. Advertisers (or anyone trying to be persuasive) will be more effective if they tailor their strategy to the processing route of their target audience. Does the audience use the central route to processing? If so, the message should be "detailed and complex." If the audience

Kevin Dietsch/Pool/Getty Images.

**Credibility Counts**
Dr. Anthony Fauci, who has served as director of the National Institute for Allergy and Infectious Diseases (NIAID) for nearly four decades, has guided six different presidents (both Republican and Democrat) on public health issues (NIAID, n.d.). When the COVID-19 pandemic gained a foothold in the United States, many people looked to Dr. Fauci for guidance on mask-wearing, social distancing, and other measures to slow disease transmission. Sources like Dr. Fauci, who are considered highly credible, are more likely to persuade people to change attitudes and beliefs.

**persuasion** Intentionally trying to make people change their attitudes and beliefs, which may lead to changes in their behaviors.

**compliance** Changes in behavior at the request or direction of another person or group, who in general does not have any true authority.

uses the peripheral route, it's best to keep things "brief and simple," as in the beer commercial (Glassman et al., 2018, p. 1416).

Following the 2018 massacre at Marjory Stoneman Douglas High School in Parkland, Florida, where 17 students and staff members lost their lives, the United States has seen an upsurge in calls for gun control and research on firearm-related deaths (Ocasio et al., 2021; Rubenstein et al., 2019). A person with strong feelings about gun control (either for or against it) might take advantage of central processing when trying to develop a persuasive argument. Consider this statement, written by pediatric trauma surgeons, who care for children wounded by firearms: "Having a firearm in the home is associated with an increased risk of injury and death. For every self-protection homicide, there were 1.3 unintentional firearm deaths, 4.6 criminal homicides and 37 gun suicides" (Petty et al., 2019, p. 10). This message, which explains the numerical relationship between different types of firearm deaths, would be more persuasive to a person using the central processing route. Someone unfamiliar with or indifferent to gun-control policy might be using the peripheral route and therefore focus on the credibility of the source, appearance of the speaker, and so on. The take-home message is this: If you want to persuade as many people as possible, make sure you take advantage of both routes.

## Compliance

**LO 5** Define compliance and explain some of the techniques used to gain it.

The results of persuasion are internal and related to a change in *attitude* (Key et al., 2009). These attitude shifts may or may not lead to changes in behavior. **Compliance,** on the other hand, occurs when people voluntarily change their *behavior* at the request or direction of another person (or group), who generally has no true authority over them. Compliance is evident in changes to "overt behavior" (Key et al., 2009; TABLE **11.1**). For example, someone might send an e-mail asking you to fill out a questionnaire. You are not obligated to respond, but perhaps you will comply. Did you know that requests sent by e-mail are less likely to achieve compliance than those made in person? Even so, people tend to place an undue amount of confidence in e-mail requests (Roghanizad & Bohns, 2017).

Surprisingly, compliance often occurs outside of our awareness. Suppose you are waiting in line at a copy machine, and a man asks if he can cut in front of you. Do you allow it? Your response may depend on the wording of the request. Researchers studying this very scenario—a person asking for permission to cut in line—have found that compliance is much more likely when the request is accompanied by a reason. Saying, "Excuse me, I have five pages. May I use the [copy] machine?" will not work as well as "Excuse me, I have five pages. May I use the [copy] machine, *because I am in a rush?*"

**TABLE 11.1**    Methods of Compliance

| Compliance Technique | What Is It? | Why It Works | Example |
|---|---|---|---|
| Foot-in-the-door technique | Making a small request followed by a larger request | If you have already said yes to a small request, chances are you will agree to a bigger request to remain consistent in your involvement. | Ask a parent for $5 and then $20. |
| Door-in-the-face technique | Making a large, sometimes unreasonable request followed by a smaller request | If the solicitor is willing to give up the large request, the person being solicited tends to give in and satisfy the smaller request. We call this *reciprocal concessions.* | Ask a parent for $100 and then $5. |

Here are two effective approaches for getting people to comply with your requests.

People are more likely to comply with a request that includes a "because" phrase, even if the reasoning is not logical. For example, "*because I am in a rush*" achieves about the same compliance as "*because I have to make copies*" (Langer et al., 1978, p. 637).

One way to achieve compliance is the **foot-in-the-door technique,** which occurs when someone makes a small request, followed by a larger request (Freedman & Fraser, 1966). If a college club is trying to enlist students to help with a service project (such as raising money for children who are starving in Yemen), its members might start by asking students to share information about Yemen's humanitarian crisis with friends on social media. If a student responds positively to this request, the club members might make a bigger request (asking for a cash donation), with the expectation that the student will comply with the second request on the grounds of having said yes to the first. Why would this technique work?

The reasoning is that if you have already said yes to a small request, you will likely agree to a bigger request in order to remain consistent in your involvement. Your prior participation leads you to believe you are the type of person who gets involved; in other words, your attitude has shifted (Cialdini & Goldstein, 2004; Freedman & Fraser, 1966). So why is such a strategy called *foot-in-the-door?* In the past, salespeople went door to door trying to sell their goods and services, and they often achieved success if they could physically get a "foot in the door," thereby keeping it open and continuing their sales pitch. This method may not work as well as it did in the past, as people are now inundated with advertising ploys (Gamian-Wilk & Dolinski, 2020).

Another method for gaining compliance is the **door-in-the-face technique,** which involves making a large, sometimes unreasonable request followed by a smaller request. With this technique, the expectation is that the person will not go along with the large request, but will comply with the smaller request because it may seem minor in comparison. There are numerous reasons people comply under these circumstances, but the main reason seems to be one of *reciprocal concessions.* If the solicitor (the person trying to obtain something) is willing to give up something (the large request), the person being solicited tends to feel that they, too, should give in and satisfy the smaller request (Cialdini & Goldstein, 2004).

Let's review these concepts using Julius as an example. After meeting the 11 orphans, Julius brought the children home and asked his parents to feed them. Once his parents *complied* with this initial request, Julius made a much larger request—he asked them to shelter the children indefinitely. This is an example of the *foot-in-the-door technique* because Julius first made a modest request ("Will you feed these children?") and then followed up with a larger one ("Will you shelter these children?"). Had these requests been flip-flopped, that is, had Julius only wanted to get the children a meal but first asked his parents to house them, we would call it the *door-in-the-face technique.*

Compliance generally occurs in response to specific requests or instructions: Will you lend me $5? Can you chop these onions? Please hold the door. But social influence needn't be explicit. Sometimes we change our behaviors and beliefs without anyone asking us to do so. We simply want to blend in with the crowd.

## Conformity

When Julius came to the United States on a college scholarship in 1995, he was struck by some of the cultural differences he observed between the United States and Uganda—the casual and revealing style of dress, for example. During the decade Julius lived in the United States, he never stopped acting like a Ugandan. Before going out in the evening, he would tuck in his shirt, comb his hair, and make sure his clothes were ironed. You might say Julius refused to *conform* to certain aspects of American culture. Resisting conformity is not always easy to do.

John Russo/Contour by Getty Images.

**Courageous Nonconformist**
In 2014, 17-year-old Malala Yousafzai became the youngest recipient of the Nobel Peace Prize. Yousafzai began her activism at age 11, blogging for the BBC about life under the Taliban in her native Pakistan. Over the next few years, she became an outspoken advocate for girls' education, but her nonconformist stance was not welcomed by all. When Yousafzai was 15, a Taliban gunman entered her school bus and shot her in the head. She recovered from her injuries and has continued to advocate for the rights of women around the world (Chotiner, 2019; NobelPrize.org, 2014).

**foot-in-the-door technique** A compliance technique that involves making a small request first, followed by a larger request.

**door-in-the-face technique** A compliance technique that involves making a large request first, followed by a smaller request.

**LO 6**   Identify the factors that influence the likelihood of someone conforming.

**WHY CONFORM?**   Have you ever found yourself turning to look in the same direction as other people, just because you see them staring at something? We seem to have a commanding urge to do what others are doing, even if it means changing our normal behavior. This tendency to modify our behaviors, attitudes, beliefs, and opinions to match those of others is known as **conformity.** Sometimes we conform to the **norms,** or standards of the social environment, which consists of family, friends, coworkers, or anyone in our social circle. Unlike compliance, which occurs in response to an explicit and direct request, conformity is generally unspoken. We often conform because we feel compelled to fit in and **belong**.

It is important to note that conformity is not always a bad thing. In many situations, we rely on conformity to ensure the smooth running of day-to-day activities. What would it be like to ride on a bus or subway if nobody conformed to common social rules?

**CONNECTIONS**

In **Chapter 9,** we described Maslow's hierarchy of needs, which includes the need to belong. When physiological and safety needs are being met, we may be motivated by the need for love and belongingness, and this can drive us to conform.

**Try This**   Next time you are outside in a crowded area, look up and keep your eyes toward the sky. Do some people change their gazes to match yours, even though there is no other indication that something is happening above?

Heather Shimmin/Shutterstock.com.

**CONFORMITY CLOUDS JUDGMENT?**   In a classic experiment by psychologist Solomon Asch (1907–1996), college-student participants were grouped with confederates working for the researchers. Each participant sat at a table with a small group of confederates (Asch, 1955). Everyone at the table was told to look at two cards: The first was marked with one vertical line, the standard line, and the second with three vertical lines of different lengths, marked 1, 2, and 3 (**FIGURE 11.2**). The group was

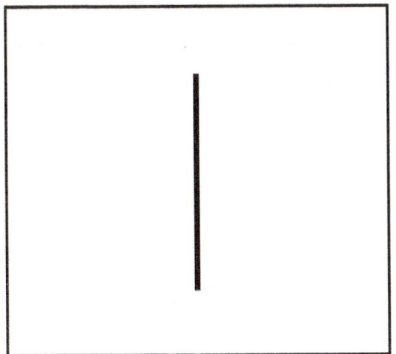

Standard line

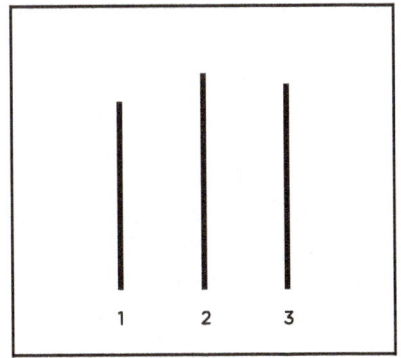

Comparison lines

**FIGURE 11.2**

**Asch's Conformity Experiment**
Participants in this experiment were asked to look at the lines on two cards and indicate which of the comparison lines was closest in length to the standard line. Imagine you are a participant, like the man wearing glasses in this photo, and everyone else at the table chooses Line 3. Would that influence your answer? If you are like many participants, it would; 76% conformed to the incorrect answer at least once. Photo by William Vandivert/ Solomon E. Asch, "Opinions and Social Pressure," *Scientific American,* Nov. 1955, Vol. 193, No. 5, 31–35.

**conformity**   The tendency to modify behaviors, attitudes, beliefs, and opinions to match those of others.

**norms**   Standards of the social environment.

**Research**
**CONNECTIONS**

In **Chapter 1,** we explained that a control group in an experiment is not exposed to the independent variable, or treatment. In this case, the control group is not exposed to confederates giving incorrect answers.

then instructed to announce, one at a time going around the table, which of the three lines was closest in length to the standard line. The first two rounds went smoothly, with everybody in agreement about which of the three lines matched the standard. But then, in the third round, the first five people (all confederates) offered what was clearly the wrong answer, one after the other (per the researchers' instructions).

Would the real participant (the sixth person to answer) follow suit and conform to the wrong answer, or would he stand his ground and report the correct answer? In roughly 37% of the trials, participants went along with the group and provided the incorrect answer. What's more, 76% of the participants conformed and gave the wrong answer at least once (Asch, 1955, 1956). When members of the **control group** made the same judgments alone in a room, they were correct 99% of the time, confirming that the differences between the standard line and the comparison lines were substantial and generally not difficult to assess. It is important to note that most participants (95%) refused to conform on at least one occasion, choosing an answer that conflicted with that of the group (Asch, 1956; Griggs, 2015c). Thus, they were capable of thinking and behaving independently. This type of study was later replicated in a variety of cultures, with mostly similar results (Bond & Smith, 1996), a significant achievement given that some research published in psychology journals has been difficult to replicate (Camerer et al., 2018; Open Science Collaboration, 2015; Schimmack, 2020).

**FOLLOWING THE CROWD**    Why did some participants in Asch's study go along with the group and provide incorrect answers? There are three major reasons for conformity. The first is *normative social influence:* Most of us want the approval of others, and this desire for acceptance may influence our behavior. If you are looking for an example of normative social influence, just think back to middle school—perhaps you remember feeling pressure to be like some of your classmates? A second reason for conformity is *informational social influence:* We follow others in order to be correct. Perhaps you have a friend who is very knowledgeable about politics or medicine. When it comes to these topics, you tend to defer to their expertise, look to them for confirmation, and follow their lead. Third, we may conform to others because they belong to a certain *reference group* we respect, admire, or long to join. Conformity is also influenced by situational circumstances (**FIGURE 11.3**).

**FIGURE 11.3**
**When Do We Conform?**

Listed here are some conditions that increase the likelihood of conforming (Aronson, 2012; Asch, 1955) and others that decrease the odds of conforming (Asch, 1955; Bond & Smith, 1996).

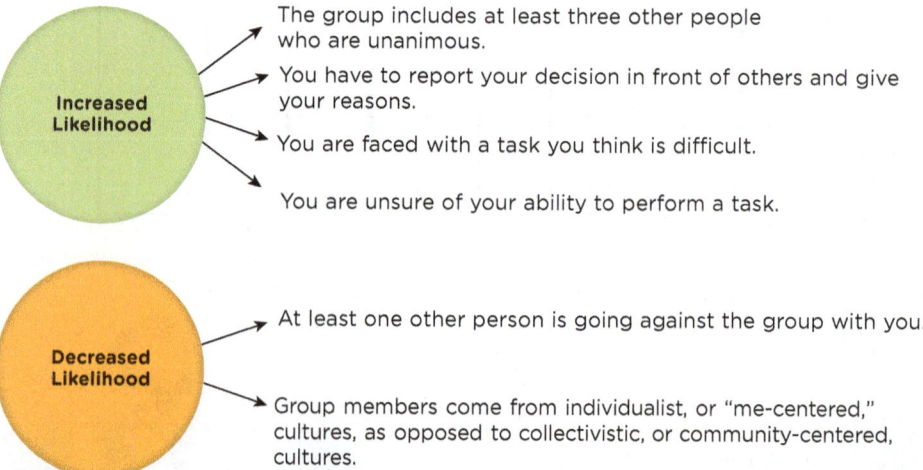

Increased Likelihood
- The group includes at least three other people who are unanimous.
- You have to report your decision in front of others and give your reasons.
- You are faced with a task you think is difficult.
- You are unsure of your ability to perform a task.

Decreased Likelihood
- At least one other person is going against the group with you.
- Group members come from individualist, or "me-centered," cultures, as opposed to collectivistic, or community-centered, cultures.

**Put Your Heads Together**

    You are running a fundraising drive to save the critically endangered Amur leopard. How would you get people to donate money? Team up and discuss ways to **A)** manipulate attitudes (cognitive, affective, and behavioral components), **B)** gain compliance (foot-in-the-door and door-in-the-face), and **C)** encourage conformity.

**TABLE 11.2    Concepts of Social Influence**

| Concept | Definition | Example |
|---------|-----------|---------|
| Persuasion | Intentionally trying to make people change their attitudes and beliefs, which may or may not lead to changes in behavior | Trust our product because it contains the purest ingredients. |
| Compliance | Voluntarily changing behavior at the request or direction of another person or group, who in general does not have any authority over you | Remove your shoes before you walk into the house because you have been asked to do so. |
| Conformity | The tendency to modify behaviors, attitudes, beliefs, and opinions to match those of others | Remove your shoes before you walk into the house because everyone else does. |
| Obedience | Changing your behavior because you have been ordered to do so by an authority figure | Follow the detour sign. |

Whether or not you realize it, other people constantly shape your thoughts, emotions, and behaviors. Here are some important types of social influence.

We have now explored three forms of social influence—persuasion, compliance, and conformity—but there is one yet to cover (**TABLE 11.2**). Let's take a trip to the darker side and examine the frightening phenomenon of obedience.

**BOY SOLDIERS**    Between 1985 and 2005, the Lord's Resistance Army (LRA) is said to have kidnapped some 66,000 youths in northern Uganda (Annan et al., 2006). While a captive of the LRA, Julius witnessed other boy soldiers assaulting innocent people and stealing property. Sometimes at the end of the day, they would laugh or brag about how many people they had beaten or killed. But these were "normal" boys from the villages, children who never would have behaved this way under regular circumstances. Julius remembers seeing other child soldiers cry alone at night after returning to the camp and reflecting on what they had done.

What drives an ordinary child to commit senseless violence? A psychologist might tell you it has something to do with *obedience*.

## Obedience

**LO 7**    Describe obedience and explain how Stanley Milgram studied it.

**Obedience** occurs when we change our behavior, or act in a way we might not normally act, because we have been ordered to do so by an authority figure. In these situations, an imbalance of power exists, and the person with more power (for example, a teacher, police officer, doctor, or boss) generally has an advantage over someone with less power, who is likely to be obedient out of respect, fear, or concern. In some cases, the person in charge demands obedience for the well-being of those less powerful (a parent demanding obedience from a child running wildly through a crowded store). Other times, the person wielding power demands obedience for their own benefit (an adult who perpetrates sexual abuses against children).

**THIS WILL SHOCK YOU: MILGRAM'S STUDY**    In the 1960s, psychologist Stanley Milgram (1933–1984) investigated the extent to which obedience can lead to behaviors that most people would consider unethical. His initial motivation for studying obedience came from learning about the horrific events of World War II and the Holocaust, which "could only have been carried out on a massive scale if a very large number of people obeyed orders" (Milgram, 1974, p. 1). To find how far ordinary people would go in obeying authority figures—particularly when it came to punishing others—Milgram (1963, 1974) conducted a series of experiments. Overall he

Vanessa Vick/Redux.

**Child Exploitation**
These boys were captured by the Lord's Resistance Army (LRA) in 2003 but later rescued. They are among the tens of thousands of children who have been exploited by military groups in Uganda. Julius was just 12 years old when he was abducted by the LRA and forced to fight and plunder on the group's behalf.

**obedience** Changing behavior because we have been ordered to do so by an authority figure.

included 780 participants, only 40 of whom were women (Martin, 2016). The samples included teachers, salespeople, post office workers, engineers, and laborers, representing a wide range of educational backgrounds, from elementary school dropouts to people with graduate degrees. Milgram conducted 24 variations of his experimental method over the course of one year, starting in the summer of 1961 (Martin, 2016). Described here is a basic outline of the method he used.

Upon arriving at Milgram's Yale University laboratory, participants were informed that they would be using punishment as part of a learning experiment (another example of research deception). Then they were asked to draw a slip of paper from a hat. All the slips read "teacher," but the participants were led to believe that the slips read either "teacher" or "learner." Thus, every study participant ended up playing the role of teacher, while confederates enlisted by the researchers played that of learner. To start, the teacher was asked to sit in the learner's chair so they could experience a 45-volt shock, just to know what the learner might be feeling. Next, the teacher was instructed to sit at a control panel and led to believe they would be delivering shocks. The panel went from 15 volts to 450 volts, labeled from "slight shock" to "XXX" (**INFOGRAPHIC 11.2**). The goal, the teacher was told, was for the learner to memorize a set of paired words. Each time the learner made a mistake, the teacher was to administer a shock, and the shock would increase by 15 volts for every mistake. The learner was located in a separate room, arms strapped to a table and electrodes attached to his wrists, apparently receiving shocks.

In reality, the learner (a confederate) did not receive any shocks, but instead followed a script of responses. The learner's behaviors, including the mistakes he made with the word pairs and his reactions to the increasing shock levels (mild complaints, screaming, references to his heart condition, pleas for the experiment to stop, and total silence as if he were unconscious or even dead), were identical for all participants. A researcher in a white lab coat (also a confederate with scripted responses) always remained in the room with the teacher, insisting the experiment proceed if the teacher questioned going any further. Meanwhile, the learner continued with appeals, such as "Experimenter, get me out of here. . . . I refuse to go on" or "I can't stand the pain" (Milgram, 1965, p. 62). The researcher would say to the teacher, "Please continue" and "You have no other choice, you *must* go on" (Milgram, 1963, p. 374).

How many participants do you think obeyed the researcher and proceeded with the experiment in spite of the learner's desperate pleas? Although some participants refused to go on (Appel, 2019), an astounding 60–65% of participants continued to the highest voltage level (Martin, 2016). Most of them showed obvious signs of discomfort (stuttering, sweating, trembling), yet they still obeyed the researcher. One person who witnessed the study reported the following: "I observed a mature and initially poised businessman enter the laboratory smiling and confident. Within 20 minutes he was reduced to a twitching, stuttering wreck, who was rapidly approaching a point of nervous collapse" (Milgram, 1963, p. 377). Even participants who eventually refused to proceed went much further than Milgram or anyone else had predicted—they all used shocks up to at least 300 volts, or "Intense Shock" (Milgram, 1963, 1964; Infographic 11.2).

**REPLICATING MILGRAM** This type of research has been replicated in the United States and other countries, and the findings have remained fairly consistent, with 61–90% of participants continuing to the highest level of shock (Aronson, 2018; Blass, 1999; Doliński et al., 2017). Not surprisingly, criticisms of Milgram's studies have been strong (Martin, 2016; Perry et al., 2020). Many were concerned that the research went too far with its deception (it would certainly not receive approval from an **Institutional Review Board** today), and some wondered if the participants were harmed by knowing that they theoretically could have killed someone

## Why Do People Join Cults?

Members of the Peoples Temple cult pose for a photo in 1975. Three years later, some 909 cult members participated in a collective suicide/murder under the direction of Reverend Jim Jones. What made these people obey their leader to the point of death? Jones used some of the same "mind control" tactics outlined in George Orwell's classic novel, *1984*, including constant surveillance, food restriction, control of sexual behaviors, and creating illusions of intense emotional bonds with followers. Members of the cult truly believed that Jones, whom they called "Dad," cared for them (Zimbardo, 2020). Attachment to charismatic leaders may be facilitated by oxytocin, a neurotransmitter and hormone that plays an important role in parent–child bonding (Gordon & Berson, 2018).

Claire Janaro/The Jonestown Institute.

**CONNECTIONS**

In **Chapter 1,** we reported that professional organizations have specific guidelines to ensure ethical treatment of research participants. They include doing no harm, safeguarding welfare, and respecting the dignity of living things. An Institutional Review Board also ensures the well-being of participants.

# Milgram's Shocking Obedience Study

Stanley Milgram's study on obedience and authority was one of the most ground-breaking and surprising experiments in all of social psychology. Milgram wanted to test the extent to which we will follow the orders of an authority figure. Would we follow orders to hurt someone else, even when that person was begging us to stop? Milgram's experiment also raises ethical issues about deception and informed consent.

Participants had to actually think they were shocking another person for the experiment to work. Creating this deception involved the use of confederates (people secretly working for the researchers) whose behaviors and spoken responses were carefully scripted. Milgram found high levels of obedience in his participants—much higher than he and others had predicted at the beginning of the study.

"Please continue."

"The experiment requires that you go on."

EXPERIMENTER (confederate)

Shock generator

TEACHER (participant)

LEARNER (confederate)

The "teacher" who operated the shock generator in Milgram's experiment was the only actual participant. The experiment involved two confederates: a "learner" who pretended to suffer shocks administered by the participant, and an "experimenter" who prompted the participant to continue (Milgram, 1965).

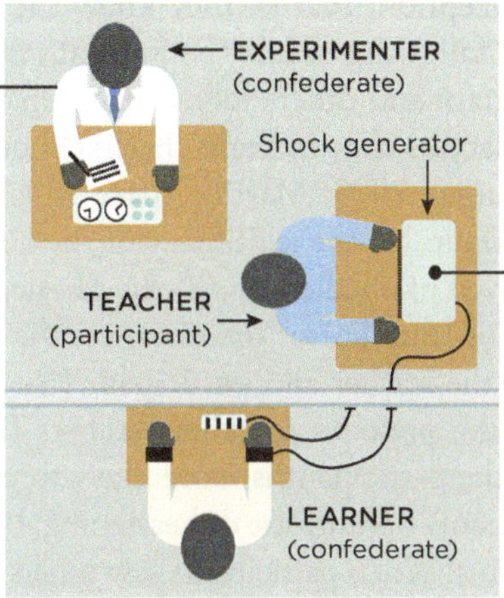

Credit: Stanley Milgram and Alexandra Milgram, distributed by Alexander Street Press.

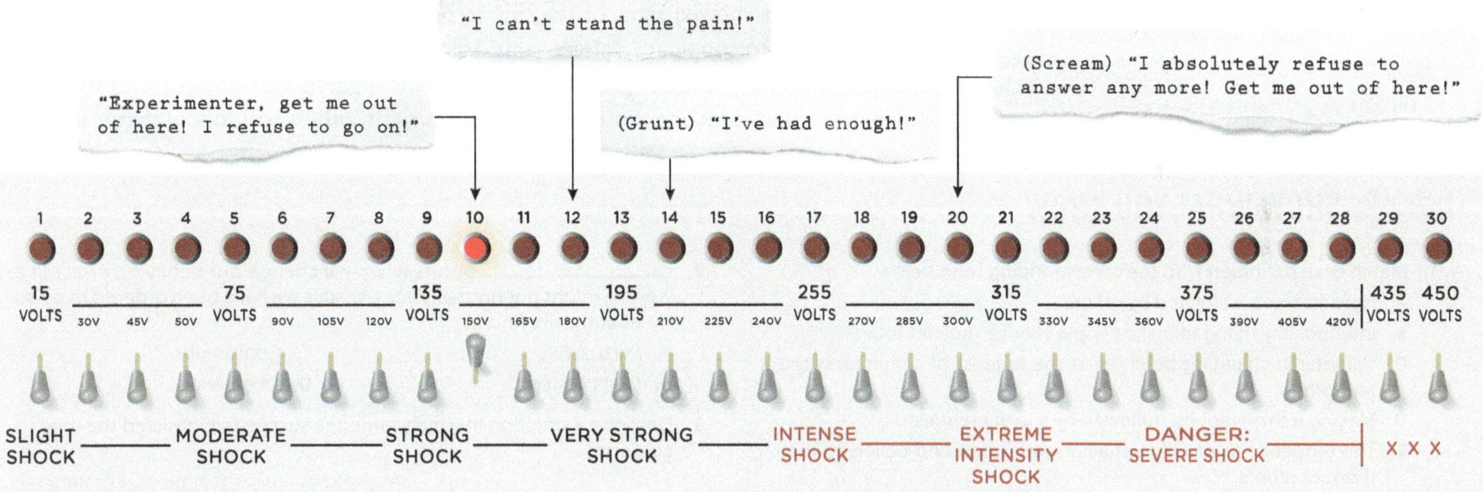

"I can't stand the pain!"

(Scream) "I absolutely refuse to answer any more! Get me out of here!"

"Experimenter, get me out of here! I refuse to go on!"

(Grunt) "I've had enough!"

| 1 | 2 | 3 | 4 | 5 | 6 | 7 | 8 | 9 | 10 | 11 | 12 | 13 | 14 | 15 | 16 | 17 | 18 | 19 | 20 | 21 | 22 | 23 | 24 | 25 | 26 | 27 | 28 | 29 | 30 |

| 15 VOLTS | 30V | 45V | 50V | 75 VOLTS | 90V | 105V | 120V | 135 VOLTS | 150V | 165V | 180V | 195 VOLTS | 210V | 225V | 240V | 255 VOLTS | 270V | 285V | 300V | 315 VOLTS | 330V | 345V | 360V | 375 VOLTS | 390V | 405V | 420V | 435 VOLTS | 450 VOLTS |

SLIGHT SHOCK • MODERATE SHOCK • STRONG SHOCK • VERY STRONG SHOCK • INTENSE SHOCK • EXTREME INTENSITY SHOCK • DANGER: SEVERE SHOCK • X X X

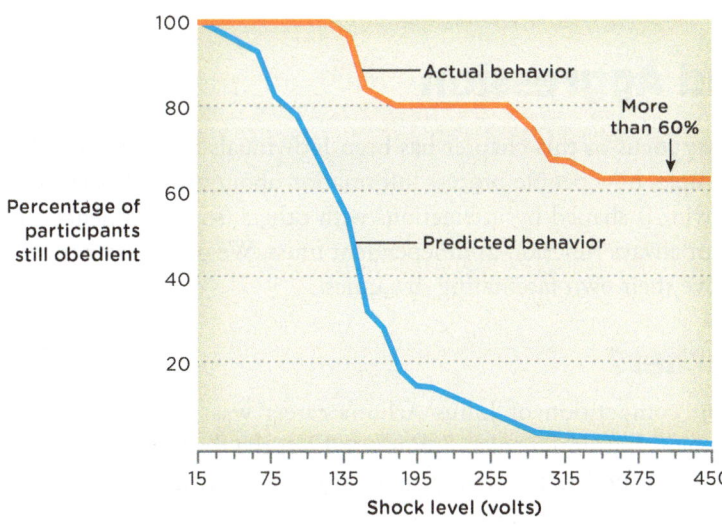

Percentage of participants still obedient

Actual behavior

More than 60%

Predicted behavior

100 / 80 / 60 / 40 / 20

15 / 75 / 135 / 195 / 255 / 315 / 375 / 450

Shock level (volts)

On the control panel of Milgram's shock generator, the participant would see 30 switches clearly labeled as delivering a range from "Slight Shock" (15 volts) to "Danger: Severe Shock" (375 volts) and beyond. The "learner" produced scripted responses at every level (Milgram, 1963).

Before the experiment, Milgram and a panel of experts predicted most participants would not proceed beyond 150 volts, when the "learner" explicitly demands to end the experiment. In fact, actual results show that many participants obeyed the experimenter's commands all the way to the highest shock level (Milgram, 1965).

with their choices during the study. Milgram (1964) spent time with participants following the study, and reported that 84% claimed to be "glad" they had participated, while only 1.3% were "sorry." The participants underwent psychiatric evaluations a year later, and none of them were said to "show signs of having been harmed by his experiences" (Milgram, 1964, p. 850). Criticisms of Milgram's research have continued, with some questioning his representation of the "seriously inadequate debriefing process," "extended prodding of participants" to continue the experiment, and "selective nonreporting" of several of his 23 studies (Griggs & Whitehead, 2015, p. 315). Others offer evidence that some participants were aware of the deception; that is, they knew the shocks were fake and thus did not have a problem following orders (Perry et al., 2020).

Milgram and others followed up on the original study to determine if there are specific factors that increase the likelihood of obedience in such a scenario (Blass, 1991; Burger, 2009; Martin, 2016; Milgram, 1965). All of the following appear to be important: (1) the legitimacy of the authority figure (more legitimate figures gain higher levels of obedience), (2) the physical distance between the authority figure and participant (the shorter the distance, the more obedience), (3) the physical distance between the learner and participant (the greater the distance, the more obedience), and (4) the presence of other teachers (if another confederate acts as an obedient teacher, the participant is more likely to obey as well).

Milgram's findings are disheartening, but one ray of hope shines through in his later experiments: When participants saw others refuse to obey, they sometimes followed suit. In a follow-up experiment, two additional confederates played the role of teacher. If these confederates showed signs of refusing to obey the authority figure, the participant was far less likely to cooperate. In fact, only 10% of participants were willing to carry on with the learning experiment (Milgram, 1974). This suggests that one person can make a difference; when someone stands up for what is right, others will follow that lead.

 **SHOW WHAT YOU KNOW**

1. Match each definition with the corresponding term below:
   **A.** How a person is affected by others
   **B.** Intentionally trying to make people change their attitudes
   **C.** Voluntarily changing behavior at the request of someone without authority
   **D.** Making a small request, followed by a larger request
   **E.** The tendency to modify behaviors, attitudes, and beliefs to match those of others

   _____ conformity      _____ persuasion      _____ social influence
   _____ compliance      _____ foot-in-the-door technique

2. _____ occurs when we change our behavior, or act in a way we might not normally act, because we have been ordered to do so by an authority figure.
   **A.** Persuasion                    **C.** Conformity
   **B.** Compliance                    **D.** Obedience

3. Describe a situation in which someone successfully resisted the urge to conform.

✓ CHECK YOUR ANSWERS AT THE BACK OF THE BOOK.

# Groups and Aggression

Thus far, the primary focus of this chapter has been individuals in social situations. We learned, for example, how people process information about others (social cognition) and how behavior is shaped by interactions with others (social influence). But human beings do not always function as independent units. We often come together in groups, which have their own fascinating dynamics.

## Better Together?

The most important competition of Julius Achon's career was probably the 1994 World Junior Championships in Portugal. Julius was 17 at the time and representing Uganda. It was his first experience traveling in an airplane, wearing running shoes, and racing on a rubber track. No one expected an unknown boy from Uganda to win, but Julius surprised everyone, including himself. Crossing the finish line strides ahead of the others, he almost looked uncertain as he raised his arms in celebration.

Julius ran the 1500 meters (the equivalent of 0.93 miles) in approximately 3 minutes and 40 seconds. Do you suppose he would have run this fast if he had been alone? Research suggests the answer is no (Worringham & Messick, 1983). In some situations, people perform better when others are observing (Steinmetz et al., 2016). This is particularly true when the task at hand is uncomplicated (running) and the individual is well prepared. (Runners may spend months training for races.) Through **social facilitation,** personal performance may improve when the activity is fairly straightforward and the person is adequately prepped. The presence of others does not always lead to higher achievement, however (Aiello & Douthitt, 2001). When people are watching, one may spend precious cognitive resources trying to pay attention to them, which can actually lead to decreases in performance (Belletier et al., 2019).

## When Two Heads Are Not Better Than One

Have you ever noticed that people on teams sometimes slack off and let others do all the work? When individual contributions to the group aren't easy to ascertain, **social loafing** may occur (Latané et al., 1979). Social loafing is the tendency for people to put forth less than their best effort when individual contributions are too complicated to measure. It often goes hand-in-hand with **diffusion of responsibility,** or the sharing of responsibilities among all group members. Diffusion of responsibility can lead to feelings of decreased accountability and motivation. If we suspect other group members are slacking, we tend to follow suit in order to keep things equal.

### Apply This ⬇

**CUT THE LOAFING**   Want some advice on how to reduce social loafing in your workgroups? Even if an instructor doesn't require it, try to get other students in your group to designate and take responsibility for specific tasks. Have team members specify their contributions to the end product, submit their part of the work to the group before the assignment is due, and participate in a group presentation (Jones, 2013; Maiden & Perry, 2011; Voyles et al., 2015). If possible, use video-conferencing technologies such as Skype or Zoom to work together, as this type of collaboration may encourage group members to do their part. Keep in mind that social loafing is less likely to occur when the assignment is challenging and group members feel they have something special to contribute (Simms & Nichols, 2014). If you do have some "free riders" in your group, don't automatically assume they are lazy or apathetic. Some group members fail to pull their weight because they feel incompetent (perhaps a result of language difficulties), or because they are not "team players" (Barr et al., 2005; Hall & Buzwell, 2012). Communicate with these individuals early in the process, and work with your group to identify a task that each person can perform with confidence and success.

**DEINDIVIDUATION**   Social loafing may be annoying and problematic, but other group dynamics can more dangerous. In the last section, we discussed how obedience played a role in the senseless violence carried out by boy soldiers in Uganda. We suspect that the actions of these children also had something to do with *deindividuation.* People in groups sometimes feel a diminished sense of personal responsibility, inhibition, or adherence to social norms. This state of **deindividuation** can

**Faster Together?**
Runners compete in the Women's 100m T42 Final during the 2016 Paralympics in Rio. Through social facilitation, competitive athletes may help each other perform better. Some research suggests that racers may actually synchronize their body movements at various points in time, without even being aware of it (Varlet & Richardson, 2015).

**social facilitation** The tendency for the presence of others to improve personal performance when the activity is fairly uncomplicated and a person is adequately prepared.

**social loafing** The tendency for group members to put forth less than their best effort when individual contributions are too complicated to measure.

**diffusion of responsibility** The sharing of duties and responsibilities among all group members that can lead to feelings of decreased accountability and motivation.

**deindividuation** The diminished sense of personal responsibility, inhibition, or adherence to social norms that occurs when group members are not treated as individuals.

occur when group members are not treated as individuals, and thus begin to exhibit a "lack of self-awareness" (Diener, 1979). As members of a group, the boy soldiers may have felt a loss of identity, social responsibility, and ability to discriminate right from wrong.

Research suggests that children are indeed vulnerable to deindividuation. In a classic study of trick-or-treaters, psychologist Ed Diener and his colleagues (Diener et al., 1976) set up an **experiment** in 27 homes throughout Seattle, Washington. Children arriving at these houses to trick-or-treat were ushered in by a woman (a confederate, of course). She told them they could take *one* piece of candy from a bowl on the table. Next to the bowl of candy was a second bowl filled with pennies and nickels. The woman then excused herself, saying she had to get back to work in another room. Unknown to the children, an experimenter was observing their behavior through a peephole, tallying up the amount of candy and/or money they took. The other variable being recorded was the number of children and adults in the hallway; the experimenters never knew how many people would show up when the doorbell rang!

The findings were fascinating. If a parent was present, the children were well behaved. (Only 8% took more than one piece of candy.) But with no adult present, events unfolded quite differently: 21% of children took more than the allotted amount when they came through the door **alone** and anonymous. (The confederate did not ask for names or other identifying information.) Perhaps more shocking, 80% of the children took extra candy and/or money when they were in a group and anonymous. The condition of being in a group combined with anonymity created a sense of deindividuation (Diener et al., 1976).

We have shown how deindividuation occurs in groups of children, but what about adults? This type of behavior has been observed in various settings and with many groups of people. Fans of soccer, football, and other sports have been known to storm playing fields and vandalize property, showing virtually no regard for the safety of others. Internet "trolls" bully people and spread inflammatory content on social media (Monakhov, 2020). Would people act this way if they weren't part of a crowd? We suspect their behaviors have something to do with deindividuation.

**MORE PEOPLE, MORE PROBLEMS?**    When people associate with like-minded individuals (think Republicans and Democrats), they tend to reinforce each other's positions. **Group polarization** is the tendency for group members to take a more extreme stance after deliberations and discussion (Myers & Lamm, 1976). Suppose you convene several individuals who strongly support universal health care. As they hear others echo their opinions and offer supporting evidence, their original beliefs and positions are reinforced, and the conversation becomes more one-sided. So is group deliberation actually useful? Perhaps not when the members are initially in agreement.

As a group becomes increasingly united, another process known as **groupthink** can occur. This is the tendency for group members to maintain cohesiveness and agreement in their decision making, and fail to consider alternatives and related viewpoints (Janis, 1972; Rose, 2011). During the COVID-19 pandemic, groups of people spread misinformation (e.g., "COVID is a lie") and acted in nonproductive ways (Forsyth, 2020, p. 140). Groupthink may have prevented protesters from asking logical questions like, *"Is it a good idea to block the entrance to a trauma treatment center during a pandemic?"* (p. 141). Instructors can help guard against groupthink in the classroom by assigning students to explore a variety of perspectives surrounding a "contentious argument"—about abortion or the death penalty, for example (Ceci & Williams, 2018). Groupthink is thought to have played a role in a variety of disasters, including the sinking of the *Titanic* in 1912, the explosion of the *Challenger* space

---

**CONNECTIONS**

In **Chapter 1**, we discussed a type of descriptive research that involves studying participants in their natural environments: Naturalistic observation requires that researchers do not disturb the participants or their surroundings. Would Diener's study be considered naturalistic observation?

**CONNECTIONS**

What motivated the children who were alone? In **Chapter 9**, we discussed various sources of motivation, ranging from instincts to the need for power. These sources of motivation might help explain why some children took more than their fair share of candy when they thought no one was watching.

**group polarization** The tendency for group members to take a more extreme stance than originally held after deliberations and discussion.

**groupthink** The tendency for group members to maintain cohesiveness and agreement in their decision making, failing to consider possible alternatives and related viewpoints.

shuttle in 1986, the Mount Everest climbing tragedy in 1996, and the U.S. decision to invade Iraq in 2003 (Badie, 2010; Burnette et al., 2011).

As you can see, groupthink can have life-or-death consequences. So, too, can the *bystander effect,* another alarming phenomenon that occurs among people in groups.

**THE BYSTANDER WHO REFUSED TO STAND BY**   Before meeting Julius in 2003, the 11 orphans spent their days begging for money. Usually, they ate scraps of food that hotels had poured onto side roads for dogs and cats. At night, they kept each other warm coiled beneath the bus, and they shared food when there was enough to go around. The older children looked after the little ones, making sure they had something to eat. Day after day, the orphans encountered hundreds of passersby. But of all those people, only three or four would typically offer food or money, nothing more—until a thin, muscular man in his mid-twenties appeared wearing the most unusual outfit. Dressed in a sleeveless top (a runner's singlet), short shorts, and fancy sneakers, Julius Achon looked different from any person the orphans had seen before (S. Mugisha, personal communication, March 9, 2012). And he was, of course, different. This man would ultimately ensure the orphans had everything they needed for a chance at a better life—food, clothing, a place to sleep, an education, and a family.

**LO 8**   Recognize factors that influence the bystander effect.

**THE BYSTANDER EFFECT**   Before meeting Julius, the orphans had been homeless for several months. Why didn't anyone try to rescue them? "Everybody was fearing responsibility," Julius says. In northern Uganda, many people cannot even afford to feed themselves, so they are reluctant to lend a helping hand.

But perhaps there was another factor at work, one that psychologists call the **bystander effect.** When a person is in trouble, bystanders have the tendency to assume (and perhaps wish) that someone else will help—and therefore stand by and do nothing. (This is partly a result of the *diffusion of responsibility.*) The bystander effect often occurs when many people are present. Strange as it seems, we are more likely to aid a person in distress if no one else is around (Darley & Latané, 1968; Eagly & Crowley, 1986; Latané & Darley, 1968). So when people encountered the orphans begging on the street, they probably assumed somebody else would take care of the problem. *These children must belong to someone; their parents will come back for them.*

Perhaps the most famous illustration of the bystander effect is the Kitty Genovese case. It was March 13, 1964, around 3:15 A.M., when Catherine "Kitty" Genovese arrived home from work in her Queens, New York, neighborhood. As she approached her apartment building, an attacker brutally stabbed her. Kitty screamed for help, but initial reports suggested that no one came to her rescue. The attacker ran away, and Kitty stumbled to her apartment building. But he soon returned, raping and stabbing her to death. *The New York Times* originally reported that 38 neighbors heard her cries for help, witnessed the attack, and did nothing to assist. But the evidence suggests there were far fewer eyewitnesses (perhaps only a half dozen), and that several people did respond (by screaming out their windows, with at least one person calling the police). What's more, the second attack occurred inside her building, where few people could have witnessed it (Griggs, 2015d; Manning et al., 2007). The attacker was arrested 5 days later when, ironically, two bystanders intervened after witnessing him commit a burglary (Kassin, 2017b).

More recently, in April 2010, a homeless man (also in Queens) was left to die after several people walked by him and decided to do nothing. The man, Hugo Tale-Yax, had been trying to help a woman under assault, but the attacker stabbed him in the chest (Livingston et al., 2010). As many as 25 people walked past

New York Daily News Archive/Getty Images.

**A Classic, but Imperfect, Example**
The murder of Kitty Genovese is frequently used to explain the bystander effect, but it is not a perfect illustration. An early news report suggested that 38 people witnessed the attack and did nothing to help, but there were actually far fewer bystanders, and some of them tried to intervene (Ferguson et al., 2018; Manning et al., 2007).

**bystander effect** The tendency for people to avoid getting involved in an emergency they witness because they assume someone else will help.

## FIGURE 11.4

**Understanding the Bystander Effect**

When you first encounter an emergency, you immediately feel personal distress and experience a reflexive response that causes you to avoid the situation or freeze. This response, which is accompanied by decreased activation in the two brain areas highlighted in the scans on the right, is enhanced when other bystanders are present. Following this initial reaction, you may feel sympathy, which increases your tendency to offer help (Hortensius & de Gelder, 2018). Hortensius, R., & de Gelder, B. (2018). From empathy to apathy: The bystander effect revisited.

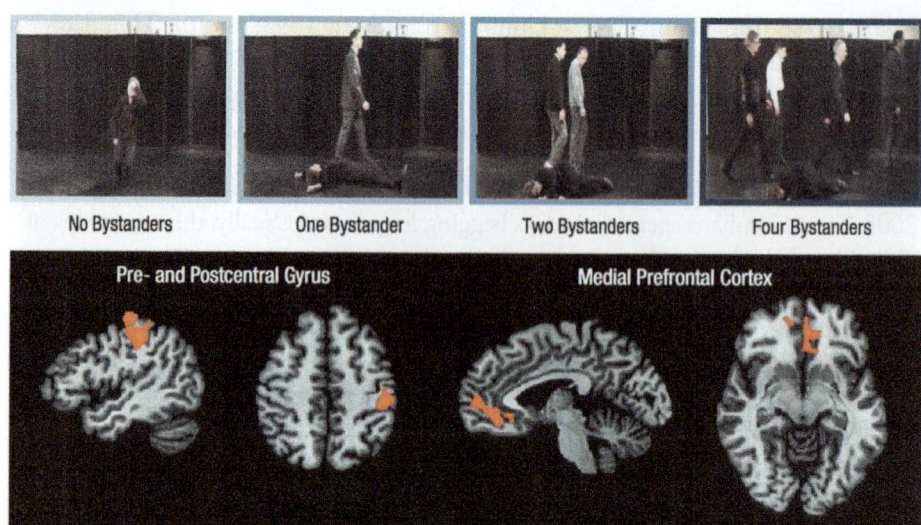

No Bystanders  One Bystander  Two Bystanders  Four Bystanders

Pre- and Postcentral Gyrus  Medial Prefrontal Cortex

Mr. Tale-Yax as he lay on the ground dying, and one even took a cell phone picture of him before walking away. The bystander effect also happens online. In one survey study, only a third of students reported that they came to the aid of cyberbullying victims (Olenik-Shemesh et al., 2017). How might the bystander effect play a role in school or workplace bullying?

More recent research suggests that things are not as bleak as these events suggest (Liebst et al., 2021; Philpot et al., 2020). Researchers report that people will lend a hand if their resources allow for it. For example, following a natural disaster, people are inclined to help others in distress, especially if they have not sustained damage to their own property (Vardy & Atkinson, 2019). In extremely dangerous situations, bystanders are actually *more* likely to help even if there is more than one person watching. More dangerous situations are recognized and interpreted quickly as being such, leading to faster intervention and help (Fischer et al., 2011). If we want to increase the likelihood of bystanders getting involved in stopping violence, we need to find ways to encourage emotional empathy. This is particularly important for boys, some of whom may need specific training on how to "recognize signs of distress in others" (Menolascino & Jenkins, 2018, p. 305). Learn more about the bystander effect in **FIGURE 11.4**, and discover factors that increase helping behavior in **TABLE 11.3**.

**TABLE 11.3**  Why Lend a Hand?

| Why People Help | Explanation |
| --- | --- |
| Kin selection | We are more likely to help those who are close relatives, as it might promote the survival of our genes (Gray & Brogdon, 2017; Hamilton, 1964). |
| Empathy | We assist others to reduce their distress (Batson & Powell, 2003). |
| Social exchange theory | We help when the benefits of our good deeds outweigh the costs (Cropanzano et al., 2017; Thibaut & Kelly, 1959). |
| Reciprocal altruism | We help those whom we believe can return the favor in the future (Brase, 2017; Trivers, 1971). |
| Mood | We tend to help others when our mood is good, but we also help when our spirits are low, knowing that this behavior can improve our mood (Batson & Powell, 2003; Schnall et al., 2010). |

Listed here are some of the reasons people assist each other in times of need.

# Aggression

**THE ULTIMATE INSULT**  When Julius attended high school in Uganda's capital city of Kampala, he never told his classmates that he had been kidnapped by the LRA. "I would not tell them, or anybody, that I was a child soldier," he says. Had the other students known, they might have called him a *rebel*—one of the most derogatory terms you can use to describe a person in Uganda. Calling someone a rebel is like saying that individual is worthless. "You're poor; you do not know anything; you're a killer," Julius says. You feel that kind of pain inside you . . . when they call you a 'rebel' within your country."

**LO 9**  Define aggression and identify some of its causes.

Using racial slurs and hurling threatening insults are forms of *aggression*. Psychologists define **aggression** as intimidating or threatening behavior or attitudes intended to hurt someone. Aggression does not always manifest as overt physical violence. It may be expressed through putdowns that are "small, common, and sometimes ambiguous" (Williams, 2020, p. 3). These *microaggressions* may seem subtle, but they accumulate and cause great pain for those on the receiving end. Being a target of repeated microaggressions can feel like "death by a thousand cuts" (Vassall, 2020, para. 10). See **TABLE 11.4** for some examples of microaggressions against people of color and other targets.

Aggressive tendencies seem to be rooted in our genes. Studies comparing identical and fraternal twins suggest that aggression runs in families. **Identical twins**, who have nearly all the same genes, are more likely than fraternal twins to share aggressive traits (Bezdjian et al., 2011; Porsch et al., 2016). Some research on identical twins suggests that approximately 50–68% of aggressive behavior in the population can be explained by genetic factors (DiLalla, 2002; Lubke et al., 2018; Tackett et al., 2009). Hormones and neurotransmitters may also play a role, with high levels of testosterone and low

**CONNECTIONS**

In previous chapters, we noted that identical twins share 100% of their genetic material at conception, whereas fraternal twins share approximately 50%. Here, we see that identical twins are more likely than fraternal twins to share aggressive traits.

## TABLE 11.4  Examples of Microaggressions

| Example | Underlying Hostile Message |
|---|---|
| Someone says to a person of color, "What are you?" or, "Where are you from?" | The person is "other" and doesn't belong in this country. |
| A coworker tells a female employee to "calm down" when she simply disagrees with a decision. | The person is emotional because she is a woman. |
| A retail employee follows a person of color around a store. | The person is assumed to be a thief because of their race. |
| A teacher assumes that an Asian student is good at math. | The person is boxed into a "smart Asian" stereotype. |
| A restaurant patron assumes that a person of color is a server or a busser. | The person is assumed to be a service employee because of their race. |
| Someone asks a gay person what made them choose to have same-sex partners. | The person is assumed to have control over their sexual orientation. |
| Someone feels uncomfortable around a person who is blind and ignores them. | The person is somehow incomplete because they have a disability. |

A microaggression is a subtle, sometimes unconscious, statement or behavior that reveals a hostile attitude toward a certain group of people. Listed here are some examples of microaggressions and the hostile messages they may reveal (Lui & Quezada, 2019). Information from Lui & Quezada, 2019.

**aggression** Intimidating or threatening behavior or attitudes intended to hurt someone.

levels of serotonin correlating with aggression in some cases (Geniole et al., 2020; Glenn et al., 2011; Montoya et al., 2012). According to the **frustration–aggression hypothesis,** we all can exhibit aggressive behavior when placed in a frustrating situation (Dollard et al., 1939).

Expressions of aggression may be influenced by gender. Some researchers have reported that men tend to show more *direct aggression* (physical displays of aggression such as hitting), while women are more likely to display *relational aggression*—behaviors such as gossip, exclusion, and ignoring, which are indirect and aimed at relationships (Ainsworth & Maner, 2012; Archer & Coyne, 2005; Denson et al., 2018). These types of sex differences have recently been called into question, however (Slawinski et al., 2019). Why might women favor relational aggression over direct aggression? One reason, according to the evolutionary perspective, is that females run a greater risk of bodily injury from a physical confrontation (Campbell, 1999). Gender disparities in aggressive behavior may appear early in life (Denson et al., 2018; Hanish et al., 2012), and result from a complex interaction of genetics and environmental factors—that is, nature and nurture (Brendgen et al., 2005; Lubke et al., 2018).

Many environmental factors seem to set the stage for aggression, among them childhood abuse and exposure to trauma. Such events could potentially trigger **epigenetic changes** that can alter the expression of genes, including those that influence behavior (Provençal et al., 2015). Risk factors for aggression can also occur on a global scale, affecting many people simultaneously. For example, hotter weather resulting from human-induced climate change may lead to increased levels of aggression around the world: "As a general trend, violence increases as climates become hotter" (Rinderu et al., 2018, p. 113). Similarly, elevated levels of air pollution may set the stage for criminal behavior. Researchers writing for *Scientific American* take a closer look at this phenomenon, below.

## CONNECTIONS

In **Chapter 8,** we introduced epigenetics, a field that examines processes involved in the development of phenotypes. Environmental factors can trigger epigenetic changes and thereby influence which genes are "turned on" or "turned off." Here, we discuss how early childhood experiences may cause epigenetic changes that could potentially pave the way for aggressive behaviors.

*From the* SCIENTIFIC *pages of* AMERICAN

# DARKER SKIES, DARKER BEHAVIORS

Why air pollution may increase crime.

Air pollution costs the world approximately $5 trillion a year, or about 7 percent of global GDP, according to the World Bank. This cost is measured in a range of metrics, including lives lost and declines in health and productivity. Such pollution can be seen, felt, smelled, and even tasted. It stings and blurs the eyes, blackens the lungs, and shortens the breath. Even in the United States, about 142 million Americans still reside in counties with dangerously polluted air. Yet air pollution affects more than just our health and our natural environment: Our research shows that air pollution also has a *moral* cost.

Without even realizing it, people around the world may be affected, morally, by air pollution. Recent data on daily changes in wind direction in Chicago and Los Angeles suggest that air pollution increases violent crime. Using both archival and lab data, we took a closer look at the link between air pollution and unethical behavior, finding that the experience of air pollution increased unethical behavior.

In our research, we first analyzed nine years of data on nearly 10,000 U.S. cities to examine how air pollution influences different crime categories, including murder, robbery, aggravated assault, and burglary. We ruled out many important factors that might explain the relationship between air pollution and unethical behavior, such as a city's population, law enforcement, demographic composition (e.g., median age, gender, race, education), income, poverty, and unemployment. Over and above these other factors, we found that high levels of air pollution were linked to increases in six crime categories, including murder, robbery, aggravated assault, and burglary. [. . .]

**frustration–aggression hypothesis**
Suggests that aggression may occur in response to frustration.

Our research offers another compelling reason to work on reducing air pollution. When environments are less polluted, they are not only healthier, but also safer. The marginal dollar invested in cleaning our collective skies appears to have larger effects than policymakers thought. And these effects are not just felt in our health and in our economic lives, but in our moral lives as well. The purer our air, the purer our actions.

Before

After

### Greener Spaces, Lower Crime

What would happen if you went into a major city and converted hundreds of abandoned land parcels into "green spaces" with freshly planted grass and trees? Researchers conducted such an experiment, and the effects were striking: Gun violence, burglary, and other crimes declined substantially, and residents felt safer and spent more time outside. The investment required was relatively minor ($5 per square meter of land), but the payoff was major: "Direct changes to vacant urban spaces may hold great promise in directly breaking the urban cycle of violence, fear, and abandonment and doing so in a cost-effective way that has broad, citywide scalability" (Branas et al., 2018, p. 2950). Citywide cluster randomized trial to restore blighted vacant land and its effects on violence, crime, and fear. Charles C. Branas, Eugenia South, Michelle C. Kondo, Bernadette C. Hohl, Philippe Bourgois, Douglas J. Wiebe, John M. MacDonald. Proceedings of the National Academy of Sciences Mar 2018, 115 (12), 2946–2951; DOI:10.1073/pnas.1718503115.

## Put Your Heads Together

Discuss the following in your groups: **A)** The study described above found a positive correlation between air pollution and violent crime. What are some possible explanations for this relationship? **B)** Can you think of any third variables that might be at work in this scenario; in other words, are there any other variables that could be driving the increases of both air pollution and crime?

## Stereotypes and Discrimination

**LO 10** Define stereotypes, prejudice, and discrimination.

Typically, we associate aggression with behavior, but it can also exist in the mind, coloring our *attitudes* about people and things. This is evidenced by the existence of **stereotypes**—the conclusions or inferences we make about people who are different from us, based on their group membership (race, religion, age, or gender, for example). Stereotypes are often negative (*blondes are airheads*), but they can also be perceived as positive (*people who wear glasses are smart*). Either way, stereotypes can be harmful (Jackson, 2020). The stereotypical college instructor is absentminded, absorbed in thought, and unapproachable. The quintessential motorcycle rider is covered in tattoos; the teenager with the tongue ring is rebelling against her parents; and most mass shooters are mentally ill. What do all these stereotypes have in common? They are not objective or grounded in empirical research. Stereotypes typically include a variety of predicted behaviors and traits that are rooted in subjective observations and value judgments.

**GROUPS AND SOCIAL IDENTITY** Evolutionary psychologists suggest that stereotypes have allowed human beings to quickly identify the group to which they belong (Liddle et al., 2012)—an adaptive trait, given that groups provide safety. But because

**stereotypes** Conclusions or inferences we make about people who are different from us based on their group membership, such as race, religion, age, or gender.

Colin Brennan.

**Violin + Viola + Hip Hop = Good Music**
When most people think of hip-hop, they don't picture classically trained musicians playing string instruments. Wil B. (left) and Kev Marcus of Black Violin are challenging stereotypes about hip-hop artists and showing the world that violins and violas do have a place in the genre. Their most recent album, "Take the Stairs," earned a Grammy nomination for Best Contemporary Instrumental Album (blackviolin.net, 2020).

we are inclined to think our group is superior, we may draw incorrect conclusions about members of other groups, or outsiders in general. We tend to see the world in terms of the **in-group** (the group to which we belong, or *us*) and the **out-group** (those outside our group, or *them*). Those in the out-group are particularly vulnerable to becoming scapegoats. A **scapegoat** is the target of negative emotions, beliefs, and behaviors. During periods of major stress (such as an economic crisis), scapegoats are often blamed for undesirable social situations (like high unemployment). In the 1930s and 1940s, German dictator Adolf Hitler blamed Jewish people for the country's problems, and this scapegoating led to unconscionable treatment of the Jewish population.

Our affiliation with an in-group helps us form a **social identity,** or view of ourselves within a social group, and this process begins at a very young age. But if we only associate with certain crowds, we may be prone to **ethnocentrism,** or seeing the world from the narrow perspective of our own group. This term is often used in reference to cultural groups, yet it can apply to any group (think of football teams, political parties, college rivals, or nations). We tend to see our own country or group as the one that is worthy of emulation. This type of group identification can lead to **discrimination,** or showing favoritism or hostility to others because of their group affiliation.

**PREJUDICE**   Discrimination is closely tied to **prejudice,** hostile or negative attitudes toward individuals or groups (**INFOGRAPHIC 11.3**). While some would argue that racial prejudice has declined in the United States over the last half-century, there is considerable evidence that racism persists (Roberts & Rizzo, 2020). *Racism* is "a system of advantage based on race that is created and maintained by an interplay between psychological factors (i.e., biased thoughts, feelings, and actions) and sociopolitical factors (i.e., biased laws, policies, and institutions)" (Roberts & Rizzo, 2020, p.2). In other words, racism is embedded in the minds of individual people and imbued through society at large. Negative attitudes also persist when it comes to sexual orientation, disabilities, and religious beliefs (Carr et al., 2012; Dovidio et al., 2002).

Most of us like to believe we are free of prejudice, but it often occurs outside of awareness. *Implicit bias* is a type of unconscious bias that reveals itself through "our behavior toward members of particular social groups, but we remain oblivious to [its] influence" (Banaji & Greenwald, 2013, p. xii). For example, a bank teller may believe they treat every client equally, be they Black, White, Asian, or Hispanic. But a closer look at their behaviors—the warmth they show in their body language, facial expressions, and subtle choices in wording—may reveal otherwise. Researchers have used a variety of tasks to uncover these unconscious attitudes (Ito et al., 2015; Jackson, 2020), some of which you can try online. (In your browser, type in key terms like "implicit association test online" and see what comes up.)

How can implicit bias be reduced? We can start by trying to view members of an out-group in a positive light—seeing a "helpful person" or a "wealthy person" as opposed to someone in "that group," for example (Gonzalez et al., 2017; Lee et al., 2018). When it comes to race, we should remember that labels like Black and White are social categories rather than biological distinctions (Gannon, 2016; Roberts & Rizzo, 2020). Indeed, scientists believe that "race is neither a relevant nor accurate way to understand or map human genetic diversity" (Yudell et al., 2016, p. 564). Did you know that two people of different races (for example, Black and White) can be more genetically similar than two people of the same race (Witherspoon et al., 2007)?

Evidence suggests that prejudice may diminish when people are forced to work together toward a common goal (Mousa, 2020; Paluck & Clark, 2020). In the early 1970s, American psychologist Eliot Aronson and colleagues developed the notion of a

**in-group**  The group to which we belong.

**out-group**  People outside the group to which we belong.

**scapegoat**  A target of negative emotions, beliefs, and behaviors; typically, a member of the out-group who receives blame for an upsetting social situation.

**social identity**  How we view ourselves within our social group.

**ethnocentrism**  Seeing the world only from the perspective of one's own group.

**discrimination**  Showing favoritism or hostility to others because of their affiliation with a group.

**prejudice**  Holding hostile or negative attitudes toward an individual or group.

# Thinking About Other People
## Stereotypes, Discrimination, and Prejudice

Attitudes are complex and only sometimes related to our behaviors. Like most attitudes, prejudicial attitudes can be connected with our *cognitions* about groups of people (also known as stereotypes), our negative *attitudes* and *feelings* about others (also referred to as prejudice), and our *behaviors* (discriminating against others). Understanding how and when these pieces connect to each other is an important goal of social psychology. Jane Elliott's classic "Blue Eyes/Brown Eyes" exercise helps demonstrate how stereotypes, discrimination, and prejudice may be connected.

**Prejudicial attitude toward others**

**Cognitive component (beliefs and ideas)**

We tend to categorize people in terms of the *in-group* (the group to which we belong) and the *out-group* (people different from us in some way). **Stereotypes** are beliefs or assumptions we hold about people, based on perceived differences we think describe members of their group.

**Affective component (emotional evaluation)**

**Prejudice,** or feelings of hostility, anger, or discomfort toward members of out-groups.

Social psychologists often use prejudice to refer to both these negative attitudes and the negative feelings tied to them.

**Behavioral component (the way we respond)**

**Discrimination,** or treating others differently because of their affiliation with a group. Can include showing hostility or anger to others, or can be more subtle, such as different body language or tone of voice.

## Stereotype

"cleaner, more civilized, smarter"

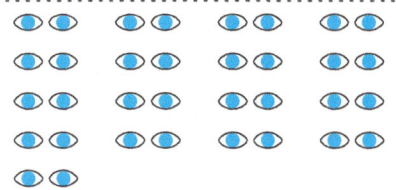

When Dr. Martin Luther King, Jr., was assassinated in 1968, a teacher named Jane Elliott gave her students a lesson about discrimination. Because no African Americans lived in their Iowa town, she knew students would have trouble understanding what motivated the terrible act. Elliott invited the class to join her in an exercise in which one set of students was segregated into a negatively stereotyped out-group: "Suppose we divided the class into blue-eyed people and brown-eyed people. . . . [B]rown-eyed people are better than blue-eyed people. They are cleaner . . . more civilized . . . smarter" (Peters, 1971, pp. 20–21).

## Prejudice

Prejudice | Discrimination

Brown-eyes dislike blue-eyes, but have to be nice while in class.

Brown-eyes dislike blue-eyes and exclude them from games at recess.

Brown-eyes, who are required to sit at the front of the room, do not sit with blue-eyes, who must sit at the back.

In her exercise, Elliott created a situation in which discrimination initially existed without the presence of actual feelings of hostility or anger. Although prejudice and discrimination often go hand in hand, either condition can exist independently.

## Discrimination

During the exercise, a list of rules governed behavior for both groups. For example, only children with brown eyes were allowed to sit at the front of the room near the teacher. The effect of this manufactured discrimination surprised even Elliott. The brown-eyed children quickly became openly hostile toward the blue-eyed children. And "[t]he blue-eyed children were miserable. . . . [T]heir entire attitudes were those of defeat. Their classroom work regressed sharply from that of the day before" (Peters, 1971, p. 25).

*jigsaw classroom.* Teachers in their study created exercises that required all students to complete individual tasks, the results of which would fit together like a jigsaw puzzle. The students began to realize the importance of working cooperatively to reach a goal. Ultimately, every contribution was an essential piece of the puzzle, and this resulted in all the students feeling valuable (Aronson, 2015).

**STEREOTYPE THREAT**    Stereotypes, discrimination, and prejudice are conceptually related to **stereotype threat,** a "situational threat" in which a person is aware of negative expectations from others. This leads to a fear of being judged or treated as inferior, and it can actually undermine performance in a specific area associated with the stereotype (Barber et al., 2020; Steele, 1997).

African American college students are often the targets of racial stereotypes about poor academic abilities. This can lead to lowered performance on tests designed to measure ability, and to a *disidentification* with the role of student (taking on the attitude *I am not a student*). Interestingly, a person does not have to believe the stereotype is accurate in order to be impacted (Steele, 1997, 2010). One way to counteract this disidentification, which disproportionately impacts male students, is by "building trusting, positive relationships among students and faculty" (McClain & Cokley, 2017, p. 131).

There is a great deal of variation in how people react to stereotype threats (Block et al., 2011). Some "fend off" the stereotype by working harder to disprove it. Others feel discouraged and respond by getting angry, either overtly or quietly. Still others seem to ignore the threats. These resilient types appear to "bounce back" and grow from the negative experience. When confronted with a stereotype, they redirect their responses to create an environment that is more inclusive and less conducive to stereotyping. Institutions can take steps to reduce the negative impact of stereotype threat. For example, colleges may include "visual representation[s] of diversity to blur group boundaries, promote social belonging, and provide in-group role models" in recruitment materials (Liu et al., 2020, p. 21).

Unfortunately, stereotypes are pervasive in our society. Just contemplate all the positive and negative stereotypes associated with certain lines of work. Lawyers are greedy, truck drivers are overweight, and (dare we say) psychologists are manipulative. Can you think of any negative stereotypes associated with prison guards? As you read the next feature, think about how stereotypes can come to life when people fail to step back and reflect on their behaviors.

## ...BELIEVE IT... OR NOT

### THE STANFORD "PRISON"

**"LOOKING BACK, I'M IMPRESSED HOW LITTLE I FELT FOR THEM."**

August 1971: Philip Zimbardo of Stanford University launched what would become one of the most controversial experiments in the history of psychology. Zimbardo and his colleagues carefully selected 24 male college students to play the roles of prisoners and guards in a simulated "prison" setup in the basement of Stanford University's psychology building. The young men chosen for the experiment were deemed "normal-average" by the researchers, who administered several psychological tests (Haney et al., 1973, p. 90).

After being "arrested" in their homes by Palo Alto Police officers, the prisoners were searched and booked at a local police station, and then sent to the "prison" at Stanford. The experiment was supposed to last for 2 weeks, but the behavior of some guards and prisoners was so disturbing that the researchers abandoned the study after just 6 days (Haney & Zimbardo, 1998). Certain guards became abusive, punishing

**stereotype threat** A "situational threat" in which individuals are aware of others' negative expectations, which leads to a fear of being judged or treated as inferior.

**social roles** The positions we hold in social groups, and the responsibilities and expectations associated with those roles.

the prisoners, stripping them naked, and confiscating their mattresses. It seemed as if they had lost sight of the prisoners' humanity, as they ruthlessly wielded their newfound power. As one guard stated, "Looking back, I'm impressed how little I felt for them" (Haney et al., 1973, p. 88). Some prisoners became passive and obedient, accepting the guards' cruel treatment; others were released early due to "extreme emotional depression, crying, rage, and acute anxiety" (p. 81).

How can we explain this fiasco? The guards and prisoners, it seemed, took their assigned **social roles** and ran way too far with them. Social roles are the positions we hold in social groups, and all the associated responsibilities and expectations. These roles guide our behavior in ways we may not even realize.

The prison experiment may have shed light on the power of social roles, but its validity has come under fire. Critics suggest that the participants were merely "acting out their stereotypic images" of guards and prisoners, and behaving in accordance with the researchers' expectations (Banuazizi & Movahedi, 1975, p. 159). As one guard explained decades later, "[Zimbardo] knew what he wanted and then tried to shape the experiment . . . to fit the conclusion that he had already worked out. He wanted to be able to say that . . . people will turn on each other just because they're given a role and given power" (Ratnesar, 2011, para. 35). Apparently, Zimbardo made his expectations quite clear, instructing the guards to deny the prisoners "privacy," "freedom," and "individuality" (Zimbardo, 2007). Without this type of guidance, do you think the study outcome would have been the same? Perhaps not, as "guards" in other prison studies exhibited very different behaviors (Griggs & Whitehead, 2014; Haslam & Reicher, 2012). In the BBC Prison Study, for instance, guards were "reluctant to impose their authority"; meanwhile, "prisoners began to mock, challenge, and undermine the guards," and some orchestrated a breakout (Haslam & Reicher, 2012, p. 159).

Complicating matters further, one of the prisoners from the original study now insists that he staged a mental meltdown just so he could get home and study for his Graduate Record Examination, or GRE (Toppi, 2018). Yet, that same participant (who went on to become a prison psychologist, interestingly) had previously indicated that the prison study caused significant distress for the participants: "The Stanford Prison was a very benign prison situation, and it still caused guards to become sadistic [and] prisoners to become hysterical" (PrisonExperiment, 2018, 2:06–2:18).

The Stanford Prison experiment has been criticized for many reasons, including questionable ethics, bias in selecting participants, and failure to adequately explain why participants responded differently to their assigned roles (Griggs, 2014a). Nevertheless, this study continues to be relevant. In 2004 news broke that U.S. soldiers and intelligence officials at Iraq's Abu Ghraib prison had beaten, sodomized, and forced detainees to commit degrading sexual acts (Hersh, 2004). The similarities between Abu Ghraib and the Stanford Prison are noteworthy (Zimbardo, 2007).

Much of this chapter has focused on negative aspects of human behavior, such as obedience, stereotyping, and discrimination. While we cannot deny the existence of these phenomena, we believe they are overshadowed by the goodness that lies within every one of us.

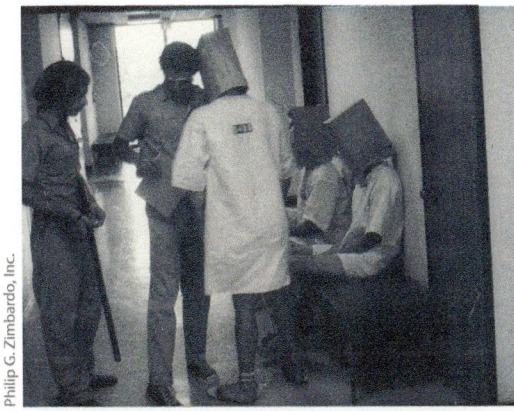

Philip G. Zimbardo, Inc.

AP Photo.

**Prison Horrors**

(Top) Prisoners in Zimbardo's 1971 prison experiment are forced to wear bags over their heads. (Bottom) In 2003 an Abu Ghraib detainee lies on the floor attached to a leash. The treatment of prisoners in the "Stanford Prison" and the Abu Ghraib facility was disturbingly similar. In both cases, authority figures threatened, abused, and forced inmates to be naked. Those in charge seemed to derive pleasure from violating and humiliating other human beings (Haney et al., 1973; Hersh, 2004).

 **SHOW WHAT YOU KNOW**

1. _____ is the tendency for people to stand by and do nothing in an emergency because they assume someone else will step in to help.
   A. Group polarization
   B. Disidentification
   C. The bystander effect
   D. Deindividuation

2. Name and describe the two types of aggression that may be influenced by gender.

3. Students often have difficulty identifying how the concepts of stereotype, discrimination, and prejudice are related. How would you explain their similarities and differences?

✓ CHECK YOUR ANSWERS AT THE BACK OF THE BOOK.

SAMSON OPUS.

**Beautiful Children**

Julius runs alongside children from Uganda's Otuke district, home to the Kristina Acuma Achon Health Center, a medical clinic created by Julius' nonprofit organization, the AUCF. The center is named after Julius' mother, who was shot by the LRA in 2004 and died from her wounds because she lacked access to proper medical care. For more information about Julius and the AUCF, please go to http://achonugandachildren.org, or read *The Boy Who Runs,* a book by John Brant (2016).

# Prosocial Behavior, Attraction, and Love

**JULIUS MAKES IT HAPPEN**   We believe that all human beings are capable of *prosocial behavior,* or behavior aimed at benefiting others. An exemplar of this ability is Julius Achon. After meeting the orphans in 2003, Julius kept his promise to assist them, wiring his family $150 a month to cover the cost of food, clothing, and other necessities—even when he and his wife were struggling to stay afloat. For 3 years, Julius was the children's sole source of financial support. Then, in 2007 he formalized his efforts by creating the Achon Uganda Children's Fund (AUCF), a nonprofit organization dedicated to improving the living conditions of children in the rural areas of northern Uganda. Julius currently lives in Uganda, where he oversees the work of the AUCF and represents his home district in the Ugandan Parliament (similar to the Senate in the United States).

As for the 11 orphans, they are flourishing. Most of them have completed high school and gone on to college, one has worked as a nurse at the medical clinic created by the AUCF, and another has run competitively like Julius.

## On the Upside

 Describe altruism.

It feels good to give to others, even when you receive nothing in return. The satisfaction of knowing you made someone feel happier, more secure, or appreciated is enough of a reward. Helping others with no expectation of payback is called **altruism.** A major component of altruism is *empathy,* the ability to recognize and understand another's emotional point of view. Humans may not be the only creatures capable of empathy; research suggests that animals as diverse as chimpanzees and mice may be able to sense and respond to the distress of others (de Waal, 2018).

**ARE TODDLERS ALTRUISTIC?**   The seeds of human altruism may be planted very early in life. One study found that the vast majority of 18-month-olds would help a researcher obtain an out-of-reach object, assist them in a book-stacking exercise, and open a door for them when their hands were full. The babies only helped when it appeared assistance was needed (Warneken & Tomasello, 2006). Although altruism is apparent in babies, it is "selective from the start." Rather than helping just anyone, they show a preference for those who are familiar and those "who have been kind to them in the past" (Wynn et al., 2018, p. 3). Findings from twin studies suggest "considerable heritability" of altruistic tendencies and other prosocial behaviors (Jiang et al., 2013). But as always, we must consider the biopsychosocial perspective, that is, recognize the interaction of genetics, environment, and culture (Knafo & Israel, 2010).

**A SECRET TO HAPPINESS?**   Helping, caring, and showing generosity toward others may reduce stress and increase happiness (Aknin et al., 2020; Cohen et al., 2015; Schwartz et al., 2003; Schwartz et al., 2009). The gestures don't have to be grand in order to be altruistic or prosocial. Consider the last time you bought coffee for a colleague without being asked, or gave a stranger a quarter to fill the parking meter. Do you recycle, conserve electricity, and take public transportation? These behaviors indicate an awareness of the need to conserve resources for the benefit of all. Promoting *sustainability* is an indirect, yet very impactful, prosocial endeavor. So, too, is changing behaviors to protect others during a disease outbreak.

**altruism** Helping others with no expectation of something in return.

## ACROSS THE WORLD

### PANDEMIC RESPONSES AND CULTURE

Research shows that social distancing, mask-wearing, and handwashing help prevent COVID-19 and other infectious diseases (Chiu et al., 2020). The Centers for Disease Control and Prevention (CDC) recommends these and other measures, yet many people don't implement them on a regular basis (CDC, 2020, December 31). Why do some people ignore public health guidelines, putting themselves and others at risk for serious illness? There are many reasons, but culture may be one of them. The United States is, generally speaking, an individualistic society: People are looking out for themselves and "appeals for altruism" may not work (Kelland & Revell, 2020, para. 7). As of late 2020, young adults (age 20–49) were driving most of the virus transmission (Monod et al., 2021), yet older adults were suffering more. About 80% of coronavirus deaths have been in people age 65 and above. "Consciously or not, this is a massive act of intergenerational betrayal" (Gerson, 2021, para. 5).

Japan is a country with a more collectivist society, where greater emphasis is placed on the community. Since the beginning of the pandemic, Japan has seen widespread use of masks, despite evidence suggesting that face coverings might not offer complete protection to the person wearing them. Perhaps this is because Japanese people are already accustomed to wearing masks from the previous SARS pandemic that impacted Asia many years ago. But the Japanese response may also be motivated by the desire to conform to social norms. "Wearing masks can be a symbol of collective confrontation against a pandemic" (Nakayachi et al., 2020, p. 3).

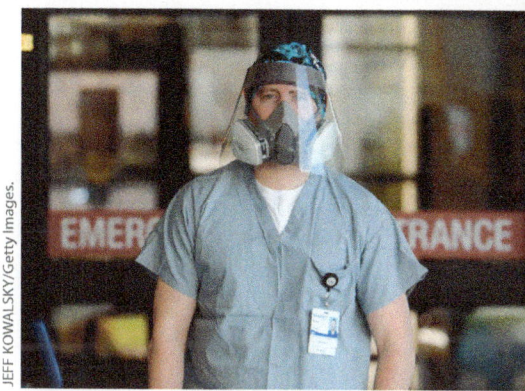

**Pandemics Bring Out the Best—and the Worst**

In the middle of a pandemic, and despite health officials' pleas to practice social distancing to protect vulnerable populations, Spring Breakers partied on (top photo). At the same time, health-care workers were coming out of retirement and crossing international borders to help in the fight against the coronavirus—putting their own health at risk to help others. This nurse from Canada (bottom photo) came to Michigan to lend a hand. "Otherness," or concern for others, is "as much a part of human nature as selfishness" (Crocker et al., 2017, p. 301).

### Put Your Heads Together

In the United States, the use of facial masks has become a political flashpoint. In this extremely diverse country, how can we find more common ground on disease prevention? Research suggests that "the key to solidarity and cooperation in heterogeneous communities is the extension of prosociality beyond close-knit networks and in-group boundaries to unknown, dissimilar others" (Baldassarri & Abascal, 2020, p. 1185). In your groups, **A)** discuss what this statement means, and **B)** identify specific behaviors that would promote more cooperation between people belonging to different groups.

Even if you're not the type to reach out to strangers, you probably demonstrate prosocial behavior toward your family and close friends. This giving of yourself allows you to experience the most magical element of human existence: love.

## The Psychology of Sexiness

**TO HAVE AND TO HOLD**    About 8 months after meeting on Tinder, Dennis and Alexa returned to the beach where they first exchanged the words "I love you." In the middle of goofing around and taking silly pictures, Dennis got down on his knee and pulled out an engagement ring. Alexa was so shocked that she took off running and came back laughing. There to witness the whole moment (in between mouthfuls of sand) was Brutus the French bulldog. It was important for Brutus to be present; after all, his photo was the main reason Alexa responded to Dennis' initial message. A few months later, the couple tied the knot in a cozy beach ceremony, with 50 of their family members and closest friends watching. Since then, marriage has been treating them well. "It is just so fun to have . . . someone to come home to who is excited to hear about all the unimportant details of my day, and to share in my victories and my defeats," Alexa says. Dennis is equally content: "I get to hang out with my best friend."

**LO 12** Identify the three major factors contributing to interpersonal attraction.

Alexa and Dennis seem to be an ideal match. Their compatibility may be explained by **interpersonal attraction,** the factors that lead us to form friendships or romantic relationships with others. Among the most important are proximity, exposure, similarity, and physical attractiveness.

**WE'RE CLOSE: PROXIMITY**    We would guess that the majority of people in your social circle live nearby. **Proximity,** or nearness, plays a significant role in the formation of our relationships. The closer people live geographically, the greater the odds they will meet, spend time together, and establish a bond (Festinger et al., 1950; Nahemow & Lawton, 1975). One study concluded that sitting in nearby seats and being assigned to the same groups in a college classroom **correlate** with the development of friendships (Back et al., 2008). In other words, sitting next to someone in class, or even in the same row, increases the chances you will become friends. Would you agree?

**MERE-EXPOSURE EFFECT**    Repeated interactions with partners may bring us closer together through the **mere-exposure effect.** In other words, the more we are exposed to people, food, jingles, songs, politics, or music, the more positive our reactions become. Researchers have also discovered that repeated *negative* exposures may lead to stronger distaste. If a person you frequently encounter has annoying habits or uncouth behavior, negative feelings might develop, even if your initial impression was positive (Cunningham et al., 2005). This can be problematic for romantic partners. All those minor irritations you overlooked early in the relationship can evolve into major headaches. For years, researchers have been asking why the mere-exposure effect occurs. The answer is complex, and we still don't have a theoretical model that fully explains the phenomenon (Montoya et al., 2017).

**SIMILARITY**    Perhaps you have heard the saying "Birds of a feather flock together." This statement alludes to the concept of *similarity,* another factor that contributes to interpersonal attraction (Moreland & Zajonc, 1982; Morry et al., 2011). We tend to prefer those who share our interests, viewpoints, values, and other characteristics. Even age, education, and occupation tend to be similar among those who are close (Brooks & Neville, 2017; Lott & Lott, 1965).

**PHYSICAL ATTRACTIVENESS**    We probably don't need to tell you that *physical attractiveness* plays a major role in interpersonal attraction (Eastwick et al., 2011; Fisher & Stinson, 2020; Lou & Zhang, 2009). Even online, men are more likely to reach out to women they find attractive. Research suggests that profile pictures play a more important role for men when it comes to making initial contact through an online dating site (Eastwick et al., 2014). But here is the question: Is beauty really in the eye of the beholder? In other words, do people from different cultures and historical periods have different concepts of beauty? There is some degree of consistency in the way people rate facial attractiveness (Langlois et al., 2000; Sutherland et al., 2018), with facial symmetry generally considered attractive (Boothroyd et al., 2014; Grammer & Thornhill, 1994). But certain aspects of beauty do appear to be culturally distinct (Gangestad & Scheyd, 2005). In some parts of the world, people go to great lengths to elongate their necks, increase their height, pierce their bodies,

**CONNECTIONS**

In **Chapter 1,** we described how researchers examine relationships between variables. A correlation does not necessarily mean one variable causes changes in the other. What other factors might be influencing the development of friendships in the classroom?

*Mike Marsland/Getty Images.*

**Sexy Stubble, or Dirty Beards?**
Actor Regé-Jean Page sports some stubble on the red carpet. What do women find most attractive—a face that is cleanly shaven, fully bearded, or somewhere in between? According to research, "heavy stubble" wins the sexiness prize. Full beards, on the other hand, tend to be associated with "parenting ability and healthiness" (Dixson & Brooks, 2013, p. 236).

**interpersonal attraction** The factors that lead us to form friendships or romantic relationships with others.

**proximity** Nearness; plays an important role in the formation of relationships.

**mere-exposure effect** The more we are exposed to someone or something, the more positive our reaction to it becomes.

augment their breasts, and enlarge or reduce the size of their waists—just so others within their culture will find them attractive. Why is physical attractiveness so important? Beauty may be a sign of health, and healthy people have greater potential for longevity and successful reproduction.

**BEAUTY PERKS**   We have discussed beauty in the context of attraction, but how does physical appearance affect other aspects of social existence? Generally speaking, physically attractive people seem to have more opportunities. Beauty is correlated with how much money people make, the type of jobs they have, and overall success (Pfeifer, 2012). Good-looking children and adults are viewed as more intelligent and popular, and are treated better in general (Langlois et al., 2000). Why would this be? From the perspective of evolutionary psychology, these beauty characteristics are good indicators of reproductive potential. Our evaluations of beautiful people may also be influenced by the *halo effect,* or the tendency to assign excessive importance to one dimension of a person. As early psychologist Edward Thorndike pointed out, people tend to form general impressions early on and then cling to them, even in the absence of supporting evidence or the presence of contradictory evidence (Aronson, 2018).

Good-looking people do not always inspire positive reactions, however. Research suggests that "other women may respond with hostility and resentment when exposed to women who are more beautiful than themselves," especially when those attractive women wear makeup (DelPriore et al., 2018, p. 363). Our initial impressions of people's beauty may lead us to assume they have positive characteristics like superior intelligence, popularity, and desirability—but it also may lead to enmity when we feel others are working too hard to be beautiful.

We have learned about some of the factors that increase the odds of romantic attraction, but how do we know whether a relationship will last beyond the dating stage? Some people think first impressions offer important clues.

## Relationships

IS "LOVE AT FIRST SIGHT" REALLY A THING?

"I knew the moment she walked into the room that I was going to marry her." You've probably heard stories like this, and perhaps you have experienced it yourself. But, is "love at first sight" a real phenomenon? Probably not, evidence suggests. If you are overcome with a feeling of immediate "love" the moment you meet someone, it's more likely you are experiencing an intense physical attraction (Zsok et al., 2017). In other words, you find the person very, very sexy.

If "love at first sight" were really a thing, you would expect the early stages of long-term relationships to look fundamentally different from those of short-term unions. The "love-at-first-sight" couples should report different experiences than those in relationships that fizzle out. Yet, the beginning stages of long- and short-term unions look very similar (Eastwick et al., 2018). Magical first impressions aren't totally meaningless, however. People who remember being swept off their feet when they met their partner tend to have "more love and passion in the relationship" (Zsok et al., 2017, p. 882). Perhaps the initial spark of physical attraction turns into a flame that sustains the couple over time.

## What Is Love?

In the United States, we are taught to believe that love is the foundation of marriage. People in Western cultures do tend to marry for love, but this is not the case everywhere. In Harare, Zimbabwe, for example, people might also marry for

**Instant Connection?**
Musical artist Ricky Martin reportedly experienced "love at first sight" when he met his husband Jwan Yosef (Boucher, 2018). But research suggests that love does not work this way (Eastwick et al., 2018; Zsok et al., 2017). Is it possible that Martin already loved Yosef when the two first met in person? For the 6 months leading up to that moment, they had been getting to know each other via Instagram (Boucher, 2018).

Jacopo Raule/Getty Images.

Courtesy Alexa Antoni.

**Young Love**

Dennis and Alexa tied the knot on a beautiful beach in San Diego on March 25, 2017. The couple has since moved to Twentynine Palms, a remote desert base in California. "The town is small, the weather is terrible, and we are miles and miles away from the comforts we're used to," says Alexa. "But we are really enjoying the uninterrupted time we get to spend together on what we're calling our 'couples retreat.'"

## CONNECTIONS

In **Chapter 3,** we discussed sensory adaptation, which occurs when sensory receptors become less sensitive to constant stimuli. In **Chapter 5,** we presented the concept of habituation, a learning process whereby an organism reduces its response to a recurring stimulus. Humans seem to be attracted to novelty, which might underlie our desire for passion.

**romantic love** Love that is a combination of connection, concern, care, and intimacy.

**companionate love** Love that consists of profound fondness, camaraderie, understanding, and emotional closeness.

**consummate love** Love that combines intimacy, commitment, and passion.

reasons associated with family needs, such as maintaining alliances and social status (Wojcicki et al., 2010), or for religious reasons (Hallfors et al., 2016). Similarly, many marriages in India and other parts of South Asia are arranged by family members. Love may not be present in the beginning stages of such unions, but it can blossom.

**STERNBERG'S THEORY OF LOVE**    In a pivotal study published in 1986, American psychologist Robert Sternberg proposed that love is made up of three elements: passion (feelings leading to romance and physical attraction), intimacy (feeling close), and commitment (the recognition of love). A combination of connection, passion, care, and intimacy is what Sternberg called **romantic love.** As a relationship grows, we see the emergence of **companionate love,** which consists of profound fondness, camaraderie, understanding, and emotional closeness. Companionate love is typical of a couple that has been together for many years. They become comfortable with each other, routines set in, and passion often fizzles (Aronson, 2018). **Consummate love** (KON-suh-mit) occurs when intimacy and commitment are accompanied by passion.

Research and life experience tell us that relationships inevitably change. Romantic love is generally what drives people to commit to one another (Berscheid, 2010), but the passion of this stage generally decreases over time. Can you think of ways that **passion** might be rekindled? Companionate love, in contrast, tends to grow over time. As we experience life with a partner, it is companionate love that seems to endear us to one another (Berscheid, 2010). Cultivating this type of love may confer both emotional and physical benefits. Did you know that having a happy spouse is associated with a longer life span (Stavrova, 2019)?

**IN IT FOR THE LONG HAUL?**    Couples stay together for many reasons, sometimes out of self-interest, other times for the sake of others (Joel et al., 2018). The *investment model of commitment* focuses on the resources at stake in relationships, including finances, possessions, time spent together, and perhaps even children (Rusbult, 1983). According to this model, decisions to stay together or separate are based on happiness with the relationship, ideas of what life would be like without it, and personal investment. Sometimes people stay in unsatisfying or unhealthy relationships because they feel they have too much to lose or no better alternatives (Rusbult & Martz, 1995). Others are reluctant to break up because they worry about their partner's level of dependence (Joel et al., 2018).

The ability to deal with relationship troubles may depend somewhat on perceptions of what the relationship represents: Do you view your relationship as something that was written in the stars (destined to happen), or more like a long journey you embark upon together (North, 2014)? "It may be romantic for lovers to think they were made for each other, but it backfires when conflicts arise and reality pokes the bubble of perfect unity" (Lee & Schwarz, 2014, p. 64). A better approach may be to consider your love a journey—one that might have "twists and turns but ultimately [is] moving toward a destination" (p. 64).

At last, we reach the end of our journey through social psychology. Hopefully you can use what you have learned in your everyday social interactions; research suggests you may be better at it than you realize (Gollwitzer & Bargh, 2018). Be conscious of the attributions you use to explain the behavior of others—are you being objective or falling prey to self-serving bias? Bear in mind that attitudes have a powerful impact on behavior—what types of attitudes do you harbor, and how do they impact your everyday decisions? Know that your behaviors are constantly being shaped by your social interactions—both as an individual and as a member of groups. Understand the dangers of prejudice, discrimination, and stereotyping, and know the human suffering caused by aggression. But perhaps most of all, be kind and helpful to others, and allow yourself to experience love.

## SHOW WHAT YOU KNOW

1. Julius sent money home every month to help cover the cost of food, clothing, and schooling for the 11 orphaned children. This is a good example of:
   A. the just-world hypothesis.
   B. deindividuation.
   C. individualistic behavior.
   D. prosocial behavior.

2. We described how the investment model of commitment can be used to predict the long-term stability of a romantic relationship. How can you use this same model to predict the long-term stability of friendships, positions at work, or loyalty to institutions?

3. What are the three major factors that play a role in interpersonal attraction?
   A. social influence; obedience; physical attractiveness
   B. proximity; similarity; physical attractiveness
   C. obedience; proximity; social influence
   D. proximity; love; social influence

4. _____ is helping others with no expectation of something in return.

CHECK YOUR ANSWERS AT THE BACK OF THE BOOK.

# Summary of Concepts

**LO 1** Define social psychology and identify how it differs from sociology. (p. 413)

Social psychology is the study of human cognition, emotion, and behavior in relation to others. Social psychology focuses on studying individuals in relation to others and groups, whereas sociology studies the groups themselves—their cultures, societies, and institutions. Social psychologists use the same general research methods as other psychologists, but their studies sometimes have an added twist of deception. This deception may involve the use of confederates, or people secretly working for the researchers. At the end of a study, researchers debrief participants, or review aspects of the research they had previously concealed.

**LO 2** Define social cognition and describe how we use attributions to explain behavior. (p. 415)

Social cognition refers to the way we think about others, attend to social information, and use this information in our lives, both consciously and unconsciously. Attributions are the beliefs we develop to explain human behaviors and characteristics, as well as situations. Because attributions rely on whatever information happens to be available (our observations of what people say and do, for example), they are vulnerable to personal bias and inaccuracies.

**LO 3** Describe several common attribution errors. (p. 416)

A situational attribution is a type of external attribution wherein behaviors are assumed to result from situational factors. A dispositional attribution is a type of internal attribution wherein behaviors are thought to result from traits or personality characteristics. Making attributions involves a certain amount of guesswork, and this leaves plenty of room for error. Common mistakes include (1) the fundamental attribution error, the tendency to favor dispositional attributions over situational attributions; (2) the just-world hypothesis, the tendency to believe the world is a fair place and people generally get what they deserve; and (3) the self-serving bias, the tendency to attribute successes to personal characteristics and failures to environmental factors.

**LO 4** Explain the meaning of social influence and recognize factors associated with persuasion. (p. 423)

Social influence refers to the way a person is affected by others, as evidenced in behavior, emotion, and cognition. Expectations are a powerful, yet often unspoken, form of social influence. Research suggests that student performance is impacted by teacher expectations. Persuasion is consciously trying to make people change their attitudes and beliefs, which may (or may not) lead to changes in their behavior. Persuasive power is determined by three factors: the source, the message, and the audience.

**LO 5** Define compliance and explain some of the techniques used to gain it. (p. 425)

Compliance occurs when people voluntarily change their behavior at the request or direction of another person (or group), who generally has no true authority over them. A common method to gain compliance is the foot-in-the-door technique, which occurs when someone makes a small request, followed by a larger request. Another method is the door-in-the-face technique, which occurs when someone makes a large request, followed by a smaller request.

**LO 6**    Identify the factors that influence the likelihood of someone conforming. (p. 427)

The tendency to modify behaviors, attitudes, beliefs, and opinions to match those of others is known as conformity. There are three major reasons we conform. Most people want approval, to be liked and accepted by others. This desire, known as normative social influence, can have a significant impact on behaviors. We also conform to be correct, looking to others for confirmation when we are uncertain about something, and then doing as they do. This is known as informational social influence. Finally, we may conform to others because they belong to a certain reference group we respect, admire, or long to join.

**LO 7**    Describe obedience and explain how Stanley Milgram studied it. (p. 429)

Obedience occurs when we change our behavior, or act in a way that we might not normally act, because we have been ordered to do so by an authority figure. Milgram conducted a series of studies examining how far people would go when urged by an authority figure to inflict punishment on others. During an early experiment, the goal was for the confederate (learner) to memorize a set of paired words. The participant (teacher) sat before a control panel for administering electrical "shocks." The teacher was told to administer a shock each time the learner made a mistake, and the shock was to increase by 15 volts for every mistake. An astonishing 60–65% of participants continued to the highest voltage level, and similar findings have been produced in subsequent studies around the world.

**LO 8**    Recognize factors that influence the bystander effect. (p. 435)

When a person is in trouble, bystanders tend to assume that someone else will help—and therefore stand by and do nothing, partly because there is a diffusion of responsibility. This bystander effect is more likely to occur when many other people are present. By contrast, individuals are more inclined to aid a person in distress if no one else is around.

**LO 9**    Define aggression and identify some of its causes. (p. 437)

Aggression is defined as intimidating or threatening behavior or attitudes intended to hurt someone. Research suggests that aggression has a biological basis. (For instance, high levels of testosterone and low levels of serotonin correlate with increased aggression.) The frustration–aggression hypothesis suggests that we can all show aggressive behavior in frustrating situations.

**LO 10**    Define stereotypes, prejudice, and discrimination. (p. 439)

We tend to see the world in terms of the in-group (the group to which we belong) and the out-group (those outside our group). Seeing the world from the narrow perspective of our own group may lead to ethnocentrism, which sets the stage for stereotyping and discrimination. Stereotypes are the conclusions or inferences we make about people based on their group membership. Discrimination means showing favoritism or hostility to others because of their affiliation with a group. People who harbor stereotypes are more likely to feel prejudice, that is, hostile or negative attitudes toward individuals or groups.

**LO 11**    Describe altruism. (p. 444)

Altruism is helping others with no expectation of something in return. Empathy, or the ability to recognize and understand another's emotional perspective, is a major component of altruism. Behavior aimed at benefiting others is known as prosocial behavior.

**LO 12**    Identify the three major factors contributing to interpersonal attraction. (p. 446)

Interpersonal attraction leads us to form friendships or romantic relationships. Important factors that influence interpersonal attraction are proximity, similarity, and physical attractiveness. The combination of connection, passion, care, and intimacy is romantic love. As a relationship grows, intimacy and commitment develop into companionate love, which consists of fondness, camaraderie, understanding, and emotional closeness. Consummate love is evident when intimacy, commitment, and passion are all present.

# Key Terms

**aggression,** p. 437

**altruism,** p. 444

**attitudes,** p. 418

**attributions,** p. 415

**bystander effect,** p. 435

**cognitive dissonance,** p. 421

**companionate love,** p. 448

**compliance,** p. 425

**conformity,** p. 427

**consummate love,** p. 448

**deindividuation,** p. 433

**diffusion of responsibility,** p. 433

**discrimination,** p. 440

**dispositional attribution,** p. 416

**door-in-the-face technique,** p. 426

**ethnocentrism,** p. 440

**false consensus effect,** p. 418

**foot-in-the-door technique,** p. 426

**frustration–aggression hypothesis,** p. 438

**fundamental attribution error,** p. 416

**group polarization,** p. 434

**groupthink,** p. 434

**in-group,** p. 440

**interpersonal attraction,** p. 446

**just-world hypothesis,** p. 417

**mere-exposure effect,** p. 446

**norms,** p. 427

**obedience,** p. 429

**out-group,** p. 440

# Test Prep Are You Ready?

1. Which of the following topics is LEAST likely to be studied by a social psychologist?
   A. children's written responses to people with disabilities
   B. teachers' reactions to children with disabilities
   C. the impact of deafness on social behaviors
   D. school board policies regarding support for children with disabilities

2. _____ refers to the way we think about others, attend to social information, and use this information in our lives.
   A. Sociology
   B. Social cognition
   C. The internal–external dimension
   D. The false consensus effect

3. Sometimes we attribute people's behaviors to their traits or personality characteristics, and underestimate the powerful influence of the environment. This is known as:
   A. the just-world hypothesis.
   B. the false consensus effect.
   C. a dispositional attribution.
   D. the fundamental attribution error.

4. The desire to help others with no expectation of payback is called:
   A. groupthink.
   B. deindividuation.
   C. altruism.
   D. conformity.

5. When it comes to decorating their house, your neighbor seems to follow the lead. If they see others hanging lights, they immediately do the same. Their urge to modify their behaviors to match those of others is known as:
   A. conformity.
   B. informational social influence.
   C. obedience.
   D. cognitive dissonance.

6. Changing your behavior at the direction of someone who generally has no true authority over you is known as:
   A. obedience.
   B. conformity.
   C. compliance.
   D. normative social influence.

7. A friend believes that suburban teenagers covered in tattoos are often troublemakers who are rebelling against their parents. These _____ are conclusions they have drawn based on their subjective observations and value judgments.
   A. norms
   B. external attributions
   C. situational attributions
   D. stereotypes

8. Psychologists define _____ as intimidating or threatening behavior, or as attitudes intended to hurt someone.
   A. prejudice
   B. discrimination
   C. aggression
   D. stereotypes

9. When teachers in a San Francisco elementary school were given a list of students likely to "show surprising gains in intellectual competence" during the next year, those "surprising gains" students achieved greater increases in test scores than their peers. This demonstrates the power of _____, a form of social influence.
   A. cognitive dissonance
   B. expectations
   C. altruism
   D. the mere-exposure effect

10. According to Sternberg, love is made up of three elements:
    A. passion, mere exposure, and proximity.
    B. proximity, similarity, and passion.
    C. romantic love, mere exposure, and similarity.
    D. passion, intimacy, and commitment.

11. Social psychology explores the way individuals behave in relation to others and groups, while sociology examines the groups themselves. Give several examples of how these two fields might approach the same overall topic (for example, prosocial behavior of college students versus the impact of social support structures in higher education).

12. Milgram's obedience experiment produced shocking results that are still relevant today. Why is it important to pay attention to your behaviors when operating under the influence of an authority figure?

13. Understanding the bystander effect is critical, particularly when it comes to responding to crises in group settings. How would you explain the bystander effect to others?

14. Identify stereotypes you might harbor about certain groups of people. How did your association with specific groups impact the development of these stereotypes?

15. Think about a close friend or partner and try to determine if—and how—proximity, similarity, and physical attractiveness played a role in your attraction to each other.

✔ CHECK YOUR ANSWERS AT THE BACK OF THE BOOK.

# 12

Gianluca Colla/Getty Images.

# Stress and Health

## What Is Stress?

### COVID COMES TO VEGAS

Summer, 2020: It was a quiet day in the Las Vegas emergency room (ER) where nurse Kaynen Brown worked. The halls and waiting areas were empty. Usually there are people milling around, but COVID-19 had changed everything. Except for caregivers of hospitalized children, family members of patients were barred from entering the hospital. Nevada was experiencing its first major wave of the coronavirus pandemic, and health-care professionals were just beginning to understand how this novel pathogen spread and created mayhem in the human body.

Despite the eerie calm, the ER was as busy as ever. Kaynen was working in the critical care section. "This day I was taking care of the sickest of the sickest patients," he recalls. Halfway through his shift, Kaynen heard a scream from

Kaynen Brown.

**Essential Worker**
Nurse Kaynen Brown was 26 years old when he began fighting on the front lines of the coronavirus pandemic. Like health-care workers all around the world, Kaynen faced an entirely new set of stressors: fighting a novel pathogen with no specific treatments, lacking adequate personal protective equipment (PPE), witnessing patients suffer and die without family members nearby, and fearing for the safety of himself and his loved ones.

down the hallway. He looked in the direction of the scream and saw a nurse running into the room of a patient who was on a ventilator. (Normally the doors would be open, but this patient was suspected of having Covid and, until proven otherwise, he would need to remain isolated.) A second nurse screamed and entered the room, and Kaynen raced down the hall to follow, his instinct being to rush toward the emergency. But he stopped in his tracks when the supervisor yelled, "Put your &*%$ gear on! Do not go in that room!"

After putting on his N95 mask, gown, gloves, and eye shield, Kaynen entered the isolation room and saw what the commotion was all about. The patient had pulled out his breathing tube. Apparently, he had woken up, realized there was a tube in his throat, and panicked. "There's obviously mucus secretions, saliva everywhere—possible Covid everywhere . . . microscopic organisms you can't see floating in the air," Kaynen recalls. The patient's oxygen saturation was 14, which is incompatible with life, according to Kaynen. After the medical team sedated the patient and re-inserted the breathing tube, his oxygen levels slowly started climbing back up. Fortunately, the patient survived, but the experience is forever seared into the memory of Kaynen and his colleagues.

"Someone is about to die . . . and he doesn't even know it, but you know," says Kaynen. "And then the second level of stress is 'oh my gosh, we're all getting exposed right now,' and I've got to go home, I have a life to live still, I have family I need to go see."

A year before this happened, Kaynen never dreamed that a novel coronavirus would upend life for populations across the planet. Even in January 2020, when Kaynen first heard about the emerging pathogen, he did not anticipate the virus gaining traction in the United States. Today, we know that COVID-19 is perhaps "the most significant public health threat the modern world has encountered" (Maraqa et al., 2020, p. 1). Millions have lost their lives, many more have been sickened and continue to experience varying and mysterious symptoms; economies have been upended; families have lost incomes; children have faced unprecedented social isolation (with consequences that will not be fully understood for years); and front line workers have risked their lives to ensure basic needs are met, often with no thanks from those they serve. As one grocery store cashier remarked, "Some customers were appreciative in the beginning, but now they're just rude" (Bhattarai, 2020, para. 11).

Needless to say, the coronavirus has created an extraordinary amount of *stress* for people around the world.

## Stressors Are to Blame

**LO 1** Define stress and stressors.

What exactly is stress, and how does it arise? We all have an intuitive sense of how stress feels, and many of us are more familiar with it than we would like. Some people report they experience the *feeling* of stress, almost as if stress were an **emotion**. Others describe it as a force that needs to be resisted. An engineer might refer to stress as the application of a force on a target, such as the wing of an airplane, to determine how much load it can handle before breaking (Lazarus, 1993). Do you ever feel you might "break" because the load you bear causes such great strain (**INFOGRAPHIC 12.1** on the next page)?

**Stress** is defined as the response to perceived threats or challenges resulting from stimuli or events that cause strain, analogous to the airplane wing bending because of an applied load. For humans, these stimuli, or **stressors,** can cause both psychological

*Note:* Quotations attributed to Kaynen Brown are personal communications.

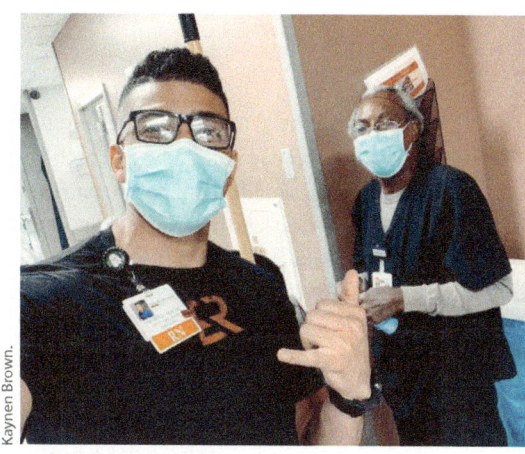

**Unsung Heroes**
Kaynen snaps a photo with an ER coworker who cleans and sanitizes the hospital. Environmental services workers have put their lives at risk to keep everyone else safe during the COVID-19 era—changing sheets, cleaning up bodily fluids, disinfecting floors and surfaces, and disposing of biohazardous waste. Such activities put these workers at great risk for contracting the virus, yet they don't always get the same recognition as doctors, nurses, and other health-care workers (Cleaning & Maintenance Management, 2020; Mejia, 2020).

**CONNECTIONS**

In **Chapter 9,** we defined emotion as a psychological state that includes a subjective or inner experience. Emotion also has a physiological component and a behavioral expression. Here, we discuss stress responses, which can have an emotional element.

**stress** The response to perceived threats or challenges resulting from stimuli or events that cause strain.

**stressors** Stimuli that cause strain, leading to both psychological and physiological reactions.

# Stressed Out

Periodically, the American Psychological Association (APA) commissions a survey investigating perceived stress among adults in the United States. In addition to measuring attitudes about stress, the survey identifies leading sources of stress and common behaviors used to manage stressors. The resulting picture shows that stress is a significant issue for many people in the United States and that we are not always managing it well (APA, 2016; 2020). Even when we acknowledge the importance of stress management and resolve to make positive lifestyle changes, many adults report barriers such as a lack of time or willpower that prevent them from achieving their goals. The good news? Our ability to manage stress appears to improve with age.

**4 OUT OF 5** Number of people reporting their **stress level has increased** or **stayed the same in the past year.**

## TOP SOURCES OF STRESS

Coronavirus pandemic **78%**

Future of our nation **77%**

Money **73%**

Healthcare **66%**

Mass shootings **62%**

Police violence toward people of color **59%**

**Number experiencing stress over the course of the pandemic.**

**NEARLY 7 IN 10**

People with high stress also report their behavior has been negatively impacted.

**21%** report increased body tension;

**20%** "snap" or get angry very quickly;

**20%** have unexpected mood swings;

**17%** scream or yell at loved ones.

## HOW STRESSFUL IS IT?

These are sample items from the College Undergraduate Stress Scale (CUSS), which rates life events according to severity. The more events you experience (particularly severe events with higher ratings), the greater your chances of developing an illness.

| Event | Rating |
| --- | --- |
| Being raped | 100 |
| Death of a close friend | 97 |
| Contracting a sexually transmitted infection (other than AIDS) | 94 |
| Finals week | 90 |
| Flunking a class | 89 |
| Financial difficulties | 84 |
| Writing a major term paper | 83 |
| Talking in front of class | 72 |
| Difficulties with a roommate | 66 |
| Maintaining a steady dating relationship | 55 |
| Commuting to campus or work, or both | 54 |
| Getting straight As | 51 |
| Falling asleep in class | 40 |

Information from SAGE Publications/APA/ LAWRENCE/ERLBAUM ASSOCIATES, INC. from Renner and Mackin (1998).

## STRESS OVER THE LIFE SPAN

People across all age groups agree that managing stress is very important. However, the ability to manage stress varies with age. Younger adults are more likely to rely on unhealthy behaviors like drinking alcohol and smoking for stress management. Older adults report more success in achieving healthy lifestyle goals such as eating healthy and getting enough sleep. They also report higher rates of religious participation (APA, 2013).

**50%** Oldest people report highest rate of meeting stress management goals.

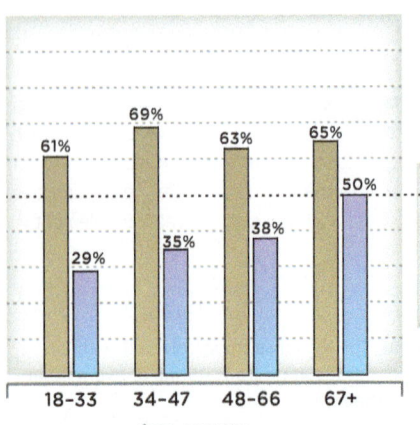

Bar chart — Age groups: 18–33: 61%, 29%; 34–47: 69%, 35%; 48–66: 63%, 38%; 67+: 65%, 50%. **Age groups**

■ Managing stress is very important
■ Doing a very good job managing stress

All information presented above, except the College Undergraduate Stress Scale, is from APA, 2020.

and physiological reactions. When Kaynen heard the scream of a fellow nurse, he instantly felt alarmed and nervous. These feelings would be considered *psychological* components of stress. He also felt a surge of energy as he ran down the hallway preparing to help; if we could have measured his heart rate and blood pressure at that moment, there is a good chance they would have been elevated. These and other bodily responses are *physiological* components of stress.

As you read this chapter, be careful not to confuse *how we react to stressors* with the *stressors* themselves; stress is the response and stressors are the cause (Harrington, 2013). Hans Selye (ZEL-yeh; 1907–1982), an **endocrinologist** who studied the impact of chronic stress, proposed that "stress is the nonspecific response of the body to any demand. A stressor is an agent that produces stress at any time" (Selye, 1976, p. 53).

We should note that not all experts agree on the definitions of stress and stressors (Cohen et al., 2019). Some contend that commonly used definitions are far too broad, and this complicates the collection and interpretation of data (Kagan, 2016; Robinson, 2018). For example, how can you create an operational definition for a "stressor" if researchers use it to describe phenomena as diverse as "a rat restrained in a tube for several hours, a mouse exposed to bright light, and an adolescent bullied by a peer, as well as an adult asked to prepare a speech to be given to strangers" (Kagan, 2016, p. 443)? What's more, the meaning of "stressor" may vary from one person to the next. Males and females experience stress in different ways, as do children and adults, and people with various personality traits (Cohen et al., 2019; Geary, 2021; Welbourne et al., 2020).

What are the stressors in your life? Some exist outside of you, like homework assignments, job demands, and credit card bills. Others are more internal, like the *thought* that your partner deceived you or the *realization* that you're not ready for your exam this afternoon. The coronavirus pandemic has introduced stressors that few of us could have anticipated. A poll taken in 2020 found that getting Covid was "a significant source of stress" for 78% of people in the United States. Around this same time, many experienced an increase in stress over discrimination and police violence. Nearly half of Black Americans (48%) reported that discrimination was a significant stressor. Overall, 59% of people in the United States were feeling stressed about "police violence toward minorities" (APA, 2020, p. 8).

Generally, we experience stress in response to stressors, but there is at least one exception to this rule: People with anxiety disorders can feel intense anxiety in the absence of any apparent stressors (Chapter 13). Which brings us to another point: Stress is very much related to how one perceives the surrounding world.

In many cases, stress results from a *perceived* threat, because what constitutes a threat differs from one person to the next. You might find the idea of working in an ER threatening; not only do you see traumatic scenes of pain and suffering; you also deal with intoxicated and belligerent people (often the family members of patients), who occasionally become violent. Perhaps you are more like Kaynen, and you thrive in exciting environments. The first time Kaynen visited an ER, shadowing his aunt during her shift as a physician assistant, he knew he wanted to work there. "I fell in love with it," Kaynen recalls. "I think what I really liked about it was that everyone was so smart . . . and at the same time, it was so action-packed."

**DISTRESS AND EUSTRESS**   When people talk about stress, they usually are referring to something unpleasant. Undesirable or disagreeable stressors lead to **distress.** This type of stress response may occur if you put off studying for your final exam, cram the night before, and show up to the exam sleep-deprived and underprepared.

**CONNECTIONS**

An endocrinologist is a scientist who studies the endocrine system. As discussed in **Chapter 2,** the endocrine system consists of glands throughout the body that secrete hormones, or chemical messengers that travel to their targets via the bloodstream. Selye studied physiological reactions to stressors, including activity of the stress hormone cortisol. His work describes human behavior from the biological perspective of psychology.

**distress**  The stress response to unpleasant or undesirable stressors.

Digital Vision/Getty Images.

**Job Stress, for Better or Worse**
Working as an airline pilot may be one of the most stressful occupations, but some former pilots "look back on their careers with fondness and a nearly childlike sense of wonder" (Vanhoenacker, 2016, para. 6). Is this because pilots and their flight crews have more eustress than distress? Research suggests that work groups experiencing eustress demonstrate more dedication and engagement (Kozusznik et al., 2015).

Not all stressors are unpleasant. For Kaynen, the science courses required for nursing school served as positive stressors. When he started taking those prerequisites at Nevada State College, he didn't have much confidence in his academic ability. "I was doubting myself, I was like, 'man, this is not going to be good, I'm wasting money here,'" says Kaynen, who had a 2.3 grade point average (GPA) in high school. "[I said to myself], Let's see what happens if I actually pay attention in class, and I actually do the homework, you know, do the stuff I didn't do in high school." What happened? He got an A- in the first science class he took. "That was such a transition point for me," says Kaynen, "because it proved to me that I can do this."

Stress caused by positive events is called **eustress** (YOO-stress) and it, too, can lead to psychological and physiological reactions. Falling in love, having kids, and planning for vacations are generally "good" stressors. Whether a stressor causes distress or eustress may depend on your interpretation of the situation: Is the anxiety before taking a final exam motivating you or paralyzing you? If it's the former, your pre-exam jitters will likely take the form of eustress (Strack et al., 2017). Distress is associated with increased heart rate, stiffness in muscles, and fatigue, while eustress is characterized by heightened energy and "butterflies in the stomach" (Branson et al., 2019, p. 322).

Now that we have a basic understanding of stress, let's explore various types of stressors and see how they impact the mind and body. We'll start big, by focusing on major life events.

## Major Life Events

**LO 2**    Describe the relationship between major life events and illness.

Tom Cooper/Getty Images News/Getty Images.

**Stressed About School Shootings**
Students and teachers leave the STEM school in Highlands Ranch, Colorado, after a shooting in May 2019. Seeing news reports about school shootings causes stress for many Americans, but particularly young people. A poll taken in 2018 found that 72% of people ages 15–21 considered school shootings "a significant source of stress" (APA, 2018, p. 2).

Any event that requires a life adjustment, such as the birth of a child, the death of a spouse, or a change in financial status, can cause a stress reaction (Holmes & Rahe, 1967). A disturbingly common life event for female college students is sexual assault; research indicates that over a quarter of women are victims of "nonconsensual sexual contact" during their undergraduate years (Brown, 2019, para. 2). Many life-changing events correlate with certain diseases (Cohen et al., 2019; Robinson, 2018), and their effect seems to be cumulative; the more events you experience in a row or within a brief period, the greater the potential for increased stress and negative health outcomes. Recall the analogy of applying a force to an airplane wing. The degree to which the wing bends (or breaks) indicates the strain it is under (Lazarus, 1993). Studies have uncovered associations between certain life events (the forces causing strain) and illnesses (the responses), including heart attacks, leukemia, diabetes, influenza, and psychiatric disorders (Hatch & Dohrenwend, 2007; Rabkin & Struening, 1976; Ridout et al., 2016). Although stress may not be the direct cause of such illnesses, it may make the body more vulnerable to disease development (Cohen et al., 2019).

**SOCIAL READJUSTMENT RATING SCALE**    Illnesses can be clearly identified and defined, but how do psychologists measure life events? The Social Readjustment Rating Scale (SRRS) was developed to do just that (Holmes & Rahe, 1967). With the SRRS, participants are asked to read through a list of events and experiences, and determine which happened during the previous year and how many times they occurred. A score is then calculated based on the severity ratings and frequency of those events. An event like the death of a spouse has a greater severity rating than

**eustress**    The stress response to agreeable or positive stressors.

something like a traffic violation. Participants are also asked to report any illnesses or accidents they experienced during the same period. This information is used to determine if there is a positive **correlation** between life events and health problems. Researchers have used this model to explore the link between these two variables for a variety of populations (Bliese et al., 2017; Kobasa, 1979; Slepecky et al., 2017). But remember, a correlation between life events and illness (or any correlation, for that matter) is not proof of causality. There is always the possibility that a third variable, such as poverty, is causing both illnesses and life-changing events. For example, children growing up in poverty tend to have poor nutrition, which impairs physical growth and cognitive development (Storrs, 2017). They are also more likely to experience stressors (Gabrielli & Lund, 2020; Steele et al., 2016). In this case, poverty is leading to stressful life events *and* poor health outcomes.

Since its introduction in the late 1960s, the SRRS has been updated and adapted for specific populations, including college students. Infographic 12.1 shows items from the College Undergraduate Stress Scale (CUSS; Renner & Mackin, 1998). Scales like the SRRS and CUSS are useful for uncovering correlations between stress levels and illness, but they are based on self-reports, which are subjective and therefore not always accurate. People tend to forget events over time, or the opposite—they tend to focus more on past events than recent ones (Pachana et al., 2011). What's more, not all negative life-changing events lead to bad outcomes. Some have even suggested that moderate exposure to stressors makes us stronger, a process described as *stress inoculation*. People with "low to moderate" levels of stress may end up with "better mental health and well-being" and a greater ability to cope with pain than those who have encountered no hardships or those who have faced overwhelming adversity (Seery, 2011, p. 393). By introducing disruptions and mild stressors, coaches and therapists may facilitate this building of stress tolerance in athletes and clients (Jackson et al., 2019; Kegelaers et al., 2020).

## Put Your Heads Together

Imagine you were tasked with updating the College Undergraduate Stress Scale (see Infographic 12.1). With your group, **A)** identify items to keep or remove, and then add your own items. **B)** Once you have created your new rating scale for college life, team up with other groups to compare your items.

## It's Nonstop: Chronic Stressors

For some of us, stressors come from balancing school and work, or taking care of children. Others face the chronic stressor of being underemployed, unemployed, or battling a chronic illness such as diabetes, asthma, or cancer (Chatzisarantis et al., 2021; Mousteri et al., 2020; Sansom-Daly et al., 2012; Sumner & Gallagher, 2017). Another cause of health-related stress is HIV, which affects nearly 38 million people and their families worldwide (UNAIDS, 2020).

**HIV AND AIDS**   One of the most feared **sexually transmitted infections (STIs)**, *human immunodeficiency virus* (HIV) is spread through the transfer of bodily fluids, such as blood, semen, vaginal fluid, or breast milk. HIV may eventually progress to *acquired immunodeficiency syndrome* (AIDS), which generally results in a severely compromised immune system and heightened vulnerability to disease. Since the virus was first identified in 1981, it has infected some 76 million people, about half of whom have died (UNAIDS, 2020). Approximately 1.2 million people in the United States have HIV, and about 1 in 7 are not aware they are infected (HIV.gov, 2020). Sub-Saharan Africa has been hit the hardest by the epidemic, though HIV prevalence can vary significantly within that area (Dwyer-Lindgren et al., 2019).

What comes to mind when you think of stressors linked to HIV? Perhaps you imagine receiving the diagnosis, losing relationships, living with a stigma, or facing

**CONNECTIONS**

In **Chapter 1,** we described what it means to have a positive correlation: As one variable increases, so does the other variable. Or, as one variable decreases, so does the other. Here, we see a positive correlation between life events and health problems: The more life events people have experienced, the more health problems they are likely to have. Likewise, the fewer life events people have experienced, the fewer health problems they are likely to have.

**CONNECTIONS**

In **Chapter 9,** we described various STIs, diseases that are passed on through sexual activity. There are many types of STIs, but most are caused by viruses or bacteria. Viral STIs such as HIV and herpes do not have cures, only treatments to reduce symptoms.

the possibility of developing AIDS. Did you think about the cost of treatment? In 2020, more than 30% of HIV sufferers around the world were not getting therapies (UNAIDS, 2020). This inability to access proper medical treatment relates to a stressor that is far more widespread than HIV: poverty.

**LO 3** Summarize how poverty, adjusting to a new culture, and daily hassles affect health.

**POVERTY** Before the coronavirus pandemic, about 1 in 10 people in the United States lived in poverty. The definition of poverty depends on the number of household residents and their ages, but to give you an idea, the poverty threshold for a family with two adults and two children is $25,926 (Semega et al., 2020). People struggling to make ends meet experience numerous stressors, including poor health care and nutrition, noisy living situations, overcrowding, violence, and underfunded schools (Blair & Raver, 2012; Mistry & Wadsworth, 2011; Schickedanz et al., 2015). The cycle of poverty is difficult to break, so these stressors often persist across generations. The longer people live in poverty, the more exposure they have to stressors, and the greater the likelihood they will become ill (Cheng et al., 2016). And we're not just talking about physical health; the brain pays a price, too.

## Think Critically

### DOES POVERTY CHANGE THE BRAIN?

The evidence is undeniable: Growing up in poverty can leave a lasting psychological imprint. Factors related to low socioeconomic status (SES) have been linked to differences in cognitive development and mental health outcomes, which can impact performance in school and at work (Blair & Raver, 2016; Drago et al., 2020; Garrison & Rodgers, 2019).

**LOW-INCOME ENVIRONMENTS MAY ADVERSELY IMPACT BRAIN DEVELOPMENT.**

"As a group, children in poverty are more likely to experience worse health and more developmental delay, lower achievement, and more behavioral and emotional problems than their more advantaged peers" (Johnson et al., 2016, p. 1). Underlying these disparities are distinct patterns of brain development. Neuroimaging evidence suggests that growing up in a low-income environment impacts the brain's ability to organize itself. As researchers explain, "Children exposed to poverty exhibit inefficient brain network organization across multiple regions," and this is more evident in girls (Kim et al., 2019, p. 414). The hippocampus, which is critical for the formation of new memories, seems particularly sensitive to the chronic stress that often goes hand in hand with poverty (Johnson et al., 2016). Specifically, the anterior hippocampus (the part closer to the front of the head) may be smaller in children and young adults from lower income backgrounds (Decker et al., 2020).

Many poverty-related variables could be causing these differences in **brain structure and function**, including poor nutrition, limited exposure to vocabulary words, and stressors like crowded living conditions and "neighborhood disorder" (Decker et al., 2020; Johnson et al., 2016). Psychologist Lisa Feldman Barrett sums up the research nicely: "The neuroscience is crystal clear: brains wire themselves to their surroundings. A developing infant brain requires wiring instructions from the world around it. Without proper nourishment, both nutritional and social, that little brain will not develop to its fullest" (Barrett, 2017, para. 6).

### CONNECTIONS

In **Chapter 7,** we discussed the relationship between poverty and cognitive abilities; studies show that SES is associated with scores on intelligence tests. Here, we highlight the link between poverty-related stressors and brain and cognitive development.

## Put Your Heads Together

In your groups, **A)** discuss why poverty is hard to escape. (*Hint:* List the stressors associated with an income of less than $25,926 for a family of four.) **B)** Consider how poverty affects the physical health and cognitive abilities of children. **C)** Use at least three of the eight perspectives introduced in Chapter 1 (Table 1.1) to explain the causes of poverty. **D)** What would you say to someone who says that people living in poverty should just "fix" their lives?

**ACCULTURATIVE STRESS**   Another common source of stress is migration. There are currently about 272 million migrants dispersed across the globe (International Organization for Migration [IOM], 2020). Moving to a new country frequently involves a process of cultural adjustment and adaptation. This **acculturation** can result in changes to language, values, cultural behaviors, and sometimes even national identity (Schwartz et al., 2014). Acculturation is often accompanied by **acculturative stress** (uh-KUHL-chur-a-tiv), or stress associated with adjusting to a new way of life. Perhaps you have experienced acculturative stress firsthand; 40 million people living in the United States (about 12% of the population) were born in another country (Budiman, 2020).

People respond to acculturative stress in a variety of ways (Berry, 1997; Cheung et al., 2020). Some try to **assimilate**, letting go of old customs and adopting those of the new culture. But assimilation can cause problems if family members or friends from the old culture reject the new one, or have trouble assimilating themselves. Other people cling to their roots and remain *separated* from the new culture—an approach that can be problematic if the new culture does not support this type of separation. A combination of these two approaches is *integration*, or holding on to some elements of the old culture but also adopting aspects of the new one.

Levels of acculturative stress vary greatly from one individual to the next. Why do some people seem to have an easier time adjusting than others?

## ACROSS THE WORLD

### THE STRESS OF STARTING ANEW

Imagine trying to get a job, pay your bills, or simply make friends in a world where most everyone speaks an unfamiliar language. Speaking the native tongue would certainly make life easier. "Language is considered one of the most central aspects for migrants' inclusion by both the receiving society and migrants themselves" (IOM, 2020, p. 192). Without verbal communication, social interactions are limited. For example, Pakistani students enrolled in universities in China report that language difficulties interfere with their social and academic adjustment (Shan et al., 2020). Another important factor is the degree of familiarity with the new culture. Latinx college students born in the United States seem to experience different effects of acculturative stress than those born abroad. Foreign-born Latinx students may display more symptoms of anxiety and depression and less altruistic behavior, perhaps because their "mental health resources are more depleted from acculturative stress" (Maiya et al., 2020, p. 11). Finally, we cannot forget the unpleasant reality of **discrimination**, which causes great stress for the world's immigrant populations. During the coronavirus pandemic, the United States saw an uptick in hate crimes against people of Asian descent (Liu, 2021). While Asian Americans have been dealing with discrimination since they first came to America in the 18th century, the pandemic seems to have amplified *xenophobia*, or fear and dislike of those perceived as being foreign. "It is likely that this rash of COVID-19 related hate crimes and incidents will have enduring deleterious psychological, emotional, and physical effects on Asian American victims and Asian communities" (Gover et al., 2020, p. 662).

Fortunately, there are ways to combat acculturative stress and cope with the challenges of living in an unfamiliar world. One of the most important defenses is **social support,** or assistance from others (Lian et al., 2020). This could mean fostering relationships with family members back home or friends who belong to the new culture (Oppedal & Idsoe, 2015). Maintaining close connections with family may actually promote prosocial (helping) behaviors in some young people dealing with acculturative stress (Davis et al., 2018).

**IMMIGRATION IS STRESSFUL, ESPECIALLY IF YOU DON'T SPEAK THE NEW LANGUAGE.**

**Celebration of Culture**
A woman participates in Brooklyn's West Indian Day Parade, a celebration of New York's diverse Caribbean cultures (Phillips et al., 2018). The United States is the number one destination for migrants from around the world (Budiman, 2020).

**CONNECTIONS**

In **Chapter 8,** we discussed Piaget's concept of assimilation, a cognitive approach to dealing with new information. With assimilation, a person attempts to understand new information using their existing knowledge base. Here, assimilation means letting go of old ways and adopting the customs of a new culture.

**CONNECTIONS**

As noted in **Chapter 11,** discrimination means showing favoritism or hostility to others because of their group affiliation. Here we describe how discrimination can be a significant stressor for those who are targeted.

**acculturation** The process of cultural adjustment and adaptation, including changes to one's language, values, cultural behaviors, and sometimes national identity.

**acculturative stress** Stress that occurs when people move to new countries or cultures and must adjust to a new way of life.

**social support** The assistance we acquire from others.

Stephanie Keith/Getty Images.

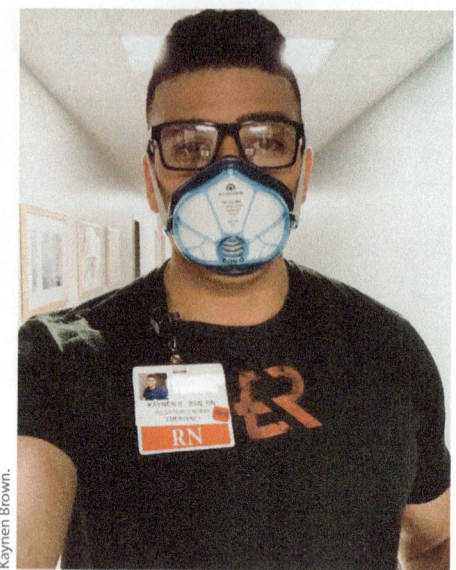

Kaynen Brown.

### Stress Over PPE

Kaynen wears personal protective equipment (PPE) to minimize exposure to the novel coronavirus. According to a survey of 15,000 nurses around the country, many hospitals did not have sufficient PPE supplies to protect their employees—after nearly a year into the pandemic (National Nurses United, 2020). Although Kaynen usually had enough PPE, he was very concerned about bringing the virus home to his family. "I was afraid for my parents," says Kaynen, who would come home from work, take off his scrubs in the garage, place them in a plastic bag for 3 days, and then wash them.

**daily hassles**  Minor, everyday problems that can act as stressors.

**uplifts**  Experiences that are positive and have the potential to make one happy.

**approach–approach conflict**  A type of conflict in which one must choose between two or more options that are attractive.

**approach–avoidance conflict**  A type of conflict that occurs when one faces a choice or situation that has favorable and unfavorable characteristics.

**avoidance–avoidance conflict**  A type of conflict in which one must choose between two or more options that are unattractive.

Now that we have described some dramatic stressors like HIV and immigration, let's shift our discussion to more mundane sources of stress. Have you ever wondered how life's little annoyances impact your mind and body?

## Hassles, Uplifts, and Conflicts

**NEW DAY, NEW RULES**    Nevada got its first COVID-19 case on March 5, 2020 (Ritter, 2020). At the time, little was known about the virus and how it was spread (*was it contaminated surfaces, sneeze and cough droplets, or smaller aerosols that linger in the air?*). Hospitals were doing the best they could with the information available, but that information was ever-changing. As new evidence rolled in, Kaynen's ER adopted new strategies. "Every day you would go into work, the rules would change," Kaynen explains. At first, the plan was to put all patients suspected of having the virus in rooms with doors closed. But soon, there were no longer enough isolation rooms to accommodate all the Covid patients. So the ER was separated into two sections—Covid, and non-Covid—and hospital managers instituted strict procedures for navigating between the two sections. Before long, that system was replaced with yet another model. "The job is already stressful enough, and you're having to worry about what rules and regulations you need to follow in order to make everyone safe," says Kaynen. "How am I supposed to know what we need to do if . . . the smartest people in the world don't even know what we're doing right now?"

**HASSLES AND UPLIFTS**    The constant procedural changes affecting Kaynen's work environment might be considered **daily hassles**—minor, everyday problems that can act as stressors. Unlike some of the major life changes described above (moving to a new country, getting an HIV diagnosis), daily hassles are small in scope. Examples in your own life may include traffic, financial worries, misplaced keys, and messy roommates.

Fortunately, the weight of our daily hassles is counterbalanced by the *uplifts* in our lives. **Uplifts** are positive experiences that have the potential to make us happy. For Kaynen, it might be a positive comment on one of his online videos. If you look at his YouTube channel, you will see thousands of responses like this: "Dude, these comments from you made my day [...] I'm gonna be in the college next year, and I think the best option is [nursing] school" (Thiago Otávio, 2018). Think about the last time you smiled; was it in response to an uplift, such as a funny comment on your Instagram post, or a surprise text from an old friend? We all experience hassles and uplifts, but how do they interact to affect our health and well-being?

Decades ago, researchers developed a scale of daily hassles and uplifts, and used it to explore the relationship between stress and illness (**FIGURE 12.1**; DeLongis et al., 1988). They asked participants to read through a list of 53 items that could be either hassles or uplifts, such as meeting deadlines, maintaining a car, interacting with fellow workers, and dealing with the weather. Participants rated these items on a 4-point scale indicating "how much of a hassle" and "how much of an uplift" each was on that particular day. They also asked participants to report any illnesses, injuries, or symptoms they experienced that same day. What did they find? Over a 6-month period, there was a significant link between hassles and health problems. The more daily stressors the participants reported, the more likely they were to suffer from sore throats, headaches, influenza, back problems, and other health issues. As subsequent research suggests, dealing with daily hassles may increase the risk of catching contagious diseases and could prolong the course of illness (Glaser & Kiecolt-Glaser, 2005). One study found that systolic blood pressure (an important indicator of cardiovascular health) tends to increase for African Americans after they move into segregated neighborhoods. "Segregation affects the quality of schools, the value of housing, and the physical access to health-promoting resources (e.g., pharmacies, full-service grocers, and gyms)" (Kershaw et al., 2017, p. E6). These resources could potentially reduce everyday stress (Kershaw et al., 2017). Apparently, the strain of managing daily hassles can take a toll on health and well-being (DeLongis et al., 1982; DeLongis et al., 1988).

How might you increase the uplifts in your life? Research suggests that people who demonstrate kindness and generosity, and act in ways that benefit others, are more likely to experience happiness and other "positive emotions." Thus, by paying it forward, you create uplifts for others and perhaps even yourself: "As people do nice things for others, they may feel greater joy, contentment, and love, which in turn promote greater overall well-being and improve social relationships and [more]" (Nelson et al., 2016, p. 856).

**FEELING CONFLICTED**   We have discussed a variety of stressors, from major life events to daily hassles. Another source of stress is conflict. The word *conflict* may conjure images of arguments and fights, but it can also refer to the discomfort one feels when making tough choices. In an **approach–approach conflict,** you must choose between two or more attractive options. For example, you have to pick between two classes you would love to take. An **approach–avoidance conflict** occurs when you face a choice or situation that has both favorable and unfavorable characteristics. You are required to take a biology lab class, and although you like biology, you do not enjoy working with other students in a lab setting. An **avoidance–avoidance conflict** occurs when you face two or more unattractive alternatives. In order to fulfill a requirement, you must choose between two courses you dread taking.

Let's see how these types of conflict might apply to Kaynen's life:

- *Approach–approach conflict:* Kaynen loves nursing. As he notes, "[It's] the best job I ever had." Yet, he is interested in going back to school and pursuing a career as a physician assistant (PA). Both options—continuing his work as a nurse and going to PA school—are positive.
- *Approach–avoidance conflict:* Kaynen sees evidence of child abuse in one of his pediatric patients. He is required by law to report this to the authorities, but the decision still creates conflict for him. Reporting the abuse means the child will be placed in foster care, an unfamiliar, often frightening environment for children. Something good will come out of the change (the child will no longer be at risk for suspected abuse), but the downside is that they will be thrust into an unfamiliar environment.
- *Avoidance–avoidance conflict:* The hospital is short of staff in both the psychiatric ward and the intensive care unit (ICU). Kaynen has a choice to help out in either department, but both options are undesirable. He is not used to working in the ICU, so being in this unfamiliar environment will cause stress, yet the psychiatric ward tends to be quiet and not as challenging for him.

Now that we have examined different types of stressors, let's explore how the brain and body respond to them.

| Hassles | | Uplifts |
|---|---|---|
| 0 1 2 3 | Your child(ren) | 0 1 2 3 |
| 0 1 2 3 | Your friend(s) | 0 1 2 3 |
| 0 1 2 3 | Your work load | 0 1 2 3 |
| 0 1 2 3 | Enough money for emergencies | 0 1 2 3 |
| 0 1 2 3 | Financial care for someone who doesn't live with you | 0 1 2 3 |
| 0 1 2 3 | Your drinking | 0 1 2 3 |
| 0 1 2 3 | Your physical appearance | 0 1 2 3 |
| 0 1 2 3 | Political or social issues | 0 1 2 3 |
| 0 1 2 3 | Amount of free time | 0 1 2 3 |
| 0 1 2 3 | Being organized | 0 1 2 3 |

**FIGURE 12.1**
**The Hassles and Uplifts Scale**
Research participants were instructed to circle a number rating the degree to which each item was a hassle (left column) and an uplift (right column). Numbers range from 0 ("none or not applicable") to 3 ("a great deal"). The scale includes 53 items, a sample of which are shown here. Information from © 1988 by the American Psychological Association.

Towfiqu Photography/Getty Images.

**Privacy or Personalization?**
You can change your phone's privacy settings to limit how much of your information is available online. But in exchange for this increase in privacy, your online experience may become less personalized, because personalization is made possible when companies collect data on people (Wirth, 2018). Which would you rather sacrifice—privacy or personalization? If both options seem undesirable, this would qualify as an avoidance–avoidance conflict.

 ## SHOW WHAT YOU KNOW

1. _____ is a response to perceived threats or challenges resulting from stimuli that cause strain.

2. The Social Readjustment Rating Scale (SRRS) was created to measure the severity and frequency of life events. This scale is most often used to examine the link between stressors and:
   **A.** aging.
   **B.** levels of eustress.
   **C.** perceived threats.
   **D.** illness.

3. _____ can occur when a person must adjust to life in a new country.
   **A.** Eustress
   **B.** Acculturative stress
   **C.** Uplifts
   **D.** Correlations

4. List three uplifts and three hassles you experienced over the last 3 days.

✓ CHECK YOUR ANSWERS AT THE BACK OF THE BOOK.

# Stress and Your Health

**EXTREME STRESS**    People who work in the ER experience stressors that are completely unfamiliar to the average person. Kaynen offers this heartbreaking example to illustrate: One day, while sitting at his desk, he heard a voice come over the intercom: "Nurse to triage." So he rushed to the triage area and found a young woman asking for help with her father, who was short of breath and needed help getting out of the car. Kaynen walked outside and found the man in his car; he was blue in the face and looking off into the distance, and his chest was not rising and falling. In the short time it had taken his daughter to go into the ER and ask for assistance, he had passed away. Kaynen grabbed the man, placed him on the ground, and started performing CPR. Despite the efforts of Kaynen and the rest of the ER team, the man could not be revived.

Only later, when the emergency was over, could Kaynen reflect on the gravity and sadness of the event. "This stuff is very traumatic," says Kaynen, who will carry memories of this man and many others for the rest of his life. But in the moment of crisis, there is no time to reflect: "This is a fight-or-flight response."

The **fight-or-flight** response that Kaynen refers to is a coordinated effort of the sympathetic nervous system and the endocrine system. It primes the body to respond to danger, either by confronting the threat head-on (in Kaynen's case, trying to save the patient's life) or by escaping (running away). Let's take a closer look at how this system works.

## CONNECTIONS

In **Chapter 2,** we introduced the sympathetic branch of the autonomic nervous system, which regulates involuntary activities. During the fight-or-flight response, the sympathetic nervous system causes blood pressure to increase, pulse and breathing rate to quicken, and the pupils to dilate. When the crisis ends, the parasympathetic system (the other branch of the autonomic nervous system) reverses the processes by reducing heart rate, blood pressure, and so on.

## Fight or Flight

**LO 4**    Identify the brain and body changes that characterize the fight-or-flight response.

When faced with a threat, portions of the brain, including the hypothalamus, activate the sympathetic nervous system, which leads to the secretion of catecholamines such as epinephrine (adrenaline) and norepinephrine (noradrenaline). These hormones cause increases in heart rate, blood pressure, respiration, and blood flow to the muscles. Such changes may explain why Kaynen felt as if his heart "dropped" the moment he realized the man had died, and why he experienced a sudden increase in energy and strength, not even noticing the weight of the man as he lifted him from the car.

There are instances when the fight-or-flight system is not adaptive. Imagine a predator–prey situation: A mouse detects a hawk flying overhead, but the hawk is not actively pursuing the mouse. Here, the mouse may be better off freezing. In some cases, the intensity of the threat may determine which response—fleeing or freezing—is more appropriate (Seo et al., 2019).

**LO 5**    Explain the function of the hypothalamic–pituitary–adrenal (HPA) system.

**HYPOTHALAMIC–PITUITARY–ADRENAL SYSTEM**    The sympathetic nervous system works with the *hypothalamic–pituitary–adrenal (HPA) system* to deal with emergencies (**INFOGRAPHIC 12.2** on page 464). When a stressful situation arises, the hypothalamus alerts the pituitary gland, prompting it to send signals to the adrenal cortex (the outside layer of the adrenal glands), which secretes corticosteroids such as cortisol. These hormones influence responses of the immune system. (The immune system defends the body from bacteria, viruses, and other types of invaders by deploying cells and chemicals to confront these threats—more on this soon.) When cortisol levels remain high for prolonged periods (as occurs with chronic stressors and threatening situations), the functioning of the immune system may decrease. How do you think this affects a person's health?

SCS Studio/Getty Images.

**Deer Me!**
If you have ever seen a "deer in the headlights" or a squirrel sitting perfectly still as a dog approaches, you have witnessed the freeze response. This fear behavior, which may precede the fight-or-flight reaction, is also seen in humans. When faced with a threat, your heart rate slows and activity increases in the midbrain, which seems to correlate with decision making (*How will I deal with this threat?*). Thus, the freeze response may serve as "a decision stage, during which the most optimal defensive action is selected" (Hashemi et al., 2019, p. 6).

**LO 6** Outline the general adaptation syndrome (GAS).

**GENERAL ADAPTATION SYNDROME**    Hans Selye, introduced earlier in the chapter, was one of the first to address this question; he suggested the human body responds to prolonged stressors in a predictable way (Selye, 1936, 1976). This specific pattern of physiological reactions is called the **general adaptation syndrome (GAS).** The GAS consists of three stages (Infographic 12.2). The first is the *alarm stage,* or the body's initial response to a threatening situation, similar to the fight-or-flight response. Arousal increases, and the body prepares to deal with the threat. Next is the *resistance stage:* The body maintains a high level of arousal (though not as high as during the *alarm stage*), but decreases its response to new stressors. It simply cannot take on additional threats. According to Selye, this is when some people start to show signs of *diseases of adaptation,* such as hypertension and arthritis (Selye, 1953; Selye & Fortier, 1950). If the threat remains and the person can no longer adapt, the *exhaustion stage* ensues. The body's resources become depleted, resulting in vulnerability to illness, physical exhaustion, and even death.

## Too Much Cortisol?

**LO 7** List some consequences of prolonged exposure to the stress hormone cortisol.

Earlier, we mentioned the stress hormone cortisol, which is released by the adrenal cortex and plays a key role in mobilizing the body to react to stressful situations. Cortisol is useful if you are responding to immediate danger, like a raging fire or ruthless assailant, but you don't want cortisol levels to remain high for too long.

**CORTISOL AND KIDS**    Prolonged exposure to cortisol can take a toll on developing brains and bodies. Infants born to mothers subjected to natural disasters, trauma, and other extreme stressors are more likely to be premature, have low birth weights, exhibit behavioral difficulties, and perhaps even show problems with cognitive development (Davis & Sandman, 2010; Levendosky et al., 2016; Tollenaar et al., 2011). Research has found that **conflicts at home** can increase cortisol levels in children (Doom et al., 2018). Imagine a child exclaiming, "No! I don't want to!" and parents saying, "You are going to shut your mouth and be quiet!" This is exactly the type of exchange associated with increased cortisol levels. Irregular cortisol activity may help explain why exposure to conflict during childhood is associated with future health problems (Oh et al., 2018; Young et al., 2019).

**CORTISOL AND COLLEGE STUDENTS**    Because cortisol enters the brain, it can have substantial effects on cognition and behavior—not only for children but also for adults (Kluen et al., 2017; Wagner et al., 2016; Wirth, 2015). Many college students experience heightened "feelings of fear, tension, and apprehension" associated with math (Jamieson et al., 2020, p. 2), which negatively correlates with achievement in the subject (Barroso et al., 2020). In other words, increased math anxiety is associated with decreased math achievement. The reason for this relationship is still under investigation, but research hints that cortisol may play a role. As one study found, students with a good working memory but high math anxiety tend to perform worse in math when cortisol levels are high. Meanwhile, those with a good working memory and lower math anxiety perform better when cortisol levels are high (Mattarella-Micke et al., 2011; Ramirez et al., 2018). This suggests that high cortisol levels may benefit people who feel comfortable with math but work against those with math anxiety.

Photo by Pete Souza/Obama Transition Office via Getty Images.
Brooks Kraft/Getty Images.
Photo courtesy of the White House/Newsmakers/Getty Images.
John Angelillo-Pool/Getty Images.

**Does Stress Make You Go Gray?**
During their 8 years in the Oval Office, President Barack Obama (top) and President George W. Bush appeared to have turned significantly grayer. Research in mammals suggests that stress contributes to the graying process. Neurons involved in the sympathetic nervous system's fight-or-flight response project into the hair follicles, releasing norepinephrine during times of stress. This appears to reduce the number of stem cells that give rise to the pigment-producing melanocytes (Zhang et al., 2020).

**CONNECTIONS**
In **Chapter 8,** we discussed how parenting behaviors impact children. Authoritarian parents who set rigid boundaries, show little warmth, and expect high control may unwittingly create stress for their children. Stress is associated with changes in cortisol activity, which could have long-term health implications.

**Is She Happy or Mad?**
How you interpret this woman's emotional state may depend on your current stress level. In one study, people were more likely to perceive negative emotions in ambiguous facial expressions when their cortisol levels were elevated (Brown et al., 2017).

drbimages/Getty Images.

# Physiological Responses to Stress

When faced with an emergency, our bodies go through a series of physiological responses that assist us in coping with a stressor. Activation of the *fight-or-flight* response and *hypothalamic–pituitary–adrenal (HPA) system* gives us the energy and resources we need to cope with a temporary stressor. Studying these physiological responses, Hans Selye (1956) found that the sequence follows the same path no matter the stressor. Selye called this sequence the general adaptation syndrome (GAS). He found that when the stressor remains, our bodies can no longer adapt.

## GENERAL ADAPTATION SYNDROME (GAS)

In the alarm stage, the short-term responses are activated, giving us the energy to combat a threat. In the resistance stage, resources remain mobilized, and we continue to cope with the stressor. But eventually we enter the exhaustion stage, becoming weak and susceptible to illness, and less able to cope with the stressor (Selye, 1956).

**STRESSOR**

Resistance to stress — high / low

normal level of resistance to stress

**Alarm stage** (stress response activated)

**Resistance stage** (coping with stressor)

**Exhaustion stage** (reserves diminished)

## SHORT-TERM RESPONSES TO STRESS

Amygdala processes information about stressor. If threat is perceived, hypothalamus triggers short-term stress response.

**STRESSOR**

Hypothalamus

Pituitary gland

Adrenal glands

kidneys

### FIGHT-OR-FLIGHT SYSTEM

**ACTIVATES**

**Sympathetic Nervous System**

**SENDS SIGNAL TO**

**Adrenal Medulla** (core of adrenal glands)

**RELEASES**

**Catecholamines** epinephrine, norepinephrine

**CAUSES**

Efficient management of bodily resources so they are available for emergency action:
• increased heart rate
• increased respiration
• increased blood flow to muscles
• digestion slows
• pupils dilate

### HYPOTHALAMIC–PITUITARY–ADRENAL (HPA) SYSTEM

**ALERTS**

**Pituitary Gland**

**SENDS SIGNAL TO**

**Adrenal Cortex** (outside layer of adrenal glands)

**RELEASES**

**Corticosteroids** including cortisol

**CAUSES**

Efficient management of bodily resources; changes in immune responses

## PROLONGED STRESS

Relative risk of a cold: 4, 3, 2, 1, 0

Duration of stressor (in months): no stressor, less than 1, 1–6, 6–24, more than 24

Prolonged stress can cause the immune system to break down. As you can see, the risk of becoming sick is directly related to the duration of a stressor. This effect is seen even when the stressor is not traumatic. Data in this study were collected from people reporting on interpersonal conflicts and problems concerning work (Cohen et al., 1998).

# How Can Stress Make You Sick?

**LO 8** Explain how stressors relate to health problems.

Before we further explore the connection between stress and illness, we must understand how the body deals with illness. Let's take a side trip into introductory biology and learn about the body's main defense against disease—the immune system, comprising the spleen, lymph nodes, bone marrow, and other tissues (FIGURE 12.2). When disease-causing invaders like viruses and bacteria threaten the body, the immune system deploys a special army of white blood cells. For example, *macrophages* ("big eaters") hunt and consume both invaders and worn-out cells of the body. *Natural killer cells* (*NK cells*) target body cells that have been affected by invaders, injecting them with a deadly chemical. NK cells also release a protein that prevents the infection from spreading. In some cases, the body must call on its "special ops" teams: the *B lymphocytes* and *T lymphocytes*. The B lymphocytes mature in the bone marrow and produce antibodies that chemically inhibit bacteria and other invaders, while T lymphocytes mature in the thymus and play an integral role in fighting cancer, viruses, and other disease-causing agents that the B lymphocytes have failed to ward off (Hickman, 2019; Straub, 2017). When the body is expending resources to deal with an ongoing stressor, the work of lymphocytes is compromised. The immune system is less powerful, and the body is more susceptible to disease.

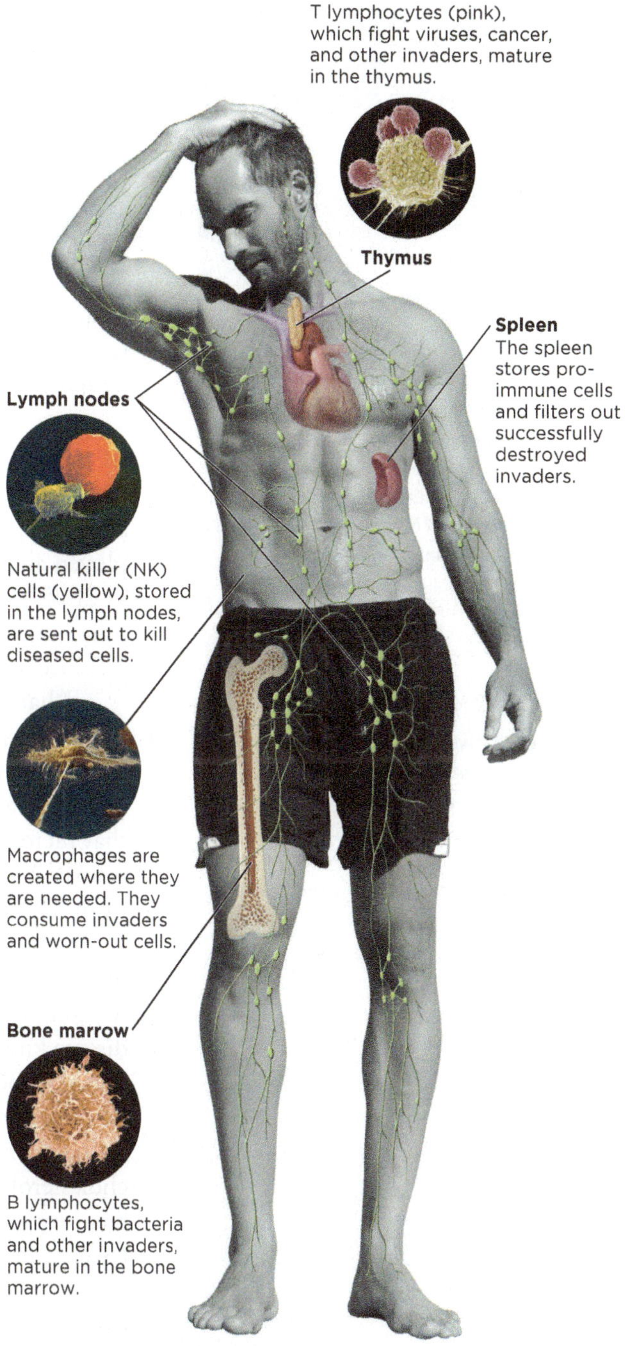

**GASTRIC ULCERS** A classic example of a stress-related ailment is the gastric ulcer. For many years, stress was assumed to be the sole culprit, but then researchers began considering other causes. They found evidence that the bacterium *H. pylori* plays an important, but not necessarily essential, role. Many "intertwined biological and psychosocial components" seem to influence the development of gastric ulcers—among them stress, smoking, family history, and the use of nonsteroidal anti-inflammatory drugs like aspirin and ibuprofen (Fink, 2011, 2017; Levenstein et al., 2015, p. 505).

**CANCER** Cancer has also been associated with stress, in terms of both risk and development. Specifically, stress has been linked to the suppression of T lymphocytes and NK cells, which help monitor immune system reactions to developing tumors (Reiche et al., 2004; Zingoni et al., 2017).

Apart from cancers of the skin, breast cancer is the greatest cancer risk for women in the United States. In fact, 1 out of every 8 American women will get breast cancer at some point in her life (American Cancer Society, 2021). Is stress to blame for this alarmingly high statistic? A study of 106,000 women in the United Kingdom found "no association of breast cancer risk overall with experienced frequency of stress" (Schoemaker et al., 2016, p. 1). Some evidence suggests that lower SES is linked to more aggressive types of breast cancer and lower survival (Coughlin, 2019). Given what you have learned about poverty and stress, do you think there could be a link between economic stressors and breast cancer outcomes?

Understanding the relationships between stressors and cancer has been a challenge for researchers. Part of the problem is that studies frequently focus on stressors of different durations. Short- and long-term stressors have distinct effects

T lymphocytes (pink), which fight viruses, cancer, and other invaders, mature in the thymus.

**Thymus**

**Spleen**
The spleen stores pro-immune cells and filters out successfully destroyed invaders.

**Lymph nodes**

Natural killer (NK) cells (yellow), stored in the lymph nodes, are sent out to kill diseased cells.

Macrophages are created where they are needed. They consume invaders and worn-out cells.

**Bone marrow**

B lymphocytes, which fight bacteria and other invaders, mature in the bone marrow.

**FIGURE 12.2**
**The Immune System**
Our immunity derives from a complex system involving structures and organs throughout the body that support the work of specialized cell types. Man: B2M Productions/Getty Images; T lymphocytes and B lymphocytes: Steve Gschmeissner/Science Source; Natural killer cells and macrophages: Eye of Science/Science Source.

**general adaptation syndrome (GAS)** A specific pattern of physiological reactions to stressors that includes the alarm stage, resistance stage, and exhaustion stage.

Scott Olson/Getty Images.

**Battling Stress**

A group of Marines practice patrolling techniques as part of their combat training. Long-term stressors such as military deployment are associated with declines in the activity of NK cells, which help the body fight infections (Dhabhar, 2014).

## CONNECTIONS

In **Chapter 11,** we discussed stereotypes, the assumptions we make about people based on their group membership (race, religion, age, or gender, for example). Stereotypes often incorporate some type of judgment. This kind of "social-evaluative threat" can cause stress in the person being stereotyped.

*Research*
## CONNECTIONS

In **Chapter 1,** we discussed meta-analysis, a statistical approach that allows researchers to combine the findings of different studies and draw general conclusions. Here we present two meta-analyses that help explain how stressors are linked to a variety of health problems.

**psychoneuroimmunology** The field that examines relationships among psychological factors, the nervous system, and immune system functioning.

on the immune system, and thus its ability to combat cancer (Dhabhar, 2014; Segerstrom & Miller, 2004). For short-lived stressors such as midterm exams, public speaking, and other activities lasting between 5 and 100 minutes, the body responds by increasing the number of NK cells and deploying other immune cells where needed. In other words, short-term stressors tend to augment immune functioning. Meanwhile, long-term stressors such as military deployment or caring for someone with dementia are associated with decreases in NK cells. To appreciate the relationship between stress, immune function, and cancer, we must consider not only the duration of stress but also a myriad of biopsychosocial factors. Variables such as age, medical history, social support, and mental health can impact the link between stressors and cancer (Özkan et al., 2017; Reiche et al., 2004; Segerstrom & Miller, 2004).

**HEART DISEASE**   Cardiovascular disease is also linked to stress (O'Connor et al., 2021). Earthquakes, unhappy marriages, caregiving burdens, and money problems are among the many stressors that may contribute. For people who became unemployed as a result of Hurricane Katrina (a devastating natural disaster that occurred in 2005), the risk of experiencing a "cardiometabolic event" jumped fivefold in the following 5 years (Joseph et al., 2014). The faster people get support to decrease "socioeconomic disruptions" related to a disaster, the better their health outcomes.

What other stressors have been linked to heart disease? "Social-evaluative threats," or concerns about being **judged by others** (about physical appearance or behaviors in a social context, for example), are associated with increases in blood pressure and consequently an elevated risk of heart disease (Smith et al., 2012). One model suggests that increased job stress can put people at greater risk for developing coronary heart disease, particularly those who perceive a significant degree of job "strain" resulting from high demands, lack of control, and other factors (Ferris et al., 2012).

The exact relationship between stressors, high blood pressure, and cardiovascular disease is not totally understood (Straub, 2019). We do know that an increase of fatty deposits containing cholesterol, calcium, clotting substances, and other material (a disease known as *atherosclerosis*) is a risk factor for stroke and heart disease (American Heart Association, n.d.-a). Researchers are not sure exactly how atherosclerosis starts, but one theory suggests that it begins with damage to the inner layer of the artery wall, which may be caused by elevated blood pressure, high blood concentrations of cholesterol and triglycerides, and cigarette use. This damage may cause blood flow in an artery to become reduced or blocked, potentially leading to a heart attack or stroke (American Heart Association, n.d.-a).

**PSYCHONEUROIMMUNOLOGY**   We have discussed how ongoing stress affects one's risk for developing gastric ulcers, cancer, and heart disease, but the list of negative health effects is much longer. According to a meta-analysis of over 300 studies, chronic stressors are associated with problematic immune system responses, which may increase the risk for various illnesses involving inflammation, including asthma, allergies, multiple sclerosis, and rheumatoid arthritis (Segerstrom & Miller, 2004). A more recent **meta-analysis** confirmed that distress is associated with adverse health effects (Barry et al., 2020). Childhood stress, in particular, may leave the "biological scar" of inflammation, which has been linked to both physical disease and psychological disorders (Halaris et al., 2019). It is an important time for those who specialize in the field of **psychoneuroimmunology** (SI-koh-NUR-oh-IM-mu-NOL-oh-gee), which examines links among psychological factors (such as coping mechanisms and beliefs), the nervous system, and immune functioning (Slavich, 2016).

## ▶▶▶ SHOW WHAT YOU KNOW

1. As an ER nurse, Kaynen has helped people in dire emergencies. When faced with a crisis, his body initially exhibits a fight-or-flight reaction, which is equivalent to the _____ of the general adaptation syndrome.

   **A.** alarm stage
   **B.** exhaustion stage
   **C.** diseases of adaptation
   **D.** acculturative stress

2. Infants of mothers subjected to extreme stressors may be born premature, have low birth weights, and exhibit behavioral difficulties. These outcomes result from increased levels of the stress hormone:

   **A.** *H. pylori.*
   **B.** lymphocytes.
   **C.** cortisol.
   **D.** NK cells.

3. _____ works with the sympathetic nervous system to deal with emergencies. The messaging cascade begins when the hypothalamus alerts the pituitary gland, prompting it to send signals to the adrenal cortex, which secretes corticosteroids such as cortisol.

   **A.** The general adaptation syndrome
   **B.** The exhaustion stage
   **C.** The hypothalamic–pituitary–adrenal system
   **D.** Eustress

4. The _____ refers to a specific pattern of physiological reactions observed in response to stressors.

5. Why are people under stress more likely to get sick?

✓ CHECK YOUR ANSWERS AT THE BACK OF THE BOOK.

# Can You Deal?

**ER EXHAUSTION**   When you work in the ER, you witness very upsetting events on a regular basis: heart attacks, strokes, knife and gunshot wounds, injuries from car accidents, life-threatening symptoms of infectious diseases like COVID-19. But with experience, "you do a better job of putting it to the side," according to Kaynen. This doesn't mean you stop caring—it just means you develop an ability to narrow your focus on what the patient needs at that moment. Rather than thinking, *this person could die,* or *I have never seen a human body injured in that way,* you go through a checklist: blood pressure, heart rate, breath sounds, and so on. During a medical emergency, a patient needs someone who can calmly and efficiently solve problems.

Kaynen seems to have the perfect disposition for nursing. He is compassionate yet able to set aside his emotions during emergencies, and he is not easily flustered. Not everyone deals with the stress of the job so easily. As one small study found, nurses who have trouble regulating emotions, taking on the perspective of others, and being fully present in the moment (mindful) may be more susceptible to *burnout* (Salvarani et al., 2019).

## Understanding Burnout

**Burnout** refers to emotional, mental, and physical fatigue that results from repeated exposure to challenges, leading to reduced motivation, enthusiasm, and performance. People who work in the helping professions, including psychologists, physicians, and child protection workers, are clearly at risk for burnout (McCormack et al., 2018; McFadden et al., 2018; Nazir et al., 2018). Before Covid, 35–54% of nurses and doctors were experiencing burnout, partly a result of excessive workload, administrative hassles, and dealing with policies and regulations that are not always compatible with providing quality care to patients (National Academies of Sciences, Engineering, and Medicine, 2019). The pandemic's effect has yet to be determined, but anecdotal reports suggest that health-care worker burnout has risen: "The impact, for now, can be measured in part by a surge of early retirements and the desperation of community hospitals struggling to hire enough workers to keep their emergency rooms running" (Jacobs, 2021, para. 7). It may take years to fully understand the mental health repercussions, but early evidence indicates high levels of depression, anxiety, and insomnia among health-care workers during the pandemic (Pappa et al., 2020).

Fortunately, Kaynen appears to have weathered the storm well. If you ask him about his emotional well-being during the pandemic, he will tell you that he was in

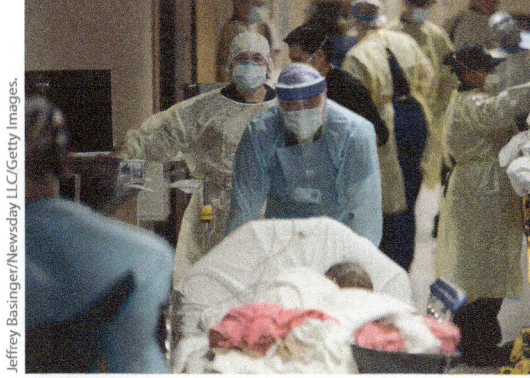

Jeffrey Basinger/Newsday LLC/Getty Images.

**Moral Injury**
COVID-19 has forced health-care professionals to make decisions that rock their sense of morality to the core. Imagine having to walk past patients struggling to breathe in the hallways of the ER where you work. These people desperately need rooms and medical care, but the hospital is overflowing with patients and you cannot help them right now. Such situations may cause *moral injury* to health-care workers, that is, "psychological distress that results from actions, or the lack thereof, that violates someone's moral or ethical code" (Litam et al., 2020, p. 1).

**burnout** Emotional, mental, and physical fatigue that results in reduced motivation, enthusiasm, and performance.

pretty good spirits. "I was more freaked out by what was happening with the rest of the country," he says, referring to the job losses, hunger, and overall economic hardship. Despite the disturbing events occurring around him, Kaynen managed to stay calm, get decent sleep, and maintain healthy relationships. How was he able to keep the stress under control, while so many others experienced burnout, anxiety, and other psychological problems? To answer this question, and many more relating to stress and health, we turn to the field of *health psychology.*

**Health psychology** explores the biological, psychological, and social factors that influence human health. Psychologists working in this area seek to explain how food choices, exercise, social interactions, and living environments affect our predisposition to illness. They study the impact of personality factors, coping style, cognitive appraisal, poverty, culture, social support, and religion (INFOGRAPHIC **12.3**). Their findings inform public policy, paving the way for changes to health-related guidelines and the promotion of positive eating and exercise habits.

## How Do You Handle Stress?

In this section, we will explore critical lessons brought to us by health psychology research. We'll start by examining some of the individual differences that influence the way people *cope* with stress.

**LO 9** Illustrate how appraisal influences coping.

**HOW DO YOU COPE?**  **Coping** refers to the cognitive, behavioral, and emotional abilities used to manage something perceived as difficult or challenging. In order to cope, you must appraise, or evaluate, the stressor. When making a **primary appraisal,** you determine how an event or situation will affect you: Is it irrelevant, positive, challenging, or harmful? Next, you form a **secondary appraisal;** that is, you decide how to respond, considering what resources are available.

Psychologist Richard Lazarus (1922–2002) suggested that stress is the result of a person's **appraisal** of a stressor, not necessarily the stressor itself (Folkman & Lazarus, 1985; Lazarus & Folkman, 1984). This viewpoint stands in contrast to Selye's suggestion (noted earlier) that we all react to stressors in a similar manner. If you believe you can cope with virtually any challenge that comes your way, the impact of stress remains low. If you think your coping abilities are poor, the impact of stress will be high. Differences in appraisal help explain why two people can react to the same event in dramatically different ways (INFOGRAPHIC **12.4** on page 470).

There are two basic types of coping. **Problem-focused coping** means taking a direct approach, confronting a problem head-on. Suppose you are having trouble in a relationship; with problem-focused coping, you might read self-help books or find a counselor. **Emotion-focused coping** involves addressing the emotions that surround a problem, rather than trying to solve it or change the situation. With a troubled relationship, you might think about your feelings, look to friends for support, or exercise to take your mind off it, instead of addressing the problem directly. When emotions interfere with daily functioning or when problems have no solutions (for example, the death of a loved one), emotion-focused coping may be better. However, problem-focused coping is usually more productive in the long run.

How we react to problems, and difficult circumstances in general, plays an important role in success. People with high levels of "grit" persevere when things get tough and continue working toward their goals. Having grit and strong self-control appears to be more important than intelligence when it comes to achieving success (Duckworth & Gross, 2014). Have you ever heard of Bethany Hamilton? At age 13, Hamilton was attacked by a tiger shark while surfing. The shark tore

**CONNECTIONS**

In **Chapter 9,** we described the cognitive appraisal theory of emotion, which suggests that emotion results from the way people appraise or interpret interactions they have. This influences our response to stressors.

**health psychology** The study of the biological, psychological, and social factors that contribute to health and illness.

**coping** The cognitive, behavioral, and emotional abilities used to manage something that is perceived as difficult or challenging.

**primary appraisal** One's initial assessment of a situation to determine its personal impact and whether it is irrelevant, positive, challenging, or harmful.

**secondary appraisal** An assessment to determine how to respond to a challenging or threatening situation.

**problem-focused coping** A coping strategy in which a person deals directly with a problem by attempting to solve and address it head-on.

**emotion-focused coping** A coping strategy in which a person addresses the emotions that surround a problem, as opposed to trying to solve it.

# Health Psychology

Health psychology is the study of the biological, psychological, and social factors that contribute to health and illness. Using the biopsychosocial perspective, health psychologists examine how a variety of factors, including diet, physical activity, and social relationships, impact our predisposition to illness. One of the primary goals is to increase positive health behaviors and decrease negative ones. Research in this field can benefit the health and well-being of individuals and the community at large through changes to public policy and health education.

## Understanding Stress: The Biopsychosocial Perspective

Stress has been linked to a variety of negative health outcomes. The biopsychosocial perspective helps us understand how the interaction among biological, psychological, and social factors contributes to our vulnerability.

Viruses, bacteria, and other disease-causing organisms invade the body, triggering an immune response and putting a strain on the body's resources.

Exercise is one of the best ways to buffer against stress and its negative effects (Alex, 2019; Milani & Lavie, 2009).

MORE STRESS **← BIOLOGY →** LESS STRESS

 OH NO!

A perceived lack of control, even in mundane aspects of life, profoundly impacts our ability to manage stress (Pagnini et al., 2016, Bercovitz, & Langer, 2016; Rodin, 1986).

Research has shown that mindfulness meditation helps ease anxiety and depression (Dimidjian et al., 2016; Iwamoto et al., 2020).

OM

MORE STRESS **← PSYCHOLOGY →** LESS STRESS

Research has shown that feeling judged on one's race, gender, income level, and other factors has a negative impact on physical health and well-being (Clark et al., 2009; Smyth et al., 2020; Williams & Mohammed, 2009).

As a species, human beings are social and benefit from interaction with other humans and even animals (Allen, 2003; Iwamoto et al., 2020; John-Henderson et al., 2015).

MORE STRESS **← SOCIAL INTERACTION →** LESS STRESS

## HEALTH PSYCHOLOGY APPLIED

### BIOLOGY
### What's in a Color?

PANTONE 448C

With public health in mind, Australia and the United Kingdom have begun requiring cigarette packs to be wrapped in "Opaque Couché" (Pantone 448C), deemed the ugliest color across the globe (Blakemore, 2016, para. 2). The packaging also features shocking images of smoking-related health consequences. Smoking rates in Australia fell after the new packaging was implemented and tobacco taxes were raised (Australian Department of Health, 2016; Blakemore, 2016).

### PSYCHOLOGY
### The Power of Thinking "Beyond the Now"

College students who were able to think about and plan for their futures showed an increase in positive health behaviors, such as exercise and conscientious eating habits (Baird et al., 2021; Visser & Hirsch, 2014).

### SOCIAL INTERACTION
### Animal Therapy in Crisis Management

Recognizing how animals can help people manage stress, professionals now use therapy dogs to facilitate coping (Allen, 2003; Associated Press, 2014, Lalonde et al., 2020; Rancilio, 2020).

# The Process of Coping

Coping refers to the cognitive, emotional, and behavioral methods we employ to manage stressful events. But we don't always rely on the same strategies to manage stressors in our lives. Coping is an individual process through which we appraise a stressor to determine how it will affect us and how we can respond.

**stressful encounter**

*I have a final exam!*

MAY **12** Math Final

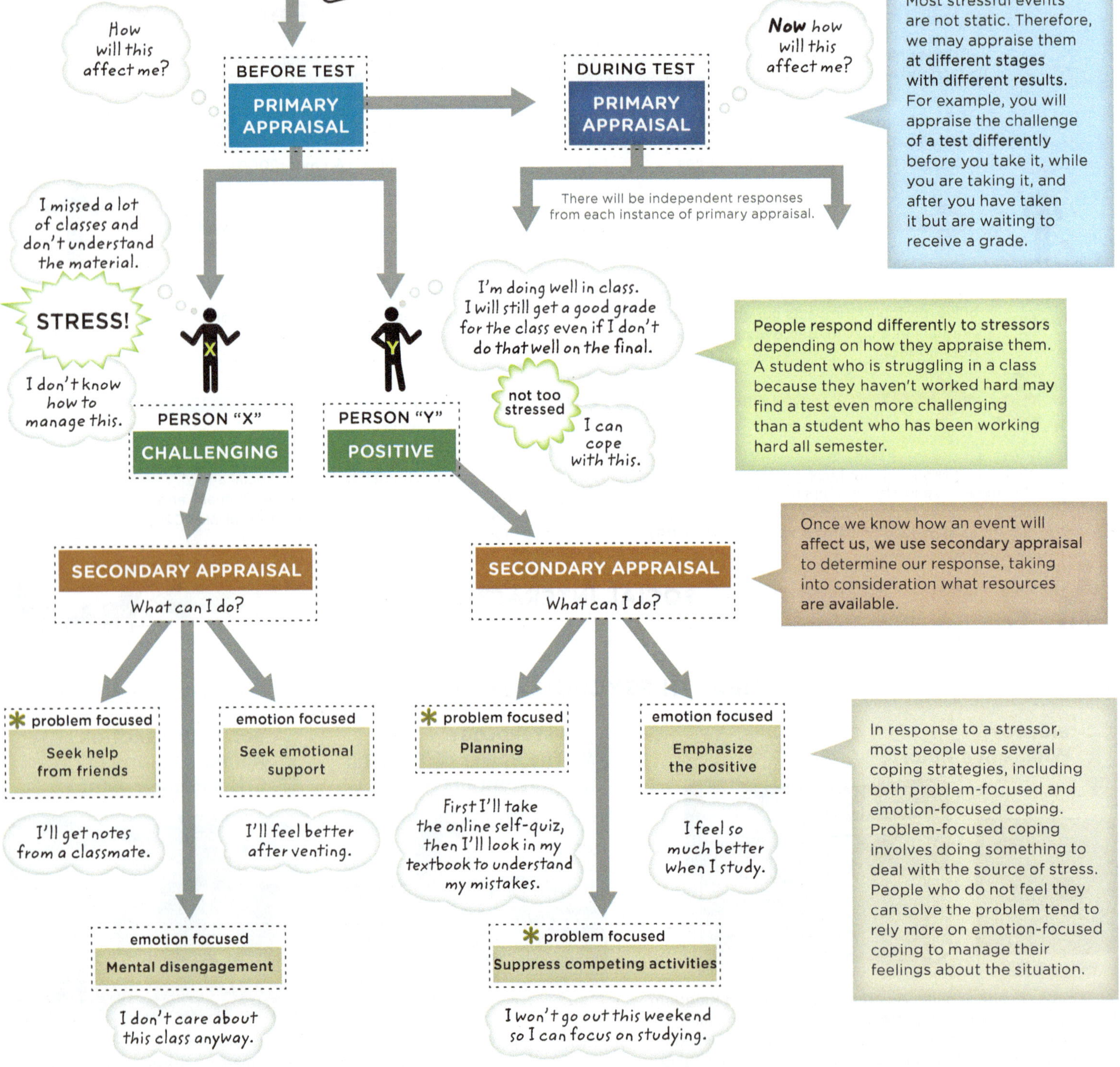

*How will this affect me?*

**BEFORE TEST**
**PRIMARY APPRAISAL**

*Now how will this affect me?*

**DURING TEST**
**PRIMARY APPRAISAL**

Most stressful events are not static. Therefore, we may appraise them at different stages with different results. For example, you will appraise the challenge of a test differently before you take it, while you are taking it, and after you have taken it but are waiting to receive a grade.

*I missed a lot of classes and don't understand the material.*

**STRESS!**

*I don't know how to manage this.*

There will be independent responses from each instance of primary appraisal.

*I'm doing well in class. I will still get a good grade for the class even if I don't do that well on the final.*

**not too stressed**

*I can cope with this.*

People respond differently to stressors depending on how they appraise them. A student who is struggling in a class because they haven't worked hard may find a test even more challenging than a student who has been working hard all semester.

**PERSON "X"**
**CHALLENGING**

**PERSON "Y"**
**POSITIVE**

**SECONDARY APPRAISAL**
*What can I do?*

**SECONDARY APPRAISAL**
*What can I do?*

Once we know how an event will affect us, we use secondary appraisal to determine our response, taking into consideration what resources are available.

**＊ problem focused**
Seek help from friends

**emotion focused**
Seek emotional support

**＊ problem focused**
Planning

**emotion focused**
Emphasize the positive

In response to a stressor, most people use several coping strategies, including both problem-focused and emotion-focused coping. Problem-focused coping involves doing something to deal with the source of stress. People who do not feel they can solve the problem tend to rely more on emotion-focused coping to manage their feelings about the situation.

*I'll get notes from a classmate.*

*I'll feel better after venting.*

*First I'll take the online self-quiz, then I'll look in my textbook to understand my mistakes.*

*I feel so much better when I study.*

**emotion focused**
Mental disengagement

**＊ problem focused**
Suppress competing activities

*I don't care about this class anyway.*

*I won't go out this weekend so I can focus on studying.*

**＊ Problem-focused coping is usually the most productive. Here are some other problem-focused strategies:**

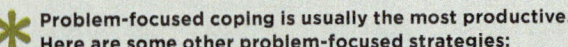 Restraint (wait to act until all relevant data have come to light)

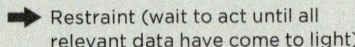 Break the problem into manageable chunks

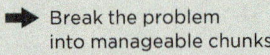 Research the situation

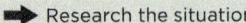 Pursue alternatives

off her left arm, but it couldn't break her passion for surfing. How did she cope? Weeks after the attack, she was paddling in the waves again, and she went on to become a champion surfer (Russell, 2020)! The fact that Hamilton built her life around surfing after such a devastating setback suggests she has considerable grit. Gritty people tend to cope well with adversity, and they have a high tolerance for frustration: "The ability to push through sustained periods of frustration might also be a key to persisting long enough to attain a long-term goal like a college degree" (Meindl et al., 2019, p. 1082).

## Put Your Heads Together

Team up and **A)** explain the meaning of primary appraisal, secondary appraisal, problem-focused coping, and emotion-focused coping. **B)** Follow the steps outlined in Infographic 12.4 using a different stressor.

**LO 10** Describe how personality characteristics relate to health.

**TYPE A AND TYPE B PERSONALITIES**   Coping styles appear to be related to personality, another area of interest for those in the field of health psychology (Segerstrom & Smith, 2019). For decades, researchers have known that people with certain personality types are prone to developing cardiovascular disease. Cardiologists Meyer Friedman (1910–2001) and Ray Rosenman (1920–2013) were among the first to suspect a link between personality type and cardiovascular problems (Friedman & Rosenman, 1974). In particular, they noted that many of the people they treated were intensely focused on time and always in a hurry. These characteristics and other behavior patterns came to be known as **Type A personality.** Someone with a Type A personality is competitive, aggressive, impatient, and often hostile (Diamond, 1982; Smith & Ruiz, 2002). Through numerous studies, Friedman and Rosenman discovered that people with Type A personality were twice as likely to develop cardiovascular disease as those with **Type B personality.** Individuals with Type B personality are often more relaxed, patient, and nonaggressive (Rosenman et al., 1975). Why would people with Type A personality suffer disproportionately from cardiovascular disease? There are various reasons, but these individuals are more likely to have high blood pressure, an elevated heart rate, and increased levels of stress hormones. They are also prone to more interpersonal problems (arguments, fights, and other hostile interactions), which increase the time their bodies are prepared for fight or flight.

For several decades, studies seemed to confirm the relationship between Type A behavior and heart disease, but then some researchers had difficulty replicating the findings (Smith & MacKenzie, 2006). This was partly the result of inconsistent methodologies; for example, some studies used samples with high-risk participants, whereas others included healthy people. As researchers continued to probe the relationship, they found that the component of *hostility* in Type A personality was the strongest predictor of coronary heart disease. While Type A and B personality types have been useful for understanding the relationship between personality characteristics and heart health, some scholars suggest this categorical approach may not capture the nuances of human personality (Wilmot et al., 2019).

**TYPE D PERSONALITY**   Another personality type associated with poor cardio-vascular outcomes is *Type D personality,* where "D" refers to distress (Denollet & Conraads, 2011). A Type D individual tends to experience worry, tension, bad moods, and social inhibition (avoids confronting others and has poor social skills). People who exhibit these Type D qualities and have heart problems are more likely to struggle with their illness. Is this because they tend to avoid dealing with issues directly and fail to take advantage of social support? Perhaps. This coping approach is

**Unbelievable Grit**
Surfer Bethany Hamilton competes in the 2020 Sydney Surf Pro in Sydney, Australia. Many years ago, Hamilton lost her left arm in a shark attack, but she returned to surfing just weeks later.
Matt Dunbar/Getty Images.

**Type A personality**  A person who exhibits a competitive, aggressive, impatient, and often hostile pattern of behaviors.

**Type B personality**  A person who exhibits a relaxed, patient, and nonaggressive pattern of behaviors.

Kaynen Brown.

**He's Resilient**

Kaynen flunked the very first exam he took in nursing school. "That was a huge ego-hitter," he recalls. "I got placed on academic probation. It was embarrassing." But instead of getting discouraged and giving up, Kaynen talked to his professor about what he needed to do and doubled down on his studying. His initiative and hard work paid off—on the next exam, he got the highest grade in the class. Kaynen's response to this setback demonstrates that he is resilient.

**hardiness** A personality characteristic indicating an ability to remain resilient and optimistic despite intensely stressful situations.

generally not effective in the long term (Habibović et al., 2020; Martin et al., 2011). Type D personality appears to be "substantially heritable," or genetically influenced (Li-Gao et al., 2021).

**THE THREE Cs OF HARDINESS**    Clearly, not everyone has the same tolerance for stress (Ganzel et al., 2010; Straub, 2019). Some people seem capable of handling intensely stressful situations, such as war and poverty. These individuals appear to have a personality characteristic called **hardiness;** they are very resilient and tend to remain positive when facing a great deal of stress. This quality seems to confer an advantage to first responders, many of whom witness traumas on a regular basis. During the coronavirus pandemic, Italian researchers asked Red Cross volunteers to fill out a questionnaire assessing hardiness. The assessment included statements such as, "By working hard you can always achieve your goals," which respondents rated with a 4-point scale (for example, 0 for "not at all true" and 3 for "completely true"; Vagni et al., 2020, p. 8). Participants who scored high in hardiness were more likely to cope effectively and less likely to experience "secondary trauma," or psychological distress as a result of witnessing the trauma of others (Vagni et al., 2020).

Researchers have also studied how some business executives seem to withstand the effects of extremely stressful jobs (Kobasa, 1979). Their hardiness appears to be associated with three characteristics: feeling a strong *commitment* to work and personal matters; believing they are in *control* of the events in their lives and not victims of circumstances; and not feeling threatened by *challenges,* but rather seeing them as opportunities for growth. Earning a college degree while balancing other responsibilities requires a certain amount of hardiness. Think about the ways you exhibit commitment and control, and how you face challenges that arise with every new semester.

**WHO'S IN CONTROL?**    Psychologists have consistently found that people who believe they have control over their lives and circumstances are less likely to experience the negative impact of stressors than those who do not feel this sense of control. For a clear illustration of this phenomenon, we turn to a series of studies on nursing home residents (Langer & Rodin, 1976). Residents in a "responsibility-induced" group were allowed to make a variety of choices about their daily activities and environments. Meanwhile, members of the "comparison" group were not given these kinds of choices; instead, the nursing home staff made all such decisions for them. (These residents were told that the staff was responsible for their happiness and care.) After following the participants for 18 months, the researchers found that members of the responsibility-induced group were more lively, socially engaged, and healthier than those in the comparison group. Perhaps more shocking, twice as many of the residents in the comparison group died during this period (Rodin & Langer, 1977).

Having a sense of personal control may impact disease outcomes and overall health of people across age groups. Cancer patients who exhibit a "helpless attitude" about their disease seem more likely to experience a recurrence of the cancer than those with perceptions of greater control. Why would this be? Women who have had breast cancer and believe they maintain control over their lifestyle, through diet and exercise, are more likely to make proactive changes related to their health (Costanzo et al., 2011). Ultimately, these changes may reduce the risk factors associated with cancer (Simon, 2015). The same type of relationship is apparent in cardiovascular disease; the less control people feel they have, the greater their risk (Shapiro et al., 1996).

Feelings of control may also have a direct effect on the body; for example, a sense of powerlessness is associated with increases in catecholamines and corticosteroids, both key players in the physiological response to stressors. Some have suggested a causal relationship between feelings of perceived control and immune system function; the greater the sense of control, the better the functioning of the immune system (Shapiro et al., 1996). But these are correlations, and the direction of causality is not clear. Could it be that better immune functioning, and thus better health, might increase one's sense of control?

We must also consider cross-cultural differences. Individual control is emphasized and valued in individualist cultures, but not necessarily in collectivistic cultures, where people may look to "powerful others" and "chance factors" to explain events and guide decision making (Cheng et al., 2013).

**LOCUS OF CONTROL**    Differences in perceived sense of control stem from beliefs about where control resides (Rotter, 1966). People with an *internal locus of control* generally feel they are in control of life; they believe it is important to take charge and make changes when problems occur. Those with an *external locus of control* generally feel that chance, luck, or fate is responsible for their circumstances; there is no point in trying to change things or make them better. Imagine that a doctor tells a patient they need to change their lifestyle and start exercising. If the patient has an internal locus of control, they will likely take charge and start walking to work or hitting the gym; they expect their actions will impact their health. If the patient has an external locus of control, they are more apt to think their actions won't make a difference and may not attempt lifestyle changes. In the 1970 British Cohort Study, researchers examined over 11,000 children at age 10, and then assessed their health at age 30. Participants with an internal locus of control, measured at 10 years of age, were less likely to be overweight or obese in adulthood, and had lower levels of psychological problems. They were also less inclined to smoke and more likely to exercise regularly than people with a more external locus of control (Gale et al., 2008). Subsequent research suggests that teens with an internal locus of control are less likely to engage in excessive drinking later in life (Cheng & Furnham, 2019).

**"I JUST DIDN'T WANT TO DO IT"**    Apart from drinking two beers at his senior prom, Kaynen has stayed away from alcohol and other drugs. Immediately after graduating, he enrolled in a police training program that strictly forbade underage drinking. Ultimately, a back injury prevented him from pursuing a career in law enforcement, but the experience kept him away from the party scene. He officially swore off alcohol after witnessing its unpleasant effects in the hospital. "I made the decision definitively to not to drink at all—ever—after volunteering in the ER and then shadowing my aunt so much in the ER."

The scenes Kaynen saw were disturbing: women who had been beaten by drunk boyfriends and husbands, people coming in paralyzed and dead from drunk driving accidents, and chronic drinkers with jaundice (yellowing of the skin and whites of eyes), a result of severe liver damage. The number of injuries and illnesses associated with alcohol use was shocking. "My family drinks. My friends drink," Kaynen says. "But for me, personally, I've just seen so much death and trauma as a result of alcohol, I just didn't want to do it."

## Substances Don't Help

Some people mistakenly view substances as stress relievers. Psychologists explain this type of behavior with the *self-medication hypothesis,* which suggests that people turn to **drugs and alcohol** to reduce anxiety (Swendsen et al., 2000). Self-medication appears to be one of the ways people in the United States have dealt with COVID-19 stress. Women, in particular, seem to have increased their alcohol intake during the pandemic. This coping strategy may provide a temporary escape, but it generally does not

**CONNECTIONS**

In **Chapter 4,** we described how people use alcohol and other drugs for recreational purposes, and how anesthesiologists rely on drugs to alleviate pain, temporarily block memories, and toy with various aspects of consciousness. Here, we discuss how people turn to substances in times of stress.

Jupiterimages/Getty Images.

**It's Not Medicine**
When faced with stressors, we may sleep poorly, eat unhealthy foods, and perhaps abuse substances. These behavioral tendencies can lead to significant health problems (Haun & Oppenauer, 2019; Liu et al., 2017; Nielsen et al., 2018). The self-medication approach is not effective. A better strategy might be going to the gym, taking a hike, or doing some deep-breathing exercises.

**CONNECTIONS**

In **Chapter 4,** we discussed the concept of tolerance. When we use drugs like nicotine, they alter the chemistry of the brain and body. Over time, the body adapts to the drug and therefore needs more and more to create the original effect.

alleviate stress in the long run (Rodriguez et al., 2020). In fact, self-medication may lead to more stress, or in some cases pave the way for the development of substance use disorders (Lin et al., 2020; Rodriguez et al., 2020; Turner et al., 2018).

**ALCOHOL AND STRESSED-OUT TEENS**     Self-medication with alcohol is particularly problematic for teens, who may use drinking to cope with daily hassles (Bailey & Covell, 2011), such as insecurities about the way they look and disagreements with family members, teachers, and peers. Drinking is not only a bad way to deal with stress; it may also cause long-term damage to the brain. The brain is especially sensitive to alcohol during three phases of life: prenatal development, older age (65 and over), and late adolescence (ages 15–19; McCarthy, 2021). During the teen years, neural synapses are being pruned and axons undergo myelination—critical processes that may be affected by alcohol use. Teenage binge drinking has been linked to "reduced neocortical volume and functional connectivity, attenuated white matter development, and small to moderate deficits in a wide range of cognitive functions" (Mewton et al., 2020, p. 1). Another way adolescents self-medicate is through problematic internet use (PIU)—using the internet to escape from stressful life events (Xiao et al., 2019). We need to help young people find new and healthier ways to handle daily hassles. This means providing more support in schools, and perhaps educating teachers and counselors about the tendency to self-medicate with substances and compulsive activities.

**SMOKING AND STRESS**     Many smokers rely on cigarettes during times of stress, but does lighting up really help them relax? In one study, participants were forced to abstain from smoking for a half day (a stressful situation for them). When they finally puffed on a cigarette, their mood improved. Yet, smoking did not have this same effect when participants were placed in other stressful situations, like getting ready to deliver a public speech (Perkins et al., 2010). These findings suggest that smoking does not reduce stress in a useful way. What's more, continued use of nicotine may interfere with the body's ability to deal with ongoing stressors (Holliday & Gould, 2016). And because it leads to severe health problems, smoking itself may become a stressor for many people and their families. Whether it comes from traditional cigarettes or e-cigarettes, nicotine is extremely addictive (Bold et al., 2018; Klein, 2018). Repeated use can lead to **tolerance**; the more you use it, the more you need to achieve the same effect.

Not everyone uses alcohol and nicotine, but we all need food, and our eating choices may change during times of stress. What kinds of food do you desire when studying for an exam, dealing with a relationship problem, or trying to resolve a conflict at work? Researcher Achim Peters explains why sugary snacks are so tempting in the following article from *Scientific American*.

From the **SCIENTIFIC** pages of **AMERICAN**

# WHY DO WE CRAVE SWEETS WHEN WE'RE STRESSED?

A brain researcher explains our desire for chocolate and other carbs during tough times.

Although our brain accounts for just 2 percent of our body weight, the organ consumes half of our daily carbohydrate requirements—and glucose is its most important fuel. Under acute stress the brain requires some 12 percent more energy, leading many to reach for sugary snacks. [. . .]

When we are hungry, a whole network of brain regions activates. At the center are the ventromedial hypothalamus (VMH) and the lateral hypothalamus. These two regions in the upper brain stem are involved in regulating metabolism, feeding behavior and digestive functions. There is, however, an upstream gatekeeper, the nucleus arcuatus (ARH) in the hypothalamus. If it registers that the brain itself lacks glucose, this gatekeeper blocks information from the rest of the body. That's why we resort to carbohydrates as soon as the brain indicates a need for energy, even if the rest of the body is well supplied.

To further understand the relationship between the brain and carbohydrates, we examined 40 subjects over two sessions. In one, we asked study participants to give a 10-minute speech in front of strangers. In the other session they were not required to give a speech. At the end of each session, we measured the concentrations of stress hormones cortisol and adrenaline in participants' blood. We also provided them with a food buffet for an hour. When the participants gave a speech before the buffet, they were more stressed, and on average consumed an additional 34 grams of carbohydrates, than when they did not give a speech. [. . .]

In order to meet the increased needs of the brain, one can either eat more of everything, as the stressed subjects did in our experiment, or make it easy for the body and just consume sweet foods. Even babies have a pronounced preference for sweets. Because their brain is extremely large compared with their tiny bodies, babies require a lot of energy. They get that energy via breast milk, which contains a lot of sugar. Over time, our preference for sweets decreases but never completely disappears, even as we become adults. The extent to which that preference is preserved varies from person to person and seems to depend, among other things, on living conditions. Studies suggest people who experience a lot of stress in childhood have a stronger preference for sweets later in life.

For some, the brain cannot get its energy from the body's reserves, even if there are enough fat deposits. The most important cause of this is chronic stress. To ensure their brains are not undersupplied, these people must always eat enough. Often the only way out of such eating habits is to leave a permanently stressful environment. So although many tend to be hard on themselves for eating too many sweets or carbs, the reasons behind such craving aren't always due to a lack of self-control and might require a deeper look into lifestyle and stressful situations—past and present. Once the root cause of stress is addressed, eating habits could ultimately resolve themselves.

## Tools for Healthy Living

Now that we have discussed some of the strategies that *don't* work well for alleviating stress, let explore some that do.

**KEEPING THE STRESS AT BAY**    Kaynen starts every day with yoga and stretching exercises. This routine, combined with some weight training, helps reduce his chronic back pain. It's also a great stress reliever. His other strategies for lowering stress and staying healthy include listening to music (country, R & B, hip hop), line-dancing (it's big in Las Vegas), and creating his extremely popular online videos and stories. Beginning in nursing school, Kaynen started posting videos to provide information to those interested in health-care careers. His YouTube videos, which include topics such as "Being a Male Nurse," "Dating in Nursing School," and "How Much Money Do Nurses Make?" have accumulated thousands, if not tens of thousands, of views. Answering people's questions and engaging such a huge base of followers has been a great way to relax and let go of his offline worries. "Oh man, it's been a blast," Kaynen says with a big smile. "It's a cool little getaway. . . . When I'm done studying, [I] make a video and talk about my opinions on something." People comment, expressing their appreciation or asking questions for him to answer. It's rewarding to help people, says Kaynen: "You feel needed."

**LO 11**   Discuss several tools for reducing stress and maintaining health.

Kaynen has just introduced us to some potent stress-fighting strategies: physical exercise and helping behaviors. Let's take a closer look at these and a few others. Some of the activities we explore not only relieve stress; they can increase your life span, too.

**EXERCISE**   You are feeling the pressure. Exam time is here, and you haven't cracked open a book because you've been so busy at work. The holidays are approaching, you have not purchased a single present, and the list of unanswered texts is growing by the minute. With so much to do, you feel paralyzed. In situations like this, the best solution may be dropping to the floor for some push-ups, or running out the door to take a jog. When you come back, you may feel a new sense of calm. *I can handle this,* you think to yourself. *One thing at a time.*

How does exercise work its magic? Physiologically, we know exercise increases blood flow, activates the autonomic nervous system, and helps initiate the release of several hormones. These reactions help the body defend against potential illnesses, especially those related to stress. Exercise also spurs the release of the body's natural painkilling and pleasure-inducing neurotransmitters, the endorphins (Daenen et al., 2015; Salmon, 2001).

When it comes to choosing an exercise regimen, the tough part is finding an activity that is intense enough to reduce the impact of stress, but sufficiently enjoyable to keep you coming back for more. Research suggests that only 30 minutes of daily exercise are needed to decrease the risk of heart disease, stroke, hypertension, diabetes, and certain types of cancer (CDC, n.d.-c; Warburton et al., 2010), not to mention improve feelings of well-being (Panza et al., 2019). Exercise needn't be a chore. Your daily 30 minutes could mean dancing with friends, raking leaves on a beautiful fall day, or shoveling snow. Exercising outdoors improves not only your physical health; it boosts your mental health in ways researchers are just beginning to understand (Klussman et al., 2021; Pasanen et al., 2014). But physical activity is just part of the story. If you want a healthy body, you need to eat nutritious foods, too.

**NUTRITION**   Earlier, we discussed the relationship between stress and food preferences: Many people reach for sweets when they are stressed out. Stress has been associated with larger waistlines and increased body mass index (BMI), and this may be partly explained by "stress-related eating," or consuming "favorite" foods and larger quantities (Cotter & Kelly, 2018, p. 518). Apparently, college students are not immune to this tendency. Perhaps you've heard of the "Freshman 15"? The popular assumption that students often put on pounds during their first year of college appears to be more than an urban myth. Approximately two thirds of students gain weight during freshman year, and this may be associated with stress, poor nutrition, inadequate exercise, and alcohol consumption. Weight gain among college freshmen is almost five times higher than that of the general population (Vadeboncoeur et al., 2015).

Stress is inevitable, but eating unhealthy food is unlikely to make it disappear. A well-balanced diet is important for long-term health. Reducing sugar and carbs, increasing lean proteins, and eating more vegetables may allow us to live longer (Jankovic et al., 2014; Lagström et al., 2020).

If you're not convinced that good nutrition and exercise will pay off in the long run, consider the following evidence.

## ACROSS THE WORLD

### WHAT'S GOING ON IN THE "BLUE ZONES"?

How long will you live, and how much control do you have over your life span? Researchers estimate that about 25% of the population-wide variability in life span can be attributed to genes (MedlinePlus, 2020). That means environmental factors play a major role in determining how long humans live. What are these longevity factors, and how can we incorporate them into our daily lives? The "blue zones" offer some valuable clues.

**LOOKING FOR THE SECRET TO A LONG AND HEALTHY LIFE ...**

Years ago, a group of researchers working with the National Geographic Society set out to identify blue zones, or regions of the world with the highest number of people living over 100 years. These locations got their name when someone used a blue pen to circle one of them on a map (Buettner, 2015). To qualify as a blue zone, an area had to be inhabited by people reaching old age without health issues such as diabetes, cancer, obesity, and heart trouble. Five areas in the world made the cut: Ikaria, Greece; Okinawa, Japan; Ogliastra Region, Sardinia; Loma Linda, California; and Nicoya Peninsula, Costa Rica (Buettner, 2015; Marston et al., 2021; FIGURE 12.3). The people in these regions are 10 times more likely than average Americans to reach the age of 100 (Buettner & Skemp, 2016). They share many characteristics (TABLE 12.1 on the next page), including the tendency to eat a diet that is largely plant-based (often featuring beans) and to "move naturally," that is, get exercise through everyday activities like yard work and gardening (Buettner & Skemp, 2016).

### FIGURE 12.3

**Blue Zones**

Pictured above are areas of the world with the highest concentrations of centenarians, or people who make it to age 100. The photo shows a centenarian from one of these "blue zones," the Nicoya Peninsula in Costa Rica. People in this region eat a lot of tropical fruits and next to no processed food. They also have a *plan de vida,* meaning a "plan" or purpose for life (Buettner & Skemp, 2016).

Photo: Gianluca Colla/Getty Images.

**TABLE 12.1    Living Longer**

| Characteristics | Benefits | Applications |
|---|---|---|
| Innate movement | You don't have to join a gym or compete in triathlons; every physical activity counts. | Walk to work or to the store; bike to school. Find ways to incorporate natural movement into your daily life. |
| Finding meaning | Purpose outside of your job makes it easier to wake up each morning; knowing your purpose can extend life expectancy. | Find your motivation for life. What energizes you? |
| Slow down | Stress affects everyone, but slowing down reduces inflammation that can lead to many age-related illnesses. | Meditate, pray, or nap. |
| "80% rule" | Helps prevent weight gain and overeating. | Stop eating when you feel 80% full. |
| Eat more plants | Plants are an inexpensive source of complex carbs, fiber, and protein. | Eat lean; make beans and vegetables the bulk of your diet. Limit your intake of meat. |
| Social support | Healthy friends encourage healthy behaviors. | Surround yourself with people who encourage healthy living and happiness. |
| Family first | Time spent with grandparents, parents, and a committed life partner can extend life expectancy. | Create strong family ties, and keep loved ones in close proximity. |

A long, healthy, low-stress life is possible, especially if you adopt these behaviors, commonly observed in "blue zone" regions of the world. Information from Buettner (2015).

**RELAX**    Exercise is all about getting the body moving, but relaxing the muscles can also relieve stress. "Just relax." We have heard it a thousand times, but do we really know how to begin? Physician and physiologist Edmund Jacobson (1888–1983) introduced a technique known as *progressive muscle relaxation,* which has since been expanded upon (Jacobson, 1938). With this technique, you begin by tensing a muscle group (for example, your toes) for about 10 seconds, and then releasing as you focus on the tension leaving. Next you progress to another muscle group, such as the calves, and then the thighs, buttocks, stomach, shoulders, arms, neck, and so on. After several weeks of practice, you will begin to recognize where you hold tension in your muscles—at least this is the goal. Once you become aware of that tension, you can focus on relaxing those specific muscles without going through the entire process. Progressive muscle relaxation may help reduce stress in pregnant women (Kantziari et al., 2019). It has also been shown to defuse anxiety in highly stressed college students. In one study, researchers found that just 20 minutes of progressive muscle relaxation had "significant short-term effects," including decreases in anxiety, blood pressure, and heart rate (Dolbier & Rush, 2012). Participants also reported a feeling of increased control and energy. Inducing this *relaxation response* may also be an effective way to reduce pain (Benson, 2000; Darnall, 2019; Dusek et al., 2008).

 Using a clock or watch to time yourself, breathe in slowly for 5 seconds. Then exhale slowly for 5 seconds. Do this for 1 minute. With each breath, you begin to slow down and relax. The key is to breathe deeply.

**BIOFEEDBACK**    One potential method for managing physiological responses to stressors is **biofeedback.** This technique builds on learning principles to teach control of seemingly involuntary physiological activities, such as heart rate, blood pressure, and skin temperature. Biofeedback equipment monitors internal responses and provides visual or auditory signals to help a person identify those that are maladaptive (for example, tense shoulder muscles). The person begins by

**biofeedback** A technique for teaching a person to control seemingly involuntary physiological activities, such as heart rate, blood pressure, and skin temperature.

focusing on a signal (a light or tone, for instance) that indicates when a desired response occurs. By controlling this biofeedback indicator, the person learns to maintain the desired response (relaxed shoulders in this example). The ultimate goal is to tap into this technique in real-life scenarios outside of the clinic or lab. Companies have created wearable biofeedback monitors that can be used with mobile apps, but the research on these technologies is still young (Peake et al., 2018). Some evidence suggests biofeedback can decrease the frequency of headaches and chronic pain (Darnall, 2019; Flor & Birbaumer, 1993). It appears to be useful for all age groups, including children, adolescents, and the elderly (Jester et al., 2019; Takacs & Kassai, 2019; Thabrew et al., 2018).

## Relationships

### STRONGER TOGETHER

One of the best ways to combat stress is by developing a strong social network. Researchers have found that cultivating positive and enduring relationships with family, friends, and religious groups can generate a health benefit similar to exercise and smoking abstinence (House et al., 1988). People who maintain close, supportive relationships have better overall health (Pietromonaco & Collins, 2017). They may have the opportunity to laugh more, too. Did you know that laughter may act as buffer against stress? One study found that college students who frequently laughed had fewer symptoms of stress (stomach aches, headaches, nervousness, and so on) following a stressor (Zander-Schellenberg et al., 2020). Most of the participants in that study were female, but other research suggests that laughter has psychological benefits for all types of people (van der Wal & Kok, 2019).

You might expect that receiving support is the key to lowering stress, but research suggests that *giving* support also makes a big difference. In a study of older married adults, researchers reported reduced mortality rates for participants who indicated that they helped or supported others, including friends, spouses, relatives, and neighbors. There were no reductions in mortality associated with receiving support from others, however (Brown et al., 2003).

Helping others and expecting nothing in return is known as *altruism,* and it appears to be an effective stress reducer and happiness booster (Hui et al., 2020; Schwartz et al., 2003; Sin et al., 2021). When we care for others, we generally don't have time to focus on our own problems; we also come to recognize that others may be dealing with more troubling circumstances than we are.

**FAITH, RELIGION, AND PRAYER** Psychologists are also discovering the health benefits of faith, religion, and prayer. Research suggests elderly people who pray or actively participate in religious services experience improved health and noticeably lower rates of depression than those who don't participate in such activities (Lawler-Row & Elliott, 2009; Powell et al., 2003). In fact, religious affiliation is associated with increased reports of happiness and physical health (Green & Elliott, 2010).

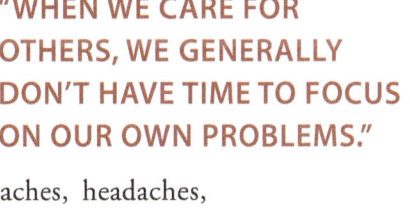

"WHEN WE CARE FOR OTHERS, WE GENERALLY DON'T HAVE TIME TO FOCUS ON OUR OWN PROBLEMS."

**Biofeedback**
Airman Aaron Street uses biofeedback at the Osan Air Base in South Korea. Biofeedback is a learning technique that enables a person to manipulate seemingly automatic functions, such as heart rate and blood pressure. With the help of a monitor that signals the occurrence of a target response, a patient can learn how to sustain this response longer.

**What Goes Around**
Volunteers pick up trash in a public park. Altruism, or helping others because it feels good, is an excellent stress reliever.

Ranta Images/Getty Images.

**Relax**

How does mindfulness meditation impact the brain? The research on meditation is relatively young and problematic in some respects (Stetka, 2017), but evidence suggests that just 10 hours of meditation training may promote change in an area of the brain called the ventral posterior cingulate cortex, "a key hub associated with self-awareness, emotion, cognition, and aging" (Tang et al., 2020, p. 1).

The link between faith and well-being may not be so clear-cut in areas where religious leaders vie for power, or where religious minorities face discrimination, however (Devine et al., 2019). And of course, not everyone participates in organized religious activities. For those who do not adhere to a particular faith, groups of friends with common interests and belief systems may offer a sense of community and belongingness many people find through religion (Galen, 2018). What's more, ordinary "spiritual experiences" (like feelings of awe and gratitude that some people feel on a daily basis) have been linked to greater well-being (Hammer & Cragun, 2019).

The proactive, stress-reducing behaviors described above reflect a certain type of attitude. You might call it a positive psychology attitude.

## Apply This ⬇

### RIGHT HERE, RIGHT NOW

In Chapter 1, we introduced *positive psychology*, "the study of positive emotions, positive character traits, and enabling institutions" (Seligman & Steen, 2005, p. 410). Rather than focusing on mental illness and abnormal behavior, positive psychology emphasizes human strengths and virtues. The goal is well-being and fulfillment, and that means "satisfaction" with the past, "hope and optimism" for the future, and "flow and happiness" at the current time (Seligman & Csikszentmihalyi, 2000, p. 5).

As we wrap up this chapter on stress and health, we encourage you to focus on that third category: flow and happiness in the present. No matter what stressors come your way, try to stay grounded in the here and now. The past is the past, the future is uncertain, but this moment is yours. Finding a way to enjoy the present is an excellent way to lift your spirits (Finkelstein-Fox et al., 2019). Easier said than done, you may be thinking.

If "being in the moment" does not come naturally, you might try **mindfulness meditation**—the practice of focusing attention on current experiences while maintaining an open mind and not passing judgment (Iwamoto et al., 2020; Schöne et al., 2018; see **FIGURE 12.4**). Research suggests that "brief mindfulness training can help college students manage their stress in response to the ubiquitous academic and cognitive challenges of college life" (Shearer et al., 2016, p. 232). This practice may reduce depression, stress, and anxiety and even promote altruistic behavior (Dimidjian et al., 2016; Iwamoto et al., 2020).

## FIGURE 12.4

**Breathe In, Breathe Out**

You don't have to be a Buddhist monk or yoga master to stay in the moment and focus your attention. Practicing meditation may be as easy as following these steps, provided by Diana Winston of the UCLA Mindful Awareness Research Center (*Fully Present: The Book,* 2010).

**mindfulness meditation** Being fully present in the moment; focusing attention on the here and now without passing judgment.

🌿 Sit on a chair or pillow. Keep your back straight but relaxed, close your eyes, and place your hands on your knees or thighs.

🌿 Feel the weight of your body and focus on whatever sensations you are experiencing right now.

🌿 Breathe naturally, and focus on the sensation of inhaling and exhaling; this might mean the rise and fall of your abdomen or chest, or the air entering and exiting your nostrils.

🌿 Continue to focus on breathing, and if a thought enters your mind, try to observe it as if you were a nonjudgmental outsider. Then calmly direct your attention back to the sensation of breathing.

🌿 Continue this practice for 5 minutes.

## Put Your Heads Together

In your group, discuss the following: **A)** A classmate insists that overeating is a sign of weakness or poor self-control. What would you say in response? **B)** What steps can you take to avoid unhealthy eating habits caused by stress? **C)** List three stress-reducing activities you could employ the next time you feel overwhelmed by academic or personal stressors.

**KAYNEN'S NEXT MOVE**  Kaynen loves nursing, but he also relishes new challenges. In the fall of 2020, Kaynen began physician assistant (PA) training at Loma Linda University in California. "Nursing school [was] hard," says Kaynen. "That was the hardest thing I had done until that point." PA school is even more demanding, both academically and clinically. In order to maintain balance in his life, Kaynen has had to let go of the "straight-A student" part of himself he discovered in nursing school. "I study hard, and I do my best, but I am not going to freak out if I [don't] get an A on the exam, I get a B+ on the exam," Kaynen says. If the difference between that A and B+ means he can be at an important birthday or family event, it's worth it to him.

What is Kaynen's advice for college students who are trying to figure out what path to take? To determine if a job is right for you, shadow a professional working in that field. Are you interested in health care? Accompany a nurse, physician assistant, or doctor on their shift. Considering a law enforcement career? Go on a ride-along with an officer. "Get involved in whatever it is you want to do," says Kaynen. Another important thing to remember is that you can succeed in more than one profession; as Kaynen notes, "There are a lot of things you can be."

Kaynen Brown.

**The Next Phase . . .**
Now a student at Loma Linda University Physician Assistant Program, Kaynen finds himself working as hard as ever. The classes are high-level and there is a mountain of information to absorb. Kaynen is doing well academically, but his real strength is applying what he has learned to clinical scenarios. "I find myself doing a little bit better in terms of implementing real knowledge than I do just regurgitating memorized information for an exam" (Kaynen Brown, 2021).

## SHOW WHAT YOU KNOW

1. _____ is apparent when you confront a problem head-on and try to solve it.
   - **A.** Emotion-focused coping
   - **B.** Positive psychology
   - **C.** Support seeking
   - **D.** Problem-focused coping

2. Describe three tools for healthy living that you could implement in your own life.

3. Individuals who are relaxed, patient, and nonaggressive are described as having a:
   - **A.** Type A personality.
   - **B.** Type B personality.
   - **C.** Type C personality.
   - **D.** Type D personality.

 CHECK YOUR ANSWERS AT THE BACK OF THE BOOK.

## Summary of Concepts

**LO 1** Define stress and stressors. (p. 453)

Stress is the response to perceived threats or challenges resulting from stimuli or events that cause strain, analogous to an airplane wing bending in response to an applied load. For humans, these stimuli, or stressors, can cause both psychological and physiological reactions. We must be careful not to confuse the cause of stress with the experience of stress. Stressors are the cause, and stress is the response.

**LO 2** Describe the relationship between major life events and illness. (p. 456)

The Social Readjustment Rating Scale (SRRS) was created to measure the impact of life events. The score is based on the severity and frequency of events. Researchers use the SRRS to examine relationships between life events and health problems. Although correlations exist, they are not necessarily indicative of cause and effect.

**LO 3**    **Summarize how poverty, adjusting to a new culture, and daily hassles affect health. (p. 458)**

People living in poverty, adjusting to a new culture, and dealing with everyday hassles face a number of stressors that increase the likelihood of illness. Moving to a new country is a major life change that can result in acculturative stress; however, cultivating social support helps combat the effects. Daily hassles are minor, everyday problems that can act as stressors. With all the stressors in our lives, we should be grateful for the positive experiences, or uplifts, that can balance them.

**LO 4**    **Identify the brain and body changes that characterize the fight-or-flight response. (p. 462)**

When faced with a threatening situation, portions of the brain, including the hypothalamus, activate the sympathetic nervous system, which then leads to the secretion of catecholamines such as epinephrine and norepinephrine. These hormones cause increases in heart rate, blood pressure, respiration, and blood flow to the muscles. At the same time, the digestive system slows and the pupils dilate. These physiological responses prepare us for emergencies.

**LO 5**    **Explain the function of the hypothalamic–pituitary–adrenal (HPA) system. (p. 462)**

The sympathetic nervous system works with the HPA system to deal with emergencies. When a stressful situation arises, the hypothalamus initiates a cascade of responses by alerting the pituitary gland, which then sends signals to the adrenal cortex, which secretes corticosteroids such as cortisol. These hormones influence responses of the immune system. When cortisol levels remain high for prolonged periods (as occurs with chronic stressors and threatening situations), the functioning of the immune system may decrease.

**LO 6**    **Outline the general adaptation syndrome (GAS). (p. 464)**

The human body responds to stressors in a predictable way. The general adaptation syndrome suggests that the body passes through three stages. The first is the alarm stage, or initial response to a threatening situation. Arousal increases, and the body prepares to deal with a threat. Next is the resistance stage; the body maintains a high level of arousal (though not as high as during the alarm stage) as it deals with a threatening situation. At this point, there is a decreased response to new stressors, and some people start to show signs of diseases of adaptation. Finally, the body enters the exhaustion stage; resources become depleted, resulting in vulnerability to illnesses, physical exhaustion, and even death.

**LO 7**    **List some consequences of prolonged exposure to the stress hormone cortisol. (p. 464)**

Cortisol prepares the body to confront a threat. Higher levels of cortisol in mothers has been associated with premature birth and low birth weight in infants. For students who feel anxious about math, elevated cortisol can hinder performance in this subject.

**LO 8**    **Explain how stressors relate to health problems. (p. 465)**

When the body is continually mobilizing its resources for fight or flight, the immune system becomes taxed, and the work of the lymphocytes is compromised. Stressors have been linked to ulcers, cancer, and cardiovascular disease. The field of psychoneuroimmunology examines links among psychological factors, the nervous system, and immune functioning.

**LO 9**    **Illustrate how appraisal influences coping. (p. 468)**

Coping refers to the cognitive, behavioral, and emotional abilities used to manage something perceived as difficult or challenging. We must decide whether an event is irrelevant, positive, challenging, or harmful (primary appraisal) and how we will respond (secondary appraisal). If we determine that we have the ability to cope, then the impact of stress will remain low. We can choose to deal directly with a problem (problem-focused coping), or to address the emotions surrounding the problem (emotion-focused coping).

**LO 10**    **Describe how personality characteristics relate to health. (p. 471)**

Personality characteristics may impact coping style and predispositions to stress-related illnesses. People with Type A personalities are competitive, aggressive, impatient, often hostile, and twice as likely to develop cardiovascular disease as people with Type B personalities, who are more relaxed, patient, and nonaggressive. The presence of Type D personality, characterized by worry, tension, bad moods, and social inhibition, may be a better predictor of how patients fare when they already have heart disease. People who exhibit a personality characteristic known as hardiness are resilient, optimistic, and better able to handle a great deal of stress. During times of stress, people may overindulge in sweets and alcohol, rely on nicotine to improve their mood, and engage in other unhealthy behaviors.

**LO 11**    **Discuss several tools for reducing stress and maintaining health. (p. 476)**

There are many ways to lower the impact of stressors. Eating healthy, getting exercise, seeking social support, developing spirituality, and using progressive muscle relaxation, biofeedback, and meditation all have positive physical and psychological effects. Helping and caring for others are also effective ways to reduce the impact of stress.

# Key Terms

**acculturation**, p. 459
**acculturative stress**, p. 459
**approach–approach conflict**, p. 461
**approach–avoidance conflict**, p. 461
**avoidance–avoidance conflict**, p. 461
**biofeedback**, p. 478
**burnout**, p. 467

**coping**, p. 468
**daily hassles**, p. 460
**distress**, p. 455
**emotion-focused coping**, p. 468
**eustress**, p. 456
**general adaptation syndrome (GAS)**, p. 465

**hardiness**, p. 472
**health psychology**, p. 468
**mindfulness meditation**, p. 480
**primary appraisal**, p. 468
**problem-focused coping**, p. 468
**psychoneuroimmunology**, p. 466
**secondary appraisal**, p. 468

**social support**, p. 459
**stress**, p. 453
**stressors**, p. 453
**Type A personality**, p. 471
**Type B personality**, p. 471
**uplifts**, p. 460

# Test Prep Are You Ready?

1. Stress is the response to perceived threats or challenges resulting from stimuli that cause strain. These stimuli are known as:
   A. conflicts.
   B. eustress.
   C. assimilation.
   D. stressors.

2. When Kaynen went on a medical mission to China, he felt happy, excited, and somewhat nervous. This kind of "good" stressor leads to a stress response known as:
   A. eustress.
   B. distress.
   C. perceived threats.
   D. optimal arousal.

3. When dealing with chronic stressors, _____ levels remain high, which can lead to a decrease in the functioning of _____.
   A. assimilation; the immune system
   B. cortisol; the immune system
   C. emotional; assimilation
   D. hassle; catecholamines

4. Once an emergency has ended, the _____ reverses the processes set in motion through the fight-or-flight reaction. Heart rate and blood pressure start to decrease, and respiration returns to normal.
   A. parasympathetic nervous system
   B. sympathetic nervous system
   C. general adaptation syndrome
   D. resistance stage

5. If a threat remains constant, the body enters the _____ of the general adaptation syndrome. Resources become depleted, resulting in a vulnerability to illness, physical exhaustion, and even death.
   A. alarm stage
   B. resistance stage
   C. exhaustion stage
   D. diseases of adaptation stage

6. When a stressful situation arises, the hypothalamus alerts the pituitary gland, prompting it to send signals to the adrenal cortex, which secretes:
   A. *H. pylori*.
   B. norepinephrine.
   C. epinephrine.
   D. cortisol.

7. Chronic stress can lead to health problems; if the body is constantly mobilizing resources for fight or flight, the work of the lymphocytes is compromised, and the _____ is less powerful.
   A. immune system
   B. *H. pylori*
   C. atherosclerosis
   D. cortisol

8. One of your classmates has been seeing a counselor all semester because of their anxiety. When it's time to take the final exam, they will use what they have learned about _____ to reduce tension in their body.
   A. the hypothalamic–pituitary–adrenal system
   B. macrophages
   C. stress inoculation
   D. progressive muscle relaxation

9. _____ refers to the cognitive, behavioral, and emotional abilities used to manage a challenging or difficult situation.
   A. Stress
   B. Coping
   C. Altruism
   D. Eustress

10. People with _____ are competitive, aggressive, and hostile, and they may face an increased risk of developing cardiovascular disease.
    A. Type A personality
    B. Type B personality
    C. Type C personality
    D. Type D personality

11. When moving to a new country, how might someone use assimilation, separation, or integration to deal with the acculturative stress of this transition?

12. List the many hassles you have faced this past week. Next, list any life events you have experienced in the past 12 months. Consider how all these stressors may have influenced your health, and explain what you can do to reduce their impact.

13. Describe a movie or television scene showing a character who appears to respond to a threat with the fight-or-flight response. What evidence suggests they are experiencing this reaction?

14. Give examples of an approach–approach conflict, an approach–avoidance conflict, and an avoidance–avoidance conflict that you have encountered in your own life.

15. Describe an acquaintance who has an internal locus of control, particularly with respect to health-related behaviors. Now describe someone who has an external locus of control, again focusing on health-related behaviors.

✓ CHECK YOUR ANSWERS AT THE BACK OF THE BOOK.

# 13

shikheigoh/Getty Images.

# Psychological Disorders

## An Introduction to Psychological Disorders

**WINTER NIGHT** It was a clear, cold night in January when 17-year-old Ross Szabo decided to end his life. Nothing bad had happened that day. Ross had woken up, gone to school, played in a basketball game (a victory for his team), and then gone to Friendly's restaurant with his buddies. But for some reason, on that winter night, Ross decided he could no longer take it. Riding home in the car, he gazed out the window at Pennsylvania's snow-blanketed cornfields. An overwhelming sense of calm descended on him.

For the four months leading to that moment, Ross had been free-falling into an abyss of sadness.

Martin Fella/Fella Studios.

**Looks Can Be Deceiving**
Ross Szabo appears happy in his senior class photo, but beneath his smile is profound pain. This was the year Ross began to have persistent thoughts of death and suicide that nearly drove him to take his own life.

Around other people, he was smiling, joking, acting like a normal teenager. But alone, he was always crying. Ross truly believed his friends and family would be happier without him. *Maybe you're the problem; maybe you'd be doing them a favor by removing the problem,* Ross remembers thinking to himself. "I didn't think I would have a funeral," he says. "I didn't think anyone should care about me."

When Ross got home, he tried calling a friend but was too upset to speak. So he walked into the bathroom and prepared to take his own life. Fortunately, his father intervened and Ross was able to say, "If you don't take me to the hospital right now, I'm going to kill myself."

## What's Normal, What's Not

**LO 1** Define psychological disorders and outline the criteria used to identify abnormal behavior.

A year and a half earlier, Ross had been diagnosed with **bipolar disorder,** a condition marked by dramatic mood swings. We all have ups and downs—periods of feeling happy, sad, anxious, or irritable—but the emotional roller coaster of bipolar disorder is something quite different. We will soon explore bipolar disorder in greater detail, but first let's familiarize ourselves with the broader focus of this chapter: *psychological disorders.*

A **psychological disorder** is a set of behavioral, emotional, and cognitive symptoms that are significantly distressing or disabling. These symptoms can interfere with social functioning, work endeavors, and other aspects of life. However, they are not the result of religious or spiritual experiences, or mere departures from cultural norms. And although stressors can trigger symptoms of psychological disorders, these conditions primarily result from disturbances in psychological, biological, and developmental processes (American Psychiatric Association, 2013).

The behaviors and symptoms associated with psychological disorders are not typical in the general population; in other words, they are *abnormal.* The academic field devoted to the study of psychological disorders is generally referred to as abnormal psychology. Researchers and scholars in this field have a variety of backgrounds, including clinical psychology, neuroscience, and psychiatry.

**WHAT IS ABNORMAL?**    Psychologists and other mental health professionals determine if a behavior is abnormal using a variety of criteria (TABLE **13.1** on the next page). Perhaps the most straightforward criterion is the degree of *typicality.* An atypical behavior is one that is rarely seen, or infrequent. The profound sadness Ross experienced is relatively rare. Most people experience sadness, even deep sadness at times, but suicidal thoughts are unusual. When assessing the typicality of a behavior, it's important to consider its duration. People frequently experience intense grief and sadness after losing a loved one, but this should resolve over time. If the duration is extended, the behavior may qualify as atypical.

While useful, the typicality criterion is not enough to confirm the existence of a psychological disorder. A child prodigy who learns to play the piano like a virtuoso by age 5 is atypical, but their rare talent does not indicate a psychological disorder. To arrive at a more definitive determination of **abnormal behavior,** mental health professionals commonly rely on three criteria (in addition to typicality): *dysfunction, distress,* and *deviance,* or the "3 Ds" (American Psychiatric Association, 2013; Wakefield, 1992).

*Note:* Ross Szabo's story is based on our personal communications with him and various passages from the book he coauthored with Melanie Hall, *Behind Happy Faces* (Szabo & Hall, 2007). Unless otherwise specified, quotations attributed to Ross Szabo and Melissa Hopely are personal communications.

**bipolar disorder** A psychological disorder marked by dramatic swings in mood, ranging from manic episodes to depressive episodes.

**psychological disorder** A set of behavioral, emotional, and cognitive symptoms that are significantly distressing or disabling in terms of social functioning, work endeavors, and other aspects of life.

**abnormal behavior** Behavior that is atypical, dysfunctional, distressful, and/or deviant.

**TABLE 13.1**    Defining Abnormal Behavior

| Criterion | What Does It Mean? |
|---|---|
| Typicality | Degree to which behavior is atypical, meaning rarely seen or statistically abnormal |
| Dysfunction | Degree to which behavior interferes with daily life and relationships |
| Distress | Degree to which behavior or emotions cause an individual to feel upset or uncomfortable |
| Deviance | Degree to which behavior is considered outside the standards or rules of society |

Psychologists typically identify abnormal behavior using the criteria outlined above.

Samuel Corum/Getty Images.

**Deviant, But Not Disordered**
People lie on the ground to protest the killing of George Floyd, who died as a result of a Minneapolis police officer kneeling on his neck for more than 9 minutes (Bogel-Burroughs, 2021). Lying down in a public walking space is a behavior that defies social norms and is therefore considered deviant. Yet in this case, deviance is not linked to a mental disorder.

**CONNECTIONS**

In **Chapter 11,** we discussed conformity, the tendency to modify our behaviors, attitudes, beliefs, and opinions to match those of others. Sometimes we conform to the norms or standards of the social environment, like a group of friends or coworkers. The protesters described here are not conforming to social norms.

The first D, *dysfunction,* indicates the degree to which a behavior interferes with daily life and relationships. Ross' depression sometimes rendered him unable to get out of bed; such a behavior certainly has the potential to interfere with daily life. But dysfunction alone does not confirm the presence of a psychological disorder. If you stay up all night to meet a deadline, you might experience temporary dysfunction in memory and attention, but that does not necessarily signal a larger problem. Dysfunctional behaviors are often maladaptive; that is, they go against one's best interests.

The second D is personal *distress.* Feeling regularly upset or uncomfortable because of unwanted behaviors or emotions is another feature of abnormality, and it's not always evident from the outside. Prior to his suicide attempt, Ross appeared to be happy and healthy, but inside he was suffering. Disorders are not always accompanied by distress, however. When Ross experienced the euphoric highs of bipolar disorder, he may not have been distressed at all. People with psychological disorders do not always have the insight to recognize that a problem exists.

The third D is *deviance,* or the degree to which a behavior is considered to be outside the standards or rules of a society. Individuals who are euphoric might talk too loudly in a place of worship where people are expected to be quiet, or become so disinhibited that they walk around naked in a public place. Yet, deviance alone does not necessarily indicate a psychological disorder. Political protesters, for example, may deliberately break **social norms** to make a statement—walking hand-in-hand with strangers, chanting at the top of their lungs, and lying on streets and sidewalks (see photo to the left).

When evaluating each of the three Ds, mental health professionals also have to consider the degree of risk or danger (both to oneself and others) associated with them. This assessment is often used to determine if a person ought to be admitted to a hospital, or what type of treatment is needed (more on this in Chapter 14).

We should note that conceptions of abnormality and definitions of psychological disorders have changed over the course of history. During the 18th century, some women were said to exhibit a psychological disorder called *hysteria,* linked to "wandering movements of the womb" and characterized by "excessive emotion, irrational speech, paralysis, and convulsions" (Wickens, 2015, p. 245). No such diagnosis exists in today's world. Always remember that the meaning of "abnormal" is relative to historical time.

**IT'S A CONTINUUM**    It's important to understand that anyone can have experiences that resemble symptoms of psychological disorders. This is because there is a continuum for many behaviors and feelings: Those at the ends are generally viewed as abnormal, and those in the middle more normal. Suppose you are afraid of spiders. Asking a housemate to remove one from the shower falls within the normal range of behaviors, but avoiding all places you have ever seen spiders (woods, parks, and basements, for example) is something quite different. At the other extreme is having no fear of spiders whatsoever—picking up a poisonous black widow spider and squeezing it between your fingers is generally not considered a normal behavior. Or consider the vastly different degrees of sadness. Ross' profound sadness would likely fall at the abnormal end of the continuum; a teary farewell to a close friend who is moving away would be considered a normal reaction in the middle; and someone with limited emotions would be at the other end of the continuum. Bear in mind that notions of normality are not the same throughout the world. As the biopsychosocial model reminds us, we must examine culture and other social influences when trying to understand psychological disorders.

**CONSIDER THE CULTURE**    Many disorders are universal, meaning they occur throughout the world and have a strong biological foundation. An example is schizophrenia, which has been documented across cultures. There are also *cultural syndromes* whose symptoms and attributions (explanations for those symptoms) appear to be unique to particular societies. *Koro,* for example, is an episode of intense anxiety observed in India, China, Thailand, and other Asian countries (Dan et al., 2017). The main feature of *Koro* is an unrealistic and intense fear that sexual organs will be pulled into the body, perhaps resulting in death. A man with *Koro* might be exceedingly anxious about the idea of his penis disappearing into his abdomen, whereas a woman may fear that her nipples will be pulled into her chest (American Psychiatric Association, 2013). Another example is *susto,* most evident in Mexico, Central America, South America, and Latinx populations of the United States. People with *susto* have extreme reactions to frightening situations; they believe their soul has left their body, which results in illness, sadness, lack of motivation, and other symptoms (American Psychiatric Association, 2013).

Even with universal disorders such as schizophrenia, culture plays an important role in determining how symptoms are viewed and interpreted. For example, people living in South Asia are more likely than those in the United States and Canada to attribute symptoms of psychological disorders to supernatural powers, such as "hexes and curses" or "punishment from God" (Knettel, 2016, p. 134). In Arab populations in the Middle East, symptoms of psychological disorders may be attributed to "God's will," the "evil eye," or other supernatural causes. Meanwhile, people in Western countries are more likely to believe that people with disorders are dangerous (Zolezzi et al., 2018). Keep in mind that the findings described above don't necessarily apply to individual members of these groups. Each person is unique, and within each category is immense diversity.

Jonathan Siegel/Getty Images.

**"Social Anxiety"?**

In Japan, social anxiety is sometimes manifested through *taijin kyofusho*, "a cultural syndrome characterized by anxiety about and avoidance of interpersonal situations due to the thought, feeling, or conviction that one's appearance and actions in social interactions are inadequate or offensive to others" (American Psychiatric Association, 2013, p. 837). *Taijin kyofusho* is more likely to affect men than women, and has been observed in Korea and other countries outside of Japan (Hofmann & Hinton, 2014).

## Put Your Heads Together

In groups, **A)** identify examples of abnormal behaviors you've seen reported in the news; **B)** show how these behaviors fit the criteria for abnormality listed in Table 13.1; **C)** give examples of some behaviors that might appear deviant, but do not fit the criteria for abnormality; and **D)** identify a behavior that might be considered abnormal in one cultural context, but not another.

We have learned how psychologists identify abnormality using the criteria of typicality, dysfunction, distress, and deviance. Now let's explore the concept of "insanity" in the judicial system.

# Think Critically

## THE INSANITY PLEA

Perhaps you have heard the term "insanity" used in a legal context. "The defendant got off on an insanity plea," or "The defense failed to demonstrate insanity." What do these statements mean? **Insanity** is a legal determination of the degree to which a person is responsible for their criminal behaviors. Those deemed legally insane are thought to have little or no control over or understanding of their behaviors at the time they committed their crimes. Therefore, they are given psychological treatment in a locked psychiatric facility rather than criminal punishment such as imprisonment or the death penalty. In America, 45 states offer a form of the insanity defense; only Alaska, Idaho, Kansas, Montana, and Utah do not. However, a 2020 Supreme Court ruling gave states the green light to "effectively eliminate" the insanity plea (Neidig, 2020).

**IT'S INVOKED IN ONLY ABOUT 1% OF CASES.**

**Many people believe** that the insanity defense is frequently used, but it's invoked in only about 1% of cases. Of those cases, just 10–25% of insanity defenses are successful (Torry & Billick, 2010). Among those who avoided prison after entering an insanity plea was John Hinckley Jr., the man who attempted to assassinate President Ronald Reagan (Perlin, 2017). The insanity plea did not work so well for the man who murdered Chris Kyle, the Navy SEAL whose memoir served as the basis for the Oscar-winning movie *American Sniper*. Kyle's killer, Eddie Ray Routh, is serving life in prison without parole (Payne et al., 2015).

Now that we have learned how psychologists identify abnormality and how the legal system characterizes "insanity," let's explore how it might feel to face a psychological disorder—and the negative judgments that sometimes accompany it.

**DISPELLING STIGMA: ROSS FINDS HIS VOICE**    After being hospitalized, Ross returned to school, where he was greeted with rumors and stares. A couple of his friends stopped spending time with him, perhaps because they were afraid of what they didn't understand. Then one day, a psychologist came to the school to give his annual presentation about helping people with psychological disorders. Most of the students thought the topic was funny and laughed throughout the presentation, but Ross did not find it one bit amusing. After class, he told his teacher that he wanted to give his own presentation. Before long, Ross was standing before his peers, heart pounding and knees wobbling, talking about life with bipolar disorder. The students listened intently, and some approached Ross after class to talk about their own struggles with psychological disorders. By coming forward to share his experiences, Ross dispelled some of his classmates' misconceptions and fears about psychological disorders. He was a real person they knew and liked, and he had a disorder.

**WHAT IS STIGMA?**    Watching his classmates laugh about people with psychological disorders, Ross bore witness to the *stigma* attached to mental illness. **Stigma** is a negative attitude or opinion about groups of people based on certain characteristics they have. Being the target of stigma may lower self-esteem, impair social functioning, and make a person less likely to seek treatment (Corrigan & Penn, 2015; DeFreitas et al., 2018; Krendl & Pescosolido, 2020). Some evidence suggests that stigma begins to take root in childhood. In one study, researchers showed that sixth graders, particularly boys and children of color, wanted more "social distance" from peers with psychological disorders. Why would this be? One possible reason is that these children face stereotypes about Black and Latino males being "prone to violence," which could make them "more inclined to avoid a mental illness label that is similarly stereotyped as violent and dangerous" (DuPont-Reyes et al., 2020, p. 203). The findings of this

---

**CONNECTIONS**

In **Chapter 7,** we discussed the availability heuristic; we often predict the probability of something happening in the future based on how easily we can recall a similar event from the past. Here, the vividness of a crime and the ensuing trial make the insanity plea more available in our memories, so we tend to overestimate the probability of it happening in the future.

**insanity** A legal determination of the degree to which a person is responsible for criminal behaviors.

**stigma** A negative attitude or opinion about a group of people based on certain traits or characteristics.

study are somewhat consistent with research in adults, with some studies suggesting that African Americans are more likely than European Americans to feel embarrassed about having mental health issues and receiving treatment, perhaps because they are "very concerned about stigma associated with mental illness" (DeFreitas et al., 2018; Ward et al., 2013, p. 186).

Stigma can lead to discrimination, stereotypes, and negative characterizations in general, although researchers are exploring strategies to counteract it (Corrigan & Penn, 2015; Cuttler & Ryckman, 2019). Surely you have heard people equate psychological disorders with violence, or perhaps you have seen TV shows portraying people with mental illness as wild and aggressive. Reality check: People with psychological disorders are usually *not* violent. A small number of disorders and symptoms (e.g., childhood conduct disorder and certain psychotic symptoms) may be associated with violent behaviors, but "an overwhelming majority of all violence is committed by individuals with no history of mental illness" (Ahonen et al., 2019, p. 622). Other factors, such as male gender, substance abuse, and previous violent behaviors, may be better predictors of violence (Ahonen et al., 2019; Bushman et al., 2016; Office of Juvenile Justice and Delinquency Program [OJJDD], 2020). The criterion of being a danger to oneself or others does determine the necessity of treatment, but given the degree of violence in our society, violent behavior is actually *atypical* of people with serious psychological disorders, and more commonly associated with substance abuse (Arkowitz & Lilienfeld, 2011; Fazel et al., 2009).

What can we do to combat stigma? One suggestion is to use "people-first language"; that is, refer to the individual affected by the disorder ("This person has been diagnosed with schizophrenia"), rather than defining the person by their disorder ("This person is *schizophrenic*"; Cuttler & Ryckman, 2019; Granello & Gibbs, 2016). We should also be cautious about using terms such as "crazy" and "insane." When used to describe people, these words are inappropriate, derogatory, and sure indicators of stigma. Another way to reduce stigma is by comparing psychological disorders to medical diseases. We don't ridicule or blame people for having asthma or diabetes, so why would we do this to those suffering from mental illness (Greenstein, 2017)? Educating others about mental illness is an important avenue for addressing stigma—don't be afraid to share what you've learned about the symptoms and causes of psychological disorders (INFOGRAPHIC **13.1** on the next page).

Thus far, our discussion has focused on overarching concepts like abnormal behavior and stigma, which relate to all psychological disorders. Now it's time to shift the discussion to more practical matters: the classification and diagnosis of mental disorders.

BIG INDIE PICTURES/Album/Alamy.

**Movie Portrayals**
Some movies portray people with mental illness as out-of-control and aggressive, but such characterizations tend to perpetuate stereotypes about people with psychological disorders, most of whom are not violent (Whiting & Fazel, 2020). Other films "can serve as useful tools for introducing the general public to the struggles people living with mental illness have to face" (Boyle, 2018, para. 7). An example is *Manchester by the Sea,* a film starring Casey Affleck and Michelle Williams that explores depression and other mental health issues (Boyle, 2018).

## Classifying Psychological Disorders

How was Ross diagnosed with bipolar disorder? He consulted with a psychiatrist. But how did this mental health professional come to the conclusion that Ross suffered from bipolar disorder, and not something else? Given the complexity of determining abnormal behavior, it probably comes as no surprise that clinicians have **not always agreed** on what qualifies as a psychological disorder. Yet, over the years, they have developed common criteria and procedures for making reliable diagnoses. These criteria and decision-making procedures are presented in manuals, which are shared across mental health professions, and are based on research findings and clinical observations.

**CONNECTIONS**

In **Chapter 1,** we presented the perspectives psychologists use to explain the complexities of human behavior. Because clinicians may have different perspectives, they don't always agree on classification criteria. Diagnostic manuals help bridge these gaps by providing standard, evidence-based criteria.

**MAKING DIAGNOSES BASED ON EVIDENCE**    Think about the last time you were ill and went to a doctor. You probably answered a series of questions about your symptoms. The nurse took your blood pressure and temperature, and the doctor

# Let's Break It Down: Stigma

The stigma of mental illness is pervasive, but with knowledge and determination, we can defeat it. To be effective, we must understand that stigma exists at multiple levels; it is present in our institutions, our communities, and sometimes even our own minds. We can target each of these levels with specific strategies (Corrigan & Al-Khouja, 2018; National Academies of Sciences, Engineering, and Medicine, 2016).

STIGMA

## Problems

prejudicial laws and policies, unfair hiring practices, housing discrimination, noninclusive cultures

## Problems

stereotypes, demeaning labels, social exclusion, negative media portrayals of mental illness

## Problems

negative self-stereotypes and shame (both barriers to seeking treatment), low self-esteem, the "why try" attitude associated with undervaluing oneself

## INSTITUTIONAL

## COMMUNITY

## SELF-STIGMA

### WHAT YOU CAN DO

+ Vote for political candidates who support equal opportunity initiatives.
+ Write letters to public officials.
+ Support businesses with fair employment practices.
+ Get involved in government.
+ Engage in peaceful protest.

(National Academies of Sciences, Engineering, and Medicine, 2016)

### WHAT YOU CAN DO

+ Talk openly about mental health and treatment.
+ Stand up for people with mental disorders.
+ If the media reinforces stigma, write a letter to the editor, or start a conversation on social media.
+ Use people-first language.
+ Show compassion and empathy.

(Cuttler & Ryckman, 2019; Greenstein, 2017, HarnEnz, 2016)

### WHAT YOU CAN DO

+ Seek peer support.
+ Educate yourself about mental health conditions.
+ Use empowerment strategies: focus on the positive, surround yourself with supportive people, believe in yourself.
+ Practice self-affirmation; attend to your own beliefs and values.

(Greenstein, 2017, HarnEnz, 2016, Lannin et al., 2019; National Academies of Sciences, Engineering, and Medicine, 2016) performed a physical exam. Using both subjective and objective findings from the exam, the doctor formulated a diagnosis. Mental health professionals must do the same—make diagnoses based on evidence. In addition to collecting information from interviews and other clinical assessments, psychologists typically rely on manuals to guide their diagnoses. Most mental health professionals in North America use the *Diagnostic and Statistical Manual of Mental Disorders* (*DSM–5*; American Psychiatric Association, 2013). The *DSM* is an evidence-based classification system of mental disorders first developed and published by the American Psychiatric Association (www.psych.org) in 1952. This manual was designed to help ensure accurate and consistent diagnoses based on the observation of symptoms. Although the *DSM* is published by the American Psychiatric Association—different from the American Psychological Association—it is used by psychiatrists, psychologists, social workers, and a variety of other clinicians. The most recent edition of the manual, the *DSM–5*, lists 157 disorders (American Psychiatric Association Division of Research, personal communication, 2013, July 26).

Classifying psychological disorders is useful because it helps therapists develop treatment plans, enables clients to obtain reimbursement from their insurance companies, and facilitates research and communication among professions. But there are some drawbacks, especially for clients, who run the risk of being labeled.

Dior Vargas.

**Disorders Do Not Discriminate**
Psychological disorders impact people from all different ethnic and cultural backgrounds, yet images of White people sometimes dominate media portrayals of mental illness. To counter the misconception that mental illness is a "White person's disease," mental health activist Dior Vargas launched the People of Color and Mental Illness Photo Project (DiorVargas.com, n.d.).

## ...BELIEVE IT...OR NOT

### A LABEL CAN CHANGE EVERYTHING

What do you think would happen if you secretly planted eight "sane" people (with no history of psychological disorders) in U.S. psychiatric hospitals? The hospital employees would immediately identify them as "normal" and send them home . . . right?

In the early 1970s, psychologist David Rosenhan and seven other mentally healthy people managed to get themselves admitted to various psychiatric hospitals by faking auditory hallucinations ("I am hearing voices"), a common symptom of schizophrenia. Such a feat would be close to impossible today, as psychiatric facilities can barely accommodate the scores of Americans with documented psychological disorders (Bojdani et al., 2020; Raphelson, 2017; Sisti et al., 2015). Upon admission, each of these pretend patients, or "pseudopatients," immediately stopped putting on an act and began behaving like their normal selves. But within the walls of a psychiatric hospital, their ordinary behavior assumed a whole new meaning. Staff members who spotted the pseudopatients taking notes concluded it must be a symptom of their psychological disorder. "Patient engaged in writing behavior," nurses wrote of one pseudopatient. "Nervous, Mr. X?" a nurse asked a pseudopatient who had been walking the halls out of sheer boredom (Rosenhan, 1973, p. 253).

**NO HOSPITAL STAFF MEMBERS IDENTIFIED THE PSEUDOPATIENTS AS FRAUDS.**

No hospital staff member identified the pseudopatients as frauds. If anyone had them figured out, it was the other patients in the hospital. "You're not crazy," they would say to the pseudopatients. "You're a journalist, or a professor. You're checking up on the hospital" (Rosenhan, 1973, p. 252). After an average stay of 19 days (the range being 7 to 52 days), the pseudopatients were discharged, but not because doctors recognized their diagnostic errors. The pseudopatients, they determined, had gone into "remission" from their fake disorders. They were released back into society—but not without their labels.

Critics have raised legitimate concerns about the scientific and ethical integrity of Rosenhan's study (Griggs et al., 2020; Lando, 1976; Spitzer, 1975). Some evidence suggests that Rosenhan ignored, manipulated, and perhaps even fabricated information in order to advance his hypothesis. He also failed to take the necessary steps to protect participants from harm (Griggs et al., 2020). The study may have been fatally flawed, but it raised awareness about the lasting impact of labels.

If eight "sane" people could be diagnosed with serious disorders like schizophrenia, you might be wondering if psychological diagnoses are **reliable or valid**. We've come a long way since 1973, but the diagnosis of psychological disorders remains a challenge, in part because it often relies on self-reports. Evaluating complex behaviors will never be as straightforward as measuring blood pressure or running a test for strep throat. Researchers continue to study the *DSM*'s utility for diagnosing a variety of disorders, reporting on improvements and pitfalls as we move forward (Boness et al., 2019; Bornstein, 2019; Rasmussen et al., 2019).

### Put Your Heads Together

In your group, discuss the following: **A)** How does being labeled with a psychological disorder affect a person's interactions with family and friends? **B)** Once a label is assigned, can it ever be fully removed? **C)** Describe three ways you can combat the stigmas associated with these labels (see Infographic 13.1).

## "Abnormal," But Not Uncommon

You probably know someone with bipolar disorder, major depressive disorder, or attention-deficit/hyperactivity disorder (ADHD). Perhaps you have experienced a disorder yourself. Psychological disorders are not uncommon (**TABLE 13.2**). Researchers estimate that approximately 50% of the U.S. population experiences the symptoms of a psychological disorder at some point in life (Kessler et al., 2005; Kessler & Wang, 2008). Yes, you read that correctly; "Nearly half the population meet criteria for a mental disorder in their life" (Kessler, 2010, p. 60). In fact, some studies suggest that figure is an underestimate (Angst et al., 2016; Schaefer et al., 2017). Among young adults, the numbers are striking: A study of 13,984 college students from eight different countries found that nearly a third of freshman met the criteria for a common psychological disorder within the past year (Auerbach et al., 2018).

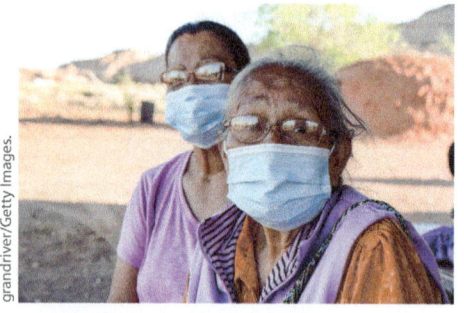

**Pandemic Anxiety**
Psychological disorders were common before the pandemic, but COVID-19 appears to have driven the numbers upward. A meta-analysis of 68 studies conducted on participants from 19 countries found evidence of depression or anxiety in approximately *one third* of adults. Factors associated with a higher risk included female gender, low socioeconomic status, younger age (less than 35 years old), more time spent in front of screens, and greater vulnerability to COVID-19 (because of a preexisting condition or local infection rates) (Wang et al., 2020).

**CONNECTIONS**
In **Chapter 10,** we discussed reliability and validity in the context of personality assessment. These concepts are also relevant to classification systems for psychological disorders. We must determine if diagnoses are reliable (providing consistent, reproducible results) and valid (measuring what they intend to measure).

**TABLE 13.2**  Yearly Rates of Psychological Disorders

| Psychological Disorder | Annual Prevalence |
|---|---|
| Anxiety disorders | 18.1% |
| Specific phobia | 8.7% |
| Social phobia | 6.8% |
| Disruptive behavior disorders | 8.9% |
| Mood disorders | 9.5% |
| Major depression | 6.7% |
| Substance disorders | 3.8% |
| Any disorder | 26.2% |

In any given year, many people are diagnosed with a psychological disorder. The numbers here represent annual prevalence: the percentage of the U.S. population affected by a disorder over a year. (Elsewhere, we have referred to lifetime prevalence, which means the percentage of the population affected by a disorder any time in life.) Information from Kessler (2010).

**A TOUGH ROAD**   With such high rates of disorders, you can be sure that many people around you are dealing with tough issues. In some cases, psychological disorders lead to greater impairment than chronic medical conditions, yet people with mental ailments are less likely to get treatment (Druss et al., 2009). Further complicating the picture is the fact that many people suffer from more than one psychological disorder at a time, a phenomenon called **comorbidity** (koh-more-BID-i-tee). A study of nearly 6 million Danish people found comorbidity to be "pervasive"; being diagnosed with one disorder was associated with an increased risk of developing yet another disorder in the following years. These findings lend evidence to the hypothesis that common genes underlie multiple disorders (Allegrini et al., 2020; Plana-Ripoll et al., 2019). Still, there is much research to be done, and cross-cultural investigations are vital: "As a field, the genetics of mental disorders has a long way to go, including a need to rectify its woeful lack of non-European samples" (Hyman, 2019, p. 236).

You already know that one psychological disorder can lead to significant impairment; now just imagine how these problems compound for a person coping with comorbidity—that is, dealing with more than one disorder. Also keep in mind that various psychological disorders are chronic (a person suffers from them continuously), others have a regular pattern (symptoms appear every winter, for example), and some are temporary.

## What Causes Psychological Disorders?

**LO 2**   Summarize the etiology of psychological disorders.

Throughout this chapter, we will discuss the causal factors, collectively referred to as the *etiology*, underlying psychological disorders. Let's familiarize ourselves with the models commonly used to explain the etiology of mental illness.

**IT'S IN YOUR BIOLOGY**   The **medical model** views psychological disorders from a biological standpoint, focusing on genes, neurochemical imbalances, and processes in the brain. This medical approach has had a long and uninterrupted history, as our culture continues to view psychological disorders as illnesses. It is evident in the language used to discuss disorders and treatment: *mental illness, therapy, remission, symptoms, patients,* and *doctors.* Some scholars criticize this approach (Szasz, 2011), in part because it fails to acknowledge how concepts of mental health and illness "may be variable across time and culture" (Kawa & Giordano, 2012, p. 7).

**IT'S IN YOUR MIND**   Another way to understand the etiology of disorders is to focus on psychological factors. Some theories propose that cognitive activities or personality characteristics contribute to the development and maintenance of disorders. Others focus on the ways that **learning** or childhood experiences might lay their foundation. For example, early trauma can increase the risk of suffering from depression, particularly among those who tend to ruminate, or "constantly focus on negative mood and on the possible causes and implications of depressed feelings" (Kim et al., 2017, p. 2).

**IT'S IN YOUR ENVIRONMENT**   Earlier, we mentioned that culture can shape definitions of "abnormal" and influence the development of psychological disorders. Social factors like poverty, racial discrimination, and community support systems, can also play a role in the development and course of these conditions (Castillo et al., 2018; Russell et al., 2018). For example, evidence suggests that people who are targets of both racism and heterosexism (prejudice against people whose orientation is not heterosexual; Salim et al., 2020) face an increased risk

**CONNECTIONS**

In **Chapter 5,** we discussed a variety of theories that explain how behaviors are learned. In this chapter, we see how learning theories help us understand the development of psychological disorders.

**comorbidity**   The occurrence of two or more disorders at the same time.

**medical model**   An approach suggesting that psychological disorders are illnesses that have underlying biological causes.

**FIGURE 13.1**
**The Biopsychosocial Perspective**
Let's consider the complex interaction of biological, psychological, and sociocultural factors that may contribute to a specific disorder.

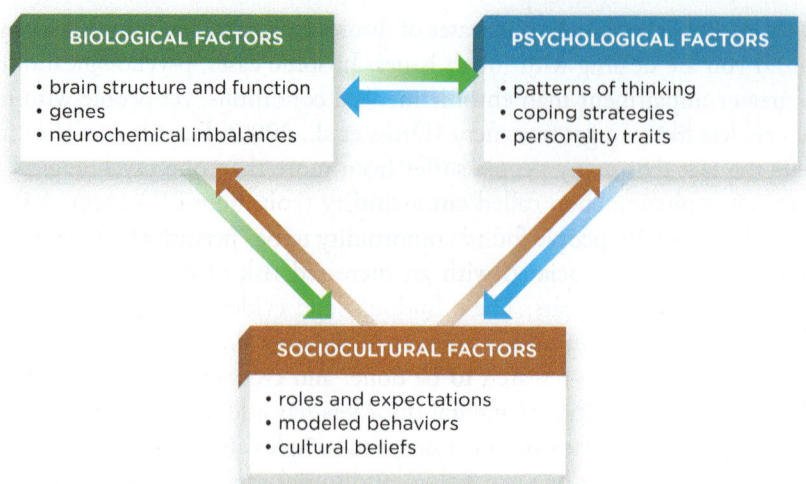

for depression, and perhaps even suicidal thoughts and behaviors: "Some initial evidence indicates that experiencing heterosexism, above and beyond racism, may explain suicidal risk among lesbian, gay, bisexual, transgender, and queer (LGBTQ) racial/ethnic minorities" (Vargas et al., 2020, p. 374).

When diagnosing disorders, psychologists must consider a variety of cultural factors that can shape the way clients experience and describe symptoms. In cases of depression, for example, European Americans tend to complain of psychological distress, while Asian clients may report physical issues like fatigue, weakness, and "imbalance." Meanwhile, people from Middle Eastern cultures may describe "heart problems" in the absence of corroborative medical evidence (Paniagua, 2018). In many cultures, opening up about mental health problems is simply taboo.

**THE BIOPSYCHOSOCIAL PERSPECTIVE**   As we have noted in previous chapters, the best way to understand human behavior is to examine it from a variety of perspectives. The *biopsychosocial perspective* suggests that psychological disorders result from a complex interaction of biological, psychological, and sociocultural factors (**FIGURE 13.1**). For example, some disorders appear to have a genetic basis, but a variety of environmental influences (many occurring during fetal and childhood development) may be involved in the nature–nurture interaction that leads to the onset of symptoms (Pedersen et al., 2018). Some of those environmental influences may surprise you.

## Didn't See That Coming

WHAT DO CATS HAVE TO DO WITH IT?

The development of psychological disorders is influenced by a number of environmental factors, one of which is a history of infection. After being hospitalized for a serious infection, a child's risk of developing a psychological disorder may be as much as 80% higher (Labrie & Brundin, 2019). One disease-causing agent that has been associated with various forms of mental illness, including schizophrenia, obsessive-compulsive disorder (OCD), and generalized anxiety disorder, is a parasite that lives in the intestines of about 40% of household cats (Sutterland et al., 2015; Suvisaari et al., 2017; Underwood, 2019). The parasite is called *Toxoplasma gondii*, and people can become infected from eating partially cooked meat, drinking unclean water, and coming into contact with cat feces. Once inside the human body, *T. gondii* can create cysts within neurons, though it is not entirely clear what the mental health consequences might be (Soleymani et al., 2020; Underwood, 2019).

A COMMON CAT PARASITE LINKED TO MENTAL ILLNESS

Does this mean owning a cat is hazardous to your brain? Current evidence suggests there is no need to panic. Infection with *T. gondii* is not very common, affecting about 1 in 10 people in the United States. It's just one of many variables that could slightly increase the risk of developing a disorder, and researchers have still not pinned down a cause-and-effect relationship (Underwood, 2019). Remember, correlation does not prove causation. If you do own a cat, just be sure to change the kitty litter often and avoid contact with cat feces. Pregnant women should not change the litter box, as infection with *T. gondii* could potentially cause miscarriage or neurological damage to the baby (de Wit et al., 2019). ⚡

graphixel/Getty Images.

Now that we have a general understanding of how psychologists conceptualize psychological disorders, let's delve into specifics. We cannot cover every disorder identified in the *DSM–5*, but we can offer an overview of those commonly discussed in introductory psychology courses.

 **SHOW WHAT YOU KNOW**

1. Which of the following is a criterion used to define abnormal behavior?
   A. dysfunction
   B. psychopathology
   C. developmental processes
   D. stigma

2. A _____ is a set of behavioral, emotional, and cognitive symptoms that are significantly distressing or disabling in terms of social functioning, work, and other aspects of life.

3. Describe the models commonly used to explain the etiology of mental illness.

✓ CHECK YOUR ANSWERS AT THE BACK OF THE BOOK.

# Anxiety Disorders, OCD, and PTSD

**UNWELCOME THOUGHTS: MELISSA'S STORY**   Melissa Hopely was about 5 years old when she began doing "weird things" to combat anxiety: flipping light switches on and off, touching the corners of tables, and running to the kitchen to make sure the oven was turned off. Taken at face value, these behaviors may not seem too strange, but for Melissa they were the first signs of a psychological disorder that eventually pushed her to the edge.

As Melissa grew older, her behaviors became increasingly regimented. She felt compelled to do everything an even number of times. Instead of entering a room once, she would enter or leave twice, four times, perhaps even 20 times—as long as the number was a multiple of 2. Some days she would sit in her bedroom for hours,

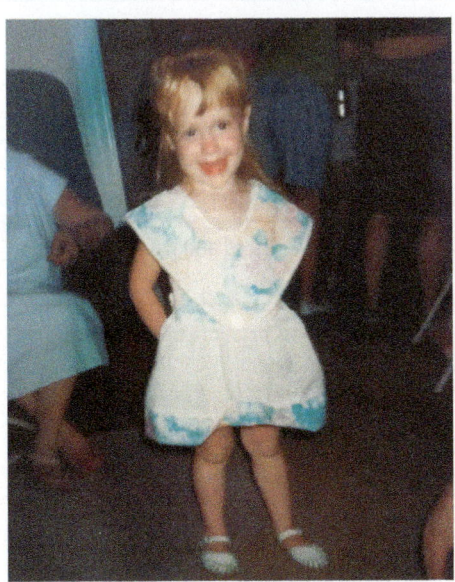

Melissa Hopely.

**What Was Melissa Battling?**

Melissa Hopely was about 3 years old when the photo on the left was taken. Within a couple of years, she began to experience the symptoms of a serious mental disorder that would continue into adulthood. Melissa was tormented by a vague feeling that something awful was about to occur. She feared that she would die, lose all her friends, or become homeless—unless she performed certain behaviors to stop these dreaded events from happening.

methodically touching all her possessions twice, then repeating the process again, and again. By performing these rituals, Melissa felt she could prevent her worst fears from becoming reality. What was she so afraid of? Dying, losing all her friends, and becoming homeless were just a few of her worries. It seemed like something dreadful was about to happen, though she couldn't put her finger on what it was. In reality, Melissa had little reason to worry. She had health, intelligence, beauty, and a loving circle of friends and family.

We all experience irrational worries from time to time, but Melissa's had become overwhelming. Where do we draw the line between normal and abnormal? This section will focus on anxiety disorders, obsessive-compulsive disorder (OCD), and posttraumatic stress disorder (PTSD).

## Anxiety Disorders

**LO 3**  Define anxiety disorders and identify their causes.

Think about the objects or situations that make you feel afraid or uneasy. Maybe you fear creepy crawly insects, slithery snakes, or crowded public spaces. A mild fear of spiders or overcrowded subways is normal, but if you become highly disturbed by the mere thought of them, or if the fear interferes with your everyday functioning, a problem may exist. People who suffer from **anxiety disorders** have extreme anxiety and/or irrational fears that are debilitating and go beyond what is commonly expected in a particular cultural context (American Psychiatric Association, 2013; TABLE 13.3). Anxiety disorders are the most common form of mental illness, affecting about 1 in 3 people at some point in life (Bandelow & Michaelis, 2015). The coronavirus pandemic appears to have sparked new levels of anxiety in the United States, as the number of people reporting symptoms tripled between early 2019 and early 2020 (Twenge & Joiner, 2020).

Let's take a look at some of the anxiety disorders identified in the *DSM–5:* panic disorder, specific phobia, agoraphobia, social anxiety disorder, and generalized anxiety disorder.

**Opening Up About Anxiety**
Actor and musician Selena Gomez has been forthright about her battle with anxiety and depression. In reference to *Anxiety,* the duet she created with Julia Michaels, she wrote, "This song is extremely close to my heart as I've experienced anxiety and know a lot of my friends do too. You're never alone if you feel this way" (Selena Gomez, 2019).

Barcroft Media/Getty Images.

**TABLE 13.3**   *Anxiety Disorders*

| Disorder | Annual Prevalence | Description |
|----------|-------------------|-------------|
| Separation anxiety disorder | 0.9–1.9% in adults; 1.6% in adolescents; 4% in children | Anxiety or fear related to "separation from home or attachment figures" (p. 191) |
| Specific phobia | 7–9% | Anxiety or fear about a specific object or situation |
| Social anxiety disorder (social phobia) | 7% | Anxiety or fear about being in a social situation that could result in scrutiny by other people |
| Panic disorder | 2–3% | Reoccurring panic attacks that are unexpected and have no apparent cue or trigger |
| Agoraphobia | 1.7% | Anxiety or fear about "using public transportation; being in open spaces; being in enclosed places; standing in line or being in a crowd; or being outside of the home" (p. 217) |
| Generalized anxiety disorder | 0.9% in adolescents; 2.9% in adults | Anxiety and worry that are out of proportion to the actual event or situation |

Anxiety disorders are relatively common among both sexes, but they are more apparent in women by an approximate 2:1 ratio. Information from the *DSM–5* (American Psychiatric Association, 2013).

**PANIC DISORDER**    What should you do if you see somebody trembling and sweating, gasping for breath, or complaining of heart palpitations? If you are concerned it's a heart attack, you may be correct; call 911 immediately if you are not sure. However, a person experiencing a *panic attack* may behave very similarly to someone having a heart attack. A **panic attack** is a sudden, extreme fear or discomfort that escalates quickly, often with no evident cause, and includes symptoms such as increased heart rate, sweating, shortness of breath, chest pain, nausea, lightheadedness, and fear of dying. A diagnosis of **panic disorder** requires such attacks to recur unexpectedly and have no obvious trigger. In addition, the person worries about losing control and having more panic attacks. People with panic disorder often make decisions that are maladaptive, like purposefully avoiding exercise or unfamiliar places, in hope of preventing a panic attack.

Panic disorder affects about 2–3% of the population (American Psychiatric Association, 2013). Research suggests it runs in families, with heritability estimates around 40–48% (Maron et al., 2010; Weber et al., 2012). People often assume heritability refers to an individual's risk for a disorder. ("Her panic disorder is 40% the result of her genes, and 60% due to her environment.") This is incorrect. Heritability explains the variation and risk *within a population.* In the example above, over 40% of the variation of panic disorder in the *population* can be attributed to genetic factors, and the remaining 60% to environmental factors. In other words, the frequency and distribution of panic disorder across people result from a combination of factors, 40% of which are genetic, and 60% nongenetic.

Women are twice as likely as men to be diagnosed with panic disorder, and this disparity is already apparent by the age of 14 (American Psychiatric Association, 2013; Craske et al., 2010; Weber et al., 2012). Such gender differences seem to result from an interaction between genes and environment (Iurato et al., 2017).

Panic disorder does appear to have a biological cause (American Psychiatric Association, 2013). Researchers have identified specific parts of the brain involved in panic attacks, including regions of the hypothalamus, which is involved in the **fight-or-flight** response, and its associated structures (Elias et al., 2020; Johnson et al., 2010). Irregularities in certain areas of the amygdala may help explain dysfunction in the fight-or-flight response, which could be associated with the physical and behavioral symptoms of panic attacks (Asami et al., 2018).

Some researchers propose that learning—particularly **classical conditioning**—can play a role in the development of panic disorder (Bouton et al., 2001; Duits et al., 2015). In a panic disorder scenario, the neutral stimulus might be something like a location (a shopping mall), the unconditioned stimulus an unexpected panic attack, and the unconditioned response the fear resulting from the panic attack. After the panic attack is paired with the shopping mall, the mall becomes the conditioned stimulus, such that every time the person thinks of this location, fear results (now the conditioned response).

**SPECIFIC PHOBIAS**    Panic attacks can occur without apparent triggers. This is not the case with a **specific phobia,** which centers on a particular object or situation, such as rats or airplane travel (TABLE **13.4** on the next page). Most people with phobias do their best to avoid the cause of their fear. If avoidance is not possible, they withstand it, but only with extreme fear and anxiousness.

As with panic disorder, phobias can be explained using the principles of learning (LeBeau et al., 2010; Rofé & Rofé, 2015). Classical conditioning may lead to the acquisition of a fear through the pairing of stimuli. Operant conditioning could maintain the phobia through negative reinforcement; if anxiety (the unpleasant stimulus) is reduced by avoiding a feared object or situation, the avoidance behavior is

**CONNECTIONS**

In **Chapter 2,** we described how the sympathetic division of the autonomic nervous system directs the body's stress response. When a stressful situation arises, the sympathetic nervous system prepares the body to react, causing the heart to beat faster, respiration to increase, and the pupils to dilate.

**CONNECTIONS**

In **Chapter 5,** we described how Little Albert acquired a conditioned emotional response: An originally neutral stimulus (a rat) was paired with an unconditioned stimulus (a loud sound), which led to an unconditioned response (fear). With repeated pairings, the conditioned stimulus (the rat) led to a conditioned response (fear).

**anxiety disorders** A group of psychological disorders associated with extreme anxiety and/or debilitating, irrational fears.

**panic attack** Sudden, extreme fear or discomfort that escalates quickly, often with no obvious trigger, and includes symptoms such as increased heart rate, sweating, shortness of breath, chest pain, nausea, lightheadedness, and fear of dying.

**panic disorder** A psychological disorder that includes recurrent, unexpected panic attacks and fear that can cause significant changes in behavior.

**specific phobia** A psychological disorder characterized by a distinct fear or anxiety related to an object or situation.

**TABLE 13.4    Are You Afraid?**

| Scientific Name | Fear of ... | Scientific Name | Fear of ... |
|---|---|---|---|
| Acrophobia | Heights | Epistemophobia | Knowledge |
| Astraphobia or keraunophobia | Lightning | Gamophobia | Marriage |
| Brontophobia | Thunder | Ophidiophobia | Snakes |
| Claustrophobia | Closed spaces | Odontophobia | Dental procedures |
| Cynophobia | Dogs | Xenophobia | Strangers |

The phobias listed in this table are not specifically included in the *DSM–5*, but they are all associated with the same general response. Also note this is not a comprehensive list, as phobias can center on virtually any object or situation. Information from Reber, Allen, and Reber (2009).

shikheigoh/Getty Images.

**Did Phobias Evolve?**
Humans seem to be biologically predisposed to fear certain threats such as snakes, spiders, and bitter foods (Shackelford & Liddle, 2014; Van Strien et al., 2014). From an evolutionary standpoint, such fears would tend to protect us from true danger (a poisonous snake bite, for example). But the link between anxiety and evolution is not always so apparent. It's hard to imagine how an intense fear of being in public, for example, would promote survival.

**agoraphobia** Extreme fear of situations involving public transportation, open spaces, or other public settings.

**generalized anxiety disorder** A psychological disorder characterized by an excessive amount of worry and anxiety about activities relating to family, health, school, and other aspects of daily life.

negatively reinforced and thus more likely to recur. Observational learning can also help explain the development of a phobia. Simply watching someone else experience its symptoms could create fear in an observer (Reynolds et al., 2017).

**AGORAPHOBIA**    A person with **agoraphobia** (ag-o-ruh-FOH-bee-uh) feels extremely uneasy in public spaces. This disorder is characterized by a distinct fear or anxiety related to public transportation, open spaces, retail stores, crowds, or being alone and away from home in general. Agoraphobia may also result in "panic-like symptoms," which can be difficult to handle. Typically, people with agoraphobia need another person to accompany them on outings, because they are unsure they can cope on their own. They may avoid situations that frighten them, or be overwhelmed with fear when avoidance or escape is not possible.

**SOCIAL ANXIETY DISORDER**    According to the *DSM–5*, a person with social anxiety disorder (social phobia) has an "intense" fear of social situations and scrutiny by others. This extreme fear could arise during a speech or presentation, while eating a meal, or simply in conversation. Social anxiety often stems from a preoccupation with offending someone or behaving in a way that reveals one's anxiety, and frequently includes an overestimation of the potential undesirable consequences. The fear is not warranted, however. Being evaluated or even mocked by others is not necessarily dangerous and should not cause debilitating stress.

**GENERALIZED ANXIETY DISORDER**    The anxiety disorders we have discussed thus far relate to specific objects and scenarios. You can predict that a person with agoraphobia will feel distressed walking through a busy college campus, and there is a good chance that someone with social phobia will feel very uncomfortable at a cocktail party. But what about anxiety that is more pervasive, affecting many aspects of life? A person with **generalized anxiety disorder** experiences an excessive amount of worry and anxiety about many activities relating to family, health, school, and other areas (American Psychiatric Association, 2013). This psychological distress is accompanied by physical symptoms such as muscle tension and restlessness. Individuals with generalized anxiety disorder may avoid activities they believe will not go smoothly, spend a great deal of time getting ready for such events, or wait until the very last minute to engage in the anxiety-producing activity.

The development of generalized anxiety disorder is influenced by both nature and nurture. Some affected individuals appear to have a genetic predisposition to developing irregularities in parts of the brain associated with fear, such as the amygdala and hippocampus (Gottschalk & Domschke, 2017; Hettema et al., 2012).

Environmental factors such as adversity in childhood and overprotective parents may also play a role (American Psychiatric Association, 2013).

**MELISSA'S STRUGGLE**   We introduced this section with the story of Melissa Hopely, a girl who struggled with anxiety and performed elaborate rituals to alleviate it. Melissa's behavior caused significant distress and dysfunction, which suggests that it was abnormal, but does it match any of the anxiety disorders described above? Her anxiety was not attached to a specific object or situation, so it doesn't appear to be a phobia. Nor was her anxiety widespread and nonspecific, as might be the case with generalized anxiety disorder. Melissa's fears emanated from nagging, dreadful thoughts generated by her own mind. She may not have been struggling with an anxiety disorder per se, but she certainly was experiencing anxiety as a result of some disorder. So what was it?

## Obsessive-Compulsive Disorder

At age 12, Melissa was diagnosed with **obsessive-compulsive disorder (OCD),** a psychological disorder characterized by unwanted thoughts, or *obsessions,* and repetitive, ritualistic behaviors known as *compulsions.*

**LO 4**   Summarize the symptoms and causes of obsessive-compulsive disorder.

An **obsession** is a thought, urge, or image that occurs repeatedly, is intrusive and unwelcome, and often causes feelings of intense anxiety and distress. Melissa's recurrent, all-consuming thoughts of disaster and death are examples of obsessions. People with OCD attempt to stop, or at least ignore, their obsessions by engaging in a replacement thought or activity. But this is not always helpful, because the replacement can become a **compulsion,** which is a behavior or "mental act" repeated over and over.

Those who suffer from OCD experience various types of obsessions and compulsions. In many cases, obsessions focus on fears of contamination with germs or dirt, and compulsions revolve around cleaning and sterilizing (Cisler et al., 2010; Jalal et al., 2020). Some people with OCD report that they repeatedly wash their hands even after abrasions have formed (Lawrence, 2020). The coronavirus pandemic seems to have exacerbated symptoms for some of these individuals (Davide et al., 2020). As the world faces a novel and highly contagious pathogen, how can one be sure which behaviors are appropriate and which are excessive: *Is it reasonable to wipe down my groceries with Clorox wipes, or is that my disorder?* Despite these challenges, people who have successfully confronted their OCD with therapy may actually "have increased abilities to accept the pandemic's uncertainty" (Lawrence, 2020, para. 5).

Other common OCD compulsions are repetitive rituals and checking behaviors. Melissa, for example, developed a compulsion about locking her car. Unlike most people, who lock their cars once and walk away, Melissa felt compelled to lock it twice. Then she would begin to wonder whether the car was really locked, so she would lock it a third time—just in case. But 3 is an odd number, and odd numbers don't sit well with Melissa, so she would lock it a fourth time. When Melissa finally felt comfortable enough to walk away, she had locked her car eight times. And sometimes that was still not enough. OCD compulsions often aim to thwart unwanted situations, and thereby **reduce** anxiety and distress. But the compulsive behaviors of OCD are either "clearly excessive" or not logically related to the event or situation the person is trying to prevent (American Psychiatric Association, 2013; FIGURE **13.2** on the next page).

Where do we draw the line between obsessive or compulsive behavior and the diagnosis of a disorder? Remember, behaviors must be significantly distressing or disabling in order to be considered symptoms. The obsessions and compulsions of OCD are very time-consuming (take more than 1 hour a day) and cause a great deal of

**obsessive-compulsive disorder (OCD)** A psychological disorder characterized by obsessions and/or compulsions that are time-consuming and cause a great deal of distress.

**obsession** A thought, an urge, or an image that happens repeatedly, is intrusive and unwelcome, and often causes anxiety and distress.

**compulsion** A behavior or "mental act" that a person repeats over and over in an effort to reduce anxiety.

## FIGURE 13.2
**Frequently Reported Obsessions and Compulsions**

While experiences with OCD vary substantially from one individual to the next, these are some of the common thoughts and behaviors associated with the disorder (American Psychiatric Association, 2013; Williams et al., 2011). Man covering face: alvarez/Getty Images; Hand washing: lostinbids/Getty Images; Colored pencils: Robert Körner/Getty Images; Hand checking stove: Misty Hull; Human head: simon2579/Getty Images.

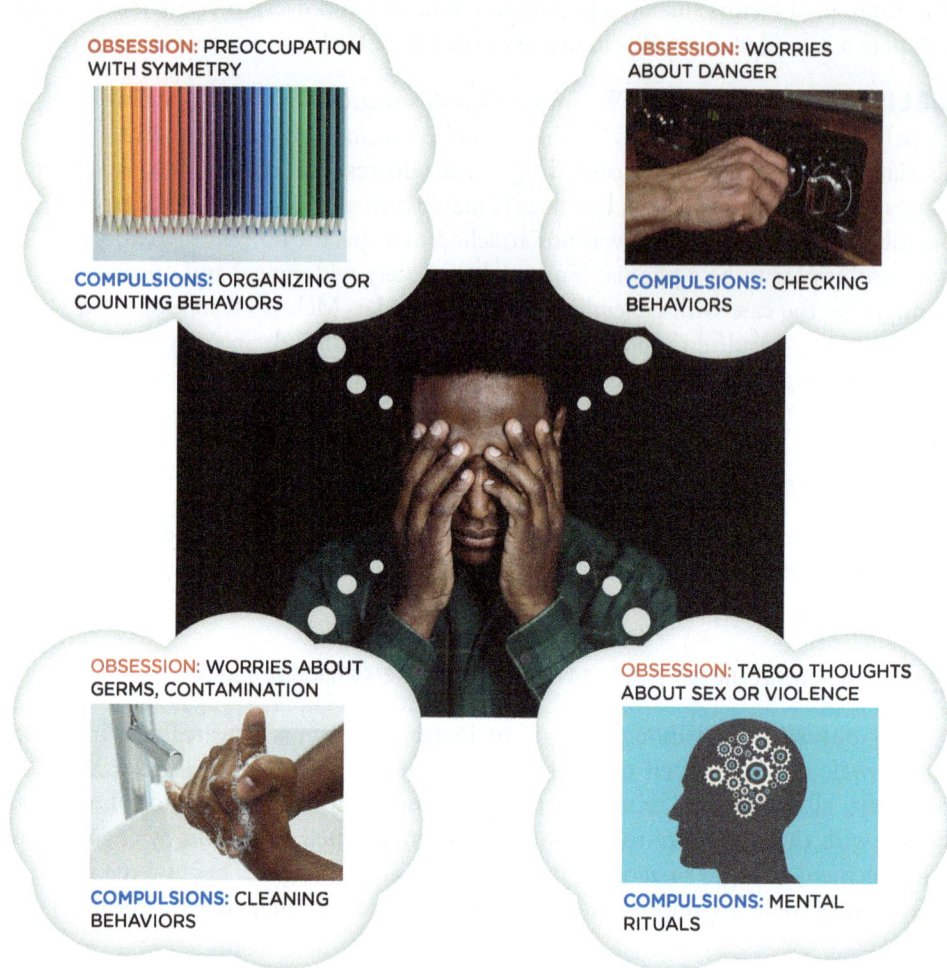

distress and disruption in daily life. Everyone has odd thoughts and quirky routines, but they don't eat up multiple hours of the day and interfere with school, work, and relationships. That's the key distinction between normal preoccupations and OCD (American Psychiatric Association, 2013). The 12-month prevalence of OCD is estimated to be 1.2% in the United States (American Psychiatric Association, 2013; Ruscio et al., 2010). The *DSM–5* identifies several disorders related to OCD, some of which are outlined in TABLE **13.5**.

### TABLE 13.5   Disorders Related to OCD

| Related Disorder | Description | Average Age of Onset |
|---|---|---|
| Body dysmorphic disorder | Focusing on perceived defects in one's appearance | 12–13 years old |
| Excoriation | Picking one's skin, including healthy areas, calluses, and pimples | Adolescence |
| Hoarding disorder | Difficulty getting rid of things, even if they have little or no worth | 11–15 years old |
| Trichotillomania | Pulling hair from the body, often from the scalp, eyebrows, and/or eyelashes | Puberty |

The disorders outlined here are related to OCD and may occur alongside OCD symptoms. While it is normal to have worries and perform rituals at various stages of development, the symptoms of these disorders go beyond what is typical and cause substantial distress and dysfunction. Information from the *DSM–5* (American Psychiatric Association, 2013).

**THE BIOLOGY OF OCD**    Evidence suggests that the symptoms of OCD are related to abnormal activity of neurotransmitters. Reduced activity of serotonin is thought to play a role, and additional neurotransmitters are being studied (Bloch et al., 2010; Karthik et al., 2020). Certain areas of the brain have been implicated, including locations in the basal ganglia, cingulate gyri, and orbital frontal cortex (American Psychiatric Association, 2013; Radua & Mataix-Cols, 2009). Normally, these regions play a role in planning and regulating movement (Rotge et al., 2009).

How do these biological differences arise? There appears to be a genetic basis for OCD. If a first-degree relative (parent, sibling, or offspring who shares about 50% of one's DNA) has an OCD diagnosis, the risk of developing OCD is twice as high as it would be if that close relative were not affected (American Psychiatric Association, 2013). However, genes do not tell the whole story. The heritability for OCD is around 40%, suggesting that environmental factors also play a substantial role in its development (Pauls et al., 2014; Smit et al., 2020).

**THE ROLE OF LEARNING**    To ease her anxiety, Melissa turned to compulsions—repetitive, ritualistic behaviors aimed at relieving or offsetting her obsessions. Because her greatest fears never came to pass, Melissa assumed that her actions had prevented them. *I didn't die because I touched all the things in my room just the right way,* she would think to herself. The more she followed through on her compulsions and saw that her fears never played out, the more convinced she became that her behaviors prevented them. As Melissa put it, "When you feed it, feed it, feed it, it gets stronger."

Melissa's case illustrates how learning can play a role in OCD. Her compulsions were negatively reinforced by the reduction in her fear, and continued to grow stronger through a "negative reinforcement cycle" (Pauls et al., 2014, p. 420). Here, we can draw a parallel with drug addiction. Taking a drug can remove unpleasant withdrawal symptoms, just like carrying out compulsions reduces fear. In both cases, the behavior increases when an unpleasant experience is removed (Abramovitch & McKay, 2016). This learning process is ongoing and potentially very powerful. In one study, researchers monitored 144 people with OCD diagnoses for more than 40 years. The participants' OCD symptoms improved, in some cases with the help of treatment, but almost half continued to show "clinically relevant" symptoms after 4 decades (Skoog & Skoog, 1999).

Anxiety disorders and OCD result from a complex interplay of genetic and environmental factors, making it difficult to identify their exact triggers. This is not the case with posttraumatic stress disorder (PTSD), which is clearly linked to a "traumatic or stressful event" (American Psychiatric Association, 2013, p. 265).

## Posttraumatic Stress Disorder

To be diagnosed with **posttraumatic stress disorder (PTSD),** a person must be exposed to or threatened by an event involving death, serious injury, or some form of violence. Someone could develop PTSD after witnessing a violent assault or accident, or upon learning about the traumatic experiences of family members, close friends, or perhaps even strangers (American Psychiatric Association, 2013; Wolf, 2018). For some people, including firefighters, police officers, and ambulance workers, the exposure to trauma is ongoing. Rates of PTSD among firefighters, for example, may be as high as 37% (Henderson et al., 2016). Others who may be disproportionately affected are COVID-19 survivors. A study of 381 patients in Italy (most of whom were sick enough to be hospitalized) found that 30.2% had symptoms of PTSD (Janiri et al., 2021). Among U.S. veterans, the lifetime rates of PTSD are 13.2% for women and 6.2% for men. Compare that to 7.9% for female civilians and 3.6% for male civilians (Lehavot et al., 2018).

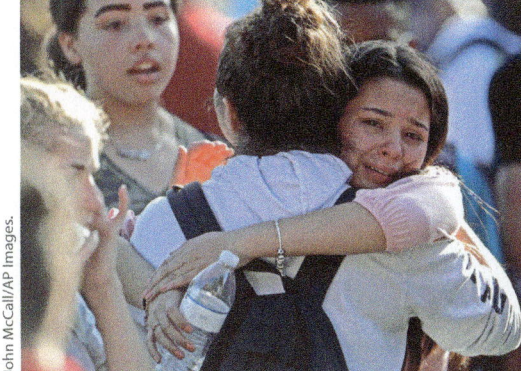

John McCall/AP Images.

**Gun Violence and PTSD**
Survivors of the school shooting in Parkland, Florida, where 17 students and staff members were killed. Shooting deaths wreak emotional havoc on family and friends. "Sudden unexpected death of a loved one is the most common traumatic cause of PTSD in the population and mass shooting incidents substantially expand the base population at risk for PTSD" (Shultz et al., 2017, p. 1753).

**posttraumatic stress disorder (PTSD)** A psychological disorder characterized by exposure to or being threatened by an event involving death, serious injury, or violence; can include disturbing memories, nightmares, flashbacks, and other distressing symptoms.

Not everyone exposed to trauma will develop PTSD. Over the course of a lifetime, most people will experience an event that qualifies as a "psychological trauma," yet the majority will not meet the diagnostic criteria for PTSD (Bonanno et al., 2011). To be diagnosed, a person must experience at least one of the following symptoms: (1) distressing, disturbing, and spontaneously recurring memories of an event; (2) dreams with content or emotions associated with the event; (3) "dissociative reactions" that include feeling as if the event is happening again (flashbacks); (4) extreme psychological distress when reminded of the event; or (5) obvious physical reactions to cues related to the event (American Psychiatric Association, 2013).

Many people with PTSD try to avoid environmental cues (people, places, or objects) linked to the trauma. Other symptoms include difficulty remembering the details of the event, unrealistic self-expectations, ongoing self-blame, and loss of interest in activities that once were enjoyable. People with PTSD might be irritable or aggressive, lashing out at loved ones for no apparent reason. They may have trouble sleeping and concentrating. *Dissociative symptoms,* which may include distorted perceptions of the world and the feeling of observing oneself from the outside, are also associated with PTSD (American Psychiatric Association, 2013; Müllerová et al., 2016; Powers et al., 2015).

## SHOW WHAT YOU KNOW

1. Someone with a diagnosis of panic disorder experiences unexpected and recurrent:
   - **A.** comorbidity.
   - **B.** medical illnesses.
   - **C.** panic attacks.
   - **D.** dramatic mood swings.

2. Melissa's therapist helped reduce the negative reinforcement of her compulsions by not allowing her to repeatedly check that her car was locked. Explain why such a technique would work.

3. Melissa demonstrated recurrent all-consuming worries. She tried to stop unwanted thoughts with a variety of behaviors that she repeated over and over. These behaviors are known as:
   - **A.** obsessions.
   - **B.** classical conditioning.
   - **C.** panic attacks.
   - **D.** compulsions.

✓ CHECK YOUR ANSWERS AT THE BACK OF THE BOOK.

# From Depression to Mania

**MELISSA'S SECOND DIAGNOSIS**    Unfortunately for Melissa, receiving a diagnosis and treatment did not solve her problems. "Every day I woke up, I wanted to die," says Melissa, who reached a breaking point during her sophomore year in high school. After a particularly difficult day at school, Melissa returned home with the intention of taking her own life. Luckily, a friend recognized that she was in distress and notified Melissa's family members, who rushed home to find Melissa curled up in a ball in the corner of her room, rocking back and forth and mumbling nonsense. They took Melissa to the hospital, where she finally met people who didn't think she was "crazy." During those 3 days in the psychiatric unit, she explains, "I realized I wasn't my disorder."

While in the hospital, Melissa received a new diagnosis in addition to OCD. Doctors told her that she was suffering from depression. Apparently, the profound sadness and helplessness she had been feeling were symptoms of *major depressive disorder,* one of the depressive disorders described in the *DSM–5.*

**The Importance of Friends**
Melissa (right) poses with childhood friend Mary Beth, whom she credits for helping to save her life. The day that Melissa arrived home intending to attempt suicide, Mary Beth recognized her friend's distress and called for help. Thanks to the intervention of friends and family, Melissa received the treatment she needed.

Melissa Hopely.

## Major Depressive Disorder

**LO5**  Summarize the symptoms and causes of major depressive disorder.

A *major depressive episode* is evident if five or more of the symptoms listed here (1) occur for at least 2 consecutive weeks and represent a change from prior functioning, (2) cause significant distress or impairment, and (3) are not due to a medical or drug-related condition:

- depressed mood, which might result in feeling sad or hopeless;
- reduced pleasure in activities almost all of the time;
- substantial loss or gain in weight without conscious effort, or changes in appetite;
- sleeping excessively or not sleeping enough;
- feeling tired, drained of energy;
- feeling worthless or extremely guilt-ridden;
- difficulty thinking or concentrating;
- persistent thoughts about death or suicide.

To be diagnosed with **major depressive disorder,** a person must have experienced at least one major depressive episode. Some people suffer a single episode, while others battle *recurrent* episodes.

Diagnosing major depressive disorder can be challenging. The clinician must be able to distinguish the symptoms from normal reactions to a "significant loss," such as the death of a loved one. This is not always easy because responses to death often resemble depression. A key distinction is that grief generally decreases with time, and comes in waves associated with memories or reminders of the loss; the sadness associated with a major depressive episode tends to remain steady (American Psychiatric Association, 2013).

Major depressive disorder is one of the most common and devastating psychological disorders. In the United States, the lifetime prevalence is between 16.6% and 20.6% (Hasin et al., 2018; Kessler et al., 2012). This means about 1 in 5 Americans experiences a major depressive episode at least once in life. Beginning in adolescence, rates of this disorder are already 1.5 to 3 times higher for females (American Psychiatric Association, 2013). Although this gender disparity reaches its maximum during adolescence, a substantial gap persists in adulthood. Women are disproportionately affected, but "it is important that clinicians do not overlook depression among men" (Salk et al., 2017, p. 808).

The effects of major depressive disorder extend far beyond the individual. For Americans ages 15 to 44, this condition is one of the main causes of disability (Greenberg et al., 2015)—and this means it impacts the productivity of the workforce. In a comprehensive study of major depressive disorder, respondents reported that their symptoms prevented them from going to work or performing day-to-day activities for an average of 35 days a year (Kessler et al., 2003). Stop and think about this statistic—we are talking about a loss of 7 work weeks! Time away from work isn't the only concern. Under performance at work, also known as "presenteeism," is observed in 13–29% of workers who are depressed (Lerner et al., n.d.).

**CULTURE**    Depression is one of the most common psychological disorders in the world, yet the symptoms experienced, the course of treatment, and the words used to describe it vary from culture to culture. For example, in Thailand, depression is commonly expressed through mental and physical symptoms such as headaches, fatigue, daydreaming, social withdrawal, irritation, and forgetfulness (Chirawatkul et al., 2011). Culture affects the way people experience emotion, and it may even impact rates of depression (Chan et al., 2015).

**SUICIDE**    The recurrent nature of major depressive disorder increases one's risk for suicide and health complications (Knorr et al., 2016; Monroe & Harkness, 2011). Around 9% of adults in 21 countries confirm they have harbored "serious thoughts of suicide" at least once (**INFOGRAPHIC 13.2** on the next page), and around 3% have attempted suicide (Borges et al., 2010). In the United States, suicide rates have been on the rise, increasing 35% between 1999 and 2018 (National Institute of Mental Health, 2021).

Steve Granitz/Getty Images.

**Dealing with Depression**
Comedian Trevor Noah has reportedly experienced the symptoms of depression for years, but hosting *The Daily Show* has helped him cope. "One of the best things for depression is routine and goal-oriented tasks," Noah said in an interview with *GQ*. "Every day I have to make a show. Every day I have to finish the show. Every day I have to let go of the show" (Lowery, 2020, para. 44).

**major depressive disorder**  A psychological disorder that includes at least one major depressive episode, with symptoms such as depressed mood, problems with sleep, and loss of energy.

# Suicide in the United States

In recent years, suicide has emerged as a leading cause of death in the United States. Non-Hispanic American Indians have been affected more than any other group, but suicide impacts all ethnicities (National Institute of Mental Health [NIMH], 2021). Researchers examine suicide rates across gender, age, and ethnicity in order to better understand risk factors and to help develop suicide prevention strategies. Let's take a look at what this means—and what you can do if you are concerned a friend or family member might be contemplating suicide.

## Suicide rates across the United States

Listed here are suicide rates per 100,000 people (age adjusted)

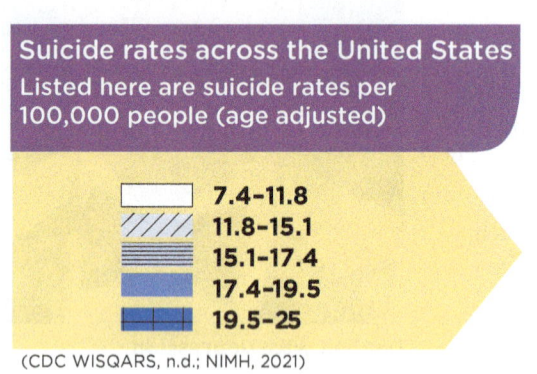

| | |
|---|---|
| ☐ | 7.4–11.8 |
| ▨ | 11.8–15.1 |
| ▤ | 15.1–17.4 |
| ▨ | 17.4–19.5 |
| ▨ | 19.5–25 |

(CDC WISQARS, n.d.; NIMH, 2021)

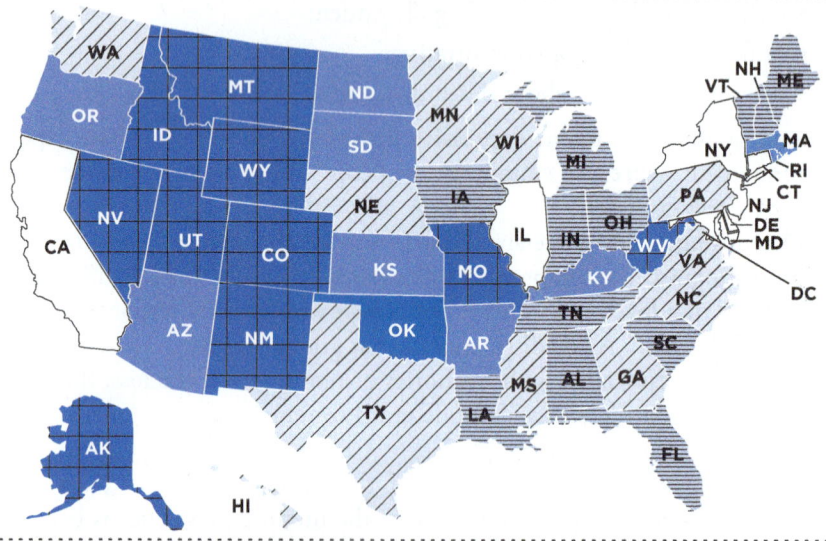

Approximately 4.8% of U.S. adults think about suicide over the course of a year. This figure increased drastically during the COVID-19 pandemic.

 The suicide rate for males is nearly 4 times higher than females.

(Czeisler et al., 2020; NIMH, 2021)

 In the United States, someone commits suicide every **12 minutes.**

(American Foundation for Suicide Prevention, n.d.)

Suicide is the second leading cause of death for people aged 10–34.

(CDC WISQARS, n.d; NIMH, 2021)

## Risk factors for suicide include:

- ✔ Previous suicide attempt(s)
- ✔ Family history of suicide or violence
- ✔ Alcohol or drug abuse
- ✔ Physical illness
- ✔ History of depression or other mental illness
- ✔ Access to firearms

(NIMH, n.d.-c)

More than half of those who complete suicide have not been diagnosed with a psychological disorder. "It is possible that mental health conditions or other circumstances could have been present and not diagnosed, known, or reported" (CDC, 2018, June 7, p. 2).

## If you believe a friend may be thinking about suicide:

- Don't be afraid to ask. Talking about suicide will not put the idea in your friend's head. Be direct and ask your friend if they are thinking about hurting themselves.

- Listen without being judgmental.

- Never agree to keep someone's thoughts about suicide a secret.

- Encourage your friend to contact a responsible person who can help. This may be a counselor, teacher, or health-care professional. Or call a suicide prevention hotline.

- If your friend admits that they have made a detailed plan or obtained a means of hurting themselves, call 911 and stay with them until help arrives.

(CDC, 2018, June 7; Mayo Clinic, 2018)

**NATIONAL SUICIDE PREVENTION LIFELINE: 1-800-273-TALK (8255)**
suicidepreventionlifeline.org

Photo is being used for illustrative purposes only; persons depicted in the photo are models.

Depression is one of many factors that have been linked to suicide; others include substance abuse, medical problems, obstacles to obtaining psychological therapy, and childhood traumas like abuse and neglect (Centers for Disease Control and Prevention [CDC], n.d.-f). For a closer look at the reasons people take their own lives, see the following article by science writer Michael Shermer, published in *Scientific American*.

# WHY DO PEOPLE KILL THEMSELVES?

## Why do people die by suicide?

Anthony Bourdain (age 61). Kate Spade (55). Robin Williams (63). Aaron Swartz (26). Junior Seau (43). Alexander McQueen (40). Hunter S. Thompson (67). Kurt Cobain (27). Sylvia Plath (30). Ernest Hemingway (61). Alan Turing (41). Virginia Woolf (59). Vincent van Gogh (37). By the time you finish reading this list of notable people who died by suicide, somewhere in the world another person will have done the same, about one every 40 seconds (around 800,000 a year), making suicide the 10th leading cause of death in the U.S. Why?

According to the prominent psychologist Jesse Bering of the University of Otago in New Zealand, in his authoritative book *Suicidal: Why We Kill Ourselves* (University of Chicago Press, 2018), "the specific issues leading any given person to become suicidal are as different, of course, as their DNA—involving chains of events that one expert calls 'dizzying in their variety.'" Indeed, my short list above includes people with a diversity of ages, professions, personality and gender. Depression is commonly fingered in many suicide cases, yet most people suffering from depression do not kill themselves (only about 5 percent Bering says), and not all suicide victims were depressed. "Around 43 percent of the variability in suicidal behavior among the general population can be explained by genetics," Bering reports, "while the remaining 57 percent is attributable to environmental factors." Having a genetic predisposition for suicidality, coupled with a particular sequence of environmental assaults on one's will to live, leads some people to try to make the pain stop.

In Bering's case, it first came as a closeted gay teenager "in an intolerant small Midwestern town" and later with unemployment at a status apex in his academic career (success can lead to unreasonably high standards for happiness, later crushed by the vicissitudes of life). [. . .] "In the vast majority of cases, people kill themselves because of other people," Bering adduces. "Social problems—especially a hypervigilant concern with what others think or will think of us if only they knew what we perceive to be some unpalatable truth—stoke a deadly fire."

Like most human behavior, suicide is a multicausal act. Teasing out the strongest predictive variables is difficult, particularly because such internal cognitive states may not be accessible even to the person experiencing them. We cannot perceive the neurochemical workings of our brain, so internal processes are typically attributed to external sources. Even those who experience suicidal ideation may not understand why or even if and when ideation might turn into action.

This observation is reinforced by Ralph Lewis, a psychiatrist at the University of Toronto, who works with cancer patients and others facing death, whom I interviewed for my Science Salon podcast about his book *Finding Purpose in a Godless World* (Prometheus Books, 2018). "A lot of people who are clinically depressed will think that the reason they're feeling that way is because of an existential crisis about the meaning of life or that it's because of such and such a relational event that happened," Lewis says. "But that's people's own subjective attribution when in fact they may be depressed for reasons they don't understand." In his clinical practice, for example, he notes, "I've seen many cases where these existential crises practically evaporated under the influence of an antidepressant."

This attributional error, Lewis says, is common: "At a basic level, we all misattribute the causes of our mental states, for example, attributing our irritability to something someone said, when in fact it's because we're hungry, tired." In consulting suicide attempt survivors, Lewis remarks, "They say, 'I don't know what came over me. I don't know what I was thinking.' This is why suicide prevention is so important: because people can be very persuasive in arguing why they believe life—their life—is not worth living. And yet the situation looks radically different months later, sometimes because of an antidepressant, sometimes because of a change in circumstances, sometimes just a mysterious change of mind."

If you have suicidal thoughts, call the National Suicide Prevention Lifeline at 800-273-8255 or phone a family member or friend. And wait it out, knowing that in time you will most likely experience one of these mysterious changes of mind and once again yearn for life. **Michael Shermer. Reproduced with permission. Copyright © 2018 Scientific American, a division of Nature America, Inc. All rights reserved.**

## What Role Does Biology Play?

About 7% of Americans battle depression in any given year (American Psychiatric Association, 2013; NIMH, 2019). What underlies this staggering statistic? There appears to be something biological at work.

**ARE GENES INVOLVED?**    Studies of twins, family pedigrees, and adoptions tell us that major depressive disorder runs in families, with heritability estimates between 37% and 50% (American Psychiatric Association, 2013; Levinson, 2006; Wray et al., 2012). This means that about 37–50% of the variability of major depressive disorder in the population can be attributed to genetic factors. The risk of having this disorder is 2 to 4 times higher if first-degree relatives are affected (American Psychiatric Association, 2013).

**DO HORMONES CONTRIBUTE?**    People with depressive disorders may have abnormal activity of cortisol, a hormone secreted by the adrenal glands (Belmaker & Agam, 2008; Dougherty et al., 2009; Herane-Vives et al., 2020). Women sufferers, in particular, appear to be affected by stress-induced brain activity and hormonal fluctuations (Holsen et al., 2011), particularly those associated with pregnancy and childbirth (Schiller et al., 2015). For both women and men, depressive symptoms may link to abnormal activity of the hypothalamic–pituitary–adrenal (HPA) system, which plays an important role in the stress response (American Psychiatric Association, 2013).

**WHAT'S GOING ON IN THE BRAIN?**    Abnormal activity of three neurotransmitters— norepinephrine, serotonin, and dopamine—may contribute to the development and progression of major depressive disorder. The relationships among these neurotransmitters are complicated, and researchers continue to explore their roles (El Mansari et al., 2010; Kambeitz & Howes, 2015; Torrente et al., 2012).

Depression also seems to be correlated with specific structural features in the brain (Andrus et al., 2012). One large analysis of brain-imaging studies suggests there are "significant differences in cortical brain structures" in both adolescents and adults with major depressive disorder (Schmaal et al., 2017). Another analysis indicates that people with this disorder (particularly those with "recurrent and early onset") experience a shrinking of the hippocampus (Schmaal et al., 2016, p. 811). Meanwhile, functional magnetic resonance imaging (fMRI) research points to disruptions in neural pathways involved in processing emotions and rewards (American Psychiatric Association, 2013).

Major depressive disorder most likely results from a complex interplay of many neural factors. What's difficult to determine is the causal direction: Do changes in the brain precede the disorder, or does the disorder lead to changes in the brain?

**Baby Blues**

Model and TV personality Chrissy Teigen feeds her baby in a New York City park. Teigen wrote an essay about her battle with postpartum depression, which was published in *Glamour*. "I'm speaking up now because I want people to know it can happen to anybody," Teigen wrote. "I don't want people who have it to feel embarrassed or to feel alone" (Teigen, 2017, para. 25). Approximately 3–6% of women experience depression starting in pregnancy or within weeks or months of giving birth (American Psychiatric Association, 2013).

 The Center for Epidemiologic Studies Depression Scale (CESD-R) is an inventory that has been used since the early 1970s. Go online to https://cesd-r.com/ and select "Start the CESD-R." If you or someone you know is struggling with depression, please call 800-273-TALK. Please call 911 if you are facing a medical emergency or suicidal crisis.

## Psychological Factors

Earlier, we mentioned that the heritability of depression is about 37–50%. What about the other 50–63% of the variability? Clearly, biology is not everything. Psychological factors also play a role in the onset and course of major depressive disorder.

**LEARNED HELPLESSNESS**    According to American psychologist Martin Seligman, people often become depressed because they believe they have no control over the consequences of their behaviors (Overmier & Seligman, 1967; Seligman, 1975; Seligman & Maier, 1967). To demonstrate this **learned helplessness,** Seligman restrained dogs in a hammock and then randomly administered **inescapable painful electric shocks** to their paws (**FIGURE 13.3**). The next day, the same dogs were put in another cage where they had the opportunity to escape the shocks, but they did not try. Seligman concluded the dogs had learned they couldn't control this painful situation; they were acting in a depressed manner. He translated this finding to people with major depressive disorder, suggesting that they, too, feel powerless to change things for the better, and therefore become passive and depressed.

**NEGATIVE THINKING**    American psychiatrist Aaron Beck suggests that depression is connected to negative thinking. Depression, according to Beck (1976), is the product of a "cognitive triad"—a negative view of experiences, self, and the future. Here's an example: A student receives a failing grade on an exam, so they begin to think they are a poor student, and that belief leads them to conclude they will fail the course. This self-defeating attitude may actually lead to them failing, reinforcing their belief that they are a poor student, and perhaps evolving into a broader belief that their life is a failure. People with this thinking style are thought to be at risk for developing a

 *Research* **CONNECTIONS**

In **Chapter 1,** we discussed the ethical treatment of living things in psychology research. Seligman's research on dogs probably would not meet the APA's current standards or be approved by an Institutional Review Board (IRB) today.

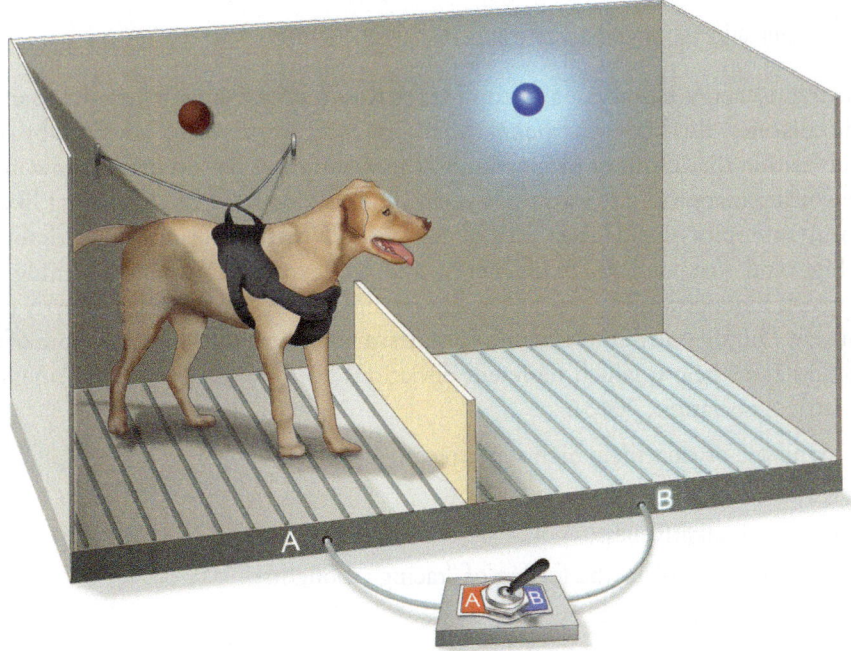

**FIGURE 13.3**
**Seligman's Research on Learned Helplessness**
Dogs restrained in a hammock were unable to escape painful shocks administered through an electrical grid on the floor of a specially designed cage called a shuttle box. The dogs soon learned that they were helpless and couldn't control these painful experiences. They did not try to escape by jumping over the barrier even when they were not restrained. The figure here shows the electrical grid activated on side B.

**learned helplessness** A tendency for people to believe they have no control over the consequences of their behaviors, resulting in passive behavior.

deep sense of hopelessness when they have negative experiences. This "hopelessness depression" can include symptoms such as sadness, suicidal behavior, self-blame, and a low sense of belonging (Fisher et al., 2015; Liu et al., 2015).

If you aren't convinced that beliefs contribute to depression, consider this: The way people respond to their experience of depression may impact the severity of the disorder. Those who repeatedly focus on this experience are much more likely to remain depressed and perhaps even descend into deeper depression (Eaton et al., 2012; Nolen-Hoeksema, 1991). Women tend to *ruminate* or constantly think about their negative emotions more than men, rather than actively trying to solve their problems (Eaton et al., 2012). We should also note that a correlation between rumination and depression is not the same as a cause-and-effect relationship. Not every negative thinker develops depression, and depression can lead to negative thoughts.

## Put Your Heads Together

Team up and **A)** consider the psychological roots of depression, such as learned helplessness and negative thinking; **B)** brainstorm some scenarios in which a person falls prey to the "cognitive triad" of negative thinking; and **C)** discuss how understanding this perspective might influence your interactions with someone who is depressed.

Now that we have explored the darkest, saddest realm of human emotion, it's time to venture to another extreme.

## Bipolar Disorders

**HIGHEST HIGHS, LOWEST LOWS**   When Ross began battling bipolar disorder, he went through periods of euphoria and excitement. Sometimes he would stay awake for 4 consecutive days, or sleep barely an hour per night for 2 weeks in a row—without feeling the least bit tired. In fact, he was exploding with energy, supercharged with confidence, and feeling high on life. Ideas flashed through his mind so fast that it was difficult to focus on any one of them. "My brain was a television," Ross says, "and someone was just constantly flipping channels." The only way he could ease his mind was by drinking—and we're not talking about a couple of beers or a few shots of vodka, but an entire case or a whole bottle. Ross was using alcohol to drown out his symptoms.

**LO 6**   Summarize the symptoms and causes of bipolar disorders.

The extreme energy, euphoria, and confidence Ross felt were most likely the result of **manic episodes,** also known as *mania.* Manic episodes are often characterized by continuous elation that is out of proportion to the situation. A person might show up to work wearing inappropriate, extravagant clothing, talking too fast, and acting like an authority on topics outside their area of expertise. Other features include irritability, very high and sustained levels of energy, and an "expansive" mood, meaning the person feels more powerful than they really are and behaves in a showy or overly confident way. During one of these manic episodes, a person exhibits three or more of the symptoms listed below, which represent deviations from normal behavior (American Psychiatric Association, 2013):

- grandiose or extremely high self-esteem;
- reduced sleep;
- increased talkativeness;
- a "flight of ideas" or the feeling of "racing" thoughts;
- being easily distracted;
- heightened activity at school or work;

**manic episode** A state of continuous elation that is out of proportion to the setting, and can include irritability, very high and sustained levels of energy, and an "expansive" mood.

- physical agitation; and
- displaying poor judgment and engaging in activities that could have serious consequences (risky sexual behavior or excessive shopping sprees, for example).

It is not unusual for a person experiencing a severe manic episode to be hospitalized. Mania is difficult to hide and can be dangerous. One may become violent or act out of character, doing things that damage important relationships or jeopardize work. Seeking help is unlikely, because mania leads to impaired judgment, feelings of grandiosity, and euphoria. (Why would you seek help if you feel on top of the world?) At these times, the support of others is essential.

There are various types of bipolar disorder. To be diagnosed with *bipolar I disorder*, a person must experience at least one *manic episode*, substantial distress, and great impairment. *Bipolar II disorder* requires at least one major depressive episode, as well as a *hypomanic episode. Hypomania* is associated with some of the same symptoms as a manic episode, but the manic behavior does not last as long and generally does not impair one's ability to function (American Psychiatric Association, 2013; TABLE **13.6**).

**BIPOLAR CYCLING**   Some people with bipolar disorder cycle between extreme highs and lows of emotion and energy that last for months, weeks, and in some cases, days. As mentioned earlier, bouts of mania are often characterized by unusually elevated, irritable, or expansive moods. At the other extreme are feelings of deep sadness, emptiness, and helplessness—the depression pole of bipolar disorder can be as severe as the major depressive episodes described earlier. Periods of mania and depression may be brought on by life changes and stressors, though some research suggests it is only the *first* episode that tends to be triggered by some sort of life event, such as the loss of a job. Subsequent episodes may not be as closely linked to such events (Belmaker, 2004; Malkoff-Schwartz et al., 1998; Weiss et al., 2015).

**WHAT CAUSES BIPOLAR DISORDER?**   Bipolar disorder is uncommon. Over the course of a lifetime, about 0.8% of the American population will receive a diagnosis of bipolar I disorder, and 1.1% bipolar II disorder (Merikangas et al., 2011). Men and women have an equal chance of being affected, but men tend to experience earlier onset of symptoms (Altshuler et al., 2010; Kennedy et al., 2005).

**TABLE 13.6**   Bipolar Disorders

| Bipolar Disorder | Description | Annual Prevalence |
|---|---|---|
| Bipolar I disorder | Episodes of mania that include an "abnormally, persistently elevated, expansive, or irritable mood and persistently increased activity or energy that is present for most of the day, nearly every day, for a period of at least 1 week" (p. 127). This may be preceded by hypomania or depression. | 0.6% |
| Bipolar II disorder | At least one major depressive episode (lasting at least 2 weeks) as well as a hypomanic episode (lasting a minimum of 4 days). | 0.8% |

Bipolar I disorder and bipolar II disorder have distinct patterns of highs and lows. Looking at the annual prevalence (yearly occurrence) of these disorders, you can see that they are relatively rare. Information from the *DSM–5* (American Psychiatric Association, 2013).

## FIGURE 13.4
### Bipolar in the Brain

This figure shows areas of the cortex that tend to show unusual thinning in people with bipolar disorder. The warmer hues (red, orange, and yellow) indicate where thinning is observed, while the gray areas are "nonsignificant." These and other anatomical differences may be related to the cognitive and behavioral symptoms associated with bipolar disorder (Hibar et al., 2018). Republished with permission of Nature Publishing Group, from Cortical abnormalities in bipolar disorder: an MRI analysis of 6503 individuals from the ENIGMA Bipolar Disorder Working Group. Hibar, D. P., Westlye, L. T., et al. *Molecular Psychiatry* volume 23, pages 932–942 (2018); permission conveyed through Copyright Clearance Center, Inc.

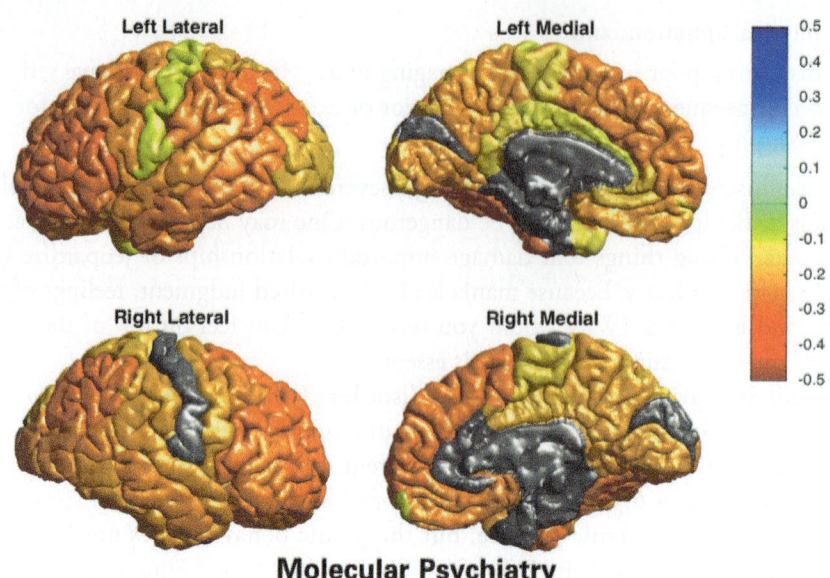

Molecular Psychiatry

Researchers have yet to determine the exact causes and biological correlates of bipolar disorder (**FIGURE 13.4**). However, evidence from twin and adoption studies underscores the importance of genes. One study pinpointed 30 different genetic factors associated with the disorder (Stahl et al., 2019). If one identical twin is diagnosed with bipolar disorder, there is a 40–70% chance that the other twin will have the disorder as well. Among fraternal twins, there is only a 5% chance that the second twin will develop the disorder (Craddock et al., 2005). The heritability estimates of bipolar disorder are high, falling somewhere between 79% and 90% (Hanford et al., 2016). According to the American Psychiatric Association (2013), "A family history of bipolar disorder is one of the strongest and most consistent risk factors for bipolar disorders" (p. 130). Adults who have a first-degree relative with bipolar disorder, on average, have a "10-fold increased risk" for developing the disorder themselves (p. 130).

But nature is not the only force at work in bipolar disorder; nurture plays a role, too. The fact that there is a higher rate of bipolar disorder in high-income countries (1.4%) than in low-income countries (0.7%; American Psychiatric Association, 2013) suggests that environment may act as a catalyst for its development. Additionally, some researchers hypothesize that exposure to viruses, poor nutrition, or stress (some of which occurs during fetal development) can spark a cascade of biological events that leads to the development of bipolar disorder. The same has been said of another serious disorder: schizophrenia (Carter, 2007; Richetto & Meyer, 2020; Yolken & Torrey, 1995).

 **SHOW WHAT YOU KNOW**

1. Li is sleeping too much, feeling tired all the time, and avoiding activities she once enjoyed. Which of the following best describes the disorder Li may be experiencing?

   **A.** obsessive-compulsive disorder

   **B.** major depressive disorder

   **C.** agoraphobia

   **D.** panic disorder

2. Many factors contribute to the etiology and course of major depressive disorder. Prepare notes for a 3-minute speech you might give on this topic.

3. Compare the symptoms of bipolar disorder with those of major depressive disorder.

4. Ross described going 4 days straight without sleeping at all, or 2 weeks in a row sleeping only 1 hour per night. He was exploding with energy, supercharged with confidence, and feeling on top of the world. It is likely that Ross was experiencing periods of euphoria and excitement, which can best be described as:

   **A.** depression.

   **B.** manic episodes.

   **C.** panic attacks.

   **D.** anxiety.

   ✓ CHECK YOUR ANSWERS AT THE BACK OF THE BOOK.

# Schizophrenia and Autism Spectrum Disorder (ASD)

## Schizophrenia: A Complex Disorder

How would it feel to see imaginary figures lurking in your peripheral vision, or to look in the mirror and see an image of your brain decomposing? What if you heard voices and ticking sounds throughout the day, and rarely felt happiness, sadness, or any type of emotion (RACHELSTARLIVE, 2018; Withers & Barnes, 2015)? These are actual symptoms reported by Rachel Star Withers, who has a disabling psychological disorder called **schizophrenia** (skit-suh-FREH-nee-uh). People with schizophrenia experience **psychosis,** a loss of contact with reality that is severe and chronic.

**LO 7** Recognize the symptoms of schizophrenia.

The hallmark features of schizophrenia are disturbances in thinking, perception, and language (**TABLE 13.7**). Psychotic symptoms include **delusions,** which are strange or false beliefs that a person maintains even when presented with evidence to the contrary. Common delusional themes are being persecuted by others, spied upon, or ridiculed. Some people have grandiose delusions; they may believe they are extraordinarily talented or famous, for example. Others are convinced that media reports, news headlines, or public announcements are about them. Delusions appear very real to those experiencing them.

People with schizophrenia may also hear voices or see things that are not actually present. This psychotic symptom is known as a **hallucination**—a "perception-like experience" that the individual believes is real but is not evident to others. Hallucinations can occur with any of the senses, but auditory hallucinations are most common. Often they manifest as voices commenting on what is happening in the environment, or voices using threatening or judgmental language (American Psychiatric Association, 2013).

The symptoms of schizophrenia are often classified as **positive and negative** (see Table 13.7). **Positive symptoms** are excesses or distortions of normal behavior, and include delusions, hallucinations, and disorganized speech—all of which are generally not observed in people without psychosis. In other words, positive symptoms indicate the *presence* of abnormal behaviors. **Negative symptoms,** on the other hand, refer to the reduction or *absence* of expected behaviors. Common negative symptoms

**Living with Schizophrenia**
Tens of thousands of YouTube viewers have watched the videos of Rachel Star Withers, a modeling and acting teacher who has schizophrenia. In her videos, Withers talks about her struggles with hallucinations, depersonalization (feeling detached from oneself), and other symptoms. "[Having schizophrenia] is not a bad thing," Withers tells *Women's Health*. "You're just different, and you have to learn how to manage that and accept it. The world wasn't made for people with mental disorders, but that doesn't mean you can't be in it and have a kickass life" (NPR, 2016; Withers & Barnes, 2015, para. 16).

Image1st/Courtesy Rachel Star Withers.

### CONNECTIONS

In **Chapter 5,** we noted that the term *positive* does not always mean "good." Positive punishment means the addition of an aversive stimulus. Positive symptoms refer to additions or excesses, not an evaluation of how "good" the symptoms are. *Negative* refers to the reduction or absence of behaviors, not an evaluation of how "bad" the symptoms are.

**TABLE 13.7　Symptoms of Schizophrenia**

| Positive Symptoms | Negative Symptoms |
|---|---|
| Delusions | Decreased emotional expression |
| Hallucinations | Lack of motivation |
| Disorganized speech | Decreased speech production |
| Grossly disorganized or catatonic behavior | Decreased functioning at work, in social situations, or in self-care |
| Abnormal motor behavior | Reduced pleasure<br>Lack of interest in interacting with others |

Schizophrenia symptoms can be grouped into two main categories: Positive symptoms are excesses or distortions of normal behavior; negative symptoms refer to a reduction in normal behaviors and mental processes. Information from the *DSM–5* (American Psychiatric Association, 2013).

**schizophrenia** A disabling psychological disorder that can include delusions, hallucinations, disorganized speech, and abnormal motor behavior.

**psychosis** Loss of contact with reality that is severe and chronic.

**delusions** Strange or false beliefs that a person firmly maintains even when presented with evidence to the contrary.

**hallucinations** Perception-like experiences that an individual believes are real, but that are not evident to others.

**positive symptoms** Excesses or distortions of normal behavior; examples are delusions, hallucinations, and disorganized speech.

**negative symptoms** Behaviors or characteristics that are limited or absent; examples are social withdrawal, diminished speech, limited or no emotions, and loss of energy and follow-up.

include social withdrawal, diminished speech or speech content, limited emotions, and loss of energy and follow-up (Fusar-Poli et al., 2015; Marder & Cannon, 2019; Tandon et al., 2009).

To be diagnosed with schizophrenia, a person must display symptoms for the majority of days in a 1-month period and experience significant dysfunction in work, school, relationships, or personal care for at least 6 months. (And it must be determined that these problems do not result from substance abuse or a serious medical condition.) Using the *DSM–5,* clinicians can rate the presence and severity of symptoms (hallucinations, delusions, disorganized speech, unusual psychomotor behaviors, and negative symptoms).

With estimates ranging from a 0.3–1% lifetime risk, schizophrenia is uncommon (American Psychiatric Association, 2013; Saha et al., 2005). Although men and women appear to face an equal risk (Abel et al., 2010; Saha et al., 2005), the onset of the disorder tends to occur earlier in men, by an average of 3–5 years (Mendrek & Mancini-Marïe, 2016). Males are typically diagnosed during their late teens or early twenties, whereas the peak age for women is the late twenties (American Psychiatric Association, 2013; Gogtay et al., 2011). In most cases, schizophrenia is a lifelong disorder that causes significant disability and a high risk of suicide. The prognosis is worse for earlier onset schizophrenia, but this may be related to the fact that men, who tend to develop symptoms earlier in life, are in poorer condition when first diagnosed (American Psychiatric Association, 2013). Schizophrenia disproportionately affects people of lower socioeconomic classes, but the **causal relationship** remains unclear (Tandon et al., 2008a, 2008b). Having the disorder makes it hard to hold down a job; up to 90% of those affected are unemployed (Evensen et al., 2016).

### CONNECTIONS

In **Chapter 1,** we discussed the direction of causality. If there is a correlation between X and Y, it is possible that X is causing Y, or that Y is causing X. In this case, we don't know if lower socioeconomic status increases the risk of developing schizophrenia, or if having schizophrenia leads to lower socioeconomic status.

## The Roots of Schizophrenia

**LO 8**   Analyze the biopsychosocial factors that contribute to schizophrenia.

Schizophrenia is a complex psychological disorder that results from an interaction of biological, psychological, and social factors, making it difficult to predict who will be affected. For many years, some experts focused the blame on environmental factors, such as unhealthy family dynamics and bad parenting. A common scapegoat was the "schizophrenogenic mother," whose poor parenting style was believed to cause the disorder in her child (Harrington, 2012). Thankfully, this belief has been shattered by our new understanding of the brain. Research on schizophrenia, particularly in the area of genetics, has made great leaps. A large body of evidence now confirms that schizophrenia runs in families (Ji et al., 2021; Schizophrenia Working Group of the Psychiatric Genomics Consortium, 2014). For a dramatic illustration of this phenomenon, we turn to the famous case of the Genain sisters.

### ...BELIEVE IT...OR NOT

FOUR SISTERS WITH SCHIZOPHRENIA

Nora, Iris, Myra, and Hester Genain were identical quadruplets born in 1930. Their mother went to great lengths to treat them equally, and in many ways the children were equals (Mirsky & Quinn, 1988). As babies, they cried in unison and teethed at the same times. As toddlers, they played with the same toys, wore the same dresses, and rode the same tricycles. The little girls were said to be so mentally in sync that they never argued (Quinn, 1963).

Mr. and Mrs. Genain kept the girls isolated. Spending most of their time at home, the quads cultivated few friendships. The Genains may have

**"EACH WOMAN EXPERIENCED THE DISORDER IN HER OWN WAY...."**

protected their daughters from the world outside, but they could not shield them from the trouble brewing inside their brains.

At age 22, one of the sisters, Nora, was hospitalized for a psychiatric disorder characterized by hallucinations, delusions, altered speech, and other symptoms. Within months, a second sister, Iris, was admitted to a psychiatric ward as well. She, too, had the symptoms of psychosis. Both Nora and Iris were diagnosed with schizophrenia, and it was only a matter of years before Myra and Hester were diagnosed as well (Mirsky & Quinn, 1988). As you can imagine, the case of the Genain quads has drawn the attention of many scientists. David Rosenthal and his colleagues at the National Institute of Mental Health studied the women when they were in their late twenties and again when they were 51. To protect the quads' identities, Rosenthal assigned them the pseudonyms Nora, Iris, Myra, and Hester, which spell out NIMH, the acronym for the National Institute of Mental Health. *Genain* is also an alias, meaning "dreadful gene" in Greek (Mirsky, 2019; Mirsky & Quinn, 1988).

Identical quads have nearly all the same genes, so the Genain case suggests that there is some heritable component to schizophrenia. Yet, each woman experienced the disorder in her own way, highlighting the importance of environmental factors, or nurture. Hester did not receive a diagnosis of schizophrenia until she was in her twenties, but she started to show signs of psychological impairment much earlier than her sisters and was never able to hold down a job or live alone. Myra, however, was employed for the majority of her life and has a family of her own (Mirsky et al., 2000; Mirsky & Quinn, 1988). She published a book about her life and, as of 2019, was still in contact with Allen F. Mirsky, one of the researchers who studied her family. Reflecting on this unique research experience, Mirsky writes the following: "For me, the contact with the Quadruplets has been the most meaningful and dynamic exposure to schizophrenia that I have had, and their story emphasizes how little we still know about the causes of the disorder" (Mirsky, 2019, p. 71).

**GENETIC FACTORS**   Overall, researchers agree that schizophrenia is "highly heritable," with genetic factors accounting for 60–80% of the population-wide risk for developing this disorder (Ji et al., 2021; Tandon et al., 2008a, 2008b). Much of the evidence derives from twin, family, and adoption studies (FIGURE **13.5**). If one

**The Quads**

Identical quadruplets (known under the fictitious surname Genain), each of whom developed symptoms of schizophrenia between the ages of 22 and 24. Schizophrenia is a highly heritable disorder that has been linked to 108 gene areas (Ji et al., 2021; Schizophrenia Working Group of the Psychiatric Genomics Consortium, 2014).

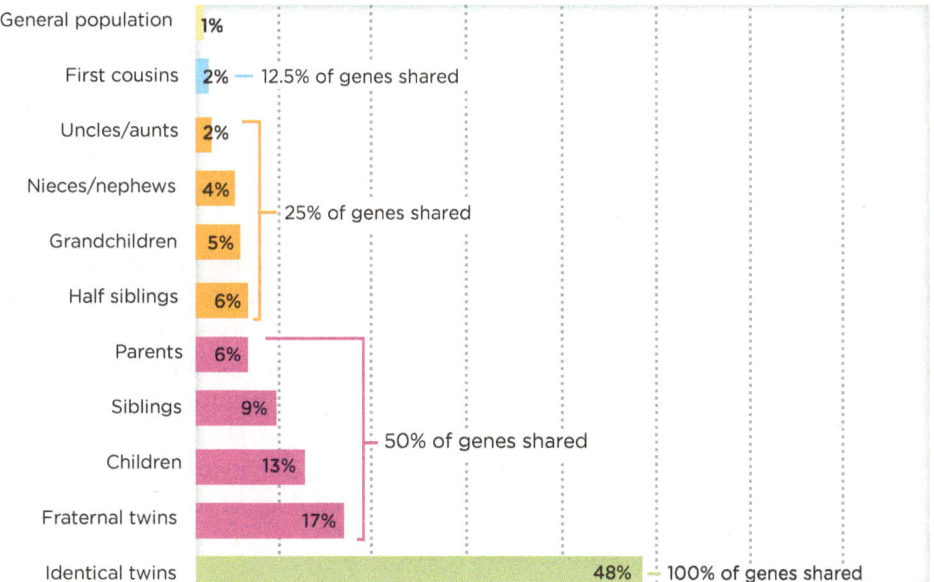

**Relationship to person with schizophrenia**

- General population — 1%
- First cousins — 2% — 12.5% of genes shared
- Uncles/aunts — 2% ⎱ 25% of genes shared
- Nieces/nephews — 4%
- Grandchildren — 5%
- Half siblings — 6%
- Parents — 6%
- Siblings — 9%
- Children — 13% } 50% of genes shared
- Fraternal twins — 17%
- Identical twins — 48% — 100% of genes shared

**Risk of developing schizophrenia**

**FIGURE 13.5**

**The Role of Genetics in Schizophrenia**

The average lifetime risk of developing schizophrenia for the general population is 1% or lower. However, for someone with a sibling diagnosed with schizophrenia, the lifetime risk increases to 9%. If that sibling is an identical twin, someone with nearly 100% of the same genes, the risk rockets to 48%. This suggests a significant role for genetic factors in the development of schizophrenia (Gottesman, 2001). More recent studies suggest multiple genes are involved (Domenici, 2017).

identical twin has schizophrenia, the risk of the other twin developing the disorder is approximately 41–65% (Petronis, 2004). Compare that to a mere 2% risk for those whose first cousins have schizophrenia (Tsuang et al., 2001). When one parent has the disorder, a person's risk of being diagnosed is 10–15% (Svrakic et al., 2013). If both parents have schizophrenia, the risk increases to 27% (Gottesman et al., 2010). Keep in mind that schizophrenia is not caused by a single gene, but by a combination of many genes interacting with the environment (Marder & Cannon, 2019; Ripke et al., 2014).

**DIATHESIS–STRESS MODEL**  Like other disorders, schizophrenia is best understood from the biopsychosocial perspective. One model that takes this perspective into account is the *diathesis–stress model,* where *diathesis* refers to the inherited disposition (to schizophrenia, for example), and *stress* refers to stressors and other factors in the environment (internal and external). Identical twins share 100% of their genetic make-up at conception (diathesis), yet the environment produces different stressors for the twins (only one of them loses a spouse, for example). This helps explain why one twin may develop the disorder, but the other does not. The diathesis–stress model suggests that developing schizophrenia involves a genetic predisposition *and* environmental triggers.

**THE BRAIN**  People with schizophrenia generally experience a thinning of the cortex, leading to enlarged ventricles, the cavities in the brain filled with cerebrospinal fluid. Research also shows that the total volume of the brain is reduced in schizophrenia (Haijma et al., 2013; Tandon et al., 2008a), and that the hippocampus, amygdala, and thalamus tend to be smaller (van Erp et al., 2016). Such abnormalities may relate to problems with cognitive functioning, psychotic symptoms, and sensory changes (Fusar-Poli et al., 2013; Glahn et al., 2008; Matheson et al., 2014). A word of caution when interpreting these findings: It is possible that differences in brain structures are not just due to schizophrenia, but may also result from long-term use of medications to control its symptoms (Chopra et al., 2021; Fusar-Poli et al., 2013).

## CONNECTIONS

In **Chapter 2,** we discussed activity at the synapse. Neurotransmitters released by the sending neuron must bind to receptor sites on the receiving neuron in order to relay their message ("fire" or "don't fire"). Medications that block or inhibit the receptor sites on the receiving neuron are referred to as antagonists, and some of these are used to reduce symptoms of schizophrenia.

**NEUROTRANSMITTER THEORIES**  Evidence suggests that abnormal neurotransmitter activity plays a role in schizophrenia. According to the **dopamine hypothesis,** the synthesis, release, and concentrations of dopamine are all elevated in people who have been diagnosed with schizophrenia and are suffering from psychosis (van Os & Kapur, 2009). Support for the dopamine hypothesis comes from the successful use of medications that **block the receptor sites** for this neurotransmitter. These drugs reduce the psychotic symptoms of schizophrenia, presumably because they decrease the potential impact of excess dopamine (van Os & Kapur, 2009). Researchers report that both positive and negative symptoms are associated with "dysfunction" in the dopamine system (Kirschner et al., 2017).

How do increased levels of dopamine impact the brain? Perhaps by influencing the "reward system." Excess dopamine may make it hard for a person to pay attention to what is rewarding in the environment, or identify which aspects are most salient, or important (van Os & Kapur, 2009). The dopamine hypothesis has evolved over the last several decades, with researchers exploring the interaction between neural activity and the environment (Edwards et al., 2016; Howes & Kapur, 2009). Emerging evidence suggests that irregular activity of the neurotransmitters glutamate and GABA may be involved in the etiology of schizophrenia, too (Marder & Cannon, 2019).

**dopamine hypothesis**  A theory suggesting that the synthesis, release, and concentrations of the neurotransmitter dopamine play a role in schizophrenia.

**ENVIRONMENTAL TRIGGERS AND SCHIZOPHRENIA** Complications during pregnancy, such as abnormal growth of the placenta, may increase the risk of developing schizophrenia later in life (Ursini et al., 2018). Some experts suspect that schizophrenia is associated with *in utero* exposure to a virus, such as human papilloma virus (HPV). Pregnant women are vulnerable to several illnesses, including genital and reproductive infections, influenza, and some parasitic diseases, that may increase their babies' risk of developing schizophrenia later in life (Brown & Patterson, 2011; Seidel, 2018). Retrospective evidence (that is, information collected much later) suggests that children of mothers who were exposed to viruses while pregnant are more likely to develop schizophrenia during adolescence. However, research exploring this theory is still ongoing and must be replicated.

Finally, sociocultural factors may play a minor role in the development and course of schizophrenia. Social stress, childhood adversity, and cannabis abuse have been associated with a slightly increased risk of schizophrenia onset, for example (Balter, 2017; Matheson et al., 2014; Tandon et al., 2008a, 2008b).

As you can see, schizophrenia is a highly complex disorder with a strong genetic component and many possible environmental causes. The same could be said of *autism spectrum disorder (ASD)*, a neurodevelopmental disorder that may share some genetic risk factors with schizophrenia and bipolar disorder (Guan et al., 2019).

## Autism Spectrum Disorder (ASD)

**LO 9**  Describe the symptoms and possible causes of autism.

Autism spectrum disorder (ASD) affects approximately 1 in 59 U.S. children (Baio et al., 2018). This disorder, which is four times more common in boys than girls, "is characterized by persistent deficits in social communication and social interaction across multiple contexts" and "restricted, repetitive patterns of behavior, interests, or activities" (American Psychiatric Association, 2013, p. 31). As the name implies, ASD refers to a vast spectrum of symptoms ranging from very mild to debilitating. With proper support, some people with ASD can communicate and function with few obvious deficiencies; others appear to be severely impaired and need a great deal of assistance carrying out daily activities. This disorder begins in childhood and typically persists into adulthood, though symptoms can improve with age, therapy, and support from others (National Institute of Neurological Disorders and Stroke, 2020).

The causes of ASD are **still under investigation**, but research demonstrates that at least 102 genes are linked to the disorder (Kosmicki et al., 2018). One large study estimated the heritability of ASD is about 50% (Sandin et al., 2014), the implication being that half of the population-wide variability in this disorder can be attributed to genes. If these findings are accurate, that leaves a lot of room for environment. Some research suggests that infections during pregnancy (those requiring hospitalization of the mother) may heighten a baby's risk for developing ASD by as much as 30% (Lee at al., 2015). Other studies offer evidence that diabetes

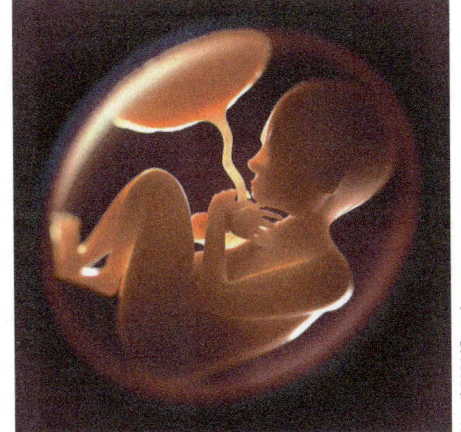

**The Role of the Placenta**
The placenta (seen in the upper left of this image) supplies the developing baby with nutrients and oxygen and disposes of waste, but problems with this organ may be involved in the etiology of schizophrenia. Research suggests that some of the genes associated with schizophrenia affect the biology of the placenta and the odds of developing pregnancy complications, which in turn can impact brain development (Ursini et al., 2018).

Henrik5000/Getty Images.

### CONNECTIONS

In **Chapter 1,** we discussed the publication of flawed research that purported a link between vaccinations and autism. Subsequent studies have found no credible support for the autism-vaccine hypothesis. Still, some parents refuse vaccines for their children, with serious consequences for the community. Here, we present the etiology of autism, suggesting that its causes include genetic and environmental factors.

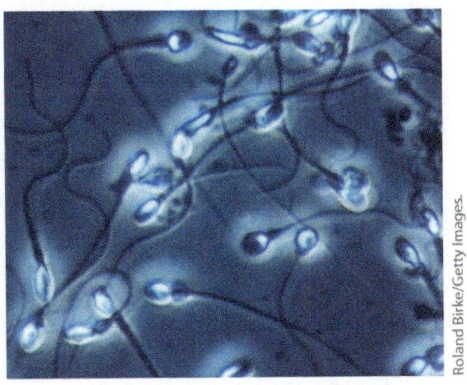

Roland Birke/Getty Images.

**Are Old Sperm Contributing?**
The etiology of autism spectrum disorder (ASD) likely involves many genetic and environmental variables. One risk factor appears to be the age of the father; as men get older, their developing sperm undergo more mutations. Some of these mutations may increase the likelihood of their children developing ASD (Bölte et al., 2019).

**CONNECTIONS**

In **Chapter 8,** we discussed epigenetic changes, or alterations to the chemical compounds surrounding DNA. Epigenetic changes can be triggered by environmental factors (exposure to toxins, for example) and may influence the expression of genes that contribute to the development of autism.

and elevated blood pressure in the pregnant mother are risk factors (Zeliadt, 2018). Still other research has focused on teratogens, or prenatal exposure to environmental toxins such as pesticides, lead, and air pollutants; however, these results are somewhat inconclusive (Arora et al., 2017; Havdahl et al., 2021). The etiology of this disorder remains a puzzle, but researchers emphasize the importance of both genes and environmental factors, and **epigenetic** changes that could mediate their interaction (Forsberg et al., 2018).

 **SHOW WHAT YOU KNOW**

1. What are some biopsychosocial factors that contribute to the development of schizophrenia?

2. A person with schizophrenia reports hearing voices saying they are ugly and worthless. This is an example of a:
   A. hallucination.
   B. delusion.
   C. negative symptom.
   D. diathesis.

3. Which may be a risk factor for autism spectrum disorder (ASD)?
   A. Poor parenting skills
   B. Childhood vaccinations
   C. Genetic and epigenetic factors
   D. Too much television

4. Loss of contact with reality is referred to as _____.

 CHECK YOUR ANSWERS AT THE BACK OF THE BOOK.

# Personality, Dissociative, and Eating Disorders

Before reading this chapter, you probably knew something about depression, bipolar disorder, and schizophrenia. But you may have been less familiar with a somewhat common group of disorders relating to personality, which can be very debilitating when it comes to work and interpersonal relationships. Across the world, approximately 8–13% of people have a *personality disorder* (Volkert et al., 2018; Winsper et al., 2020).

## Personality Disorders

People with **personality disorders** exhibit "an enduring pattern of inner experience and behavior that deviates markedly from the expectations of the individual's culture, is pervasive and inflexible, has an onset in adolescence or early adulthood, is stable over time, and leads to distress or impairment" (American Psychiatric Association, 2013, p. 645). Specifically, someone with a personality disorder behaves in a way that deviates substantially in the following areas: (1) cognition, including perceptions of self, others, and events; (2) emotional responses; (3) interpersonal functioning; and (4) impulse control. To be diagnosed with a personality disorder, one must struggle in at least two of these four categories. In addition, these problems must be resistant to change and have far-reaching consequences for interpersonal relationships.

Like personality traits in general, the core qualities of people with personality disorders (as well as the problems that result) are fairly stable over a lifetime and across situations. When diagnosing this type of disorder, the clinician must focus on troublesome personality traits—and be very careful not to confuse them with problems resulting from developmental changes, culture, drug use, or medical conditions.

The *DSM–5* includes 10 personality disorders (TABLE **13.8**). Here, we direct the spotlight onto two that have received considerable research attention: *antisocial personality disorder* and *borderline personality disorder.*

**personality disorders** A group of psychological disorders that can include impairments in cognition, emotional responses, interpersonal functioning, and impulse control.

**TABLE 13.8**  Personality Disorders

| Personality Disorder | Description |
| --- | --- |
| Paranoid | Widespread distrust of others without basis |
| Schizoid | Detachment from relationships and a limited range of emotional expression |
| Schizotypal | Difficulty in establishing relationships, limited ability to maintain close relationships, and eccentric or strange behavior |
| Antisocial | Unethical behavior, deceitfulness, impulsivity, irritability, aggressiveness, disregard for others, and lack of remorse |
| Borderline | Incomplete sense of self, extreme self-criticism, unstable emotions, and feelings of emptiness |
| Histrionic | Extreme emotions used to gain attention |
| Narcissistic | Self-absorbed, needs to be admired, lack of empathy |
| Avoidant | Social self-consciousness, hypersensitive to negative feedback |
| Dependent | Clingy, needs to be cared for by others |
| Obsessive-compulsive | Fixation with order, perfection, and control |

Listed here are the 10 personality disorders identified by the *DSM–5*. Information from the *DSM–5* (American Psychiatric Association, 2013).

**LO 10**  Differentiate between antisocial and borderline personality disorders.

**ANTISOCIAL PERSONALITY DISORDER**    Many shows and films, including *Mind Hunters* and *No Country for Old Men,* feature characters who behave in ways most people find incomprehensible. The qualities of these characters often parallel a diagnosis of **antisocial personality disorder.**

People with antisocial personality disorder may seek personal gratification even when it means violating ethical standards and breaking laws. They sometimes lie or con others, and exhibit aggressive, impulsive, or irritable behaviors. These individuals have difficulty feeling empathy, and may not show concern for others or feel remorse upon hurting them. Other common behavior patterns include carelessness in sexual relationships, and the use of intimidation to control others (American Psychiatric Association, 2013). Around 1–4% of U.S. adults are diagnosed with antisocial personality disorder, which is more common in men than women (Lenzenweger et al., 2007; Werner et al., 2015) and may be as high as 50% among prison inmates (Azevedo et al., 2020).

How does antisocial personality disorder develop? Heredity appears to play a role, as first-degree biological relatives of people with this disorder are more likely to be affected than those in the general population (American Psychiatric Association, 2013). There is some evidence for family risk factors, but it is unclear how much of this risk is transmitted through genes, and how much results from learning. Heritability estimates for antisocial personality disorder range from 38–69%, but environmental factors seem to play an important role. "Adverse childhood experiences" like sexual abuse have been associated with this diagnosis (Delisi et al., 2019). Like most mental health problems, antisocial personality disorder seems to result from a complex interaction of genes and environment (Ferguson, 2010; Werner et al., 2015).

Photo 12/Alamy.

**Antisocial Personality Disorder?**
Actor Adam Driver plays "Kylo Ren" in *Star Wars: The Force Awakens*. Both movie fans and psychologists have wondered what psychological disorder this fictitious character may be battling (Langley, 2016; Plata, 2017). Does Kylo Ren have antisocial personality disorder? He certainly manipulates, hurts, and uses people in order to gain power, going so far as to kill his own father. Yet (spoiler alert), he seems to display a "speck of empathy" when he decides to spare his mother in *The Last Jedi* (Plata, 2017, para. 8).

**antisocial personality disorder**  A psychological disorder distinguished by unethical behavior, deceitfulness, impulsivity, irritability, aggressiveness, disregard for others, and lack of remorse.

Is there anything unique about the brain of a person with antisocial personality disorder? Some studies point to irregularities in the frontal lobes. For example, reduced tissue volume in the prefrontal cortex (11% less than expected) is apparent in some men with antisocial personality disorder. This deficit might be linked to reduced morality, and problems with decision making, planning, and developing normal responses to fear and punishment, all potentially associated with antisocial behavior. The fact that the prefrontal cortex plays a role in controlling arousal may explain why people with this disorder tend to seek out stimulation, including aggressive and antisocial activities (Raine et al., 2000). That being said, not everyone with this diagnosis has frontal lobe abnormalities, and the development of this disorder likely involves biological, psychological, and social factors (Paris, 2014).

**BORDERLINE PERSONALITY DISORDER**    People with **borderline personality disorder** suffer from feelings of emptiness and an incomplete sense of self. According to the *DSM–5*, individuals with borderline personality disorder experience emotions that are unstable, intense, and inappropriate for the situation at hand. They may feel extreme anxiety and insecurity, concern about being rejected one moment, worry about being too dependent the next. Depressed moods are common, along with feelings of hopelessness, pessimism, and shame. Writing for the National Alliance on Mental Illness, Ashley Nestler offers an inside perspective: "Having BPD feels like my emotions are constantly amplified. Being sad feels like being suicidal, anger feels like I am burning from the inside out and fear sends my heart into a pounding fit" (Nestler, 2020, para. 3).

Behaviors associated with borderline personality disorder can be unpredictable. The person may act without thinking and frequently change plans. They may exhibit intense anger, have difficulty controlling their temper, and get into physical fights. When it comes to sexual activity, substance abuse, and spending money, impulses may prevail over rational thought. Recurrent suicide threats or attempts are not uncommon. Emotionally unstable and extremely needy, people with this disorder may struggle to develop intimacy, and their relationships tend to be unstable, tainted with feelings of mistrust and fear of abandonment. Those with borderline personality disorder may see the world in terms of black and white, rather than different shades of gray. This tendency to perceive extremes may lead a person to become overinvolved or totally withdrawn in relationships (American Psychiatric Association, 2013).

Seventy-five percent of people diagnosed with borderline personality disorder are female, and research suggests that some traits associated with this disorder have a genetic component (American Psychiatric Association, 2013; Gunderson et al., 2018). There is also evidence that childhood trauma sets the stage for the development of this condition. A biosocial developmental model has been proposed, indicating an early vulnerability that includes impulsive behavior and increased "emotional sensitivity." If the environment is right, this susceptibility can lead to problems with emotions, behaviors, and cognitive processes (Crowell et al., 2009). In addition to the potential contributions of childhood trauma and temperament, overprotective parenting may inhibit a developing child's ability to independently handle emotions (Sharp & Kim, 2015, p. 3).

People with personality disorders have traits that are relatively easy to characterize. This is *not* the case for those with dissociative disorders, whose personal identities may be very difficult to pin down.

## Dissociative Disorders

**LO 11**    Identify differences among dissociative disorders.

**Dissociative disorders** are disturbances in normal psychological functioning that can include problems with memory, identity, consciousness, emotion, perception,

**Mozart's Mystery**
Did the great composer suffer from a psychological disorder? Some scholars believe his mood swings were indicative of depression or bipolar disorder, while others speculate he had a personality disorder. Mozart's symptoms included "efforts to avoid real or imagined abandonment, impulsiveness, affective instability due to a marked reactivity of mood . . . a feeling of emptiness, and identity disturbance" (Huguelet & Perroud, 2005, p. 137). What disorder do these characteristics suggest? DEA/A. DAGLI ORTI/Getty Images.

**borderline personality disorder** A psychological disorder distinguished by an incomplete sense of self, extreme self-criticism, unstable emotions, and feelings of emptiness.

**dissociative disorders** Psychological disorders distinguished by disturbances in normal psychological functioning; may include problems with memory, identity, consciousness, perception, and motor control.

and motor control (American Psychiatric Association, 2013). The main feature of these disorders is **dissociation,** or a disturbance in the normally unified experience of psychological functions involved in memory, consciousness, perception, or identity (Spiegel et al., 2011; Vesuna et al., 2020). Dissociation may lead to difficulty recalling personal information (for example, where I live, who I am), or the feeling of being detached from one's body. Here, we focus our discussion on two dissociative disorders: *dissociative amnesia* and *dissociative identity disorder.*

**DISSOCIATIVE AMNESIA**   People with **dissociative amnesia** have difficulty remembering important personal information. In some cases, the amnesia is fixed around a certain event, often one that is traumatic or stressful. Other times, the amnesia spans a lifetime. Those affected typically report a great deal of distress or impairment in work, relationships, and other important areas of life, and put a lot of effort into managing the mundane details of daily existence (Staniloiu & Markowitsch, 2012). Some individuals with dissociative amnesia experience **dissociative fugue** (fyoog), that is, they wander in a confused and disorganized manner (Spiegel et al., 2011).

**DISSOCIATIVE IDENTITY DISORDER**   Dissociative fugue is also seen in people with **dissociative identity disorder,** once referred to as "multiple personality disorder." This rare condition is characterized by the presence of two or more distinct personalities within the same person (American Psychiatric Association, 2013), and it is considered the most complicated and persistent of the dissociative disorders (Sar, 2011). One of its key features is a lack of connection among behavior, awareness, memory, and cognition. There is often a reported gap in remembering day-to-day events and personal details. These symptoms are not related to substance use or medical issues, and they may cause distress in relationships, work, and other areas of life.

People with dissociative identity disorder have been misrepresented as violent and dangerous in some movies and TV shows, but the film *Frankie & Alice* makes a sincere effort to tell the story of a real person who has lived with this disorder. Set in 1970s Los Angeles, the movie draws upon the experiences of "Frankie Murdoch," a woman who worked as a go-go dancer in this era. Frankie, portrayed by Halle Berry, is dealing with two personalities on top of her own: a white supremacist named "Alice," and a timid little girl named "Genius." All three personalities—Frankie, Alice, and Genius—have distinct accents, mannerisms, and personal histories. Unaware that she is shifting between personalities, Frankie alienates friends and family with her contradictory behaviors; she forgets important events; and she struggles to function in society. Ultimately, Frankie finds a therapist and gains insight on her disorder. As Berry said in an interview, "Frankie manages to find her journey of recovery, to live her life and to eventually achieve a full life" (National Alliance on Mental Illness [NAMI] Film Discussion Guide, n.d., p. 13).

Dissociative identity disorder has been observed all over the world and in many cultures (Dorahy et al., 2014). But, when it comes to understanding dissociative states, clinicians must consider cross-cultural and religious differences. For example, some characteristics associated with dissociative identity disorder seem to present themselves in Brazilian spiritist mediums, and it is important to distinguish between a culturally accepted religious practice and disordered behavior (Delmonte et al., 2016; Moreira-Almeida et al., 2008).

**WHAT CAUSES DISSOCIATIVE DISORDERS?**   Historically, there has been controversy around the diagnosis of dissociative identity disorder in the United States. Some suggest that clinicians have been reinforcing the development of these dissociations. In other words, by suggesting the possibility of alternate personalities or

**Trance Dance**
A young man in São Paulo, Brazil, dances in a trance state during a religious ceremony. Behaviors observed in this type of context may resemble those of dissociative identity disorder, so it is important to differentiate between religious practices and disordered behaviors (de Oliveira Maraldi et al., 2021; Moreira-Almeida et al., 2008).

**dissociation** A disturbance in the normally integrated experience of psychological functions involved in memory, consciousness, perception, or identity.

**dissociative amnesia** A psychological disorder marked by difficulty remembering important personal information and life events.

**dissociative fugue** A condition in which a person with dissociative amnesia or dissociative identity disorder wanders about in a confused and unexpected manner.

**dissociative identity disorder** A psychological disorder that involves the occurrence of two or more distinct personalities within an individual.

using hypnosis to "recover" lost memories, the clinician "cues" the individual to believe an alternate personality is responsible for behaviors (Lynn et al., 2012). There is now general agreement that trauma plays a causal role in experiences of dissociation, as do factors like fantasy proneness, suggestibility, and neurological deficits (Dalenberg et al., 2014; Lynn et al., 2014). We should also note that these disorders are often linked to childhood abuse and neglect, war, and terrorism in regions throughout the world (American Psychiatric Association, 2013).

We've covered a lot of material in this chapter, and it's almost time to wrap things up. But first, let's explore one more category of abnormal behavior: eating disorders.

# Eating Disorders

**LO 12** Outline the characteristics of the major eating disorders.

Eating disorders are serious dysfunctions in eating behavior that can involve restricting food consumption, obsessing over weight or body shape, eating too much, and purging (American Psychiatric Association, 2013). These disorders usually begin in the early teens and typically affect girls, though boys make up a substantial proportion of cases (Raevuori et al., 2014).

**ANOREXIA NERVOSA**    One eating disorder that has received considerable media attention is **anorexia nervosa,** which is characterized by self-imposed restrictions on calories needed to maintain a healthy weight. These restrictions lead to extremely low body weight in relation to age, sex, development, and physical health. People with anorexia nervosa have an extreme fear of getting heavier, even though their body weight is very low. They often have a distorted sense of body weight and figure, and fail to recognize the severity of their condition (American Psychiatric Association, 2013). Some women stop getting their menstrual periods, a condition called *amenorrhea* (Mehler & Brown, 2015). Other severe symptoms may include brain damage, multi-organ failure, infertility, and thinning of the bones (Mehler & Brown, 2015; NIMH, n.d.-b). Anorexia has one of the highest death rates of all psychological disorders, second only to substance use disorder (Couzin-Frankel, 2020). Over half the deaths associated with anorexia result from medical complications (Mehler & Brown, 2015), and approximately 20% are suicides (Joy et al., 2016; Smink et al., 2012). Although anorexia nervosa is typically seen in women and adolescent girls, males can also be affected, particularly those involved in wrestling, running, dancing, and other activities where it is important to maintain a certain weight.

**BULIMIA NERVOSA**    Another eating disorder is **bulimia nervosa,** which involves recurrent episodes of binge eating, or consuming large amounts of food in short periods (more than most people would eat in the same time frame). While bingeing, the person feels a lack of control and thus engages in purging behaviors to prevent weight gain—for example, self-induced vomiting, misuse of laxatives, fasting, or excessive exercise (American Psychiatric Association, 2013). Like anorexia, bulimia more often affects women and girls, but it can also impact males (Peschel et al., 2016). Bulimia carries serious health risks, such as high blood pressure, heart disease, and type 2 diabetes (Haedt-Matt & Keel, 2011). Other consequences include decaying teeth, damage to the throat, gastrointestinal disorders, and electrolyte imbalance, which can lead to a heart attack (Joy et al., 2016; NIMH, n.d.-b). Research indicates that 23% of deaths associated with bulimia nervosa result from suicide (Joy et al., 2016; Smink et al., 2012).

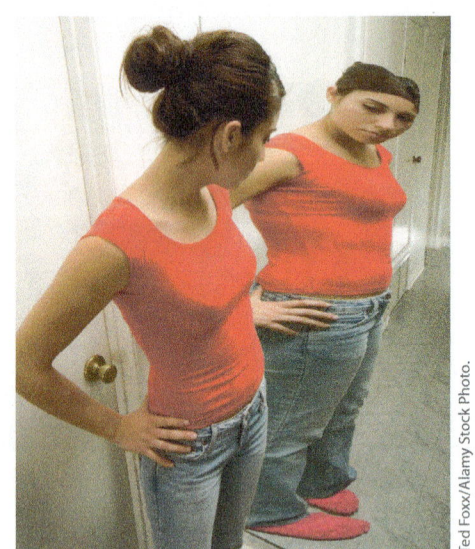

*Ted Foxx/Alamy Stock Photo.*

**Distorted Perceptions**
People with anorexia nervosa may look in the mirror and behold a version of themselves that others never see. Altered perceptions of body size and shape are common features of this disorder (American Psychiatric Association, 2013).

**anorexia nervosa** An eating disorder identified by significant weight loss, an intense fear of being overweight, a false sense of body image, and a refusal to eat the proper amount of calories to achieve a healthy weight.

**bulimia nervosa** An eating disorder characterized by extreme overeating followed by purging, with serious health risks.

**binge-eating disorder** An eating disorder characterized by episodes of extreme overeating, during which a larger amount of food is consumed than most people would eat in a similar amount of time under similar circumstances.

**BINGE-EATING DISORDER** Less commonly known, **binge-eating disorder** is characterized by episodes of excessive food consumption—eating more than most people would in the same amount of time and under similar circumstances (American Psychiatric Association, 2013). As in bulimia, one feels unable to control the bingeing, but the excessive weight control and purging behaviors are not present. Psychological effects may include embarrassment about the quantity of food consumed, depression, and guilt after overeating.

We know that eating disorders occur in the United States—we see evidence of them on television, in magazines, and in everyday life. But are these disorders also observed in India, South Africa, Egypt, and other parts of the world?

## ACROSS THE WORLD

### A CROSS-CULTURAL LOOK AT EATING DISORDERS

 Eating disorders like anorexia and bulimia are most commonly diagnosed and treated in Western societies such as the United States (Kolar et al., 2016; Mayhew et al., 2018). Psychologists once believed these disorders were mainly seen in "wealthy, white, educated, young women in industrialized Western nations" (Pike & Dunne, 2015, p. 1). But evidence suggests that men and women of all backgrounds living in countries around the world, from China to Fiji to Pakistan, are impacted (Agüera et al., 2017; Gerbasi et al., 2014; Pike & Dunne, 2015).

In recent decades, eating disorders have become increasingly common in non-Western countries. This trend often coincides with industrialization, urbanization, and "media-exposure promoting the Western beauty-ideal" (Smink et al., 2012, p. 412). For women, this Western beauty ideal implies thinness; for men, a muscular physique (Pike & Dunne, 2015). As researchers studying teens in Arab countries explain, "The Western standard of beauty has contributed to the preoccupation with thinness and body image dissatisfaction" (Musaiger et al., 2013, p. 165). This influence may be important, but researchers caution against viewing eating disorders as an "export of Western culture" (Pike & Dunne, 2015, p. 11). These disorders generally result from an interaction between many genetic, psychological, and environmental factors (Bulik et al., 2016; Mayhew et al., 2018).

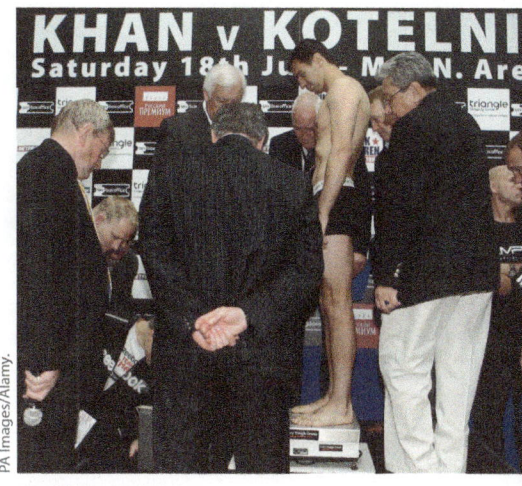

PA Images/Alamy.

**Making Weight**
A boxer "weighs in" before a match. For some athletes, pressure to maintain a certain body weight may set the stage for the development of eating disorders. Although eating disorders are often associated with "affluent, middle class, young Caucasian females," a substantial proportion of those affected are male. In fact, eating disorders "have been reported in male patients for as long as they have been reported in females" (Murray et al., 2017, p. 1).

### Put Your Heads Together

 This chapter has provided an overview of many psychological disorders. In your group, read the case study below and discuss **A)** what disorder is being described, **B)** the most surprising things you learned about abnormal behaviors and psychological disorders, and **C)** how your perspective on mental illness has changed as a result of taking this class.

A college sophomore reports going several days with little to no sleep, yet she seems to have a *lot* of energy. Often irritable and easily distracted, she has trouble getting to class and eventually stops going.

## ➤➤➤ SHOW WHAT YOU KNOW

1. Individuals with _____ are likely to anger easily, feel a sense of emptiness, and maintain intense but unstable relationships.

2. Distress and dysfunction are two identifiers of abnormal behavior. How might these criteria manifest themselves in a person with borderline personality disorder?

3. _____ is characterized by two or more distinct personalities within an individual, and a lack of connection among behavior, awareness, memory, and cognition.

4. Bulimia nervosa is an eating disorder characterized by:
   A. restrictions of energy intake.
   B. extreme fear of gaining weight, although one's body weight is extremely low.
   C. a distorted sense of body weight and figure.
   D. extreme overeating followed by purging.

 ✓ CHECK YOUR ANSWERS IN APPENDIX C.

**Making a Difference**

Ross celebrates graduation day at a center for people with disabilities in Botswana, Africa, where he served in the Peace Corps. After completing his work with the Peace Corps, Ross returned to the United States and founded a consulting group that designs mental health curricula. For more information on Ross' Human Power Project, visit http://humanpowerproject.com.

**Voice of Inspiration**

As a presenter for the mental health organization Minding Your Mind, Melissa traveled across the country, educating students about mental health issues. She has also published *The People You Meet in Real Life* (Hopely, 2014), which provides first-person accounts of resilient individuals facing a variety of trials and tribulations. The book addresses issues related to mental health, bullying, suicide, cancer, and HIV, sending a message of hope and inspiration. It is available through Amazon and Barnes & Noble websites; proceeds support a youth suicide prevention scholarship.

**DEFYING STIGMA: ROSS AND MELISSA LEARN TO THRIVE**   It took years of hard work for Ross to get on top of his bipolar disorder. He quit using alcohol, caffeine, nicotine, and marijuana, and imposed a new structure on his life—waking up and going to sleep at the same time each day, eating regular meals, and exercising. He also started being open and honest in relationships with friends, family, and his therapist. Most important, he confronted his self-hatred, working hard to identify and appreciate things he liked about himself. "What was missing was me being an active member in my treatment," Ross says, "and doing things outside of treatment [to get better]." After graduating cum laude from American University, Ross became a mental health advocate, giving presentations at high schools and colleges across the United States. Today, he is busy running his own consulting group, Human Power Project, which designs cutting-edge mental health curricula for middle and high schools. His battle with bipolar disorder is ongoing ("I'm not cured," says Ross), but he continues learning better ways to cope.

Shortly after leaving the hospital, Melissa found a therapist who introduced her to cognitive behavioral therapy (CBT), an approach you can learn about in Chapter 14. "He taught me how to live with OCD," says Melissa. "He basically saved my life." Like Ross, Melissa discovered she had a gift for public speaking. She started a mental health awareness group on her college campus, opening a chapter

of the national organization Active Minds, and later became a speaker for Minding Your Mind, an organization devoted to educating school communities and families about mental health issues. Melissa is now married and busy caring for her two young children, but she manages to squeeze in public speaking engagements from time to time. Her OCD is still present, but it's under control. Instead of walking through a doorway 20 times, she passes through it twice. And the time she once spent sitting alone in her room meticulously touching objects in sets of 2s, she now spends loving and nurturing her two children, Hope and Parker.

# Summary of Concepts

**LO 1**   Define psychological disorders and outline the criteria used to identify abnormal behavior. (p. 485)

A psychological disorder is a set of behavioral, emotional, and cognitive symptoms that are significantly distressing in terms of social functioning, work endeavors, and other aspects of life. Human behaviors and feelings fall along a continuum. Those at the ends are generally viewed as abnormal, and those in the middle are more normal. Mental health professionals identify abnormal behavior using the criteria of typicality and the 3 Ds: dysfunction, distress, and deviance. Conceptions of normal and abnormal are partly determined by culture.

**LO 2**   Summarize the etiology of psychological disorders. (p. 493)

The biopsychosocial perspective provides a model for explaining the causes of psychological disorders, which are complicated and often result from interactions among biological, psychological, and sociocultural factors. Examples of these factors include neurochemical imbalances and genetic predispositions (biological); cognitive activities, personality, and childhood experiences (psychological); and poverty and community support systems (sociocultural).

### LO 3 Define anxiety disorders and identify their causes. (p. 496)

Anxiety disorders are a group of psychological disorders associated with extreme anxiety and/or irrational and debilitating fears. People with panic disorder worry about losing control and having unexpected panic attacks; those with specific phobias fear certain objects or situations; and individuals with agoraphobia are afraid of public transportation, open spaces, retail stores, crowds, or being alone and away from home in general. Social anxiety disorder (social phobia) is characterized by extreme fear of social situations and scrutiny by others. With generalized anxiety disorder, worries and fears are more widespread, often relating to family, health, school, and other aspects of daily life. Anxiety disorders can develop as a result of environmental factors and genetic predisposition, and are more prevalent in women. They can be culture specific and shaped by learning processes.

### LO 4 Summarize the symptoms and causes of obsessive-compulsive disorder. (p. 499)

Obsessive-compulsive disorder (OCD) is characterized by obsessions and/or compulsions that are very time-consuming (taking more than 1 hour a day) and cause a great deal of distress and disruptions in daily life. An obsession is a thought, urge, or image that occurs repeatedly, is intrusive and unwelcome, and often causes feelings of intense anxiety and distress. Compulsions are behaviors or "mental acts" that a person repeats over and over in an attempt to neutralize obsessions. Sociocultural factors, learning, and biological causes are all involved in the course and maintenance of OCD.

### LO 5 Summarize the symptoms and causes of major depressive disorder. (p. 502)

Symptoms of major depressive disorder include feelings of sadness or hopelessness, reduced pleasure, sleeping excessively or not enough, loss of energy, feelings of worthlessness, or difficulties thinking and concentrating. Symptoms are severe and accompanied by impairment in the ability to perform expected roles. Biological theories suggest the disorder results from a genetic predisposition and irregular activity of neurotransmitters and hormones. Psychological theories focus on feelings of learned helplessness and negative thinking.

### LO 6 Summarize the symptoms and causes of bipolar disorders. (p. 508)

A diagnosis of bipolar I disorder requires that a person experience at least one manic episode, substantial distress, and great impairment. Bipolar II disorder involves at least one major depressive episode as well as a hypomanic episode, which is associated with some of the same symptoms as a manic episode, but is not as severe and does not impair functioning. People with bipolar disorder cycle between extreme highs and lows of emotion and energy that last for months, weeks, and in some cases, days.

### LO 7 Recognize the symptoms of schizophrenia. (p. 511)

Schizophrenia is a disabling disorder that can involve delusions, hallucinations, abnormal psychomotor behavior, limited emotions, loss of energy, and disorganized or diminished speech. Delusions are strange and false beliefs that a person maintains even when presented with contradictory evidence. Hallucinations are "perception-like experiences" that the individual believes are real but are not evident to others.

### LO 8 Analyze the biopsychosocial factors that contribute to schizophrenia. (p. 512)

Schizophrenia is a complex psychological disorder that results from biological, psychological, and social factors. Because this disorder stems from an interaction of genes and environment, researchers have a hard time predicting who will be affected. The diathesis–stress model takes these factors into account, with diathesis referring to an inherited disposition, and stress referring to stressors in the environment (internal and external). Genes, neurotransmitter activity, differences in the brain, and *in utero* exposure to viruses are all factors that may contribute to the development of schizophrenia.

### LO 9 Describe the symptoms and possible causes of autism. (p. 515)

Autism spectrum disorder (ASD) refers to a vast spectrum of symptoms ranging from mild to debilitating. This disorder, which begins in childhood and typically persists into adulthood, is characterized by repetitive actions, problems with communication and social skills, and other symptoms. The causes of ASD are still being researched, but evidence suggests there is a genetic component. Environmental factors, such as infections, diabetes, and elevated blood pressure in the pregnant mother, may also play a role.

### LO 10 Differentiate between antisocial and borderline personality disorders. (p. 517)

People with antisocial personality disorder may seek personal gratification even when it means violating ethics and breaking laws. They sometimes deceive people, and exhibit aggressive, impulsive, or irritable behavior. These individuals lack empathy, and may not show concern for others or feel remorse upon hurting them. Borderline personality disorder is distinguished by an incomplete sense of self and feelings of emptiness. Those affected may exhibit intense anger, have difficulty controlling their temper, and get into physical fights. They can be impulsive, especially where sexual activity, substance abuse, and spending money are concerned. Suicide threats and attempts may occur repeatedly. Both of these personality disorders may result in issues with intimacy and trust.

**LO 11** Identify differences among dissociative disorders. (p. 518)

People suffering from dissociative amnesia seem unable to remember important information about their lives. Dissociative identity disorder, the most complicated and persistent of the dissociative disorders, occurs when an individual experiences two or more distinct personalities. People with either of these disorders may experience dissociative fugue; that is, they wander in a confused and disorganized manner. The commonality in this group of disorders is dissociation, or a disturbance in the normally unified experience of psychological functions involved in memory, consciousness, perception, or identity.

**LO 12** Outline the characteristics of the major eating disorders. (p. 520)

Anorexia nervosa is a serious, life-threatening eating disorder characterized by a significantly low body weight in relation to age, sex, development, and physical health; an extreme fear of gaining weight; an altered and distorted sense of body weight and figure; and self-imposed restrictions on calories needed to maintain a healthy weight. Bulimia nervosa is characterized by recurrent episodes of binge eating followed by purging (self-induced vomiting, misuse of laxatives, fasting, or excessive exercise). Binge-eating disorder is characterized by episodes of eating very large amounts of food (more than most people would eat in a similar amount of time under similar circumstances).

## Key Terms

abnormal behavior, p. 485
agoraphobia, p. 498
anorexia nervosa, p. 520
antisocial personality disorder, p. 517
anxiety disorders, p. 496
binge-eating disorder, p. 521
bipolar disorder, p. 485
borderline personality disorder, p. 518
bulimia nervosa, p. 520

comorbidity, p. 493
compulsion, p. 499
delusions, p. 511
dissociation, p. 519
dissociative amnesia, p. 519
dissociative disorders, p. 518
dissociative fugue, p. 519
dissociative identity disorder, p. 519
dopamine hypothesis, p. 514
generalized anxiety disorder, p. 498

hallucination, p. 511
insanity, p. 488
learned helplessness, p. 507
major depressive disorder, p. 503
manic episodes, p. 508
medical model, p. 493
negative symptoms, p. 511
obsession, p. 499
obsessive-compulsive disorder (OCD), p. 499
panic attack, p. 497

panic disorder, p. 497
personality disorders, p. 516
positive symptoms, p. 511
posttraumatic stress disorder (PTSD), p. 501
psychological disorder, p. 485
psychosis, p. 511
schizophrenia, p. 511
specific phobia, p. 497
stigma, p. 488

## Test Prep Are You Ready?

1. A researcher studying psychological disorders from a biological standpoint, focusing on genes, neurochemical imbalances, and problems in the brain, is using an approach known as:
   A. comorbidity.
   B. the medical model.
   C. the diathesis–stress model.
   D. heritability.

2. Melissa experienced recurrent, all-consuming thoughts of disaster and death. These _____ were accompanied by her _____, repetitive behaviors like locking her car or entering a room an even number of times.
   A. obsessions; compulsions
   B. compulsions; obsessions
   C. compulsions; contamination
   D. negative reinforcers; obsessions

3. To help explain the causes of psychological disorders, researchers often use the _____ perspective, which examines the complex interaction of biological, psychological, and sociocultural factors.
   A. medical model
   B. biopsychosocial
   C. etiological
   D. learning

4. An individual is extremely anxious when they are unaccompanied in public. They no longer use public transportation, refuse to go to the mall, and do not like being away from home. Perhaps they should get evaluated for which of the following diagnoses?
   A. panic disorder
   B. agoraphobia
   C. social anxiety disorder
   D. specific phobia

5. A neighbor describes a newspaper article about someone in their twenties known to lie and con others, act aggressive and impulsive, and show little empathy or remorse. These are long-standing traits, so it is possible that the person has:
   A. borderline personality disorder.
   B. antisocial personality disorder.
   C. dissociative identity disorder.
   D. dissociative amnesia.

6. Rhonda routinely eats large amounts of food that most people could not eat in similar situations or in a similar amount of time. She often feels unable to control her eating and frequently eats alone because she is embarrassed by how much she eats. It is likely that Rhonda has a diagnosis of:

   **A.** anorexia nervosa.

   **B.** bulimia nervosa.

   **C.** amenorrhea.

   **D.** binge-eating disorder.

7. A symptom shared by both major depressive disorder and bipolar disorder is:

   **A.** hypomania.

   **B.** manic episodes.

   **C.** problems associated with sleep.

   **D.** extremely high self-esteem.

8. An individual with schizophrenia has hallucinations and delusions, and seems to be out of touch with reality. A psychologist explains that the client is experiencing:

   **A.** mania.

   **B.** psychosis.

   **C.** dissociative identity disorder.

   **D.** hypomania.

9. Someone in your neighborhood develops a reputation for being emotionally unstable, intense, and extremely needy. They also don't seem to have a sense of themselves and complain of feeling empty. They struggle with intimacy, and their relationships are unstable. If these are long-standing traits, which of the following might they be evaluated for?

   **A.** borderline personality disorder

   **B.** antisocial personality disorder

   **C.** bipolar II disorder

   **D.** major depressive disorder

10. Dissociative identity disorder involves two or more distinct _____ within an individual.

   **A.** hypomanic episodes    **C.** panic disorders

   **B.** personalities    **D.** psychotic episodes

11. Describe the 3 Ds, and give an example of how each may apply to a psychological disorder.

12. What is wrong with the following statement? "My friend is anorexic."

13. How can classical conditioning be used to explain the development of panic disorder?

14. How does negative thinking lead to depression?

15. Briefly summarize the theories of schizophrenia's etiology.

✓ CHECK YOUR ANSWERS AT THE BACK OF THE BOOK.

# 14

BSIP/Getty Images.

# Treatment of Psychological Disorders

## An Introduction to Treatment

**VOICES**  It's a beautiful evening on the Rosebud Indian Reservation in south-central South Dakota. Oceans of prairie grass roll in the wind. The scene could not be more tranquil. But for Chepa, a young Lakota woman living in this Northern Plains sanctuary, life has been anything but tranquil. For days, Chepa has been tormented by the voice of a deceased uncle. Hearing voices is nothing unusual in the Lakota spiritual tradition; ancestors visit the living often. But in the case of this young woman, the voice is telling her to kill herself. Chepa has tried to make peace with her uncle's spirit using prayer, pipe ceremony, and other forms of traditional medicine, but he will not be appeased. Increasingly paranoid and withdrawn, Chepa is making her relatives uneasy, so they take her to the home of a trusted neighbor, Dr. Dan Foster. A sun

Robert VAN DER HILST/Gamma-Rapho via Getty Images.

**Breathtaking**
The Rosebud Indian Reservation is a vast and beautiful land, but its residents struggle with economic hardship. The poverty rate for American Indians and Alaska Natives is 26.2%, exceeding that of any other racial group in the United States (U.S. Census Bureau, 2017). Poverty-related stressors can interfere with work, strain personal relationships, and possibly trigger the symptoms of psychological disorders.

dancer and pipe carrier, Dr. Foster is a respected member of the community. He also happens to be the reservation's lead clinical psychologist.

Upon meeting with Chepa and her family, Dr. Foster realizes that she is having *hallucinations*, **perception-like experiences** she thinks are real, but that are not evident to anyone else. Chepa is also experiencing *delusions*, strange or false beliefs that a person firmly maintains even when presented with evidence to the contrary. And because she is vulnerable to acting on these hallucinations and delusions, she poses a risk to herself and possibly others. Chepa needs to go to the hospital, and it is Dr. Foster's responsibility to make sure she gets there. "I'm going to make an intervention," Dr. Foster says, "and I'm going to have to do it in a way that's respectful to that person and to the culture, but still respectful to the body of literature and training that I come from as a psychologist."

An ambulance arrives and transports Chepa to the emergency room, where she finds Dr. Foster waiting. He is there to make a diagnosis and develop a treatment plan, but also to provide her with a sense of security, and to do so in the context of a nurturing relationship. "First of all my concern is safety, and secondly my concern is that you realize I am concerned about you," Dr. Foster says. "Whatever it is that we're facing, we are going to make it so that it comes out better than it is right now."

Dr. Foster's observations and assessments point to a rare and complex psychological disorder known as schizophrenia. Because Chepa poses an imminent risk to herself, Dr. Foster and his colleagues arrange a transfer to a psychiatric hospital, where she may stay for several days. The medical staff will stabilize her with a drug to help reduce her symptoms, the first of many doses likely to be administered in years to come. When Chepa returns to the reservation, Dr. Foster and his colleagues will offer her treatment designed with her specific needs in mind.*

As we learn more about Dr. Foster's work on the Rosebud Reservation, be mindful that therapists have clients with a broad spectrum of psychological issues. Dr. Foster tends to work with people in severe distress, often related to the conditions of extreme poverty that exist on Northern Plains Indian reservations. Some of his clients do not seek therapy, but end up in his care only because friends and relatives intervene. There are also therapists who spend much of their time helping people with issues such as self-esteem, chronic illness, relationship problems, career challenges, or major life changes like immigration and divorce. Therapy is not just for those with psychological disorders, but for anyone wishing to live a more fulfilling existence.

*The story of Chepa, a Lakota woman with schizophrenia, is hypothetical, but it is based on actual scenarios Dr. Foster has encountered. *Note:* Quotations attributed to Dr. Dan Foster and Dr. Nneka Jones Tapia are personal communications.

**CONNECTIONS**

In **Chapter 3,** we described sensation as the detection of stimuli by sensory organs. Perception is the process through which sensory data are organized, interpreted, and transformed into something meaningful. With hallucinations, the first step does not occur (no apparent physical stimuli).

Macmillan Learning.

**The Sun Dancer**
Dr. Dan Foster is the lead clinical psychologist on the Rosebud Reservation. He frequently works with clients suffering from severe emotional trauma, but he maintains a positive outlook. "I feel like the crucible of poverty and pain also is the crucible for transformation," says Dr. Foster, who is a respected member of the Lakota community he serves.

**CONNECTIONS**

In **Chapter 13,** we discussed the etiology of psychological disorders. The medical model assumes that disorders have biological causes. The biopsychosocial perspective suggests disorders result from an interaction of biological, psychological, and sociocultural factors.

Historic Images/Alamy Stock Photo.

**The Reformer**

U.S. schoolteacher Dorothea Dix led the nation's "mental hygiene movement," an effort to improve the treatment of people living in institutions. Her advocacy began in the mid-1800s, when people with psychological disorders were sometimes chained, beaten, and "housed in darkness without heat or sanitation" (Strickler & Farmer, 2019, p. 50).

**CONNECTIONS**

In **Chapter 13,** we noted that most mental health professionals in the United States use the *DSM–5.* The *DSM–5* is a classification system designed to help clinicians form accurate and consistent diagnoses based on the observation of symptoms. This manual does not include information on treatment.

**deinstitutionalization** The mass movement of patients with psychological disorders out of institutions, and the attempt to reintegrate them into the community.

# A Primitive Past

**LO 1**   Outline the history of treatment for psychological disorders.

Over the course of history, people have used various **models** to explain abnormal behavior and psychological disorders. As our understanding of disorders has changed, so have methods of treatment. Many early attempts to cure mental illness were inhumane and unproven. According to one theory, Stone Age people believed psychological disorders were caused by possession with demons and evil spirits. They may have practiced *trephination,* or drilling holes in the skull, perhaps to create exit routes for evil spirits (Maher & Maher, 2003; Staudt et al., 2019). Trephination was used beyond the Stone Age, and some have speculated this "earliest known" surgical procedure was intended to treat "madness, idiocy, moral degeneration, headache, [and used for] the removal of foreign bodies, and the release of pressures, airs, vapours, and humours" (Wickens, 2015, p. 8).

**ASYLUMS OR PRISONS?**   A major shift came in the 16th century. Religious groups began creating *asylums,* special places to house and treat people with psychological disorders. However, these asylums were overcrowded and resembled prisons, with inmates chained in dungeonlike cells, starved, and subjected to sweltering heat and frigid cold. During the French Revolution, physician Philippe Pinel (1745–1826) began working in Paris asylums. Horrified by the conditions he observed, Pinel removed the inmates' chains and insisted they be treated more humanely (Frances, 2016; Maher & Maher, 2003). The idea of using "moral treatment," or respect and kindness instead of harsh methods, spread throughout Europe and the United States (Frances, 2016; Routh & Reisman, 2003). In the mid- to late 1800s, a U.S. schoolteacher named Dorothea Dix (1802–1887) vigorously championed the "mental hygiene movement," a campaign to reform asylums in the United States. Appalled by what she witnessed in prisons and institutions housing the poor, including the caging of naked inmates, Dix helped establish and upgrade dozens of state mental hospitals (Strickler & Farmer, 2019; Whitaker, 2015). Despite the good intentions of reformers like Pinel and Dix, many institutions eventually deteriorated into overcrowded warehouses for people with psychological disorders.

In the early 1900s, psychiatrists began to realize that mental health problems existed outside asylums—among people who appeared to be fully functioning. By midcentury, psychotherapy was common and touched the lives of most Americans; they either received therapy themselves or knew people who received or provided mental health services (Rosner, 2018). Mental health professionals were starting to view mental health as a continuum. Their effort to classify psychological disorders based on symptoms and progression ultimately led to the creation of the first *Diagnostic and Statistical Manual of Mental Disorders* in 1952 (*DSM;* American Psychiatric Association, 1952; Pierre, 2012; Shorter, 2015).

**RETURN TO THE COMMUNITY**   In the 1950s and 1960s, the United States saw a mass exodus of patients out of institutions and back into the community (**FIGURE 14.1**). This **deinstitutionalization** was partly the result of a movement to reduce the social isolation of people with psychological disorders and integrate them into society. Deinstitutionalization was also made possible by the introduction of medications that eased some symptoms of severe psychological disorders (Sisti et al., 2015). Thanks to these new drugs, some people who had previously needed constant care and supervision began caring for themselves and managing their own medications (Harrington, 2012). But this arrangement did not work out for everyone. Many people stopped taking

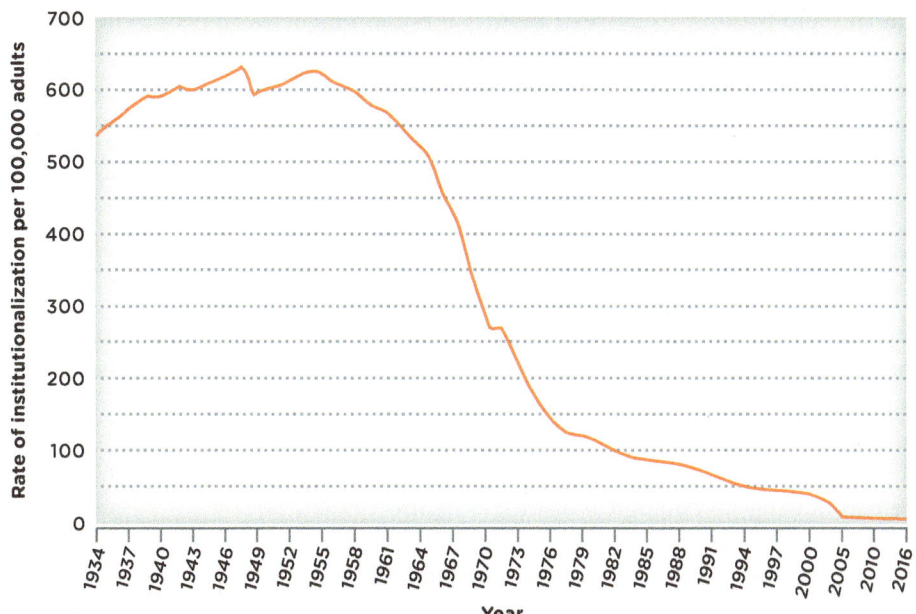

FIGURE 14.1
**Deinstitutionalization**
Since the 1950s, the rate of institutionalization has declined dramatically. Information from: Copyright 2011 by the University of Chicago Press from Harcourt (2011); 2005, 2010, 2016 data from Fuller et al., 2016.

their medication and ended up back in the hospitals, only to be discharged without adequate follow-up. Often, they would return again, "creating what some began to call a 'revolving door' of care" (Harrington, 2019, p. 115). Lack of long-term care continues to be an issue for people with serious and "treatment-resistant psychotic disorders" (often severe schizophrenia or bipolar disorder), who comprise about 4% of the adult population (Sisti et al., 2015).

## Where to Now?

In spite of the deinstitutionalization movement, psychiatric hospitals and institutions continue to play an important role in the treatment of psychological disorders. The scenario involving Dr. Foster and Chepa may be unusual in some respects, but not when it comes to the initiation of treatment. For someone experiencing a dangerous **psychotic episode**, the standard approach includes a stay in a psychiatric facility. Some of these admissions are voluntary; others are not.

Typically, a person is ready to leave the hospital after a few days or weeks, but many people in crisis are released after just a few hours, due to the high cost of treatment and financial pressures on hospitals. As critics contend, patients are being "held hostage" by the financial needs of insurance companies and physicians (Decker, 2016a). The length of a hospital stay is often determined by what insurance will cover rather than what a person needs, and restricted by the severe shortage of available beds (Sisti et al., 2015). The coronavirus pandemic has only served to add pressure to an already strained system. Maintaining social distance requires additional space, but space is in scarce supply when psychiatric beds are co-opted for treating COVID-19 patients. Meanwhile, the demand for psychological care continues to increase (Rapoport, 2020).

With such a shortage of mental health facilities, where else do people needing treatment end up? A substantial number have no place to live. An estimated 18.8% of homeless people in "developed" countries have psychotic disorders (Ayano et al., 2019). Given that the U.S. homeless population may be as high as 1.5 million (Population Reference Bureau [PRP], 2020), that translates to about 282,000 people. A much larger number of individuals with psychological disorders are locked

**CONNECTIONS**

In **Chapter 13,** we described psychotic symptoms, such as hallucinations and delusions. Psychotic episodes can be risky for people experiencing them— as well as those nearby. Individuals experiencing psychosis may be admitted to a hospital against their will, but hospitals have procedures in place to ensure that involuntary admissions are ethical.

up in jails and prisons: Every year, about 1.8 million mentally ill people are arrested and processed by U.S. law enforcement, and one in five prisoners has severe mental illness. "Prisons appear to have replaced mental hospitals as the largest institutions housing people with [severe disorders]" (Allison et al., 2018, p. 798). Inmates have limited access to treatment, but things may be changing, thanks to visionaries like Dr. Nneka Jones Tapia.

**JAIL OR MENTAL HOSPITAL?**    Dr. Jones Tapia is the executive director of the Cook County Jail in Chicago. Home to about 6,100 inmates at any given time, Cook County is "one of the largest single-site jails in the country" (Cook County Sheriff's Office, n.d., para. 1). According to Dr. Jones Tapia, about 20–24% of the detainees have a history of mental illness or are currently exhibiting symptoms. There is nothing unusual about this statistic. As noted earlier, about one in five U.S. inmates (20% of the jail and prison population) have debilitating psychological disorders (Allison et al., 2018).

"We have a crisis at hand right now with the number of individuals with mental illness coming into correctional institutions," says Dr. Jones Tapia, one of the first clinical psychologists to be placed in charge of a U.S. jail. Most correctional facilities are not set up to provide psychological treatment on a large scale (many do not even have a full-time psychologist), but Cook County is setting an inspiring example. With the support of Sheriff Tom Dart and the Cook County Health and Hospitals System, Dr. Jones Tapia has created a comprehensive system for identifying and treating psychological disorders among inmates. Every person admitted to the facility undergoes a psychological assessment performed by a licensed mental health professional. (Mental health screening occurs at other correctional facilities but is often done by correctional officers or nurses.) The detainee is then assigned to a living arrangement appropriate for their level of functioning and, if necessary, a psychological treatment plan. Inmates participate in a variety of mental health programs, including anger management, art therapy, yoga, and meditation. Some of these individuals continue receiving care after they have left jail, as Dr. Jones Tapia and her team have set up two clinics to provide ongoing care to former detainees in need.

We will learn more about Dr. Jones Tapia and her work in the pages to come, but first let's explore what psychological treatment is all about.

**Inspiring Psychologist**
Dr. Nneka Jones Tapia stands in a cell of Chicago's Cook County Jail. Unlike most jail wardens, who have backgrounds in criminal justice, Dr. Jones Tapia is a doctorate-level clinical psychologist (Decker, 2016b). Her training is invaluable in this setting, as U.S. correctional institutions have absorbed much the country's mental health burden. "Today the three largest mental health providers in the United States are jails: Illinois's Cook County Jail, the Los Angeles County Jail, and New York's Rikers Island" (Harrington, 2019, p. 118).

JOSHUA LOTT/The New York Times/Redux.

## Treatment Today

**LO 2**   Explain how the main approaches to therapy differ and identify their common goal.

The word "psychotherapy" derives from the Ancient Greek *psychē*, meaning "soul," and *therapeuō*, meaning "to heal" (Brownell, 2010), and there are many ways to go about this healing of the soul. Therapies can be categorized along three major dimensions (**INFOGRAPHIC 14.1**). The first is the manner of delivery—whether therapy is administered to an *individual* or a *group*. The second dimension is the treatment approach, which can be biomedical or psychological. **Biomedical therapy** refers to drugs and other medical interventions that target the biological basis of a disorder. **Psychotherapy,** or "talk therapy," zeroes in on psychological factors. The third dimension of therapy is the theoretical perspective, or approach. We can group the various approaches into two broad categories: **insight therapies,** which aim to increase awareness of self and environment, and **behavior therapy,** which focuses on behavioral change.

**biomedical therapy** Drugs and other physical interventions that target the biological processes underlying psychological disorders; primary goal is to reduce symptoms.

**psychotherapy** "Talk therapy"; a treatment approach wherein a client works with a mental health professional to reduce psychological symptoms and improve quality of life.

**insight therapies** Psychotherapies aimed at increasing awareness of self and environment.

**behavior therapy** A type of therapy that focuses on behavioral change.

# Major Approaches to Therapy

According to some estimates, there exist at least 500 specific types of psychotherapy (Lilienfeld & Arkowitz, 2012). Therapies can be categorized along three major dimensions: manner of delivery, treatment approach, and theoretical perspective. Here we see where different therapies fall along these dimensions. Note that today's therapists often work with teams of medical experts and other professionals to formulate treatment plans for clients (Wedding & Corsini, 2019). All therapies share the common goal of reducing symptoms and increasing the quality of life.

## MANNER OF DELIVERY

**INDIVIDUAL**
Involves a one-on-one relationship with a therapist

**GROUP**
Involves one or more therapists working with multiple people

## TREATMENT APPROACH

**BIOMEDICAL**
Using drugs or other medical interventions, focuses on the biological basis of a disorder

**PSYCHOLOGICAL**
Focuses on psychological factors

**PSYCHOLOGICAL**
Focuses on psychological factors

## THEORETICAL PERSPECTIVE

**BEHAVIOR THERAPIES**
Focus on behavioral change

**INSIGHT THERAPIES**
Focus on increasing awareness of self and environment

**INSIGHT THERAPIES**
Focus on increasing awareness of self and environment

## MAJOR FORMS OF THERAPY

**BEHAVIOR THERAPY**
Using principles of learning, seeks to replace maladaptive behaviors

**PSYCHOANALYSIS**
Seeks to increase awareness of unconscious conflicts

**FAMILY**
Focuses on the family as an integrated system

**PSYCHOPHARMACOLOGY**
Uses medicine to alter perceptions, moods, and behaviors

**PSYCHODYNAMIC**
New approach to psychoanalysis

**GROUP**
Preferred approach for interpersonal issues

**ELECTROCONVULSIVE THERAPY**
Induces seizures in the brain

**HUMANISTIC**
Emphasizes positive nature

**NEUROSURGERY**
Destroys some portion of the brain or connections between different areas of the brain

**COGNITIVE**
Seeks to change maladaptive thoughts

BSIP/Getty Images.

### What Is Art Therapy?

Art therapy is "the use of artistic activities, such as painting and clay modeling, in psychotherapy and rehabilitation" (APA, n.d.-a). During the COVID-19 pandemic, many people used art to relax and enjoy the moment, whether it was baking bread, making colorful signs for health-care workers, or using chalk to write messages of hope and inspiration on sidewalks. "In art therapy, mindfulness is what allows an individual to receive the therapeutic benefit of 'tuning out' the daily stress and anxiety and to focus on a single task" (Braus & Morton, 2020, p. S267).

These approaches share many common features: The relationship between the client and the treatment provider, or *therapeutic alliance,* is critical. In other words, the therapist must connect with the client in a meaningful way. "The therapy relationship accounts for client improvement (or lack of improvement) as much as, and probably more than, the particular treatment method" (Norcross & Lambert, 2018, p. 308). Another commonality across treatment methods is the hope that things will get better (Feinstein et al., 2015; Goldfried, 2019). Finally, all therapies aim to reduce symptoms and increase the quality of life.

As you learn about the many forms of therapy, keep in mind that there are a multitude of perspectives (far more than we can cover here), and that most psychologists use a combined approach (Goldfried, 2019). Even those who are trained in one discipline may integrate multiple methods, tailoring treatment for each client with an **eclectic approach to therapy.** In fact, "integrating techniques from different clinical approaches is now the norm for practitioners and no longer the exception" (Safran & Hunter, 2020b, p. 154). The American Psychological Association (APA) highlights the importance of using **evidence-based practice,** that is, choosing treatment that integrates the "best available" research findings, "clinical expertise," and knowledge of a patient's culture, values, and preferences (APA Presidential Task Force on Evidence-Based Practice, 2006; Bufka & Halfond, 2016).

In addition to describing the various approaches to treatment, we will examine how well they work. *Outcome research,* which evaluates the success of therapies, is a complicated endeavor. First, it is not always easy to pinpoint the meaning of success, or operationalize it. Should we measure self-esteem, happiness, or some other benchmark? Second, it can be difficult for clinicians to remain **free of bias** (both positive and negative) when reporting on the successes and failures of clients. One relatively new approach to measuring success is feedback-informed treatment (FIT). Clients answer questionnaires before and after sessions, and the data are used to determine how well the therapy is working and identify areas that need improvement (DeAngelis, 2018). Current evidence suggests that FIT does not have a major impact on client well-being or tendency to stay in treatment, but more high-quality studies are needed (Pejtersen et al., 2020).

### CONNECTIONS

In **Chapter 11,** we discussed the self-serving bias, which is the tendency for people to attribute their successes to internal characteristics and their failures to environmental factors. Clinicians may fall prey to this type of bias, taking credit for their clients' successes but blaming them for failures.

## ▶▶▶ SHOW WHAT YOU KNOW

1. A therapist writes a letter to the editor in support of more funding for mental health facilities, stating that all therapies share the same goal of reducing _____ and increasing the quality of life.
   - **A.** symptoms
   - **B.** combined approaches
   - **C.** biomedical therapy
   - **D.** the number of asylums

2. Dorothea Dix championed the _____, a campaign to reform asylums in the United States.

3. What were some of the consequences of deinstitutionalization?

   ✓ CHECK YOUR ANSWERS AT THE BACK OF THE BOOK.

## Insight Therapies

### "IMPROVEMENTS, MINOR AS THEY MAY BE"    Before becoming the

warden at Cook County, Dr. Jones Tapia worked as the jail's staff psychologist, and later as its chief psychologist. It was not easy providing therapy in this setting, because clients tend to come and go without much warning. Unlike prison, where inmates live for years at a time, jail is only intended for people who are awaiting trial or serving sentences for less than 365 days. Most inmates at Cook County are awaiting trial, which means they are presumed innocent. Eventually, they will be convicted and sent to prison, or acquitted and released back into the community. "Here, you don't know how much time you have with an individual, and so you want to be careful not to open up wounds that you're unable to close," says Dr. Jones Tapia. For inmates who are ready and willing, the therapist can help them piece together the past and figure out where things went wrong. The goal, according to Dr. Jones Tapia, is to "develop some insight on how they can make some improvements, minor as they may be, but improvements to give them a better outlook on life, and a better trajectory, even if they go to prison."

Developing this type of self-awareness is one of the unifying goals of the insight therapies, which we will now explore.

## Taking It to the Couch: Psychoanalysis

**LO3** Describe how psychoanalysis differs from psychodynamic therapy.

When imagining the stereotypical therapy session, many people picture a person reclining on a couch and talking about dreams and childhood memories. Modern-day therapy generally does not resemble this image. But if we could travel back in time to 1930s Vienna, Austria, and sit on Sigmund Freud's sofa, we just might see this stereotype come to life.

**FREUD AND THE UNCONSCIOUS**    Freud (1900/1953) proposed that humans are motivated by animal-like drives that are aggressive and sexual in nature. But acting on these drives is not always compatible with social norms, so they create conflict and get pushed below the surface, or **repressed**. These drives simmer beneath conscious awareness, affecting our moods and behaviors. And when we can no longer keep them at bay, the result may be disordered behavior, as seen with phobias, obsessions, and panic attacks (Solms, 2006). To help patients deal with these drives, Freud created *psychoanalysis,* the first formal system of psychotherapy. Psychoanalysis attempts to increase awareness of unconscious conflicts, thus making it possible to address and work through them.

Dreams, according to Freud, are a pathway to unconscious thoughts and desires (Freud, 1900/1953). The overt material of a dream (what we remember upon waking) is called the *manifest content,* and it can disguise a deeper meaning, or *latent content.* Because this latent content often consists of uncomfortable issues and desires, it is hidden from awareness. But with the help of a therapist, it can be unearthed. Freud would often use dreams as a launching pad for **free association,** a therapy technique in which a patient says anything and everything that comes to mind, regardless of how silly, bizarre, or inappropriate it may seem. Freud believed this seemingly directionless train of thought would lead to clues about the patient's unconscious. Piecing together the hints he gathered from dreams, free association, and other parts of therapy sessions, Freud would make inferences about the unconscious conflicts driving the patient's behavior. He called this investigative work **interpretation.** When the time seemed right, Freud would share his interpretations, increasing his patients' self-awareness and helping them come to terms with conflicts (Freud, 1900/1953).

You might be wondering what behaviors Freud considered signs of unconscious conflict. One indicator is **resistance,** a patient's unwillingness to cooperate in therapy. Examples of resistance might include arriving late, "forgetting" appointments, or becoming angry or agitated when certain topics arise. Resistance is a crucial step in psychoanalysis because it means the discussion might be veering close to something that makes the patient feel uncomfortable or threatened, like a critical memory or conflict causing distress. If resistance occurs, the job of the therapist is to help the patient identify its unconscious roots.

**CONNECTIONS**

In **Chapter 10,** we introduced the concept of repression, a defense mechanism whereby the ego moves anxiety-provoking thoughts, memories, or feelings from the conscious to unconscious level. Here, we will see how psychoanalysis helps uncover some of these unconscious processes.

**eclectic approach to therapy** Drawing on multiple theories and approaches to tailor treatment for a client.

**evidence-based practice** Making treatment decisions that integrate valuable research findings, clinical expertise, and knowledge of a patient's culture, values, and preferences.

**free association** A psychoanalytic technique in which a patient says anything that comes to mind.

**interpretation** A psychoanalytic technique used to explore unconscious conflicts driving behavior.

**resistance** A patient's unwillingness to cooperate in therapy; a sign of unconscious conflict.

**CONNECTIONS**

In **Chapter 10,** we presented projective personality tests. These assessments are based on the premise that the test taker will project unconscious conflicts onto the test material. It is up to the therapist to try to uncover these underlying issues. In the context of therapy, a patient may project conflicts onto the therapist.

Another sign of unconscious conflict is **transference,** which occurs when patients react to therapists as if they were parents or other important people from childhood. Suppose a client relates to Dr. Jones Tapia as if she were their mother. The client hated letting their mom down, so they resist telling Dr. Jones Tapia things they suspect would disappoint her. Transference can be a good thing, especially when it illuminates the unconscious conflicts fueling a patient's behaviors (Hoffman, 2009). One of the reasons Freud sat off to the side and out of a patient's sight was to encourage transference. With Freud in this neutral position, patients would have an easier time **projecting** their unconscious conflicts and feelings onto him.

## Goodbye, Couch: Psychodynamic Therapy

Freudian theories have been heavily criticized, and many contemporary psychologists do not identify themselves as psychoanalysts. Still, Freud left an indelible mark on the field of psychology, and his work paved the way for a briefer approach called **psychodynamic therapy.** This newer form of insight therapy has been evolving over the last 40 to 50 years, incorporating many of Freud's core themes, including the idea that personality and behaviors often can be traced to unconscious conflicts and experiences from the past.

However, psychodynamic therapy breaks from traditional psychoanalysis in important ways. Psychoanalysts may meet with clients many times a week for years (an expensive arrangement, as you might imagine), while psychodynamic therapists tend to see clients once a week for several months. (The duration may be longer or shorter depending on the severity of the disorder and limitations of insurance; Lazar, 2018.) And rather than sitting quietly off to the side as the client reclines on a couch, the psychodynamic therapist sits face-to-face with the client, giving feedback and sometimes advice. Frequently, the goal of psychodynamic therapy is to understand and resolve a specific, current problem.

**CONNECTIONS**

In **Chapter 1,** we described the experimental method, a research design that can uncover cause-and-effect relationships. Here, we see how this method is used to study therapy outcomes. In randomized controlled trials, participants are randomly assigned to treatment and control groups. The independent variable is the type of treatment, and the dependent variables measure the effectiveness of the treatment.

For many years, psychodynamic therapists treated clients without much evidence to back up their approach (Levy & Ablon, 2010). More recently, researchers have been testing the effects of psychoanalysis and psychodynamic therapy with rigorous scientific methods, and their results are encouraging (Gazzillo et al., 2018; Leichsenring et al., 2015; Levy et al., 2015). **Randomized controlled trials** suggest that psychodynamic psychotherapy is effective for treating an array of disorders, including depression, anxiety disorders, and some personality disorders (Fonagy et al., 2020; Keefe et al., 2019; Keefe et al., 2020), and the benefits may last long after treatment has ended (Shedler, 2010).

## You Can Do It! Humanistic Therapy

**GREATNESS IN ALL OF US**   Growing up in a small North Carolina town, Dr. Jones Tapia was always aware that her family did not look "perfect" from the outside. "[My father] was arrested for possession of marijuana a few times and spent a considerable amount of my early childhood in prison," she says. "But that did not take away from my sense of family, and it definitely did not negatively impact my relationship with my dad." On the weekends, her mother would prepare food and the whole family would go to the prison for Sunday dinner. "That was our version of normal," says Dr. Jones Tapia, who credits her unyielding optimism to a strong sense of spirituality and the love and support she has received from friends, teachers, and especially her mother and father. "They taught us very early on that, despite what anyone says, despite what our life looks like in the here and now, we can be successful." This sense of hope, along with her extraordinary capacity for empathy, has driven Dr. Jones Tapia's work as a therapist. In many ways, she exemplifies the humanistic perspective of psychology.

Courtesy Dr. Nneka Jones Tapia.

**On Her Way**

When Dr. Jones Tapia was applying to graduate school, a professor told her she would never make it through her master's program while working full-time. "For me that wasn't an option," says Dr. Jones Tapia. "I needed to make money." Not only did she manage to balance a full-time job with her master's program; she was essentially a straight-A student.

**LO 4** Outline the principles and characteristics of humanistic therapy.

For the first half of the 20th century, most psychotherapists leaned on Freud's theoretical framework. But in the 1950s, some psychologists began to question his dark view of human nature and his approach to treating clients. A new perspective began to take shape, one that focused on the positive aspects of human nature. This **humanistic movement** was championed by U.S. psychotherapist Carl Rogers, who believed that human beings are inherently good and inclined toward growth. "It has been my experience that persons have a basically positive direction," he wrote in his widely popular book *On Becoming a Person* (Rogers, 1961, p. 26). Rogers recognized that people have basic biological "demands" for food and sex, but he also saw that we have powerful desires to form close relationships, treat others with warmth and tenderness, and grow and mature as individuals (Rogers, 1961).

With this optimistic spirit, Rogers and others pioneered several types of insight therapy collectively known as **humanistic therapy,** which emphasizes the positive nature of humankind. Unlike psychoanalysis, which tends to focus on the distant past, humanistic therapy concentrates on the present, seeking to identify and address current problems. And rather than digging up unconscious thoughts and feelings, humanistic therapy emphasizes the conscious experience: What's going on in your mind right now?

**LO 5** Describe person-centered therapy.

**PERSON-CENTERED THERAPY**    Rogers' distinct form of humanistic therapy is known as **person-centered therapy,** and it closely follows his theory of personality. According to Rogers, humans have an innate drive to become fully functioning. We all have a natural tendency toward growth and *self-actualization,* or achieving our full potential. But expectations from family and society can stifle the process. Such external factors often cause an *incongruence,* or a mismatch, between the client's *ideal self* (often involving unrealistic expectations of who they should be) and *real self* (the way the client views themselves). One of the main goals of treatment is to reduce the incongruence between these two selves. Person-centered therapy also aims to create a warm and accepting relationship between therapist and client, and to help clients see they have the power to make changes in their lives and follow a path of positive growth.

Person-centered therapy is **nondirective,** meaning the therapist follows the lead of the client. As Rogers once wrote, "It is the *client* who knows what hurts, what directions to go, what problems are crucial, what experiences have been deeply buried" (Rogers, 1961, pp. 11–12). Sitting face-to-face with a client, the therapist's main job is to "be there" for that person through **empathy,** unconditional positive regard, **genuineness,** and **active listening**—all essential components of the therapeutic alliance (TABLE 14.1 on the next page). This **therapeutic alliance** is based on mutual respect and caring between therapist and client, and it provides a safe place for self-exploration.

Part of Rogers' philosophy was his refusal to identify the people he worked with as "patients" (Rogers, 1951). Patients depend on doctors to make decisions for them, or at least give them instructions. In Rogers' mind, it was the patient who had the answers, not the therapist. So he began using the term *client* and eventually settled on the term *person.*

"To me, Rogerian therapy is the essence of good clinical work in a correctional institution," says Dr. Jones Tapia. Detainees are often defined by their alleged crimes, she notes: "If you're accused of a murder, people will see you as a murderer, and people will respond to you as such." To remain as neutral as possible, Dr. Jones Tapia does not try to find out what charges inmates are facing before she meets with them. She also employs unconditional positive regard—total acceptance of a person regardless of their behaviors, beliefs, and words. "Everybody has a story, and it's not meant for me to judge that person based off of whatever reason they are in my custody,"

**transference** An unconscious conflict that occurs when a patient reacts to a therapist as if dealing with parents or other caregivers from childhood.

**psychodynamic therapy** A type of insight therapy that incorporates core psychoanalytic themes, including the idea that personality and behaviors frequently can be traced to unconscious conflicts and experiences from the past.

**humanistic therapy** A type of insight therapy that emphasizes the positive nature of humankind.

**person-centered therapy** A form of humanistic therapy developed by Rogers; aimed at helping clients achieve their full potential.

**nondirective** A technique used in person-centered therapy whereby the therapist follows the lead of the client during treatment sessions.

**empathy** The ability to feel what a person is experiencing by attempting to observe the world through their eyes.

**genuineness** The ability to respond to a client in an authentic way rather than hiding behind a polite or professional mask.

**active listening** The ability to pick up on the content and emotions behind words in order to understand a client's perspective, often by echoing the main point of what the client says.

**therapeutic alliance** A warm and accepting client–therapist relationship that serves as a safe place for self-exploration.

**I Believe in You**
Carl Rogers leads a group therapy session in 1966. One of the founders of humanistic therapy, Rogers firmly believed that all people are fundamentally good and capable of self-actualization, or becoming all that they can be.

says Dr. Jones Tapia. "Many of the detainees that I encounter have had histories of severe abuse and neglect, and so just beyond their crimes, they have had circumstances and interactions with people that are negative at best." Some inmates have never experienced unconditional positive regard, she notes, but this approach makes them feel more comfortable, enables them to talk openly, and ultimately helps them develop more self-awareness.

**TAKING STOCK: AN APPRAISAL OF INSIGHT THERAPY**   The insight therapies we have explored—psychoanalysis, psychodynamic therapy, and humanistic therapy— have had a profound impact on the field. Freudian theories help therapists understand how past experiences and unconscious conflicts influence behavior, and psychoanalysis continues to evolve (Safran & Hunter, 2020b). Psychodynamic therapy may be effective for treating a variety of disorders (Fonagy et al., 2020; Keefe et al., 2020). Humanistic therapy is useful for people dealing with complex and diverse problems, and in many cases its success rivals that of other methods (Angus et al., 2015; Corey, 2017). Humanistic techniques, in particular, have helped therapists of all persuasions build stronger relationships with clients and create positive therapeutic environments.

As with all approaches, the insight therapies have their limitations. Freud's theories, in particular, have drawn controversy. Some experts claim they lack scientific support, while others contend the opposite. How does a therapist (or client) know if they are tapping into the client's unconscious? The thoughts, memories, and desires contained within are often beyond awareness and hard to operationalize (Parth & Loeffler-Stastka, 2015). Humanistic therapy is difficult to study for similar reasons: The methodology has not been operationalized, and its use varies from one therapist to the next. Finally, insight therapies demand high levels of verbal expression and awareness of self and environment. Symptoms like hallucinations or delusions might interfere with these requirements.

**TABLE 14.1**  **Building a Therapeutic Alliance**

| Components | Description |
|---|---|
| Empathy | The ability to feel what a client is experiencing; seeing the world through the client's eyes (Rogers, 1951); therapist perceives feelings and experiences from "inside" the client (Rogers, 1961) |
| Unconditional positive regard | Total acceptance of a client no matter how distasteful the client's behaviors, beliefs, and words may be (see Chapter 10) |
| Genuineness | Being authentic, responding to a client in a way that is real rather than hiding behind a polite or professional mask; the client knows exactly where the therapist stands, which makes it easier to feel secure and open up (Rogers, 1961) |
| Active listening | Picking up on the content and emotions behind words in order to understand a client's point of view; includes reflection, or echoing the main point of what a client says |

Humanistic psychologist Carl Rogers believed it was critical to establish a strong and trusting therapist–client relationship. The key elements of a therapeutic alliance are listed above.

 **SHOW WHAT YOU KNOW**

1. _____ therapy focuses on the positive nature of human beings and on the here and now.
   A. Humanistic
   B. Psychoanalytic
   C. Psychodynamic
   D. Free association

2. How do psychoanalytic and psychodynamic therapies differ?

3. Seeing the world through a client's eyes and understanding how it feels to be that person is referred to as:
   A. interpretation.
   B. genuineness.
   C. empathy.
   D. self-actualization.

✓ CHECK YOUR ANSWERS AT THE BACK OF THE BOOK.

# Behavior and Cognitive Therapies

Insight therapies help clients develop a deeper understanding of self, which often leads to positive changes in behavior and mental processes. But is it possible to alter behavior and mental processes directly? This is the goal of behavior and cognitive therapies.

## Get to Work! Behavior Therapy

**LO 6** Outline the principles and characteristics of behavior therapy.

Using the principles of classical conditioning, operant conditioning, and observational learning (Chapter 5), behavior therapy aims to replace maladaptive behaviors with those that are adaptive. If behaviors are learned, who says they can't be changed through the same mechanisms?

**EXPOSURE AND RESPONSE PREVENTION**   To help a person overcome a fear or phobia, a behavior therapist might use **exposure,** a technique of placing clients in the situations they fear—without any physical risks involved. Take, for example, a client struggling with a dog phobia. Dogs cause this person extreme anxiety; the mere thought of seeing one being walked down the street causes considerable distress. The client usually goes to great lengths to avoid dogs, which allays the anxiety. The reduced anxiety **negatively reinforces** the client's avoidance behavior. With exposure therapy, the therapist might arrange for the client to be in a room with a very friendly Labrador Retriever. After a positive experience with the animal, the client's anxiety diminishes (along with efforts to avoid it), and the client learns that the situation needn't be anxiety-provoking. Ideally, both the anxiety and the avoidance behavior are extinguished. This process of stamping out learned associations is called *extinction.* The theory behind this *response prevention* technique is that if you encourage someone to confront a feared object or situation, and prevent them from responding the way they normally do, the fear response eventually diminishes or disappears.

A particularly intense form of exposure is to *flood* the client with an anxiety-provoking stimulus that cannot be escaped, causing a high degree of arousal. In one study, for example, women with snake phobias sat very close to a garter snake in a glass aquarium for 30 minutes without a break (Girodo & Henry, 1976). Flooding is potentially stressful for some therapists, which may be one reason this technique is not commonly used (Schumacher et al., 2015). Just imagine being a therapist and watching your client become extremely anxious or frightened during a flooding session you orchestrated.

For some clients, it's better to approach a feared scenario with "baby steps," upping the exposure with each movement forward (Prochaska & Norcross, 2018). This can be accomplished with an *anxiety hierarchy,* which is essentially a list of experiences ordered from least to most anxiety-provoking. If dogs are the focus of fear, the process might go something like this. Step 1: Think about a dog in a crate. Step 2: Look at a dog in a crate from afar. Step 3: Walk toward the crate, and so on.

But take note: Working up the anxiety hierarchy needn't involve actual dogs. With technologies available today, you could put on some fancy goggles and travel into a virtual "dog world," where it is possible to reach out and "touch" these animals. Virtual reality exposure therapy has become a popular way of reducing anxiety associated with various disorders, including specific phobias. Let's see how it works.

**CONNECTIONS**

In **Chapter 5,** we learned about negative reinforcement; behaviors followed by a reduction in something unpleasant are likely to recur. If avoiding a feared object leads to a decrease in anxiety, the avoidance will likely be repeated.

**exposure** A therapeutic technique that brings a person into contact with a feared object or situation in a safe environment, with the goal of extinguishing or eliminating the fear response.

**Everyone Is Looking at Me—But Not Really**

Wearing a headset like the one on shown in the top photo, a client can enter a virtual reality and face feared objects or situations—in this case, giving a presentation to a group of people. The goal of exposure therapy (virtual or otherwise) is to reduce the fear response by exposing clients to situations they fear. When nothing bad happens, their anxiety diminishes, and they are less likely to avoid the feared situations in the future.

**CONNECTIONS**

In **Chapter 12,** we described progressive muscle relaxation for relieving stress. Here, we see it can also be used in the treatment of anxiety.

**systematic desensitization**  A treatment that combines anxiety hierarchies with relaxation techniques.

## Didn't See That Coming

### VIRTUAL REALITY EXPOSURE THERAPY

Imagine you suffer from an intense and irrational fear of airplane travel (aviophobia), and your therapist develops a treatment plan that includes virtual reality exposure therapy. Wearing a head-mounted display (HMD), you are suddenly transported into the virtual interior of an airplane (Shiban et al., 2017; Wechsler et al., 2019). The rows of seats, the overhead luggage compartments, everything seems so real. So, too, do the movements of the plane, thanks to the hydraulic chair supporting you. Turn your head to the side or look toward the ceiling, and the computer creating this experience automatically adjusts to show you the part of the "plane" you are viewing (Shiban et al., 2017).

**SOUNDS LIKE A GREAT IDEA, BUT DOES IT WORK?**

Your therapist sits a few feet away, clicking on a keyboard or swiping and typing on a screen; they are moving you through the virtual airplane and monitoring your reports of anxiety every step of the way (Krijn et al., 2004). It's time to take your seat. Next, prepare for takeoff. If you're really feeling comfortable, your therapist might simulate some turbulence or a bumpy landing.

At this point, you may be wondering if a virtual reality plane ride can actually inspire true anxiety. "People often think virtual reality won't scare them, since they know it's not real. But it doesn't take a whole lot to tap into that fear," said Emory University psychologist Barbara Rothbaum in an interview with *Monitor on Psychology*. "Their brains and bodies fill in the details, and suddenly they are shaking and hyperventilating" (Weir, 2018, p. 52).

Studies indicate that virtual reality exposure therapy may be effective for treating a variety of disorders, among them agoraphobia, social anxiety disorder, and phobias of public speaking, heights, and spiders (Chesham et al., 2018; Lindner et al., 2021; Wechsler et al., 2019). The field is in need of systematic training for clinicians and more rigorous studies, including randomized controlled trials. But, researchers seem optimistic: "Virtual reality has emerged as a viable tool to help in a number of different disorders. . . . Overall, meta-analyses have indicated that [virtual reality] is an efficacious tool, compares favorably to comparison conditions, and has lasting effects that generalize to the real world" (Maples-Keller et al., 2017, p. 110).

**SYSTEMATIC DESENSITIZATION**   Virtual reality exposure therapy and other behavioral approaches may incorporate **systematic desensitization,** which takes advantage of the fact that we can't be relaxed and anxious at the same time. The therapist begins by teaching clients how to relax their muscles. This can be accomplished through **progressive muscle relaxation**, the process of tensing and then relaxing muscle groups, starting at the head and ending at the toes. Using this method, clients can learn to release all the tension in their body. It's very simple—want to try it?

 **Try This**   Sit in a comfortable chair in a quiet room. Start by tensing the muscles controlling your scalp: After 10 seconds, relax the muscles and focus on the tension dissipating. Next, follow the same procedure for the muscles in your face. Continue tensing and releasing muscles all the way down to your toes and see what happens.

Once a client has learned how to relax, it's time to face an anxiety hierarchy (either in the real world or via imagination) while trying to maintain a sense of calm. Imagine a client who fears flying, moving through an anxiety hierarchy with their therapist. Starting with the least-feared scenario at the bottom of their hierarchy, they imagine purchasing a ticket online. If they can stay relaxed through the first step, then they move to the second item in the hierarchy, thinking about boarding a plane.

At some point in the process, they might start to feel jittery or unable to take the next step. If this happens, the therapist guides them back a step or two in the hierarchy, or as many steps as they need to feel calm again, using progressive muscle relaxation. Then it's back up the hierarchy they go. This process does not happen in one session, but over the course of many.

**AVERSION THERAPY**    Exposure therapy focuses on *extinguishing* or eliminating associations, but there is another behavior therapy aimed at producing them. It's called **aversion therapy.** Seizing on the power of classical conditioning, aversion therapy seeks to link problematic behaviors, such as drug use, to unpleasant physical reactions like sickness and pain (**INFOGRAPHIC 14.2** on the next page). One type of aversion therapy uses the drug Antabuse, which has helped some people with alcoholism stop drinking, at least temporarily (Cannon et al., 1986; Gaval-Cruz & Weinshenker, 2009). Antabuse interferes with the body's ability to break down alcohol, so combining this drug with even a small amount of alcohol brings on an immediate unpleasant reaction (vomiting, throbbing headache, and so on). With repeated pairings of alcohol consumption and physical misery, one is less inclined to drink in the future. But aversion therapies like this are only effective if the client is motivated to change and complies with treatment (Newton-Howes et al., 2016).

**IT'S ABOUT CHANGING BEHAVIOR**    Another form of behavior therapy is **behavior modification,** which draws on the principles of operant conditioning. Therapists practicing behavior modification use **positive and negative reinforcement**, as well as punishment, to help clients increase adaptive behaviors and reduce maladaptive ones. In difficult cases, therapists might use successive approximations, that is, reinforce incremental changes toward the desired behaviors. Some will incorporate observational learning (that is, learning by watching and imitating others) to help clients change their behaviors.

In a **token economy,** people are given tokens as positive reinforcement for desired behaviors. **Tokens** can be exchanged for candy, outings, privileges, and other perks. They can also be taken away as a punishment to reduce undesirable behaviors. This behavior modification approach has proven successful for a variety of populations, including psychiatric patients in residential treatment facilities and hospitals, children in classrooms, and prison inmates (Dickerson et al., 2005; Walker et al., 2016; Yassine & Tipton-Fisler, 2021). In a residential treatment facility, for example, patients with schizophrenia may earn tokens for socializing with each other or cleaning up after themselves. One might argue that token economies manipulate the people they intend to help. (Maybe you would agree that giving adults play money for good behavior is degrading.) We also have to consider what happens to those residents who move on to less structured settings—do the changes in their behavior persist? Despite these drawbacks, token economies can help people adopt healthier behaviors.

## You Are What You Think: Cognitive Therapies

**FOLLOW-UP**    Earlier in the chapter, we described Dr. Foster's initial encounter with Chepa, a young woman facing schizophrenia. After being discharged from the psychiatric hospital, Chepa returns to the reservation, where Dr. Foster and his colleagues from Indian Health Service follow her progress. Every month, she goes to the medical clinic for an injection to quell her psychosis. This is also when she is most likely to have a therapy session with Dr. Foster.

Psychologists on the reservation typically don't have the luxury of holding more than two or three sessions with a client, so Dr. Foster has to make the most of every minute. For someone who has just received a new diagnosis, a good portion of

**CONNECTIONS**

In **Chapter 5,** we described how positive reinforcement (a desirable consequence) increases the likelihood of a behavior being repeated. With behavior modification, therapists use reinforcers to replace maladaptive behaviors with adaptive ones.

**CONNECTIONS**

Tokens are an excellent example of secondary reinforcers. In **Chapter 5,** we reported that secondary reinforcers derive their power from their connection with primary reinforcers, which satisfy biological needs.

Jon Schulte/Getty Images.

**aversion therapy**  A therapeutic approach that uses the principles of classical conditioning to link problematic behaviors to unpleasant physical reactions.

**behavior modification**  A therapeutic approach in which behaviors are shaped through reinforcement and punishment.

**token economy**  A type of behavior modification that uses tokens to reinforce desired behaviors.

# Classical Conditioning in Behavior Therapy

Behavior therapists believe that most behaviors—either desirable or undesirable—are learned. When a behavior is maladaptive, a new, more adaptive behavior can be learned to replace it. Behavior therapists use learning principles to help clients eliminate unwanted behaviors. The two behavior therapies highlighted here rely upon classical conditioning techniques. In exposure therapy, a therapist might use an approach known as *systematic desensitization* to reduce an unwanted response, such as a fear of needles, by pairing it with relaxation. In *aversion therapy*, an unwanted behavior such as excessive drinking is paired with unpleasant reactions, creating an association that prompts avoidance of that behavior.

## SYSTEMATIC DESENSITIZATION

A client practices relaxation techniques while engaging in situations listed on their anxiety hierarchy, beginning with the least anxiety-provoking situation. After repeated pairings, the client learns to associate the anxiety-provoking situation with the desirable, conditioned response (calm), which is incompatible with fear or anxiety. The process is repeated for every step on the hierarchy.

During conditioning, two stimuli that produce incompatible responses are repeatedly paired.

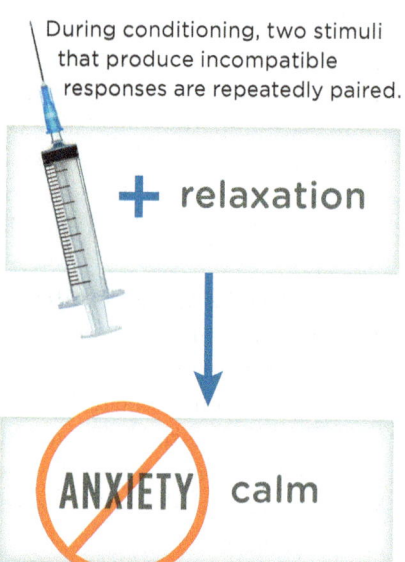

**+ relaxation**

ANXIETY calm

Because the responses are incompatible, one response will eventually be extinguished. Starting at the bottom of the hierarchy with the least anxiety-provoking situation enables the desired response (calm) to prevail.

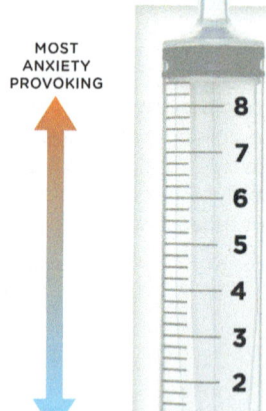

MOST ANXIETY PROVOKING

LEAST ANXIETY PROVOKING

### Anxiety Hierarchy for Fear of Needles

8 Getting a flu shot.

7 Allowing someone to prep your arm for a shot.

6 Visiting a health clinic to discuss getting a shot.

5 Watching someone get a shot.

4 Holding a hypodermic needle.

3 Touching a hypodermic needle in its packaging.

2 Looking at an actual hypodermic needle.

1 Looking at a photo of a hypodermic needle.

**Before conditioning**

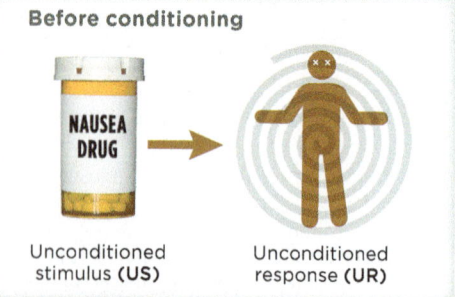

Unconditioned stimulus (US)

Unconditioned response (UR)

**During conditioning**

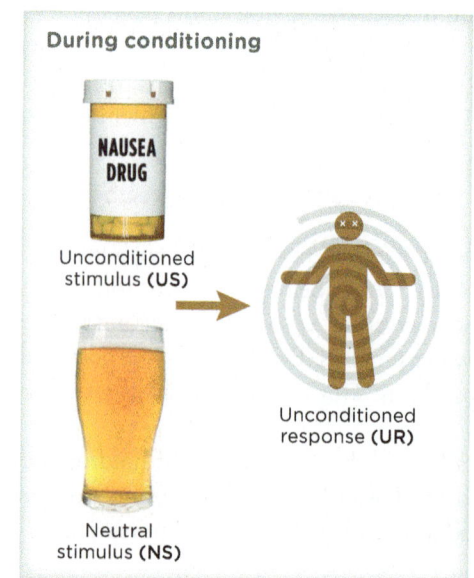

Unconditioned stimulus (US)

Unconditioned response (UR)

Neutral stimulus (NS)

**After conditioning**

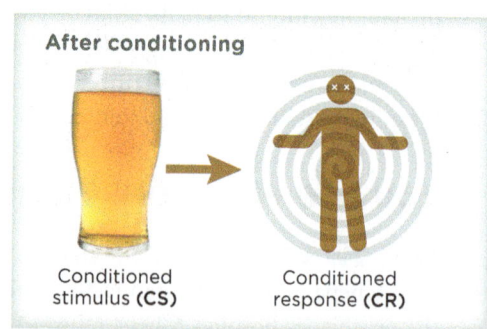

Conditioned stimulus (CS)

Conditioned response (CR)

## AVERSION THERAPY

Aversion therapy seeks to diminish a behavior by linking it with an unpleasant reaction. To reduce alcohol consumption, alcohol is consumed with a drug that causes feelings of nausea. Eventually, alcohol becomes a conditioned stimulus, prompting the unpleasant physical reaction all on its own.

the session is spent on *psychoeducation,* or learning more about a disorder: *What is schizophrenia, and how will it affect my life?* Dr. Foster and the client might go over some of the user-friendly literature on schizophrenia published by the National Alliance on Mental Illness (NAMI; www.nami.org).

Another main goal is to turn Chepa's negative thought patterns into healthier ones. To help clients recognize the maladaptive nature of their thoughts, Dr. Foster might provide an analogy, as he does here:

**Dr. Foster:**   If we had a blizzard in February and it's 20 degrees below for 4 days in a row, would you consider that a strange winter?

**Chepa:**   No.

**Dr. Foster:**   If we had a day that's 105 degrees in August, would you consider that an odd summer?

**Chepa:**   Well, no.

**Dr. Foster:**   Yet you're talking about a difference of 125 degrees, and we're in the same place and we're saying this is normal weather. . . . We're part of nature. You and I are part of this natural world, and so you might have a day today where you're very distressed, upset, and a week from now where you're very calm and at peace, and both of those are normal. Both of those are appropriate.

Dr. Foster might also remind Chepa that her symptoms result from her psychological condition. "Your response is a normal response [for] a human being with this [psychological disorder]," he says, "and so of course you're scared, of course you're upset."

**LO 7**   Outline the principles and characteristics of cognitive therapy.

Dr. Foster has identified his client's maladaptive thoughts and is beginning to help her change the way she views her world and her relationships. This is the basic goal of **cognitive therapy,** an approach advanced by psychiatrist Aaron Beck.

**BECK'S COGNITIVE THERAPY**   Beck was trained in psychoanalysis, but he opted to develop his own approach after trying (without luck) to produce scientific evidence showing that Freud's methods work (Beck, 2019). Beck believes that patterns of *automatic thoughts* lie at the root of psychological disturbances. These *cognitive distortions,* or errors, cause individuals to misinterpret events in their lives and are associated with psychological problems like depression (Beck et al., 1979; TABLE **14.2** on the next page). One such distortion is **overgeneralization,** or thinking that self-contained events will have major repercussions in life (Prochaska & Norcross, 2018). For example, a person assumes that something is always true just because it happens to be true under one set of circumstances. (*I have had difficulty working for a male boss, so I will never be able to work effectively under a male supervisor.*) Beck suggests that cognitive **schemas** underlie such patterns of automatic thoughts, directing the way we interpret events (Beck, 2019). His cognitive therapy aims to dismantle, or take apart, the schemas harboring these errors and replace them with beliefs that nurture more positive, realistic thoughts.

The restructuring of schemas can be facilitated by client homework. For example, the therapist may challenge clients to test "hypotheses" related to their dysfunctional thinking. ("If it's true you don't work effectively under male bosses, then why did your previous boss give you a promotion?") Client homework is an important component of cognitive therapy. So, too, is psychoeducation, which might include sharing websites and reading materials that help clients understand their disorders and thus adopt more realistic attitudes and expectations.

**Beck's Cognitive Approach**
Aaron Beck, who has spent the last 60 years working as a psychiatrist and mental health researcher, helped pioneer the field of cognitive therapy (Beck, 2019). Beck believes that distorted thought processes lie at the heart of psychological problems.

**CONNECTIONS**

In **Chapter 8,** we presented Piaget's concept of the schema, a collection of ideas or notions representing a basic unit of understanding. Young children form schemas based on functional relationships they observe in the environment. Beck suggests that schemas can also direct the way we interpret events, not always in a realistic or rational manner.

**cognitive therapy** A type of therapy aimed at addressing the maladaptive thinking that leads to maladaptive behaviors and feelings.

**overgeneralization** A cognitive distortion that assumes self-contained events will have major repercussions.

**TABLE 14.2    Cognitive Distortions**

| Cognitive Distortion | Explanation | Example |
| --- | --- | --- |
| Arbitrary inference | Coming to a conclusion even when there is no evidence to support it | *I am a horrible student.* |
| Selective abstraction | Ignoring information and assuming something has happened based on details taken out of context | *I know he is cheating because he is e-mailing a woman at work.* |
| Overgeneralizing | Belief that something may always occur because it has occurred before | *My boss doesn't like me; I will never be liked.* |
| Magnification/minimization | Belief that something is more or less critical than it really is | *If I don't pass this first quiz, I will fail the course.* |
| Dichotomous thinking | Viewing experiences in extremes | *I can either be at the top of my class, or I can get married and have a family.* |
| Personalizing | Taking other people's behaviors too personally | *I waved at her, but she didn't even acknowledge me. I must have upset her.* |

Aaron Beck contends that psychological problems stem from distorted patterns of thought. Cognitive therapy aims to replace these cognitive distortions with more realistic and constructive ways of thinking. Information from Beck and Weishaar (2014).

**ELLIS' RATIONAL EMOTIVE BEHAVIOR THERAPY**    The other major figure in cognitive therapy is psychologist Albert Ellis (1913–2007). Like Beck, Ellis was trained in psychoanalysis and was disappointed by its results, so he created his own treatment approach: **rational emotive behavior therapy (REBT).** The goal of REBT is to help people identify their irrational or illogical thoughts and convert them into rational ones (Ellis & Ellis, 2019). An REBT therapist uses the ABC model to understand a client's problems. Point A represents an *activating* event in the client's life: "My boss fired me." Point B stands for the irrational *beliefs* that follow: "I will never be able to hold a steady job." And point C represents the emotional *consequences:* "I feel hopeless and depressed." Therapy focuses on addressing point B, the irrational beliefs causing distress. If all goes well, the client successfully reaches point D, *disputing* flawed beliefs: "Losing one job does not spell the end of my career." That leads to point E, an *effective* new philosophy: "I am capable of being successful in another job" (Ellis & Dryden, 1997; FIGURE **14.2**).

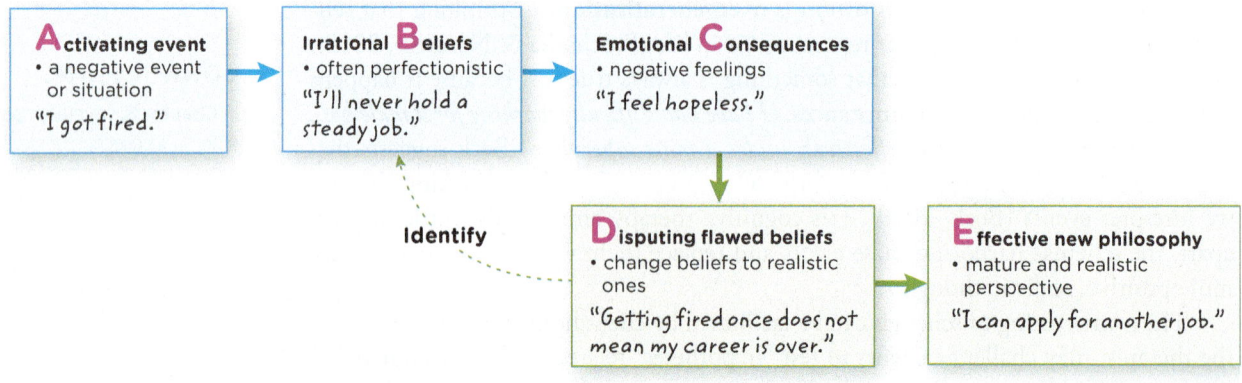

**FIGURE 14.2**
**The ABCs of REBT**
A rational emotive behavior therapist uses the ABC model (depicted in blue) to understand a client's problems. Therapy, shown in green, helps a client identify and address irrational beliefs—and ultimately develop a mature and realistic perspective.

**rational emotive behavior therapy (REBT)**
A type of cognitive therapy, developed by Ellis, that identifies illogical thoughts and attempts to convert them into rational ones.

According to Ellis, people tend to have unrealistic beliefs, often perfectionist in nature, about how they and others should think and act. This inevitably leads to disappointment, as no one is perfect. The ultimate goal of REBT is to change these irrational thoughts to realistic ones, and arrive at self-acceptance. This often involves letting go of the "I shoulds" and "I musts," what Ellis called "musturbatory thinking" (Prochaska & Norcross, 2018, p. 241). Through REBT, one develops a rational way of thinking that helps reduce suffering and amplify enjoyment: "The purpose of life," as Ellis was known to say, "is to have a $&%#@ good time" (p. 239). Ellis took a hard line with clients, forcefully challenging them to provide evidence for their irrational ideas and often shocking people with his direct manner (Kaufman, 2007; Prochaska & Norcross, 2018).

As Ellis developed his therapy throughout the years, he realized it was important to focus on behavior as well as cognitive processing. Thus, REBT therapists aim to change both cognitions and behaviors, assigning homework to implement the insights clients gain during therapy. Because Ellis and Beck incorporated both cognitive and behavior therapy methods, their approaches are commonly referred to as **cognitive behavioral therapy (CBT)**. CBT is supported by a strong research base, and it is now one of the most popular therapeutic approaches across the world (Beck, 2019). It is action-oriented, requiring clients to confront and resist their illogical thinking. CBT also tends to work relatively fast—or, in some cases, very fast. *Scientific American* reports:

# PSYCHOTHERAPY IN A FLASH

Brief but intensive treatments are proving to be effective for many anxiety disorders.

From the SCIENTIFIC
pages of AMERICAN

Psychotherapy is not what most people think of as a quick fix. From its early Freudian roots, it has taken the form of 50- to 60-minute sessions repeated weekly (or more often) over a period of months or even years. For modern cognitive-behavioral therapy (CBT), 10 to 20 weekly sessions is typical. But must it be so? "Whoever told us that one 50-minute session a week is the best way to help people get over their problems?" asks Thomas Ollendick, director of the Child Study Center at Virginia Tech.

For nearly 20 years Ollendick has been testing briefer, more intensive forms of CBT for childhood anxiety disorders and getting results that closely match those of slower versions. His center often has a waiting list for treatments that include a four-day therapy for obsessive-compulsive disorder (OCD) and a three-hour intervention for specific phobias (such as fear of flying, heights or dogs). Around the U.S. and Europe, short-course therapies for anxiety disorders have begun to catch on, creating a nascent movement in both adult and child psychology.

The idea originated with Swedish psychologist Lars-Göran Öst, now professor emeritus at Stockholm University. Some 40 years ago Öst got the impression that not all his phobia patients needed multiple weeks of therapy and decided to ask if they would like to try a single, three-hour session. His first taker was a 35-year-old spider-phobic woman. "She lived five hours away, so she was happy," he recalls, to be treated in one go. He later showed the efficacy of the approach in a clinical trial, although it took four years to recruit 20 participants. "People with a specific phobia rarely apply for treatment," he explains. "They adjust their lives [say, avoiding spiders] or think they can't be helped." Öst went on to work with a team in Bergen, Norway, to test an intensive therapy for OCD known as the Bergen four-day treatment. By the early 2000s Ollendick was adapting brief therapies for adolescents and kids.

The details vary, but the quick treatments have some common features. They generally begin with "psychoeducation," in which patients learn about their condition and the catastrophic thoughts that keep it locked in place. In Bergen, this is done in a small group. With children, the lessons may be more hands-on and concrete. For instance, Ollendick might help a snake-phobic kid grasp why the creature moves in a

**cognitive behavioral therapy (CBT)** An action-oriented type of therapy that requires clients to confront and resist their illogical thinking.

creepy, slithering way by having the child lie on the floor and try to go forward without using any limbs.

A second part usually involves "exposure and response prevention," in which patients confront in incremental steps whatever triggers their anxiety: perhaps shopping, for agoraphobics, or having dirty hands, for people with OCD. With support from the therapist, they learn to tolerate it and see it as less threatening. Patients leave with homework to reinforce the lessons. Parents may be taught how to support a child's progress.

How well do these approaches work? A 2017 meta-analysis by Öst and Ollendick looked at 23 randomized controlled studies and found that "brief, intensive, or concentrated" therapies for childhood anxiety disorders were comparable to standard CBT. With the quicker therapies, 54 percent of patients were better immediately post-treatment, and that rose to 64 percent on follow-up—presumably because they continued to practice and apply what they had learned. With standard therapy, 57 percent were better after the final session and 63 percent on follow-up. The severity of symptoms and whether the patient was also taking antianxiety medication did not seem to impact outcomes.

An obvious advantage to quick therapy is that it accelerates relief. Children with panic disorder, for instance, may refuse to leave home for fear of triggering an episode of shortness of breath, a racing heart and nausea. "They start to avoid places like the mall, the movies, the school dance," says child psychologist Donna Pincus of Boston University. Pincus developed an eight-day treatment for the disorder as an alternative to three months of CBT, which, she observes, "is a long time if you are not going to school or are avoiding doing things that are fun or healthy."

Making these briefer therapies more widely available could help address the sad fact that only about a third of patients with anxiety disorders get any kind of treatment. A weeklong therapy could be completed over a school or work vacation. Rural patients who cannot find CBT nearby could be treated during a short out-of-town stay. The intensive approach requires special training and a big shift for therapists—and health insurers—accustomed to the tradition of 50-minute blocks. But is there really anything sacred about that? Claudia Wallis. Reproduced with permission.

## Put Your Heads Together

Now that you have read the above, consider these questions with your group: **A)** The quick and intensive treatments described generally incorporate psychoeducation. Why do you think it is helpful for people to learn about their disorders? **B)** Another important component is exposure: Clients are placed in situations they fear, and their anxiety eventually diminishes. How can you explain this phenomenon from a learning perspective? *Hint:* Think reinforcement.

### TAKING STOCK: AN APPRAISAL OF BEHAVIOR AND COGNITIVE THERAPIES

Behavior therapy tends to work fast, producing quick resolutions to stressful situations, sometimes in a single session (Oar et al., 2015; Öst, 1989). And reduced time in therapy typically translates to a lower cost. What's more, the procedures used in behavior therapy are often easy to operationalize (remember, the focus is on modifying observable behavior), so evaluating the outcome is more straightforward. There are some drawbacks to behavior therapy, however. The goal is to change learned behaviors, but not all behaviors and symptoms are learned. (For example, you can't "learn" to have hallucinations.) And because the reinforcement comes from an external source, newly learned behaviors may disappear when reinforcement stops. Finally, the emphasis on observable behavior may downplay the social, biological, and cognitive roots of psychological disorders. This narrow approach works well for treating phobias and other behavior problems, but not as well for addressing far-reaching, complex issues arising from disorders such as schizophrenia and depression.

As with behavior therapy, the cognitive approaches of Beck and Ellis have the advantage of being short term. CBT typically involves 10–20 one-hour sessions, but as you learned from the *Scientific American* article, the duration can be even shorter (Wallis, 2019). For clients with obsessive-compulsive disorder (OCD), major depressive disorder, and posttraumatic stress disorder (PTSD), CBT is not only effective—it also produces measurable changes in the brain (Moody et al., 2017; Shou et al., 2017). Even when administered online, CBT may benefit clients with a variety of psychological problems (Carlbring et al., 2018). Still, every approach has its limitations. Cognitive models that focus on flawed assumptions and attitudes may present a chicken-and-egg problem. People experiencing depression often have distorted beliefs, but are distorted beliefs causing their depression or is depression causing their distorted beliefs? Perhaps it is a combination of both.

## Put Your Heads Together

Before you team up, **A)** outline the major approaches to therapy we have discussed. Then, in your group, **B)** imagine someone who is terrified of flying, and consider the obstacles they face getting over their fear. **C)** Explain how one of the therapy approaches described above might be used for this individual.

All the therapies we have discussed thus far involve interactions among therapists and clients. But in many cases, psychotherapy is not enough; a biological approach is needed, too.

## SHOW WHAT YOU KNOW

1. The goal of _____ therapy is to replace maladaptive behaviors with more adaptive ones.
   **A.** behavior
   **B.** exposure
   **C.** humanistic
   **D.** psychodynamic

2. Describe the similarities and differences between cognitive and behavior therapy.

3. The basic goal of _____ is to help clients identify maladaptive thoughts and change the way they view the world and their relationships.

✓ CHECK YOUR ANSWERS AT THE BACK OF THE BOOK.

# Biomedical Therapies

**LO 8** Identify biomedical treatments for psychological disorders and describe their common goal.

People with severe disorders like depression, schizophrenia, and bipolar disorder can benefit from talk therapy, but this may not be enough. Their symptoms are driven by biological processes that can be directly targeted with biomedical therapies. These treatments take three basic forms: (1) drugs, or *psychotropic* medications; (2) electroconvulsive therapy; and (3) surgery.

## Medicines That Help

Psychotropic medications are used to treat psychological disorders and their symptoms. Prescribing these drugs is generally the domain of *psychiatrists,* physicians who specialize in treating people with disorders. (Psychiatrists are medical doctors, whereas clinical psychologists have PhDs or PsyDs and generally cannot prescribe medication. To learn more about these professions, see the online appendix Careers in Psychology.) *Psychopharmacology* is the scientific study of how psychotropic medications alter perceptions, moods, behaviors, and other aspects of psychological functioning. These drugs can be divided into four categories: *antidepressant, mood-stabilizing, antipsychotic,* and *anti-anxiety.*

Wavebreakmedia Ltd/Getty Images.

**Psychologists Who Prescribe**
Psychotropic medications are typically prescribed by psychiatrists, but a small number of psychologists have prescription privileges as well. New Mexico, Louisiana, Iowa, Illinois, and Idaho have passed laws giving psychologists the green light to prescribe, provided they have "advanced specialized training," including a postdoctoral master's degree in clinical psychopharmacology (APA, 2017b, para. 1).

## CONNECTIONS

In **Chapter 2,** we described how sending neurons release neurotransmitters into the synapse, where they bind to receptors on the receiving neuron. Neurotransmitters that do not immediately attach are reabsorbed by the sending neuron (reuptake) or broken down in the synapse. Here, we see how medications can influence this process.

**ANTIDEPRESSANT DRUGS**    Major depressive disorder is commonly treated with **antidepressant drugs,** medication used to improve mood (and to treat anxiety and eating disorders in certain individuals). Essentially, there are three classes of antidepressant drugs: monoamine oxidase inhibitors (MAOIs), such as Nardil (phenelzine); tricyclic antidepressants, such as Elavil (amitriptyline); and selective serotonin reuptake inhibitors (SSRIs), such as Prozac (fluoxetine). All these antidepressants are thought to work by influencing the activity of **neurotransmitters** hypothesized to be involved in depression and other disorders (**INFOGRAPHIC 14.3** on page 549). (Keep in mind, no one has pinpointed the exact neurological mechanisms underlying depression.)

The MAOIs help people with major depressive disorder by slowing the breakdown of certain neurotransmitters called monoamines: norepinephrine, serotonin, and dopamine. MAOIs extend the amount of time these neurotransmitters remain in the synapse by hindering the normal activity of monoamine oxidase, whose natural role is to break them down. By making these neurotransmitters more available (that is, allowing them more time in the synapse), MAOIs might lessen symptoms of depression. These drugs have fallen out of use due to safety concerns and side effects, as they require great attention to diet. MAOIs can trigger a life-threatening jump in blood pressure when ingested alongside tyramine, a substance found in many everyday foods, including cheddar cheese, salami, and wine (Anastasio et al., 2010; Horwitz et al., 1964; Larsen et al., 2016).

The tricyclic antidepressants, named for their three-ringed molecular structure, inhibit the reuptake of serotonin and norepinephrine in the synaptic gap. This allows these neurotransmitters more time to be active, which appears to reduce symptoms. The tricyclic drugs are not always well tolerated by patients and can cause a host of side effects, including sexual dysfunction, confusion, and increased risk of heart attack (Cohen et al., 2000; Coupland et al., 2016; Higgins et al., 2010). Overdoses can be fatal.

Newer, more popular pharmaceutical interventions include SSRIs—brands such as Prozac, Paxil (paroxetine), and Zoloft (sertraline)—that inhibit the reuptake of serotonin specifically. SSRIs may reduce the potentially devastating symptoms of depression and are generally safer and have fewer negative effects than the older generation of antidepressants, but they are far from perfect. Weight gain, fatigue, hot flashes, chills, insomnia, nausea, and sexual dysfunction are all possible side effects. Some research suggests that SSRIs are not better than a **placebo** when it comes to treating mild to moderate depression (Fournier et al., 2010; Khan & Brown, 2015). An analysis of studies concluded that antidepressants of various types (not just SSRIs) "were more efficacious than placebo in adults with major depressive disorder," although these effects were "mostly modest" (Cipriani et al., 2018, p. 1362).

## Research
## CONNECTIONS

In **Chapter 1,** we stated that a placebo is a fake treatment used to explore the effectiveness of an actual treatment. The placebo effect is the tendency to feel better if we believe we are being treated with a real medication. Expectations about getting better can change treatment outcomes.

## CONNECTIONS

In **Chapter 4,** we described hallucinogens—drugs that produce hallucinations, altered moods, and distorted perception and thought. Ketamine falls into this category, but it also shows promise for reducing the symptoms of treatment-resistant depression.

**antidepressant drugs** Psychotropic medications used for the treatment of depression.

In 2019, the U.S. Food and Drug Administration (FDA) approved two medications that could potentially impact the lives of many people experiencing symptoms of depression: Zulresso (brexanolone) and Spravato (esketamine). Zulresso is the first FDA-approved drug specifically indicated for postpartum depression. The drug is given as "a continuous IV infusion over a total of 60 hours (2.5 days)" in a health-care facility, where patients can be closely monitored for side effects such as "sudden loss of consciousness" (FDA, 2019, March 19, para. 4). The other recent approval, Spravato, is a nasal spray for people whose depression symptoms fail to resolve with other medications. This drug is a chemical component of *ketamine,* a **hallucinogen** used to dampen pain in surgical patients. Spravato can have serious side effects, among them "disassociation, dizziness, nausea, sedation, [and] vertigo," and it must be administered in a clinical setting and taken alongside another antidepressant (FDA, 2019, March 6, para. 7). The approval of this nasal spray offers new hope for people facing "treatment-resistant depression" (Daly et al., 2019, p. 894), but questions remain about how frequently the drug should be administered and how long it should be given (Salahudeen et al., 2020).

**MOOD-STABILIZING DRUGS**   People with bipolar disorder may find some degree of symptom relief in **mood-stabilizing drugs.** Lithium, for instance, helps smooth the mood swings of people with bipolar disorder, leveling out the dramatic peaks (mania) and valleys (depression) (Amare et al., 2020). Considered by some to be the "gold standard" for treating bipolar disorder, lithium has been a mainstay treatment for decades. It doesn't work for everyone, but 30% of people show a "full response" (Amare et al., 2020). Doctors must be very careful when prescribing lithium, monitoring the blood levels of their patients. Too small a dose will fall short of controlling bipolar symptoms, while too large a dose can be lethal.

Scientists have yet to determine the cause of bipolar disorder and how its symptoms might be lessened with lithium. Some research suggests that lithium alters gene expression in certain parts of the brain, which are linked to structural changes that could potentially explain the drug's effects (Anand et al., 2020). Lithium also seems to be effective in lowering suicide risk among people with bipolar disorder (Amare et al., 2020; Hayes et al., 2016), who are 20 times more likely than people in the general population to take their own lives (Inder et al., 2016; Tondo et al., 2003).

Anticonvulsant medications are also used to treat bipolar disorder. These drugs were originally created to alleviate symptoms of seizure disorders, but scientists discovered they might also function as mood stabilizers (Bowden et al., 2000; López-Muñoz et al., 2018). Unfortunately, certain anticonvulsants may increase the risk of suicide or possible suicide masked as violent death through injury or accident (Muller et al., 2015; Patorno et al., 2010). For this reason, the FDA (2008) requires drug companies to place warnings on their labels.

**ANTIPSYCHOTIC DRUGS**   The hallucinations and delusions of people with disorders like schizophrenia can be subdued with **antipsychotic drugs.** Both *traditional antipsychotics* and *atypical antipsychotics* seek to reduce dopamine activity in certain areas of the brain, as abnormal activity of this neurotransmitter is believed to contribute to the psychotic symptoms of schizophrenia and other disorders (Blasi et al., 2015; Cheng et al., 2020; Schnider et al., 2010). Antipsychotics accomplish this by acting as dopamine **antagonists**, meaning they "pose" as dopamine, binding to receptors normally reserved for dopamine (sort of like stealing someone's parking space). By blocking dopamine's receptors, antipsychotic drugs reduce dopamine's excitatory effect on neurons. The main difference between atypical antipsychotics and the traditional variety is that atypical antipsychotics *also* interfere with neural pathways involving other neurotransmitters, such as serotonin, whose activity is associated with psychotic symptoms (Xu & Zhuang, 2019).

Antipsychotics have helped many people achieve higher levels of functioning, but these drugs have unwanted side effects. After about a year of taking traditional antipsychotics, some patients develop a neurological condition called *tardive dyskinesia,* whose symptoms include shaking, restlessness, and bizarre facial grimaces. Atypical antipsychotics like Risperdal (risperidone) usually do not cause tardive dyskinesia (Correll et al., 2004; Jacobsen, 2015), but they have other potential side effects, such as weight gain, increased risk for Type 2 diabetes, sexual dysfunction, and heart disease (Üçok & Gaebel, 2008; Xu & Zhuang, 2019). And although these drugs reduce symptoms in 60–85% of patients, they do not provide a cure.

**ANTI-ANXIETY DRUGS**   Most of today's **anti-anxiety drugs** are *benzodiazepines* such as Xanax (alprazolam) and Ativan (lorazepam). Also called "minor tranquilizers,"

Tuned_In/Getty Images.

**FDA Warning**
A growing number of children and teenagers are taking SSRIs to combat depression, but these medications may increase the risk of suicidal behaviors and thoughts for a small percentage of youth. For this reason, the FDA requires manufacturers to include a boxed warning on the packaging of these drugs (National Institute of Mental Health, n.d.-a).

**CONNECTIONS**

In **Chapter 2,** we described how drugs influence behavior by changing what is happening in the synapse. Agonists increase the normal activity of a neurotransmitter, and antagonists block normal neurotransmitter activity. Here, we see how antipsychotics can act as antagonists.

**mood-stabilizing drugs** Psychotropic medications that minimize the lows of depression and the highs of mania.

**antipsychotic drugs** Psychotropic medications used in the treatment of psychotic symptoms, such as hallucinations and delusions.

**anti-anxiety drugs** Psychotropic medications used for treating the symptoms of anxiety.

**Community in Pain**

A young man stands among the graves of relatives on the Pine Ridge Indian Reservation in South Dakota. In the United States, the suicide rate among American Indian and Alaska Native youth (ages 10 to 24) exceeds that of all other racial groups. Both youth and adult suicides have increased substantially over the last two decades (Leavitt et al., 2018; Willis et al., 2014). Traumatic incidents like suicides inevitably have witnesses, and those witnesses suffer from what they see and hear. Their pain may manifest itself in the form of anxiety.

Matthew Ryan Williams/Redux.

these anti-anxiety drugs are used for a continuum of anxiety, from fear of flying to extreme panic attacks. In high doses, benzodiazepines promote sleep, so they can also be used to treat insomnia.

Benzodiazepines ease anxiety by enhancing the effect of GABA, an inhibitory neurotransmitter that decreases or stops some types of neural activity. By giving GABA a boost, these drugs inhibit the firing of neurons that normally induce anxiety reactions. Dangerously addictive and fast-acting, benzodiazepines are potentially lethal when mixed with alcohol, opioids, and other drugs. Between 2010 and 2017, the number of fatal overdoses involving benzodiazepines rose by about 780% (Brooks, 2020). "To address the serious risks of abuse, addiction, physical dependence, and withdrawal reactions," the FDA requires manufacturers to place a boxed warning on the packaging of these drugs (FDA, 2020, para. 1).

**MEDICATION PLUS PSYCHOTHERAPY** Psychotropic medications have helped countless people get back on their feet and enjoy life, but drugs alone don't produce the best long-term outcomes. Studies suggest that psychotropic drugs are most effective when used alongside talk therapy. For example, combining medication with an integrative approach to psychotherapy, including cognitive, behavioral, and psychodynamic perspectives, may reduce major depressive symptoms faster than either approach alone (Cuijpers et al., 2015; Manber et al., 2008). With therapy, Dr. Foster says, "The person feels greater self-efficacy. They're not relying on a pill to manage depression."

Another key point to remember: Medications affect people in different ways. A drug that works for one person may have no impact on another, and could produce distinct side effects. We metabolize (break down) drugs at different rates, which means dosages must be assessed on a case-by-case basis. To complicate matters further, many people take multiple medications at once, and some drugs interact in harmful ways.

## Other Biomedical Therapies

Sometimes, the symptoms of psychological disorders do not improve with medication. In these extreme cases, there are other biomedical options.

**REPETITIVE TRANSCRANIAL MAGNETIC STIMULATION (rTMS)** For example, repetitive transcranial magnetic stimulation (rTMS) appears to be effective in treating symptoms of depression, some types of pain, and stroke symptoms. This technology is also being investigated for other conditions, including PTSD, anxiety disorders, and substance use disorders (Lefaucheur et al., 2020). With rTMS, electromagnetic coils are put on (or above) a person's head, directing brief electrical current into a particular area of the brain (Slotema et al., 2010). The FDA has approved rTMS for treating major depressive disorder, but its effects vary from person to person. Researchers are just beginning to understand why this is the case (Castrillon et al., 2020), and more studies are needed.

**electroconvulsive therapy (ECT)** A biomedical treatment for severe disorders that induces seizures in the brain through electrical currents.

**ELECTROCONVULSIVE THERAPY** Another treatment for severe depression that has not improved with medication or therapy is **electroconvulsive therapy (ECT)**, which essentially causes seizures in the brain. If you've ever seen ECT, or "shock therapy," portrayed in movies, you might think it's a barbaric form of abuse. Truth be told, ECT was a brutal and overused treatment in the mid-20th century (Glass, 2001; Smith, 2001). Doctors jolted patients (in some cases, a dozen times a day)

# Biomedical Therapies

Biomedical therapies use physical interventions to treat psychological disorders. These therapies can be categorized according to the method by which they influence the brain's functioning: structural, electrical, or chemical.

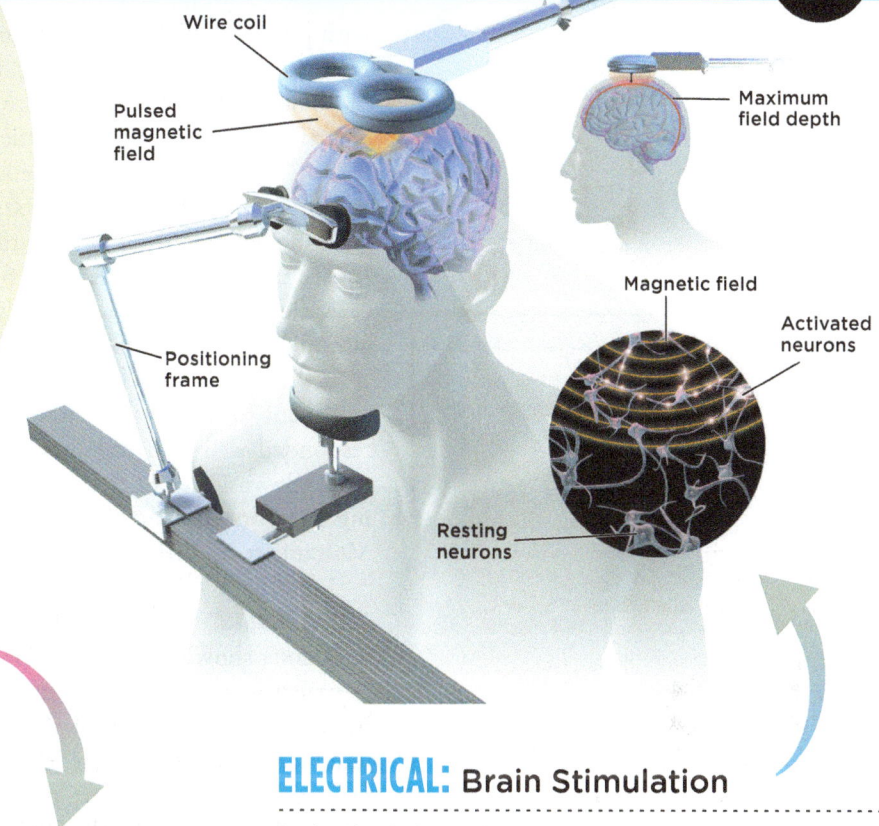

Wire coil

Pulsed magnetic field

Maximum field depth

Positioning frame

Magnetic field

Activated neurons

Resting neurons

## STRUCTURAL: Neurosurgery

Modern surgical techniques are able to target a very precise area of the brain known to be directly involved in the condition being treated. For example, the black circles on these scans mark areas typically targeted for a form of surgery known as anterior cingulotomy, which has been shown to reduce symptoms in patients with severe cases of major depression (Volpini et al., 2017). Using radio frequencies emitted from a 6-millimeter probe, the surgeon destroys part of the anterior cingulate cortex, an area known to be associated with emotions (Faria, 2013).

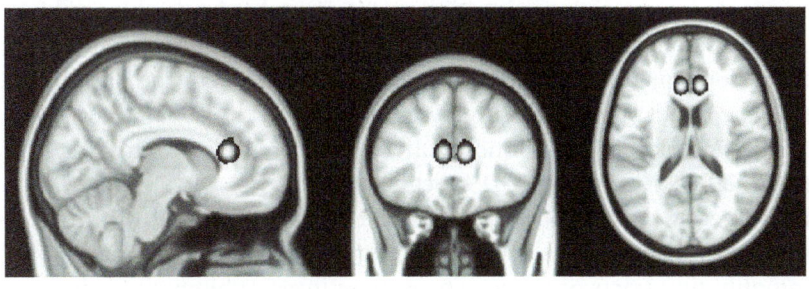

## ELECTRICAL: Brain Stimulation

Brain stimulation techniques can be used to relieve symptoms by affecting the electrical activity of the brain. Electroconvulsive therapy, which involves delivering electric current to certain areas of the brain, may work better than medication for some patients with treatment-resistant depression (Ross et al., 2018). Repetitive transcranial magnetic stimulation (rTMS), shown above, is a noninvasive procedure. A coil pulses a magnetic field that passes painlessly through scalp and bone, penetrating just to the outer cortex. The field induces electric currents in nearby neurons, activating targeted regions in the brain (National Institute of Mental Health, 2016).

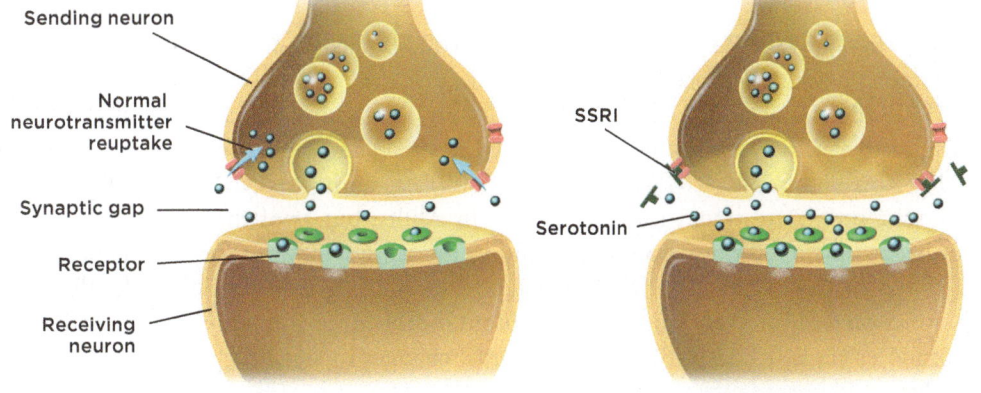

Sending neuron

Normal neurotransmitter reuptake

Synaptic gap

Receptor

Receiving neuron

SSRI

Serotonin

## CHEMICAL:
## Psychotropic Medications

Drug therapies, which alter the brain's chemistry, are the most commonly prescribed biomedical treatment. Each works to influence neurotransmitters thought to be associated with certain disorders. This illustration shows the action of a class of antidepressants known as selective serotonin reuptake inhibitors (SSRIs).

In normal communication between neurons, neurotransmitters released into the synaptic gap bind to the receiving neuron, sending a message. Excess neurotransmitters are reabsorbed into the sending neurons through the process of reuptake.

As indicated by their name, SSRIs inhibit the reuptake of the neurotransmitter serotonin. Allowed to remain longer in the synapse, serotonin can achieve a greater effect.

Credits: (Illustration) Reproduced with permission. Graphic by Bryan Christie Design. Stimulating the Brain by Mark S. George. Copyright 2003 *Scientific American*, Sept. 2003, page 69. A division of Nature America, Inc. All rights reserved; (Brain scans) Reprinted by permission from Macmillan Publishers Ltd: Tractographic analysis of historical lesion surgery for depression. Schoene-Bake JC, Parpaley Y, Weber B, Panksepp J, Hurwitz TA, Coenen VA. *Neuropsychopharmacology*. 2010 December; 35(13): 2553–2563.

with powerful electric currents, creating seizures violent enough to break bones and erase weeks or months of memories (Smith, 2001). ECT has since become much more humane, administered according to guidelines developed by the American Psychiatric Association (2001). Patients take painkillers and muscle relaxants before the treatment, and general anesthesia can be used during the procedure. The electrical currents are weaker, inducing seizures only in the brain. In the United States, patients typically undergo three treatments per week for up to a month (Glass, 2001; National Institute of Mental Health, 2016).

Scientists don't know exactly how ECT reduces the symptoms of depression, although a variety of theories have been proposed (Cyrzyk, 2013; Harrington, 2019; Pirnia et al., 2016). And despite its enduring "bad rap," ECT can be an effective treatment for depression, bipolar disorder, and schizophrenia in people who haven't responded well to psychotherapy or drugs (Glass, 2001; Oremus et al., 2015). The major downside of ECT is its tendency to induce confusion and memory loss, including **anterograde and retrograde amnesia** (American Psychiatric Association, 2001; Moirand et al., 2018; Read & Bentall, 2010).

### CONNECTIONS

In **Chapter 6,** we discussed amnesia, which is memory loss due to physical or psychological conditions. Retrograde amnesia is the inability to access old memories; anterograde amnesia is the inability to make new memories. ECT can cause these types of amnesia, which is one reason the American Psychiatric Association developed guidelines for its use.

**THE EVOLUTION OF NEUROSURGERY** Another extreme option for patients who don't show substantial improvement with psychotherapy or psychotropic drugs is **neurosurgery,** which destroys some portion of the brain or severs connections between different areas of the brain. Like ECT, neurosurgery is tarnished by an unethical past. During the 1930s, 1940s, and 1950s, doctors performed *prefrontal lobotomies,* destroying part of the frontal lobes or disconnecting them from lower areas of the brain (Kucharski, 1984; Wickens, 2015). But lobotomies often had severe side effects, including permanent impairments in everyday functioning. This procedure lacked precision, frequently resulting in personality changes and diminished function. The consequences of lobotomy were often worse than the disorders they aimed to fix. The popularity of this surgery plummeted in the 1950s when the first-generation antipsychotics were introduced, offering a safer alternative to surgery (Caruso & Sheehan, 2017; Harrington, 2019; Schlich, 2015).

Today, brain surgeries are a last-resort treatment for psychological disorders, and they are far more precise than the archaic lobotomy. Surgeons focus on a small target, destroying only tiny tracts of tissue. These more invasive biomedical therapies are seldom used, but they can make a difference in the quality of life for some individuals.

### Stimulate the Brain

An X-ray image of a person undergoing deep brain stimulation (DBS) reveals two electrodes—one implanted in each hemisphere. These electrodes send electrical impulses through certain neural networks, inducing changes that may lead to reduced symptoms. DBS has produced promising results in patients with OCD and depression, but further research is needed to identify its long-term effects (Bergfeld et al., 2016; Lozano et al., 2019).

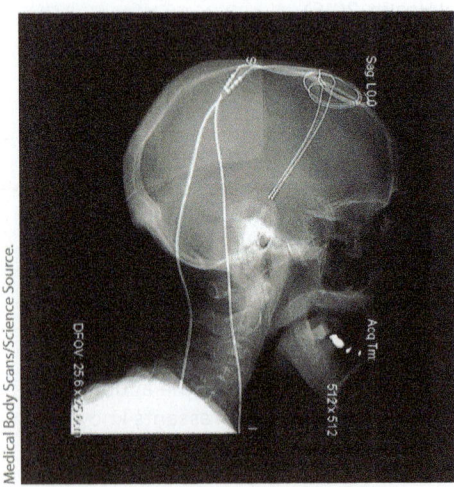

Medical Body Scans/Science Source.

**DEEP BRAIN STIMULATION (DBS)** Some 160,000 people around the world have undergone a surgical procedure called deep brain stimulation (DBS; Lozano et al., 2019). DBS involves implanting electrodes in the brain and sending electrical currents to specific areas thought to be linked to OCD and depression (Lozano et al., 2019; Riva-Posse et al., 2018). The FDA (2009) has authorized the use of DBS for "chronic, severe, treatment-resistant" OCD in adults, but as of this printing it has not been approved for depression. In addition to easing symptoms for some patients, DBS has helped scientists better understand the brain, by revealing that "localized dysfunction and intervention can have profound influences on brain-wide networks" (Lozano et al., 2019, p. 148). In other words, changes in small regions of the brain can have widespread effects.

**neurosurgery** A biomedical therapy that involves the destruction of some portion of the brain or connections between different areas of the brain.

### Put Your Heads Together

In your group, **A)** identify the pros and cons of using psychotropic medications, **B)** describe the circumstances in which other biomedical therapies (rTMS or ECT, for example) might be needed, and **C)** consider how biomedical approaches to treating psychological disorders differ across cultures.

## SHOW WHAT YOU KNOW

1. A young man is taking psychotropic medications for major depression, but the drugs do not seem to be alleviating his symptoms. Which of the following biomedical approaches might his psychiatrist try next?

   **A.** split-brain operation    **C.** prefrontal lobotomy

   **B.** tardive dyskinesia    **D.** electroconvulsive therapy

2. Psychotropic drugs can be divided into four categories: mood-stabilizing, antipsychotic, anti-anxiety, and

   **A.** mood normalizer.    **C.** antagonist.

   **B.** antidepressant.    **D.** atypical antipsychotic.

3. Patients with serious disorders who don't show substantial improvement with psychotherapy or psychotropic drugs may benefit from _____, which involves destroying some portion of the brain or severing connections between different areas of the brain.

4. How do biomedical interventions differ from psychotherapy? Compare their goals.

✓ CHECK YOUR ANSWERS AT THE BACK OF THE BOOK.

# Psychotherapy: Who's in the Mix?

**LO 9** Describe how culture interacts with the therapy process.

**WHEN TO LISTEN, WHEN TO TALK**   One of the challenges of providing therapy in an ethnically diverse country like the United States is meeting the needs of clients from vastly different cultures. For Dr. Foster, this part of the job is relatively straightforward. All his clients are Northern Plains Indians, which means they follow similar social rules. And because Dr. Foster belongs to this culture, its norms are second nature to him. He has come to expect, for example, that a young Lakota client will not begin talking until he, the therapist, has spoken first. Dr. Foster is an elder, and elders are shown respect. Thus, he might begin a session by talking for 3 or 4 minutes. Once the client does open up, he limits his verbal and nonverbal feedback, sitting quietly and avoiding eye contact. In mainstream U.S. culture, people continuously respond to each other with facial animation and filler words like "wow" and "uh-huh," but the Lakota find this ongoing feedback intrusive.

Another facet of Lakota communication—one that often eludes therapists from outside the culture—is the tendency to pause for long periods in the middle of a conversation. If Dr. Foster poses the question "How are you doing?" a client might take 20 to 30 seconds to respond. These long pauses make some non-Indians very uncomfortable, according to Dr. Foster. "I've found that an outside provider will feel awkward, will start talking within 3 to 5 seconds," he adds. "The client will feel that they never have a chance to speak, and they'll leave frustrated because the person wouldn't be quiet [and] listen."

**The Power of Culture**
Residents of the Rosebud Reservation gather for a cultural event. Dr. Foster believes and hopes that Indian language, spiritual ceremony, and culture can act somewhat like a shield, protecting people from psychological problems. But centuries of assaults by Western society have eroded American Indian cultures.

*Robert VAN DER HILST/Gamma-Rapho via Getty Images.*

## ACROSS THE WORLD

### KNOW THY CLIENT

Clearly, it is important for therapists to understand the cultural context in which they work. But does that mean therapists and clients should be matched according to ethnicity? Some clients prefer to discuss private thoughts and feelings with a therapist who shares their experience—someone who knows firsthand how it feels to be, say, an African American male (Cabral & Smith, 2011; Steinfeldt et al., 2020). For clients with certain disorders (like severe PTSD), treatment outcomes may be better when the therapist and client belong to the same ethnicity. However, it's important to remember that a common ethnic background does not always translate to shared experiences and perspectives. People of the same ethnicity may belong to different religions and socioeconomic groups, and their views on psychotherapy may conflict (Ruglass et al., 2014). "Culturally

**SHOULD THERAPISTS AND CLIENTS BE MATCHED ACCORDING TO ETHNICITY?**

Thierry Falise/LightRocket via Getty Images.

**Culture-Conscious**
A psychologist meets with two young Muslim women at the Centre for Needy Orphans and Poor Children in Thailand. Psychologists must always be mindful of cultural factors that may come into play during therapy.

sensitive treatment needs to be aware of differences between racial groups, but it also requires an appreciation of differences among members within each racial group" (Steinfeldt et al., 2020, p. 6). Working with a therapist of the same background may be helpful, but it is not always essential.

When the therapist and client do come from different worlds, it is the therapist's job to get in touch with the client's unique perspective and adjust their treatment approach accordingly (Soto et al., 2018). That includes respecting cultural norms. Western therapists working in Sri Lanka, for example, should be aware that mental illness is highly stigmatized in this cultural setting, and that intense emotional displays, such as crying in group therapy, are taboo (Christopher et al., 2014). Similarly, a therapist working with Syrian refugees must appreciate not only their experience with armed conflict and trauma, but also the role that Islam may play in their lives (Soto et al., 2018).

It is also critical that therapists be cognizant of their own cultural biases and sensitive to the many forms of prejudice and discrimination people experience. In addition to their personal problems, some clients may be dealing with the larger specter of racism. Suppose an African American client is already facing depression. Seeing media reports about police officers shooting Black men could potentially exacerbate the client's sense of isolation and hopelessness (Soto et al., 2018).

Within any group, there is vast variation from one individual to the next, but cultural themes do emerge. The Sioux and Blackfeet Indians, for example, are very relationship-oriented. "What kind of car you drive or how nice your home is, and so forth, is not even important," Dr. Foster says. "Relationships matter." Some therapists working with American Indian groups report that entire families may show up at sessions to express support for the client (Prochaska & Norcross, 2018). Similarly, Latinx and Polynesian cultures tend to place a high value on family, often prioritizing relationships with relatives over individual needs (Allen et al., 2016; Greenfield & Quiroz, 2013). Keep in mind that these are only general trends; assuming they apply to an entire population promotes stereotyping (Wong et al., 2018).

When it comes to psychological treatment, there is no "one-size-fits-all" approach. Every client has a unique story and a singular set of psychological needs. Responding to the needs of the person—their culture, religious beliefs, and unique personality traits—is essential for successful therapy (Anestis et al., 2021; Norcross & Wampold, 2018; Soto el al., 2018). 💬

## Let's Get Through This Together

For some people, group therapy is a better fit than individual therapy. First developed in the 1940s, group therapy has adapted to the ever-changing demands of clinical work (Brabender & Fallon, 2019; Yalom & Leszcz, 2005). Usually, group therapy is led by one or two therapists trained in any of the various approaches (for example, psychoanalytic or cognitive). Sessions typically include 5–15 clients, and members share their problems as openly as possible (APA, 2019). There are groups to help people cope with shyness, panic disorder, compulsive gambling, grief, and sexual identity issues, just to name a few. Working in a group, clients often realize that they are not alone in their struggles to improve. It is not always a psychological disorder that brings people to group therapy, but instead a desire to work on a specific issue.

**LO 10**  Identify the benefits and challenges of group therapy.

**GROUP THERAPY**    Research shows that group therapy is as effective as individual therapy for addressing many problems. In fact, it is the preferred approach for interpersonal issues, because it allows therapists to observe clients interacting with others.

The therapist's skills play an important role in the success of group sessions, and the dynamics between clients and therapists may be similar to those that arise in individual therapy. (Clients may demonstrate resistance or transference, for example.)

**SELF-HELP GROUPS\*** Another type of group that offers opportunities for personal growth is the *self-help group*. Alcoholics Anonymous (AA), Al-Anon, Parents Without Partners, and Weight Watchers are commonly known examples, but self-help groups provide support for people facing a host of issues, including bereavement, divorce, infertility, HIV/AIDS, and cancer. Many of these groups have organically sprung up on the internet. For example, during the coronavirus pandemic, people with lingering COVID-19 symptoms (also known as "long-haul Covid") shared information and provided emotional support for each other through online forums (Callard & Perego, 2021).

With more than 2 million active members in 181 countries, AA is the most widely used self-help group in the world (AA, 2019; Kelly et al., 2020). Group meetings are open to anyone who wants help overcoming an alcohol problem. AA does not provide counseling but does offer one-on-one support called "sponsorship." Known as a "12-step program," AA bases its model on 12 steps that members must follow in order to take control of their drinking problem (Kelly et al., 2020). Groups like Al-Anon and Alateen are based on the 12 steps of AA but provide support for friends and family of people with alcohol problems. Other 12-step programs include Debtors Anonymous, Narcotics Anonymous, Overeaters Anonymous, and Sex Addicts Anonymous. These groups strive to ensure a high level of confidentiality for all participants.

Self-help groups are *not* typically run by a psychiatrist, licensed psychologist, or other mental health professional, but by a mental health advisor or *paraprofessional* trained to run the groups. The typical AA leader, for example, is a "recovering alcoholic" who grasps the complexities of alcoholism and recovery but is not necessarily a mental health professional. How effective are 12-step programs like AA? One large review concluded that AA and similar programs run by mental health professionals "performed at least as well as established active comparison treatments (e.g., CBT) on all outcomes except for abstinence where it often outperformed other treatments" (Kelly et al., 2020, p. 621). In simple terms, the AA approach seems to work just as well as psychological treatments when it comes to getting people to drink less, and it may be more effective for maintaining abstinence (Kelly et al., 2020).

**FAMILY THERAPY** Introduced in North America in the 1940s, **family therapy** focuses on the family as an integrated system, recognizing how the interactions within can create instability or lead to collapse of the entire unit (Corey, 2017). Family therapy explores relationship problems rather than the symptoms of particular disorders, teaching communication skills in the process. The family is viewed as a dynamic, holistic entity, and the goal is to understand each person's role in the system, not to root out troublemakers, assign blame, or identify one member who must be "fixed." Because families typically seek the resolution of a specific problem, the course of therapy tends to be brief (Corey, 2017). Suppose a teenage girl has become withdrawn at home and is acting out in school, and the whole family decides to participate in therapy. The therapist begins by helping the parents identify ways they encourage her behaviors (not following through with consequences, for example), and may examine how their marital dynamics affect their children. If it becomes evident that the marriage is in trouble, the parents might seek therapy without the rest of the family, which brings us to the next topic: *couples therapy.*

**family therapy** A type of therapy that focuses on the family as an integrated system, recognizing that the interactions within it can create instability or lead to the breakdown of the family unit.

---

\*You can learn more about self-help groups in your area from the National Mental Health Consumers' Self-Help Clearinghouse, at www.mhselfhelp.org.

**COUPLES THERAPY**    What are some common problems plaguing marriages? Trust issues are not unusual, especially if there have been betrayals in the past. Another source of conflict is the "baggage" each person brings to the relationship—childhood traumas, unhappy family dynamics, and other life experiences. Stress can test relationships, too. Chronic medical conditions, infertility, and money problems are just a few circumstances that create strain (Bradbury & Bodenmann, 2020). When these problems begin to cause significant distress, couples therapy is a smart choice. Couples therapists are trained in many of the therapeutic approaches described earlier, and they tend to focus on conflict management. A key goal of couples therapy and relationship education programs is to provide guidance on how to communicate within relationships (Roddy et al., 2020; Scott et al., 2013).

**TAKING STOCK: AN APPRAISAL OF GROUP THERAPIES**    Like any treatment, group therapies have their strengths and limitations (TABLE **14.3**). Group members may not get along, or they may feel uncomfortable discussing sensitive issues. But conflict and discomfort are not necessarily bad when it comes to therapy (group or otherwise), because such feelings often motivate people to reevaluate how they interact with others, and perhaps try new approaches.

Evaluating group therapies can be difficult because there is so much variation in approach (psychodynamic, cognitive behavioral, and so on). For many types of clients and problems, the outcomes of group therapy rival those of individual therapy (Barrera et al., 2013; Burlingame & Baldwin, 2011; Yalom & Leszcz, 2005). As with individual therapies, the role of the therapist is of critical importance: Empathy, good facilitation skills, listening, and careful observation are important predictors of successful outcomes. So, too, are the preparation of the group members, the therapist's verbal style, and the "climate" and cohesion of the group (Burlingame & Baldwin, 2011).

Joshua Lott/The New York Times/Redux.

**Finding Strength in Others**

Cook County inmates participate in a class at the jail's Mental Health Transition Center. There are over a dozen mental health professionals working at the jail, and they often provide therapy in group settings. "We have such a large number of people that receive mental health treatment services here . . . while they may have individualized treatment plans, it's very difficult to individualize the actual care that they receive," Dr. Jones Tapia explains. "So you have to do more group work and rely on group activities to really get the person to the level of stability that they should be at."

## Put Your Heads Together

Team up and **A)** discuss the advantages and disadvantages of group therapy. **B)** Looking back at Chapter 13, identify which psychological disorders would be best addressed through group therapy, and explain your reasoning. **C)** Identify disorders that would be best addressed in private sessions, again explaining your reasoning.

**TABLE 14.3    Evaluating Group Therapy**

| Strengths | Weaknesses |
|---|---|
| Sessions generally cost about half as much as individual therapy (Helliker, 2009). | Not everyone feels at ease discussing personal troubles in a room full of people. |
| People find relief and comfort knowing that others face similar struggles. | Group members may not always get along (Parks & Tasca, 2021). This friction can inhibit the therapeutic process. |
| Group members offer support and encouragement. They also challenge one another to think and behave in new ways (APA, 2019). | Group therapy may not be enough for those with complex problems and significant impairment (Tasca et al., 2021). |
| Seeing others improve offers hope and inspiration. | Some group therapy participants have had negative family experiences, and thus maintain negative expectations of the group setting (Yalom & Leszcz, 2005). |

Listed above are some of the pros and cons of group therapy.

# Does Psychotherapy Work?

**LO 11**  Evaluate the effectiveness of psychotherapy.

So far, we have familiarized ourselves with the strengths and weaknesses of various therapeutic approaches, but now let's direct our attention to overall outcomes. How effective is psychotherapy in general? This question is not easily answered, partly because therapeutic "success" is so difficult to quantify. What constitutes success in one context may not be the same in another. And for therapists trying to measure the efficacy of their own methods, eliminating bias can be very challenging. But there is reason to be optimistic.

Decades of research have established that psychotherapy is indeed effective (Norcross & Lambert, 2018; Rathgeber et al., 2019). For many disorders, the benefits derived from psychotherapy may actually surpass those provided by medication (Decker, 2016a). In one large study investigating the effects of psychotherapy, all therapeutic approaches performed equally well across disorders. But there is one caveat: Individuals who were limited by their insurance companies in terms of therapist choice and treatment duration did not see the same improvement as those who were less restricted by insurance (Seligman, 1995). Perhaps this is not surprising, since people who start therapy but then quit prematurely tend to experience less successful outcomes (Swift & Greenberg, 2012; Windle et al., 2020). Given the many therapeutic approaches, the unique qualities of each client, and the variety of therapists, identifying the best type of therapy can be challenging (Pope & Wedding, 2014). But it is relatively safe to say that psychotherapy is "cost-effective, reduces disability, morbidity, and mortality, improves work functioning, decreases use of psychiatric hospitalization, and . . . leads to reduction in unnecessary use of medical and surgical services" (APA, 2012c, para. 19).

How much therapy is enough? The answer to this question depends on the specific needs of the client and the ability of the therapist to help reduce symptoms and improve functioning (Owen et al., 2016). Around 50% of clients show "clinically significant improvement" after 21 psychotherapy sessions, whereas some 75% show the same degree of improvement after twice as many sessions (Lambert et al., 2001).

# Help When You Need It

If you or someone in your life is showing signs of a psychological disorder or needs support coping with a divorce, death, or major life change, do not hesitate to seek professional help. The first step is figuring out what kind of therapy best fits the person and the situation (individual, family, group, and so on). Then there is the issue of cost: Therapy can be expensive. These days, one 60-minute therapy session can cost anywhere from $80 to $250 (or more). If you attend a college or university, however, your student fees may cover services at a student counseling center.

Many people have health insurance that helps pay for medication and psychotherapy. In 2010 the Mental Health Parity and Addiction Equity Act (MHPAEA) took effect, requiring all group health insurance plans (with 50 employees or more) to provide mental health treatment benefits equal to those provided for medical treatment. Essentially, this means that mental health problems merit the same attention and resources as physical health problems. Copayments must be the same, limits on treatment must be the same, and so on. If your insurance plan does not restrict the number of times you can see your family physician, it also cannot limit the number of visits you have with a psychologist (APA, 2014, May). For those without insurance, community-based mental health centers provide quality care to all in need, often with a sliding scale for fees.

The next step is finding the right therapist, that is, the right qualified therapist. Helping others manage their mental health issues is a tremendous responsibility that only licensed professionals should take on. Licensing requirements differ from state to state, so we encourage you to verify the standing of a therapist's license with your state's Department of Regulatory Agencies. The pool of potential therapists might include clinical psychologists with PhDs or PsyDs, counseling psychologists, psychiatrists, psychiatric nurses, social workers, marriage and family therapists, pastoral counselors, people with EdDs (doctorates in education), and more. (See the online appendix Careers in Psychology for additional information.)

## From Self-Help to Smartphones

Type "psychology" or "self-help" into your search engine, and you will find thousands of books, articles, and YouTube channels designed to reduce stress, boost self-esteem, and beat depression. Some self-help resources contain valuable information, but others make claims that lack scientific support or propagate myths (Kayes & Bailey, 2018). Keep an open mind, but proceed with skepticism, especially when it comes to the research cited by self-help purveyors. As you have learned, determining the efficacy of therapy is a difficult business, even when studies are impeccably designed. Consumer beware.

**LO 12** Summarize the strengths and weaknesses of telepsychology.

### Didn't See That Coming

HAS COVID CHANGED THERAPY FOREVER?

With 90% of U.S. adults connected to the internet and 81% owning smartphones (Anderson et al., 2019; Pew Research Center, 2019), many therapists and clients were already taking advantage of digital technologies before COVID-19. But the pandemic really thrust these tools into mainstream use. *Telepsychology*, or psychological care delivered with the help of communication technologies such as video conferencing, phone calls, and e-mail (APA, 2014m), became the obvious choice for many therapists and clients when in-person visits were no longer feasible (Greenbaum, 2020). "The whole paradigm of sitting in a room with a clinician and receiving an intervention in a 45-minute session has essentially been flipped on its head," said psychologist Adam Haim in a 2020 interview with *Monitor on Psychology* (Greenbaum, 2020, p. 46).

Fortunately for those who used (and continue to use) telepsychology, this approach seems to work quite well for treating a variety of mental health issues, among them depression, anxiety, and PTSD (Greenbaum, 2020; Turgoose et al., 2018; Varker et al., 2019). There are some clear advantages to this approach, even in the absence of a pandemic. For example, it completely eliminates the hassle of traveling to a therapist's office. This is particularly helpful for clients who have limited mobility or live in rural and remote areas. Telepsychology also saves money, as it has "the potential to reduce healthcare costs for patients, therapists, and society as a whole" (Stoll et al., 2020, p. 5). There are some potential drawbacks, including concerns about privacy and reimbursement: *Is the video conferencing app adequately encrypted? Will my insurance company pay for this type of treatment?* (Calkins, 2021). Navigating the therapist–client relationship presents new challenges as well (Glass & Bickler, 2021). But such issues are being worked out, and many psychologists feel

Rawpixel.com/Shutterstock.com.

**Telepsychology**

With digital communication technologies such as Zoom and Google Meet, therapists can conduct sessions with clients on the opposite side of the globe. But problems may arise when therapy occurs online; for example, certain types of nonverbal communication may be difficult to detect (de Bitencourt Machado et al., 2016; Glass & Bickler, 2021).

**Can Instagram Help Diagnose Depression?**
Which photo is more likely to be posted by a person experiencing depression? One group of researchers used "machine learning tools" to identify signs of depression in Instagram posts. They found that "photos posted by depressed individuals tended to be bluer, darker, and grayer" than those posted by nondepressed people (Reece & Danforth, 2017, p. 7). Republished with permission of Springer Science from Instagram photos reveal predictive markers of depression, Reece and Danforth, from EPJ Data Science (2017) 6:15. doi:10.1140/epjds/s13688-017-0110-z; permission conveyed through Copyright Clearance Center, Inc.

positive about incorporating online therapy into their practice (Békés & Aafjes-van Doorn, 2020). More research is needed to fully understand the advantages and limitations of telepsychology, but one thing seems certain: The pandemic catapulted it into widespread use, and it's likely "here to stay" (Calkins, 2021). ⊕

**MENTAL HEALTH APPS**    Some mental health experts believe that smartphones can help identify mental health issues and facilitate the treatment of psychological disorders. Unlike therapists, who only see their clients once or twice a week, smartphones stay with their owners almost all hours of the day. Phones also have built-in technologies (GPS, movement trackers, and sound and video recorders) that can be used to monitor behaviors associated with mental health, such as sleep patterns, physical activity, and social interactions (Bush et al., 2019). For example, a person who is becoming depressed may be less likely to leave home, respond to phone calls, and be active on social media—all activities that could be recorded by a smartphone. What's more, that same smartphone could be used to connect people to peer support networks and therapists (Dobbs, 2017). Research suggests that some mental health apps can be useful in the treatment of depression, anxiety, and substance use problems, but there is a mismatch between the speed at which apps are developed and the rate at which researchers can evaluate them. An app can be developed in 18 weeks, but conducting a randomized controlled trial may take 3 to 5 years (Bush et al., 2019). With some 10,000 mental health apps to choose from, how do consumers know which ones are high-quality and appropriate for their circumstances? At this point, the field is in great need of rigorous research and standard quality control practices (Torous et al., 2019).

**PASSIONATE PROVIDERS**    Before wrapping up, we thought you might like to know what Dr. Dan Foster and Dr. Nneka Jones Tapia are doing these days. Dr. Foster is currently working full-time at Fort Belknap Tribal Health in Montana. He and his wife Becky (also a doctorate-level psychologist) consult for the Rosebud Tribe Methamphetamine Program, in addition to raising their younger children. (They have 10 in all.) One of their daughters, also a clinical psychologist, provides care to clients at the Great Falls VA Clinic. The Covid pandemic has been terribly painful, as many in their community have been lost to the virus, but the Fosters continue to find "much meaning, purpose, fulfillment in parenting and [their] vocations," according to Dr. Foster.

After many years of service at Cook County Jail, Dr. Jones Tapia has decided to take her career in a new direction. She is currently Managing Director of

Macmillan Learning.

Dr. Dan Foster with his wife, Dr. Becky Foster.

Courtesy Dr. Nneka Jones Tapia.

Dr. Nneka Jones Tapia.

Justice Initiatives at Chicago Beyond, an organization devoted to promoting equity and creating opportunities for Chicago's youth. Looking back on her days at the jail, Dr. Jones Tapia thinks about the remarkable changes she witnessed in some of the men and women confined there. She remembers how they appeared in their mugshots when they first came into custody. "I can't even describe it. It's almost like they look humiliated; they look angry; it's every negative emotion you can think of," she says. Helping these men and women change their outlook and move in a more positive direction, and seeing that transformation in their faces, is "an intrinsic reward that is like none other," Dr. Jones Tapia says. "I try to encourage as many clinical professionals as I can to work with people who have been justice-involved. . . . To me, there is true value in really helping a human being to actualize their great potential."

## SHOW WHAT YOU KNOW

1. Studies indicate that psychotherapy is generally effective, but which of the following factors has been linked to less successful outcomes?
   A. type of therapeutic approach
   B. client's disorder
   C. limits imposed by an insurance company
   D. Mental Health Parity and Addiction Equity Act

2. Under what circumstances might group therapy fail or be inappropriate?

3. What are some concerns regarding online psychotherapy?

4. If you were trying to convince a friend that psychological treatment works for many people, what evidence would you provide? What would you say about the role of culture in its outcome?

✓ CHECK YOUR ANSWERS AT THE BACK OF THE BOOK.

## Summary of Concepts

### LO 1   Outline the history of treatment for psychological disorders. (p. 528)

Early "treatments" for psychological disorders were often inhumane. According to one theory, Stone Age people may have used trephination (drilling holes through the skull) to let demons escape. In the late 1700s, Philippe Pinel advanced the idea of "moral treatment," which eventually spread throughout Europe and the United States. In the mid- to late 1800s, Dorothea Dix supported the "mental hygiene movement," a campaign to reform asylums in the United States. The mid-1900s

witnessed deinstitutionalization, a mass movement of people with psychological disorders out of U.S. mental institutions and into the community.

### LO 2   Explain how the main approaches to therapy differ and identify their common goal. (p. 530)

The insight therapies—psychoanalysis, psychodynamic therapy, and humanistic therapy—aim to increase awareness of self and environment. Behavior therapy focuses on behavioral change. Cognitive therapy seeks to change maladaptive thoughts. Biomedical therapy targets the biological basis of disorders, often with the use of medication. All these approaches share a common goal: to reduce symptoms and increase quality of life, whether the person suffers from a debilitating psychological disorder or simply wants to lead a happier existence.

### LO 3 Describe how psychoanalysis differs from psychodynamic therapy. (p. 533)

Psychoanalysis, the first formal system of psychotherapy, attempts to uncover unconscious conflicts, making it possible to address and work through them. Psychodynamic therapy is an updated form of psychoanalysis that incorporates many of Freud's core themes, including the notion that personality characteristics and behavior problems often can be traced to unconscious conflicts. With psychodynamic therapy, therapists see clients once a week for several months rather than many times a week for years. And instead of sitting quietly off to the side, therapists face clients and engage in dialogue.

### LO 4 Outline the principles and characteristics of humanistic therapy. (p. 535)

Humanistic therapy concentrates on the positive aspects of human nature: our powerful desires to form close relationships, treat others with warmth and empathy, and grow as individuals. Instead of digging up unconscious thoughts and feelings, humanistic therapy emphasizes conscious experiences and problems in the present.

### LO 5 Describe person-centered therapy. (p. 535)

Person-centered therapy aims to help clients reach their full potential. Sitting face-to-face with the client, the therapist's main job is to "be there" for the client through empathy, unconditional positive regard, genuineness, and active listening, all important components of building a therapeutic alliance. The goal of treatment is to reduce incongruence between the ideal self and real self, to create a warm and accepting relationship between therapist and client, and to help clients see they have the power to make changes in their lives and follow a path of positive growth.

### LO 6 Outline the principles and characteristics of behavior therapy. (p. 537)

Using the principles of classical conditioning, operant conditioning, and observational learning, behavior therapy aims to replace maladaptive behaviors with more adaptive behaviors. It incorporates a variety of techniques, including exposure therapy, aversion therapy, systematic desensitization, and behavior modification. Behavior therapy focuses on observable behaviors in the present.

### LO 7 Outline the principles and characteristics of cognitive therapy. (p. 541)

The goal of cognitive therapy is to identify maladaptive thinking and help clients change the way they view the world and thoughts. relationships. Aaron Beck believes patterns of automatic thoughts, or cognitive distortions, lie at the root of psychological disturbances. The aim of cognitive therapy is to help clients recognize and challenge cognitive distortions. Sessions are short-term, action-oriented, and homework-intensive. Albert Ellis created rational emotive behavior therapy (REBT), another form of cognitive therapy, to help people identify and correct irrational and illogical ways of thinking.

### LO 8 Identify biomedical treatments for psychological disorders and describe their common goal. (p. 545)

Psychopharmacology is the scientific study of how psychotropic medications alter perception, mood, behavior, and other aspects of psychological functioning. Psychotropic drugs include antidepressant, mood-stabilizing, antipsychotic, and anti-anxiety medications. When severe symptoms do not improve with medication and psychotherapy, other biomedical options are available: electroconvulsive therapy (ECT), which causes seizures in the brain; and neurosurgery, which destroys some portion of the brain or severs connections between different brain areas. Biomedical interventions target the biological roots of psychological disorders.

### LO 9 Describe how culture interacts with the therapy process. (p. 551)

Therapists work with clients from a vast array of cultures. Every client has a unique story and a singular set of psychological needs, but therapists should know the cultural context in which they work. This includes being respectful of cultural norms and sensitive to the many forms of prejudice and discrimination people can experience.

### LO 10 Identify the benefits and challenges of group therapy. (p. 552)

The benefits of group therapy include cost-effectiveness, identification with others, accountability, support, encouragement, and a sense of hope. Challenges include potential conflict among group members and discomfort expressing feelings in the presence of others.

### LO 11 Evaluate the effectiveness of psychotherapy. (p. 555)

Psychotherapy generally works with different approaches achieving comparable success across disorders. Clients with insurance plans that limit choice of therapists and duration of therapy do not see the same improvement as those with less restrictive insurance. In addition, people who start therapy but then quit prematurely experience less successful outcomes.

### LO 12 Summarize the strengths and weaknesses of telepsychology. (p. 556)

With more people connected to the internet and owning smartphones, many therapists and clients are taking advantage of digital technologies. Telepsychology, or psychological care delivered with the help of communication technologies such as video conferencing, phone calls, and e-mail, is a good choice for many therapists and clients when in-person visits are not feasible. For example, these digital tools are valuable for serving rural areas and providing treatment to those who would otherwise have no access. There are some potential drawbacks, including concerns about privacy, reimbursement from insurance companies, and communication with nonverbal cues.

## Key Terms

active listening, p. 535
anti-anxiety drugs, p. 547
antidepressant drugs, p. 546
antipsychotic drugs, p. 547
aversion therapy, p. 539
behavior modification, p. 539
behavior therapy, p. 530
biomedical therapy, p. 530
cognitive behavioral therapy (CBT), p. 543
cognitive therapy, p. 541

deinstitutionalization, p. 528
eclectic approach to therapy, p. 532
electroconvulsive therapy (ECT), p. 548
empathy, p. 535
evidence-based practice, p. 532
exposure, p. 537
family therapy, p. 553
free association, p. 533

genuineness, p. 535
humanistic therapy, p. 535
insight therapies, p. 530
interpretation, p. 533
mood-stabilizing drugs, p. 547
neurosurgery, p. 550
nondirective, p. 535
overgeneralization, p. 541
person-centered therapy, p. 535

psychodynamic therapy, p. 534
psychotherapy, p. 530
rational emotive behavior therapy (REBT), p. 542
resistance, p. 533
systematic desensitization, p. 538
therapeutic alliance, p. 535
token economy, p. 539
transference, p. 534

## Test Prep Are You Ready?

1. Philippe Pinel worked to improve the living conditions of people in mental institutions, removing their chains and showing them respect and care. This _____ eventually spread throughout Europe and the United States.
   A. trephination
   B. moral treatment
   C. psychoanalysis
   D. deinstitutionalization

2. Which of the following goals are shared by the main approaches to therapy?
   A. increasing awareness of self and environment
   B. using medications to target biological basis of disorder
   C. focusing on behavioral change
   D. reducing symptoms and increasing quality of life

3. Lorena has three weekly sessions with her therapist. She generally lies on a couch while her therapist sits off to the side, out of Lorena's sight. The goal of her therapy is to uncover unconscious conflicts influencing her behavior. Which type of therapy is Lorena receiving?
   A. psychodynamic
   B. psychoanalysis
   C. behavioral
   D. humanistic

4. A friend tells you about their therapist, who is nondirective, uses active listening, and shows empathy and unconditional positive regard. This therapist is most likely conducting:
   A. cognitive therapy.
   B. behavior therapy.
   C. psychoanalysis.
   D. person-centered therapy.

5. Systematic desensitization uses _____ that represent(s) gradual increases in clients' anxiety.
   A. hierarchies
   B. token economies
   C. behavior modification
   D. free association

6. Which of the following statements would not qualify as one of Beck's cognitive errors?
   A. My friend stole from me; therefore, everyone will steal from me.
   B. Getting fired once does not mean my career is over.
   C. I forgot to vote; that's why the president lost.
   D. My hairdresser added $20 to my Visa charge. You can't trust salons.

7. Which of the following claims about group therapy is true?
   A. It generally costs twice as much as one-on-one therapy.
   B. Everyone feels comfortable sharing their troubles with a group.
   C. Group members avoid supporting each other.
   D. Seeing others improve offers hope and inspiration.

8. Humanistic therapy emphasizes the positive nature of humans, with a focus on:
   A. the unconscious.
   B. rational emotive behavior.
   C. past problems.
   D. the present.

9. _____ is the scientific study of how medication alters perceptions, moods, behaviors, and other aspects of psychological functioning.
   A. Biomedical therapy
   B. Psychoeducation
   C. Therapeutic alliance
   D. Psychopharmacology

10. Overall, psychotherapy is cost-effective and helps to decrease disability, hospitalization, and problems at work. Which of the following factors may reduce its effectiveness?

    A. unlimited number of sessions

    B. insurance-mandated limitations on choice of therapist

    C. number of people in a therapy session

    D. gender of therapist

11. Compare and contrast cognitive behavioral therapy and insight therapies.

12. Beck identified a collection of common cognitive distortions. Describe two of these distortions and give examples of each.

13. How might a behavior therapist help someone overcome a fear of spiders?

14. How does culture influence the therapeutic process?

15. Describe the strengths and weaknesses of telepsychology.

✓ CHECK YOUR ANSWERS AT THE BACK OF THE BOOK.

# Check Your Answers

 SHOW WHAT YOU KNOW

## What Is Psychology and How Did It Begin?

1. basic research; applied research
2. D. change
3. B. functionalism.
4. Answers will vary. The *sociocultural* and *biopsychosocial* perspectives are similar in that both examine how interactions with other people influence behaviors and mental processes. The *cognitive* and *biological* perspectives differ in that the cognitive perspective focuses on the thought processes underlying behavior, while the biological perspective emphasizes physiological processes.

## How Do Psychologists Do Research?

1. C. representative sample
2. hypothesis
3. Answers will vary. If the population is large, the researcher will need to select a sample. A random sample is a subset of the population chosen through a procedure that ensures all members have an equal chance of being selected. Random sampling increases the likelihood of achieving a representative sample, or subgroup, whose characteristics are similar to the population of interest. If the sample is small relative to the population size, we must be careful about drawing inferences from sample to population. It is important for researchers to choose representative samples, because this allows them to generalize their findings, or apply information from a sample to the population at large.

## Descriptive and Correlational Methods

1. C. new or unexplored topics.
2. The correlational method is useful for illuminating links between variables, and it helps researchers make predictions, but it cannot determine cause and effect. Even if variables $X$ and $Y$ are strongly correlated, we cannot assume that changes in $X$ are driving changes in $Y$ (or vice versa); there may be some third variable influencing both $X$ and $Y$. Some possible third variables that may be involved in the correlation between smartphone use and absenteeism might include: boredom on the job, an ill family member, or apathy about work.
3. naturalistic observation

## The Experimental Method

1. D. cause-and-effect relationship
2. debriefing
3. At any major research institution, experiments on humans and animals must be approved by an Institutional Review Board (IRB). An IRB is a committee that reviews research proposals to ensure that the rights and welfare of all participants are protected.

## Test Prep Are You Ready?

1. B. applied research.
2. B. critical thinking.
3. C. the nature side of the nature–nurture issue.
4. D. humanistic
5. C. the scientific method
6. C. variables.
7. A. positive correlation.
8. B. case study
9. A. double-blind
10. D. random sample
11. Answers will vary. The goals of psychology are to describe, explain, predict, and change behavior. These goals lay the foundation for the scientific approach and the research designs used to carry out experiments in psychology. A researcher might conduct a study to describe differences in children's food preferences. If the researcher saw a pattern of food preferences among children within families, she might explain it by considering the children's home environment. She might conduct a study that predicted children's food preferences based on other close family members. The researcher might apply the findings to help experts create a campaign for healthy eating.
12. Answers will vary. They will need to read through other studies on aggression and exposure to media violence to see how they ensured ethical treatment. The researchers will also need to read through the ethical guidelines of the professional organizations and submit their proposal to the Institutional Review Board.
13. Answers will vary. See Table 1.1.
14. Answers will vary. Look for studies on topics that would be very hard for researchers to manipulate in an ethical manner (for example, breast-feeding, amount of television watched, attitudes). Also check to see how the sample participants were selected.

15. Answers will vary. In the SpongeBob study, the researchers used the experimental method to establish a cause-and-effect relationship between watching the cartoons and changes in cognitive function. The children were randomly assigned to the groups, and the researchers manipulated the activities they were involved in. Other variables were held constant. One way to change the study is to use a different age group.

# 2 Biology and Behavior

 SHOW WHAT YOU KNOW

## Introducing the Brain

1. D: creates cross-sectional images using X-rays

   B: records electrical activity from the brain

   A: tracks changes of radioactive substances

   E: tracks changes in blood oxygen levels

   C: creates cross-sectional images with the help of magnetic fields

2. neuroscience

## Neurons and Neural Communication

1. B. Neurotransmitters; synaptic gap

2. myelin sheath

3. Answers will vary. See Table 2.1 for some surprising facts about neurotransmitters.

## The Brain Can't Do It Alone

1. C. autonomic nervous system

2. pituitary

3. Yes, Brandon would display a reflex. Remember that a reflex is an involuntary reaction carried out by neurons outside of the brain.

## The Amazing Brain

1. D. lateralization.

2. B. Broca's area.

3. A. neuroplasticity.

4. The *corpus callosum* is a bundle of nerve fibers that allows the two halves of the brain to communicate and work together to process information. For example, with visual information each eye receives visual sensations, but that information is sent to the opposite hemisphere, and shared between the hemispheres via the corpus callosum. Specifically, information presented in the right visual field is processed in the left hemisphere, and information presented in the left visual field is processed in the right hemisphere. Because the hemispheres are disconnected through the surgery, researchers can study each hemisphere separately to explore its own unique capabilities (or specializations). In a *split-brain* individual, communication between the hemispheres is limited.

5. association areas

6. The *frontal lobes* direct higher-level cognitive activities, such as language, emotions, control of social behavior, and decision making. The *occipital lobes* process visual information, and help us see. The *parietal lobes* receive and process sensory information, and orient the body in space. The *temporal lobes* are instrumental in the comprehension of hearing and language. They process auditory stimuli, recognize visual objects, and play a key role in language comprehension and memory.

## Let's Dig a Little Deeper

1. amygdala

2. cerebellum

3. A. relay sensory information.

## Test Prep Are You Ready?

1. C. Neurons

2. A. an action potential

3. 1. acetylcholine: C. movement; 2. GABA: B. sleep and wakefulness; 3. endorphins: A. reduction of pain; 4. serotonin: D. mood, aggression, appetite

4. A. central nervous system.

5. B. spinal cord

6. D. peripheral nervous system

7. B. endocrine system; glands

8. D. Wernicke's area

9. B. The right hemisphere is more competent handling visual-spatial tasks.

10. 1. association areas; B. integration of information from all over the brain; 2. temporal lobes: C. hearing and language comprehension; 3. meninges: A. protection of the brain; 4. occipital lobes: E. process visual information; 5. parietal lobes: D. receive sensory information, such as touch

11. *Neuroplasticity* is the brain's ability to heal, grow new connections, and reorganize in order to adapt to the environment. Examples of neuroplasticity will vary, but Brandon Burns and Christina Santhouse provide compelling examples.

12. *Neurotransmitters* are chemical messengers produced by neurons, which enable those neurons to communicate with each other. *Hormones* are chemical messengers produced by the endocrine system and released into the bloodstream. The effects of neurotransmitters are almost instantaneous, whereas those of hormones are usually delayed and longer-lasting. Both influence thoughts, emotions, and behaviors. Neurotransmitters and hormones can work together, for example, directing the fight-or-flight response.

13. Answers will vary. The limbic system includes the hippocampus, amygdala, thalamus, and hypothalamus. In addition to processing emotions and memories, the limbic system fuels the most basic drives, such as hunger, sex, and aggression. The stalklike trio of

structures is called the brainstem, which includes the midbrain, pons, and medulla. The midbrain plays a role in arousal levels. The hindbrain includes areas responsible for fundamental life-sustaining processes. The cerebellum is responsible for muscle coordination and balance.

14. Sperry and Gazzaniga's research demonstrated that the hemispheres of the human brain, while strikingly similar in appearance, specialize in different functions. The left hemisphere excels in language processing, and the right hemisphere excels at visual-spatial tasks. The corpus callosum normally allows the two hemispheres to share and integrate information.

15. The *EEG* detects electrical impulses in the brain. The *CAT* uses X-rays to create many cross-sectional images of the brain. The *MRI* uses powerful magnets to produce more detailed cross-sectional images than those of a CAT scan, but both MRI and CAT scan are used to study the structure of the brain. The *PET* uses radioactivity to track glucose consumption and construct a map of brain activity. The *fMRI* also captures changes in brain activity, but instead of tracking glucose consumption, it reveals patterns of blood flow in the brain, which is a good indicator of how much oxygen is being used.

# 3 Sensation and Perception

## SHOW WHAT YOU KNOW

### An Introduction to Sensation and Perception

1. A. perception.

2. Answers will vary, but can include examples such as hearing the honking of a car outside, or smelling food cooking in the kitchen, or the lamp illuminating the book that enables you to see the words on the page.

3. D. sensory adaptation.

### Vision

1. D. rods.

2. wavelength

3. The trichromatic theory of color vision suggests there are three types of cones, each sensitive to particular wavelengths in the red, green, and blue spectrums. The brain identifies a precise hue by calculating patterns of excitement among the three types of cones, that is, the relative activity of the three types.

The opponent-process theory of color vision suggests that in addition to the color-sensitive cones, we also have neurons that respond to opponent colors (for example, red–green, blue–yellow). This type of neuron fires in response to red but not green, for example. Both the trichromatic and opponent-process theories clarify different aspects of color vision, as color perception occurs in the light-sensing cones in the retina and in the opponent cells serving the brain.

### Hearing

1. A. frequency

2. place

3. B. transduction.

### Smell, Taste, Touch

1. olfaction

2. B. transduction.

3. Answers will vary, but may include examples such as typing on your keyboard, holding your head upright, sitting upright in your chair, and moving your hand to scratch your head.

4. C. the gate-control theory

### Perception: Is It All in Your Head?

1. A. convergence

2. Gestalt

## Test Prep Are You Ready?

1. C. sensation.

2. A. transduction.

3. D. cornea

4. B. wavelength

5. A. afterimage effect; trichromatic

6. C. neural impulses firing

7. A. thalamus

8. A. proprioceptors

9. A. tension of the muscles focusing the eyes

10. D. proximity.

11. Answers will vary. Tastes push us toward foods we need and away from those that could harm us. We gravitate toward sweet, calorie-rich foods for their life-sustaining energy. We are also drawn to salty foods, which tend to contain valuable minerals, and to umami, which signals the presence of proteins essential for cellular health and growth. Bitter and sour tastes we tend to avoid. This also gives us an evolutionary edge because poisonous plants or rancid foods are often bitter or sour.

12. Answers will vary. Rods are extremely sensitive to light; they enable vision in dim lighting but do not provide the sensation of color. If you are in a dark room, your rods will allow you to see the outline of furniture or other objects in your path. Cones enable us to sense color and discern details, but they are not used when ambient light is low. When trying to read an electrical wiring manual in a bright room, your cones enable you to make out the details of the fine print and color coding. Rods are found throughout the retina, but not in the fovea; this is where the cones are concentrated.

13. Diagrams will vary; see Infographic 3.2. The pinna funnels sound waves into the auditory canal, focusing them toward the

eardrum. Vibrations in the eardrum cause the malleus to push the incus, which moves the stapes, which presses on the oval window, amplifying waves. Pressure on the oval window causes fluid in the cochlea to vibrate and bend the hair cells on the basilar membrane. If the vibration is sufficiently strong, the hair cells bend enough to initiate the firing of nearby nerve cells. The auditory nerve carries signals to the auditory cortex in the brain, where sounds are given meaning.

14. The sharp immediate pain is caused by signaling of the fast nerve fibers made up of large myelinated neurons. The dull aching pain that lingers is caused by the slow nerve fibers, made up of smaller, unmyelinated neurons.

15. An absolute threshold is the weakest stimuli that can be detected 50% of the time. Difference thresholds indicate the minimum difference between two stimuli noticed 50% of the time. Weber's law states the ratios that determine these difference thresholds.

# 4 Consciousness

 ## SHOW WHAT YOU KNOW

## An Introduction to Consciousness

1. A. Consciousness

2. Answers will vary. The ability to focus awareness on a small segment of information that is available through our sensory systems is called *selective attention*. Although we are exposed to many different stimuli at once, we tend to pay particular attention to abrupt or unexpected changes in the environment. Such events may pose a danger, and we need to be aware of them. However, selective attention can cause us to be blind to objects directly in our line of vision. This "looking without seeing" can have serious consequences, as we fail to see important occurrences in our surroundings. Our advice would be to try to remain aware of the potential for inattentional blindness, particularly when you are in situations that could involve serious injury.

3. automatic processing

## Sleep

1. D. retinal ganglion cells.

2. cataplexy

3. B. Stage N2

4. Drawings will vary; see Infographic 4.1. A normal adult sleeper begins in non-rapid eye movement sleep. Stage N1, the lightest sleep, is associated with theta waves. Stage N2 includes evidence of sleep spindles. Stage N3, or deep sleep, is associated with delta waves. The depth of sleep then decreases as the sleeper works back from Stages N3 to N2. Then, instead of waking up, the sleeper enters rapid eye movement sleep (REM). Each cycle lasts about 90 minutes, with the average adult sleeper looping through five cycles per night.

## Dreams

1. C. activation–synthesis model

2. manifest content; latent content

3. Electroencephalogram (EEG) and PET scan technologies can demonstrate neural activity of the sleeping brain. During REM sleep, the motor areas of the brain are inhibited, but a great deal of neural activity is occurring in the sensory areas of the brain. The *activation–synthesis model* suggests dreams result when the brain responds to this random neural activity as if it has meaning. The creative human mind makes up stories to match the neural activity. The vestibular system is also active during REM sleep, resulting in sensations of floating or flying. The *neurocognitive theory of dreams* proposes that a network of neurons in the brain (including some areas in the limbic system and forebrain) is necessary for dreaming to occur.

## What Are Altered States?

1. I. depressant: B. slows down activity in the CNS; II. opioid: A. blocks pain; III. alcohol: D. cirrhosis of the liver; IV. cocaine: C. increases activity in the CNS

2. To determine if behaviors should be considered problematic, one could evaluate the presence of tolerance or withdrawal, both signs of physiological dependence. With *tolerance,* one's system adapts to a drug over time and therefore needs more and more of the substance to re-create the original effect. *Withdrawal* can occur with constant use of some psychoactive drugs, when the body has become dependent and then reacts when the drug is withheld. *Psychological dependence* is indicated by a host of problematic symptoms distinct from tolerance and withdrawal. It is a strong urge or craving, not a physical need to continue using the substance. If an individual harms themselves or others around them as a result of their behaviors, it is a problem. Overuse is maladaptive and causes significant impairment or distress to the user and/or their family. This might include difficulties at work or school, neglect of children and household duties, and physically dangerous behaviors.

3. C. LSD

4. psychoactive drugs

## Test Prep Are You Ready?

1. B. selective attention.

2. D. circadian rhythm.

3. A. insomnia

4. B. hallucinogen

5. D. REM sleep

6. A. REM rebound.

7. B. wish fulfillment.

8. C. Psychoactive drugs

9. A. dopamine

10. C. Physiological; withdrawal

11. Answers will vary. If someone walks into your room while you are asleep, you wake up immediately if there is a noise. You hear a text message come in during the night and immediately wake up to answer the message.

12. Without one's awareness, the brain determines what is important, what requires immediate attention, and what can be processed and stored for later use if necessary. This *automatic processing* happens involuntarily, with little or no conscious effort, and is important because our sensory systems absorb large amounts of information that need to be processed. But it would not be possible to be consciously aware of all of it. Automatic processing also enables *sensory adaption,* which is the tendency to become less sensitive to and less aware of constant stimuli after a period of time.

13. We might not want a doctor with such a schedule to care for us because staying up for 48 hours can result in problems with memory, attention, reaction time, and decision making, all important processes that doctors use in caring for patients. Sleep deprivation impairs the ability to focus attention on a single activity, such as delivering medical care.

14. Answers will vary. See Table 4.2 for information on sleep disturbances and their defining characteristics.

15. Answers will vary. There are many different drugs that people use legally on an everyday basis. Caffeine is a psychoactive drug found in coffee, soda, tea, and some medicines. Over-the-counter painkillers are legal drugs used to treat minor aches and pains. Nicotine is a highly addictive drug found in cigarettes, e-cigarettes, cigars, and other products. Alcohol is a legal psychoactive drug used on a daily basis by many people, as they drink a glass of wine or beer with an evening meal.

# 5 Learning

 ## SHOW WHAT YOU KNOW

## An Introduction to Learning

1. Answers will vary. Learning that your tongue will get burned if you put your coffee in the microwave for too long; studying hard for a test after getting a good score on the last test you studied for.

2. behavior or thinking; experiences

## Classical Conditioning

1. Classical conditioning

2. biological preparedness

3. When Little Albert heard the loud bang, it was an unconditioned stimulus (US) that elicited fear, the unconditioned response (UR). Through conditioning, the sight of the rat became paired with the loud noise, and thus the rat went from being a *neutral stimulus* to a conditioned stimulus (CS). Little Albert's fear of the rat became a conditioned response (CR). Little Albert exhibited stimulus generalization, as he not only began to fear rats, but also generalized this fear to other furry objects, including a sealskin coat and rabbit.

4. A. salmonella

## Operant Conditioning

1. D. stimulus generalization.

2. Answers will vary, but can be based on the following definitions. *Reinforcers* are consequences that increase the likelihood of a behavior recurring. *Positive reinforcement* is the process by which pleasant reinforcers are presented following a target behavior. *Negative reinforcement* occurs with the removal of an unpleasant stimulus following a target behavior. *Successive approximation* is a method that uses reinforcers to condition a series of small steps that gradually approach the target behavior. We could consider using food as a primary reinforcer (meeting a biological need). Good grades, or money, are examples of secondary reinforcers.

3. law of effect

4. A. positive punishment

5. *Continuous reinforcement* is a schedule of reinforcement in which every target behavior is reinforced. *Partial reinforcement* is a schedule of reinforcement in which target behaviors are reinforced intermittently, not continuously. Continuous reinforcement is generally more effective for establishing a behavior, whereas learning through partial reinforcement is more resistant to extinction and useful for maintaining behavior.

## Observational Learning and Cognition

1. Answers will vary, but can be based on the following definitions. A *model* is an individual or character whose behavior is being imitated. *Observational learning* occurs as a result of watching the behavior of others.

2. A. observational learning.

3. C. latent learning.

## Test Prep Are You Ready?

1. B. habituation

2. C. ability to learn through positive reinforcement.

3. A. involuntary; voluntary

4. B. conditioned response.

5. C. a conditioned emotional response.

6. D. The law of effect

7. C. a dog whining in the morning, which prompts the owner to wake up and take it outside

8. B. positive reinforcement.

9. A. were more likely to display aggressive behavior.

10. A. latent learning.

11. With stimulus generalization, once an association is forged between a conditioned stimulus and a conditioned response, the learner often responds to similar stimuli as if they were the conditioned stimulus.

Stimulus discrimination is the ability to differentiate between the conditioned stimulus and other sufficiently different stimuli.

12. Answers will vary. See Infographics 5.2 through 5.4, and Table 5.2.

13. Answers will vary, but can be based on the following definitions. *Primary reinforcers* are reinforcers that satisfy biological needs, such as food, water, or physical contact. *Secondary reinforcers* do not satisfy biological needs, but often gain their power through their association with primary reinforcers. A primary reinforcer used to change behavior might be food. A college tries to increase student participation by providing food at important school functions. Money can be used as a secondary reinforcer. Employees are paid money, which increases attendance at work.

14. Answers will vary, but can be based on the following definitions. *Punishment decreases* the likelihood of a behavior recurring. On the other hand, *negative reinforcement increases* the likelihood of a behavior recurring. See Table 5.2 for examples.

15. Answers can vary. A conditioned taste aversion is a form of classical conditioning that occurs when an organism learns to associate the taste of a particular food or drink with illness. Avoiding foods that induce sickness increases the odds the organism will survive and reproduce, passing its genes along to the next generation. Imagine a grizzly bear that avoids poisonous berries after it vomits from eating them. In this case, the unconditioned stimulus (US) is the poison in the berries; the unconditioned response (UR) is the vomiting. After acquisition, the conditioned stimulus (CS) would be the sight of the berries, and the conditioned response (CR) would be a nauseous feeling.

**Try This    p. 178**

ANSWER: The neutral stimulus (NS) is the sight of a hot dog, the unconditioned stimulus (US) is the virus, the unconditioned response (UR) is the upset stomach, the conditioned stimulus (CS) is the sight or thought of a hot dog, and the conditioned response (CR) is the sick feeling you get even after you have recovered.

**Try This    p. 198**

ANSWER: Independent variable: exposure to an adult displaying aggressive or nonaggressive behavior. Dependent variable: child's level of aggression. Ideas for altering the study: conducting the same study with older or younger children; exposing the children to other children (as opposed to adults) behaving aggressively; pairing children with adults of the same and different ethnicities to determine the impact of ethnic background.

# 6 Memory

 **SHOW WHAT YOU KNOW**

## What is Memory?

1. A. Retrieval failure

2. Memory

3. Paying little attention to data entering our sensory system results in *shallow processing*. For example, you remember seeing a word that has been boldfaced in the text while studying. You might even be able to recall the page that it appears on, and where on the page it is located. *Deeper-level processing* relies on characteristics related to patterns and meaning, and generally results in longer-lasting and easier to retrieve memories. As we study, if we contemplate incoming information and relate it to memories we already have, deeper processing occurs and the new memories are more likely to persist.

## Stages of Memory

1. B. 30 seconds

2. B. working memory.

3. chunking

4. Answers will vary. **Ex**quisitely **S**erious **Ep**isodes **F**lashed **Im**possible **P**roteins **L**ightning **S**tyle.

   **Ex**plicit memory, **S**emantic memory, **Ep**isodic memory, **F**lashbulb memory, **Im**plicit memory, **P**rocedural memory, **L**ong-term memory, **S**ensory memory.

5. No. This definition of short-term memory is not accurate from a psychological perspective. Short-term memory usually lasts about 30 seconds.

## Retrieval and Forgetting

1. A. context-dependent memory.

2. B. curve of forgetting.

3. D. rich false memory.

4. misinformation effect

## The Biology of Memory

1. A. Anterograde amnesia

2. C. hippocampus

3. A. Long-term potentiation

4. Answers will vary, but can be based on the following information. *Infantile amnesia* is the inability to remember events from one's earliest years. Most adults cannot remember events that occurred before the age of 3.

# Test Prep Are You ready?

1. D. retrieval

2. C. iconic memory.

3. D. chunking

4. B. working memory

5. A. the encoding specificity principle.

6. C. Proactive interference; retroactive interference

7. B. rich false memory

8. B. access memories of events created before the trauma.

9. B. Long-term potentiation

10. D. hippocampus

11. Information enters sensory memory, which includes an overwhelming array of sensory stimuli. If it is not lost in sensory memory, it enters the short-term memory stage. The amount of time information is maintained and processed in short-term memory can be about 30 seconds. And short-term memory has a limited capacity. Because short-term memories cannot last for a couple of hours, it is more likely his grandmother is having difficulty encoding, storing, and/or recalling information that would normally be held in long-term memory.

12. *Iconic memories* are visual impressions that are photograph-like in their accuracy but dissolve in less than a second. *Echoic memories* are exact copies of the sounds we hear, lasting about 1–10 seconds. Iconic memory uses our visual system, whereas echoic memory uses our auditory system.

13. *Short-term memory* is a stage of memory that temporarily maintains and processes a limited amount of information. *Working memory* is the active processing of information in short-term memory. Working memory refers to what is going on in short-term memory.

14. Answers will vary. **E**very **S**tudent **R**emembers.

15. The teacher should list the most important rules first and last in the list. The *serial position effect* suggests items at the beginning and at the end of a list are more likely to be recalled. The *primacy effect* suggests we are more likely to remember items at the beginning of a list, because they have a better chance of moving into long-term memory. The *recency effect* suggests we are more likely to remember items at the end of a list because they linger in short-term memory. Students are likely to remember rules at the beginning of the list, as these would be encoded into long-term memory.

## 7 Cognition, language, and intelligence

 **SHOW WHAT YOU KNOW**

### What Is Cognition?

1. Cognition

2. B. concept

3. C. formal concept

### Problem Solving and Decision Making

1. C. trial and error.

2. heuristic

3. D. availability heuristic.

4. Answers will vary. A *heuristic* uses a "rule of thumb" or broad application of a strategy to solve a problem, but it can also be used to help predict the probability of an event occurring. However, heuristics can lead us astray in our assessment of situations or predictions of outcomes. In the current example, you can present information to your friend that indicates flying is the safest form of travel. But you can also describe how the *availability heuristic* might lead your friend to believe that air travel is not safe. The vividness of airplane crashes can influence your friend's recall; even though they are rare events, your friend is likely to overestimate the probability of them happening again due to the ease with which your friend recalls similar events. Highly detailed media reports of an airplane crash are likely to linger in your friend's memory.

### The Power of Language

1. B. thinking and perception.

2. Phonemes

### Intelligence

1. C. analytic, creative, practical.

2. The *intelligence quotient (IQ)* is a score from an intelligence assessment, which provides a way to compare levels of intelligence across ages. Originally, an IQ score was derived by dividing mental age by chronological age and multiplying that number by 100. Modern intelligence tests still assign a numerical score, although they no longer use the actual quotient score.

3. aptitude; achievement

4. originality

### Test Prep Are You Ready?

1. D. Cognition; thinking

2. A. Concepts

3. C. natural concepts

4. D. an algorithm

5. D. linguistic relativity hypothesis

6. B. heuristic

7. D. confirmation bias.

8. C. the framing effect.

9. B. phonemes

10. B. validity

11. *Formal concepts* are created through rigid and logical rules, or features of a concept. *Natural concepts* are acquired through everyday experience, and they do not have the same types of rigid rules for identification that formal concepts have.

   Examples will vary. An example of a formal concept is an isosceles triangle, which refers to a three-sided polygon with at least two equal-length sides. The concept of family is an example of a natural concept. Is a family a group of people who just live together, or do they have to be related genetically? Family is a natural concept that can change based on individual experiences.

12. See Table 7.2. Charles Spearman speculated that intelligence consists of a *general intelligence* (or *g*-factor), which refers to a singular underlying aptitude or intellectual ability. Howard

Gardner suggested we have *multiple intelligences,* proposing eight different types of intelligences or "frames of mind": linguistic (verbal), logical-mathematical, spatial, bodily-kinesthetic, musical, intrapersonal, interpersonal, and naturalist. Robert Sternberg proposed three kinds of intelligences. His *triarchic theory of intelligence* suggests that humans have varying degrees of analytical, creative, and practical abilities.

13. Using the *availability heuristic,* we predict the probability of something happening in the future based on how easily we can recall a similar type of event from the past. The availability heuristic is essentially a decision-making strategy that relies on memory. They remembered a recent storm in which they did not have to leave their homes, so they decided it was safe to stay.

14. *Reliability* is the ability of an assessment to provide consistent, reproducible results. *Validity* is the degree to which an assessment measures what it intends to measure. An unreliable IQ test might result in getting different scores for the IQ test taken now and the same test taken again in a few months; it would not be consistent across time, which is counter to what you would expect (we expect level of intelligence to remain fairly stable over time). An IQ test that is not valid would not be able to predict future performance on tasks related to intellectual ability.

15. Answers will vary. *Divergent thinking* is the ability to devise many solutions to a problem.

    Possible solutions: as a door stop, icebreaker, paper weight, shovel, or axe; for putting out cigarettes; for breaking glass; for crushing ingredients for a recipe; for putting out a candle; and so on.

# 8 Human Development

 ## SHOW WHAT YOU KNOW

## Why Study Human Development?

1. development

2. Developmental psychologists' longstanding discussions have centered on three major themes: stages and continuity; nature and nurture; and stability and change. Each of these themes relates to a basic question: (1) Does development occur in separate or discrete stages, or is it a steady, continuous process? (2) What are the relative roles of heredity and environment in human development? (3) How stable is one's personality over a lifetime and across situations?

3. C. cross-sectional

## Inside the Womb

1. D. Chromosomes

2. Genotype; phenotype

3. A. embryonic period

## Infants and Children

1. rooting; sucking

2. D. assimilation.

3. There is a universal sequence of language development. At around 2–3 months, infants typically start to produce vowel-like sounds known as *cooing.* At 4–6 months, in the *babbling stage,* infants combine consonants with vowels. Around their first birthday, many babies utter their first word, and at about 18 months, many are using two-word phrases (*telegraphic speech*). As children mature, they start to use more complete sentences. Infants pay more attention to adults who use infant-directed speech and are more likely to provide them with chances to learn and interact, thus allowing more exposure to language. Parents and caregivers should talk with their infants and children as much as possible, as babies benefit from a lot of chatter.

4. C. developmental tasks or emotional crises.

5. scaffolding

## The Teenage Years

1. A. formal operational stage.

2. B. secondary sex characteristics.

3. C. gender role

4. Answers will vary. During the stage of *ego identity versus role confusion,* adolescents seek to define themselves through their values, beliefs, and goals. If helicopter or drone parents have been troubleshooting all their children's problems, the children have never had to learn to take care of themselves. Thus, they may feel helpless and unsure of how to handle problems that arise. The parents might also have ensured the children were successful in every endeavor, but this, too, could cause the children to be unable to identify their true strengths, again interfering with the creation of an adult identity.

5. Preconventional

## Adulthood

1. A. physical exercise

2. integrity; despair

3. Information processing and long-term memory begin to decline in midlife. However, decreases in general cognitive abilities cannot be reliably measured before age 60.

## Test Prep Are You Ready?

1. B. longitudinal research.

2. D. nature and nurture

3. D. genes

4. A. epigenetics.

5. C. synaptic pruning

6. B. scaffolding

7. D. Teratogens

8. C. Primary sex characteristics

9. A. formal operational stage.

10. A. babbling stage.

11. Answers will vary, but can be based on the following. Gender refers to the categories or dimensions of masculinity and femininity based on social, cultural, and psychological characteristics. Men are expected to be masculine, while women are expected to be more feminine. We learn how to behave in gender-conforming ways through the gender roles designated by our cultures, and from observations of people around us, particularly those of the same gender. One component of identity is gender identity, which is the feeling or sense of being either male, female, or an alternative gender, and the compatibility, contentment, and conformity one feels with one's gender. Adolescents explore who they are by trying out different ideas in a variety of categories, including politics and religion. Then they begin to commit to a particular set of beliefs and attitudes, making decisions to engage in activities related to their evolving identity. Concepts of masculine and feminine vary according to culture, social context, and the individual.

12. Answers will vary. See Infographics 8.3 and 8.4, and Table 8.4.

13. We typically reach our physical peak in early adulthood, and then decline as we approach late adulthood. Gradual changes occur, including hearing and vision loss, wrinkles, graying hair, reduced stamina, menopause for women, and reduced fertility for men. Lifestyle can have a significant impact on health. Heavy drinking, drug use, poor eating habits, and sleep deprivation can make one look, feel, and function like someone much older.

14. Answers will vary. According to Erikson, young adults face the crisis of *intimacy versus isolation,* and failure to create meaningful, deep relationships may lead to a life of isolation. During middle adulthood, people face the crisis of *generativity versus stagnation.* Positive resolution at this stage includes feeling that one has made a valuable impact on the next generation. Late adulthood is characterized by the crisis of *integrity versus despair;* people look back on life and evaluate how they have done.

15. Practical abilities seem to increase. Experiences allow people to develop a more balanced understanding of the world surrounding them. What's more, aging may be accompanied by increases in knowledge gained through learning and experience.

# 9 Motivation and Emotion

 ## SHOW WHAT YOU KNOW

## Motivation

1. Motivation

2. B. intrinsic motivation

3. hierarchy of needs

4. The *drive-reduction theory* of motivation suggests that human behaviors are driven by the need to maintain homeostasis—that is, to fulfill basic biological needs. If a need is not fulfilled, this creates a drive, or state of tension, that pushes us or motivates behaviors to meet the need. Once a need is met, the drive is reduced, at least temporarily, because this is an ongoing process, as the need inevitably returns. *Arousal theory* suggests that humans seek an optimal level of arousal, and what is optimal is based on individual differences. Behaviors can arise out of the simple desire for stimulation, or arousal, which is a level of alertness and engagement in the world, and people are motivated to seek out activities that fulfill this need. Drive-reduction theory suggests that the motivation is to reduce tension, but arousal theory suggests that in some cases the motivation is to increase tension.

## Sexuality

1. A. excitement, plateau, orgasm, and resolution.

2. fraternal birth order effect

## Hunger

1. A. stomach was contracting.

2. When glucose levels dip, the stomach and liver send signals to the brain that something must be done about this reduced energy source. The brain, in turn, initiates a sense of hunger. When the lateral hypothalamus is activated, appetite increases. On the other hand, if the ventromedial hypothalamus becomes activated, appetite declines, causing an animal to stop eating.

## Emotion

1. Answers will vary, but can be based on the following definitions. *Emotion* is a psychological state that includes a subjective or inner experience. It also has a physiological component and entails a behavioral expression. Emotions are quite strong, but they don't generally last as long as moods. In addition, emotions are more likely to have an identifiable cause (that is, a reaction to a stimulus that provoked it), which has a greater probability of motivating a person to take some sort of action. *Moods* are longer-term emotional states that are less intense than emotions and do not appear to have distinct beginnings or ends. It is very likely that on your way to a wedding you are in a happy mood, and you have been that way for quite a while. If you were to get mud on your clothing, it is likely that you would experience an emotion such as anger, which might have been triggered by someone jumping in a large mud puddle and splashing you. Your anger would have a subjective experience (your feeling of anger), a physiological component (you felt your face flush with heat), and a behavioral expression (you glared angrily at the person who splashed you).

2. B. Display rules

3. Answers may vary. See Infographic 9.2. The *Cannon–Bard* theory of emotion suggests that environmental stimuli are the starting point for emotions, and that body changes and emotions happen together. The *Schachter–Singer* theory of emotion suggests there is a general pattern of physiological arousal caused by the sympathetic nervous system, and this pattern is common to a variety of emotions. Unlike the Cannon–Bard theory, the Schachter–Singer theory suggests our thoughts about our body changes can lead to emotions. The experience of emotion is the result of two factors: physiological arousal and a cognitive label for this physiological state (the arousal). Cannon–Bard did not suggest that a cognitive label is necessary for emotions to be experienced.

4. Darwin suggested that interpreting facial expressions is not something we learn, but rather is an innate ability that evolved

because it promotes survival. Sharing the same facial expressions allows for communication. Research on an isolated group of indigenous people in New Guinea suggests that the same facial expressions represent the same basic emotions across cultures. In addition, the fact that children born deaf and blind have the same types of emotional expressions as children with normal sensory abilities indicates that these displays, and the emotions behind them, may be universal.

5. amygdala

6. *Heritability* is the degree to which heredity is responsible for a particular characteristic in a population. In this case, the heritability for happiness is as high as 80%, indicating that around 80% of the variation in happiness can be attributed to genes, and 20% to environmental influences. In other words, we can explain a high proportion of the variation in happiness, life satisfaction, and well-being by considering genetic make-up, as opposed to environmental factors.

# Test Prep Are You Ready?

1. D. an incentive

2. A. extrinsic motivation

3. B. drive-reduction

4. A. sensation seekers

5. A. excitement

6. C. behavioral expression.

7. B. could identify the facial expressions common across the world.

8. C. physiological arousal and cognitive labeling.

9. B. cognitive-appraisal approach

10. B. heritability estimates

11. Because monozygotic twins share nearly 100% of their genetic make-up, we expect them to share more genetically influenced characteristics than dizygotic twins, who only share about 50% of their genes. Using twins, researchers explored the impact of genes and environment on same-sex sexual behavior. Monozygotic twins were moderately more likely than dizygotic twins to have the same sexual orientation. They found men and women differ in terms of the heritability of same-sex sexual behavior. These studies highlight that the influence of the environment is substantial with regard to same-sex sexual behavior.

12. Answers will vary, but can be based on the following. Maslow's hierarchy of needs is considered universal. Needs are ordered according to the strength of their associated drives, with more critical needs at the base of the hierarchy and nonessential, higher-level needs at the top: physiological needs; safety needs; love and belongingness needs; esteem needs; self-actualization; self-transcendence. Maslow suggested that one's most basic needs must be met before higher-level needs motivate behavior. An example of someone not following the prescribed order of needs might be a martyr who is motivated by self-transcendence needs, ignoring safety needs altogether.

13. Answers will vary. Stomach contractions accompany feelings of hunger, and the stomach (and liver) send signals to the brain when glucose levels in the blood decrease. The brain, in turn, initiates a sense of hunger. When the lateral hypothalamus is activated, appetite increases. If the ventromedial hypothalamus becomes activated, appetite declines, causing an animal to stop eating. A variety of social and cultural factors, including exposure to large portion sizes and the presence of eating companions, may impact eating behaviors.

14. The amygdala is found in the limbic system and appears to be central to our experience of fear. When people view threatening images, or even look at an image of a frightened face, the amygdala is activated. When confronted with a fear-provoking situation, the amygdala enables an ultrafast and unconscious response. The direct route (thalamus to amygdala, causing an emotional reaction) enables us to react quickly to threats for which we are biologically prepared (snakes, spiders, aggressive faces). The other pathway allows us to evaluate more complex threats (such as nuclear weapons, job layoffs) with our cortex, overriding the fast-response pathway when necessary.

15. Answers will vary but may be based on the following. There is relatively little fluctuation in adult weight over time. The communication between the brain and the appetite hormones helps regulate the body's set point, or stable weight that we tend to maintain despite variability in day-to-day exercise and intake of food. The set point helps to maintain a consistent weight in part through changes in metabolism. Research suggests that the biological basis of happiness may include a "set point," similar to the set point for body weight. Happiness tends to fluctuate around a fixed level, which is influenced by genes and related to temperament. We may experience periodic ups and downs, but ultimately we move back toward that fixed level of happiness. However, the set points for body weight and happiness may not be as powerful as researchers once suspected. To some degree, they depend on our conscious choices and behaviors.

# 10 Personality

 SHOW WHAT YOU KNOW

## An Introduction to Personality

1. Heritability estimates help us gauge the extent to which genes influence different characteristics in a given population. If the heritability of humor styles is 30–47%, that means 30–47% of the population-wide variability for this characteristic can be attributed to genes. The biological perspective of personality development is most relevant in this example because it helps us understand how genetic and physiological factors shape personality characteristics.

2. Personality

## Psychoanalytic Theories

1. D. topographical model of the mind

2. psychosexual; fixation

3. Answers will vary, but could include the following. Some of *Freud's followers* branched out on their own due to disagreements

about certain issues, such as his focus on the instincts of sex and aggression, his idea that personality is determined by the end of childhood, and his somewhat negative view of human nature. *Adler* proposed that humans are conscious and intentional in their behaviors. *Jung* suggested that we are driven by a psychological energy (as opposed to sexual energy), which encourages positive growth, self-understanding, and balance. *Horney* emphasized the role of relationships between children and their caregivers, not erogenous zones and psychosexual stages.

## Humanistic, Learning, and Trait Theories

1. D. unconditional positive regard.

2. learning theory

3. B. locus of control

4. Answers will vary (also see Table 10.4). The *Big Five* traits are openness, conscientiousness, extraversion, agreeableness, and neuroticism. Three decades of twin and adoption studies point to a genetic (and therefore biological) basis of these five factors. The proportion of variation in the Big Five traits attributed to genetic make-up is substantial (ranging from .41 to .61), suggesting that the remainder can be attributed to environmental influences.

5. A. traits.

6. Answers will vary, but can be based on the following definition (also see Infographic 10.2). *Reciprocal determinism* refers to the multidirectional interactions among cognition, behaviors, and the environment guiding our behavior patterns and personality.

## Personality Tests

1. B. Projective

2. Answers will vary, but can be based on the following definitions. A *valid measure* is one that can be shown to measure what it intends to measure. If a measure is not valid, a client might be given information that is not meaningful because the findings have not been shown to measure their intended topic. A *reliable measure* provides consistent results across time as well as across raters or people scoring the measure. If findings from a personality test are not reliable, a client may be given information that will not reflect a consistent pattern, or may be questionable due to problems with scoring.

3. A. standardization

## Test Prep Are You Ready?

1. D. behavioral

2. A. reciprocal determinism.

3. A. psychosexual stages; fixation

4. A. incongruent

5. C. self-efficacy

6. A. Personality

7. A. source traits

8. B. the stability of personality characteristics over time.

9. C. Reliability

10. C. his intense emphasis on sex and aggression

11. Answers will vary, but can be based on the following information. According to behaviorists and learning theory, the *environment* shapes personality through *operant* conditioning. *Observation* and *modeling* also play a role in personality development.

12. Answers will vary. The *humanistic perspective* suggests that we are innately good and that we have capabilities we can and should take advantage of as we strive for personal growth. The choices we make in life influence our personalities. The *social-cognitive perspective* focuses on relationships, environmental influences, cognitive activity, and individual behavior as they come together to form personality. The humanistic perspective views personality as what we are able to do, whereas the social-cognitive perspective views personality, in part, as how we react to the environment.

13. Both the Oedipus (for boys) and the Electra (for girls) complex represent an important conflict that occurs during the phallic stage. For both boys and girls, the conflict can be resolved through the process of identification. Although basic urges and developmental processes underlie both of these complexes, there are several important differences. The *Oedipus complex* is the attraction a boy feels toward his mother, along with resentment or envy directed toward his father. When a little boy becomes aware of his attraction to his mother, he realizes his father is a formidable rival and experiences jealousy and anger toward him. With the *Electra complex,* a little girl feels an attraction to her father and becomes jealous and angry toward her mother. Realizing she doesn't have a penis, she may respond with anger, blaming her mother for her missing penis.

14. Answers will vary, but can be based on the following definitions. An *internal locus of control* suggests that the causes of life events reside within an individual, and that one has some control over them. An *external locus of control* suggests that causes for outcomes reside outside of an individual, and there is little control over them.

15. *Objective assessments* of personality are based on a standardized procedure in which the scoring is free of opinions, beliefs, expectations, and values. Critics of objective assessments contend they do not allow flexibility or fully appreciate individual differences in experiences. Findings from *subjective assessments* of personality are based, in part, on personal intuition, opinions, and interpretations. Critics of the subjective assessments suggest there is not enough consistency across findings because of nonstandard scoring procedures.

# 11 Social Psychology

 SHOW WHAT YOU KNOW

## An Introduction to Social Psychology

1. B. Social psychology; sociology

2. A. Attributions

3. D. disposition of the person.

4. Social psychology studies often involve confederates who are working for the researchers. Playing the role of participants, confederates say what the researchers tell them to say and do what the researchers tell them to do. They are, unknown to the other participants, just part of the researchers' experimental manipulation. In a double-blind study, neither participants nor researchers administering a treatment know who is getting the real treatment. Participants are told ahead of time that they might receive a placebo, but they do not necessarily know about confederates until after the study is complete.

## Social Influence

1. A. social influence; B. persuasion; C. compliance; D. foot-in-the-door technique; E. conformity

2. D. Obedience

3. Answers will vary. Examples may include resisting the urge to eat dessert when others at the table are doing so, saying no to a cigarette when others offer one, and so forth.

## Groups and Aggression

1. C. The bystander effect

2. Males tend to show more direct aggression (physical displays of aggression), whereas females are more likely to engage in relational aggression (gossip, exclusion, ignoring), perhaps because females have a higher risk for physical or bodily harm than males do.

3. Answers will vary, but may be based on the following information. *Discrimination* is showing favoritism or hostility to others because of their affiliation with a group. *Prejudice* is holding hostile or negative attitudes toward an individual or group. *Stereotypes* are conclusions or inferences we make about people who are different from us based on their group membership, such as their race, religion, age, or gender. Discrimination, prejudice, and stereotypes involve making assumptions about others we may not know. They often lead to unfair treatment of others.

## Prosocial Behavior, Attraction, and Love

1. D. prosocial behavior.

2. According to this model, decisions to stay together or part ways are based on how happy people are in their relationship, their notion of what life would be like without it, and their investment in the relationship. People may stay in unsatisfying or unhealthy relationships if they feel there are no better alternatives or believe they have too much to lose. This model helps us understand why people remain in destructive relationships. These principles also apply to friendships, positions at work, or loyalty to institutions.

3. B. proximity; similarity; physical attractiveness

4. Altruism

## Test Prep Are You Ready?

1. D. school board policies regarding support for children with disabilities

2. B. Social cognition

3. D. the fundamental attribution error.

4. C. altruism.

5. A. conformity.

6. C. compliance.

7. D. stereotypes

8. C. aggression

9. B. expectations

10. D. passion, intimacy, and commitment.

11. Answers will vary, but may be based on the following information. Social psychology is the study of human cognition, emotion, and behavior in relation to others. This includes how we perceive and react to others, and how we behave in social settings. Social psychology focuses on studying individuals in relation to others and groups, whereas sociology studies the groups themselves—their cultures, societies, and institutions.

12. Answers will vary. *Obedience* occurs when we change our behavior, or act in a way that we might not normally, because we have been ordered to do so by an authority figure. An imbalance of power exists, and the person with more power generally has an advantage over a person with less power. It is important for us to pay attention to how we react when under the influence of an authority figure, as we could inflict harm on others. One person can make a difference when they stand up for what is right.

13. Answers will vary. When a person is in trouble, bystanders have the tendency to assume that someone else will help—and therefore they stand by and do nothing, a phenomenon that is partly due to the diffusion of responsibility. This bystander effect is particularly common when there are many other people present. Individuals are more likely to aid a person in distress if no one else is present.

14. Answers will vary, but can be based on the following. *Stereotypes* are the conclusions or inferences we make about people who are different from us, based on their group membership (such as race, religion, age, or gender). We tend to see the world in terms of *in-groups* (the group to which we belong) and *out-groups* (people who are outside the group to which we belong), which can impact the stereotypes we hold.

15. Answers will vary, but can be based on the following definitions. *Proximity* means nearness, which may play an important role in the formation of relationships. *Similarity* has to do with how much you have in common with someone else. We tend to prefer those who share our interests, viewpoints, ethnicity, values, and other characteristics.

## 12 Stress and Health

 **SHOW WHAT YOU KNOW**

## What is Stress?

1. Stress

2. D. illness.

3. B. Acculturative stress

4. Answers will vary, but can be based on the following definitions. *Daily hassles* are the minor, everyday problems or irritants we deal

with on a regular basis (for example, heavy traffic, financial worries, and messy roommates). *Uplifts* are positive experiences that have the potential to make us happy (for example, a humorous text message or a small gift).

## Stress and Your Health

1. A. alarm stage

2. C. cortisol.

3. C. The hypothalamic–pituitary–adrenal system

4. general adaptation syndrome (GAS)

5. When the body is expending its resources to deal with an ongoing stressor, the immune system is less powerful, and the work of the lymphocytes is compromised. During times of stress, people tend to sleep poorly and eat erratically, and they may increase their drug and alcohol use, along with other poor behavioral choices. These tendencies can lead to health problems.

## Can You Deal?

1. D. Problem-focused coping

2. Answers may vary. *Stress management* incorporates tools to lower the impact of possible stressors. Exercise, meditation, progressive muscle relaxation, biofeedback, and social support all have positive physical and psychological effects on the response to stressors. In addition, looking out for the well-being of others by caring and giving of yourself is an effective way to reduce the impact of stress.

3. B. Type B personality.

## Test Prep Are You Ready?

1. D. stressors.

2. A. eustress.

3. B. cortisol; the immune system

4. A. parasympathetic nervous system

5. C. exhaustion stage

6. D. cortisol.

7. A. the immune system

8. D. progressive muscle relaxation

9. B. Coping

10. A. Type A personality

11. Answers will vary, but can be based on the following explanation. There are various ways people respond to acculturative stress. Some try to assimilate into the culture, letting go of old ways and adopting those of the new culture. Another approach is to cling to one's roots and remain separated from the new culture. Such an approach can be very problematic if the new culture does not support this type of separation and requires assimilation. A combination of these two approaches is integration, or holding onto some elements of the old culture, but also adopting aspects of the new one.

12. Answers will vary, but can be based on the following definitions. *Daily hassles* are the minor problems or irritants we deal with on a regular basis. *Life-changing events* are occurrences that require a life adjustment (for example, marriage or change in school status). During times of stress, people tend to sleep poorly and eat erratically, and they may increase their drug and alcohol use, along with other poor behavioral choices. These tendencies can lead to health problems. Exercise, meditation, progressive muscle relaxation, biofeedback, and social support all have positive physical and psychological effects on the response to stressors.

13. Answers will vary, but can be based on the following information. Reactions associated with the fight-or-flight response include increased pulse, breathing rate, and mental alertness. A coordinated effort of the sympathetic nervous system and the endocrine system, the fight-or-flight reaction primes the body to respond to danger, either by escaping or by confronting the threat head-on.

14. Answers will vary, but can be based on the following definitions. One major source of stress is conflict, which can be defined as the discomfort felt when making tough choices. Often two choices presented are both attractive to you (*approach–approach conflict*); at times, a choice or situation has favorable and unfavorable characteristics (*approach–avoidance conflict*); and at other times, the two alternatives are both unattractive (*avoidance–avoidance conflict*).

15. Answers will vary, but can be based on the following definitions. Someone with an *internal locus of control* generally feels as if they are in control of life and its circumstances; they probably believe it is important to take charge and make changes when problems occur. A person with an *external locus of control* generally feels as if chance, luck, or fate is responsible for their circumstances; there is no need to try to change things or make them better. Any decisions related to healthy choices can be influenced by locus of control.

# 13 Psychological Disorders

 ## SHOW WHAT YOU KNOW

## An Introduction to Psychological Disorders

1. A. dysfunction

2. psychological disorder

3. Answers will vary, but can be based on the following information (see Figure 13.1). The *biopsychosocial perspective* suggests that psychological disorders result from a complex interaction of factors: *biological* (for example, neurotransmitters, hormones), *psychological* (for example, thinking, coping, personality traits), and *sociocultural* (for example, media, cultural beliefs).

## Anxiety Disorders, OCD, and PTSD

1. C. panic attacks.

2. Repeatedly locking the car temporarily reduced Melissa's anxiety, making her more likely to perform this behavior in the future; thus, negative reinforcement promoted this maladaptive behavior. The therapist probably expected that if Melissa was not able to repeatedly check the locks and nothing bad happened, eventually Melissa would not need to continue locking her car repeatedly.

3. D. compulsions.

## From Depression to Mania

1. B. major depressive disorder

2. Answers will vary, but can be based on the following information. The symptoms of major depressive disorder can include feelings of sadness or hopelessness, reduced pleasure, sleeping excessively or not at all, loss of energy, feelings of worthlessness, or difficulties thinking or concentrating. The hallmarks of major depressive disorder are the "substantial" severity of symptoms and impairment in the ability to perform expected roles. *Biological theories* suggest the disorder results from a genetic predisposition, neurotransmitters, and hormones. *Psychological theories* suggest that feelings of learned helplessness and negative thinking may play a role. Not just one factor is involved in major depressive disorder, but rather the interplay of several.

3. A diagnosis of *bipolar I disorder* requires that a person experience at least one manic episode, substantial distress, and great impairment. *Bipolar II disorder* requires at least one major depressive episode as well as a hypomanic episode, which is associated with some of the same symptoms as a manic episode, but is not as severe and does not impair one's ability to function. People with bipolar disorder cycle between extreme highs and lows of emotion and energy that last for months, weeks, or in some cases, days. Individuals with *major depressive disorder,* on the other hand, tend to experience a persistent low mood, loss of energy, and feelings of worthlessness.

4. B. manic episodes.

## Schizophrenia and Autism Spectrum Disorder (ASD)

1. Answers will vary, but can be based on the following information. Schizophrenia is a complex psychological disorder that results from a combination of biological, psychological, and social factors. This disorder springs from a complex interaction of genes and environment. The diathesis–stress model takes these factors into account, with *diathesis* referring to an inherited disposition (for example, to schizophrenia) and *stress* referring to the stressors in the environment (internal and external). Genes, neurotransmitters, differences in the brain, and exposure to a virus *in utero* are all possible influences in the development of schizophrenia. There are some sociocultural and environmental factors that may play a minor role in one's risk for developing the disorder, as well as the severity of symptoms. Evidence exists, for instance, that complications at birth, social stress, and cannabis abuse are related to a slightly increased risk of schizophrenia onset.

2. A. hallucination.

3. C. Genetic and epigenetic factors

4. psychosis

## Personality, Dissociative, and Eating Disorders

1. borderline personality disorder

2. Answers will vary, but can be based on the following information (see Table 13.1). *Distress* is the degree to which behavior or emotions cause an individual to feel upset or uncomfortable. *Impairment* or *dysfunction* is the degree to which behavior interferes with daily life and relationships. *Deviance* means violating the norms, or rules, of society. Personality disorders are a group of psychological disorders that can include impairments in cognition, emotional responses, interpersonal functioning, and impulse control. Thus, they involve issues that can meet three of the criteria of abnormal behavior: dysfunction (they interfere with daily life and relationships), distress (from problems in interpersonal relationships, anxiety), and deviance (behaviors often considered outside the standards of society).

3. Dissociative identity disorder

4. D. extreme overeating followed by purging.

## Test Prep Are You Ready?

1. B. the medical model.

2. A. obsessions; compulsions

3. B. biopsychosocial

4. B. agoraphobia

5. B. antisocial personality disorder.

6. D. binge-eating disorder.

7. C. problems associated with sleep.

8. B. psychosis.

9. A. borderline personality disorder

10. B. personalities

11. Answers will vary, but can be based on the following information. *Dysfunction* is the degree to which a behavior interferes with one's life or ability to function (for example, washing one's hands to the point of making them raw). *Distress* is feeling regularly upset or uncomfortable because of unwanted behaviors or emotions (for example, continually feeling sad and hopeless). *Deviance* is the degree to which a behavior is considered to be outside of the standards or rules of a society (for example, removing one's clothes in inappropriate settings).

12. Answers will vary. This statement does not follow the suggestion of using "people-first language." Instead, it is defining an individual by their disorder. People are much more than their diagnoses. The diagnosis does not describe who your friend is, but only what is causing their distress or discomfort.

13. Classical conditioning can play a role in the development of a panic disorder by pairing an initially neutral stimulus (for example, a mall) with an unexpected panic attack (the unconditioned stimulus). The panic attack location then becomes a conditioned stimulus. When the location is visited or even considered, a panic attack can ensue (now the conditioned response).

14. Cognitive therapist Aaron Beck suggests that depression is a product of a cognitive triad, which includes a negative view of experiences, self, and the future. Negative thinking may lead to self-defeating behaviors, which, in turn, reinforce the beliefs.

15. Answers will vary, but can be based on the following information. Schizophrenia is a complex psychological disorder that results from

biological, psychological, and social factors. Because this disorder springs from a complex interaction of genes and environment, researchers have a hard time predicting who will be affected. The diathesis–stress model takes these factors into account, with *diathesis* referring to an inherited disposition (for example, to schizophrenia) and *stress* referring to the stressors in the environment (internal and external). Genes, neurotransmitters, differences in the brain, and exposure to a virus *in utero* are all possible biological factors. Neurotransmitters are also thought to play a role in schizophrenia. The *dopamine hypothesis,* for example, suggests that the synthesis, release, and concentrations of dopamine are all elevated in people who have been diagnosed with schizophrenia and are suffering from psychosis. There are several environmental triggers thought to be involved in one's risk for developing the disorder as well as the severity of symptoms (for example, complications at birth, social stress, and cannabis abuse are related to a slightly increased risk of schizophrenia onset).

# 14 Treatment of Psychological Disorders

 **SHOW WHAT YOU KNOW**

## An Introduction to Treatment

1. A. symptoms

2. "mental hygiene movement"

3. *Deinstitutionalization* was the mass movement of patients with psychological disorders out of mental institutions, in an attempt to reintegrate them into the community. Deinstitutionalization was partially the result of a movement to reduce the social isolation of people with psychological disorders. This movement marked the beginning of new treatment modalities that allowed some individuals to better care for themselves and function in society. However, many former patients ended up living on the streets or behind bars. Many people locked up in U.S. jails and prisons are suffering from mental health problems.

## Insight Therapies

1. A. Humanistic

2. *Psychoanalysis,* the first formal system of psychotherapy, attempts to increase awareness of unconscious conflicts, making it possible to address and work through them. The therapist's goal is to uncover these unconscious conflicts. *Psychodynamic therapy* is an updated form of psychoanalysis; it incorporates many of Freud's core themes, including the notion that personality characteristics and behavior problems often can be traced to unconscious conflicts. In psychodynamic therapy, therapists see clients once a week for several months rather than many times a week for years. And instead of sitting quietly off to the side, therapists and clients sit face-to-face and engage in a two-way dialogue.

3. C. empathy.

## Behavior and Cognitive Therapies

1. A. behavior

2. Answers will vary, but may be based on the following information. *Behavior therapies* focus on behavioral change. Using the learning principles of classical conditioning, operant conditioning, and observational learning, behavior therapy aims to replace maladaptive behaviors with more adaptive behaviors. It incorporates a variety of techniques, including exposure therapy, aversion therapy, systematic desensitization, and behavior modification. Behavior therapy covers a broad range of treatment approaches and focuses on observable behaviors in the present. *Cognitive therapy* is a type of therapy aimed at addressing the maladaptive thinking that leads to negative behaviors and feelings. The aim of cognitive therapy is to help clients recognize and resist their own cognitive distortions and illogical thoughts in short-term, action-oriented, and homework-intensive therapy sessions. The goal of both approaches is to change the way an individual works or functions in the world. One major difference is that behavioral therapy focuses on behaviors, whereas cognitive therapy focuses on thinking—the way an individual views the world, and views themselves in the world.

3. cognitive therapy

## Biomedical Therapies

1. D. electroconvulsive therapy

2. B. antidepressant.

3. neurosurgery

4. Answers will vary. *Biomedical therapies* use physical interventions to treat psychological disorders. These therapies can be categorized according to the method by which they influence the brain's functioning: chemical, electrical, or structural. *Psychotherapy* is a treatment approach wherein a client works with a mental health professional to reduce psychological symptoms and increase quality of life. These approaches share common features: The relationship between the client and the treatment provider is of utmost importance, as is a sense of hope that things will get better. Also, both of these approaches seek to reduce symptoms and increase quality of life, whether a person is struggling with a psychological disorder or simply wants to be more fulfilled.

## Psychotherapy: Who's in the Mix?

1. C. limits placed by insurance company

2. Answers will vary (see Table 14.3). Group therapy would be inappropriate for an individual who is not comfortable talking or interacting with others and is unwilling to share their own thoughts, feelings, or problems. A group may fail if group members do not get along or have problems too complex to address in a group setting. The skills of the group therapist also play a role in the success of treatment (for example, empathy, facilitation skills, and observation skills).

3. privacy issues; questions about reimbursement from insurance; more empirical support needed

4. Answers will vary, but may be based on the following information. In general, therapy works, and some research suggests all approaches to psychotherapy perform equally well across disorders. But individuals whose insurance companies limit their choice of therapists and how long they can receive treatment do not

experience the same improvement as those who are less restricted. In addition, people who start therapy but then decide to stop it experience less successful outcomes. The client's cultural experience is important to keep in mind. Within any group, there is vast variation from one individual to the next, but it is still necessary for therapists to understand the cultural context in which they work. This includes being respectful of cultural norms and sensitive to the many forms of prejudice and discrimination that people can experience.

## Test Prep Are You Ready?

1. B. moral treatment
2. D. reducing symptoms and increasing quality of life
3. B. psychoanalysis
4. D. person-centered therapy.
5. A. hierarchies
6. B. Getting fired once does not mean my career is over.
7. D. Seeing others improve offers hope and inspiration.
8. D. the present.
9. D. Psychopharmacology
10. B. insurance-mandated limitations on choice of therapist
11. Answers will vary, but may be based on the following information. *Cognitive behavior therapy* is an action-oriented type of therapy that requires clients to confront and resist their illogical thinking. *Insight therapies* aim to increase awareness of self and the environment. These approaches share common features: The relationship between the client and the treatment provider is of utmost importance, as is a sense of hope that things will get better. Also, these approaches generally seek to reduce symptoms and increase the quality of life, whether a person is struggling with a psychological disorder or simply wants to be more fulfilled.
12. Answers will vary (see Table 14.2).
13. Answers will vary, but may be based on the following information. *Exposure* is a therapeutic technique that brings a person into contact with a feared object or situation while in a safe environment, with the goal of extinguishing or eliminating the fear response. An anxiety hierarchy (a list of activities ordered from least to most anxiety provoking) can be used to help with exposure. *Aversion therapy* is an approach that uses principles of classical conditioning to link problematic behaviors to unpleasant physical reactions.
14. Answers will vary, but may be based on the following information. One challenge of providing therapy is to meet the needs of clients from vastly different cultures. Within any group, there is great variation from one individual to the next, but it is still necessary for the therapist to keep in mind the client's cultural experience. This includes being respectful of cultural norms and sensitive to the many forms of prejudice and discrimination that people can experience. Every client has a unique story and a singular set of psychological needs. Responding to those needs and determining which approach will be most effective are key to successful therapy.
15. Answers will vary, but may be based on the following information. With more people connected to the internet and owning smartphones, many therapists and clients are taking advantage of digital technologies. Telepsychology, or psychological care delivered with the help of communication technologies such as video conferencing, phone calls, and e-mail, is a good choice for many therapists and clients when in-person visits are not feasible. For example, these digital tools are valuable for serving rural areas and providing treatment to those who would otherwise have no access. There are some potential drawbacks, including concerns about privacy, reimbursement from insurance companies, and communication with nonverbal cues.

# A Introduction to Statistics

## Test Prep Are You Ready?

1. Statistics
2. A. summarize data.
3. D. statistical significance
4. A. 2; B. 2; C. 1; D. 1.
5. C. frequency distribution
6. A. normal curve.
7. negatively skewed; positively skewed
8. B. measures of central tendency.
9. B. 5
10. A. 4
11. A. 4
12. C. outlier; mean
13. A. range
14. A. 2
15. Answers will vary, but it is important to consider what is being measured, how that measurement is actually being depicted, where the data come from, and the purpose of gathering the data.

**page APP A-3**

Answers will vary, but here are examples from Chapter 4: *Quantitative variables:* frequency of sound waves, pitch of sound, number of hair cells, color wavelength
*Qualitative variables*: gender, religious affiliation, supertaster status, carpentered worlds versus traditional settings

**page APP A-13**

The mean for the sample is 38.6, the median is 38, the range is 65, and the standard deviation is 16.5. A stem-and-leaf plot would be as shown, and it appears the sample data might be positively skewed.

| | |
|---|---|
| 1 | 0 0 1 6 8 8 |
| 2 | 0 0 4 4 5 5 6 9 9 |
| 3 | 0 1 1 2 3 6 8 9 |
| 4 | 0 1 1 2 3 6 8 9 |
| 5 | 0 0 1 2 3 6 7 9 |
| 6 | 1 1 6 |
| 7 | 1 5 |

# Glossary

**abnormal behavior** Behavior that is atypical, dysfunctional, distressful, and/or deviant. (p. 485)

**absolute thresholds** The weakest stimuli that can be detected 50% of the time. (p. 87)

**accommodation** A restructuring of old ideas to make a place for new information. (p. 305)

**accommodation** The process by which the lens changes shape in order to focus on objects near and far. (p. 92)

**acculturation** The process of cultural adjustment and adaptation, including changes to one's language, values, cultural behaviors, and sometimes national identity. (p. 459)

**acculturative stress** Stress that occurs when people move to new countries or cultures and must adjust to a new way of life. (p. 459)

**achievement** Acquired knowledge, or what has been learned. (p. 272)

**acquisition** The initial learning phase in both classical and operant conditioning. (p. 175)

**action potential** The spike in voltage that passes through the axon of a neuron, the result of which is to convey information. (p. 49)

**activation–synthesis model** A theory proposing that humans respond to random neural activity while in REM sleep as if it has meaning. (p. 146)

**active listening** The ability to pick up on the content and emotions behind words in order to understand a client's perspective, often by echoing the main point of what the client says. (p. 535)

**adaptive value** The degree to which a trait or behavior helps an organism survive. (p. 178)

**adolescence** The transition period between late childhood and early adulthood. (p. 314)

**adrenal glands** Endocrine glands involved in responses to stress and the regulation of salt balance. (p. 62)

**afterimage** An image that appears to linger in the visual field after its stimulus, or source, is removed. (p. 97)

**aggression** Intimidating or threatening behavior or attitudes intended to hurt someone. (p. 437)

**agoraphobia** Extreme fear of situations involving public transportation, open spaces, or other public settings. (p. 498)

**algorithm** An approach to problem solving using a formula or set of rules that, if followed, ensures a solution. (p. 257)

**all-or-none** A neuron either fires or does not fire; action potentials are always the same strength. (p. 49)

**alpha waves** Brain waves that indicate a relaxed, drowsy state. (p. 135)

**altruism** Helping others with no expectation of something in return. (p. 444)

**amphetamines** Stimulant drugs; methamphetamine falls in this class of drugs. (p. 155)

**amplitude** The height of a wave; distance from midpoint to peak, or from midpoint to trough. (p. 91)

**amygdala** A pair of almond-shaped structures in the limbic system that processes aggression and basic emotions such as fear, as well as associated memories. (p. 75)

**androgens** The male hormones secreted by the testes in males and by the adrenal glands in both males and females. (p. 293)

**androgyny** The tendency to cross gender-role boundaries, exhibiting behaviors associated with different genders. (p. 321)

**anorexia nervosa** An eating disorder identified by significant weight loss, an intense fear of being overweight, a false sense of body image, and a refusal to eat the proper amount of calories to achieve a healthy weight. (p. 520)

**anterograde amnesia** A type of memory loss; an inability to create new memories following damage to the brain. (p. 238)

**anti-anxiety drugs** Psychotropic medications used for treating the symptoms of anxiety. (p. 548)

**antidepressant drugs** Psychotropic medications used for the treatment of depression. (p. 546)

**antipsychotic drugs** Psychotropic medications used in the treatment of psychotic symptoms, such as hallucinations and delusions. (p. 548)

**antisocial personality disorder** A psychological disorder distinguished by unethical behavior, deceitfulness, impulsivity, irritability, aggressiveness, disregard for others, and lack of remorse. (p. 517)

**anxiety disorders** A group of psychological disorders associated with extreme anxiety and/or debilitating, irrational fears. (p. 496)

**approach–approach conflict** A type of conflict in which one must choose between two or more options that are attractive. (p. 461)

**approach–avoidance conflict** A type of conflict that occurs when one faces a choice or situation that has favorable and unfavorable characteristics. (p. 461)

**aptitude** An individual's potential for learning. (p. 272)

**archetypes** Primal images, patterns of thought, and story lines stored in the collective unconscious, with themes that may be found in art, literature, music, dreams, and religions. (p. 388)

**arousal theory** Suggests that humans are motivated to seek an optimal level of arousal, or alertness and engagement in the world. (p. 338)

**assimilation** Using existing knowledge and ideas to understand new information and experiences. (p. 304)

**association areas** Regions of the cortex that integrate information from all over the brain, allowing us to learn, think in abstract terms, and carry out complex behaviors. (p. 73)

**attachment** The degree to which an infant feels an emotional connection with primary caregivers. (p. 309)

**attitudes** The relatively stable thoughts, feelings, and responses one has toward people, situations, ideas, and things. (p. 418)

**attributions** Beliefs one develops to explain human behaviors and characteristics, as well as situations. (p. 415)

**audition** The sense of hearing. (p. 99)

**authoritarian parenting** A rigid parenting style characterized by strict rules and poor communication skills. (p. 327)

**authoritative parenting** A parenting style characterized by high expectations, strong support, and respect for children. (p. 327)

**automatic processing** Attending to information with little or no conscious effort or awareness. (p. 129)

**autonomic nervous system** The branch of the peripheral nervous system that controls involuntary processes within the body, such as contractions in the digestive tract and activity of glands. (p. 58)

**availability heuristic** A decision-making strategy that predicts the likelihood of something happening based on how easily a similar type of event from the past can be recalled. (p. 261)

**aversion therapy** A therapeutic approach that uses the principles of classical conditioning to link problematic behaviors to unpleasant physical reactions. (p. 539)

**avoidance–avoidance conflict** A type of conflict in which one must choose between two or more options that are unattractive. (p. 461)

**axon** Skinny tube-like structure of a neuron that extends from the cell body and sends messages to other neurons through its terminals. (p. 46)

**barbiturates** Depressant drugs that decrease neural activity and reduce anxiety; a type of sedative. (p. 149)

**bar graph** Displays qualitative data with categories of interest on the *x*-axis and frequency on the *y*-axis. (p. APP A-7)

**behavioral perspective** An approach suggesting that behavior is primarily learned through associations, reinforcers, and observation. (p. 9)

**behaviorism** The scientific study of observable behavior. (p. 8)

**behavior modification** A therapeutic approach in which behaviors are shaped through reinforcement and punishment. (p. 539)

**behavior therapy** A type of therapy that focuses on behavioral change. (p. 530)

**beta waves** Brain waves that indicate an alert, awake state. (p. 135)

**bimodal distribution** A distribution with two modes, which are the two most frequently occurring values. (p. APP A-9)

**binge-eating disorder** An eating disorder characterized by episodes of extreme overeating, during which a larger amount of food is consumed than most people would eat in a similar amount of time under similar circumstances. (p. 521)

**binocular cues** Information gathered from both eyes to help judge depth and distance. (p. 118)

**biofeedback** A technique for teaching a person to control seemingly involuntary physiological activities, such as heart rate, blood pressure, and skin temperature. (p. 478)

**biological perspective** An approach that uses knowledge about underlying physiology to explain behavior and mental processes. (p. 10)

**biological preparedness** The tendency for animals to be predisposed or inclined to form certain kinds of associations through classical conditioning. (p. 179)

**biological psychology** The branch of psychology that focuses on how the brain and other biological systems influence human behavior. (p. 43)

**biomedical therapy** Drugs and other physical interventions that target the biological processes underlying psychological disorders; primary goal is to reduce symptoms. (p. 530)

**biopsychosocial perspective** Explains behavior through the interaction of biological, psychological, and sociocultural factors. (p. 10)

**bipolar disorder** A psychological disorder marked by dramatic swings in mood, ranging from manic episodes to depressive episodes. (p. 485)

**bisexual** Being attracted to more than one sex or gender. (p. 346)

**blind spot** A hole in the visual field caused by the optic disc (the location where the optic nerve exits the retina). (p. 93)

**borderline personality disorder** A psychological disorder distinguished by an incomplete sense of self, extreme self-criticism, unstable emotions, and feelings of emptiness. (p. 518)

**bottom-up processing** Taking basic information about incoming sensory stimuli and processing it for further interpretation. (p. 84)

**Broca's area** A region of the cortex that is critical for speech production. (p. 66)

**bulimia nervosa** An eating disorder characterized by extreme overeating followed by purging, with serious health risks. (p. 520)

**burnout** Emotional, mental, and physical fatigue that results in reduced motivation, enthusiasm, and performance. (p. 467)

**bystander effect** The tendency for people to avoid getting involved in an emergency they witness because they assume someone else will help. (p. 435)

**Cannon–Bard theory of emotion** Suggests that environmental stimuli are the starting point for emotions, and physiological or behavioral responses occur at the same time emotions are felt. (p. 359)

**case study** A type of descriptive research that closely examines an individual or small group. (p. 21)

**cell body** The region of the neuron that includes structures that nourish the cell, and a nucleus containing DNA. (p. 46)

**central nervous system (CNS)** A major component of the human nervous system; includes the brain and spinal cord. (p. 56)

**cerebellum** A hindbrain structure located behind the brainstem that is responsible for muscle coordination and balance; Latin for "little brain." (p. 77)

**cerebral cortex** The wrinkled outermost layer of the cerebrum, responsible for higher mental functions, such as decision making, language, and processing visual information. (p. 68)

**cerebrum** The largest area of the brain; includes virtually all parts of the brain except brainstem structures; has two distinct hemispheres. (p. 62)

**chromosomes** Inherited threadlike structures composed of deoxyribonucleic acid (DNA). (p. 292)

**chronic traumatic encephalopathy (CTE)** A neurodegenerative disease that leads to atypical deposits of tau protein throughout various regions in the brain as a result of traumatic brain injury. (p. 244)

**chunking** Grouping numbers, letters, or other items into recognizable subsets as a strategy for increasing the quantity of information that can be maintained in short-term memory. (p. 216)

**circadian rhythm** The daily patterns roughly following the 24-hour cycle of daylight and darkness; a 24-hour cycle of physiological and behavioral functioning. (p. 132)

**classical conditioning** A learning process in which two stimuli become associated with each other; when an originally neutral stimulus is conditioned to elicit an involuntary response. (p. 173)

**cochlea** Fluid-filled, snail-shaped organ of the inner ear that is lined with the basilar membrane. (p. 101)

**cognition** The mental activity associated with obtaining, converting, and using knowledge. (p. 251)

**cognitive appraisal approach** Suggests that the appraisal or interpretation of interactions with surroundings causes an emotional reaction. (p. 361)

**cognitive behavioral therapy (CBT)** An action-oriented type of therapy that requires clients to confront and resist their illogical thinking. (p. 543)

**cognitive dissonance** A state of tension that results when behaviors are inconsistent with attitudes. (p. 421)

**cognitive map** A mental representation of physical space. (p. 203)

**cognitive perspective** An approach examining the mental processes that direct behavior. (p. 9)

**cognitive psychology** The scientific study of mental processes such as thinking, problem solving, and language. (p. 128)

**cognitive therapy** A type of therapy aimed at addressing the maladaptive thinking that leads to maladaptive behaviors and feelings. (p. 541)

**cohort effect** The differences across groups that result from common experiences within the groups. (p. 290)

**collective unconscious** According to Jung, the universal experiences of humankind passed from generation to generation. (p. 388)

**color constancy** Objects are perceived as maintaining their color, even with changing sensory data. (p. 120)

**comorbidity** The occurrence of two or more disorders at the same time. (p. 493)

**companionate love** Love that consists of profound fondness, camaraderie, understanding, and emotional closeness. (p. 448)

**compliance** Changes in behavior at the request or direction of another person or group, who in general does not have any true authority. (p. 425)

**compulsion** A behavior or "mental act" that a person repeats over and over in an effort to reduce anxiety. (p. 499)

**concepts** Mental representations of categories of objects, situations, and ideas that belong together based on their central features or characteristics. (p. 251)

**concrete operational stage** Piaget's stage of cognitive development during which children begin to think more logically, but mainly in reference to concrete objects and circumstances. (p. 306)

**conditioned emotional response** An emotional reaction acquired through classical conditioning; process by which an emotional reaction becomes associated with a previously neutral stimulus. (p. 180)

**conditioned response (CR)** A learned response to a conditioned stimulus. (p. 175)

**conditioned stimulus (CS)** A previously neutral stimulus that an organism learns to associate with an unconditioned stimulus. (p. 175)

**conditioned taste aversion** A form of classical conditioning that occurs when an organism learns to associate the taste of a particular food or drink with illness. (p. 178)

**cones** Photoreceptors that enable us to sense color and details. (p. 93)

**confirmation bias** The tendency to look for evidence that upholds our beliefs and to overlook evidence that runs counter to them. (p. 262)

**conformity** The tendency to modify behaviors, attitudes, beliefs, and opinions to match those of others. (p. 427)

**confounding variable** A type of extraneous variable that changes in sync with the independent variable, making it difficult to discern which one is causing changes in the dependent variable. (p. 31)

**consciousness** The state of being aware of oneself, one's thoughts, and/or the environment. (p. 126)

**conservation** Refers to the unchanging properties of volume, mass, or amount in relation to appearance. (p. 305)

**consummate love** Love that combines intimacy, commitment, and passion. (p. 448)

**continuous reinforcement** A schedule of reinforcement in which every target behavior is reinforced. (p. 189)

**control group** The participants in an experiment who are not exposed to the treatment variable; this is the comparison group. (p. 29)

**convergence** A binocular cue used to judge distance and depth based on the tension of the muscles that direct where the eyes are focusing. (p. 118)

**convergent thinking** A conventional approach to problem solving that focuses on finding a single best solution to a problem by using previous experience and knowledge. (p. 282)

**coping** The cognitive, behavioral, and emotional abilities used to manage something that is perceived as difficult or challenging. (p. 468)

**cornea** The clear, outer layer of the eye that shields it from damage and focuses incoming light waves. (p. 92)

**corpus callosum** The thick band of nerve fibers connecting the right and left cerebral hemispheres; principal structure for information sharing between the two hemispheres. (p. 63)

**correlation** An association or relationship between two (or more) variables. (p. 24)

**correlational method** A type of research examining relationships among variables. (p. 24)

**correlation coefficient** The statistical measure (symbolized as $r$) that indicates the strength and direction of the relationship between two variables. (p. 25)

**creativity** In problem solving, the ability to construct valuable results in innovative ways; the ability to generate original ideas. (p. 282)

**critical period** Specific time frame in which an organism is sensitive to environmental factors, and certain behaviors and abilities are readily shaped or altered by events or experiences. (p. 289)

**critical thinking** The process of weighing pieces of evidence, synthesizing them, and evaluating the contributions of each; disciplined thinking that is clear, rational, openminded, and informed by evidence. (p. 16)

**cross-sectional method** A research design that examines people of different ages at a single point in time. (p. 290)

**cross-sequential method** A research design that examines groups of people of different ages, following them across time. (p. 290)

**culture-fair intelligence tests** Assessments designed to minimize cultural bias. (p. 277)

**daily hassles** Minor, everyday problems that can act as stressors. (p. 460)

**dark adaptation** Process by which the eyes adjust to dark after exposure to bright light. (p. 95)

**debriefing** Sharing information with participants after their involvement in a study has ended, including the purpose of the research and any deception used. (p. 35)

**decision making** The cognitive process of choosing from alternatives that might be used to reach a goal. (p. 261)

**deindividuation** The diminished sense of personal responsibility, inhibition, or adherence to social norms that occurs when group members are not treated as individuals. (p. 433)

**deinstitutionalization** The mass movement of patients with psychological disorders out of institutions, and the attempt to reintegrate them into the community. (p. 528)

**delirium tremens (DTs)** Withdrawal symptoms that can occur when a person who is physiologically dependent on alcohol suddenly stops drinking; can include sweating, restlessness, hallucinations, severe tremors, and seizures. (p. 162)

**delta waves** Brain waves that indicate a deep sleep. (p. 136)

**delusions** Strange or false beliefs that a person firmly maintains even when presented with evidence to the contrary. (p. 511)

**dendrites** Tiny, branchlike fibers extending from the cell body that receive messages from other neurons and send information in the direction of the cell body. (p. 46)

**deoxyribonucleic acid (DNA)** A molecule that provides instructions for the development of an organism. (p. 292)

**dependent variable (DV)** In the experimental method, the characteristic or response that is measured to determine the effect of the researcher's manipulation. (p. 29)

**depressants** A class of psychoactive drugs that depress or slow down activity in the central nervous system. (p. 149)

**depth perception** The ability to perceive three-dimensional objects and judge distances. (p. 118)

**descriptive research** Research methods that describe and explore behaviors, but whose findings cannot definitively state cause-and-effect relationships. (p. 20)

**developmental psychology** A field of psychology that examines age-related physical, cognitive, and socioemotional changes across the life span. (p. 288)

**difference threshold** The minimum difference between two stimuli that can be noticed 50% of the time. (p. 87)

**diffusion of responsibility** The sharing of duties and responsibilities among all group members that can lead to feelings of decreased accountability and motivation. (p. 433)

**discrimination** Showing favoritism or hostility to others because of their affiliation with a group. (p. 440)

**display rules** Framework or guidelines for when, how, and where an emotion is expressed. (p. 364)

**dispositional attribution** A type of internal attribution where behaviors are assumed to result from traits or personality characteristics. (p. 416)

**dissociation** A disturbance in the normally integrated experience of psychological functions involved in memory, consciousness, perception, or identity. (p. 519)

**dissociative amnesia** A psychological disorder marked by difficulty remembering important personal information and life events. (p. 519)

**dissociative disorders** Psychological disorders distinguished by disturbances in normal psychological functioning; may include problems with memory, identity, consciousness, perception, and motor control. (p. 518)

**dissociative fugue** A condition in which a person with dissociative amnesia or dissociative identity disorder wanders about in a confused and unexpected manner. (p. 519)

**dissociative identity disorder** A psychological disorder that involves the occurrence of two or more distinct personalities within an individual. (p. 519)

**distress** The stress response to unpleasant or undesirable stressors. (p. 455)

**distributed practice** Spreading out study sessions over time with breaks in between. (p. 223)

**distribution shape** How the frequencies of the values are spread along the x-axis. (p. APP A-5)

**divergent thinking** The ability to devise many solutions to a problem; a component of creativity. (p. 282)

**dizygotic twins** Fraternal twins who develop from two eggs inseminated by two sperm, and are as genetically similar as any sibling pair. (p. 293)

**dominant gene** One of a pair of genes that has power over the expression of an inherited characteristic. (p. 294)

**door-in-the-face technique** A compliance technique that involves making a large request first, followed by a smaller request. (p. 426)

**dopamine hypothesis** A theory suggesting that the synthesis, release, and concentrations of the neurotransmitter dopamine play a role in schizophrenia. (p. 514)

**double-blind study** Type of study in which neither the participants nor the researchers administering the independent variable know which participants are receiving the treatment and which are getting the placebo. (p. 32)

**drive** A state of tension that pushes us (motivates our behaviors) to meet a need. (p. 337)

**drive-reduction theory** Suggests that homeostasis motivates us to meet biological needs. (p. 337)

**echoic memory** Exact copies of the sounds we hear; a form of sensory memory. (p. 214)

**eclectic approach to therapy** Drawing on multiple theories and approaches to tailor treatment for a client. (p. 532)

**effortful processing** The encoding and storage of information with conscious effort, or awareness. (p. 221)

**ego** According to Freud, the structure of the mind that uses the reality principle to manipulate situations, plan for the future, solve problems, and make decisions to satisfy the needs of the id. (p. 381)

**egocentrism** When a person is only able to imagine the world from their own perspective. (p. 305)

**ego defense mechanisms** Unconscious processes the ego uses to distort perceptions and memories and thereby reduce anxiety created by the id–superego conflict. (p. 382)

**elaborative rehearsal** The method of connecting incoming information to knowledge in long-term memory; a deep level of encoding. (p. 221)

**electroconvulsive therapy (ECT)** A biomedical treatment for severe disorders that induces seizures in the brain through electrical currents. (p. 549)

**embryo** The unborn human from the beginning of the third week of pregnancy, lasting through the eighth week of prenatal development. (p. 296)

**emerging adulthood** A phase of life between 18 and 25 years that includes exploration and opportunity. (p. 322)

**emotion** A psychological state that includes a subjective or inner experience, physiological component, and behavioral expression. (p. 356)

**emotional intelligence** The capacity to perceive, understand, regulate, and use emotions to adapt to social situations. (p. 279)

**emotion-focused coping** A coping strategy in which a person addresses the emotions that surround a problem, as opposed to trying to solve it. (p. 468)

**empathy** The ability to feel what a person is experiencing by attempting to observe the world through their eyes. (p. 535)

**empirical method** A process that uses objective observation to measure and collect data. (p. 5)

**encoding** The process through which information enters our memory system. (p. 210)

**encoding specificity principle** States that memories are more easily recalled when the context and cues at the time of encoding are similar to those at the time of retrieval. (p. 227)

**endocrine system** The communication system that uses glands to convey messages by releasing hormones into the bloodstream. (p. 60)

**epigenetics** A field of study that examines the processes involved in the development of phenotypes. (p. 295)

**episodic memory** The record of memorable experiences or "episodes" including when and where they occurred; a type of explicit memory. (p. 219)

**estrogens** The female hormones secreted primarily by the ovaries and by the adrenal glands in both males and females. (p. 293)

**ethnocentrism** Seeing the world only from the perspective of one's own group. (p. 440)

**eustress** The stress response to agreeable or positive stressors. (p. 456)

**evidence-based practice** Making treatment decisions that integrate valuable research findings, clinical expertise, and knowledge of a patient's culture, values, and preferences. (p. 532)

**evolutionary perspective** An approach that uses knowledge about evolutionary forces, such as natural selection, to understand behavior. (p. 9)

**expectancy** The predictions we make about the outcomes or consequences of our behaviors. (p. 394)

**experiment** A controlled procedure that involves careful examination through the use of scientific observation and/or manipulation of variables (measurable characteristics). (p. 12)

**experimental group** The participants in an experiment who are exposed to the treatment variable or manipulation by the researcher; represents the treatment group. (p. 29)

**experimental method** A type of research that manipulates a variable of interest (independent variable) to uncover cause-and-effect relationships. (p. 28)

**experimenter bias** Researcher expectations that influence the outcome of a study. (p. 32)

**explicit memory** A type of memory you are aware of having and can consciously express in words or declare, including memories of facts and experiences. (p. 219)

**exposure** A therapeutic technique that brings a person into contact with a feared object or situation in a safe environment, with the goal of extinguishing or eliminating the fear response. (p. 537)

**extinction** In classical conditioning, the process by which the conditioned response decreases after repeated exposure to the conditioned stimulus in the absence of the unconditioned stimulus; in operant conditioning, the disappearance of a learned behavior through the removal of its reinforcer. (p. 176)

**extraneous variable** A characteristic of participants or the environment that could unexpectedly influence the outcome of a study. (p. 31)

**extrinsic motivation** The drive or urge to continue a behavior because of external reinforcers. (p. 336)

**facial feedback hypothesis** Suggests that the facial expression of an emotion can affect the experience of that emotion. (p. 365)

**false consensus effect** The tendency to overestimate the degree to which others think or act like we do. (p. 418)

**family therapy** A type of therapy that focuses on the family as an integrated system, recognizing that the interactions within it can create instability or lead to the breakdown of the family unit. (p. 553)

**feature detectors** Neurons in the visual cortex specialized in detecting specific features of the visual experience, such as angles, lines, and movements. (p. 95)

**fetal alcohol syndrome (FAS)** Delays in development that result from moderate to heavy alcohol use during pregnancy. (p. 297)

**figure-ground** A central principle of Gestalt psychology, involving the shifting of focus; as attention is focused on one object, all other features drop or recede into the background. (p. 116)

**five-factor model of personality** A trait approach to explaining personality, including dimensions of openness to experience, conscientiousness, extraversion, agreeableness, and neuroticism; also known as the "Big Five." (p. 398)

**fixation** Being stuck in a particular psychosexual stage of development; occurs when one is unsuccessful at resolving the conflict associated with that stage. (p. 384)

**fixed-interval schedule** A schedule in which the reinforcer comes after a preestablished interval of time; the behavior is only reinforced after the given interval is over. (p. 192)

**fixed-ratio schedule** A schedule in which the subject must exhibit a predetermined number of desired behaviors before a reinforcer is given. (p. 190)

**flashbulb memory** A detailed account of circumstances surrounding an emotionally significant or shocking, sometimes historic, event. (p. 220)

**foot-in-the-door technique** A compliance technique that involves making a small request first, followed by a larger request. (p. 426)

**forebrain** The largest part of the brain; includes the cerebrum and the limbic system. (p. 76)

**formal concepts** The mental representations of categories that are created through rigid and logical rules, or features. (p. 253)

**formal operational stage** Piaget's stage of cognitive development during which children begin to think more logically and systematically. (p. 306)

**free association** A psychoanalytic technique in which a patient says anything that comes to mind. (p. 533)

**frequency** The number of sound waves passing a given point per unit of time; higher frequency is perceived as higher pitch, and lower frequency is perceived as lower pitch. (p. 99)

**frequency distribution** A simple way to portray data that displays how often various values in a data set are present. (p. APP A-3)

**frequency polygon** A type of graphic display that uses lines to represent the frequency of data values. (p. APP A-4)

**frequency theory** States that pitch is determined by the vibrating frequency of the sound wave, basilar membrane, and associated neural impulses. (p. 103)

**frontal lobes** The area of the cortex that directs higher-level cognitive activities, such as language, emotions, control of social behavior, and decision making. (p. 69)

**frustration–aggression hypothesis** Suggests that aggression may occur in response to frustration. (p. 438)

**functional fixedness** A barrier to problem solving that occurs when familiar objects can only be imagined to function in their usual way. (p. 258)

**functionalism** An early school of psychology that focused on the function of thoughts, feelings, and behaviors and how they help us adapt to the environment. (p. 7)

**fundamental attribution error** The tendency to overestimate the degree to which the characteristics of an individual are the cause of an event, and to underestimate the involvement of situational factors. (p. 416)

**gate-control theory** Suggests that the perception of pain will either increase or decrease through the interaction of biopsychosocial factors; signals are sent to open or close "gates" that control the neurological pathways for pain. (p. 111)

**gender** The dimension of masculinity and femininity based on social, cultural, and psychological characteristics. (p. 319)

**gender identity** The feeling or sense of being male, female, or an alternative gender, and compatibility, contentment, and conformity with one's gender. (p. 319)

**gender roles** The collection of actions, beliefs, and characteristics that a culture associates with masculinity and femininity. (p. 319)

**gender schemas** The psychological or mental guidelines that dictate how to be masculine and feminine. (p. 320)

**gene** Specified segment of a DNA molecule. (p. 292)

**general adaptation syndrome (GAS)** A specific pattern of physiological reactions to stressors that includes the alarm stage, resistance stage, and exhaustion stage. (p. 463)

**general intelligence (*g*-factor)** A singular underlying aptitude or intellectual ability that drives capabilities in many areas, including verbal, spatial, and reasoning competencies. (p. 270)

**generalized anxiety disorder** A psychological disorder characterized by an excessive amount of worry and anxiety about activities relating to family, health, school, and other aspects of daily life. (p. 498)

**genotype** An individual's complete collection of genes. (p. 294)

**genuineness** The ability to respond to a client in an authentic way rather than hiding behind a polite or professional mask. (p. 535)

**gestalt** The natural tendency for the brain to organize stimuli into a whole, rather than perceiving the parts and pieces. (p. 116)

**gifted** Highly intelligent; defined as having an IQ score of 130 or above. (p. 278)

**glial cells** Cells of the nervous system that support, nourish, and protect neurons. (p. 46)

**grammar** The rules associated with word and sentence structure. (p. 267)

**group polarization** The tendency for group members to take a more extreme stance than originally held after deliberations and discussion. (p. 434)

**groupthink** The tendency for group members to maintain cohesiveness and agreement in their decision making, failing to consider possible alternatives and related viewpoints. (p. 434)

**gustation** The sense of taste. (p. 107)

**habituation** A basic form of learning evident when an organism does not respond as strongly or as often to an event following multiple exposures to it. (p. 171)

**hallucinations** Perception-like experiences that an individual believes are real, but that are not evident to others. (p. 511)

**hallucinogens** A group of psychoactive drugs that can produce hallucinations, distorted sensory experiences, alterations of mood, and distorted thinking. (p. 157)

**hardiness** A personality characteristic indicating an ability to remain resilient and optimistic despite intensely stressful situations. (p. 472)

**health psychology** The study of the biological, psychological, and social factors that contribute to health and illness. (p. 468)

**heritability** The degree to which hereditary factors (genes) are responsible for a particular characteristic observed within a population. (p. 279)

**heterosexual** Attraction to members of the opposite sex. (p. 345)

**heuristics** Problem-solving shortcuts that incorporate a rule of thumb, guideline, or strategy. (p. 257)

**hierarchy of needs** A continuum of needs that are universal and ordered in terms of the strength of their associated drives. (p. 339)

**higher order conditioning** With repeated pairings of a conditioned stimulus and a second neutral stimulus, that second neutral stimulus becomes a conditioned stimulus as well. (p. 176)

**hindbrain** Includes areas of the brain responsible for fundamental life-sustaining processes. (p. 77)

**hindsight bias** The mistaken belief that an outcome could have been predicted easily; the "I knew it all along" feeling. (p. 263)

**hippocampus** A pair of sea-horse shaped structures located in the limbic system; primarily responsible for creating new memories. (p. 75)

**histogram** Displays the classes of a variable on the *x*-axis and the frequency of the data on the *y*-axis; frequency is indicated by the height of the vertical bars. (p. APP A-3)

**homeostasis** The tendency for bodies to maintain constant states through internal controls. (p. 337)

**homosexual** An antiquated and derogatory term referring to those who are attracted to members of the same sex. (p. 346)

**hormones** Chemical messengers released into the bloodstream that influence mood, cognition, appetite, and many other processes and behaviors. (p. 60)

**hue** The color of an object, determined by the wavelength of light it reflects. (p. 91)

**humanistic psychology** An approach suggesting that human nature is by and large positive, and the human direction is toward growth. (p. 9)

**humanistic therapy** A type of insight therapy that emphasizes the positive nature of humankind. (p. 535)

**hypnosis** An altered state of consciousness allowing for changes in perceptions and behaviors, which result from suggestions made by a hypnotist. (p. 164)

**hypothalamus** A small structure located below the thalamus that maintains the internal environment within a healthy range; helps regulate sleep–wake cycles, sexual behavior, and appetite. (p. 74)

**hypothesis** A statement that can be used to test a prediction. (p. 12)

**hypothesis testing** Mathematical procedures used to explore whether data support a hypothesis or result from chance. (p. APP A-11)

**iconic memory** Visual impressions that are photograph-like in their accuracy but dissolve in less than a second; a form of sensory memory. (p. 213)

**id** According to Freud, the most primitive structure of the mind, the activities of which occur at the unconscious level and are guided by the pleasure principle. (p. 381)

**ideal self** The self-concept a person strives for and fervently wishes to achieve. (p. 392)

**identity** A sense of self based on values, beliefs, and goals. (p. 316)

**illusion** A perception that is inconsistent with sensory data. (p. 114)

**implicit memory** A memory of something you know or know how to do, which may be automatic, unconscious, and difficult to bring to awareness and express. (p. 219)

**incentive** An association established between a behavior and its consequences, which then motivates that behavior. (p. 335)

**independent variable (IV)** In the experimental method, the variable manipulated by the researcher to determine its effect on the dependent variable. (p. 29)

**informed consent** Acknowledgment from study participants that they understand what their participation will entail. (p. 35)

**in-group** The group to which we belong. (p. 440)

**insanity** A legal determination of the degree to which a person is responsible for criminal behaviors. (p. 488)

**insight** An understanding or solution that occurs in a sudden stroke of clarity (the "aha!" feeling). (p. 258)

**insight therapies** Psychotherapies aimed at increasing awareness of self and environment. (p. 530)

**insomnia** Sleep disturbance characterized by an inability to fall asleep or stay asleep, impacting both the quality and quantity of sleep. (p. 141)

**instinctive drift** The tendency for animals to revert to instinctual behaviors after a behavior pattern has been learned. (p. 189)

**instincts** Complex behaviors that are fixed, unlearned, and consistent within a species. (p. 337)

**Institutional Review Board (IRB)** A committee that reviews research proposals to protect the rights and welfare of all participants. (p. 36)

**intelligence** Innate ability to solve problems, adapt to the environment, and learn from experiences. (p. 270)

**intelligence quotient (IQ)** A score from an intelligence assessment; originally based on mental age divided by chronological age, multiplied by 100. (p. 273)

**interneurons** Neurons that reside exclusively in the brain and spinal cord; act as a bridge connecting sensory and motor neurons. (p. 57)

**interpersonal attraction** The factors that lead us to form friendships or romantic relationships with others. (p. 446)

**interpretation** A psychoanalytic technique used to explore unconscious conflicts driving behavior. (p. 533)

**intersexual** Having ambiguous or inconsistent biological indicators of male or female in the sexual structures and organs. (p. 294)

**intrinsic motivation** The drive or urge to continue a behavior because of internal reinforcers. (p. 336)

**introspection** The examination of one's own conscious activities. (p. 6)

**iris** The part of the eye responsible for changing the size of the pupil. (p. 92)

**James–Lange theory of emotion** Suggests that a stimulus initiates the experience of a physiological and/or behavioral reaction, and this reaction leads to the feeling of an emotion. (p. 358)

**just-world hypothesis** The tendency to believe the world is a fair place and individuals generally get what they deserve. (p. 417)

**kinesthesia** Sensory system that conveys information about body position and movement. (p. 112)

**language** A system for using symbols to think and communicate. (p. 267)

**latent content** The hidden meaning of a dream, often concealed by the manifest content of the dream. (p. 145)

**latent learning** Learning that occurs without awareness and regardless of reinforcement, and is not evident until needed. (p. 202)

**lateralization** The idea that each cerebral hemisphere processes certain types of information and excels in certain activities. (p. 65)

**law of effect** Thorndike's principle stating that behaviors are more likely to be repeated when followed by pleasurable outcomes, and less likely to be repeated when followed by unpleasant outcomes. (p. 183)

**learned helplessness** A tendency for people to believe they have no control over the consequences of their behaviors, resulting in passive behavior. (p. 507)

**learning** A relatively enduring change in behavior or thinking that results from experiences. (p. 170)

**light adaptation** Process by which the eyes adjust to light after being in the dark. (p. 95)

**limbic system** A collection of structures that regulates emotions and basic drives such as hunger, and aids in the creation of memories. (p. 74)

**longitudinal method** A research design that examines one sample of people over a period of time to determine age-related changes. (p. 290)

**long-term memory** A stage of memory with essentially unlimited capacity and the ability to store information indefinitely. (p. 212)

**long-term potentiation** The increased efficiency of neural communication over time, resulting in learning and the formation of memories. (p. 242)

**lysergic acid diethylamide (LSD)** A synthetically produced, odorless, tasteless, and colorless hallucinogen that is very potent; produces extreme changes in sensations and perceptions. (p. 157)

**maintenance rehearsal** Technique of repeating information to be remembered, increasing the length of time it can be held in short-term memory. (p. 215)

**major depressive disorder** A psychological disorder that includes at least one major depressive episode, with symptoms such as depressed mood, problems with sleep, and loss of energy. (p. 503)

**manic episode** A state of continuous elation that is out of proportion to the setting, and can include irritability, very high and sustained levels of energy, and an "expansive" mood. (p. 508)

**manifest content** The apparent meaning of a dream; the remembered story line of a dream. (p. 145)

**massed practice** Studying for long periods of time without breaks. (p. 221)

**maturation** Physical growth beginning with conception and ending when the body stops growing. (p. 288)

**mean** The arithmetic average of a data set; a measure of central tendency. (p. APP A-8)

**measures of central tendency** Numbers that represent the middle of a data set. (p. APP A-8)

**measures of position** Numbers that represent where particular data values fall in relation to other values in the data set. (p. APP A-10)

**measures of variation** Numbers that describe the variation or dispersion in a data set. (p. APP A-10)

**median** A number that represents the position in the data set for which 50% of the values are above it, and 50% are below it; a measure of central tendency. (p. APP A-8)

**medical model** An approach suggesting that psychological disorders are illnesses that have underlying biological causes. (p. 493)

**medulla** A hindbrain structure that oversees vital functions, including breathing, digestion, and heart rate. (p. 77)

**memory** The processes involved in the encoding, storage, and retrieval of information. (p. 210)

**memory trace** The physical spot where memories are etched in the brain, also called an *engram.* (p. 239)

**menarche** The point at which menstruation begins. (p. 315)

**menopause** The time when a woman no longer ovulates, her menstrual cycle stops, and she is no longer capable of reproduction. (p. 324)

**mental age (MA)** A score representing the mental abilities of an individual in relation to others of a similar chronological age. (p. 272)

**mere-exposure effect** The more we are exposed to someone or something, the more positive our reaction to it becomes. (p. 446)

**meta-analysis** A type of statistical analysis that combines findings from many studies on a single topic; statistics used to merge the outcomes of many studies. (p. APP A-12)

**methylenedioxymethamphetamine (MDMA)** A synthetic drug that produces a combination of stimulant and hallucinogenic effects. (p. 158)

**midbrain** The part of the brainstem involved in levels of arousal; responsible for generating movement patterns in response to sensory input. (p. 76)

**mindfulness meditation** Being fully present in the moment; focusing attention on the here and now without passing judgment. (p. 480)

**misinformation effect** The tendency for new and misleading information obtained after an incident to distort one's memory of it. (p. 233)

**mnemonic** Techniques to improve memory. (p. 221)

**mode** The value of the data set that is most frequent; a measure of central tendency. (p. APP A-9)

**model** An individual or character whose behavior is being imitated. (p. 197)

**monocular cues** Depth and distance cues that require the use of only one eye. (p. 119)

**monozygotic twins** Identical twins who develop from one egg inseminated at conception, which then splits into two separate zygotes. (p. 293)

**mood-stabilizing drugs** Psychotropic medications that minimize the lows of depression and the highs of mania. (p. 548)

**morphemes** The fundamental units that bring meaning to language. (p. 267)

**motivation** A stimulus that can direct behavior, thinking, and feeling. (p. 335)

**motor cortex** A strip of brain tissue toward the rear of the frontal lobes that works with other brain regions to plan and execute voluntary movements. (p. 71)

**motor neurons** Neurons that transmit information from the central nervous system to the muscles and glands. (p. 57)

**myelin sheath** A fatty substance that insulates the axon and speeds the transmission of neural messages. (p. 46)

**narcolepsy** A neurological disorder characterized by excessive daytime sleepiness, which includes lapses into sleep and napping. (p. 138)

**natural concepts** The mental representations of categories developed through everyday experiences. (p. 252)

**naturalistic observation** A type of descriptive research that studies participants in their natural environment through systematic observation. (p. 20)

**natural selection** The process through which inherited traits in a given population either increase in frequency because they are adaptive, or decrease in frequency because they are maladaptive. (p. 9)

**nature** The inherited biological factors that shape behaviors, personality, and other characteristics. (p. 4)

**need for achievement (n-Ach)** A drive to reach attainable and challenging goals, especially in the face of competition. (p. 342)

**need for power (n-Pow)** A drive to control and influence others. (p. 342)

**needs** Physiological or psychological requirements that must be maintained at some baseline or constant state. (p. 337)

**negatively skewed** A nonsymmetrical distribution with a longer tail to the left side of the distribution; left-skewed distribution. (p. APP A-6)

**negative punishment** The removal of something desirable following an unwanted behavior, with the intention of decreasing that behavior. (p. 193)

**negative reinforcement** The removal of an unpleasant stimulus following a target behavior, which increases the likelihood of that behavior occurring again. (p. 185)

**negative symptoms** Behaviors or characteristics that are limited or absent; examples are social withdrawal, diminished speech, limited or no emotions, and loss of energy and follow-up. (p. 511)

**nerves** Bundles of neurons that carry information to and from the central nervous system; enable communication between the central nervous system and the muscles, glands, and sensory receptors. (p. 58)

**neurogenesis** The generation of new neurons in the brain. (p. 68)

**neurons** Specialized cells of the nervous system that transmit electrical and chemical signals in the body. (p. 42)

**neuroplasticity** The brain's ability to heal, grow new connections, and reorganize in order to adapt to the environment. (p. 67)

**neuroscience** The study of the brain and other parts of the nervous system. (p. 43)

**neurosurgery** A biomedical therapy that involves the destruction of some portion of the brain or connections between different areas of the brain. (p. 550)

**neurotransmitters** Chemical messengers that neurons use to communicate at the synapse. (p. 51)

**neutral stimulus (NS)** A stimulus that does not cause a relevant automatic or reflexive response. (p. 173)

**nightmares** Frightening dreams that occur during REM sleep. (p. 142)

**nondirective** A technique used in person-centered therapy whereby the therapist follows the lead of the client during treatment sessions. (p. 535)

**non-rapid eye movement (non-REM or NREM)** The nondreaming sleep that occurs during sleep Stages N1 to N3. (p. 136)

**normal curve** Depicts the frequency of values of a variable along a continuum; bell-shaped symmetrical distribution, with the highest point reflecting the average score. (p. 275)

**norms** Standards of the social environment. (p. 427)

**nurture** The environmental factors that shape behaviors, personality, and other characteristics. (p. 4)

**obedience** Changing behavior because we have been ordered to do so by an authority figure. (p. 429)

**object permanence** A milestone of the sensorimotor stage of cognitive development; an infant's realization that objects and people still exist even when out of sight or touch. (p. 305)

**observational learning** Learning that occurs as a result of watching the behavior of others. (p. 197)

**observer bias** Errors in the recording of observations, which result from the researcher's value system, expectations, or attitudes. (p. 21)

**obsession** A thought, an urge, or an image that happens repeatedly, is intrusive and unwelcome, and often causes anxiety and distress. (p. 499)

**obsessive-compulsive disorder (OCD)** A psychological disorder characterized by obsessions and/or compulsions that are time-consuming and cause a great deal of distress. (p. 499)

**obstructive sleep apnea hypopnea** A serious disturbance of non-REM sleep characterized by complete absence of air flow (apnea) or reduced air flow (hypopnea). (p. 140)

**occipital lobes** The area of the cortex in the back of the head that processes visual information. (p. 69)

**Oedipus complex** According to Freud, the attraction a boy feels toward his mother, along with resentment or envy directed toward his father. (p. 385)

**olfaction** The sense of smell. (p. 104)

**operant conditioning** Learning that occurs when voluntary actions become associated with their consequences. (p. 184)

**operational definition** The precise manner in which variables of interest are defined and measured. (p. 14)

**opiates** A class of psychoactive drugs that cause a sense of euphoria; drugs that imitate the endorphins naturally produced in the brain. (p. 151)

**opponent-process theory** Suggests that perception of color derives from a special group of neurons that respond to opponent colors (red–green, blue–yellow). (p. 97)

**optic nerve** The bundle of axons from ganglion cells leading to the visual cortex. (p. 93)

**orgasm** A powerful combination of extremely gratifying sensations and a series of rhythmic muscular contractions. (p. 345)

**out-group** People outside the group to which we belong. (p. 440)

**overgeneralization** A cognitive distortion that assumes self-contained events will have major repercussions. (p. 541)

**panic attack** Sudden, extreme fear or discomfort that escalates quickly, often with no obvious trigger, and includes symptoms such as increased heart rate, sweating, shortness of breath, chest pain, nausea, lightheadedness, and fear of dying. (p. 497)

**panic disorder** A psychological disorder that includes recurrent, unexpected panic attacks and fear that can cause significant changes in behavior. (p. 497)

**parameters** Numbers that describe characteristics of a population. (p. APP A-2)

**parasympathetic nervous system** The division of the autonomic nervous system that orchestrates the "rest-and-digest" response to bring the body back to a noncrisis mode. (p. 59)

**parietal lobes** The area of the cortex that receives and processes sensory information such as touch, pressure, temperature, and spatial orientation. (p. 69)

**partial reinforcement** A schedule of reinforcement in which target behaviors are reinforced intermittently, not continuously. (p. 189)

**partial reinforcement effect** The tendency for behaviors acquired through intermittent reinforcement to be more resistant to extinction than those acquired through continuous reinforcement. (p. 190)

**perception** The organization and interpretation of sensory stimuli by the brain. (p. 84)

**perceptual constancy** The tendency to perceive objects in our environment as stable in terms of shape, size, and color, regardless of changes in the sensory data received. (p. 119)

**perceptual set** The tendency to perceive stimuli in a specific manner based on past experiences and expectations. (p. 120)

**peripheral nervous system (PNS)** The part of the nervous system that connects the central nervous system to the rest of the body. (p. 56)

**permissive parenting** A parenting style characterized by low demands of children and few limitations. (p. 327)

**personality** The unique, core set of characteristics that influence the way one thinks, acts, and feels, which are relatively consistent and enduring throughout the life span. (p. 376)

**personality disorders** A group of psychological disorders that can include impairments in cognition, emotional responses, interpersonal functioning, and impulse control. (p. 516)

**person-centered therapy** A form of humanistic therapy developed by Rogers; aimed at helping clients achieve their full potential. (p. 535)

**persuasion** Intentionally trying to make people change their attitudes and beliefs, which may lead to changes in their behaviors. (p. 424)

**phenotype** The observable expression or characteristics of one's genetic inheritance. (p. 295)

**phonemes** The basic building blocks of spoken language. (p. 267)

**photoreceptors** Specialized cells in the retina that absorb light energy and turn it into electrical and chemical signals for the brain to process. (p. 93)

**phrenology** An early approach to explaining the functions of the brain by trying to link the physical structure of the skull with a variety of characteristics. (p. 43)

**physiological dependence** With constant use of some psychoactive drugs, the body no longer functions normally without the drug. (p. 162)

**pie chart** Displays qualitative data with categories of interest represented by slices of the pie. (p. APP A-7)

**pitch** The degree to which a sound is high or low, determined by the frequency of its sound wave. (p. 99)

**pituitary gland** The small endocrine gland located in the center of the brain just under the hypothalamus; known as the master gland. (p. 61)

**place theory** States that pitch corresponds to the location of the vibrating hair cells along the cochlea. (p. 103)

**placebo** An inert substance or fake treatment given to members of the control group. (p. 32)

**pleasure principle** A principle that guides the id, directing behavior toward instant gratification and away from contemplating consequences. (p. 381)

**pons** A hindbrain structure that helps regulate sleep–wake cycles and coordinate movement between the right and left sides of the body. (p. 77)

**population** All members of an identified group about which a researcher is interested. (p. 18)

**positively skewed** A nonsymmetrical distribution with a longer tail to the right side of the distribution; right-skewed distribution. (p. APP A-6)

**positive psychology** An approach that focuses on human flourishing and the positive aspects of human nature, seeking to understand the roots of happiness, creativity, humor, and other strengths. (p. 38)

**positive punishment** The addition of something unpleasant following an unwanted behavior, with the intention of decreasing that behavior. (p. 193)

**positive reinforcement** The process by which reinforcers are added or presented following a target behavior, increasing the likelihood of it occurring again. (p. 184)

**positive symptoms** Excesses or distortions of normal behavior; examples are delusions, hallucinations, and disorganized speech. (p. 511)

**posttraumatic stress disorder (PTSD)** A psychological disorder characterized by exposure to or being threatened by an event involving death, serious injury, or violence; can include disturbing memories, nightmares, flashbacks, and other distressing symptoms. (p. 501)

**pragmatics** The social rules that help to organize language. (p. 267)

**prejudice** Holding hostile or negative attitudes toward an individual or group. (p. 440)

**preoperational stage** Piaget's stage of cognitive development during which children can start to use language to explore and understand their worlds. (p. 305)

**primacy effect** The tendency to remember items at the beginning of a list. (p. 225)

**primary appraisal** One's initial assessment of a situation to determine its personal impact and whether it is irrelevant, positive, challenging, or harmful. (p. 468)

**primary reinforcer** A reinforcer that satisfies a biological need; innate reinforcer. (p. 186)

**primary sex characteristics** Organs associated with reproduction, including the ovaries, uterus, vagina, penis, scrotum, and testes. (p. 315)

**priming** The stimulation of memories as a result of retrieval cues in the environment. (p. 225)

**proactive interference** The tendency for information learned in the past to interfere with the retrieval of new material. (p. 230)

**problem-focused coping** A coping strategy in which a person deals directly with a problem by attempting to solve and address it head-on. (p. 468)

**problem solving** The variety of approaches that can be used to achieve a goal. (p. 256)

**procedural memory** The unconscious memory of how to carry out a variety of skills and activities; a type of implicit memory. (p. 220)

**projective personality tests** Assessments used to explore characteristics that might not be accessible through interview or observation; the test taker is presented with ambiguous stimuli and then projects meaning onto them. (p. 404)

**proprioceptors** Specialized nerve endings primarily located in the muscles and joints that provide information about body location and orientation. (p. 113)

**prosocial behaviors** Actions that are kind, generous, and beneficial to others. (p. 200)

**prototype** The ideal or most representative example of a natural concept; helps us categorize or identify specific members of a concept. (p. 253)

**proximity** Nearness; plays an important role in the formation of relationships. (p. 446)

**psychoactive drugs** Substances that can cause changes in psychological activities such as sensation, perception, attention, judgment, memory, self-control, emotion, thinking, and behavior; substances that cause changes in conscious experiences. (p. 148)

**psychoanalysis** Freud's theories of personality as well as his system of psychotherapy and tools for the exploration of the unconscious. (p. 379)

**psychoanalytic perspective** An approach developed by Freud suggesting that behavior and personality are shaped by unconscious conflicts. (p. 8)

**psychodynamic therapy** A type of insight therapy that incorporates core psychoanalytic themes, including the idea that personality and behaviors frequently can be traced to unconscious conflicts and experiences from the past. (p. 534)

**psychological dependence** With constant use of some psychoactive drugs, a strong desire or need to continue using the substance occurs without the evidence of tolerance or withdrawal symptoms. (p. 162)

**psychological disorder** A set of behavioral, emotional, and cognitive symptoms that are significantly distressing or disabling in terms of social functioning, work endeavors, and other aspects of life. (p. 485)

**psychologists** Scientists who study behavior and mental processes. (p. 2)

**psychology** The scientific study of behavior and mental processes. (p. 2)

**psychoneuroimmunology** The field that examines relationships among psychological factors, the nervous system, and immune system functioning. (p. 466)

**psychosexual stages** According to Freud, the stages of development of sexuality and personality, from birth to adulthood, each of which has an erogenous zone and a conflict that must be dealt with. (p. 384)

**psychosis** Loss of contact with reality that is severe and chronic. (p. 511)

**psychotherapy** "Talk therapy"; a treatment approach wherein a client works with a mental health professional to reduce psychological symptoms and improve quality of life. (p. 530)

**puberty** The period of development during which the body changes and becomes sexually mature and capable of reproduction. (p. 315)

**punishment** The application of a consequence that decreases the likelihood of a behavior recurring. (p. 193)

**random assignment** The process of appointing study participants to experimental or control groups, ensuring that every person has an equal chance of being assigned to either. (p. 29)

**random sample** A subset of the population chosen through a procedure that ensures all members of the population have an equal chance of being selected to participate in the study. (p. 18)

**range** A number that represents the length of the data set and is a rough depiction of dispersion; a measure of variation. (p. APP A-10)

**rapid eye movement (REM)** The stage of sleep associated with dreaming; sleep characterized by bursts of eye movements, with brain activity similar to that of a waking state, but with a lack of muscle tone. (p. 136)

**rational emotive behavior therapy (REBT)** A type of cognitive therapy, developed by Ellis, that identifies illogical thoughts and attempts to convert them into rational ones. (p. 542)

**reality principle** A principle that guides the ego as it negotiates between the id and the environment, directing behavior to follow society's rules. (p. 381)

**recall** The process of retrieving information held in long-term memory without the help of explicit retrieval cues. (p. 225)

**recency effect** The tendency to remember items at the end of a list. (p. 225)

**receptor sites** Locations on the receiving neuron's dendrites where neurotransmitters attach. (p. 51)

**recessive gene** One of a pair of genes that is overpowered by a dominant gene. (p. 294)

**reciprocal determinism** According to Bandura, multidirectional interactions among cognition, behaviors, and the environment. (p. 395)

**recognition** The process of matching incoming data to information stored in long-term memory. (p. 225)

**reflex arc** An automatic response to a sensory stimulus, using a simple pathway of communication from sensory neurons through interneurons in the spinal cord and back out through motor neurons. (p. 58)

**refractory period** An interval of time during which a man cannot attain another orgasm. (p. 345)

**reinforcement** Process of increasing the frequency of behaviors with consequences. (p. 183)

**reinforcers** Events, stimuli, and other consequences that increase the likelihood of a behavior recurring. (p. 183)

**relearning** Material learned previously is acquired more quickly in subsequent exposures. (p. 228)

**reliability** The ability of an assessment to provide consistent, reproducible results. (p. 274)

**REM rebound** An increased amount of time spent in REM after sleep deprivation. (p. 143)

**REM sleep behavior disorder** A sleep disturbance in which the mechanism responsible for paralyzing the body during REM sleep is not functioning, resulting in the acting out of dreams. (p. 140)

**replicate** To repeat an experiment, generally with a new sample and/or other changes to the procedures, the goal of which is to provide further support for the findings of the first study. (p. 16)

**representativeness heuristic** A decision-making strategy that evaluates the degree to which the primary characteristics of a person or situation are similar to our prototype of that kind of person or situation. (p. 262)

**representative sample** A subgroup of a population selected so that its members have characteristics similar to those of the population of interest. (p. 19)

**resistance** A patient's unwillingness to cooperate in therapy; a sign of unconscious conflict. (p. 533)

**resting potential** The electrical potential of a cell "at rest"; the state of a cell when it is not activated. (p. 49)

**reticular formation** A network of neurons running through the midbrain that controls levels of arousal and quickly analyzes sensory information on its way to the cortex. (p. 76)

**retina** The layer of the eye containing photoreceptor cells, which transduce light energy into neural activity. (p. 93)

**retinal disparity** A binocular cue used to determine the distance of objects; the difference between the images seen by the right and left eyes. (p. 118)

**retrieval** The process of accessing information encoded and stored in memory. (p. 211)

**retrieval cues** Stimuli that help in the retrieval of stored information that is difficult to access. (p. 224)

**retroactive interference** The tendency for recently learned information to interfere with the retrieval of things learned in the past. (p. 230)

**retrograde amnesia** A type of memory loss; an inability to access memories formed prior to damage to the brain. (p. 238)

**reuptake** A process by which neurotransmitters are reabsorbed by the sending axon terminal. (p. 51)

**rich false memories** Detailed recollections of events that never occurred, which are expressed with emotions and confidence. (p. 235)

**rods** Photoreceptors that enable us to see in dim lighting; not sensitive to color, but useful for night vision. (p. 93)

**romantic love** Love that is a combination of connection, concern, care, and intimacy. (p. 448)

**sample** A subset of a population chosen for inclusion in an experiment. (p. 18)

**saturation** Color purity. (p. 91)

**scaffolding** Pushing children to go just beyond what they are competent and comfortable doing, while providing help in a decreasing manner. (p. 308)

**scapegoat** A target of negative emotions, beliefs, and behaviors; typically, a member of the outgroup who receives blame for an upsetting social situation. (p. 440)

**Schachter–Singer theory of emotion** Suggests that the experience of emotion is the result of physiological arousal and a cognitive label for this physiological state. (p. 359)

**schema** A collection of ideas that represents a basic unit of understanding. (p. 304)

**schizophrenia** A disabling psychological disorder that can include delusions, hallucinations, disorganized speech, and abnormal motor behavior. (p. 511)

**scientific method** The process scientists use to conduct research, which includes a continuing cycle of exploration, critical thinking, and systematic observation. (p. 12)

**secondary appraisal** An assessment to determine how to respond to a challenging or threatening situation. (p. 468)

**secondary reinforcer** A reinforcer that does not satisfy a biological need but often gains power through its association with a primary reinforcer. (p. 186)

**secondary sex characteristics** Body characteristics, such as pubic hair, underarm hair, and enlarged breasts, that develop in puberty but are not associated with reproduction. (p. 315)

**selective attention** The ability to focus awareness on a small segment of information that is available through our sensory systems. (p. 130)

**self-actualization** The need to be one's best and strive for one's fullest potential. (p. 340)

**self-concept** The knowledge an individual has about their strengths, abilities, behavior patterns, and temperament. (p. 392)

**self-determination theory (SDT)** Suggests that humans are born with the needs for competence, relatedness, and autonomy, which are always driving us in the direction of growth and optimal functioning. (p. 342)

**self-efficacy** Beliefs about our ability and effectiveness in reaching goals. (p. 394)

**self-serving bias** The tendency to attribute our successes to personal characteristics and our failures to environmental factors. (p. 418)

**semantic memory** The memory of information theoretically available to anyone, which pertains to general facts about the world; a type of explicit memory. (p. 219)

**semantics** The rules used to bring meaning to words and sentences. (p. 267)

**sensation** The process by which receptors in the sensory organs (the eyes, ears, nose, mouth, skin, and other tissues) receive and detect stimuli. (p. 84)

**sensorimotor stage** Piaget's stage of cognitive development during which infants use their sensory capabilities and motor skills to learn about the surrounding world. (p. 305)

**sensory adaptation** The process through which sensory receptors become less sensitive to constant stimuli. (p. 87)

**sensory memory** A stage of memory that captures near-exact copies of vast amounts of sensory stimuli for a very brief period of time. (p. 212)

**sensory neurons** Neurons that receive information from the sensory systems and convey it to the brain for further processing. (p. 57)

**serial position effect** The ability to recall items in a list depends on where they are in the series. (p. 225)

**set point** The stable weight that is maintained despite variability in exercise and food intake. (p. 354)

**sexual dysfunction** A significant disturbance in the ability to respond sexually or to gain pleasure from sex. (p. 349)

**sexuality** A dimension of human nature encompassing everything that makes us sexual beings: sexual activities, attitudes, and behaviors. (p. 344)

**sexually transmitted infections (STIs)** Diseases or illnesses transmitted through sexual activity. (p. 350)

**sexual orientation** A person's enduring sexual attraction to others; a continuum that includes dimensions of sexuality, attraction, desire, and emotions. (p. 345)

**shape constancy** An object is perceived as maintaining its shape, regardless of the image projected on the retina. (p. 120)

**shaping** A process by which a person observes the behaviors of another organism, providing reinforcers if the organism performs at a required level. (p. 187)

**short-term memory** A stage of memory that temporarily maintains and processes a limited amount of information. (p. 212)

**signal detection theory** Explains how internal and external factors influence our ability to detect weak signals in the environment. (p. 88)

**situational attribution** A type of external attribution where behaviors are assumed to result from situational factors. (p. 417)

**size constancy** An object is perceived as maintaining its size, regardless of the image projected on the retina. (p. 120)

**skewed distribution** Nonsymmetrical frequency distribution. (p. APP A-6)

**sleep terrors** A disturbance of non-REM sleep, generally occurring in children; characterized by screaming, staring fearfully, and usually no memory of the episode the following morning. (p. 141)

**social cognition** The way people think about others, attend to social information, and use this information in their lives, both consciously and unconsciously. (p. 415)

**social-cognitive perspective** Suggests that personality results from relationships and other environmental factors (social) and patterns of thinking (cognitive). (p. 394)

**social facilitation** The tendency for the presence of others to improve personal performance when the activity is fairly uncomplicated and a person is adequately prepared. (p. 433)

**social identity** How we view ourselves within our social group. (p. 440)

**social influence** How a person is affected by others as evidenced in behaviors, emotions, and cognition. (p. 423)

**social loafing** The tendency for group members to put forth less than their best effort when individual contributions are too complicated to measure. (p. 433)

**social psychology** The study of human cognition, emotion, and behavior in relation to others. (p. 413)

**social roles** The positions we hold in social groups, and the responsibilities and expectations associated with those roles. (p. 443)

**social support** The assistance we acquire from others. (p. 459)

**sociocultural perspective** An approach examining how social interactions and culture influence behavior and mental processes. (p. 10)

**somatic nervous system** The branch of the peripheral nervous system that includes sensory nerves and motor nerves; gathers information from sensory receptors and controls the skeletal muscles responsible for voluntary movement. (p. 58)

**somatosensory cortex** A strip of brain tissue running parallel to the motor cortex that receives and integrates sensory information from all over the body. (p. 72)

**source traits** Basic underlying or foundational characteristics of personality. (p. 397)

**specific phobia** A psychological disorder characterized by a distinct fear or anxiety related to an object or situation. (p. 497)

**spermarche** A boy's first ejaculation. (p. 315)

**spinal cord** The bundle of neurons that allows communication between the brain and the peripheral nervous system. (p. 56)

**split-brain operation** A rare procedure used to disconnect the right and left hemispheres; involves cutting the corpus callosum. (p. 63)

**spontaneous recovery** The reappearance of a conditioned response following its extinction. (p. 176)

**standard deviation** A number that represents the average distance the values in a data set are from their mean; a measure of variation. (p. APP A-10)

**standardization** Occurs when test developers administer a test to a large sample and then publish the average scores for specified groups. (p. 274)

**statistical significance** The probability that the findings of a study were due to chance. (p. APP A-12)

**statistics** A science that focuses on how to collect, organize, analyze, display, and interpret data; numbers that describe characteristics of a sample. (p. APP A-1)

**stem-and-leaf plot** A type of graphical display that uses the actual data values in the form of leading digits and trailing digits. (p. APP A-5)

**stem cells** Cells responsible for producing new neurons. (p. 68)

**stereotypes** Conclusions or inferences we make about people who are different from us based on their group membership, such as race, religion, age, or gender. (p. 439)

**stereotype threat** A "situational threat" in which individuals are aware of others' negative expectations, which leads to a fear of being judged or treated as inferior. (p. 442)

**stigma** A negative attitude or opinion about a group of people based on certain traits or characteristics. (p. 488)

**stimulants** A class of drugs that increase neural activity in the central nervous system. (p. 154)

**stimulus** An event or object that generally leads to a response. (p. 171)

**stimulus discrimination** The ability to differentiate between a conditioned stimulus and other stimuli sufficiently different from it. (p. 176)

**stimulus generalization** The tendency for stimuli similar to the conditioned stimulus to elicit the conditioned response. (p. 175)

**storage** The process of preserving information for possible recollection in the future. (p. 211)

**stress** The response to perceived threats or challenges resulting from stimuli or events that cause strain. (p. 453)

**stressors** Stimuli that cause both psychological and physiological reactions. (p. 453)

**structuralism** An early school of psychology that used introspection to determine the structure and most basic elements of the mind. (p. 6)

**successive approximations** A method that uses reinforcers to condition a series of small steps that gradually approach the target behavior. (p. 187)

**superego** According to Freud, the structure of the mind that guides behavior to follow the rules of society, parents, or other authority figures. (p. 381)

**surface traits** Easily observable characteristics that derive from source traits. (p. 397)

**survey method** A type of descriptive research that uses questionnaires or interviews to gather data. (p. 22)

**sympathetic nervous system** The division of the autonomic nervous system that mobilizes the "fight-or-flight" response to stressful or crisis situations. (p. 58)

**synapse** The place where the axon terminal of a sending neuron meets the dendrite of a neighboring neuron or other type of cell receiving its signal; junction between neurons where communication occurs. (p. 46)

**syntax** The collection of rules concerning where to place words or phrases. (p. 267)

**systematic desensitization** A treatment that combines anxiety hierarchies with relaxation techniques. (p. 538)

**temperament** Characteristic differences in behavioral patterns and emotional reactions that are evident from birth. (p. 308)

**temporal lobes** The area of the cortex that processes auditory stimuli and language. (p. 69)

**teratogens** Environmental agents that can damage the growing embryo or fetus. (p. 296)

**tetrahydrocannabinol (THC)** The psychoactive ingredient in marijuana. (p. 160)

**thalamus** A structure in the limbic system that processes and relays sensory information to the appropriate areas of the cortex. (p. 74)

**theory** Synthesizes observations in order to explain phenomena and guide predictions to be tested through research. (p. 12)

**therapeutic alliance** A warm and accepting client–therapist relationship that serves as a safe place for self-exploration. (p. 535)

**theta waves** Brain waves that indicate light sleep. (p. 136)

**thinking** Mental activity associated with coming to a decision, reaching a solution, or forming a belief. (p. 251)

**third variable** An unaccounted for characteristic of participants or the environment that explains changes in the variables of interest. (p. 25)

**thyroid gland** The endocrine gland that regulates the rate of metabolism by secreting thyroxin. (p. 61)

**token economy** A type of behavior modification that uses tokens to reinforce desired behaviors. (p. 539)

**tolerance** With constant use of some psychoactive drugs, the body requires more and more of the drug to create the original effect; a sign of physiological dependence. (p. 162)

**top-down processing** Drawing on past experiences and knowledge to decipher and interpret sensory information. (p. 84)

**traits** The relatively stable properties that describe elements of personality. (p. 395)

**trait theories** Theories that focus on personality dimensions and their influence on behavior; can be used to predict behaviors. (p. 395)

**transduction** The process of transforming stimuli into neural signals. (p. 86)

**transference** An unconscious conflict that occurs when a patient reacts to a therapist as if dealing with parents or other caregivers from childhood. (p. 534)

**transgender** Refers to people whose gender identity and expression do not match the sex assigned to them at birth. (p. 321)

**transsexual** Describes a person who undergoes a social transition from male to female or female to male, often by making changes to the body through surgery and/or medical treatment. (p. 321)

**trial and error** An approach to problem solving that involves finding a solution through a series of attempts and eliminating those that do not work. (p. 257)

**triarchic theory of intelligence** Theory suggesting that humans have varying degrees of analytical, creative, and practical abilities. (p. 271)

**trichromatic theory** Suggests that perception of color results from the activation of three cone types, which are sensitive to wavelengths in the red, green, and blue spectrums. (p. 96)

**Type A personality** A person who exhibits a competitive, aggressive, impatient, and often hostile pattern of behaviors. (p. 471)

**Type B personality** A person who exhibits a relaxed, patient, and nonaggressive pattern of behaviors. (p. 471)

**unconditional positive regard** According to Rogers, the total acceptance or valuing of a person, regardless of behavior. (p. 392)

**unconditioned response (UR)** A reflexive, involuntary response to an unconditioned stimulus. (p. 173)

**unconditioned stimulus (US)** A stimulus that automatically triggers an involuntary response without any learning needed. (p. 173)

**unconscious** According to Freud, the level of consciousness outside of awareness, which is difficult to access without effort or therapy. (p. 380)

**uninvolved parenting** A parenting style characterized by a parent's indifference to a child, including a lack of emotional involvement. (p. 327)

**uplifts** Experiences that are positive and have the potential to make one happy. (p. 460)

**validity** The degree to which an assessment measures what it intends to measure. (p. 274)

**variable-interval schedule** A schedule in which the reinforcer comes after an interval of time, but the length of the interval changes from trial to trial. (p. 192)

**variable-ratio schedule** A schedule in which the number of desired behaviors that must occur before a reinforcer is given changes across trials and is based on an average number of behaviors to be reinforced. (p. 192)

**variables** Measurable characteristics that can vary over time or across people. (p. 18)

**vestibular sense** The sense of balance and equilibrium. (p. 113)

**volley principle** States that neurons work together so their combined firing reaches frequencies higher than one neuron can achieve alone. (p. 103)

**wavelength** The distance between wave peaks (or troughs). (p. 90)

**Weber's law** States that each of the senses has its own constant ratio determining difference thresholds. (p. 88)

**Wernicke's area** A region of the cortex that plays a pivotal role in language comprehension. (p. 66)

**withdrawal** With constant use of some psychoactive drugs, the body becomes dependent and then reacts when the drug is withheld; a sign of physiological dependence. (p. 162)

**working memory** The active processing of information in short-term memory; the maintenance and manipulation of information in the memory system. (p. 216)

**zone of proximal development** The range of cognitive tasks that can be accomplished alone and those that require the guidance and help of others. (p. 308)

**zygote** A single cell formed by the union of a sperm and egg. (p. 292)

# References

**AAA.** (2015, October 22). New hands-free technologies pose hidden dangers for drivers. https://newsroom.aaa.com/2015/10/new-hands-free-technologies-pose-hidden-dangers-for-drivers/

**Abdellaoui, A., Ehli, E. A., Hottenga, J. J., Weber, Z., Mbarek, H., Willemsen, G., Van Beijsterveldt, T., Brooks, A., Hudziak, J. J., Sullivan, P. F., De Geus, E. J., & Davies, G. E., Boomsma, D. I.** (2015). CNV concordance in 1,097 MZ twin pairs. *Twin Research and Human Genetics, 18,* 1–12.

**Abel, A., Hayes, A. M., Henley, W., & Kuyken, W.** (2016). Sudden gains in cognitive-behavior therapy for treatment-resistant depression: Processes of change. *Journal of Consulting and Clinical Psychology, 84,* 726–737. https://doi.org/10.1037/ccp0000101

**Abel, K. M., Drake, R., & Goldstein, J. M.** (2010). Sex differences in schizophrenia. *International Review of Psychiatry, 22,* 417–428.

**Abramovitch, A., & McKay, D.** (2016). Behavioral impulsivity in obsessive–compulsive disorder. *Journal of Behavioral Addictions, 5*(3), 395–397. https://doi.org/10.1556/2006.5.2016.029

**Acevedo, B. P., Aron, A., Fisher, H. E., & Brown, L. L.** (2012). Neural correlates of long-term intense romantic love. *Social Cognitive and Affective Neuroscience, 7*(2), 145–159.

**Ackerman, D.** (2018, October). Heading off injury. *Scientific American, 319,* 20.

**Adam, K.** (2018, July 3). Meet the British "A-team" divers at the center of Thailand cave rescue. *The Washington Post.* https://www.washingtonpost.com/news/worldviews/wp/2018/07/03/meet-the-british-a-team-divers-at-the-center-of-thailand-cave-rescue/

**Adams, L., & Bourke, P.** (2020). Examining the triggers of lucid insight. *Dreaming, 30*(2), 120–139. https://doi.org/10.1037/drm0000139

**Adams, M.** (2020). The kingdom of dogs: Understanding Pavlov's experiments as human–animal relationships. *Theory & Psychology, 30*(1), 121–141. https://doi.org/10.1177/0959354319895597

**Adams, M.** (2020, June 1). The kingdom of dogs: Matthew Adams revisits Pavlov's labs from a dog's perspective. *Leicester: The British Psychological Society, 33,* 76–79. https://thepsychologist.bps.org.uk/volume-33/june-2020/kingdom-dogs

**Adinolfi, B., & Gava, N.** (2013). Controlled outcome studies of child clinical hypnosis. *Acta Bio Medica Atenei Parmensis, 84,* 94–97.

**Adler, A.** (1927/1994). *Understanding human nature.* Oneworld.

**Adolphs, R.** (2008). Fear, faces, and the human amygdala. *Current Opinion in Neurobiology, 18,* 166–172.

**Adolphs, R.** (2013). The biology of fear. *Current Biology, 23,* R79–R93.

**Advokat, C. D., Comaty, J. E., & Julien, R. M.** (2019). *Julien's primer of drug action* (14th ed.). Worth Publishers.

**Agüera, Z., Brewin, N., Chen, J., Granero, R., Kang, Q., Fernandez-Aranda, F., & Arcelus, J.** (2017). Eating symptomatology and general psychopathology in patients with anorexia nervosa from China, UK and Spain: A cross-cultural study examining the role of social attitudes. *PLOS one, 12,* Article e0173781. https://doi.org/10.1371/journal.pone.0173781

**Ahonen, L., Loeber, R., & Brent, D. A.** (2019). The association between serious mental health problems and violence: Some common assumptions and misconceptions. *Trauma, Violence, & Abuse, 20*(5), 613–625. https://doi.org/10.1177/1524838017726423

**Aidelbaum, R., Labelle, A., Choueiry, J., & Knott, V.** (2021). The acute dose and baseline amplitude-dependent effects of CDP-choline on deviance detection (MMN) in chronic schizophrenia: A pilot study. *Experimental and Clinical Psychopharmacology.* Advance online publication. https://doi.org/10.1037/pha0000418

**Aiello, J. R., & Douthitt, E. A.** (2001). Social facilitation from Triplett to electronic performance monitoring. *Group Dynamics: Theory, Research, and Practice, 5,* 163–180.

**Ainsworth, M. D. S.** (1979). Infant–mother attachment. *American Psychologist, 34,* 932–937.

**Ainsworth, M. D. S.** (1985). Patterns of attachment. *Clinical Psychologist, 38,* 27–29.

**Ainsworth, M. D. S., & Bell, S. M.** (1970). Attachment, exploration, and separation: Illustrated by the behavior of one-year-olds in a strange situation. *Child Development, 41,* 49–67.

**Ainsworth, M. D. S., Blehar, M. C., Waters, E., & Wall, S.** (1978). *Patterns of attachment: A psychological study of the strange situation.* Lawrence Erlbaum Associates.

**Ainsworth, S. E., & Maner, J. K.** (2012). Sex begets violence: Mating motives, social dominance, and physical aggression in men. *Journal of Personality and Social Psychology, 103,* 819–829.

**Ajzen, I.** (2001). Nature and operation of attitudes. *Annual Review of Psychology, 52,* 27–58.

**Akcay, O., Dalgin, M. H., & Bhatnagar, S.** (2011). Perception of color in product choice among college students: A cross-national analysis of USA, India, China and Turkey. *International Journal of Business and Social Science, 2,* 42–48.

**Akhtar, S., Justice, L. V., Morrison, C. M., & Conway, M. A.** (2018). Fictional first memories. *Psychological Science, 29*(10), 1612–1619. https://doi.org/10.1177/0956797618778831

**Akin-Little, A., & Little, S. G.** (2019). Effect of extrinsic reinforcement on "intrinsic" motivation: Separating fact from fiction. In S. G. Little & A. Akin-Little (Eds.), *Applying psychology in the schools book series. Behavioral interventions in schools: Evidence-based positive strategies* (p. 113–132). American Psychological Association. https://doi.org/10.1037/0000126-007

**Aknin, L. B., Dunn, E. W., Proulx, J., Lok, I., & Norton, M. I.** (2020). Does spending money on others promote happiness? A registered replication report. *Journal of Personality and Social Psychology, 119*(2), e15–e26. https://doi.org/10.1037/pspa0000191

**Aktar, E., Nikolić, M., & Bögels, S. M.** (2017). Environmental transmission of generalized anxiety disorder from parents to children: Worries, experiential avoidance, and intolerance of uncertainty. *Dialogues in Clinical Neuroscience, 19*(2), 137–146.

**Al Firdaus, M. M.** (2012). SQ3R strategy for increasing students' retention of reading and written information. *Majalah Ilmiah Dinamika, 31,* 49–63.

**Alberini, C. M., & Kandel, E. R.** (2015). The regulation of transcription in memory consolidation. *Cold Spring Harbor Perspectives in Biology, 7*(1), a021741.

**Albert, D., Chein, J., & Steinberg, L.** (2013). The teenage brain: Peer influences on adolescent decision making. *Current Directions in Psychological Science, 22,* 114–120.

**Albertazzi, L.** (2020). Experimental phenomenology for consciousness. *Psychology of Consciousness: Theory, Research, and Practice.* Advance online publication. https://doi.org/10.1037/cns0000238

**Albuquerque, D., Stice, E., Rodríguez-López, R., Manco, L., & Nóbrega, C.** (2015). Current review of genetics of human obesity: From molecular mechanisms to an evolutionary perspective. *Molecular Genetics and Genomics, 290,* 1191–1221.

**Alcoholics Anonymous (AA).** (2019, March). Estimated worldwide A.A. individual and group membership. Service Material from the General Service Office. http://www.aa.org/assets/en_US/smf-132_en.pdf

**Alex, B.** (2019, June 21). What science says about why you're stressed and how to cope. *Discover.* http://discovermagazine.com/2019/july/ewk-stress

**Alexander, G. M., & Hines, M.** (2002). Sex differences in response to children's toys in nonhuman primates (*Cercopithecus aethiops sabaeus*). *Evolution and Human Behavior, 23,* 467–479.

**Alexander, G. M., Wilcox, T., & Woods, R.** (2009). Sex differences in infants' visual interest in toys. *Archives of Sexual Behavior, 38,* 427–433.

**Alexander, W. H., & Brown, J. W.** (2018). Frontal cortex function as derived from hierarchical predictive coding. *Scientific Reports, 8*(3843), 1–11. https://doi.org/10.1038/s41598-018-21407-9

**Alexandrou, A. M., Saarinen, T., Mäkelä, S., Kujala, J., & Salmelin, R.** (2017). The right hemisphere is highlighted in connected natural speech production and perception. *NeuroImage, 152,* 628–638. https://doi.org/10.1016/j.neuroimage.2017.03.006

**Algoe, S. B., Kurtz, L. E., & Grewen, K.** (2017). Oxytocin and social bonds: The role of oxytocin in perceptions of romantic partners' bonding behavior. *Psychological Science, 28*(12), 1763–1772. https://doi.org/10.1177/0956797617716922

**Allegrini, A. G., Cheesman, R., Rimfeld, K., Selzam, S., Pingault, J. B., Eley, T. C., & Plomin, R.** (2020). The p factor: Genetic analyses support a general dimension of psychopathology in childhood and adolescence. *Journal of Child Psychology and Psychiatry, 61*(1), 30–39. https://doi.org/10.1111/jcpp.13113

**Allen, G. E., Kim, B., Smith, T. B., & Hafoka, O.** (2016). Counseling attitudes and stigma among Polynesian Americans. *The Counseling Psychologist, 44,* 6–27. https://doi.org/10.1177/0011000015618762

Allen, K. (2003). Are pets a healthy pleasure? The influence of pets on blood pressure. *Current Directions in Psychological Science, 12,* 236–239.

Allen, M. S., & McCarthy, P. J. (2016). Be happy in your work: The role of positive psychology in working with change and performance. *Journal of Change Management, 16,* 55–74. https://doi.org/10.1080/14697017.2015.1128471

Allen, N. J., & Lyons, D. A. (2018). Glia as architects of central nervous system formation and function. *Science, 362*(6411), 181–185. https://doi.org/10.1126/science.aat0473

Allik, J., Church, A. T., Ortiz, F. A., Rossier, J., Hřebíčková, M., de Fruyt, F., Realo, A., & McCrae, R. R. (2017). Mean profiles of the NEO Personality Inventory. *Journal of Cross-Cultural Psychology, 48*(3), 402–420. https://doi.org/10.1177/0022022117692100

Allik, J., & McCrae, R. R. (2004). Toward a geography of personality traits patterns of profiles across 36 cultures. *Journal of Cross-Cultural Psychology, 35,* 13–28.

Allison, S., Bastiampillai, T., Licinio, J., Fuller, D. A., Bidargaddi, N., & Sharfstein, S. S. (2018). When should governments increase the supply of psychiatric beds? *Molecular Psychiatry, 23*(4), 796–800. https://doi.org/10.1038/mp.2017.139

Allport, G. W., & Odbert, H. S. (1936). Trait-names: A psycho-lexical study. *Psychological Monographs, 47*(211), i–171.catt

Alosco, M. L., Kasimis, A. B., Stamm, J. M., Chua, A. S., Baugh, C. M., Daneshvar, D. H., Robbins, C. A., Mariani, M., Hayden, J., Conneely, S., Au, R., Torres, A., McClean, M. D., McKee, A. C., Cantu, R. C., Mez, J., Nowinski, C. J., Martin, B. M., Chaisson, C. E., . . . Stern, R. A. (2017). Age of first exposure to American football and long-term neuropsychiatric and cognitive outcomes. *Translational Psychiatry, 7*(9), e1236. https://doi.org/10.1038/tp.2017.197

Altschul, D. M., Hopkins, W. D., Herrelko, E. S., Inoue-Murayama, M., Matsuzawa, T., King, J. E., Ross, S. R., & Weiss, A. (2018). Personality links with lifespan in chimpanzees. *eLife, 7,* e33781. https://doi.org/10.7554/eLife.33781

Altshuler, L. L., Kupka, R. W., Hellemann, G., Frye, M. A., Sugar, C. A., McElroy, S. L., Nolen, W. A., Grunze, H., Leverich, G. S., Keck, P. E., Jr., Zermeno, M., Post, R. M., & Suppes, T. (2010). Bipolar disorder evaluated prospectively in the Stanley Foundation Bipolar Treatment Outcome Network. *American Journal of Psychiatry, 167,* 708–715.

Alvarez, L. D. C., Leach, J. L., Rodriguez, J. L., & Jones, K. N.

(2020). Unsung psychology pioneers: A content analysis of who makes history (and who doesn't). *The American Journal of Psychology, 133*(2), 241–262.

Aly, M. (2020). Brain dynamics underlying memory for lifetime experiences. *Trends in Cognitive Sciences, 24*(10), 780–781. https://doi.org/10.1016/j.tics.2020.06.010

Amare, A. T., Schubert, K. O., Hou, L., Clark, S. R., Papiol, S., Cearns, M., Heilbronner, U., Degenhardt, F., Tekola-Ayele, F., Hsu, Y.-H., Shekhtman, T., Adli, M., Akula, N., Akiyama, K., Ardau, R., Arias, B., Aubry, J.-M., Backlund, L., Bhattacharjee, A. K., . . . Stamm, T. (2020). Association of polygenic score for major depression with response to lithium in patients with bipolar disorder. *Molecular Psychiatry.* Advance online publication. https://doi.org/10.1038/s41380-020-0689-5

America's Got Talent. (2017, June 6). *Mandy Harvey: Deaf singer earns Simon's golden buzzer with original song* [Video]. https://www.youtube.com/watch?v=ZKSWXzAnVe0

American Academy of Pediatrics. (2016a). Media and young minds. *Pediatrics, 138,* e20162399. https://doi.org/10.1542/peds.2016-2591

American Academy of Pediatrics. (2016b). Media use in school-aged children and adolescents. *Pediatrics, 138,* e20162592. https://doi.org/10.1542/peds.2016-2592

American Academy of Pediatrics. (n.d.). Media and children. https://www.aap.org/en-us/advocacy-and-policy/aap-health-initiatives/pages/media-and-children.aspx

American Academy of Sleep Medicine. (2017, February 9). *Healthy sleep habits.* http://sleepeducation.org/essentials-in-sleep/healthy-sleep-habits

American Cancer Society. (2021, January 12). *How common is breast cancer?* https://www.cancer.org/cancer/breast-cancer/about/how-common-is-breast-cancer.html

American College of Obstetricians and Gynecologists, & Society for Maternal-Fetal Medicine. (2017). Obstetric care consensus No. 6: Periviable birth. *Obstetrics and Gynecology, 130*(4), e187–e199. https://doi.org/10.1097/AOG.0000000000002352.

American Foundation for Suicide Prevention. (n.d.). *Suicide: Facts and figures.* https://afsp.org/wp-content/uploads/2017/06/US_FactsFigures_Flyer.pdf

American Heart Association. (n.d.-a). *Atherosclerosis.* http://www.heart.org/HEARTORG/Conditions/Cholesterol/AboutCholesterol/Atherosclerosis_UCM_305564_Article.jsp#.WiV6_raZOks

American Heart Association. (n.d.-b). *Can processed food be part of a healthy diet?*

https://www.heart.org/en/healthy-living/healthy-eating/eat-smart/nutrition-basics/processed-foods

American Heart Association News. (2019, May 24). *Drinking red wine for heart health? Read this before you toast.* https://www.heart.org/en/news/2019/05/24/drinking-red-wine-for-heart-health-read-this-before-you-toast

American Medical Association (AMA). (2018). *Physicians' progress to reverse the nation's opioid epidemic.* http://www.end-opioid-epidemic.org/wp-content/uploads/2018/05/AMA2018-OpioidReport-FINAL-updated.pdf

American Optometric Association. (n.d.). *Infant vision: Birth to 24 months of age.* https://www.aoa.org/healthy-eyes/eye-health-for-life/infant-vision?sso=y

American Psychiatric Association. (1952). *Diagnostic and statistical manual of mental disorders.*

American Psychiatric Association. (2001). *The practice of ECT: A task force report* (2nd ed.).

American Psychiatric Association. (2013). *Diagnostic and statistical manual of mental disorders* (DSM-5; 5th ed.).

American Psychological Association (APA). (1998). Final conclusions of the American Psychological Association's working group on investigation of memories of childhood abuse. *Psychology, Public Policy, and Law, 4,* 933–940.

American Psychological Association (APA). (2011). *Careers in psychology: Some of the subfields in psychology.* http://www.apa.org/careers/resources/guides/careers.aspx?item=3#

American Psychological Association (APA). (2012a). *Francis Sumner, PhD, and Inez Beverly Prosser, PhD.* https://www.apa.org/pi/oema/resources/ethnicity-health/psychologists/sumner-prosser

American Psychological Association (APA). (2012b). Guidelines for psychological practice with lesbian, gay, and bisexual clients. *American Psychologist, 67,* 10–42.

American Psychological Association (APA). (2012c). *Resolution on the recognition of psychotherapy effectiveness.* http://www.apa.org/about/policy/resolution-psychotherapy.aspx

American Psychological Association (APA). (2012, March). *Understanding alcohol use disorders and their treatment.* http://www.apa.org/helpcenter/alcohol-disorders.aspx

American Psychological Association (APA). (2013a). *APA guidelines for the undergraduate psychology major: Version 2.0.* https://www.apa.org/ed/precollege/about/undergraduate-major.aspx

American Psychological Association (APA). (2013b). *Margaret Floy Washburn, PhD: 1921 APA President.* http://www.apa.org/about/governance/president/

American Psychological Association (APA). (2013c). *Roper v. Simmons.* http://www.apa.org/about/offices/ogc/amicus/roper.aspx

American Psychological Association (APA). (2013d). *Stress in America: Missing the health care connection.* http://www.apa.org/news/press/releases/stress/2012/full-report.pdf

American Psychological Association (APA). (2014a). *Answers to your questions about transgender people, gender identity, and gender expression.* http://www.apa.org/topics/lgbt/transgender.aspx

American Psychological Association (APA). (2014b). *Psychology: Science in action. Pursuing a career in clinical or counseling psychology.* http://www.apa.org/action/science/clinical/education-training.pdf

American Psychological Association (APA). (2014c). *Psychology: Science in action. Pursuing a career in developmental psychology.* http://www.apa.org/action/science/developmental/education-training.pdf

American Psychological Association (APA). (2014d). *Psychology: Science in action. Pursuing a career in experimental psychology.* http://www.apa.org/action/science/experimental/education-training.pdf

American Psychological Association (APA). (2014e). *Psychology: Science in action. Pursuing a career in forensic and public service psychology.* http://www.apa.org/action/science/forensic/education-training.pdf

American Psychological Association (APA). (2014f). *Psychology: Science in action. Pursuing a career in health psychology.* http://www.apa.org/action/science/health/education-training.pdf

American Psychological Association (APA). (2014g). *Psychology: Science in action. Pursuing a career in human factors and engineering psychology.* http://www.apa.org/action/science/human-factors/education-training.pdf

American Psychological Association (APA). (2014h). *Psychology: Science in action. Pursuing a career in industrial and organizational psychology.* http://www.apa.org/action/science/organizational/education-training.pdf

American Psychological Association (APA). (2014i). *Psychology: Science in action. Pursuing a career in the psychology of teaching and learning.* http://www.apa.org/action/science/teaching-learning/education-training.pdf

American Psychological Association (APA). (2014j). *Psychology: Science in action. Pursuing a career in rehabilitation psychology.* http://www.apa.org/action/science/rehabilitation/education-training.pdf

American Psychological Association (APA). (2014k). *Psychology: Science in action. Pursuing a career in social psychology.* http://www.apa.org/action/science/social/education-training.pdf

American Psychological Association (APA). (2014l). *Psychology: Science in action. Pursuing a career in sport and performance psychology.* http://www.apa.org/action/science/performance/education-training.pdf

American Psychological Association (APA). (2014m). *What are telehealth and telepsychology?* https://www.apa.org/pi/disability/resources/publications/telepsychology

American Psychological Association (APA). (2014, May). *Resources on mental health parity law.* http://www.apa.org/helpcenter/parity-lawresources.aspx

American Psychological Association (APA). (2015a). *Demographics of the U.S. psychology workforce: Findings from the American Community Survey.*

American Psychological Association (APA). (2015b). Guidelines for psychological practice with transgender and gender nonconforming people. *American Psychologist, 70*(9), 832–864.

American Psychological Association (APA). (2015c). *Key terms and concepts in understanding gender diversity and sexual orientation among students.* https://doi.org/10.1037/e527502015-001

American Psychological Association (APA). (2015d). Proceedings of the American Psychological Association for the legislative year 2014. Minutes of the annual meeting of the Council of Representatives and minutes of the meetings of the Board of Directors. *American Psychologist, 70*, 386–430.

American Psychological Association (APA). (2016). Guidelines for the undergraduate psychology major: Version 2.0. *The American Psychologist, 71*(2), 102–111. https://doi.org/10.1037/a0037562

American Psychological Association (APA). (2017a). *Ethical principles of psychologists and code of conduct.* http://www.apa.org/ethics/code/?item=6#21

American Psychological Association (APA). (2017b). *Idaho becomes fifth state to allow psychologists to prescribe medications* [Press release]. http://www.apa.org/news/press/releases/2017/04/idaho-psychologists-medications.aspx

American Psychological Association (APA). (2017c). *Salaries in psychology: Findings from the National Science Foundation's 2015 National Survey of College Graduates.* https://www.apa.org/workforce/publications/2015-salaries/report.pdf

American Psychological Association (APA). (2017, March). *Ethical principles of psychologists and code of conduct.* https://www.apa.org/ethics/code

American Psychological Association (APA). (2017, November). *Understanding bisexuality.* https://www.apa.org/pi/lgbt/resources/bisexual

American Psychological Association (APA). (2018). *Demographics of the U.S. psychology workforce: Findings from the 2007–16 American Community Survey.*

American Psychological Association (APA). (2018, August 10). *Why we're susceptible to fake news, how to defend against it* [Press release]. https://www.apa.org/news/press/releases/2018/08/fake-news

American Psychological Association (APA). (2018, October). *Stress in America: Generation Z.* https://www.apa.org/news/press/releases/stress/2018/stress-gen-z.pdf

American Psychological Association (APA). (2019). *Graduate study in psychology, 2019 edition.*

American Psychological Association (APA). (2019, October 31). *Psychotherapy: Understanding group therapy.* https://www.apa.org/topics/psychotherapy/group-therapy

American Psychological Association (APA). (2020). *Publication manual of the American Psychological Association* (7th ed.).

American Psychological Association (APA). (2020, March). *Speaking of psychology: Psychologically sound tips for better sleep.* https://www.apa.org/research/action/speaking-of-psychology/better-sleep-tips

American Psychological Association (APA). (2020, March 25). *Combatting bias and stigma related to COVID-19.* https://www.apa.org/topics/covid-19-bias

American Psychological Association (APA). (2020, October). *Stress in America 2020: A national mental health crisis.* https://www.apa.org/news/press/releases/stress/2020/sia-mental-health-crisis.pdf

American Psychological Association (APA). (n.d.-a). *APA dictionary of psychology: Art therapy.* https://dictionary.apa.org/art-therapy

American Psychological Association (APA). (n.d.-b). *APA style blog.* https://apastyle.apa.org/blog

American Psychological Association (APA). (n.d.-c). *Clinical psychology solves complex human problems.* http://www.apa.org/action/science/clinical/index.aspx

American Psychological Association (APA). (n.d.-d). *Divisions of the APA.* http://www.apa.org/about/division/index.aspx

American Psychological Association (APA). (n.d.-e). *A career in counseling psychology.* http://www.apa.org/action/science/counseling/index.aspx

American Psychological Association (APA). (n.d.-f). *Cognitive psychology explores our mental processes.* http://www.apa.org/action/science/brain-science/index.aspx

American Psychological Association (APA). (n.d.-g). *Developmental psychology studies humans across the lifespan.* http://www.apa.org/action/science/developmental/index.aspx

American Psychological Association (APA). (n.d.-h). *Environmental psychology makes a better world.* http://www.apa.org/action/science/environment/index.aspx

American Psychological Association (APA). (n.d.-i). *Experimental psychology studies humans and animals.* http://www.apa.org/action/science/experimental/index.aspx

American Psychological Association (APA). (n.d.-j). *Frequently asked questions about graduate school.* http://www.apa.org/education/grad/faqs.aspx

American Psychological Association (APA). (n.d.-k). *Health psychology promotes wellness.* http://www.apa.org/action/science/health/index.aspx

American Psychological Association (APA). (n.d.-l). *Human factors psychology studies humans and machines.* http://www.apa.org/action/science/human-factors/index.aspx

American Psychological Association (APA). (n.d.-m). *I/O psychology provides workplace solutions.* http://www.apa.org/action/science/organizational/index.aspx

American Psychological Association (APA). (n.d.-n). *Pursuing a career in counseling psychology.* http://www.apa.org/action/science/counseling/education-training.aspx

American Psychological Association (APA). (n.d.-o). *Questions and answers about memories of childhood abuse.* http://apa.org/topics/trauma/memories.aspx

American Psychological Association (APA). (n.d.-p). *Rehabilitation psychology tackles challenges.* http://www.apa.org/action/science/rehabilitation/index.aspx

American Psychological Association (APA). (n.d.-q). *Social psychology studies human interactions.* http://www.apa.org/action/science/social/index.aspx

American Psychological Association (APA). (n.d.-r). *What is media psychology?* http://www.apadivisions.org/division-46/about/what-is.aspx

American Psychological Association, APA Task Force on Race and Ethnicity Guidelines in Psychology. (2019). *Race and ethnicity guidelines in psychology: Promoting responsiveness and equity.* http://www.apa.org/about/policy/race-and-ethnicity-in-psychology.pdf

American Speech-Language-Hearing Association. (n.d.). *Noise.* http://www.asha.org/public/hearing/Noise/

Amesbury, E. C., & Schallhorn, S. C. (2003). Contrast sensitivity and limits of vision. *International Ophthalmology Clinics, 43*, 31–42.

Amso, D. (2017, January/February). Ask the brains: When do children start making long-term memories? *Scientific American Mind, 28*, 72–73.

Anand, A., Nakamura, K., Spielberg, J. M., Cha, J., Karne, H., & Hu, B. (2020). Integrative analysis of lithium treatment associated effects on brain structure and peripheral gene expression reveals novel molecular insights into mechanism of action. *Translational Psychiatry, 10*(1), Article 103. https://doi.org/10.1038/s41398-020-0784-z

Anastasi, A., & Urbina, S. (1997). *Psychological testing* (7th ed.). Prentice Hall.

Anastasio, A., Draisci, R., Pepe, T., Mercogliano, R., Quadri, F. D., Luppi, G., & Cortesi, M. L. (2010). Development of biogenic amines during the ripening of Italian dry sausages. *Journal of Food Protection, 73*, 114–118.

Anderson, C. A., Bushman, B. J., Bartholow, B. D., Cantor, J., Christakis, D., Coyne, S., M., Donnerstein, E., Funk Brockmyer, J., Gentile, D. A., Green, C. S., Huesmann, R., Hummer, T., Krahé, B., Strasburger, V. C., Warburton, W., Wilson, B. J., & Ybarra, M. (2017). Screen violence and youth behavior. *Pediatrics, 140*(Suppl. 2), S142–S147. https://doi.org/10.1542/peds.2016-1758T

Anderson, M., Perrin, A., Jiang, J., & Kumar, M. (2019, April 22). *10% of Americans don't use the internet. Who are they?* Pew Research Center. https://www.pewresearch.org/fact-tank/2019/04/22/some-americans-dont-use-the-internet-who-are-they/

Anderson, M., Vogel, E. A., & Turner, E. (2020, February 6). The virtues and downsides of online dating. *Pew Research Center.* https://www.pewresearch.org/internet/2020/02/06/the-virtues-and-downsides-of-online-dating/

Anderson, W. E. (2017, August 23). Herpes simplex encephalitis. *Medscape.* https://emedicine.medscape.com/article/1165183-overview#a5

Ando, K. (2020). Umami and salt reduction. *Hypertension Research, 43*(6), 569–570. https://doi.org/10.1038/s41440-020-0414-4

Andrus, B. M., Blizinsky, K., Vedell, P. T., Dennis, K., Shukla, P. K., Schaffer, D. J., Radulovic, J., Churchill, G. A., & Redei, E. E. (2012). Gene expression patterns in the hippocampus and amygdala of endogenous depression and chronic stress models. *Molecular Psychiatry, 17*, 49–61.

Anestis, J. C., Rodriguez, T. R., Preston, O. C., Harrop, T. M., Arnau, R. C., & Finn, J. A. (2021). Personality assessment and psychotherapy preferences: Congruence between client personality and therapist personality preferences. *Journal of Personality Assessment, 103*(3), 416–426. https://doi.org/10.1080/00223891.2020.1757459

Angst, J., Paksarian, D., Cui, L., Merikangas, K. R., Hengartner, M. P., Ajdacic-Gross, V., & Rössler, W. (2016). The epidemiology of common mental disorders from age 20 to 50: Results from the prospective Zurich cohort Study. *Epidemiology and Psychiatric Sciences, 25,* 24–32.

Angus, L., Watson, J. C., Elliott, R., Schneider, K., & Timulak, L. (2015). Humanistic psychotherapy research 1990–2015: From methodological innovation to evidence-supported treatment outcomes and beyond. *Psychotherapy Research, 25,* 330–347.

Annan, J., Blattman, C., & Horton, R. (2006). *The state of youth and youth protection in northern Uganda: Findings from the Survey for War Affected Youth* (Report for UNICEF Uganda, pp. ii–89). http://chrisblattman.com /documents/policy/sway/SWAY.Phase1 .FinalReport.pdf

Anokhin, A. P., Grant, J. D., Mulligan, R. C., & Heath, A. C. (2015). The genetics of impulsivity: Evidence for the heritability of delay discounting. *Biological Psychiatry, 77*(10), 887–894.

Ansbacher, H. L., & Ansbacher, R. R. (Eds.). (1956). *The individual psychology of Alfred Adler.* Harper and Row.

Anton, M. T., Jones, D. J., & Youngstrom, E. A. (2015). Socioeconomic status, parenting, and externalizing problems in African American single-mother homes: A person-oriented approach. *Journal of Family Psychology, 29,* 405–415.

APA Center for Workforce Studies. (2017). Table 3: Current major field of APA members by membership status. APA Directory. Retrieved from https:// www.apa.org/workforce/publications /17-member-profiles/table-3.pdf

APA Presidential Task Force on Evidence-Based Practice. (2006). Evidence-based practice in psychology. *American Psychologist, 61,* 271–285.

APA Style. (2019, September). *Sexual orientation.* https://apastyle.apa.org /style-grammar-guidelines/bias-free -language/sexual-orientation

Appel, J. M. (2019, December 9). Rethinking the infamous Milgram experiment in authoritarian times. *Scientific American.* https://blogs .scientificamerican.com/observations /rethinking-the-infamous-milgram -experiment-in-authoritarian-times/

Arab, L., & Ang. A. (2015). A cross sectional study of the association between walnut consumption and cognitive function among adult US populations represented in NHANES. *Journal of Nutrition, Health & Aging, 19*(3), 284–290.

Aranake, A., Mashour, G. A., & Avidan, M. S. (2013). Minimum alveolar concentration: Ongoing relevance and clinical utility. *Anaesthesia, 68,* 512–522.

Archer, J., & Coyne, S. M. (2005). An integrated review of indirect, relational, and social aggression. *Personality and Social Psychology Review, 9,* 212–230.

Arganini, C., & Sinesio, F. (2015). Chemosensory impairment does not diminish eating pleasure and appetite in independently living older adults. *Maturitas, 82,* 241–244.

Arkes, H. R. (2013). The consequences of the hindsight bias in medical decision making. *Current Directions in Psychological Science, 22,* 356–360.

Arkowitz, H., & Lilienfeld, S. O. (2011, July/August). Deranged and dangerous? *Scientific American Mind, 22,* 64–65.

Arlin, P. K. (1975). Cognitive development in adulthood: A fifth stage? *Developmental Psychology, 11,* 602–606.

Armstrong, G. B. (2020, April 29). Can high-intensity exercise improve your memory? *Scientific American.* https://www.scientificamerican.com /article/can-high-intensity-exercise -improve-your-memory/

Arnett, J. J. (2000). Emerging adulthood: A theory of development from the late teens through the twenties. *American Psychologist, 55,* 469–480.

Aron, A., Fisher, H., Mashek, D. J., Strong, G., Li, H., & Brown, L. L. (2005). Reward, motivation, and emotion systems associated with early-stage intense romantic love. *Journal of Neurophysiology, 94*(1), 327–337.

Aronson, E. (2012). *The social animal* (11th ed.). Worth Publishers.

Aronson, E. (2015). *Jigsaw classroom.* http://www.jigsaw.org

Aronson, E. (2018). *The social animal* (12th ed.). Worth Publishers.

Aronson, E., & Festinger, L. (1958). *Some attempts to measure tolerance for dissonance* (WADC.TR-58.492ASTIA Document No. AD 207 337). Lackland Air Force Base.

Arora, M., Reichenberg, A., Willfors, C., Austin, C., Gennings, C., Berggren, S., Lichtenstein, P., Anckarsäter, H., Tammimies, K., & Bölte, S. (2017). Fetal and postnatal metal dysregulation in autism. *Nature Communications, 8.* Article 15493. https://doi.org/10.1038/ncomms15493

Asami, T., Nakamura, R., Takaishi, M., Yoshida, H., Yoshimi, A., Whitford, T. J., & Hirayasu, Y. (2018). Smaller volumes in the lateral and basal nuclei of the amygdala in patients with panic disorder. *PLOS ONE, 13*(11), Article e0207163. https://doi.org/10 .1371/journal.pone.0207163

Asch, S. E. (1955). Opinions and social pressure. *Scientific American, 193*(5), 31–35.

Asch, S. E. (1956). Studies of independence and conformity: I. A minority of one against a unanimous majority. *Psychological Monographs: General and Applied, 70,* 1–70.

Ascoli, G. A. (2015). On synaptic circuits, memory, and kumquats. *New England Journal of Medicine, 373*(12), 1170–1172.

Assaf, Y. (2018). New dimensions for brain mapping. *Science, 362*(6418), 994–995. https://doi.org/10.1126 /science.aav7357

Assari, S. (2019). Race, education attainment, and happiness in the United States. *International Journal of Epidemiologic Research, 6*(2), 76–82. https://doi.org/10.15171/ijer.2019.14

Assefa, S. Z., Diaz-Abad, M., Wickwire, E. M., & Scharf, S. M. (2015). The functions of sleep. *AIMS Neuroscience, 2*(3), 155–171.

Assistant Secretary for Public Affairs (ASPA), U.S. Department of Health and Human Services. (2017). *The opioid epidemic in the U.S.* https://www.hhs.gov/opioids/about -the-epidemic/index.html

Associated Press. (2014, May 8). Therapy dogs help troops deal with postwar stress. *CBS News.* http://www .cbsnews.com/news/therapy-dog-help -stroops-deal-with-postwar-stress/

Association for Psychological Science (APS). (n.d.-a). *Psychological science links.* http://www.psychologicalscience.org /index.php/about/psychology-links

Association for Psychological Science (APS). (n.d.-b). *Psychology links.* http://www.psychologicalscience .org/index.php/about/psychology-links

Atance, C. M., & Caza, J. S. (2018). "Will I know more in the future than I know now?" Preschoolers' judgments about changes in general knowledge. *Developmental Psychology, 54*(5), 857–865. https://doi.org/10.1037 /dev0000480

Athanasopoulos, P., Bylund, E., Montero-Melis, G., Damjanovic, L., Schartner, A., Kibbe, A., Riches, N., & Thierry, G. (2015). Two languages, two minds: Flexible cognitive processing driven by language of operation. *Psychological Science, 26*(4), 518–526. https://doi.org/10.1177 /0956797614567509

Atkinson, R. C., & Shiffrin, R. M. (1968, January 31–February 2). *Some speculations on storage and retrieval processes in long-term memory* (Technical Report No. 127). Paper presented at Conference on Research on Human Decision Making sponsored by NASA-Ames Research Center, Moffett Field, CA.

Attarian, H. P., Schenck, C. H., & Mahowald, M. W. (2000). Presumed REM sleep behavior disorder arising from cataplexy and wakeful dreaming. *Sleep Medicine, 1,* 131–133.

Auerbach, R. P., Mortier, P., Bruffaerts, R., Alonso, J., Benjet, C., Cuijpers, P., Demyttenaere, K., Ebert, D. D., Green, J. G., Hasking, P., Murray, E., Nock, M. K., Pinder-Amaker, S., Sampson, N. A., Stein, D. J., Vilagut, G., Zaslavsky, A. M., Kessler, R. C., & WHO WMH-ICS Collaborators. (2018). WHO World Mental Health Surveys International College Student Project: Prevalence and distribution of mental disorders. *Journal of Abnormal Psychology, 127*(7), 623–638. https://doi.org/10.1037/abn0000362

Aurora, R. N., Zak, R. S., Maganti, R. K., Auerbach, S. H., Casey, K. R., Chowdhuri, S., Karippot, A., Ramar, K., Kristo, D. A., & Morgenthaler, T. I. (2010). Best practice guide for the treatment of REM sleep behavior disorder (RED). *Journal of Clinical Sleep Medicine, 6*(1), 85–95. https://jcsm.aasm.org /doi/10.5664/jcsm.27717

Auster, C. J., & Mansbach, C. S. (2012). The gender marketing of toys: An analysis of color and type of toy on the Disney store website. *Sex Roles, 67,* 375–388.

Australian Department of Health. (2016, May 27). *Tobacco control key facts and figures.* http://www.health .gov.au/internet/main/publishing.nsf /Content/tobacco-kff

Axelrod, V., Bar, M., Rees, G., & Yovel, G. (2014). Neural correlates of subliminal language processing. *Cerebral Cortex, 25,* 2160–2169. https://doi.org/10.1093/cercor /bhu022

Ayano, G., Tesfaw, G., & Shumet, S. (2019). The prevalence of schizophrenia and other psychotic disorders among homeless people: A systematic review and meta-analysis. *BMC Psychiatry, 19,* Article 370. https://doi.org/10.1186 /s12888-019-2361-7

Aydin, B. K., Saka, N., Bas, F., Bas, E. K., Coban, A., Yildirim, S., Guran, T., & Darendeliler, F. (2019). Frequency of ambiguous genitalia in 14,177 newborns in Turkey. *Journal of the Endocrine Society, 3*(6), 1185–1195. https://doi.org/10 .1210/js.2018-00408

Azevedo, J., Vieira-Coelho, M., Castelo-Branco, M., Coelho, R., & Figueiredo-Braga, M. (2020). Impulsive and premeditated aggression in male offenders with antisocial personality disorder. *PLOS ONE, 15*(3), Article e0229876. https://doi.org/10.1371/journal .pone.0229876

Azucar, D., Marengo, D., & Settanni, M. (2018). Predicting the Big 5 personality traits from digital footprints on social media: A meta-analysis. *Personality and Individual Differences, 124,* 150–159. https://doi.org/10.1016/j .paid.2017.12.018

**Back, M. D., Schmukle, S. C., & Egloff, B.** (2008). Becoming friends by chance. *Psychological Science, 19,* 439–440.

**Backeljauw, P., & Hwa, V.** (2016). Growth hormone physiology. In L. E. Cohen (Ed.), *Growth hormone deficiency: Physiology and clinical management* (pp. 7–20). Springer International.

**Bacon, J.** (2018, July 5). "Hero or zero?": Thailand abuzz over coach who led boys into cave—then kept them alive. *USA Today.* https://www.usatoday.com /story/news/world/2018/07/05 /thailand-cave-rescue-coach/759510002/

**Baddeley, A.** (1995). Working memory. In M. S. Gazzaniga (Ed.), *The cognitive neurosciences* (pp. 755–764). MIT Press.

**Baddeley, A.** (1999). *Essentials of human memory.* Psychology Press.

**Baddeley, A.** (2000). The episodic buffer: A new component of working memory? *Trends in Cognitive Sciences, 4,* 417–423.

**Baddeley, A.** (2002). Is working memory still working? *European Psychologist, 7,* 85–97.

**Baddeley, A.** (2006). Working memory: An overview. In S. J. Pickering (Ed.), *Working memory in education* (pp. 3–31). Elsevier.

**Baddeley, A.** (2012). Working memory: Theories, models, and controversies. *Annual Review of Psychology, 63,* 1–29.

**Baddeley, A. D., & Hitch, G. J.** (1974). Working memory. In G. Bower (Ed.), *Recent advances in learning and memory* (Vol. 8, pp. 47–90). Academic Press.

**Baddeley, A. D., & Hitch, G. J.** (2019). The phonological loop as a buffer store: An update. *Cortex: A Journal Devoted to the Study of the Nervous System and Behavior, 112,* 91–106. https://doi .org/10.1016/j.cortex.2018.05.015

**Baddeley, A. D., Hitch, G. J., & Allen, R. J.** (2019). From short-term store to multicomponent working memory: The role of the modal model. *Memory & Cognition, 47*(4), 575–588. https://doi .org/10.3758/s13421-018-0878-5

**Badie, D.** (2010). Groupthink, Iraq, and the war on terror: Explaining US policy shift toward Iraq. *Foreign Policy Analysis, 6,* 277–296.

**Baer, J. M.** (1993). *Creativity and divergent thinking.* Erlbaum.

**Bahrick, H. P., Hall, L. K., & Da Costa, L. A.** (2008). Fifty years of memory of college grades: Accuracy and distortions. *Emotion, 8,* 13–22.

**Bahrick, L. E., Gogate, L. J., & Ruiz, I.** (2002). Attention and memory for faces and actions in infancy: The salience of actions over faces in dynamic events. *Child Development, 73,* 1629–1643. https:// doi.org/10.1111/1467-8624.00495

**Bailey, S. J., & Covell, K.** (2011). Pathways among abuse, daily hassles, depression and substance use in adolescents. *The New School Psychology Bulletin, 8,* 4–14.

**Baillargeon, R., Spelke, E. S., & Wasserman, S.** (1985). Object permanence in five-month-old infants. *Cognition, 20,* 191–208.

**Baio, J., Wiggins, L., Christensen, D. L., Maenner, M. J., Daniels, J., Warren, Z., Kurzius-Spencer, M., Zahorodny, W., Robinson Rosenberg, C., White, T., Durkin, M. S., Imm, P., Nikolaou, L., Yeargin-Allsopp, M., Lee, L-C., Harrington, R., Lopez, M., Fitzgerald, R. T., Hewitt, A., . . . Dowling, N. F.** (2018). Prevalence of autism spectrum disorder among children aged 8 years—autism and developmental disabilities monitoring network, 11 sites, United States, 2014. *MMWR Surveillance Summaries, 67*(SS-6), 1–23. https://doi.org/10 .15585/mmwr.ss6706a1

**Baird, H. M., Webb, T. L., Sirois, F. M., & Gibson-Miller, J.** (2021). Understanding the effects of time perspective: A meta-analysis testing a self-regulatory framework. *Psychological Bulletin, 147*(3), 233–267. https://doi .org/10.1037/bul0000313

**Baker, L. R., Kane, M. J., & Russell, V. M.** (2020). Romantic partners' working memory capacity facilitates relationship problem resolution through recollection of problem-relevant information. *Journal of Experimental Psychology: General, 149*(3), 580–584. https://doi .org/10.1037/xge0000659

**Bakker, E. A., van Bakel, B. M., Aengevaeren, W. R., Meindersma, E. P., Snoek, J. A., Waskowsky, W. M., van Kuijk, A. A., Jacobs, M. M. L. M., Hopman, M. T. E., Thijssen, D. H. J., & Eijsvogels, T. M. H.** (2020). Sedentary behaviour in cardiovascular disease patients: Risk group identification and the impact of cardiac rehabilitation. *International Journal of Cardiology.* https://doi.org /10.1016/j.ijcard.2020.11.014

**Baldassarri, D., & Abascal, M.** (2020). Diversity and prosocial behavior. *Science, 369*(6508), 1183–1187. https://doi.org/10.1126 /science.abb2432

**Ball, P.** (2020, May 13). Anti-vaccine movement could undermine efforts to end coronavirus pandemic, researchers warn. *Nature.* https://www.nature.com /articles/d41586-020-01423-4

**Balliet, D., & Ferris, D. L.** (2013). Ostracism and prosocial behavior: A social dilemma perspective. *Organizational Behavior and Human Decision Processes, 120,* 298–308.

**Balter, M.** (2017, July/August). Schizophrenia's unyielding mysteries. *Scientific American Mind, 28,* 50–60.

**Banaji, M. R., & Greenwald, A. G.** (2013). *Blindspot: Hidden biases of good people.* Delacorte Press.

**Bandell, M., Macpherson, L. J., & Patapoutian, A.** (2007). From chills to chilis: Mechanisms for thermosensation and chemesthesis via thermoTRPs. *Current Opinion in Neurobiology, 17,* 490–497.

**Bandelow, B., & Michaelis, S.** (2015). Epidemiology of anxiety disorders in the 21st century. *Dialogues in Clinical Neuroscience, 17*(3), 327–335.

**Bandura, A.** (1977a). Self-efficacy: Toward a unifying theory of behavioral change. *Psychological Review, 84,* 191–215.

**Bandura, A.** (1977b). *Social learning theory.* Prentice Hall.

**Bandura, A.** (1978). The self system in reciprocal determinism. *American Psychologist, 33,* 344–358.

**Bandura, A.** (1986). *Social foundations of thought and action: A social cognitive theory.* Prentice Hall.

**Bandura, A.** (2001). Social cognitive theory: An agentic perspective. *Annual Review of Psychology, 52,* 1–26.

**Bandura, A.** (2006). Toward a psychology of human agency. *Perspectives on Psychological Science, 1,* 164–180.

**Bandura, A., & Cherry, L.** (2020). Enlisting the power of youth for climate change. *American Psychologist, 75*(7), 945–951. https://doi.org/10 .1037/amp0000512

**Bandura, A., Ross, D., & Ross, S. A.** (1961). Transmission of aggression through imitation of aggressive models. *Journal of Abnormal and Social Psychology, 63,* 575–582.

**Banks, M. S., & Salapatek, P.** (1978). Acuity and contrast sensitivity in 1-, 2-, and 3-month-old human infants. *Investigative Ophthalmology & Visual Science, 17,* 361–365.

**Banuazizi, A., & Movahedi, S.** (1975). Interpersonal dynamics in a simulated prison: A methodological analysis. *American Psychologist, 30,* 152–160.

**Baraona, E., Abittan, C. S., Dohmen, K., Moretti, M., Pozzato, G., Chayes, Z. W., Schaefer, C., & Lieber, C. S.** (2001). Gender differences in pharmacokinetics of alcohol. *Alcoholism: Clinical and Experimental Research, 25,* 502–507. https://doi.org/10.1111/j .1530-0277.2001.tb02242.x

**Barash, P. G., Cullen, B. F., Stoelting, R. K., & Cahalan, M.** (2009). *Clinical anesthesia* (6th ed.). Lippincott Williams & Wilkins.

**Barber, R.** (2012, October 27). Yes, I give dogs electric shocks and use spike chokers . . . but I'm NOT cruel, says Hollywood's favourite pet guru. *Daily Mail.* http://www .dailymail.co.uk/news/article-2224252 /Yes-I-dogs-electric-shocks-use-spike -chokers--Im-NOT-cruel-says -Hollywoods-favourite-pet-guru-Cesar -Millan.html

**Barber, S. J., Hamel, K., Ketcham, C., Lui, K., & Taylor-Ketcham, N.** (2020). The effects of stereotype threat on older adults' walking performance as a function of task difficulty and resource evaluations. *Psychology and Aging, 35*(2), 250–266. https://doi .org/10.1037/pag0000440

**Bard, P.** (1934). Emotion I: The neuro-humoral basis of emotional reactions. In C. Murchison, (Ed.), *Handbook of general experimental psychology* (International University Series in Psychology, pp. 264–311). Clark University Press.

**Bardach, L., Oczlon, S., Pietschnig, J., & Lüftenegger, M.** (2020). Has achievement goal theory been right? A meta-analysis of the relation between goal structures and personal achievement goals. *Journal of Educational Psychology, 112*(6), 1197–1220. https://doi.org/10 .1037/edu0000419

**Bar-Hillel, M.** (2015). Position effects in choice from simultaneous displays: A conundrum solved. *Perspectives on Psychological Science, 10,* 419–433.

**Barlow, R.** (2017, November 10). *Aaron Hernandez's CTE worst seen by BU experts in a young person.* Boston University Research. http://www.bu.edu /research/articles/aaron-hernandez -cte-worst-seen-in-young-person/

**Barnes, R.** (2020, June 15). Supreme Court says gay, transgender workers protected by federal law forbidding discrimination. *The Washington Post.* https://www.washingtonpost.com /politics/courts_law/supreme-court -says-gay-transgender-workers-are -protected-by-federal-law-forbidding -discrimination-on-the-basis-of-sex /2020/06/15/2211d5a4-655b-11ea -acca-80c22bbee96f_story.html

**Barr, T. F., Dixon, A. L., & Gassenheimer, J. B.** (2005). Exploring the "lone wolf" phenomenon in student teams. *Journal of Marketing Education, 27,* 81–90.

**Barredo, J. L., & Deeg, K. E.** (2009, February 24). Could living in a mentally enriching environment change your genes? *Scientific American.* http://www.scientificamerican.com /article.cfm?id=enriched-environments -memory

**Barrera, T. L., Mott, J. M., Hofstein, R. F., & Teng, E. J.** (2013). A meta-analytic review of exposure in group cognitive behavioral therapy for posttraumatic stress disorder. *Clinical Psychology Review, 33,* 24–32.

**Barrett, L. F.** (2017, June 4). *Poverty on the brain* [Web log post]. https:// lisafeldmanbarrett.com/2017/06/04 /poverty-on-the-brain/

Barrett, T. S., & White, K. R. (2017). Trends in hearing loss among adolescents. *Pediatrics, 140*(6), e20170619. https://doi.org/10.1542/peds.2017-0619

Barrington-Trimis, J. L., & Leventhal, A. M. (2018). Adolescents' use of "pod mod" e-cigarettes—urgent concerns. *New England Journal of Medicine, 379*(12), 1099–1102. https://doi.org/10.1056/NEJMp1805758

Barroso, C., Ganley, C. M., McGraw, A. L., Geer, E. A., Hart, S. A., & Daucourt, M. C. (2020). A meta-analysis of the relation between math anxiety and math achievement. *Psychological Bulletin. 147*(2), 134–168. https://doi.org/10.1037/bul0000307

Barrouillet, P., Gorin, S., & Camos, V. (2020). Simple spans underestimate verbal working memory capacity. *Journal of Experimental Psychology: General.* Advance online publication. https://doi.org/10.1037/xge0000957

Barry, C. T., Doucette, H., Loflin, D. C., Rivera-Hudson, N., & Herrington, L. L. (2017). "Let me take a selfie": Associations between self-photography, narcissism, and self-esteem. *Psychology of Popular Media Culture, 6*(1), 48–60. https://doi.org/10.1037/ppm0000089

Barry, C. T., Reiter, S. R., Anderson, A. C., Schoessler, M. L., & Sidoti, C. L. (2019). "Let me take another selfie": Further examination of the relation between narcissism, self-perception, and Instagram posts. *Psychology of Popular Media Culture, 8*(1), 22–33. https://doi.org/10.1037/ppm0000155

Barry, V., Stout, M. E., Lynch, M. E., Mattis, S., Tran, D. Q., Antun, A., Ribeiro, M. J. A., Stein, S. F., & Kempton, C. L. (2020). The effect of psychological distress on health outcomes: A systematic review and meta-analysis of prospective studies. *Journal of Health Psychology, 25*(2), 227–239. https://doi.org/10.1177/1359105319842931

Barsalou, L. W. (2020). Challenges and opportunities for grounding cognition. *Journal of Cognition, 3*(1), 31. https://doi.org/10.5334/joc.116

Barss, T. S., Pearcey, G. E., & Zehr, E. P. (2016). Cross-education of strength and skill: An old idea with applications in the aging nervous system. *Yale Journal of Biology and Medicine, 89*(1), 81–86.

Bartels, M. (2015). Genetics of wellbeing and its components satisfaction with life, happiness, and quality of life: A review and meta-analysis of heritability studies. *Behavior Genetics, 45*, 137–156.

Bartels, M., Saviouk, V., De Moor, M. H. M., Willemsen, G., van Beijsterveldt, T. C. E. M., Hottenga, J.-J., de Geus, E. J. C., & Boomsma, D. I. (2010). Heritability and genome-wide linkage scan of subjective happiness. *Twin Research and Human Genetics, 13*, 135–142.

Bartlett, T. (2014). The search for psychology's lost boy. *Chronicle of Higher Education, 60*(38). http://chronicle.com/interactives/littlealbert

Barton, R. A., & Capellini, I. (2016). Sleep, evolution and brains. *Brain, Behavior and Evolution, 87*, 65–68. https://doi.org/10.1159/000443716

Barwich, A.-S. (2019). A critique of olfactory objects. *Frontiers in Psychology, 10*, Article 1337. https://doi.org/10.3389/fpsyg.2019.01337

Baselmans, B. M., Yengo, L., van Rheenen, W., & Wray, N. R. (2020). Risk in relatives, heritability, SNP-based heritability and genetic correlations in psychiatric disorders: A review. *Biological Psychiatry.* https://doi.org/10.1016/j.biopsych.2020.05.034

Bastos, A. P., & Taylor, A. H. (2020). Kea show three signatures of domain-general statistical inference. *Nature Communications, 11*(1), 1–8. https://doi.org/10.1038/s41467-020-14695-1

Bates, M. (2012, September 18). Super powers for the blind and deaf. *Scientific American.* https://www.scientificamerican.com/article/superpowers-for-the-blind-and-deaf/

Batiuk, M. Y., Martirosyan, A., Wahis, J., de Vin, F., Marneffe, C., Kusserow, C., Koeppen, J., Viana, J. F., Oliveira, J. F., Voet, T., Ponting, C. P., Belgard, T. G., & Holt, M. G. (2020). Identification of region-specific astrocyte subtypes at single cell resolution. *Nature Communications, 11*(1), 1–15. https://doi.org/10.1038/s41467-019-14198-8

Batsell, W. R., Jr., Perry, J. L., Hanley, E., & Hostetter, A. B. (2017). Ecological validity of the testing effect: The use of daily quizzes in introductory psychology. *Teaching of Psychology, 44*(1), 18–23. https://doi.org/10.1177/0098628316677492

Batson, C. D., & Powell, A. A. (2003). Altruism and prosocial behavior. In I. B. Weiner, T. Millon, & M. J. Lerner (Eds.), *Handbook of psychology: Vol. 5. Personality and social psychology* (pp. 463–484). John Wiley & Sons.

Bauer, P. J. (2006). Constructing a past in infancy: A neuro-developmental account. *Trends in Cognitive Sciences, 10*, 175–181.

Bauer, P. J. (2015). A complementary processes account of the development of childhood amnesia and a personal past. *Psychological Review, 122*, 204–231.

Bauer, P. J., & Larkina, M. (2014). The onset of childhood amnesia in childhood: A prospective investigation of the course and determinants of forgetting of early-life events. *Memory, 22*, 907–924.

Baughman, H. M., Giammarco, E. A., Veselka, L., Schermer, J. A., Martin, N. G., Lynskey, M., & Vernon, P. A. (2012). A behavioral genetic study of humor styles in an Australian sample. *Twin Research and Human Genetics, 15*, 663–667.

Baumrind, D. (1966). Effects of authoritative parental control on child behavior. *Child Development, 37*, 887–907.

Baumrind, D. (1971). Current patterns of parental authority. *Developmental Psychology Monograph, 4*, 1–103.

Baumrind, D. (1991). The influence of parenting style on adolescent competence and substance use. *Journal of Early Adolescence, 11*, 56–95.

Baumrind, D. (2013). Is a pejorative view of power assertion in the socialization process justified? *Review of General Psychology, 17*, 420–427.

Bayley, N. (1993). *The Bayley Scales of Infant Development* (2nd ed.). Psychological Test Corporation.

Bazzano, A. N., Anderson, C. E., Hylton, C., & Gustat, J. (2018). Effect of mindfulness and yoga on quality of life for elementary school students and teachers: Results of a randomized controlled school-based study. *Psychology Research and Behavior Management, 11*, 81–89.

BBC. (2018, July 14). The full story of Thailand's extraordinary cave rescue. https://www.bbc.com/news/world-asia-44791998

BBC News. (2017, May 12). *Singer finds her sound after going deaf* [Video]. http://www.bbc.com/news/av/world-us-canada-39901298/mandy-harvey-singer-finds-her-sound-after-going-deaf

BBC Newsbeat. (2015, June 25). We know what LGBT means but here's what LGBTQQIAAP stands for. http://www.bbc.co.uk/newsbeat/article/33278165/we-know-what-lgbt-means-but-heres-what-lgbtqqiaap-stands-for

Beauchamp, M. H., & Anderson, V. (2010). Social: An integrative framework for the development of social skills. *Psychological Bulletin, 136*, 39–64. https://doi.org/10.1037/a0017768

Beck, A. (2019). A 60-year evolution of cognitive theory and therapy. *Perspectives on Psychological Science, 14*(1), 16–20. https://doi.org/10.1177/1745691618804187

Beck, A. T. (1976). *Cognitive therapy and the emotional disorders.* International Universities Press.

Beck, A. T., & Weishaar, M. E. (2014). Cognitive therapy. In R. J. Corsini & D. Wedding (Eds.), *Current psychotherapies* (10th ed., pp. 231–264). Brooks/Cole, Cengage Learning.

Beck, A. T., Rush, A. J., Shaw, B. F., & Emory, G. (1979). *Cognitive therapy of depression.* Guilford Press.

Beck, H. P., Levinson, S., & Irons, G. (2009). Finding Little Albert: A journey to John B. Watson's infant laboratory. *American Psychologist, 64*, 605–614. https://doi.org/10.1037/a0017234

Becker, K. A. (2003). History of the Stanford-Binet intelligence scales: Content and psychometrics. In *Stanford-Binet intelligence scales: Fifth edition assessment service bulletin* (No. 1). Riverside.

Becker, M., Sommer, T., & Kühn, S. (2020a). Inferior frontal gyrus involvement during search and solution in verbal creative problem solving: A parametric fMRI study. *Neuroimage, 206*, 116294. https://doi.org/10.1016/j.neuroimage.2019.116294

Becker, M., Sommer, T., & Kühn, S. (2020b). Verbal insight revisited: fMRI evidence for early processing in bilateral insulae for solutions with AHA! experience shortly after trial onset. *Human Brain Mapping, 41*(1), 30–45. https://doi.org/10.1002/hbm.24785

Bedrosian, T. A., Fonken, L. K., & Nelson, R. J. (2016). Endocrine effects of circadian disruption. *Annual Review of Physiology, 78*, 1.1–1.23. https://doi.org/10.1146/annurev-physiol-021115-105102

Beebe-Center, J. G. (1951). Feeling and emotion. In H. Helson (Ed.), *Theoretical foundations of psychology* (pp. 254–317). Van Nostrand.

Beech, H., Paddock, R. C., & Suhartono, M. (2018, July 12). "Still can't believe it worked": The story of the Thailand cave rescue. *The New York Times.* https://www.nytimes.com/2018/07/12/world/asia/thailand-cave-rescue-seals.html

Békés, V., & Aafjes-van Doorn, K. (2020). Psychotherapists' attitudes toward online therapy during the COVID-19 pandemic. *Journal of Psychotherapy Integration, 30*(2), 238–247. https://doi.org/10.1037/int0000214

Belgrave, F. Z., & Allison, K. W. (2019). *African American psychology* (4th ed.). Sage.

Belletier, C., Normand, A., & Huguet, P. (2019). Social-facilitation-and-impairment effects: From motivation to cognition and the social brain. *Current Directions in Psychological Science, 28*(3), 260–265. https://doi.org/10.1177/0963721419829699

Bellieni, C. V., Alagna, M. G., & Buonocore, G. (2013). Analgesia for infants' circumcision. *Italian Journal of Pediatrics, 39*(38). https://doi.org/10.1186/1824-7288-39-38

Belmaker, R. H. (2004). Bipolar disorder. *New England Journal of Medicine, 351*, 476–486.

Belmaker, R. H., & Agam, G. (2008). Major depressive disorder. *New England Journal of Medicine, 358*, 55–68.

Bem, S. L. (1981). Gender schema theory: A cognitive account of sex typing. *Psychological Review, 88*, 354–364.

**Bench, S. W., & Lench, H. C.** (2019). Boredom as a seeking state: Boredom prompts the pursuit of novel (even negative) experiences. *Emotion, 19*(2), 242–254. https://doi.org /10.1037/emo0000433

**Benedek, M., Franz, F., Heene, M., & Neubauer, A. C.** (2012). Differential effects of cognitive inhibition and intelligence on creativity. *Personality and Individual Differences, 53*, 480–485.

**Benjamin, G. A. H., & Kaslow, F. W.** (2020). Custody case family consultation. In C. A. Falender & E. P. Shafranske (Eds.), *Consultation in psychology: A competency-based approach* (pp. 253–277). American Psychological Association. https://doi.org/10.1037/0000153-015

**Benjamin, L. T.** (2007). *A brief history of modern psychology.* Blackwell.

**Benjamin, S., MacGillivray, L., Schildkrout, B., Cohen-Oram, A., Lauterbach, M. D., & Levin, L. L.** (2018). Six landmark case reports essential for neuropsychiatric literacy. *The Journal of Neuropsychiatry and Clinical Neurosciences, 30*(4), 279–290. https://doi.org/10.1176/appi .neuropsych.18020027

**Bennett, A. T. D., Cuthill, I. C., Partridge, J. C., & Maier, E. J.** (1996). Ultraviolet vision and mate choice in zebra finches. *Nature, 380,* 433–435.

**Ben-Porath, Y. S.** (2012). *Interpreting the MMPI 2 RF.* University of Minnesota Press.

**Benson, H.** (2000). *The relaxation response.* Avon Books.

**Berenbaum, S. A., Blakemore, J. E. O., & Beltz, A. M.** (2011). A role for biology in gender-related behavior. *Sex Roles, 64,* 804–825.

**Bergfeld, I. O., Mantione, M., Hoogendoorn, M. L., Ruhé, H. G., Notten, P., van Laarhoven, J., Visser, I., Figee, M., de Kwaasteniet, B. P., Horst, F., Schene, A. H., van den Munckhof, P., Beute, G., Schuurman, R., & Denys, D.** (2016). Deep brain stimulation of the ventral anterior limb of the internal capsule for treatment-resistant depression: A randomized clinical trial. *JAMA Psychiatry, 73,* 456–464. https://doi .org/10.1001/jamapsychiatry.2016.0152

**Bergh, C., Sjöstedt, S., Hellers, G., Zandian, M., & Södersten, P.** (2003). Meal size, satiety and cholecystokinin in gastrectomized humans. *Physiology &* **Bridgman, T., Cummings** *Behavior, 78,* 143–147.

**Bering, J.** (2018). *Suicidal: Why we kill ourselves.* University of Chicago Press.

**Bernard, L. L.** (1926). *An introduction to social psychology.* Henry Holt.

**Berry, J. W.** (1997). Immigration, acculturation, and adaptation. *Applied Psychology: An International Review, 46,* 5–68.

**Berry, R. B., Brooks, R., Gamald, C. E., Harding, S. M., Lloyd, R. M., Marcus, C. L., & Vaughn, B. V., for the American Academy of Sleep Medicine.** (2016). *The AASM manual for the scoring of sleep and associated events: Rules, terminology, and technical specifications, Version 2.3.* American Academy of Sleep Medicine.

**Berry, R. B., & Wagner, M. H.** (2015). *Sleep medicine pearls* (3rd ed.). Elsevier Saunders.

**Berry, T. D., Mitteer, D. R., & Fournier, A. K.** (2015). Examining hand-washing rates and durations in public restrooms: A study of gender differences via personal, environmental, and behavioral determinants. *Environment and Behavior, 47,* 923–944.

**Berscheid, E.** (2010). Love in the fourth dimension. *Annual Review of Psychology, 61,* 1–25.

**Berwick, R. C., Friederici, A. D., Chomsky, N., & Bolhuis, J. J.** (2013). Evolution, brain, and the nature of language. *Trends in Cognitive Sciences, 17*(2), 89–98.

**Besedovsky, L., Lange, T., & Born, J.** (2012). Sleep and immune function. *Pflügers Archiv—European Journal of Physiology, 463, 121–137.* https://doi .org/10.1007/s00424-011-1044-0

**Beyens, I., Pouwels, J. L., van Driel, I. I., Keijsers, L., & Valkenburg, P. M.** (2020). The effect of social media on well-being differs from adolescent to adolescent. *Scientific Reports, 10*(1). https://doi.org/10.1038/s41598-020 -67727-7

**Bezdjian, S., Tuvblad, C., Raine, A., & Baker, L. A.** (2011). The genetic and environmental covariation among psychopathic personality traits, and reactive and proactive aggression in childhood. *Child Development, 82,* 1267–1281.

**Bhattarai, A.** (2020, August 12). Grocery workers say morale is at an all-time low: "They don't even treat us like humans anymore." *The Washington Post.* https://www.washingtonpost.com/ business/2020/08/12/grocery-workers -coronavirus/

**Bhavsar, V., Dean, K., Hatch, S. L., MacCabe, J. H., & Hotopf, M.** (2019). Psychiatric symptoms and risk of victimisation: A population-based study from Southeast London. *Epidemiology and Psychiatric Sciences, 28*(2), 168–178.

**Biderman, N., Bakkour, A., & Shohamy, D.** (2020). What are memories for? The hippocampus bridges past experience with future decisions. *Trends in Cognitive Sciences, 24*(7), 542–556. https://doi.org/10 .1016/j.tics.2020.04.004

**Bihm, E. M., Gillaspy, J. A., Lammers, W. J., & Huffman, S. P.** (2010). IQ zoo and teaching operant concepts. *Psychological Record, 60,* 523–526.

**Bikle, D. D.** (2004). Vitamin D and skin cancer. *Journal of Nutrition, 134,* 3472S–3478S.

**Binda, P., Pereverzeva, M., & Murray, S. O.** (2013). Pupil constrictions to photographs of the sun. *Journal of Vision, 13.* https://doi.org/10.1167/13.6.8

**Birch, J.** (2012). Worldwide prevalence of red-green color deficiency. *Journal of the Optical Society of America A, 29,* 313–320.

**Birch, J., Schnell, A. K., & Clayton, N. S.** (2020). Dimensions of animal consciousness. *Trends in Cognitive Sciences, 24*(10), 789–801. https://doi .org/10.1016/j.tics.2020.07.007

**Blackmore, S. J.** (2005). *Consciousness: A very short introduction.* Oxford University Press.

**Blackmore, S. J.** (2018, September). The hardest problem. *Scientific American, 319,* 48–53.

**blackviolin.net.** (2020, December 3). Black Violin Grammy nomination for "Take the Stairs" album. https:// blackviolin.net/news/

**Blair, C., & Raver, C. C.** (2012). Child development in the context of adversity: Experiential canalization of brain and behavior. *American Psychologist, 67,* 309–318.

**Blair, C., & Raver, C. C.** (2016). Poverty, stress, and brain development: New directions for prevention and intervention. *Academic Pediatrics, 16*(3), S30–S36. https://doi.org/10 .1016/j.acap.2016.01.010

**Blake, A. B., Nazarian, M., & Castel, A. D.** (2015). The Apple of the mind's eye: Everyday attention, metamemory, and reconstructive memory for the Apple logo. *Quarterly Journal of Experimental Psychology, 68,* 858–865.

**Blakemore, E.** (2016, June 9). The world's "ugliest" color could help people quit smoking. *Smithsonian.com.* http://www.smithsonianmag.com /smartnews/worlds-ugliest-color-could -help-people-quit-smoking-180959364 /?no-ist

**Blanchard, R.** (2008). Review and theory of handedness, birth order, and homosexuality in men. *Laterality, 13,* 51–70.

**Blanchard, R., Krupp, J., VanderLaan, D. P., Vasey, P. L., & Zucker, K. J.** (2020). A method yielding comparable estimates of the fraternal birth order and female fecundity effects in male homosexuality. *Proceedings of the Royal Society B, 287*(1923), 20192907. https://doi.org /10.1098/rspb.2019.2907

**Blasi, A.** (1980). Bridging moral cognition and moral action: A critical review of the literature. *Psychological Bulletin, 88,* 1–45.

**Blasi, G., Selvaggi, P., Fazio, L., Antonucci, L. A., Taurisano,** P., Masellis, R., Romano, R., Mancini, M., Zhang, F., Caforio, G., Popolizio, T., Apud, J., Weinberger, D. R., & Bertolino, A. (2015). Variation in dopamine D2 and serotonin 5-HT2A receptor genes is associated with working memory processing and response to treatment with antipsychotics. *Neuropsychopharmacology, 40,* 1600–1608.

**Blasiman, R. N., Larabee, D., & Fabry, D.** (2018). Distracted students: A comparison of multiple types of distractions on learning in online lectures. *Scholarship of Teaching and Learning in Psychology, 4*(4), 222–230. https://doi.org/10.1037/stl0000122

**Blass, T.** (1991). Understanding behavior in the Milgram obedience experiment: The role of personality, situations, and their interactions. *Journal of Personality and Social Psychology, 60,* 398–413.

**Blass, T.** (1999). The Milgram paradigm after 35 years: Some things we now know about obedience to authority. *Journal of Applied Social Psychology, 25,* 955–978.

**Blatchley, B., & O'Brien, K. R.** (2007). Deceiving the participant: Are we creating the reputational spillover effect? *North American Journal of Psychology, 9,* 519–534.

**Bleidorn, W., Hopwood, C. J., Ackerman, R. A., Witt, E. A., Kandler, C., Riemann, R., Samuel, D. B, & Donnellan, M. B.** (2020). The healthy personality from a basic trait perspective. *Journal of Personality and Social Psychology, 118*(6), 1207–1225. https://doi.org/10.1037/pspp0000231

**Bliese, P. D., Edwards, J. R., & Sonnentag, S.** (2017). Stress and well-being at work: A century of empirical trends reflecting theoretical and societal influences. *Journal of Applied Psychology, 102,* 389–402. https://doi .org/10.1037/apl0000109

**Bliss-Moreau, E., Bauman, M. D., & Amaral, D. G.** (2011). Neonatal amygdala lesions result in globally blunted affect in adult rhesus macaques. *Behavioral Neuroscience, 125,* 848–858.

**Bloch, M. H., McGuire, J., Landeros-Weisenberger, A., Leckman, J. F., & Pittenger, C.** (2010). Meta-analysis of the dose-response relationship of SSRI in obsessive-compulsive disorder. *Molecular Psychiatry, 15,* 850–855.

**Block, C. J., Koch, S. M., Liberman, B. E., Merriweather, T. J., & Roberson, L.** (2011). Contending with stereotype threat at work: A model of long-term responses. *Counseling Psychologist, 39,* 570–600.

**Boccella, K.** (2012, May 6). Blindness is no barrier for Center City triathlete. *The Philadelphia Inquirer.* http:// articles.philly.com/2012-05-06/news /31587179_1_husband-retinal-cancer -guide/3

Boerner, K., Jopp, D. S., Kim, K., Butt, A., Ribeiro, Ó., Araújo, L., & Rott, C. (2018). Thinking about the end of life when it is near: A comparison of German and Portuguese centenarians. *Research on Aging, 41*(3), 265–285. https://doi.org/10.1177/0164027518807919

Bogaard, G., Meijer, E. H., Vrij, A., & Merckelbach, H. (2016). Strong, but wrong: Lay people's and police officers' beliefs about verbal and nonverbal cues to deception. *PLOS ONE, 11*(6). e0156615. https://doi.org/10.1371/journal.pone.0156615

Bogel-Burroughs, N. (2021, March 30). Prosecutors say Derek Chauvin knelt on George Floyd for 9 minutes 29 seconds, longer than initially reported. *The New York Times*. https://www.nytimes.com/2021/03/30/us/derek-chauvin-george-floyd-kneel-9-minutes-29-seconds.html

Bojdani, E., Rajagopalan, A., Chen, A., Gearin, P., Olcott, W., Shankar, V., Cloutier, A., Solomon, H., Naqvi, N. Z., Batty, N., Festin, F. D., Tahera, D., Chang, G., & DeLisi, L. E. (2020). COVID-19 pandemic: Impact on psychiatric care in the United States, a review. *Psychiatry Research, 289*, Article 113069. https://doi.org/10.1016/j.psychres.2020.113069

Bold, K. W., Kong, G., Camenga, D. R., Simon, P., Cavallo, D. A., Morean, M. E., & Krishnan-Sarin, S. (2018). Trajectories of e-cigarette and conventional cigarette use among youth. *Pediatrics, 141*(1), Article e20171832. https://doi.org/10.1542/peds.2017-1832

Bold, K. W., Yoon, H., Chapman, G. B., & McCarthy, D. E. (2013). Factors predicting smoking in a laboratory-based smoking-choice task. *Experimental and Clinical Psychopharmacology, 21*, 133–143. https://doi.org/10.1037/a0031559

Bolhuis, K., Tiemeier, H., Jansen, P. R., Muetzel, R. L., Neumann, A., Hillegers, M. H., van den Akker, E. T. L., van Rossum, E. F. C., Jaddoe, V. W. V., Vernooij, M. W., White, T., & Kushner, S. A. (2019). Interaction of schizophrenia polygenic risk and cortisol level on pre-adolescent brain structure. *Psychoneuroendocrinology, 101*, 295–303. https://doi.org/10.1016/j.psyneuen.2018.12.231

Bölte, S., Girdler, S., & Marschik, P. B. (2019). The contribution of environmental exposure to the etiology of autism spectrum disorder. *Cellular and Molecular Life Sciences, 76*(7), 1275–1297. https://doi.org/10.1007/s00018-018-2988-4

Bonanno, G. A., Westphal, M., & Mancini, A. D. (2011). Resilience to loss and potential trauma. *Annual Review of Clinical Psychology, 7*, 1.1–1.25.

Bond, R., & Smith, P. B. (1996). Culture and conformity: A meta-analysis of studies using Asch's (1952b, 1956) line judgment task. *Psychological Bulletin, 119*, 111–137.

Boness, C. L., Lane, S. P., & Sher, K. J. (2019). Not all alcohol use disorder criteria are equally severe: Toward severity grading of individual criteria in college drinkers. *Psychology of Addictive Behaviors, 33*(1), 35–49. https://doi.org/10.1037/adb0000443

Bongers, P., van den Akker, K., Havermans, R., & Jansen, A. (2015). Emotional eating and Pavlovian learning: Does negative mood facilitate appetitive conditioning? *Appetite, 89*, 226–236.

Bonnet, L., Comte, A., Tatu, L., Millot, J. L., Moulin, T., & de Bustos, E. M. (2015). The role of the amygdala in the perception of positive emotions: An "intensity detector." *Frontiers in Behavioral Neuroscience, 9*. https://doi.org/10.3389/fnbeh.2015.00178

Bonnie, R. J., & Scott, E. S. (2013). The teenage brain: Adolescent brain research and the law. *Current Directions in Psychological Science, 22*, 158–161.

Boomsma, D. I., Helmer, Q., Nieuwboer, H. A., Hottenga, J. J., de Moor, M. H., van den Berg, S. M., Davies, G. E., Vink, J. M., Schouten, M. J., Dolan, C. V., Willemsen, G., Bartels, M., van Beijsterveldt, T. C. E. M., Ligthart, L., & de Geus, E. J. (2018). An extended twin-pedigree study of neuroticism in the Netherlands Twin Register. *Behavior Genetics, 48*(1), 1–11. https://doi.org/10.1007/s10519-017-9872-0

Boothroyd, L. G., Meins, E., Vukovic, J., & Burt, D. M. (2014). Developmental changes in children's facial preferences. *Evolution and Human Behavior, 35*, 376–383.

Borbély, A. A., Daan, S., Wirz-Justice, A., & Deboer, T. (2016). The two-process model of sleep regulation: A reappraisal. *Journal of Sleep Research, 25*, 131–143. https://doi.org/10.1111/jsr.12371

Bordier, A., Futerman, S., & Pulitzer, L. (2014). *Separated @ birth: A true love story of twin sisters reunited.* G.P. Putnam's Sons.

Borges, G., Nock, M. K., Abad, J. M. H., Hwang, I., Sampson, N. A., Alonso, J., Andrade, L. H., Angermeyer, M. C., Beautrais, A., Bromet, E., Bruffaerts, R., de Girolamo, G., Florescu, S., Gureje, O., Hu, C., Karam, E. G., Kovess-Masfety, V., Lee, S., Levinson, D., . . . Kessler, R. C. (2010). Twelve month prevalence of and risk factors for suicide attempts in the WHO world mental health surveys. *Journal of Clinical Psychiatry, 71*, 1617–1628.

Boring, E. G. (1953). A history of introspection. *Psychological Bulletin, 50*, 169–189.

Bornstein, R. F. (2019). The trait–type dialectic: Construct validity, clinical utility, and the diagnostic process. *Personality Disorders: Theory, Research, and Treatment, 10*(3), 199–209. https://doi.org/10.1037/per0000299

Borota, D., Murray, E., Keceli, G., Chang, A., Watabe, J. M., Ly, M., Toscano, J. P., & Yassa, M. A. (2014). Post-study caffeine administration enhances memory consolidation in humans. *Nature Neuroscience, 17*, 201–203.

Borra, J. E. (2005). *Roper v. Simmons. Journal of Gender, Social Policy, & the Law, 13*, 707–715.

Boscamp, E. (2013, July 11). Dining etiquette from around the world. *Huffington Post*. http://www.huffingtonpost.com/2013/07/11/dining-etiquette-around-the-world_n_3567015.html

Botta, P., Demmou, L., Kasugai, Y., Markovic, M., Xu, C., Fadok, J. P., Lu, T., Poe, M. M., Xu, L., Cook, J. M., Rudolph, U., Sah, P., Ferraguti, F., & Lüthi, A. (2015). Regulating anxiety with extrasynaptic inhibition. *Nature Neuroscience, 18*, 1493–1500.

Botzet, L. J., Rohrer, J. M., & Arslan, R. C. (2021). Analysing effects of birth order on intelligence, educational attainment, Big Five, and risk aversion in an Indonesian sample. *35*(2), 234–248. *European Journal of Personality*, doi.org/10.1002/per.2285

Bouchard, T. J., Jr., Lykken, D. T., McGue, M., Segal, N. L., & Tellegen, A. (1990). Sources of human psychological differences: The Minnesota Study of Twins Reared Apart. *Science, 250*, 223–228.

Boucher, P. (2018, March 29). Ricky Martin admits to love at first sight with husband Jwan Yosef: "I lost my breath." *People*. https://people.com/music/ricky-martin-husband-jwan-yosef-love-at-first-sight/

Bourgeois, A., Neveu, R., & Vuilleumier, P. (2016). How does awareness modulate goal-directed and stimulus-driven shifts of attention triggered by value learning? *PLOS ONE, 11*(8), e0160469. https://doi.org/10.1371/journal.pone.0160469

Bouton, C. E., Shaikhouni, A., Annetta, N. V., Bockbrader, M. A., Friedenberg, D. A., Nielson, D. M., Sharma, G., Sederberg, P. B., Glenn, B. C., Mysiw, W. J., Morgan, A. G., Deogaonkar, M., & Rezai, A. R. (2016). Restoring cortical control of functional movement in a human with quadriplegia. *Nature, 533*, 247–250. https://doi.org/10.1038/nature17435

Bouton, M. E., Mineka, S., & Barlow, D. H. (2001). A modern learning theory perspective on the etiology of panic disorder. *Psychological Review, 108*, 4–32.

Bowden, C. L., Calabrese, J. R., McElroy, S. L., Gyulai, L., Wassef, A., Petty, F., Pope, H. G., Jr., Chou, J. C.-Y., Keck, P. E., Jr., Rhodes, L. J., Swann, A. C., Hirschfeld, R. M. A., Wozniak, P. J., & Divalproex Maintenance Study Group. (2000). A randomized, placebo-controlled 12-month trial of divalproex and lithium in treatment of outpatients with bipolar I disorder. *Archives of General Psychiatry, 57*, 481–489.

Bower, G. H., Clark, M. C., Lesgold, A. M., & Winzenz, D. (1969). Hierarchical retrieval schemes and recall of categorized word lists. *Journal of Verbal Learning and Verbal Behavior, 8*, 323–343.

Bower, G. H., Gilligan, S. G., & Menteiro, K. P. (1981). Selectivity of learning caused by affective states. *Journal of Experimental Psychology: General, 110*, 451–473.

Bower, J. M., & Parsons, L. M. (2003, July 14). Rethinking "the lesser brain." *Scientific American, 289*, 51–57.

Bowers, J. S., Mattys, S. L., & Gage, S. H. (2009). Preserved implicit knowledge of a forgotten childhood language. *Psychological Science, 20*, 1064–1069.

Bowler, J., & Bourke, P. (2019). Facebook use and sleep quality: Light interacts with socially induced alertness. *British Journal of Psychology, 110*(3), 519–529. https://doi.org/10.1111/bjop.12351

Bowman, C. R., & Zeithamova, D. (2020). Training set coherence and set size effects on concept generalization and recognition. *Journal of Experimental Psychology: Learning, Memory, and Cognition, 46*(8), 1442–1464. https://doi.org/10.1037/xlm0000824

Boyd, K. (2020, January 16). *Smoking and eye disease.* American Academy of Ophthalmology. https://www.aao.org/eye-health/tips-prevention/smokers

Boyle, M. (2018, December 19). 5 Films that address mental health [Web log post]. National Alliance on Mental Illness. https://www.nami.org/Blogs/NAMI-Blog/December-2018/5-Films-That-Address-Mental-Health

Braat, M., Engelen, J., van Gemert, T., & Verhaegh, S. (2020). The rise and fall of behaviorism: The narrative and the numbers. *History of Psychology, 23*(3), 252–280. https://doi.org/10.1037/hop0000146

Brabender, V., & Fallon, A. (2019). *Group psychotherapy in inpatient, partial hospital, and residential care settings.* American Psychological Association. https://doi.org/10.1037/0000113-002

Bradbury, T. N., & Bodenmann, G. (2020). Interventions for couples. *Annual Review of Clinical Psychology, 16*, 99–123. https://doi.org/10.1146/annurev-clinpsy-071519-020546

**Bradley, L. A.** (2011). Culture, gender and clothing. *Paideusis—Journal for Interdisciplinary and Cross-Cultural Studies, 5*, A1–A6.

**Bradshaw, M. J., & Venkatesan, A.** (2016). Herpes simplex virus-1 encephalitis in adults: Pathophysiology, diagnosis, and management. *Neurotherapeutics, 13*(3), 493–508. https://doi.org/10.1007/s13311-016 -0433-7

**Brady, S. T., Reeves, S. L., Garcia, J., Purdie-Vaughns, V., Cook, J. E., Taborsky-Barba, S., Tomasetti, S., Davis, E. M., & Cohen, G. L.** (2016). The psychology of the affirmed learner: Spontaneous self-affirmation in the face of stress. *Journal of Educational Psychology, 108*, 353–373. https://doi .org/10.1037/edu0000091

**Brainard, J., & You, J.** (2018, October 26). Rethinking retractions. *Science, 362*(6413), 390–393.

**Branas, C. C., South, E., Kondo, M. C., Hohl, B. C., Bourgois, P., Wiebe, D. J., & MacDonald, J. M.** (2018). Citywide cluster randomized trial to restore blighted vacant land and its effects on violence, crime, and fear. *Proceedings of the National Academy of Sciences, 115*(12), 2946–2951. https:// doi.org/10.1073/pnas.1718503115

**Branch, J.** (2016, March 3). Brandi Chastain to donate her brain for C.T.E. research. *The New York Times.* http:// www.nytimes.com/2016/03/04/sports /soccer/brandi-chastain-to-donate -her-brain-for-cte-research.html?_r=0

**Brandone, A. C., Salkind, S. J., Golinkoff, R. M., & Hirsh-Pasek, K.** (2006). Language development. In G. G. Bear & K. M. Minke (Eds.), *Children's needs III: Development, prevention, and intervention* (pp. 499–514). National Association of School Psychologists.

**Brandt, J., & Benedict, R. H. B.** (1993). Assessment of retrograde amnesia: Findings with a new public events procedure. *Neuropsychology, 7*, 217–227.

**Branje, S.** (2018). Development of parent–adolescent relationships: Conflict interactions as a mechanism of change. *Child Development Perspectives, 12*(3), 171–176. https:// doi.org/10.1111/cdep.12278

**Brann, D. H., Tsukahara, T., Weinreb, C., Lipovsek, M., Van den Berge, K., Gong, B., Chance, R., Macaulay, I. C., Chou, H.-J., Fletcher, R. B., Das, D., Street, K., Roux de Bezieux, H., Choi, Y. G., Risso, D., Dudoit, S., Purdom, E., Mill, J., Hachem, R. A., . . . Datta, S. R.** (2020). Non-neuronal expression of SARS-CoV-2 entry genes mechanisms underlying COVID-19-associated anosmia. *Science Advances, 6*(31), Article eabc5801. https://doi.org/10.1126/sciadv.abc5801

**Branson, V., Turnbull, D., Dry, M. J., & Palmer, E.** (2019). How do young people experience stress? A qualitative examination of the indicators of distress and eustress in adolescence. *International Journal of Stress Management, 26*(3), 321–329. https://doi.org/10.1037/str0000102

**Branstetter, R.** (2020, October 20). How parents can support children with special needs during distance learning. *Greater Good Magazine.* https:// greatergood.berkeley.edu/article/item /how_parents_can_support_children _with_special_needs_during_distance _learning

**Brant, J.** (2016). *The boy who runs: The odyssey of Julius Achon.* Ballantine.

**Brase, G. L.** (2017). Emotional reactions to conditional rules of reciprocal altruism. *Evolutionary Behavioral Sciences, 11*, 294–308. https://doi.org/10.1037/ebs0000092

**Braus, M., & Morton, B.** (2020). Art therapy in the time of COVID-19. *Psychological Trauma: Theory, Research, Practice, and Policy, 12*(S1), S267–S268. https://doi.org/10.1037/tra0000746

**Bravo, A. J., Villarosa-Hurlocker, M. C., Pearson, M. R., & Protective Strategies Study Team.** (2018). College student mental health: An evaluation of the DSM-5 self-rated Level 1 cross-cutting symptom measure. *Psychological Assessment, 30*, 1382–1389. https://doi .org/10.1037/pas0000628

**Breakstone, J., Smith, M., Wineburg, S., Rapaport, A., Carle, J., Garland, M., & Saavedra, A.** (2019). Students' civic online reasoning: A national portrait. Stanford History Education Group & Gibson Consulting. https://purl.stanford .edu/gf151tb4868

**Breeden, P.** (n.d.). Dog whispering in the 20th century [Web log post]. https:// biologyofbehavior.wordpress.com/dog -whispering-in-the-21st-century/

**Breedlove, S. M.** (2017). Prenatal influences on human sexual orientation: Expectations versus data. *Archives of Sexual Behavior, 46*, 1583–1592. https:// doi.org/10.1007/s10508-016-0904-2

**Breland, K., & Breland, M.** (1951). A field of applied animal psychology. *American Psychologist, 6*, 202–204.

**Breland, K., & Breland, M.** (1961). The misbehavior of organisms. *American Psychologist, 16*, 681–684.

**Bremner, J. G., Slater, A., & Johnson, S.** (2015). Perception of object persistence: The origins of object permanence in infancy. *Child Development Perspectives, 9*, 7–13.

**Brendgen, M., Dionne, G., Girard, A., Boivin, M., Vitaro, F., & Pérusse, D.** (2005). Examining genetic and environmental effects on social aggression: A study of 6-year-old twins. *Child Development, 76*, 930–946.

**Brent, R. L.** (2004). Environmental causes of human congenital malformations: The pediatrician's role in dealing with these complex clinical problems caused by a multiplicity of environmental and genetic factors. *Pediatrics, 113*, 957–968.

**Brewin, C. R.** (2020). Tilting at windmills: Why attacks on repression are misguided. *Perspectives on Psychological Science,* 1745691620927674. https://doi .org/10.1177/1745691620927674

**Brewin, C. R., Andrews, B., & Mickes, L.** (2020). Regaining consensus on the reliability of memory. *Current Directions in Psychological Science, 29*(2), 121–125. https://doi .org/10.1177/0963721419898122

**Bridge, H., Harrold, S., Holmes, E. A., Stokes, M., & Kennard, C.** (2012). Vivid visual mental imagery in the absence of the primary visual cortex. *Journal of Neurology, 259*, 1062–1070.

**Bridgman, T., Cummings, S., & Ballard, J.** (2019). Who built Maslow's pyramid? A history of the creation of management studies' most famous symbol and its implications for management education. *Academy of Management Learning & Education, 18*(1), 81–98. https://doi.org/10.5465 /amle.2017.0351

**Briggs, K. C., & Myers, I. B.** (1998). *Myers–Briggs type indicator.* Consulting Psychologists Press.

**Briley, D. A., & Tucker-Drob, E. M.** (2014). Genetic and environmental continuity in personality development: A meta-analysis. *Psychological Bulletin, 140*, 1303–1331.

**Brimdyr, K., Cadwell, K., Widström, A. M., Svensson, K., & Phillips, R.** (2019). The effect of labor medications on normal newborn behavior in the first hour after birth: A prospective cohort study. *Early Human Development, 132*, 30–36. https://doi.org/10.1016/j .earlhumdev.2019.03.019

**Brito, C.** (2020, October 14). Cougar follows and lunges at Utah hiker in terrifying six-minute video. *CBS News.* https://www.cbsnews.com /news/cougar-utah-mountain-lion -man-chased/

**Broadbelt, K. G., Paterson, D. S., Rivera, K. D., Trachtenberg, F. L., & Kinney, H. C.** (2010). Neuroanatomic relationships between the GABAergic and serotonergic systems in the developing human medulla. *Autonomic Neuroscience: Basic & Clinical, 154*, 30–41.

**Brogaard, B., & Gatzia, D. E.** (2017). Cortical color and the cognitive sciences. *Topics in Cognitive Science, 9*(1), 135–150. https://doi .org/10.1111/tops.12241

**Brogaard, P., & Marlow, K.** (2012, December 11). Kim Peek, the real rain man [Web log post]. *Psychology Today.* http://www.psychologytoday.com /blog/the-superhuman-mind/201212 /kim-peek-the-real-rain-man

**Brooks, J. E., & Neville, H. A.** (2017). Interracial attraction among college men: The influence of ideologies, familiarity, and similarity. *Journal of Social and Personal Relationships, 34*(2), 166–183. https://doi.org/10.1177 /0265407515627508

**Brooks, M.** (2020, November 24). FDA orders stronger warnings on benzodiazepines. *Medscape.* https://www .medscape.com/viewarticle/937997

**Brothers, J. R., & Lohmann, K. J.** (2018). Evidence that magnetic navigation and geomagnetic imprinting shape spatial genetic variation in sea turtles. *Current Biology, 28*(8), 1325–1329. https://doi.org/10.1016/j .cub.2018.03.022

**Brotto, L. A.** (2010). The DSM diagnostic criteria for hypoactive sexual desire disorder in men. *Journal of Sexual Medicine, 7*, 2015–2030.

**Brown, A. S., & Nix, L. A.** (1996). Age-related changes in the tip-of-the-tongue experience. *American Journal of Psychology, 109*, 79–91.

**Brown, A. S., & Patterson, P. H.** (2011). Maternal infection and schizophrenia: Implications for prevention. *Schizophrenia Bulletin, 37*, 284–290.

**Brown, C. C., Raio, C. M., & Neta, M.** (2017). Cortisol responses enhance negative valence perception for ambiguous facial expressions. *Scientific Reports, 7*, Article 15107. https://doi.org/10.1038 /s41598-017-14846-3

**Brown, K.** (2021, February 5). *Is PA school what I expected?* [Video]. YouTube. https://www.youtube.com /watch?v=vElog10-Uys

**Brown, P. K., & Wald, G.** (1964). Visual pigments in single rods and cones of the human retina. *Science, 144*, 45.

**Brown, R., & Kulik, J.** (1977). Flashbulb memories. *Cognition, 5*, 73–99.

**Brown, S.** (2019). More than 1 in 4 undergraduate women experience sexual misconduct in college. *Chronicle of Higher Education, 66*(8).

**Brown, S. L, Nesse, R. M., Vinokur, A. D., & Smith, D. M.** (2003). Providing social support may be more beneficial than receiving it: Results from a prospective study of mortality. *Psychological Science, 14*, 320–327.

**Brownell, P.** (2010). *Gestalt therapy: A guide to contemporary practice.* Springer.

**Brownlee, W. J., Hardy, T. A., Fazekas, F., & Miller, D. H.** (2017). Diagnosis of multiple sclerosis: Progress and challenges. *The Lancet, 389*, 1336–1346. https://doi.org/10.1016/S0140 -6736(16)30959-X

**Bruett, H., Calloway, R. C., Tokowicz, N., & Coutanche, M. N.** (2020). Neural pattern similarity across concept exemplars predicts memory after a long delay. *NeuroImage, 219,* 117030. https://doi.org/10.1016/j.neuroimage.2020.117030

**Bruine de Bruin, W., Galesic, M., Parker, A. M., & Vardavas, R.** (2020). The role of social circle perceptions in "false consensus" about population statistics: Evidence from a national flu survey. *Medical Decision Making, 40*(2), 235–241. https://doi.org/10.1177/0272989X20904960

**Brummelman, E., & Sedikides, C.** (2020). Raising children with high self-esteem (but not narcissism). *Child Development Perspectives, 14*(2), 83–89. https://doi.org/10.1111/cdep.12362

**Brummelman, E., Thomaes, S., Nelemans, S. A., Orobio de Castro, B., Overbeek, G., & Bushmane, B. J.** (2015). Origins of narcissism in children. *Proceedings of the National Academy of Sciences, 112,* 3659–3662.

**Buchanan, L. R., Rooks-Peck, C. R., Finnie, R. K., Wethington, H. R., Jacob, V., Fulton, J. E., Johnson, D. B., Kahwati, L. C., Pratt, C. A., Ramirez, G., Mercer, S. L., Glanz, K., & Community Preventive Services Task Force.** (2016). Reducing recreational sedentary screen time: A community guide systematic review. *American Journal of Preventive Medicine, 50,* 402–415. https://doi.org/10.1016/j.amepre.2015.09.030

**Buchanan, T. W., Tranel, D., & Adolphs, R.** (2004). Anteromedial temporal lobe damage blocks startle modulation by fear and disgust. *Behavioral Neuroscience, 188,* 429–437.

**Buck, R.** (1980). Nonverbal behavior and the theory of emotion: The facial feedback hypothesis. *Journal of Personality and Social Psychology, 38,* 811–824.

**Budiman, A.** (2020, August 20). *Key findings about U.S. immigrants.* Pew Research Center. https://www.pewresearch.org/fact-tank/2020/08/20/key-findings-about-u-s-immigrants/

**Buettner, D.** (2015). *The Blue Zones solution.* National Geographic.

**Buettner, D., & Skemp, S.** (2016). Blue Zones: Lessons from the world's longest lived. *American Journal of Lifestyle Medicine, 10*(5), 318–321. https://doi.org/10.1177/1559827616637066

**Bufka, L. F., & Halfond, R.** (2016). Professional standards and guidelines. In J. C. Norcross, G. R. VandenBos, D. K. Freedheim, & L. E. Campbell (Eds.), *APA handbook of clinical psychology: Education and profession* (Vol. 5, pp. 355–373). American Psychological Association.

**Bulik, C. M., Kleiman, S. C., & Yilmaz, Z.** (2016). Genetic epidemiology of eating disorders. *Current Opinion in Psychiatry, 29*(6),

383–388. https://doi.org/10.1097/YCO.0000000000000275

**Bulpitt, C. J., Markowe, H. L. J., & Shipley, M. J.** (2001). Why do some people look older than they should? *Postgraduate Medical Journal, 77,* 578–581.

**Burda, J. E., Bernstein, A. M., & Sofroniew, M. V.** (2016). Astrocyte roles in traumatic brain injury. *Experimental Neurology, 275,* 305–315. https://doi.org/10.1016/j.expneurol.2015.03.020

**Bureau of Labor Statistics.** (2018). Employment by industry, occupation, and percent distribution, 2018 and projected 2028. 19-3030 Psychologists. Retrieved from https://www.bls.gov/ooh/life-physical-and-social-science/psychologists.htm#tab-6

**Bureau of Labor Statistics.** (2019a). *Occupational outlook handbook: Childcare workers.* https://www.bls.gov/ooh/personal-care-and-service/childcare-workers.htm

**Bureau of Labor Statistics.** (2019b). *Occupational outlook handbook: Customer service representatives.* https://www.bls.gov/ooh/office-and-administrative-support/customer-servicerepresentatives.htm

**Bureau of Labor Statistics.** (2019c). *Occupational outlook handbook: High school teachers.* https://www.bls.gov/ooh/education-training-and-library/high-school-teachers.htm

**Bureau of Labor Statistics.** (2019d). *Occupational outlook handbook: Human resources specialists.* https://www.bls.gov/ooh/business-and-financial/human-resources-specialists.htm **Bureau of Labor Statistics.** (2019e). *Occupational Outlook handbook: Insurance sales agents.* https://www.bls.gov/ooh/sales/insurance-sales-agents.htm

**Bureau of Labor Statistics.** (2019f). *Occupational outlook handbook: Medical and health services managers.* https://www.bls.gov/ooh/management/medical-and-health-services-managers.htm

**Bureau of Labor Statistics.** (2019g). *Occupational outlook handbook: Police and detectives.* https://www.bls.gov/ooh/protective-service/police-and-detectives.htm

**Bureau of Labor Statistics.** (2019h). *Occupational outlook handbook: Probation officers and correctional treatment specialists.* https://www.bls.gov/ooh/community-and-social-service/probation-officers-and-correctional-treatment-specialists.htm

**Bureau of Labor Statistics.** (2019i). *Occupational outlook handbook: Psychologists.* https://www.bls.gov/ooh/life-physical-and-social-science/psychologists.htm

**Bureau of Labor Statistics.** (2019j). *Occupational outlook handbook: Public relations specialists.* https://www.bls.gov/ooh/media-and-communication/public-relations-specialists.htm

**Bureau of Labor Statistics.** (2019k). *Occupational outlook handbook: Recreation workers.* https://www.bls.gov/ooh/personal-care-and-service/recreation-workers.htm

**Bureau of Labor Statistics.** (2019l). *Occupational outlook handbook: Secretaries and administrative assistants.* https://www.bls.gov/ooh/office-and-administrative-support/secretaries-and-administrative-assistants.htm

**Bureau of Labor Statistics.** (2019m). *Occupational outlook handbook: Social and community service managers.* https://www.bls.gov/ooh/management/social-and-community-service-managers.htm

**Bureau of Labor Statistics.** (2019n). *Occupational outlook handbook: Social and human service assistants.* https://www.bls.gov/ooh/community-and-social-service/social-and-human-service-assistants.htm

**Bureau of Labor Statistics.** (2019o). *Occupational outlook handbook: Substance abuse, behavioral disorder, and mental health counselors.* https://www.bls.gov/ooh/community-and-social-service/substance-abuse-behavioral-disorder-and-mental-health-counselors.htm

**Burger, J. M.** (2009). Replicating Milgram: Would people still obey today? *American Psychologist, 64,* 1–11.

**Burger, J. M.** (2015). *Personality* (9th ed.). Wadsworth, Cengage Learning.

**Burlingame, G. M., & Baldwin, S.** (2011). Group therapy. In J. C. Norcross, G. R. VandenBos, & D. K. Freedheim (Eds.), *History of psychotherapy: Continuity and change* (2nd ed., pp. 505–515). American Psychological Association.

**Burnette, J. L., Pollack, J. M., & Forsyth, D. R.** (2011). Leadership in extreme contexts: A groupthink analysis of the May 1996 Mount Everest disaster. *Journal of Leadership Studies, 4,* 29–40.

**Burns, K. C., & Gurung, R. A. R.** (2020). A longitudinal multisite study of the efficacy of retrieval and spaced practice in introductory psychology. *Scholarship of Teaching and Learning in Psychology.* Advance online publication. https://doi.org/10.1037/stl0000206

**Burstein, A. G., & Loucks, S.** (1989). *Rorschach's test: Scoring and interpretation.* Hemisphere.

**Burt, D. M., & Hausmann, M.** (2019). Hemispheric asymmetries in categorical facial expression perception. *Emotion, 19*(4), 584–592. https://doi.org/10.1037/emo0000460

**Burton, H.** (2003). Visual cortex activity in early and late blind people. *Journal of Neuroscience, 23,* 4005–4011.

**Burton, J. Z., & Warne, R. T.** (2020). The neglected intelligence

course: Needs and suggested solutions. *Teaching of Psychology, 47*(2), 130–140. https://doi.org/10.1177/0098628320901381

**Burton, N.** (2017, July 12). Gender variation and same-sex relations in precolonial times [Web log post]. *Psychology Today.* https://www.psychologytoday.com/us/blog/hide-and-seek/201707/gender-variation-and-same-sex-relations-in-precolonial-times

**Bush, N. E., Armstrong, C. M., & Hoyt, T. V.** (2019). Smartphone apps for psychological health: A brief state of the science review. *Psychological Services, 16*(2), 188–195. https://doi.org/10.1037/ser0000286

**Bushdid, C., Magnasco, M. O., Vosshall, L. B., & Keller, A.** (2014). Humans can discriminate more than 1 trillion olfactory stimuli. *Science, 343,* 1370–1372.

**Bushman, B. J., Newman, K., Calvert, S. L., Downey, G., Dredze, M., Gottfredson, M., Jablonski, N. G., Masten, A. S., Morrill, C., Neill, D. B., Romer, D., & Webster, D. W.** (2016). Youth violence: What we know and what we need to know. *American Psychologist, 71*(1), 17–39. https://doi.org/10.1037/a0039687

**Buss, D. M.** (2018). Sexual and emotional infidelity: Evolved gender differences in jealousy prove robust and replicable. *Perspectives on Psychological Science, 13,* 155–160. https://doi.org/10.1177/1745691617698225

**Buss, D. M., & Penke, L.** (2015). Evolutionary personality psychology. In M. Mikulincer, P. R. Shaver, M. L. Cooper, & R. J. Larsen (Eds.), *APA handbook of personality and social psychology* (Vol. 4, pp. 3–29). American Psychological Association.

**Bussey, K., & Bandura, A.** (1999). Social cognitive theory of gender development and differentiation. *Psychological Review, 106,* 676–713.

**Butcher, J. N., & Rouse, S. V.** (1996). Personality: Individual differences and clinical assessment. *Annual Review of Psychology, 47,* 87–111.

**Butler, J.** (2015). Hypnosis for dental professionals. *BDJ Team, 41*(1). https://doi.org/10.1038/bdjteam.2015.28

**Bzdok, D., & Dunbar, R. I.** (2020). The neurobiology of social distance. *Trends in Cognitive Sciences, 24*(9), 717–733. https://doi.org/10.1016/j.tics.2020.05.016

**Bzdok, D., Varoquaux, G., & Steyerberg, E. W.** (2020). Prediction, not association, paves the road to precision medicine. *JAMA Psychiatry.* https://doi.org/10.1001/jamapsychiatry.2020.2549

**Cabral, R. R., & Smith, T. B.** (2011). Racial/ethnic matching of clients and therapists in mental health services: A meta-analytic review of preferences, perceptions, and outcomes. *Journal of Counseling Psychology, 58,* 537–554.

Caldwell, J. A., Caldwell, J. L., Thompson, L. A., & Lieberman, H. R. (2019). Fatigue and its management in the workplace. *Neuroscience & Biobehavioral Reviews, 96,* 272–289. https://doi.org/10.1016/j.neubiorev.2018.10.024

Callan, M. J., Ferguson, H. J., & Bindemann, M. (2013). Eye movements to audiovisual scenes reveal expectations of a just world. *Journal of Experimental Psychology: General, 142,* 34–40. https://doi.org/10.1037/a0028261

Callard, F., & Perego, E. (2021). How and why patients made Long Covid. *Social Science & Medicine, 268,* Article 113426. https://doi.org/10.1016/j.socscimed.2020.113426

Calkins, H. (2021, January 1). Online therapy is here to stay. *Monitor on Psychology, 52,* 78. https://www.apa.org/monitor/2021/01/trends-online-therapy

Callier, V. (2018, December 10). Yes, it is getting harder to publish in prestigious journals if you haven't already. *Science.* https://doi.org/10.1126/science.caredit.aaw3380

Calvert, S. L., Appelbaum, M., Dodge, K. A., Graham, S., Nagayama Hall, G. C., Hamby, S., Fasig-Caldwell, L. G., Citkowicz, M., Galloway, D. P., & Hedges, L. V. (2017). The American Psychological Association Task Force assessment of violent video games: Science in the service of public interest. *American Psychologist, 72*(2), 126–143. https://doi.org/10.1037/a0040413

Camerer, C. F., Dreber, A., Holzmeister, F., Ho, T. H., Huber, J., Johannesson, M., Kirchler, M., Nave, G., Nosek, B. A., Pfeiffer, T., Altmejd, A., Buttrick, N., Chan, T., Chen, Y., Forsell, E., Gampa, A., Heikensten, E., Hummer, L., Imai, T., I, . . . Wu, H. (2018). Evaluating the replicability of social science experiments in *Nature* and *Science* between 2010 and 2015. *Nature Human Behaviour, 2*(9), 637–644. https://doi.org/10.1038/s41562-018-0399-z

Campbell, A. (1999). Staying alive: Evolution, culture, and women's intrasexual aggression. *Behavioral and Brain Sciences, 22,* 203–252.

Campbell, D. T., & Stanley, J. C. (1963). Experimental and quasi-experimental designs for research. In N. L. Gage (Ed.), *Handbook of research on teaching* (pp. 171–246). Houghton, Mifflin.

Campbell, G. A., & Rosner, M. H. (2008). The agony of ecstasy: MDMA (3,4-methylenedioxymethamphetamine) and the kidney. *Clinical Journal of the American Society of Nephrology, 3,* 1852–1860.

Campos, F., Sobrino, T., Ramos-Cabrer, P., Argibay, B., Agulla, J., Pérez-Mato, M., Rodríguez-González, R., Brea, D., & Castillo, J. (2011). Neuroprotection by glutamate oxaloacetate transaminase in ischemic stroke: An experimental study. *Journal of Cerebral Blood Flow & Metabolism, 31,* 1378–1386.

Cannon, D. S., Baker, T. B., Gino, A., & Nathan, P. E. (1986). Alcohol-aversion therapy: Relation between strength of aversion and abstinence. *Journal of Consulting and Clinical Psychology, 54,* 825–830.

Cannon, W. B. (1927). The James-Lange theory of emotions: A critical examination and an alternative theory. *American Journal of Psychology, 39,* 106–124.

Cannon, W. B., & Washburn, A. L. (1912). An explanation of hunger. *American Journal of Physiology, 29,* 441–454.

Cantero, J. L., Atienza, M., Salas, R. M., & Gómez, C. M. (1999). Alpha EEG coherence in different brain states: An electrophysiological index of the arousal level in human subjects. *Neuroscience Letters, 271,* 167–170.

Caporro, M., Haneef, Z., Yeh, H. J., Lenartowicz, A., Buttinelli, C., Parvizi, J., & Stern, J. M. (2012). Functional MRI of sleep spindles and K-complexes. *Clinical Neurophysiology, 123*(2), 303–309.

Carbon, C. C. (2014). Understanding human perception by human-made illusions. *Frontiers in Human Neuroscience, 8,* art. 566.

Cardeña, E. (2020). Derangement of the senses or alternate epistemological pathways? Altered consciousness and enhanced functioning. *Psychology of Consciousness: Theory, Research, and Practice, 7*(3), 242–261. https://doi.org/10.1037/cns0000175

Cardno, A. G., & Owen, M. J. (2014). Genetic relationships between schizophrenia, bipolar disorder, and schizoaffective disorder. *Schizophrenia Bulletin, 40,* 504–515.

Carey, B. (2008, December 4). H.M., an unforgettable amnesiac, dies at 82. *The New York Times.* http://www.nytimes.com/2008/12/05/us/05hm.html?pagewanted=all&_r=0

Carlbring, P., Andersson, G., Cuijpers, P., Riper, H., & Hedman-Lagerlöf, E. (2018). Internet-based vs. face-to-face cognitive behavior therapy for psychiatric and somatic disorders: An updated systematic review and meta-analysis. *Cognitive Behaviour Therapy, 47,* 1–18. https://doi.org/10.1080/16506073.2017.1401115

Carlson, A. (2018, November 15). Thai soccer team Rescued after weeks in cave don't seem to be "traumatized in any way." *People.* https://people.com/human-interest/thai-soccer-team-psychological-recovery-after-rescue/

Carr, M., Konkoly, K., Mallett, R., Edwards, C., Appel, K., & Blagrove, M. (2020). Combining presleep cognitive training and REM-sleep stimulation in a laboratory morning nap for lucid dream induction. *Psychology of Consciousness: Theory, Research, and Practice.* Advance online publication. https://doi.org/10.1037/cns0000227

Carr, P. B., Dweck, C. S., & Pauker, K. (2012). "Prejudiced" behavior without prejudice? Beliefs about the malleability of prejudice affect interracial interactions. *Journal of Personality and Social Psychology, 103,* 452–471.

Carrier, L. M., Rosen, L. D., Cheever, N. A., & Lim, A. F. (2015). Causes, effects, and practicalities of everyday multitasking. *Developmental Review, 35,* 64–78.

Carroll, Y. I., Eichwald, J., Scinicariello, F., Hoffman, H. J., Deitchman, S., Radke, M. S., Themann, C. L., & Breysse, P. (2017). Vital signs: Noise-induced hearing loss among adults—United States 2011–2012. *MMWR: Morbidity and Mortality Weekly Report, 66*(5), 139–144. https://doi.org/10.15585/mmwr.mm6605e3

Carson, H. (2011). *Captain for life: My story as a hall of fame linebacker.* St. Martin's Press.

Carstensen, L. L., Turan, B., Scheibe, S., Ram, N., Ersner-Hershfield, H., Samanez-Larkin, G. R., Brooks, K. P., & Nesselroade, J. R. (2011). Emotional experience improves with age: Evidence based on over 10 years of experience sampling. *Psychology and Aging, 26,* 21–33.

Carter, B. D., Abnet, C. C., Feskanich, D., Freedman, N. D., Hartge, P., Lewis, C. D., Ockene, J. K., Prentice, R. L., Speizer, F. E., Thun, M. J., & Jacobs, E. J. (2015). Smoking and mortality—beyond established causes. *New England Journal of Medicine, 372,* 631–640. https://doi.org/10.1056/NEJMsa1407211

Carter, C. J. (2007). eIF2B and oligodendrocyte survival: Where nature and nurture meet in bipolar disorder and schizophrenia? *Schizophrenia Bulletin, 33,* 1343–1353.

Carter, K. (2020, July 14). School psychologists adapt to help students during COVID-19. *American Psychological Association.* https://www.apa.org/members/content/school-psychologists-covid-19

Caruso, J. P., & Sheehan, J. P. (2017). Psychosurgery, ethics, and media: A history of Walter Freeman and the lobotomy. *Neurosurgical Focus, 43*(3), Article E6. https://doi.org/10.3171/2017.6.FOCUS17257

Caspi, A., Roberts, B. W., & Shiner, R. L. (2005). Personality development: Stability and change. *Annual Review of Psychology, 56,* 453–484.

Cassidy, J. (2001). Truth, lies, and intimacy: An attachment perspective. *Attachment & Human Development, 3,* 121–155.

Castillo, E. G., Chung, B., Bromley, E., Kataoka, S. H., Braslow, J. T., Essock, S. M., Young, A. S., Greenberg, J. M., Miranda, J., Dixon, L. B., & Wells, K. B. (2018). Community, public policy, and recovery from mental illness: Emerging research and initiatives. *Harvard Review of Psychiatry, 26*(2), 70–81. https://doi.org/10.1097/HRP.0000000000000178

Castrillon, G., Sollmann, N., Kurcyus, K., Razi, A., Krieg, S. M., & Riedl, V. (2020). The physiological effects of noninvasive brain stimulation fundamentally differ across the human cortex. *Science Advances, 6*(5), Article eaay2739. https://advances.sciencemag.org/content/6/5/eaay2739

Catalino, L. I., & Fredrickson, B. L. (2011). A Tuesday in the life of a flourisher: The role of positive emotional reactivity in optimal mental health. *Emotion, 11,* 938–950.

Cattell, R. B. (1950). *Personality: A systematic theoretical and factual study.* McGraw-Hill.

Cattell, R. B. (1973a). *Personality and mood by questionnaire.* Jossey-Bass.

Cattell, R. B. (1973b). Personality pinned down. *Psychology Today, 7,* 40–46

Cattell, R. B., Eber, H. W., & Tatsuoka, M. M. (1970). *Handbook for the sixteen personality factor questionnaire (16PF).* Institute for Personality and Ability Testing.

Catts, V. S., Lai, Y. L., Weickert, C. S., Weickert, T. W., & Catts, S. V. (2016). A quantitative review of the postmortem evidence for decreased cortical N-methyl-d-aspartate receptor expression levels in schizophrenia: How can we link molecular abnormalities to mismatch negativity deficits? *Biological Psychology, 116,* 57–67. https://doi.org/10.1016/j.biopsycho.2015.10.013

Cavadel, E. W., & Frye, D. A. (2017). Not just numeracy and literacy: Theory of mind development and school readiness among low-income children. *Developmental Psychology, 53,* 2290–2303. https://doi.org/10.1037/dev0000409

CBS/AP. (2018, July 18). Thai soccer team opens up about dramatic cave rescue. *CBS News.* https://www.cbsnews.com/live-news/thailand-soccer-team-leaves-hospital-speaks-in-chiang-rai-today-2018-07-18/

**CBS News.** (2018, July 13). Father of youngest Thai cave survivor describes how boys became trapped, coach's response. https://www.cbsnews.com/news/thailand-cave-rescue-father-of-youngest-survivor-describes-how-team-became-trapped/

**Ceci, S., & Williams, W. M.** (2009). Yes: The scientific truth must be pursued. *Nature, 457,* 788–789.

**Ceci, S. J., & Williams, W. M.** (2018). Who decides what is acceptable speech on campus? Why restricting free speech is not the answer. *Perspectives on Psychological Science, 13*(3), 299–323. https://doi.org/10.1177/1745691618767324

**Center for Behavioral Health Statistics and Quality.** (2015). *Behavioral health trends in the United States: Results from the 2014 National Survey on Drug Use and Health* (HHS Publication No. SMA 15-4927, NSDUH Series H-50). https://www.samhsa.gov/data/sites/default/files/NSDUH-FRR1-2014/NSDUH-FRR1-2014.pdf

**Center on Budget and Policy Priorities.** (2021, January 8). Tracking the COVID-19 recession's effects on food, housing, and employment hardships. https://www.cbpp.org/research/poverty-and-inequality/tracking-the-covid-19-recessions-effects-on-food-housing-and

**Centers for Disease Control and Prevention (CDC).** (2017). *Genital herpes—CDC Fact Sheet* (detailed). https://www.cdc.gov/std/herpes/stdfact-herpes-detailed.htm

**Centers for Disease Control and Prevention (CDC).** (2017, May 15). *Health effects of cigarette smoking.* https://www.cdc.gov/tobacco/data_statistics/fact_sheets/health_effects/effects_cig_smoking/index.htm

**Centers for Disease Control and Prevention (CDC).** (2018, June 7). Suicide rising across the US. CDC Vitalsigns. https://www.cdc.gov/vitalsigns/pdf/vs-0618-suicide-H.pdf

**Centers for Disease Control and Prevention (CDC).** (2020, January 31). *Antibiotic resistance questions and answers.* https://www.cdc.gov/antibiotic-use/community/about/antibiotic-resistance-faqs.html

**Centers for Disease Control and Prevention (CDC).** (2020, February 27). *Health effects of secondhand smoke.* https://www.cdc.gov/tobacco/data_statistics/fact_sheets/secondhand_smoke/health_effects/index.htm

**Centers for Disease Control and Prevention (CDC).** (2020, March 19). *Drug overdose deaths.* https://www.cdc.gov/drugoverdose/data/statedeaths.html

**Centers for Disease Control and Prevention (CDC).** (2020, April 28). Tobacco-related mortality. https://www.cdc.gov/tobacco/data_statistics/fact_sheets/health_effects/tobacco_related_mortality/index.htm

**Centers for Disease Control and Prevention (CDC).** (2020, May 21). *Smoking and tobacco use: Fast facts.* https://www.cdc.gov/tobacco/data_statistics/fact_sheets/fast_facts/index.htm#cigarette-smoking

**Centers for Disease Control and Prevention (CDC).** (2020, July 28). *Sexually transmitted disease surveillance 2018.* https://www.cdc.gov/std/stats18/default.htm

**Centers for Disease Control and Prevention (CDC).** (2020, October 1). *Deaths from excessive alcohol use in the U.S.* https://www.cdc.gov/alcohol/features/excessive-alcohol-deaths.html

**Centers for Disease Control and Prevention (CDC).** (2020, December 31). *How to protect yourself and others.* https://www.cdc.gov/coronavirus/2019-ncov/prevent-getting-sick/prevention.html

**Centers for Disease Control and Prevention (CDC).** (n.d.-a). *About teen pregnancy.* http://www.cdc.gov/teenpregnancy/about/index.htm

**Centers for Disease Control and Prevention (CDC).** (n.d.-b). *Common questions about vaccines.* https://www.cdc.gov/vaccines/parents/FAQs.html

**Centers for Disease Control and Prevention (CDC).** (n.d.-c). *How much physical activity do adults need?* https://www.cdc.gov/physicalactivity/basics/adults/index.htm

**Centers for Disease Control and Prevention (CDC).** (n.d.-d). *Important milestones: Your baby at six months.* http://www.cdc.gov/ncbddd/actearly/milestones/milestones-6mo.html

**Centers for Disease Control and Prevention (CDC).** (n.d.-e). *Sexually transmitted diseases: Adolescents and young adults.* https://www.cdc.gov/std/life-stages-populations/adolescents-youngadults.htm

**Centers for Disease Control and Prevention (CDC).** (n.d.-f). *Suicide prevention: Risk and protective factors.* https://www.cdc.gov/suicide/factors/index.html?CDC_AA_refVal=https%3A%2F%2Fwww.cdc.gov%2Fviolenceprevention%2Fsuicide%2Friskprotectivefactors.html

**Centers for Disease Control and Prevention and National Center for Health Statistics (CDC/NCHS), National Vital Statistics System, Mortality.** (2016). *Overdose deaths involving opioids, United States, 2000–2015.* CDC WONDER. US Department of Health and Human Services, CDC. https://www.cdc.gov/drugoverdose/data/index.html

**Centers for Disease Control and Prevention (CDC), WISQARS.** (n.d.). *Leading causes of death reports, 1981–2018.* https://webappa.cdc.gov/sasweb/ncipc/leadcause.html

**Centre for Addiction and Mental Health.** (2010). *LSD: What's LSD?* http://www.camh.ca/en/hospital/health_information/a_z_mental_health and_addiction_information/LSD/Pages/default.aspx

**Cerda-Molina, A. L., Hernández-López, L., de la O, C. E., Chavira-Ramírez, R., & Mondragón-Ceballos, R.** (2013). Changes in men's salivary testosterone and cortisol levels, and in sexual desire after smelling female axillary and vulvar scents. *Frontiers in Endocrinology, 28*(4), art. 159. https://doi.org/10.3389/fendo.2013.00159

**Cesana-Arlotti, N., Martín, A., Téglás, E., Vorobyova, L., Cetnarski, R., & Bonatti, L. L.** (2018). Precursors of logical reasoning in preverbal human infants. *Science, 359*(6381), 1263–1266. https://doo.org/10.1126/science.aao3539

**Chae, Y., Goodman, M., Goodman, G. S., Troxel, N., McWilliams, K., Thompson, R. A., Shaver, P. R., & Widaman, K. F.** (2018). How children remember the Strange Situation: The role of attachment. *Journal of Experimental Child Psychology, 166,* 360–379. https://doi.org/10.1016/j.jecp.2017.09.001

**Chaiken, S., & Eagly, A. H.** (1976). Communication modality as a determinant of message persuasiveness and message comprehensibility. *Journal of Personality and Social Psychology, 34,* 605–614.

**Chamberlain, R., Drake, J. E., Kozbelt, A., Hickman, R., Siev, J., & Wagemans, J.** (2019). Artists as experts in visual cognition: An update. *Psychology of Aesthetics, Creativity, and the Arts, 13*(1), 58–73. https://doi.org/10.1037/aca0000156

**Chan, D. K., Zhang, X., Fung, H. H., & Hagger, M. S.** (2015). Does emotion and its daily fluctuation correlate with depression? A cross-cultural analysis among six developing countries. *Journal of Epidemiology and Global Health, 5,* 65–74.

**Chan, Y. C., Hsu, W. C., Liao, Y. J., Chen, H. C., Tu, C. H., & Wu, C. L.** (2018). Appreciation of different styles of humor: An fMRI study. *Scientific Reports, 8*(1), 15649. https://doi.org/10.1038/s41598-018-33715-1

**Charlesworth, T. E., & Banaji, M. R.** (2019). Patterns of implicit and explicit attitudes: I. Long-term change and stability from 2007 to 2016. *Psychological Science, 30*(2), 174–192. https://doi.org/10.1177/0956797618813087

**Charlton, B., & Verghese, A.** (2010). Caring for Ivan Ilyich. *Journal of General Internal Medicine, 25,* 93–95.

**Chatterjee, R.** (2015). Out of the darkness. *Science, 350*(6259), 372–375.

**Chatzisarantis, N. L. D., Kamarova, S., Twomey, C., Hansen, G., Harris, M., Windus, J., Bateson, A., & Hagger, M. S.** (2021). Relationships between health promoting activities, life satisfaction, and depressive symptoms in unemployed individuals. *European Journal of Health Psychology, 28*(1), 1–12. https://doi.org/10.1027/2512-8442/a000058

**Chawla, J.** (2018, June 14). Neurologic effects of caffeine. *Medscape.* https://emedicine.medscape.com/article/1182710-overview

**Chechik, G., Meilijson, I., & Ruppin, E.** (1998). Synaptic pruning in development: A computational account. *Neural Computation, 10,* 1759–1777.

**Chen, A.** (2018, October 10). How accurate are personality tests? *Scientific American.* https://www.scientificamerican.com/article/how-accurate-are-personality-tests/

**Chen, A. C. H., Chang, R. Y. H., Besherat, A., & Baack, D. W.** (2013). Who benefits from multiple brand celebrity endorsements? An experimental investigation. *Psychology & Marketing, 30,* 850–860.

**Chen, E. H., & Bailey, D. H.** (2021). Dual-task studies of working memory and arithmetic performance: A meta-analysis. *Journal of Experimental Psychology: Learning, Memory, and Cognition, 47*(2), 220–233. https://doi.org/10.1037/xlm0000822

**Chen, H., Chen, S., Zeng, L., Zhou, L., & Hou, S.** (2014). Revisiting Einstein's brain in Brain Awareness Week. *Bioscience Trends, 8*(5), 286–289.

**Chen, H., Kwong, J. C., Copes, R., Hystad, P., van Donkelaar, A., Tu, K., Brook, J. R., Goldberg, M. S., Martin, R. V., Murray, B. J., Wilton, A. S., Kopp, A., & Burnett, R. T.** (2017). Exposure to ambient air pollution and the incidence of dementia: A population-based cohort study. *Environment International, 108,* 271–277. https://doi.org/10.1016/j.envint.2017.08.020

**Chen, P., Chavez, O., Ong, D. C., & Gunderson, B.** (2017). Strategic resource use for learning: A self-administered intervention that guides self-reflection on effective resource use enhances academic performance. *Psychological Science, 28,* 774–785. https://doi.org/10.1177/0956797617696456

**Chen, Q., Larochelle, M. D., Weaver, D. T., Lietz, A. P., Mueller, P. P., Mercaldo, S., Wakeman, S. E., Freedberg, K. A., Raphel, T. J., Knudsen, A. B., Pandharipande, P. V., & Chhatwal, J.** (2019). Prevention of prescription opioid misuse and projected overdose deaths in the United States. *JAMA Network Open, 2,* e187621. https://doi.org/10.1001/jamanetworkopen.2018.7621

Chen, R., McIntosh, S., Hemby, S. E., Sun, H., Sexton, T., Martin, T. J., & Childers, S. R. (2018). High and low doses of cocaine intake are differentially regulated by dopamine D2 receptors in the ventral tegmental area and the nucleus accumbens. *Neuroscience Letters, 671*, 133–139. https://doi.org/10.1016/j.neulet.2018.02.026

Chen, T., Su, H., Zhong, N., Tan, H., Li, X., Meng, Y., Duan, C., Zhang, C., Bao, J., Xu, D., Song, W., Zou, J., Liu, T., Zhan, Q., Jiang, H., & Song, W. (2020). Disrupted brain network dynamics and cognitive functions in methamphetamine use disorder: Insights from EEG microstates. *BMC Psychiatry, 20*(1), 1–11. https://doi.org/10.1186/s12888-020-02743-5

Cheng, C., Cheung, S.-F., Chio, J. H.-M., & Chan, M.-P. S. (2013). Cultural meaning of perceived control: A meta-analysis of locus of control and psychological symptoms across 18 cultural regions. *Psychological Bulletin, 139*, 152–188.

Cheng, D. T., Knight, D. C., Smith, C. N., & Helmstetter, F. J. (2006). Human amygdala activity during the expression of fear responses. *Behavioral Neuroscience, 120*, 1187–1195.

Cheng, H., & Furnham, A. (2019). Teenage locus of control, psychological distress, educational qualifications and occupational prestige as well as gender as independent predictors of adult binge drinking. *Alcohol, 76*, 103–109. https://doi.org/10.1016/j.alcohol.2018.08.008

Cheng, P. W. C., Chang, W. C., Lo, G. G., Chan, K. W. S., Lee, H. M. E., Hui, L. M. C., Suen, Y. N., Leung, Y. L. E., Yeung, K. M. P. A., Chen, S., Mak, K. F. H., Sham, P. C., Santangelo, B., Veronese, M., Ho, C.H., Chen, Y. H. E., & Howes, O. D. (2020). The role of dopamine dysregulation and evidence for the transdiagnostic nature of elevated dopamine synthesis in psychosis: A positron emission tomography (PET) study comparing schizophrenia, delusional disorder, and other psychotic disorders. *Neuropsychopharmacology, 45*(11), 1870–1876. https://doi.org/10.1038/s41386-020-0740-x

Cheng, P., Tallent, G., Burgess, H. J., Tran, K. M., Roth, T., & Drake, C. L. (2018). Daytime sleep disturbance in night shift work and the role of PERIOD3. *Journal of Clinical Sleep Medicine, 14*(03), 393–400. https://doi.org/10.5664/jcsm.6984

Cheng, S. Y., Suh, S. Y., Morita, T., Oyama, Y., Chiu, T. Y., Koh, S. J., Kim, H. S., Hwang, S.-J., Yoshie, T., & Tsuneto, S. (2015). A cross-cultural study on behaviors when death is approaching in East Asian countries: What are the physician-perceived common beliefs and practices?

*Medicine, 94*, e1573. https://doi.org/10.1097/MD.0000000000001573

Cheng, T. L., Johnson, S. B., & Goodman, E. (2016). Breaking the intergenerational cycle of disadvantage: The three generation approach. *Pediatrics, 136*(6), Article e20152467. https://doi.org/10.1542/peds.2015-2467

Cherry, K. (2020, December 30). What does LGBTQ+ mean? *Verywell Mind.* https://www.verywellmind.com/what-does-lgbtq-mean-5069804

Chesham, R. K., Malouff, J. M., & Schutte, N. S. (2018). Meta-analysis of the efficacy of virtual reality exposure therapy for social anxiety. *Behaviour Change, 35*(3), 152–166.

Cheung, R. Y. M., Bhowmik, M. K., & Hue, M.-T. (2020). Why does acculturative stress elevate depressive symptoms? A longitudinal study with emotion regulation as a mediator. *Journal of Counseling Psychology, 67*(5), 645–652. https://doi.org/10.1037/cou0000412

Cheyne, J. A. (2002). Situational factors affecting sleep paralysis and associated hallucinations: Position and timing effects. *Journal of Sleep Research, 11*, 169–177.

Chiandetti, C., & Turatto, M. (2017). Context-specific habituation of the freezing response in newborn chicks. *Behavioral Neuroscience, 131*, 437–446. https://doi.org/10.1037/bne0000212

Chiao, J. Y., Iidka, T., Gordon, H. L., Nogawa, J., Bar, M., Aminoff, E., Sadato, N., & Ambady, N. (2008). Cultural specificity in amygdala response to fear faces. *Journal of Cognitive Neuroscience, 20*, 2167–2174.

Chiras, D. D. (2015). *Human biology* (8th ed.). Jones & Bartlett Learning.

Chirawatkul, S., Prakhaw, P., & Chomnirat, W. (2011). Perceptions of depression among people of Khon Kaen City: A gender perspective. *Journal of Nursing Science & Health, 34*, 66–75.

Chiu, N. C., Chi, H., Tai, Y. L., Peng, C. C., Tseng, C. Y., Chen, C. C., Tan, B. F., & Lin, C. Y. (2020). Impact of wearing masks, hand hygiene, and social distancing on influenza, enterovirus, and all-cause pneumonia during the coronavirus pandemic: Retrospective national epidemiological surveillance study. *Journal of Medical Internet Research, 22*(8), e21257. https://doi.org/10.2196/21257

Choi, C. Q. (2008, March). Do you need only half your brain? *Scientific American, 298*, 104.

Chomsky, N. (2000). *New horizons in the study of language and mind.* Cambridge University Press.

Chomsky, N. (2000). *New horizons in the study of language and mind.* Cambridge University Press.

Chong, E., Moroni, M., Wilson, C., Shoham, S., Panzeri, S., & Rinberg, D. (2020). Manipulating synthetic optogenetic odors reveals the coding logic of olfactory perception. *Science, 368*(6497). Article eaba2357. https://doi.org/10.1126/science.aba2357

Chopik, W. J., Newton, N. J., Ryan, L. H., Kashdan, T. B., & Jarden, A. J. (2019). Gratitude across the life span: Age differences and links to subjective well-being. *The Journal of Positive Psychology, 14*(3), 292–302. https://doi.org/10.1080/17439760.2017.1414296

Chopra, S., Fornito, A., Francey, S. M., O'Donoghue, B., Cropley, V., Nelson, B., Graham, J., Baldwin, L., Tahtalian, S., Yuen, H. P., Allott, K., Alvarez-Jimenez, Harrigan, S., Sabaroedin, K., Pantelis, C., Wood, S. J., & McGorry, P. (2021). Differentiating the effect of antipsychotic medication and illness on brain volume reductions in first-episode psychosis: A longitudinal, randomised, triple-blind, placebo-controlled MRI study. *Neuropsychopharmacology.* https://doi.org/10.1038/s41386-021-00980-0

Chotiner, I. (2019, January 12). How close should an activist icon get to power? An interview with Malala Yousafzai. *The New Yorker.* https://www.newyorker.com/news/q-and-a/how-close-should-an-activist-icon-get-to-power-an-interview-with-malala-yousafzai

Chouchou, F., Khoury, S., Chauny, J. M., Denis, R., & Lavigne, G. J. (2014). Postoperative sleep disruptions: A potential catalyst of acute pain? *Sleep Medicine Reviews, 18*, 273–282.

Christakis, D. A., Garrison, M. M., Herrenkohl, T., Haggerty, K., Rivara, F. P., Zhou, C., & Liekweg, K. (2013). Modifying media content for preschool children: A randomized controlled trial. *Pediatrics, 131*, 431–438. https://doi.org/10.1542/peds.2012-1493

Christiani, D. C. (2020). Vaping-induced acute lung injury. *New England Journal of Medicine, 382*, 960–962. https://doi.org/10.1056/NEJMe1912032

Christopher, J. C., Wendt, D. C., Marecek, J., & Goodman, D. M. (2014). Critical cultural awareness: Contributions to a globalizing psychology. *American Psychologist, 69*, 645–655.

Chu, D. K., Akl, E. A., Duda, S., Solo, K., Yaacoub, S., Schünemann, H. J., El-harakeh, A., Bognanni, A., Lotfi, T., Loeb, M., Hajizadeh, A., Bak, A., Izcovich, A., Cuello-Garcia, C. A., Chen, C., Harris, D. J., Borowiack, E.,

. . . Reinap, M. (2020). Physical distancing, face masks, and eye protection to prevent person-to-person transmission of SARS-CoV-2 and COVID-19: A systematic review and meta-analysis. *The Lancet, 395*(10242), 1973–1987. https://doi.org/10.1016/S0140-6736(20)31142-9

Chua, E. C. P., Fang, E., & Gooley, J. J. (2017). Effects of total sleep deprivation on divided attention performance. *PLOS ONE, 12*(11), e0187098. https://doi.org/10.1371/journal.pone.0187098

Chung, F., & Elsaid, H. (2009). Screening for obstructive sleep apnea before surgery: Why is it important? *Current Opinion in Anesthesiology, 22*, 405–411.

Cialdini, R. B., & Goldstein, N. J. (2004). Social influence: Compliance and conformity. *Annual Review of Psychology, 55*, 591–621.

Cimpian, J. R., Kim, T. H., & McDermott, Z. T. (2020). Understanding persistent gender gaps in STEM. *Science, 368*(6497), 1317–1319. https://doi.org/10.1126/science.aba7377

Cipriani, A., Furukawa, T. A., Salanti, G., Chaimani, A., Atkinson, L. Z., Ogawa, Y., Y., Leucht, S., Ruhe, H. G., Turner, E. H., Higgins, J. P. T., Egger, M., Takeshima, N., Hayasaka, Y., Imai, H., Shinohara, K., Tajika, A., Ioannidis, J. P. A., & Geddes, J. R. (2018). Comparative efficacy and acceptability of 21 antidepressant drugs for the acute treatment of adults with major depressive disorder: A systematic review and network meta-analysis. *The Lancet, 391*, 1357–1366. https://doi.org/10.1016/S0140-6736(17)32802-7

Cirelli, C. (2012). Brain plasticity, sleep and aging. *Gerontology, 58*(5), 441–445.

Cirelli, C., & Tononi, G. (2019). Linking the need to sleep with synaptic function. *Science, 366*(6462), 189–190. https://doi.org/10.1126/science.aay5304

Cisler, J. M., Brady, R. E., Olatunji, B. O., & Lohr, J. M. (2010). Disgust and obsessive beliefs in contamination-related OCD. *Cognitive Therapy Research, 34*, 439–448.

Clark, A. M., DesMeules, M., Luo, W., Duncan, A. S., & Wielgosz, A. (2009). Socioeconomic status and cardiovascular disease: Risk and implications for care. *Nature Reviews Cardiology, 6*, 712–722.

Clark, I., & Landolt, H. P. (2017). Coffee, caffeine, and sleep: A systematic review of epidemiological studies and randomized controlled trials. *Sleep Medicine Reviews, 31*, 70–78. https://doi.org/10.1016/j.smrv.2016.01.006

Clark, M., & Adams, D. (2020). The self-identified positive attributes and favourite activities of children on the autism spectrum. *Research in Autism Spectrum Disorders, 72*, Article 101512. https://doi.org/10.1016/j.rasd.2020.101512

Cleaning & Maintenance Management. (2020, December 7). *Hospital custodians express COVID-19 concerns.* https://www.cmmonline.com/news/hospital-custodians-express-covid-19-concerns

Clement, J. (2020, May 19). Social media usage in the United States—statistics & facts. *Statista.* https://www.statista.com/topics/3196/social-media-usage-in-the-united-states

Coan, J. A. (2010). Emergent ghosts of the emotion machine. *Emotion Review, 2*, 274–285.

Coffey, J. K. (2020). Cascades of infant happiness: Infant positive affect predicts childhood IQ and adult educational attainment. *Emotion, 20*(7), 1255–1265. https://doi.org/10.1037/emo0000640

Cohen, D. J., & Jones, H. E. (2008). How shape constancy relates to drawing accuracy. *Psychology of Aesthetics, Creativity, and the Arts, 2*, 8–19.

Cohen, H. W., Gibson, G., & Alderman, M. H. (2000). Excess risk of myocardial infarction in patients treated with antidepressant medications: Association with use of tricyclic agents. *American Journal of Medicine, 108*, 2–8.

Cohen, S., Doyle, W., Frank, E., Gwaltney, J. M., Jr., Rabin, B. S., & Skoner, D. P. (1998). Types of stressors that increase susceptibility to the common cold in healthy adults. *Health Psychology, 17*, 214–223.

Cohen, S., Janicki-Deverts, D., Turner, R. B., & Doyle, W. J. (2015). Does hugging provide stress-buffering social support? A study of susceptibility to upper respiratory infection and illness. *Psychological Science, 26*, 135–147.

Cohen, S., Murphy, M. L. M., & Prather, A. A. (2019). Ten surprising facts about stressful life events and disease risk. *Annual Review of Psychology, 70*, 577–597. https://doi.org/10.1146/annurev-psych-010418-102857

Cole, C. F., Labin, D. B., & del Rocio Galarza, M. (2008). Begin with the children: What research on Sesame Street's international coproductions reveals about using media to promote a new more peaceful world. *International Journal of Behavioral Development, 32*(4), 359–365.

Coleman-Jensen, A., Rabbitt, M. P., Gregory, C. A., & Singh, A. (2020). *Household food security in the United States in 2019 (ERR-275).* United States Department of Agriculture. https://ers.usda.gov/webdocs/publications/99282/err-275.pdf?v=2745

Coles, N. A., Larsen, J. T., & Lench, H. C. (2019). A meta-analysis of the facial feedback literature: Effects of facial feedback on emotional experience are small and variable. *Psychological Bulletin, 145*(6), 610–651. https://doi.org/10.1037/bul0000194

Collins, K. L., Russell, H. G., Schumacher, P. J., Robinson-Freeman, K. E., O'Conor, E. C., Gibney, K. D., Yambem, O., Dykes, R. W., Waters, R. S., & Tsao, J. W. (2018). A review of current theories and treatments for phantom limb pain. *The Journal of Clinical Investigation, 128*(6), 2168–2176. https://doi.org/10.1172/JCI94003

Collisson, B., McCutcheon, L. E., Johnston, M., & Edman, J. (2021). How popular are pop stars? The false consensus of perceived celebrity popularity. *Psychology of Popular Media, 10*(1), 14–20. https://doi.org/10.1037/ppm0000271

Colloca, L. (2017). Nocebo effects can make you feel pain. *Science, 358*(6359), 44. https://doi.org/10.1126/science.aap8488

Compton, R. (2017, July). *Marijuana-impaired driving: A report to Congress* (DOT HS 812 440). National Highway Traffic Safety Administration.

Compton, W. C. (2018). Self-actualization myths: What did Maslow really say? *Journal of Humanistic Psychology.* OnlineFirst. https://doi.org/10.1177/0022167818761929

Contrera, J. (2017, September 4). "These are all fake news," said the honor student. He was wrong. *The Washington Post.* https://www.washingtonpost.com/lifestyle/style/these-are-all-fake-news-said-the-honor-student-he-was-wrong/2017/09/01/e2db60be-890a-11e7-961d-2f373b3977ee_story.html?utm_term=.443dc7161372

Convento, S., Russo, C., Zigiotto, L., & Bolognini, N. (2016). Transcranial electrical stimulation in post-stroke cognitive rehabilitation. *European Psychologist, 21*, 55–64. https://doi.org/10.1027/1016-9040/a000238

Conway, G. S. (2014). Disorders of sex development (DSD): An overview of recent scientific advances. *Psychology & Sexuality, 5*(1), 28–33.

Conway, M. A., Cohen, G., & Stanhope, N. (1991). On the very long-term retention of knowledge acquired through formal education: Twelve years of cognitive psychology.

*Journal of Experimental Psychology: General, 120*, 395–409.

Cook County Sheriff's Office. (n.d.). *Corrections.* https://www.cookcountysheriff.org/cook-county-department-of-corrections/

Cooper, A. B., Blake, A. B., Pauletti, R. E., Cooper, P. J., Sherman, R. A., & Lee, D. I. (2020). Personality assessment through the situational and behavioral features of Instagram photos. *European Journal of Psychological Assessment, 36*(6), 959–972. https://doi.org/10.1027/1015-5759/a000596

Cooper, H. L., Cloud, D. H., Young, A. M., & Freeman, P. R. (2020). When prescribing isn't enough—pharmacy-level barriers to buprenorphine access. *The New England Journal of Medicine, 383*(8), 703–705. https://doi.org/10.1056/NEJMp2002908

Copur-Gencturk, Y., Cimpian, J. R., Lubienski, S. T., & Thacker, I. (2020). Teachers' bias against the mathematical ability of female, Black, and Hispanic students. *Educational Researcher, 49*(1), 30–43. https://doi.org/10.3102/0013189X19890577

Corballis, M. C. (2014). Left brain, right brain: Facts and fantasies. *PLOS Biology, 12*(1), e1001767. https://doi.org/10.1371/journal.pbio.1001767

Cordi, M. J., & Rasch, B. (2021). How robust are sleep-mediated memory benefits? *Current Opinion in Neurobiology, 67.* https://doi.org/10.1016/j.conb.2020.06.002

Corey, G. (2017). *Theory and practice of counseling and psychotherapy* (10th ed.). Brooks/Cole, Cengage Learning.

Corkin, S. (2002). What's new with the amnesic patient H.M.? *Nature Reviews Neuroscience, 3*, 153–160.

Correia, I., Alves, H., Morais, R., & Ramos, M. (2015). The legitimation of wife abuse among women: The impact of belief in a just world and gender identification. *Personality and Individual Differences, 76*, 7–12.

Correll, C. U., Leucht, S., & Kane, J. M. (2004). Lower risk for tardive dyskinesia associated with second-generation antipsychotics: A systematic review of 1-year studies. *American Journal of Psychiatry, 161*, 414–425.

Corrigan, P. W., & Al-Khouja, M. A. (2018). Three agendas for changing the public stigma of mental illness. *Psychiatric Rehabilitation Journal, 41*(1), 1–7. https://doi.org/10.1037/prj0000277

Corrigan, P. W., & Penn, D. L. (2015). Lessons from social

psychology on discrediting psychiatric stigma. *Stigma and Health, 1*(Suppl.), 2–15.

Cortes, J. (2020, May 1). *Study claims eating meat can help improve mental health.* Medical Daily. https://www.medicaldaily.com/study-claims-eating-meat-can-help-improve-mental-health-mental-health-science-452533

Costa, P. T., Jr., McCrae, R. R., & Löckenhoff, C. E. (2019). Personality across the life span. *Annual Review of Psychology, 70*, 423–448. https://doi.org/10.1146/annurev-psych-010418-103244

Costa, P. T., Jr., Terracciano, A., & McCrae, R. R. (2001). Gender differences in personality traits across cultures: Robust and surprising findings. *Journal of Personality and Social Psychology, 81*, 322–331.

Costandi, M. (2009, February 10). Where are old memories stored in the brain? *Scientific American Online.* http://www.scientificamerican.com/article/the-memory-trace/

Costanzo, E. S., Lutgendorf, S. K., & Roeder, S. L. (2011). Common-sense beliefs about cancer and health practices among women completing treatment for breast cancer. *Psychooncology, 20*, 53–61.

Cotter, E. W., & Kelly, N. R. (2018). Stress-related eating, mindfulness, and obesity. *Health Psychology, 37*(6), 516–525. https://doi.org/10.1037/hea0000614

Cottrell, J. M., Newman, D. A., & Roisman, G. I. (2015). Explaining the Black–White gap in cognitive test scores: Toward a theory of adverse impact. *Journal of Applied Psychology, 100*, 1713–1736.

Coughlin, S. S. (2019). Social determinants of breast cancer risk, stage, and survival. *Breast Cancer Research and Treatment, 177*(3), 537–548. https://doi.org/10.1007/s10549-019-05340-7

Coulson, J. (2018, November 27). The fallacy of the "I turned out fine" argument. *The New York Times.* https://www.nytimes.com/2018/11/27/well/family/the-fallacy-of-the-i-turned-out-fine-argument.html

County of Los Angeles, Department of Medical Examiner-Coroner. (2017, May 15). *Autopsy report* (Case No. 09419). http://documents.latimes.com/read-carrie-fishers-autopsy/

Coupland, C., Hill, T., Morriss, R., Moore, M., Arthur, A., & Hippisley-Cox, J. (2016). Antidepressant use and risk of cardiovascular outcomes in people aged 20 to 64: Cohort study using primary care database. *BMJ Open, 352*, Article i1350. https://doi.org/10.1136/bmj.i1350

Courtney, J. A., & Nowakowski-Sims, E. (2019). Technology's impact on the parent–infant attachment relationship: Intervening through FirstPlay® therapy. *International Journal of Play Therapy, 28*(2), 57–68. https://doi.org/10.1037/pla0000090

Couzin-Frankel, J. (2020, April 10). Rethinking anorexia. *Science, 368*(6487), 124–127. https://doi.org/10.1126/science.368.6487.124

Covre, P., Baddeley, A. D., Hitch, G. J., & Bueno, O. F. A. (2019). Maintaining task set against distraction: The role of working memory in multitasking. *Psychology & Neuroscience, 12*(1), 38–52. https://doi.org/10.1037/pne0000152

Cowan, N. (1988). Evolving conceptions of memory storage, selective attention, and their mutual constraints within the human information-processing system. *Psychological Bulletin, 104,* 163–191.

Cowan, N. (2001). The magical number 4 in short-term memory: A reconsideration of mental storage capacity. *Behavioral and Brain Sciences, 24*(1), 87–185. https://doi.org/10.1017/S0140525X01003922

Cowan, N. (2015). George Miller's magical number of immediate memory in retrospect: Observations on the faltering progression of science. *Psychological Review, 122,* 536–541.

Cowan, N., Chen, Z., & Rouder, J. N. R. (2004). Constant capacity in an immediate serial-recall task: A logical sequel to Miller (1956). *Psychological Science, 15,* 634–640.

Cowen, A. S., & Keltner, D. (2020). Universal facial expressions uncovered in art of the ancient Americas: A computational approach. *Science Advances, 6*(34), eabb1005. https://doi.org/10.1126/sciadv.abb1005

Coyne, S. M. (2016). Effects of viewing relational aggression on television on aggressive behavior in adolescents: A three-year longitudinal study. *Developmental Psychology, 52*(2), 284–295. https://doi.org/10.1037/dev0000068

Coyne, S. M., Padilla-Walker, L. M., Holmgren, H. G., & Stockdale, L. A. (2019). Instagrowth: A longitudinal growth mixture model of social media time use across adolescence. *Journal of Research on Adolescence, 29*(4), 897–907. https://doi.org/10.1111/jora.12424

Coyne, S. M., Warburton, W. A., Essig, L. W., & Stockdale, L. A. (2018). Violent video games, externalizing behavior, and prosocial behavior: A five-year longitudinal study during adolescence. *Developmental Psychology, 54*(10), 1868–1880. https://doi.org/10.1037/dev0000574

Craddock, N., O'Donovan, M. C., & Owen, M. J. (2005). The genetics of schizophrenia and bipolar disorder: Dissecting psychosis. *Journal of Medical Genetics, 42,* 193–204.

Craik, F. I. M. (2020). Remembering: An activity of mind and brain. *Annual Review of Psychology, 71,* 1–24. https://doi.org/10.1146/annurev-psych-010419-051027

Craik, F. I. M., & Lockhart, R. S. (1972). Levels of processing: A framework for memory research. *Journal of Verbal Learning and Verbal Behavior, 11,* 671–684.

Craik, F. I. M., & Tulving, E. (1975). Depth of processing and the retention of words in episodic memory. *Journal of Experimental Psychology, 104,* 268–294.

Cramer, P. (2000). Defense mechanisms in psychology today: Further processes for adaptation. *American Psychologist, 55,* 637–646.

Cramer, P. (2008). Identification and the development of competence: A 44-year longitudinal study from late adolescence to late middle age. *Psychology and Aging, 23,* 410–421.

Cramer, P. (2015). Defense mechanisms: 40 years of empirical research. *Journal of Personality Assessment, 97,* 114–122.

Craske, M. G., Kircanski, K., Epstein, A., Wittchen, H.-U., Pine, D. S., Lewis-Fernández, R., Hinton, D., & DSM V Anxiety, OC Spectrum, Posttraumatic and Dissociative Disorder Work Group. (2010). Panic disorder: A review of DSM-IV panic disorder and proposals for DSM-V. *Depression and Anxiety, 27*(2), 93–112.

Crisco, J. J., Fiore, R., Beckwith, J. G., Chu, J. J., Brolinson, P. G., Duma, S., McAllister, T. W., Duhaimer, A.-C., & Greenwald, R. M. (2010). Frequency and location of head impact exposures in individual collegiate football players. *Journal of Athletic Training, 45,* 549–559. https://doi.org/10.4085/1062-6050-45.6.549

Crocker, J., Canevello, A., & Brown, A. A. (2017). Social motivation: Costs and benefits of selfishness and otherishness. *Annual Review of Psychology, 68,* 299–325. https://doi.org/10.1146/annurev-psych-010416-044145

Crooks, R., & Baur, K. (2021). *Our sexuality* (14th ed.). Cengage Learning.

Cropanzano, R., Anthony, E. L., Daniels, S. R., & Hall, A. V. (2017). Social exchange theory: A critical review with theoretical remedies. *The Academy of Management Annals, 11,* 479–516. https://doi.org/10.5465/annals.2015.0099

Crosby, L. E., Quinn, C. T., & Kalinyak, K. A. (2015). A biopsychosocial model for the management of patients with sickle-cell disease transitioning to adult medical care. *Advances in Therapy, 32,* 293–305.

Crouch, T. A., Verdi, E. K., & Erickson, T. M. (2020). Gratitude is positively associated with quality of life in multiple sclerosis. *Rehabilitation Psychology, 65*(3), 231–238. https://doi.org/10.1037/rep0000319

Crowell, S. E., Beauchaine, T. P., & Linehan, M. M. (2009). A biosocial developmental model of borderline personality: Elaborating and extending Linehan's theory. *Psychological Bulletin, 135,* 495–510.

Crowley, R., Kirschner, N., Dunn, A. S., & Bornstein, S. S. (2017). Health and public policy to facilitate effective prevention and treatment of substance use disorders involving illicit and prescription drugs: An American College of Physicians position paper. *Annals of Internal Medicine, 166,* 733–736. https://doi.org/10.7326/M16-2953

Cserép, C., Pósfai, B., Lénárt, N., Fekete, R., László, Z. I., Lele, Z., Orsolits, B., Molnár, G., Heindl, S., Schwarcz, A. D., Ujvári, K., Környei, Z., Tóth, K., Szabadits, E., Sperlágh, B., Baranyi, M., Csiba, L., Hortobágyi, T., Maglóczky, Z., Martinecz, B., . . . Dénes, A. (2020). Microglia monitor and protect neuronal function through specialized somatic purinergic junctions. *Science, 367*(6477), 528–537. https://doi.org/10.1126/science.aax6752

Csikszentmihalyi, M. (1975). Play and intrinsic rewards. *Journal of Humanistic Psychology, 15,* 41–63.

Csikszentmihalyi, M. (1990). *Flow: The psychology of optimal experience.* Harper Perennial.

Csikszentmihalyi, M. (1999). If we are so rich, why aren't we happy? *American Psychologist, 54,* 821–827.

Cuijpers, P., De Wit, L., Weitz, E., Andersson, G., & Huibers, M. J. H. (2015). The combination of psychotherapy and pharmacotherapy in the treatment of adult depression: A comprehensive meta-analysis. *Journal of Evidence-Based Psychotherapies, 15,* 147–168.

Culbertson, S. S., Fullagar, C. J., Simmons, M. J., & Zhu, M. (2015). Contagious flow antecedents and consequences of optimal experience in the classroom. *Journal of Management Education, 39,* 319–349.

Cullen, K. A., Ambrose, B. K., Gentzke, A. S., Apelberg, B. J., Jamal, A., & King, B. A. (2018). Notes from the field: Use of electronic cigarettes and any tobacco product among middle and high school students—United States, 2011–2018. *MMWR: Morbidity and Mortality Weekly Report, 67*(45), 1276–1277. https://doi.org/10.15585/mmwr.mm6745a5

Cummins, R. A., Li, N., Wooden, M., & Stokes, M. (2014). A demonstration of set-points for subjective wellbeing. *Journal of Happiness Studies, 15,* 183–206.

Cunha, J. P., & Stöppler, M. C. (Eds.). (2016, June 6). *Jetlag. MedicineNet.com.* http://www.medicinenet.com/jet_lag/article.htm

Cunningham, M. R., Shamblen, S. R., Barbee, A. P., & Ault, L. K. (2005). Social allergies in romantic relationships: Behavioral repetition, emotional sensitization, and dissatisfaction in dating couples. *Personal Relationships, 12,* 273–295.

Currin, J. M., Gibson, L., & Hubach, R. D. (2015). Multidimensional assessment of sexual orientation and the fraternal birth order effect. *Psychology of Sexual Orientation and Gender Diversity, 2,* 113–122.

Curtiss, S., Fromkin, V., Krashen, S., Rigler, D., & Rigler, M. (1974). The linguistic development of Genie. *Language, 50,* 528–554.

Cuttler, C., & Ryckman, M. (2019). Don't call me delusional: Stigmatizing effects of noun labels on people with mental disorders. *Stigma and Health, 4*(2), 118–125. https://doi.org/10.1037/sah0000132

Cyranoski, D. (2018, November 14). Reprogrammed stem cells implanted into patient with Parkinson's disease. *Nature News.* https://www.nature.com/articles/d41586-018-07407-9

Cyryk, T. (2013). Electroconvulsive therapy: Why it is still controversial. *Mental Health Practice, 16,* 22–27.

Czarnowski, C., Bailey, J., & Bal, S. (2007). Curare and a Canadian connection. *Canadian Family Physician, 53,* 1531–1532.

Czeisler, M. É., Lane, R. I., Petrosky, E., Wiley, J. F., Christensen, A., Njai, R., Weaver, M. D., Robbins, R., Facer-Childs, E. R., Barger, L. K., Czeisler, C. A., Howard, M. E., & Rajaratnam, S. M. (2020). Mental health, substance use, and suicidal ideation during the COVID-19 pandemic—United States, June 24–30, 2020. *Morbidity and Mortality Weekly Report, 69*(32), 1049. https://doi.org/10.15585/mmwr.mm6932a1

d'Apice, K., Latham, R. M., & von Stumm, S. (2019). A naturalistic home observational approach to children's language, cognition, and behavior. *Developmental Psychology, 55*(7), 1414–1427. https://doi.org/10.1037/dev0000733

Dadds, M. R., & Tully, L. A. (2019). What is it to discipline a child: What should it be? A reanalysis of time-out from the perspective of child mental health, attachment, and trauma. *American Psychologist, 74*(7), 794–808. https://doi.org/10.1037/amp0000449

Daenen, L., Varkey, E., Kellmann, M., & Nijs, J. (2015). Exercise, not to exercise, or how to exercise in patients with chronic pain? Applying science to practice. *Clinical Journal of Pain, 31,* 108–114.

Daffner, K. R., Chong, H., Riis, J., Rentz, D. M., Wolk, D. A., Budson, A. E., & Holcomb, P. J. (2007). Cognitive status impacts age-related changes in attention to novel and target events. *Neuropsychology, 21,* 291–300.

Dahlhamer, J., Lucas, J., Zelaya, C., Nahin, R., Mackey, S., DeBar, L., Kerns, R., Van Korff, M., Porter, L., & Helmick, C. (2018). Prevalence of chronic pain and high-impact chronic pain among adults—United States, 2016. *Morbidity and Mortality Weekly Report, 67*(36), 1001–1006. https://doi.org/10.15585/mmwr.mm6736a2

Dajches, L., & Terán, L. (2020). Hetero-(sex)pectations: Exploring the link between compulsive pornography consumption, heterosexual script endorsement, and hookups among emerging adults. *Psychology of Popular Media.* Advance online publication. https://doi.org/10.1037/ppm0000332

Dalenberg, C. J., Brand, B. L., Loewenstein, R. J., Gleaves, D. H., Dorahy, M. J., Cardeña, E., Frewen, P. A., Carlson, E. B., & Spiegel, D. (2014). Reality versus fantasy: Reply to Lynn et al. (2014). *Psychological Bulletin, 140,* 911–920.

Daly, E. J., Trivedi, M. H., Janik, A., Li, H., Zhang, Y., Li, X., Lane, R., Lim, P., Duca, A. R., Hough, D., Thase, M. E., Zajecka, J., Winokur, A., Divacka, I., Fagiolini, A., Cubała, W. J., Bitter, I., Blier, P., Shelton, R. C., . . . Singh, J. B. (2019). Efficacy of esketamine nasal spray plus oral antidepressant treatment for relapse prevention in patients with treatment-resistant depression: A randomized clinical trial. *JAMA Psychiatry, 76*(9), 893–903. https://doi.org/10.1001/jamapsychiatry.2019.1189

Damasio, H., Grabowski, T., Frank, R., Galaburda, A. M., & Damasio, A. R. (1994). The return of Phineas Gage: Clues about the brain from the skull of a famous patient. *Science, 264,* 1102–1105.

Damian, R. I., & Roberts, B. W. (2015). Settling the debate on birth order and personality. *Proceedings of the National Academy of Sciences, 112,* 14119–14120.

Dan, A., Mondal, T., Chakraborty, K., Chaudhuri, A., & Biswas, A. (2017). Clinical course and treatment outcome of *Koro:* A follow up study from a *Koro* epidemic reported from West Bengal, India. *Asian Journal of Psychiatry, 26,* 14–20. https://doi.org/10.1016/j.ajp.2016.12.016

Daneshfard, B., Dalfardi, B., & Nezhad, G. S. M. (2016). Ibn

al-Haytham (965–1039 AD), the original portrayal of the modern theory of vision. *Journal of Medical Biography, 24*(2), 227–231.

Daniels, L. A. (2019). Feeding practices and parenting: A pathway to child health and family happiness. *Annals of Nutrition and Metabolism, 74*(2), 29–42. https://doi.org/10.1159/000499145

Darley, J. M., & Latané, B. (1968). Bystander intervention in emergencies: Diffusion of responsibility. *Journal of Personality and Social Psychology, 8,* 377–383.

Darnall, B. D. (2019). Mindfulness interventions, hypnosis, and biofeedback. In B. D. Darnall (Ed.), *Psychological treatment for patients with chronic pain* (pp. 99–106). American Psychological Association. https://doi.org/10.1037/0000104-008

Darnall, B. D. (2019). Overview of evidence-based psychobehavioral interventions for pain. In B. D. Darnall, 2019. *Psychological treatment for patients with chronic pain* (pp. 77–84). American Psychological Association. https://doi.org/10.1037/0000104-006

Darwin, C. (1872/2002). *The expression of the emotions in man and animals.* Oxford University Press.

Das, S., Tran, L. N., & Theel, M. (2021). Understanding patterns in marijuana impaired traffic crashes. *Journal of Substance Use.* Advance online publication. https://doi.org/10.1080/14659891.2020.1760381

Davide, P., Andrea, P., Martina, O., Andrea, E., Davide, D., & Mario, A. (2020). The impact of the COVID-19 pandemic on patients with OCD: Effects of contamination symptoms and remission state before the quarantine in a preliminary naturalistic study. *Psychiatry Research, 291,* Article 113213. https://doi.org/10.1016/j.psychres.2020.113213

Davidson, R. J., Scherer, K. R., & Goldsmith, H. H. (Eds.). (2002). *Handbook of affective sciences.* Oxford University Press.

Davies, G., Tenesa, A., Payton, A., Yang, J., Harris, S. E., Liewald, D., Ke, X., Hellard, S. L., Christoforou, A., Luciano, M., McGhee, K., Lopez, L., Gow, A. J., Corley, J., Redmond, P., Frox, H. C., Haggarty, P., Whalley, L. J., McNeill, G., . . . Deary, I. J. (2011). Genome-wide association studies establish that human intelligence is highly heritable and polygenic. *Molecular Psychiatry, 16,* 996–1005.

Davies, M. (2015). A model of critical thinking in higher education. In M. B. Paulsen (Ed.), *Higher education: Handbook of theory and research* (Vol. 30, pp. 41–92). Springer International.

Davis, A. N., Carlo, G., Schwartz, S. J., Zamboanga, B. L., Armenta, B., Kim, S. Y., Opal, D., & Streit, C. (2018). The roles of familism and emotion reappraisal in the relations between acculturative stress and prosocial behaviors in Latino/a college students. *Journal of Latina/o Psychology, 6*(3), 175–189. https://doi.org/10.1037/lat0000092

Davis, E. P., & Sandman, C. A. (2010). The timing of prenatal exposure to maternal cortisol and psychosocial stress is associated with human infant cognitive development. *Child Development, 81,* 131–148.

Davis, K. (2012, November). Brain trials: Neuroscience is taking a stand in the courtroom. *ABA Journal.* http://www.abajournal.com/magazine/article/brain_trials_neuroscience_is_taking_a_stand_in_the_courtroom/

Davis, K. (2015, October 20). Federal judge says neuroscience is not ready for the courtroom—yet. *ABA Journal.* http://www.abajournal.com/news/article/federal_judge_says_neuroscience_is_not_ready_for_the_courtroom_yet

Davis, K. (2020, June 1). Millions have been invested in the emerging field of neurolaw. Where is it leading? *ABA Journal.* https://www.abajournal.com/magazine/article/millions-have-been-invested-in-the-emerging-field-of-neurolaw.-where-is-it-leading

Dawidziak, M. (2018, August 4). *Twins Days Festival celebrates relative happiness for a 43rd year.* Cleveland.com. https://www.cleveland.com/metro/2018/08/twins_days_festival_celebrates.html

DeAngelis, T. (2018, January). Practice makes perfect: Strategies that hone practitioners' skills. *Monitor on Psychology, 29*(1). http://www.apa.org/monitor/2018/01/ce-corner.aspx

de Bitencourt Machado, D., Braga Laskoski, P., Trelles Severo, C., Margareth Bassols, A., Sfoggia, A., & Kowacs, C. (2016). A psychodynamic perspective on a systematic review of online psychotherapy for adults. *British Journal of Psychotherapy, 32,* 79–108. https://doi.org/10.1111/bjp.12204

de Boysson-Bardies, B., Halle, P., Sagart, L., & Durand, C. (1989). A cross-linguistic investigation of vowel formats in babbling. *Journal of Child Language, 16,* 1–17.

De Brey, C., Snyder, T. D., Zhang, A., & Dillow, S. A. (2021). *Digest of education statistics 2019* (NCES 2021-009). National Center for Education Statistics, Institute of Education Sciences, U.S. Department of Education. https://nces.ed.gov/pubs2021/2021009.pdf

de Bruin, E. J., Meijer, A., & Bögels, S. M. (2020). The contribution of

a body scan mindfulness meditation to effectiveness of internet-delivered CBT for insomnia in adolescents. *Mindfulness, 11*(4), 872–882.

DeCaro, M. S., Van Stockum Jr., C. A., & Wieth, M. B. (2016). When higher working memory capacity hinders insight. *Journal of Experimental Psychology: Learning, Memory, and Cognition, 42,* 39–49. https://doi.org/10.1037/xlm0000152

DeCasper, A. J., & Fifer, W. P. (1980). Of human bonding: Newborns prefer their mothers' voices. *Science, 208,* 1174–1176.

Deci, E. L., & Ryan, R. M. (2008). Self-determination theory: A macrotheory of human motivation, development, and health. *Canadian Psychology, 49,* 182–185.

Deci, E. L., Koestner, R., & Ryan, R. M. (1999). A meta-analytic review of experiments examining the effects of extrinsic rewards on intrinsic motivation. *Psychological Bulletin, 125,* 627–668.

Deci, E. L., Koestner, R., & Ryan, R. M. (2001). Extrinsic rewards and intrinsic motivation in education: Reconsidered once again. *Review of Educational Research, 71,* 1–27.

Deci, E. L., Olafsen, A. H., & Ryan, R. M. (2017). Self-determination theory in work organizations: The state of a science. *Annual Review of Organizational Psychology and Organizational Behavior, 4,* 19–43. https://doi.org/10.1146/annurev-orgpsych-032516-113108

Decker, A. L., Duncan, K., Finn, A. S., & Mabbott, D. J. (2020). Children's family income is associated with cognitive function and volume of anterior not posterior hippocampus. *Nature Communications, 11*(1). Article 4040. https://doi.org/10.1038/s41467-020-17854-6

Decker, H. S. (2016a). Cyclical swings: The bête noire of psychiatry. *History of Psychology, 19,* 52–56. https://doi.org/10.1037/hop0000017

Decker, H. S. (2016b). Professor Decker replies. *History of Psychology, 19,* 66–67. https://doi.org/10.1037/hop0000022

Deeb, S. S. (2005). The molecular basis of variation in human color vision. *Clinical Genetics, 67,* 369–377.

Deemyad, T., Lüthi, J., & Spruston, N. (2018). Astrocytes integrate and drive action potential firing in inhibitory subnetworks. *Nature Communications, 9*(1), 4336. https://doi.org/10.1038/s41467-018-06338-3

Deer, B. (2011). How the case against the MMR vaccine was fixed. *British Medical Journal, 342,* 77–82.

Deese, J., & Kaufman, R. A. (1957). Serial effects in recall of unorganized and sequentially organized verbal material. *Journal of Experimental Psychology, 54,* 180–187.

DeFreitas, S. C., Crone, T., DeLeon, M., & Ajayi, A. (2018). Perceived and personal mental health stigma in Latino and African American college students. *Frontiers in Public Health, 6,* Article 49. https://doi.org/10.3389/fpubh.2018.00049

de Gelder, D. B., Hortensius, R., & Tamietto, M. (2012). Attention and awareness each influence amygdala activity for dynamic bodily expressions—a short review. *Frontiers in Integrative Neuroscience, 6.* https://doi.org/10.3389/fnint.2012.00054

de Haan, E. H. F., Corballis, P. M., Hillyard, S. A., Marzi, C. A., Seth, A., Lamme, V. A. F., Volz, L., Fabri, M., Schechter, E., Bayne, T., Corballis, M., & Pinto, Y. (2020). Split-brain: What we know now and why this is important for understanding consciousness. *Neuropsychology Review, 30*(2), 224–233. https://doi.org/10.1007/s11065-020-09439-3

Deisseroth, K. (2015). Optogenetics: 10 years of microbial opsins in neuroscience. *Nature Neuroscience, 18*(9), 1213–1225. https://doi.org/10.1038/nn.4091

Deisseroth, K. (2015). Optogenetics: 10 years of microbial opsins in neuroscience. *Nature Neuroscience, 18*(9), 1213–1225.

DeJesus, J. M., Du, K. M., Shutts, K., & Kinzler, K. D. (2019). How information about what is "healthy" versus "unhealthy" impacts children's consumption of otherwise identical foods. *Journal of Experimental Psychology: General, 148*(12), 2091–2103. https://doi.org/10.1037/xge0000588

DeJong, K., Olyaei, A., & Lo, J. O. (2019). Alcohol use in pregnancy. *Clinical Obstetrics and Gynecology, 62*(1), 142–155. https://doi.org/10.1097/GRF.0000000000000414

DeKosky, S. T., & Williamson, J. B. (2020). The long and the short of benzodiazepines and sleep medications: Short-term benefits long-term harms? *Neurotherapeutics, 17*(1), 153–155. https://doi.org/10.1007/s13311-019-00827-z

Del Missier, F., Hansson, P., Parker, A. M., Bruine de Bruin, W., & Mäntylä, T. (2020). Decision-making competence in older adults: A rosy view from a longitudinal investigation. *Psychology and Aging, 35*(4), 553–564. https://doi.org/10.1037/pag0000443

DeLisi, M., Drury, A. J., & Elbert, M. J. (2019). The etiology of antisocial personality disorder: The differential roles of adverse childhood experiences and childhood psychopathology. *Comprehensive Psychiatry, 92,* 1–6. https://doi.org/10.1016/j.comppsych.2019.04.001

Delmonte, R., Lucchetti, G., Moreira-Almeida, A., & Farias, M. (2016). Can the *DSM-5* differentiate between nonpathological possession and dissociative identity disorder? A case study from an Afro-Brazilian religion. *Journal of Trauma & Dissociation, 17*(3), 322–337. https://doi.org/10.1080/15299732.2015.1103351

DeLongis, A., Coyne, J. C., Dakof, G., Folkman, S., & Lazarus, R. S. (1982). Relationship of daily hassles, uplifts, and major life events to health status. *Health Psychology, 1,* 119–136.

DeLongis, A., Folkman, S., & Lazarus, R. S. (1988). The impact of daily stress on health and mood: Psychological and social resources as mediators. *Journal of Personality and Social Psychology, 54,* 486–495.

DelPriore, D. J., Bradshaw, H. K., & Hill, S. E. (2018). Appearance enhancement produces a strategic beautification penalty among women. *Evolutionary Behavioral Sciences, 12*(4), 348–366. https://doi.org/10.1037/ebs0000118

Dement, W. C., & Vaughan, C. (1999). *The promise of sleep.* Delacorte Press.

Dement, W., & Kleitman, N. (1957). The relation of eye movements during sleep to dream activity: An objective method for the study of dreaming. *Journal of Experimental Psychology, 53,* 339–346.

Demiral, Ş. B., Tomasi, D., Sarlls, J., Lee, H., Wiers, C. E., Zehra, A., Srivastava, T., Ke, K., Shokri-Kojori, E., Freeman, C. R., Lindgren, E., Ramirez, V., Miller, G., Bandettini, P., Horovitz, S., Wang, G.-J., Benveniste, H., & Volkow, N. D. (2019). Apparent diffusion coefficient changes in human brain during sleep—Does it inform on the existence of a glymphatic system? *NeuroImage, 185,* 263–273. https://doi.org/10.1016/j.neuroimage.2018.10.043

Denning, A., Pewonka, B., Grunspan, D., & Marin, A. J. (2018). Digital textbooks: The effects of input modality and distraction on student learning at a Hispanic-serving institution. *Scholarship of Teaching and Learning in Psychology, 4,* 127–139. https://doi.org/10.1037/stl0000115

Denollet, J., & Conraads, V. M. (2011). Type D personality and vulnerability to adverse outcomes in heart disease. *Cleveland Clinic Journal of Medicine, 78,* S13–S19.

Denson, T. F., O'Dean, S. M., Blake, K. R., & Beames, J. R. (2018). Aggression in women: Behavior, brain and hormones. *Frontiers in Behavioral Neuroscience, 12,* Art. ID 81. https://doi.org/10.3389/fnbeh.2018.00081

Denworth, L. (2019, November). The kids are alright. *Scientific American, 321*(5), 44–49.

Denworth, L. (2020, April 8). How people with autism forge friendships. *Scientific American.* https://www.scientificamerican.com/article/how-people-with-autism-forge-friendships/

Denworth, L. (2020, May 14). Masks reveal new social norms: What a difference a plague makes. *Scientific American.* https://www.scientificamerican.com/article/masks-reveal-new-social-norms-what-a-difference-a-plague-makes/

de Oliveira Maraldi, E., Costa, A., Cunha, A., Flores, D., Hamazaki, E., de Queiroz, G. P., Martinez, M., Siqueira, S., & Reichow, J. (2021). Cultural presentations of dissociation: The case of possession trance experiences. *Journal of Trauma & Dissociation, 22*(1), 11–16. https://doi.org/10.1080/15299732.2020.1821145

DePaulo, B. M., Lindsay, J. J., Malone, B. E., Muhlenbruck, L., Charlton, K., & Cooper, H. (2003). Cues to deception. *Psychological Bulletin, 129*(1), 74–118.

Depner, C. M., Melanson, E. L., Eckel, R. H., Snell-Bergeon, J. K., Perreault, L., Bergman, B. C., Higgens, J. A., Guerin, M. K., Stothard, E. R., Morton, S. J., & Wright Jr, K. P. (2019). Ad libitum weekend recovery sleep fails to prevent metabolic dysregulation during a repeating pattern of insufficient sleep and weekend recovery sleep. *Current Biology, 29*(6), 957–967. https://doi.org/10.1016/j.cub.2019.01.069

de Raad, B., & Mlačić, B. (2017). The lexical foundation of the Big Five Factor Model. In T. A. Widiger (Ed.), *Oxford library of psychology. The Oxford handbook of the Five Factor Model* (pp. 191–216). Oxford University Press.

DeRobertis, E. M. (2016). On framing the future of humanistic psychology. *The Humanistic Psychologist, 44*(1), 18–41. https://doi.org/10.1037/hum0000014

Derogatis, L. R., Revicki, D. A., & Clayton, A. H. (2020). Instruments for screening, diagnosis, and management of patients with generalized acquired hypoactive sexual desire disorder. *Journal of Women's Health, 20*(6), 806–814. https://doi.org/10.1089/jwh.2019.7917

Derr, M. (2016, March 9). Cesar Millan crosses the line again. *Psychology Today.* https://www.psychologytoday.com/blog/dogs-best-friend/201603/cesar-millan-crosses-the-line-again

Desco, M., Navas-Sanchez, F. J., Sanchez-González, J., Reig, S., Robles, O., Franco, C., Guzmán-De-Villoria, J. A., García-Barreno, P., & Arango, C. (2011). Mathematically gifted adolescents use more extensive and more bilateral areas of the fronto-parietal network than controls during executive functioning and fluid reasoning tasks. *NeuroImage, 57,* 281–292.

deShazo, R. D., Hall, J. E., & Skipworth, L. B. (2015). Obesity bias, medical technology, and the hormonal hypothesis: Should we stop demonizing fat people? *American Journal of Medicine, 128,* 456–460.

Deslauriers, L., McCarty, L. S., Miller, K., Callaghan, K., & Kestin, G. (2019). Measuring actual learning versus feeling of learning in response to being actively engaged in the classroom. *Proceedings of the National Academy of Sciences, 116*(39), 19251–19257.

Desmarais, S. L., Van Dom, R. A., Johnson, K. L., Grimm, K. J., Douglas, K. S., & Swartz, M. S. (2014). Community violence perpetration and victimization among adults with mental illness. *American Journal of Public Health, 104,* 2342–2349.

Desmond, M. (2018, September 11). Americans want to believe jobs are the solution to poverty. They're not. *The New York Times Magazine.* https://www.nytimes.com/2018/09/11/magazine/americans-jobs-poverty-homeless.html

Detrick, P., & Chibnall, J. T. (2014). Underreporting on the MMPI—2-RF in a high-demand police officer selection context: An illustration. *Psychological Assessment, 26,* 1044–1049.

DeValois, R. L., & DeValois, K. K. (1975). Neural coding of color. *Handbook of Perception, 5,* 117–166.

Devine, J., Hinks, T., & Naveed, A. (2019). Happiness in Bangladesh: The role of religion and connectedness. *Journal of Happiness Studies, 20*(2), 351–371. https://doi.org/10.1007/s10902-017-9939-x

Devore, E. E., Kang, J. H., Breteler, M. M., & Grodstein, F. (2012). Dietary intake of berries and flavonoids in relation to cognitive decline. *Annals of Neurology, 72*(1), 135–143.

de Waal, F. B. M. (2018, September). Do animals feel empathy? *Scientific American, 27,* 92–99.

DeWall, C. N., Baumeister, R. F., & Vohs, K. D. (2008). Satiated with belongingness? Effects of acceptance, rejection, and task framing on self-regulatory performance. *Journal of Personality Social Psychology, 95,* 1367–1382.

Dewar, M., Alber, J., Butler, C., Cowan, N., & Della Sala, S. (2012). Brief wakeful resting boosts new memories over the long term. *Psychological Science, 23,* 955–960.

de Wit, L. A., Croll, D. A., Tershy, B., Correa, M. D., Luna-Pasten, H., Quadri, P., & Kilpatrick, A. M. (2019). Potential public health benefits from cat eradications on islands. *PLOS Neglected Tropical Diseases, 13*(2), Article e0007040. https://doi.org /10.1371/journal.pntd.0007040

DeYoung, C. G., Carey, B. E., Krueger, R. F., & Ross, S. R. (2016). Ten aspects of the Big Five in the Personality Inventory for DSM–5. *Personality Disorders: Theory, Research, and Treatment, 7*(2), 113–123. https:// doi.org/10.1037/per0000170

de Zambotti, M., Willoughby, A. R., Franzen, P. L., Clark, D. B., Baker, F. C., & Colrain, I. M. (2016). K-complexes: Interaction between the central and autonomic nervous systems during sleep. *Sleep, 39,* 1129–1137. https://doi.org/10.5665 /sleep.5770

de Zeeuw, E. L., van Beijsterveldt, C. E., Hoekstra, R. A., Bartels, M., & Boomsma, D. I. (2017). The etiology of autistic traits in preschoolers: A population-based twin study. *Journal of Child Psychology and Psychiatry, 58*(8), 893–901.

Dhabhar, F. S. (2014). Effects of stress on immune function: The good, the bad, and the beautiful. *Immunologic Research, 58,* 193–210.

Di Lorenzo, L., De Pergola, G., Zocchetti, C., L'Abbate, N., Basso, A., Pannacciulli, N., Cignarelli, M., Giorgino, R., & Soleo, L. (2003). Effect of shift work on body mass index: Results of a study performed in 319 glucose-tolerant men working in a southern Italian industry. *International Journal of Obesity, 21,* 1353–1358. https://doi.org/10.1038/sj.ijo.0802419

Diamond, E. L. (1982). The role of anger and hostility in essential hypertension and coronary heart disease. *Psychological Bulletin, 92,* 410–433.

Diamond, R. M., Brown, K. S., & Miranda, J. (2020). Impact of COVID-19 on the perinatal period through a biopsychosocial systemic framework. *Contemporary Family Therapy: An International Journal, 42,* 205–216. https://doi.org/10.1007 /s10591-020-09544-8

Dickens, W. T., & Flynn, J. R. (2001). Heritability estimates vs. large environmental effects: The IQ paradox resolved. *Psychological Review, 108,* 346–369.

Dickens, W. T., & Flynn, J. R. (2006). Black Americans reduce the racial IQ gap: Evidence from standardization samples. *Psychological Science, 17,* 913–920.

Dickerson, F. B., Tenhula, W. N., & Green-Paden, L. D. (2005). The token economy for schizophrenia: Review of the literature and

recommendations for future research. *Schizophrenia Research, 75,* 405–416.

Dickinsin, K. (2019, February 22). Do participation trophies hinder child development? *Big Think Edge.* https:// bigthink.com/culture-religion /participation-trophy-and-child-develo pment?rebelltitem=1#rebelltitem1

Diehl, M., & Wahl, H.-W. (2020). *Personality development in adulthood and aging.* In M. Diehl & H.-W. Wahl, *The psychology of later life: A contextual perspective* (pp. 61–89). American Psychological Association. https://doi .org/10.1037/0000185-004

Diener, E. (1979). Deindividuation, self-awareness, and disinhibition. *Journal of Personality and Social Psychology, 3,* 1160–1171.

Diener, E., Fraser, S. C., Beaman, A. L., & Kelem, R. T. (1976). Effects of deindividuation variables on stealing among Halloween trick-or-treaters. *Journal of Personality and Social Psychology, 33,* 178–183.

Diener, E., Lucas, R. E., & Scollon, C. N. (2006). Beyond the hedonic treadmill. *American Psychologist, 6,* 305–314.

Dienes, Z., Lush, P., Palfi, B., Roseboom, W., Scott, R., Parris, B., Seth, A., & Lovell, M. (2020). Phenomenological control as cold control. *Psychology of Consciousness: Theory, Research, and Practice.* Advance online publication. https://doi.org/10 .1037/cns0000230

Digdon, N. (2020). The Little Albert controversy: Intuition, confirmation bias, and logic. *History of Psychology, 23*(2), 122–131. https://doi.org/10 .1037/hop0000055

Digdon, N., Powell R. A., & Harris, B. (2014). Little Albert's alleged neurological impairment: Watson, Rayner, and historical revision. *History of Psychology, 17*(4), 312–324.

DiLalla, L. F. (2002). Behavior genetics of aggression in children: Review and future directions. *Developmental Review, 22,* 593–622.

Dimberg, U., Thunberg, M., & Elmehed, K. (2000). Unconscious facial reactions to emotional facial expressions. *Psychological Science, 11,* 86–89.

Dimidjian, S., Goodman, S. H., Felder, J. N., Gallop, R., Brown, A. P., & Beck, A. (2016). Staying well during pregnancy and the postpartum: A pilot randomized trial of mindfulness-based cognitive therapy for the prevention of depressive relapse/ recurrence. *Journal of Consulting and Clinical Psychology, 84,* 134–145. https://doi.org/10.1037/ccp0000068

DiorVargas.com. (n.d.). People of color & mental illness photo project. http://diorvargas.com/poc-mental -illness/

Distefano, G., & Goodpaster, B. H. (2018). Effects of exercise and aging on skeletal muscle. *Cold Spring Harbor Perspectives in Medicine, 8*(3), a029785. https://doi.org/10.1101/cshperspect .a029785

Dixson, B. J., & Brooks, R. C. (2013). The role of facial hair in women's perceptions of men's attractiveness, health, masculinity and parenting abilities. *Evolution and Human Behavior, 34,* 236–241.

Dobbs, D. (2017, July/August). The smartphone psychiatrist. *The Atlantic.* https://www.theatlantic.com/magazine /archive/2017/07/the-smartphone -psychiatrist/528726/

Dobbs, P. D., Clawson, A. H., Gowin, M., & Cheney, M. K. (2020). Where college students look for vaping information and what information they believe. *Journal of American College Health, 68*(4), 347–356. https://doi.org/10.1080 /07448481.2018.1549557

Dobersek, U., Wy, G., Adkins, J., Altmeyer, S., Krout, K., Lavie, C. J., & Archer, E. (2020). Meat and mental health: A systematic review of meat abstention and depression, anxiety, and related phenomena. *Critical Reviews in Food Science and Nutrition.* 1–14. https://doi.org/10.1080/10408398 .2020.1741505

Dockterman, E. (2020, October 15). Women are deciding not to have babies because of the pandemic. That's bad for all of us. *Time.* https://time.com /5892749/covid-19-baby-bust/

Doerig, A., Schurger, A., & Herzog, M. H. (2020). Hard criteria for empirical theories of consciousness. *Cognitive Neuroscience.* Advance online publication. https//doi.org/10.1080 /17588928.2020.1772214

Dolbier, C. L., & Rush, T. E. (2012). Efficacy of abbreviated progressive muscle relaxation in a high-stress college sample. *International Journal of Stress Management, 19,* 48–68.

Doliński, D., Grzyb, T., Folwarczny, M., Grzybała, P., Krzyszycha, K., Martynowska, K., & Trojanowski, J. (2017). Would you deliver an electric shock in 2015? Obedience in the experimental paradigm developed by Stanley Milgram in the 50 years following the original studies. *Social Psychological and Personality Science, 8,* 927–933. https:// doi.org/10.1177/1948550617693060

Dollard, J., Miller, N. E., Doob, L. W., Mowrer, O. H., & Sears, R. R. (1939). *Frustration and aggression.* Yale University Press.

Dollion, N., Paulus, A., Champagne, N., St-Pierre, N., St-Pierre, É., Trudel, M., & Plusquellec, P. (2019). Fear/ reactivity in working dogs: An analysis of 37 years of behavioural data from

the Mira Foundation's future service dogs. *Applied Animal Behaviour Science, 221,* Article 104864. https:// doi.org/10.1016/j.applanim.2019 .104864

Domenici, E. (2017). Schizophrenia genetics comes to translation. *NPJ Schizophrenia, 3.* https://doi.org /10.1038/s41537-017-0011-y

Domhoff, G. W. (2001). A new neurocognitive theory of dreams. *Dreaming, 11,* 13–33.

Domhoff, G. W. (2017a). The invasion of the concept snatchers: The origins, distortions, and future of the continuity hypothesis. *Dreaming, 27,* 14–39. https://doi.org/10.1037 /drm0000047

Domhoff, G. W. (2017b). Now an invasion by a Freudian concept-snatcher: Reply to Erdelyi. *Dreaming, 27,* 345–350. https://doi.org/10.1037 /drm0000068

Domhoff, G. W. (2018). *The emergence of dreaming: Mind-wandering, embodied simulation, and the default network.* Oxford University Press.

Domhoff, G. W., & Fox, K. C. (2015). Dreaming and the default network: A review, synthesis, and counterintuitive research proposal. *Consciousness and Cognition, 33,* 342–353.

Domoff, S. E., Foley, R. P., & Ferkel, R. (2020). Addictive phone use and academic performance in adolescents. *Human Behavior and Emerging Technologies, 2*(1), 33–38. https://doi.org/10.1002/hbe2.171

Donaldson, S. I., Dollwet, M., & Rao, M. A. (2015). Happiness, excellence, and optimal human functioning revisited: Examining the peer-reviewed literature linked to positive psychology. *The Journal of Positive Psychology, 10,* 185–195.

Donnelly, G. E., Ksendzova, M., Howell, R. T., Vohs, K. D., & Baumeister, R. F. (2016). Buying to blunt negative feelings: Materialistic escape from the self. *Review of General Psychology, 20*(3), 272–316. https://doi .org/10.1037/gpr0000078

Doom, J. R., Cook, S. H., Sturza, J., Kaciroti, N., Gearhardt, A. N., Vazquez, D. M., Lumeng, J. C., & Miller, A. L. (2018). Family conflict, chaos, and negative life events predict cortisol activity in low-income children. *Developmental Psychobiology, 60,* 364–379. https://doi.org/10.1002 /dev.21602

Dorahy, M. J., Brand, B. L., Şar, V., Krüger, C., Stavropoulos, P., Martínez-Taboas, A., Lewis-Fernández, R., & Middleton, W. (2014). Dissociative identity disorder: An empirical overview. *Australian & New Zealand Journal of Psychiatry, 48,* 402–417.

Doran, J. M., Kraha, A., Marks, L. R., Ameen, E. J., & El-Ghoroury, N. H. (2016). Graduate debt in psychology: A quantitative analysis. *Training and Education in Professional Psychology, 10*(1), 3–13. https://doi.org/10.1037/tep0000112

Dorfman, H. M., Bhui, R., Hughes, B. L., & Gershman, S. J. (2019). Causal inference about good and bad outcomes. *Psychological Science, 30*(4), 516–525. https://doi.org/10.1177/0956797619828724

Dorman, M. F., Natale, S. C., Zeitler, D. M., Baxter, L., & Noble, J. H. (2019). Looking for Mickey Mouse™ but finding a Munchkin: The perceptual effects of frequency upshifts for single-sided deaf, cochlear implant patients. *Journal of Speech, Language, and Hearing Research, 62*(9), 3493–3499. https://doi.org/10.1044/2019_JSLHR-H-18-0389

Doron, R., Sterkin, A., Fried, M., Yehezkel, O., Lev, M., Belkin, M., Rosner, M., Solomon, A. S., Mandel, Y., & Polat, U. (2019). Spatial visual function in anomalous trichromats: Is less more? *PLOS ONE, 14*(1), e0209662. https://doi.org/10.1371/journal.pone.0209662

Dossett, M. L., Fricchione, G. L., & Benson, H. B. (2020). A new era for mind–body medicine. *The New England Journal of Medicine, 382*(15), 1390–1391.

Dougherty, L. R., Klein, D. N., Olino, T. M., Dyson, M., & Rose, S. (2009). Increased waking salivary cortisol and depression risk in preschoolers: The role of maternal history of melancholic depression and early child temperament. *Journal of Child Psychology and Psychiatry, 50,* 1495–1503.

Dovidio, J. F., Kawakami, K., & Gaertner, S. L. (2002). Implicit and explicit prejudice and interracial interaction. *Journal of Personality and Social Psychology, 82,* 62–68.

Drace, S., Ric, F., & Desrichard, O. (2010). Affective biases in likelihood perception: A possible role of experimental demand in mood-congruence effects. *International Review of Social Psychology, 23*(1), 93–109.

Drago, F., Scharf, R. J., Maphula, A., Nyathi, E., Mahopo, T. C., Svensen, E., Mduma, E., Bessong, P., & Rogawski McQuade, E. T. (2020). Psychosocial and environmental determinants of child cognitive development in rural South Africa and Tanzania: Findings from the mal-ed cohort. *BMC Public Health, 20,* Article 505. https://doi.org/10.1186/s12889-020-08598-5.

Dreuning, K. M., Barendsen, R. W., van Trotsenburg, A. P., Twisk, J. W., Sleeboom, C., van Heurn, L. E., & Derikx, J. P. (2020). Inguinal hernia in girls: A retrospective analysis of over 1000 patients. *Journal of Pediatric Surgery, 55*(9), 908–1913. https://doi.org/10.1016/j.jpedsurg.2020.03.015

Drew, T., Vo, M. L. H., & Wolfe, J. M. (2013). The invisible gorilla strikes again: Sustained inattentional blindness in expert observers. *Psychological Science, 24,* 1848–1853.

Drexler, B., Zinser, S., Huang, S., Poe, M. M., Rudolph, U., Cook, J. M., & Antkowiak, B. (2013). Enhancing the function of alpha5-subunit-containing GABAA receptors promotes action potential firing of neocortical neurons during upstates. *European Journal of Pharmacology, 702,* 18–24.

drjilltaylor.com. (n.d.). *About Dr. Jill Bolte Taylor.* http://drjilltaylor.com/about.html

Drougard, A., Fournel, A., Valet, P., & Knauf, C. (2015). Impact of hypothalamic reactive oxygen species in the regulation of energy metabolism and food intake. *Frontiers in Neuroscience, 9,* 1–12. https://doi.org/10.3389/fnins.2015.00056

Druckman, D., & Bjork, R. A. (Eds.). (1994). *Learning, remembering, believing: Enhancing human performance* [Study conducted by the National Research Council]. National Academy Press.

Drug Enforcement Administration (DEA). (2020a, April). *Rohypnol.* U.S. Department of Justice. https://www.dea.gov/sites/default/files/2020-06/Rohypnol-2020.pdf

Drug Enforcement Administration (DEA). (2020b, April). *Synthetic opioids.* https://www.dea.gov/sites/default/files/2020-06/Synthetic%20Opioids-2020.pdf

Drug Enforcement Administration (DEA). (n.d.). *Drug schedules.* U.S. Department of Justice. https://www.dea.gov/druginfo/ds.shtml

Druss, B. G., Hwang, I., Petukhova, M., Sampson, N. A., Wang, P. S., & Keller, R. C. (2009). Impairment in role functioning in mental and chronic medical disorders in the United States: Results from the National Comorbidity Survey Replication. *Molecular Psychiatry, 14,* 728–737.a

Ducharme, J. (2020, January 10). Forget what you think you know about blue light and sleep. *Time.* https://time.com/5752454/blue-light-sleep/

Duckworth, A., & Gross, J. J. (2014). Self-control and grit: Related but separable determinants of success. *Current Directions in Psychological Science, 23*(5), 319–325.

Duckworth, A. L., & Seligman, M. E. P. (2005). Self-discipline outdoes IQ in predicting academic performance of adolescents. *Psychological Science, 16,* 939–944.

Duckworth, A. L., Gendler, T. S., & Gross, J. J. (2016). Situational strategies for self-control. *Perspectives on Psychological Science, 11,* 35–55. https://doi.org/10.1177/1745691615623247

Duckworth, A. L., Weir, D., Tsukayama, E., & Kwok, D. (2012). Who does well in life? Conscientious adults excel in both objective and subjective success. *Frontiers in Psychology, 3,* 356. https://doi.org/10.3389/fpsyg.2012.00356

Duggal, N. A., Pollock, R. D., Lazarus, N. R., Harridge, S., & Lord, J. M. (2018). Major features of immunesenescence, including reduced thymic output, are ameliorated by high levels of physical activity in adulthood. *Aging Cell, 17*(2), e12750. https://doi.org/10.1111/acel.12750

Duits, P., Cath, D. C., Lissek, S., Hox, J. J., Hamm, A. O., Engelhard, I. M., van den Hout, M. A., & Baas, J. M. (2015). Updated meta-analysis of classical fear conditioning in the anxiety disorders. *Depression and Anxiety, 32,* 239–253.

Dulka, B. N. (2020, January 13). Glutamate built the brain—Can it treat it, too? *Scientific American.* https://blogs.scientificamerican.com/observations/glutamate-built-the-brain-can-it-treat-it-too/

Dunbar, R. I. M. (1993). Co-evolution of neocortex size, group size and language in humans. *Behavioral and Brain Sciences, 16*(4), 681–735.

Dunlop, G. (2017, January 19). Saroo Brierley: The real-life search behind the film Lion. *BBC News.* http://www.bbc.com/news/world-australia-38645840

Dunlosky, J., Rawson, K. A., Marsh, E. J., Nathan, M. J., & Willingham, D. T. (2013). Improving students' learning with effective learning techniques promising directions from cognitive and educational psychology. *Psychological Science in the Public Interest, 14,* 4–58.

Dunn, E. W., Aknin, L. B., & Norton, M. I. (2014). Prosocial spending and happiness: Using money to benefit others pays off. *Current Directions in Psychological Science, 23*(1), 41–47.

DuPont-Reyes, M. J., Villatoro, A. P., Phelan, J. C., Painter, K., & Link, B. G. (2020). Adolescent views of mental illness stigma: An intersectional lens. *American Journal of Orthopsychiatry, 90*(2), 201–211. https://doi.org/10.1037/ort0000425

Duregotti, E., Zanetti, G., Scorzeto, M., Megighian, A., Montecucco, C., Pirazzini, M., & Rigoni, M. (2015). Snake and spider toxins induce a rapid recovery of function of botulinum neurotoxin paralysed neuromuscular junction. *Toxins, 7,* 5322–5336.

Duschinsky, R., & Solomon, J. (2017). Infant disorganized attachment: Clarifying levels of analysis. *Clinical Child Psychology and Psychiatry, 22*(4), 524–538. https://doi.org/10.1177/1359104516685602

Dusek, J. A., Out, H. H., Wohlhueter, A. L., Bhasin, M., Zerbini, L. F., Joseph, M. G., Benson, H., & Libermann, T. A. (2008). Genomic counter-stress changes induced by the relaxation response. *PLOS ONE, 3,* Article e2576. https://doi.org/10.1371/journal.pone.0002576

Dutta, D. J., Woo, D. H., Lee, P. R., Pajevic, S., Bukalo, O., Huffman, W. C., Wake, H., Basser, P. J., SheikhBahaei, S., Lazarevic, V., Smith, J. C., & Fields, R. D. (2018). Regulation of myelin structure and conduction velocity by perinodal astrocytes. *Proceedings of the National Academy of Sciences, 115*(46), 11832–11837. https://doi.org/10.1073/pnas.1811013115

Dwyer, C., Sowerby, l., & Rotenberg, B. W. (2016). Is cocaine a safe topical agent for use during endoscopic sinus surgery? *Laryngoscope, 126,* 1721–1723. https://doi.org/10.1002/lary.25836

Dwyer-Lindgren, L., Cork, M. A., Sligar, A., Steuben, K. M., Wilson, K. F., Provost, N. R., Mayala, B. K., VanderHeide, J. D., Collison, M. L., Hall, J. B., Biehl, M. H., Carter, A., Frank, T., Douwes-Schultz, D., Burstein, R., Casey, D. C., Deshpande, A., Earl, L., El Bcheraoui, C., . . . Hay, S. I. (2019). Mapping HIV prevalence in sub-Saharan Africa between 2000 and 2017. *Nature, 570,* 189–193. https://doi.org/10.1038/s41586-019-1200-9

Dzau, V. J., Inouye, S. K., Rowe, J. W., Finkelman, E., & Yamada, T. (2019). Enabling healthful aging for all—The National Academy of Medicine Grand Challenge in Healthy Longevity. *The New England Journal of Medicine, 381*(18), 1699–1701.

Eagly, A. H., & Crowley, M. (1986). Gender and helping behavior: A meta-analytic review of the social psychological literature. *Psychological Bulletin, 100,* 283–308.

Eastside College Preparatory School. (n.d.). *History.* http://www.eastside.org/_about/history.html

Eastwick, P. W., Eagly, A. H., Finkel, E. J., & Johnson, S. E. (2011). Implicit and explicit preferences for physical attractiveness in a romantic partner: A double dissociation in predictive validity. *Journal of Personality and Social Psychology, 101,* 993–1011.

Eastwick, P. W., Keneski, E., Morgan, T. A., McDonald, M. A., & Huang, S. A. (2018). What do short-term and long-term relationships look like? Building the relationship coordination and strategic timing (ReCAST) model. *Journal of Experimental Psychology: General, 147*(5), 747–781. https://doi.org/10.1037/xge0000428

Eastwick, P. W., Luchies, L. B., Finkel, E. J., & Hunt, L. L. (2014). The predictive validity of ideal partner preferences: A review and meta-analysis. *Psychological Bulletin, 140,* 623–665.

Eaton, N. R., Keyes, K. M., Krueger, R. F., Balsis, S., Skodol, A. E., Markon, K. E., Grant, B. F., & Hasin, D. S. (2012). An invariant dimensional liability model of gender differences in mental disorder prevalence: Evidence from a national sample. *Journal of Abnormal Psychology, 121,* 282–288.

Ebbinghaus, H. (1885/1913). *Memory: A contribution to experimental psychology* (H. A. Ruger & C. E. Bussenius, Trans.). Teachers College, Columbia University.

Eccleston, C., Fisher, E., Howard, R. F., Slater, R., Forgeron, P., Palermo, T. M., Birnie, K. A., Anderson, B. J., Chambers, C. T., Crombez, G., Ljungman, G. Jordan, I., Jordan, Z., Roberts, C., Schechter, N., Sieberg, C. B., Tibboel, D., Walker, S. M., Wilkinson, D., & Wood, C. (2020). Delivering transformative action in paediatric pain: A Lancet Child & Adolescent Health Commission. *The Lancet. Child & Adolescent Health, 5*(1), 47–87. https://doi.org/10.1016/S2352-4642(20)30277-7

Eckstein, D., Aycock, K. J., Sperber, M. A., McDonald, J., Van Wiesner, V., III, Watts, R. E., & Ginsburg, P. (2010). A review of 200 birth-order studies: Lifestyle characteristics. *Journal of Individual Psychology, 6,* 408–434.

Editors of *The Lancet*. (2010). Retraction—Ileal-lymphoid-nodular hyperplasia, non-specific colitis, and pervasive developmental disorder in children. *The Lancet, 375,* 445.

Edwards, A. C., Bigdeli, T. B., Docherty, A. R., Bacanu, S., Lee, D., De Candia, T. R., Moscati, A., Thiselton, D. L., Maher, B. S., Wormley, B. K., Walsh, D., O'Neill, F. A., Kendler, K. S., Riley, B. P., Fanous, A. H., & Molecular Genetics of Schizophrenia Collaboration (MGS). (2016). Meta-analysis of positive and negative symptoms reveals schizophrenia modifier genes. *Schizophrenia Bulletin, 42*(2), 279–287. https://doi.org/10.1093/schbul/sbv119

Eichenbaum, H. (2004). Hippocampus: Cognitive processes and neural representations that underlie declarative memory. *Neuron, 44,* 109–120.

Eikenberry, S. E., Mancuso, M., Iboi, E., Phan, T., Eikenberry, K., Kuang, Y., Kostelich, E., & Gumel, A. B. (2020). To mask or not to mask: Modeling the potential for face mask use by the general public to curtail the COVID-19 pandemic. *Infectious Disease Modelling, 5,* 293–308. https://doi.org/10.1016/j.idm.2020.04.001

Eisenberg, M. J., Hébert-Losier, A., Windle, S. B., Greenspoon, T., Brandys, T., Fülöp, T., Nguyen, T., Elkouri, S., Montigny, M., Wilderman, I., Bertrand, O. F., Bostwick, J. A., Abrahamson, J., Lacasse, Y., Pakhale, S., Cabaussel, J. &, Filion, K. B. (2020) Effect of e-cigarettes plus counseling vs counseling alone on smoking cessation: A randomized clinical trial. *Journal of the American Medical Association, 324*(18), 1844–1854. https://doi.org/10.1001/jama.2020.18889

Ekman, P. (1992). Are there basic emotions? *Psychological Review, 99,* 550–553.

Ekman, P. (2003). *Emotions revealed.* Times Books.

Ekman, P. (2016). What scientists who study emotion agree about. *Perspectives on Psychological Science, 11,* 31–34. https://doi.org/10.1177/1745691615596992

Ekman, P., & Friesen, W. V. (1971). Constants across cultures in the face and emotion. *Journal of Personality and Social Psychology, 17,* 124–129.

Ekman, P., & Keltner, D. (2014, April 10). Darwin's claim of universals in facial expressions not challenged. *Huffington Post.* http://www.huffingtonpost.com/paul-ekman/darwins-claim-of-universals-in-facial-expression-not-challenged_b_5121383.html

El Hayek, L., Khalifeh, M., Zibara, V., Abi Assaad, R., Emmanuel, N., Karnib, N., El-Ghandour, R., Nasrallah, P., Bilen, M., Ibrahim, P., Younes, J., Abou Haidar, E., Barmo, N., Jabre, V., Stephan, J. S., & Sleiman, S. F. (2019). Lactate mediates the effects of exercise on learning and memory through SIRT1-dependent activation of hippocampal brain-derived neurotrophic factor (BDNF). *Journal of Neuroscience, 39*(13), 2369–2382. https://doi.org/10.1523/JNEUROSCI.1661-18.2019

El Mansari, M., Guiard, B. P., Chernoloz, O., Ghanbari, R., Katz, N., & Blier, P. (2010). Relevance of norepinephrine-dopamine interactions in the treatment of major depressive disorder. *CNS Neuroscience & Therapeutics, 16*(3), e1–e17. https://doi.org/10.1111/j.1755-5949.2010.00146.x

Elder, B. L., Ammar, E. M., & Pile, D. (2015). Sleep duration, activity levels, and measures of obesity in adults. *Public Health Nursing, 33,* 200–205.

Elder, C. R., Gullion, C. M., Funk, K. L., DeBar, L. L., Lindberg, N. M., & Stevens, V. J. (2012). Impact of sleep, screen time, depression and stress on weight change in the intensive weight loss phase of the LIFE study. *International Journal of Obesity, 36,* 86–92.

Elias, G. J., Giacobbe, P., Boutet, A., Germann, J., Beyn, M. E., Gramer, R. M., Pancholi, A., Joel, S. E., & Lozano, A. M. (2020). Probing the circuitry of panic with deep brain stimulation: Connectomic analysis and review of the literature. *Brain Stimulation, 13*(1), 10–14. https://doi.org/10.1016/j.brs.2019.09.010

Eling, P., & Finger, S. (2019). Franz Joseph Gall on the cerebellum as the organ for the reproductive drive. *Frontiers in Neuroanatomy, 13,* 40. https://doi.org/10.3389/fnana.2019.00040

Elkind, D. (1967). Egocentrism in adolescence. *Child Development, 38,* 1025–1034.

Ellentube. (2018). Ellen talks to Thai soccer team in their first in-studio interview since cave rescue [Video]. https://www.ellentube.com/video/ellen-talks-to-thai-soccer-team-in-their-first-in-studio-interview-since-cave-rescue.html#time=352

Ellis, A., & Dryden, W. (1997). *The practice of rational emotive behavior therapy* (2nd ed.). Springer.

Ellis, A., & Joffe Ellis, D. (2019). *Theories of psychotherapy series. Rational emotive behavior therapy* (2nd ed.). American Psychological Association. https://doi.org/10.1037/0000134-000

Ellis, W. E., Dumas, T. M., & Forbes, L. M. (2020). Physically isolated but socially connected: Psychological adjustment and stress among adolescents during the initial COVID-19 crisis. *Canadian Journal of Behavioural Science, 52*(3), 177–187. https://doi.org/10.1037/cbs0000215

Ellis-Petersen, H. (2020, February 5). "Honk more, wait more": Mumbai tests traffic lights that reward the patient driver. *The Guardian.* https://www.theguardian.com/world/2020/feb/05/honk-more-wait-more-mumbai-tests-traffic-lights-that-reward-the-patient-driver

Elsawaf, Y., Rynearson, K. D., Tanzi, R. E., & Wagner, S. L. (2019). Comparative pathophysiology, biomarkers and gross anatomical changes in chronic traumatic encephalopathy and Alzheimer's disease suggest a common therapeutic rationale. *Current Trends in Neurology, 13,* 91–100.

El-Sayes, J., Harasym, D., Turco, C. V., Locke, M. B., & Nelson, A. J. (2019). Exercise-induced neuroplasticity: A mechanistic model and prospects for promoting plasticity. *The Neuroscientist, 25*(1), 65–85. https://doi.org/10.1177/1073858418771538

Else-Quest, N. M., Higgins, A., Allison, C., & Morton, L. C. (2012). Gender differences in self-conscious emotional experience: A meta-analysis. *Psychological Bulletin, 138,* 947–981.

Emmons, R. A., & McCullough, M. E. (2003). Counting blessings versus burdens: An experimental investigation of gratitude and subjective well-being in daily life. *Journal of Personality and Social Psychology, 84,* 377–389. https://doi.org/10.1037/0022-3514.84.2.377

Emmons, R. A., Froh, J., & Rose, R. (2019). Gratitude. In M. W. Gallagher & S. J. Lopez (Eds.), *Positive psychological assessment: A handbook of models and measures* (pp. 317–332). American Psychological Association. https://doi.org/10.1037/0000138-020

Emotion. (n.d.). In *Online etymology dictionary.* http://www.etymonline.com/index.php?term=emotion

Endicott, L., Bock, T., & Narvaez, D. (2003). Moral reasoning, intercultural development, and multicultural experiences: Relations and cognitive underpinnings. *International Journal of Intercultural Relations, 27,* 403–419.

Enea, V., & Dafinoiu, I. (2009). Motivational/solution-focused intervention for reducing school truancy among adolescents. *Journal of Cognitive and Behavioral Psychotherapies, 9,* 185–198.

Engler, J. N., Druen, P. B., Steck, L. W., Ligon, M., Jacob, S., & Arseneau, L. J. (2020). Enhancing advocacy for individuals in poverty: The role of a poverty simulation training. *Psychological Services, 17*(S1), *110–119.* https://doi.org/10.1037/ser0000348

Ensink, K., Borelli, J. L., Normandin, L., Target, M., & Fonagy, P. (2020). Childhood sexual abuse and attachment insecurity: Associations with child psychological difficulties. *American Journal of Orthopsychiatry, 90*(1), 115–124. https://doi.org/10.1037/ort0000407

Epstein, L., & Mardon, S. (2007). *The Harvard Medical School guide to a good night's sleep.* McGraw-Hill.

Epstein, R. (2016). Do gays have a choice? *Scientific American, 25,* 56–63.

Epstein, R., McKinney, P., Fox, S., & Garcia, C. (2012). Support for a fluid-continuum model of sexual orientation: A large-scale Internet study. *Journal of Homosexuality, 59,* 1356–1381.

Erdberg, P. (1990). Rorschach assessment. In G. Goldstein &

M. Hersen (Eds.), *Handbook of psychological assessment* (2nd ed.). Pergamon.

Erickson, K. I., Voss, M. W., Prakash, R. S., Basak, C., Szabo, A., Chaddock, L., Kim, J. S., Heo, S., Alves, H., White, S. M., Wojcicki, T. R., Mailey, E., Vieira, V. J., Martin, S. A., Pence, B. D., Woods, J. A., McAuley, E., & Kramer, A. F. (2011). Exercise training increases size of hippocampus and improves memory. *Proceedings of the National Academy of Sciences, 108*(7), 3017–3022.

Ericsson, K. A. (2003). The acquisition of expert performance as problem solving. In J. E. Davidson & R. J. Sternberg (Eds.), *The psychology of problem solving* (pp. 31–83). Cambridge University Press.

Erikson, E. H. (1993). *Childhood and society*. W. W. Norton.

Erikson, E. H., & Erikson, J. M. (1997). *The life cycle completed*. W. W. Norton.

Eriksson, P. S., Perfilieva, E., Bjork-Eriksson, T., Alborn, A. M., Nordborg, C., Peterson, D. A., & Gage, F. H. (1998). Neurogenesis in the adult human hippocampus. *Nature Medicine, 4*, 1313–1317.

Erland, L. A., & Saxena, P. K. (2017). Melatonin natural health products and supplements: Presence of serotonin and significant variability of melatonin content. *Journal of Clinical Sleep Medicine, 13*, 275–281. https://doi.org/10.5664/jcsm.6462

Erol, A., & Karpyak, V. M., (2015). Sex and gender-related differences in alcohol use and its consequences: Contemporary knowledge and future research considerations. *Drug and Alcohol Dependence, 156*, 1–13. https://doi.org/10.1016/j.drugalcdep.2015.08.023

Escobar-Viera, C. G., Shensa, A., Bowman, N. D., Sidani, J. E., Knight, J., James, A. E., & Primack, B. A. (2018). Passive and active social media use and depressive symptoms among United States adults. *Cyberpsychology, Behavior, and Social Networking, 21*(7), 437–443. https://doi.org/10.1089/cyber.2017.0668

Etaugh, C. (2008). Women in the middle and later years. In F. L. Denmark & M. Paludi (Eds.), *Psychology of women: Handbook of issues and theories* (2nd ed., pp. 271–302). Praeger.

Evans, V., & Green, M. (2006). *Cognitive linguistics: An introduction*. Erlbaum.

Evensen, S., Wisløff, T., Lystad, J. U., Bull, H., Ueland, T., & Falkum, E. (2016). Prevalence, employment rate, and cost of schizophrenia in a high-income welfare society: A population-based study using comprehensive health and welfare

registers. *Schizophrenia Bulletin, 42*(2), 476–483. https://doi.org/10.1093/schbul/sbv141

Exner, J. E. (1980). But it's only an inkblot. *Journal of Personality Assessment, 44*, 562–577.

Exner, J. E. (1986). *The Rorschach: A comprehensive system* (Vol. 1, 2nd ed.). John Wiley & Sons.

Eysenck, H. J. (1967). *The biological basis of personality*. C.C. Thomas.

Eysenck, H. J. (1990). Biological dimensions of personality. In L. A. Pervin (Ed.), *Handbook of personality: Theory of research* (pp. 244–276). Guilford Press.

Eysenck, H. J., & Eysenck, B. G. (1968). *Manual for the Eysenck Personality Inventory*. Educational Industrial Testing Service.

Fabian, J. (2015, June 19). Obama goofs in speech at Tyler Perry's house. *The Hill*. http://thehill.com/homenews/administration/245512-obama-goofs-in-speech-at-tyler-perrys-house

Fainaru, S. (2016, March 15). *NFL acknowledges, for first time, link between football, brain disease*. ESPN. https://www.espn.com/espn/otl/story/_/id/14972296/top-nfl-official-acknowledges-link-football-related-head-trauma-cte-first

Fainaru-Wada, M. (2013, February 15). League of denial: The NFL's concussion crisis. In M. Kirk (Producer & Director), J. Gilmore (Producer), & M. Wiser (Producer), *The Frontline interviews*. PBS. http://www.pbs.org/wgbh/pages/frontline/sports/league-of-denial/the-frontline-interview-sydney-seau-2/

Fairbairn, C. E., Velia, B. A., Creswell, K. G., & Sayette, M. A. (2020). A dynamic analysis of the effect of alcohol consumption on humor enjoyment in a social context. *Journal of Experimental Social Psychology, 86*, Article 103903. https://doi.org/10.1016/j.jesp.2019.103903

Falcon, B., Zivanov, J., Zhang, W., Murzin, A. G., Garringer, H. J., Vidal, R., Crowther, R. A., Newell, K. L., Ghetti, B., Goedert, M., & Scheres, S. H. (2019). Novel tau filament fold in chronic traumatic encephalopathy encloses hydrophobic molecules. *Nature, 568*(7752), 420–423. https://doi.org/10.1038/s41586-019-1026-5

Falk, D., Lepore, F. E., & Noe, A. (2013). The cerebral cortex of Albert Einstein: A description and preliminary analysis of unpublished photographs. *Brain, 136*, 1304–1327.

Falk, E., & Platt, M. (2018, July 9). What your Facebook network reveals about how you use your brain. *Scientific American Mind, 29*(5), 45–47.

Fancher, R. E., & Rutherford, A. (2012). *Pioneers of psychology: A history* (4th ed.). W. W. Norton.

Fantini, M. L., Corona, A., Clerici, S., & Ferini-Strambi, L. (2005). Aggressive dream content without daytime aggressiveness in REM sleep behavior disorder. *Neurology, 65*, 1010–1015.

Farb, N. A., Chapman, H. A., & Anderson, A. K. (2013). Emotions: Form follows function. *Current Opinion in Neurobiology, 23*, 393–398.

Faria, M. A. (2013). Violence, mental illness, and the brain. A brief history of psychosurgery: Part 2—from the limbic system and cingulotomy to deep brain stimulation. *Surgical Neurology International, 4*. http://doi.org/10.4103/2152-7806.112825

Farmer, T. A., & Matlin, M. W. (2019). *Cognition* (10th ed.). John Wiley & Sons.

Farthing, G. W. (1992). *The psychology of consciousness*. Prentice Hall.

Faymonville, M. E., Laureys, S., Degueldre, C., DelFiore, G., Luxen, A., Franck, G., Lamy, M., & Maquet, P. (2000). Neural mechanisms of antinociceptive effects of hypnosis. *Anesthesiology, 2*, 1257–1267. https://doi.org/10.1097/00000542-200005000-00013

Fazel, S., Gulati, G., Linsell, L., Geddes, J. R., & Grann, M. (2009). Schizophrenia and violence: Systematic review and meta-analysis. *PLOS Medicine, 6*, Article e1000120. https://doi.org/10.1371/journal.pmed.1000120

FBI Uniform Crime Reports. (n.d.). *Crime in the United States 2001, Section II—Crime index offenses reported*. https://ucr.fbi.gov/crime-in-the-u.s/2001/01sec2.pdf

Feigelman, S. (2011). The first year. In R. M. Kliegman, R. E. Behrman, H. B. Jenson, & B. F. Stanton (Eds.), *Nelson textbook of pediatrics* (19th ed., pp. 26–30). Saunders Elsevier.

Feinstein, J. S., Adolphs, R., Damasio, A., & Tranel, D. (2011). The human amygdala and the induction and experience of fear. *Current Biology, 21*, 34–38.

Feinstein, R., Heiman, N., & Yager, J. (2015). Common factors affecting psychotherapy outcomes: Some implications for teaching psychotherapy. *Journal of Psychiatric Practice, 21*, 180–189.

Feist, G. J. (2004). Creativity and the frontal lobes. *Bulletin of Psychology and the Arts, 5*, 21–28.

Feng, P., Huang, L., & Wang, H. (2013). Taste bud homeostasis in health, disease, and aging. *Chemical Senses, 39*, 3–16.

Fennell, A. B., Benau, E. M., & Atchley, R. A. (2016). A single session of meditation reduces of physiological indices of anger in both experienced and novice meditators. *Consciousness and Cognition, 40*, 54–66. https://doi.org/10.1016/j.concog.2015.12.010

Ferguson, C. J. (2010). Genetic contributions to antisocial personality and behavior: A meta-analytic review from an evolutionary perspective. *Journal of Social Psychology, 150*, 160–180.

Ferguson, C. J. (2015a). Do angry birds make for angry children? A meta-analysis of video game influences on children's and adolescents' aggression, mental health, prosocial behavior, and academic performance. *Perspectives on Psychological Science, 10*(5), 646–666. https://doi.org/10.1177/1745691615592234

Ferguson, C. J. (2015b). "Everybody knows psychology is not a real science": Public perceptions of psychology and how we can improve our relationship with policymakers, the scientific community, and the general public. *American Psychologist, 70*, 527–542. https://doi.org/10.1037/a0039405

Ferguson, C. J., Brown, J. M., & Torres, A. V. (2018). Education or indoctrination? The accuracy of introductory psychology textbooks in covering controversial topics and urban legends about psychology. *Current Psychology, 37*(3), 574–582. https://doi.org/10.1007/s12144-016-9539-7

Ferguson, C. J., Copenhaver, A., & Markey, P. (2020). Reexamining the findings of the American Psychological Association's 2015 Task Force on Violent Media: A meta-analysis. *Perspectives on Psychological Science, 15*(6), 1423–1443. https://doi.org/10.1177/1745691620927666

Ferland, G. (2013). Vitamin K status and cognitive function in healthy older adults. *Neurobiology of Aging, 34*(12), 2777–2783.

Fernald, A., Marchman, V. A., & Weisleder, A. (2014). SES differences in language processing skill and vocabulary are evident at 18 months. *Developmental Science, 16*, 234–248.

Ferrante, A., Gellerman, D., Ay, A., Woods, K. P., Filipowica, A. M., Jain, K., Bearden, N., & Ingram, K. K. (2015). Diurnal preference predicts phase differences in expression of human peripheral circadian clock genes. *Journal of Circadian Rhythms, 13*, 1–7. https://doi.org/10.5334/jcr.ae

Ferris, P. A., Kline, T. J. B., & Bourdage, J. S. (2012). He said, she said: Work, biopsychosocial, and lifestyle contributions to coronary heart disease risk. *Health Psychology, 31*, 503–511.

Fesharaki-Zadeh, A. (2019). Chronic traumatic encephalopathy: A brief overview. *Frontiers in Neurology, 10*, 713. https://doi.org/10.3389/fneur.2019.00713

**Fessler, L.** (2017, June 22). Good managers give constructive criticism—but truly masterful leaders offer constructive praise. *Quartz.* https://qz.com/1010784/good-managers-give-constructive-criticism-but-truly-masterful-leaders-give-constructive-praise/

**Festinger, L.** (1957). *A theory of cognitive dissonance.* Harper & Row.

**Festinger, L., & Carlsmith, J. M.** (1959). Cognitive consequences of forced compliance. *Journal of Abnormal and Social Psychology, 58,* 203–210.

**Festinger, L., Schachter, S., & Back, K.** (1950). *Social pressures in informal groups: A study of human factors in housing.* Stanford University Press.

**Fichera, A.** (2020, October 23). *Posts target Trump with false claim on MAGA hats.* FactCheck.org. https://www.factcheck.org/2020/10/posts-target-trump-with-false-claim-on-maga-hats/

**Fichera, A., & Spencer, S. H.** (2020, October 15). *Conspiracy theory baselessly claims Biden dad Navy SEALs killed.* FactCheck.org. https://www.factcheck.org/2020/10/conspiracy-theory-baselessly-claims-biden-had-navy-seals-killed/

**Field, T.** (1996). Attachment and separation in young children. *Annual Review of Psychology, 47,* 541–561.

**Filkins, D.** (2004, November 21). In Falluja, young Marines saw the savagery of an urban war. *The New York Times.* http://www.nytimes.com/2004/11/21/international/middleeast/21battle.html?_r=0

**Finch, L. E., Cummings, J. R., & Tomiyama, A. J.** (2019). Cookie or clementine? Psychophysiological stress reactivity and recovery after eating healthy and unhealthy comfort foods. *Psychoneuroendocrinology, 107,* 26–36.

**Fincham, F. D., & May, R. W.** (2017). Infidelity in romantic relationships. *Current Opinion in Psychology, 13,* 70–74.

**Fine, J.** (2013, February 7). Rescuing Cesar Millan. *Men's Journal.* http://www.mensjournal.com/magazine/rescuing-dog-whisperer-cesar-millan-20130207

**Finger, S.** (2001). *Origins of neuroscience: A history of explorations into brain function.* Oxford University Press.

**Fink, G.** (2011). Stress controversies: Post-traumatic stress disorder, hippocampal volume, gastroduodenal ulceration. *Journal of Neuroendocrinology, 23,* 107–117.

**Fink, G.** (2017). Selye's general adaptation syndrome: Stress-induced gastro-duodenal ulceration and inflammatory bowel disease. *Journal of Endocrinology, 232,* F1–F5. https://doi.org/10.1530/JOE-16-0547

**Finkelstein-Fox, L., Park, C. L., & Riley, K. E.** (2019). Mindfulness' effects on stress, coping, and mood: A daily diary goodness-of-fit study. *Emotion, 19*(6), 1002–1013. https://doi.org/10.1037/emo0000495

**Finucane, A. M.** (2011). The effect of fear and anger on selective attention. *Emotion, 11*(4), 970–974. https://doi.org/10.1037/a0022574

**Firestein, S.** (2001). How the olfactory system makes sense of scents. *Nature, 413,* 211–218.

**Firth, S.** (2005). End-of-life: A Hindu view. *The Lancet, 366,* 682–686.

**Fischer, P., Krueger, J. I., Greitemeyer, T., Vogrincic, C., Kastenmüller, A., Frey, D., Heene, M., Wicher, M., & Kainbacher, M.** (2011). The bystander-effect: A meta-analytic review on bystander intervention in dangerous and non-dangerous emergencies. *Psychological Bulletin, 137,* 517–537.

**Fisher, A. N., & Stinson, D. A.** (2020). Ambivalent attraction: Beauty determines whether men romantically desire or dismiss high status women. *Personality and Individual Differences, 154*(1). https://doi.org/10.1016/j.paid.2019.109681

**Fisher, H. E., Aron, A., & Brown, L. L.** (2006). Romantic love: A mammalian brain system for mate choice. *Philosophical Transactions of the Royal Society B: Biological Sciences, 361*(1476), 2173–2186.

**Fisher, J. P., Steele, J., Gentil, P., Giessing, J., & Westcott, W. L.** (2017). A minimal dose approach to resistance training for the older adult; the prophylactic for aging. *Experimental Gerontology, 99,* 80–86. https://doi.org/10.1016/j.exger.2017.09.012

**Fisher, L. B., Overholser, J. C., Ridley, J., Braden, A., & Rosoff, C.** (2015). From the outside looking in: Sense of belonging, depression, and suicide risk. *Psychiatry, 78,* 29–41.

**Fisher, T. D., & Brunell, A. B.** (2014). A bogus pipeline approach to studying gender differences in cheating behavior. *Personality and Individual Differences, 61,* 91–96.

**Fitzpatrick, M. J., & McPherson, B. J.** (2010). Coloring within the lines: Gender stereotypes in contemporary coloring books. *Sex Roles, 62,* 127–137.

**Flanigan, A. E., & Kiewra, K. A.** (2018). What college instructors can do about student cyber-slacking. *Educational Psychology Review, 30*(2), 585–597. https://doi.org/10.1007/s10648-017-9418-2

**Flor, H., & Birbaumer, N.** (1993). Comparison of the efficacy of electromyographic biofeedback, cognitive-behavioral therapy, and conservative medical interventions in the treatment of chronic musculoskeletal pain. *Journal of Consulting and Clinical Psychology, 61,* 653–658.

**Flor, H., Nikolajsen, L., & Jensen, T. S.** (2006). Phantom limb pain: A case of maladaptive CNS plasticity? *Nature Reviews Neuroscience, 7,* 873–881.

**Flora, C.** (2018). Are smartphones really destroying the adolescent brain? *Scientific American, 318,* 30–37.

**Flueck, J. L., Schaufelberger, F., Lienert, M., Schäfer Olstad, D., Wilhelm, M., & Perret, C.** (2016). Acute effects of caffeine on heart rate variability, blood pressure and tidal volume in paraplegic and tetraplegic compared to able-bodied individuals: A randomized, blinded trial. *PLOS ONE, 11*(10), e0165034. https://doi.org/10.1371/journal.pone.0165034

**Flynn, J. R.** (2009). *What is intelligence? Beyond the Flynn effect.* Cambridge University Press.

**Flynn, J. R.** (2012). *Are we getting smarter? Rising IQ in the twenty-first century.* Cambridge University Press.

**Flynn, J. R., & Shayer, M.** (2018). IQ decline and Piaget: Does the rot start at the top? *Intelligence, 66,* 112–121. https://doi.org/10.1016/j.intell.2017.11.010

**Flynn, R. M., Richert, R. A., & Wartella, E.** (2019). Play in a digital world: How interactive digital games shape the lives of children. *American Journal of Play, 12*(1), 54–73.

**Fogel, S. M., & Smith, C. T.** (2011). The function of the sleep spindle: A psychological index of intelligence and a mechanism for sleep-dependent memory consolidation. *Neuroscience & Biobehavioral Reviews, 35,* 1154–1165.

**Fog-Poulsen, K., Jacobs, T., Høyer, S., Rohde, C., Vermande, A., De Wachter, S., & De Win, G.** (2020). PD28-09: Can time to ejaculation be affected by pornography? *The Journal of Urology, 203*(Supplement 4), e615–e615. https://doi.org/10.1097/JU.0000000000000892.09

**Folkman, S., & Lazarus, R. S.** (1985). If it changes it must be a process: Study of emotion and coping during three stages of a college examination. *Journal of Personality and Social Psychology, 48,* 150–170.

**Fonagy, P., Lemma, A., Target, M., O'Keeffe, S., Constantinou, M. P., Wurman, T. V., Luyten, P., Allison, E., Roth, A., Cape, J., & Pilling, S.** (2020). Dynamic interpersonal therapy for moderate to severe depression: A pilot randomized controlled and feasibility trial. *Psychological Medicine, 50*(6), 1010–1019. https://doi.org/10.1017/S0033291719000928

**Foos, P. W., & Goolkasian, P.** (2008). Presentation format effects in a levels-of-processing task. *Experimental Psychology, 55,* 215–227.

**Forbes, C. E., Poore, J. C., Krueger, F., Barbey, A. K., Solomon, J., & Grafman, J.** (2014). The role of executive function and the dorsolateral prefrontal cortex in the expression of neuroticism and conscientiousness. *Social Neuroscience, 9*(2), 139–151.

**Forchuk, C. A., Plouffe, R. A., & Saklofske, D. H.** (2020). Do you "like" me? The roles of Facebook reassurance seeking and attachment style on depression. *Psychology of Popular Media.* Advance online publication. https://doi.org/10.1037/ppm0000312

**Ford, M., Acosta, A., & Sutcliffe, T. J.** (2013). Beyond terminology: The policy impact of a grassroots movement. *Intellectual and Developmental Disabilities, 51,* 108–112.

**Forder, L., & Lupyan, G.** (2019). Hearing words changes color perception: Facilitation of color discrimination by verbal and visual cues. *Journal of Experimental Psychology: General, 148*(7), 1105–1123. https://doi.org/10.1037/xge0000560

**Forgas, J. P.** (2008). Affect and cognition. *Perspectives on Psychological Science, 3,* 94–101.

**Forsberg, S. L., Ilieva, M., & Michel, T. M.** (2018). Epigenetics and cerebral organoids: Promising directions in autism spectrum disorders. *Translational Psychiatry, 8*(1), Article 14. https://doi.org/10.1038/s41398-017-0062-x

**Forster, S., & Spence, C.** (2018). "What smell?" Temporarily loading visual attention induces a prolonged loss of olfactory awareness. *Psychological Science, 29*(10), 1642–1652. https://doi.org/10.1177/0956797618781325

**Forsyth, D. R.** (2020). Group-level resistance to health mandates during the COVID-19 pandemic: A groupthink approach. *Group Dynamics: Theory, Research, and Practice, 24*(3), 139–152. https://doi.org/10.1037/gdn0000132

**Foss, D. J., & Pirozzolo, J. W.** (2017). Four semesters investigating frequency of testing, the testing effect, and transfer of training. *Journal of Educational Psychology, 109*(8), 1067–1083.

**Fournier, J. C., DeRubeis, R. J., Hollon, S. D., Dimidjian, S., Amsterdam, J. D., Shelton, R. C., & Fawcett, J.** (2010). Antidepressant drug effects and depression severity. *Journal of the American Medical Association, 303,* 47–53.

**Fowlkes, C. C., Martin, D. R., & Malik, J.** (2007). Local figure–ground cues are valid for natural images. *Journal of Vision, 7,* 1–9.

Fox, M. (2013, July 25). Virginia Johnson, Masters' collaborator in sex research, dies at 88. *The New York Times.* http://www.nytimes.com/2013/07/26/us/virginia-johnson-masterss-collaborator-in-sex-research-dies-at-88.html?pagewanted=all&_r=0

Fox, N. A., Snidman, N., Haas, S. A., Degnan, K. A., & Kagan, J. (2015). The relations between reactivity at 4 months and behavioral inhibition in the second year: Replication across three independent samples. *Infancy, 20,* 98–114.

Frances, A. (2016). Entrenched reductionisms: The bête noire of psychiatry. *History of Psychology, 19*(1), 57–59. https://doi.org/10.1037/hop0000018

Francis, W. S., & Gutiérrez, M. (2012). Bilingual recognition memory: Stronger performance but weaker levels-of-processing effects in the less fluent language. *Memory Cognition, 40,* 496–503.

Frankenburg, W. K., Dodds, J., Archer, P., Shapiro, H., & Bresnick, B. (1992). The Denver II: A major revision and restandardization of the Denver Developmental Screening Test. *Pediatrics, 89,* 91–97.

Franklin, K. A., & Lindberg, E. (2015). Obstructive sleep apnea is a common disorder in the population—a review on the epidemiology of sleep apnea. *Journal of Thoracic Disease, 7,* 1311–1322.

Franz, S. (2020) Deciding what to cover in intro psych: The neighbor test. In T. M. Ober, E. Che, J. E. Brodsky, C. Raffaele, & P. J. Brooks (Eds.), *How we teach now: The GSTA guide to transformative teaching* (pp. 86–94). Society for the Teaching of Psychology. http://teachpsych.org/ebooks/howweteachnow-transformative

Frederick, E. (2019, October 4). What makes people happy when skies are gray? The color yellow. *Science.* https://www.sciencemag.org/news/2019/10/what-makes-people-happy-when-skies-are-gray-color-yellow

Frederick, E. (2019, November 6). Bad dog? Think twice before yelling, experts say. *Science.* https://www.sciencemag.org/news/2019/11/bad-dog-think-twice-yelling-experts-say

Fredrickson, B. L., & Joiner, T. (2018). Reflections on positive emotions and upward spirals. *Perspectives on Psychological Science, 13*(2), 194–199.

Freedman, J. L., & Fraser, S. C. (1966). Compliance without pressures: The foot-in-the-door technique. *Journal of Personality and Social Psychology, 4,* 195–202.

Frequently Asked Questions About Chronic Traumatic Encephalopathy. (n.d.). https://www.bu.edu/cte/about/frequently-asked-questions/

Freud Museum. (n.d.). *About the museum.* http://www.freud.org.uk/about/

Freud, S. (1900/1953). The interpretation of dreams. In J. Strachey (Ed. & Trans.), *The standard edition of the complete psychological works of Sigmund Freud* (Vol. 4, pp. 1–338; Vol. 5, pp. 339–621). Hogarth Press.

Freud, S. (1905/1953). Three essays on the theory of sexuality. In J. Strachey (Ed. & Trans.), *The standard edition of the complete psychological works of Sigmund Freud* (Vol. 7, pp. 123–245). Hogarth Press.

Freud, S. (1917/1966). *Introductory lectures on psycho-analysis: The standard edition.* W. W. Norton.

Freud, S. (1923/1960). *The ego and the id* (Joan Riviere, Trans., & James Strachey, Ed.). W. W. Norton.

Freud, S. (1923/1961). The ego and the id. In J. Strachey (Ed. & Trans.), *The standard edition of the complete psychological works of Sigmund Freud* (Vol. 19, pp. 1–66). Hogarth Press.

Freud, S. (1933/1964). New introductory lectures on psycho-analysis. In J. Strachey (Ed. & Trans.), *The standard edition of the complete psychological works of Sigmund Freud* (Vol. 22, pp. 1–182). Hogarth Press.

Freud, S. (1940/1949). *An outline of psychoanalysis.* (James Strachey, Trans.). W. W. Norton.

Frewen, P., Schroeter, M. L., Riva, G., Cipresso, P., Fairfield, B., Padulo, C., Kemp, A. H., Palaniyappan, L., Owolabi, M., Kusi-Mensah, K., Polyakova, M., Fehertoi, N., D'Andrea, W., Lowe, L., & Northoff, G. (2020). Neuroimaging the consciousness of self: Review, and conceptual-methodological framework. *Neuroscience & Biobehavioral Reviews, 112,* 164–212. https://doi.org/10.1016/j.neubiorev.2020.01.023

Fridlund, A. J., Beck, H. P., Goldie, W. D., & Irons, G. (2012). Little Albert: A neurologically impaired child. *History of Psychology, 15*(4), 302–327.

Fridlund, A. J., Beck, H. P., Goldie, W. D., & Irons, G. (2020). The case for Douglas Merritte: Should we bury what is alive and well? *History of Psychology, 23*(2), 132–148. https://doi.org/10.1037/hop0000142

Friedman, B. H., Stephens, C. L., & Thayer, J. F. (2014). Redundancy analysis of autonomic and self-reported, responses to induced emotions. *Biological Psychology, 98,* 19–28.

Friedman, H. (2014). Are humanistic and positive psychology really incommensurate? *American Psychologist, 69,* 89–90. https://doi.org/10.1037/a0034865

Friedman, M., & Rosenman, R. H. (1974). *Type A behavior and your heart.* Knopf.

Friedman, R. A. (2017, February 13). LSD to cure depression? Not so fast. *The New York Times.* https://www.nytimes.com/2017/02/13/opinion/lsd-to-cure-depression-not-so-fast.html?_r=0

Friedmann, N., & Rusou, D. (2015). Critical period for first language: The crucial role of language input during the first year of life. *Current Opinion in Neurobiology, 35,* 27–34.

Friedrich, A., & Schlarb, A. A. (2018). Let's talk about sleep: A systematic review of psychological interventions to improve sleep in college students. *Journal of Sleep Research, 27,* 4–22. https://doi.org/10.1111/jsr.12568

Friedrich, P., Anderson, C., Schmitz, J., Schlüter, C., Lor, S., Stacho, M., Ströckens, F., Grimshaw, G., & Ocklenburg, S. (2019). Fundamental or forgotten? Is Pierre Paul Broca still relevant in modern neuroscience? *Laterality: Asymmetries of Body, Brain and Cognition, 24*(2), 125–138. https://doi.org/10.1080/1357650X.2018.1489827

Fukada, M., Kano, E., Miyoshi, M., Komaki, R., & Watanabe, T. (2012). Effect of "rose essential oil" inhalation on stress-induced skin-barrier disruption in rats and humans. *Chemical Senses, 37,* 347–356.

Fuller, D. A., Sinclair, E., Geller, J., Quanbeck, C., & Snook, J. (2016). *Going, going, gone: Trends and consequences of eliminating state psychiatric beds, 2016.* Treatment Advocacy Center.

*Fully Present: The Book.* (2010, August 3). Fully present: The book—meditation [Video file]. https://www.youtube.com/watch?v=k8ARntepT6g

Funk, C., & Kennedy, B. (2020, April 21). *For Earth Day, how Americans see climate change and the environment in 7 charts.* Pew Research Center. https://www.pewresearch.org/fact-tank/2020/04/21/how-americans-see-climate-change-and-the-environment-in-7-charts/

Furnham, A., & Hughes, D. J. (2014). Myths and misconceptions in popular psychology: Comparing psychology students and the general public. *Teaching of Psychology, 4,* 256–261. https://doi.org/10.1177/0098628314537984

Fusar-Poli, P., Papanastasiou, E., Stahl, D., Rocchetti, M., Carpenter, W., Shergill, S., & McGuire, P. (2015). Treatments of negative symptoms in schizophrenia: Meta-analysis of 168 randomized placebo-controlled trials. *Schizophrenia Bulletin, 41,* 892–899.

Fusar-Poli, P., Smieskova, R., Kempton, M. J., Ho, B. C., Andreasen, N. C., & Borgwardt, S. (2013). Progressive brain changes in schizophrenia related to antipsychotic treatment? A meta-analysis of longitudinal MRI studies. *Neuroscience & Biobehavioral Reviews, 37,* 1680–1691.

Füzesi, T., & Bains, J. S. (2015). A tonic for anxiety. *Nature Neuroscience, 18,* 1434–1435.

Fymat, A. L. (2018). Alzheimer's disease: A review. *Current Opinions in Neurological Science, 2,* 415–436.

Gabrieli, J. D. E., Corkin, S., Mickel, S. F., & Growdon, J. H. (1993). Intact acquisition and long-term retention of mirror-tracing skill in Alzheimer's disease and in global amnesia. *Behavioral Neuroscience, 107,* 899–910.

Gabrielli, J., & Lund, E. (2020). Acute-on-chronic stress in the time of COVID-19: Assessment considerations for vulnerable youth populations. *Pediatric Research, 88*(6), 829–831. https://doi.org/10.1038/s41390-020-1039-7

Gackenbach, J., & LaBerge, S. (Eds.). (1988). *Conscious mind, sleeping brain: Perspectives on lucid dreaming.* Plenum Press.

Gaillard, D., & Kinnamon, S. C. (2019). New evidence for fat as a primary taste quality. *Acta Physiologica (Oxford, England), 226*(1), Article e13246. https://doi.org/10.1111/apha.13246

Gainotti, G. (2019). The role of the right hemisphere in emotional and behavioral disorders of patients with frontotemporal lobar degeneration: An updated review. *Frontiers in Aging Neuroscience, 11,* 55. https://doi.org/10.3389/fnagi.2019.00055

Galanter, E. (1962). Contemporary psychophysics. In R. Brown, E. Galanter, E. H. Hess, & G. Mandler (Eds.), *New directions in psychology* (pp. 87–156). Holt, Rinehart & Winston.

Galati, D., Scherer, K. R., & Ricci-Bitti, P. E. (1997). Voluntary facial expression of emotion: Comparing congenitally blind with normally sighted encoders. *Journal of Personality and Social Psychology, 73,* 1363–1379.

Gale, C. R., Batty, G. D., & Deary, I. J. (2008). Locus of control at age 10 years and health outcomes and behaviors at age 30 years: The 1970 British Cohort Study. *Psychosomatic Medicine, 70,* 397–403.

Galen, L. W. (2018). Focusing on the nonreligious reveals secular mechanisms underlying well-being and prosociality. *Psychology of Religion and Spirituality, 10*(3), 296–306. https://doi.org/10.1037/rel0000202

Gamian-Wilk, M., & Dolinski, D. (2020). The foot-in-the-door phenomenon 40 and 50 years later: A direct replication of the original Freedman and Fraser study in Poland and in Ukraine. *Psychological Reports, 123*(6), 2582–2596. https://doi.org/10.1177/0033294119872208

Gandhi, T., Kalia, A., Ganesh, S., & Sinha, P. (2015). Immediate susceptibility to visual illusions after sight onset. *Current Biology, 25*(9), R358–R359.

Gandolphe, M. C., & El Haj, M. (2017). Flashbulb memories of the Paris attacks. *Scandinavian Journal of Psychology, 58*, 199–204. https://doi.org/10.1111/sjop.12364

Gangestad, S. W., & Haselton, M. G. (2015). Human estrus: Implications for relationship science. *Current Opinion in Psychology, 1*, 45–51.

Gangestad, S. W., & Scheyd, G. J. (2005). The evolution of human physical attractiveness. *Annual Review of Anthropology, 34*, 523–548.

Ganis, G., Thompson, W. L., & Kosslyn, S. M. (2004). Brain areas underlying visual mental imagery and visual perception: An fMRI study. *Cognitive Brain Research, 20*, 226–241.

Ganna, A., Verweij, K. J., Nivard, M. G., Maier, R., Wedow, R., Busch, A. S., Abdellaoui, A., Guo, S., Sathirapongsasuti, J. F., Lichtenstein, P., Lundström, S., Långström, N., Auton, A., Harris, K. M., Beecham, G. W., Martin, E. R., Sanders, A. R., Perry, J. R. B., Neale, B. M., . . . 23andMe Research Team. (2019). Large-scale GWAS reveals insights into the genetic architecture of same-sex sexual behavior. *Science, 365*(6456). https://doi.org/10.1126/science.aat7693

Gannon, M. (2016, February 5). Race is a social construct, scientists argue. *Scientific American.* https://www.scientificamerican.com/article/race-is-a-social-construct-scientists-argue/

Ganzel, B. L., Morris, P. A., & Wethington, E. (2010). Allostasis and the human brain: Integrating models of stress from the social and life sciences. *Psychological Review, 117*, 134–174.

Garcia, J., Ervin, F. R., & Koelling, R. A. (1966). Learning with prolonged delay of reinforcement. *Psychonomic Science, 5*, 121–122.

García-Lázaro, H., Ramirez-Carmona, R., Lara-Romero, R., & Roldan-Valadez, E. (2012). Neuroanatomy of episodic and semantic memory in humans: A brief review of neuroimaging studies. *Neurology India, 60*, 613–617.

Gardner, D. M., & Alanis, J. M. (2020). Together we stand: Ally training for discrimination and harassment reduction. *Industrial and Organizational Psychology: Perspectives on Science and Practice, 13*(2), 196–199. https://doi.org/10.1017/iop.2020.35

Gardner, H. (1999). *Intelligence reframed: Multiple intelligences for the 21st century.* Basic Books.

Gardner, H. (2003). Multiple intelligences after twenty years. Paper presented at the American Educational Research Association, Chicago, IL.

Gardner, H. (2011). *Frames of mind: The theory of multiple intelligences.* Basic Books.

Gardner, H. (2020). *A synthesizing mind: A memoir from the creator of multiple intelligences theory.* The MIT Press.

Gardner, H., & Hatch, T. (1989). Educational implications of the theory of multiple intelligences. *Educational Researcher, 18*, 4–10.

Garg, A. K., Li, P., Rashid, M. S., & Callaway, E. M. (2019). Color and orientation are jointly coded and spatially organized in primate primary visual cortex. *Science, 364*(6447), 1275–1279. https://doi.org/10.1126/science.aaw5868

Garrett-Bakelman, F. E., Darshi, M., Green, S. J., Gur, R. C., Lin, L., Macias, B. R., McKenna, M. J., Meydan, C., Mishra, T., Nasrini, J., Piening, B. D., Rizzardi, L. F., Sharma, K., Siamwala, J. H., Taylor, L., Vitaterna, M. H., Afkarian, M., Afshinnekoo, E., Ahadi, S., . . . Turek, F. W. (2019). The NASA Twins Study: A multidimensional analysis of a year-long human spaceflight. *Science, 364*(6436), eaau8650.

Garrison, S. M., & Rodgers, J. L. (2019). Decomposing the causes of the socioeconomic status-health gradient with biometrical modeling. *Journal of Personality and Social Psychology, 116*(6), 1030–1047. https://doi.org/10.1037/pspp0000226

Garry, M., & Gerrie, M. P. (2005). When photographs create false memories. *Current Directions in Psychological Science, 14*, 321–325.

Gastil, J. (1990). Generic pronouns and sexist language: The oxymoronic character of masculine generics. *Sex Roles, 23*, 629–643.

Gat, A. (2018, July 1). Daily horoscope: July 2, 2018. *Broadly.* https://broadly.vice.com/en_us/article/pavjgn/daily-horoscope-july-2-2018

Gatchel, R. J., Haggard, R., Thomas, C., & Howard, K. J. (2013). Biopsychosocial approaches to understanding chronic pain and disability. In R. J. Moore (Ed.), *Handbook of pain and palliative care* (pp. 1–16). Springer.

Gatchel, R. J., & Maddrey, A. M. (2004). The biopsychosocial perspective of pain. In J. M. Raczynski & L. C. Leviton (Eds.), *Handbook of clinical health psychology: Vol. 2. Disorders of behavior and health* (pp. 357–378). American Psychological Association.

Gaval-Cruz, M., & Weinshenker, D. (2009). Mechanisms of disulfiram-induced cocaine abstinence: Antabuse and cocaine relapse. *Molecular Interventions, 9*, 175–187.

Gavie, J., & Revonsuo, A. (2010). The future of lucid dreaming treatment [Commentary on "The neurobiology of consciousness: Lucid dreaming wakes up" by J. Allan Hobson]. *International Journal of Dream Research, 3*, 13–15.

Gay, P. (1988). *Freud: A life for our time.* W. W. Norton.

Gazzaniga, M. S. (1967). The split brain in man. *Scientific American, 217*, 24–29.

Gazzaniga, M. S. (1998). The split brain revisited. *Scientific American, 279*, 50–55.

Gazzaniga, M. S. (2005). Forty-five years of split-brain research and still going strong. *Nature Reviews Neuroscience, 6*, 653–659.

Gazzaniga, M. S., Bogen, J. E., & Sperry, R. W. (1965). Observations on visual perception after disconnection of the cerebral hemispheres in man. *Brain, 88*, 221–236.

Gazzillo, F., Waldron, S., Gorman, B. S., Stukenberg, K., Genova, F., Ristucci, C., Faccini, F., & Mazza, C. (2018). The components of psychoanalysis: Factor analyses of process measures of 27 fully recorded psychoanalyses. *Psychoanalytic Psychology, 35*(2), 184–195. https://doi.org/10.1037/pap0000155

Geary, D. C. (2021). *Sex differences in the modern world.* In D. C. Geary, *Male, female: The evolution of human sex differences* (pp. 421–453). American Psychological Association. https://doi.org/10.1037/0000181-014

Gendelman, D. (2018, July 10). Why does every soccer player do this? *The New York Times.* https://www.nytimes.com/2018/07/10/sports/world-cup/england-croatia-france-belgium.html

Genetics Home Reference. (2020a, August 17). *Congenital insensitivity to pain with anhidrosis.* U.S. National Library of Medicine, U.S. Department of Health and Human Services, National Institutes of Health. https://ghr.nlm.nih.gov/condition/congenital-insensitivity-to-pain-with-anhidrosis

Genetics Home Reference. (2020b, August 17). *Narcolepsy.* U.S. National Library of Medicine, U.S. Department of Health and Human Services, National Institutes of Health. https://ghr.nlm.nih.gov/condition/narcolepsy

Geniole, S. N., Bird, B. M., McVittie, J. S., Purcell, R. B., Archer, J., & Carré, J. M. (2020). Is testosterone linked to human aggression? A meta-analytic examination of the relationship between baseline, dynamic, and manipulated testosterone on human aggression. *Hormones and Behavior, 123*, Article 104644. https://doi.org/10.1016/j.yhbeh.2019.104644

Genzel, L., Rossato, J. I., Jacobse, J., Grieves, R. M., Spooner, P. A., Battaglia, F. P., Fernández, G., & Morris, R. G. (2017). The yin and yang of memory consolidation: Hippocampal and neocortical. *PLOS Biology, 15*(1), e2000531. https://doi.org/10.1371/journal.pbio.2000531

George, M. J., Russell, M. A., Piontak, J. R., & Odgers, C. L. (2018). Concurrent and subsequent associations between daily digital technology use and high risk adolescents' mental health symptoms. *Child Development, 89*, 78–88. https://doi.org/10.1111/cdev.12819

Georgiadis, J. R., Reinders, A. A. T., Paans, A. M., Renken, R., & Kortekaas, R. (2009). Men versus women on sexual brain function: Prominent differences during tactile genital stimulation, but not during orgasm. *Human Brain Mapping, 30*, 3089–3101.

Gerbasi, M. E., Richards, L. K., Thomas, J. J., Agnew-Blais, J. C., Thompson-Brenner, H., Gilman, S. E., & Becker, A. E. (2014). Globalization and eating disorder risk: Peer influence, perceived social norms, and adolescent disordered eating in Fiji. *International Journal of Eating Disorders, 47*, 727–737.

Gerhart, B., & Fang, M. (2015). Pay, intrinsic motivation, extrinsic motivation, performance, and creativity in the workplace: Revisiting long-held beliefs. *Annual Reviews of Organizational Psychology and Organizational Behavior, 2*, 489–521.

Gerkin, R. C., & Castro, J. B. (2015). The number of olfactory stimuli that humans can discriminate is still unknown. *Elife, 4*, e08127. https://doi.org/10.7554/eLife.08127.001

German, T. P., & Defeyter, M. A. (2000). Immunity to functional fixedness in young children. *Psychonomic Bulletin & Review, 7*, 707–712.

Gershoff, E. T., Goodman, G. S., Miller-Perrin, C. L., Holden, G. W., Jackson, Y., & Kazdin, A. E. (2018). The strength of the causal evidence against physical punishment of children and its implications for parents, psychologists, and policymakers. *American Psychologist, 73*(5), 626–638. https://doi.org/10.1037/amp0000327

Gerson, M. (2021, February 18). Opinion: Six takeaways from Covid-19 that could shape our future. *The Washington Post.* https://www.washingtonpost.com/opinions/six-takeaways-from-covid-19-that-could-shape-our-future/2021/02/18/667c5196-722b-11eb-85fa-e0ccb3660358_story.html

Gerstorf, D., Ram, N., Hoppmann, C., Willis, S. L., & Schaie, K. W. (2011). Cohort differences in cognitive aging and terminal decline in the Seattle Longitudinal Study. *Developmental Psychology, 47,* 1026–1041.

Gettleman, J. (2018, February 17). The peculiar position of India's third gender. *The New York Times.* https://www.nytimes.com/2018/02/17/style/india-third-gender-hijras-transgender.html

Gibbons, A., & Warne, R. T. (2019). First publication of subtests in the Stanford-Binet 5, WAIS-IV, WISC-V, and WPPSI-IV. *Intelligence, 75,* 9–18. https://doi.org/10.1016/j.intell.2019.02.005

Gibson, E. J., & Walk, R. D. (1960). The "visual cliff." *Scientific American, 202,* 80–92.

Giedd, J. N., Lalonde, F. M., Celano, M. J., White, S. L., Wallace, G. L., Lee, N. R., & Lenroot, R. K. (2009). Anatomical brain magnetic resonance imaging of typically developing children and adolescents. *Journal of the American Academy of Child and Adolescent Psychiatry, 48,* 465–475.

Gillath, O., & Collins, T. (2016). Unconscious desire: The affective and motivational aspects of subliminal sexual priming. *Archives of Sexual Behavior, 45*(1), 5–20. https://doi.org/10.1007/s10508-015-0609-y

Gilligan, C. (1982). *In a different voice: Psychological theory and women's development.* Harvard University Press.

Gillin, J. C. (2002, March 25). How long can humans stay awake? *Scientific American.* http://www.scientificamerican.com/article.cfm?id=how-long-can-humans-stay

Gilovich, T., & Kumar, A. (2015). We'll always have Paris: The hedonic payoff from experiential and material investments. *Advances in Experimental Social Psychology, 51,* 147–187.

Girodo, M., & Henry, D. R. (1976). Cognitive, physiological and behavioural components of anxiety in flooding. *Canadian Journal of Behavioural Science/Revue Canadienne des Sciences du Comportement, 8,* 224–231.

GLAAD. (n.d.). *GLAAD media reference guide—lesbian / gay / bisexual glossary of terms.* https://www.glaad.org/reference/lgbtq

Glahn, D. C., Laird, A. R., Ellison-Wright, I., Thelen, S. M., Robinson, J. L., Lancaster, J. L., Bullmore, E., & Fox, P. (2008). Meta-analysis of gray matter anomalies in schizophrenia: Application of anatomic likelihood estimation and network analysis. *Biological Psychiatry, 64,* 774–781.

Glaser, R., & Kiecolt-Glaser, J. K. (2005). Stress-induced immune dysfunction: Implications for health. *Nature Reviews Immunology, 5,* 243–251.

Glass, R. M. (2001). Electroconvulsive therapy: Time to bring it out of the shadows. *Journal of the American Medical Association, 285,* 1346–1348.

Glass, S. T., Lingg, E., & Heuberger, E. (2015). Do ambient urban odors evoke basic emotions? *Frontiers in Psychology, 5,* Article 340. https://doi.org/10.3389/fpsyg.2014.00340

Glass, V. Q., & Bickler, A. (2021). Cultivating the therapeutic alliance in a telemental health setting. *Contemporary Family Therapy: An International Journal, 43,* 189–198. https://doi.org/10.1007/s10591-021-09570-0

Glassman, T., Paprzycki, P., Castor, T., Wotring, A., Wagner-Greene, V., Ritzman, M., Diehr, A. J., & Kruger, J. (2018). Using the elaboration likelihood model to address Drunkorexia among college students. *Substance Use & Misuse, 53*(9), 1411–1418. https://doi.org/10.1080/10826084.2017.1409766

Glenn, A. L., Raine, A., Schug, R. A., Gao, Y., & Granger, D. A. (2011). Increased testosterone-to-cortisol ration in psychopathy. *Journal of Abnormal Psychology, 120,* 389–399.

Gobbi, G., Atkin, T., Zytynski, T., Wang, S., Askari, S., Boruff, J., Ware, M., Marmorstein, N., Cipriani, A., Dendukuri, N., & Mayo, N. (2019). Association of cannabis use in adolescence and risk of depression, anxiety, and suicidality in young adulthood: A systematic review and meta-analysis. *JAMA Psychiatry, 76*(4), 426–434. https://doi.org/10.1001/jamapsychiatry.2018.4500

Goddard, M. J. (2018). Extending B. F. Skinner's selection by consequences to personality change, implicit theories of intelligence, skill learning, and language. *Review of General Psychology, 22*(4), 421–426. https://doi.org/10.1037/gpr0000168

Godden, D. R., & Baddeley, A. D. (1975). Context-dependent memory in two natural environments: On land and underwater. *British Journal of Psychology, 66,* 325–331.

Godlee, F., Smith, J., & Marcovitch, H. (2011). Wakefield's article linking MMR vaccine and autism was fraudulent. *British Medical Journal, 342,* c7452.

Goel, N., Rao, H., Durmer, J. S., & Dinges, D. F. (2009, September). Neurocognitive consequences of sleep deprivation. *Seminars in Neurology, 29,* 320–339.

Gogtay, N., Vyas, N. S., Testa, R., Wood, S. J., & Pantelis, C. (2011). Age of onset of schizophrenia: Perspectives from neural structural neuroimaging studies. *Schizophrenia Bulletin, 37,* 504–513.

Goksan, S., Hartley, C., Emery, F., Cockrill, N., Poorun, R., Moultrie, F., Rogers, R., Campbell, J., Sanders, M., Adams, E., Clare, S., Jenkinson, M., Tracey, I., & Slater, R. (2015). fMRI reveals neural activity overlap between adult and infant pain. *eLife, 4,* e06356. https://doi.org/10.7554/eLife.06356

Gold, M. (2019, June 21). The ABCs of L.G.B.T.Q.I.A.+. *The New York Times.* https://www.nytimes.com/2018/06/21/style/lgbtq-gender-language.html

Gold, R. B. (2005). The implications of defining when a woman is pregnant. *Guttmacher Report on Public Policy, 8*(2), 7–10.

Goldberg, A. E., & Kuvalanka, K. A. (2018). Navigating identity development and community belonging when "there are only two boxes to check": An exploratory study of nonbinary trans college students. *Journal of LGBT Youth, 15*(2), 106–131. https://doi.org/10.1080/19361653.2018.1429979

Goldfried, M. R. (2019). Obtaining consensus in psychotherapy: What holds us back? *American Psychologist, 74*(4), 484–496. https://doi.org/10.1037/amp0000365

Goldin-Meadow, S. (1978). Review: A study in human capacities. *Science, 200,* 649–651.

Goldman, J. G. (2019, February 1). Killer whales and chimpanzees have similar personalities. *Scientific American.* https://www.scientificamerican.com/article/killer-whales-and-chimpanzees-have-similar-personalities/

Goldsmith, H. H., Buss, A. H., Plomin, R., Rothbart, M. K., Chess, S., Hinde, R. A., & McCall, R. B. (1987). What is temperament? Four approaches. *Child Development, 58,* 505–529.

Goldstein, E. B. (2011). *Cognitive psychology: Connecting mind, research, and everyday experience* (3rd ed.). Wadsworth, Cengage Learning.

Goleman, D. (1995). *Emotional intelligence.* Bantam Books.

Golinkoff, R. M., Can, D. D., Soderstrom, M., & Hirsh-Pasek, K. (2015). (Baby) Talk to me: The social context of infant-directed speech and its effects on early language acquisition. *Current Directions in Psychological Science, 24,* 339–344.

Golinkoff, R. M., Hoff, E., Rowe, M. L., Tamis-LeMonda, C. S., & Hirsh-Pasek, K. (2019). Language matters: Denying the existence of the 30-million-word gap has serious consequences. *Child Development, 90*(3), 985–992. https://doi.org/10.1111/cdev.13128

Gollwitzer, A., & Bargh, J. A. (2018). Social psychological skill and its correlates. *Social Psychology, 49*(2), 88–102. https://doi.org/10.1027/1864-9335/a000332

Golumbic, E. M. Z., Ding, N., Bickel, S., Lakatos, P., Schevon, C. A., McKhann, G. M., Goodman, R. R., Emerson, R., Mehta, A. D., Simon, J. Z., Poeppel, D., & Schroeder, C. E. (2013). Mechanisms underlying selective neuronal tracking of attended speech at a "cocktail party." *Neuron, 77*(5), 980–991. https://doi.org/10.1016/j.neuron.2012.12.037

Gonzalez, A. M., Steele, J. R., & Baron, A. S. (2017). Reducing children's implicit racial bias through exposure to positive out-group exemplars. *Child Development, 88,* 123–130. https://doi.org/10.1111/cdev.12582

Good, C. H., Brager, A. J., Capaldi, V. F., & Mysliwiec, V. (2020). Sleep in the United States military. *Neuropsychopharmacology, 45*(1), 176–191. https://doi.org/10.1038/s41386-019-0431-7

Goodwin, M. A., Stange, K. C., Zyzanski, S. J., Crabtree, B. F., Borawski, E. A., & Flocke, S. A. (2017). The Hawthorne effect in direct observation research with physicians and patients. *Journal of Evaluation in Clinical Practice, 23*(6), 1322–1328.

Gordon, B. (2013, January 1). Does photographic memory exist? *Scientific American Mind, 23.* http://www.scientificamerican.com/article/i-developed-what-appears-to-be-a-ph/

Gordon, I., & Berson, Y. (2018). Oxytocin modulates charismatic influence in groups. *Journal of Experimental Psychology: General, 147*(1), 132–138. https://doi.org/10.1037/xge0000375

Gottesman, I. I. (2001). Psychopathology through a life span–genetic prism. *American Psychologist, 56,* 867–878.

Gottesman, I. I., Laursen, T. M., Bertelsen, A., & Mortensen, P. B. (2010). Severe mental disorders in offspring with 2 psychiatrically ill parents. *Archives of General Psychiatry, 67,* 252–257.

Gottlieb, B., & Trifiro, M. A. (2017, May 11). Androgen insensitivity syndrome. In M. P. Adam, H. H. Ardinger, R. A. Pagon, et al. (Eds.), *GeneReviews.* https://www.ncbi.nlm.nih.gov/books/NBK1429/

Gottlieb, B., Beitel, L. K., & Trifiro, M. A. (2014). Androgen insensitivity syndrome. In R.A. Pagon, M. P. Adam, H. H. Ardinger, et al., (Eds.), *GeneReviews [Internet]*. University of Washington, Seattle. http://www.ncbi.nlm.nih.gov/books/NBK1429/

Gottschalk, M. G., & Domschke, K. (2017). Genetics of generalized anxiety disorder and related traits. *Dialogues in Clinical Neuroscience, 19*(2), 159–168.

Gould, E., Beylin, A., Tanapat, P., Reeves, A., & Shors, T. J. (1999). Learning enhances adult neurogenesis in the hippocampal formation. *Nature Neuroscience, 2*, 260–265.

Gover, A. R., Harper, S. B., & Langton, L. (2020). Anti-Asian hate crime during the COVID-19 pandemic: Exploring the reproduction of inequality. *American Journal of Criminal Justice, 45*(4), 647–667. https://doi.org/10.1007/s12103-020-09545-1

Göz, İ., Çeven, Z. İ., & Tekcan, A. İ. (2017). Urban–rural differences in children's earliest memories. *Memory, 25*(2), 214–219. https://doi.org/10.1080/09658211.2016.1150490

Grabner, R. H., Ansari, D., Reishofer, G., Stern, E., Ebner, F., & Neuper, C. (2007). Individual differences in mathematical competence predict parietal brain activation during mental calculation. *NeuroImage, 38*, 346–356.

Grabowska, A. (2017). Sex on the brain: Are gender-dependent structural and functional differences associated with behavior? *Journal of Neuroscience Research, 95*(1–2), 200–212. https://doi.org/10.1002/jnr.23953

Gracheva, E. O., Ingolia, N. T., Kelly, Y. M., Cordero-Morales, J. F., Hollopeter, G., Chesler, A. T., Sánchez, E. E., Perez, J. C., Weissman, J. S., & Julius, D. (2010). Molecular basis of infrared detection by snakes. *Nature, 464*, 1006–1011. https://doi.org/10.1038/nature08943

Graham, L. C., Harder, J. M., Soto, I., de Vries, W. N., John, S. W., & Howell, G. R. (2016). Chronic consumption of a Western diet induces robust glial activation in aging mice and in a mouse model of Alzheimer's disease. *Scientific Reports, 6*, 1–13. https://doi.org/10.1038/srep21568

Graiver, I. (2019). The late antique history of psychology: The test case of introspection. *History of Psychology, 22*(2), 130–148. https://doi.org/10.1037/hop0000118

Grammer, K., & Thornhill, R. (1994). Human (*Homo sapiens*) facial attractiveness and sexual selection: The role of symmetry and averageness. *Journal of Comparative Psychology, 108*, 233–242.

Granello, D. H., & Gibbs, T. A. (2016). The power of language and labels: "The mentally ill" versus "people with mental illnesses." *Journal of Counseling & Development, 94*(1), 31–40. https://doi.org/10.1002/jcad.12059

Granrud, C. E. (2009). Development of size constancy in children: A test of the metacognitive theory. *Perception & Psychophysics, 71*, 644–654.

Grant, B. F., Chou, S. P., Saha, T. D., Pickering, R. P., Kerridge, B. T., Ruan, W. J., Huang, B., Jung, J., Zhang, H., Fan, A., & Hasin, D. S. (2017). Prevalence of 12-month alcohol use, high-risk drinking, and DSM-IV alcohol use disorder in the United States, 2001–2002 to 2012–2013: Results from the National Epidemiologic Survey on Alcohol and Related Conditions. *JAMA Psychiatry, 74*(9), 911–923. https://doi.org/10.1001/jamapsychiatry.2017.2161

Grant, J. A., & Zeidan, F. (2019). Employing pain and mindfulness to understand consciousness: A symbiotic relationship. *Current Opinion in Psychology, 28*, 192–197. https://doi.org/10.1016/j.copsyc.2018.12.025

Gray, P. B., & Brogdon, E. (2017). Do step- and biological grandparents show differences in investment and emotional closeness with their grandchildren? *Evolutionary Psychology, 15*, Article 1474704917694367. https://doi.org/10.1177/1474704917694367

Gray, P. B., Garcia, J. R., & Gesselman, A. N. (2019). Age-related patterns in sexual behaviors and attitudes among single U.S. adults: An evolutionary approach. *Evolutionary Behavioral Sciences, 13*(2), 111–126. https://doi.org/10.1037/ebs0000126

Gray, P. B., Straftis, A. A., Bird, B. M., McHale, T. S., & Zilioli, S. (2020). Human reproductive behavior, life history, and the Challenge Hypothesis: A 30-year review, retrospective and future directions. *Hormones and Behavior, 123*, Article 104530. https://doi.org/10.1016/j.yhbeh.2019.04.017

Graziano, M. S. A., Guterstam, A., Bio, B. J., & Wilterson, A. I. (2020). Toward a standard model of consciousness: Reconciling the attention schema, global workspace, higher-order thought, and illusionist theories. *Cognitive Neuropsychology, 37*(3-4), 155–172. https://doi.org/10.1080/02643294.2019.1670630

Green, C. B. (2019). Many paths to preserve the body clock. *Science, 363*(6423), 124–125. https://doi.org/10.1126/science.aav9706

Green, C. S., & Bavelier, D. (2015). Action video game training for cognitive enhancement. *Current Opinion in Behavioral Sciences, 4*, 103–108.

Green, J. P. (1999). Hypnosis and the treatment of smoking cessation and weight loss. In I. Kirsch, A. Capafons, E. Cardeña-Buelna, & S. Amigó (Eds.), *Clinical hypnosis and self-regulation: Cognitive-behavioral perspectives* (Dissociation, Trauma, Memory, and Hypnosis Book Series, pp. 249–276). American Psychological Association.

Green, M., & Elliott, M. (2010). Religion, health, and psychological well-being. *Journal of Religious Health, 49*, 149–163.

Greenbaum, Z. (2020, March 20). *Psychologists' advice for newly remote workers*. American Psychological Association. https://www.apa.org/news/apa/2020/03/newly-remote-workers

Greenbaum, Z. (2020, July 1). How well is telepsychology working? *Monitor on Psychology, 51*, 46. https://www.apa.org/monitor/2020/07/cover-telepsychology

Greenberg, P. E., Fournier, A. A., Sisitsky, T., Pike, C. T., & Kessler, R. C. (2015). The economic burden of adults with major depressive disorder in the United States (2005 and 2010). *Journal of Clinical Psychiatry, 76*, 155–162.

Greenfield, P. M., & Quiroz, B. (2013). Context and culture in the socialization and development of personal achievement values: Comparing Latino immigrant families, European American families, and elementary schoolteachers. *Journal of Applied Developmental Psychology, 34*, 108–118.

Greenstein, L. (2017, October 11). 9 Ways to fight mental health stigma [Web log post]. National Alliance on Mental Illness. https://www.nami.org/blogs/nami-blog/october-2017/9-ways-to-fight-mental-health-stigma

Grigalavicius, M., Moan, J., Dahlback, A., & Juzeniene, A. (2015). Daily, seasonal, and latitudinal variations in solar ultraviolet A and B radiation in relation to vitamin D production and risk for skin cancer. *International Journal of Dermatology, 55*, e23–e28.

Griggs, R. A. (2014a). Coverage of the Stanford prison experiment in introductory psychology textbooks. *Teaching of Psychology, 41*, 195–203.

Griggs, R. A. (2014b). The continuing saga of Little Albert in introductory psychology textbooks. *Teaching of Psychology, 41*, 309–317. https://doi.org/10.1177/0098628314549702

Griggs, R. A. (2015a). Coverage of the Phineas Gage story in introductory psychology textbooks: Was Gage no longer Gage? *Teaching of Psychology, 42*, 195–202.

Griggs, R. A. (2015b). Psychology's lost boy. Will the real Little Albert please stand up? *Teaching of Psychology, 42*, 14–18. https://doi.org/10.1177/0098628314562668

Griggs, R. A. (2015c). The disappearance of independence in textbook coverage of Asch's social pressure experiments. *Teaching of Psychology, 42*, 137–142.

Griggs, R. A. (2015d). The Kitty Genovese story in introductory psychology textbooks fifty years later. *Teaching of Psychology, 42*, 149–152.

Griggs, R. A., Blyler, J., & Jackson, S. L. (2020). New revelations about Rosenhan's pseudopatient study: Scientific integrity in remission. *Scholarship of Teaching and Learning in Psychology*. Advance online publication. https://doi.org/10.1037/stl0000202

Griggs, R. A., & Christopher, A. N. (2016). Who's who in introductory psychology textbooks: A citation analysis redux. *Teaching of Psychology, 43*, 108–119.

Griggs, R. A., & Whitehead, G. I., III. (2014). Coverage of the Stanford prison experiment in introductory social psychology textbooks. *Teaching of Psychology, 41*, 318–324.

Griggs, R. A., & Whitehead, G. I., III. (2015). Coverage of Milgram's obedience experiments in social psychology textbooks: Where have all the criticisms gone? *Teaching of Psychology, 42*, 315–322.

Grinstein, J. D. (2018, October 16). How exercise might "clean" the Alzheimer's brain. *Scientific American*. https://www.scientificamerican.com/article/how-exercise-might-clean-the-alzheimers-brain1/

Griskevicius, V., Haselton, M, G., & Ackerman, J. M. (2015). Evolution and close relationships. In M. Mikulincer, P. R. Shaver, J. A. Simpson, & J. F. Dovidio (Eds.), *APA handbook of personality and social psychology, Volume 3: Interpersonal relations* (APA Handbooks in Psychology, pp. 3–32). American Psychological Association.

Griswold, A. (2013, December 27). 20 low-paying jobs that workers love. *Business Insider*. http://www.businessinsider.com/happy-low-paying-jobs-2013-12

Groopman, J. (2008). *How doctors think*. Houghton Mifflin.

Gross, C. G. (2007). The discovery of motor cortex and its background. *Journal of the History of the Neurosciences, 16*, 320–331.

Grossman, A. J. (2012, June 9). The science of Cesar Millan's dog training: Good timing and hard kicks in the stomach. *The Huffington Post*. http://www.huffingtonpost.com/anna-jane-grossman/the-dog-whisperer-technique_b_1406337.html

Grossman, R. P., & Till, B. D. (1998). The persistence of classically conditioned brand attitudes. *Journal of Advertising, 21*, 23–31.

Grosso, G., Godos, J., Galvano, F., & Giovannucci, E. L. (2017). Coffee, caffeine, and health outcomes: An umbrella review. *Annual Review of Nutrition, 37*, 131–156. https://doi.org/10.1146/annurev-nutr-071816-064941

Grover, S., & Helliwell, J. F. (2019). How's life at home? New evidence on marriage and the set point for happiness. *Journal of Happiness Studies: An Interdisciplinary Forum on Subjective Well-Being, 20*(2), 373–390.

Gruber, D. F. (2009). Three's company. *Nature Medicine, 15*, 232–235.

Gruber, J., Mendle, J., Lindquist, K. A., Schmader, T., Clark, L. A., Bliss-Moreau, E., Akinola, M., Atlas, L., Barch, D. M., Barrett, L. F., Borelli, J. L., Brannon, T. N., Bunge, S. A., Campos, B., Cantlon, J., Carter, R., Carter-Sowell, A. R., Chen, S., Craske, M. G., . . . Williams, L. A. (2020). The future of women in psychological science. *Perspectives on Psychological Science.* https://doi.org/10.1177/1745691620952789

Gruber, S. A., Dahlgren, M. K., Sagar, K. A., Gönenç A., & Lukas, S. E. (2014). Worth the wait: Effects of age of onset of marijuana use on white matter and impulsivity. *Psychopharmacology, 231*, 1455–1465.

Grunberg, N. E., McManigle, J. E., & Barry, E. S. (2020). Using social psychology principles to develop emotionally intelligent healthcare leaders. *Frontiers in Psychology, 11.* https://doi.org/10.3389/fpsyg.2020.01917

Grusec, J. E., & Goodnow, J. J. (1994). Impact of parental discipline methods on the child's internalization of values: A reconceptualization of current points of view. *Developmental Psychology, 30*, 4–19.

Grusec, J. E., Goodnow, J. J., & Kuczynski, L. (2000). New directions in analyses of parenting contributions to children's acquisition of values. *Child Development, 71*, 205–211.

Guan, J., Cai, J. J., Ji, G., & Sham, P. C. (2019). Commonality in dysregulated expression of gene sets in cortical brains of individuals with autism, schizophrenia, and bipolar disorder. *Translational Psychiatry, 9*(1), Article 152. https://doi.org/10.1038/s41398-019-0488-4

Guilford, J. P. (1967). *The nature of human intelligence.* McGraw-Hill.

Guilford, J. P., Christensen, P. R., Merrifield, P. R., & Wilson, R. C. (1960). *Alternate uses.* Sheridan Psychological Services.

Guillot, C. (2007). Is recreational ecstasy (MDMA) use associated with higher levels of depressive symptoms? *Journal of Psychoactive Drugs, 39*, 31–39.

Gulevich, G., Dement, W., & Johnson, L. (1966). Psychiatric and EEG observations on a case of prolonged (264 hours) wakefulness. *Archives of General Psychiatry, 15*, 29–35.

Gundersen, C., Hake, M., Dewey, A., & Engelhard, E. (2020). Food Insecurity during COVID-19. *Applied Economic Perspectives and Policy.* https://doi.org/10.1002/aepp.13100

Gunderson, E. A., Ramirez, G., Levine, S. C., & Beilock, S. L. (2012). The role of parents and teachers in the development of gender-related math attitudes. *Sex Roles, 66*, 153–166.

Gunderson, J. G., Fruzzetti, A., Unruh, B., & Choi-Kain, L. (2018). Competing theories of borderline personality disorder. *Journal of Personality Disorders, 32*(2), 148–167. https://doi.org/10.1521/pedi.2018.32.2.148

Gundlach, H. (2018). William James and the Heidelberg fiasco. *History of Psychology, 21*(1), 47–72. https://doi.org/10.1037/hop0000083

Gürel, C., & Brummelman, E. (2020, April 7). The problem with telling children they're better than others. *Scientific American.* https://www.scientificamerican.com/article/the-problem-with-telling-children-theyre-better-than-others/

Gurung, R. A. R., Hackathorn, J., Enns, C., Frantz, S., Cacioppo, J. T., Loop, T., & Freeman, J. E. (2016). Strengthening introductory psychology: A new model for teaching the introductory course. *American Psychologist, 71*(2), 112–124. https://doi.org/10.1037/a0040012

Gurven, M., von Rueden, C., Massenkoff, M., Kaplan, H., & Lero Vie, M. (2013). How universal is the Big Five? Testing the five-factor model of personality variation among forager-farmers in the Bolivian Amazon. *Journal of Personality and Social Psychology, 104*, 354–370.

Gustavson, D. E., Friedman, N. P., Fontanillas, P., Elson, S. L., Palmer, A. A., Sanchez-Roige, S., & 23andMe Research Team. (2020). The latent genetic structure of impulsivity and its relation to internalizing psychopathology. *Psychological Science, 31*(8), 1025–1035. https://doi.org/10.1177/0956797620938160

Guterres, A. (2020, March 10). *Opening remarks at press conference on WMO State of the Climate 2019 Report.* United Nations Secretary-General. https://www.un.org/sg/en/content/sg/speeches/2020-03-10/wmo-state-of-the-climate-2019-report-remarks

Gutman, M., & Winsor, M. (2018, July 12). Water rushed back into Thailand cave soon after boys soccer team was rescued: Official. *ABC News.* https://abcnews.go.com/International/News/water-rushed-back-thailand-cave-boys-soccer-team/story?id=56506736

Gutzeit, V. A., Ahuna, K., Santos, T. L., Cunningham, A. M., Sadsad Rooney, M., Muñoz Zamora, A., Denny, C. A., & Donaldson, Z. R. (2020). Optogenetic reactivation of prefrontal social neural ensembles mimics social buffering of fear. *Neuropsychopharmacology, 45*(6), 1068–1077. https://doi.org/10.1038/s41386-020-0631-1

Habibović, M., Gavidia, G., Broers, E., Wetzels, M., Ayoola, I., Ribas, V., Piera-Jimenez, J., Widdershoven, J., & Denollet, J. (2020). Type D personality and global positioning system tracked social behavior in patients with cardiovascular disease. *Health Psychology, 39*(8), 711–720. https://doi.org/10.1037/hea0000823

Háden, G. P., Mády, K., Török, M., & Winkler, I. (2020). Newborn infants differently process adult directed and infant directed speech. *International Journal of Psychophysiology, 147*, 107–112. https://doi.org/10.1016/j.ijpsycho.2019.10.011

Haedt-Matt, A. A., & Keel, P. K. (2011). Revisiting the affect regulation model of binge eating: A meta-analysis of studies using ecological momentary assessment. *Psychological Bulletin, 137*, 660–681.

Hagan, L. K. (2016). History of child development. In W. D. Woody, R. L. Miller, & W. J. Wozniak (Eds.), *Psychological specialties in historical context: Enriching the classroom experience for teachers and students.* Society for the Teaching of Psychology http://teachpsych.org/ebooks/

Haijma, S. V., Van Haren, N., Cahn, W., Koolschijn, P. C. M., Pol, H. E. H., & Kahn, R. S. (2013). Brain volumes in schizophrenia: A meta-analysis in over 18,000 subjects. *Schizophrenia Bulletin, 39*, 1129–1138.

Halaris, A., Bechter, K., Haroon, E., Leonard, B. E., Miller, A., Pariante, C., & Zunszain, P. (2019). The future of psychoneuroimmunology: Promises and challenges. In A. Javed & K. N. Fountoulakis (Eds.), *Advances in psychiatry* (pp. 235–266). Springer-Verlag.

Halberda, J. (2018). Logic in babies. *Science, 359*(6381), 1214–1215. https://doi.org/10.1126/science.aas9183

Hale, L., Kirschen, G. W., LeBourgeois, M. K., Gradisar, M., Garrison, M. M., Montgomery-Downs, H., Kirschen, H., McHale, S. M., Change, A.-M., & Buton, O. M. (2018). Youth screen media habits and sleep: Sleep-friendly screen behavior recommendations for clinicians, educators, and parents. *Child and Adolescent Psychiatric Clinics, 27*(2), 229–245. https://doi.org/10.1016/j.chc.2017.11.014

Hales, C. M., Carroll, M. D., Fryar, C. D., & Ogden, C. L. (2020). Prevalence of obesity and severe obesity among adults: United States, 2017–2018. *NHS Data Brief,* no. 360. National Center for Health Statistics.

Hall, D., & Buzwell, S. (2012). The problem of free-riding in group projects: Looking beyond social loafing as reason for non-contribution. *Active Learning in Higher Education, 14*, 37–49.

Hall, G., & Rodríguez, G. (2020). When the stimulus is predicted and what the stimulus predicts: Alternative accounts of habituation. *Journal of Experimental Psychology: Animal Learning and Cognition, 46*(3), 327–340. https://doi.org/10.1037/xan0000237

Hall, J. W., Smith, S. D., & Popelka, G. R. (2004). Newborn hearing screening with combined otoacoustic emissions and auditory brainstem responses. *Journal of the American Academy of Audiology, 15*, 414–425.

Hallfors, D. D., Iritani, B. J., Zhang, L., Hartman, S., Lueseno, W. K., Mpofu, E., & Rusakaniko, S. (2016). "I thought if I marry the prophet I would not die": The significance of religious affiliation on marriage, HIV testing, and reproductive health practices among young married women in Zimbabwe. *Journal of Social Aspects of HIV/AIDS, 13*(1), 178–189.

Halpern, D. F. (2014). It's complicated—in fact, it's complex: Explaining the gender gap in academic achievement in science and mathematics. *Psychological Science in the Public Interest, 15*(3), 72–74.

Hambrick, D. Z., & Katsumata, D. S. (2020, January/February). How research on working memory can improve your romantic relationship. *Scientific American Mind, 31*(1), 4–5.

Hameed, M. A., & Lewis, A. J. (2016). Offspring of parents with schizophrenia: A systematic review of developmental features across childhood. *Harvard Review of Psychiatry, 24*(2), 104–117. https://doi.org/10.1097/HRP.0000000000000076

Hamilton, W. D. (1964). The genetical evolution of social behavior. *Journal of Theoretical Biology, 12*, 12–45.

Hamm, J. M., Heckhausen, J., Shane, J., & Lachman, M. E. (2020). Risk of cognitive declines with retirement: Who declines and why? *Psychology and Aging, 35*(3), 449–457. https://doi.org/10.1037/pag0000453

Hammer, J. H., & Cragun, R. T. (2019). Daily spiritual experiences and well-being among the nonreligious, spiritual, and religious: A bifactor analysis. *Psychology of Religion and Spirituality, 11*(4), 463–473. https://doi.org/10.1037/rel0000248

Hammond, S. I., Müller, U., Carpendale, J. I. M., Bibok, M. B., & Liebermann-Finestone, D. P. (2012). The effects of parental scaffolding on preschoolers' executive function. *Developmental Psychology, 48,* 271–281.

Hampton, J. A. (1998). Similarity-based categorization and fuzziness of natural categories. *Cognition, 65,* 137–165.

Hamzelou, J. (2015, January 26). Is MSG a silent killer or useful flavour booster? *NewScientist.* https://www.newscientist.com/article/dn26854-ismsg-a-silent-killer-or-useful-flavour-booster/

Haney, C., Banks, C., & Zimbardo, P. (1973). Interpersonal dynamics in a simulated prison. *International Journal of Criminology and Penology, 1,* 69–97.

Haney, C., & Zimbardo, P. (1998). The past and future of U.S. prison policy: Twenty-five years after the Stanford prison experiment. *American Psychologist, 53,* 709–727.

Hanford, L. C., Nazarov, A., Hall, G. B., & Sassi, R. B. (2016). Cortical thickness in bipolar disorder: A systematic review. *Bipolar Disorders, 18*(1), 4–18. https://doi.org/10.1111/bdi.12362

Hanish, L. D., Sallquist, J., DiDonato, M., Fabes, R. A., & Martin, C. L. (2012). Aggression by whom–aggression toward whom: Behavioral predictors of same- and other-gender aggression in early childhood. *Developmental Psychology, 48,* 1450–1462.

Hanley, J. R., & Chapman, E. (2008). Partial knowledge in a tip-of-the-tongue state about two- and three-word proper names. *Psychonomic Bulletin & Review, 15,* 156–160.

Hanna-Pladdy, B., & MacKay, A. (2011). The relation between instrumental musical activity and cognitive aging. *Neuropsychology, 25,* 378–386.

Hannon, E., Dempster, E., Viana, J., Burrage, J., Smith, A. R., Macdonald, R., St. Clair, D., Mustard, C., Breen, G, Therman, S., Kaprio, J., Toulopoulou, T., Hulshoff Pol, H. E., Bohlken, M. M., Kahn, R. S., Nenadic, I., Hultman, C. M., Murray, R. M., Collier, D. A., . . . Mill, J. (2016). An integrated genetic-epigenetic analysis of schizophrenia: Evidence for co-localization of genetic associations and differential DNA methylation. *Genome Biology, 17*(1), 176. https://doi.org/10.1186/s13059-016-1041-x

Hanscombe, K. B., Trzaskowski, M., Haworth, C. M. A., Davis, O. S. P., Dale, P. S., & Plomin, R. (2012). Socioeconomic status (SES) and children's intelligence (IQ): In a UK-representative sample SES moderates the environmental, not genetic, effect on IQ. *PLOS ONE, 7,* e30320. https://doi.org/10.1371/journal.pone.0030320

Hard, B. M., Lovett, J. M., & Brady, S. T. (2019). What do students remember about introductory psychology, years later? *Scholarship of Teaching and Learning in Psychology, 5*(1), 61–74. https://doi.org/10.1037/stl0000136

Hardman, R. J., Kennedy, G., Macpherson, H., Scholey, A. B., & Pipingas, A. (2016). Adherence to a Mediterranean-style diet and effects on cognition in adults: A qualitative evaluation and systematic review of longitudinal and prospective trials. *Frontiers in Nutrition, 3,* 22. https://doi.org/10.3389/fnut.2016.00022

Hare, R. M., Schlatter, S., Rhodes, G., & Simmons, L. W. (2017). Putative sex-specific human pheromones do not affect gender perception, attractiveness ratings or unfaithfulness judgements of opposite sex faces. *Royal Society Open Science, 4*(3), 160831. https://doi.org/10.1098/rsos.160831

Hareli, S., Kafetsios, K., & Hess, U. (2015). A cross-cultural study on emotion expression and the learning of social norms. *Frontiers in Psychology, 6.* https://doi.org/10.3389/fpsyg.2015.01501

Hariri, A. R., Tessitore, A., Mattay, V. S., Fera, F., & Weinberger, D. R. (2002). The amygdala response to emotional stimuli: A comparison of faces and scenes. *NeuroImage, 17,* 317–323.

Harlow, H. F. (1958). The nature of love. *American Psychologist, 13,* 673–685.

Harlow, H. F., Harlow, M. K., & Suomi, S. J. (1971). From thought to therapy: Lessons from a primate laboratory. *American Scientist, 59,* 538–549.

Harlow, H. F., & Zimmerman, R. R. (1959). Affectional responses in the infant monkey. *Science, 130,* 421–432.

HarnEnz, Z. (November 14, 2016). Fighting stigma: How to respond to inappropriate and insensitive comments about mental health [Web log post]. https://www.psychiatry.org/news-room/apa-blogs/apa-blog/2016/11/fi...ond-to-inappropriate-and-insensitive-comments-about-mental-health

Harper, R. S. (1950). The first psychological laboratory. *Isis, 41,* 158–161.

Harrington, A. (2012). The fall of the schizophrenogenic mother. *The Lancet, 379,* 1292–1293.

Harrington, A. (2019). *Mind fixers: Psychiatry's troubled search for the biology of mental illness.* W. W. Norton & Company.

Harrington, R. (2013). *Stress, health and well-being: Thriving in the 21st century.* Wadsworth, Cengage Learning.

Harris, B. (1979). Whatever happened to Little Albert? *American Psychologist, 34,* 151–160.

Harris, B. (2020). Journals, referees, and gatekeepers in the dispute over Little Albert, 2009–2014. *History of Psychology, 23*(2), 103–121. https://doi.org/10.1037/hop0000087

Hart, B., & Risley, T. R. (1992). American parenting of language learning children: Persisting differences in family-child interactions observed in natural home environments. *Developmental Psychology, 28*(6), 1096–1105.

Hart, B., & Risley, T. R. (2003). The early catastrophe: The 30 million word gap by age 3. *American Educator, 27*(1), 4–9.

Hart, C. L. (2020, January 14). Do lie detector tests really work? [Web log post]. *Psychology Today.* https://www.psychologytoday.com/us/blog/the-nature-deception/202001/do-lie-detector-tests-really-work

Harter, J., & Adkinds, A. (2015, April 8). Employees want a lot more from their managers. *Gallop.* http://www.gallup.com/businessjournal/182321/employees-lot-managers.aspx

Hartig, H., & Geiger, A. (2018, October 8). *About six-in-ten Americans support marijuana legalization.* Pew Research Center. http://www.pewresearch.org/fact-tank/2018/10/08/americans-support-marijuana-legalization/

Hartmann, C., & Goudarzi, S. (2019, August 8). Does birth order affect personality? *Scientific American.* https://www.scientificamerican.com/article/does-birth-order-affect-personality/

Hartmann Rasmussen, L. J., Caspi, A., Ambler, A., Broadbent, J. M., Cohen, H. J., d'Arbeloff, T., Elliott, M., Hancox, R. J., Harrington, H., Hogan, S., Houts, R., Ireland, D., Knodt, A. R., Meredith-Jones, K., Morey, M. C., Morrison, L., Poulton, R., Ramrakha, S., Richmond-Rakerd, L., . . . Moffitt, T. R. (2019). Association of neurocognitive and physical function with gait speed in midlife. *JAMA Network Open, 2*(10), e1913123–e1913123. https://doi.org/10.1001/jamanetworkopen.2019.13123

Hartwell, M., & Kaplan, A. (2018). Students' personal connection with science: Investigating the multidimensional phenomenological structure of self-relevance. *Journal of Experimental Education, 86*(1), 86–104. https://doi.org/10.1080/00220973.2017.1381581

Harvard Health Publishing. (2016, May 12). Hearing loss: A guide to prevention and treatment. https://www.health.harvard.edu/diseases-and-conditions/hearing-loss-a-guide-to-prevention-and-treatment

Harvard Health Publishing. (2020, July 21). *Exercising to relax.* https://www.health.harvard.edu/staying-healthy/exercising-to-relax

Hashemi, M. M., Gladwin, T. E., de Valk, N. M., Zhang, W., Kaldewaij, R., van Ast, V., Koch, S. B. J., Klumpers, F., & Roelofs, K. (2019). Neural dynamics of shooting decisions and the switch from freeze to fight. *Scientific Reports, 9*(1), Article 4240. https://doi.org/10.1038/s41598-019-40917-8

Hasher, L., & Zacks, R. T. (1979). Automatic and effortful processes in memory. *Journal of Experimental Psychology: General, 108,* 356–388.

Hasher, L., & Zacks, R. T. (1984). Automatic processing of fundamental information: The case of frequency of occurrence. *American Psychologist, 39,* 1372–1388.

Hasin, D. S., Sarvet, A. L., Meyers, J. L., Saha, T. D., Ruan, W. J., Stohl, M., & Grant, B. F. (2018). Epidemiology of adult *DSM-5* major depressive disorder and its specifiers in the United States. *JAMA Psychiatry, 75*(4), 336–346. https://doi.org/10.1001/jamapsychiatry.2017.4602

Haslam, N. (2006). Dehumanization: An integrative review. *Personality and Social Psychology Review, 10*(3), 252264. https://doi.org/10.1207/s15327957pspr1003_4

Haslam, S. A., & Reicher, S. D. (2012). When prisoners take over the prison: A social psychology of resistance. *Personality and Social Psychology Review, 16,* 154–179.

Hassett, J. M., Siebert, E. R., & Wallen, K. (2008). Sex differences in rhesus monkey toy preferences parallel those of children. *Hormones and Behavior, 54,* 359–364.

Hassin, R. R., Bargh, J. A., & Zimerman, S. (2009). Automatic and flexible: The case of non-conscious goal pursuit. *Social Cognition, 27,* 20–36.

Hasson, U., Andric, M., Atilgan, H., & Collignon, O. (2016). Congenital blindness is associated with large-scale reorganization of anatomical networks. *NeuroImage, 128,* 362–372. https://doi.org/10.1016/j.neuroimage.2015.12.048

Hatch, S. L., & Dohrenwend, B. P. (2007). Distribution of traumatic and other stressful life events by race/ethnicity, gender, SES and age: A review of the research. *American Journal of Community Psychology, 40,* 313–332.

**Hatemi, P. K., McDermott, R., & Eaves, L.** (2015). Genetic and environmental contributions to relationships and divorce attitudes. *Personality and Individual Differences, 72*, 135–140.

**Hatemi, P. K., Medland, S. E., Klemmensen, R., Oskarsson, S., Littvay, L., Dawes, C. T., Verhulst, B., McDermott, R., Nørgaard, A. S., Klofstad, C. A., Christensen, K., Johannesson, M., Magnusson, P. K. E., Eaves, L. J., & Martin, N. G.** (2014). Genetic influences on political ideologies: Twin analyses of 19 measures of political ideologies from five democracies and genome-wide findings from three populations. *Behavior Genetics, 44*, 282–294.h

**Hauck, C., Weiß, A., Schulte, E. M., Meule, A., & Ellrott, T.** (2017). Prevalence of "food addiction" as measured with the Yale Food Addiction Scale 2.0 in a representative German sample and its association with sex, age and weight categories. *Obesity Facts, 10*(1), 12–24. https://doi.org/10.1159/000456013

**Haun, V. C., & Oppenauer, V.** (2019). The role of job demands and negative work reflection in employees' trajectory of sleep quality over the workweek. *Journal of Occupational Health Psychology, 24*(6), 675–688. *https://doi.org/10.1037/ocp0000156*

**Häuser, W., Hagl, M., Schmierer, A., & Hansen, E.** (2016). The efficacy, safety and applications of medical hypnosis: A systematic review of meta-analyses. *Deutsches Ärzteblatt International, 113*, 289. https://doi.org/10.3238/arztebl.2016.0289

**Havdahl, A., Niarchou, M., Starnawska, A., Uddin, M., van der Merwe, C., & Warrier, V.** (2021). Genetic contributions to autism spectrum disorder. *Psychological Medicine*, 1–14. https://doi.org/10.1017/S0033291721000192

**Hawk, S. T., van den Eijnden, R. J., van Lissa, C. J., & ter Bogt, T. F.** (2019). Narcissistic adolescents' attention-seeking following social rejection: Links with social media disclosure, problematic social media use, and smartphone stress. *Computers in Human Behavior, 92*, 65–75. https://doi.org/10.1016/j.chb.2018.10.032

**Hayashi, Y., & Modico, J. G.** (2019). Effect of response-independent delivery of positive and negative reinforcers on the development of superstitious behavior and belief in humans. *Behavior Analysis: Research and Practice, 19*(4), 327–342. https://doi.org/10.1037/bar0000147

**Hayes, J. E., & Keast, R. E.** (2011). Two decades of supertasting: Where do we stand? *Physiology & Behavior, 104*, 1072–1074.

**Hayes, J. F., Pitman, A., Marston, L., Walters, K., Geddes, J. R., King, M., & Osborn, D. P.** (2016). Self-harm, unintentional injury, and suicide in bipolar disorder during maintenance mood stabilizer treatment: A UK population-based electronic health records study. *JAMA Psychiatry, 73*, 630–637. https://doi.org/10.1001/jamapsychiatry.2016.0432

**He, Z., Guo, J. L., McBride, J. D., Narasimhan, S., Kim, H., Changolkar, L., Zhang, B., Gathagan, R. J., Yue, C., Dengler, C., Stieber, A., Nitla, M., Coulter, D. A., Abel, T., Brunden, K. R., Trojanowski, J. Q., & Lee, V. M.-Y.** (2018). Amyloid-β plaques enhance Alzheimer's brain tau-seeded pathologies by facilitating neuritic plaque tau aggregation. *Nature Medicine, 24*(1), 29–38. https://doi.org/10.1038/nm.4443

**Hecht, S., & Mandelbaum, J.** (1938). Rod-cone dark adaptation and vitamin A. *Science, 88*, 219–221.

**Hedegaard, H., Miniño, A. M., & Warner, M.** (2020). Drug overdose deaths in the United States, 1999-2018. NCHS Data Brief, no 356. Hyattsville, MD: National Center for Health Statistics. https://www.cdc.gov/nchs/products/databriefs/db356.htm

**Hedegaard, H., Warner, M., & Miniño, A. M.** (2018). *Drug overdose deaths in the United States, 1999–2017* (NCHS Data Brief No. 329). Centers for Disease Control and Prevention. https://www.cdc.gov/nchs/data/databriefs/db329-h.pdf

**Hegarty, P., & Buechel, C.** (2006). Androcentric reporting of gender differences in APA journals: 1965–2004. *Review of General Psychology, 10*, 377–389.

**Heijnen, S., Hommel, B., Kibele, A., & Colzato, L. S.** (2015). Neuromodulation of aerobic exercise—a review. *Frontiers in Psychology, 6*. https://doi.org/10.3389/fpsyg.2015.0189

**Heil, M., Krüger, M., Krist, H., Johnson, S. P., & Moore, D. S.** (2018). Adults' sex difference in a dynamic Mental Rotation Task: Validating infant results. *Journal of Individual Differences, 39*, 48–52. https://doi.org/10.1027/1614-0001/a000248

**Hein, S., Thomas, T., Naumova, O. Y., Luthar, S. S., & Grigorenko, E. L.** (2019). Negative parenting modulates the association between mother's DNA methylation profiles and adult offspring depression. *Developmental Psychobiology, 61*(2), 304–310. https://doi.org/10.1002/dev.21789

**Helliker, K.** (2009, March 24). No joke: Group therapy offers savings in numbers. *The Wall Street Journal.* http://www.wsj.com/articles/SB123785686766020551

**Helliwell, J. F., Layard, R., & Sachs, J.** (Eds.). (2018). *World happiness report 2018.* Sustainable Development Solutions Network.

**Henderson, S. N., Van Hasselt, V. B., LeDuc, T. J., & Couwels, J.** (2016). Firefighter suicide: Understanding cultural challenges for mental health professionals. *Professional Psychology: Research and Practice, 47*(3), 224–230. https://doi.org/10.1037/pro0000072

**Hendricks, M. L., & Testa, R. J.** (2012). A conceptual framework for clinical work with transgender and gender nonconforming clients: An adaptation of the minority stress model. *Professional Psychology: Research and Practice, 43*, 460–467.

**Henley, J,** (2020, November 4). US elects first trans state senator and first black gay congressman. *The Guardian.* https://www.theguardian.com/us-news/2020/nov/04/us-elects-first-trans-state-senator-and-first-black-gay-congressman

**Hennefield, L., Hwang, H. G., Weston, S. J., & Povinelli, D. J.** (2018). Meta-analytic techniques reveal that corvid causal reasoning in the Aesop's fable paradigm is driven by trial-and-error learning. *Animal Cognition, 21*(6), 735–748. https://doi.org/10.1007/s10071-018-1206-y

**Henrich, J., & Muthukrishna, M.** (2021). The origins and psychology of human cooperation. *Annual Review of Psychology, 72*, 207–240. https://doi.org/10.1146/annurev-psych-081920-042106

**Henry, C. D.** (2017). Humanistic psychology and introductory textbooks: A 21st-century reassessment. *The Humanistic Psychologist, 45*(3), 281–294. https://doi.org/10.1037/hum0000056

**Hensch, T. K.** (2004). Critical period regulation. *Annual Review of Neuroscience, 27*, 549–579.

**Herane-Vives, A., Young, A. H., Wise, T., Aguirre, J., de Angel, V., Arnone, D., Papadopoulos, A., & Cleare, A. J.** (2020). Comparison of short-term (saliva) and long-term (hair) cortisol levels in out-patients with melancholic and non-melancholic major depression. *BJPsych Open, 6*(3), Article E41. https://doi.org/10.1192/bjo.2020.8

**Herbenick, D., Reece, M., Schick, V., Sanders, S. A., Dodge, B., & Fortenberry, J. D.** (2010). Sexual behavior in the United States: Results from a national probability sample of men and women ages 14–94. *Journal of Sexual Medicine, 7*(Suppl. 5), 255–265.

**Herman, C. P., Roth, D. A., & Polivy, J.** (2003). Effects of the presence of others on food intake: A normative interpretation. *Psychological Bulletin, 129*, 873–886.

**Hernandez, D.** (2017, April 10). How I learned to take the SAT like a rich kid. *The New York Times.* https://www.nytimes.com/2017/04/10/opinion/how-i-learned-to-take-the-sat-like-a-rich-kid.html?mcubz=0&_r=0

**Herring, D., & Scott, M.** (2020, February 3). *Isn't there a lot of disagreement among climate scientists about global warming?* NOAA Climate.gov. https://www.climate.gov/news-features/climate-qa/isnt-there-lot-disagreement-among-climate-scientists-about-global-warming

**Hersh, S. M.** (2004, May 10). Torture at Abu Ghraib. *The New Yorker.* http://www.newyorker.com/archive/2004/05/10/040510fa_fact?printable=true&currentPage=all

**Hertenstein, M. J., & McCullough, M. A.** (2005). Separation anxiety. In N. J. Salkind (Ed.), *Encyclopedia of human development* (Vol. 3, pp. 1146–1147). Sage.

**Hertz-Picciotto, I., Sass, J. B., Engel, S., Bennett, D. H., Bradman, A., Eskenazi, B., Lanphear, B., & Whyatt, R.** (2018). Organophosphate exposures during pregnancy and child neurodevelopment: Recommendations for essential policy reforms. *PLOS Medicine, 15*(10), e1002671. https://doi.org/10.1371/journal.pmed.1002671

**Herz, R.** (2007). *The scent of desire: Discovering our enigmatic sense of smell.* William Morrow/HarperCollins.

**Herzog, T. K., Hill-Chapman, C., Hardy, T. K., Wrighten, S. A., & El-Khabbaz, R.** (2015). Trait emotion, emotional regulation, and parenting styles. *Journal of Educational and Developmental Psychology, 5*, 119–135.

**Hettema, J. M., Kettenmann, B., Ahluwalia, V., McCarthy, C., Kates, W. R., Schmitt, J. E., Silberg, J. L., Neale, M. C., Kendler, K. S., & Fatouros, P.** (2012). Pilot multimodal twin imaging study of generalized anxiety disorder. *Depression and Anxiety, 29*, 202–209.

**Hey, J.** (2009). Why should we care about species? *Nature Education, 2*, 2.

**Hibar, D. P., Westlye, L. T., Doan, N. T., Jahanshad, N., Cheung, J. W., Ching, C. R. K., Versace, A., Bilderbeck, A. C., Uhlmann, A., Mwangi, B., Krämer, B., Overs, B., Hartberg, C. B., Abé, C., Dima, D., Grotegerd, D., Sprooten, E., Bøen, E., Jimenez, E., . . . ENIGMA Bipolar Disorder Working Group.** (2018). Cortical abnormalities in bipolar disorder: An MRI analysis of 6503 individuals from the ENIGMA Bipolar Disorder Working Group. *Molecular Psychiatry, 23*(4), 932–942. https://doi.org/10.1038/mp.2017.73

**Hickman, H. D.** (2019). Slowing blood flow to fight viral infection. *Science, 363*(6427), 585–586. https://doi.org/10.1126/science.aaw3618

**Hickok, G., & Poeppel, D.** (2000). Towards a functional neuroanatomy of speech perception. *Trends in Cognitive Sciences, 4,* 131–138.

**Hidden Curriculum.** (2015, July 13). In S. Abbott (Ed.), *The glossary of education reform.* http://edglossary.org/hidden-curriculum

**Higgins, A., Nash, M., & Lynch, A. M.** (2010, September 8). Antidepressant-associated sexual dysfunction: Impact, effects, and treatment. *Drug, Healthcare and Patient Safety, 2,* 141–150.

**Hilgard, E. R.** (1987). *Psychology in America: A historical survey.* Harcourt Brace Jovanovich.

**Hilgard, E. R., Morgan, A. H., & Macdonald, H.** (1975). Pain and dissociation in the cold pressor test: A study of hypnotic analgesia with "hidden reports" through automatic key pressing and automatic talking. *Journal of Abnormal Psychology, 84,* 280–289.

**Hines, M.** (2011a). Gender development and the human brain. *Annual Review of Neuroscience, 34,* 69–88.

**Hines, M.** (2011b). Prenatal endocrine influences on sexual orientation and on sexually differentiated childhood behavior. *Frontiers in Neuroendocrinology, 32,* 170–182.

**Hirshkowitz, M., Whiton, K., Albert, S. M., Alessi, C., Bruni, O., DonCarlos, L., Hazen, N., Herman, J., Adams Hillard, P. J., Katz, E. S., Kheirandish-Gozal, L., Neubauer, D. N., O'Donnell, A. E., Ohayon, M., Peever, J., Rawding, R., Sachdeva, R. C., Setters, B., Vitiello, M. V., & Ware, J. C.** (2015). National Sleep Foundation's updated sleep duration recommendations: Final report. *Sleep Health, 1,* 233–243. https://doi.org/10.1016/j.sleh.2015.10.004

**Hirsh-Pasek, K., Golinkoff, R. M., & Eyer, D.** (2003). *Einstein never used flash cards.* Rodale.

**Hirst, W., & Phelps, E. A.** (2016). Flashbulb memories. *Current Directions in Psychological Science, 25,* 36–41. https://doi.org/10.1177/0963721415622487

**Hirst, W., Phelps, E. A., Meksin, R., Vaidya, C. J., Johnson, M. K., Mitchell, K. J., Buckner, R. L., Budson, A. E., Gabrieli, J. D. E., Lustig, C., Mather, M., Ochsner, K. N., Schacter, D., Simons, J. S., Lyle, K. B., Cuc, A. F., & Olsson, A.** (2015). A ten-year follow-up of a study of memory for the attack of September 11, 2001: Flashbulb memories and memories for flashbulb events. *Journal of Experimental Psychology: General, 144,* 604–623. https://doi.org/10.1037/xge0000055

**HIV.gov.** (2020, June 20). *U.S. statistics.* https://www.hiv.gov/hiv-basics/overview/data-and-trends/statistics

**Hobson, J. A.** (1989). *Sleep.* Scientific American Library.

**Hobson, J. A.** (2006, April/May). Freud returns? Like a bad dream. *Scientific American Mind, 17,* 35.

**Hobson, J. A.** (2009). REM sleep and dreaming: Towards a theory of protoconsciousness. *Nature Reviews Neuroscience, 10,* 803–813.

**Hobson, J. A., & Friston, K. J.** (2012). Waking and dreaming consciousness: Neurobiological and functional considerations. *Progress in Neurobiology, 98,* 82–98.

**Hobson, J. A., & McCarley, R. W.** (1977). The brain as a dream state generator: An activation–synthesis hypothesis of the dream process. *American Journal of Psychiatry, 134,* 1335–1348.

**Hobson, J. A., & Pace-Schott, E. F.** (2002). The cognitive neuroscience of sleep: Neuronal systems, consciousness and learning. *Nature Reviews Neuroscience, 3,* 679–693.

**Hochard, K. D., Heym, N., & Townsend, E.** (2016). The behavioral effects of frequent nightmares on objective stress tolerance. *Dreaming, 26,* 42–49. https://doi.org/10.1037/drm0000013

**Hock, R. R.** (2016). *Human sexuality* (4th ed.). Pearson Education.

**Hodgson, A. B., Randell, R. K., & Jeukendrup, A. E.** (2013). The metabolic and performance effects of caffeine compared to coffee during endurance exercise. *PLOS ONE, 8,* e59561. https://doi.org/10.1371/journal.pone.0059561

**Hoeft, F., Gabrieli, J. D., Whitfield-Gabrieli, S., Haas, B. W., Bammer, R., Menon, V., & Spiegel, D.** (2012). Functional brain basis of hypnotizability. *Archives of General Psychiatry, 69,* 1064–1072.

**Høeg, B. L., Johansen, C., Christensen, J., Frederiksen, K., Dalton, S. O., Dyregrov, A., Bøge, P., Dencker, A., & Bidstrup, P. E.** (2018). Early parental loss and intimate relationships in adulthood: A nationwide study. *Developmental Psychology, 54*(5), 963–974. https://doi.org/10.1037/dev0000483

**Hoffman, I. Z.** (2009). Therapeutic passion in the countertransference. *Psychoanalytic Dialogues, 19,* 617–636.

**Hoffman, S. J., & Tan, C.** (2013). Following celebrities' medical advice: Metanarrative analysis. *British Medical Journal, 347,* f7151. https://doi.org/10.1136/bmj.f7151

**Hofmann, L., & Palczewski, K.** (2015). Advances in understanding the molecular basis of the first steps in color vision. *Progress in Retinal and Eye Research, 49,* 46–66.

**Hofmann, S. G., & Doan, S. N.** (2018). Defining emotions. In S. G. Hofmann & S. N. Doan, *The social foundations of emotion: Developmental, cultural, and clinical dimensions* (p. 11–21). American Psychological Association. https://doi.org/10.1037/0000098-002

**Hofmann, S. G., & Hinton, D. E.** (2014). Cross-cultural aspects of anxiety disorders. *Current Psychiatry Reports, 16,* Article 450. https://doi.org/10.1007/s11920-014-0450-3

**Hofstra, E., Elfeddali, I., Bakker, M., de Jong, J. J., Van Nieuwenhuizen, C., & van der Feltz-Cornelis, C. M.** (2018). Springtime peaks and Christmas troughs: A national longitudinal population-based study into suicide incidence time trends in the Netherlands. *Frontiers in Psychiatry, 9,* 45. https://doi.org/10.3389/fpsyt.2018.00045

**Holahan, C. K., & Sears, R. R.** (1995). *The gifted group in later maturity.* Stanford University Press.

**Holbrook, E. H., & Leopold, D.** (2020, July 7). *Disorders of taste and smell.* Medscape. https://emedicine.medscape.com/article/861242-overview#a3.

**Holliday, E., & Gould, T. J.** (2016). Nicotine, adolescence, and stress: A review of how stress can modulate the negative consequences of adolescent nicotine abuse. *Neuroscience & Biobehavioral Reviews, 65,* 173–184. https://doi.org/10.1016/j.neubiorev.2016.04.003

**Holmes, R.** (2020, April 24). Is COVID-19 social media's levelling up moment? *Forbes.* https://www.forbes.com/sites/ryanholmes/2020/04/24/is-covid-19-social-medias-levelling-up-moment/?sh=240b4a646c60

**Holmes, T. H., & Rahe, R. H.** (1967). The Social Readjustment Rating Scale. *Journal of Psychosomatic Research, 11,* 213–318.

**Holsen, L. M., Spaeth, S. B., Lee, J.-H., Ogden, L. A., Klibanski, A., Whitfield-Gabrieli, S., & Goldstein, J. M.** (2011). Stress response circuitry hypoactivation related to hormonal dysfunction in women with major depression. *Journal of Affective Disorders, 131,* 379–387.

**Holtgraves, T.** (2015). I think I am doing great but I feel pretty bad about it: Affective versus cognitive verbs and self-reports. *Personality & Social Psychology Bulletin, 41,* 677–686.

**Homa, D. M., Neff, L. J., King, B. A., Caraballo, R. S., Bunnell, R. E., Babb, S. D., Garrett, B. E., Sosnoff, C. S., & Want, L.** (2015, February 6). Vital signs: Disparities in nonsmokers' exposure to secondhand smoke—United States, 1999–2012. *MMWR Morbidity and Mortality Weekly Report, 64,* 103–108.

**Honda, H., Shimizu, Y., & Rutter, M.** (2005). No effect of MMR withdrawal on the incidence of autism: A total population study. *Journal of Child Psychology and Psychiatry, 46,* 572–579.

**Hong, S., Jahng, M. R., Lee, N., & Wise, K. R.** (2020). Do you filter who you are?: Excessive self-presentation, social cues, and user evaluations of Instagram selfies. *Computers in Human Behavior, 104,* 106159. https://doi.org/10.1016/j.chb.2019.106159

**Hooper, J., Sharpe, D., & Roberts, S. G. B.** (2016). Are men funnier than women, or do we just think they are? *Translational Issues in Psychological Science, 2*(1), 54–62. https://doi.org/10.1037/tps0000064

**Hopely, M.** (2014). *The people you meet in real life.* Brighton Publishing.

**Hopwood, C. J., Bleidorn, W., Schwaba, T., & Chen, S.** (2020). Health, environmental, and animal rights motives for vegetarian eating. *PLOS ONE, 15*(4), e0230609.

**Horgan, J.** (2017, March 10). Why Freud still isn't dead [Web log post]. *Scientific American.* https://blogs.scientificamerican.com/cross-check/why-freud-still-isnt-dead/

**Horne, J.** (2006). *Sleepfaring.* Oxford University Press.

**Horney, K.** (1926/1967). The flight from womanhood: The masculinity-complex in women as viewed by men and by women. In H. Kelman (Ed.), *Feminine psychology* (pp. 54–70). W. W. Norton.

**Horney, K.** (1945). *Our inner conflicts: A constructive theory of neurosis.* W. W. Norton.

**Hornsey, M. J.** (2020). Why facts are not enough: Understanding and managing the motivated rejection of science. *Current Directions in Psychological Science, 29*(6), 583–591. https://doi.org/10.1177/0963721420969364

**Horsley, R. R., Osborne, M., Norman, C., & Wells, T.** (2012). High-frequency gamblers show increased resistance to extinction following partial reinforcement. *Behavioural Brain Research, 229,* 438–442.

**Hortensius, R., & de Gelder, B.** (2018). From empathy to apathy: The bystander effect revisited. *Current Directions in Psychological Science, 27*(4), 249–256. https://doi.org/10.1177/0963721417749653

**Horwitz, D., Lovenberg, W., Engelman, K., & Sjoerdsma, A.** (1964). Monoamine oxidase inhibitors, tyramine, and cheese. *Journal of the American Medical Association, 188,* 1108–1110.

Hothersall, D. (2004). *History of psychology* (4th ed.). McGraw-Hill.

Houlihan, A. E. (2019). Patient prototypes: Perceptions of others who have an illness and associations with other health cognitions and behavior. *European Journal of Health Psychology, 26*(4), 129–145. https://doi.org/10.1027/2512-8442/a000041

House, J. S., Landis, K. R., & Umberson, D. (1988). Social relationships and health. *Science, 241,* 540–545.

Hovland, C. I., Janis, I. L., & Kelley, H. H. (1953). *Communication and persuasion: Psychological studies of opinion change.* Yale University Press.

Hovland, C. I., & Weiss, W. (1951). The influence of source credibility on communication effectiveness. *Public Opinion Quarterly, 15,* 635–650.

Howard, J. (2018, July 5). Thailand cave rescue: The health toll of waiting for freedom. *CNN.* https://www.cnnamerican psychologi.com/2018/07/03/health/cave-rescue-psychological-toll-explainer/index.html

Howes, O. D., & Kapur, S. (2009). The dopamine hypothesis of schizophrenia: Version III—the final common pathway. *Schizophrenia Bulletin, 35,* 549–562.

Howland, J., Rohsenow, D. J., Greece, J. A., Littefield, C. A., Almeida, A., Heeren, T., Winter, M., Bliss, C. A., Hunt, S., & Hermos, J. (2010). The effects of binge drinking on college students' next-day academic test-taking performance and mood state. *Addiction, 105,* 655–665. https://doi.org/10.1111/j.1360-0443.2009.02880.x

Hřebíčková, M., Mõttus, R., Graf, S., Jelínek, M., & Realo, A. (2018). How accurate are national stereotypes? A test of different methodological approaches. *European Journal of Personality, 32*(2), 87–99. https://doi.org/10.1002/per.2146

Hsu, P. J., Shoud, H., Benzinger, T., Marcus, D., Durbin, T., Morris, J. C., & Sheline, Y. I. (2015). Amyloid burden in cognitively normal elderly is associated with preferential hippocampal subfield volume loss. *Journal of Alzheimer's Disease, 45,* 27–33.

Hu, M. T. (2020). REM sleep behavior disorder (RBD). *Neurobiology of Disease, 143.* https://doi.org/10.1016/j.nbd.2020.104996

Huang, Y., & Zhao, N. (2020). Generalized anxiety disorder, depressive symptoms and sleep quality during COVID-19 outbreak in China: A web-based cross-sectional survey. *Psychiatry Research, 228,* Article 112954. https://doi.org/10.1016/j.psychres.2020.112954

Huang, Z. J., & Luo, L. (2015). It takes the world to understand the brain. *Science, 350*(6256), 42–44.

Hubel, D. H., & Wiesel, T. N. (1979, September). Brain mechanisms of vision. *Scientific American, 241,* 150–162.

Hufer, A., Kornadt, A. E., Kandler, C., & Riemann, R. (2020). Genetic and environmental variation in political orientation in adolescence and early adulthood: A Nuclear Twin Family analysis. *Journal of Personality and Social Psychology, 118*(4), 762–776. https://doi.org/10.1037/pspp0000258

Huffman, J. C., Beale, E. E., Celano, C. M., Beach, S. R., Belcher, A. M., Moore, S. V., Suarez, L., Motiwala, S. R., Gandhi, P. U., Gaggin, H. K., & Januzzi, J. L. (2016). Effects of optimism and gratitude on physical activity, biomarkers, and readmissions after an acute coronary syndrome: The gratitude research in acute coronary events study. *Circulation: Cardiovascular Quality and Outcomes, 9,* 55–63.

Huguelet, P., & Perroud, N. (2005). Wolfgang Amadeus Mozart's psychopathology in light of the current conceptualization of psychiatric disorders. *Psychiatry, 68,* 130–139.

Hui, B. P. H., Ng, J. C. K., Berzaghi, E., Cunningham-Amos, L. A., & Kogan, A. (2020). Rewards of kindness? A meta-analysis of the link between prosociality and well-being. *Psychological Bulletin, 146*(12), 1084–1116. https://doi.org/10.1037/bul0000298

Huizink, A. C. (2014). Prenatal cannabis exposure and infant outcomes: Overview of studies. *Progress in Neuro-Psychopharmacology and Biological Psychiatry, 52,* 45–52.

Hull, C. L. (1952). *A behavior system: An introduction to behavior theory concerning the individual organism.* Yale University Press.

Hulsegge, G., Looman, M., Smit, H. A., Daviglus, M. L., van der Schouw, Y. T., & Verschuren, W. M. (2016). Lifestyle changes in young adulthood and middle age and risk of cardiovascular disease and all-cause mortality: The Doetinchem Cohort Study. *Journal of the American Heart Association, 5.* https://doi.org/10.1161/JAHA.115.002432

Humphreys, H., Fitzpatrick, F., & Harvey, B. J. (2015). Gender differences in rates of carriage and bloodstream infection caused by methicillin-resistant *Staphylococcus aureus:* Are they real, do they matter and why? *Clinical Infectious Diseases, 61,* 1708–1714.

Hunsley, J., Lee, C. M., & Wood, J. M. (2003). Controversial and questionable assessment techniques.

In S. O. Lilienfeld, J. M. Lohr, & S. J. Lynn (Eds.), *Science and pseudoscience in clinical psychology* (pp. 39–76). Guilford Press.

Hunt, W. A. (1939). A critical review of current approaches to affectivity. *Psychological Bulletin, 36,* 807–828.

Hunter, S. C., Fox, C. L., & Jones, S. E. (2016). Humor style similarity and difference in friendship dyads. *Journal of Adolescence, 46,* 30–37. https://doi.org/10.1016/j.adolescence.2015.10.015

Hurley, S. W., & Johnson, A. K. (2014). The role of the lateral hypothalamus and orexin in ingestive behavior: A model for the translation of past experience and sensed deficits into motivated behaviors. *Frontiers in Systems Neuroscience, 8.* http://dx.doi.org/10.3389/fnsys.2014.00216

Hustá, C., Dalmaijer, E., Belopolsky, A., & Mathôt, S. (2019). The pupillary light response reflects visual working memory content. *Journal of Experimental Psychology: Human Perception and Performance, 45*(11), 1522–1528. https://doi.org/10.1037/xhp0000689

Hutson, M. (2018, March). Ineffective geniuses? *Scientific American, 318*(3), 20.

Hyman, I. E., Jr., Husband, T. H., & Billings, F. J. (1995). False memories of childhood experiences. *Applied Cognitive Psychology, 3,* 181–197.

Hyman, S. E. (2019). New evidence for shared risk architecture of mental disorders. *JAMA Psychiatry, 76*(3), 235–236. https://doi.org/10.1001/jamapsychiatry.2018.4269

Iacono, W. G., & Ben-Shakhar, G. (2019). Current status of forensic lie detection with the comparison question technique: An update of the 2003 National Academy of Sciences report on polygraph testing. *Law and Human Behavior, 43*(1), 86–98. https://doi.org/10.1037/lhb0000307

Ilias, I., Tayeh, L. S., & Pachoundakis, I. (2016). Diversity in endocrinology practice: The case of Ramadan. *Hormones, 15,* 147–148.

Ilse, A., Donohue, S. E., Schoenfeld, M. A., Hopf, J. M., Heinze, H. J., & Harris, J. A. (2020). Unseen food images capture the attention of hungry viewers: Evidence from event-related potentials. *Appetite, 155,* 104828. https://doi.org/10.1016/j.appet.2020.104828

Im, S. H., Cho, J. Y., Dubinsky, J. M., & Varma, S. (2018). Taking an educational psychology course improves neuroscience literacy but does not reduce belief in neuromyths. *PLOS ONE, 13*(2). https://doi.org/10.1371/journal.pone.0192163

iminmotion.net. (n.d.). *Ivonne Marcela Mosquera-Schmidt.* http://www.iminmotion.net

Impey, C., Buxner, S., & Antonellis, J. (2012). Non-scientific beliefs among undergraduate students. *Astronomy Education Review, 11.* https://doi.org/10.3847/AER2012016

Inder, M. L., Crowe, M. T., Luty, S. E., Carter, J. D., Moor, S., Frampton, C. M., & Joyce, P. R. (2016). Prospective rates of suicide attempts and nonsuicidal self-injury by young people with bipolar disorder participating in a psychotherapy study. *Australian and New Zealand Journal of Psychiatry, 50,* 167–173. https://doi.org/10.1177/0004867415622268

Indigo, N., Smith, J., Webb, J. K., & Phillips, B. (2018). Not such silly sausages: Evidence suggests northern quolls exhibit aversion to toads after training with toad sausages. *Austral Ecology, 43*(5), 592–601. https://doi.org/10.1111/aec.12595

Ingalhalikar, M., Smith, A., Parker, D., Satterthwaite, T. D., Elliott, M. A., Ruparel, K., Hakonarson, H., Gur, R. E., Gur, R. C., & Verma, R. (2014). Sex differences in the structural connectome of the human brain. *PNAS Proceedings of the National Academy of Sciences of the United States of America, 111*(2), 823–828. https://doi.org/10.1073/pnas.1316909110

Ingraham, C. (2020, October 23). A powerful argument for wearing a mask, in visual form. *The Washington Post.* https://www.washingtonpost.com/business/2020/10/23/pandemic-data-chart-masks/

Insurance Institute for Highway Safety, Highway Loss Data Institute. (2018, October 18). *Status Report, 53*(6). https://www.iihs.org/iihs/sr/statusreport/article/53/6/1

International Organization for Migration (IOM). (2020). *World migration report 2020.* https://publications.iom.int/system/files/pdf/wmr_2020.pdf

Intersex Justice Project (IJP). (n.d.) About IJP. https://www.intersexjusticeproject.org/about.html

Inui, K., Urakawa, T., Yamahiro, K., Otsuru, N., Takeshima, Y., Nishihara, M., Motomura, E., Kida, T., & Kakigi, R. (2010). Echoic memory of a single pure tone by change-related brain activity. *BMS Neuroscience, 11,* 135–145.

Isen, A. (2008). Some ways in which positive affect influences decision making and problem solving. In M. Lewis, J. M. Haviland-Jones, & L. F. Barrett (Eds.), *Handbook of emotions* (3rd ed., pp. 548–573). Guilford Press.

Ito, T. A., Friedman, N. P., Bartholow, B. D., Correll, J., Loersch, C., Altamirano, L. J., & Miyake, A. (2015). Toward a comprehensive understanding of executive cognitive function in implicit racial bias. *Journal of Personality and Social Psychology, 108*, 187–218.

Iurato, S., Carrillo-Roa, T., Arloth, J., Czamara, D., Diener-Hölzl, L., Lange, J., Müller-Myhsok, B., Binder, E. B., & Erhardt, A. (2017). DNA methylation signatures in panic disorder. *Translational Psychiatry, 7*, Article 1287. https://doi.org/10.1038/s41398-017-0026-1

Iwamoto, S. K., Alexander, M., Torres, M., Irwin, M. R., Christakis, N. A., & Nishi, A. (2020). Mindfulness meditation activates altruism. *Scientific Reports, 10*, Article 6511.

Izadi, E. (2017, July 27). Justin Bieber 'purpose' timeline: Pinkeye, punching dudes and posing with controversial tigers. *The Washington Post.* https://www.washingtonpost.com/news/arts-and-entertainment/wp/2017/07/26/justin-bieber-purpose-timeline-pink-eye-punching-dudes-and-posing-with-controversial-tigers/?utm_term=.433868b68a3a

Izard, C. E. (1992). Basic emotions, relations among emotions, and emotion-cognition relations. *Psychological Review, 99*, 561–565.

Izard, C. E. (2007). Basic emotions, natural kinds, emotion schemas, and a new paradigm. *Perspectives on Psychological Science, 2*, 260–280.

Izbicki, P. (2020, April 9). Your brain will thank you for being a musician. *Scientific American.* https://blogs.scientificamerican.com/observations/your-brain-will-thank-you-for-being-a-musician/

Jaarsveld, S., Fink, A., Rinner, M., Schwab, D., Benedek, M., & Lachmann, T. (2015). Intelligence in creative processes: An EEG study. *Intelligence, 49*, 171–178.

Jack, R. E., Sun, W., Delis, I., Garrod, O. G., & Schyns, P. G. (2016). Four not six: Revealing culturally common facial expressions of emotion. *Journal of Experimental Psychology, 145*, 708–730. https://doi.org/10.1037/xge0000162

Jackson, L. M. (2020). *Defining prejudice.* In L. M. Jackson, *The psychology of prejudice: From attitudes to social action* (pp. 9–25). American Psychological Association. https://doi.org/10.1037/0000168-002

Jackson, S., Baity, M. R., Bobb, K., Swick, D., & Giorgio, J. (2019). Stress inoculation training outcomes among veterans with PTSD and TBI. *Psychological Trauma: Theory, Research, Practice, and Policy, 11*(8), 842–850. https://doi.org/10.1037/tra0000432

Jacobs, A. (2021, February 8). A parallel pandemic hits health care workers: Trauma and exhaustion. *New York Times.* https://www.nytimes.com/2021/02/04/health/health-care-workers-burned-out-quitting.html

Jacobs, H. (2012). Don't ask, don't tell, don't publish. *EMBO Reports, 13*, 393.

Jacobsen, F. M. (2015). Second-generation antipsychotics and tardive syndromes in affective illness: A public health problem with neuropsychiatric consequences. *American Journal of Public Health, 105*, e10–e16.leavitt

Jacobson, E. (1938). *Progressive relaxation.* University of Chicago Press.

Jahanshad, N., & Thompson, P. M. (2017). Multimodal neuroimaging of male and female brain structure in health and disease across the life span. *Journal of Neuroscience Research, 95*(1–2), 371–379. https://doi.org/10.1002/jnr.23919

Jain, A., Marshall, J., Buikema, A., Bancroft, T., Kelly J. P., & Newschaffer, C. J. (2015). Autism occurrence by MMR vaccine status among US children with older siblings with and without autism. *Journal of the American Medical Association, 313*, 1534–1540.

Jäkel, S., & Dimou, L. (2017). Glial cells and their function in the adult brain: A journey through the history of their ablation. *Frontiers in Cellular Neuroscience, 11.* https://doi.org/10.3389/fncel.2017.00024

Jalal, B., Chamberlain, S. R., Robbins, T. W., & Sahakian, B. J. (2020). Obsessive–compulsive disorder—contamination fears, features, and treatment: Novel smartphone therapies in light of global mental health and pandemics (COVID-19). *CNS Spectrums.* https://doi.org/10.1017/S1092852920001947

Jalal, B., & Ramachandran, V. S. (2014). Sleep paralysis and "the bedroom intruder": The role of the right superior parietal, phantom pain and body image projection. *Medical Hypotheses, 83*, 755–757.

Jalal, B., Taylor, C. T., & Hinton, D. E. (2014). A comparison of self-report and interview methods for assessing sleep paralysis: Pilot investigations in Denmark and the United States. *Journal of Sleep Disorders: Treatment & Care, 3.* https://doi.org/10.4172/2325-9639.1000131

James, L. E., & Burke, D. M. (2000). Phonological priming effects on word retrieval and tip-of-the-tongue experiences in young and older adults. *Journal of Experimental Psychology: Learning, Memory, and Cognition, 26*, 1378–1391.

James, S. M., Honn, K. A., Gaddameedhi, S., & Van Dongen, H. P. (2017). Shift work: Disrupted circadian rhythms and sleep—implications for health and well-being. *Current Sleep Medicine Reports, 3*(2), 104–112. https://doi.org/10.1007/s40675-017-0071-6

James, W. J. (1890/1983). *The principles of psychology.* Harvard University Press.

Jameson, D., & Hurvich, L. M. (1989). Essay concerning color constancy. *Annual Review of Psychology, 40*, 1–24.

Jamieson, J. P., Black, A. E., Pelaia, L. E., & Reis, H. T. (2020). The impact of mathematics anxiety on stress appraisals, neuroendocrine responses, and academic performance in a community college sample. *Journal of Educational Psychology.* Advance online publication. https://doi.org/10.1037/edu0000636

Jamkhande, P. G., Chintawar, K. D., & Chandak, P. G. (2014). Teratogenicity: A mechanism based short review on common teratogenic agents. *Asian Pacific Journal of Tropical Disease, 4*, 421–432.

Janak, P. H., & Tye, K. M. (2015). From circuits to behaviour in the amygdala. *Nature, 517*, 284–292.

Jang, K. L., Livesley, W. J., & Vernon, P. A. (1996). Heritability of the Big Five personality dimensions and their facets: A twin study. *Journal of Personality, 64*, 577–592.

Janiri, D., Carfì, A., Kotzalidis, G. D., Bernabei, R., Landi, F., Sani, G., & Gemelli Against COVID-19 Post-Acute Care Study Group. (2021). Posttraumatic stress disorder in patients after severe COVID-19 infection. *JAMA Psychiatry.* https://jamanetwork.com/journals/jamapsychiatry/fullarticle/2776722

Janis, I. J., Kaye, D., & Kirschner, P. (1965). Facilitating effects of "eating-while-reading" on responsiveness to persuasive communication. *Journal of Personality and Social Psychology, 1*, 181–186.

Janis, I. L. (1972). *Victims of groupthink: A psychological study of foreign-policy decisions and fiascoes.* Houghton Mifflin.

Janis, I. L., & Feshbach, S. (1953). Effects of fear-arousing communications. *Journal of Abnormal and Social Psychology, 48*, 78–92.

Jankovic, N., Geelen, A., Streppel, M. T., de Groot, L. C., Orfanos, P., van den Hooven, E. H., Pikhart, H., Boffetta, P., Trichopoulou, A., Bobak, M., Bueno-de-Mesquita, H. B., Kee, F., Franco, O. H., Park, Y., Hallmans, G., Tjønneland, A., May, A. M., Pajak, A., Malyutina, S., . . . Feskens, E. J. (2014). Adherence to a healthy diet according to the World Health Organization guidelines and all-cause mortality in elderly men and women from Europe and the United States. *American Journal of Epidemiology, 180*, 978–988.

Japan-guide.com. (2020, February 23). *Japanese table manners.* https://www.japan-guide.com/e/e2005.html

Jeanfreau, M. M., Herring, A., & Jurich, A. P. (2016). Permission-giving and marital infidelity. *Marriage and Family Review, 52*(6), 535–547. https://doi.org/10.1080/01494929.2015.1124354

Jerald, C. D. (2009). Defining a 21st century education. Center for Public Education. http://www.centerforpubliceducation.org/LearnAbout/21st-Century/Defining-a-21st-CenturyEducation-Full-Report-PDF.pdf

Jeste, D. V., Savla, G. N., Thompson, W. K., Vahia, I. V., Glorioso, D. K., Palmer, B. W., Rock, D., Golshan, S., Kraemer, H. C., & Depp, C. A. (2013). Association between older age and more successful aging: Critical role of resilience and depression. *American Journal of Psychiatry, 170*, 188–196. https://doi.org/10.1176/appi.ajp.2012.12030386

Jester, D. J., Rozek, E. K., & McKelley, R. A. (2019). Heart rate variability biofeedback: Implications for cognitive and psychiatric effects in older adults. *Aging & Mental Health, 23*(5), 574–580. https://doi.org/10.1080/13607863.2018.1432031

Ji, Y., Zhang, X., Wang, Z., Qin, W., Liu, H., Xue, K., Tang, J., Xu, Q., Zhu, D., Liu, F., & Yu, C. (2021). Genes associated with gray matter volume alterations in schizophrenia. *NeuroImage, 225*, Article 117526. https://doi.org/10.1016/j.neuroimage.2020.117526

Jiang, Y., Chew, S. H., & Ebstein, R. P. (2013). The role of D4 receptor gene exon III polymorphisms in shaping human altruism and prosocial behavior. *Frontiers in Human Neuroscience, 7*, 1–7.

Joel, D., Persico, A., Salhov, M., Berman, Z., Oligschläger, S., Meilijson, I., & Averbuch, A. (2018). Analysis of human brain structure reveals that the brain "types" typical of males are also typical of females, and vice versa. *Frontiers in Human Neuroscience, 12*, Article 399. https://doi.org/10.3389/fnhum.2018.00399

Joel, S., Impett, E. A., Spielmann, S. S., & MacDonald, G. (2018). How interdependent are stay/leave decisions? On staying in the relationship for the sake of the romantic partner. *Journal of Personality and Social Psychology, 115*(5), 805–824. https://doi.org/10.1037/pspi0000139

Johannsson, M., Snaedal, J., Johannesson, G. H., Gudmundsson, T. E., & Johnsen, K. (2015). The acetylcholine index: An electroencephalographic marker of cholinergic activity in the living human brain applied to Alzheimer's disease and other dementias. *Dementia and Geriatric Cognitive Disorders, 39,* 132–142.

John-Henderson, N. A., Stellar, J. E., Mendoza-Denton, R., & Francis, D. D. (2015). Socioeconomic status and social support: Social support reduces inflammatory reactivity for individuals whose early-life socioeconomic status was low. *Psychological Science, 26,* 1620–1629.

Johnson, H. D., McNair, R., Vojick, A., Congdon, D., Monacelli, J., & Lamont, J. (2006). Categorical and continuous measurement of sex-role orientation: Differences in associations with young adults' reports of well-being. *Social Behavior and Personality, 34,* 59–76.

Johnson, P. L., Truitt, W., Fitz, S. D., Minick, P. E., Dietrich, A., Sanghani, S., Träskman-Bendz, L., Goddard, A. W., Brundin, L., & Shekhar, A. (2010). A key role for orexin in panic anxiety. *Nature Medicine, 16,* 111–115.

Johnson, R. D. (1987). Making judgments when information is missing: Inferences, biases, and framing effects. *Acta Psychologica, 66,* 69–72.

Johnson, S. B., Riis, J. L., & Noble, K. G. (2016). State of the art review: Poverty and the developing brain. *Pediatrics, 137*(4), Article e20153075. https://doi.org/10.1542/peds.2015 -3075

Johnson, S. P., & Moore, D. S. (2020). Spatial thinking in infancy: Origins and development of mental rotation between 3 and 10 months of age. *Cognitive Research: Principles and Implications, 5*(10), 1–14. https://doi .org/10.1186/s41235-020-00212-x

Johnson, W., & Bouchard, T. J. (2011). The MISTR A data: Forty-two mental ability tests in three batteries. *Intelligence, 39,* 82–88.

Johnston, M. V. (2009). Plasticity in the developing brain: Implications for rehabilitation. *Developmental Disabilities Research Reviews, 15,* 94–101.

Joly, J., Soroka, S., & Loewen, P. (2019). Nice guys finish last: Personality and political success. *Acta Politica, 54,* 667–683. https://doi .org/10.1057/s41269-018-0095-z

Jonauskaite, D., Abdel-Khalek, A. M., Abu-Akel, A., Al-Rasheed, A. S., Antonietti, J. P., Ásgeirsson, Á. G., Kokou, A. A., Barma, M., Barratt, D., Bogushevskaya, V., Meziane, M. K. B., Chamseddine, A., Charernboom, T., Chkonia, E., Ciobanua, T., Corona, V., Creed, A., Dael, N., Daoud, H., . . . Mohr, C. (2019). The sun is no fun without rain: Physical environments affect how we feel about yellow across 55 countries. *Journal of Environmental Psychology, 66,* 101350. https://doi.org/10.1016/j .jenvp.2019.101350

Jonauskaite, D., Dael, N., Chèvre, L., Althaus, B., Tremea, A., Charalambides, L., & Mohr, C. (2019). Pink for girls, red for boys, and blue for both genders: Colour preferences in children and adults. *Sex Roles, 80*(9–10), 630–642. https://doi .org/10.1007/s11199-018-0955-z

Jones, K. (2013). Discouraging social loafing during team-based assessments. *Teaching Innovation Projects, 3,* Art. 13.

Jones, O. P., Alfaro-Almagro, F., & Jbabdi, S. (2018). An empirical, 21st century evaluation of phrenology. *Cortex, 106,* 26–35. https://doi.org /10.1016/j.cortex.2018.04.011

Jonsson, B., Wiklund-Hörnqvist, C., Stenlund, T., Andersson, M., & Nyberg, L. (2020). A learning method for all: The testing effect is independent of cognitive ability. *Journal of Educational Psychology.* Advance online publication. https:// doi.org/10.1037/edu0000627

Jordan-Young, R. M. (2012). Hormones, context, and "brain gender": A review of evidence from congenital adrenal hyperplasia. *Social Science & Medicine, 74,* 1738–1744.

Joseph, D. L., Jin, J., Newman, D. A., & O'Boyle, E. H. (2015). Why does self-reported emotional intelligence predict job performance? A meta-analytic investigation of mixed EI. *Journal of Applied Psychology, 100,* 298–342.

Joseph, N. T., Matthews, K. A., & Myers, H. F. (2014). Conceptualizing health consequences of Hurricane Katrina from the perspective of socioeconomic status decline. *Health Psychology, 33,* 139–146.

Josselyn, S. A., & Tonegawa, S. (2020). Memory engrams: Recalling the past and imagining the future. *Science, 367*(6473). https://doi.org/10 .1126/science.aaw4325

Jouvet, M. (1979). What does a cat dream about? *Trends in Neurosciences, 2,* 280–282.

Joy, E., Kussman, A., & Nattiv, A. (2016). 2016 update on eating disorders in athletes: A comprehensive narrative review with a focus on clinical assessment and management. *British Journal of Sports Medicine, 50,* 154–162. https://doi.org/10.1136 /bjsports-2015-095735

Juberg, D. R., Alfano, K., Coughlin, R. J., & Thompson, K. M. (2001). An observational study of object mouthing behavior by young children. *Pediatrics, 107,* 135–142.

Judge, T. A., Piccolo, R. F., Podsakoff, N. P., Shaw, J. C., & Rich, B. L. (2010). The relationship between pay and job satisfaction: A meta-analysis of the literature. *Journal of Vocational Behavior, 77,* 157–167.

Jung, C. G. (1969). *Collected works: Vol. 8. The structure and dynamics of the psyche* (R. F. C. Hull, Ed., 2nd ed.). Princeton University Press.

Jung, H., Seo, E., Han, E., Henderson, M. D., & Patall, E. A. (2020). Prosocial modeling: A meta-analytic review and synthesis. *Psychological Bulletin, 146*(8), 635–663. https://doi.org/10.1037/bul0000235

Jurkowski, M. P., Bettio, L., K Woo, E., Patten, A., Yau, S. Y., & Gil-Mohapel, J. (2020). Beyond the hippocampus and the SVZ: Adult neurogenesis throughout the brain. *Frontiers in Cellular Neuroscience, 14,* 293. https://doi.org/10.3389/fncel .2020.576444

Jussim, L., & Harber, K. D. (2005). Teacher expectations and self-fulfilling prophecies: Knowns and unknowns, resolved and unresolved controversies. *Personality and Social Psychology Review, 9,* 131–155.

Kaczmarek, M. (2015). On the doorstep to senility: Physical changes, health status and well-being in midlife. *Anthropological Review, 78,* 269–287.

Kagan, J. (1985). The human infant. In A. M. Rogers & C. J. Scheirer (Eds.), *The G. Stanley Hall lecture series* (Vol. 5., pp. 55–86). American Psychological Association.

Kagan, J. (2003). Biology, context, and developmental inquiry. *Annual Review of Psychology, 54,* 1–23.

Kagan, J. (2016). An overly permissive extension. *Perspectives on Psychological Science, 11,* 442–450. https://doi .org/10.1177/1745691616635593

Kahlenberg, S. G., & Hein, M. M. (2010). Progression on Nickelodeon? Gender-role stereotypes in toy commercials. *Sex Roles, 62,* 830–847.

Kahn, J. (2018, June 21). Born to run back. *Runner's World.* https://www .runnersworld.com/runners-stories /a21750581/born-to-run-back/

Kahneman, D., & Tversky, A. (1984). Choices, values, and frames. *American Psychologist, 39,* 341–350.

Kahneman, D., & Tversky, A. (1996). On the reality of cognitive illusions. *Psychological Review, 103,* 582–591.

Kaiser, J. (2019, August 29). Genetics may explain up to 25% of same-sex behavior, giant analysis reveals. *Science.* https://www.sciencemag.org/news/2019 /08/genetics-may-explain-25-same-sex -behavior-giant-analysis-reveals

Kajonius, P. J., & Johnson, J. (2018). Sex differences in 30 facets of the five factor model of personality in the large public (*N* = 320,128). *Personality and Individual Differences, 129,* 126–130.

https://doi.org/10.1016/j.paid.2018 .03.026

Kambeitz, J. P., & Howes, O. D. (2015). The serotonin transporter in depression: Meta-analysis of in vivo and post mortem findings and implications for understanding and treating depression. *Journal of Affective Disorders, 186,* 358–366.

Kamenetz, A. (2018, June 1). Let's stop talking about the "30 million word gap." *NPR Ed.* https://www .npr.org/sections/ed/2018/06/01 /615188051/lets-stop-talking-about -the-30-million-word-gap

Kamilar-Britt, P., & Bedi, G. (2015). The prosocial effects of 3,4-methylene-dioxymethamphetamine (MDMA): Controlled studies in humans and laboratory animals. *Neuroscience & Biobehavioral Reviews, 57,* 433–446.

Kamimori, G. H., McLellan, T. M., Tate, C. M., Voss, D. M., Niro, P., & Lieberman, H. R. (2015). Caffeine improves reaction time, vigilance and logical reasoning during extended periods with restricted opportunities for sleep. *Psychopharmacology, 232,* 2031–2042.

Kanai, R., Bahrami, B., Roylance, R., & Rees, G. (2012). Online social network size is reflected in human brain structure. *Proceedings of the Royal Society B, 279,* 1327–1334.

Kandel, E. R. (2009). The biology of memory: A forty-year perspective. *Journal of Neuroscience, 29,* 12748–12756.

Kandel, E. R., & Pittenger, C. (1999). The past, the future and the biology of memory storage. *Philosophical Transactions: Biological Sciences, 354,* 2027–2052.

Kandler, C., Bleidorn, W., Riemann, R., Spinath, F. M., Thiel, W., & Angleitner, A. (2010). Sources of cumulative continuity in personality: A longitudinal multiple-rater twin study. *Journal of Personality and Social Psychology, 98,* 995–1008.

Kandler, C., Kornadt, A. E., Hagemeyer, B., & Neyer, F. J. (2015). Patterns and sources of personality development in old age. *Journal of Personality and Social Psychology, 109,* 175–191.

Kaneda, H., Maeshima, K., Goto, N., Kobayakawa, T., Ayabe-Kanamura, S., & Saito, S. (2000). Decline in taste and odor discrimination abilities with age, and relationship between gustation and olfaction. *Chemical Senses, 25,* 331–337.

Kang, Y., Rahrig, H., Eichel, K., Niles, H. F., Rocha, T., Lepp, N. E., Gold, J., & Britton, W. B. (2018). Gender differences in response to a school-based mindfulness training intervention for early adolescents. *Journal of School Psychology, 68,* 163–176. https://doi.org/10.1016/j .jsp.2018.03.004

Kanherkar, R. R., Bhatia-Dey, N., & Csoka, A. B. (2014). Epigenetics across the human lifespan. *Frontiers in Cell and Developmental Biology, 2,* 49. https://doi.org/10.3389/fcell.2014 .00049

Kanny, D., Naimi, T. S., Liu, Y., & Brewer, R. D. (2020). Trends in total binge drinks per adult who reported binge drinking—United States, 2011–2017. *Morbidity and Mortality Weekly Report, 69*(2), 30–34. https://doi.org /10.15585/mmwr.mm6902a2

Kantziari, M. A., Nikolettos, N., Sivvas, T., Bakoula, C. T., Chrousos, G. P., & Darviri, C. (2019). Stress management during the second trimester of pregnancy. *International Journal of Stress Management, 26*(1), 102–105. https:// doi.org/10.1037/str0000078

Kaplan, R. M., & Saccuzzo, D. P. (2018). *Psychological testing: Principles, applications, and issues* (9th ed.). Cengage Learning.

Kapler, I. V., Weston, T., & Wiseheart, M. (2015). Spacing in a simulated undergraduate classroom: Long-term benefits for factual and higher-level learning. *Learning and Instruction, 36,* 38–45.

Kaptchuk, T. J., & Miller, F. G. (2015). Placebo effects in medicine. *New England Journal of Medicine, 373,* 8–9.

Karandashev, V., Zarubko, E., Artemeva, V., Evans, M., Morgan, K. A. D., Neto, F., Feybesse, C., Surmanidze, L., & Purvis, J. (2020). Cross-cultural comparison of sensory preferences in romantic attraction. *Sexuality and Culture, 24*(1), 23–53. https://doi.org/10.1007/s12119-019 -09628-0

Karanicolas, P. J., Graham, D., Gönen, M., Strong, V. E., Brennan, M. F., & Coit, D. G. (2013). Quality of life after gastrectomy for adenocarcinoma: A prospective cohort study. *Annals of Surgery, 257,* 1039–1046.

Karlen, S. J., Kahn, D. M., & Krubitzer, L. (2006). Early blindness results in abnormal cortico-cortical and thalamocortical connections. *Neuroscience, 142,* 843–858.

Karremans, J. C., Stroebe, W., & Claus, J. (2006). Beyond Vicary's fantasies: The impact of subliminal priming and brand choice. *Journal of Experimental Social Psychology, 42,* 792–798.

Karthik, S., Sharma, L. P., & Narayanaswamy, J. C. (2020). Investigating the role of glutamate in obsessive-compulsive disorder: Current perspectives. *Neuropsychiatric Disease and Treatment, 16,* 1003–1013. https:// doi.org/10.2147/NDT.S211703

Karwowski, M., & Lebuda, I. (2016). The Big Five, the Huge Two, and creative self-beliefs: A meta-analysis. *Psychology of Aesthetics, Creativity, and the Arts, 10*(2), 214–232. https://doi.org/10.1037 /aca0000035

Kassin, S. M. (2017a). False confessions: How can psychology so basic be so counterintuitive? *American Psychologist, 72*(9), 951–964. https:// doi.org/10.1037/amp0000195

Kassin, S. M. (2017b). The killing of Kitty Genovese: What else does this case tell us? *Perspectives on Psychological Science, 12*(3), 374–381. https://doi .org/10.1177/1745691616679465

Kassin, S., Fein, S., & Markus, H. R. (2017). *Social psychology* (10th ed.). Wadsworth, Cengage Learning.

Kastenbaum, R., & Costa, P. T., Jr. (1977). Psychological perspectives on death. *Annual Review of Psychology, 28,* 225–249.

Katz, J. (2017, April 14). You draw it: Just how bad is the drug overdose epidemic? *The New York Times.* https:// www.nytimes.com/interactive/2017 /04/14/upshot/drug-overdose-epidemic -you-draw-it.html

Kaufman, M. T. (2007, July 25). Albert Ellis, 93, influential psychotherapist, dies. *The New York Times.* http://www.nytimes.com /2007/07/25/nyregion/25ellis.html ?pagewanted=all&_r=0

Kaufman, S. B. (2018, January/ February). There is no one way to live a good life. *Scientific American Mind, 29,* 24–32.

Kaufman, S. B. (2019, January 18). There is no nature–nurture war. *Scientific American.* https://blogs .scientificamerican.com/beautiful -minds/there-is-no-nature-nurture -war/

Kaufman, S. B. (2019, December 12). Taking sex differences in personality seriously. *Scientific American.* https:// blogs.scientificamerican.com/beautiful -minds/taking-sex-differences-in -personality-seriously/

Kaufman, S. B. (2020, May 11). Finding inner harmony: The underappreciated legacy of Karen Horney. *Scientific American.* https://blogs.scientificamerican.com /beautiful-minds/finding-inner-harmony -the-underappreciated-legacy-of-karen -horney/

Kaul, G. (2017, July 17). How Minnesota determines who's fit—and unfit—to be a police officer. *MinnPost.* https://www.minnpost.com/politics -policy/2017/07/how-minnesota -determines-who-s-fit-and-unfit-be -police-officer

Kavšek, M., & Granrud, C. E. (2012). Children's and adults' size estimates at near and far distances: A test of the perceptual learning theory of size constancy development. *i-Perception, 3*(7), 459–466.

Kawa, S., & Giordano, J. (2012). A brief historicity of the *Diagnostic and Statistical Manual of Mental Disorders:* Issues and implications for the future of psychiatric canon and practice. *Philosophy, Ethics, and Humanities in Medicine, 7 Article 2.* https://doi.org /10.1186/1747-5341-7-2

Kayes, D. C., & Bailey, J. R. (2018, February 2). 4 self-improvement myths that may be holding you back. *Harvard Business Review.* https://hbr.org/2018 /02/4-self-improvement-myths-that -may-be-holding-you-back

Kearney, M. S., & Levine, P. B. (2020, June 15). Half a million fewer children? The coming COVID baby bust. *The Brookings Institution.* https:// www.brookings.edu/research/half-a -million-fewer-children-the-coming -covid-baby-bust/

Keating, D. P. (2018, July 13). The boys from the cave: The case for resilience [Blog post]. https:// www.psychologytoday.com/us/blog /stressful-lives/201807/the-boys-the -cave-the-case-resilience

Keefe, J. R., Chambless, D. L., Barber, J. P., & Milrod, B. L. (2019). Treatment of anxiety and mood comorbidities in cognitive-behavioral and psychodynamic therapies for panic disorder. *Journal of Psychiatric Research, 114,* 34–40. https://doi.org/10.1016/j .jpsychires.2019.04.009

Keefe, J. R., McMain, S. F., McCarthy, K. S., Zilcha-Mano, S., Dinger, U., Sahin, Z., Graham, K., & Barber, J. P. (2020). A meta-analysis of psychodynamic treatments for borderline and cluster C personality disorders. *Personality Disorders: Theory, Research, and Treatment, 11*(3), 157–169. https:// doi.org/10.1037/per0000382

Keefe, P. R. (2012, July 13). The uncannily accurate depiction of the meth trade in "Breaking Bad." *The New Yorker.* https://www.newyorker .com/culture/culture-desk/the -uncannily-accurate-depiction-of-the -meth-trade-in-breaking-bad

Keenan, T. D., Agrón, E., Mares, J. A., Clemons, T. E., van Asten, F., Swaroop, A., Chew, E. Y., & AREDS and AREDS2 Research Groups. (2020). Adherence to a Mediterranean diet and cognitive function in the Age-Related Eye Disease Studies 1 & 2. *Alzheimer's & Dementia, 16*(6), 831–842. https://doi .org/10.1002/alz.12077

Keesey, R. E., & Hirvonen, M. D. (1997). Body weight set-points: Determination and adjustment. *Journal of Nutrition, 127,* 1875S–1883S.

Kegelaers, J., Wylleman, P., & Oudejans, R. R. D. (2020). A coach perspective on the use of planned disruptions in high-performance sports. *Sport, Exercise, and Performance Psychology, 9*(1), 29–44. https://doi .org/10.1037/spy0000167

Keirstead, H. S., Nistor, G., Bernal, G., Totoiu, M., Cloutier, F., Sharp, K., & Oswald, S. (2005). Human embryonic stem cell-derived oligodendrocyte progenitor cell transplants remyelinate and restore locomotion after spinal cord injury. *Journal of Neuroscience, 25,* 4694–4705.

Keith, S. E., Michaud, D. S., & Chiu, V. (2008). Evaluating the maximum playback sound levels from portable digital audio players. *Journal of the Acoustical Society of America, 123,* 4227–4237.

Kelland, M., & Revell, M. (2020, August 13). Pandemic behaviour: Why some people don't play by the rules. *Reuters.* https://www.reuters.com /article/us-health-coronavirus-behavioral -science/pandemic-behaviour-why -some-people-dont-play-by-the-rules -idUSKCN2590NH?il=0

Keller, A., & Malaspina, D. (2013). Hidden consequences of olfactory dysfunction: A patient report series. *BMC Ear, Nose and Throat Disorders, 13*(8). https://doi.org/10.1186/1472 -6815-13-8

Kelley, M. R., Neath, I., & Surprenant, A. M. (2015). Serial position functions in general knowledge. *Journal of Experimental Psychology: Learning, Memory, and Cognition, 41,* 1715–1727.

Kelly, J. F., Abry, A., Ferri, M., & Humphreys, K. (2020). Alcoholics Anonymous and 12-step facilitation treatments for alcohol use disorder: A distillation of a 2020 Cochrane review for clinicians and policy makers. *Alcohol & Alcoholism, 55*(6), 641–651. https://doi.org/10.1093/alcalc/agaa050

Kember, D., Ho, A., & Hong, C. (2008). The importance of establishing relevance in motivating student learning. *Active Learning in Higher Education, 9,* 249–263.

Kemeny, M. E., & Shestyuk, A. (2008). Emotions, the neuroendocrine and immune systems, and health. In M. Lewis, J. M. Haviland-Jones, & L. F. Barrett (Eds.), *Handbook of emotions* (3rd ed., pp. 661–675). Guilford Press.

Kempermann, G., Gage, F. H., Aigner, L., Song, H., Curtis, M. A., Thuret, S., Kuhn, H. G., Jessberger, S., Frankland, P. W., Cameron, H. A., Gould, E., Hen, R., Abrous, D. N., Toni, N., Schinder, A. F., Zhao, X., Lucassen, P. J., & Frisén, J. (2018). Human adult neurogenesis: Evidence and remaining questions. *Cell Stem Cell, 23,* 25–30. https://doi.org /10.1016/j.stem.2018.04.004

Kennedy, N., Boydell, J., Kalidindi, S., Fearon, P., Jones, P. B., van Os, J., & Murray, R. M. (2005). Gender differences in incidence and age at onset of mania and bipolar disorder over a 35-year period in Camberwell, England. *American Journal of Psychiatry, 162,* 257–262.

Kennedy, P. (2017, April 7). To be a genius, think like a 94-year-old. *The New York Times*. https://www.nytimes.com/2017/04/07/opinion/sunday/to-be-a-genius-think-like-a-94-year-old.html?mcubz=0

Kennison, S. M. (2020). *Individual differences in humor*. In S. M. Kennison (Ed.), *The cognitive neuroscience of humor* (pp. 95–107). American Psychological Association. https://doi.org/10.1037/0000203-008

Kerr, B. A., & Stull, O. A. (2019). Measuring creativity in research and practice. In M. W. Gallagher & S. J. Lopez (Eds.), *Positive psychological assessment: A handbook of models and measures* (p. 125–138). American Psychological Association. https://doi.org/10.1037/0000138-009

Kershaw, K. N., Robinson, W. R., Gordon-Larsen, P., Hicken, M. T., Goff, D. C., Carnethon, M. R., Kiefe, C. I., Sidney, S., & Roux, A. V. D. (2017). Association of changes in neighborhood-level racial residential segregation with changes in blood pressure among black adults: The CARDIA study. *JAMA Internal Medicine, 177*, 996–1002. https://doi.org/10.1001/jamainternmed.2017.1226

Kersten, A. W., Meissner, C. A., Lechuga, J., Schwartz, B. L., Albrechtsen, J. S., & Iglesias, A. (2010). English speakers attend more strongly than Spanish speakers to manner of motion when classifying novel objects and events. *Journal of Experimental Psychology: General, 139*, 638–653.

Kessler, R. C. (2010). The prevalence of mental illness. In T. L. Scheid & T. N. Brown (Eds.), *A handbook for the study of mental health: Social contexts, theories, and systems* (2nd ed., pp. 46–63). Cambridge University Press.

Kessler, R. C., Berglund, P., Demler, O., Jin, R., Koretz, D., Merikangas, K. R., Rush, A. J., Walters, E. E., & Wang, P. S. (2003). The epidemiology of major depressive disorder: Results from the National Comorbidity Survey Replication (NCS-R). *Journal of the American Medical Association, 289*, 3095–3105.

Kessler, R. C., Berglund, P., Demler, O., Jin, R., Merikangas, K. R., & Walters, E. E. (2005). Lifetime prevalence and age-of-onset distributions of *DSM-IV* disorders in the National Comorbidity Survey Replication. *Archives of General Psychiatry, 62*, 593–602.

Kessler, R. C., Petukhova, M., Sampson, N. A., Zaslavsky, A. M., & Wittchen, H. U. (2012). Twelve-month and lifetime prevalence and lifetime morbid risk of anxiety and mood disorders in the United States. *International Journal of Methods in Psychiatric Research, 21*, 169–184.

Kessler, R. C., & Wang, P. S. (2008). The descriptive epidemiology of commonly occurring mental disorders in the United States. *Annual Review of Public Health, 29*, 115–129.

Kessler, S. (2016, January 8). What I learned in 12 weeks of therapy for social media addiction. *Fast Company*. https://www.fastcompany.com/3055149/what-i-learned-in-12-weeks-of-therapy-for-social-media-addiction

Key, M. S., Edlund, J. E., Sagarin, B. J., & Bizer, G. Y. (2009). Individual differences in susceptibility to mindlessness. *Personality and Individual Differences, 46*, 261–264.

Keys, T. E. (1945). *The history of surgical anesthesia*. Schuman's.

Khan, A., & Brown, W. A. (2015). Antidepressants versus placebo in major depression: An overview. *World Psychiatry, 14*, 294–300.

Khan, N. A., & Hillman, C. H. (2014). The relation of childhood physical activity and aerobic fitness to brain function and cognition: A review. *Pediatric Exercise Science, 26*, 138–146.

Khanna, S., Briggs, Z., & Rink, C. (2015). Inducible glutamate oxaloacetate transaminase as a therapeutic target against ischemic stroke. *Antioxidants and Redox Signaling, 22*(2), 175–186.

Kibenge, O. (2020, May 27). *STPF Fellow Luis Rivera Tackles psychology of bias and stereotyping*. American Association for the Advancement of Science (AAAS). https://www.aaas.org/membership/member-spotlight/stpf-fellow-luis-rivera-tackles-psychology-bias-and-stereotyping

Kidd, S. A., Eskenazi, B., & Wyrobek, A. J. (2001). Effects of male age on semen quality and fertility: A review of the literature. *Fertility and Sterility, 75*, 237–248.

Kieny, C., Flores, G., Ingenhaag, M., & Maurer, J. (2020). Healthy, wealthy, wise, and happy? Assessing age differences in evaluative and emotional well-being among mature adults from five low-and middle-income countries. *Social Indicators Research*. https://doi.org/10.1007/s11205-020-02515-4

Kihlstrom, J. F. (1985). Hypnosis. *Annual Review of Psychology, 36*, 385–418.

Kihlstrom, J. F. (2014). Hypnosis and cognition. *Psychology of Consciousness: Theory, Research, and Practice, 1*, 139–152.

Kilmartin, C. T., & Dervin, D. (1997). Inaccurate representation of the Electra complex in psychology textbooks. *Teaching of Psychology, 24*, 269–270.

Kim, D. J., Davis, E. P., Sandman, C. A., Glynn, L., Sporns, O., O'Donnell, B. F., & Hetrick, W. P. (2019). Childhood poverty and the organization of structural brain connectome. *NeuroImage, 184*, 409–416. https://doi.org/10.1016/j.neuroimage.2018.09.041

Kim, H., & Anderson, B. A. (2020, July 27). How does the attention system learn from aversive outcomes? *Emotion*. Advance online publication. https://doi.org/10.1037/emo0000757

Kim, J., & Anagondahalli, D. (2017). The effects of temporal perspective on college students' energy drink consumption. *Health Psychology, 36*, 898–906. https://doi.org/10.1037/hea0000536

Kim, J. S., Jin, M. J., Jung, W., Hahn, S. W., & Lee, S. H. (2017). Rumination as a mediator between childhood trauma and adulthood depression/anxiety in non-clinical participants. *Frontiers in Psychology, 8*, Article 1597. https://doi.org/10.3389/fpsyg.2017.01597

Kim, S., & Kochanska, G. (2019). Evidence for childhood origins of conscientiousness: Testing a developmental path from toddler age to adolescence. *Developmental Psychology, 55*(1), 196–206. https://doi.org/10.1037/dev0000608

Kindred. (n.d). Mission. http://www.kindredadoption.org

King, B. M. (2006). The rise, fall, and resurrection of the ventromedial hypothalamus in the regulation of feeding behavior and body weight [Invited review]. *Physiology & Behavior, 87*, 221–244.

Kingsbury, M. K., & Coplan, R. J. (2012). Mothers' gender-role attitudes and their responses to young children's hypothetical display of shy and aggressive behaviors. *Sex Roles, 66*, 506–517.

Kinsella, E. L., Ritchie, T. D., & Igou, E. R. (2015). Zeroing in on heroes: A prototype analysis of hero features. *Journal of Personality and Social Psychology, 108*, 114–127.

Kinsey, A. C., Pomeroy, W. B., & Martin, C. E. (1948). *Sexual behavior in the human male*. W. B. Saunders Co.

Kinsey, A. C., Pomeroy, W. B., Martin, C. E., & Gebhard, P. H. (1953). *Sexual behavior in the human female*. W. B. Saunders Co.

Kirby, J. N., & Kirby, P. G. (2017). An evolutionary model to conceptualise masculinity and compassion in male teenagers: A unifying framework. *Clinical Psychologist, 21*(2), 74–89. https://doi.org/10.1111/cp.12129

Kircher, M. (2017, February 28). This baffling picture of strawberries actually doesn't contain any red pixels. *New York Magazine*. http://nymag.com/intelligencer/2017/02/strawberries-look-red-without-red-pixels-color-constancy.html

Kirk, M. (Interviewer), & Carson, H. (Interviewee). (2013, September 4). Harry Carson [Interview transcript]. *Frontline*. PBS. http://www.pbs.org/wgbh/pages/frontline/sports/league-of-denial/the-frontline-interview-harry-carson/#seg10

Kirschner, M., Aleman, A., & Kaiser, S. (2017). Secondary negative symptoms—A review of mechanisms, assessment and treatment. *Schizophrenia Research, 186*, 29–38. https://doi.org/10.1016/j.schres.2016.05.003

Kishida, M., & Rahman, Q. (2015). Fraternal birth order and extreme right-handedness as predictors of sexual orientation and gender nonconformity in men. *Archives of Sexual Behavior, 44*, 1493–1501.

Kisilevsky, B. S., Hains, S. M. J., Lee, K., Xie, X., Huang, H., Ye, H. H., Zhang, K., & Wang, Z. (2003). Effects of experience on fetal voice recognition. *Psychological Science, 14*, 220–224.

Kitamura, T., Ogawa, S. K., Roy, D. S., Okuyama, T., Morrissey, M. D., Smith, L. M., Redondo, R. L., & Tonegawa, S. (2017). Engrams and circuits crucial for systems consolidation of a memory. *Science, 356*, 73–78. https://doi.org/10.1126/science.aam6808

Klaver, C. C., Wolfs, R. C., Vingerling, J. R., Hoffman, A., & de Jong, P. T. (1998). Age-specific prevalence and causes of blindness and visual impairment in an older population: The Rotterdam Study. *Archives Opthamology, 116*, 653–658.

Klein, J. D. (2018). E-cigarettes: A 1-way street to traditional smoking and nicotine addiction for youth. *Pediatrics, 141*(1), Article e20172850. https://doi.org/10.1542/peds.2017-2850

Klein, S. B. (2020). Thoughts on the scientific study of phenomenal consciousness. *Psychology of Consciousness: Theory, Research, and Practice*. Advance online publication. https://doi.org/10.1037/cns0000231

Kliemann, D., Adolphs, R., Tyszka, J. M., Fischl, B., Yeo, B. T., Nair, R., Dubois, J., & Paul, L. K. (2019). Intrinsic functional connectivity of the brain in adults with a single cerebral hemisphere. *Cell Reports, 29*(8), 2398–2407. https://doi.org/10.1016/j.celrep.2019.10.067

Klimstra, T. A., Luyckx, K., Hale, W. W., III, Frijns, T., van Lier, P. A. C., & Meeus, W. H. J. (2010). Short-term fluctuations in identity: Introducing a micro-level approach to identity formation. *Journal of Personality and Social Psychology, 99*, 191–202.

Kluen, L. M., Agorastos, A., Wiedemann, K., & Schwabe, L. (2017). Cortisol boosts risky decision-making behavior in men but not in women. *Psychoneuroendocrinology, 84*, 181–189. https://doi.org/10.1016/j.psyneuen.2017.07.240

Klugman, A., & Gruzelier, J. (2003). Chronic cognitive impairment in users of "ecstasy" and cannabis. *World Psychiatry, 2,* 184–190.

Klussman, K., Langer, J., & Nichols, A. L. (2021). The relationship between physical activity, health, and well-being: Type of exercise and self-connection as moderators. *European Journal of Health Psychology, 28*(2), 59–70. https://doi.org/10.1027/2512-8442/a000070

Kluver, H., & Bucy, P. (1939). Preliminary analysis of function of the temporal lobe in monkeys. *Archives of Neurology, 42,* 979–1000.

Knafo, A., & Israel, S. (2010). Genetic and environmental influences on prosocial behavior. In M. Mikulincer & P. R. Shaver (Eds.), *Prosocial motives, emotions, and behavior: The better angels of our nature* (pp. 149–167). American Psychological Association.

Knettel, B. A. (2016). Exploring diverse mental illness attributions in a multinational sample: A mixed-methods survey of scholars in international psychology. *International Perspectives in Psychology: Research, Practice, Consultation, 5*(2), 128–140. https://doi.org/10.1037/ipp0000048

Knoester, M., & Au, W. (2017). Standardized testing and school segregation: Like tinder for fire? *Race Ethnicity and Education, 20*(1), 1–14. https://doi.org/10.1080/13613324.2015.1121474

Knoll, J., & Matthes, J. (2017). The effectiveness of celebrity endorsements: A meta-analysis. *Journal of the Academy of Marketing Science, 45*(1), 55–75. https://doi.org/10.1007/s11747-016-0503-8

Knorr, A. C., Tull, M. T., Anestis, M. D., Dixon-Gordon, K. L., Bennett, M. F., & Gratz, K. L. (2016). The interactive effect of major depression and nonsuicidal self-injury on current suicide risk and lifetime suicide attempts. *Archives of Suicide Research, 20*(4), 539–552. https://doi.org/10.1080/13811118.2016.1158679

Knudsen, E. I. (2004). Sensitive periods in the development of the brain and behavior. *Journal of Cognitive Neuroscience, 16,* 1412–1425.

Ko, K. H. (2015). Brain reorganization allowed for the development of human language: Lunate sulcus. *International Journal of Biology, 7,* 59–65.

Ko, K., Byun, M. S., Yi, D., Lee, J. H., Kim, C. H., & Lee, D. Y. (2018). Early-life cognitive activity is related to reduced neurodegeneration in Alzheimer signature regions in late life. *Frontiers in Aging Neuroscience, 10,* 70. https://doi.org/10.3389/fnagi.2018.00070

Kobasa, S. C. (1979). Stressful life events, personality, and health: An inquiry into hardiness. *Journal of Personality and Social Psychology, 37,* 1–11.

Koch, C. (2018, June). What is consciousness? *Scientific American, 318*(6), 60–64.

Koch, I., Lawo, V., Fels, J., & Vorländer, M. (2011). Switching in the cocktail party: Exploring intentional control of auditory selective attention. *Journal of Experimental Psychology: Human Perception and Performance, 37,* 1140–1147.

Kohda, M., Hotta, T., Takeyama, T., Awata, S., Tanaka, H., Asai, J. Y., & Jordan, A. L. (2019). If a fish can pass the mark test, what are the implications for consciousness and self-awareness testing in animals? *PLOS Biology, 17*(2), Article e3000021. https://doi.org/10.1371/journal.pbio.3000021

Kohlberg, L. (1981). *The philosophy of moral development: Vol. 1. Essays on moral development.* Harper & Row.

Kohlberg, L., & Hersh, R. H. (1977). Moral development: A review of the theory. *Theory into Practice, 16,* 53–59.

Köhler, W. (1925). *The mentality of apes.* Harcourt Brace Jovanovich.

Kolar, D. R., Rodriguez, D. L. M., Chams, M. M., & Hoek, H. W. (2016). Epidemiology of eating disorders in Latin America: A systematic review and meta-analysis. *Current Opinion in Psychiatry, 29*(6), 363–371. https://doi.org/10.1097/YCO.0000000000000279

Kolb, B., & Gibb, R. (2011). Brain plasticity and behaviour in the developing brain. *Journal of the Canadian Academy of Child and Adolescent Psychiatry, 20,* 265–276.

Kolb, B., & Whishaw, I. Q. (1998). Brain plasticity and behavior. *Annual Review of Psychology, 49,* 43–64.

Kolb, B., & Whishaw, I. Q. (2015). *Fundamentals of human neuropsychology* (7th ed.). Worth Publishers.

Kolb, B., Whishaw, I. Q., & Teskey, G. C. (2019). *An introduction to brain and behavior* (6th ed.). Worth Publishers.

Koopman, P., Sinclair, A., & Lovell-Badge, R. (2016). Of sex and determination: Marking 25 years of Randy, the sex-reversed mouse. *Development, 143,* 1633–1637. https://doi.org/10.1242/dev.137372

Koopmann-Holm, B., & Matsumoto, D. (2011). Values and display rules for specific emotions. *Journal of Cross-Cultural Psychology, 42,* 355–371.

Koopmann-Holm, B., & Tsai, J. L. (2014). Focusing on the negative: Cultural differences in expressions of sympathy. *Journal of Personality and Social Psychology, 107,* 1092–1115.

Kornheiser, A. S. (1976). Adaptation to laterally displaced vision: A review. *Psychological Bulletin, 5,* 783–816.

Kosmicki, J., Satterstrom, F. K., Kosmicki, J. A., Wang, J., Breen, M. S., Gerges, S., Peng, M., Xu, X., Stevens, C., Grove, J. J., Børglum, A. D., Buxbaum, J. D., Cutler, D. J., Devlin, B., Roeder, K., Sanders, S. J., Talkowski, M. E., Daly, M. J., & Autism Sequencing Consortium. (2018, October 16). *Discovery and characterization of 102 genes associated with autism from exome sequencing of 37,269 individuals.* Paper presented at the American Society of Human Genetics 2018 annual meeting. San Diego, CA.

Kosslyn, S. M., Ball, T. M., & Reiser, B. J. (1978). Visual images preserve metric spatial information: Evidence from studies of image scanning. *Journal of Experimental Psychology: Human Perception and Performance, 4,* 47–60.

Kosslyn, S. M., Thompson, W. L., Costantini-Ferrando, M. F., Alpert, N. M., & Spiegel, D. (2000). Hypnotic visual illusion alters color processing in the brain. *American Journal of Psychiatry, 157,* 1279–1284.

Kostopoulou, O., Nurek, M., Cantarella, S., Okoli, G., Fiorentino, F., & Delaney, B. C. (2019). Referral decision making of general practitioners: A signal detection study. *Medical Decision Making, 39,* 21–31. https://doi.org/10.1177/0272989X18813357

Kostora, N. (2012, May 16). 25 craziest football terms and where they come from. *Bleacher Report.* http://bleacherreport.com/articles/1184750-25-craziest-football-terms-and-where-they-come-from

Kothandapani, A., Lewis, S. R., Noel, J. L., Zacharski, A., Krellwitz, K., Baines, A., Winske, S., Vezina, C. M., Kaftanovskaya, E. M., Agoulnik, Merton, E. M., Cohn, M. J., & Jorgensen, J. S. (2020). GLI3 resides at the intersection of hedgehog and androgen action to promote male sex differentiation. *PLOS Genetics, 16*(6), Article e1008810. https://doi.org/10.1371/journal.pgen.1008810

Kotsoglou, K. N. (2021). Zombie forensics: The use of the polygraph and the integrity of the criminal justice system in England and Wales. *The International Journal of Evidence and Proof, 25*(1), 16–35. https://doi.org/10.1177/1365712720983929

Kounios, J., & Beeman, M. (2009). The *Aha!* moment: The cognitive neuroscience of insight. *Current Directions in Psychological Science, 18,* 210–216.

Kozusznik, M. W., Rodríguez, I., & Peiró, J. M. (2015). Eustress and distress climates in teams: Patterns and outcomes. *International Journal of Stress Management, 22,* 1–23.

Kraft, D. (2012). Successful treatment of heavy smoker in one hour using split screen imagery, aversion, and suggestions to eliminate cravings. *Contemporary Hypnosis and Integrative Therapy, 29,* 175–188.

Krebs, D. L., & Denton, K. (2005). Toward a more pragmatic approach to morality: A critical evaluation of Kohlberg's model. *Psychological Review, 112,* 629–649.

Krejtz, I., Nezlek, J. B., Michnicka, A., Holas, P., & Rusanowska, M. (2016). Counting one's blessings can reduce the impact of daily stress. *Journal of Happiness Studies, 17*(1), 25–39. https://doi.org/10.1007/s10902-014-9578-4

Kremen, W. S., Panizzon, M. S., & Cannon, T. D. (2016). Genetics and neuropsychology: A merger whose time has come. *Neuropsychology, 30*(1), 1–5. https://doi.org/10.1037/neu0000254

Krendl, A. C., & Pescosolido, B. A. (2020). Countries and cultural differences in the stigma of mental illness: The east–west divide. *Journal of Cross-Cultural Psychology, 51*(2), 149–167. https://doi.org/10.1177/0022022119901297

Krijn, M., Emmelkamp, P. M. G., Olafsson, R. P., & Biemond, R. (2004). Virtual reality exposure therapy of anxiety disorders: A review. *Clinical Psychology Review, 24,* 259–281.

Kripke, D. F., Langer, R. D., & Kline, L. E. (2012). Hypnotics' association with mortality or cancer: A matched cohort study. *BMJ Open, 2,* e000850.

Krishnakumar, P., & Kannan, S. (2020, September 15). The worst fire season ever. Again. *Los Angeles Times.* https://www.latimes.com/projects/california-fires-damage-climate-change-analysis/

Krizan, Z., & Windschitl, P. D. (2007). The influence of outcome desirability on optimism. *Psychological Bulletin, 133,* 95–121.

Kroencke, L., Harari, G. M., Katana, M., & Gosling, S. D. (2019). Personality trait predictors and mental well-being correlates of exercise frequency across the academic semester. *Social Science & Medicine, 236,* Article 112400. https://doi.org/10.1016/j.socscimed.2019.112400

Krogsrud, S. K., Fjell, A. M., Tamnes, C. K., Grydeland, H., Due-Tønnessen, P., Bjørnerud, A., Sampaio-Baptista, C., Andersson, J., Johansen-Berg, H., & Walhovd, K. B. (2018). Development of white matter microstructure in relation to verbal and visuospatial working memory—A longitudinal study. *PLOS ONE, 13*(4), e0195540. https://doi.org/10.1371/journal.pone.0195540

Kroneisen, M., Kriechbaumer, M., Kamp, S.-M., & Erdfelder, E. (2020). How can I use it? The role of functional fixedness in the survival-processing paradigm. *Psychonomic Bulletin & Review, 28,* 324–332. https://doi.org/10.3758/s13423-020-01802-y

Krueger, E. T., & Reckless, W. C. (1931). The theory of human motivation. In *Social psychology* (Longmans' Social Science Series, pp. 142–170). Longmans, Green and Co.

Kübler-Ross, E. (2009). *On death and dying. What the dying have to teach doctors, nurses, clergy, and their own families* (40th anniversary ed.). Routledge.

Kucharski, A. (1984). History of frontal lobotomy in the United States, 1935–1955. *Neurosurgery, 14,* 765–772.

Kuhl, P. K. (2015). Baby talk. *Scientific American, 313,* 64–69.

Kuhl, P. K., Conboy, B. T., Padden, D., Nelson, T., & Pruitt, J. (2005). Early speech perception and later language development: Implications for the "Critical Period." *Language Learning and Development, 1,* 237–264.

Kujawa, S. G., & Liberman, M. C. (2006). Acceleration of age-related hearing loss by early noise exposure: Evidence of a misspent youth. *Journal of Neuroscience, 26,* 2115–2123.

Kuo, Z. Y. (1921). Giving up instincts in psychology. *Journal of Philosophy, 18,* 654–664.

Kupferschmidt, K. (2019). Psychologist aims to study diverse minds, not WEIRDos. *Science, 365*(6449), 110.

Kupferschmidt, K. (2019, April). Atmospheric scientists join pheromone quest. *Science, 364*(6436), 112. https://doi.org/10.1126/science.364.6436.112

Kushlev, K., Heintzelman, S. J., Lutes, L. D., Wirtz, D., Kanippayoor, J. M., Leitner, D., & Diener, E. (2020). Does happiness improve health? Evidence from a randomized controlled trial. *Psychological Science, 31*(7), 807–821. https://doi.org/10.1177/0956797620919673

Kuznetsov, I. A., & Kuznetsov, A. V. (2018). How the formation of amyloid plaques and neurofibrillary tangles may be related: A mathematical modelling study. *Proceedings of the Royal Society A: Mathematical, Physical and Engineering Sciences, 474*(2210). https://doi.org/10.1098/rspa.2017.0777

Kwon, D. (2019, January 18). The cerebellum is your "little brain"—and it does some pretty big things. *Scientific American.* https://www.scientificamerican.com/article/the-cerebellum-is-your-little-brain-mdash-and-it-does-some-pretty-big-things1/

LaBerge, S. (2014). Lucid dreaming: Paradoxes of dreaming consciousness. In C. Etzel, S. J. Lynn, & S. Krippner (Eds.), *Dissociation, Trauma, Memory, and Hypnosis Series: Varieties of anomalous experience: Examining the scientific evidence* (2nd ed.,

pp. 145–173). American Psychological Association.

Labrie, V., & Brundin, L. (2019). Harbingers of mental disease: Infections associated with an increased risk for neuropsychiatric illness in children. *JAMA Psychiatry, 76*(3), 237–238. https://doi.org/10.1001/jamapsychiatry.2018.3333

Lackner, J. R. (2014). Motion sickness: More than nausea and vomiting. *Experimental Brain Research, 232,* 2493–2510.

Ladouceur, C. D. (2012). Neural systems supporting cognitive-affective interactions in adolescence: The role of puberty and implications for affective disorders. *Frontiers in Integrative Neuroscience, 6,* 1–11.

Laeng, B., Profeti, I., Sæther, L., Adolfsdottir, S., Lundervold, A. J., Vangberg, T., Øvervoll, M., Johnsen, S. H., & Waterloo, K. (2010). Invisible expressions evoke core impressions. *Emotion, 10,* 573–386.

Lafferty, C. K., Yang, A. K., Mendoza, J. A., & Britt, J. P. (2020). Nucleus accumbens cell type- and input-specific suppression of unproductive reward seeking. *Cell Reports, 30*(11), 3729–3742. https://doi.org/10.1016/j.celrep.2020.02.095

Lagström, H., Stenholm, S., Akbaraly, T., Pentti, J., Vahtera, J., Kivimäki, M., & Head, J. (2020). Diet quality as a predictor of cardiometabolic disease–free life expectancy: The Whitehall II cohort study. *The American Journal of Clinical Nutrition, 111*(4), 787–794. https://doi.org/10.1093/ajcn/nqz329

Lahav, O., & Mioduser, D. (2008). Construction of cognitive maps of unknown spaces using a multi-sensory virtual environment for people who are blind. *Computers in Human Behavior, 24,* 1139–1155.

Laird, J. D., & Lacasse, K. (2014). Bodily influences on emotional feelings: Accumulating evidence and extensions of William James's theory of emotion. *Emotion Review, 6,* 27–34.

Lake, B. B., Chen, S., Sos, B. C., Fan, J., Kaeser, G. E., Yung, Y. C., Duong, T. E., Gao, D., Chun, J., Kharchenko, P. V., & Zhang, K. (2018). Integrative single-cell analysis of transcriptional and epigenetic states in the human adult brain. *Nature Biotechnology, 36*(1), 70–80. https://doi.org/10.1038/nbt.4038

Lalonde, R., Dell, C., & Claypool, T. (2020). PAWS your stress: The student experience of therapy dog programming. *Canadian Journal for New Scholars in Education/Revue canadienne des jeunes chercheures et chercheurs en éducation, 11*(2), 78–90.

Lambert, M. J., Hansen, N. B., & Finch, A. E. (2001). Patient-focused research: Using patient outcome data

to enhance treatment effects. *Journal of Consulting and Clinical Psychology, 69,* 159–172.

Lamont, P. (2020). The construction of "critical thinking": Between how we think and what we believe. *History of Psychology, 23*(3), 232–251. https://doi.org/10.1037/hop0000145

Lamport, D. J., Christodoulou, E., & Achilleos, C. (2020). Beneficial effects of dark chocolate for episodic memory in healthy young adults: A parallel-groups acute intervention with a white chocolate control. *Nutrients, 12*(2), 483. https://doi.org/10.3390/nu12020483

Lanagan-Leitzel, L. K., Skow, E., & Moore, C. M. (2015). Great expectations: Perceptual challenges of visual surveillance in lifeguarding. *Applied Cognitive Psychology, 29,* 425–435.

Lanciano, T., Curci, A., Matera, G., & Sartori, G. (2018). Measuring the flashbulb-like nature of memories for private events: The flashbulb memory checklist. *Memory, 26*(8), 1053–1064. https://doi.org/10.1080/09658211.2018.1428348

Landgren, M. (2017). How much is too much? The implication of recognizing alcohol as a teratogen. *Acta Paediatrica, 106,* 353–355. https://doi.org/10.1111/apa.13696

Landrum, R. E. (2001). I'm getting my bachelor's degree in psychology—what can I do with it? *Eye on Psi Chi, 6,* 22–24.

Landrum, R. E. (2016). The history of the teaching of psychology: Or, what was old is new again. In W. D. Woody, R. L. Miller, & W. J. Wozniak (Eds.), *Psychological specialties in historical context: Enriching the classroom experience for teachers and students.* Society for the Teaching of Psychology. http://teachpsych.org/ebooks/

Landrum, R. E. (2018, January). *What can you do with a bachelor's degree in psychology? Like this title, the actual answer is complicated.* Psychology Student Network. http://www.apa.org/ed/precollege/psn/2018/01/bachelors-degree.aspx

Lando, H. A. (1976). On being sane in insane places: A supplemental report. *Professional Psychology, 7,* 47–52.

Lang, A., Del Giudice, R., & Schabus, M. (2020). Sleep, little baby: The calming effects of prenatal speech exposure on newborns' sleep and heartrate. *Brain Sciences, 10*(8), Article 511. https://doi.org/10.3390/brainsci10080511

Lange, C. G., & James, W. (1922). The emotions. In K. Dunlap (Ed.), *Psychology classics: A series of reprints and translations.* Williams & Wilkins.

Langer, E., Blank, A., & Chanowitz, B. (1978). The mindlessness of

ostensibly thoughtful action: The role of "placebic" information in interpersonal interaction. *Journal of Personality and Social Psychology, 36,* 635–642.

Langer, E. J., & Rodin, J. (1976). The effects of choice and enhanced personal responsibility for the aged: A field experiment in an institutional setting. *Journal of Personality and Social Psychology, 34,* 191–198.

Langeslag, S. J. E., & van Strien, J. W. (2018). Early visual processing of snakes and angry faces: An ERP study. *Brain Research, 1678,* 297–303.

Langley, T. (2016, February 10). Star Wars psychology: The problems with diagnosing Kylo Ren [Web log post]. *Psychology Today.* https://www.psychologytoday.com/blog/beyond-heroes-and-villains/201602/star-wars-psychology-the-problems-diagnosing-kylo-ren

Langlois, J. H., Kalakanis, L., Rubenstein, A. J., Larson, A., Hallam, M., & Smoot, M. (2000). Maxims or myths of beauty? A meta-analytic and theoretical review. *Psychological Bulletin, 126,* 390–423.

Långström, N., Rahman, Q., Carlström, E., & Lichtenstein, P. (2010). Genetic and environmental effects on same-sex sexual behavior: A population study of twins in Sweden. *Archives of Sexual Behavior, 39,* 75–80.

Lannin, D. G., Ludwikowski, W. M. A., Vogel, D. L., Seidman, A. J., & Anello, K. (2019). Reducing psychological barriers to therapy via contemplation and self-affirmation. *Stigma and Health, 4*(3), 247–255. https://doi.org/10.1037/sah0000139

Lansford, J. E., Godwin, J., Al-Hassan, S. M., Bacchini, D., Bornstein, M. H., Chang, L., Chen, B.-B., Deater-Deckard, K., Di Giunta, L., Dodge, K. A., Malone, P. S., Oburu, P., Pastorelli, C., Skinner, A. T., Sorbring, E., Steinberg, L., Tapanya, S., Alampay, L. P., Uribe Tirado, L. M., & Zelli, A. (2018). Longitudinal associations between parenting and youth adjustment in twelve cultural groups: Cultural normativeness of parenting as a moderator. *Developmental Psychology, 54*(2), 362–377. https://doi.org/10.1037/dev0000416

Lara, D. R. (2010). Caffeine, mental health, and psychiatric disorders. *Journal of Alzheimer's Disease, 20,* S239–S248.

Larsen, J. K., Krogh-Nielsen, L., & Brøsen, K. (2016). The monoamine oxidase inhibitor isocarboxazid is a relevant treatment option in treatment-resistant depression-experience-based strategies in Danish psychiatry. *Health Care: Current Reviews, 4*(2), Article 1000168. https://doi.org/10.4172/2375-4273.1000168

Larsen, L., Hartmann, P., & Nyborg, H. (2008). The stability of general intelligence from early adulthood to middle-age. *Intelligence, 36*, 29–34.

Larsson, M., & Willander, J. (2009). Autobiographical odor memory. *Annals of the New York Academy of Sciences, 1170*, 318–323.

Larzelere, R. E., Gunnoe, M. L., Ferguson, C. J., & Roberts, M. W. (2019). The insufficiency of the evidence used to categorically oppose spanking and its implications for families and psychological science: Comment on Gershoff et al. (2018). *American Psychologist, 74*(4), 497–499. https://doi.org/10.1037/amp0000461

Lashley, K. D. (1950). In search of the engram. *Symposia of the Society for Experimental Biology, 4*, 454–482.

Lasser, J., Ryser, G., Borrego, D., Ham, E., Fierros, K. R., Pruin, J., & Randolph, P. (2020). Contemporary college students' attitudes about deception in research. *Ethics & Human Research, 42*(1), 14–21. https://doi.org/10.1002/eahr.500039

Latané, B., & Darley, J. M. (1968). Group inhibition of bystander intervention in emergencies. *Journal of Personality and Social Psychology, 10*, 215–221.

Latané, B., Williams, K., & Harkins, S. (1979). Many hands make light the work: The causes and consequences of social loafing. *Journal of Personality and Social Psychology, 37*, 822–832.

Lathia, N., Sandstrom, G. M., Mascolo, C., & Rentfrow, P. J. (2017). Happier people live more active lives: Using smartphones to link happiness and physical activity. *PLOS ONE, 12*(1), e0160589. https://doi.org/10.1371/journal.pone.0160589

Latreille, V., von Ellenrieder, N., Peter-Derex, L., Dubeau, F., Gotman, J., & Frauscher, B. (2020). The human k-complex: Insights from combined scalp-intracranial EEG recordings. *NeuroImage, 213*, Article 116748. https://doi.org/10.1016/j.neuroimage.2020.116748

Laumann, E. O., Gagnon, J. H., Michael, R. T., & Michaels, S. (1994). *The social organization of sexuality: Sexual practices in the United States.* University of Chicago Press.

Laumann, E. O., Paik, A., & Rosen, R. C. (1999). Sexual dysfunction in the United States: Prevalence and predictors. *JAMA, 281*, 537–544.

Lawler-Row, K. A., & Elliott, J. (2009). The role of religious activity and spirituality in the health and well-being of older adults. *Journal of Health Psychology, 14*, 43–52.

Lawrence, E. (2020, June 18). COVID-19 worsens obsessive-compulsive disorder—but therapy offers coping skills. *Scientific American.* https://www.scientificamerican.com/article/covid-19-worsens-obsessive-compulsive-disorder-but-therapy-offers-coping-skills1/

Laxton, V., & Crundall, D. (2018). The effect of lifeguard experience upon the detection of drowning victims in a realistic dynamic visual search task. *Applied Cognitive Psychology, 32*(1), 14–23. https://doi.org/10.1002/acp.3374

Lazar, S. G. (2018). The place for psychodynamic therapy and obstacles to its provision. *Psychiatric Clinics, 41*(2), 193–205. https://doi.org/10.1016/j.psc.2018.01.004

Lazarus, R. S. (1984). On the primacy of cognition. *American Psychologist, 39*, 124–129.

Lazarus, R. S. (1991a). Cognition and motivation in emotion. *American Psychologist, 46*, 352–367.

Lazarus, R. S. (1991b). Progress on a cognitive-motivational-relational theory of emotion. *American Psychologist, 46*, 819–834.

Lazarus, R. S. (1993). From psychological stress to the emotions: A history of changing outlooks. *Annual Review of Psychology, 44*, 1–21.

Lazarus, R. S., & Folkman, S. (1984). *Stress, appraisal, and coping.* Springer.

Lazer, D. M., Baum, M. A., Benkler, Y., Berinsky, A. J., Greenhill, K. M., Menczer, F., Metzger, J. M., Nyhan, B., Pennycook, G., Rothschild, D., Schudson, M., Sloman, S. A., Sunstein, C. R., Thorson, E. A., Watts, D. J., & Zittrain, J. L. (2018). The science of fake news. *Science, 359*(6380), 1094–1096. https://doi.org/10.1126/science.aao2998

Lazzouni, L., & Lepore, F. (2014). Compensatory plasticity: Time matters. *Frontiers in Human Neuroscience, 8*, art. 340.

le Clercq, C. M., Goedegebure, A., Jaddoe, V. W., Raat, H., de Jong, R. J. B., & van der Schroeff, M. P. (2018). Association between portable music player use and hearing loss among children of school age in the Netherlands. *JAMA Otolaryngology–Head & Neck Surgery, 144*(8), 668–675. https//doi.org/10.1001/jamaoto.2018.0646

Leavitt, R. A., Ertl, A., Sheats, K., Petrosky, E., Ivey-Stephenson, A., & Fowler, K. A. (2018). Suicides among American Indian/Alaska Natives—National Violent Death Reporting System, 18 states, 2003–2014. *Morbidity and Mortality Weekly Report, 67*(8), 237–242. https://doi.org/10.15585/mmwr.mm6708a1

LeBeau, R. T., Glenn, D., Liao, B., Wittchen, H.-U., Beesdo-Baum, K., Ollendick, T., & Craske, M. G. (2010). Specific phobia: A review of DSM-IV specific phobia and preliminary recommendations for *DSM-V. Depression and Anxiety, 27*, 148–167.

Lebel, C., & Deoni, S. (2018). The development of brain white matter microstructure. *NeuroImage, 182*, 207–218. https://doi.org/10.1016/j.neuroimage.2017.12.097

Lecendreux, M., Churlaud, G., Pitoiset, F., Regnault, A., Tran, T. A., Liblau, R., Klatzmann, D., & Rosenzwajg, M. (2017). Narcolepsy type 1 is associated with a systemic increase and activation of regulatory T Cells and with a systemic activation of global T cells. *PLOS ONE, 12*, e0169836. https://doi.org/10.1371/journal.pone.0169836

LeDoux, J. E. (1996). *The emotional brain: The mysterious underpinnings of emotional life.* Simon & Schuster.

LeDoux, J. E. (2000). Emotion circuits in the brain. *Annual Review of Neuroscience, 23*, 155–184.

LeDoux, J. E. (2012). Rethinking the emotional brain. *Neuron, 73*, 653–676.

Lee, B. K., Magnusson, C., Gardner, R. M., Blomström, Å., Newschaffer, C. J., Burstyn I., Karlsson, H., & Dalman, C. (2015). Maternal hospitalization with infection during pregnancy and risk of autism spectrum disorders. *Brain, Behavior, and Immunity, 44*, 100–105.

Lee, D. S., & Way, B. M. (2019). Perceived social support and chronic inflammation: The moderating role of self-esteem. *Health Psychology, 38*(6), 563–566. https://doi.org/10.1037/hea0000746

Lee, H., Xie, L., Yu, M., Kang, H., Feng, T., Deane, R., Logan, J., Nedergaard, M., & Benveniste, H. (2015). The effect of body posture on brain glymphatic transport. *Journal of Neuroscience, 35*(31), 11034–11044. https://doi.org/10.1523/JNEUROSCI.1625-15.2015

Lee, H., & Müllensiefen, D. (2020). The Timbre Perception Test (TPT): A new interactive musical assessment tool to measure timbre perception ability. *Attention, Perception, and Psychophysics.* Advance online publication. https://doi.org/10.3758/s13414-020-02058-3

Lee, J., Hardin, A., Parmar, B., & Gino, F. (2020, January/February). How dishonesty drains you. *Scientific American Mind, 31*(1), 20–22.

Lee, J., & Harley, V. R. (2012). The male fight-flight response: A result of SRY regulation of catecholamines? *BioEssays, 34*(6), 454–457.

Lee, J. J., Hardin, A. E., Parmar, B., & Gino, F. (2019, July 15). The interpersonal costs of dishonesty: How dishonest behavior reduces individuals' ability to read others' emotions. *Journal of Experimental Psychology: General, 148*(9), 1557–1574. http://dx.doi.org/10.1037/xge0000639

Lee, K. M., Lindquist, K. A., & Payne, B. K. (2018). Constructing bias: Conceptualization breaks the link between implicit bias and fear of Black Americans. *Emotion, 18*, 855–871. https://doi.org/10.1037/emo0000347

Lee, P. A., Houk, C. P., Ahmed, S. F., & Hughes, I. A. (2006). Consensus statement on management of intersex disorders. *Pediatrics, 118*, e488–e500.

Lee, S. W. S., & Schwarz, N. (2014). Framing love: When it hurts to think we were made for each other. *Journal of Experimental Social Psychology, 54*, 61–67.

Lefaucheur, J. P., Aleman, A., Baeken, C., Benninger, D. H., Brunelin, J., Di Lazzaro, V., Filipovic, S. R., Grefkes, C., Hasan, A., Hummel, F. C., Jääskeläinen, S. K., Langguth, B., Leocani, L., Londero, A., Nardone, R., Nguyen, J.-P., Nyffeler, T., Oliveira-Maia, A. J., Oliviero., A., . . . Ziemann, U. (2020). Evidence-based guidelines on the therapeutic use of repetitive transcranial magnetic stimulation (rTMS): An update (2014–2018). *Clinical Neurophysiology, 131*(2), 474–528. https://doi.org/10.1016/j.clinph.2019.11.002

Lehavot, K., Katon, J. G., Chen, J. A., Fortney, J. C., & Simpson, T. L. (2018). Post-traumatic stress disorder by gender and veteran status. *American Journal of Preventive Medicine, 54*(1), e1–e9. https://doi.org/10.1016/j.amepre.2017.09.008

Leibowitz, K. A., Hardebeck, E. J., Goyer, J. P., & Crum, A. J. (2019). The role of patient beliefs in open-label placebo effects. *Health Psychology, 38*(7), 613–622. https://doi.org/10.1037/hea0000751

Leichsenring, F., Luyten, P., Hilsenroth, M. J., Abbass, A., Barber, J. P., Keefe, J. R., Leweke, F., Rabung, S., & Steinert, C. (2015). Psychodynamic therapy meets evidence-based medicine: A systematic review using updated criteria. *The Lancet Psychiatry, 2*, 648–660.

Leighty, K. A., Grand, A. P., Pittman Courte, V. L., Maloney, M. A., & Bettinger, T. L. (2013). Relational responding by eastern box turtles (*Terrapene carolina*) in a series of color discrimination tasks. *Journal of Comparative Psychology, 127*, 256–264. https://doi.org/10.1037/a0030942

Leinninger, G. (2011). Lateral thinking about leptin: A review of leptin action via the lateral hypothalamus. *Physiology & Behavior, 104*, 572–581.

Leiserowitz, A., Feinberg, G., Rosenthal, S., Smith, N., Anderson A., Roser-Renouf, C., & Maibach, E.

(2014). *What's in a name? Global warming vs. climate change.* Yale University and George Mason University. Yale Project on Climate Change Communication.

**Lembke, A., Papac, J., & Humphreys, K.** (2018). Our other prescription drug problem. *New England Journal of Medicine, 378,* 693–695. https://doi.org/10.1056 /NEJMp1715050.

**Lenzenweger, M. F., Lane, M. C., Loranger, A. W., & Kessler, R. C.** (2007). *DSM-IV* personality disorders in the national comorbidity survey replication. *Biological Psychiatry, 62,* 553–564.

**Leo, J.** (1987, January 12). Behavior: Exploring the traits of twins. *Time.* http://content.time.com/time/magazine /article/0,9171,963211,00.html

**Leontovich, O.** (2016). Garlic and love: Gastronomic communication in an intercultural family. *Procedia— Social and Behavioral Sciences, 236,* 89–94. https://doi.org/10.1016/j .sbspro.2016.12.039

**Leptourgos, P., Notredame, C. E., Eck, M., Jardri, R., & Denève, S.** (2020). Circular inference in bistable perception. *Journal of Vision, 20*(4), Article 12. https://doi.org/10.1167 /jov.20.4.12

**Lerner, D., Lyson, M., Sandberg, E., & Rogers, W. H.** (n.d.). The high cost of mental disorders: Facts for employers. *One Mind Initiative.* https://oneminditiative.org/wp -content/uploads/2018/02/OMI -White-Paper-R18.pdf

**Lerner, J. S., Li, Y., Valdesolo, P., & Kassam, K. S.** (2015). Emotion and decision making: Online supplement. *Annual Review of Psychology, 66,* 799–823.

**Leung, H., Pakpour, A. H., Strong, C., Lin, Y. C., Tsai, M.-C., Griffiths, M. D., Lin, Y.-C., & Chen, I.-H.** (2020). Measurement invariance across young adults from Hong Kong and Taiwan among three internet-related addiction scales: Bergen Social Media Addiction Scale (BSMAS), Smartphone Application-Based Addiction Scale (SABAS), and Internet Gaming Disorder Scale-Short Form (IGDS-SF9) (Study Part A). *Addictive Behaviors, 101,* Article 105969. https://doi.org/10.1016/j .addbeh.2019.04.027

**Levendosky, A. A., Bogat, G. A., Lonstein, J. S., Martinez-Torteya, C., Muzik, M., Granger, D. A., & Von Eye, A.** (2016). Infant adrenocortical reactivity and behavioral functioning: Relation to early exposure to maternal intimate partner violence. *Stress, 19,* 37–44. https://doi.org/10 .3109/10253890.2015.1108303

**Levenstein, S., Rosenstock, S., Jacobsen, R. K., & Jorgensen, T.**

(2015). Psychological stress increases risk for peptic ulcer, regardless of *Helicobacter pylori* infection or use of nonsteroidal anti-inflammatory drugs. *Clinical Gastroenterology and Hepatology, 13*(3), 498–506.

**Levett-Jones, T., Sundin, D., Bagnall, M., Hague, K., Schuman, W., Taylor, C., & Wink, J.** (2010). Learning to think like a nurse. *HNE Handover: For Nurses and Midwives, 3,* 15–20.

**Levi-Belz, Y., Krysinska, K., & Andriessen, K.** (2021). "Turning personal tragedy into triumph": A systematic review and meta-analysis of studies on posttraumatic growth among suicide-loss survivors. *Psychological Trauma: Theory, Research, Practice, and Policy, 13*(3), 322–332. https://doi.org/10.1037/tra0000977

**Levin, D.** (2020, February 24). "Open, insert, squirt." In this town, children are taught to administer Narcan. *Boston Globe.* https://www .boston.com/news/national-news /2020/02/24/open-insert-squirt-in -this-town-children-are-taught-to -administer-narcan

**Levine, B.** (2002, September 25). Redeeming Rover. *Los Angeles Times.* http://articles.latimes.com/2002 /sep/25/news/lv-dogtherapy25

**Levinson, D. F.** (2006). The genetics of depression: A review. *Biological Psychiatry, 60,* 84–92.

**Levit, A., Hachinski, V., & Whitehead, S. N.** (2020). Neurovascular unit dysregulation, white matter disease, and executive dysfunction: The shared triad of vascular cognitive impairment and Alzheimer disease. *GeroScience, 42,* 445–465. https://doi.org/10.1007 /s11357-020-00164-6

**Levy, F., & Rodkin, J.** (2015). The Bloomberg recruiter report: Job skills companies want but can't get. *Bloomberg.* http://www.bloomberg .com/graphics/2015-job-skills-report/

**Levy, R. A., & Ablon, S. J.** (2010, February 23). Talk therapy: Off the couch and into the lab. *Scientific American.* http://www .scientificamerican.com/article/talk -therapy-off-couch-into-lab/

**Levy, S. R., Hilsenroth, M. J., & Owen, J. J.** (2015). Relationship between interpretation, alliance, and outcome in psychodynamic psychotherapy: Control of therapist effects and assessment of moderator variable impact. *Journal of Nervous and Mental Disease, 203,* 418–424.

**Lew, S. M.** (2014). Hemispherectomy in the treatment of seizures: A review. *Translational Pediatrics, 3,* 208–217.

**Lewis, D. J., & Duncan, C. P.** (1956). Effect of different percentages of money reward on extinction of a lever-pulling response. *Journal of Experimental Psychology, 52,* 23–27.

**Lewis, R.** (2018). *Finding purpose in a godless world.* Prometheus Books.

**Li, H., Zhang, C., Cai, X., Wang, L., Luo, F., Ma, Y., Li, M., & Xiao, X.** (2020). Genome-wide association study of creativity reveals genetic overlap with psychiatric disorders, risk tolerance, and risky behaviors. *Schizophrenia Bulletin, 46*(5), 1317–1326. https://doi.org/10 .1093/schbul/sbaa025

**Li, J.** (2005). Mind or virtue: Western and Chinese beliefs about learning. *Current Directions in Psychological Science, 14,* 190–194.

**Li, J. (J.), Chen, X.-P., Kotha, S., & Fisher, G.** (2017). Catching fire and spreading it: A glimpse into displayed entrepreneurial passion in crowdfunding campaigns. *Journal of Applied Psychology, 102,* 1075–1090. https://doi.org/10.1037/apl0000217

**Li, Q.** (2018, May 1). "Forest bathing" is great for your health. Here's how to do it. *Time.* http://time.com/5259602 /japanese-forest-bathing/

**Lian, Z., Wallace, B. C., & Fullilove, R. E.** (2020). Mental health help-seeking intentions among Chinese international students in the U.S. higher education system: The role of coping self-efficacy, social support, and stigma for seeking psychological help. *Asian American Journal of Psychology, 11*(3), 147–157. https://doi.org/10 .1037/aap0000183

**Liao, J., Shen, S., & Eisemann, E.** (2018). Depth annotations: Designing depth of a single image for depth-based effects. *Computers & Graphics, 71,* 180–188. https://doi.org/10.1016/j.cag .2017.11.005

**Liberles, S. B.** (2015). Mammalian pheromones. *Annual Review of Physiology, 76,* 151–175.

**Liberman, M. C.** (2015). Hidden hearing loss. *Scientific American, 313,* 48–53.

**Libourel, P. A., & Herrel, A.** (2016). Sleep in amphibians and reptiles: A review and a preliminary analysis of evolutionary patterns. *Biological Reviews, 91,* 833–866. https://doi.org /10.1111/brv.12197

**Lichtwarck-Aschoff, A., Kunnen, S. E., & van Geert, P. L. C.** (2009). Here we go again: A dynamic systems perspective on emotional rigidity across parent-adolescent conflicts. *Developmental Psychology, 45,* 1364–1375.

**Licis, A. K., Desruisseau, D. M., Yamada, K. A., Duntley, S. P., & Gurnett, C. A.** (2011). Novel findings in an extended family pedigree with sleepwalking. *Neurology, 76,* 49–52.

**Liddle, J. R., Shackelford, T. K., & Weekes-Shackelford, V. A.** (2012). Why can't we all just get along? Evolutionary perspectives on violence, homicide, and war. *Review of General Psychology, 16,* 24–36.

**Lieberman, H. R., Agarwal, S., & Fulgoni III, V. L.** (2019). Daily patterns of caffeine intake and the association of intake with multiple sociodemographic and lifestyle factors in US adults based on the NHANES 2007–2012 surveys. *Journal of the Academy of Nutrition and Dietetics, 119*(1), 106–114. https://doi.org/10.1016/j.jand.2018 .08.152

**Liebst, L. S., Philpot, R., Levine, M., & Lindegaard, M. R.** (2021). Cross-national CCTV footage shows low victimization risk for bystander interveners in public conflicts. *Psychology of Violence, 11*(1), 11–18. https://doi.org/10 .1037/vio0000299

**Li-Gao, R., Boomsma, D. I., de Geus, E. J. C., Denollet, J., & Kupper, N.** (2021). The heritability of type D personality by an extended twin-pedigree analysis in the Netherlands twin register. *Behavior Genetics, 51*(1), 1–11. https://doi .org/10.1007/s10519-020-10023-x

**Likhtik, E., Stujenske, J. M., Topiwala, M. A., Harris, A. Z., & Gordon, J. A.** (2014). Prefrontal entrainment of amygdala activity signals safety in learned fear and innate anxiety. *Nature Neuroscience, 17*(1), 106–113.

**Lilienfeld, S. O.** (2012). Public skepticism of psychology: Why many people perceive the study of human behavior as unscientific. *American Psychologist, 67,* 111–129.

**Lilienfeld, S. O., & Arkowitz, H.** (2012, September 1). Are all psychotherapies created equal? *Scientific American.* http://www .scientificamerican.com/article/are -all-psychotherapies-created-equal/

**Lilienfeld, S. O., Lynn, S. J., Ruscio, J., & Beyerstein, B. L.** (2010). Busting big myths in popular psychology. *Scientific American Mind, 21,* 42–49.

**Lilienfeld, S. O., Wood, J. M., & Garb, H. N.** (2005). What's wrong with this picture? *Scientific American Mind, 16,* 50–57.

**Lillard, A. S., Drell, M. B., Richey, E. M., Boguszewski, K., & Smith, E. D.** (2015). Further examination of the immediate impact of television on children's executive function. *Developmental Psychology, 51,* 792–805. doi:10.1037/a0039097

**Lillard, A. S., & Peterson, J.** (2011). The immediate impact of different types of television on young children's executive function. *Pediatrics, 128,* 644–649.

**Lim, J., & Dinges, D. F.** (2010). A meta-analysis of the impact of short-term sleep deprivation on cognitive variables. *Psychological Bulletin, 136,* 375–389.

Lin, J., Jiang, Y., Wang, G., Meng, M., Zhu, Q., Mei, H., Liu, A., & Jiang, F. (2020). Associations of short sleep duration with appetite-regulating hormones and adipokines: A systematic review and meta-analysis. *Obesity Reviews, 21*(11), e13051. https://doi.org/10.1111/obr.13051

Lin, P. (2016). Risky behaviors: Integrating adolescent egocentrism with the theory of planned behavior. *Review of General Psychology, 20,* 392–398. https://doi.org/10.1037/gpr0000086

Lin, S.-Y., Fried, E. I., & Eaton, N. R. (2020). The association of life stress with substance use symptoms: A network analysis and replication. *Journal of Abnormal Psychology, 129*(2), 204–214. https://doi.org/10.1037/abn0000485

Lina, J., Epel, E., & Blackburn, E. (2012). Telomeres and lifestyle factors: Roles in cellular aging. *Mutation Research, 730,* 85–89.

Lind, O., & Delhey, K. (2015). Visual modelling suggests a weak relationship between the evolution of ultraviolet vision and plumage coloration in birds. *Journal of Evolutionary Biology, 28,* 715–722.

Lindau, S. T., Schumm, L. P., Laumann, E. O., Levinson, W., O'Muircheartaigh, C. A., & Waite, L. J. (2007). A study of sexuality and health among older adults in the United States. *New England Journal of Medicine, 357,* 762–774.

Lindner, P., Dagöö, J., Hamilton, W., Miloff, A., Andersson, G., Schill, A., & Carlbring, P. (2021). Virtual reality exposure therapy for public speaking anxiety in routine care: A single-subject effectiveness trial. *Cognitive Behaviour Therapy, 50*(1), 67–87. https://doi.org/10.1016/j.janxdis.2018.07.003

Lindquist, K. A., Satpute, A. B., & Gendron, M. (2015). Does language do more than communicate emotion? *Current Directions in Psychological Science, 24,* 99–108.

Lindqvist, A., Renström, E. A., & Sendén, M. G. (2019). Reducing a male bias in language? Establishing the efficiency of three different gender-fair language strategies. *Sex Roles, 81*(1–2), 109–117. https://doi.org/10.1007/s11199-018-0974-9

Lineberry, T. W., & Bostwick, J. M. (2006). Methamphetamine abuse: A perfect storm of complications. *Mayo Clinic Proceedings, 81,* 77–84.

Linhares, J. M., Pinto, P. D., & Nascimento, S. M. (2008). The number of discernible colors in natural scenes. *Journal of the Optical Society of America, 25,* 2918–2924.

Lisman, J. (2015). The challenge of understanding the brain: Where we stand in 2015. *Neuron, 86,* 864–882.

Liszewski, W., Peebles, J. K., Yeung, H., & Arron, S. (2018). Persons of nonbinary gender—awareness, visibility, and health disparities. *New England Journal of Medicine, 379*(25), 2391–2393. https://doi.org/10.1056/NEJMp1812005

Litam, S. D. A., & Balkin, R. S. (2020). Moral injury in health-care workers during COVID-19 pandemic. *Traumatology.* Advance online publication. https://doi.org/10.1037/trm0000290

Liu, J. (2021, February 20). How to support Asian American colleagues amid the recent wave of anti-Asian violence. *CNBC.* https://www.cnbc.com/2021/02/19/how-to-support-asian-american-colleagues-amid-anti-asian-violence.html

Liu, K., Daviglus, M. L., Loria, C. M., Colangelo, L. A., Spring, B., Moller, A. C., & Lloyd-Jones, D. M. (2012). Healthy lifestyle through young adulthood and the presence of low cardiovascular disease risk profile in middle age: The coronary artery risk development in (young) adults (cardia) study. *Circulation, 125,* 996–1004.

Liu, L., Preotiuc-Pietro, D., Samani, Z. R., Moghaddam, M. E., & Ungar, L. H. (2016). Analyzing personality through social media profile picture choice. In *Proceedings of the Tenth International AAAI Conference on Web and Social Media* (pp. 211–220). Association for the Advancement of Artificial Intelligence.

Liu, R. T., Kleiman, E. M., Nestor, B. A., & Cheek, S. M. (2015). The hopelessness theory of depression: A quarter-century in review. *Clinical Psychology: Science and Practice, 22,* 345–365.

Liu, S., Liu, P., Wang, M., & Zhang, B. (2020). Effectiveness of stereotype threat interventions: A meta-analytic review. *Journal of Applied Psychology.* Advance online publication. https://doi.org/10.1037/apl0000770

Liu, Y., Song, Y., Koopmann, J., Wang, M., Chang, C. H. D., & Shi, J. (2017). Eating your feelings? Testing a model of employees' work-related stressors, sleep quality, and unhealthy eating. *Journal of Applied Psychology, 102*(8), 1237–1258. https://doi.org/10.1037/apl0000209

Liu, Y., Wheaton, A. G., Chapman, D. P., Cunningham, T. J., Lu, H., & Croft, J. B. (2016). Prevalence of healthy sleep duration among adults—United States, 2014. *Morbidity and Mortality Weekly Report (MMWR), 65,* 137–141. https://www.jstor.org/stable/24857917

Liu, Y., Yu, C., Liang, M., Li, J., Tian, L., Zhou, Y., Qin, W., Li, K., & Jiang, T. (2007). Whole brain functional connectivity in the early blind. *Brain, 130,* 2085–2096. https://doi.org/10.1093/brain/awm121

Livingston, I., Doyle, J., & Mangan, D. (2010, April 25). Stabbed hero dies as more than 20 people stroll past him. *New York Post.* http://www.nypost.com/p/news/local/queens/passers_by_let_good_sam_die_5SGkf5XDP5ooudVuEd8fbI

LoBue, C., Schaffert, J., Cullum, C. M., Peters, M. E., Didehbani, N., Hart, J., & White, C. L. (2020). Clinical and neuropsychological profile of patients with dementia and chronic traumatic encephalopathy. *Journal of Neurology, Neurosurgery & Psychiatry, 91*(6), 586–592. https://doi.org/10.1136/jnnp-2019-321567

Loftfield, E., Cornelis, M. C., Caporaso, N., Yu, K., Sinha, R., & Freedman, N. (2018). Association of coffee drinking with mortality by genetic variation in caffeine metabolism: Findings from the UK Biobank. *JAMA Internal Medicine, 178*(8), 1086–1097. https://doi:10.1001/jamainternmed.2018.2425

Loftus, E. F. (1994). The repressed memory controversy. *American Psychologist, 49,* 443–445.

Loftus, E. F. (1997). Creating false memories. *Scientific American, 277,* 70–75.

Loftus, E. F. (2005). Planting misinformation in the human mind: A 30-year investigation of the malleability of memory. *Learning and Memory, 12,* 361–366.

Loftus, E. F., & Bernstein, D. M. (2005). Rich false memories. In A. F. Healy (Ed.), *Experimental cognitive psychology and its applications* (pp. 101–113). American Psychological Association Press.

Loftus, E., & Ketcham, K. (1994). *The myth of repressed memory.* St. Martin's Griffin.

Loftus, E. F., Miller, D. G., & Burns, H. J. (1978). Semantic integration of verbal information into a visual memory. *Journal of Experimental Psychology: Human Learning and Memory, 4,* 19–31.

Loftus, E. F., & Palmer, J. C. (1974). Reconstruction of automobile destruction. *Journal of Verbal Learning and Verbal Behavior, 13,* 585–589.

Loftus, E. F., & Pickrell, J. E. (1995). The formation of false memories. *Psychiatric Annals, 25,* 720–725.

Logan, J. A. R., Justice, L. M., Yumuş, M., & Chaparro-Moreno, L. J. (2019). When children are not read to at home: The million word gap. *Journal of Developmental and Behavioral Pediatrics, 40*(5), 383–386. https://doi.org/10.1097/DBP.0000000000000657

Lohr, J. (2015, September/October). Does napping really help cognitive function? *Scientific American Mind, 26,* 70.

Lonsdorf, E. V. (2017). Sex differences in nonhuman primate behavioral development. *Journal of Neuroscience Research, 95*(1–2), 213–221. https://doi.org/10.1002/jnr.23862

Lopez, F. G., Ramos, K., & Kim, M. (2018). Development and initial validation of a measure of attachment security in late adulthood. *Psychological Assessment, 30*(9), 1214–1225. https://doi.org/10.1037/pas0000568

Lopez, R. (2012, March 18). "Dog whisperer" Cesar Millan grooms his canine-training empire. *Los Angeles Times.* http://articles.latimes.com/2012/mar/18/business/la-fi-himi-millan-20120318

López-Muñoz, F., Shen, W. W., D'ocon, P., Romero, A., & Álamo, C. (2018). A history of the pharmacological treatment of bipolar disorder. *International Journal of Molecular Sciences, 19*(7), Article 2143. https://doi.org/10.3390/ijms19072143

Lorenz, K. Z. (1937). The companion in the bird's world. *The Auk, 54,* 245–273.

Lott, A. J., & Lott, B. E. (1965). Group cohesiveness as interpersonal attraction: A review of relationships with antecedent and consequent variables. *Psychological Bulletin, 64,* 259–309.

Lotze, M., Domin, M., Gerlach, F. H., Gaser, C., Lueders, E., Schmidt, C. O., & Neumann, N. (2019). Novel findings from 2,838 adult brains on sex differences in gray matter brain volume. *Scientific Reports, 9*(1), 1–7. https://doi.org/10.1038/s41598-018-38239-2

Lou, S., & Zhang, G. (2009). What leads to romantic attractions: Similarity, reciprocity, security, or beauty? Evidence from a speed-dating study. *Journal of Personality, 77,* 933–964.

Loudin, A. (2020, February 14). Strength training is vital in avoiding injuries and staying independent as you age. *The Washington Post.* https://www.washingtonpost.com/health/strength-training-is-vital-in-avoiding-injuries-and-staying-independent-as-you-age/2020/02/07/88694832-3888-11ea-bf30-ad313e4ec754_story.html

Loughrey, D. G., Kelly, M. E., Kelley, G. A., Brennan, S., & Lawlor, B. A. (2018). Association of age-related hearing loss with cognitive function, cognitive impairment, and dementia: A systematic review and meta-analysis. *JAMA Otolaryngology–Head & Neck Surgery, 144*(2), 115–126. https://doi.org/10.1001/jamaoto.2017.2513

Louie, J. F., Kurtz, J. E., & Markey, P. M. (2018). Evaluating circumplex structure in the interpersonal scales for the NEO-PI-3. *Assessment, 25*(5), 589–595. https://doi.org/10.1177/1073191116665697

Louie, J. Y., Oh, B. J., & Lau, A. S. (2013). Cultural differences in the links between parental control and children's emotional expressivity. *Cultural Diversity and Ethnic Minority Psychology, 19,* 424–434.

Lourida, I., Hannon, E., Littlejohns, T. J., Langa, K. M., Hyppönen, E., Kuźma, E., & Llewellyn, D. J. (2019). Association of lifestyle and genetic risk with incidence of dementia. *Journal of the American Medical Association, 322*(5), 430–437. https://doi.org/10.1001/jama.2019.9879

Lowery, W. (2020, November 18). Trevor Noah is still trying to explain America to itself. It's getting harder. *GQ.* https://www.gq.com/story/trevor-noah-newsman-of-the-year-2020

Lowy, J. (2017, October 5). Technology crammed into cars worsens driver distraction. *Associated Press.* https://apnews.com/23e2fbcf837348b69e5b5a8d1e3f2963

Lozano, A. M., Lipsman, N., Bergman, H., Brown, P., Chabardes, S., Chang, J. W., Keith Matthews, K., McIntyre, C. C., Schlaepfer, T. E., Schulder, M., Temel, Y., Volkmann, J., & Krauss, J. K. (2019). Deep brain stimulation: Current challenges and future directions. *Nature Reviews Neurology, 15*(3), 148–160. https://doi.org/10.1038/s41582-018-0128-2

Lozano, A. V. (2020, November 4). "A tipping point": Psychedelics, cannabis win big across the country on election night. *NBC News.* https://www.nbcnews.com/politics/2020-election/tipping-point-psychedelics-cannabis-win-big-across-country-election-night-n1246469

Lu, J., Lee, J., Gino, F., & Galinsky, A. (2018). Darker skies, darker behaviors. *Scientific American.* https://www.scientificamerican.com/article/darker-skies-darker-behaviors/

Lu, Z.-L., Williamson, S. J., & Kaufman, L. (1992). Behavioral lifetime of human auditory sensory memory predicted by physiological measures. *Science, 258,* 1668–1670.

Lubke, G. H., McArtor, D. B., Boomsma, D. I., & Bartels, M. (2018). Genetic and environmental contributions to the development of childhood aggression. *Developmental Psychology, 54*(1), 39–50. https://doi.org/10.1037/dev0000403

Lucasfilm (Producer), & Marquand, R. (Director). (1983). *Star wars: Episode VI – return of the Jedi* [Motion picture]. Twentieth Century Fox Film Corporation.

Ludden, D. C. (2021). *A history of modern psychology: The quest for a science of the mind.* Sage.

Ludel, J. (1978). *Introduction to sensory processes.* W. H. Freeman.

Luers, J. C., & Hüttenbrink, K.-B. (2016). Surgical anatomy and pathology of the middle ear. *Journal of Anatomy, 228,* 338–353. https://doi.org/10.1111/joa.12389

Lui, P. P., & Quezada, L. (2019). Associations between microaggression and adjustment outcomes: A meta-analytic and narrative review. *Psychological Bulletin, 145*(1), 45–78. https://doi.org/10.1037/bul0000172

Lundin, R. W. (1963). Personality theory in behavioristic psychology. In J. M. Wepman & R. W. Heine (Eds.), *Concepts of personality* (pp. 257–290). Aldine.

Luo, S. X., van Horen, F., Millet, K., & Zeelenberg, M. (2020, July 2). What we talk about when we talk about hope: A prototype analysis. *Emotion.* Advance online publication. http://dx.doi.org/10.1037/emo0000821

Luo, Y. H-L., & da Cruz, L. (2014). A review and update on the current status of retinal prostheses (bionic eye). *British Medical Bulletin, 109,* 31–44.

Lupo, M., Troisi, E., Chiricozzi, F. R., Clausi, S., Molinari, M., & Leggio, M. (2015). Inability to process negative emotions in cerebellar damage: A functional transcranial Doppler sonographic study. *The Cerebellum, 14,* 663–669.

Lussier, K. (2018). Temperamental workers: Psychology, business, and the Humm-Wadsworth Temperament Scale in interwar America. *History of Psychology, 21*(2), 79–99. https://doi.org/10.1037/hop0000081

Luyster, F. S., Strollo Jr., P. J., Zee, P. C., & Walsh, J. K. (2012). Sleep: A health imperative. *SLEEP, 35,* 727–734.

Lyamin, O. I., Kosenko, P. O., Korneva, S. M., Vyssotski, A. L., Mukhametov, L. M., & Siegel, J. M. (2018). Fur seals suppress REM sleep for very long periods without subsequent rebound. *Current Biology, 28.* https://doi.org/10.1016/j.cub.2018.05.022

Lyckholm, L. J. (2004). Thirty years later: An oncologist reflects on Kübler-Ross's work. *American Journal of Bioethics, 4,* 29–31.

Lynch, G. (2002). Memory enhancement: The search for mechanism-based drugs. *Nature Neuroscience, 5*(Suppl.), 1035–1038.

Lynch, K. (1960). *The image of the city.* MIT Press.

Lynn, S. J., Lilienfeld, S. O., Merckelbach, H., Giesbrecht, T., McNally, R. J., Loftus, E. F., Bruck, M., Garry, M., & Malaktaris, A. (2014). The trauma model of dissociation: Inconvenient truths and stubborn fictions: Comment on Dalenberg et al. (2012). *Psychological Bulletin, 140,* 896–910.

Lynn, S. J., Lilienfeld, S. O., Merckelbach, H., Giesbrecht, T., & van der Kloet, D. (2012). Dissociation and dissociative disorders: Challenging conventional wisdom. *Current Directions in Psychological Science, 21,* 48–53.

Lyons, K. (2020, October 11). Twitter flags, limits sharing on Trump tweet about being "immune" to coronavirus. *The Verge.* https://www.theverge.com/2020/10/11/21511682/twitter-disables-sharing-trump-tweet-coronavirus-misinformation

Lyoo, I. K., Yoon, S., Kim, T. S., Lim, S. M., Choi, Y., Kim, J.E., Hwang, J., Jeong, H. S., Cho, H. B., Chung, Y. A., & Renshaw, P. F. (2015). Predisposition to and effects of methamphetamine use on the adolescent brain. *Molecular Psychiatry, 20,* 1516–1524. https://doi.org/10.1038/mp.2014.191

Lyubomirsky, S., Dickerhoof, R., Boehm, J. K., & Sheldon, K. M. (2011). Becoming happier takes both a will and a proper way: An experimental longitudinal intervention to boost well-being. *Emotion, 11,* 391–402.

Lyubomirsky, S., & Layous, K. (2013). How do simple positive activities increase well-being? *Current Directions in Psychological Science, 22,* 57–62.

Lyubomirsky, S., Sheldon, S. M., & Schkade, D. (2005). Pursuing happiness: The architecture of sustainable change. *Review of General Psychology, 9,* 111–131.

Maass, A., Düzel, S., Brigadski, T., Goerke, M., Becke, A., Sobieray, U., Neumann, K., Lövdén, M., Lindenberger, U., Bäckman, L., Braun-Dullaeus, R., Ahrens, D., Heinze, H.-J., Müller, N. G., Lessmann, V., Sendtner, M., & Düzel, E. (2016). Relationships of peripheral IGF-1, VEGF and BDNF levels to exercise-related changes in memory, hippocampal perfusion and volumes in older adults. *NeuroImage, 131,* 142–154. https://doi.org/10.1016/j.neuroimage.2015.10.084

Maaswinkel, I. M., van der Aa, H. P. A., van Rens, G. H. M. B., Beekman, A. T. F., Twisk, J. W. R., & van Nispen, R. M. A. (2020). Mastery and self-esteem mediate the association between visual acuity and mental health: A population-based longitudinal cohort study. *BMC Psychiatry, 20*(1), 1–9. https://doi.org/10.1186/s12888-020-02853-0

MacCann, C., Fogarty, G. J., Zeidner, M., & Roberts, R. D. (2011). Coping mediates the relationship between emotional intelligence (EI) and academic achievement. *Contemporary Educational Psychology, 36,* 60–70.

Maccoby, E. E., & Martin, J. A. (1983). Socialization in the context of the family: Parent–child interaction. In P. Mussen & E. M. Hetherington (Eds.), *Handbook of child psychology: Vol. IV. Socialization, personality and social development* (pp. 1–101). John Wiley & Sons.

Macdonald, K., Germine, L., Anderson, A., Christodoulou, J., & McGrath, L. M. (2017). Dispelling the myth: Training in education or neuroscience decreases but does not eliminate beliefs in neuromyths. *Frontiers in Psychology, 8,* 1314. https://doi.org/10.3389/fpsyg.2017.01314

Mack, A. (2003). Inattentional blindness: Looking without seeing. *Current Directions in Psychological Science, 12,* 180–184.

Mackes, N. K., Golm, D., Sarkar, S., Kumsta, R., Rutter, M., Fairchild, G., Mehta, M. A., Sonuga-Barke, E. J. S., & ERA Young Adult Follow-up team. (2020). Early childhood deprivation is associated with alterations in adult brain structure despite subsequent environmental enrichment. *Proceedings of the National Academy of Sciences, 117*(1), 641–649. https://doi.org/10.1073/pnas.1911264116

MacLean, E. L., & Hare, B. (2015). Dogs hijack the human bonding pathway. *Science, 348*(6232), 280–281. https://doi.org/10.1126/science.aab1200

MacLean, E. L., Snyder-Mackler, N., VonHoldt, B. M., & Serpell, J. A. (2019). Highly heritable and functionally relevant breed differences in dog behaviour. *Proceedings of the Royal Society B, 286*(1912), 20190716. https://doi.org/10.1098/rspb.2019.0716

MacLeod, C. M., Jonker, T. R., & James, G. (2013). Individual differences in remembering. In T. J. Perfect & D. S. Lindsay (Eds.), *The SAGE handbook of applied memory* (pp. 385–403). Sage.

Macmillan, C. (2020, June 24). Drinking more than usual during the COVID-19 pandemic? *Yale Medicine.* https://www.yalemedicine.org/stories/alcohol-covid/

Macmillan, M. (2000). Restoring Phineas Gage: A 150th retrospective. *Journal of the History of the Neurosciences, 9,* 46–66.

Madeira, C., Alheira, F. V., Calcia, M. A., Silva, T. C., Tannos, F. M., Vargas-Lopes, C., Fisher, M., Goldenstein, N., Brasil, M. A., Vinogradov, S., Ferreira, S. T., & Panizzutti, R. (2018). Blood levels of glutamate and glutamine in recent onset and chronic schizophrenia. *Frontiers in Psychiatry, 9.* https://doi.org/10.3389/fpsyt.2018.00713

Madigan, S., Browne, D., Racine, N., Mori, C., & Tough, S. (2019). Association between screen time and children's performance on a developmental screening test. *JAMA Pediatrics, 173*(3), 244–250. https://doi.org/10.1001/jamapediatrics.2018.5056

Madsen, K. M., Hviid, A., Vestergaard, M., Schendel, D., Wohlfahrt, J., Thorsen, P., Olsen, J., & Melbye, M. (2002). A population-based study of measles, mumps, and rubella vaccination and autism. *New England Journal of Medicine, 347,* 1477–1482.

Maguire, E. A., Woollett, K., & Spiers, H. J. (2006). London taxi drivers and bus drivers: A structural MRI and neuropsychological analysis. *Hippocampus, 16,* 1091–1101.

Mah, K., & Binik, Y. M. (2001). Do all orgasms feel alike? Evaluating a two-dimensional model of orgasm experience across gender and sexual context. *Journal of Sex Research, 39,* 104–113.

Maher, B. A., Ahmed, I. A., Karloukovski, V., MacLaren, D. A., Foulds, P. G., Allsop, D., Mann, D. M. A., Torres-Jardón, R., & Calderon-Garciduenas, L. (2016). Magnetite pollution nanoparticles in the human brain. *Proceedings of the National Academy of Sciences, 113*(39), 10797–10801. https://doi.org/10.1073/pnas.1605941113

Maher, W. B., & Maher, B. A. (2003). Abnormal psychology. In D. K. Freedheim (Ed.), *Handbook of psychology: History of psychology* (Vol. 1, pp. 303–336). John Wiley & Sons.

Mahmut, M. K., Stevenson, R. J., & Stephen, I. (2019). Do women love their partner's smell? Exploring women's preferences for and identification of male partner and non-partner body odor. *Physiology & Behavior, 210,* Article 112517. https://doi.org/10.1016/j.physbeh.2019.04.006

Mahoney, C. R., Giles, G. E., Marriott, B. P., Judelson, D. A., Glickman, E. L., Geiselman, P. J., & Lieberman, H. R. (2019). Intake of caffeine from all sources and reasons for use by college students. *Clinical Nutrition, 38*(2), 668–675. https://doi.org/10.1016/j.clnu.2018.04.004

Mahtani, S., & Wutwanich, P. (2018, July 10). "A miracle, a science, or what": How the world came together to save 12 boys trapped in a Thai cave. *The Washington Post.* https://www.washingtonpost.com/world/thai-authorities-prepare-to-rescue-remaining-four-boys-and-their-coach-from-a-flooded-cave-as-the-eight-freed-boys-start-laughing-joking-with-doctors/2018/07/10/1af52f52-83b5-11e8-9e06-4db52ac42e05_story.html?utm_term=.f6cae9ad7899

Mai, E., & Buysse, D. J. (2008). Insomnia: Prevalence, impact, pathogenesis, differential diagnosis, and evaluation. *Sleep Medicine Clinics, 3,* 167–174.

Maiden, B., & Perry, B. (2011). Dealing with free-riders in assessed group work: Results from a study at a UK university. *Assessment & Evaluation in Higher Education, 36,* 451–464.

Maiya, S., Carlo, G., Davis, A. N., & Streit, C. (2020). Relations among acculturative stress, internalizing symptoms, and prosocial behaviors in Latinx college students. *Journal of Latinx Psychology.* Advance online publication. https://doi.org/10.1037/lat0000177

Majid, A. (2012). Current emotion research in the language sciences. *Emotion Review, 4,* 432–443.

Makin, J. W., & Porter, R. H. (1989). Attractiveness of lactating females' breast odors to neonates. *Child Development, 60,* 803–810.

Makin, S. (2020, March 2). Born ready: Babies are prewired to perceive the world. *Scientific American.* https://www.scientificamerican.com/article/born-ready-babies-are-prewired-to-perceive-the-world/

Makin, T. R., Scholz, J., Slater, D. H., Johansen-Berg, H., & Tracey, I. (2015). Reassessing cortical reorganization in the primary sensorimotor cortex following arm amputation. *Brain, 138,* 2140–2146.

Malani, P., Clark, S., Solway, E., Singer, D., & Kirch, M. (2018, May). Let's talk about sex. National Poll on Healthy Aging, University of Michigan. https://www.healthyagingpoll.org/sites/default/files/2018-05/NPHA-Sexual-Health-Report_050118_final2.pdf

Malenka, R. C., & Nicoll, R. A. (1999). Long-term potentiation—a decade of progress? *Science, 285,* 1870–1874.

Malinowski, J., & Horton, C. L. (2014). Evidence for the preferential incorporation of emotional waking-life experiences into dreams. *Dreaming, 24,* 18–31.

Malkemus, S. A. (2015). Reclaiming instinct: Exploring the phylogenetic unfolding of animate being. *Journal of Humanistic Psychology, 55,* 3–29

Malkoff-Schwartz, S., Frank, E., Anderson, B., Sherrill, J. T., Siegel, L., Patterson, D., & Kupfer, D. J. (1998). Stressful life events and social rhythm disruption in the onset of manic and depressive bipolar episodes. *Archives of General Psychiatry, 55,* 702–707.

Malmberg, K. J., Raaijmakers, J. G. W., & Shiffrin, R. M. (2019). 50 years of research sparked by Atkinson and Shiffrin (1968). *Memory & Cognition, 47*(4), 561–574. https://doi.org/10.3758/s13421-019-00896-7

Manber, R., Kraemer, H. C., Arnow, B. A., Trivedi, M. H., Rush, A. J., Thase, M. E., Rothbaum, B. O., Klein, D. N., Kocsis, J. H., Gelenberg, A. J., & Keller, M. E. (2008). Faster remission of chronic depression with combined psychotherapy and medication than with each therapy alone. *Journal of Consulting and Clinical Psychology, 76,* 459–467.

Mancini, A. D., Bonanno, G. A., & Clark, A. E. (2011). Stepping off the hedonic treadmill: Individual differences in response to major life events. *Journal of Individual Differences, 32,* 144–152.

Mandler, J. M. (2008). On the birth and growth of concepts. *Philosophical Psychology, 21,* 207–230.

Mandoki, M. W., Sumner, G. S., Hoffman, R. P, & Riconda, D. L. (1991). A review of Klinefelter's syndrome in children and adolescents. *Psychiatry, 30,* 167–172.

Mann, S., Vrij, A., Leal, S., Granhag, P. A., Warmelink, L., & Forrester, D. (2012). Windows to the soul? Deliberate eye contact as a cue to deceit. *Journal of Nonverbal Behavior, 36*(3), 205–215.

Manning, J. T., Kilduff, L. P., & Trivers, R. (2013). Digit ratio (2D:4D) in Klinefelter's syndrome. *Andrology, 1,* 1–6.

Manning, R., Levine, M., & Collins, A. (2007). The Kitty Genovese murder and the social psychology of helping: The parable of the 38 witnesses. *American Psychologist, 62,* 555–562.

Manns, J. R., Hopkins, R. O., & Squire, L. R. (2003). Semantic memory and the human hippocampus. *Neuron, 38,* 127–133.

Maples-Keller, J. L., Bunnell, B. E., Kim, S. J., & Rothbaum, B. O. (2017). The use of virtual reality technology in the treatment of anxiety and other psychiatric disorders. *Harvard Review of Psychiatry, 25*(3), 103–113. https://doi.org/10.1097/HRP.0000000000000138

Maraldi, E. d. O., & Krippner, S. (2019). Cross-cultural research on anomalous experiences: Theoretical issues and methodological challenges. *Psychology of Consciousness: Theory, Research, and Practice, 6*(3), 306–319. https://doi.org/10.1037/cns0000188

Maraqa, B., Nazzal, Z., & Zink, T. (2020). Palestinian health care workers' stress and stressors during COVID-19 pandemic: A cross-sectional study. *Journal of Primary Care & Community Health, 11.* https://doi.org/10.1177/2150132720955026

March, E., & McBean, T. (2018). New evidence shows self-esteem moderates the relationship between narcissism and selfies. *Personality and Individual Differences, 130,* 107–111.

https://doi.org/10.1016/j.paid.2018.03.053

Marczinski, C. A., Fillmore, M. T., Maloney, S. F., & Stamates, A. L. (2017). Faster self-paced rate of drinking for alcohol mixed with energy drinks versus alcohol alone. *Psychology of Addictive Behaviors, 31,* 154–161. https://doi.org/10.1037/adb0000229

Marczinski, C. A., Stamates, A. L., & Maloney, S. F. (2018, January 15). Differential development of acute tolerance may explain heightened rates of impaired driving after consumption of alcohol mixed with energy drinks versus alcohol alone. *Experimental and Clinical Psychopharmacology, 26,* 147–155. http://dx.doi.org/10.1037/pha0000173

Marder, S. R., & Cannon, T. D. (2019). Schizophrenia. *New England Journal of Medicine, 38,* 1753–1761. https://www.nejm.org/doi/10.1056/NEJMra1808803

Mariën, P., Ackermann, H., Adamaszek, M., Barwood, C. H., Beaton, A., Desmond, J., De Witte, E., Fawcett, A. J., Hertrich, I., Küper, M., Leggio, M., Marvel, C., Molinari, M., Murdoch, B. E., Nicolson, R. I., Schmahmann, J. D., Stoodley, C. J., Thürling, M., Timmann, D., . . . Ziegler, W. (2014). Consensus paper: Language and the cerebellum: An ongoing enigma. *The Cerebellum, 13*(3), 386–410. https://doi.org/10.1007/s12311-013-0540-5

Marin, M. M., Rapisardi, G., & Tani, F. (2015). Two-day-old newborn infants recognise their mother by her axillary odour. *Acta Paediatrica, 104,* 237–240.

Markovitch, N., Luyckx, K., Klimstra, T., Abramson, L., & Knafo-Noam, A. (2017). Identity exploration and commitment in early adolescence: Genetic and environmental contributions. *Developmental Psychology, 53,* 2092–2102. https://doi.org/10.1037/dev0000318

Marks, D. F. (2019). The Hans Eysenck affair: Time to correct the scientific record. *Journal of Health Psychology, 24*(4), 409–420. https://doi.org/10.1177/1359105318820931

Marmurek, H. C., & Grant, R. D. (1990). Savings in a recognition test. *Canadian Journal of Psychology, 44,* 414–419.

Maron, D. F. (2018, March 5). "My brain made me do it" is becoming a more common criminal defense. *Scientific American.* https://www.scientificamerican.com/article/my-brain-made-me-do-it-is-becoming-a-more-common-criminal-defense/

Maron, E., Hettema, J. M., & Shlik, J. (2010). Advances in molecular genetics of panic disorder. *Molecular Psychiatry, 15,* 681–701.

Maroon, J. C., Winkelman, R., Bost, J., Amos, A., Mathyssek, C., & Miele, V. (2015). Chronic traumatic encephalopathy in contact sports: A systematic review of all reported pathological cases. *PLOS ONE, 10,* e0117338.

Marsh, A. A., Rhoads, S. A., & Ryan, R. M. (2019). A multisemester classroom demonstration yields evidence in support of the facial feedback effect. *Emotion, 19*(8), 1500–1504. https://doi.org/10.1037/emo0000532

Marsh, H. W., Nagengast, B., & Morin, A. J. (2013). Measurement invariance of Big-Five factors over the life span: ESEM tests of gender, age, plasticity, maturity, and La Dolce Vita effects. *Developmental Psychology, 49,* 1194–1218.

Marston, H. R., Niles-Yokum, K., & Silva, P. A. (2021). A commentary on Blue Zones®: A critical review of age-friendly environments in the 21st century and beyond. *International Journal of Environmental Research and Public Health, 18*(2), Article 837. https://doi.org/10.3390/ijerph18020837

Martin, C. (2013). Memorable outliers. *Current Biology, 23*(17), R731–R733.

Martin, C. L., & Cook, R. E. (2018). Cognitive perspectives on children's toy choices. In E. S. Weisgram & L. M. Dinella (Eds.), *Gender typing of children's toys: How early play experiences impact development* (pp. 141–164). American Psychological Association.

Martin, J. (2016). Ernest Becker and Stanley Milgram: Twentieth-century students of evil. *History of Psychology, 19*(1), 3–21. https://doi.org/10.1037/hop0000016

Martin, L. A., Doster, J. A., Critelli, J. W., Purdum, M., Powers, C., Lambert, P. L., & Miranda, V. (2011). The "distressed" personality, coping and cardiovascular risk. *Stress and Health, 27,* 64–72.

Martin, R., & Kuiper, N. A. (2016). Three decades investigating humor and laughter: An interview with Professor Rod Martin. *Europe's Journal of Psychology, 12*(3), 498–512. https://doi.org/10.5964/ejop.v12i3.1119

Martin, R. A., Puhlik-Doris, P., Larsen, G., Gray, J., & Weir, K. (2003). Individual differences in uses of humor and their relation to psychological well-being: Development of the Humor Styles Questionnaire. *Journal of Research in Personality, 37,* 48–75.

Martinez, G. M. (2020, September 10). Trends and patterns in menarche in the United States: 1995 through 2013–2017. *National Health Statistics Reports.* https://www.cdc.gov/nchs/data/nhsr/nhsr146-508.pdf

Martinez-Conde, S. (2019, November 12). Lions see these illusions the same way you do: And then they rip them to shreds. *Scientific American.* https://blogs.scientificamerican.com/illusion-chasers/lions-see-these-illusions-the-same-way-you-do/#

Martinez-Conde, S., & Macknik, S.L. (2020). A pair of crocs to match the dress. *Scientific American Mind, 31*(1), 35–36. https://doi.org/10.1038/scientificamericanmind0120-35

Marx, V., & Nagy, E. (2015). Fetal behavioural responses to maternal voice and touch. *PLOS ONE, 10*(6), e0129118.

Masaoka, K., Berns, R. S., Fairchild, M. D., & Moghareh Abed, F. (2013). Number of discernible object colors is a conundrum. *Journal of the Optical Society of America A, 30,* 264–277.

Masiulis, S., Desai, R., Uchański, T., Martin, I. S., Laverty, D., Karia, D., Malinauskas, T., Zivanov, J., Pardon, E., Kotecha, A., Steyaert, J., Miller, K. W., & Aricescu, A. R. (2019). GABA A receptor signalling mechanisms revealed by structural pharmacology. *Nature, 565*(7740), 454–459. https://doi.org/10.1038/s41586-018-0832-5

Maslow, A. H. (1943). A theory of human motivation. *Psychological Review, 50,* 370–396.

Massen, J. J., Dusch, K., Eldakar, O. T., & Gallup, A. C. (2014). A thermal window for yawning in humans: Yawning as a brain cooling mechanism. *Physiology & Behavior, 130,* 145–148.

Masters, W., & Johnson, V. (1966). *Human sexual response.* Little, Brown.

Masuda, T., Batdorj, B., & Senzaki, S. (2020). Culture and attention: Future directions to expand research beyond the geographical regions of WEIRD cultures. *Frontiers in Psychology, 11,* 1394. https://doi.org/10.3389/fpsyg.2020.01394

Mathes, J., Schredl, M., & Göritz, A. S. (2014). Frequency of typical dream themes in most recent dreams: An online study. *Dreaming, 24,* 57–66.

Matheson, S. L., Shepherd, A. M., & Carr, V. J. (2014). How much do we know about schizophrenia and how well do we know it? Evidence from the schizophrenia library. *Psychological Medicine, 44,* 3387–3405.

Mathur, M. B., & VanderWeele, T. J. (2019). Finding common ground in meta-analysis "wars" on violent video games. *Perspectives on Psychological Science, 14*(4), 705–708. https://doi.org/10.1177/1745691619850104

Matsumoto, D., & Willingham, B. (2009). Spontaneous facial expressions of emotion of congenitally and noncongenitally blind individuals. *Journal of Personality and Social Psychology, 96,* 1–10.

Mattarella-Micke, A., Mateo, J., Kozak, M. N., Foster, K., & Beilock, S. L. (2011). Choke or thrive? The relation between salivary cortisol and math performance depends on individual differences in working memory and math-anxiety. *Emotion, 11*(4), 1000–1005. https://doi.org/10.1037/a0023224

May, C. (2018, May 29). The problem with "learning styles." *Scientific American.* https://www.scientificamerican.com/article/the-problem-with-learning-styles/

Mayhew, A. J., Pigeyre, M., Couturier, J., & Meyre, D. (2018). An evolutionary genetic perspective of eating disorders. *Neuroendocrinology, 106*(3), 292–306. https://doi.org/10.1159/000484525

Mayo Clinic. (2017, December 6). *Presbyopia.* https://www.mayoclinic.org/diseases-conditions/presbyopia/symptoms-causes/syc-20363328

Mayo Clinic. (2018, January 31). Suicide: What to do when someone is suicidal. https://www.mayoclinic.org/diseases-conditions/suicide/in-depth/suicide/art-20044707

Mayo Clinic. (2020, October 6). *Persistent post-concussive symptoms (post-concussion syndrome).* https://www.mayoclinic.org/diseases-conditions/post-concussion-syndrome/symptoms-causes/syc-20353352

Mayo Clinic. (n.d.). *Cochlear implants.* https://www.mayoclinic.org/tests-procedures/cochlear-implants/about/pac-20385021

Mayo Clinic Staff. (2019, December 18). Weight loss: 6 strategies for success. https://www.mayoclinic.org/healthy-lifestyle/weight-loss/in-depth/weight-loss/art-20047752

Mazza, S., Gerbier, E., Gustin, M. P., Kasikci, Z., Koenig, O., Toppino, T. C., & Magnin, M. (2016). Relearn faster and retain longer: Along with practice, sleep makes perfect. *Psychological Science, 27*(10), 1321–1330. https://doi.org/10.1177/0956797616659930

McAdams, D. P., & Olson, B. D. (2010). Personality development: Continuity and change over the life course. *Annual Review of Psychology, 61,* 5.1–5.26.

McCarthy, C. (2021, January 15). Alcohol harms the brain in teen years—before and after that, too. Harvard Health Blog. https://www.health.harvard.edu/blog/alcohol-harms-the-brain-in-teen-years-before-and-after-that-too-2021011521758

McClain, S., & Cokley, K. (2017). Academic disidentification in Black college students: The role of teacher trust and gender. *Cultural Diversity and Ethnic Minority Psychology, 23,* 125–133. https://doi.org/10.1037/cdp0000094

McClelland, D. C., Atkinson, J. W., Clark, R. W., & Lowell, E. L. (1976). *The achievement motive.* Irvington.

McClintock, M. K. (1971). Menstrual synchrony and suppression. *Nature, 229,* 244–245.

McCoach, D. B., & Flake, J. K. (2018). The role of motivation. In S. I. Pfeiffer, E. Shaunessy-Dedrick, & M. Foley-Nicpon (Eds.), *APA handbooks in psychology®. APA handbook of giftedness and talent* (pp. 201–213). American Psychological Association. https://doi.org/10.1037/0000038-013

McCormack, H. M., MacIntyre, T. E., O'Shea, D., Herring, M. P., & Campbell, M. J. (2018). The prevalence and cause(s) of burnout among applied psychologists: A systematic review. *Frontiers in Psychology, 9,* Article 1897. https://doi.org/10.3389/fpsyg.2018.01897

McCrae, R. R., Chan, W., Jussim, L., De Fruyt, F., Löckenhoff, C. E., De Bolle, M., Costa, P. T., Jr., Hřebíčková, M., Graf, S., Realo, A., Allik, J., Nakazato, K., Shimonaka, Y., Yik, M., Ficková, E., Brunner-Sciarra, M., Reátigui, N., de Figueora, N. L., Schmidt, V., . . . Terracciano, A. (2013). The inaccuracy of national character stereotypes. *Journal of Research in Personality, 47*(6), 831–842. https://doi.org/10.1016/j.jrp.2013.08.006

McCrae, R. R., & Costa, P. T., Jr. (1987). Validation of the five-factor model of personality across instruments and observers. *Journal of Personality and Social Psychology, 49,* 81–90.

McCrae, R. R., & Costa, P. T., Jr. (1990). *Personality in adulthood.* Guilford Press.

McCrae, R. R., Costa, P. T., Jr., Ostendorf, F., Angleitner, A., Hřebíčková, M., Avia, M. D., Sanz, J., Sánchez-Bernardos, M. L., Kusdil, M. E., Woodfield, R., Saunders, P. R., & Smith, P. B. (2000). Nature over nurture: Temperament, personality, and life span development. *Journal of Personality and Social Psychology, 78*(1), 173–186. https://doi.org/10.1037/0022-3514.78.1.173

McCrae, R. R., Scally, M., Terracciano, A., Abecasis, G. R., & Costa, P. T., Jr. (2010). An alternative to the search for single polymorphisms: Toward molecular personality scales for the five-factor model. *Journal of Personality and Social Psychology, 99,* 1014–1024.

McCrae, R. R., Terracciano, A., & 78 Members of the Personality Profiles of Cultures Project. (2005). Universal features of personality traits from the observer's perspective: Data from 50 cultures. *Journal of Personality and Social Psychology, 88,* 547–561.

McDougall, W. (1912). *An introduction to social psychology* (Rev. 4th ed.). John W. Luce.

McEwen, B. S. (2000). The neurobiology of stress: From serendipity to clinical relevance. *Brain Research, 886*, 172–189.

McFadden, P., Mallett, J., & Leiter, M. (2018). Extending the two-process model of burnout in child protection workers: The role of resilience in mediating burnout via organizational factors of control, values, fairness, reward, workload, and community relationships. *Stress and Health, 34*, 72–83. https://doi.org/10.1002/smi.2763

McGann, J. P. (2017). Poor human olfaction is a 19th-century myth. *Science, 356*(6338), eaam7263. https://doi.org/10.1126/science.aam7263

McGaugh, J. L., & LePort, A. (2014). Remembrance of all things past. *Scientific American, 310*, 40–45.

McGue, M., Bouchard, T. J. Jr., Iacono, W. G., & Lykken, D. T. (1993). Behavioral genetics of cognitive ability: A life-span perspective. In R. Plomin & G. E. McClearn (Eds.), *Nature, nurture and psychology* (pp. 59–76). American Psychological Association.

McKee, A. C., Cairns, N. J., Dickson, D. W., Folkerth, R. D., Keene, C. D., Litvan, I., Perl, D. P., Stein, T. D., Vonsatte, J.-P., Stewart, W., Tripodis, Y., Crary, J. F., Bieniek, K. F., Dams-O'Connor, K., Alvarez, V. E., Gordon, W. A., & the TBI/CTE group. (2016). The first NINDS/NIBIB consensus meeting to define neuropathological criteria for the diagnosis of chronic traumatic encephalopathy. *Acta Neuropathologica, 131*, 75–86. https://doi.org/10.1007/s00401-015-1515-z

McKee, A. C., Stein, T. D., Nowinski, C. J., Stern, R. A., Daneshvar, D. H., Alvarez, V. E., Lee, H.-S., Hall, G., Wojtowicz, S. M., Baugh, C. M., Riley, D. O., Kubilus, C. A., Cormier, K. A., Jacobs, M. A., Martin, B. R., Abraham, C. R., Ikezu, T., Reichard, R. R., Wolozin, B. L., . . . Cantu, R. C. (2013). The spectrum of disease in chronic traumatic encephalopathy. *Brain, 136*, 43–64. https://doi.org/10.1093/brain/aws307

McKinney, A., & Coyle, K. (2006). Alcohol hangover effects on measures of affect the morning after a normal night's drinking. *Alcohol & Alcoholism, 41*, 54–60.

McLean, W. J., Yin, X., Lu, L., Lenz, D. R., McLean, D., Langer, R. D., Karp, J. M., & Edge, A. S. (2017). Clonal expansion of Lgr5-positive cells from mammalian cochlea and high-purity generation of sensory hair cells. *Cell Reports, 18*, 1917–1929. https://doi.org/10.1016/j.celrep.2017.01.066

McLellan, T. M., Caldwell, J. A., & Lieberman, H. R. (2016). A review of caffeine's effects on cognitive, physical and occupational performance. *Neuroscience & Biobehavioral Reviews, 71*, 294–312. https://doi.org/10.1016/j.neubiorev.2016.09.001

McMurray, B. (2007). Defusing the childhood vocabulary explosion. *Science, 317*, 631.

McNally, R. J., & Clancy, S. A. (2005). Sleep paralysis, sexual abuse, and space alien abduction. *Transcultural Psychiatry, 42*, 113–122.

McPherson, M., Smith-Lovin, L., & Cook, J. M. (2001). Birds of a feather: Homophily in social networks. *Annual Review of Sociology, 27*, 415–444.

McRae, A. F., Visscher, P. M., Montgomery, G. W., & Martin, N. G. (2015). Large autosomal copy-number differences within unselected monozygotic twin pairs are rare. *Twin Research and Human Genetics, 18*, 13–18.

McRobbie, L. R. (2017, February 8). Total recall: The people who never forget. *The Guardian*. https://www.theguardian.com/science/2017/feb/08/total-recall-the-people-who-never-forget

Meczkowski, E. J., Dillard, J. P., & Shen, L. (2016). Threat appeals and persuasion: Seeking and finding the elusive curvilinear effect. *Communication Monographs, 83*, 373–395. https://doi.org/10.1080/03637751.2016.1158412

Medeiros-Ward, N., Watson, J. M., & Strayer, D. L. (2015). On supertaskers and the neural basis of efficient multitasking. *Psychonomic Bulletin & Review, 22*, 876–883.

Medline Plus. (2020, June 18). *Is longevity determined by genetics?* https://medlineplus.gov/genetics/understanding/traits/longevity/

Medline Plus. (2020, August 18). *Androgen insensitivity syndrome.* https://medlineplus.gov/genetics/condition/androgen-insensitivity-syndrome/

Medline Plus. (2020, September 17). *What is a gene?* https://medlineplus.gov/genetics/understanding/basics/gene/

Medline Plus. (2020, September 21). *What is epigenetics?* https://medlineplus.gov/genetics/understanding/howgeneswork/epigenome/

Medline Plus. (n.d.). *Infant-newborn development.* U.S. National Library of Medicine, U.S. Department of Health and Human Services, National Institutes of Health. https://medlineplus.gov/ency/article/002004.htm

Meerwijk, E. L., & Sevelius, J. M. (2017). Transgender population size in the United States: A meta-regression of population-based probability samples. *American Journal of Public Health, 107*, e1–e8. https://doi.org/10.2105/AJPH.2016.303578

Mehler, P. S., & Brown, C. (2015). Anorexia nervosa—Medical complications. *Journal of Eating Disorders, 3*, Article 11. https://doi.org/10.1186/s40337-015-0040-8

Meier, M. H., Caspi, A., Ambler, A., Harrington, H., Houts, R., Keefe, R. S., McDonald, K., Ward, A., Poulton, R., & Moffitt, T. E. (2012). Persistent cannabis users show neuropsychological decline from childhood to midlife. *Proceedings of the National Academy of Sciences, 109*(40), E2657–E2664. https://doi.org/10.1073/pnas.1206820109

Meindl, P., Yu, A., Galla, B. M., Quirk, A., Haeck, C., Goyer, J. P., Lejuez, C. W., D'Mello, S. K., & Duckworth, A. L. (2019). A brief behavioral measure of frustration tolerance predicts academic achievement immediately and two years later. *Emotion, 19*(6), 1081–1092. https://doi.org/10.1037/emo0000492

Mejia, B. (2020, December 19). They risk their lives cleaning hospitals. Now, they are getting vaccinated. "I want people to know that we exist." *Los Angeles Times*. https://www.latimes.com/california/story/2020-12-19/covid-vaccine-california-hospital-custodial-workers

Melchert, T. P. (2015). Physical health. In T. P. Melchert, *Biopsychosocial practice: A science-based framework for behavioral health care* (pp. 123–132). APA Books.

Melin, A. D., Hiramatsu, C., Parr, N. A., Matsushita, Y., Kawamura, S., & Fedigan, L. M. (2014). The behavioral ecology of color vision: Considering fruit conspicuity, detection distance and dietary importance. *International Journal of Primatology, 35*, 258–287

Melnikova, N., Welles, W. L., Wilburn, R. E., Rice, N., Wu, J., & Stanbury, M. (2011). Hazards of illicit methamphetamine production and efforts at reduction: Data from the hazardous substances emergency events surveillance system. *Public Health Reports, 126*, 116–123.

Melzack, R. (1993). Pain: Past present and future. *Canadian Journal of Experimental Psychology, 47*, 615–629.

Melzack, R. (2008). The future of pain. *Nature Reviews, 7*, 629.

Melzack, R., & Wall, P. D. (1965). Pain mechanisms: A new theory. *Science, 150*, 971–979.

Méndez-Bértolo, C., Moratti, S., Toledano, R., Lopez-Sosa, F., Martínez-Alvarez, R., Mah, Y. H., Vuilleumier, P., Gil-Nagel, A., & Strange, B. A. (2016). A fast pathway for fear in human amygdala. *Nature Neuroscience, 19*, 1041–1049. https://doi.org/10.1038/nn.4324

Mendle, J., Harden, K. P., Brooks-Gunn, J., & Graber, J. A. (2010). Development's tortoise and hare: Pubertal timing, pubertal tempo, and depressive symptoms in boys and girls. *Developmental Psychology, 46*, 1341–1353.

Mendrek, A., & Mancini-Marïe, A. (2016). Sex/gender differences in the brain and cognition in schizophrenia. *Neuroscience & Biobehavioral Reviews, 67*, 57–78. https://doi.org/10.1016/j.neubiorev.2015.10.013

Menéndez-Aller, Á., Postigo, Á., Montes-Álvarez, P., González-Primo, F. J., & García-Cueto, E. (2020). Humor as a protective factor against anxiety and depression. *International Journal of Clinical and Health Psychology, 20*(1), 38–45. https://doi.org/10.1016/j.ijchp.2019.12.002

Meng, X., Deng, Y., Dai, Z., & Meng, Z. (2020). COVID-19 and anosmia: A review based on up-to-date knowledge. *American Journal of Otolaryngology, 41*(5), Article 102581. https://doi.org/10.1016/j.amjoto.2020.102581

Menken, J., Trussell, J., & Larsen, U. (1986). Age and infertility. *Science, 233*, 1389–1394.

Mennella, J. A., Coren P., Jagnow, M. S., & Beauchamp, G. K. (2001). Prenatal and postnatal flavor learning by human infants. *Pediatrics, 107*, e88.

Menni, C., Sudre, C. H., Steves, C. J., Ourselin, S., & Spector, T. D. (2020). Quantifying additional COVID-19 symptoms will save lives. *The Lancet, 395*(10241), e107–e108. https://doi.org/10.1016/S0140-6736(20)31281-2

Menolascino, N., & Jenkins, L. N. (2018). Predicting bystander intervention among middle school students. *School Psychology Quarterly, 33*, 305–313. https://doi.org/10.1037/spq0000262

Mercado, D. (2020, November 4). Voters chose to legalize and tax recreational marijuana in these 4 states. *CNBC*. https://www.cnbc.com/2020/11/04/voters-chose-to-legalize-tax-recreational-marijuana-in-these-4-states.html

Merikangas, K. R., Jin, R., He, J. P., Kessler, R. C., Lee, S., Sampson, N. A., Viana, M. C., Andrade, L. H., Hu, C., Karam, E. G., Ladea, M., Medina-Mora, M. E., Ono, Y., Posada-Villa, J., Sagar, R., Wells, E., & Zarkov, Z. (2011). Prevalence and correlates of bipolar spectrum disorder in the world mental health survey initiative. *Archives of General Psychiatry, 68*(3), 241–251.

Mervis, C. B., & Rosch, E. (1981). Categorization of natural objects. *Annual Review of Psychology, 32*, 89–115.

Mewton, L., Lees, B., & Rao, R. T. (2020). Lifetime perspective on alcohol and brain health. *BMJ, 371*(8272), Article m4691. https://www.bmj.com/content/371/bmj.m4691

Mez, J., Daneshvar, D. H., Kiernan, P. T., Abdolmohammadi, B., Alvarez, V. E., Huber, B. R., Alosco, M. L., Solomon, T. M., Nowinski, C. J., McHale, L., Cormier, K. A., Kubilus, C. A., Martin, B. M., Murphy, L., Baugh, C. M., Montenigro, P. H., Chaisson, C. E., Tripodis, Y., Kowall, N. W., . . . McKee, A. C. (2017). Clinicopathological evaluation of chronic traumatic encephalopathy in players of American football. *JAMA, 318,* 360–370. https://doi.org/10.1001/jama.2017.8334

Michael, R. T., Laumann, E. O., Kolata, G. B., & Gagnon, J. H. (1994). *Sex in America: A definitive survey.* Little, Brown.

Michaelson, L. E., & Munakata, Y. (2020). Same data set, different conclusions: Preschool delay of gratification predicts later behavioral outcomes in a preregistered study. *Psychological Science, 31*(2), 193–201. https://doi.org/10.1177/0956797619896270

Michals, D. (Ed.). (2015). *Harriet Tubman.* National Women's History Museum. http://www.nwhm.org/education-resources/biography/biographies/harriet-tubman/

Miech, R., Johnston, L., O'Malley, P. M., Bachman, J. G., & Patrick, M. E. (2019). Adolescent vaping and nicotine use in 2017–2018—US national estimates. *New England Journal of Medicine, 380*(2), 192–193. https://doi.org/10.1056/NEJMc1814130

Milani, R. V., & Lavie, C. J. (2009). Reducing psychosocial stress: A novel mechanism of improving survival from exercise training. *The American Journal of Medicine, 122,* 931–938. https://doi.org/10.1016/j.amjmed.2009.03.028

Milar, K. S. (2016). Unknown, untold, unsung: Women in the history of psychology. In W. D. Woody, R. L. Miller, & W. J. Wozniak (Eds.), *Psychological specialties in historical context: Enriching the classroom experience for teachers and students.* Society for the Teaching of Psychology. http://teachpsych.org/ebooks/

Milgram, S. (1963). Behavioral study of obedience. *Journal of Abnormal and Social Psychology, 67,* 371–378.

Milgram, S. (1964). Issues in the study of obedience: A reply to Baumrind. *American Psychologist, 19,* 848–852.

Milgram, S. (1965). Some conditions of obedience and disobedience to authority. *Human Relations, 18*(1), 57–76.

Milgram, S. (1974). *Obedience to authority: An experimental view.* Harper & Row.

Millan, C. (2013). *Cesar Millan's short guide to a happy dog.* National Geographic Society.

Millan, C. (2013, March 26). It isn't always about the dog. *Huffington Post.* https://www.huffpost.com/entry/it-isnt-always-about-the_b_2541801

Millan, C. (n.d.). The Dog Psychology Center: Evolution of a dream [Web log comment]. https://www.cesarsway.com/cesar-millan/cesars-blog/dog-psychology-center-evolution-of-a-dream

Millan, C., & Peltier, M. J. (2006). *Cesar's way: The natural, everyday guide to understanding & correcting common dog problems.* Random House.

Millan, C., & Peltier, M. J. (2010). *Cesar's rules: Your way to train a well-behaved dog.* Three Rivers Press.

Miller, B. L. & Cummings, J. L. (2018). The human frontal lobes: An introduction. In B. L. Miller & J. L. Cummings (Eds.), *The human frontal lobes: Functions and disorders* (3rd ed.) (pp. 1–9). Guilford Press.

Miller, G. (1956). The magical number seven, plus or minus two: Some limits on our capacity for processing information. *Psychological Review, 63,* 81–97.

Miller, R., Mach, K., & Field. C. (2020, October 29). Climate change is central to California's wildfires. *Scientific American.* https://www.scientificamerican.com/article/climate-change-is-central-to-californias-wildfires/

Miller, S. L., & Maner, J. K. (2010). Scent of a woman: Men's testosterone responses to olfactory ovulation cues. *Psychological Science, 21,* 276–283.

Miller-Perrin, C., & Rush, R. (2018). Attitudes, knowledge, practices, and ethical beliefs of psychologists related to spanking: A survey of American Psychological Association division members. *Psychology, Public Policy, and Law, 24*(4), 405–417. https://doi.org/10.1037/law0000184

Minnesota Center for Twin and Family Research. (2016, September 1). Other twin research at the U of M. https://mctfr.psych.umn.edu/research/UM%20research.html

Mirsky, A. F. (2019). Monte S. Buchsbaum and the Genain quadruplets. *Psychiatry Research, 277,* 70–71. https://doi.org/10.1016/j.psychres.2019.02.031

Mirsky, A. F., & Quinn, O. W. (1988). The Genain triplets. *Schizophrenia Bulletin, 14,* 595–612.

Mirsky, A. F., Bieliauskas, L. A., French, L. M., Van Kammen, D. P.,

Jönsson, E., & Sedvall, G. A. (2000). A 39-year followup of the Genain quadruplets. *Schizophrenia Bulletin, 26,* 699–708.

Mischel, W., & Shoda, Y. (1995). A cognitive-affective system theory of personality: Reconceptualizing the invariances in personality and the role of situations. *Psychological Review, 102,* 229–258.

Mistry, R. S., & Wadsworth, M. E. (2011). Family functioning and child development in the context of poverty. *Prevention Researcher, 18,* 11–15.

Mitchell, A. S., Sherman, S. M., Sommer, M. A., Mair, R. G., Vertes, R. P., & Chudasama, Y. (2014). Advances in understanding mechanisms of thalamic relays in cognition and behavior. *Journal of Neuroscience, 34*(46), 15340–15346.

Mitchell, H. A., & Weinshenker, D. (2010). Good night and good luck: Norepinephrine in sleep pharmacology. *Biochemical Pharmacology, 79,* 801–809.

Miyatsu, T., Nguyen, K., & McDaniel, M. A. (2018). Five popular study strategies: Their pitfalls and optimal implementations. *Perspectives on Psychological Science, 13,* 390–407. https://doi.org/10.1177/1745691617710510

Moeck, E. K., Thomas, N. A., & Takarangi, M. K. T. (2020). Lateralized processing of emotional images: A left hemisphere memory deficit. *Emotion, 20*(2), 236–247. https://doi.org/10.1037/emo0000554

Moed, A., Gershoff, E. T., Eisenberg, N., Hofer, C., Losoya, S., Spinrad, T. L., & Liew, J. (2015). Parent–adolescent conflict as sequences of reciprocal negative emotion: Links with conflict resolution and adolescents' behavior problems. *Journal of Youth and Adolescence, 44,* 1607–1622.

Mogilner, C., & Norton, M. I. (2016). Time, money, and happiness. *Current Opinion in Psychology, 10,* 12–16. https://doi.org/10.1016/j.copsyc.2015.10.018

Moirand, R., Galvao, F., Lecompte, M., Poulet, E., Haesebaert, F., & Brunelin, J. (2018). Usefulness of the Montreal Cognitive Assessment (MoCA) to monitor cognitive impairments in depressed patients receiving electroconvulsive therapy. *Psychiatry Research, 259,* 476–481. https://doi.org/10.1016/j.psychres.2017.11.022

Moller, A. C., Roth, G., Niemiec, C. P., Kanat-Maymon, Y., & Deci, E. L. (2019). Mediators of the associations between parents' conditional regard and the quality of their adult-children's peer-relationships. *Motivation and Emotion, 43*(1), 35–51. https://doi.org/10.1037/hum0000168

Moller, A. C., & Sheldon, K. M. (2020). Athletic scholarships are negatively associated with intrinsic motivation for sports, even decades later: Evidence for long-term undermining. *Motivation Science, 6*(1), 43–48. https://doi.org/10.1037/mot0000133

Mollon, J. D. (1982). Color vision. *Annual Review of Psychology, 33,* 41–85.

Molloy, K., Lavie, N., & Chait, M. (2019). Auditory figure–ground segregation is impaired by high visual load. *The Journal of Neuroscience, 39*(9), 1699–1708. https://doi.org/10.1523/JNEUROSCI.2518-18.2018

Monakhov, S. (2020). Early detection of internet trolls: Introducing an algorithm based on word pairs/single words multiple repetition ratio. *PLOS ONE, 15*(8). https://doi.org/10.1371/journal.pone.0236832

Monod, M., Blenkinsop, A., Xi, X., Hebert, D., Bershan, S., Tietze, S., Baguelin, M., Bradley, V. C., Chen, Y., Coupland, H., Filippi, S., Ish-Horowicz, J., McManus, M., Mellan, T., Gandy, A., Hutchinson, M., Unwin, H. J. T., van Elsland, S. L., Vollmer, M. A. C., Weber, S., Zhu, H., Bezancon, A., Ferguson, N. M., Mishra, S., Flaxman, S., Bhatt, S., & Ratmann, O. (2021). Age groups that sustain resurging COVID-19 epidemics in the United States. *Science.* https://doi.org/10.1126/science.abe8372

Monroe, S. M., & Harkness, K. L. (2011). Recurrence in major depression: A conceptual analysis. *Psychological Review, 118,* 655–674.

Montano, C., Taub, M. A., Jaffe, A., Briem, E., Feinberg, J. I., Trygvadottir, R., Idrizi, A., Runarsson, A., Berndsen, B., Gur, R. C., Moore, T. M., Perry, R. T., Fugman, D., Sabunciyan, S., Yolken, R. H., Hyde, T. M., Kleinman, J. E., Sobell, J. L., Pato, C. N., . . . Feinberg, A. P. (2016). Association of DNA methylation differences with schizophrenia in an epigenome-wide association study. *JAMA Psychiatry, 73*(5), 506–514. https://doi.org/10.1001/jamapsychiatry.2016.0144

Montemayor, R. (1983). Parents and adolescents in conflict: All families some of the time and some families most of the time. *Journal of Early Adolescence, 3,* 83–103.

Monthly Aquarius horoscope. (2020, April). https://www.horoscope.com/us/horoscopes/general/horoscope-general-monthly.aspx?sign=11

Montoya, E. R., Terburg, D., Bos, P. A., & van Honk, J. (2012). Testosterone, cortisol, and serotonin as key regulators of social aggression: A review and theoretical perspective. *Motivation and Emotion, 36,* 65–73.

Montoya, R. M., Horton, R. S., Vevea, J. L., Citkowicz, M., & Lauber, E. A. (2017). A re-examination of the mere exposure effect: The influence of repeated exposure on recognition, familiarity, and liking. *Psychological Bulletin, 143,* 459–498. https://doi.org/10.1037/bul0000085

Moody, T. D., Morfini, F., Cheng, G., Sheen, C., Tadayonnejad, R., Reggente, N., O-Neill, J., & Feusner, J. D. (2017). Mechanisms of cognitive-behavioral therapy for obsessive-compulsive disorder involve robust and extensive increases in brain network connectivity. *Translational Psychiatry, 7, Article* e1230. https://doi.org/10.1038/tp.2017.192

Moon, C., Lagercrantz, H., & Kuhl, P. K. (2013). Language experienced in utero affects vowel perception after birth: A two-country study. *Acta Paediatrica, 102*(2), 156–160.

Moon, C., Zernzach, R. C., & Kuhl, P. K. (2015). Mothers say "baby" and their newborns do not choose to listen: A behavioral preference study to compare with ERP results. *Frontiers in Human Neuroscience, 9.* http://journal.frontiersin.org/article/10.3389/fnhum.2015.00153/full

Moore, D. S. (2013). Current thinking about nature and nurture. In K. Kampourakis (Ed.), *The philosophy of biology: A companion for educators* (pp. 629–652). Springer Science.

Moore, S. R., & Depue, R. A. (2016). Neurobehavioral foundation of environmental reactivity. *Psychological Bulletin, 142,* 107–164. https://doi.org/10.1037/bul0000028

Moosa, A. N., Jehi, L., Marashly, A., Cosmo, G., Lachhwani, D., Wyllie, E., Kotagal, P., Bingaman, W., & Gupta, A. (2013). Long-term functional outcomes and their predictors after hemispherectomy in 115 children. *Epilepsia, 54,* 1771–1779. https://doi.org/10.1111/epi.12342

Morales, A., Heaton, J. P. W., & Carson, C. C., III. (2000). Andropause: A misnomer for a true clinical entity. *Journal of Urology, 163,* 705–712.

Morales Ayma, E. (2009, March 13). Let me chew my coca leaves. *The New York Times.* http://www.nytimes.com/2009/03/14/opinion/14morales.html

Morehead, K., Dunlosky, J., & Rawson, K. A. (2019). How much mightier is the pen than the keyboard for note-taking? A replication and extension of Mueller and Oppenheimer (2014). *Educational Psychology Review, 31*(3), 753–780.

Moreira-Almeida, A., Neto, F. L., & Cardeña, E. (2008). Comparison of Brazilian spiritist mediumship and dissociative identity disorder. *Journal of Nervous and Mental Disease, 196,* 420–424.

Moreland, R. L., & Zajonc, R. B. (1982). Exposure effects in person perception: Familiarity, similarity, and attraction. *Journal of Experimental Social Psychology, 18,* 395–415.

Morell, V. (2020, March 3). New Zealand birds show humanlike ability to make predictions. *Science.* https://www.sciencemag.org/news/2020/03/new-zealand-birds-show-humanlike-ability-make-predictions

Moreno-Jiménez, E. P., Flor-García, M., Terreros-Roncal, J., Rábano, A., Cafini, F., Pallas-Bazarra, N., Ávila, J., & Llorens-Martín, M. (2019). Adult hippocampal neurogenesis is abundant in neurologically healthy subjects and drops sharply in patients with Alzheimer's disease. *Nature Medicine, 25,* 554–560. https://doi.org/10.1038/s41591-019-0375-9

Morling, B., & Calin-Jageman, R. J. (2020). What psychology teachers should know about open science and the new statistics. *Teaching of Psychology, 47*(2), 169–179. https://doi.org/10.1177/0098628320901372

Morris, M. C., Tangney, C. C., Wang, Y., Sacks, F. M., Bennett, D. A., & Aggarwal, N. T. (2015). MIND diet associated with reduced incidence of Alzheimer's disease. *Alzheimer's & Dementia, 11*(9), 1007–1014.

Morry, M. M., Kito, M., & Ortiz, L. (2011). The attraction-similarity model and dating couples: Projection, perceived similarity, and psychological benefits. *Personal Relationships, 18,* 125–143.

Morsy, L., & Rothstein, R. (2019). *Toxic stress and children's outcomes: African American children growing up poor are at greater risk of disrupted physiological functioning and depressed academic achievement.* Economic Policy Institute. https://files.eric.ed.gov/fulltext/ED598149.pdf

Moss, D. (2015). The roots and genealogy of humanistic psychology. In K. J. Schneider, J. F. Pierson, & J. F. T. Bugental (Eds.), *The handbook of humanistic psychology: Theory, research, and practice* (2nd ed., pp. 5–20). Sage.

Most, S. B., Simons, D. J., Scholl, B. J., Jimenez, R., Clifford, E., & Chabris, C. F. (2001). How not to be seen: The contribution of similarity and selective ignoring to sustained inattentional blindness. *Psychological Science, 12,* 9–17.

Motive. (n.d.). In *Online etymology dictionary.* https://www.etymonline.com/word/motive

Mõttus, R., Sinick, J., Terracciano, A., Hřebíčková, M., Kandler, C., Ando, J., Mortensen, E. L., Colodro-Conde, L., & Jang, K. L. (2019). Personality characteristics below facets: A replication and meta-analysis of cross-rater agreement, rank-order stability, heritability, and utility of personality nuances. *Journal of Personality and Social Psychology, 117*(4), e35–e50. https://doi.org/10.1037/pspp0000202

Mouland, J. W., Martial, F., Watson, A., Lucas, R. J., & Brown, T. M. (2019). Cones support alignment to an inconsistent world by suppressing mouse circadian responses to the blue colors associated with twilight. *Current Biology, 29*(24), 4260–4267. https://doi.org/10.1016/j.cub.2019.10.028

Mousa, S. (2020). Building social cohesion between Christians and Muslims through soccer in post-ISIS Iraq. *Science, 369*(6505), 866–870.

Mousteri, V., Daly, M., & Delaney, L. (2020). Underemployment and psychological distress: Propensity score and fixed effects estimates from two large UK samples. *Social Science & Medicine, 244,* Article 112641. https://doi.org/10.1016/j.socscimed.2019.112641

Moyle, P., & Hackston, J. (2018). Personality assessment for employee development: Ivory tower or real world? *Journal of Personality Assessment, 100*(5), 507–517. https://doi.org/10.1080/00223891.2018.1481078

Mueller, P. A., & Oppenheimer, D. M. (2014). The pen is mightier than the keyboard: Advantages of longhand over laptop note taking. *Psychological Science, 25,* 1159–1168. https://doi.org/10.1177/0956797614524581

Müller, K. W., Dreier, M., Beutel, M. E., Duven, E., Giralt, S., & Wölfling, K. (2016). A hidden type of internet addiction? Intense and addictive use of social networking sites in adolescents. *Computers in Human Behavior, 55,* 172–177. https://doi.org/10.1016/j.chb.2015.09.007

Muller, P. Y., Dambach, D., Gemzik, B., Hartmann, A., Ratcliffe, S., Trendelenburg, C., & Urban, L. (2015). Integrated risk assessment of suicidal ideation and behavior in drug development. *Drug Discovery Today, 20,* 1135–1142.

Müllerová, J., Hansen, M., Contractor, A. A., Elhai, J. D., & Armour, C. (2016). Dissociative features in posttraumatic stress disorder: A latent profile analysis. *Psychological Trauma: Theory, Research, Practice, and Policy, 8*(5), 601–608. https://doi.org/10.1037/tra0000148

Mulvey, S. (2006, May 15). Cakes and jokes at Cafe d'Europe. *BBC News.* http://news.bbc.co.uk/2/hi/europe/4755659.stm

Murdoch, D. D. (2016). Psychological literacy: Proceed with caution, construction ahead. *Psychology Research and Behavior Management, 9,* 189–199.

Murdock, B. (1962). The serial position effect of free recall. *Journal of Experimental Psychology, 64,* 482–488.

Murkar, A., Smith, C., Dale, A., & Miller, N. (2014). A neuro-cognitive model of sleep mentation and memory consolidation. *International Journal of Dream Research, 7,* 85–89.

Murphy, D., & Joseph, S. (2016). Person-centered therapy: Past, present, and future orientations. In D. J. Cain, K. Keenan, & S. Rubin (Eds.), *Humanistic psychotherapies: Handbook of research and practice* (2nd ed., pp. 185–218). American Psychological Association.

Murphy, K. (2020, April 29). Why Zoom is terrible. *The New York Times.* https://www.nytimes.com/2020/04/29/sunday-review/zoom-video-conference.html

Murray, R. M., Morrison, P. D., Henquet, C., & Di Forti, M. (2007). Cannabis, the mind and society: The hash realities. *Nature Reviews Neuroscience, 8,* 885–895.

Murray, S. B., Nagata, J. M., Griffiths, S., Calzo, J. P., Brown, T. A., Mitchison, D., Blashill, A. J., & Mond, J. M. (2017). The enigma of male eating disorders: A critical review and synthesis. *Clinical Psychology Review, 57,* 1–11. https://doi.org/10.1016/j.cpr.2017.08.001

Murre, J. M., & Dros, J. (2015). Replication and analysis of Ebbinghaus' forgetting curve. *PLOS ONE, 10,* e0120644. https://doi.org/10.1371/journal.pone.0120644

Musaiger, A. O., Al-Mannai, M., Tayyem, R., Al-Lalla, O., Ali, E. Y., Kalam, F., Benhamed, M. M., Saghir, S., Halahleh, I., Djoudi, Z., & Chirane, M. (2013). Risk of disordered eating attitudes among adolescents in seven Arab countries by gender and obesity: A cross cultural study. *Appetite, 60,* 162–167.

Musto, D. F. (1991). Opium, cocaine and marijuana in American history. *Scientific American, 265,* 41–47.

Muthukrishna, M., Bell, A. V., Henrich, J., Curtin, C. M., Gedranovich, A., McInerney, J., & Thue, B. (2020). Beyond western, educated, industrial, rich, and democratic (WEIRD) psychology: Measuring and mapping scales of cultural and psychological distance. *Psychological Science,* http://10.1177/0956797620916782

Myers, B. J. (2014). Mother–infant bonding as a critical period. In M. H. Bornstein (Ed.), *Sensitive periods in development: Interdisciplinary perspectives* (pp. 223–245). Psychology Press. (Original work published in 1987.)

Myers, D. G., & Lamm, H. (1976). The group polarization phenomenon. *Psychological Bulletin, 83,* 602–627.

Nabity-Grover, T., Cheung, C. M., & Thatcher, J. B. (2020). Inside out and outside in: How the COVID-19 pandemic affects self-disclosure on social media. *International Journal of Information Management, 55.* https://doi.org/10.1016/j.ijinfomgt.2020.102188

Nadorff, M. R., Nadorff, D. K., & Germain, A. (2015). Nightmares: Underreported, undetected, and therefore untreated. *Journal of Clinical Sleep Medicine, 11*(7), 747–750.

Naftulin, J. (2020, May 29). The coronavirus "baby boom" is only for the rich and famous. Most people are too terrified to think about having kids right now. *Insider.* https://www.insider.com/coronavirus-baby-boom-rich-famous-celebrity-pregnancy-2020-5

Nagasawa, M., Mitsui, S., En, S., Ohtani, N., Ohta, M., Sakuma, Y., Onaka, T., Mogi, K., & Kikusui, T. (2015). Oxytocin-gaze positive loop and the coevolution of human–dog bonds. *Science, 348*(6232), 333–336. https://doi.org/10.1126/science.1261022

Nahemow, L., & Lawton, M. P. (1975). Similarity and propinquity in friendship formation. *Journal of Personality and Social Psychology, 32,* 205–213.

Nakayachi, K., Ozaki, T., Shibata, Y., & Yokoi, R. (2020). Why do Japanese people use masks against COVID-19, even though masks are unlikely to offer protection from infection?. *Frontiers in Psychology, 11.* https://doi.org/10.3389/fpsyg.2020.01918

Nancekivell, S. E., Shah, P., & Gelman, S. A. (2020). Maybe they're born with it, or maybe it's experience: Toward a deeper understanding of the learning style myth. *Journal of Educational Psychology, 112*(2), 221–235.

Nash, M. R. (2001). The truth and the hype of hypnosis. *Scientific American, 285,* 44–55.

National Academies of Sciences, Engineering, and Medicine. (2016). *Ending discrimination against people with mental and substance use disorders: The evidence for stigma change.* National Academies Press.

National Academies of Sciences, Engineering, and Medicine. (2017, January). *The health effects of cannabis and cannabinoids: Committee's conclusions.* http://nationalacademies.org/hmd/~/media/Files/Report%20Files/2017/Cannabis-Health-Effects/cannabis-conclusions.pdf?_ga=2.247507972.2083320254.1499706356-1581552225.1499706356

National Academies of Sciences, Engineering, and Medicine. (2019). *Taking action against clinician burnout:*

*A systems approach to professional well-being.* The National Academies Press. https://doi.org/10.17226/25521.

National Alliance on Mental Illness (NAMI) Film Discussion Guide. (n.d.). *Frankie & Alice: Inspired by an amazing true story.* https://www.nami.org/getattachment/Get-Involved/What-Can-I-Do/Movies-to-Watch/frankie-alice-viewingguide.pdf

National Center for Health Statistics. (2019, February). *Long-term care providers and services users in the United States, 2015–2016.* https://www.cdc.gov/nchs/data/series/sr_03/sr03_43-508.pdf

National Geographic. (2015). *Dia de los Muertos.* http://education.nationalgeographic.com/education/media/dia-de-los-muertos/?ar_a=1

National Highway Traffic Safety Administration (NHTSA). (n.d.) *What is distracted driving?* United States Department of Transportation. https://www.nhtsa.gov/risky-driving/distracted-driving

National Institute for Allergy and Infectious Diseases (NIAID). (n.d.). *Anthony S. Fauci, M. D.* https://www.niaid.nih.gov/about/anthony-s-fauci-md-bio

National Institute of Mental Health (NIMH). (2016). *Brain stimulation therapies.* https://www.nimh.nih.gov/health/topics/brain-stimulation-therapies/brain-stimulation-therapies.shtml

National Institute of Mental Health (NIMH). (2019, February). *Major depression.* https://www.nimh.nih.gov/health/statistics/major-depression.shtml

National Institute of Mental Health (NIMH). (2021, January). *Suicide.* https://www.nimh.nih.gov/health/statistics/suicide.shtml

National Institute of Mental Health (NIMH). (n.d.-a). *Antidepressant medications for children and adolescents: Information for parents and caregivers.* http://www.nimh.nih.gov/health/topics/child-and-adolescent-mental-health/antidepressant-medications-for-children-and-adolescents-information-for-parents-and-caregivers.shtml

National Institute of Mental Health (NIMH). (n.d.-b). *Eating disorders.* http://www.nimh.nih.gov/health/topics/eating-disorders/index.shtml

National Institute of Mental Health (NIMH). (n.d.-c). *Suicide in America: Frequently asked questions.* https://www.nimh.nih.gov/health/publications/suicide-faq/index.shtml

National Institute of Neurological Disorders and Stroke (NINDS). (2013, January 10). *NIH statement.* http://espn.go.com/pdf/2013/0110/espn_otl_NIH_Statement.pdf

National Institute of Neurological Disorders and Stroke (NINDS).

(2019). *Arteriovenous malformations and other vascular lesions of the central nervous system fact sheet.* https://www.ninds.nih.gov/Disorders/Patient-Caregiver-Education/Fact-Sheets/Arteriovenous-Malformation-Fact-Sheet#3052_1

National Institute of Neurological Disorders and Stroke (NINDS). (2019a, March 27). *Chronic pain information page.* National Institutes of Health. https://www.ninds.nih.gov/Disorders/All-Disorders/Chronic-pain-Information-Page

National Institute of Neurological Disorders and Stroke (NINDS). (2019b, March 27). *Prosopagnosia information page.* https://www.ninds.nih.gov/Disorders/All-Disorders/Prosopagnosia-Information-Page

National Institute of Neurological Disorders and Stroke (NINDS). (2020, February 13). Brain basics: Know your brain. https://www.ninds.nih.gov/disorders/patient-caregiver-education/know-your-brain#The%20Inner%20Brain

National Institute of Neurological Disorders and Stroke (NINDS). (2020, March 13). *Autism spectrum disorder fact sheet.* https://www.ninds.nih.gov/disorders/patient-caregiver-education/fact-sheets/autism-spectrum-disorder-fact-sheet

National Institute of Neurological Disorders and Stroke (NINDS). (2020, September 30). *Narcolepsy fact sheet.* https://www.ninds.nih.gov/Disorders/Patient-Caregiver-Education/fact-Sheets/Narcolepsy-Fact-Sheet#3201_2

National Institute on Aging. (n.d.). About Alzheimer's disease: Alzheimer's basics. http://www.nia.nih.gov/alzheimers/topics/alzheimers-basics

National Institute on Alcohol Abuse and Alcoholism. (n.d.). *Alcohol use disorder.* https://www.niaaa.nih.gov/alcohol-health/overview-alcohol-consumption/alcohol-use-disorders

National Institute on Drug Abuse (NIDA). (2012, July). *Nationwide trends.* http://www.drugabuse.gov/sites/default/files/drugfactsnationtrends_1.pdf

National Institute on Drug Abuse (NIDA). (2018, June). *What is methamphetamine?* https://www.drugabuse.gov/publications/drugfacts/methamphetamine

National Institute on Drug Abuse (NIDA). (2018, July). *What is cocaine?* https://www.drugabuse.gov/publications/drugfacts/cocaine

National Institute on Drug Abuse (NIDA). (2019). How legal is marijuana? https://archives.drugabuse.gov/blog/post/how-legal-marijuana

National Institute on Drug Abuse (NIDA). (2020, January). *Vaping*

*devices (electronic cigarettes) DrugFacts.* https://www.drugabuse.gov/publications/drugfacts/vaping-devices-electronic-cigarettes

National Institute on Drug Abuse (NIDA). (2020, April 8). *What is the scope of marijuana use in the United States?* https://www.drugabuse.gov/publications/research-reports/marijuana/what-scope-marijuana-use-in-united-states on 2020, September 15

National Institute on Drug Abuse (NIDA). (2020a, June). *MDMA (Ecstasy/molly) DrugFacts.* https://www.drugabuse.gov/publications/drugfacts/mdma-ecstasymolly

National Institute on Drug Abuse (NIDA). (2020b, June). *Synthetic cannabinoids (K2/Spice) DrugFacts.* https://www.drugabuse.gov/publications/drugfacts/synthetic-cannabinoids-k2spice

National Institutes of Health. (2017, May 17). *Study finds tens of millions of Americans drink alcohol at dangerously high levels* [Press release]. https://www.nih.gov/news-events/news-releases/study-finds-tens-millions-americans-drink-alcohol-dangerously-high-levels

National Institutes of Health. (2020, April 4). *Diet may help preserve cognitive function* [Press release]. https://www.nih.gov/news-events/news-releases/diet-may-help-preserve-cognitive-function

National Nurses United. (2020, November 12). National nurse survey exposes hospitals' knowing failure to prepare for a Covid-19 surge during flu season [Press release]. https://www.nationalnursesunited.org/covid-19-survey

National Organization on Fetal Alcohol Syndrome. (n.d.). *Living with FASD.* https://www.nofas.org/living-with-fasd/

National Public Radio (NPR). (2016, June 13). *How YouTube videos help people cope with mental illness.* https://www.npr.org/sections/health-shots/2016/06/13/481547500/how-seeing-youtube-videos-helped-me-understand-my-schizophrenia

National Public Radio (NPR) Staff. (2014, June 22). With memories and online maps, a man finds his "way home." *NPR.* http://www.npr.org/2014/06/22/323355643/with-memories-and-online-maps-a-man-finds-his-way-home

National Safety Council. (n.d.). Preventable deaths: Odds of dying. https://injuryfacts.nsc.org/all-injuries/preventable-death-overview/odds-of-dying/

National Science Foundation. (2019, March 8). *Women, minorities, and persons with disabilities in science and engineering—field of degree: Women.* https://ncses.nsf.gov/pubs/nsf19304/digest/field-of-degree-women#computer-sciences

**National Science Foundation, National Center for Science and Engineering Statistics.** (2019). Doctorate recipients from U.S. universities: 2018. In *Special report NSF 20-301.* https://ncses.nsf.gov /pubs/nsf20301/report

**National Sleep Foundation.** (2009). *Sleep in America poll: Highlights and key findings.* http://sleepfoundation.org /sites/default/files/2009%20POLL%20 HIGHLIGHTS.pdf

**National Sleep Foundation.** (2020, August 6). *Melatonin and sleep.* A OneCare Media Company. https:// www.sleepfoundation.org/articles /melatonin-and-sleep

**National Sleep Foundation.** (2020, July 28). *Why electronics may stimulate you before you go to bed.* A OneCare Media Company. https://www .sleepfoundation.org/articles/why -electronics-may-stimulate-you-bed

**National Sleep Foundation.** (2020, July 31). *How much sleep do we really need?* A OneCare Media Company. https://www.sleepfoundation.org /articles/how-much-sleep-do-we-really -need

**National Sleep Foundation.** (n.d.). *See: A great night's sleep can depend on the visual conditions in your bedroom environment.* http://sleepfoundation .org/bedroom/see.php

**Nazir, A., Smalbrugge, M., Moser, A., Karuza, J., Crecelius, C., Hertogh, C., Feldman, S., & Katz, P. R.** (2018). The prevalence of burnout among nursing home physicians: An international perspective. *Journal of the American Medical Directors Association, 19,* 86–88. https://doi.org/10.1016/j .jamda.2017.10.019

**Neal, T. M., Slobogin, C., Saks, M. J., Faigman, D. L., & Geisinger, K. F.** (2019). Psychological assessments in legal contexts: Are courts keeping "junk science" out of the courtroom? *Psychological Science in the Public Interest, 20*(3), 135–164. https://doi .org/10.1177/1529100619888860

**Nebel, R.** (2018, September 1). Alzheimer's hits men and women differently, and we need to understand why. *Scientific American.* https:// www.scientificamerican.com/article /alzheimers-hits-men-and-women -differently-and-we-need-to -understand-why/

**Neidig, H.** (2020, March 23). Supreme Court rules states can eliminate insanity defense. *The Hill.* https://thehill.com/regulation/court -battles/488996-supreme-court-rules -states-can-eliminate-insanity-defense

**Neisser, U.** (1979). The control of information pickup in selective looking. In A. D. Pick (Ed.), *Perception and its development: A tribute to Eleanor J. Gibson* (pp. 201–219). Erlbaum.

**Neisser, U.** (1991). A place of misplaced nostalgia. *American Psychologist, 46,* 34–36.

**Neisser, U., & Becklen, R.** (1975). Selective looking: Attending to visually specified events. *Cognitive Psychology, 7,* 480–494.

**Nekmat, E., Gower, K. K., Zhou, S., & Metzger, M.** (2019). Connective-collective action on social media: Moderated mediation of cognitive elaboration and perceived source credibility on personalness of source. *Communication Research, 46*(1), 62–87. https://doi.org/10.1177 /0093650215609676

**Nelson, C. A., III, & Gabard-Durnam, L. J.** (2020). Early adversity and critical periods: Neurodevelopmental consequences of violating the expectable environment. *Trends in Neurosciences, 43*(3), 133–143. https://doi.org/10.1016/j.tins .2020.01.002

**Nelson, R.** (2014). Scientific basis for polygraph testing. *Polygraph, 44,* 28–61.

**Nelson, R., & Handler, M.** (2013). A brief history of scientific reviews of polygraph accuracy research. *APA Magazine, 46,* 22–28.

**Nelson, S. K., Layous, K., Cole, S. W., & Lyubomirsky, S.** (2016). Do unto others or treat yourself? The effects of prosocial and self-focused behavior on psychological flourishing. *Emotion, 16*(6), 850–861. https://doi .org/10.1037/emo0000178

**Nelson, S. M., Telfer, E. E., & Anderson, R. A.** (2013). The ageing ovary and uterus: New biological insights. *Human Reproduction Update, 19,* 67–83.

**Nes, R. B., Czajkowski, N., & Tambs, K.** (2010). Family matters: Happiness in nuclear families and twins. *Behavioral Genetics, 40,* 577–590.

**Nestler, A.** (2020, October 5). What I want you to know as someone with BPD. *National Alliance on Mental Illness.* https://www.nami.org/Blogs /NAMI-Blog/October-2020/What-I -Want-You-to-Know-as-Someone-with -BPD

**Newell, A., Shaw, J. C., & Simon, H. A.** (1958). Elements of a theory of human problem solving. *Psychological Review, 65,* 151–166.

**Newell, B. R., & Andrews, S.** (2004). Levels of processing effects on implicit and explicit memory tasks: Using question position to investigate the lexical-processing hypothesis. *Experimental Psychology, 51,* 132–144.

**Newton-Howes, G., Levack, W. M., McBride, S., Gilmor, M., & Tester, R.** (2016). Non-physiological mechanisms influencing disulfiram treatment of alcohol use disorder: A grounded theory study. *Drug and Alcohol Dependence, 165,* 126–131. https://doi.org/10.1016/j .drugalcdep.2016.05.027

**Neylan, T. C.** (1999). Frontal lobe function: Mr. Phineas Gage's famous injury. *Journal of Neuropsychiatry and Clinical Neurosciences, 11,* 280–281.

**Ngun, T. C., Ghahramani, N., Sánchez, F. J., Bocklandt, S., & Vilain, E.** (2011). The genetics of sex differences in brain and behavior. *Frontiers in Neuroendocrinology, 32,* 227–248.

**Nichols, A. L., & Edlund, J. E.** (2015). Practicing what we preach (and sometimes study): Methodological issues in experimental laboratory research. *Review of General Psychology, 19,* 191–202. https://doi.org/10.1037 /gpr0000027

**Nichols, H.** (2020, February 24). Everything you need to know about Botox. *Medical News Today.* https:// www.medicalnewstoday.com/articles /158647

**Nielsen, J. A., Zielinski, B. A., Ferguson, M. A., Lainhart, J. E., & Anderson, J. S.** (2013). An evaluation of the left-brain vs. right-brain hypothesis with resting state functional connectivity magnetic resonance imaging. *PLOS ONE, 8,* e71275.

**Nielsen, M. B., Gjerstad, J., & Frone, M. R.** (2018). Alcohol use and psychosocial stressors in the Norwegian workforce. *Substance Use & Misuse, 53*(4), 574–584. https://doi.org/10 .1080/10826084.2017.1349797

**Nisbett, R. E., Aronson, J., Blair, C., Dickens, W., Flynn, J., Halpern, D. F., & Turkheimer, E.** (2012). Intelligence: New findings and theoretical developments. *American Psychologist, 67,* 130–159.

**Niskar, A. S., Kieszak, S. M., Holmes, A. E., Esteban, E., Rubin, C., & Brody, D. J.** (2001). Estimated prevalence of noise-induced hearing threshold shifts among children 6 to 19 years of age: The Third National Health and Nutrition Examination Survey, 1988–1994, United States. *Pediatrics, 108,* 40–43.

**No Barriers (No Barriers USA).** (2015, July 29). No Barriers Summit 2015—Mandy Harvey singing "Try" [Video file]. https://www.youtube.com /watch?v=z-DRYk0OxCo

**Nobel Media.** (2018). The Nobel Peace Prize for 2018 [Press release]. https://www.nobelprize.org/prizes /peace/2018/press-release/

**NobelPrize.org.** (2009, October 9). *Facts on the Nobel Prize in Literature.* https://www.nobelprize.org/nobel _prizes/facts/literature/

**NobelPrize.org.** (2014). *Malala Yousafzai—biographical.* https://www .nobelprize.org/nobel_prizes/peace /laureates/2014/yousafzai-bio.html

**Noël, R. A.** (2018, May 1). *Race, economics, and social status.* Bureau of Labor Statistics. https://www.bls.gov /spotlight/2018/race-economics-and -social-status/pdf/race-economics-and -social-status.pdf

**Nolen-Hoeksema, S.** (1991). Responses to depression and their effects on the duration of depressive episodes. *Journal of Abnormal Psychology, 100,* 569–582.

**Nonnemaker, J., Hersey, J., Homsi, G., Busey, A., Hyland, A., Juster, H., & Farrelly, M.** (2011). Self-reported exposure to policy and environmental influences on smoking cessation and relapse: A 2-year longitudinal population-based study. *International Journal of Environmental Research and Public Health, 8,* 3591–3608.

**Nooij, S. A., Pretto, P., Oberfeld, D., Hecht, H., & Bülthoff, H. H.** (2017). Vection is the main contributor to motion sickness induced by visual yaw rotation: Implications for conflict and eye movement theories. *PLOS ONE, 12*(4), e0175305. https://doi .org/10.1371/journal.pone.0175305

**Norcross, J. C., & Lambert, M. J.** (2018). Psychotherapy relationships that work III. *Psychotherapy, 55*(4), 303–315. https://doi.org/10.1037 /pst0000193

**Norcross, J. C., & Wampold, B. E.** (2018). A new therapy for each patient: Evidence-based relationships and responsiveness. *Journal of Clinical Psychology, 74*(11), 1889–1906. https:// doi.org/10.1002/jclp.22678

**Norris, D., Kalm, K., & Hall, J.** (2020). Chunking and redintegration in verbal short-term memory. *Journal of Experimental Psychology: Learning, Memory, and Cognition, 46*(5), 872–893. https://doi.org/10.1037/xlm0000762

**North, A.** (2014, August 1). Here's the thing that "lasting love" is really about [Web log post]. *The New York Times.* http://op-talk.blogs.nytimes.com/2014 /08/01/heres-the-thing-that-lasting -love-is-really-about/?_r=0

**Northoff, G., Schneider, F., Rotte, M., Matthiae, C., Tempelmann, C., Wiebking, C., Bermpohl, F., Heinzel, A., Danos, P., Heinze, H.-J., Bogerts, B., Walter, M., & Panksepp, J.** (2009). Differential parametric modulation of self-relatedness and emotions in different brain regions. *Human Brain Mapping, 30,* 369–382.

**Northside Center.** (n.d.). *[Home page].* https://www.northsidecenter.org

**Nowicki, S., Ellis, G., Iles-Caven, Y., Gregory, S., & Golding, J.** (2018). Events associated with stability and change in adult locus of control orientation over a six-year period. *Personality and Individual Differences, 126,* 85–92. https://doi.org/10.1016/j .paid.2018.01.017

**NPR.** (2014, March 30). *Cesar Millan's long walk to becoming the "Dog Whisperer."* http://www.npr.org/2014/03/30/295796786/cesar-millans-long-walk-to-becoming-the-dog-whisperer

**Nusbaum, E. C., & Silvia, P. J.** (2011). Are intelligence and creativity really so different? Fluid intelligence, executive processes, and strategy use in divergent thinking. *Intelligence, 39,* 36–45.

**Nutt, D. J., Lingford-Hughes, A., Erritzoe, D., & Stokes, P. R. A.** (2015). The dopamine theory of addiction: 40 years of highs and lows. *Nature Reviews Neuroscience, 16,* 305–312.

**Nuwer, R.** (2019, April). Failing successfully. *Scientific American, 320*(4), 16.

**Nuwer, R.** (2020, July 10). Americans increase LSD use—and a bleak outlook for the world may be to blame. *Scientific American.* https://www.scientificamerican.com/article/americans-increase-lsd-use-and-a-bleak-outlook-for-the-world-may-be-to-blame1/

**Oar, E. L., Farrell, L. J., & Ollendick, T. H.** (2015). One session treatment for specific phobias: An adaptation for paediatric blood-injection-injury phobia in youth. *Clinical Child and Family Psychology Review, 18,* 370–394.

**Oatley, K., Keltner, D., & Jenkins, J.** (2006). *Understanding emotions.* Blackwell.

**O'Brien, D.** (2013). *How to develop a brilliant memory week by week: 50 Proven ways to enhance your memory skills.* Watkins.

**O'Brien, E.** (2019). Enjoy it again: Repeat experiences are less repetitive than people think. *Journal of Personality and Social Psychology, 116*(4), 519–540. https://doi.org/10.1037/pspa0000147

**Ocasio, B. P., Ceballos, A., & Daugherty, A.** (2021, February 12). Three years after Parkland massacre, what has student activism changed? *Tampa Bay Times.* https://www.tampabay.com/news/florida-politics/2021/02/13/three-years-after-parkland-massacre-what-has-student-activism-changed/

**Occupational Safety & Health Administration.** (n.d.). Occupational noise exposure. https://www.osha.gov/SLTC/noisehearingconservation/hearingprograms.html

**O'Connor, D. B., Thayer, J. F., & Vedhara, K.** (2021). Stress and health: A review of psychobiological processes. *Annual Review of Psychology, 72,* 663–688. https://doi.org/10.1146/annurev-psych-062520-122331

**Oda, R., Matsumoto-Oda, A., & Kurashima, O.** (2005). Effects of belief in genetic relatedness on resemblance judgments by Japanese raters. *Evolution of Human Behavior, 26,* 441–450.

**O'Donnell, S., & Epstein, L. H.** (2019). Smartphones are more reinforcing than food for students. *Addictive Behaviors, 90,* 124–133. https://doi.org/10.1016/j.addbeh.2018.10.018

**Oexman, R.** (2013, May 5). Better sleep month: Top 10 sleep myths debunked. *Huffpost Life.* https://www.huffpost.com/entry/sleep-myths_b_3177375

**Office of Disease Prevention and Health Promotion.** (n.d.). *Dietary guidelines 2015–2020: Appendix 2. Estimated calorie needs per day, by age, sex, and physical activity level.* https://health.gov/our-work/food-nutrition/2015-2020-dietary-guidelines/guidelines/appendix-2/

**Office of Juvenile Justice and Delinquency Program (OJJDD).** (2020, November 16). *Statistical briefing book: Law enforcement & juvenile crime, arrest trends by offense, age, and gender.* https://www.ojjdp.gov/ojstatbb/crime/ucr_trend.asp?table_in=1&selOffenses=35&rdoGroups=3&rdoDataType=1

**O'Grady, C.** (2020, July 15). Misconduct allegations push psychology hero off his pedestal. *Science.* https://www.sciencemag.org/news/2020/07/misconduct-allegations-push-psychology-hero-his-pedestal

**Oh, D. L., Jerman, P., Marques, S. S., Koita, K., Boparai, S. K. P., Harris, N. B., & Bucci, M.** (2018). Systematic review of pediatric health outcomes associated with childhood adversity. *BMC Pediatrics, 18*(1), Article 83. https://doi.org/10.1186/s12887-018-1037-7

**Ohayon, M., Carskadon, M. A., Guilleminault, C., & Vitiello, M. V.** (2004). Meta-analysis of quantitative sleep parameters from childhood to old age in healthy individuals: Developing normative sleep values across the human lifespan. *Sleep, 21,* 1255–1273.

**Oishi, S., Talhelm, T., & Lee, M.** (2015). Personality and geography: Introverts prefer mountains. *Journal of Research in Personality, 58,* 55–68.

**Olenik-Shemesh, D., Heiman, T., & Eden, S.** (2017). Bystanders' behavior in cyberbullying episodes: Active and passive patterns in the context of personal–socio-emotional factors. *Journal of Interpersonal Violence, 32,* 23–48. https://doi.org/10.1177/0886260515585531

**Olson, J. M., Vernon, P. A., Harris, J. A., & Jang, K. L.** (2001). The heritability of attitudes: A study of twins. *Journal of Personality and Social Psychology, 80,* 845–860.

**Olson, R., Verley, J., Santos, L., & Salas, C.** (2004). What we teach students about the Hawthorne studies: A review of content within a sample of introductory IO and OB textbooks. *The Industrial-Organizational Psychologist, 41*(3), 23–39.

**Oluwole, O. S. A.** (2019). Recurrent dreams of Nigerian undergraduates. *Dreaming, 29*(4), 339–357. https://doi.org/10.1037/drm0000112

**Omalu, B. I., DeKosky, S. T., Minster, R. L., Kamboh, M. I., Hamilton, R. L., & Wecht, C. H.** (2005). Chronic traumatic encephalopathy in a National Football League player. *Neurosurgery, 57,* 128–134.

**Open Science Collaboration.** (2015). Estimating the reproducibility of psychological science. *Science, 349*(6251), aac4716. https://doi.org/10.1126/science.aac4716

**Oppedal, B. & Idsoe, T.** (2015). The role of social support in the acculturation and mental health of unaccompanied minor asylum seekers. *Scandinavian Journal of Psychology, 56,* 203–211.

**Oremus, C., Oremus, M., McNeely, H., Losier, B., Parlar, M., King, M., Hasey, G., Fervaha, G., Graham, A. C., Gregory, C., Hanford, L., Nazarov, A., Restivo, M., Tatham, E., Truong, W., Hall, G. B. C., Lanius, R., & McKinnon, M.** (2015). Effects of electroconvulsive therapy on cognitive functioning in patients with depression: Protocol for a systematic review and meta-analysis. *BMJ Open, 5,* e006966.

**Ormerod, T. C., & Dando, C. J.** (2015). Finding a needle in a haystack: Toward a psychologically informed method for aviation security screening. *Journal of Experimental Psychology: General, 144*(1), 76–84.

**Ornish, D., Lin, J., Chan, J. M., Epel, E., Kemp, C., Weidner, G., Marlin, R., Frenda, S. J., Magbanua, M. J. M., Daubenmier, J., Estay, I., Hills, N. K., Chainani-Wu, N., Carroll, P. R., & Blackburn, E. H.** (2013). Effect of comprehensive lifestyle changes on telomerase activity and telomere length in men with biopsy-proven low-risk prostate cancer: 5-year follow-up of a descriptive pilot study. *The Lancet Oncology, 14,* 1112–1120.

**Orzeł-Gryglewska, J.** (2010). Consequences of sleep deprivation. *International Journal of Occupational Medicine & Environmental Health, 23,* 94–114.

**Öst, L. G.** (1989). One-session treatment for specific phobias. *Behaviour Research and Therapy, 27,* 1–7.

**Ostrofsky, J., Kozbelt, A., & Seidel, A.** (2012). Perceptual constancies and visual selection as predictors of realistic drawing skill. *Psychology of Aesthetics, Creativity, and the Arts, 6,* 124–136.

**O'Sullivan, E. D., & Schofield, S. J.** (2018). Cognitive bias in clinical medicine. *Journal of the Royal College of Physicians of Edinburgh, 48*(3), 225–232. https://doi.org/10.4997/JRCPE.2018.306

**Otgaar, H., Howe, M. L., Patihis, L., Merckelbach, H., Lynn, S. J., Lilienfeld, S. O., & Loftus, E. F.** (2019). The return of the repressed: The persistent and problematic claims of long-forgotten trauma. *Perspectives on Psychological Science, 14*(6), 1072–1095. https://doi.org/10.1177/1745691619862306

**Otgaar, H., Wang, J., Dodier, O., Howe, M. L., Lilienfeld, S. O., Loftus, E. F., Lynn, S. J., Merckelbach, H., & Patihis, L.** (2020). Skirting the issue: What does believing in repression mean? *Journal of Experimental Psychology: General, 149*(10), 2005–2006. https://doi.org/10.1037/xge0000982

**Oudin, A., Forsberg, B., Adolfsson, A. N., Lind, N., Modig, L., Nordin, M., Nordin, S., Adolfsson, R., & Nilsson, L.-G.** (2016). Traffic-related air pollution and dementia incidence in northern Sweden: A longitudinal study. *Environmental Health Perspectives, 124*(3), 306–312. https://doi.org/10.1289/ehp.1408322

**Overmier, J. B., & Seligman, M. E. P.** (1967). Effects of inescapable shock upon subsequent escape and avoidance responding. *Journal of Comparative and Physiological Psychology, 63,* 28–33.

**Owen, J. J., Adelson, J., Budge, S., Kopta, S. M., & Reese, R. J.** (2016). Good-enough level and dose-effect models: Variation among outcomes and therapists. *Psychotherapy Research, 26,* 22–30. https://doi.org/10.1080/10503307.2014.966346

**Owen, P. R., & Padron, M.** (2016). The language of toys: Gendered language in toy advertisements. *Journal of Research on Women and Gender, 6,* 67–80.

**Oxford Royale Academy.** (2014, October 15). 11 Great jokes to help you remember English grammar rules. https://www.oxford-royale.co.uk/articles/11-great-jokes-remember-english-grammar-rules.html

**Özkan, M., Yıldırım, N., Dişçi, R., İlgün, A. S., Sarsenov, D., Alço, G., Aktepe, F., Kalyoncu, N., İzci, F., Selamoğlu, D., Ordu, Ç., Pilancı K. N., Erdoğan, Z. İ., Eralp, Y., & Özmen, V.** (2017). Roles of biopsychosocial factors in the development of breast cancer. *European Journal of Breast Health, 13*(4), 206–212. https://doi.org/10.5152/ejbh.2017.3519

Pace, A., Alper, R., Burchinal, M. R., Golinkoff, R. M., & Hirsh-Pasek, K. (2019). Measuring success: Within and cross-domain predictors of academic and social trajectories in elementary school. *Early Childhood Research Quarterly, 46,* 112–125. https://doi.org/10.1016/j.ecresq.2018.04.001

Pace, A., Luo, R., Hirsh-Pasek, K., & Golinkoff, R. M. (2017). Identifying pathways between socioeconomic status and language development. *Annual Review of Linguistics, 3,* 285–308.

Pachana, N. A., Brilleman, S. L., & Dobson, A. J. (2011). Reporting of life events over time: Methodological issues in a longitudinal sample of women. *Psychological Assessment, 23,* 277–281.

Paddock, R. C., & Ives, M. (2018, July 10). Freed from Thai cave, boys may still face health problems. *The New York Times.* https://www.nytimes.com/2018/07/10/world/asia/thai-cave-boys-health.html

Paddock, R. C., & Jirenuwat, R. (2018, July 27). As search for Thai boys lost in cave hits day 5, a nation holds its breath. *The New York Times.* https://www.nytimes.com/2018/06/27/world/asia/thailand-cave-soccer-search.html

Paddock, R. C., Suhartono, M., & Ives, M. (2018, July 6). Thai cave rescue will be a murky and desperate ordeal, divers say. *The New York Times.* https://www.nytimes.com/2018/07/06/world/asia/thai-cave-rescue-divers.html

Pagnini, F., Bercovitz, K., & Langer, E. (2016). Perceived control and mindfulness: Implications for clinical practice. *Journal of Psychotherapy Integration, 26,* 91–102. https://doi.org/10.1037/int0000035

Paikoff, R. L., & Brooks-Gunn, J. (1991). Do parent–child relationships change during puberty? *Psychological Bulletin, 110,* 47–66.

Palermo, E. (2013, June 25). How far away is lightening? *LiveScience.* https://www.livescience.com/37734-how-far-away-is-lightning-distance.html

Palmer, C. (2020, May 11). Researchers mobilize to study impact of COVID-19. *Monitor on Psychology.* https://www.apa.org/monitor/2020/06/covid-researchers

Palombo, D. J., Sheldon, S., & Levine, B. (2018). Individual differences in autobiographical memory. *Trends in Cognitive Sciences, 22*(7), 583–597. https://doi.org/10.1016/j.tics.2018.04.007

Paluck, E. L., & Clark, C. S. (2020). Can playing together help us live together? *Science, 369*(6505), 769–770.

Paniagua, F. A. (2018). *ICD-10 versus DSM-5 on cultural issues. Sage Open, 8*(1). https://doi.org//10.1177/2158244018756165

Panza, G. A., Taylor, B. A., Thompson, P. D., White, C. M., & Pescatello, L. S. (2019). Physical activity intensity and subjective well-being in healthy adults. *Journal of Health Psychology, 24*(9), 1257–1267. https://doi.org/10.1177/1359105317691589

Papadatou-Pastou, M., Ntolka, E., Schmitz, J., Martin, M., Munafò, M. R., Ocklenburg, S., & Paracchini, S. (2020). Human handedness: A meta-analysis. *Psychological Bulletin, 146*(6), 481–524. https://doi.org/10.1037/bul0000229

Pape, H.-C., & Pare, D. (2010). Plastic synaptic networks of the amygdala for the acquisition, expression, and extinction of conditioned fear. *Physiological Review, 90,* 419–463.

Pappa, S., Ntella, V., Giannakas, T., Giannakoulis, V. G., Papoutsi, E., & Katsaounou, P. (2020). Prevalence of depression, anxiety, and insomnia among healthcare workers during the COVID-19 pandemic: A systematic review and meta-analysis. *Brain, Behavior, and Immunity, 88,* 901–907. https://doi.org/10.1016/j.bbi.2020.05.026

Pappas, S. (2020, April 1). What do we really know about kids and screens? *Monitor on Psychology, 51*(3), 42–48. https://www.apa.org/monitor/2020/04/cover-kids-screens

Paris, J. (2014). Modernity and narcissistic personality disorder. *Personality Disorders: Theory, Research, and Treatment, 5,* 220–226. https://doi.org/10.1037/a0028580

Parivesh, A., Barseghyan, H., Delot, E., & Vilain, E. (2019). Translating genomics to the clinical diagnosis of disorders/differences of sex development. In B. Capel (Ed.), *Current Topics in Developmental Biology, 134.* (pp.317–375). Academic Press. https://doi.org/10.1016/bs.ctdb.2019.01.005

Park, S. Q., Kahnt, T., Dogan, A., Strang, S., Fehr, E., & Tobler, P. N. (2017). A neural link between generosity and happiness. *Nature Communications, 8,* 15964. https://doi.org/10.1038/ncomms15964

Parker, C. B. (2016, June 15). *Stanford big data study finds racial disparities in Oakland, Calif., police behavior, offers solutions* [Press release]. https://news.stanford.edu/2016/06/15/stanford-big-data-study-finds-racial-disparities-oakland-calif-police-behavior-offers-solutions/

Parkin, S. (2018, March 4). Has dopamine got us hooked on tech? *The Guardian.* https://www.theguardian.com/technology/2018/mar/04/has-dopamine-got-us-hooked-on-tech-facebook-apps-addiction

Parks, C. D., & Tasca, G. A. (Eds.). (2021). The psychology of groups:

The intersection of social psychology and psychotherapy research. *American Psychological Association.* https://doi.org/10.1037/0000201-000

Parmar, M., Grealish, S., & Henchcliffe, C. (2020). The future of stem cell therapies for Parkinson disease. *Nature Reviews Neuroscience,* 21, 103–115. https://doi.org/10.1038/s41583-019-0257-7

Parmentier, F. B. R., & Andrés, P. (2010). The involuntary capture of attention by sound: Novelty and postnovelty distraction in young and older adults. *Experimental Psychology, 57,* 68–76.

Parrill, F. (2020). Using cognitive science to teach cognitive science: Embodied teaching and learning in the cognitive science classroom. *Scholarship of Teaching and Learning in Psychology.* Advance online publication. https://doi.org/10.1037/stl0000196

Parrott, A. C. (2015). Why all stimulant drugs are damaging to recreational users: An empirical overview and psychobiological explanation. *Human Psychopharmacology: Clinical and Experimental, 30*(4), 213–224.

Partanen, E., Kujala, T., Näätänen, R., Liitola, A., Sambeth, A., & Huotilainen, M. (2013). Learning-induced neural plasticity of speech processing before birth. *Proceedings of the National Academy of Sciences, 110*(37), 15145–15150.

Parth, K., & Loeffler-Stastka, H. (2015). Psychoanalytic core competence. *Frontiers in Psychology, 6, Article 356.* https://doi.org/10.3389/fpsyg.2015.00356

Partisan Pictures (Producer). (2012). *Cesar Millan: The real story* [DVD]. https://www.amazon.com/Cesar-Millan-Real-Story-Milan/dp/B00A4Y61SC

Pasanen, T. P., Tyrväinen, L., & Korpela, K. M. (2014). The relationship between perceived health and physical activity indoors, outdoors in built environments, and outdoors in nature. *Applied Psychology: Health and Well-Being, 6,* 324–346.

Pashler, H., Rohrer, D., Cepeda, N. J., & Carpenter, S. K. (2007). Enhancing learning and retarding forgetting: Choices and consequences. *Psychonomic Bulletin & Review, 14,* 187–193.

Patihis, L. (2016). Individual differences and correlates of highly superior autobiographical memory. *Memory, 24,* 961–978. https://doi.org/10.1080/09658211.2015.1061011

Patihis, L., Frenda, S. J., LePort, A. K., Petersen, N., Nichols, R. M., Stark, C. E. L., McGaugh, J. L., & Loftus, E. F. (2013). False memories in highly superior autobiographical memory individuals. *Proceedings of the National Academy of Sciences, 110,*

20947–20952. https://doi.org/10.1073/pnas.1314373110

Patihis, L., Ho, L. Y., Loftus, E. F., & Herrera, M. E. (2019). Memory experts' beliefs about repressed memory. *Memory.* https://doi.org/10.1080/09658211.2018.1532521

Patihis, L., Ho, L. Y., Tingen, I. W., Lilienfeld, S. O., & Loftus, E. F. (2014). Are the "Memory Wars" over? A scientist-practitioner gap in beliefs about repressed memory. *Psychological Science, 25,* 519–530.

Patihis, L., Lilienfeld, S. O., Ho, L. Y., & Loftus, E. F. (2014). Unconscious repressed memory is scientifically questionable. *Psychological Science, 25,* 1967–1968.

Patihis, L., & Pendergrast, M. H. (2019). Reports of recovered memories of abuse in therapy in a large age-representative U.S. national sample: Therapy type and decade comparisons. *Clinical Psychological Science, 7*(1), 3–21. https://doi.org/10.1177/2167702618773315

Patil, K., Pressnitzer, D., Shamma, S., & Elhilali, M. (2012). Music in our ears: The biological bases of musical timbre perception. *PLOS Computational Biology, 8*(11), e1002759. https://doi.org/10.1371/journal.pcbi.1002759

Patorno, E., Bohn, R. L., Wahl, P. M., Avorn, J., Patrick, A. R., Liu, J., & Schneeweiss, S. (2010). Anticonvulsant medications and the risk of suicide, attempted suicide, or violent death. *Journal of the American Medical Association, 303,* 1401–1409.

Patrick, M. E., & Schulenberg, J. E. (2014). Prevalence and predictors of adolescent alcohol use and binge drinking in the United States. *Alcohol Research: Current Reviews, 35,* 193–200.

Pauls, D. L., Abramovitch, A., Rauch, S. L., & Geller, D. A. (2014). Obsessive compulsive disorder: An integrative genetic and neurobiological perspective. *Nature Reviews Neuroscience, 15,* 410–424.

Pavlos, P., Vasilios, N., Antonia, A., Dimitrios, K., Georgios, K., & Georgios, A. (2009). Evaluation of young smokers and non-smokers with electrogustometry and contact endoscopy. *BMC Ear, Nose and Throat Disorders, 9*(9). https://doi.org/10.1186/1472-6815-9-9

Pavlov, I. (1906). The scientific investigation of the psychical faculties or processes in the higher animals. *Science, 24,* 613–619.

Pavlov, I. (1927/1960). *Conditioned reflexes.* Dover.

Payne, E. Ford, D., & Morris, J. (2015, February 25). Jury finds Eddie Ray Routh guilty in "American Sniper" case. *CNN.* http://www.cnn.com/2015/02/24/us/american-sniper-chris-kyle-trial/

Pazzaglia, M. (2015). Body and odors not just molecules, after all. *Current Directions in Psychological Science, 24,* 329–333.

PBS. (2005, January 27). Kinsey. *American Experience.* http://www.pbs.org/wgbh/amex/kinsey/peopleevents/p_kinsey.html

Peake, J. M., Kerr, G., & Sullivan, J. P. (2018). A critical review of consumer wearables, mobile applications, and equipment for providing biofeedback, monitoring stress, and sleep in physically active populations. *Frontiers in Physiology, 9,* Article 743. https://doi.org/10.3389/fphys.2018.00743

Pebsworth, P., & Radhakrishna, S. (2020). Using conditioned taste aversion to reduce human–nonhuman primate conflict: A comparison of four potentially illness-inducing drugs. *Applied Animal Behaviour Science, 225,* Article 104948. https://doi.org/10.1016/j.applanim.2020.104948

Pedersen, C. B., Bybjerg-Grauholm, J., Pedersen, M. G., Grove, J., Agerbo, E., Baekvad-Hansen, M., Poulsen, J. B., Hansen, C. S., McGrath, J. J., Als, T. D., Goldstein, J. I., Neale, B. M., Daly, M. J., Hougaard, D. M., Mors, O., Nordentoft, M., Børglum, A. D., Werge, T., & Mortensen, P. B. (2018). The iPSYCH2012 case–cohort sample: New directions for unravelling genetic and environmental architectures of severe mental disorders. *Molecular Psychiatry, 23*(1), 6–14. https://doi.org/10.1038/mp.2017.196

Peever, J., Luppi, P. H., & Montplaisir, J. (2014). Breakdown in REM sleep circuitry underlies REM sleep behavior disorder. *Trends in Neuroscience, 7,* 279–288.

Pejtersen, J. H., Viinholt, B. C. A., & Hansen, H. (2020). Feedback-informed treatment: A systematic review and meta-analysis of the partners for change outcome management system. *Journal of Counseling Psychology, 67*(6), 723–735. https://doi.org/10.1037/cou0000420

Pelosi, A. J. (2019). Personality and fatal diseases: Revisiting a scientific scandal. *Journal of Health Psychology, 24*(4), 421–439. https://doi.org/10.1177/1359105318822045

Penfield, W., & Boldrey E. (1937). Somatic motor and sensory representation in the cerebral cortex of man as studied by electrical stimulation. *Brain, 60,* 389–443.

Pennisi, E. (2019, January 7). Dog breeds really do have distinct personalities—and they're rooted in DNA. *Science.* https://www.sciencemag.org/news/2019/01/dog-breeds-really-do-have-distinct-personalities-and-they-re-rooted-dna

Pennisi, E. (2020, April 16). Male lemurs may spread fruity 'love potions'

with their tails. *Science: Plants & Animals.* https://doi.org/10.1126/science.abc2923

Pennycook, G., McPhetres, J., Zhang, Y., Lu, J. G., & Rand, D. G. (2020). Fighting COVID-19 misinformation on social media: Experimental evidence for a scalable accuracy-nudge intervention. *Psychological Science.* https://doi.org/10.1177/0956797620939054.

Peplau, L. A. (2003). Human sexuality: How do men and women differ? *Current Directions in Psychological Science, 12,* 37–40.

Perkins, K. A., Karelitz, J. L., Conklin, C. A., Sayette, M. A., & Giedgowd, G. E. (2010). Acute negative affect relief from smoking depends on the affect measure and situation, but not on nicotine. *Biological Psychiatry, 67,* 707–714.

Perlin, M. L. (2017). The insanity defense: Nine myths that will not go away. https://digitalcommons.nyls.edu/fac_articles_chapters/1128

Perone, P., Becker, D. V., & Tybur, J. M. (2020). Visual disgust elicitors produce an attentional blink independent of contextual and trait-level pathogen avoidance. *Emotion.* Advance online publication. https://doi.org/10.1037/emo0000751

Perry, G., Brannigan, A., Wanner, R. A., & Stam, H. (2020). Credibility and incredulity in Milgram's obedience experiments: A reanalysis of an unpublished test. *Social Psychology Quarterly, 83*(1), 88–106. https://doi.org/10.1177/0190272519861952

Perry, N. B., Dollar, J. M., Calkins, S. D., Keane, S. P., & Shanahan, L. (2018). Childhood self-regulation as a mechanism through which early over-controlling parenting is associated with adjustment in preadolescence. *Developmental Psychology, 54*(8), 1542–1554. https://doi.org/10.1037/dev0000536

Peschel, S. K., Feeling, N. R., Vögele, C., Kaess, M., Thayer, J. F., & Koenig, J. (2016). A systematic review on heart rate variability in bulimia nervosa. *Neuroscience & Biobehavioral Reviews, 63,* 78–97. https://doi.org/10.1016/j.neubiorev.2016.06.019

Peter-Hagene, L. C., & Ullman, S. E. (2018). Longitudinal effects of sexual assault victims' drinking and self-blame on posttraumatic stress disorder. *Journal of Interpersonal Violence, 33*(1), 83–93. https://doi.org/10.1177/0886260516636394

Peters, A. (2019, February 27). Why do we crave sweets when we're stressed? *Scientific American.* https://www.scientificamerican.com/article/why-do-we-crave-sweets-when-were-stressed/

Peters, W. (1971). *A class divided: Then and now.* Yale University Press.

Peterson, G. B. (2000). The discovery of shaping: B. F. Skinner's big surprise. *The Clicker Journal: The Magazine for Animal Trainers, 43,* 6–13.

Peterson, G. B. (2004). A day of great illumination: B. F. Skinner's discovery of shaping. *Journal of the Experimental Analysis of Behavior, 82,* 317–328.

Peterson, L. R., & Peterson, M. J. (1959). Short-term retention of individual verbal items. *Journal of Experimental Psychology, 58,* 193–198.

Peterson, M. J., Meagher, R. B., Jr., & Ellsbury, S. W. (1970). Repetition effects in sensory memory. *Journal of Experimental Psychology, 84,* 15–23.

Petit, D., Pennestri, M. H., Paquet, J., Desautels, A., Zadra, A., Vitaro, F., Tremblay, R. E., Boivin, M., & Montplaisir, J. (2015). Childhood sleepwalking and sleep terrors: A longitudinal study of prevalence and familial aggregation. *JAMA Pediatrics, 169,* 653–658. https://doi.org/10.1001/jamapediatrics.2015.127

Petitto, L. A., & Marentette, P. F. (1991). Babbling in the manual mode: Evidence for the ontogeny of language. *Science, 251,* 1493–1496.

Petronis, A. (2004). The origin of schizophrenia: Genetic thesis, epigenetic antithesis, and resolving synthesis. *Biological Psychiatry, 55,* 965–970.

Petty, J. K., Henry, M. C., Nance, M. L., Ford, H. R., & APSA Board of Governors. (2019, February 15). *Firearm injuries and children: Position statement of the American Pediatric Surgical Association.* https://eapsa.org/getattachment/Resources/For-Professionals/APSA-Statements-Guidelines/American-Pediatric-Surgical-Association-Firearm-Statement-2018.pdf

Petty, R. E., & Cacioppo, J. T. (1986). The elaboration likelihood model of persuasion. *Advances in Experimental Social Psychology, 19,* 123–205.

Pew Research Center. (2019, June 12). *Mobile fact sheet.* https://www.pewinternet.org/fact-sheet/mobile/

Pfeifer, C. (2012). Physical attractiveness, employment and earnings. *Applied Economics Letters, 19,* 505–510.

Pfungst, O. (1911). *Clever Hans (the horse of Mr. Von Osten): A contribution to experimental, animal, and human psychology* (C. L. Rahn, Trans.). Holt.

Phelps, S. M., & Wedow, R. (2019, August 29). What genetics is teaching us about sexuality. *The New York Times.* https://www.nytimes.com/2019/08/29/opinion/genetics-sexual-orientation-study.html

Phillips, R. G., & LeDoux, J. E. (1992). Differential contribution of amygdala and hippocampus to cued and contextual fear conditioning. *Behavioral Neuroscience, 106,* 274–285.

Phillips, T., Time Out New York contributors, & Picht, J. (2018, August 1). West Indian Day Parade 2019 guide. *Time Out New York.* https://www.timeout.com/newyork/west-indian-american-day-carnival-new-york

Philpot, R., Liebst, L. S., Levine, M., Bernasco, W., & Lindegaard, M. R. (2020). Would I be helped? Cross-national CCTV footage shows that intervention is the norm in public conflicts. *American Psychologist, 75*(1), 66–75. https://doi.org/10.1037/amp0000469

Piaget, J. (1936/1952). *The origins of intelligence in children.* Norton.

Piazza, E. A., Hasenfratz, L., Hasson, U., & Lew-Williams, C. (2020). Infant and adult brains are coupled to the dynamics of natural communication. *Psychological Science, 31*(1), 6–17. https://doi.org/10.1177/0956797619878698

Pich, E. M., Pagliusi, S. R., Tessari, M., Talabot-Ayer, D., Van Huijsduijnen, R. H., & Chiamulera, C. (1997). Common neural substrates for the addictive properties of nicotine and cocaine. *Science, 275,* 83–86.

Pickren, W. E., & Burchett, C. (2014). Making psychology inclusive: A history of education and training for diversity in American psychology. In F. T. L. Leong, L. Comas-Díaz, G. C. Nagayama Hall, V. C. McLoyd, & J. E. Trimble (Eds.), *APA handbooks in psychology. APA handbook of multicultural psychology: Vol. 2. Applications and training.* (pp. 3–18). American Psychological Association.

Pierre, J. M. (2012). Mental illness and mental health: Is the glass half empty or half full? *Canadian Journal of Psychiatry, 57,* 651–658.

Pietromonaco, P. R., & Collins, N. L. (2017). Interpersonal mechanisms linking close relationships to health. *American Psychologist, 72*(6), 531–542. https://doi.org/10.1037/amp0000129

Pike, K. M., & Dunne, P. E. (2015). The rise of eating disorders in Asia: A review. *Journal of Eating Disorders, 3,* Article 33. https://doi.org/10.1186/s40337-015-0070-2

Pilcher, J. J., & Morris, D. M. (2020). Sleep and organizational behavior: Implications for workplace productivity and safety. *Frontiers in Psychology, 11,* Article 45. https://doi.org/10.3389/fpsyg.2020.00045

Pines, A. (2011). Male menopause: Is it a real clinical syndrome? *Climacteric, 14,* 15–17.

Pinker, S. (1994). *The language instinct.* Harper Perennial.

Pinker, S. (2007). *The stuff of thought: Language as a window into human nature.* Penguin Books Ltd.

Pinkstone, J. (2020, April 29). Eating meat may IMPROVE mental health and one in three vegetarians are depressed, study suggests. *Daily Mail.* https://www.dailymail.co.uk/sciencetech/article-8270125/Eating-meat-improves-mental-health-study-claims.html

Pinquart, M., & Kauser, R. (2018). Do the associations of parenting styles with behavior problems and academic achievement vary by culture? Results from a meta-analysis. *Cultural Diversity and Ethnic Minority Psychology, 24*(1), 75–100. https://doi.org/10.1037/cdp0000149

Pinto, Y., Neville, D. A., Otten, M., Corballis, P. M., Lamme, V. A. F., de Haan, E. H. F., Foschi, N., & Fabri, M. (2017). Split brain: Divided perception but undivided consciousness. *Brain, 140,* 1231–1237. https://doi.org/10.1093/brain/aww358

Pirnia, T., Joshi, S. H., Leaver, A. M., Vasavada, M., Njau, S., Woods, R. P., Espinoza, R., & Narr, K. L. (2016). Electroconvulsive therapy and structural neuroplasticity in neocortical, limbic and paralimbic cortex. *Translational Psychiatry, 6,* Article e832. https://doi.org/10.1038/tp.2016.102

Pisano, S., Muratori, P., Senese, V. P., Gorga, C., Siciliano, M., Carotenuto, M., Iuliano, R., Bravaccio, C., Signoriello, S., Gritti, A., Pascotto, A., & Catone, G. (2019). Phantom phone signals in youths: Prevalence, correlates and relation to psychopathology. *PLOS ONE, 14*(1), e0210095. https://doi.org/10.1371/journal.pone.0210095

Pittenger, D. J. (1993, November). Measuring the MBTI and coming up short. *Journal of Career Planning & Placement, 54*(1), 48–52.

Pittenger, D. J. (2005). Cautionary comments regarding the Myers-Briggs Type Indicator. *Consulting Psychology Journal: Practice and Research, 57,* 210–221.

Pittman, M., & Reich, B. (2016). Social media and loneliness: Why an Instagram picture may be worth more than a thousand Twitter words. *Computers in Human Behavior, 62,* 155–167. https://doi.org/10.1016/j.chb.2016.03.084

Pitts, M. A., Lutsyshyna, L. A., & Hillyard, S. A. (2018). The relationship between attention and consciousness: An expanded taxonomy and implications for "no-report" paradigms. *Philosophical Transactions of the Royal Society B: Biological Sciences, 373*(1755), Article 20170348. https://doi.org/10.1098/rstb.2017.0348

Plana-Ripoll, O., Pedersen, C. B., Holtz, Y., Benros, M. E., Dalsgaard, S., De Jonge, P., Fan, C. C., Degenhardt, L., Ganna, A., Greve, A. N., Gunn, J., Iburg, K. M., Kessing, L. V., Lee, B. K., Lim,

C. C. W., Mors, O., Nordentoft, M., Prior, A., Roest, A. M., . . . McGrath, J. J. (2019). Exploring comorbidity within mental disorders among a Danish national population. *JAMA Psychiatry, 76*(3), 259–270. https://doi.org/10.1001/jamapsychiatry.2018.3658

Plante, C., & Anderson, C. A. (2017, February). Global warming and violent behavior. *Observer, 30*(2). https://www.psychologicalscience.org/observer/global-warming-and-violent-behavior

Plata, M. (2017, December 19). 3 narcissistic traits in Kylo Ren [Web log post]. *Psychology Today.* https://www.psychologytoday.com/blog/the-gen-y-psy/201712/3-narcissistic-traits-in-kylo-ren

Platt, J. R. (2011, December 27). Lions vs. cattle: Taste aversion could solve African predator problem [Web log post]. *Scientific American.* http://blogs.scientificamerican.com/extinction-countdown/lions-vs-cattle-taste-aversion/

Platt, J. R. (2015, June 24). African lion populations drop 42 percent in past 21 years [Web log post]. *Scientific American.* http://blogs.scientificamerican.com/extinction-countdown/african-lion-populations-drop-42-percent-in-past-21-years/

Plessen, C. Y., Franken, F. R., Ster, C., Schmid, R. R., Wolfmayr, C., Mayer, A.-M., Sobisch, M., Kathofer, M., Rattner, K., Kotlyar, E., Maierwieser, R. J., & Tran, U. S. (2020). Humor styles and personality: A systematic review and meta-analysis on the relations between humor styles and the Big Five personality traits. *Personality and Individual Differences, 154,* Article 109676. https://doi.org/10.1016/j.paid.2019.109676

Plomin, R., & DeFries, J. C. (1998). Genetics of cognitive abilities and disabilities. *Scientific American, 218*(5), 62–69.

Plomin, R., DeFries, J. C., Knopik, V. S., & Neiderhiser, J. M. (2013). *Behavioral genetics* (6th ed.). Worth Publishers.

Plomin, R., DeFries, J. C., Knopik, V. S., & Neiderhiser, J. M. (2016). Top 10 replicated findings from behavioral genetics. *Perspectives on Psychological Science, 11,* 3–23. https://doi.org/10.1177/1745691615617439

Poels, K., & Dewitte, S. (2019). The role of emotions in advertising: A call to action. *Journal of Advertising, 48*(1), 81–90. https://doi.org/10.1080/00913367.2019.1579688

Polat, B. (2017). Before attachment theory: Separation research at the Tavistock Clinic, 1948–1956. *Journal of the History of the Behavioral Sciences, 53,* 48–70. https://doi.org/10.1002/jhbs.21834

Polderman, T. J., Benyamin, B., de Leeuw, C. A., Sullivan, P. F., van

Bochoven, A., Visscher, P. M., & Posthuma, D. (2015). Meta-analysis of the heritability of human traits based on fifty years of twin studies. *Nature Genetics, 47*(7), 702–709.

Poly, C., Massaro, J. M., Seshadri, S., Wolf, P. A., Cho, E., Krall, E., Jacques, P. F., & Au, R. (2011). The relation of dietary choline to cognitive performance and white-matter hyperintensity in the Framingham Offspring Cohort. *American Journal of Clinical Nutrition, 94*(6), 1584–1591. https://doi.org/10.3945/ajcn.110.008938

Pongrácz, P., Ujvári, V., Faragó, T., Miklósi, Á., & Péter, A. (2017). Do you see what I see? The difference between dog and human visual perception may affect the outcome of experiments. *Behavioural Processes, 140,* 53–60. https://doi.org/10.1016/j.beproc.2017.04.002

Poole, S. (2016, April 20). 20 things you probably didn't know about Harriet Tubman. *The Atlanta Journal-Constitution.* http://www.ajc.com/news/lifestyles/think-you-know-everything-about-harriet-tubman-thi/nq8Xd/

Pope, K. S., & Wedding, D. (2014). Contemporary challenges and controversies. In R. J. Corsini & D. Wedding (Eds.), *Current psychotherapies* (10th ed., pp. 569–604). Brooks/Cole, Cengage Learning.

Popova, S., Lange, S., Probst, C., Gmel, G., & Rehm, J. (2017). Estimation of national, regional, and global prevalence of alcohol use during pregnancy and fetal alcohol syndrome: A systematic review and meta-analysis. *The Lancet Global Health, 5,* 290–299. https://doi.org/10.1016/S2214-109X(17)30021-9

Population Reference Bureau (PRP). (2020, September 22). *How many people in the United States are experiencing homelessness?* https://www.prb.org/how-many-people-in-the-united-states-are-experiencing-homelessness/#

Porsch, R. M., Middeldorp, C. M., Cherny, S. S., Krapohl, E., van Beijsterveldt, C. E. M., Loukola, A., Korhonen, T., Pulkkinen, L., Corley, R., Rhee, S., Kaprio, J., Rose, R. R., Hewitt, J. K., Sham, P., Plomin, R., Boomsma, D. I., & Bartels, M. (2016). Longitudinal heritability of childhood aggression. *American Journal of Medical Genetics Part B: Neuropsychiatric Genetics, 171*(5), 697–707. https://doi.org/10.1002/ajmg.b.32420

Porter, R. H., & Winberg, J. (1999). Unique salience of maternal breast odors for newborn infants. *Neuroscience & Biobehavioral Reviews, 23,* 439–449.

Portnuff, C. D. F. (2016). Reducing the risk of music-induced hearing loss from overuse of portable listening

devices: Understanding the problems and establishing strategies for improving awareness in adolescents. *Adolescent Health, Medicine and Therapeutics, 7,* 27–35. https://doi.org/10.2147/AHMT.S74103

Posey, A. J., & Cushing, J. (2019). Little Freudian slippage: Coverage of the psychodynamic perspective in the undergraduate personality course. *Teaching of Psychology, 46*(3), 251–259. https://doi.org/10.1177/0098628319853941

Postuma, R. B., Gagnon, J. F., Vendette, M., Fantini, M. L., Massicotte-Marquez, J., & Montplaisir, J. (2009). Quantifying the risk of neurodegenerative disease in idiopathic REM sleep behavior disorder. *Neurology, 72,* 1296–1300.

Pottala, J. V., Yaffe, K., Robinson, J. G., Espeland, M. A., Wallace, R., & Harris, W. S. (2014). Higher RBC EPA + DHA corresponds with larger total brain and hippocampal volumes: WHIMS-MRI Study. *Neurology, 82*(5), 435–442.

Potter, R. H. (2006). "As firecrackers to atom bombs": Kinsey, science, and authority. *Sexuality and Culture, 10,* 29–38.

Potter, S., Drewelies, J., Wagner, J., Duezel, S., Brose, A., Demuth, I., Steinhagen-Thiessen, E., Lindenberger, U., Wagner, G. G., & Gerstorf, D. (2020). Trajectories of multiple subjective well-being facets across old age: The role of health and personality. *Psychology and Aging, 35*(6), 894–909. https://doi.org/10.1037/pag0000459

Poulter, S. (2012, October 18). Cadbury cuts the size of Dairy Milk chocolate bar (but keeps the price exactly the same!). *Daily Mail.* https://www.dailymail.co.uk/news/article-2219775/Cadbury-cuts-size-Dairy-Milk-chocolate-bar-keeps-price-exactly-same.html

Poulton, E. C. (1967). Population norms of top sensory magnitudes and SS Stevens' exponents. *Perception & Psychophysics, 2,* 312–316.

Powell, L. H., Shahabi, L., & Thoresen, C. E. (2003). Religion and spirituality: Linkages to physical health. *American Psychologist, 58,* 36–52.

Powell, R. A. (2010). Little Albert still missing. *American Psychologist, 65,* 299–300.

Powell, R. A., Digdon, N., Harris, B., & Smithson, C. (2014). Correcting the record on Watson, Rayner and Little Albert: Albert Barger as "Psychology's Lost Boy." *American Psychologist, 69,* 600–611.

Powers, A., Cross, D., Fani, N., & Bradley, B. (2015). PTSD, emotion dysregulation, and dissociative symptoms in a highly traumatized sample. *Journal of Psychiatric Research, 61,* 174–179.

Pratte, M. S. (2018). Iconic memories die a sudden death. *Psychological Science, 29*(6), 877–887. https://doi.org/10.1177/09567976177471

Prescott, A. T., Sargent, J. D., & Hull, J. G. (2018). Metaanalysis of the relationship between violent video game play and physical aggression over time. *Proceedings of the National Academy of Sciences, 115*(40), 9882–9888. https://doi.org/10.1073/pnas.1611617114

Presse, N., Belleville, S., Gaudreau, P., Greenwood, C. E., Kergoat, M. J., Morais, J. A., Payette, H., Shatenstein, B., & Ferland, G. (2013). Vitamin K status and cognitive function in healthy older adults. *Neurobiology of Aging, 34*(12), 2777–2783. https://doi.org/10.1016/j.neurobiolaging.2013.05.031

Pressman, S. D., Cohen, S., Miller, G. E., Barkin, A., Rabin, B. S., & Treanor, J. J. (2005). Loneliness, social network size, and immune response to influenza vaccination in college freshmen. *Health Psychology, 24*(3), 297–306.

Pribis, P., Bailey, R. N., Russell, A. A., Kilsby, M. A., Hernandez, M., Craig, W. J., Grajales T., Shavlik, D. J., & Sabatè, J. (2012). Effects of walnut consumption on cognitive performance in young adults. *British Journal of Nutrition, 107*(9), 1393–1401. https://doi.org/10.1017/S0007114511004302

Prieto, L. R., Siegel, Z. D., & Kaiser, D. J. (2021). One fish, two fish; red fish (or green fish?): Assisting students with color vision deficiency. *Teaching of Psychology, 48*(1), 90–94. https://doi.org/10.1177/0098628320959946

PrisonExperiment. (2018, June 26). Stanford Prison Experiment: Prisoner 8612's emotional breakdown [Video file]. https://www.youtube.com/watch?v=kXOM8IK4HOs

Pro Football Hall of Fame. (n.d.). Harry Carson enshrinement speech. http://www.profootballhof.com/players/harry-carson/enshrinement/

Prochaska, J. O., & Norcross, J. C. (2018). *Systems of psychotherapy* (9th ed.). Oxford University Press.

Provençal, N., Booij, L., & Tremblay, R. E. (2015). The developmental origins of chronic physical aggression: Biological pathways triggered by early life adversity. *Journal of Experimental Biology, 218*(1), 123–133.

Prunas, A., Di Pierro, R., Huemer, J., & Tagini, A. (2019). Defense mechanisms, remembered parental caregiving, and adult attachment style. *Psychoanalytic Psychology, 36*(1), 64–72. https://doi.org/10.1037/pap0000158

Przybylski, A. K., & Weinstein, N. (2019). Violent video game

engagement is not associated with adolescents' aggressive behaviour: Evidence from a registered report. *Royal Society Open Science, 6*(2), 171474. https://doi.org/10.1098/rsos.171474

PubMed Health. (2016, August 17). How does our sense of taste work? https://www.ncbi.nlm.nih.gov/pubmedhealth/PMH0072592/

Puig, J., Englund, M. M., Simpson, J. A., & Collins, W. A. (2013). Predicting adult physical illness from infant attachment: A prospective longitudinal study. *Health Psychology, 32*, 409–417.

Pullum, G. K. (1991). *The great Eskimo vocabulary hoax and other irreverent essays on the study of language.* University of Chicago Press.

Purves, D., Augustine, G. J., Fitzpatrick, D., Hall, W. C., LaMantia, A.-S., Mooney, R. D., Platt, M. L., & White, L. E. (Eds.) (2018). *Neuroscience* (6th ed.). Oxford University Press.

Qian, M. K., Quinn, P. C., Heyman, G. D., Pascalis, O., Fu, G., & Lee, K. (2017). Perceptual individuation training (but not mere exposure) reduces implicit racial bias in preschool children. *Developmental Psychology, 53*(5), 845–859.

Quick, V. B. S., Wang, B., & State, M. W. (2020). Leveraging large genomic datasets to illuminate the pathobiology of autism spectrum disorders. *Neuropsychopharmacology, 46*, 55–69. https://doi.org/10.1038/s41386-020-0768-y

Quinn, O. W. (1963). The public image of the family. In D. Rosenthal (Ed.), *The Genain quadruplets: A case study and theoretical analysis of heredity and environment in schizophrenia* (pp. 355–372). Basic Books.

Quintana, D. S., & Guastella, A. J. (2020). An allostatic theory of oxytocin. *Trends in Cognitive Sciences, 24*, 515–528. https://doi.org/10.1016/j.tics.2020.03.008

Rabkin, J. G., & Struening, E. L. (1976). Life events, stress, and illness. *Science, 194*, 1013–1020.

RACHELSTARLIVE. (2018, January 11). I feel nothing—anhedonia [Video file]. https://www.youtube.com/watch?v=5oD7gKfCL6w

Radua, J., & Mataix-Cols, D. (2009). Voxel-wise meta-analysis of grey matter changes in obsessive-compulsive disorder. *British Journal of Psychiatry, 195*, 393–402.

Raevuori, A., Keski-Rahkonen, A., & Hoek, H. W. (2014). A review of eating disorders in males. *Current Opinion in Psychiatry, 27*, 426–430.

Ragelienė, T., & Grønhøj, A. (2020). The influence of peers' and siblings' on children's and adolescents' healthy eating behavior. A systematic literature review. *Appetite, 148*(1), Article 104592. https://doi.org/10.1016/j.appet.2020.104592

Rahhal, N. (2020, March 25). New York enlists more than 6,000 therapists to man free mental health care hotline amid coronavirus lockdown that's left millions in the state isolated and anxious. *DailyMail.* https://www.dailymail.co.uk/health/article-8149961/They-anxiety-disorder-Now-comes-pandemic.html

Raichlen, D. A., & Alexander, G. E. (2017). Adaptive capacity: An evolutionary neuroscience model linking exercise, cognition, and brain health. *Trends in Neurosciences, 40*, 408–421. https://doi.org/10.116/j.tins.2017.05.001

Raichlen, D. A., & Alexander, G. E. (2020, January). Why your brain needs exercise. *Scientific American, 322*, 1, 26–31.

Raine, A., Lencz, T., Bihrle, S., LaCasse, L., & Colletti, P. (2000). Reduced prefrontal gray matter volume and reduced autonomic activity in antisocial personality disorder. *Archives of General Psychiatry, 57*, 119–127.

Rainville, P., Duncan, G. H., Price, D. D., Carrier, B., & Bushnell, M. C. (1997, August 15). Pain affect encoded in human anterior cingulate but not somatosensory cortex. *Science, 277* (5328), 968–971.

Ramachandran, V. S., & Rogers-Ramachandran, D. (2008). Right side up. *Scientific American, 18*, 22–25.

Ramchandran, K., & Hauser, J. (2010). Phantom limb pain #212. *Journal of Palliative Medicine, 13*, 1285–1287.

Ramirez, G., Shaw, S. T., & Maloney, E. A. (2018). Math anxiety: Past research, promising interventions, and a new interpretation framework. *Educational Psychologist, 53*(3), 145–164. https://doi.org/10.1080/00461520.2018.1447384

Ramnerö, J., Molander, O., Lindner, P., & Carlbring, P. (2019). What can be learned about gambling from a learning perspective? A narrative review. *Nordic Psychology, 71*(4), 303–322. https://doi.org/10.1080/19012276.2019.1616320

Rancilio, A. (2020, April 14). Cats, dogs, Quillie the hedgehog source of comfort in crisis. *Associated Press.* https://apnews.com/article/4543537314c6e8a9a9643ddbecc5a9f9

Ransom, J. (2019, January 24). He spent 19 years in prison for murder. Now prosecutors say his confession was coerced. *The New York Times.* https://www.nytimes.com/2019/01/24/nyregion/huwe-burton-exoneration-bronx-murder.html

Raphelson, S. (2017, November 30). How the loss of U.S. psychiatric hospitals led to a mental health crisis. *NPR.* https://www.npr.org/2017/11/30/567477160/how-the-loss-of-u-s-psychiatric-hospitals-led-to-a-mental-health-crisis

Rapoport, R. (2020, December 23). "Every day is an emergency": The pandemic is worsening psychiatric bed shortages nationwide. *STAT.* https://www.statnews.com/2020/12/23/mental-health-covid19-psychiatric-beds/

Rasch, B., & Born, J. (2013). About sleep's role in memory. *Physiological Reviews, 93*, 681–766.

Rasmussen, A., Verkuilen, J., Jayawickreme, N., Wu, Z., & McCluskey, S. T. (2019). When did posttraumatic stress disorder get so many factors? Confirmatory factor models since *DSM–5. Clinical Psychological Science, 7*(2), 234–248. https://doi.org/10.1177/2167702618809370

Rasmussen, E. E., Strouse, G. A., Colwell, M. J., Johnson, C. R., Holiday, S., Brady, K., Flores, I., Troseth, G., Wright, H. D., Densley, R. L., & Norman, M. S. (2019). Promoting preschoolers' emotional competence through prosocial TV and mobile app use. *Media Psychology, 22*(1), 1–22. https://doi.org/10.1080/15213269.2018.1476890

Rathgeber, M., Bürkner, P. C., Schiller, E. M., & Holling, H. (2019). The efficacy of emotionally focused couples therapy and behavioral couples therapy: A meta-analysis. *Journal of Marital and Family Therapy, 45*(3), 447–463. https://doi.org/10.1111/jmft.12336

Ratiu, P., Talos, I. F., Haker, S., Lieberman, D., & Everett, P. (2004). The tale of Phineas Gage, digitally remastered. *Journal of Neurotrauma, 21*, 637–643.

Ratnesar, R. (2011, July/August). The menace within. *Stanford Magazine.* http://alumni.stanford.edu/get/page/magazine/article/?article_id=40741

Rauh, V. A. (2018). Polluting developing brains—EPA failure on chlorpyrifos. *New England Journal of Medicine, 378*, 1171–1174. https://doi.org/10.1056/NEJMp1716809h

Read, J., & Bentall, R. (2010). The effectiveness of electroconvulsive therapy: A literature review. *Epidemiologia e Psichiatria Sociale, 19*, 333–347.

Reas, E. (2014). Exercise counteracts genetic risk for Alzheimer's. *Scientific American Mind, 25*, 12.

Reber, S., Allen, R., & Reber, E. S. (2009). Appendix A: Simple phobias. In S. Reber, R. Allen, & E. S. Reber (Eds.), *The Penguin dictionary of psychology* (4th ed.). Penguin.

Reby, D., Levréro, F., Gustafsson, E., & Mathevon, N. (2016). Sex stereotypes influence adults' perception of babies' cries. *BioMed Central Psychology, 4*(19). https://doi.org/10.1186/s40359-016-0123-6

Rechtschaffen, A., & Bergmann, B. M. (1995). Sleep deprivation in the rat by the disk-over-water method. *Behavioural Brain Research, 69,* 55–63.

Reece, A. G., & Danforth, C. M. (2017). Instagram photos reveal predictive markers of depression. *EPJ Data Science, 6,* Article 15. https://doi.org/10.1140/epjds/s13688-017-0110-z

Rees, J. L. (2003). Genetics of hair and skin color. *Annual Review of Genetics, 37,* 67–90.

Reese, H. W. (2010). Regarding Little Albert. *American Psychologist, 65,* 300–301.

Regaiolli, B., Rizzo, A., Ottolini, G., Miletto Petrazzini, M. E., Spiezio, C., & Agrillo, C. (2019). Motion illusions as environmental enrichment for zoo animals: A preliminary investigation on lions (*Panthera leo*). *Frontiers in Psychology, 10,* 2220. https://doi.org/10.3389/fpsyg.2019.02220

Rehm, J., Shield, K. D., Roerecke, M., & Gmel, G. (2016). Modelling the impact of alcohol consumption on cardiovascular disease mortality for comparative risk assessments: An overview. *BMC Public Health, 16,* 363–372. https://doi.org/10.1186/s12889-016-3026-9

Reiche, E. M. V., Nunes, S. O. V., & Morimoto, H. K. (2004). Stress, depression, the immune system, and cancer. *The Lancet Oncology, 5,* 617–625.

Reichert, J. L., & Schöpf, V. (2018). Olfactory loss and regain: Lessons for neuroplasticity. *The Neuroscientist, 24,* 22–35. https://doi.org/10.1177/1073858417703910

Reifsteck, E. J., Gill, D. L., & Labban, J. D. (2016). "Athletes" and "exercisers": Understanding identity, motivation, and physical activity participation in former college athletes. *Sport, Exercise, and Performance Psychology, 5,* 25–38. https://doi.org/10.1037/spy0000046

Reisenzein, R. (1983). The Schachter theory of emotion: Two decades later. *Psychological Bulletin, 94,* 239–264.

Ren, J., Wu, Y. D., Chan, J. S., & Yan, J. H. (2013). Cognitive aging affects motor performance and learning. *Geriatrics & Gerontology International, 13,* 19–27. https://doi.org/10.1111/j.1447-0594.2012.00914.x

Reneman, L., Booij, J., de Bruin, K., Reitsma, J. B., de Wolff, F. A., Gunning, W. B., den Heeten, G. J., & van den Brink, W. (2001). Effects of dose, sex, and long-term abstention from use on toxic effects of MDMA (ecstasy) on brain serotonin neurons. *The Lancet, 358,* 1864–1869. https://doi.org/10.1016/S0140-6736(01)06888-X

Renner, M. J., & Mackin, R. S. (1998). A life stress instrument for classroom use. *Teaching of Psychology, 25,* 46–48.

Rentzeperis, I., Nikolaev, A. R., Kiper, D. C., & van Leeuwen, C. (2014). Distributed processing of color and form in the visual cortex. *Frontiers in Psychology, 5,* Art. 932.

Rethorn, Z. D., Pettitt, R. W., Dykstra, E., & Pettitt, C. D. (2020). Health and wellness coaching positively impacts individuals with chronic pain and pain-related interference. *PLOS ONE, 15*(7), Article e0236589. https://doi.org/10.1371/journal.pone.0236734

Reynolds, G., Field, A. P., & Askew, C. (2017). Learning to fear a second-order stimulus following vicarious learning. *Cognition and Emotion, 31*(3), 572–579. https://doi.org/10.1080/02699931.2015.1116978

Rheinberg, F. (2020). Intrinsic motivation and flow. *Motivation Science, 6*(3), 199–200. https://doi.org/10.1037/mot0000165

Riccelli, R., Toschi, N., Nigro, S., Terracciano, A., & Passamonti, L. (2017). Surface-based morphometry reveals the neuroanatomical basis of the five-factor model of personality. *Social Cognitive and Affective Neuroscience, 12*(4), 671–684. https://doi.org/10.1093/scan/nsw175

Richards, S. E. (2018, September 29). Scientists see twins as the perfect laboratory to examine the impact of nature vs. nurture. *The Washington Post.* https://www.washingtonpost.com/national/health-science/scientists-see-twins-as-the-perfect-laboratory-to-examine-the-impact-of-nature-vs-nurture/2018/09/28/d8423d16-9bfc-11e8-b60b-1c897f17e185_story.html

Richetto, J., & Meyer, U. (2020). Epigenetic modifications in schizophrenia and related disorders: Molecular scars of environmental exposures and source of phenotypic variability. *Biological Psychiatry, 89*(3), 215–226. https://doi.org/10.1016/j.biopsych.2020.03.008

Richtel, M. (2017, March 13). Are teenagers replacing drugs with smartphones? *The New York Times.* https://www.nytimes.com/2017/03/13/health/teenagers-drugs-smartphones.html?mcubz=0&_r=0

Ridout, K. K., Carpenter, L. L., & Tyrka, A. R. (2016). The cellular sequelae of early stress: Focus on aging and mitochondria. *Neuropsychopharmacology, 41,* 388–389. https://doi.org/10.1038/npp.2015.301

Rieke, F., & Baylor, D. A. (1998). Single-photon detection by rod cells of the retina. *Reviews of Modern Physics, 70,* 1027–1036.

Riemer, A. R., Gervais, S. J., Skorinko, J. L., Douglas, S. M., Spencer, H., Nugai, K., Karapanagou, A., & Miles-Novelo, A. (2019). She looks like she'd be an animal in bed: Dehumanization of drinking women in social contexts. *Sex Roles, 80*(9-10), 617–629. https://doi.org/10.1111/j.1465-3362.2011.00296.x

Riener, C. (2019). New approaches and debates on top-down perceptual processing. *Teaching of Psychology, 46*(3), 267–272. https://doi.org/10.1177/0098628319853943

Rietman, E. A., Taylor, S., Siegelmann, H. T., Deriu, M. A., Cavaglia, M., & Tuszynski, J. A. (2020). Using the Gibbs function as a measure of human brain development trends from fetal stage to advanced age. *International Journal of Molecular Sciences, 21*(3), 1116. https://doi.org/10.3390/ijms21031116

Riggio, H. R., & Garcia, A. L. (2009). The power of situations: Jonestown and the fundamental attribution error. *Teaching of Psychology, 36,* 108–112.

Rinderu, M. I., Bushman, B. J., & Van Lange, P. A. (2018). Climate, aggression, and violence (CLASH): A cultural-evolutionary approach. *Current Opinion in Psychology, 19,* 113–118. https://doi.org/10.1016/j.copsyc.2017.04.010

Ripke, S., Neale, B. M., Corvin, A., Walters, J. T., Farh, K. H., Holmans, P. A., Lee, P., Bulik-Sullivan, B., Collier, D. A., Huang, H., Pers, T. H., Agartz, I., Agerbo, E., Albus, M., Alexander, M., Amin, F., Bacanu, S. A., Begemann, M., Belliveau Jr., R. A., Bene, J., Bergen, S. E., Bevilacqua, E., Bigdeli, T. B., . . . O'Donovan, M. C. (2014). Biological insights from 108 schizophrenia-associated genetic loci. *Nature, 511,* 421–427.

Ritchie, J. (2009, January 12). Fact or fiction: Elephants never forget. *Scientific American Online.* http://www.scientificamerican.com/article.cfm?id=elephants-never-forget

Ritter, K. (2020, March 5). Tourist mecca Las Vegas sees Nevada's first coronavirus case. *US News & World Report.* https://www.usnews.com/news/best-states/nevada/articles/2020-03-05/nevada-reports-its-1st-coronavirus-case-in-las-vegas

Riva-Posse, P., Choi, K. S., Holtzheimer, P. E., Crowell, A. L., Garlow, S. J., Rajendra, J. K., McIntyre, C. C., Gross, R. E., & Mayberg, H. S. (2018). A connectomic approach for subcallosal cingulate deep brain stimulation surgery: Prospective targeting in treatment-resistant depression. *Molecular Psychiatry, 23*(4), 843–849. https://doi.org/10.1038/mp.2017.59

Robb, K. A., Gatting, L., & Wardle, J. (2017). What impact do questionnaire length and monetary incentives have on mailed health psychology survey response? *British Journal of Health Psychology, 22*(4), 671–685. https://doi.org/10.1111/bjhp.12239

Robbins, B. D. (2008). What is the good life? Positive psychology and the renaissance of humanistic psychology. *The Humanistic Psychologist, 36,* 96–112.

Robbins, R. N., & Bryan, A. (2004). Relationships between future orientation, impulsive sensation seeking, and risk behavior among adjudicated adolescents. *Journal of Adolescent Research, 19,* 428–445.

Roberson, R. (2013, September). Helping students find relevance. *Psychology Teacher Network, 23,* 18–20. http://apa.org/ed/precollege/ptn/2013/09/students-relevance.aspx

Roberti, J. W. (2004). A review of behavioral and biological correlates of sensation seeking. *Journal of Research in Personality, 38,* 256–279.

Roberts, B. W., & DelVecchio, W. F. (2000). The rank-order consistency of personality traits from childhood to old age: A quantitative review of longitudinal studies. *Psychological Bulletin, 126,* 3–25.

Roberts, C. A., Jones, A., & Montgomery, C. (2016). Meta-analysis of molecular imaging of serotonin transporters in Ecstasy/polydrug users. *Neuroscience & Biobehavioral Reviews, 63,* 158–167. https://doi.org/10.1016/j.neubiorev.2016.02.003

Roberts, J. A., & David, M. E. (2017). Put down your phone and listen to me: How boss phubbing undermines the psychological conditions necessary for employee engagement. *Computers in Human Behavior, 75,* 206–217. https://doi.org/10.1016/j.chb.2017.05.021

Roberts, J. A., & David, M. E. (2020). Boss phubbing, trust, job satisfaction and employee performance. *Personality and Individual Differences, 155,* Article 109702. https://doi.org/10.1016/j.paid.2019.109702ch

Roberts, S. O., & Rizzo, M. T. (2020). The psychology of American racism. *American Psychologist.* Advance online publication. https://doi.org/10.1037/amp0000642

Robino, A., Concas, M. P., Catamo, E., & Gasparini, P. (2019). A brief review of genetic approaches to the study of food preferences: Current knowledge and future directions.

*Nutrients, 11*(8), Article 1735. https://doi.org/10.3390/nu11081735

Robinson, A. M. (2018). Let's talk about stress: History of stress research. *Review of General Psychology, 22,* 334–342. https://doi.org/10.1037/gpr0000137

Robinson, E., Oldham, M., Cuckson, I., Brunstrom, J. M., Rogers, P. J., & Hardman, C. A. (2016). Visual exposure to large and small portion sizes and perceptions of portion size normality: Three experimental studies. *Appetite, 98,* 28–34. https://doi.org/10.1016/j.appet.2015.12.010

Rocheleau, M. (2017, March 7). Chart: The percentage of women and men in each profession. *Boston Globe.* https://www.bostonglobe.com/metro/2017/03/06/chart-the-percenta…women-and-men-each-profession/GBX22YsWl0XaeHghwXfE4H/story.html

Roddy, M. K., Walsh, L. M., Rothman, K., Hatch, S. G., & Doss, B. D. (2020). Meta-analysis of couple therapy: Effects across outcomes, designs, timeframes, and other moderators. *Journal of Consulting and Clinical Psychology, 88*(7), 583–596. https://doi.org/10.1037/ccp0000514

Rodin, J. (1986). Aging and health: Effects of the sense of control. *Science, 233,* 1271–1276. https://doi.org/10.1126/science.3749877

Rodin, J., & Langer, E. J. (1977). Long-term effects of a control-relevant intervention with the institutionalized aged. *Journal of Personality and Social Psychology, 12,* 897–902.

Rodkey, E. N. (2015). The visual cliff's forgotten menagerie: Rats, goats, babies, and myth-making in the history of psychology. *Journal of the History of the Behavioral Sciences, 51,* 113–140.

Rodriguez, L. M., Litt, D. M., & Stewart, S. H. (2020). Drinking to cope with the pandemic: The unique associations of COVID-19-related perceived threat and psychological distress to drinking behaviors in American men and women. *Addictive Behaviors, 110,* Article 106532. https://doi.org/10.1016/j.addbeh.2020.106532

Roediger, H. L., & Bergman, E. T. (1998). The controversy over recovered memories. *Psychology, Public Policy, and Law, 4,* 1091–1109.

Roediger, H. L., III, Putnam, A. L., & Smith, M. A. (2011). Ten benefits of testing and their applications to educational practice. *Psychology of Learning and Motivation: Advances in Research and Theory, 55,* 1–36.

Röer, J. P., & Cowan, N. (2020). A preregistered replication and extension of the cocktail party phenomenon: One's name captures attention, unexpected words do not. *Journal of Experimental Psychology: Learning, Memory, and Cognition.* Advance online publication. https://doi.org/10.1037/xlm0000874

Rofé, Y., & Rofé, Y. (2015). Fear and phobia: A critical review and the rational choice theory of neurosis. *International Journal of Psychological Studies, 7,* 37–73.

Rogers, C. R. (1951). *Client-centered therapy: Its current practice, implications, and theory.* Houghton Mifflin.

Rogers, C. R. (1959). A theory of therapy, personality, and interpersonal relationships as developed in the client-centered framework. In S. Koch (Ed.), *Psychology: A study of a science: Vol. 3. Formulations of the person and the social context* (pp. 184–256). McGraw-Hill.

Rogers, C. R. (1961). *On becoming a person.* Houghton Mifflin.

Rogers, C. R. (1979). The foundations of the person-centered approach. *Education, 100,* 98–107.

Roghanizad, M. M., & Bohns, V. K. (2017). Ask in person: You're less persuasive than you think over email. *Journal of Experimental Social Psychology, 69,* 223–226. https://doi.org/10.1016/j.jesp.2016.10.002

Rohrer, D., & Taylor, K. (2006). The effects of overlearning and distributed practice on the retention of mathematics knowledge. *Applied Cognitive Psychology, 20,* 1209–1224.

Rohrer, J. M., Egloff, B., & Schmukle, S. C. (2015). Examining the effects of birth order on personality. *Proceedings of the National Academy of Sciences, 112,* 14224–14229.

Rohwedder, S., & Willis, R. J. (2010). Mental retirement. *Journal of Economic Perspective, 24,* 119–138.

Roid, G. H. (2003). *Stanford-Binet Intelligence Scales* (5th ed.). Riverside.

Roitblat, Y., Burger, J., Vaiman, M., Nehuliaieva, L., Buchris, N., & Shterenshis, M. (2020). Owls and larks do not exist: COVID-19 quarantine sleep habits. *Sleep Medicine.* Advance online publication. https://doi.org/10.1016/j.sleep.2020.09.003

Ros, E., Izquierdo-Pulido, M., & Sala-Vila, A. (2018). Beneficial effects of walnut consumption on human health: Role of micronutrients. *Current Opinion in Clinical Nutrition & Metabolic Care, 21*(6), 498–504. https://doi: 10.1097/MCO.0000000000000508

Rosales-Lagarde, A., Armony, J. L., del Rio-Portilla, Y., Trejo-Mardnez, D., Conde, R., & Corsi-Cabrera, M. (2012). Enhanced emotional reactivity after selective REM sleep deprivation in humans: An fMRI study. *Frontiers in Behavioral Neuroscience, 6,* 1–13.

Rosch, E. (1973). Natural categories. *Cognitive Psychology, 4,* 328–350.

Rosch, E., & Mervis, C. B. (1975). Family resemblances: Studies in the internal structure of categories. *Cognitive Psychology, 7,* 573–605.

Rosch, E., Mervis, C. B., Gray, W. D., Johnson, D. M., & Boyes-Braem, P. (1976). Basic objects in natural categories. *Cognitive Psychology, 8,* 382–439.

Rose, J. D. (2011). Diverse perspectives on the groupthink theory—A literary review. *Emerging Leadership Journeys, 4,* 37–57.

Rosen, J. (2014, November 10). The knowledge, London's legendary taxi-driver test, puts up a fight in the age of GPS. *The New York Times.* http://www.nytimes.com/2014/11/10/t-magazine/london-taxi-test-knowledge.html

Rosen, M. L., Meltzoff, A. N., Sheridan, M. A., & McLaughlin, K. A. (2019). Distinct aspects of the early environment contribute to associative memory, cued attention, and memory-guided attention: Implications for academic achievement. *Developmental Cognitive Neuroscience, 40,* 100731. https://doi.org/10.1016/j.dcn.2019.100731

Rosenblum, L. D. (2010). *See what I'm saying: The extraordinary powers of our five senses.* W. W. Norton.

Rosenhan, D. L. (1973). On being sane in insane places. *Science, 179,* 250–258.

Rosenman, R. H., Brand, R. J., Jenkins, D., Friedman, M., Straus, R., & Wurm, M. (1975). Coronary heart disease in the Western Collaborative Group Study: Final follow-up experience of 8 ½ years. *Journal of the American Medical Association, 233,* 872–877.

Rosenthal, R. (1965). *Clever Hans: A case study of scientific method, introduction to Clever Hans.* Holt, Rinehart & Winston.

Rosenthal, R. (1966). *Experimenter effects in behavioral research.* Appleton-Century-Crofts.

Rosenthal, R. (2002a). Covert communication in classrooms, clinics, courtrooms, and cubicles. *American Psychologist, 57,* 839–849.

Rosenthal, R. (2002b). Experimenter and clinician effects in scientific inquiry and clinical practice. *Prevention & Treatment, 5,* 1–12.

Rosenthal, R. (2003). Covert communication in laboratories, classrooms, and the truly real world. *Current Directions in Psychological Science, 12,* 151–154.

Rosenthal, R., & Jacobson, L. (1966). Teachers' expectancies: Determinants of pupils' IQ gains. *Psychological Reports, 19,* 115–118.

Rosenthal, R., & Jacobson, L. (1968). *Pygmalion in the classroom: Teacher expectation and pupils' intellectual development.* Holt, Rinehart, & Winston.

Rosenzweig, M. R. (1984). Experience, memory, and the brain. *American Psychologist, 39,* 365–376.

Roseth, C. J., Johnson, D. W., & Johnson, R. T. (2008). Promoting early adolescents' achievement and peer relationships: The effects of cooperative, competitive, and individualistic goal structures. *Psychological Bulletin, 134,* 223–246.

Rosky, J. W. (2013). The (f)utility of post-conviction polygraph testing. *Sexual Abuse, 25,* 259–281.

Rosner, R. I. (2018). History and the topsy-turvy world of psychotherapy. *History of Psychology, 21*(3), 177–186. https://doi.org/10.1037/hop0000102

Ross, E. L., Zivin, K., & Maixner, D. F. (2018). Cost-effectiveness of electroconvulsive therapy vs pharmacotherapy/psychotherapy for treatment-resistant depression in the United States. *JAMA Psychiatry, 75*(7), 713–722. https://doi.org/10.1001/jamapsychiatry.2018.0768

Ross, L. (1977). The intuitive psychologist and his shortcomings: Distortions in the attribution process. In L. Berkowitz (Ed.), *Advances in experimental social psychology* (Vol. 10, pp. 173–220). Academic Press.

Ross, L. (2018). From the fundamental attribution error to the truly fundamental attribution error and beyond: My research journey. *Perspectives on Psychological Science, 13*(6), 750–769. https://doi.org/10.1177/1745691618769855

Ross, L., Greene, D., & House, P. (1977). The "false consensus effect": An egocentric bias in social perception and attribution processes. *Journal of Experimental Social Psychology, 13,* 279–301.

Ross, L. D., Amabile, T. M., & Steinmetz, J. L. (1977). Social roles, social control, and biases in social-perception processes. *Journal of Personality and Social Psychology, 33,* 485–494.

Rossen, L. M., Ahrens, K. A., & Branum, A. M. (2017). Trends in risk of pregnancy loss among US women, 1990–2011 [Abstract]. *Paediatric and Perinatal Epidemiology, 32,* 19–29. https://doi.org/10.1111/ppe.12417

Rosso, A., Mossey, J., & Lippa, C. F. (2008). Review: Caffeine: Neuroprotective functions in cognition and Alzheimer's disease. *American Journal of Alzheimer's Disease and Other Dementias, 23,* 417–422.

Rotge, J.-Y., Guehl, D., Dilharreguy, B., Tignol, J., Bioulac, B., Allard, M., Burbaud, P., & Aouizerate, B. (2009). Meta-analysis of brain volume changes in obsessive-compulsive disorder. *Biological Psychiatry, 65,* 75–83.

Roth, T. (2007). Insomnia: Definition, prevalence, etiology, and consequences. *Journal of Clinical Sleep Medicine, 3*, 7–10.

Rothbaum, F., Weisz, J., Pott, M., Miyake, K., & Morelli, G. (2000). Attachment and culture: Security in the United States and Japan. *American Psychologist, 55*, 1093–1104.

Rotter, J. B. (1966). Generalized expectancies for internal versus external control of reinforcement. *Psychological Monographs: General and Applied, 80*, 1–28.

Rotter, J. B. (1990). Internal versus external control of reinforcement: A case history of a variable. *American Psychologist, 45*, 489–493.

Routh, D. K., & Reisman, J. M. (2003). Clinical psychology. In D. K. Freedheim (Ed.), *Handbook of psychology: Vol. 1. History of psychology* (pp. 337–355). John Wiley & Sons.

Rubenstein, A., Wood, S. K., Levine, R. S., & Hennekens, C. H. (2019). Alarming trends in mortality from firearms among United States schoolchildren. *American Journal of Medicine, 132*(8) 992–994. https://doi.org/10.1016/j.amjmed.2019.02.012

Rubin, Z., & Peplau, L. A. (1975). Who believes in a just world? *Journal of Social Issues, 31*, 65–89.

Ruglass, L. M., Hien, D. A., Hu, M. C., Campbell, A. N., Caldeira, N. A., Miele, G. M., & Chang, D. F. (2014). Racial/ethnic match and treatment outcomes for women with PTSD and substance use disorders receiving community-based treatment. *Community Mental Health Journal, 50*, 811–822.

Ruisch, I. H., Dietrich, A., Klein, M., Faraone, S. V., Oosterlaan, J., Buitelaar, J. K., & Hoekstra, P. J. (2020). Aggression based genome-wide, glutamatergic, dopaminergic and neuroendocrine polygenic risk scores predict callous-unemotional traits. *Neuropsychopharmacology, 45*(5), 761–769. https://doi.org/10.1038/s41386-020-0608-0

Ruiz, J., Gutiérrez, F., Peri, J. M., Aluja, A., Baillés, E., Gutiérrez-Zotes, A., Vall, G., Edo Villamón, S., Meliá de Alba, A., & Ruipérez Rodríguez, M. Á. (2020). Mean-level change in pathological personality dimensions over 4 decades in clinical and community samples: A cross-sectional study. *Personality Disorders: Theory, Research, and Treatment, 11*(6), 409–417. https://doi.org/10.1037/per0000384

Running, C. A., Craig, B. A., & Mattes, R. D. (2015). Oleogustus: The unique taste of fat. *Chemical Senses, 40*, 507–516. https://doi.org/10.1093/chemse/bjv036

Rupp, R. (2014, September 30). Are you a supertaster? *National Geographic.* http://theplate.nationalgeographic.com/2014/09/30/are-you-a-supertaster/

Rusbult, C. E. (1983). A longitudinal test of the investment model: The development (and deterioration) of satisfaction and commitment in heterosexual involvements. *Journal of Personality and Social Psychology, 45*, 101–117.

Rusbult, C. E., & Martz, J. M. (1995). Remaining in an abusive relationship: An investment model analysis of nonvoluntary dependence. *Personality and Social Psychology Bulletin, 21*, 558–571.

Ruscio, A. M., Stein, D. J., Chiu, W. T., & Kessler, R. C. (2010). The epidemiology of obsessive-compulsive disorder in the National Comorbidity Survey Replication. *Molecular Psychiatry, 15*, 53–63.

Rushton, J. P., & Jensen, A. R. (2010). Race and IQ: A theory-based review of the research in Richard Nisbett's *Intelligence and how to get it. Open Psychology Journal, 3*, 9–35.

Russell, D. W., Clavél, F. D., Cutrona, C. E., Abraham, W. T., & Burzette, R. G. (2018). Neighborhood racial discrimination and the development of major depression. *Journal of Abnormal Psychology, 127*(2), 150–159. https://doi.org/10.1037/abn0000336

Russell, G. (2020, March 6). Bethany Hamilton: "My fear of losing surfing was greater than my fear of sharks." *The Guardian.* https://www.theguardian.com/sport/2020/mar/07/bethany-hamilton-unstoppable-film-my-fear-of-losing-surfing-was-greater-than-my-fear-of-sharks

Ryan, R. M., & Deci, E. L. (2017). *Self-determination theory: Basic psychological needs in motivation, development, and wellness.* Guilford Press.

Ryan, R. M., & Deci, E. L. (2020). Intrinsic and extrinsic motivation from a self-determination theory perspective: Definitions, theory, practices, and future directions. *Contemporary Educational Psychology, 61*, Article 101860. https://doi.org/10.1016/j.cedpsych.2020.101860

Sabia, S., Dugravot, A., Dartigues, J.-F., Abell, J., Elbaz, A., Kivimäki, M., & Singh-Manoux, A. (2017). Physical activity, cognitive decline, and risk of dementia: 28 year follow-up of Whitehall II cohort study. *British Medical Journal, 357*, Article ID j2709. https://doi.org/10.1136/bmj.j2709

Sable, P., & Akcay, O. (2011). Response to color: Literature review with cross-cultural marketing perspective. *International Bulletin of Business Administration, 11*, 34–41.

Sabra, A. I. (2003, September–October). Ibn al-Haytham. *Harvard Magazine.* https://harvardmagazine.com/2003/09/ibn-al-haytham-html

Sabri, O., Meyer, P. M., Gräf, S., Hesse, S., Wilke, S., Becker, G. A., Rullmann, M., Patt, M., Luthardt, J., Wagenknecht, G., Hoepping, A., Smits, R., Franke, A., Sattler, B., Tiepolt, S., Fischer, S., Deuther-Conrad, W., Hegerl, U., Barthel, H., . . . Brust, P. (2018). Cognitive correlates of α4β2 nicotinic acetylcholine receptors in mild Alzheimer's dementia. *Brain, 141*(6), 1840–1854. https://doi.org/10.1093/brain/awy099

Sacks, O. (2007, September 24). The abyss. *The New Yorker.* https://www.newyorker.com/reporting/2007/09/24/070924fa_fact_sacks

Safran, A. B., & Sanda, N. (2015). Color synesthesia. Insight into perception, emotion, and consciousness. *Current Opinion in Neurology, 28*(1), 36–44. https://doi.org/10.1097/WCO.0000000000000169

Safran, J. D., & Hunter, J. (2020a). History. In J. D. Safran & J. Hunter (Eds.), *Theories of psychotherapy series. Psychoanalysis and psychoanalytic therapies* (pp. 17–36). American Psychological Association. https://doi.org/10.1037/0000190-002

Safran, J. D., & Hunter, J. (2020b). *Theories of psychotherapy series. Psychoanalysis and psychoanalytic therapies.* American Psychological Association. https://doi.org/10.1037/0000190-006

Saha, S., Chant, D., Welham, J., & McGrath, J. (2005). A systematic review of the prevalence of schizophrenia. *PLOS Medicine, 2*, Article e141.

Saikia, G. (2017, April 19). Addiction to internet and social media on the rise. *NewsBytes.* https://www.newsbytesapp.com/timeline/Science/6273/37962/the-dark-world-of-internet-addiction

Sailor, K. A., Schinder, A. F., & Lledo, P. M. (2017). Adult neurogenesis beyond the niche: Its potential for driving brain plasticity. *Current Opinion in Neurobiology, 42*, 111–117. https://doi.org/10.1016/j.conb.2016.12.001

Sakai, J. (2020). Core concept: How synaptic pruning shapes neural wiring during development and, possibly, in disease. *Proceedings of the National Academy of Sciences, 117*(28), 16096–16099. https://doi.org/10.1073/pnas.2010281117

Sakaki, M., Yagi, A., & Murayama, K. (2018). Curiosity in old age: A possible key to achieving adaptive aging. *Neuroscience & Biobehavioral Reviews, 88*, 106–116. https://doi.org/10.1016/j.neubiorev.2018.03.007

Salahudeen, M. S., Wright, C. M., & Peterson, G. M. (2020). Esketamine: New hope for the treatment of treatment-resistant depression? A narrative review. *Therapeutic Advances in Drug Safety, 11*, 71–93. https://doi.org/10.1177/2042098620937899

Salim, S. R., McConnell, A. A., & Messman-Moore, T. L. (2020). Bisexual women's experiences of stigma and verbal sexual coercion: The roles of internalized heterosexism and outness. *Psychology of Women Quarterly, 44*(3), 362–376. https://doi.org/10.1177/0361684320917391

Salk, R. H., Hyde, J. S., & Abramson, L. Y. (2017). Gender differences in depression in representative national samples: Meta-analyses of diagnoses and symptoms. *Psychological Bulletin, 143*, 783–822. https://doi.org/10.1037/bul0000102

Salmon, C., Cuthbertson, A. M., & Figueredo, A. J. (2016). The relationship between birth order and prosociality: An evolutionary perspective. *Personality and Individual Differences, 96*, 18–22. https://doi.org/10.1016/j.paid.2016.02.066

Salmon, P. (2001). Effects of physical exercise on anxiety, depression, and sensitivity to stress: A unifying theory. *Clinical Psychology Review, 21*, 33–61.

Salovey, P., Mayer, J. D., & Caruso, D. (2002). The positive psychology of emotional intelligence. In C. R. Snyder & S. J. Lopez (Eds.), *Handbook of positive psychology* (pp. 159–171). Oxford University Press.

Salthouse, T. A. (2006). Mental exercise and mental aging: Evaluating the validity of the "use it or lose it" hypothesis. *Perspectives on Psychological Science, 1*, 68–87.

Salva, O. R., Farroni, T., Regolin, L., Vallortigara, G., & Johnson, M. H. (2011). The evolution of social orienting: Evidence from chicks (*Gallus gallus*) and human newborns. *PLOS ONE, 6*, e18802. https://doi.org/10.1371/journal.pone.0018802

Salvarani, V., Rampoldi, G., Ardenghi, S., Bani, M., Blasi, P., Ausili, D., Di Mauro, S., & Strepparava, M. G. (2019). Protecting emergency room nurses from burnout: The role of dispositional mindfulness, emotion regulation and empathy. *Journal of Nursing Management, 27*(4), 765–774. https://doi.org/10.1111/jonm.12771

Samaha, A. (2014, August 7). The rise and fall of crime in New York City: A timeline. *The Village Voice.* https://www.villagevoice.com/2014/08/07/the-rise-and-fall-of-crime-in-new-york-city-a-timeline/

Samaha, M., & Hawi, N. S. (2016). Relationships among smartphone addiction, stress, academic performance, and satisfaction with life. *Computers in Human Behavior, 57*, 321–325.

Samhita, L., & Gross, H. J. (2013). The "Clever Hans phenomenon" revisited. *Communicative & Integrative Biology, 6,* e27122.

Sandin, S., Lichtenstein, P., Kuja-Halkola, R., Larsson, H., Hultman, C. M., & Reichenberg, A. (2014). The familial risk of autism. *Journal of the American Medical Association, 311,* 1770–1777.

Sangha, S., Diehl, M. M., Bergstrom, H. C., & Drew, M. R. (2020). Know safety, no fear. *Neuroscience & Biobehavioral Reviews, 108,* 218–230. https://doi.org/10.1016/j.neubiorev.2019.11.006

Sansom-Daly, U. M., Peate, M., Wakefield, C. E., Bryant, R. A., & Cohn, R. (2012). A systematic review of psychological interventions for adolescents and young adults living with chronic illness. *Health Psychology, 31,* 380–393.

Santa Cruz, N. (2020, June 30). How to keep your pets safe during Fourth of July fireworks. *Los Angeles Times.* https://www.latimes.com/california/story/2020-06-30/pets-fireworks-july-4th

Santangelo, V., Pedale, T., Macrì, S., & Campolongo, P. (2020). Enhanced cortical specialization to distinguish older and newer memories in highly superior autobiographical memory. *Cortex, 129,* 476–483. https://doi.org/10.1016/j.cortex.2020.04.029

Santoro, N., Roeca, C., Peters, B. A., & Neal-Perry, G. (2021). The menopause transition: Signs, symptoms, and management options. *The Journal of Clinical Endocrinology & Metabolism, 106*(1), 1–16. https://doi.org/10.1210/clinem/dgaa764

Saper, C. B., Scammell, T. E., & Lu, J. (2005). Hypothalamic regulation of sleep and circadian rhythms. *Nature, 437,* 1257–1263.

Sar, V. (2011). Epidemiology of dissociative disorders: An overview. *Epidemiology Research International, 2011,* Article 404538. https://doi.org/10.1155/2011/404538

Saryazdi, R., Bak, K., & Campos, J. L. (2019). Inattentional blindness during driving in younger and older adults. *Frontiers in Psychology, 10,* Article 880. https://doi.org/10.3389/fpsyg.2019.00880

Sastre, J. P., & Jouvet, M. (1979). Le comportement onirique du chat [Oneiric behavior in cats]. *Physiology & Behavior, 22,* 979–989.

Sattler, J. M. (1990). *Assessment of children* (3rd ed.). Author.

Sauce, B., & Matzel, L. D. (2018). The paradox of intelligence: Heritability and malleability coexist in hidden gene–environment interplay. *Psychological Bulletin, 144*(1), 26–47. https://doi.org/10.1037/bul0000131

Sawangjit, A., Oyanedel, C. N., Niethard, N., Salazar, C., Born, J., & Inostroza, M. (2018). The hippocampus is crucial for forming nonhippocampal long-term memory during sleep. *Nature, 564*(7734), 109–113. https://doi.org/10.1038/s41586-018-0716-8

Sawangjit, A., Oyanedel, C. N., Niethard, N., Salazar, C., Born, J., & Inostroza, M. (2018). The hippocampus is crucial for forming non-hippocampal long-term memory during sleep. *Nature, 564*(7734), 109–113. https://doi.org/10.1038/s41586-018-0716-8

Saxbe, D. E. (2017). Birth of a new perspective? A call for biopsychosocial research on childbirth. *Current Directions in Psychological Science, 26,* 81–86. https://doi.org/10.1177/0963721416677096

Sayette, M. A., Creswell, K. G., Fairbairn, C. E., Dimoff, J. D., Bentley, K., & Lazerus, T. (2019). The effects of alcohol on positive emotion during a comedy routine: A facial coding analysis. *Emotion, 19*(3), 480–488. https://doi.org/10.1037/emo0000451

Sayette, M. A. & Norcross, J. C. (2020). *Insider's guide to graduate programs in clinical and counseling psychology 2020/2021 edition.* Guilford Press.

Scarf, D., & Hinten, A. E. (2018). Television format and children's executive function. *Pediatrics, 141*(3), e20172674. https://doi.org/10.1542/peds.2017-2674

Scarr, S., & McCartney, K. (1983). How people make their own environments: A theory of genotype–environment effects. *Child Development, 54,* 424–435.

Schaal, B., Saxton, T. K., Loos, H., Soussignan, R., & Durand, K. (2020). Olfaction scaffolds the developing human from neonate to adolescent and beyond. *Philosophical Transactions of the Royal Society B, 375*(1800), 20190261. https://doi.org/10.1098/rstb.2019.0261

Schaarschmidt, T. (2018, September/October). The art of lying. *Scientific American Mind, 29,* 18–25.

Schachner, A., & Hannon, E. E. (2011). Infant-directed speech drives social preferences in 5-month-old infants. *Developmental Psychology, 47,* 19–25.

Schachter, S., & Singer, J. E. (1962). Cognitive, social, and physiological determinants of emotional state. *Psychological Review, 69,* 379–399.

Schacter, D. L. (2019). Implicit memory, constructive memory, and imagining the future: A career perspective. *Perspectives on Psychological Science, 14*(2), 256–272. https://doi.org/10.1177/1745691618803640

Schaefer, J. D., Caspi, A., Belsky, D. W., Harrington, H., Houts, R., Horwood, L. J., Hussong, A., Ramrakha, S., Poulton, R., & Moffitt, T. E. (2017). Enduring mental health: Prevalence and prediction. *Journal of Abnormal Psychology, 126,* 212–224. https://doi.org/10.1037/abn0000232

Schaffner, K. F. (2020). A comparison of two neurobiological models of fear and anxiety: A "construct validity" application? *Perspectives on Psychological Science, 15*(5), 1214–1227. https://doi.org/10.1177/1745691620920860

Schaie, K. W. (1993). The Seattle longitudinal studies of adult intelligence. *Current Directions in Psychological Science, 2,* 171–175.

Schaie, K. W. (2008). Historical processes and patterns of cognitive aging. In S. M. Hofer & D. F. Alwin (Eds.), *Handbook of cognitive aging: Interdisciplinary perspectives.* Sage.

Schalock, R. L., Borthwick-Duffy, S., Bradley, V. J., Bunting, W. H. E., Coulter, D. L., & Craig, E. M. (2010). *Intellectual disability: Definition classification, and systems of supports* (11th ed.). American Association on Intellectual and Developmental Disabilities.

Schenck, C. H., & Mahowald, M. W. (2002). REM sleep behavior disorder: Clinical, developmental, and neuroscience perspectives 16 years after its formal identification in SLEEP. *SLEEP, 25,* 120–138.

Scherer, A. M., Windschitl, P. D., O'Rourke, J., & Smith, A. R. (2012). Hoping for more: The influence of outcome desirability on information seeking and predictions about relative quantities. *Cognition, 125,* 113–117.

Scherr, S., Mares, M. L., Bartsch, A., & Goetz, M. (2019). Parents, television, and children's emotional expressions: A cross-cultural multilevel model. *Journal of Cross-Cultural Psychology, 50*(1), 22–46. https://doi.org/10.1177/0022022118806585

Scheufele, D. A., & Krause, N. M. (2019). Science audiences, misinformation, and fake news. *Proceedings of the National Academy of Sciences, 116*(16), 7662–7669. https://doi.org/10.1073/pnas.1805871115

Schickedanz, A., Dreyer, B. P., & Halfon, N. (2015). Childhood poverty: Understanding and preventing the adverse impacts of a most-prevalent risk to pediatric health and well-being. *Pediatric Clinics of North America, 62,* 1111–1135.

Schiller, C. E., Meltzer-Brody, S., & Rubinow, D. R. (2015). The role of reproductive hormones in postpartum depression. *CNS Spectrums, 20,* 48–59.

Schilling, O. K., Wahl, H. W., Boerner, K., Horowitz, A., Reinhardt, J. P., Cimarolli, V. R., Brennan-Ing, M., & Heckhausen, J. (2016). Developmental regulation with progressive vision loss: Use of control strategies and affective well-being. *Developmental Psychology, 52,* 679–694. http://doi.org/10.1037/dev0000099

Schimmack, U. (2020). A meta-psychological perspective on the decade of replication failures in social psychology. *Canadian Psychology/Psychologie canadienne, 61*(4), 364–376. https://doi.org/10.1037/cap0000246

Schizophrenia Working Group of the Psychiatric Genomics Consortium. (2014). Biological insights from 108 schizophrenia-associated genetic loci. *Nature, 511,* 421–427.

Schlaug, G. (2015). Musicians and music making as a model for the study of brain plasticity. *Progress in Brain Research, 217,* 37–55.

Schleppenbach, M., Flevares, L. M., Sims, L. M., & Perry, M. (2007). Teachers' responses to student mistakes in Chinese and U.S. mathematics classrooms. *The Elementary School Journal, 108,* 131–147.

Schlich, T. (2015, May). Cutting the body to cure the mind. *The Lancet, 2,* 390–392.

Schlichting, A., & Bäuml, K. H. T. (2017). Brief wakeful resting can eliminate directed forgetting. *Memory, 25,* 254–260. https://doi.org/10.1080/09658211.2016.1153659

Schmaal, L., Hibar, D. P., Sämann, P. G., Hall, G. B., Baune, B. T., Jahanshad, N., Cheung, J. W., van Erp, T. G. M., Bos, D., Ikram, M. A., Vernooij, M. W., Niessen, W. J., Tiemeier, H., Hofman, A., Wittfeld, K., Grabe, H. J., Janowitz, D., Bülow, R., Selonke, M., . . . ENIGMA-Major Depressive Disorder Working Group. (2017). Cortical abnormalities in adults and adolescents with major depression based on brain scans from 20 cohorts worldwide in the ENIGMA Major Depressive Disorder Working Group. *Molecular Psychiatry, 22,* 900–909. https://doi.org/10.1038/mp.2016.60

Schmaal, L., Veltman, D. J., van Erp, T. G., Sämann, P. G., Frodl, T., Jahanshad, N., Loehrer, E., Tiemeier, H., Hofman, A., Niessen, W. J., Vernooij, M. W., Ikram, M. A., Wittfeld, K., Grabe, H. J., Block, A., Hegenscheid, K., Völzke, H., Hoehn, D., Czisch, M., . . . ENIGMA–Major Depressive Disorder Working Group. (2016). Subcortical brain alterations in major depressive disorder: Findings from the ENIGMA Major Depressive Disorder working group. *Molecular Psychiatry, 21,* 806–812. https://doi.org/10.1038/mp.2015.69

**Schmaltz, R., & Lilienfeld, S. O.** (2014). Hauntings, homeopathy, and the Hopkinsville Goblins: Using pseudoscience to teach scientific thinking. *Frontiers in Psychology, 5,* 1–5. https://doi.org/10.3389/fpsyg .2014.00336

**Schmerling, R. H.** (2017, August). Right brain/left brain, right? *Harvard Health Blog.* https://www.health .harvard.edu/blog/right-brainleft-brain -right-2017082512222

**Schmidt, H. G., Peeck, V. H., Paas, F., & van Breukelen, G. J. P.** (2000). Remembering the street names of one's childhood neighbourhood: A study of very long-term retention. *Memory, 8,* 37–49.

**Schmidt, S. R., & Qiao, L.** (2020). A comparison of Chinese and American memories for public events. *Applied Cognitive Psychology, 34*(1), 217–227. https://doi.org/10.1002/acp.3611

**Schmitt, D. P., Realo, A., Voracek, M., & Allik, J.** (2008). Why can't a man be more like a woman? Sex differences in Big Five personality traits across 55 cultures. *Journal of Personality and Social Psychology, 94,* 168–182.

**Schnall, S., Roper, J., & Fessler, D. M.** (2010). Elevation leads to altruistic behavior. *Psychological Science, 21,* 315–320.

**Schneidman, E. S.** (1973). *Deaths of man.* Quadrangle/The New York Times Book Co.

**Schnider, A., Guggisberg, A., Nahum, L., Gabriel, D., & Morand, S.** (2010). Dopaminergic modulation of rapid reality adaptation in thinking. *Neuroscience, 167,* 583–587.

**Schoemaker, M. J., Jones, M. E., Wright, L. B., Griffin, J., McFadden, E., Ashworth, A., & Swerdlow, A. J.** (2016). Psychological stress, adverse life events and breast cancer incidence: A cohort investigation in 106,000 women in the United Kingdom. *Breast Cancer Research, 18,* Article 72. https://doi.org /10.1186/s13058-016-0733-1

**Schoenborn, C. A., Adams, P. F., & Peregoy, J. A.** (2013). Health behaviors of adults: United States, 2008–2010. *Vital Health Stat, 10*(257), 1–184.

**Scholl, L., Seth, P., Kariisa, M., Wilson, N., & Baldwin, G.** (2019). Drug and opioid-involved overdose deaths—United States, 2013–2017. *Morbidity and Mortality Weekly Report (MMWR), 67*(51-52), 1419–1427. https://doi.org/10.15585/mmwr .mm675152e1

**Schöne, B., Gruber, T., Graetz, S., Bernhof, M., & Malinowski, P.** (2018). Mindful breath awareness meditation facilitates efficiency gains in brain networks: A steady-state visually evoked potentials study. *Scientific Reports, 8*(1), Article 13687. https:// doi.org/10.1038/s41598-018-32046-5

**Schouten, A. P., Janssen, L., & Verspaget, M.** (2019). Celebrity vs. influencer endorsements in advertising: The role of identification, credibility, and product-endorser fit. *International Journal of Advertising: The Review of Marketing Communications, 39*(2), 258–281. https://doi.org/10.1080 /02650487.2019.1634898

**Schredl, M., & Erlacher, D.** (2020). Fever dreams: An online study. *Frontiers in Psychology, 11,* Article 53. https://doi .org/10.3389/fpsyg.2020.00053

**Schrempft, S., van Jaarsveld, C. H., Fisher, A., Herle, M., Smith, A. D., Fildes, A., & Llewellyn, C. H.** (2018). Variation in the heritability of child body mass index by obesogenic home environment. *JAMA Pediatrics, 172*(12), 1153–1160. https://doi .org/10.1001/jamapediatrics.2018.1508

**Schultz, D. P., & Schultz, S. E.** (2016). *A history of modern psychology* (11th ed.). Wadsworth, Cengage Learning.

**Schultz, D. P., & Schultz, S. E.** (2017). *Theories of personality* (11th ed.). Cengage Learning.

**Schumacher, S., Miller, R., Fehm, L., Kirschbaum, C., Fydrich, T., & Ströhle, A.** (2015). Therapists' and patients' stress responses during graduated versus flooding in vivo exposure in the treatment of specific phobia: A preliminary observational study. *Psychiatry Research, 230,* 668–675.

**Schurz, M., Radua, J., Tholen, M. G., Maliske, L., Margulies, D. S., Mars, R. B., Sallet, J., & Kanske, P.** (2020). Toward a hierarchical model of social cognition: A neuroimaging meta-analysis and integrative review of empathy and theory of mind. *Psychological Bulletin.* Advance online publication. https://doi.org/10.1037 /bul0000303

**Schutte, N. M., Nederend, I., Hudziak, J. J., de Geus, E. J., & Bartels, M.** (2016). Differences in adolescent physical fitness: A multivariate approach and meta-analysis. *Behavior Genetics, 46,* 217–227.

**Schwartz, B. L.** (2012). *Tip-of-the-tongue states: Phenomenology, mechanism, and lexical retrieval.* Psychology Press.

**Schwartz, C., Meisenhelder, J. B., Yunsheng, M., & Reed, G.** (2003). Altruistic social interest behaviors are associated with better mental health. *Psychosomatic Medicine, 65,* 778–785.

**Schwartz, C. E., Keyl, P. M., Marcum, J. P., & Bode, R.** (2009). Helping others shows differential benefits on health and well-being for male and female teens. *Journal of Happiness Studies, 10,* 431–448.

**Schwartz, S. J.** (2001). The evolution of Eriksonian and neo-Eriksonian identity theory and research: A review and integration. *Identity: An International Journal of Theory and Research, 1,* 7–58.

**Schwartz, S. J., Benet-Martínez, V., Knight, G. P., Unger, J. B., Zamboanga, B. L., Des Rosiers, S. E., Stephens, D. P., Huang, S., & Szapocznik, J.** (2014). Effects of language of assessment on the measurement of acculturation: Measurement equivalence and cultural frame switching. *Psychological Assessment, 26,* 100–114.

**Schweizer, K., Brunner, F., Handford, C., & Richter-Appelt, H.** (2014). Gender experience and satisfaction with gender allocation in adults with diverse intersex conditions (divergences of sex development, DSD). *Psychology & Sexuality, 5*(1), 56–82.

**Scoboria, A., Wade, K. A., Lindsay, D. S., Azad, T., Strange, D., Ost, J., & Hyman, I. E.** (2017). A mega-analysis of memory reports from eight peer-reviewed false memory implantation studies. *Memory, 25,* 146–163. https://doi.org/10.1080 /09658211.2016.1260747

**Scott, K. E., Shutts, K., & Devine, P. G.** (2020). Parents' role in addressing children's racial bias: The case of speculation without evidence. *Perspectives on Psychological Science, 15*(5), 1178–1186. https://doi.org/10 .1177/1745691620927702

**Scott, S. B., Rhoades, G. K., Stanley, S. M., Allen, E. S., & Markman, H. J.** (2013). Reasons for divorce and recollections of premarital intervention: Implications for improving relationship education. *Couple and Family Psychology: Research and Practice, 2,* 131–145.

**Scott, S. K., Blank, C. C., Rosen, S., & Wise, R. J. S.** (2000). Identification of a pathway for intelligible speech in the left temporal lobe. *Brain, 123,* 2400–2406.

**Scoville, W. B., & Milner, B.** (1957). Loss of recent memory after bilateral hippocampal lesions. *Journal of Neurology, Neurosurgery, & Psychiatry, 20,* 11–21.

**Scullin, M. K., & Bliwise, D. L.** (2015). Sleep, cognition, and normal aging integrating a half century of multidisciplinary research. *Perspectives on Psychological Science, 10,* 97–137.

**Searleman, A.** (2007, March 12). Is there such a thing as a photographic memory? And if so, can it be learned? *Scientific American Online.* http://www .scientificamerican.com/article/is-there -such-a-thing-as/

**Seery, M. D.** (2011). Resilience: A silver lining to experiencing adverse life events? *Current Directions in Psychological Science, 20,* 390–394.

**Segal, D. L., Coolidge, F. L., & Mizuno, H.** (2007). Defense mechanism differences between younger and older adults: A cross-sectional investigation. *Aging and Mental Health, 11,* 415–422.

**Segal, N.** (1984). Cooperation, competition, and altruism within twin sets: A reappraisal. *Ethology and Sociobiology, 5,* 163–177.

**Segal, N. L.** (1999). *Entwined lives: Twins and what they tell us about human behavior.* Dutton/Penguin Books.

**Segal, N. L.** (2012). *Born together—reared apart: The landmark Minnesota Twin Study.* Harvard University Press.

**Segal, N. L.** (2017). Twins reared together and apart: The science behind the fascination. *Proceedings of the American Philosophical Society, 161*(1), 1–17.

**Segal, N. L., & Cortez, F. A.** (2014). Born in Korea—adopted apart: Behavioral development of monozygotic twins raised in the United States and France. *Personality and Individual Differences, 70,* 97–104.

**Segall, M. H., Campbell, D. T., & Herskovits, M. J.** (1968). The influence of culture on visual perception. In H. Toch & C. Smith (Eds.), *Social perception* (pp. 1–5). Bobbs-Merrill.

**Segerstrom, S. C., & Miller, G. E.** (2004). Psychological stress and the human immune system: A meta-analytic study of 30 years of inquiry. *Psychological Bulletin, 130,* 601–630.

**Segerstrom, S. C., & Smith, G. T.** (2019). Personality and coping: Individual differences in responses to emotion. *Annual Review of Psychology, 70,* 651–671. https://doi.org/10.1146 /annurev-psych-010418-102917

**Segraves, R. T.** (2010). Considerations for a better definition of male orgasmic disorder in *DSM V. Journal of Sexual Medicine, 7,* 690–699.

**Seidel, J.** (2018). Convergence of placenta biology and genetic risk for schizophrenia. *Nature Medicine, 24*(6), 792–801. https://doi.org/10.1038 /s41591-018-0021-y

**Sekara, V., Deville, P., Ahnert, S. E., Barabási, A. L., Sinatra, R., & Lehmann, S.** (2018). The chaperone effect in scientific publishing. *Proceedings of the National Academy of Sciences, 115*(50), 12603–12607.

**Selena Gomez** [@selenagomez]. (2019, January 24). "My sweet soul sister. Julia you have been a huge part of my life. You have taught me how to" [Photograph]. Instagram. https:// .instagram.com/p/BtBuE0Hg-6j/?utm _source=ig_embed

**Seligman, M. E.** (2019). Positive psychology: A personal history. *Annual Review of Clinical Psychology, 15,* 1–23. https://doi.org/10.1146/annurev -clinpsy-050718-095653

Seligman, M. E. P. (1975). *Helplessness: On depression, development, and death.* W. H. Freeman.

Seligman, M. E. P. (1995). The effectiveness of psychotherapy: The *Consumer Reports* study. *American Psychologist, 50,* 965–974.

Seligman, M. E. P., & Csikszentmihalyi, M. (2000). Positive psychology: An introduction. *American Psychologist, 55,* 5–14.

Seligman, M. E. P., & Maier, S. F. (1967). Failure to escape traumatic shock. *Journal of Experimental Psychology, 74,* 1–9.

Seligman, M. E. P., & Steen, T. A. (2005). Positive psychology progress. *American Psychologist, 60,* 410–421.

Seltenrich, N. (2015, October). POPs and pubertal timing: Evidence of delayed development. *Environmental Health Perspectives, 123,* A266.

Selye, H. (1936). A syndrome produced by diverse nocuous agents. *Nature, 138,* 32.

Selye, H. (1953). The general-adaptation-syndrome in its relationships to neurology, psychology, and psychopathology. In A. Weider (Ed.), *Contributions toward medical psychology: Vol. 1. Theory and psychodiagnostic methods* (pp. 234–274). Ronald Press.

Selye, H. (1956). *The stress of life.* McGraw-Hill.

Selye, H. (1976). Forty years of stress research: Principal remaining problems and misconceptions. *Canadian Medical Association Journal, 115,* 53–56.

Selye, H., & Fortier, C. (1950). Adaptive reaction to stress. *Psychosomatic Medicine, 12,* 149–157.

Semega, J., Kollar, M., Shrider, E. A., & Creamer, J. (2020, September 15). *Income and poverty in the United States: 2019.* United States Census Bureau. https://www.census.gov /library/publications/2020/demo/p60 -270.html

Semple, R. J., Droutman, V., & Reid, B. A. (2017). Mindfulness goes to school: Things learned (so far) from research and real-world experiences. *Psychology in the Schools, 54,* 29–52.

Seo, C., Guru, A., Jin, M., Ito, B., Sleezer, B. J., Ho, Y.-Y., Wang, E., Boada, C., Krupa, N. A., Kullakanda, D. S., Shen, C. X., & Warden, M. R. (2019). Intense threat switches dorsal raphe serotonin neurons to a paradoxical operational mode. *Science, 363*(6426), 538–542. https://doi.org/10.1126/science .aau8722

Serrano, R. A. (2002, November 26). Hate crimes against Muslims soar, report says. *Los Angeles Times.* http:// articles.latimes.com/2002/nov/26 /nation/na-hate26

Servick, K. (2019, December). Doubts persist for claimed Alzheimer's drug. *Science, 366*(6471), 1298. https://doi.org/10.1126/science.366 .6471.1298

Seubert, J., Freiherr, J., Djordjevic, J., & Lundström, J. N. (2013). Statistical localization of human olfactory cortex. *Neuroimage, 66,* 333–342.

Shackelford, T. K., & Liddle, J. R. (2014). Understanding the mind from an evolutionary perspective: An overview of evolutionary psychology. *Wiley Interdisciplinary Reviews: Cognitive Science, 5,* 247–260.

Shafer, M., & Schiller, D. (2020, February 1). In search of the brain's social road maps. *Scientific American.* https://www.scientificamerican.com /article/in-search-of-the-brains-social -road-maps/

Shah, A. K., & Oppenheimer, D. M. (2008). Heuristics made easy: An effort-reduction framework. *Psychological Bulletin, 134,* 207–222.

Shahani, A. (2017, June 9). Changing pay rates keep Uber drivers on the road longer. *NPR.* http://www.npr.org /2017/06/09/532196932/changing-pay -rates-keep-uber-drivers-on-the-road -longer

Shahkhase, M. S., Gharaei, A., Fathi, M., Yaghoobi, H., & Bayazi, M. H. (2014). The study of hypnosis effectiveness in the treatment of headaches. *Reef Resources Assessment and Management Technical Paper, 40,* 426–432.

Shain, C., Blank, I. A., van Schijndel, M., Schuler, W., & Fedorenko, E. (2020). fMRI reveals language-specific predictive coding during naturalistic sentence comprehension. *Neuropsychologia, 138,* 107307. https://doi.org/10.1016/j .neuropsychologia.2019.107307

Shakeshaft, N. G., Trzaskowski, M., McMillan, A., Krapohl, E., Simpson, M. A., Reichenberg, A., Cederlöf, M., Larsson, H., Lichtenstein, P., & Plomin, R. (2015). Thinking positively: The genetics of high intelligence. *Intelligence, 48,* 123–132. https://doi .org/10.1016/j.intell.2014.11.005

Shams, M. [Mansoor Shams]. (2016, December 2). Stories of Muslims in US Armed Forces (Ibrahim Hashi) [Video file]. https://www.youtube.com /watch?v=EV38RkjljhA

Shan, C., Hussain, M., & Sargani, G. R. (2020). A mix-method investigation on acculturative stress among Pakistani students in China. *PLOS ONE, 15*(10), Article e0240103. https://doi.org/10 .1371/journal.pone.0240103

Shanok, N. A., Reive, C., Mize, K. D., & Jones, N. A. (2020). Mindfulness meditation intervention alters neurophysiological symptoms of anxiety and depression in preadolescents. *Journal of Psychophysiology, 34*(3), 159–170.

https://doi.org/10.1027/0269-8803 /a000244

Shapiro, D. H., Jr., Schwartz, C. E., & Astin, J. A. (1996). Controlling ourselves, controlling our world: Psychology's role in understanding positive and negative consequences of seeking and gaining control. *American Psychologist, 51,* 1213–1230.

Sharp, C., & Kim, S. (2015). Recent advances in the developmental aspects of borderline personality disorder. *Current Psychiatry Reports, 17* Article 21. https://doi.org/10.1007/s11920 -015-0556-2

Sharpless, B. A., & Barber, J. P. (2011). Lifetime prevalence rates of sleep paralysis: A systematic review. *Sleep Medicine Reviews, 15,* 311–315.

Shaw, J. (2016, January 8). 9 Things you probably didn't know about Sigmund Freud [Web log post]. *Scientific American.* https://blogs .scientificamerican.com/mind-guest -blog/9-things-you-probably-didn-t -know-about-sigmund-freud/

Shaw, J. (2020). Do false memories look real? Evidence that people struggle to identify rich false memories of committing crime and other emotional events. *Frontiers in Psychology, 11,* 650. https://doi.org/10.3389/fpsyg.2020 .00650

Shaw, J., & Porter, S. (2015). Constructing rich false memories of committing crime. *Psychological Science, 26,* 291–301.

Shea, B. (n.d.). Karl Popper: Philosophy of science. *Internet Encyclopedia of Philosophy.* http://www .iep.utm.edu/pop-sci/

Shearer, A., Hunt, M., Chowdhury, M., & Nicol, L. (2016). Effects of a brief mindfulness meditation intervention on student stress and heart rate variability. *International Journal of Stress Management, 23,* 232–254. https://doi.org/10.1037/a0039814

Shearer, C. B. (2020). A resting state functional connectivity analysis of human intelligence: Broad theoretical and practical implications for multiple intelligences theory. *Psychology & Neuroscience, 13*(2), 127–148. https:// doi.org/10.1037/pne0000200

Shearer, C. B., & Karanian, J. M. (2017). The neuroscience of intelligence: Empirical support for the theory of multiple intelligences? *Trends in Neuroscience and Education, 6,* 211–223. https://doi.org/10.1016/j.tine .2017.02.002

Shedler, J. (2010). The efficacy of psychodynamic psychotherapy. *American Psychologist, 63,* 98–109.

Shell, E. R. (2020, May 1). The new Alzheimer's–air pollution link. *Scientific American.* https://www .scientificamerican.com/article /the-new-alzheimers-air-pollution-link/

Shelton, J. F., Geraghty, E. M., Tancredi, D. J., Delwiche, L. D., Schmidt, R. J., Ritz, B., Hansen, R. L., & Hertz-Picciotto, I. (2014). Neurodevelopmental disorders and prenatal residential proximity to agricultural pesticides: The CHARGE study. *Environmental Health Perspectives, 122,* 1103–1109.

Shen, H. (2018, March 14). Portrait of a memory. *Scientific American.* https:// www.scientificamerican.com/article /portrait-of-a-memory/

Shepard, R. N., & Metzler, J. (1971). Mental rotation of three-dimensional objects. *Science, 171,* 701–703.

Sher, L. (2020). COVID-19, anxiety, sleep disturbances and suicide. *Sleep Medicine, 70*(124). https://doi.org/10 .1016/j.sleep.2020.04.019

Sherman, L. E., Payton, A. A., Hernandez, L. M., Greenfield, P. M., & Dapretto, M. (2016). The power of the like in adolescence: Effects of peer influence on neural and behavioral responses to social media. *Psychological Science, 27*(7), 1027–1035. https://doi.org/10.1177 /0956797616645673

Shermer, M. (2018, October 1). Why do people kill themselves? *Scientific American.* https://www.scientificamerican .com/article/why-do-people-kill -themselves/

Shernoff, D. J., Csikszentmihalyi, M., Shneider, B., & Shernoff, E. S. (2003). Student engagement in high school classrooms from the perspective of flow theory. *School Psychology Quarterly, 18,* 158–176.

Sherwood, L. (2016). *Human physiology: From cells to systems* (9th ed.). Cengage Learning.

Shi, F., Yap, P.-T., Wu, G., Jia, H., Gilmore, J. H., Lin, W., & Shen, D. (2011). Infant brain atlases from neonates to 1- and 2-year-olds. *PLOS ONE, 6.* https://doi.org/10.1371 /journal.pone.0018746

Shiban, Y., Diemer, J., Müller, J., Brütting-Schick, J., Pauli, P., & Mühlberger, A. (2017). Diaphragmatic breathing during virtual reality exposure therapy for aviophobia: Functional coping strategy or avoidance behavior? A pilot study. *BMC Psychiatry, 17*(1), Article 29. https://doi.org/10.1186 /s12888-016-1181-2

Shorter, E. (2015). The history of nosology and the rise of the *Diagnostic and Statistical Manual of Mental Disorders. Dialogues in Clinical Neuroscience, 17,* 59–67.

Shou, H., Yang, Z., Satterthwaite, T. D., Cook, P. A., Bruce, S. E., Shinohara, R. T., Rosenberg, B., & Sheline, Y. I. (2017). Cognitive behavioral therapy increases amygdala connectivity with the cognitive control network in both MDD and PTSD. *NeuroImage: Clinical, 14,* 464–470. https://doi.org/10.1016/j .nicl.2017.01.030

Shteynberg, G., Hirsh, J. B., Bentley, R. A., & Garthoff, J. (2020). Shared worlds and shared minds: A theory of collective learning and a psychology of common knowledge. *Psychological Review, 127*(5), 918–931. https://doi.org/10.1037/rev0000200

Shulman, H. C., Dixon, G. N., Bullock, O. M., & Colón Amill, D. (2020). The effects of jargon on processing fluency, self-perceptions, and scientific engagement. *Journal of Language and Social Psychology, 39*(5-6), 579–597. https://doi.org/10.1177/0261927X20902177

Shultz, J. M., Thoresen, S., & Galea, S. (2017). The Las Vegas shootings—underscoring key features of the firearm epidemic. *JAMA, 318*(18), 1753–1754. https://doi.org/10.1001/jama.2017.16420

Siciliano, C. A., Saha, K., Calipari, E. S., Fordahl, S. C., Chen, R., Khoshbouei, H., & Jones, S. R. (2018). Amphetamine reverses escalated cocaine intake via restoration of dopamine transporter conformation. *Journal of Neuroscience, 38*(2), 484–497. https://doi.org/10.1523/JNEUROSCI.2604-17.2017

Siclari, F., Baird, B., Perogamvros, L., Bernardi, G., LaRocque, J. J., Riedner, B., Boly, M., Postle, B. R., & Tononi, G. (2017). The neural correlates of dreaming. *Nature Neuroscience, 20*, 872–878. https://doi.org/10.1038/nn.4545

Siegel, J. M. (2005). Clues to the functions of mammalian sleep. *Nature, 437*, 1264–1271.

Sierp, A., & Karner, C. (2017). National stereotypes in the context of the European crisis. *National Identities, 19.* http://doi.org/10.1080/14608944.2016.1209646

Sifferlin, A. (2018, February 12). Fatal car crashes happen more often than usual on 4/20, study finds. *Time.* http://time.com/5143828/420-april-20-marijuana-day-car-crashes/

Signs, T. L., & Woods, S. B. (2020). Linking family and intimate partner relationships to chronic pain: An application of the biobehavioral family model. *Families, Systems, & Health, 38*(1), 38–50. https://doi.org/10.1037/fsh0000459

Silber, M. H., Ancoli-Israel, S., Bonnet, M. H., Chokroverty, S., Grigg-Damberger, M. M., Hirshkowitz, M., Kapen, S., Keenan, S. A., Kryger, M. H., Penzel, T., Pressman, M. R., & Iber, C. (2007). The visual scoring of sleep in adults. *Journal of Clinical Sleep Medicine, 3*(2), 121–131. https://doi.org/10.5664/jcsm.26814

Silva, C. E., & Kirsch, I. (1992). Interpretive sets, expectancy, fantasy proneness, and dissociation predictors of hypnotic response. *Journal of Personality and Social Psychology, 63,* 847–856.

Simion, F., & Di Giorgio, E. (2015). Face perception and processing in early infancy: Inborn predispositions and developmental changes. *Frontiers in Psychology, 6.* https://doi.org/10.3389/fpsyg.2015.00969

Simms, A., & Nichols, T. (2014). Social loafing: A review of the literature. *Journal of Management Policy and Practice, 15,* 58–67.

Simon, E. B., Rossi, A., Harvey, A. G., & Walker, M. P. (2020). Overanxious and underslept. *Nature Human Behaviour, 4*(1), 100–110. https://doi.org/10.1038/s41562-019-0754-8

Simon, S. (2015, January 16). *6 steps to help lower your cancer risk.* American Cancer Society. http://www.cancer.org/cancer/news/features/6-steps-to-help-lower-your-cancer-risk

Simons, D. J. (2010). Monkeying around with the gorillas in our midst: Familiarity with an inattentional-blindness task does not improve the detection of unexpected events. *i-Perception, 1,* 3–6.

Simonton, D. K. (2000). Creativity: Cognitive, personal, developmental, and social aspects. *American Psychologist, 55,* 151–158.

Simonton, D. K. (2012, November/December). The science of genius. *Scientific American Mind, 23,* 35–41.

Simpson, J. A., & Rholes, W. S. (2010). Attachment and relationships: Milestones and future directions. *Journal of Social and Personal Relationships, 27,* 173–180.

Sin, N. L., Klaiber, P., Wen, J. H., & DeLongis, A. (2021). Helping amid the pandemic: Daily affective and social implications of COVID-19-related prosocial activities. *The Gerontologist, 61*(1), 59–70. https://doi.org/10.1093/geront/gnaa140

Singh, L., Nestor, S., Parikh, C., & Yull, A. (2009). Influences of infant-directed speech on early word recognition. *Infancy, 14,* 654–666.

Singh, S., & Ilyayeva, S. (2020). Androgen insensitivity syndrome. *StatPearls [Internet].* https://www.ncbi.nlm.nih.gov/books/NBK542206/

Singh-Manoux, A., Kivimaki, M., Glymour, M. M., Elbaz, A., Berr, C., Ebmeier, K. P., Ferrie, A., & Dugravot, A. (2012). Timing of onset of cognitive decline: Results from Whitehall II prospective cohort study. *British Medical Journal, 334,* 1–8.

Sinn, D. L., & Moltschaniwskyj, N. A. (2005). Personality traits in dumpling squid (*Euprymna tasmania*): Context-specific traits and their correlation with biological characteristics. *Journal of Comparative Psychology, 119,* 99–110.

Sio, U. N., & Ormerod, T. C. (2009). Does incubation enhance problem solving? A meta-analytic review. *Psychological Bulletin, 135,* 94–120.

Sisti, D. A., Segal, A. G., & Emanuel, E. J. (2015). Improving long-term psychiatric care: Bring back the asylum. *Journal of the American Medical Association, 313,* 243–244.

Sivacek, J., & Crano, W. D. (1982). Vested interest as a moderator of attitude-behavior consistency. *Journal of Personality and Social Psychology, 43,* 210–221.

Skeem, J., Kennealy, P., Monahan, J., Peterson, J., & Appelbaum, P. (2016). Psychosis uncommonly and inconsistently precedes violence among high risk individuals. *Clinical Psychological Science, 4,* 40–49. https://doi.org/10.1177/2167702615575879

Skeldon, A. C., Derks, G., & Dijk, D. J. (2016). Modelling changes in sleep timing and duration across the lifespan: Changes in circadian rhythmicity or sleep homeostasis? *Sleep Medicine Reviews, 28,* 92–103. https://doi.org/10.1016/j.smrv.2015.05.011

Skinner, A. C., Ravanbakht, S. N., Skelton, J. A., Perrin, E. M., & Armstrong, S. C. (2018). Prevalence of obesity and severe obesity in US children, 1999–2016. *Pediatrics, 141*(3). https://doi.org/10.1542/peds.2017-3459

Skinner, B. F. (1953). *Science and human behavior.* Macmillan.

Skinner, B. F. (1956). A case history in scientific method. *American Psychologist, 11,* 221–233.

Skinner, B. F. (1957). *Verbal behavior.* Macmillan.

Skinner, B. F. (1976). *Particulars of my life.* Knopf.

Skinner, N. F. (2009). Academic folk wisdom: Fact, fiction and falderal. *Psychology Learning and Teaching, 8,* 46–50.

Skoog, G., & Skoog, I. (1999). A 20-year follow-up of patients with obsessive compulsive disorder. *Archives of General Psychiatry, 56,* 121–127.

Slavich, G. M. (2016). Life stress and health: A review of conceptual issues and recent findings. *Teaching of Psychology, 43,* 346–355. https://doi.org/10.1177/0098628316662768

Slawinski, B. L., Klump, K. L., & Burt, S. A. (2019). No sex differences in the origins of covariation between social and physical aggression. *Psychological Medicine, 49*(15), 2515–2523. https://doi.org/10.1017/S0033291718003392

Slepecky, M., Kotianova, A., Prasko, J., Majercak, I., Gyorgyova, E., Kotian, M., Zatkova, M., Popelkova, M., Ociskova, M., & Tonhajzerova, I. (2017). Which psychological, psychophysiological, and anthropometric factors are connected with life events, depression, and quality of life in patients with cardiovascular disease. *Neuropsychiatric Disease and Treatment, 13,* 2093–2104. https://doi.org/10.2147/NDT.S141811

Slife, B. D. (1990). Introduction and overview of the special issue on Aristotle. *Theoretical & Philosophical Psychology, 10,* 3–6.

Slotema, C. W., Blom, J. D., Hoek, H. W., & Sommer, I. E. C. (2010). Should we expand the toolbox of psychiatric treatment methods to include repetitive transcranial magnetic stimulation (rTMS)? A meta-analysis of the efficacy of rTMS in psychiatric disorders. *Journal of Clinical Psychiatry, 71,* 873–884.

Sloter, E., Schmid, T. E., Marchetti, F., Eskenazi, B., Nath, J., & Wyrobek, A. J. (2006). Quantitative effects of male age on sperm motion. *Human Reproduction, 21,* 2868–2875.

Smalarz, L., Douglass, A., & Chang, A. (2020). Eyewitness-identification decisions as Brady material: Disclosing information about prior decisions affects evaluations of eyewitnesses. *Psychology, Public Policy, and Law, 26*(1), 10–21.

Small, D. M., & DiFeliceantonio, A. G. (2019). Processed foods and food reward. *Science, 363*(6425), 346–347. https://doi.org/10.1126/science.aav0556

Smink, F. R., van Hoeken, D., & Hoek, H. W. (2012). Epidemiology of eating disorders: Incidence, prevalence and mortality rates. *Current Psychiatry Reports, 14,* 406–414.

Smit, D. J., Cath, D., Zilhão, N. R., Ip, H. F., Denys, D., den Braber, A., de Geus, E. J. C., Verweij, K. J. H., Hottenga, J.-J., & Boomsma, D. I. (2020). Genetic meta-analysis of obsessive–compulsive disorder and self-report compulsive symptoms. *American Journal of Medical Genetics Part B: Neuropsychiatric Genetics, 183*(4), 208–216. https://doi.org/10.1002/ajmg.b.32777

Smith, A. C., Marty-Dugas, J., Ralph, B. C. W., & Smilek, D. (2020). Examining the relation between grit, flow, and measures of attention in everyday life. *Psychology of Consciousness: Theory, Research, and Practice.* Advance online publication. https://doi.org/10.1037/cns0000226

Smith, C. N., & Squire, L. R. (2009). Medial temporal lobe activity during retrieval of semantic memory is related to the age of the memory. *Journal of Neuroscience, 29,* 930–938.

Smith, D. (2001). Shock and disbelief. *Atlantic Monthly, 287,* 79–90.

Smith, D. H., Johnson, V. E., Trojanowski, J. Q., & Stewart, W. (2019). Chronic traumatic encephalopathy—confusion and controversies. *Nature Reviews Neurology, 15*(3), 179–183. https://doi.org/10.1038/s41582-018-0114-8

Smith, R., Lane, R. D., Alkozei, A., Bao, J., Smith, C., Sanova, A., Nettles, M., & Killgore, W. D. (2018). The role of medial prefrontal cortex in the working memory maintenance of one's own emotional responses. *Scientific Reports, 8,* 3460. https://doi.org/10.1038/s41598-018-21896-8

Smith, S. M., Glenberg, A. M., & Bjork, R. A. (1978). Environmental context and human memory. *Memory & Cognition, 6,* 342–353.

Smith, T. W., Birmingham, W., & Uchino, B. N. (2012). Evaluative threat and ambulatory blood pressure: Cardiovascular effects of social stress in daily experience. *Health Psychology, 31,* 763–766.

Smith, T. W., & MacKenzie, J. (2006). Personality and risk of physical illness. *Annual Review of Clinical Psychology, 2,* 435–467.

Smith, T. W., & Ruiz, J. M. (2002). Psychosocial influences on the development and course of coronary heart disease: Current status and implications for research and practice. *Journal of Consulting and Clinical Psychology, 70,* 548–568.

Smolen, P., Baxter, D. A., & Byrne, J. H. (2019). How can memories last for days, years, or a lifetime? Proposed mechanisms for maintaining synaptic potentiation and memory. *Learning and Memory, 26*(5), 133–150. https://doi.org/10.1101/lm.049395.119

Smyth, A. P., Gammage, K. L., Lamarche, L., & Muir, C. (2020). Examining university men's psychobiological and behavioral response-recovery profile from a social-evaluative body image threat. *American Journal of Men's Health, 14*(2). https://doi.org/10.1177/1557988320910831

Snyder, T. D., de Brey, C., & Dillow, S. A. (2019). *Digest of education statistics 2017* (NCES 2018-070). National Center for Education Statistics, Institute of Education Sciences, U.S. Department of Education. https://nces.ed.gov/pubs2018/2018070.pdf

Soat, M. (2015). Social media triggers a dopamine high. *Marketing News, 49*(11), 20–21.

Socci, V., Tempesta, D., Desideri, G., De Gennaro, L., & Ferrara, M. (2017). Enhancing human cognition with cocoa flavonoids. *Frontiers in Nutrition, 4,* 19. https://doi.org/10.3389/fnut.2017.00019

Sohn, E. (2018, July 25). How the evidence stacks up for preventing Alzheimer's disease. *Nature, 559,* S18–S20. https://doi.org10.1038/d41586-018-05724-7.

Soleymani, E., Faizi, F., Heidarimoghadam, R., Davoodi, L., & Mohammadi, Y. (2020). Association of T. gondii infection with suicide: A systematic review and meta-analysis. *BMC Public Health, 20,* Article 766. https://doi.org/10.1186/s12889-020-08898-w

Solivan, A. E., Wallace, M. E., Kaplan, K. C., & Harville, E. W. (2015). Use of a resiliency framework to examine pregnancy and birth outcomes among adolescents: A qualitative study. *Families, Systems, & Health, 33,* 349–355.

Solms, M. (2006, April/May). Freud returns. *Scientific American,* 82–88.

Solomon, B. C., & Jackson, J. J. (2014). The long reach of one's spouse: Spouses' personality influences occupational success. *Psychological Science, 25,* 2189–2198.

Solomon, S. G., & Lennie, P. (2007). The machinery of color vision. *Nature Reviews Neuroscience, 8,* 276–286.

Song, C., & Knöpfel, T. (2016). Optogenetics enlightens neuroscience drug discovery. *Nature Reviews Drug Discovery, 15,* 97–109. https://doi.org/10.1038/nrd.2015.15

Song, C. G., Zhang, Y. Z., Wu, H. N., Cao, X. L., Guo, C. J., Li, Y. Q., Zheng, M.-H., & Han, H. (2018). Stem cells: A promising candidate to treat neurological disorders. *Neural Regeneration Research, 13*(7), 1294–1304. https://doi.org/10.4103/1673-5374.235085

Song, W., Torous, J., Kossowsky, J., Chen, C. Y., Huang, H., & Wright, A. (2020). Genome-wide association analysis of insomnia using data from partners Biobank. *Scientific Reports, 10*(1), 6928. https://doi.org/10.1038/s41598-020-63792-0

Sorhagen, N. S. (2013). Early teacher expectations disproportionately affect poor children's high school performance. *Journal of Educational Psychology, 105,* 465–477.

Sorokowski, P., Sorokowska, A., & Witzel, C. (2014). Sex differences in color preferences transcend extreme differences in culture and ecology. *Psychonomic Bulletin & Review, 21*(5), 1195–1201.

Sorrells, S. F., Paredes, M. F., Cebrian-Silla, A., Sandoval, K., Qi, D., Kelley, K. W., James, D., Mayer, S., Chang, J., Auguste, K. I., Chang, E. F., Gutierrez, A. J., Kriegstein, A. R., Mathern, G. W., Oldham, M. C., Huang, E. J., Garcia-Verdugo, J. M., Yang, Z., & Alvarez-Buylla, A. (2018). Human hippocampal neurogenesis drops sharply in children to undetectable levels in adults. *Nature, 555*(7696), 377–381. https://doi.org/10.1038/nature25975

Soto, A., Smith, T. B., Griner, D., Domenech Rodríguez, M., & Bernal, G. (2018). Cultural adaptations and therapist multicultural competence: Two meta-analytic reviews. *Journal of Clinical Psychology: In Session, 74,* 1907–1923. https://doi.org/10.1002/jclp.22679

Soto, C. J. (2019). How replicable are links between personality traits and consequential life outcomes? The Life Outcomes of Personality Replication Project. *Psychological Science, 30,* 711–727. https://doi.org/10.1177/0956797619831612

Soto, C. J., & John, O. P. (2017). The next Big Five Inventory (BFI-2): Developing and assessing a hierarchical model with 15 facets to enhance bandwidth, fidelity, and predictive power. *Journal of Personality and Social Psychology, 113,* 117–143. https://doi.org/10.1037/pspp0000096

Soto, C. J., & Tackett, J. L. (2015). Personality traits in childhood and adolescence structure, development, and outcomes. *Current Directions in Psychological Science, 24,* 358–362.

Spagna, A., Kim, T. H., Wu, T., & Fan, J. (2020). Right hemisphere superiority for executive control of attention. *Cortex, 122,* 263–276. https://doi.org/10.1016/j.cortex.2018.12.012

Spanos, B. (2018, April 26). Janelle Monáe frees herself. *Rolling Stone.* https://www.rollingstone.com/music/music-features/janelle-monae-frees-herself-629204/

Sparling, J., Wilder, D. A., Kondash, J., Boyle, M., & Compton, M. (2011). Effects of interviewer behavior on accuracy of children's responses. *Journal of Applied Behavior Analysis, 44,* 587–592.

Speakman, J. R., Levitsky, D. A., Allison, D. B., Bray, M. S., de Castro, J. M., Clegg, D. J., Clapham, J. C., Dulloo, A. G., Gruer, L., Haw, S., Hebebrand, J., Hetherington, M. M., Higgs, S., Jebb, S. A., Loos, R. J. F., Luckman, S., Luke, A., Mohammed-Ali, V., O'Rahilly, S., . . . Westerterp-Plantenga, M. S. (2011). Set points, settling points and some alternative models: Theoretical options to understand how genes and environments combine to regulate body adiposity. *Disease Models & Mechanisms, 4,* 733–745.

Spear, L. P. (2013). Adolescent neurodevelopment. *Journal of Adolescent Health, 52,* S7–S13.

Specht, J., Egloff, B., & Schmukle, S. C. (2011). Stability and change of personality across the life course: The impact of age and major life events on mean-level and rank-order stability of the Big Five. *Journal of Personality and Social Psychology, 101,* 862–882.

Spence, C. (2020). Wine psychology: Basic & applied. *Cognitive Research: Principles and Implications, 5,* Article 22(2020). https://doi.org/10.1186/s41235-020-00225-6

Sperling, G. (1960). The information available in brief visual presentations. *Psychological Monographs: General and Applied, 74,* 1–29.

Sperry, D. E., Sperry, L. L., & Miller, P. J. (2019). Reexamining the verbal environments of children from different socioeconomic backgrounds. *Child Development, 90*(4), 1303–1318. https://doi.org/10.1111/cdev.13072

Spiegel, D., Loewenstein, R. J., Lewis-Fernández, R., Sar, V., Simeon, D., Vermetten, E., Simeon, D., & Dell, P. F. (2011). Dissociative disorders in *DSM-5. Depression and Anxiety, 28,* 824–852.

Spinelli, M., Fasolo, M., & Mesman, J. (2017). Does prosody make the difference? A meta-analysis on relations between prosodic aspects of infant-directed speech and infant outcomes. *Developmental Review, 44,* 1–18. https://doi.org/10.1016/j.dr.2016.12.001

Spinner, L., Cameron, L., & Calogero, R. (2018). Peer toy play as a gateway to children's gender flexibility: The effect of (counter) stereotypic portrayals of peers in children's magazines. *Sex Roles, 79,* 314–328. https://doi.org/10.1007/s11199-017-0883-3

Spitzer, R. L. (1975). On pseudoscience in science, logic in remission, and psychiatric diagnosis: A critique of Rosenhan's "On Being Sane in Insane Places." *Journal of Abnormal Psychology, 84,* 442–451.

Spong, C. Y. (2013). Defining "term" pregnancy: Recommendations from the Defining "Term" Pregnancy Workgroup. *Journal of the American Medical Association, 309*(23), 2445–2446.

Squire, L. R. (2009). The legacy of patient HM for neuroscience. *Neuron, 61*(1), 6–9.

Squire, L. R., Stark, C. E. L., & Clark, R. E. (2004). The medial temporal lobe. *Annual Review of Neuroscience, 27,* 279–306.

Squire, L. R., & Wixted, J. T. (2011). The cognitive neuroscience of human memory since HM. *Annual Review of Neuroscience, 34,* 259–288.

Stahl, E. A., Breen, G., Forstner, A. J., McQuillin, A., Ripke, S., Trubetskoy, V., Mattheisen, M., Wang, Y., Coleman, J. R. I., Gaspar, H. A., de Leeuw, C. A., Steinberg, J. S., Whitehead Pavlides, J. M., Trzaskowski, M., Byrne, E. M., Pers, T. H., Holmans, P. A., Richards, A. L., Abbott, L., . . . The Bipolar Working Group of the Psychiatric Genomics Consortium. (2019). Genome-wide association study identifies 30 loci associated with bipolar disorder. *Nature Genetics, 51,* 793–803. https://doi.org/10.1038/s41588-019-0397-8

**Stahre, M., Roeber, J., Kanny, D., Brewer, R. D., & Zhang, X.** (2014). Contribution of excessive alcohol consumption to deaths and years of potential life lost in the United States. *Preventing Chronic Disease, 11.* https://doi.org/10.5888/pcd11.130293

**Stajkovic, A. D., Bandura, A., Locke, E. A., Lee, D., & Sergent, K.** (2018). Test of three conceptual models of influence of the big five personality traits and self-efficacy on academic performance: A meta-analytic path-analysis. *Personality and Individual Differences, 120,* 238–245. https://doi.org/10.1016/j.paid.2017.08.014

**Stamatakis, A. M., Van Swieten, M., Basiri, M. L., Blair, G. A., Kantak, P., & Stuber, G. D.** (2016). Lateral hypothalamic area glutamatergic neurons and their projections to the lateral habenula regulate feeding and reward. *Journal of Neuroscience, 36,* 302–311. https://doi.org/10.1523/JNEUROSCI.1202-15.2016

**Stanbrook, M. B., & Drazen, J. M.** (2020). Vaping-induced lung disease—a look forward by looking back. *New England Journal of Medicine, 382,* 1649–1650. https://doi.org/10.1056/NEJMe2004876

**Staniloiu, A., & Markowitsch, H. J.** (2012). The remains of the day in dissociative amnesia. *Brain Sciences, 2,* 101–129.

**Stanley, T. D., Carter, E. C., & Doucouliagos, H.** (2018). What meta-analyses reveal about the replicability of psychological research. *Psychological Bulletin, 144*(12), 1325–1346. https://doi.org/10.1037/bul0000169

**Stanovich, K. E.** (2019). *How to think straight about psychology* (11th ed.). Pearson.

**Starr, D.** (2019, June 13). This psychologist explains why people confess to crimes they didn't commit. *Science.* https://www.sciencemag.org/news/2019/06/psychologist-explains-why-people-confess-crimes-they-didn-t-commit

**Starr, D.** (2020, March 26). Meet the psychologist exploring unconscious bias—and its tragic consequences for society. *Science.* https://www.sciencemag.org/news/2020/03/meet-psychologist-exploring-unconscious-bias-and-its-tragic-consequences-society

**Staub, M. E.** (2016). The other side of the brain: The politics of split-brain research in the 1970s–1980s. *History of Psychology, 19,* 259–273. https://doi.org/10.1037/hop0000035

**Staudt, M. D., Herring, E. Z., Gao, K., Miller, J. P., & Sweet, J. A.** (2019). Evolution in the treatment of psychiatric disorders: From psychosurgery to psychopharmacology to neuromodulation. *Frontiers in Neuroscience, 13,* Article 108. https://doi.org/10.3389/fnins.2019.00108

**Stavrova, O.** (2019). Having a happy spouse is associated with lowered risk of mortality. *Psychological Science, 30,* 798–803. https://doi.org/10.1177/0956797619835147

**Steele, C. M.** (1997). A threat in the air: How stereotypes shape intellectual identity and performance. *American Psychologist, 52,* 613–629.

**Steele, C. M.** (2010). *Whistling Vivaldi: How stereotypes affect us and what we can do.* W. W. Norton.

**Steele, H., Bate, J., Steele, M., Dube, S. R., Danskin, K., Knafo, H., Nikitiades, A., Bonuck, K., Meissner, P., & Murphy, A.** (2016). Adverse childhood experiences, poverty, and parenting stress. *Canadian Journal of Behavioural Science/Revue Canadienne des Sciences du Comportement, 48*(1), 32–38. https://doi.org/10.1037/cbs0000034

**Steenhuis, I., & Poelman, M.** (2017). Portion size: Latest developments and interventions. *Current Obesity Reports, 6*(1), 10–17. https://doi.org/10.1007/s13679-017-0239-x

**Stein, B. E., Stanford, T. R., & Rowland, B. A.** (2009). The neural basis of multisensory integration in the midbrain: Its organization and maturation. *Hearing Research, 258,* 4–15.

**Stein, R., & Swan, A. B.** (2019). Evaluating the validity of Myers-Briggs Type Indicator theory: A teaching tool and window into intuitive psychology. *Social and Personality Psychology Compass, 13*(2), e12434. https://doi.org/10.1111/spc3.12441

**Steinberg, L.** (2010). Commentary: A behavioral scientist looks at the science of adolescent brain development. *Brain and Cognition, 72,* 160–164.

**Steinberg, L.** (2012). Should the science of adolescent brain development inform public policy? *Issues in Science & Technology, 28,* 76–78.

**Steinberg, L., Icenogle, G., Shulman, E. P., Breiner, K., Chein, J., Bacchini, D., Chang, L., Chaudhary, N., Di Giunta, L., Dodge, K. A., Fanti, K. A., Lansford, J. E., Malone, P. S., Oburu, P., Pastorelli, C., Skinner, A. T., Sorbring, E., Tapanya, S., Tirado, L. M. U., . . . Takash, H. M. S.** (2018). Around the world, adolescence is a time of heightened sensation seeking and immature self-regulation. *Developmental Science, 21*(2), e12532. https://doi.org/10.1111/desc.12532

**Steindl, C., & Jonas, E.** (2015). The dynamic reactance interaction—How vested interests affect people's experience, behavior, and cognition in social interactions. *Frontiers in Psychology, 6.* https://doi.org/10.3389/fpsyg.2015.01752

**Steiner, M.** (2012, September 4). *The importance of pragmatic communication.* Monocacy Neurodevelopmental Center. http://monocacycenter.com/the-importance-of-pragmatic-communication/

**Steinfeldt, J. A., Clay, S. L., & Priester, P. E.** (2020). Prevalence and perceived importance of racial matching in the psychotherapeutic dyad: A national survey of addictions treatment clinical practices. *Substance Abuse Treatment, Prevention, and Policy, 15*(1), Article 76. https://doi.org/10.1186/s13011-020-00318-x

**Steinmetz, J., Xu, Q., Fishbach, A., & Zhang, Y.** (2016). Being observed magnifies action. *Journal of Personality and Social Psychology, 111,* 852–865. https://doi.org/10.1037/pspi0000065

**Stenseng, F., Belsky, J., Skalicka, V., & Wichstrøm, L.** (2014). Preschool social exclusion, aggression, and cooperation: A longitudinal evaluation of the need-to-belong and the social-reconnection hypotheses. *Personality and Social Psychology Bulletin, 40,* 1637–1647.

**Stern, E. M.** (2016). Foreword to the second edition. In K. J. Schneider, J. F. Pierson, & J. F. T. Bugental (Eds.), *The handbook of humanistic psychology: Theory, research, and practice* (2nd ed., p. xi). Sage.

**Stern, K., & McClintock, M. K.** (1998). Regulation of ovulation by human pheromones. *Nature, 392,* 177–179.

**Stern, R. A., Adler, C. H., Chen, K., Navitsky, M., Luo, J., Dodick, D. W., Alosco, M. L., Tripodis, Y., Goradia, D. D., Martin, B., Mastroeni, D., Fritts, N. G., Jarnagin, J., Devous, M. D., Mintun, M. A., Pontecorvo, M. J., Shenton, M. E., & Reiman, E. M.** (2019). Tau positron-emission tomography in former national football league players. *New England Journal of Medicine, 380*(18), 1716–1725. https://doi.org/10.1056/NEJMoa1900757

**Sternberg, R. J.** (1988). *The triarchic mind: A new theory of human intelligence.* Viking.

**Sternberg, R. J.** (2004). Culture and intelligence. *American Psychologist, 59,* 325–338.

**Sternberg, R. J.** (2006a). Creating a vision of creativity: The first 25 years. *Psychology of Aesthetics, Creativity, and the Arts, S*(1), 2–12.

**Sternberg, R. J.** (2006b). The nature of creativity. *Creativity Research Journal, 18,* 87–98.

**Stetka, B.** (2017, October 11). Where's the proof that mindfulness meditation works? *Scientific American.* https://www.scientificamerican.com/article/wheres-the-proof-that-mindfulness-meditation-works1/

**Stetka, B.** (2020, June 18). The brain interprets smell like the notes of a song. *Scientific American.* https://www.scientificamerican.com/article/the-brain-interprets-smell-like-the-notes-of-a-song/

**Steventon, J. J., Foster, C., Furby, H., Helme, D., Wise, R. G., & Murphy, K.** (2020). Hippocampal blood flow is increased after 20 min of moderate-intensity exercise. *Cerebral Cortex, 30*(2), 525–533. https://doi.org/10.1093/cercor/bhz104

**Stieff, M., Origenes, A., DeSutter, D., Lira, M., Banevicius, L., Tabang, D., & Cabel, G.** (2018). Operational constraints on the mental rotation of STEM representations. *Journal of Educational Psychology, 110,* 1160–1174. https://doi.org/10.1037/edu0000258

**Stierwalt, S.** (2020, June 25). Is astrology real? Here's what science says. *Scientific American.* https://www.scientificamerican.com/article/is-astrology-real-heres-what-science-says/?print=true

**Stix, G.** (2020, January 30). What's in kale (or a pear) that seems to lower Alzheimer's risk? *Scientific American.* https://www.scientificamerican.com/article/whats-in-kale-or-a-pear-that-seems-to-lower-alzheimers-risk1/?print=true

**Stoet, G., & Geary, D. C.** (2013). Sex differences in mathematics and reading achievement are inversely related: Within- and across-nation assessment of 10 years of PISA data. *PLOS ONE, 8,* e57988. https://doi.org/10.1371/journal.pone.0057988

**Stoica, T.** (2019, January 25). Why do we sleep? *Scientific American.* https://blogs.scientificamerican.com/observations/why-do-we-sleep/#googDisableSync

**Stojanoski, B., Wild, C. J., Battista, M. E., Nichols, E. S., & Owen, A. M.** (2020). Brain training habits are not associated with generalized benefits to cognition: An online study of over 1000 "brain trainers." *Journal of Experimental Psychology: General.* Advance online publication. https://doi.org/10.1037/xge0000773

**Stoll, J., Müller, J. A., & Trachsel, M.** (2020). Ethical issues in online psychotherapy: A narrative review. *Frontiers in Psychiatry, 10,* Article 993. https://doi.org/10.3389/fpsyt.2019.00993

**Stoltenborgh, M., Bakermans-Kranenburg, M. J., Alink, L. R. A., & van IJzendoorn, M. H.** (2015). The prevalence of child maltreatment across the globe: Review of a series of meta-analyses. *Child Abuse Review, 24,* 37–50.

**Stone, D. N., Deci, E. L., & Ryan, R. M.** (2009). Beyond talk: Creating autonomous motivation through self-determination theory. *Journal of General Management, 34,* 75–102.

Storm, B. C., Bjork, E. L., & Bjork, R. A. (2008). Accelerated relearning after retrieval-induced forgetting: The benefit of being forgotten. *Journal of Experimental Psychology: Learning, Memory, and Cognition, 34,* 230–236.

Storrs, C. (2017, July 13). How poverty affects the brain. *Nature News, 547,* 150–152.

Strack, F., Martin, L. L., & Stepper, S. (1988). Inhibiting and facilitating conditions of the human smile: A nonobtrusive test of the facial feedback hypothesis. *Journal of Personality and Social Psychology, 54,* 768–777.

Strack, J., Lopes, P., Esteves, F., & Fernandez-Berrocal, P. (2017). Must we suffer to succeed? When anxiety boosts motivation and performance. *Journal of Individual Differences, 38*(2), 113–124. https://doi.org/10.1027/1614-0001/a000228

Strain, G. M. (2003). How well do dogs and other animals hear? Department of Comparative Biomedical Sciences, School of Veterinary Medicine, Louisiana State University. http://www.lsu.edu/deafness/HearingRange.html

Stratton, G. (1896, August). *Some preliminary experiments on vision without inversion of the retinal image.* Paper presented at the Third International Congress for Psychology, Munich.

Straub, R. O. (2017). *Health psychology: A biopsychosocial approach* (5th ed.). Worth Publishers.

Straub, R. O. (2019). *Health psychology: A biopsychosocial approach* (6th ed.). Worth Publishers.

Strawser, M. G., & McCormick, J. K. (2017). Adapting the basic communication course for a globally and technologically mediated 21st century context. *Basic Communication Course Annual, 29,* 83–89.

Strayer, D. L., Getty, D., Biondi, F., & Cooper, J. M. (2021). The multitasking motorist and the attention economy. In S. M. Lane & P. Atchley (Eds.), *Human capacity in the attention economy* (pp. 135–156). American Psychological Association. https://doi.org/10.1037/0000208-007

Streit, W. J. (2000). Microglial response to brain injury: A brief synopsis. *Toxicologic Pathology, 28,* 28–30.

Strelan, P. (2018). Justice and forgiveness in interpersonal relationships. *Current Directions in Psychological Science, 27,* 20–24. https://doi.org/10.1177/0963721417734311

Strenger, C. (2015). Can psychoanalysis reclaim the public sphere? *Psychoanalytic Psychology, 32,* 293–306.

Strickland, B. R. (2014). Julian B. Rotter (1916–2014). *American Psychologist, 69,* 545–546.

Strickler, J., & Farmer, T. (2019). Dorothea Dix: Crusader for

patients with mental illness. *Nursing 2019, 49*(1), 49–51. https://doi.org/10.1097/01.NURSE.0000549724.14939.d8

Stroebe, W., van Koningsbruggen, G. M., Papies, E. K., & Aarts, H. (2013). Why most dieters fail but some succeed: A goal conflict model of eating behavior. *Psychological Review, 120,* 110–138.

Stull, A. T., & Hegarty, M. (2016). Model manipulation and learning: Fostering representational competence with virtual and concrete models. *Journal of Educational Psychology, 108,* 509–527. https://doi.org/10.1037/edu0000077

Stumm, S., Smith-Woolley, E., Ayorech, Z., McMillan, A., Rimfeld, K., Dale, P. S., & Plomin, R. (2020). Predicting educational achievement from genomic measures and socioeconomic status. *Developmental Science, 23.* Article e12925. https://doi.org/10.1111/desc.12925

Stuss, D. T., & Alexander, M. P. (2000). Executive functions and the frontal lobes: A conceptual view. *Psychological Research, 63,* 289–298.

Su, Y. S., Veeravagu, A., & Grant, G. (2016). Neuroplasticity after traumatic brain injury. In D. Laskowitz & G. Grant (Eds.), *Translational research in traumatic brain injury* (Chap. 8). CRC Press/Taylor and Francis Group. https://www.ncbi.nlm.nih.gov/books/NBK326735/

Substance Abuse and Mental Health Services Administration (SAMHSA). (2020). *Key substance use and mental health indicators in the United States: Results from the 2019 National Survey on Drug Use and Health* (HHS Publication No. PEP20-07-01-001, NSDUH Series H-55). Center for Behavioral Health Statistics and Quality, Substance Abuse and Mental Health Services Administration. https://www.samhsa.gov/data/

Sullivan, E. (2018, October 5). Nobel Peace Prize goes to Denis Mukwege and Nadia Murad for fighting sexual violence. *NPR.* https://www.npr.org/2018/10/05/654675123/denis-mukwege-and-nadia-murad-win-nobel-peace-prize-for-fighting-sexual-violence

Summa, K. C., & Turek, F. W. (2015, February). The clocks within us. *Scientific American, 312,* 50–55.

Sumner, R. C., & Gallagher, S. (2017). Unemployment as a chronic stressor: A systematic review of cortisol studies. *Psychology & Health, 32,* 289–311. https://doi.org/10.1080/08870446.2016.1247841

Sunderam, S., Kissin, D. M., Zhang, Y., Folger, S. G., Boulet, S. L., Warner, L., Callaghan, W. M., & Barfield, W. D. (2019). Assisted reproductive technology surveillance—United States, 2016. *MMWR Surveillance Summaries, 68*(4). https://doi.org/10.15585/mmwr.ss6804a1

Suni, E. (2020, July 31). How much sleep do we really need? *SleepFoundation.org.* https://www.sleepfoundation.org/articles/how-much-sleep-do-we-really-need

Sutherland, C. A., Liu, X., Zhang, L., Chu, Y., Oldmeadow, J. A., & Young, A. W. (2018). Facial first impressions across culture: Data-driven modeling of Chinese and British perceivers' unconstrained facial impressions. *Personality and Social Psychology Bulletin, 44,* 521–537. https://doi.org/10.1177/0146167217744194

Sutherland, S. (2017, May/June). Rethinking relief. *Scientific American Mind, 28,* 28–35.

Sutterland, A. L., Fond, G., Kuin, A., Koeter, M. W. J., Lutter, R., Van Gool, T., Yolken, R., Szoke, A., Leboyer, M., & de Haan, L. (2015). Beyond the association. *Toxoplasma gondii* in schizophrenia, bipolar disorder, and addiction: Systematic review and meta-analysis. *Acta Psychiatrica Scandinavica, 132*(3), 161–179.

Sutton, C. (2018, July 6). Dark and treacherous: Perils of the Thai cave rescue. *news.com.au.* https://www.news.com.au/world/asia/dark-and-treacherous-perils-of-the-thai-cave-rescue/news-story/b8e636f74ddd342f275835bdfd8dc99d

Suvisaari, J., Torniainen-Holm, M., Lindgren, M., Härkänen, T., & Yolken, R. H. (2017). *Toxoplasma gondii* infection and common mental disorders in the Finnish general population. *Journal of Affective Disorders, 223,* 20–25. https://doi.org/10.1016/j.jad.2017.07.020

Suwanrath, C., & Suntharasaj, T. (2010). Sleep–wake cycles in normal fetuses. *Archives of Gynecology and Obstetrics, 281,* 449–454.

Svoboda, E. (2020, August 22). How our brains numb us to COVID-19's risks—and what we can do about it. *The Washington Post.* https://www.washingtonpost.com/health/covid-risks-stop-seeming-so-scary/2020/08/21/09c286c4-cc49-11ea-bc6a-6841b28d9093_story.html

Svrakic, D. M., Zorumski, C. F., Svrakic, N. M., Zwir, I., & Cloninger, C. R. (2013). Risk architecture of schizophrenia: The role of epigenetics. *Current Opinion in Psychiatry, 26,* 188–195.

Swan, S. H., Liu, F., Hines, M., Kruse, R. L, Wang, C., Redmon, J. B., Sparks, A., & Weiss, B. (2010). Prenatal phthalate exposure and reduced masculine play in boys. *International Journal of Andrology, 3,* 259–269.

Swendsen, J. D., Tennen, H., Carney, M. A., Affleck, G., Willard, A., & Hromi, A. (2000). Mood and alcohol consumption: An experience sampling test of the self-medication

hypothesis. *Journal of Abnormal Psychology, 109,* 198–204.

Swift, J. K., & Greenberg, R. P. (2012). Premature discontinuation in adult psychotherapy: A meta-analysis. *Journal of Consulting and Clinical Psychology, 80,* 547–559.

Syracuse University. (n.d.). InclusiveU. http://taishoffcenter.syr.edu/inclusiveu/

Szabo, B., Noble, D. W., & Whiting, M. J. (2020). Learning in non-avian reptiles 40 years on: Advances and promising new directions. *Biological Reviews.* https://doi.org/10.1111/brv.12658

Szabo, R., & Hall, M. (2007). *Behind happy faces: Taking charge of your mental health—a guide for young adults.* Taylor Trade.

Szasz, T. (2011). The myth of mental illness: 50 years later. *Psychiatrist Online, 35,* 179–182.

Tackett, J. L., Waldman, I. D., & Lahey, B. B. (2009). Etiology and measurement of relational aggression: A multi-informant behavior genetic investigation. *Journal of Abnormal Psychology, 118,* 722–733.

Tai, N. C. (2015). Computational investigation of the illusory depth effect of luminance contrast on a three-dimensional architectural scene with binocular vision. *Journal of Asian Architecture and Building Engineering, 14*(2), 331–338. https://doi.org/10.3130/jaabe.14.331

Takacs, Z. K., & Kassai, R. (2019). The efficacy of different interventions to foster children's executive function skills: A series of meta-analyses. *Psychological Bulletin, 145,* 653–697. https://doi.org/10.1037/bul0000195

Takahashi, K., Mizuno, K., Sasaki, A. T., Wada, Y., Tanaka, M., Ishii, A., Tajima, K., Tsuyuguchi, N., Watanabe, K., Zeki, S., & Watanabe, Y. (2015). Imaging the passionate stage of romantic love by dopamine dynamics. *Frontiers in Human Neuroscience, 9.* https://doi.org/10.3389/fnhum.2015.00191

Talarico, J. M., Bohn, A., & Wessel, I. (2019). The role of event relevance and congruence to social groups in flashbulb memory formation. *Memory, 27*(7), 985–997. https://doi.org/10.1080/09658211.2019.1616097

Talhelm, T., Zhang, X., & Oishi, S. (2018). Moving chairs in Starbucks: Observational studies find rice-wheat cultural differences in daily life in China. *Science Advances, 4*(4), eaap8469.

Tallandini, M. A., & Caudek, C. (2010). Defense mechanisms development in typical children. *Psychotherapy Research, 20,* 535–545.

Tammen, S. A., Friso, S., & Choi, S. W. (2013). Epigenetics: The link between nature and nurture. *Molecular Aspects of Medicine, 34*(4), 753–764.

Tan, R., & Goldman, M. S. (2015). Exposure to female fertility pheromones influences men's drinking. *Experimental and Clinical Psychopharmacology, 23*(3), 139–146.

Tandon, R., Keshavan, M. S., & Nasrallah, H. A. (2008a). Schizophrenia, "just the facts": What we know in 2008. Part 1: Overview. *Schizophrenia Research, 100*, 4–19.

Tandon, R., Keshavan, M. S., & Nasrallah, H. A. (2008b). Schizophrenia, "just the facts": What we know in 2008. Part 2: Epidemiology and etiology. *Schizophrenia Research, 102*, 1–18.

Tandon, R., Nasrallah, H. A., & Keshavan, M. S. (2009). Schizophrenia, "just the facts." Part 4: Clinical features and conceptualization. *Schizophrenia Research, 110*, 1–23.

Tang, A., Crawford, H., Morales, S., Degnan, K. A., Pine, D. S., & Fox, N. A. (2020). Infant behavioral inhibition predicts personality and social outcomes three decades later. *Proceedings of the National Academy of Sciences, 117*(18), 9800–9807. https://doi.org/10.1073/pnas.1917376117

Tang, R., Friston, K. J., & Tang, Y. Y. (2020). Brief mindfulness meditation induces gray matter changes in the brain hub. *Neural Plasticity, 2020*, Article 8830005. https://doi.org/10.1155/2020/8830005

Tanis, M., Beukeboom, C. J., Hartmann, T., & Vermeulen, I. E. (2015). Phantom phone signals: An investigation into the prevalence and predictors of imagined cell phone signals. *Computers in Human Behavior, 51*, 356–362.

Tasca, G. A., Mikail, S. F., & Hewitt, P. L. (2021). Group psychodynamic-interpersonal psychotherapy. *American Psychological Association.* https://doi.org/10.1037/0000213-000

Tate, M. C., Herbet, G., Moritz-Gasser, S., Tate, J. E., & Duffau, H. (2014). Probabilistic map of critical functional regions of the human cerebral cortex: Broca's area revisited. *Brain, 137*, 2773–2782.

Tauer, J. (2009). Monday morning quarterbacking: The case of the hindsight bias. *Psychology Today.* https://www.psychologytoday.com/blog/goal-posts/200911/monday-morning-quarterbacking-the-case-the-hindsight-bias

Taylor, C., Clifford, A., & Franklin, A. (2013). Color preferences are not universal. *Journal of Experimental Psychology: General, 142*, 1015–1027.

Taylor, J. B. (2006). *My stroke of insight.* Plume.

Taylor, J. B. (2008, February). Jill Bolte Taylor: My stroke of insight [Video file]. *TED 2008.* http://www.ted.com/talks/jill_bolte_taylor_s_powerful_stroke_of_insight

Taylor, S. E., & Master, S. L. (2011). Social responses to stress: The tend-and-befriend model. In R. J. Contrada & A. Baum (Eds.), *The handbook of stress science: Biology, psychology, and health* (pp. 101–109). Springer.

Taylor, S. E., Klein, L. C., Lewis, B. P., Gruenewald, T. L., Gurung, R. A., & Updegraff, J. A. (2000). Biobehavioral responses to stress in females: Tend-and-befriend, not fight-or-flight. *Psychological Review, 107*(3), 411–429.

Teghtsoonian, R. (1971). On the exponents in Stevens' law and the constant in Ekman's law. *Psychological Review, 78*, 71–80.

Teigen, C. (2017, March 6). Chrissy Teigen opens up for the first time about her postpartum depression. *Glamour.* https://www.glamour.com/story/chrissy-teigen-postpartum-depression

Teigen, K. H. (1994). Yerkes-Dodson: A law for all seasons. *Theory & Psychology, 4*, 525–547.

Tenenbaum, H. R., & Leaper, C. (2002). Are parents' gender schemas related to their children's gender-related cognitions? A meta-analysis. *Developmental Psychology, 38*, 615–630.

Teng, Z., Nie, Q., Guo, C., Zhang, Q., Liu, Y., & Bushman, B. J. (2019). A longitudinal study of link between exposure to violent video games and aggression in Chinese adolescents: The mediating role of moral disengagement. *Developmental Psychology, 55*(1), 184–195. https://doi.org/10.1037/dev0000624

Teodorescu, M., Barnet, J. H., Hagen, E. W., Palta, M., Young, T. B., & Peppard, P. E. (2015). Association between asthma and risk of developing obstructive sleep apnea. *Journal of the American Medical Association, 313*, 156–164.

Terman, L. M. (1916). *The measurement of intelligence.* Houghton Mifflin.

Terman, L. M. (1925). *Genetic studies of genius. Mental and physical traits of a thousand gifted children.* Stanford University Press.

Terman, L. M., & Oden, M. H. (1947). *The gifted child grows up: Twenty-five years' follow-up of a superior group.* Stanford University Press.

Terracciano, A., Abdel-Khalek, A. M., Ádám, N., Adamovová, L., Ahn, C. K., Ahn, H. N., Alansari, B. M., Alcalay, L., Allik, J., Angleitner, A., Avia, M. D., Ayearst, L. E., Barbaranelli, C., Beer, A., Borg-Cunen, M. A., Bratko, D., Brunner-Sciarra, M., Budzinski, L., Camart, N., . . . McCrae, R. R. (2005). National character does not reflect mean personality trait levels in 49 cultures. *Science, 310*(5745), 96–100. https://doi.org/10.1126/science.1117199

Terracciano, A., Costa, P. T., & McCrae, R. R. (2006). Personality plasticity after age 30. *Personality and Social Psychology Bulletin, 32*, 999–1009.

Thabrew, H., Ruppeldt, P., & Sollers, J. J. (2018). Systematic review of biofeedback interventions for addressing anxiety and depression in children and adolescents with long-term physical conditions. *Applied Psychophysiology and Biofeedback, 43*, 179–192. https://doi.org/10.1007/s10484-018-9399-z

Thai NavySEAL. (2018, July 2). *Hooyah. . . . . Wild Boar team* [Video]. https://www.facebook.com/ThaiSEAL/videos/1631228493667210/

Thai NavySEAL. (n.d.). *Posts* [Facebook page]. Facebook. https://www.facebook.com/ThaiSEAL/

Thelen, E., & Fisher, D. M. (1982). Newborn stepping: An explanation for a "disappearing" reflex. *Developmental Psychology, 18*, 760–775.

Thiago Otávio. (2018). Re: *Being a male nurse?* https://www.youtube.com/watch?v=iXfjOB8sTMA

Thibaut, J., & Kelly, H. (1959). *The social psychology of groups.* John Wiley & Sons.

Thomas, A., & Chess, S. (1986). The New York Longitudinal Study: From infancy to early adult life. In R. Plomin & J. Dunn (Eds.), *The study of temperament: Changes, continuities, and challenges* (pp. 39–52). Lawrence Erlbaum Associates.

Thompson, P. M., Giedd, J. N., Woods, R. P., MacDonald, D., Evans, A. C., & Toga, A. W. (2000). Growth patterns in the developing brain detected by using continuum mechanical tensor maps. *Nature, 404*, 190–193.

Thompson, R. F., & Kim, J. J. (1996). Memory systems in the brain and localization of a memory. *Proceedings of the National Academy of Sciences, USA, 93*, 13438–13444.

Thompson, R. F., & Steinmetz, J. E. (2009). The role of the cerebellum in classical conditioning of discrete behavioral responses. *Neuroscience, 162*, 732–755.

Thompson, T., Terhune, D. B., Oram, C., Sharangparni, J., Rouf, R., Solmi, M., Veronese, N., & Stubbs, B. (2019). The effectiveness of hypnosis for pain relief: A systematic review and meta-analysis of 85 controlled experimental trials. *Neuroscience & Biobehavioral Reviews, 99*, 298–310. https://doi.org/10.1016/j.neubiorev.2019.02.013

Thorndike, E. L. (1898). Animal intelligence: An experimental study of the associative process in animals. *Psychological Review Monograph Supplement, 2*(8).

Thorndike, E. L. (1936). Edward Lee Thorndike. In C. Murchison (Ed.), *The International University Series in Psychology: A history of psychology in autobiography* (Vol. 3, pp. 263–270). Clark University Press.

Thorne, M., & Henley, T. B. (2005). *Connections in the history and systems of psychology* (3rd ed.). Houghton Mifflin.

Thoß, M., Luzynski, K. C., Enk, V. M., Razzazi-Fazeli, E., Kwak, J., Ortner, I., & Penn, D. J. (2019). Regulation of volatile and non-volatile pheromone attractants depends upon male social status. *Scientific Reports, 9*, Article 489. https://doi.org/10.1038/s41598-018-36887-y

Thurfjell, H., Ciuti, S., & Boyce, M. S. (2017). Learning from the mistakes of others: How female elk (*Cervus elaphus*) adjust behaviour with age to avoid hunters. *PLOS ONE, 12*, e0178082. https://doi:10.1371/journal.pone.0178082

Tik, M., Sladky, R., Luft, C. D. B., Willinger, D., Hoffmann, A., Banissy, M. J., Bhattacharya, J., & Windischberger, C. (2018). Ultra-high-field fMRI insights on insight: Neural correlates of the Aha!-moment. *Human Brain Mapping, 39*(8), 3241–3252. https://doi.org/10.1002/hbm.24073

Tilot, A. K., Kucera, K. S., Vino, A., Asher, J. E., Baron-Cohen, S., & Fisher, S. E. (2018). Rare variants in axonogenesis genes connect three families with sound–color synesthesia. *Proceedings of the National Academy of Sciences, 115*(12), 3168–3173. https://doi.org/10.1073/pnas.1715492115

Tin, E. (2004, February). APA fellow Brenda Milner receives NAS award. *Psychological Science Agenda.* https://www.apa.org/science/about/psa/2004/02/milner

Tinder. (2020, December 7). Gen Z never stopped dating in 2020.

Tirindelli, R., Dibattista, M., Pifferi, S., & Menini, A. (2009). From pheromones to behavior. *Physiological Reviews, 89*(3), 921–956.

Tobin, M. K., Musaraca, K., Disouky, A., Shetti, A., Bheri, A., Honer, W. G., Kim, N., Dawe, R. J., Bennett, D. A., Arfanakis, K., & Lazarov, O. (2019). Human hippocampal neurogenesis persists in aged adults and Alzheimer's disease patients. *Cell Stem Cell, 24*(6), 974–982. https://doi.org/10.1016/j.stem.2019.05.003

Todd, A. R., Johnson, D. J., Lassetter, B., Neel, R., Simpson, A. J., & Cesario, J. (2020). Category salience and racial bias in weapon identification: A diffusion modeling approach. *Journal of Personality and Social Psychology.* Advance online publication. https://doi.org/10.1037/pspi0000279

Todes, D. P. (2014). *Ivan Pavlov: A Russian life in science.* Oxford University Press.

Toga, A. W., Thompson, P. M., & Sowell, E. R. (2006). Mapping brain maturation. *Trends in Neuroscience, 29,* 148–159.

Toledo, S., Shohami, D., Schiffner, I., Lourie, E., Orchan, Y., Bartan, Y., & Nathan, R. (2020). Cognitive map–based navigation in wild bats revealed by a new high-throughput tracking system. *Science, 369*(6500), 188–193. https://doi.org/10.1126/science.aax6904

Tollenaar, M. S., Beijers, R., Jansen, J., Riksen-Walraven, J. M. A., & De Weerth, C. (2011). Maternal prenatal stress and cortisol reactivity to stressors in human infants. *Stress, 14,* 53–65.

Tolman, E. C. (1948). Cognitive maps in rats and men. *Psychological Review, 55*(4), 189–208.

Tolman, E. C., & Honzik, C. H. (1930). Introduction and removal of reward, and maze performance in rats. *University of California Publications in Psychology, 4,* 257–275.

Tomanney, S. (2019, March 1). 6 Best bets this weekend in Houston: Azaleas, dancing dogs and skating fun. *Houston Press.* https://www.houstonpress.com/arts/things-to-do-best-bets-for-a-great-weekend-in-houston-march-1-3-2019-11222139

Tomova, L., Wang, K., Thompson, T., Matthews, G., Takahashi, A., Tye, K., & Saxe, R. (2020). Acute social isolation evokes midbrain craving responses similar to hunger. *Nature Neuroscience, 23*(12), 1597–1605. https://doi.org/10.1038/s41593-020-00742-z

Tondo, L., Isacsson, G., & Baldessarini, R. J. (2003). Suicidal behaviour in bipolar disorder: Risk and prevention. *CNS Drugs, 17,* 491–511.

Tononi, G., & Cirelli, C. (2014). Sleep and the price of plasticity: From synaptic and cellular homeostasis to memory consolidation and integration. *Neuron, 81,* 12–34.

Topp, S. S. (2013). Against the quiet revolution: The rhetorical construction of intersex individuals as disordered. *Sexualities, 16,* 180–194.

Toppi, G. (2018, June 20). Time to dismiss the Stanford Prison experiment? *Inside Higher Ed.* https://www.insidehighered.com/news/2018/06/20/new-stanford-prison-experiment-revelations-question-findings

Torous, J., Andersson, G., Bertagnoli, A., Christensen, H., Cuijpers, P., Firth, J., Haim, A., Hsin, H., Hollis, C., Lewis, S., Mohr, D. C., Pratap, A., Roux, S., Sherrill, J., & Arean, P. A. (2019). Towards a consensus around standards for smartphone apps and digital mental health. *World Psychiatry, 18*(1), 97–98. https://doi.org/10.1002/wps.20592

Torrente, M. P., Gelenberg, A. J., & Vrana, K. E. (2012). Boosting serotonin in the brain: Is it time to revamp the treatment of depression? *Journal of Psychopharmacology, 26,* 629–635.

Torry, Z. D., & Billick, S. B. (2010). Overlapping universe: Understanding legal insanity and psychosis. *Psychiatric Quarterly, 81,* 253–262.

Tracy, J. L., & Matsumoto, D. (2008). The spontaneous expression of pride and shame: Evidence for biologically innate nonverbal displays. *Proceedings of the National Academy of Sciences, 105*(33), 11655–11660.

Treffers-Daller, J., & Milton, J. (2013). Vocabulary size revisited: The link between vocabulary size and academic achievement. *Applied Linguistics Review, 4,* 151–172.

Treffert, D. A. (2015). Accidental genius. *Scientific American, 23,* 54–59.

Trent, J. D., Barron, L. G., Rose, M. R., & Carretta, T. R. (2020). Tailored Adaptive Personality Assessment System (TAPAS) as an indicator for counterproductive work behavior: Comparing validity in applicant, honest, and directed faking conditions. *Military Psychology, 32*(1), 51–59. https://doi.org/10.1080/08995605.2019.1652481

Trimmer, C., Keller, A., Murphy, N. R., Snyder, L. L., Willer, J. R., Nagai, M. H., Katsanis, N., Vosshall, L. B., Matsunami, H., & Mainland, J. D. (2019). Genetic variation across the human olfactory receptor repertoire alters odor perception. *Proceedings of the National Academy of Sciences, 116*(19), 9475–9480. https://doi.org/10.1073/pnas.1804106115

Trivers, R. L. (1971). The evolution of reciprocal altruism. *Quarterly Review of Biology, 46,* 35–57.

Tsai, M. N., Wu, C. L., Chang, Y. L., & Chen, H. C. (2019). Humor styles in marriage: How similar are husband and wife? *Psychological Reports, 122*(6), 2331–2347. https://doi.org/10.1177/0033294118805008

Tsuang, M. T., Stone, W. S., & Faraone, S. V. (2001). Genes, environment and schizophrenia. *British Journal of Psychiatry, 178,* s18–s24.

Tsuji, O., Sugai, K., Yamaguchi, R., Tashiro, S., Nagoshi, N., Kohyama, J., Iida, T., Ohkubo, T., Itakura, G., Isoda, M., Shinozaki, M., Fujiyoshi, K., Kanemura, Y., Yamanaka, S., Nakamura, M., & Okano, H. (2019). Concise review: Laying the groundwork for a first-in-human study of an induced pluripotent stem cell-based intervention for spinal cord injury. *Stem Cells, 37*(1), 6–13. https://doi.org/10.1002/stem.2926

Tullis, J. G., & Benjamin, A. S. (2015). Cue generation: How learners flexibly support future retrieval. *Memory & Cognition, 43,* 922–938.

Tulving, E. (1972). Episodic and semantic memory. In E. Tulving & W. Donaldson (Eds.), *Organization of memory* (pp. 381–403). Academic Press.

Tulving, E. (1985). Memory and consciousness. *Canadian Psychology/Psychologice Canadienne, 26,* 1–11.

Tulving, E., & Osler, S. (1968). Effectiveness of retrieval cues in memory for words. *Journal of Experimental Psychology, 77,* 593–601.

Tulving, E., & Thomson, D. M. (1973). Encoding specificity and retrieval processes in episodic memory. *Psychological Review, 80,* 352–373.

Tummala-Narra, P. (2016). A historical overview and critique of the psychoanalytic approach to culture and context. In P. Tummala-Narra, *Psychoanalytic theory and cultural competence in psychotherapy* (pp. 7–29). American Psychological Association. https://doi.org/10.1037/14800-002

Turbert, D. (2019, March 23). *Eye injury prevention.* American Academy of Ophthalmology. https://www.aao.org/eye-health/tips-prevention/preventing-injuries

Turbert, D. (2020, June 11). *The sun, UV light and your eyes.* American Academy of Ophthalmology. https://www.aao.org/eye-health/tips-prevention/sun

Turgoose, D., Ashwick, R., & Murphy, D. (2018). Systematic review of lessons learned from delivering tele-therapy to veterans with post-traumatic stress disorder. *Journal of Telemedicine and Telecare, 24*(9), 575–585. https://doi.org/10.1177/1357633X17730443

Turnbull, P. R., & Phillips, J. R. (2017). Ocular effects of virtual reality headset wear in young adults. *Scientific Reports, 7,* Article 16172. https://doi.org/10.1038/s41598-017-16320-6

Turner, S., Mota, N., Bolton, J., & Sareen, J. (2018). Self-medication with alcohol or drugs for mood and anxiety disorders: A narrative review of the epidemiological literature. *Depression and Anxiety, 35*(9), 851–860. https://doi.org/10.1002/da.22771

Tversky, A., & Kahneman, D. (1981). The framing of decisions and the psychology of choice. *Science, 211,* 453–458.

Tversky, A., & Kahneman, D. (1982). Judgment under uncertainty: Heuristics and biases. In D. Kahneman, P. Slovic, & A. Tversky (Eds.), *Judgment under uncertainty: Heuristics and biases* (pp. 3–20). Cambridge University Press.

Twenge, J. M., Baumeister, R. F., DeWall, C. N., Ciarocco, N. J., & Bartels, J. M. (2007). Social exclusion decreases prosocial behavior. *Journal of Personality and Social Psychology, 92,* 56–66.

Twenge, J. M., & Campbell, W. K. (2018). Associations between screen time and lower psychological well-being among children and adolescents: Evidence from a population-based study. *Preventive Medicine Reports, 12,* 271–283. https://doi.org/10.1016/j.pmedr.2018.10.003

Twenge, J. M., & Joiner, T. E. (2020). US Census Bureau-assessed prevalence of anxiety and depressive symptoms in 2019 and during the 2020 COVID-19 pandemic. *Depression and Anxiety, 37*(10), 954–956. https://doi.org/10.1002/da.23077

Twenge, J. M., Martin, G. N., & Spitzberg, B. H. (2019). Trends in US adolescents' media use, 1976–2016: The rise of digital media, the decline of TV, and the (near) demise of print. *Psychology of Popular Media Culture, 8*(4), 329–345. https://doi.org/10.1037/ppm0000203

Twenge, J. M., & Park, H. (2019). The decline in adult activities among US adolescents, 1976–2016. *Child Development, 90*(2), 638–654. https://doi.org/10.1111/cdev.12930

Twenge, J. M., Sherman, R. A., & Wells, B. E. (2017). Declines in sexual frequency among American adults, 1989–2014. *Archives of Sexual Behavior, 46,* 2389–2401. https://doi.org/10.1007/s10508-017-0953-1

Tyler, K. L. (2018). Acute viral encephalitis. *New England Journal of Medicine, 379*(6), 557–566. https://doi.org/10.1056/NEJMra1708714

U.S. Census Bureau. (2017). *Facts for features: American Indian and Alaska Native Heritage Month: November 2017.* https://www.census.gov/newsroom/facts-for-features/2017/aian-month.html

U.S. Department of Health and Human Services. (2019). What is the U.S. opioid epidemic? https://www.hhs.gov/opioids/about-the-epidemic/index.html

U.S. Fish and Wildlife Service. (n.d.). *Endangered species.* https://www.fws.gov/endangered/

U.S. Food and Drug Administration (FDA). (2008). *Trileptal (oxcarbazepine) FDA drug safety communication.* https://www.pdr.net/fda-drug-safety-communication/trileptal?druglabelid=1806

U.S. Food and Drug Administration (FDA). (2009). *Humanitarian device exemption (HDE).* https://www.accessdata.fda.gov/scripts/cdrh/cfdocs/cfhde/hde.cfm?id=H050003

U.S. Food and Drug Administration (FDA). (2018, June 25). *FDA approves first drug comprised of an active ingredient derived from marijuana to treat rare, severe forms of epilepsy* [Press release]. https://www.fda.gov/newsevents/newsroom/pressannouncements/ucm611046.htm

**U.S. Food and Drug Administration (FDA).** (2019). *Vaporizers, e-cigarettes, and other electronic nicotine delivery systems (ENDS).* https://www.fda.gov/tobaccoproducts/labeling/productsingredientscomponents/ucm456610.htm#references

**U.S. Food and Drug Administration (FDA).** (2019, March 6). FDA approves new nasal spray medication for treatment-resistant depression; available only at a certified doctor's office or clinic [Press release]. https://www.fda.gov/news-events/press-announcements/fda-approves-new-nasal-spray-medication-treatment-resistant-depression-available-only-certified

**U.S. Food and Drug Administration (FDA).** (2019, March 19). FDA approves first treatment for post-partum depression [Press release]. https://www.fda.gov/news-events/press-announcements/fda-approves-first-treatment-post-partum-depression

**U.S. Food and Drug Administration (FDA).** (2020). *FDA requiring boxed warning updated to improve safe use of benzodiazepine drug class.* https://www.fda.gov/drugs/drug-safety-and-availability/fda-requiring-boxed-warning-updated-improve-safe-use-benzodiazepine-drug-class

**U.S. Food and Drug Administration (FDA).** (2020, September 23). *FDA requiring boxed warning updated to improve safe use of benzodiazepine drug class.* https://www.fda.gov/drugs/drug-safety-and-availability/fda-requiring-boxed-warning-updated-improve-safe-use-benzodiazepine-drug-class

**U.S. Food and Drug Administration (FDA).** (n.d.). *For consumers: Side effects of sleep drugs.* http://www.fda.gov/forconsumers/consumerupdates/ucm107757.htm

**Uchino, B. N., Ruiz, J. M., Smith, T. W., Smyth, J. M., Taylor, D. J., Allison, M., & Ahn, C.** (2016). Ethnic/racial differences in the association between social support and levels of C-reactive proteins in the North Texas Heart Study. *Psychophysiology, 53*(1), 64–70.

**UCLA Health.** (n.d.). Coping with shift work. https://www.uclahealth.org/sleepcenter/coping-with-shift-work

**Üçok, A., & Gaebel, W.** (2008). Side effects of atypical antipsychotics: A brief overview. *World Psychiatry, 7,* 58–62.

**Uhls, Y. T., Ellison, N. B., & Subrahmanyam, K.** (2017). Benefits and costs of social media in adolescence. *Pediatrics, 140*(Suppl. 2), S67–S70. https://doi.org/10.1542/peds.2016-1758E

**Ujvari, B., & Madsen, T.** (2009). Increased mortality of naive varanid lizards after the invasion of non-native can toads (*Bufo marinus*). *Herpetological Conservation and Biology, 4,* 248–251.

**Ulmer-Yaniv, A., Avitsur, R., Kanat-Maymon, Y., Schneiderman, I., Zagoory-Sharon, O., & Feldman, R.** (2016). Affiliation, reward, and immune biomarkers coalesce to support social synchrony during periods of bond formation in humans. *Brain, Behavior, and Immunity, 56,* 130–139. https://doi.org/10.1016/j.bbi.2016.02.017

**UNAIDS.** (2020). *Global HIV & AIDS statistics—2020 fact sheet.* https://www.unaids.org/en/resources/fact-sheet

**Underwood, E.** (2014). The taste of things to come. *Science, 345*(6198), 750–751.

**Underwood, E.** (2019, February 15). Reality check: Can cat poop cause mental illness? *Science.* https://www.sciencemag.org/news/2019/02/reality-check-can-cat-poop-cause-mental-illness

**Union of Concerned Scientists.** (2020, March 11). *The connection between climate change and wildfires.* https://www.ucsusa.org/resources/climate-change-and-wildfires

**United Nations.** (2019, January 11). Shattering stereotypes—Jillian Mercado, model and disability rights advocate. https://www.un.org/sustainabledevelopment/blog/2019/01/shattering-stereotypes-jillian-mercado-model-and-disability-rights-advocate/

**United States Census Bureau.** (2019). *Historical marital status tables.* https://www.census.gov/data/tables/time-series/demo/families/marital.html

**University of Maryland Medical Center.** (n.d.). *Corneal disease.* https://www.umms.org/ummc/health-services/ophthalmology/cornea

**University of Notre Dame.** (n.d.). *Blood alcohol concentration.* https://mcwell.nd.edu/your-well-being/physical-well-being/alcohol/blood-alcohol-concentration/

**Ursini, G., Punzi, G., Chen, Q., Marenco, S., Robinson, J. F., Porcelli, A., Hamilton, E. G., Mitjans, M., Maddalena, G., Begemann, M., Seidel, J., Yanamori, H., Jaffe, A. E., Berman, K. F., Egan, M. F., Straub, R. E., Colantuoni, C., Blasi, G., Hashimoto, R., . . . Weinberger, D. R.** (2018). Convergence of placenta biology and genetic risk for schizophrenia. *Nature Medicine, 24*(6), 792–801. https://doi.org/10.1038/s41591-018-0021-y

**Usher, K., Bhullar, N., & Jackson, D.** (2020). Life in the pandemic: Social isolation and mental health. *Journal of Clinical Nursing, 29,* 2756–2757. https://doi.org/10.1111/jocn.15290

**Vadeboncoeur, C., Townsend, N., & Foster, C.** (2015). A meta-analysis of weight gain in first year university students: Is freshman 15 a myth? *BMC Obesity, 2,* Article 22. https://doi.org/10.1186/s40608-015-0051-7

**Vagni, M., Maiorano, T., Giostra, V., & Pajardi, D.** (2020). Hardiness and coping strategies as mediators of stress and secondary trauma in emergency workers during the COVID-19 pandemic. *Sustainability, 12*(18), Article 7561. https://doi.org/10.3390/su12187561

**Vaillant, G. E.** (1992). *Ego mechanisms of defense: A guide for clinicians and researchers.* American Psychiatric Association.

**Vaillant, G. E.** (2000). Adaptive mental mechanisms: Their role in a positive psychology. *American Psychologist, 55,* 89–98.

**Vainchtein, I. D., Chin, G., Cho, F. S., Kelley, K. W., Miller, J. G., Chien, E. C., Liddelow, S. A., Nguyen, P. T., Nakao-Inoue, H., Dorman, L. C., Akil, O., Joshita, S., Barres, B. A., Paz, J. T., Molofsky, A. B., & Molofsky, A. V.** (2018). Astrocyte-derived interleukin-33 promotes microglial synapse engulfment and neural circuit development. *Science, 359*(6381), 1269–1273. https://doi.org/10.1126/science.aal3589

**Valenza, E., Leo, I., Gava, L., & Simion, F.** (2006). Perceptual completion in newborn human infants. *Child Development, 77,* 1810–1821.

**Vall, O., Salat-Batlle, J., & Garcia-Algar, O.** (2015). Alcohol consumption during pregnancy and adverse neurodevelopmental outcomes. *Journal of Epidemiology and Community Health, 69*(10), 927–929.

**Van Dam, N. T., van Vugt, M. K., Vago, D. R., Schmalzl, L., Saron, C. D., Olendzki, A., Meissner, T., Lazar, S. W., Kerr, C. E., Gorchov, J., Fox, K. C., Field, B. A., Britton, W. B., Brefczynski-Lewis, J. A., & Meyer, D. E.** (2018). Mind the hype: A critical evaluation and prescriptive agenda for research on mindfulness and meditation. *Perspectives on Psychological Science, 13*(1), 36–61. https://doi.org/10.1177/1745691617709589

**Van den Akker, A. L., Deković, M., Asscher, J., & Prinzie, P.** (2014). Mean-level personality development across childhood and adolescence: A temporary defiance of the maturity principle and bidirectional associations with parenting. *Journal of Personality and Social Psychology, 107*(4), 736–750.

**Van den Bergh, B. R. H., van den Heuvel, M. I., Lahti, M., Braeken, M., de Rooij, S. R., Entringer, S., Hoyer, D., Roseboom, T., Räikkönen, K., King, S., & Schwab, M.** (2020). Prenatal developmental origins of behavior and mental health: The influence of maternal stress in pregnancy. *Neuroscience & Biobehavioral Reviews, 117,* 26–64. https://doi.org/10.1016/j.neubiorev.2017.07.003

**van den Eijnden, R. J. J. M., Lemmens, J. S., & Valkenburg, P. M.** (2016). The social media disorder scale. *Computers in Human Behavior, 61,* 478–487. https://doi.org/10.1016/j.chb.2016.03.038

**van der Linden, D., Dunkel, C. S., Figueredo, A. J., Gurven, M., von Rueden, C., & Woodley of Menie, M. A.** (2018). How universal is the general factor of personality? An analysis of the Big Five in forager farmers of the Bolivian Amazon. *Journal of Cross-Cultural Psychology, 49*(7), 1081–1097. https://doi.org/10.1177/0022022118774925

**van der Linden, D., Schermer, J. A., de Zeeuw, E., Dunkel, C. S., Pekaar, K. A., Bakker, A. B., Vernon, P. A., & Petrides, K. V.** (2018). Overlap between the general factor of personality and trait emotional intelligence: A genetic correlation study. *Behavior Genetics, 48*(2), 147–154.

**van der Wal, C. N., & Kok, R. N.** (2019). Laughter-inducing therapies: Systematic review and meta-analysis. *Social Science & Medicine, 232,* 473–488. https://doi.org/10.1016/j.socscimed.2019.02.018

**Van Doorn, M. D., Branje, S. J. T., & Meeus, W. H.** (2011). Developmental changes in conflict resolution styles in parent–adolescent relationships: A four-wave longitudinal study. *Journal of Youth and Adolescence, 40,* 97–107.

**van Erp, T. G. M., Hibar, D. P., Rasmussen, J. M., Glahn, D. C., Pearlson, G. D., Andreassen, O. A., Agartz, I., Westlye, L. T., Haukvik, U. K., Dale, A. M., Melle, I., Hartberg, C. B., Gruber, O., Kraemer, B., Zilles, D., Donohoe, G., Kelly, S., McDonald, C., Morris, D. W., . . . ENIGMA Schizophrenia Working Group.** (2016). Subcortical brain volume abnormalities in 2028 individuals with schizophrenia and 2540 healthy controls via the ENIGMA consortium. *Molecular Psychiatry, 21,* 547–553. https://doi.org/10.1038/mp.2015.63

**van Harmelen, A. L., Kievit, R. A., Ioannidis, K., Neufeld, S., Jones, P. B., Bullmore, E., Dolan, R., NSPN Consortium, Fonagy, G., & Goodyer, I.** (2017). Adolescent friendships predict later resilient functioning across psychosocial domains in a healthy community cohort. *Psychological Medicine, 47*(13), 2312–2322.

**Vanhoenacker, M.** (2016, May 31). Become a pilot. *Slate.* http://www.slate.com/articles/technology/technology/2016/05/become_a_pilot_seriously_it_s_a_great_job.html

Van Horn, J. D., Irinia, A., Torgerson, C. M., Chambers, M., Kikinis, R., & Toga, A. W. (2012). Mapping connectivity damage in the case of Phineas Gage. *PLOS ONE, 7,* e37454. https://doi.org/10.1371/journal.pone.0037454

Vanini, G., Lydic, R., & Baghdoyan, H. A. (2012). GABA-to-ACh ratio in basal forebrain and cerebral cortex varies significantly during sleep. *SLEEP, 35,* 1325–1334.

van Os, J., & Kapur, S. (2009). Schizophrenia. *The Lancet, 374,* 635–645.

Van Petegem, S., Soenens, B., Vansteenkiste, M., & Beyers, W. (2015). Rebels with a cause? Adolescent defiance from the perspective of reactance theory and self-determination theory. *Child Development, 86,* 903–918.

van Praag, H., Kempermann, G., & Gage, F. H. (2000). Neural consequences of environmental enrichment. *Nature Reviews Neuroscience, 1,* 191–198.

Vaquero, L., Hartmann, K., Ripollés, P., Rojo, N., Sierpowska, J., François, C., Càmara, E., van Vugt, F. T., Mohammadi, B., Samii, A., Münte, T. F., Rodríguez-Fornellsa, A., & Altenmüller, E. (2016). Structural neuroplasticity in expert pianists depends on the age of musical training onset. *NeuroImage, 126,* 106–119. https://doi.org/10.1016/j.neuroimage.2015.11.008

van Rooij, A. J., Ferguson, C. J., van de Mheen, D., & Schoenmakers, T. M. (2017). Time to abandon internet addiction? Predicting problematic internet, game, and social media use from psychosocial well-being and application use. *Clinical Neuropsychiatry, 14,* 113–121.

Van Rosmalen, L., van der Horst, F. C., & Van der Veer, R. (2016). From secure dependency to attachment: Mary Ainsworth's integration of Blatz's security theory into Bowlby's attachment theory. *History of Psychology, 19,* 22–39. https://doi.org/10.1037/hop0000015

van Schalkwijk, F. J., Hauser, T., Hoedlmoser, K., Ameen, M. S., Wilhelm, F. H., Sauter, C., Klösch, G., Moser, D., Gruber, G., Anderer, P., Saletu, B., Parapatics, S., Zeitlhofer, J., & Schabus, M. (2020). Procedural memory consolidation is associated with heart rate variability and sleep spindles. *Journal of Sleep Research, 29*(3), Article e12910. https://doi.org/10.1111/jsr.12910

Van Someren, E. J. W., Cirelli, C., Dijk, D. J., Van Cauter, E., Schwartz, S., & Chee, M. W. (2015). Disrupted sleep: From molecules to cognition. *Journal of Neuroscience, 35,* 13889–13895.

Van Strien, J. W., Franken, I. H., & Huijding, J. (2014). Testing the snake-detection hypothesis: Larger early posterior negativity in humans to pictures of snakes than to pictures of other reptiles, spiders and slugs. *Frontiers in Human Neuroscience, 8,* Article 691. https://doi.org/10.3389/fnhum.2014.00691

Varadkar, S., Bien, C. G., Kruse, C. A., Jensen, F. E., Bauer, J., Pardo, C. A., Vincent, A., Mathern, G. W., & Cross, J. H. (2014). Rasmussen's encephalitis: Clinical features, pathobiology, and treatment advances. *The Lancet Neurology, 13,* 195–205. https://doi.org/10.1016/S1474-4422(13)70260-6

Vardy, T., & Atkinson, Q. D. (2019). Property damage and exposure to other people in distress differentially predict prosocial behavior after a natural disaster. *Psychological Science, 30,* 563–575. https://doi.org/10.1177/0956797619826972

Vargas, S. M., Huey, S. J., Jr., & Miranda, J. (2020). A critical review of current evidence on multiple types of discrimination and mental health. *American Journal of Orthopsychiatry, 90*(3), 374–390. https://doi.org/10.1037/ort0000441

Varker, T., Brand, R. M., Ward, J., Terhaag, S., & Phelps, A. (2019). Efficacy of synchronous telepsychology interventions for people with anxiety, depression, posttraumatic stress disorder, and adjustment disorder: A rapid evidence assessment. *Psychological Services, 16*(4), 621–635. https://doi.org/10.1037/ser0000239

Varlet, M., & Richardson, M. J. (2015). What would be Usain Bolt's 100-meter sprint world record without Tyson Gay? Unintentional interpersonal synchronization between the two sprinters. *Journal of Experimental Psychology: Human Perception and Performance, 41,* 36–41.

Vartanian, L. R. (2015). Impression management and food intake. Current directions in research. *Appetite, 86,* 74–80.

Vartanian, L. R., Herman, C. P., & Polivy, J. (2016). What does it mean to eat an appropriate amount of food? *Eating Behaviors, 23,* 24–27. https://doi.org/10.1016/j.eatbeh.2016.07.002

Vartanian, L. R., Spanos, S., Herman, C. P., & Polivy, J. (2015). Modeling of food intake: A meta-analytic review. *Social Influence, 10,* 119–136.

Vassall, N. (2020, June 17). "Like death by a thousand cuts": How microaggressions play a traumatic part in everyday racism. *Independent.* https://www.independent.co.uk/life-style/microaggression-meaning-definition-racism-black-lives-matter-george-floyd-a9568506.html

Vejpongsa, T., & Peck, G. (2018, July 5). Trapped in Thai cave, youngsters must grapple with stress. *Chicago Tribune.* https://www.chicagotribune.com/news/nationworld/ct-soccer-team-trapped-thai-cave-20180705-story.html

Velagaleti, G. V. N., & Moore, C. M. (2011). Role of array comparative genomic hybridization of cytogenetic causes of pregnancy loss. *Pathology Case Reviews, 16,* 214–221.

Vemuri, B., Malik, A., Asbeutah, A. A. A., & Welty, F. K. (2019). A plasma phospholipid omega-3 fatty acid index > 4% prevents cognitive decline in cognitively healthy subjects with coronary artery disease. *Circulation, 140*(Suppl_1), A10723-A10723.

Vennard, M. (2011, November 21). How can musicians keep playing despite amnesia? *BBC World Service.* http://www.bbc.co.uk/news/magazine-15791973

Verduyn, P., Lee, D. S., Park, J., Shablack, H., Orvell, A., Bayer, J., Ybarra, O., Jonides, J., & Kross, E. (2015). Passive Facebook usage undermines affective well-being: Experimental and longitudinal evidence. *Journal of Experimental Psychology: General, 144,* 480–488.

Vergunst, F. (2019, September 19). A simple test predicts what kindergartners will earn as adults. *Scientific American.* https://www.scientificamerican.com/article/a-simple-test-predicts-what-kindergartners-will-earn-as-adults/

Verhulst, B. (2020). Sociopolitical attitudes through the lens of behavioral genetics: Contributions from Dr Nicholas Martin. *Twin Research and Human Genetics, 23*(2), 125–126. https://doi.org/10.1017/thg.2020.30

Vernon, P. A., Martin, R. A., Schermer, J. A., Cherkas, L. F., & Spector, T. D. (2008). Genetic and environmental contributions to humor styles: A replication study. *Twin Research and Human Genetics, 11,* 44–47.

Vervecken, D., & Hannover, B. (2015). Effects of gender fair job descriptions on children's perceptions of job status, job difficulty, and vocational self-efficacy. *Social Psychology, 46*(2), 76–92.

Vespia, K. M. (2019). Psychology, careers, and workforce readiness: A curricular infusion approach. *Scholarship of Teaching and Learning in Psychology, 6,* 163–173. http://dx.doi.org/10.1037/stl0000180

Vesuna, S., Kauvar, I. V., Richman, E., Gore, F., Oskotsky, T., Sava-Segal, C., Luo, L., Malenka, R. C., Henderson, J. M., Nuyujukian, P., Parvizi, J., & Deisseroth, K. (2020). Deep posteromedial cortical rhythm in dissociation. *Nature, 586*(7827),

87–94. https://doi.org/10.1038/s41586-020-2731-9

Vicedo, M. (2017). Putting attachment in its place: Disciplinary and cultural contexts. *European Journal of Developmental Psychology, 14,* 684–699. https://doi.org/10.1080/17405629.2017.1289838

Vilain, E. J. N. (2008). Genetics of sexual development and differentiation. In D. L. Rowland & L. Incrocci (Eds.), *Handbook of sexual and gender identity disorders* (pp. 329–353). John Wiley & Sons.

Villar, J., Fernandes, M., Purwar, M., Staines-Urias, E., Di Nicola, P., Ismail, L. C., Ochieng, R., Barros, F., Albernaz, E., Victora, C., Kunnawar, N., Temple, S., Giuliani, F., Sandells, T., Carvalho, M., Ohuma, E., Jaffer, Y., Noble, A., Gravett, M., . . . Kennedy, S. (2019). Neurodevelopmental milestones and associated behaviours are similar among healthy children across diverse geographical locations. *Nature Communications, 10*(1), 511. https://doi.org/10.1038/s41467-018-07983-4

Vishwanath, D. (2020). Advancing a new theory of stereopsis: Reply to Rogers (2019). *Psychological Review, 127*(1), 146–152.

Visser, B. A., Ashton, M. C., & Vernon, P. A. (2006). Beyond *g*: Putting multiple intelligences theory to the test. *Intelligence, 34,* 487–502.

Visser, P. L., & Hirsch, J. K. (2014). Health behaviors among college students: The influence of future time perspective and basic psychological need satisfaction. *Health Psychology and Behavioral Medicine, 2,* 88–99.

Volkert, J., Gablonski, T. C., & Rabung, S. (2018). Prevalence of personality disorders in the general adult population in Western countries: Systematic review and meta-analysis. *The British Journal of Psychiatry, 213*(6), 709–715. https://doi.org/10.1192/bjp.2018.202

Volkow, N. D. (2020, September). The stigma of addiction. *Scientific American, 323*(3), 10.

Volkow, N. D., Wise, R. A., & Baler, R. (2017). The dopamine motive system: Implications for drug and food addiction. *Nature Reviews Neuroscience, 18*(12), 741–752. https://doi.org/10.1038/nrn.2017.130

Vollbehr, N. K., Hoenders, H. R., Bartels-Velthuis, A. A., Nauta, M. H., Castelein, S., Schroevers, M. J., Stant, A. D., de Jong, P. J., & Ostafin, B. D. (2020). A mindful yoga intervention for young women with major depressive disorder: Design and baseline sample characteristics of a randomized controlled trial. *International Journal of Methods in Psychiatric Research,* e1820. https://doi.org/10.1002/mpr.1820

Volpini, M., Giacobbe, P., Cosgrove, G. R., Levitt, A., Lozano, A. M., & Lipsman, N. (2017). The history and future of ablative neurosurgery for major depressive disorder. *Stereotactic and Functional Neurosurgery, 95*(4), 216–228. https://doi.org/10.1159/000478025

von Dawans, B., Ditzen, B., Trueg, A., Fischbacher, U., & Heinrichs, M. (2019). Effects of acute stress on social behavior in women. *Psychoneuroendocrinology, 99*, 137–144. https://doi.org/10.1016/j.psyneuen.2018.08.031

von Dawans, B., Fischbacher, U., Kirschbaum, C., Fehr, E., & Heinrichs, M. (2012). The social dimension of stress reactivity: Acute stress increases prosocial behavior in humans. *Psychological Science, 23*(6), 651–660.

Voyles, E. C., Bailey, S. F., & Durik, A. M. (2015). New pieces of the jigsaw classroom: Increasing accountability to reduce social loafing in student group projects. *The New School Psychology Bulletin, 13*, 11–20.

Vredeveldt, A., Baddeley, A. D., & Hitch, G. J. (2014). The effectiveness of eye-closure in repeated interviews. *Legal and Criminological Psychology, 19*, 282–295.

Vrij, A., Hartwig, M., & Granhag, P. A. (2019). Reading lies: Nonverbal communication and deception. *Annual Review of Psychology, 70*, 295-317. https://doi.org/10.1146/annurev-psych-010418-103135

Vukasović, T., & Bratko, D. (2015). Heritability of personality: A meta-analysis of behavior genetic studies. *Psychological Bulletin, 141*(4), 769–785.

Vygotsky, L. S. (1934/1962). *Thought and language* (Eugenia Hanfmann & Gertrude Vakar, Eds. & Trans.). Massachusetts Institute of Technology.

Wagner, H. S., Ahlstrom, B., Redden, J. P., Vickers, Z., & Mann, T. (2014). The myth of comfort food. *Health Psychology, 33*, 1552–1557.

Wagner, J., Orth, U., Bleidorn, W., Hopwood, C. J., & Kandler, C. (2020). Toward an integrative model of sources of personality stability and change. *Current Directions in Psychological Science, 29*(5), 438–444. https://doi.org/10.1177/0963721420924751

Wagner, S. L., Cepeda, I., Krieger, D., Maggi, S., D'Angiulli, A., Weinberg, J., & Grunau, R. E. (2016). Higher cortisol is associated with poorer executive functioning in preschool children: The role of parenting stress, parent coping and quality of daycare. *Child Neuropsychology, 22*, 853–869. https://doi.org/10.1080/09297049.2015.1080232

Wakefield, A. J., Murch, S. H., Anthony, A., A., Linnell, J., Casson, D. M., Malik, M., Berelowitz, M., Dhillon, A. P., Thomson, M. A., Harvey, P., Valentine, A., Davies, S. E., & Walker-Smith, J. A. (1998). Ileal-lymphoid-nodular hyperplasia, non-specific colitis, and pervasive developmental disorder in children. *The Lancet, 28*, 637–641.

Wakefield, J. C. (1992). The concept of mental disorder: On the boundary between biological facts and social values. *American Psychologist, 47*, 373–388.

Wakeman, S. E., & Barnett, M. L. (2018). Primary care and the opioid-overdose crisis—buprenorphine myths and realities. *New England Journal of Medicine, 379*(1), 1–4. https://doi.org/10.1056/NEJMp1802741

Waldrop, M. M. (2017). News feature: The genuine problem of fake news. *Proceedings of the National Academy of Sciences, 114*(48), 12631–12634. https://doi.org/10.1073/pnas.1719005114

Walker, L. E., Pann, J. M., Shapiro, D. L., & Van Hasselt, V. B. (2016). A review of best practices for the treatment of persons with mental illness in jail. In *Best practices for the mentally ill in the criminal justice system* (pp. 57–69). Springer International.

Wall, S. S. (2015). Standing at the intersections: Navigating life as a Black intersex man. *Narrative Inquiry in Bioethics, 5*, 117–119.

Wallin, P. (1949). An appraisal of some methodological aspects of the Kinsey report. *American Sociological Review, 14*, 197–210.

Wallis, C. (2017, December 1). What pot really does to the teen brain. *Scientific American.* https://www.scientificamerican.com/article/what-pot-really-does-to-the-teen-brain/

Wallis, C. (2019, April). Psychotherapy in a flash. *Scientific American, 320*(4), 20.

Wang, Q. (2016). Remembering the self in cultural contexts: A cultural dynamic theory of autobiographical memory. *Memory Studies, 9*, 295–304. https://doi.org/10.1177/1750698016645238

Wang, Q. (2019). Culture in the organization of autobiographical memory. In J. Mace (Ed.), *The organization and structure of autobiographical memory* (pp. 72–92). Oxford University Press.

Wang, Q., & Conway, M. A. (2004). The stories we keep: Autobiographical memory in American and Chinese middle-aged adults. *Journal of Personality, 72*, 911–938.

Wang, Q. J., & Spence, C. (2019). Drinking through rosé-coloured glasses: Influence of wine colour on the perception of aroma and flavour in wine experts and novices. *Food Research International, 126*, Article 108678. https://doi.org/10.1016/j.foodres.2019.108678

Wang, Y., Kala, M. P., & Jafar, T. H. (2020). Factors associated with psychological distress during the coronavirus disease 2019 (COVID-19) pandemic on the predominantly general population: A systematic review and meta-analysis. *PLOS ONE, 15*(12), Article e0244630. https://doi.org/10.1371/journal.pone.0244630

Warburton, D. E. R., Charlesworth, S., Ivey, A., Nettlefold, L., & Bredin, S. S. D. (2010). A systematic review of the evidence for Canada's physical activity guidelines for adults. *International Journal of Behavioral Nutrition and Physical Activity, 7*, 1–220.

Ward, E., Wiltshire, J. C., Detry, M. A., & Brown, R. L. (2013). African American men and women's attitude toward mental illness, perceptions of stigma, and preferred coping behaviors. *Nursing Research, 62*, 185–194.

Ward-Fear, G., Pearson, D. J., Brown, G. P., Rangers, B., & Shine, R. (2016). Ecological immunization: In situ training of free-ranging predatory lizards reduces their vulnerability to invasive toxic prey. *Biology Letters, 12*, 20150863. https://doi.org/10.1098/rsbl.2015.0863

Ward-Fear, G., Thomas, J., Webb, J. K., Pearson, D. J., & Shine, R. (2017). Eliciting conditioned taste aversion in lizards: Live toxic prey are more effective than scent and taste cues alone. *Integrative Zoology, 12*(2), 112–120. https://doi.org/10.1111/1749-4877.12226

Warne, R. T. (2019). An evaluation (and vindication?) of Lewis Terman: What the father of gifted education can teach the 21st century. *Gifted Child Quarterly, 63*(1), 3–21. https://doi.org/10.1177/0016986218799433

Warne, R. T., Astle, M. C., & Hill, J. C. (2018). What do undergraduates learn about human intelligence? An analysis of introductory psychology textbooks. *Archives of Scientific Psychology, 6*(1), 32–50. https://doi.org/10.1037/arc0000038

Warneken, F., & Tomasello, M. (2006). Altruistic helping in human infants and young chimpanzees. *Science, 311*, 1301–1303.

Washburn, D. A. (2010). Book reviews: *The Animal Mind* at 100. *Psychological Record, 60*, 369–376.

Watanabe, K., Masaoka, Y., Kawamura, M., Yoshida, M., Koiwa, N., Yoshikawa, A., Kubota, S., Ida, M., Ono, K., & Izumizaki, M. (2018). Left posterior orbitofrontal cortex is associated with odor-induced autobiographical memory: An fMRI study. *Frontiers in Psychology, 9*. https://doi.org/10.3389/fpsyg.2018.00687

Watcharasakwet, W., Dvorak, P., & Chomchuen, W. (2018, July 18). Thai boys moved from dark to light, physically and mentally, after being trapped in cave. *The Wall Street Journal.* https://www.wsj.com/articles/thailand-boys-recount-their-ordeal-in-cave-1531922987

Waterhouse, L. (2006). Multiple intelligences, the Mozart effect, and emotional intelligence: A critical review. *Educational Psychologist, 41*, 207–225.

Watson, J. B., & Rayner, R. (1920). Conditioned emotional reactions. *Journal of Experimental Psychology, 3*, 1–14. (Reprinted in *American Psychologist, 55*, 313–317.)

Watson, J. M., & Strayer, D. L. (2010). Supertaskers: Profiles in extraordinary multi-tasking ability. *Psychonomic Bulletin & Review, 17*, 479–485.

Watson, N. F., Morgenthaler, T., Chervin, R., Carden, K., Kirsch, D., Kristo, D., Malhotra, R., Martin, J., Ramar, K., Rosen, I., Weaver, T., & Wise, M. (2015). Confronting drowsy driving: The American Academy of Sleep Medicine perspective. *Journal of Clinical Sleep Medicine, 11*(11), 1335–1336. https://doi.org/10.5664/jcsm.5200

Watson, R. I. (1968). *The great psychologists* (2nd ed.). J. B. Lippincott.

Watts, T. W., Duncan, G. J., & Quan, H. (2018). Revisiting the marshmallow test: A conceptual replication investigating links between early delay of gratification and later outcomes. *Psychological Science, 29*(7), 1159–1177. https://doi.org/10.1177/0956797618761661

Waugh, N. C., & Norman, D. A. (1965). Primary memory. *Psychological Review, 72*, 89–104.

Wearing, D. (2005). *Forever today: A memoir of love and amnesia.* Corgi Books.

Webb, A., Matsuno, E. P., Budge, S. L., Krishnan, M. C., & Balsam, K. F. (2015). *Non-binary gender identities.* The Society for the Psychological Study of Lesbian, Gay, Bisexual, and Transgender Issues. https://www.apadivisions.org/division-44/resources/advocacy/non-binary-facts.pdf

Webb, S. J., Monk, C. S., & Nelson, C. A. (2001). Mechanisms of postnatal neurobiological development: Implications for human development. *Developmental Neuropsychology, 19*, 147–171.

Weber, H., Scholz, C. J., Domschke, K., Baumann, C., Klauke, B., Jacob, C. P., Maier, W., Fritze, J., Bandelow, B., Zwanzger, P. M., Lang, T., Fehm, L., Ströhle, A., Hamm, A., Gerlach, A. L., Alpers, G. W., Kircher, T., Wittchen, H.-U., Arolt, V., . . . Reif, A. (2012). Gender differences in associations of glutamate decarboxylase 1 gene (GAD1) variants with panic disorder. *PLOS ONE, 7*, Article e37651.

*Webster's New International Dictionary of the English Language.* (1925). W. T. Harris & F. Sturges Allen (Eds.). G. & C. Merriam.

Wechsler, T. F., Kümpers, F., & Mühlberger, A. (2019). Inferiority or even superiority of virtual reality exposure therapy in phobias?—A systematic review and quantitative meta-analysis on randomized controlled trials specifically comparing the efficacy of virtual reality exposure to gold standard in vivo exposure in agoraphobia, specific phobia, and social phobia. *Frontiers in Psychology, 10,* Article 1758. https://doi.org/10.3389/fpsyg.2019.01758

Wedding, D., & Corsini, R. J. (2019). *Current psychotherapies* (11th ed.). Cengage.

Weidner, R., Plewan, T., Chen, Q., Buchner, A., Weiss, P. H., & Fink, G. R. (2014). The moon illusion and size–distance scaling—evidence for shared neural patterns. *Journal of Cognitive Neuroscience, 26,* 1871–1882.

Weintraub, K. (2017, January 4). How to control aging. *Scientific American.* https://www.scientificamerican.com/article/how-to-control-aging/

Weintraub, K. (2019, March 25). The adult brain does grow new neurons after all. *Scientific American.* https://www.scientificamerican.com/article/the-adult-brain-does-grow-new-neurons-after-all-study-says/

Weir, F. W., Hatch, J. L., Muus, J. S., Wallace, S., & Meyer, T. A. (2016). Audiologic outcomes in Ehlers-Danlos syndrome. *Otology & Neurotology, 37,* 748–752. 10.1097/MAO.0000000000001082

Weir, K. (2015, November). Marijuana and the developing brain. *Monitor on Psychology, 46,* 48.

Weir, K. (2018, February). Virtual reality expands its reach. *Monitor in Psychology, 49*(2), 52.

Weir, K. (2020, March 16). Seven crucial research findings that can help people deal with COVID-19. *American Psychological Association.* https://www.apa.org/news/apa/2020/03/covid-19-research-findings

Weisberg, D. S., Ilgaz, H., Hirsh-Pasek, K., Golinkoff, R., Nicolopoulou, A., & Dickinson, D. K. (2015). Shovels and swords: How realistic and fantastical themes affect children's word learning. *Cognitive Development, 35,* 1–14.

Weisgram, E. S., Fulcher, M., & Dinella, L. M. (2014). Pink gives girls permission: Exploring the roles of explicit gender labels and gender-typed colors on preschool children's toy preferences. *Journal of Applied Developmental Psychology, 35*(5), 401–409.

Weiss, A., Wilson, M. L., Collins, D. A., Mjungu, D., Kamenya. S., Foerster, S., & Pusey, A. E. (2017).

Personality in the chimpanzees of Gombe National Park. *Scientific Data, 4.* https://doi.org/10.1038/sdata.2017.146

Weiss, R. B., Stange, J. P., Boland, E. M., Black, S. K., LaBelle, D. R., Abramson, L. Y., & Alloy, L. B. (2015). Kindling of life stress in bipolar disorder: Comparison of sensitization and autonomy models. *Journal of Abnormal Psychology, 124,* 4–16.

Welbourne, J. L., Miranda, G., & Gangadharan, A. (2020). Effects of employee personality on the relationships between experienced incivility, emotional exhaustion, and perpetrated incivility. *International Journal of Stress Management, 27*(4), 335–345. https://doi.org/10.1037/str0000160

Welch, S. (2019). An evaluation of Macmillan Education's LaunchPad as a textbook technology supplement when teaching introductory psychology. *Scholarship of Teaching and Learning in Psychology, 5*(3), 236–246. https://doi.org/10.1037/stl0000162

Welhaf, M. S., Smeekens, B. A., Gazzia, N. C., Perkins, J. B., Silvia, P. J., Meier, M. E., Kwapil, T. R., & Kane, M. J. (2020). An exploratory analysis of individual differences in mind wandering content and consistency. *Psychology of Consciousness: Theory, Research, and Practice, 7*(2), 103–125. https://doi.org/10.1037/cns0000180

Wells, G. L., Kovera, M. B., Douglass, A. B., Brewer, N., Meissner, C. A., & Wixted, J. T. (2020). Policy and procedure recommendations for the collection and preservation of eyewitness identification evidence. *Law and Human Behavior, 44*(1), 3–36. https://doi.org/10.1037/lhb0000359

Wentzel, K. R., McNamara Barry, C., & Caldwell, K. A. (2004). Friendships in middle school: Influences on motivation and school adjustment. *Journal of Educational Psychology, 96,* 195–203.

Werker, J. F., & Hensch, T. K. (2015). Critical periods in speech perception: New directions. *Annual Review of Psychology, 66,* 173–196.

Werker, J. F., & Tees, R. C. (1984). Cross-language speech perception: Evidence for perceptual reorganization during the first year of life. *Infant Behavior and Development, 7,* 49–63.

Werner, K. B., Few, L. R., & Bucholz, K. K. (2015). Epidemiology, comorbidity, and behavioral genetics of antisocial personality disorder and psychopathy. *Psychiatric Annals, 45,* 195–199.

Wernig, M., Zhao, J. P., Pruszak, J., Hedlund, E., Fu, D., Soldner, F., Broccoli, V., Constantine-Paton, M., Isacson, O., & Jaenisch, R. (2008). Neurons derived from reprogrammed fibroblasts functionally integrate into the fetal brain and

improve symptoms of rats with Parkinson's disease. *Proceedings of the National Academy of Sciences, 105,* 5856–5861. https://doi.org/10.1073/pnas.0801677105

Wertheimer, M. (2012). *A brief history of psychology* (5th ed.). Taylor & Francis.

Wertheimer, M. (2014). Music, thinking, perceived motion: The emergence of Gestalt theory. *History of Psychology, 17,* 131–133.

Wertheimer, M., & Puente, A. E. (2020). *A brief history of psychology* (6th ed.). Routledge.

Westbrook, A., & Braver, T. S. (2015). Cognitive effort: A neuroeconomic approach. *Cognitive, Affective & Behavioral Neuroscience, 15,* 395–415.

Westen, D. (1990). Psychoanalytic approaches to personality. In L. A. Pervin (Ed.), *Handbook of personality* (pp. 21–65). Guilford Press.

Westen, D., Gabbard, G. O., & Ortigo, K. M. (2008). Psychoanalytic approaches to personality. In O. P. John, R. W. Robins, & L. A. Pervin (Eds.), *Handbook of personality: Theory of research* (pp. 61–113). Guilford Press.

Wetzel, E., Frick, S., & Brown, A. (2021). Does multidimensional forced-choice prevent faking? Comparing the susceptibility of the multidimensional forced-choice format and the rating scale format to faking. *Psychological Assessment, 33*(2), 156–170. https://doi.apa.org/doiLanding?doi=10.1037%2Fpas0000971

Whillans, A. V., Dunn, E. W., Smeets, P., Bekkers, R., & Norton, M. I. (2017). Buying time promotes happiness. *Proceedings of the National Academy of Sciences, 114*(32), 8523–8527. https://doi.org/10.1073/pnas.1706541114

Whitaker, R. (2015). The triumph of American psychiatry: How it created the modern therapeutic state. *European Journal of Psychotherapy & Counselling, 17,* 326–341.

White, A. M., Slater, M. E., Ng, G., Hingson, R., & Breslow, R. (2018). Trends in alcohol-related emergency department visits in the United States: Results from the Nationwide Emergency Department Sample, 2006 to 2014. *Alcoholism: Clinical and Experimental Research, 42*(2), 352–359. https://doi.org/10.1111/acer.13559

Whiting D., & Fazel, S. (2020) Epidemiology and risk factors for violence in people with mental disorders. In Carpiniello B., Vita A., & Mencacci C. (Eds.), *Violence and mental disorders. Comprehensive approach to psychiatry* (Vol. 1, pp. 49–62). Springer. https://doi.org/10.1007/978-3-030-33188-7_3

Whiting, P. F., Wolff, R. F., Deshpande, S., Di Nisio, M., Duffy, S., Hernandez, A. V., Keurentjes, C., Lang, S., Misso, K., Ryder, S., Schmidlkofer, S., Westwood, M., & Kleijnen, J. (2015). Cannabinoids for medical use: A systematic review and meta-analysis. *JAMA, 313*(24), 2456–2473. https://doi:10.1001/jama.2015.6358

Whitlock, J. R., Heynen, A. J., Shuler, M. G., & Bear, M. F. (2006). Learning induces long-term potentiation in the hippocampus. *Science, 313,* 1093–1097.

Whittington, B. L. (2019). Benefits of a voluntary cell phone abstinence intervention in general psychology courses. *Teaching of Psychology, 46*(4), 299–305. https://doi.org/10.1177/0098628319872575

Whorf, B. L. (1956). *Language, thought, and reality.* MIT Press.

Whyte, A. R., Cheng, N., Butler, L. T., Lamport, D. J., & Williams, C. M. (2019). Flavonoid-rich mixed berries maintain and improve cognitive function over a 6 h period in young healthy adults. *Nutrients, 11,* 2685. https://doi.org/10.3390/nu11112685

Wickens, A. P. (2015). *A history of the brain: From stone age surgery to modern neuroscience.* Psychology Press.

Wicker, A. W. (1969). Attitudes versus actions: The relationship of verbal and overt behavioral responses to attitude objects. *Journal of Social Issues, 24,* 41–78.

Wickman, F. (2013, September 26). 10 things *Breaking Bad* has actually gotten wrong [Web log post]. *Slate.* http://www.slate.com/blogs/browbeat/2013/09/26/breaking_bad_accuracy_the_show_s_biggest_errors_and_mistakes_from_blue_meth.html

Wielgosz, J., Goldberg, S. B., Kral, T. R., Dunne, J. D., & Davidson, R. J. (2019). Mindfulness meditation and psychopathology. *Annual Review of Clinical Psychology, 15,* 285–316.

Wikoff, D., Welsh, B. T., Henderson, R., Brorby, G. P., Britt, J., Myers, E., Goldberger, J., Lieberman, H. R., O'Brien, C., Peck, J., Tenenbein, M., Weaver, C., Harvey, S., Urban, J., & Doepker, C. (2017). Systematic review of the potential adverse effects of caffeine consumption in healthy adults, pregnant women, adolescents, and children. *Food and Chemical Toxicology, 109,* 585–648. https://doi.org/10.1016/j.fct.2017.04.002

Wilcox, M. M., Barbaro-Kukade, L., Pietrantonio, K. R., Franks, D. N., & Davis, B. L. (2021). It takes money to make money: Inequity in psychology graduate student borrowing and financial stressors. *Training and Education in Professional Psychology, 15*(1), 2–17. https://doi.org/10.1037/tep0000294

Wilhelmus, M. M., Hay, J. L., Zuiker, R. G., Okkerse, P., Perdrieu, C., Sauser, J., Beaumont, M., Schmitt, J., van Gerven, J. M. A., & Silber, B. Y. (2017). Effects of a single, oral 60 mg caffeine dose on attention in healthy adult subjects. *Journal of Psychopharmacology, 31*, 222–232. https://doi.org/0269881116668593

Wilke, J. (2020). Functional high-intensity exercise is more effective in acutely increasing working memory than aerobic walking: An exploratory randomized, controlled trial. *Scientific Reports, 10*, Article 12335. https://doi.org/10.1038/s41598-020-69139-z

Wilkie, G., Sakr, B., & Rizack, T. (2016). Medical marijuana use in oncology: A review. *JAMA Oncology, 2*(5), 670–675. https://doi.org/10.1001/jamaoncol.2016.0155

Williams, C. (Writer), & Whittingham, K. (Director). (2007, February 8). Phyllis' wedding (G. Daniels, Producer). In *The Office* [Television series]. Los Angeles, CA: NBC.

Williams, C. L., & Lally, S. J. (2017). MMPI-2, MMPI-2-RF, and MMPI-A administrations (2007–2014): Any evidence of a "new standard"? *Professional Psychology: Research and Practice, 48*(4), 267–274. https://doi.org/10.1037/pro0000088

Williams, D. R., & Mohammed, S. A. (2009). Discrimination and racial disparities in health: Evidence and needed research. *Journal of Behavioral Medicine, 32*, 20–47. https://doi.org/10.1007/s10865-008-9185-0

Williams, M., Hong, S. W., Kang, M.-S., Carlisle, N. B., & Woodman, G. F. (2013). The benefit of forgetting. *Psychonomic Bulletin & Review, 20*, 348–355.

Williams, M. T. (2020). Microaggressions: Clarification, evidence, and impact. *Perspectives on Psychological Science, 15*(1), 3–26. https://doi.org/10.1177/1745691619827499

Williams, M. T., Farris, S. G., Turkheimer, E., Pinto, A., Ozanick, K., Franklin, M. E., Liebowitz, M., Simpson, H. B., & Foa, E. B. (2011). Myth of the pure obsessional type in obsessive–compulsive disorder. *Depression and Anxiety, 28*(6), 495–500.

Williams, P. G., Suchy, Y., & Kraybill, M. L. (2010). Five-factor model personality traits and executive functioning among older adults. *Journal of Research in Personality, 44*, 485–491.

Williams, V. (2018, December 25). Mayo Clinic Minute: What is hearing loss. *Mayo Clinic News Network.* https://newsnetwork.mayoclinic.org/discussion/mayo-clinic-minute-what-is-hearing-loss/

Williamson, A. A., Meltzer, L. J., & Fiks, A. G. (2020). A stimulus package to address the pediatric sleep debt crisis in the United States. *JAMA Pediatrics, 174*(2), 115–116.

Williamson, A. A., Mindell, J. A., Hiscock, H., & Quach, J. (2020). Longitudinal sleep problem trajectories are associated with multiple impairments in child well-being. *Journal of Child Psychology and Psychiatry, 61*(10), 1092–1103. https://doi.org/10.1111/jcpp.13303

Williamson, A. M., & Feyer, A. M. (2000). Moderate sleep deprivation produces impairments in cognitive and motor performance equivalent to legally prescribed levels of alcohol intoxication. *Occupational and Environmental Medicine, 57*, 649–655.

Williamson, D. A., & Chen, M. Y. (2020). Emerging and reemerging sexually transmitted infections. *New England Journal of Medicine, 382*(21), 2023–2032. https://doi.org/10.1056/NEJMra1907194

Willis, D. J., DeLeon, P. H., Haldane, S., & Heldring, M. B. (2014). A policy article—personal perspectives on the public policy process: Making a difference. *Professional Psychology: Research and Practice, 45*, 143–151.

Willoughby, K. A., Desrocher, M., Levine, B., & Rovet, J. F. (2012). Episodic and semantic autobiographical memory and everyday memory during late childhood and early adolescence. *Frontiers in Psychology, 3*, 1–15. https://doi.org/10.3389/fpsyg.2012.00053

Wilmot, M. P., Haslam, N., Tian, J., & Ones, D. S. (2019). Direct and conceptual replications of the taxometric analysis of type A behavior. *Journal of Personality and Social Psychology, 116*(3), e12–e26. https://doi.org/10.1037/pspp0000195

Wilson, B. A., & Wearing, D. (1995). Prisoner of consciousness: A state of just awakening following herpes simplex encephalitis. In R. Campbell & M. Conway (Eds.), *Broken memories: Case studies in memory impairment* (pp. 14–30). Blackwell.

Wilson, B. A., Baddeley, A. D., & Kapur, N. (1995). Dense amnesia in a professional musician following herpes simplex virus encephalitis. *Journal of Clinical and Experimental Neuropsychology, 17*, 668–681.

Wilson, B. A., Kopelman, M., & Kapur, N. (2008). Prominent and persistent loss of past awareness in amnesia: Delusion, impaired consciousness or coping strategy. *Neuropsychological Rehabilitation, 18*, 527–540.

Wilson, M. (2018, January 29). How Ikea's Ingvar Kamprad built the first global design giant. *Fast Company.* https://www.fastcompany.com/90158487/how-ikeas-ingvar-kamprad-built-the-first-global-design-giant

Wimber, M., Alink, A., Charest, I., Kriegeskorte, N., & Anderson, M. C. (2015). Retrieval induces adaptive forgetting of competing memories via cortical pattern suppression. *Nature Neuroscience, 18*, 582–589.

Windham, G. C., Pinney, S. M., Voss, R. W., Sjödin, A., Biro, F. M., Greenspan, L. C., Stewart, S., Hiatt, R. A., & Kushi, L. H. (2015). Brominated flame retardants and other persistent organohalogenated compounds in relation to timing of puberty in a longitudinal study of girls. *Environmental Health Perspectives, 123*, 1046–1052.

Windle, E., Tee, H., Sabitova, A., Jovanovic, N., Priebe, S., & Carr, C. (2020). Association of patient treatment preference with dropout and clinical outcomes in adult psychosocial mental health interventions: A systematic review and meta-analysis. *JAMA Psychiatry, 77*(3), 294–302. https://doi.org/10.1001/jamapsychiatry.2019.3750

Winsper, C., Bilgin, A., Thompson, A., Marwaha, S., Chanen, A. M., Singh, S. P., Wang, A., & Furtado, V. (2020). The prevalence of personality disorders in the community: A global systematic review and meta-analysis. *The British Journal of Psychiatry, 216*(2), 69–78. https://doi.org/10.1192/bjp.2019.166

Winter, U., LeVan, P., Borghardt, T. L., Akin, B., Wittmann, M., Leyens, Y., & Schmidt, S. (2020). Content-free awareness: EEG-fcMRI correlates of consciousness as such in an expert meditator. *Frontiers in Psychology, 10*, 3064. https://doi.org/10.3389/fpsyg.2019.03064

Winton, W. M. (1987). Do introductory textbooks present the Yerkes-Dodson Law correctly? *American Psychologist, 42*, 202–203.

Wipfli, B., Landers, D., Nagoshi, C., & Ringenbach, S. (2011). An examination of serotonin and psychological variables in the relationship between exercise and mental health. *Scandinavian Journal of Medicine and Science in Sports, 21*(3), 474–481.

Wirth, K. (2018, June 22). Personalization and privacy in a GDPR world. *Entrepreneur.* https://www.entrepreneur.com/article/314611

Wirth, M. M. (2015). Hormones, stress, and cognition: The effects of glucocorticoids and oxytocin on memory. *Adaptive Human Behavior and Physiology, 1*, 177–201.

Wise, N. J., Frangos, E., & Komisaruk, B. R. (2017). Brain activity unique to orgasm in women: An fMRI analysis. *Journal of Sexual Medicine, 14*, 1380–1391. https://doi.org/10.1016/j.jsxm.2017.08.014

Wisman, A., & Shrira, I. (2020). Sexual chemosignals: Evidence that men process olfactory signals of women's sexual arousal. *Archives of Sexual Behavior.* Advance online publication. https://doi.org/10.1007/s10508-019-01588-8

Witelson, S., Kigar, D., & Harvey, T. (1999). The exceptional brain of Albert Einstein. *The Lancet, 353*, 2149–2153.

Withers, R. S., & Barnes, Z. (2015, September 11). What it's really like to live with schizophrenia. *Women's Health.* https://www.womenshealthmag.com/health/living-with-schizophrenia

Witherspoon, D. J., Wooding, S., Rogers, A. R., Marchani, E. E., Watkins, W. S., Batzer, M. A., & Jorde, L. B. (2007). Genetic similarities within and between human populations. *Genetics, 176*, 351–359.

Wittig, S. M., & Rodriguez, C. M. (2019). Emerging behavior problems: Bidirectional relations between maternal and paternal parenting styles with infant temperament. *Developmental Psychology, 55*(6), 1199–1210. https://doi.org/10.1037/dev0000707

Wixted, J., & Mickes, L. (2017, November/December). Eyewitness memory is a lot more reliable than you think. *Scientific American Mind, 28*, 35–38.

Wixted, J. T. (2020). The forgotten history of signal detection theory. *Journal of Experimental Psychology: Learning, Memory, and Cognition, 46*(2), 201–233. https://doi.org/10.1037/xlm0000732

Wixted, J. T., Mickes, L., Clark, S. E., Gronlund, S. D., & Roediger, H. L. III. (2015). Initial eyewitness confidence reliably predicts eyewitness identification accuracy. *American Psychologist, 70*, 515–526.

Wobst, A. H. K. (2007). Hypnosis and surgery: Past, present, and future. *Anesthesia & Analgesia, 104*, 1199–1208.

Wohlfahrt-Veje, C., Korsholm Mouritsen, A., Hagen, C. P., Tinggaard, J., Grunnet Mieritz, M., Boas, M., Petersen, J. H., Skakkebæk, N. E., & Main, K. M. (2016). Pubertal onset in boys and girls is influenced by pubertal timing of both parents. *Journal of Clinical Endocrinology & Metabolism, 101*, 2667–2674. https://doi.org/10.1210/jc.2016-1073

Wojcicki, J. M., van der Straten, A., & Padian, N. (2010). Bridewealth and sexual and reproductive practices among women in Harare, Zimbabwe. *AIDS Care, 22*, 705–710.

**Wolf, C.** (2018, October 3). Post-traumatic stress disorder can be contagious. *Scientific American.* https://www.scientificamerican.com/article/post-traumatic-stress-disorder-can-be-contagious/

**Wolfe, U., & Ali, N.** (2015). Dark adaptation and Purkinje shift: A laboratory exercise in perceptual neuroscience. *Journal of Undergraduate Neuroscience Education, 13*(2), A59–A63.

**Wolman, D.** (2012, March 15). The split brain: A tale of two halves. *Nature, 483,* 260–263.

**Wolpert, D. M., Goodbody, S. J., & Husain, M.** (1998). Maintaining internal representations: The role of the human superior parietal lobe. *Nature Neuroscience, 1,* 529–533.

**Wong, B.** (2011). Point of view: Color blindness. *Nature Methods, 8,* 441.

**Wong, Y. J., Wang, S.-Y., & Klann, E. M.** (2018). The emperor with no clothes: A critique of collectivism and individualism. *Archives of Scientific Psychology, 6*(1), 251–260. http://dx.doi.org/10.1037/arc0000059

**Wongcha-um, P., & Pearson, J.** (2018, July 14). Thailand's cave boys to be discharged from hospital on Thursday. *Reuters.* https://www.reuters.com/article/us-thailand-accident-cave/thailands-cave-boys-to-be-discharged-from-hospital-on-thursday-idUSKBN1K4051

**Wood, G., & Pennington, J.** (1973). Encoding and retrieval from long-term storage. *Journal of Experimental Psychology, 99,* 243–254.

**Wood, W., & Eagly, A. H.** (2015). Two traditions of research on gender identity. *Sex Roles, 73,* 461–473.

**Woolley, J. D., & Kelley, K. A.** (2020). "When something like a ladybug lands on you": Origins and development of the concept of luck. *Developmental Psychology, 56*(10), 1866–1878. https://doi.org/10.1037/dev0001104

**Woolley, K., & Fishbach, A.** (2018). It's about time: Earlier rewards increase intrinsic motivation. *Journal of Personality and Social Psychology, 114,* 877–890. https://doi.org/10.1037/pspa0000116

**World Health Organization (WHO).** (2018). *Deafness and hearing loss.* https://www.who.int/news-room/fact-sheets/detail/deafness-and-hearing-loss

**World Health Organization (WHO).** (2019). *Sexually transmitted infections (STIs): Key facts.* https://www.who.int/news-room/fact-sheets/detail/sexually-transmitted-infections-(stis)

**World Health Organization (WHO).** (2019, December 5). *More than 140,000 die from measles as cases surge worldwide* [Press release]. https://www.who.int/news-room/detail/05-12-2019-more-than-140-000-die-from-measles-as-cases-surge-worldwide

**World Health Organization (WHO).** (2020, August 28). *Opioid overdose.* https://www.who.int/news-room/fact-sheets/detail/opioid-overdose

**Worringham, C. J., & Messick, D. M.** (1983). Social facilitation of running: An unobtrusive study. *Journal of Social Psychology, 121,* 23–29.

**Wray, N. R., Pergadia, M. L., Blackwood, D. H. R., Penninx, B. W. J. H., Gordon, S. D., Nyholt, D. R., Ripke, S., MacIntyre, D. J., McGhee, K. A., Maclean, A. W., Smit, J. H., Hottenga, J. J., Willemsen, G., Middeldorp, C. M., de Geus, E. J. C., Lewis, C. M., McGuffin, P., Hickie, I. B., van den Oord, E. J. C. G., . . . Sullivan, P. F** (2012). Genome-wide association study of major depressive disorder: New results, meta-analysis, and lessons learned. *Molecular Psychiatry, 17,* 36–48.

**Wright, K.** (2002). The times of our lives. *Scientific American, 287,* 59–65.

**Wright, K. P., Bogan, R. K., & Wyatt, J. K.** (2013). Shift work and the assessment and management of shift work disorder (SWD). *Sleep Medicine Reviews, 17,* 41–54.

**Wu, C., Odden, M. C., Fisher, G. G., & Stawski, R. S.** (2016). Association of retirement age with mortality: A population-based longitudinal study among older adults in the USA. *Journal of Epidemiology and Community Health, 70,* 917–923. http://dx.doi.org/10.1136/jech-2015-207097

**Wu, J.** (2020, May 21). Why oxytocin is incredible and how to get more of It. *Scientific American.* https://www.scientificamerican.com/article/why-oxytocin-is-incredible-and-how-to-get-more-of-it/

**Wyatt, T. D.** (2015). The search for human pheromones: The lost decades and the necessity of returning to first principles. *Proceedings of the Royal Society B, 282,* 20142994. https://doi.org/10.1098/rspb.2014.2994

**Wynn, K., Bloom, P., Jordan, A., Marshall, J., & Sheskin, M.** (2018). Not noble savages after all: Limits to early altruism. *Current Directions in Psychological Science, 27,* 3–8. https://doi.org/10.1177/0963721417734875

**Xiao, J., Li, D., Jia, J., Wang, Y., Sun, W., & Li, D.** (2019). The role of stressful life events and the Big Five personality traits in adolescent trajectories of problematic internet use. *Psychology of Addictive Behaviors, 33*(4), 360–370. https://doi.org/10.1037/adb0000466

**Xie, L., Kang, H., Xu, Q., Chen, M. J., Liao, Y., Thiyagarajan, M., O'Donnell, J., Christensen, D. J., Nicholson, C., Iliff, J. J., Takano, T., Deane, R., & Nedergaard, M.** (2013). Sleep drives metabolite clearance from the adult brain. *Science, 342*(6156), 373–377. https://doi.org/10.1126/science.1241224

**Xu, H., & Zhuang, X.** (2019). Atypical antipsychotics-induced metabolic syndrome and nonalcoholic fatty liver disease: a critical review. *Neuropsychiatric Disease and Treatment, 15,* 2087–2099. http://doi.org/10.2147/NDT.S208061

**Xu, H., Wen, L. M., Hardy, L. L., & Rissel, C.** (2016). Associations of outdoor play and screen time with nocturnal sleep duration and pattern among young children. *Acta Paediatrica, 105,* 297–303. https://doi.org/10.1111/apa.13285

**Xu, J, Q., Murphy, S. L., Kochanek, K. D., & Arias, E.** (2020). Mortality in the United States, 2018. NCHS data brief, no 355. *National Center for Health Statistics.* https://www.cdc.gov/nchs/data/databriefs/db355-h.pdf

**Xu, J., Gannon, P. J., Emmorey, K., Smith, J. F., & Braun, A. R.** (2009). Symbolic gestures and spoken language are processed by a common neural system. *Proceedings of the National Academy of Sciences USA, 106,* 20664–20669.

**Xu, M., Chung, S., Zhang, S., Zhong, P., Ma, C., Chang, W.-C., Weissbourd, B., Sakai, N,, Luo, L., Nishino, S., & Dan, Y.** (2015). Basal forebrain circuit for sleep–wake control. *Nature Neuroscience, 18,* 1641–1647. https://doi.org/10.1038/nn.4143

**Xu, X., & Tart-Zelvin, A.** (2017, July 19). What goes on in our brains when we are in love? *Scientific American.* https://www.scientificamerican.com/article/what-goes-on-in-our-brains-when-we-are-in-love/

**Xu, Y., Norton, S., & Rahman, Q.** (2019). Early life conditions and adolescent sexual orientation: A prospective birth cohort study. *Developmental Psychology, 55*(6), 1226–1243. https://doi.org/10.1037/dev0000704

**Xu, Y., & Zheng, Y.** (2017). Fraternal birth order, handedness, and sexual orientation in a Chinese population. *The Journal of Sex Research, 54,* 10–18. https://doi.org/10.1080/00224499.2015.1104530

**Yaghmaian, R., & Miller, S. S.** (2019). A feminist, biopsychosocial subjective well-being framework for women with fibromyalgia. *Rehabilitation Psychology, 64*(2), 154–166. https://doi.org/10.1037/rep0000226

**Yale University.** (n.d.). Weight management strategies for success. https://beingwell.yale.edu/programs/weight-management-nutrition/weight-management-options/your-own/weight-management-strategies

**Yalom, I. D., & Leszcz, M.** (2005). *The theory and practice of group psychotherapy* (5th ed.). Basic Books.

**Yamagata, S., Suzuki, A., Ando, J., Ono, Y., Kijima, N., Yoshimura, K., Ostendorf, F., Angleitner, A., Riemann, R., Spinath, F. M., Livesley, W. J., & Jang, K. L.** (2006). Is the genetic structure of human personality universal? A cross-cultural twin study from North America, Europe, and Asia. *Journal of Personality and Social Psychology, 90*(6), 987–998. https://doi.org/10.1037/0022-3514.90.6.987

**Yanchar, S. C., Slife, B. D., & Warne, R.** (2008). Critical thinking as disciplinary practice. *Review of General Psychology, 12,* 265–281.

**Yang, C., Luo, L., Vadillo, M. A., Yu, R., & Shanks, D. R.** (2021). Testing (quizzing) boosts classroom learning: A systematic and meta-analytic review. *Psychological Bulletin.* Advance online publication. https://doi.org/10.1037/bul0000309

**Yang, C., Sun, B., Potts, R., Yu, R., Luo, L., & Shanks, D. R.** (2020, June 4). Do working memory capacity and test anxiety modulate the beneficial effects of testing on new learning? *Journal of Experimental Psychology: Applied, 26*(4), 724–738. https://doi.org/10.1037/xap0000278

**Yang, F., Knobe, J., & Dunham, Y.** (2020, June 18). Happiness is from the soul: The nature and origins of our happiness concept. *Journal of Experimental Psychology: General, 150*(2), 276–288. https://doi.org/10.1037/xge0000790

**Yassine, J., & Tipton-Fisler, L. A.** (2021). Independent contingency and token economy at recess to reduce aggression. *Contemporary School Psychology.* Advance online publication. https://doi.org/10.1007/s40688-021-00364-7

**Yee, E.** (2019). Abstraction and concepts: When, how, where, what and why? *Language, Cognition and Neuroscience, 34*(10), 1257–1265. https://doi.org/10.1080/23273798.2019.1660797

**Yee, E., & Thompson-Schill, S. L.** (2016). Putting concepts into context. *Psychonomic Bulletin & Review, 23,* 1015–1027. https://doi.org/10.3758/s13423-015-0948-7

**Yee, M., & Brown, R.** (1994). The development of gender differentiation in young children. *British Journal of Social Psychology, 33,* 183–196.

**Yerkes, R. M., & Dodson, J. D.** (1908). The relation of strength of stimulus to rapidity of habit-formation. *Journal of Comparative Neurology, 18,* 459–482.

**Yogman, M., Garner, A., Hutchinson, J., Hirsh-Pasek, K., Golinkoff, R. M., & Committee on Psychosocial Aspects of Child and Family Health.** (2018). The power of play: A pediatric role in enhancing development in young children. *Pediatrics, 142*(3), Article e20182058. https://doi.org/10.1542/peds.2018-2058

**Yolken, R. H., & Torrey, E. F.** (1995). Viruses, schizophrenia, and bipolar disorder. *Clinical Microbiology Reviews, 8,* 131–145.

**Yoon, S. H., Choi, J., Lee, W. J., & Do, J. T.** (2020). Genetic and epigenetic etiology underlying autism spectrum disorder. *Journal of Clinical Medicine, 9*(4), 966. https://doi.org/10.3390/jcm9040966

**Young, C. C., Williams, J. R., Feroze, A. H., McGrath, M., Ravanpay, A. C., Ellenbogen, R. G., Ojemann, J. G., & Hauptman, J. S.** (2020). Pediatric functional hemispherectomy: Operative techniques and complication avoidance. *Neurosurgical Focus, 48*(4), E9. https://doi.org/10.3171/2020.1.FOCUS19889

**Young, E. S., Farrell, A. K., Carlson, E. A., Englund, M. M., Miller, G. E., Gunnar, M. R., Roisman, G. I., & Simpson, J. A.** (2019). The dual impact of early and concurrent life stress on adults' diurnal cortisol patterns: A prospective study. *Psychological Science, 30*(5), 739–747. https://doi.org/10.1177/0956797619833664

**Young, M. E., Mizzau, M., Mai, N. T., Sirisegaram, A., & Wilson, M.** (2009). Food for thought: What you eat depends on your sex and eating companions. *Appetite, 53,* 268–271.

**Youyou, W., Stillwell, D., Schwartz, H. A., & Kosinski, M.** (2017). Birds of a feather do flock together: Behavior-based personality assessment method reveals personality similarity among couples and friends. *Psychological Science, 28,* 276–284. https://doi.org/10.1177/0956797616678187

**Yu, C. K. C.** (2015). One hundred typical themes in most recent dreams, diary dreams, and dreams spontaneously recollected from last night. *Dreaming, 25,* 206–219.

**Yu, C. K. C., & Fu, W.** (2011). Sex dreams, wet dreams, and nocturnal emissions. *Dreaming, 21,* 197–212.

**Yuan, Z., & Park, Y.** (2020, July 21). The psychological toll of rude e-mails. *Scientific American.* https://www.scientificamerican.com/article/the-psychological-toll-of-rude-e-mails/

**Yuan, Z., Park, Y., & Sliter, M. T.** (2020). Put you down versus tune you out: Further understanding active and passive e-mail incivility. *Journal of Occupational Health Psychology, 25*(5), 330–344. https://doi.org/10.1037/ocp0000215

**Yudell, M., Roberts, D., DeSalle, R., & Tishkoff, S.** (2016). Taking race out of human genetics. *Science, 351,* 564–565. https://doi.org/10.1126/science.aac4951

**Yule, G.** (1996). *Pragmatics.* Oxford University Press.

**Zabelina, D. L., & Silvia, P. J.** (2020). Percolating ideas: The effects of caffeine on creative thinking and problem solving. *Consciousness and Cognition, 79,* Article 102899. https://doi.org/10.1016/j.concog.2020.102899

**Zafeiriou, D. I.** (2004). Primitive reflexes and postural reactions in the neurodevelopmental examination. *Pediatric Neurology, 31,* 1–8.

**Zajonc, R. B.** (1980). Feeling and thinking: Preferences need no inferences. *American Psychologist, 35,* 151–175.

**Zajonc, R. B.** (1984). On the primacy of affect. *American Psychologist, 39,* 117–123.

**Zander-Schellenberg, T., Collins, I. M., Miché, M., Guttmann, C., Lieb, R., & Wahl, K.** (2020). Does laughing have a stress-buffering effect in daily life? An intensive longitudinal study. *PLOS ONE, 15*(7), Article e0235851. https://doi.org/10.1371/journal.pone.0235851

**Zaretskii, V. K.** (2009). The zone of proximal development: What Vygotsky did not have time to write. *Journal of Russian and East European Psychology, 47,* 70–93.

**Zeliadt, N.** (2018, July 20). Study ties autism to maternal high blood pressure, diabetes. *Scientific American.* https://www.scientificamerican.com/article/study-ties-autism-to-maternal-high-blood-pressure-diabetes/

**Zenger, J., & Folkman, J.** (2017, May 2). Why do so many managers avoid giving praise? *Harvard Business Review.* https://hbr.org/2017/05/why-do-so-many-managers-avoid-giving-praise

**Zhang, B., Ma, S., Rachmin, I., He, M., Baral, P., Choi, S., Gonçalves, W. A., Shwartz, Y., Fast, E. M., Su, Y., Zon, L. I., Regev, A., Buenrostro, J. D., Cunha, T. M., Chiu, I. M., Fisher D. E., & Hsu, Y. C.** (2020). Hyperactivation of sympathetic nerves drives depletion of melanocyte stem cells. *Nature, 577*(7792), 676–681.

https://doi.org/10.1038/s41586-020-1935-3

**Zhang, F., Li, W., Li, H., Gao, S., Sweeney, J. A., Jia, Z., & Gong, Q.** (2020). The effect of jet lag on the human brain: A neuroimaging study. *Human Brain Mapping, 41*(9), 2281–2291. https://doi.org/10.1002/hbm.24945

**Zhang, L., Dong, Y., Doyon, W. M., & Dani, J. A.** (2012). Withdrawal from chronic nicotine exposure alters dopamine signaling dynamics in the nucleus accumbens. *Biological Psychiatry, 71,* 184–191.

**Zhang, T., Feng, S., Han, B., & Sun, S.** (2018). Red color in flags: A signal for competition. *Color Research & Application, 43*(1), 114–118. https://doi.org/10.1002/col.22165

**Zhang, T.-Y., & Meaney, M. J.** (2010). Epigenetics and the environmental regulation of the genome and its function. *Annual Review of Psychology, 61,* 439–466.

**Zhang, X., Chen, X., & Zhang, X.** (2018). The impact of exposure to air pollution on cognitive performance. *Proceedings of the National Academy of Sciences, 115*(37), 9193–9197. https://doi.org/10.1073/pnas.180947411

**Zhao, H.** (2017). Recent progress of development of optogenetic implantable neural probes. *International Journal of Molecular Sciences, 18,* 1751. https://doi.org/10.3390/ijms18081751

**Zhou, W. X., Sornette, D., Hill, R. A., & Dunbar, R. I.** (2005). Discrete hierarchical organization of social group sizes. *Proceedings of the Royal Society of London B: Biological Sciences, 272*(1561), 439–444.

**Zhou, X., Wu, X., & Zhen, R.** (2017). Understanding the relationship between social support and posttraumatic stress disorder/posttraumatic growth among adolescents after Ya'an earthquake: The role of emotion regulation. *Psychological trauma: Theory, Research, Practice, and Policy, 9*(2), 214–221.

**Zhou, Y., Shao, A., Xu, W., Wu, H., & Deng, Y.** (2019). Advance of stem cell treatment for traumatic brain injury. *Frontiers in Cellular Neuroscience, 13.* https://doi.org/10.3389/fncel.2019.00301

**Zimbardo, P.** (2007). *The Lucifer effect: Understanding how good people turn evil.* Random House.

**Zimbardo, P. G.** (2020). How Orwell's *1984* has influenced Rev. Jim Jones to dominate and then destroy his followers: With extensions to current political leaders. *Peace and Conflict: Journal of Peace Psychology, 26*(1), 4–8. https://doi.org/10.1037/pac0000428

**Zimmerman, A., Bai, L., & Ginty, D. D.** (2014). The gentle touch receptors of mammalian skin. *Science, 346*(6212), 950–954.

**Zimmerman, T. N., Porcerelli, J. H., & Arterbery, V. E.** (2019). Defensive functioning in cancer patients, cancer survivors, and controls. *Psychoanalytic Psychology, 36,* 259–262. https://doi.org/10.1037/pap0000225

**Zingoni, A., Fionda, C., Borrelli, C., Cippitelli, M., Santoni, A., & Soriani, A.** (2017). Natural killer cell response to chemotherapy-stressed cancer cells: Role in tumor immunosurveillance. *Frontiers in Immunology, 8,* Article 1194. https://doi.org/10.3389/fimmu.2017.01194

**Zlatevska, N., Dubelaar, C., & Holden, S.** (2014). Sizing up the effect of portion size on consumption: A meta-analytic review. *Journal of Marketing, 78*(3), 140–154.

**Zolezzi, M., Alamri, M., Shaar, S., & Rainkie, D.** (2018). Stigma associated with mental illness and its treatment in the Arab culture: A systematic review. *International Journal of Social Psychiatry, 64*(6), 597–609. https://doi.org/10.1177/0020764018789200

**Zosuls, K. M., Miller, C. F., Ruble, D. N., Martin, C. L., & Fabes, R. A.** (2011). Gender development research in *Sex Roles*: Historical trends and future directions. *Sex Roles, 64,* 826–842.

**Zsok, F., Haucke, M., De Wit, C. Y., & Barelds, D. P.** (2017). What kind of love is love at first sight? An empirical investigation. *Personal Relationships, 24*(4), 869–885. https://doi.org/10.1111/pere.12218

**Zucker, J. R., Rosen, J. B., Iwamoto, M., Arciuolo, R. J., Langdon-Embry, M., Vora, N. M., Rakeman, J. L., Isaac, B. M., Jean, A., Asfaw, M., Hawkins, S. C., Merrill, T. G., Kennelly, M. O., Maldin Morgenthau, B., Daskalakis, D. C., & Barbot, O.** (2020). Consequences of undervaccination: Measles outbreak, New York City, 2018–2019. *New England Journal of Medicine, 382*(11), 1009–1017. https://doi.org/10.1056/NEJMoa1912514

**Zuckerman, M.** (1979). *Sensation seeking: Beyond the optimal level of arousal.* Lawrence Erlbaum Associates.

**Zuckerman, M.** (1994). *Behavioral expressions and biosocial bases of sensation seeking.* Cambridge University Press.

**Zuckerman, M.** (2015). Behavior and biology: Research on sensation seeking and reactions to the media. In L. Donohew, H. Sypher, & E. T. Higgins (Eds.), *Communication, social cognition and affect* (pp. 173–194). Psychology Press.

# Name Index

# Subject Index

Note: **Boldface** indicates key terms; *italics* indicate features; f indicates figures; t indicates tables; i indicates *Infographics*; c indicates *Connections* or *Research Connections*

This index includes entries for Online Appendix A: Introduction to Statistics and Online Appendix B: Careers in Psychology, which are included in the Achieve e-book.